THE 1970 Compton Yearbook

A summary and interpretation of the events of 1969 to supplement Compton's Encyclopedia

F. E. Compton Co.
Division of Encyclopædia Britannica, Inc.

William Benton
PUBLISHER

CHICAGO · LONDON
TORONTO · GENEVA
SYDNEY · TOKYO
MANILA

Contents

Library of Congress Catalog Card Number: 58-26525
International Standard Book Number: 0-85229-143-4

Printed in U.S.A.

How to Use the Yearbook

In order to make the best possible use of the Yearbook, the reader is advised to make frequent use of the Index and of the cross-references within articles. The Index can save a great deal of time and effort for a reader who is looking for specific information. In addition to cataloguing all the articles in the current Yearbook (see below), the Index notes whether a given topic has been covered in Yearbooks of the past five years. Many articles in the Yearbook contain cross-references to other articles of related interest within the Yearbook—for example, the VIETNAM article might have a cross-reference to INTERNATIONAL RELATIONS. At the end of an article, the reader will usually find a cross-reference to articles in Compton's Encyclopedia, which should be consulted if more background information is needed or wanted—for example, (*See in* CE: Honduras.).

The Yearbook is divided into several sections—feature articles and special reports, main text, new words, reprints, index, and family record.

FEATURE ARTICLES AND SPECIAL REPORTS
The feature articles discuss topics of especial current interest. Each one is written by an expert in his field. Each is a full-length survey piece. The special reports are two- or three-page supplements to nine main-text articles—covering the news in greater depth.

MAIN TEXT
The main text of the 1970 Compton Yearbook is an alphabetical arrangement of articles on all the subjects that made news during the year. At the end of this section is a useful 1970 calendar.
Most of the articles are accompanied by outstanding news pictures, diagrams, maps, or graphs.

NEW WORDS
The New Words section in this Yearbook comes in two parts. The first is a list of words newly accepted for inclusion in Merriam-Webster dictionaries. This list is a valuable reference source and could be a great aid in schoolwork. The second part of this section is an interesting essay on some of the new words of the 1960's and how they came to be used—for example, many of the new words that were introduced to the general reader during the Apollo 11 and 12 moon-landing missions.

INDEX
The Index lists alphabetically all the subjects and illustrations in the Yearbook. It shows the exact page on which information can be found. In addition, bracketed numbers, such as [68], [66], indicate that material on this subject can also be found in the Yearbooks of those years.

FAMILY RECORD
The last section of the Yearbook is a unique one with Compton's. Family affairs can be recorded under convenient headings.

THE 1970 COMPTON YEARBOOK

Feature Authors

Steve Allen, Television Humorist, Author, and Composer, *WHAT ARE WE LAUGHING AT?*

J. W. Fulbright, U.S. Senator (D, Ark.); Chairman, Senate Committee on Foreign Relations, *CHINA AND THE UNITED STATES: DISTORTED IMAGES*

William Barry Furlong, Reporter and Author; Special Correspondent for *Sports Illustrated, RUN FOR YOUR SUPPER*

Marion Kaplan, Free-Lance Writer and Photographer in Africa for 14 years, *BLACK AFRICA SAVES THE GAME*

Max Kozloff, Art Editor and Critic; Contributing Editor of *Art Forum;* Author, 'Renderings' and 'Jasper Johns', *COLOR: The Artist Experiments*

Contributors and Consultants

These authorities either wrote the articles listed or supplied information and data that were used in writing them.

Stener Mørch Aarsdal, Economic Editor, 'Børsen', and Press Officer, Chamber of Commerce, Copenhagen, *Denmark*

Joseph John Accardo, Washington Editor, Chilton Publications, and Columnist, 'Gas', *Fuel and Power* (in part)

Betty Claire Agree, Assistant Director, Public Relations, American Nurses' Association, *Nursing*

Jacob Bernard Agus, Rabbi, Beth El Congregation, Baltimore, Md., *Religion* (in part)

Ann M. Anderson, Acting Director, Peace Corps Office of Public Information, *Peace Corps*

Gustavo Arthur Antonini, Assistant Professor, Department of Geography, College of Social Sciences, University of Puerto Rico, *Dominican Republic*

Miguel Aranguren, Deputy Director, Department of Information and Public Affairs, Pan American Union, *Latin America* (in part)

Bruce Arnold, Free-Lance Journalist and Writer, Dublin, *Ireland*

John C. Baker, Public Information Officer, Bureau of the Census, U.S. Department of Commerce, *Population*

Robert M. Ball, Commissioner of Social Security, Department of Health, Education, and Welfare, *Social Services* (in part)

Kenneth de la Barre, Director, Montreal Office, Arctic Institute of North America, *Arctic*

James P. Barrett, Public Relations Director, Junior Achievement, Inc., *Youth Organizations* (in part)

Howard Bass, Winter Sports Correspondent, 'The Daily Telegraph' (London) and 'The Christian Science Monitor', *Ice Skating; Skiing*

Richard Herbert Beddoes, Sports Columnist, 'The Globe and Mail' of Toronto, Ont., *Ice Hockey*

David H. Beetle, Special Correspondent, Gannett Newspapers, Albany, N.Y., *State Governments, United States*

Clyde Richard Bergwin, Chief of Information, Headquarters, First Air Force Reserve Region, Andrews Air Force Base, Md., *Aircraft*

Mark Berke, President, American Hospital Association, and Executive Director, Mount Zion Hospital and Medical Center, San Francisco, Calif., *Hospitals*

Victor Gordon Charles Blackman, Staff Photographer, 'Daily Express', London, and Columnist, 'Amateur Photographer', *Photography*

Allan Geoffrey Blyth, Music Critic, London, *Music; Opera*

William Charles Boddy, Editor, 'Motor Sport', and Full Member, Guild of Motoring Writers, *Auto Racing* (in part)

Kooman Boycheff, Supervisor of Physical Education and Coordinator of Recreation, University of California at Berkeley, *Hobbies; Toys and Games*

Arnold C. Brackman, Writer and Consultant on Asian Affairs, *Indonesia*

Elston Gordon Bradfield, Editor Emeritus, 'The Numismatist'; Co-editor, 'Selections from The Numismatist'; and Editor, 'Introduction to Numismatics', *Coin Collecting*

Robert J. Braidwood, Professor of Old World Prehistory, Oriental Institute and Department of Anthropology, University of Chicago, *Archaeology* (in part)

William A. Bresnahan, Managing Director, American Trucking Associations, Inc., Washington, D.C., *Transportation* (in part)

Jack Brickhouse, Manager of Sports, WGN, Chicago, Ill., *Baseball* (in part)

John C. G. Brooks, Editor, 'Fortnightly Review', Bank of London and South America Ltd., London, *Costa Rica; Venezuela*

D. A. Brown, Agriculture Librarian, University of Illinois, *Animals and Wildlife; Conservation*

Leonard Ralph Buckley, Formerly Assistant Editor, 'The Times Educational Supplement', London, *Colleges and Universities; Education*

Ardath Walter Burks, Professor, Department of Political Science, Rutgers, The State University, New Brunswick, N.J., *Japan*

M. Dallas Burnett, Associate Professor of Communications, Brigham Young University, Provo, Utah, *Newspapers*

Allen D. Bushong, Associate Professor of Geography, University of South Carolina, *Honduras*

Frank Butler, Sports Editor, 'News of the World', London, *Boxing*

Joanna A. Carey, Assistant Director, Bureau of Public Information, American Dental Association, *Dentistry*

Lucien Chalmey, Adviser, International Union of Producers and Distributors of Electrical Energy, Paris, *Fuel and Power* (in part)

Kenneth Francis Chapman, Editor, 'Stamp Collecting', and Philatelic Correspondent, 'The Times', London, *Stamps*

Robin Chapman, Economic Research Officer, Bank of London and South America Ltd., London, *Cuba; Haiti; Portugal*

Loriene Eck Chase, Clinical Psychologist in Private Practice, *Psychology SPECIAL REPORT: If Stars Could Talk . . .*

Richard Christenson, Public Relations Assistant, American Bowling Congress, *Bowling*

Hung-Ti Chu, Expert in Far Eastern Affairs, Area Specialist and Chief of Asia-Africa Section and Trusteeship Council Section of the United Nations Secretariat, 1946–67, and Professor of Government, Texas Tech University, 1968–69, *China, People's Republic of; Taiwan*

Ivor Cecil Coffin, Economic Research Officer, Bank of London and South America Ltd., London, *Argentina*

Max Coiffait, Correspondent, Agence France-Presse, Vientiane, *Laos*

Rufus William Crater, Editorial Director, 'Broadcasting', New York City, *Television and Radio* (in part)

Norman Crossland, Bonn Correspondent, 'Manchester Guardian', *Germany, West*

Gloria Clare Cumper, Chairman, Council of Voluntary Social Services, and Member, Judicial Services Commission, Kingston, *Jamaica*

Hiroshi Daifuku, Chief, Section for the Development of the Cultural Heritage, United Nations Educational, Scientific, and Cultural Organization, Paris, *Landmarks and Monuments*

Ernest Albert John Davies, Editor, 'Traffic Engineering and Control', 'Roads and Their Traffic', and 'Traffic Engineering Practice', *Transportation* (in part)

Alfred Dawber, Chairman and Editorial Director, Emmott and Company, Ltd., Kennedy Press Ltd., Technical Publishers, Manchester; Editor, 'Textile Manufacturer'; and Compiler, 'Mechanical World Year Book', 'Electrical Year Book', *Textiles* (in part)

Antony King Deacon, Menswear Editor, 'The Times', *Fashion SPECIAL REPORT: The Peacock Revolution*

Philippe Decraene, Member, Editorial Staff, 'Le Monde', Paris, *Cameroon; Central African Republic; Chad; Congo, Republic of; Dahomey; Gabon; Guinea; Ivory Coast; Malagasy Republic; Mali; Mauritania; Niger; Senegal; Togo; Tunisia; Upper Volta*

Frances C. Dickson, Youth Information Specialist, Federal Extension Service, U.S. Department of Agriculture, *Youth Organizations* (in part)

Elfriede Dirnbacher, Austrian Civil Servant, *Austria*

Alton F. Doody, Professor of Marketing, The Ohio State University, *Retail Trade*

Jim Dunne, Detroit Editor, 'Popular Science Monthly', *Automobiles*

François Duriaud, Reuter's Correspondent, Algiers, *Algeria*

Raul d'Eca, Formerly Fulbright Visiting Lecturer on American History, University of Minas Gerais, *Brazil*

Jonathan R. Eley, Assistant Instructor of Illinois Aikido Club; Member of Board of Directors of Midwest Aikido Federation; 2d Dan (Degree) Black Belt, Aikido, and 3d Kyu Brown Belt, Judo, *Sports Champions SPECIAL REPORT: The Art of Self-Defense* (in part)

Eric George Ellis, Petroleum Technologist and Consultant, *Fuel and Power* (in part)

N. R. Ellis, Formerly of the Agricultural Research Service, U.S. Department of Agriculture, *Agriculture* (in part)

Jan Robert Engels, Editor, 'P.V.V. Flitsen' (Journal of the Belgian Party for Freedom and Progress), *Belgium*

Environmental Science Services Administration, Office of Public Information, *Weather*

Gerrit Hendrik van Es, Associate, Institute for Political Science, University of Amsterdam, *Netherlands*

David M. L. Farr, Professor of History, Carleton University, Ottawa, Ont., *Canada*

Jacques Fauchart, Engineer of Bridges and Highways, Department of Technical Studies on Roads and Highways, Ministry of Equipment and Housing, Paris, *Engineering Projects* (in part)

Robert Joseph Fendell, New York Editor, 'Automotive News', New York City, *Auto Racing* (in part)

Morris Fishbein, Editor, 'Medical World News', *Medicine* (in part)

Robert Moore Fisher, Senior Economist, Board of Governors, Federal Reserve System, and Lecturer, American University, Washington, D.C., *Building Construction*

David Fouquet, Staff Writer, 'Congressional Quarterly', *Immigration and Citizenship; Laird, Melvin R.*

Peter William Gaddum, Chairman, H. T. Gaddum and Company Ltd., Silk Merchants, Macclesfield, Cheshire, England, *Textiles* (in part)

Fabio Galvano, Correspondent, 'Epoca', London, *Italy*

Albert Ganado, Lawyer, Malta, *Malta*

S. N. Geal, Retired Assistant Director, American Camping Association, *Camping*

Thayil Jacob Sony George, Assistant Editor, 'Far Eastern Economic Review', Hong Kong, *Asia; Cambodia; Korea; Vietnam* (in part)

Arch C. Gerlach, Chief Geographer, U.S. Geological Survey, Washington, D.C., and Editor, 'The Professional Geographer', *Earth Sciences* (in part)

Paul Glikson, Secretary, Division of Jewish Demography and Statistics, Institute of Contemporary Jewry, The Hebrew University, Israel, *Religion* (in part)

Harry Golombek, British Chess Champion, 1947, 1949, and 1955, and Chess Correspondent, 'The Times' and 'Observer', London, *Chess*

John T. Goodman, Assistant Professor of Psychiatry (Psychology), Department of Psychiatry, McMaster University, Hamilton, Ont., *Psychology*

Robert Goralski, Correspondent, NBC News, Pentagon, Washington, D.C., *Vietnam* (in part)

Jarlath John Graham, Editor, 'Advertising Age', *Advertising*

The Rev. Arthur R. Green, Religion and Education Consultant, *Religion* (in part)

Benny Green, Jazz Critic, 'Observer', London, and Record Reviewer, British Broadcasting Corporation, *Popular Music* (in part)

Ernst Clark Griffin, Fellow, Michigan State University, *Uruguay*

Anthony Royston Grant Griffiths, Lecturer in History, Flinders University of South Australia, *Australia; Nauru*

John Austin Guinan, Bureau of Commercial Fisheries, U.S. Department of the Interior, *Fish and Fisheries*

Donald Douglas Hanson, Head of Department of Architecture, Chicago Circle Campus, University of Illinois, *Architecture* (in part)

Mac Harrelson, Chief of United Nations Bureau, The Associated Press, *Lindsay, John V.*

Philip Morris Hauser, Professor of Sociology, and Director, Population Research Center, University of Chicago, *Cities and Urban Affairs*

William D. Hawkland, Provost and Professor of Law, School of Law, State University of New York, Buffalo, *Supreme Court of the United States*

John Arnfield Heap, Member of the British Antarctic Survey, *Antarctica*

Phyllis West Heathcote, Correspondent on Women's Topics, 'Manchester Guardian', Paris, *Cosmetics; Fashion*

The Rev. Peter Anthony Hebblethwaite, Editor, 'The Month', *Religion* (in part)

William Dale Hickman, Jr., News Correspondent, McGraw-Hill Publications, Inc., Washington, D.C., *Telephones*

Edison L. Hoard, Attorney at Law, *Law*

John Hockin, Formerly London Editor, 'Times of Ceylon', *Ceylon*

Robert David Hodgson, Assistant Geographer, U.S. Department of State, *Luxemburg; Monaco*

Jerome Holtzman, Sportswriter, 'Chicago Sun-Times', *Basketball; Football*

Oscar H. Horst, Professor of Geography, Western Michigan University, *Guatemala*

Louis Hotz, Formerly Editorial Writer, 'The Johannesburg Star', *South Africa*

Audrey M. Hudson, Assistant to National Public Relations Director, Camp Fire Girls, Inc., *Youth Organizations* (in part)

David Huelin, Manager, Economic Intelligence Department, Bank of London and South America Ltd., London, *Latin America* (in part)

Stephen Hughes, Reuter's Correspondent, *Morocco*

Kenneth Ingham, Professor of Modern History, University of Bristol, England, *Congo, Democratic Republic of the; Equatorial Guinea; Kenya; Malawi; Rhodesia; Tanzania; Uganda; Zambia*

John Edward Ingle, Law and Justice Topic Editor, 'National Journal', *Burger, Warren E.*

(William) Harold Ingrams, Formerly Adviser on Overseas Information, Colonial Office, London, *Gambia; Sierra Leone*

Stanley S. Jados, Professor of Political Science, De Paul University, Chicago, *United States* (in part)

Bernard R. Kantor, Chairman, Division of Cinema, and Associate Dean, School of Performing Arts, University of Southern California, *Motion Pictures*

Maud Karpeles, Honorary President, International Folk Music Council, Kingston, Ont., *Popular Music* (in part)

William A. Katz, Professor, School of Library Science, State University of New York, *Magazines*

John Arnold Kelleher, Editor, 'The Dominion', Wellington, *New Zealand*

Peter Kilner, Editor, 'Arab Report and Record', *Sudan*

Jon Kimche, Editor, 'The New Middle East', and Expert on Middle East Affairs, 'Evening Standard', London, *Israel; Meir, Golda*

Joshua B. Kind, Associate Professor of Art History, Northern Illinois University, De Kalb, *Museums*

Resa W. King, Contributing Editor, 'Business Week', *Business and Industry*

Hugh John Klare, Secretary, Howard League for Penal Reform, London, *Prisons*

Alfred Paul Klausler, Executive Secretary, Associated Church Press, *Religion* (in part)

Jean Marcel Knecht, Assistant Foreign Editor, 'Le Monde', Paris, *France*

Ole Ferdinand Knudsen, Editor, 'Norway Exports', Oslo, *Norway*

Hans Kohn, Emeritus Professor of History, City College of New York, *Communist Movement*

Richard Kostelanetz, Author, Critic, and Cultural Historian, *Popular Music SPECIAL REPORT: Today's Rock Sound*

Valdimar Kristinsson, Editor, 'Fjármálatidindi', *Iceland*

Geoffrey Charles Last, Adviser, Imperial Ethiopian Ministry of Education and Fine Arts, Addis Ababa, *Ethiopia*

Wilma Laws, Journalist, London, and Member of International Association of Art Critics, *Painting and Sculpture*

Chapin R. Leinbach, Information Services, Air Transport Association of America, *Transportation* (in part)

Arnold E. Levitt, Senior Associate Editor, 'Chemical and Engineering News', *Chemistry*

Ioan Myrddin Lewis, Professor of Anthropology, London School of Economics, University of London, *Somalia*

Raymond Basil Lewry, Economic Research Officer, Bank of London and South America Ltd., London, *Colombia; Ecuador*

Jerry Lipson, Reporter, 'Chicago Daily News', *Post Office, United States*

Frank Litsky, Assistant to the Sports Editor, 'The New York Times', *Swimming*

Herbert R. Lottman, Contributing Editor, 'Publishers' Weekly', and Contributor to 'The New York Times Book Review', 'Cultural Affairs', *Publishing, Book* (in part)

Commander Terry McDonald, Chief, Public Information Division, U.S. Coast Guard, *Armed Forces, United States* (in part)

Irene McManus, Assistant Editor, 'American Forests' Magazine, *Forest Products; Recreation*

Tom McNally, Outdoor Editor, 'Chicago Tribune', *Fishing and Hunting*

Norris McWhirter, Television Commentator, British Broadcasting Corp., London, *Track and Field* (in part)

Katharine A. Mahon, Public Relations Director, Girls Clubs of America, Inc., *Youth Organizations* (in part)

Hugh Michael Finer Mallett, Editor, 'Weekly Wool Chart', Bradford, England, *Textiles* (in part)

Andrew J. A. Mango, Orientalist and Broadcaster, *Turkey*

William Arthur Peete Manser, Consultant, International Iron and Steel Institute, Brussels, *Metals; Mines and Mining; World Trade*

Peter (John) Mansfield, Formerly Middle East Correspondent, 'The Sunday Times', London, *Iraq; Jordan; Lebanon; Middle East; Saudi Arabia; Southern Yemen; Syria; United Arab Republic; Yemen*

Aldo Marcello, Civil Engineer, *Engineering Projects* (in part)

Marine Corps, Division of Information, *Armed Forces, United States* (in part)

Joseph William Marlow, Lawyer, *Chronology* (in part)

Jerome Mazzaro, Author and Professor of English, State University of New York at Buffalo, *Literature*

Michael G. Messer, District Editor, 'The Oil and Gas Journal', *Fuel and Power* (in part)

The Rev. John Meyendorff, Professor of Church History and Patristics, St. Vladimir's Seminary, Tuckahoe, N.Y., *Religion* (in part)

Arthur M. Mikesell, Assistant Director of Public Relations, American Bankers Association, *Banks*

Raymond Spencer Millard, Deputy Director, Road Research Laboratory, Ministry of Transport, Crowthorne, Berkshire, England, *Engineering Projects* (in part)

Sandra Millikin, Assistant Curator of Drawings, Royal Institute of British Architects, London, *Architecture* (in part)

Mario (S.) Modiano, Correspondent, 'The Times' (London), Athens, *Greece*

Evelyn Monte, Director, Gaines Dog Research Center, *Pets* (in part)

Hazel Romola Morgan, Assistant to Administrative Manager, International Sales Division, E.M.I. Records, London, *Popular Music* (in part)

Horace Denton Morgan, Senior Partner, Sir William Halcrow and Partners, *Engineering Projects* (in part)

Molly Mortimer, Journalist on Commonwealth and International Affairs, *Botswana; Burundi; Commonwealth of Nations; Ghana; Lesotho; Maldives, Republic of; Mauritius; Nigeria; Rwanda; Swaziland; West Indies* (in part)

George Saul Mottershead, Director-Secretary, Chester Zoo, England, *Zoo*

Pauline G. Mower, Information Director, Future Homemakers of America, Washington, D.C., *Youth Organizations* (in part)

Stephanie Mullins, Historian, *West Indies* (in part)

Martin Patrick Myrieckes, Shodan (First Degree), Kendo and Karate-Do, *Sports Champions SPECIAL REPORT: The Art of Self-Defense* (in part)

Edward Harwood Nabb, Vice-President, Union of International Motorboating, *Boats and Boating*

Raymond K. Neal, Assistant to the Director, Editorial Service, Boy Scouts of America, *Youth Organizations* (in part)

John Neill, Chemical Engineer and Author of Climbers' Club Guides 'Cwm Silyn and Tremadoc' and 'Snowdon South' and Alpine Club Guide 'Selected Climbs in the Pennine Alps', *Mountain Climbing*

Bert Nelson, Publisher, 'Track and Field News', *Track and Field* (in part)

Bruce Carlton Netschert, Director, National Economic Research Associates, Inc., Washington, D.C., *Fuel and Power* (in part)

Blake T. Newton, Jr., President, Institute of Life Insurance, *Insurance*

Edwin Bohannon Newton, Formerly Manager, Advanced Rubber Technology, B. F. Goodrich Co., *Rubber*

Laurence H. Nobles, Professor of Geology, Northwestern University, *Earth Sciences* (in part)

Julius Novick, Assistant Professor of English, New York University, Guest Lecturer, Drama Division, Juilliard School, and Drama Critic, 'Village Voice', *Theater*

Arden W. Ohl, Instructor of Geography, Modesto (Calif.) Junior College, *Nicaragua*

Frederick I. Ordway, Director, Science and Technology Applications and Evaluation Research Institute, University of Alabama, *Space Exploration* (in part)

Jane H. Overton, Associate Professor of Biology, University of Chicago, *Biology*

Rafael Pargas, Computer Operator, National Geographic Society, *Philippines*

Sandy Parker, Fur Editor, 'Women's Wear Daily', *Furs*

Vernon John Parry, Reader in the History of the Near and Middle East, School of Oriental and African Studies, University of London, *Cyprus*

Alexander Paton, *Medicine* (in part)

Oglesby Paul, Chief, Division of Medicine, Passavant Memorial Hospital, Chicago, *Medicine* (in part)

Robin Charles Penfold, Public Relations Executive, Carl Byior and Associates Ltd., London, *Synthetics*

Virgil W. Peterson, Executive Director, Chicago Crime Commission, *Crime; Police*

Eugene Edwin Pfaff, Professor of History, University of North Carolina at Greensboro, *Europe* (in part); *International Relations*

David Kemsley Robert Phillips, Assistant Editor, 'World Sports', *Sports Champions of 1969*

Otto Pick, Reader in International Relations, University of Surrey, England, *Union of Soviet Socialist Republics*

Frederick P. Pittera, Chairman, International Exposition Consultants Co., and Director, New Nations Exposition and Development Corp., *Fairs and Shows*

Dan Q. Posin, Professor of Physics and Physical Sciences, and Chairman of the Department of Interdisciplinary Sciences, San Francisco State College, *Physics*

Martin C. Powers, Chief, Creative Services, Public Affairs, U.S. Office of Economic Opportunity, *Poverty, War on*

Holenarasipur Y. Sharada Prasad, Deputy Information Adviser, Prime Minister's Secretariat, New Delhi, *India*

Manuel Pulgar, Senior Economic Research Officer, Bank of London and South America Ltd., London, *Mexico; Spain*

Howard Pyle, President, National Safety Council, *Safety*

Margaret H. Quinn, Reporter, 'Sun-Gazette', Williamsport, Pa., *Baseball* (in part)

Charles Edgar Randall, Assistant Editor, 'Journal of Forestry', *Forest Products*

Mahinder Singh Randhava, Sub-editor, 'The Straits Times', Kuala Lumpur, *Malaysia; Singapore*

Robert John Ranger, Lecturer in Politics, University of Aberdeen, *Defense*

Vivian Foster Raven, Editor, 'Tobacco', *Tobacco*

Randolph Richard Rawlins, Research Associate, Instituto para la Integración de América Latina, Buenos Aires, *Guyana*

Joseph Lee Reid, Research Oceanographer, Scripps Institution of Oceanography, La Jolla, Calif., *Oceanography*

A. Daniel Reuwee, Director of Information, Future Farmers of America, *Youth Organizations* (in part)

Richard K. Richards, Professor of Pharmacology, Northwestern University Medical School, Chicago, and Editor of 'Clinical Evaluation of Drugs', *Drugs; Medicine* (in part)

Francis Allen Riddell, State Archaeologist for California, *Archaeology* (in part)

Wallace B. Riley, Computers Editor, 'Electronics', McGraw-Hill Publications, Inc., *Computers; Electronics*

David Jonathan Robinson, Economic Research Officer, Bank of London and South America Ltd., London, *Peru*

David Julien Robinson, Film Critic, 'The Financial Times', *Motion Pictures* (in part)

Leif J. Robinson, Associate Editor, 'Sky and Telescope', Sky Publishing Corp., *Astronomy*

Alan Raymond Roe, Research Officer, Department of Applied Economics, Cambridge University, England, *Money and International Finance*

Evelyn Gita Rose, Cookery Editor, 'Jewish Chronicle'; Home Economics Consultant; Broadcaster; and Food Historian, *Home Economics; Interior Decoration*

Robert L. Ross, Manager, Adela Investment Company, Lima, Peru, *Chile*

Philip Morton Rowe, Press Officer, British Man-Made Fibres Federation, Manchester, *Textiles* (in part)

Frank Ferdinand Roxborough, Lecturer in Mining Engineering, University of Newcastle upon Tyne, *Fuel and Power* (in part)

Nicholas Ruggieri, Assistant Public Affairs Adviser, U.S. Arms Control and Disarmament Agency, *Disarmament*

Al Salerno, Director, American Heart Association, Inc., *Medicine* (in part)

Carl Fredrik Sandelin, Foreign News Editor, Finnish News Agency, and President, Society of Swedish-Speaking Writers in Finland, *Finland*

Hidehiko Sazanami, Chief, Urban Facilities Research Group, Building Research Institute, Ministry of Construction, Tokyo, *Housing*

Stephan E. Schattmann, Economist, London, *Germany, East*

Gretchen Knief Schenk, Library Consultant, *Libraries* (in part)

William Scholz, Director of Public Relations, American Hotel & Motel Association, *Hotels and Motels*

Byron T. Scott, Editor, 'Today's Health' Magazine, American Medical Association, *Medicine* (in part)

Joel Segall, Professor of Finance, Graduate School of Business, University of Chicago, *Business and Industry SPECIAL REPORT: The Conglomerate*

Peter Shackleford, Research Officer, International Union of Official Travel Organizations, Geneva, *Travel*

Mitchell R. Sharpe, Jr., Science Writer, *Armstrong, Neil A.; Space Exploration* (in part)

Harvey R. Sherman, Research Associate, Legislative Reference, Library of Congress, *Agriculture* (in part); *Food*

Robert Sherrill, Washington Correspondent, 'The Nation' Magazine, *Defense SPECIAL REPORT: Military Values Revisited*

Frank Silvey, Journalist 2nd Class, U.S. Navy, and Staff Writer, 'All Hands' Magazine, The Bureau of Naval Personnel Career Publication, *Armed Forces, United States* (in part)

Elaine C. Smith, Assistant Director of Information, Cooperative League of the USA, *Cooperatives*

John Jervis Smith, Research Officer, Economic Intelligence Department, Bank of London and South America Ltd., London, *Bolivia; Paraguay*

Raymond Daniel Smith, Publisher, 'Cats Magazine', *Pets* (in part)

J. Frederick Smithcors, Associate Editor, American Veterinary Publications, Inc., Santa Barbara, Calif., *Veterinary Medicine*

Kazimierz Maciej Smogorzewski, Founder and Editor, 'Free Europe', London, and Writer on Contemporary History, *Albania; Bulgaria; Hungary; Intelligence Operations; Mongolian People's Republic; Poland; Romania*

Ida Sloan Snyder, Associate and News Director, Bureau of Communications, Young Women's Christian Association of the United States of America, *Youth Organizations* (in part)

Leonard M. Snyder, Director, Interpretation Services, Young Men's Christian Association, *Youth Organizations* (in part)

Wallace Sokolsky, Assistant Professor, History Department, Bronx Community College, the New School for Social Research, New York University, Division of Adult Education, *Africa*

Melanie F. Staerk, Head, Press Service, Swiss National Commission for UNESCO, *Switzerland*

Sam Stanley, Program Coordinator, Center for the Study of Man, Smithsonian Institution, *Indians, American*

E. J. Stapleton, Director of Public Information, Boys' Clubs of America, *Youth Organizations* (in part)

Phyllis B. Steckler, Director of Bibliography, R. R. Bowker Co., and Editor, 'Textbooks in Print' and 'Children's Books for Schools and Libraries', *Publishing, Book* (in part)

Douglas R. Stephenson, Manager, Information Services, Public Relations Department, Association of American Railroads, *Transportation* (in part)

Geoffrey Howard Stern, Lecturer in International Relations, London School of Economics and Political Science, University of London, *Yugoslavia*

Tom Stevenson, Garden Columnist, 'Baltimore News American', 'Washington Post', and 'Los Angeles Times', *Flowers and Gardens*

Zena Bailey Sutherland, Editor, 'Bulletin of the Center for Children's Books', University of Chicago, and Editor, Books for Young People, 'Saturday Review', *Literature, Children's*

Richard N. Swift, Head, Department of Politics, New York University, New York City, *United Nations*

Sol Taishoff, President, Editor, and Publisher, 'Broadcasting', *Television and Radio* (in part)

Arthur Tattersall, Cotton Trade Expert and Statistician, Manchester, England, *Textiles* (in part)

Harold Anthony Taylor, Air Transport Editor, 'Flight International', London, 1964–69, *Transportation* (in part)

Walter Terry, Dance Critic, 'Saturday Review', *Dance*

William Harford Thomas, Managing Editor, 'Manchester Guardian', *Great Britain*

Anthony Thompson, General Secretary, International Federation of Library Associations, *Libraries* (in part)

Norman Samuel Thompson, Professor of Business Education and Chairman, Department of Business Education, Eastern Washington State College, *Consumer Protection; Economy*

Lancelot Oliver Tingay, Lawn Tennis Correspondent, 'The Daily Telegraph', London, *Tennis*

Jack F. Tolbert, Public Affairs Officer, U.S. Air Force, *Armed Forces, United States* (in part)

Jeanne Toomey, Media Specialist, Public Affairs Division, Girl Scouts of the U.S.A., *Youth Organizations* (in part)

Edward Townsend, Associate Editor of 'Business Week', *Labor Unions*

John Trevelyan, Secretary, British Board of Film Censors, *Motion Pictures SPECIAL REPORT: How Far Can We Go?*

Melvin M. Tumin, Professor of Sociology and Anthropology, Princeton University, *Race Relations*

Govindan Unny, Correspondent, Agence France-Presse, Bangkok, *Thailand*

Pierre Viansson-Ponté, Political News Editor, 'Le Monde', Paris, *Pompidou, Georges*

John R. Vosburgh, Chief, Branch of Features, Division of Information, National Park Service, U.S. Department of the Interior, *National Park Service*

David McCall Walsten, Senior Editor, 'Britannica Junior Encyclopaedia', *Insects and Pesticides; Ships and Shipping; Stocks and Bonds*

Percy Ainsworth Ward-Thomas, Golf Correspondent, 'Manchester Guardian', *Golf*

Laurence Frederic Rushbrook Williams, C. B. E., Professor of Modern Indian History, Allahabad, India, 1914–19, and Editor of 'Handbook to India, Pakistan, Burma, and Ceylon', *Afghanistan; Iran; Pakistan*

Murat Willis Williams, Formerly U.S. Ambassador to El Salvador, *El Salvador*

Trevor Williamson, Sports Sub-editor, 'The Daily Telegraph', London, *Soccer*

David K. Willis, Tokyo Bureau, 'The Christian Science Monitor', *Chronology* (in part); *Japan SPECIAL REPORT: Expo '70*

Alan David Wilson, Assistant Editor, 'Sweden Now', *Sweden*

Dorothy Woodman, Contributor on Asian Affairs, 'New Statesman', London, *Burma; Nepal*

Richard Worsnop, Writer, Editorial Research Reports, Washington, D.C., *Foreign Policy, United States; Kissinger, Henry A.; Liberia; Nixon, Richard M.; United States*

Almon R. Wright, Retired Senior Historian, U.S. Department of State, *Panama*

Stanley Faust Yolles, M.D., Director, National Institute of Mental Health, Chevy Chase, Md., *Mental Health*

Paul Ziemer, Copy Editor, 'Chicago Today', *Congress, United States; Political Parties*

Arnold J. Zurcher, Professor of Comparative Politics, Graduate School of Arts and Sciences, New York University, *Europe* (in part)

Compton's Pictured Highlights and Chronology of 1969

ABOVE: DAN MCCOY FROM BLACK STAR
FACING PAGE—TOP LEFT: FRED WARD FROM BLACK STAR. TOP RIGHT: CONSTANTINE MANOS FROM MAGNUM.
BOTTOM: JAMES PICKERELL FROM BLACK STAR

DICK SWANSON FROM BLACK STAR

Crew members of the intelligence ship USS Pueblo *enter a helicopter, following their release by North Korea in late December 1968. A Navy court of inquiry, convened in January 1969 to determine whether any of the crew had violated the Code of Conduct for servicemen, recommended that two officers be court-martialed. Secretary of the Navy John H. Chafee stated that no action would be taken.*

JANUARY

1 France's President Charles de Gaulle condemns the 1968 Israeli raid on the Beirut, Lebanon, airport.

2 Fidel Castro, premier of Cuba, celebrates the tenth anniversary of the Cuban revolution.

3 Senator Edward M. Kennedy of Massachusetts defeats Senator Russell B. Long of Louisiana for the post of U.S. Senate Democratic whip.

A draft of the new Chinese Communist party constitution reaches Western sources; the document names Defense Minister Lin Piao as heir apparent to Politburo Chairman Mao Tse-tung.

4 Protestant extremists battle Roman Catholics in Northern Ireland; some 100 persons are injured.

5 Henry Cabot Lodge is named by U.S. President-elect Richard M. Nixon to head the U.S. negotiating team at the Vietnam peace talks in Paris, France.

The Soviet Union launches a 2,500-pound unmanned spacecraft on a four-month journey to Venus; the capsule is expected to make a soft landing.

7 A representative assembly of Dutch Roman Catholics challenges the pope's right to decide on the morality of birth control.

In Los Angeles, Calif., Sirhan Bishara Sirhan goes on trial, charged with first-degree murder in the June 5, 1968, assassination of Senator Robert F. Kennedy.

Major U.S. banks increase their prime interest rate to 7%.

8 The government of Czechoslovakia imposes new "voluntary" controls on press, radio, and television.

10 Sweden becomes the first West European nation to extend diplomatic recognition to North Vietnam.

14 South Vietnam suggests that the United States begin a gradual withdrawal of troops from South Vietnam at the rate of 10,000 to 20,000 per month.

16 In his annual economic message to Congress, U.S. President Lyndon B. Johnson warns that restraints on inflation should not be the cause of a depression.

Jan Palach, a Czechoslovak student, sets himself on fire in Prague, Czechoslovakia, to protest the Soviet-led occupation of his country.

18 President Johnson approves a bill raising the presidential salary to $200,000 a year.

Bolivia's President René Barrientos Ortuño declares a state of siege and suspends constitutional guarantees.

20 Richard M. Nixon is inaugurated as 37th president of the United States.

Police prevent University of Wisconsin students from entering a campus building following a student strike and riot in February. The disturbances began when students boycotted classes in support of black students' demands.

IRA BLOCK—PIX FROM PUBLIX

24 Senator Kennedy urges that the United States take new steps toward friendly relations with Communist China.

Italy announces a decision to seek diplomatic ties with Communist China.

Antigovernment rioting erupts in Dacca, capital of East Pakistan.

27 Fourteen Iraqi prisoners, including nine Jews, are executed at public hangings in Iraq. The 14 men were charged with spying for Israel.

28 Antigovernment rioting continues in Pakistan.

FEBRUARY

1 Peru and the Soviet Union establish diplomatic relations for the first time since 1917.

2 France's President De Gaulle announces a spring referendum on Senate and regional reform.

3 Eduardo Chivambo Mondlane, president of the Mozambique Liberation Front, is assassinated in Dar es Salaam, Tanzania.

5 President Nixon asks the U.S. Senate to ratify the Treaty on the Non-Proliferation of Nuclear Weapons.

The United States agrees to a French proposal for a "big four" approach to the Middle East crisis.

Oil and gas bubble to the surface from a leaking well in the Santa Barbara Channel off the coast of California in January. The leak resulted in a huge oil slick that covered beaches and threatened wildlife in many shoreline areas.

PETER BURSARI FOR CAMERA 5

A British frigate lies at anchor off the coast of Anguilla after carrying British paratroops from Antigua to occupy the Caribbean island in March. Troops were sent to restore order and stability after Anguilla declared itself a republic.

LYNN PELHAM FROM RAPHO GUILLUMETTE

7 Brazil's President Artur da Costa e Silva recesses the legislatures of five states and expels 33 federal legislators.

9 East Germany announces restrictions barring land travel to West Berlin by all delegates to West Germany's presidential election.

11 The death toll rises to 43 persons on the third day of rioting in Bombay, India.

13 India's ruling Congress party suffers defeats in state elections in the Punjab and West Bengal but retains some strength in Uttar Pradesh and Bihar.

The Soviet Union again warns West Germany not to hold its presidential election in West Berlin.

14 President Mohammed Ayub Khan of Pakistan agrees to lift the state of emergency imposed in 1965 and to release opposition leader Zulfikar Ali Bhutto.

15 Ian D. Smith, prime minister of Rhodesia, unveils a new constitution, creating a racially segregated electorate.

The United States announces a balance-of-payments surplus for 1968—the first in 11 years.

17 The price of gold in Paris reaches a new high of $46.32 per ounce.

18 Six persons are injured as Arab guerrillas fire on an

Israeli El Al jet liner at the Zurich, Switzerland, airport.

19 The United States calls for restraint in the Middle East and asks for new ways to prevent attacks on commercial airliners.

20 In defiance of Soviet threats, Heinrich Lübke, president of West Germany, is flown to West Berlin in a U.S. Air Force plane.

23 President Nixon leaves Washington, D.C., for Brussels, Belgium, his first stop in an eight-day visit to Europe.

24 The United States launches an unmanned Mariner 6 spacecraft on a 220-million-mile flight toward Mars.

26 Israel's Prime Minister Levi Eshkol, 73, dies following a heart attack. Deputy Prime Minister Yigal Allon is named as acting prime minister.

27 President Nixon visits West Berlin and reaffirms the U.S. commitment there.

28 Paris demonstrators stage hit-and-run stone-throwing raids to protest the visit of President Nixon.

Cuba announces full diplomatic recognition of the National Liberation Front (NLF) of South Vietnam, becoming the first country to do so.

23 In the face of mounting violence, President Ayub Khan of Pakistan appeals to his people to save their country.

24 Joseph Kasavubu, first president of the Democratic Republic of the Congo, dies in Boma, the Congo.

25 Pakistan's President Ayub Khan steps down and turns the government over to army commander Gen. Agha Mohammed Yahya Khan.

28 Dwight David Eisenhower, 34th president of the United States, dies in Washington, D.C., at the age of 78.

29 The Soviet Union asks Communist China to negotiate differences on border problems.

31 General Yahya Khan becomes president of Pakistan, declaring that he will step down as soon as constitutional rule is restored in the country.

MARCH

1 A New Orleans, La., jury acquits Clay L. Shaw of the charge of conspiring to assassinate the late U.S. President John F. Kennedy.

2 Following a meeting with Pope Paul VI, President Nixon returns to Washington, D.C., from his European tour.

3 Three U.S. astronauts aboard Apollo 9 are launched into earth orbit to test the lunar-landing craft.

5 Gustav Heinemann, a Social Democrat, is elected president of West Germany.

7 In Moscow, U.S.S.R., huge crowds surround the Communist Chinese Embassy to protest alleged Chinese attacks on Soviet troops at the Ussuri River border.

The Apollo 9 lunar module docks successfully with the "mother" craft.

9 In a second day of fighting along the Suez Canal, Gen. Abdel Moneim Riad, chief of staff of the United Arab Republic (UAR), or Egypt, is killed.

10 Before a Memphis, Tenn., jury, James Earl Ray pleads guilty to the charge of slaying the Rev. Martin Luther King, Jr. Ray is sentenced to 99 years in jail.

Communist forces fire heavy rockets into Hue, South Vietnam, the former imperial capital.

11 Workers in France stage a 24-hour strike to support demands for a wage increase of up to 12%.

13 The three Apollo 9 astronauts make a near-perfect landing in the Atlantic Ocean.

The U.S. Senate ratifies the nuclear nonproliferation treaty by a vote of 83–15.

14 President Nixon announces that he has approved plans for a modified ABM (antiballistic missile) system.

Communist forces rain rockets on Hue and stage mortar attacks on other South Vietnamese cities.

17 Golda Meir, former foreign minister, is sworn in as prime minister of Israel, succeeding the late Levi Eshkol.

APRIL

1 The long-delayed Ninth Congress of the Chinese Communist Party opens in Peking, People's Republic of China.

2 Twenty-one members of the U.S. Black Panther party are indicted in New York City on charges of planning to bomb stores and police headquarters.

3 The U.S. Federal Reserve System's Board of Governors raises its discount rate from 5.5% to 6%—the highest in 40 years.

Canada announces it will reduce its troop strength in Western Europe but will remain in the North Atlantic Treaty Organization (NATO).

Israel expresses opposition to the "big four" Middle East peace talks beginning at United Nations (UN) headquarters in New York City.

7 At his first press conference, Secretary of State William P. Rogers declares that the United States does not expect to withdraw unilaterally from South Vietnam.

8 President Nixon confers in Washington, D.C., with King Hussein I of Jordan.

9 At Harvard University, Cambridge, Mass., about 300 students seize the main administration building.

10 NATO announces a major series of maneuvers in the Mediterranean Sea as the Soviet Union increases its Mediterranean fleet to about 40 ships.

Jordan's King Hussein proposes a six-point plan for peace in the Middle East. Israel rejects the plan the following day.

11 An Ecuadorian airliner is hijacked to Cuba.

15 Great Britain unveils a new budget increasing taxes for an already heavily taxed public.

17 Gustav Husak replaces Alexander Dubcek as Czechoslovak Communist party first secretary.

Sirhan B. Sirhan is found guilty of first-degree murder in the 1968 slaying of Senator Kennedy.

Bernadette Devlin, from Londonderry, Northern Ireland, at 21 becomes the youngest member of Britain's House of Commons.

20 Armed black students end their occupation of the student Union at Cornell University, Ithaca, N.Y.

In Athens, Greece, military leaders celebrate the second anniversary of their seizure of power.

A meeting of the Organization of African Unity (OAU) Consultative Committee on Nigeria fails in an effort toward ending the Nigerian civil war.

21 British troops are sent to guard public utilities in Northern Ireland.

23 The Nigerian federal government announces the capture of Umuahia, the administrative center of Biafra.

Jurors pronounce a death sentence for Sirhan B. Sirhan, convicted of the murder of Senator Kennedy.

Dissident black and Puerto Rican students close down City College in New York City.

27 Bolivia's President Barrientos dies in a helicopter accident in the Bolivian interior.

28 France's President De Gaulle resigns after defeat in a national referendum; Senate President Alain Poher becomes interim president pending an election.

30 Prince Norodom Sihanouk of Cambodia rejects U.S. recognition of Cambodia's frontiers and asks for a seat at the Paris peace talks on Vietnam.

MAY

1 Major James D. Chichester-Clark is elected prime minister of Northern Ireland.

James Forman, representing the National Black Economic Development Conference, meets with Episcopal church leaders and demands that U.S. churches and synagogues pay $500 million in reparations to the nation's black people.

2 UN Secretary-General U Thant proposes that a "safe perimeters" plan be put into effect around UN observer posts along the Suez Canal.

3 President Zakir Husain of India, the first Muslim to hold that office, dies at the age of 72.

6 U.S. Secretary of the Navy John H. Chafee overrules a Navy court of inquiry and states that no action will be taken against any crewman of the USS *Pueblo*, seized by North Koreans in January 1968.

7 Indonesia announces it has quelled a revolt by 30,000 Papuans in West Irian.

9 The Vatican eliminates 200 saints from the Roman Catholic liturgical calendar, including St. Valentine and St. Christopher.

12 Communist forces launch their biggest wave of attacks in South Vietnam since February 1968.

13 More than a week of Malay-Chinese fighting begins in Kuala Lumpur, Federation of Malaysia, following the elections of May 10.

15 Abe Fortas becomes the first U.S. Supreme Court associate justice to resign under public pressure focused on unethical behavior.

16 The Soviet Venera 5 spacecraft descends toward the surface of Venus, then loses radio contact. Venera 6 does likewise the following day.

18 The U.S. Apollo 10 astronauts relay the first live color telecast of the earth as they speed toward the moon after blast-off from Cape Kennedy, Fla.

WIDE WORLD

Armed black students file out of Cornell University's student Union, which they seized in April to protest university treatment of black demonstrators. Students occupying the building demanded that all judicial proceedings against the demonstrators be dropped.

20 Allied forces in South Vietnam capture Ap Bia Mountain (Hamburger Hill), touching off protests by war critics in Washington, D.C.

21 Judge Herbert V. Walker refuses to reverse the death sentence for Sirhan B. Sirhan, convicted of the murder of Senator Kennedy.

President Nixon nominates Warren Earl Burger as chief justice of the United States. The U.S. Senate confirms the appointment on June 9.

The Soviet Union displays its needle-nosed TU-144, the world's first commercial supersonic airliner, to the foreign press.

23 Peru cancels a planned visit by New York's Gov. Nelson A. Rockefeller after the United States suspends sales of military equipment to that country.

Pierre Elliott Trudeau, Canada's prime minister, speaks out against the U.S. ABM system.

Japan and the Mongolian People's Republic are invited to become members of the 18-Nation Committee on Disarmament.

25 President Nguyen Van Thieu of South Vietnam forms a six-party coalition group in Saigon, the capital.

Prime Minister Mohammed Ahmed Mahgoub of Sudan is overthrown by a leftist military coup.

26 James Earl Ray's request for a new trial is denied following his conviction on charges of killing the Rev. Martin Luther King, Jr.

28 U.S. troops abandon Hamburger Hill in South Vietnam.

30 Riots begin on the island of Curaçao, Netherlands Antilles, resulting in the downfall of the government of Prime Minister Ciro de Kroon.

JUNE

2 Governor Rockefeller returns from a second fact-finding visit to Latin America after encountering riots in Colombia, Ecuador, and Bolivia.

The destroyer USS *Frank E. Evans* collides with the Australian aircraft carrier HMAS *Melbourne* in the South China Sea; 73 men lose their lives.

4 Several bombs fall on Port-au-Prince, Haiti; the government places the blame on Cuba.

Mexican tennis star Rafael Osuna is among 79 persons killed in an airline crash near Monterrey, Mexico.

5 The Conference of Communist and Workers' Parties, attended by 75 delegations, opens in Moscow.

Kiichi Aichi, Japan's foreign minister, ends a four-day visit to Washington, D.C., to open talks on the return of Okinawa to Japanese administration.

6 The Soviet Union warns Arab guerrillas against using force to recapture land lost in the Arab-Israeli war of 1967.

7 Communist China agrees to meet with the Soviet Union on June 18 to discuss navigation on border rivers.

8 President Nixon announces at Midway island that 25,000 U.S. troops will be withdrawn from South Vietnam by August 31.

10 Pope Paul VI visits Geneva, Switzerland, and addresses the World Council of Churches.

The National Liberation Front (NLF) announces a new provisional revolutionary government in South Vietnam.

13 The Soviet Union recognizes the NLF provisional revolutionary government in South Vietnam.

15 Georges Pompidou is elected president of France with 58.2% of the vote, against 41.8% for Alain Poher.

16 The U.S. Supreme Court rules 7–1 that the House of Representatives acted unconstitutionally in excluding Representative Adam Clayton Powell (D, N.Y.) from the 90th Congress in 1967.

Communist China and Czechoslovakia sign a 1969 trade agreement increasing trade flows by 11%.

17 South Korea announces the killing or capture of 15 North Korean commandos who tried to infiltrate that country.

20 Jacques Chaban-Delmas is appointed premier of France by President Pompidou.

Voters in Rhodesia approve a new constitution that

In June 1969 Charles Evers was elected mayor of Fayette, Miss. He was the first black mayor of a racially mixed town in the state since reconstruction. His platform included promises to attempt to attract new employers to the area and to obtain federal aid for the city.
WIDE WORLD

COURTESY, CUNARD STEAM-SHIP CO. LTD.

The crew of the new British superliner Queen Elizabeth 2 *tests the ship prior to its first commercial cruise in April. This view of the stern shows the liner's two outdoor swimming pools and its expansive deck space.*

would maintain white supremacy and set up a full-fledged republic.

23 Le Duc Tho, North Vietnam's chief negotiator in Paris, rejects any compromise or setting up of special elections in South Vietnam.

24 A group of African nations are defeated in the UN Security Council in their attempt to urge Great Britain to use force against Rhodesia. The General Assembly, however, passes a similar resolution in November.

25 The U.S. Senate passes a nonbinding resolution opposing any commitment of troops or financial resources abroad without Congressional approval.

26 El Salvador breaks diplomatic relations with Honduras; Honduras reciprocates on June 27.

28 Racial violence flares again between Malays and Chinese in Malaysia; 12 die.

29 Moise Tshombe, former premier of the Democratic Republic of the Congo, dies in an Algerian prison.

JULY

1 Britain's Prince Charles is invested as prince of Wales in ceremonies at Caernarvon Castle, Caernarvon, Wales.

3 Ronald L. Ziegler, White House press secretary, announces that President Nixon has decided not to establish formal diplomatic relations with the Vatican.

5 Tom Mboya, Kenya's minister of economic planning and development, is assassinated on a Nairobi street.

7 Ethiopia's Emperor Haile Selassie I arrives in Washington, D.C., for talks with President Nixon.

8 The first contingent of U.S. troops to pull out of South Vietnam arrives in the United States.

Communist China charges that Soviet gunboats, troops, and planes have crossed the Amur River into Manchuria.

12 A fresh outbreak of clashes between Protestants and Roman Catholics sweeps Northern Ireland.

14 Troops from El Salvador are reported to have invaded Honduras.

16 El Salvador claims the capture of several Honduran towns and calls for the surrender of the Honduran army.

The U.S. Apollo 11 spacecraft is successfully launched, heading for the first manned moon landing.

17 Denmark, Finland, Norway, and Sweden agree to a draft treaty aimed at the eventual formation of a Nordic economic union.

18 A peace mission from the Organization of American States (OAS) obtains the agreement of El Salvador and Honduras to a four-point peace proposal.

19 Senator Edward Kennedy reports that he accidentally drove his car off a bridge on Chappaquiddick Island in Massachusetts. Mary Jo Kopechne, a 28-year-old passenger, drowned in the accident.

20 Apollo 11 astronauts Neil A. Armstrong and Edwin E. Aldrin, Jr., land successfully on the moon. A few hours later, they leave the lunar module; Armstrong is the first man to walk on the moon.

21 Astronauts Armstrong and Aldrin blast off from the moon and link up with the Apollo 11 command module, piloted by astronaut Michael Collins.

22 The U.S. Department of Defense reveals for the first time that lethal nerve-gas munitions have been shipped to U.S. forces overseas.

23 Prince Juan Carlos of Bourbon is formally invested as Spain's future king.

24 The Apollo 11 spacecraft splashes down near its target in the Pacific Ocean and is picked up by the aircraft carrier USS *Hornet.*

Israeli and UAR forces clash along the Suez Canal in the heaviest fighting since the war of June 1967.

26 On the first leg of a nine-day tour of Asia, President Nixon arrives in Manila, Philippines.

28 A $3.1-billion surplus for the fiscal year ending June 30, 1969, is reported by the Nixon Administration.

30 President Nixon pays an unannounced 5½-hour visit to South Vietnam.

31 Pope Paul VI flies to Uganda to address the closing session of the all-African bishops' conference.

AUGUST

1 The U.S. Department of Justice files suit against the state of Georgia to end racial segregation in public schools.

2 President Nixon arrives in Bucharest, Romania, becoming the first U.S. president to visit a Communist country during peacetime.

5 Italy's caretaker Premier Mariano Rumor organizes a

Thousands of Viennese citizens line the streets for a procession to welcome Queen Elizabeth II as she arrived on May 5 to begin a state visit to Austria—the first by a British sovereign since 1903. Austria's President Franz Jonas presented the queen with a pair of Hoflinger horses as a symbol of friendship between the two countries.
KEYSTONE

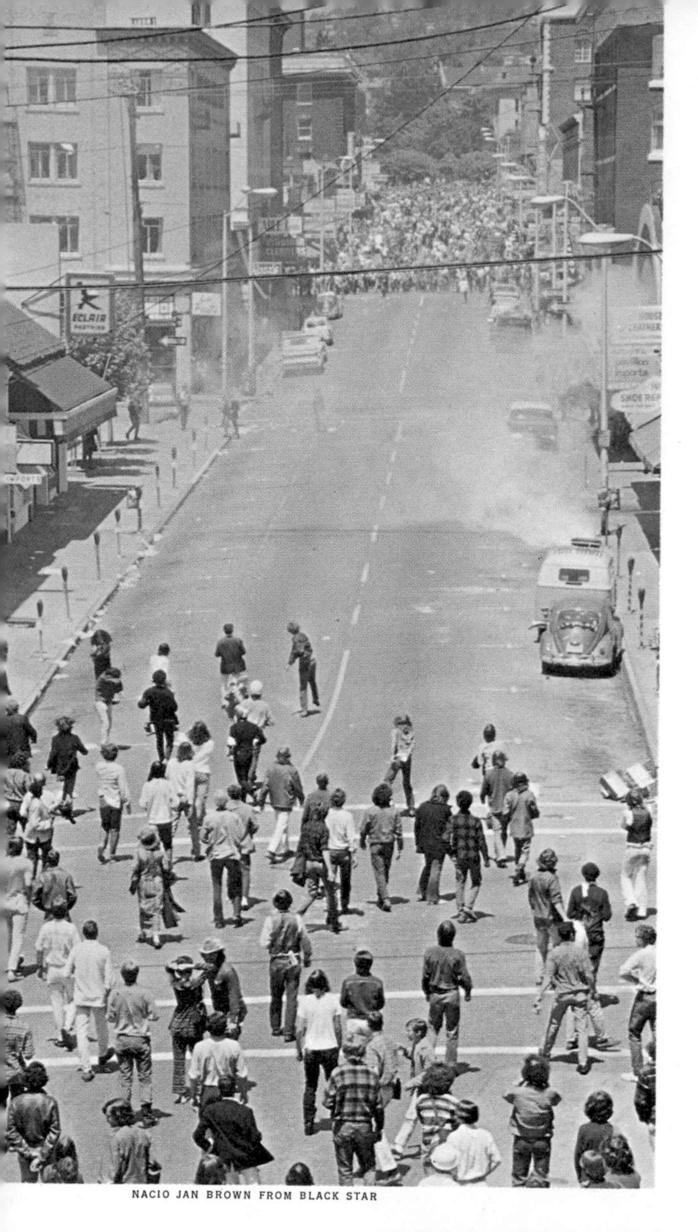

NACIO JAN BROWN FROM BLACK STAR

minority cabinet consisting entirely of Christian Democrats.

6 The U.S. Senate narrowly approves the Nixon Administration's plan for a modified ABM system.

8 In a nationwide address, President Nixon reveals plans for a sweeping overhaul of the U.S. welfare system. The new system would more than double the number of citizens eligible for public assistance.

11 President Kenneth Kaunda of Zambia announces plans for the nationalization of Zambia's copper industry.

13 Violence continues for the second night in the Catholic Bogside area in Londonderry, Northern Ireland.

15 Britain flies troops to Northern Ireland following a night of gunfire in Belfast that has left 4 persons dead and at least 120 injured.

17 Philip Blaiberg, the world's longest-surviving heart-transplant patient, dies in a Cape Town, South Africa, hospital.

18 Hurricane Camille rips through the Gulf coast of Mississippi, leaving some 200 persons dead and causing millions of dollars in damage. President Nixon declares Mississippi a disaster area.

Britain discloses plans to boost its troop strength in Northern Ireland by about 2,000 men.

20 Jamaica becomes the 24th member of the OAS.

21 On the first anniversary of the Soviet-led invasion, thousands of Czechoslovaks gather in Prague's Wenceslaus Square shouting, "Long live Dubcek!" Tear gas and armored cars are used to disperse the crowd.

In Israeli-occupied Jerusalem, the Al Aksa Mosque—

Tear gas spreads across a street near the campus of the University of California at Berkeley as police and National Guard troops opened fire on demonstrators protesting the university's take-over of "People's Park" in May. The tract was owned by the university but was improved into a park by students, hippies, and other nonstudents.

U.S. President Richard M. Nixon stands with Earl Warren (left), who retired in June as chief justice of the United States, and Warren E. Burger (right), who was sworn in as Warren's successor.

FRED WARD FROM BLACK STAR

one of Islam's most sacred shrines—is badly damaged by fire.

22 Denis Michael Rohan, a 28-year-old Australian Christian, is arrested by Israeli police and charged with arson in connection with the fire in the Al Aksa Mosque.

23 Ronald Ziegler announces that as a result of new enemy attacks in South Vietnam, President Nixon has postponed further U.S. troop withdrawals.

25 Foreign ministers of the Arab League nations meet in Cairo, UAR, to consider the implications of Al Aksa Mosque fire.

27 Workers in Argentina defy a warning by the military government and stage a 24-hour nationwide strike.

29 Two commandos of the Popular Front for the Liberation of Palestine hijack a Trans World Airlines (TWA) jet and force it to land in Damascus, Syria.

30 The Syrian government releases 107 of the 113 passengers aboard the hijacked TWA jet.

Brazil's President Costa e Silva suffers a stroke; the government is taken over by a three-member military junta the following day.

This footprint was left in the Sea of Tranquillity on July 20, 1969, when two U.S. astronauts became the first men to set foot on the surface of the moon. Personnel for the Apollo 11 mission included Neil A. Armstrong and Edwin E. Aldrin, Jr., who descended to the lunar surface, and Michael Collins, who remained in the command module as it circled the moon.
COURTESY, NASA

KEYSTONE

A British soldier armed with an automatic rifle guards an intersection in Belfast, Northern Ireland, amid rubble left by riots between militant Catholic and Protestant factions which local police could not control. Troops were called in at first to guard key installations and, finally in August, to keep the opposing groups apart.

CHRISTOPHERSON—AMBASSADOR COLLEGE

SEPTEMBER

1 A revolutionary council takes control of Libya after overthrowing the conservative regime of King Idris I.

2 Official sources state that Communist China is believed to have withdrawn all its labor and engineer battalions from North Vietnam.

3 Israeli jets blast the slopes of Mount Hermon, in Lebanon, where 800 Arab guerrillas are reported to be poised for attack.

North Vietnam's President Ho Chi Minh dies.

4 A three-day cease fire is declared by the Viet Cong to mourn the death of President Ho.

6 Yemeni radio reports that republican forces have captured the royalist rebel stronghold of Sa 'ada, near the Saudi Arabian border.

9 An Israeli armored task force crosses the Gulf of Suez and conducts a ten-hour destructive sweep of UAR coastal positions.

11 Soviet Premier Aleksei N. Kosygin makes an unex-

Buildings along the Gulf coast of Mississippi lie shattered after the area was hit by Hurricane Camille in August. More than 200 deaths there were caused by the storm, the second most violent hurricane ever recorded in the United States.

pected visit to Communist China to confer with China's Premier Chou En-lai.

Israel reports it has shot down 11 UAR planes after UAR air attacks in the Sinai Peninsula set off the heaviest air combat since the 1967 war.

15 The UN Security Council adopts, by a vote of 11–0, a resolution demanding that Israel rescind all measures aimed at altering the status of Jerusalem.

17 Laos government troops are reported to have seized two strategic areas of Laos, long held by pro-Communist forces.

19 Soviet Foreign Minister Andrei A. Gromyko, in a speech to the UN General Assembly, rejects a U.S. call for talks on an arms embargo in the Middle East.

20 Foreign ministers of Australia, New Zealand, the Philippines, South Korea, and Thailand announce that their combined force of 70,000 combat troops in South Vietnam will not be reduced, despite President Nixon's decision to withdraw about 60,000 U.S. soldiers.

22 The premier of Laos, Prince Souvanna Phouma, denies that U.S. forces are fighting in Laos on behalf of his government or that U.S. planes are flying combat missions in tactical support of his armed forces.

24 The trial of eight persons charged with conspiracy to foment a riot during the 1968 Democratic National Convention in Chicago, Ill., begins in a federal district court in Chicago before Judge Julius J. Hoffman.

26 A military junta in Bolivia overthrows the civilian government of President Luis Adolfo Siles Salinas and announces that Gen. Alfredo Ovando Candia, commander in chief of the armed forces, has assumed the presidency.

28 The Czechoslovak Communist party says that Alexander Dubcek, its former chief, has been excluded from the ruling Presidium and will also be removed from chairmanship of the Federal Assembly.

29 Secretary of the Army Stanley R. Resor announces the dropping of charges against six U.S. Special Forces troops (Green Berets) accused of killing an alleged South Vietnamese double agent.

OCTOBER

1 Lebanon expels two Soviet diplomats, shot and arrested by Beirut police for an alleged spy plot on September 30.

Nigeria's leader, Maj. Gen. Yakubu Gowon, an-

Members of the Black P Stone Nation confront Chicago, Ill., police during a "Black Monday" rally at the Civic Center Plaza in September. More than 4,000 Negroes gathered to emphasize their demands for more skilled jobs in the construction trades. A Building Trades Council offer of 1,000 journeyman jobs was turned down on the grounds that it would not meet the needs of the black community.

CHESTER SHEARD

Abbie Hoffman (left) and Jerry Rubin were two of the "Chicago eight" accused of conspiring to incite riots at the 1968 Democratic National Convention. The eight defendants were brought to trial in September in the first test of a new federal law prohibiting interstate travel with the intent to incite riots.
PAUL FENTON FROM NANCY PALMER AGENCY

nounces a collective pardon of Biafran civilians and prisoners of war.

3 The Greek government lifts press censorship and restores some civil rights removed in April 1967.

4 Anthony Grey, Reuter's correspondent in Peking, is freed by Communist China after 26 months in solitary confinement.

Israeli jet planes join a major artillery battle across the Suez Canal in the wake of one of the largest UAR commando raids since the 1967 war.

5 A Cuban pilot lands a Soviet-built MiG-17 near Miami, Fla., and asks for asylum.

7 General Emílio Garrastazú Médici is appointed president of Brazil.

Montreal, Que., police and firemen stage a 20-hour strike; looters and arsonists move in.

8 The "Weatherman" faction of Students for a Democratic Society (SDS) begins a series of violent incidents in Chicago.

12 More British troops are flown to Northern Ireland after shots are fired at soldiers in new rioting.

14 Olof Palme is sworn in to succeed Tage Erlander as prime minister of Sweden.

15 Somalia's President Abdirashid Ali Shermarke is assassinated by a member of the national police.

16 The New York Mets baseball team defeats the Baltimore Orioles 5–3 to win the 1969 World Series.

Three U.S. scientists are awarded the Nobel prize for physiology or medicine.

18 The U.S. Department of Health, Education, and Welfare orders removal of the artificial sweetener cyclamate from the consumer market by Feb. 1, 1970, following tests by the Food and Drug Administration.

20 The Nobel peace prize is awarded to the UN International Labor Organization.

21 Willy Brandt, leader of the Social Democratic party, is elected chancellor of West Germany.

Following army revolts, the Chilean government imposes a state of siege and suspends Congress.

22 Premier Rashid Karami of Lebanon resigns after clashes between Lebanese troops and Palestinian guerrillas.

26 Portugal's ruling National Union wins every National Assembly seat in parliamentary elections allowing opposition candidates for the first time since 1926.

27 Kenyan opposition leader Oginga Odinga is put under house arrest on charges of organizing an antigovernment riot in which 11 persons died on October 25.

28 The Israel Labor party, led by Golda Meir, is returned to power in elections in Israel.

29 The U.S. Supreme Court unanimously rules that school districts must end racial segregation at once.

30 President Nixon asks the U.S. Congress for measures to protect consumers against deceptive sales practices and inferior products.

NOVEMBER

1 Police in Italy arrest U.S. Marine Lance Corp. Raffaele Minichiello, who staged one of the world's most spectacular airplane hijackings—from California to Rome.

India's Congress party formally splits into two factions, one headed by Prime Minister Indira Gandhi and the other by old-guard political leaders.

The National Commission on the Causes and Prevention of Violence issues a report urging drastic revision of the U.S. system of justice, which it calls fragmental, inadequate, and archaic.

3 President Nixon asks the nation for support of his efforts toward peace in Vietnam. He unfolds a plan for the gradual withdrawal of all U.S. combat ground troops from South Vietnam.

Negotiators for Lebanon and the Palestinian commandos announce that they have reached an agreement on ending the discord stemming from commando operations in Lebanon.

4 John V. Lindsay is reelected mayor of New York City.

5 Judge Hoffman convicts Bobby G. Seale, one of the eight "conspiracy" defendants in Chicago, of contempt of court and sentences him to four years in prison.

7 The 52d anniversary of the Bolshevist Revolution is celebrated in Moscow with a traditional military parade in Red Square.

10 Israel reports that all UAR ground-to-air missile sites along the Suez Canal have been destroyed by continuous Israeli air attacks.

11 The UN General Assembly rejects for the 20th time a proposal to expel Nationalist China and give its seat to Communist China.

Torsten Nilsson, Sweden's minister of foreign affairs,

Richard Cragun as Petruchio courts Katherine, danced by Marcia Haydée, in the Stuttgart Ballet's production of 'The Taming of the Shrew', which had its world premiere in March. The company received rave reviews during its tour of the United States later in 1969. Cragun was born in Sacramento, Calif., and took up ballet when he was 11 years old.

COURTESY, HUROK CONCERTS, INC.

DAVID GAHR

More than a thousand peace marchers crowd into New York City's Wall Street on the way from a memorial service at Trinity Church on moratorium day, Oct. 15, 1969. At the service, bankers and brokerage-house executives read from the pulpit the names of U.S. troops killed in Vietnam.

announces that Sweden will begin its three-year economic-aid program to North Vietnam in July 1970.

13 Vice-President Spiro T. Agnew assails news presentations by three major U.S. television networks.

Two Chicago policemen are killed and six others wounded during a gun battle between police and members of the Black Panther party.

14 The U.S. Apollo 12 spacecraft bearing astronauts Alan L. Bean, Charles Conrad, Jr., and Richard F. Gordon, Jr., is successfully launched on its journey to the moon.

17 The United States and the Soviet Union begin preliminary strategic-arms-limitation talks (SALT) in Helsinki, Finland.

18 The appointment of Canada's Undersecretary of State for External Affairs Marcel Cadieux as ambassador to the United States is announced.

19 The UN General Assembly endorses the "act of free choice" decision by West Irian to become part of Indonesia.

Astronauts Conrad and Bean land on the moon in the lunar module and begin the first of two exploring excursions on foot.

20 White House spokesmen announce that Henry Cabot Lodge has resigned as head of the U.S. delegation to the Paris peace talks on Vietnam.

21 President Nixon and Japan's Premier Eisaku Sato reach agreement on the return of Okinawa to Japanese administration in 1972.

The U.S. Senate refuses, by a vote of 55–45, to confirm the nomination of Judge Clement F. Haynsworth, Jr., as an associate justice of the U.S. Supreme Court.

22 Secretary of Defense Melvin R. Laird announces that the January 1970 U.S. draft call, the first to be held under the new lottery system, will total 12,500 men rather than the estimated 35,000.

25 West Germany formally proposes talks with Poland in an effort aimed at improving relations between the two countries.

26 President Nixon signs a bill providing for a lottery system within the U.S. selective service.

27 Arab terrorists throw a hand grenade into the Athens passenger terminal of El Al, the Israeli airline; 15 persons are injured, none of them Israelis.

30 Foreign ministers of Austria and Italy reach an agreement to end a long-standing dispute over Alto Adige, part of South Tyrol.

DECEMBER

1 The U.S. command in Saigon reports that the last of the 60,000 men to be withdrawn by Dec. 15, 1969, have already left Vietnam.

2 A U.S. Army board of inquiry begins closed hearings on the alleged massacre of South Vietnamese civilians at Song My in March 1968.

Leaders of the European Economic Community, or Common Market, agree to begin negotiations during 1970 on membership for Britain.

3 Israeli commandos report that they have destroyed an Arab guerrilla camp in southern Lebanon as a reprisal for the ambush of three Israeli vehicles in the Golan Heights, Syria, several hours earlier.

COURTESY, NASA

4 Two Black Panther party leaders, Fred Hampton and Mark Clark, are killed in a pre-dawn raid by police in Chicago.

5 Military spokesmen for the United States in Saigon confirm that tear gas is being used routinely in South Vietnam.

7 Lebanon's parliament approves the new cabinet of Rashid Karami, ending a political crisis that has lasted for 214 days.

8 Soviet Foreign Minister Gromyko meets with West Germany's Ambassador Helmut Allardt for 90 minutes to discuss their countries' mutual renunciation of the use of force.

10 President Emile Derlin Zinsou of Dahomey is ousted by an army coup d'etat.

11 For the first time in two years, U.S. and Communist Chinese diplomats meet in Warsaw, Poland, to discuss the resumption of ambassadorial talks.

12 Soviet and UAR officials conclude a high-level conference on the Middle East, held in Moscow.

Greece announces its withdrawal from the Council of Europe.

13 The British Foreign and Commonwealth Office discloses that Britain has agreed to withdraw all its forces from Libya by March 31, 1970.

15 Mrs. John Letts, an Englishwoman who has taken fertility drugs, gives birth to sextuplets, five of whom survive.

An Apollo 12 astronaut deploys scientific experiments during man's second landing on the moon, in November 1969. A highlight of the mission was locating the Surveyor 3 spacecraft, which landed on the moon in 1967, and detaching a number of parts to take back to earth for scientific examination.

Riot police with shields face militant students who halted train service and forced offices and stores to close in Tokyo, Japan, on "international antiwar day," in October. The students demanded abrogation of the Japanese-U.S. security treaty, closure of U.S. bases in Japan, and withdrawal of all U.S. troops from Vietnam.

PICTORIAL PARADE

ALAN COPELAND FROM BLACK STAR

American Indians invaded Alcatraz island in San Francisco Bay in November and planned to establish a center for native American studies on the island. The purpose of the take-over, reflecting a new militance among Indians, was to dramatize the injustices suffered by Indians at the hands of the government's Bureau of Indian Affairs. Many sympathetic area residents donated food, and a resolution was introduced to Congress to transfer Alcatraz to Indian ownership.

Los Angeles, Calif., police officers escort Charles M. Manson, described as the leader of a hippie cult, to the city jail in December. Manson and five members of his group were charged with murdering seven persons, including the actress Sharon Tate.
UPI COMPIX

16 Brigadier Gen. Omar Torrijos, the power behind Panama's ruling junta, returns to Panama from Mexico to foil an attempted coup d'etat that would make Col. Ramiro Silvera the new strong man.

18 Britain's House of Lords completes Parliamentary action on a bill to ban the death penalty for murder.

19 The United States eases restrictions on trade with Communist China through a partial lifting of the embargo imposed in 1950.

21 Israeli jets stage a five-hour raid deep into Jordan.

22 The United States and the Soviet Union agree to begin full-scale SALT meetings on April 16, 1970, in Vienna, Austria.

25 Israeli jets raid Egyptian positions along the Suez Canal for 8½ hours.

Pope Paul VI, in his annual Christmas message, warns that humanism without Christianity is futile and self-defeating.

26 Vice-President Agnew begins a 23-day goodwill mission to the Far East.

27 In countrywide elections, controlling power in Japan's House of Representatives is maintained by Premier Sato's Liberal-Democratic party.

30 Negotiators for the United States at the Paris peace talks confront North Vietnam's delegates with a list of 1,046 U.S. men missing in action.

Government officials of France come under public attack for what is termed collusion in allowing Israel to obtain five French-built gunboats despite an arms embargo.

31 The U.S. Army announces that Staff Sgt. David Mitchell will be tried by a general court-martial on charges of assault with intent to murder 30 South Vietnamese civilians during the alleged massacre at Song My.

Bullet holes and a bloodstained bed mark the room where Black Panther Fred Hampton was killed in a police raid in Chicago in December. Police claimed self-defense but black leaders claimed murder.
"CHICAGO SUN-TIMES"

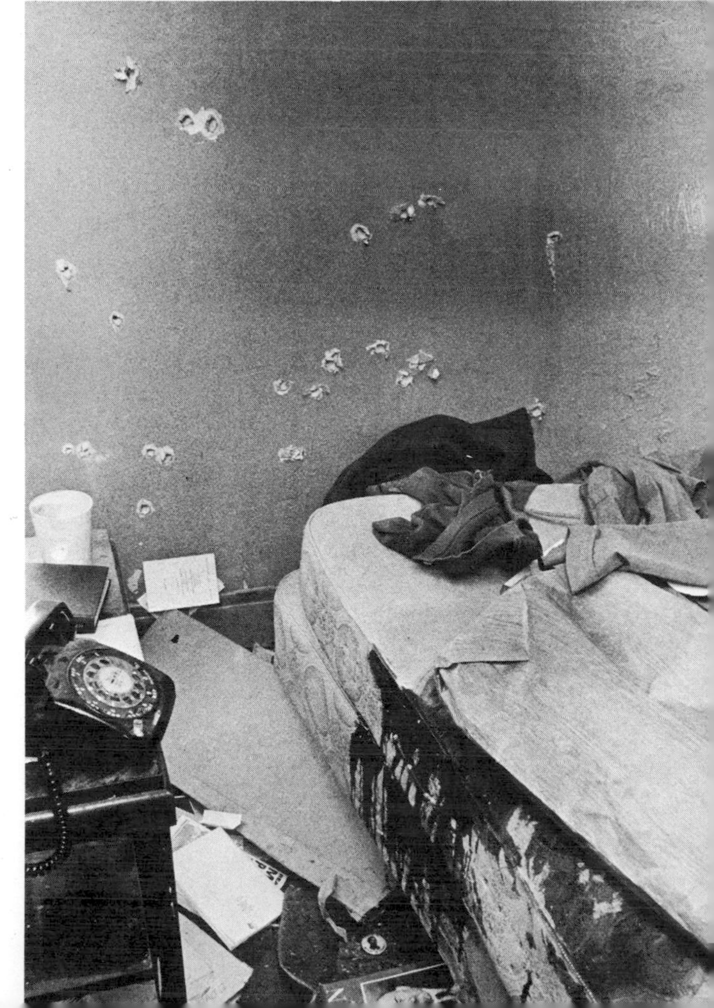

China and the United States: Distorted Images

by SENATOR J. W. FULBRIGHT,
Chairman, Senate Committee on Foreign Relations

At the outset of U.S. President Richard M. Nixon's trip to Asia in July 1969, the U.S. government announced a relaxation in its restrictions on travel and trade with the People's Republic of China. In the official U.S. government announcement, it was also stated that "we would not be surprised if these present decisions were dismissed out of hand." Several days later, without even bothering to comment on the U.S. announcement, the Chinese Communist press agency denounced President Nixon as a "god of plague and war" visiting Asian capitals on a "trip for conducting aggressive activities."

This episode is representative of the hostility of the Chinese leaders toward the United States. It is true, of course, that in the mid-1950's, when the Peking government was encouraging travel to China by U.S. correspondents, U.S. Secretary of State John Foster Dulles was as rigid in his determination to maintain an absolute boycott of Communist China as the Chinese have been in their attitude toward the United States in recent years. (The U.S. policy has been slightly more flexible since the John F. Kennedy Administration.) With the onset of the "cultural revolution" and the Red Guard movement in 1966, however, all travel to China has been radically curtailed and China has withdrawn into self-imposed isolation.

The Chinese leaders have repeatedly rejected U.S. initiatives toward a degree of communication, if not exactly friendship, with insult and invective. In early 1969, for example, the Chinese government canceled a renewal of the long-suspended series of meetings between the Chinese and U.S. ambassadors in Poland. The Chinese took the opportunity to note the inauguration of a new U.S. Administration by describing Presidents Nixon and Lyndon B. Johnson as "jackals of the same lair." The Chinese are intensely hostile to the U.S. intervention in Vietnam and have become convinced—so they say—that the U.S. "imperialists" and the Soviet "revisionists" are in secret collusion for the encirclement, and perhaps even the destruction, of China.

Shall we conclude, as many Americans seem to have concluded, that the Chinese Communists are mad fanatics who can be kept at bay only by superior force? Or is it possible that there are things we do not know, motives that do not meet the eye, which might give us an altered picture of the seemingly fearsome Chinese dragon? Is it not possible, for instance, that the Chinese may sincerely believe that the United States plans to make war on them, even though it is not true? Or that the Soviet Union and the United States are in secret collusion against them, planning their destruction, even though that too has no basis in fact?

Because we have confidence in our own good intentions, it may seem to us that any who accuse us of such monstrous designs must be lying outright. Possibly they are, but before we conclude that the Chinese leaders are liars or madmen, we ought to ask ourselves two questions. First, are our intentions toward China, as reflected in our behavior, really as friendly and generous as we believe them to be? And second, even if our intentions are as good as we think they are, can the Chinese be expected to know that we wish them no harm and to put their trust in us just because we say they should?

After 20 years of mutual fear and hostility China and the United States have profoundly distorted images of each other. It is probably not an exaggeration to say that what each perceives of the other is determined as much by subjective fears as by objective fact. Before we can suggest new policies we must try as best we can to separate fact from fear, identifying and hopefully eliminating the distorted images.

Old and new China meet at the ancient Gate of Heavenly Peace, now covered with political signs and Mao Tse-tung's portrait.

Facts and Images

To most Americans it must seem inexplicable that the Chinese have chosen to regard the United States as an enemy. We have always considered ourselves to be China's true friend, its one Western defender against the greed of the old imperial powers—Russia, Great Britain, France, Germany, and Japan. In the years around the turn of the century these nations were eagerly seizing Chinese territory and, through the "unequal treaties," reducing China to the status of a semicolony. At that time the United States proclaimed its "open-door policy," which called for the preservation of China's territorial integrity and for equal commercial access to Chinese markets.

After World War I the United States tried hard, though unsuccessfully, to prevent Japan from taking over the old German leasehold of the Shantung Peninsula. In 1922 the United States took the lead in drawing the potential predators, especially Japan, into the Nine-Power Treaty committing them to support the open-door policy. The United States condemned Japanese aggression against China in the 1930's, fought as China's ally in World War II, voluntarily gave up the privileges of the "unequal treaties," sponsored China as one of the world's "Big Five" nations with a permanent seat on the United Nations (UN) Security Council, and, after World War II, even tried to persuade Nationalist China's leader Chiang Kai-shek to accept the Communists in a coalition government.

Americans recall these events as part of a record of benevolence toward China. What we do not take into account, however, is that the Chinese Communists see the past from a different point of view. What their eyes perceive is not American benevolence but American condescension, combined with a greed differing from that of the European predators only in degree. Can we be certain that their viewpoint is one of malicious distortion while ours is cold reality? Or is it not possible that our image also may be clouded by pride, by cultural predisposition, and by the tendency of all nations to portray themselves in self-congratulatory terms?

The traditional U.S. attitude toward China seems to have been marked by a number of illusions. One illusion is the supposition of U.S. moral superiority compared with the Europeans in dealing with China. It is true that we did not extract territory and leaseholds or make war on China as the Europeans did. We did join, however, in the punitive expedition following the Boxer Rebellion, and we shared in many of the privileges which the Europeans forced China to concede. We can fairly say that we were less aggressive than others in our relations with China but, in moral terms, what that adds up to is not greater morality but, instead, only a lesser degree of immorality.

Another illusion—or at the very least an unfounded assumption—is the belief that a Chinese Communist design exists for the conquest of Asia. Former U.S. Secretary of State Dean Rusk, in his efforts to justify the Vietnam conflict, invoked the specter of a world "cut in two by Asian Communism." By this he apparently meant to suggest that North Vietnam and the Viet Cong were merely pawns in a Chinese strategy of conquest. No one knows what goes on in the minds of China's leaders—perhaps they do dream of conquering Asia. All we can conclude from their behavior, however, is that whatever their dreams may be they are not at present trying to conquer anybody, nor has their past behavior indicated a design for territorial conquest. This view is sustained by the following facts.

In 1969 the Chinese had no combat forces stationed outside of their borders. Prior to the halt in U.S. bombing the Chinese had engineer and air defense units in North Vietnam. Most of these, according to official U.S. government information, have now been removed.

In 1962 China fought a border war with India, for which, according to knowledgeable observers, the Indians were not entirely innocent of responsibility. After defeating the Indian army the Chinese halted their advance, confining their acquisitions to the disputed borderlands—territory that even the exiled government of President Chiang Kai-shek claimed to be Chinese. The same can be said for China's takeover of Tibet. Despite what the Tibetans might feel, not only the Chinese Nationalists but even the Indians have traditionally regarded Tibet as Chinese territory.

At the end of the Korean War there were a million Chinese soldiers in North Korea with nothing to stop them from, if they chose, subjugating or annexing North Korea. In 1958, however, the entire Chinese army was withdrawn from North Korea. There are still 50,000 U.S. troops in South Korea.

Closely examined, even the theory of "wars of national liberation," as defined by Communist China's Defense Minister Lin Piao, cannot be read as a blueprint for conquest. The Lin Piao doctrine is much closer to being a prescription

A Chinese poster, encouraging the Vietnamese to fight on, shows U.S. soldiers crushed by the power of the people's revolution.

MARC RIBOUD FROM MAGNUM

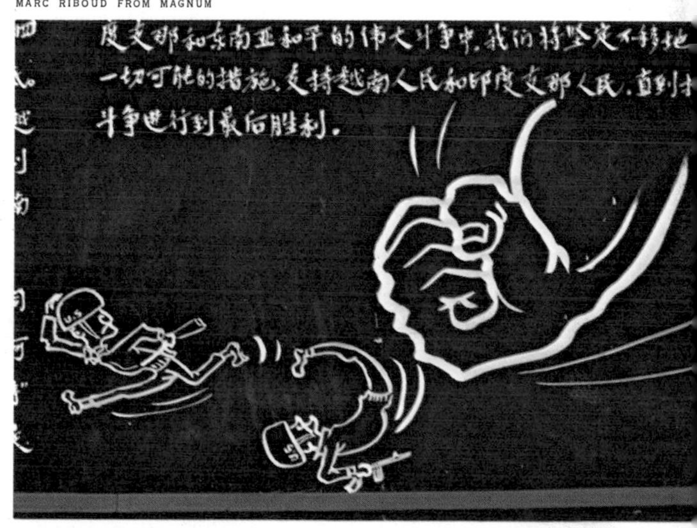

for "doing-it-yourself" and therefore, perhaps, a warning to the Vietnamese Communists not to expect too much of China. This is what Lin Piao wrote in part in 1965:

> In order to make a revolution and to fight a people's war and be victorious, it is imperative to adhere to the policy of self-reliance, rely on the strength of the masses in one's own country and prepare to carry on the fight independently even when all material aid from outside is cut off. If one does not operate by one's own

PAOLO KOCH FROM BLACK STAR

Under a blaze of waving banners, members of the militant Red Guard youth movement take a moment's rest from their task—revitalizing the revolutionary spirit of the country.

> efforts, does not independently ponder and solve the problems of the revolution in one's own country and does not rely on the strength of the masses, but leans wholly on foreign aid—even though this be aid from socialist countries which persist in revolution (i.e., China)—no victory can be won, or be consolidated even if it is won.

The Chinese Communists have encouraged and supported "wars of national liberation" in Vietnam and Laos and presumably would do so in other countries. The Chinese have not, however, participated in these insurrections with their own combat forces, nor, if they still adhere to the Lin Piao doctrine, do they regard their participation as feasible.

I think it is time for us to be sensible about these so-called "wars of national liberation" and to stop treating them as if they were the work of Communist supermen in Peking. It is true that insurrections can be and are supported from outside, just as efforts to suppress them can be and are supported from outside. Essentially, however, they have been home-grown products, nourished as in Vietnam by the corruption and incompetence of unpopular governments.

Though not wholly unfounded, the fear of Chinese intervention by several Asian regimes is largely an effort to put the blame for their countries' internal problems on the Chinese. The Chinese appear to have no such illusions of their own omnipotence. As Lin Piao states, when a revolutionary movement leans wholly on foreign support, "no victory can be won, or be consolidated even if it is won."

None of what I have said is meant to suggest that China poses no dangers for the United States. As the dominant power of the West we are regarded by the Chinese with hostility. With nuclear weapons and ballistic missiles, China will be a potential threat to us as long as it remains hostile. Strategically, however, the Chinese are decades away from having a nuclear capacity comparable to that of the Soviet Union. With our superior nuclear power, our mastery of the sea and air, and our ring of bases around China, we have a more than adequate deterrent to Chinese attack. The Chinese Communist leaders have shown themselves to be as sane as anybody and saner than many governments in matters affecting their own survival.

In strategic terms and in terms of actual Chinese policy on the Asian mainland, it seems clear that our fears have been exaggerated, as much the product of images in our minds as of hard, observable facts. Thus we would do well to recognize that China's fear of us is the product of a mixed bag of illusions and facts. We have heard a great deal about China's misconceptions of America, and I will not take up space to repeat them here. We hear less, however, of reasons why the Chinese may genuinely fear the United States.

We have vast military power along China's borders, including 500,000 men in Vietnam, 50,000 in South Korea, 40,000 in Thailand, the Seventh Fleet in the Taiwan Strait, and military installations in Japan, the Philippines, Taiwan, Okinawa, and Guam. The Chinese, so far as we know, have no combat forces at all anywhere outside their borders. Nonetheless, we regard Chinese power as a major threat to our security. If we are afraid of them, despite their lack of strategic capacity for aggressive warfare, is it any great wonder that they fear us, with our vast and sophisticated arsenal of weapons?

Since the Communist victory in the Chinese civil war 20 years ago, the United States has been as hostile to the Chinese Communists as they have been to us. In 1950, following North Korea's invasion of South Korea, U.S. Gen. Douglas MacArthur launched a counteroffensive that overran North Korea and brought U.S. forces to China's border. The Chinese then intervened, and U.S. and Chinese armies fought each other to a bloody stalemate in Korea. The Korean War froze Chinese-American relations in a state of bitter hostility. In the words of Kenneth Young, president of the Asia Society, since 1950 the United States "has treated Peking as an aggressor and outlaw, refused it diplomatic recognition, blocked its membership in the United Nations, prevented its taking over Taiwan, encouraged its 'passing away', isolated it diplomatically and economically, confronted it with overwhelming force, and undertaken military operations along China's west and near China's southern flank."

Another factor in China's fear of the United States is the agitated state of the Chinese public mind. Fear, tension, anxiety, suspicion, and hostility are characteristic of revolutionary societies. After six decades of civil war, foreign invasion, and social revolution, China is a nation that, as UN Secretary-General U Thant once put it, has had a kind of "nervous breakdown." The high level of tension in Chinese life—deliberately fostered by the Communist leadership—naturally generates strong feelings of fear and hostility. These in turn give rise to behavior that seems inexplicable to foreigners. As the distinguished psychiatrist Jerome D. Frank once commented: "Frightened, hostile individuals tend to behave in ways which aggravate their difficulties instead of resolving them, and frightened, hostile nations seem to behave similarly."

Another possible factor in China's hostility to the United States is that the Chinese leadership may find our hostility useful for their own purposes. To bring about radical changes in a traditional society a revolutionary government must sustain the dedication of the population. This task becomes increasingly difficult as the revolution recedes into the past. Nothing serves better to prolong revolutionary fervor than a foreign enemy who can be characterized as enormously powerful and dangerous. An editorial in the Chinese Communist party newspaper in 1966 spelled out this thesis:

> The Chinese people's great enemy is U.S. imperialism. The enemy is indeed most hateful and harmful to us; but we must see that its existence also has a beneficial effect on us. To have a ferocious enemy like U.S. imperialism glowering at us and threatening us day and night will make the Chinese people always bear in mind the danger of war while living in

A poster depicts a frightened Uncle Sam overcome by worldwide Communism.

MARC RIBOUD FROM MAGNUM

Huge, eye-catching billboards confront passersby with rousing political slogans to inspire them in their daily lives.

MAX SCHELER FROM BLACK STAR

> peace and raise our vigilance a hundredfold; will keep us always on the alert and enable our enthusiasm to burst forth; can help the Chinese people to maintain preparedness and sharpen our fighting spirit. Wanton U.S. imperialist aggression and intimidation can further raise our political consciousness, strengthen our unity, and enhance our combat readiness.

U.S. hostility may well serve the purposes of the Peking government, but it is not clear that it serves any purposes of ours. We are indeed acting against our own best interests insofar as we may be helping the Chinese Communist leaders to prolong their revolution. Having reconciled ourselves to the improbability of a Chinese Nationalist return to the mainland, and to the probable permanence of Communist rule in China, it makes no sense whatever—as the Nixon Administration has wisely acknowledged—to sustain a bankrupt policy of "isolating" Communist China.

Our interests concerning China are approximately as follows: to liquidate existing quarrels, notably those over Vietnam and Taiwan; to create a zone of neutrality or "strategic distance" between Chinese and U.S. military power; and, insofar as possible, to draw China into a cooperative role in the world community. To advance these aims it will be necessary to shape a new policy based on facts rather than images born of fear and ideology.

A New China Policy

A radical change in Sino-American relations—from hostility to friendship—is most unlikely under present circumstances. After 20 years of hostility, as well as for ideological reasons, the Chinese most probably do not want our friendship. This being so, I think it would be unrewarding for us to press ourselves upon the Chinese with eager offers of reconciliation. No matter how sincere, U.S. proposals for an immediate transformation in Sino-American relations would in all likelihood be rejected by the Chinese. That would be even more likely if we seemed unduly eager, or tried to reap a propaganda harvest by trumpeting our "generous" offers for the world to see and admire.

Between hostility and friendship a period of gradual thaw is desirable—a period in which tensions can abate and animosities decrease, a period in which China and the United States would simply leave each other alone. I emphasize the need of a cautious, gradual approach because I think we Americans have a tendency to veer extravagantly between extremes of hostility and affection for foreign nations that sometimes gets us into trouble. Only 25 years ago, for example, Germany and Japan, now esteemed allies, were hated enemies, while China and the Soviet Union, whom we now fear so greatly, were then being patriotically hailed as our heroic brothers-in-arms.

I do not mean to suggest that in this period of gradual thaw we should do nothing with respect to China. There are certain initiatives we can take in our direct policy toward China and in our policy toward Asia outside of mainland China, particularly with respect to Vietnam and Taiwan. I turn now to suggest some specific courses of action, cautioning only that, whatever we propose, we do so quietly and without ballyhoo and that we must not expect an immediate favorable Chinese response.

Travel, Trade, and Diplomacy

After 19 years of maintaining a total embargo on travel and trade with China, the U.S. government announced in July 1969 that U.S. citizens with specific professional reasons to travel in

China—such as scholars and journalists—would be permitted to do so if the Chinese would let them in. Furthermore, U.S. tourists would be permitted to bring into the United States up to $100 worth of goods of Chinese Communist origin.

I see no reason why this intelligent initiative should not be followed by the removal of all restrictions on travel. The U.S. government has already indicated that it would welcome Chinese visitors to the United States. The next step would be to announce that hereafter the Department of State will validate any U.S. citizen's passport for travel in China.

In the field of trade, I propose the lifting of our embargo on all nonmilitary commodities. The embargo was imposed almost two decades ago in the belief that it would have such disastrous economic effects that the Chinese would be willing to make concessions or would be weakened to the point of exhaustion or even expiration. It is doubtful that a general embargo would in fact have brought China to heel. We shall never know, however, because our non-Communist allies were unwilling to join in an embargo. In fact, China now has most of its trade with our major allies—Great Britain, Japan, West Germany, Australia, Canada, and France. Our attempted embargo thus has had little economic effect.

Nor can we use the Vietnam conflict as an excuse for this bankrupt policy of embargo. If we did, we would not trade with any Communist countries. The Soviets and other European Communist nations are providing North Vietnam with sophisticated military equipment that far exceeds the assistance being given by the Chinese. For these reasons, then, I propose the immediate removal of the U.S. trade embargo against China.

In the field of diplomacy the outstanding issues are the recognition of the People's Republic of China and China's admission to the UN. It is possible that the Chinese government would reject both U.S. recognition and UN membership. It would be appropriate nonetheless for the U.S. government to state without qualification that it is willing to recognize that the government of the People's Republic of China controls the mainland of China, that we look forward to the time when that government will be willing to enter into diplomatic, trade, and cultural relations with us and will also be willing to join the UN, and that we are willing to meet and discuss these questions at any time and at any level.

Official U.S. policy on the recognition of new governments has been equivocal in recent years. It is officially held that diplomatic recognition is only the acknowledgment of a fact,

Children of the Young Pioneer movement practice marching in step as a lesson in discipline.
MARC RIBOUD FROM MAGNUM

having nothing to do with approval of the government. In practice the U.S. government has repeatedly withheld recognition from Communist governments of which it disapproved while readily granting recognition to non-Communist governments of which it professed disapproval. This distinction makes neither logical nor political sense.

In 1969 the Senate Committee on Foreign Relations recommended the adoption by the Senate of a resolution declaring that the extension of recognition to a foreign government and the exchange of diplomatic representatives with it "does not of itself imply that the United States approves of the form, ideology, or policy" of that government. Adherence to this principle in the recognition of Communist as well as non-Communist states would eliminate the ambivalence of U.S. government practice. Admittedly, there are difficulties about its immediate implementation with respect to China. Having withheld recognition for 20 years as an expression of our disapproval, we cannot extend recognition now without its taking on a significance that it would not have had 20 years ago. In that time other issues, notably Taiwan and Vietnam, have intervened. It may be necessary to move toward some resolution of these issues before diplomatic relations can be established between China and the United States.

As to Chinese membership in the UN, I recommend that the United States drop its opposition to the admittance of Communist China. Because of our relationship with the Chiang Kai-shek government on Taiwan, we might prefer not to vote for the seating of the Chinese Communist delegates as the representatives of China unless prior agreement is reached for the preservation of separate representation for Taiwan—or the Chinese Nationalist government of Taiwan. This of course involves the single most intractable issue in Sino-American relations—the question of "two Chinas." Since an agreement on this matter is almost inconceivable at present, it might be well for the United States simply to abstain when the question of seating Communist China is raised again. At the same time the United States should abandon its efforts to secure the votes of other countries against Communist China.

Taiwan

The idea of "two Chinas" makes perfectly good sense to Americans. On the one hand it is absurd to pretend that the Chinese Nationalist fugitives who were driven from the Chinese mainland 20 years ago are the "legitimate" government of China. On the other hand we cannot, as the Chinese Communists have demanded, stand altogether aside while they seize Taiwan. The obvious and logical solution to the dilemma would seem to be acceptance and formalization of the status quo of "two Chinas."

The trouble with this obvious and logical solution is that it is violently opposed by the interested parties, each of whom is adamant in its claim to be the sole legitimate government of a unified China. One can argue forever that acceptance of the status quo is the only course of political "realism." The governing fact of the situation, however, is that neither Communist Party Politburo Chairman Mao Tse-tung nor Chiang Kai-shek has the slightest interest in being politically "realistic" about Taiwan. Nor has either shown the slightest willingness to honor the principle of self-determination. If the Taiwanese (who number about 11 million) had their way, they would probably reject the rule of both the Communists and the minority of Nationalist fugitives (some 2.5 million) who now dominate their island.

The "two Chinas" solution, which seems so sensible to many Americans, will probably never be acceptable to the Chinese. However divided they may be on other things, they are united in their belief in a single Chinese identity. This being the case, I think there is nothing for the United States to do as to the status of Taiwan except to leave it to the Chinese to resolve—or to leave unresolved—in their own way.

Leaving Taiwan to the Chinese does not mean "selling out" the Chiang Kai-shek government, to which we are allied. What it does mean is the gradual reduction and elimination of direct U.S. military involvement. We have already ended most economic assistance and have substantially reduced our military assistance to Nationalist China. We can continue to lessen our involvement by further reducing military assistance and, most important, by transferring the responsibility for patrolling the Taiwan Strait from the U.S. Seventh Fleet to the Chinese Nationalists themselves.

This course of action will not resolve the question of the status of Taiwan. It will serve only to remove the United States as an intruder in the Chinese civil conflict. It is by no means clear that the Chinese themselves can resolve this issue, but it is quite clear that, if it can be solved, it is only the Chinese who can solve it.

While Taiwan may be the most intractable issue between the United States and China, Vietnam is the most dangerous. The ending of the U.S. bombing of North Vietnam and the beginning of military de-escalation has removed the immediate danger of Chinese intervention. But as long as the war goes on, as long as there is a massive U.S. military involvement in Southeast Asia, there can be little prospect of promoting a general accommodation between the United States and China.

China, as I pointed out earlier, has done little if anything to suggest that it aspires to the military conquest of Asia. At the same time it seems obvious that China genuinely fears U.S. military power in Asia. The Chinese profess—and undoubtedly feel—considerable gratification over the attrition of U.S. resources in a futile war. But I think it likely that they would forgo that satisfaction for the removal of U.S. military power from the Asian mainland. Surrounded by U.S. military forces, China must surely suffer apprehensions that we can begin to appreciate by recalling our own extreme agitation over the Soviet missiles in Cuba and the great risk we took to secure their removal.

To remove this major cause of Sino-American hostility and to achieve peace in Southeast Asia, we would do well to direct our policy toward the neutralization of Southeast Asia. The first requirement is the termination of the Vietnam conflict. Whatever the peace settlement might provide for the internal regime of South Vietnam, it would be highly desirable if the settlement were accompanied by a general agreement for the neutralization of Southeast Asia, subscribed to by China and the United States and other major powers as well as by the Asian nations directly concerned.

It is not likely that such an agreement, formally subscribed to by both China and the United States, could be reached in the near future. Even if a formal agreement cannot be made in connection with a Vietnam peace settlement, it will still be in our interests to initiate a general U.S. military withdrawal from the Asian mainland. We have already pledged to withdraw all U.S. military forces from Vietnam within six months from the date of a peace settlement. The only other country in the region in which there is a sizable U.S. military presence is Thailand, and the Thais have said that they will want the U.S. forces withdrawn when the Vietnam conflict is over.

The removal of U.S. military power from the Asian mainland would not impair our own security or leave the Chinese free to overrun their neighbors should they come to feel so inclined.

MARC RIBOUD FROM MAGNUM

An anti-American demonstration in Peking, China's capital, features an open-air mime drama with paint-daubed amateur actors. They portray a humiliated U.S. soldier followed by a defeated, cowering Uncle Sam.

We would still have our deterrent missile and air power, our island bases in the western Pacific, and our highly mobile striking force. On the basis of past experiences, moreover, there is reason to believe that U.S. military withdrawal would reduce the likelihood of Chinese intervention in the internal affairs of its Asian neighbors. The countries in which China has supported domestic insurgencies have been exactly those—Vietnam, Laos, and Thailand—in which there has been a U.S. military presence. Those Asian countries that have avoided military connections with the United States—notably Burma and Cambodia—by and large, and in comparison, have been left alone by the Chinese. It seems reasonable to conclude that U.S. military involvement in Asia has been more of an inducement than a deterrent to Chinese support of domestic insurgencies.

U.S. military withdrawal from Southeast Asia, along with the reduction of the American involvement with Taiwan, would remove the two most important causes of Chinese hostility to the United States. Nonetheless, I would not expect an era of Sino-American friendship to follow. That, however, ought not to give us undue concern. After 20 years of mutual fear and hostility a period of separation—of just leaving each other alone—would be healthy for both countries. There will be time enough, once present tensions have faded into memory, to renew the association of two great civilizations.

Trophy
STOP WATCHES
COMPETE
AFTER SHAVE
ROBUST
ANTI-PERSPIRANT
SMOKE
DYNAMOS
SUPER STAR
SOCKS
TRIUMPH
BAR-BELLS
FESTIVAL
AIRLINES
STAMINA
SHORTS
STRIVE
TOOTHPASTE
Drink
SPRINT

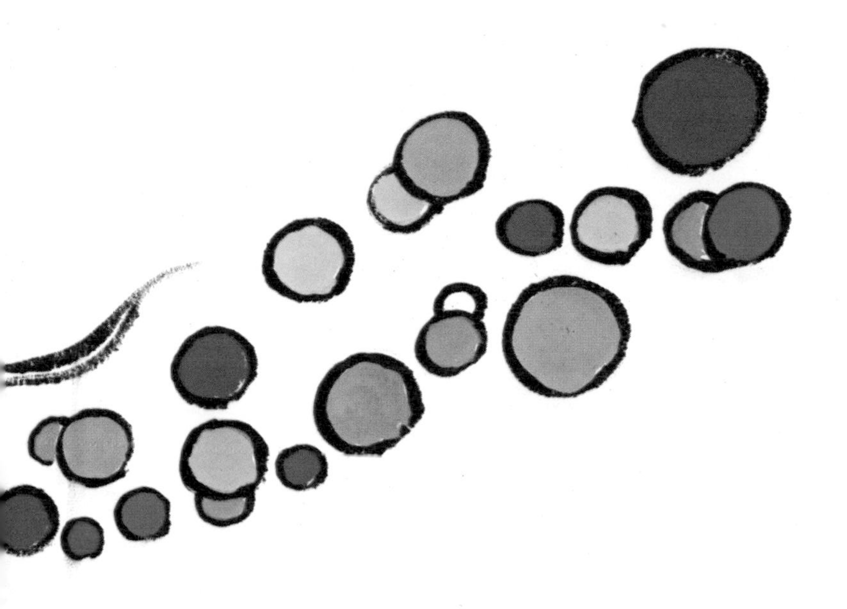

Are there any
amateurs in sports?

Run For Your Supper

by WILLIAM BARRY FURLONG
reporter and author

He is a tough-talking, tough-thinking man with pink skin and wisps of white hair. He is a man of regular habits: he has an egg-and-bacon sandwich with a tomato on the side for lunch every day. He is a man of outrageous opinions: "Too many women athletes," he says, "shave every morning." He is a man of cherished anachronisms: he still believes in sport for its own sake rather than for the dollar that can be made out of it. At 82 years of age, square-cut, blunt-talking Avery Brundage, president of the International Olympic Committee (IOC), is a man embattled, but not defeated, by the growing professionalism of "amateur" sports. Yet he stands virtually helpless while all over the world promoters and politicians use amateur sports for their own gain.

THE PROFIT MOTIVE

In West Germany it was revealed that 85% of the medal winners in the track and field events of the 1968 Olympic Games had been paid by a company making track shoes. And that the payments ranged as high as $10,000 for a particularly attractive "amateur." In France the Fédération Internationale de Ski (FIS) was asked to return all medals won by victors in the Alpine skiing events of the 1968 Olympics because of what Brundage regarded as blatant commercialization—and possible payoffs to the "amateur" skiers. ("Come and try to get them," challenged triple gold-medal winner Jean-Claude Killy.) Instead of responding, the FIS approved a neoprofessional system whereby amateur skiers could earn income from television appearances, from commercial endorsement of products, and for articles appearing in the press under their names.

All over the world, the demands of the modern, well-paid amateur have aroused great concern and cynicism. In football, subsidized athletes at several universities—living on the payment of their tuition, books, fees, food, and housing—threatened to strike for better working conditions. In tennis, a famous amateur player who was paid $1,200 for appearing in a "middle-level" tournament embittered his employers by failing to survive even the first round—and then hoped to make 10 or 20 times as much in open competition. In basketball, a professional player told of the "amateur" days when he was a high school senior being sought by various colleges: several institutions mentioned paying him a monthly salary (under the table, of course); another offered him a large weekly income for keeping the football field clear of seaweed (the nearest ocean was 1,000 miles away); and vast numbers of recruiters agreed to give him "expense money" when he appeared in amateur tournaments, or they took him to dinner and coyly slipped $10 bills under his napkin.

An International Problem

The growing professionalism of amateur sports is not a problem in the United States alone. In West Germany athletes receive help from the national Olympic Association. In France many skiers are aided by the French government, which believes that skiing is an aid to tourism. In Pakistan many members of the Olympic field-hockey team worked for an international airway that made sure they had the time and opportunity to practice. In Japan all of the members of the crack women's volleyball team work quite coincidentally in the same textile plant near Osaka, where they get together for practice every day. In certain African countries, an amateur athlete with sufficient skill might be employed by the army or constabulary and spend up to 90% of his time practicing his sport. In the Soviet Union and the other Communist-bloc countries, the top athletes are employed directly by the state, which provides them with a very comfortable living while they spend most of their time polishing and honing their athletic skills.

In all of this, one thing becomes clear: the amateur athlete is corrupted by the hypocrisies of his society and by the goals it seeks most urgently. Professionalism in amateur athletics, therefore, is inspired as much by political prestige in some parts of the world as by financial gain in others.

Vocal Critics

In the face of all this, Brundage remains the most indomitable foe of professionalism in sports. His throaty insistence on the highest standards of amateurism have earned him the reputation of being everything from a tiresome scold to—in the words of sports columnist Red Smith—"the greatest practicing patsy, or sitting duck, of this century." But he has never yielded. Indeed, he has become more militant. He insists, for example, that the high-pressure professional sports—football, baseball, and basketball—should be reviewed on the entertainment pages, not on the sports pages. "They're no different from a circus," he once said. He disdains college sports with their systems for subsidizing athletes, many of whom should not even be in college. His view of amateur sport is almost as celestial as it is eloquent: "Sport is a pastime and a diversion. The minute it becomes more than that, it's business or work. Amateurism is a thing of the spirit—it's inside a person. The devotion of the true amateur athlete is the same devotion that makes an artist starve in his garret rather than commercialize his work. If a man has the ability to succeed in any other field, he has no business taking part in professional athletics." It would be hard, but not impossible, to find a man with this amateur "spirit." In Brundage's view, Roger Bannister, who ran the first sub-four-minute mile in history, stands as an example of such spirit. He was dedicated to running, and running well. But he never let this devotion to sports divert him from an even nobler career in medicine.

If Brundage is the most vocal critic of the growing professionalism in amateur sports, he is not the only one. The late A. Whitney Griswold, when he was president of Yale University, branded the handing out of athletic scholarships as "the greatest swindle ever perpetrated on American youth." Reuel Denny, the sociologist who collaborated with David Riesman on 'The Lonely Crowd', observed that in highly commercialized sports the amateur athlete is "first turned into a robot, and then sometimes the robot becomes a burglar. I think the first stage, when the human being is turned into a robot, is far worse." Even some of the better athletes are deeply concerned. Bill Toomey, the 1968 Olympic decathlon champion, says, "The hypocrisy is what's killing us, not the money."

It's Ancient History

As it happens, hypocrisy and money have long been a major problem in amateur sports. The ancient Greeks, who were the first to organize the Olympics, were also the first to corrupt it. It took 61 Olympiads, but in the end Greek society had to reward the athletes who triumphed in the games. At first the rewards were intangible: a three-time winner had a statue erected to him in his hometown. But, as time passed, the rewards increased materially. The winners were entertained at public expense. They were made exempt from paying taxes. They were given homes. They were given free meals for the rest of their lives. And if they still lacked money, wealthy townspeople got together and provided funds to help them live in the style to which they had become accustomed.

If sufficient rewards were not forthcoming, the athlete exacted his own revenge. One such Olympic winner, Oebotas of Achaea, felt so unhappy over his lack of reimbursement that he placed a curse upon his city and for 300 years not one Achaean won an Olympic event. Then, on the advice of the oracle at Delphi, the city built a statue to the memory of Oebotas, and in the very next Olympics an Achaean was the winner of the sprint for boys. This was an impressive example of the productive value of a payoff, even a posthumous one, to a so-called "amateur" athlete.

In a short time the people of these ancient city-states hit on a principle now common in U.S. colleges and universities. The city fathers began to import good athletes, reward them handsomely for representing the community, and send them into competition disguised as amateurs. In short, the payoff came before the competition, not after it. And the athlete was rewarded whether he won or not.

A desire for national prestige was the primary motivating force for this emphasis on winning. A feeling began to arise that one community was better than another because the athletes who represented it were better. It was a false notion but a crucial one. As Greece came under the rule of foreign conquerors, the people hungered even more to build their fading prestige by success in athletics. The Greeks became bolder and bolder in matters of professionalism—but so did their conquerors, the Romans. Eventually the Olympic Games degenerated into a sham and a shame. Just before 400 A.D, the Olympics were brought to an end, after 1,170 years, by a combination of corrupt ideals, an invasion of the Olympic site by a gang of marauding Goths, and a decree of the Roman emperor, Theodosius.

The games were revived in 1896. By 1908 an element of prestige and political one-upmanship again violently intruded. To the surprise of the European world, the United States—then just beginning to emerge as a world power—surged to victory in the 1904 Olympics. As the host country in 1908, Great Britain did not want to be defeated again by its former colonials. The English announced, therefore, that they would run the games by English rules and that, among other things, the scores of all British possessions and countries within the British Empire would count in the English total. (Several of the most talented Irish athletes immediately quit the Olympics.) For the United States and the other countries, this was almost like being invited to be guest of honor at a public execution. A great many quarrels broke out, many athletes were disqualified, certain races had to be run over, and, according to one observer, "there was almost open warfare between the U.S. and English teams."

When it appeared that Americans would take the first three places in the 400-meter run, for example, one British official raced onto the track to grab and slow down one of the Americans; another raced to the finish line and cut the tape before the Americans could get there, apparently hoping to force the race into being run over again so that someone else would win. In the marathon, the leader, an Italian named Dorando Pietri, collapsed not far from the finish line. Less than a minute behind him was an American named Johnny Hayes, who had won fame as a youth who trained while working as a shipping clerk for a New York department store. The horrified British officials took prompt action. They rushed onto the course, picked up Pietri, and literally dragged him across the finish line some 34 seconds in front of Johnny Hayes. Unfortunately for the British, the gambit did not work. Pietri was disqualified, and Hayes was declared the winner.

The Hand That Feeds

At about the same time that the Olympics were experiencing rebirth pains, corruption began to seep into sports in U.S. colleges. Seven members of the University of Michigan's 1893 football team were not even enrolled at the university. In 1902, when Yale managed to lure a tackle named James Hogan, a future all-American, to New Haven (Conn.), it was by guaranteeing him free tuition, a suite in Vanderbilt Hall, a ten-day trip to Cuba, and a monopoly on the sale of scorecards. By the 1920's, some of the college football players were playing their own "Sunday schedules" on the side for more money than the colleges were giving them. Notre Dame and the University of Illinois were not meeting on the playing field yet, but some of their players were battling in memorable games in the small towns of central and southern Illinois for $100 and $200 a game.

For a long time, there were efforts to disguise payments to amateurs. As late as the 1950's, one sprinter told of how he watched a track official reject another trackman's demand for a payoff of $250 to compete. It would be against the rules simply to give him $250, said the official. But he would make a bet that the athlete could not jump over a folding chair laid flat on

the track. After the athlete promptly jumped over the chair, the official clucked that he'd lost another bet and handed over the $250.

Another deceit of the athletes was to over-collect their expenses. If they were in a town for one day for a track meet, they would collect expenses for five days. Or they would receive airline tickets for trips they did not take. Or if two meets were held in the Midwest on one weekend, for instance, athletes from the West coast would collect two round-trip tickets between Los Angeles, Calif., and the Midwest—one from the promoter of each meet—even though they obviously could make only one of the air trips. Then they would cash in the extra ticket and pocket the money.

Eventually the world of amateur track made outright payments to the competitors. In fact, the runners seemed to be put on a time rate. Sprinters would get only $50 to $100 a night; they were actually running only 10 to 20 seconds depending on the number of heats. But a good miler could command $1,000 or more a night since he would be running for as long as four minutes. Other athletes set their own standards. One famous middle-distance runner customarily demanded $1 a yard for his appearance. In one meet—according to another competitor—he was offered $400 for a 440-yard race. He led the race from the start. But at exactly 400 yards, he suddenly pulled up and ran off the track, apparently with a pulled muscle. Later the promoter of the meet told him that he was sorry about his injured leg. "Injured leg! Man, you paid for 400 yards and you got exactly what you paid for!"

Not all athletes subscribe to the payoff system, of course. And those who do know that it is hypocritical in the extreme. "But almost every meet, here and abroad, is dirty, if you want to call it that," said one U.S. track star early in 1969. Another athlete of international stature

concedes: "I get paid at about 70% of the meets, indoors and outdoors. I don't ask for anything, but if I'm offered, I accept. If it's $100, I take it. If it's $500, I take it. But I don't ask."

In many other countries, either athletic officials or equipment manufacturers are only too eager to give without being asked. In the world of international track, Scandinavia is said to be the best—that is, the most profitable—place to run. Payments are said to be as high as $2,000 a meet. Some athletes even hire agents to book them into these richly rewarding competitions.

All's Fair

At times, the athlete has found not only hypocrisy, but also inconsistency and even foolishness, in the arbitrary rulings of officials on money and amateurism. In the late 1950's, for example, one of the top amateur golfers in the United States was suspended for a year because he accepted travel expenses to certain tournaments. These expenses had been paid for him by his regular employer, who had no interest in the sports business. Had the employer given the golfer a raise instead and allowed him to pay the expenses out of his own pocket, there would have been no objection. It was all a matter of bookkeeping.

Amateur tennis, too, has a sullied reputation. It was revealed in the mid-1960's that the U.S. Lawn Tennis Association (USLTA), the guardian of amateur tennis in the United States, was quietly paying members of the Davis Cup team from $7,000 to $9,000 a year for their efforts. The surprise was the large amount of the payments and the fact that the USLTA was not eager to make them public. It was known that the tennis players had long been permitted a certain amount of money for expenses—$28 a day and transportation costs was then the maximum —and that the USLTA had also provided ex-

pense money to Davis Cup players in the past while they were in training. The rationale behind the salary increase was that the period of training and competition had been vastly expanded. The captain of the Davis Cup team said, "A player has to live, whether he's competing or not."

The players, in 1968, were asking for and receiving as much as $1,000 to $1,500 a week while making the tournament officials miserable at the same time. "Discussing money matters with the kids is very disagreeable," said the chairman of a prominent East coast tournament. "I come out of it thinking they're holdup men and they regard me as an ogre." Not only that, but they regard him as a pinchpenny. Just four years ago, two accomplished Australian tennis players received at least $500 a week for playing the summer circuit in the United States. A skilled Latin American player got the same amount for competing at Forest Hills, on Long Island, N.Y. At that time, however, U.S. players were under close supervision; they were not being paid much beyond their expenses. This led one former Davis Cup player to complain, "When the clamping down is done, it is always on us. We live simon-pure at our own tournaments and even get shortchanged a little—all in the name of amateurism—while the foreign players come in here and grab the big money."

In track, the sheer pressure of the Olympics causes all kinds of hypocrisy to rise to the surface. A year or so ago, Jurgen May of West Germany, one of the best middle-distance runners in the world, accepted $100 to wear the shoes of a particular manufacturer in a track meet. Then he thought better of it and gave the money back—all within about ten hours. But he was found out and the officials of amateurism righteously banned him from competing in the 1968 Olympics. By the time the games were actually under way, systems of high payment were common. One athlete who shopped around a bit was paid $10,000 to wear a particular pair of shoes in competition. Another got $6,000. Two German shoe manufacturers were accused by *Sports Illustrated* of giving an estimated $100,000 in cash and $350,000 in equipment to "amateur" athletes in 1968. All of this information was delivered to various amateur and Olympic officials, yet no action was taken against the athletes. To some people, it seemed that Jurgen May's only crimes were that he was early, obvious, and lacking in greed.

A College Education

Nothing arouses so many cynical remarks as the "aid" that is given to college athletes. Grants-in-aid given top athletes—covering tuition, fees, books, board, and certain incidentals over a four-year period—are estimated at $15,000 to $20,000 in some universities. In many institutions of higher learning, the athlete lives in a luxurious environment that may not be shared with other students. One example of this is the palatial "Hilton Bryant" at the University of Alabama—the athletic dormitories nicknamed after Alabama's football coach and reserved for athletes on aid. In other instances, colleges provide "extra pay" for athletes. Sometimes this is outright and illegal: one university was put on probation for giving $200 down and $50 a month for certain athletes. In most cases, the money is feebly disguised as earned income: one athlete reported that he was offered $110 a month to water the track occasionally; another was offered $50 a month to answer the coach's phone when no one else was there (somebody was always there; the coach had a secretary); still another was offered $50 a month "to keep the coach's desk clean." When this isn't enough, the alumni can be expected to chip in with clothes, car, or a cash "job."

In addition, the athlete is sometimes in college on a free pass academically as well as economically. It's not that certain athletes aren't qualified for college; it's that some of them aren't even qualified for grade school. One somewhat renowned athlete of the last decade couldn't get a driver's license because he couldn't read well enough to understand the written test. Yet he got into a Big Ten university. Everybody—including a good many college authorities—seems to accept the fact that athletes are in college to perform, not to study. Studies, therefore, are often made easy for them. One Olympic shot-putter of a few years ago found he couldn't quite make the academic grade at the University of Southern California. So he transferred to a less stringent college in the same area and soon found he could do quite well in all five of his courses: dance, first aid, methods of track and field, methods of baseball, and safety education.

The attitude of college authorities toward the professionalism of amateur athletics is enough to confuse—and outrage—anyone. At the University of Michigan, the better athletes found that part of the unspoken "deal" was a series of gifts offered by the businessmen and townspeople of Ann Arbor to cover minor expenses: cut-rate movie tickets, discounts on clothes bought in Ann Arbor shops, and free meals in certain local restaurants. When this was brought to public attention, the Big Ten Conference dismissed it as not falling within the intent of its rules. But at the University of Illinois, when certain athletes were given "expense money" for transportation home on weekends, telephone charges, and other expenses out of a secret fund maintained by several of the coaches, the Big Ten swooped down, banned the athletes—at least those still in school—and forced the college to fire the coaches involved. Apparently it was not a matter of the amount of money involved, or even how it was used. The policy of the officials seemed to be that money was "legal" if it came from the fans and "illegal" if it came from the coaches. ("As far as I'm concerned, it's all 'legal' when it comes to spending it," said one athlete.)

Second-Class Citizens

To the amateur athlete, it sometimes appears that everyone profits from his skill except him. In 1969, for instance, the National Collegiate Athletic Association signed a television contract that would bring in $12 million over the next two years. Television rights for the next Olympic Games were sold for $6.5 million. The Amateur Athletic Union (AAU) sold television rights for ten track meets for $440,000. The U.S. Ski Association devised a couple of television races against a French team and got $65,000 for the idea. The U.S. ski team—made up of amateur performers—has a budget of about $365,000 a year, most of which was raised in 1969 through television and other commercial contracts. In face of all of this, the performer is expected to get nothing and want nothing.

But as he warms up before his event, he must look around a stadium steadily filling up with paying customers and realize that he is the only unpaid laborer in an arena filled with promoters hoping to get richer: television announcers, program hawkers, ticket takers, sportswriters, beer salesmen, and, most of all, the men who run the event.

Soon, the athlete comes to realize that the officials who guard amateurism are really enjoying the fruits of the athletes' labor. They travel all over the world, live in the best hotels, eat in the best restaurants, and drink the best wine—all on money earned by amateur athletes. Meanwhile, the athlete finds he must scuttle around for under-the-table payments if he wants to bring his wife or mother to the Olympics. When sprinter Tommie Smith and decathlon champion Bill Toomey were invited to a meet in Australia, the AAU said that they could not go without a "chaperon." However, the sponsor of the meet in Australia could not afford a third round-trip air fare from the United States. Toomey decided, therefore, that he would stay home and give his ticket to the official; in that way, at least Tommie Smith could go to Australia. The AAU apparently didn't even appreciate the irony of this: an athlete was being shunted aside so that a nonathlete could represent the United States at an overseas track meet. As it turned out, the nonathlete was 70 years old and not too knowledgeable about sports. As he was about to board the plane to Australia, he turned to Smith—certainly one of the most famous sprinters in the world—and asked, "What event do you run, son?"

As the drive toward professionalism heightens, certain organizations have begun to make compromises. For example, in the spring of 1969, the French FIS approved payments to amateurs for noncompetitive activities. In 1968 the International Lawn Tennis Association approved open competition between amateurs and professionals. As it worked out, three classes of players were officially recognized: the true professional, the true amateur, and the "registered amateur," who existed somewhere in between. By registering, an amateur could collect prize money from certain tournaments while remaining classified an "amateur"—retaining the right to take part in other nonpaying amateur tournaments.

In the first U.S. Open, all of the true professionals were eliminated before the finals, and two amateurs met for the championship. Arthur Ashe, a "true" amateur, took the title—but he did not take the money that went with it. Tom Okker, a young Dutch "registered" amateur who lost to Ashe in the finals, was awarded the top prize money of $14,000. However curious this arrangement seems, it is likely to endure until tennis evolves to where golf is today—with amateurs and professionals competing and the profits of commercialism growing so fast that the best players all became professional.

THE POLITICAL MOTIVE

If financial gain is behind the professionalizing of amateur athletics in some parts of the world, political prestige is responsible in much of the rest of the world. In the Caribbean Games a few years ago, Cuba—then eager to flex its international muscle—found that its soccer team was beaten by the tiny Dutch West Indies, its water polo team was humiliated 23–4 by Panama, its volleyball team had been beaten by the hated Dominican Republic, and four weight lifters, one basketball player, two coaches, and the second in command were all plotting ways to elude Premier Fidel Castro's secret police (even the bat boy was one) so that they could defect.

At this point, the Castroites discerned that things were coming to a head. So the chief of Cuba's delegation to the games called an emergency meeting and exhorted his men to follow the high standards urged on them by their leader. "You have been told by Fidel to break the bones of the agitators! So remember your duty!" Sure enough, in a baseball game against Puerto Rico—whom the Cubans described cordially as "worms at the service of Yankee imperialism"—a bat-wielding, chair-throwing, fist-swinging riot broke out in which seven persons were hurt. Cuba also lost the baseball game 4–3.

State Aid

In the Soviet Union and many other Communist countries, the top athletes are placed on the payroll of the Red army or the secret police or some state industrial complex where they will have plenty of time to concentrate on preparing themselves for international competition. To be sure, in such countries one cannot earn a living unless he works for the state. But the state could set up sports organizations that would support and reward the athletes openly. Such action, however, would probably be regarded as professionalism and would arouse the wrath of men like Brundage. So these nations indulge in a deceit as hypocritical and ill-concealed as those in the profit-oriented nations.

It is a peculiar blind spot in the president of the IOC that he recognizes the profit motive in commercialization of sports, but not the political motive. At the Winter Games in Grenoble, France, in 1968, Brundage grumbled openly, "We had 'Olympic' butter, 'Olympic' liquor, 'Olympic' petrol"; and he worried over the brazen efforts of many skiers to get equipment trademarks on television or news photos, perhaps because they had been paid by the manufacturers to do so. ("If I had my way, we wouldn't have given them any medals. I didn't even go to those events in Alpine skiing—it was the only thing I could do: stay away.") But he tends to ignore, or excuse the "state amateurism" of the politically motivated societies. Indeed, he refuses to recognize politics as an urgent motive in international sports. Instead, Brundage prefers to believe that amateur sport is the only thing that has kept half the world from giving the other half 24 hours to get out. "Sports transcend politics," he insists. "They are international phenomena, like science or music."

Out of Tune

The 1962 Asian Games (which are regional games held between Olympic years) were to be held in Djakarta, Indonesia. When the entry forms sent to the athletes of Nationalist China

turned out to be blank pieces of paper, the Taiwan government was angered and blamed the slight on Communist influence in Indonesia. When the entries for Israel got lost, the government of Prime Minister David Ben-Gurion was angered and blamed it on Arab influence in Indonesia. To smooth things over, the delegate from India suggested that perhaps the games should be stripped of their status as "Asian Games" and simply be designated as an "international competition." Then it was Indonesia's turn to feel slighted: the trade minister angrily urged his government not to enter into any new trade agreements with India. Eventually, the International Weight-Lifting Federation withdrew its sanction of the games; the International

Amateur Athletic Association did the same; Japan debated quitting the games for fear of jeopardizing its status as host for the 1964 Olympic Games; and the IOC suspended Indonesia, thus giving it the distinction of being the first member to be barred altogether from the 1964 Olympics. All in all, it was a rich, winy example of the goodwill and fellowship that can be fostered through sports.

It is obvious that something must be done about such a situation. It must be recognized that the trend toward professionalizing amateur sports is worldwide and that it affects the politically motivated countries as deeply as the profit-oriented ones. The age-old myth that the amateur athlete reflects the basic fiber of the people of a society—that the amateur is of the people in a way that the professional is not—must be exposed for what it is.

The ancient Greeks believed in the myth and took every means possible to make sure that their city-states achieved success. The Soviet Union finally accepted the myth after nearly 40 years of spurning the Olympics as a bourgeois pastime. When they decided to go into them in 1952, they did it in a big way: they placed second in the unofficial standings that year in the Summer Games, then went on to win the Winter and Summer Games of 1956 and 1960 and the Winter Games of 1964. All this represented not only an athletic triumph for the Soviet Union but supposedly a political defeat for the United States as well. Because the United States had won six of the preceding seven Summer Olympics, it could now be made to appear that the basic fabric of Western society was in decline. There were even those on both sides of the iron curtain who felt that the Soviet success reflected darkly on the U.S. economic system and its political viability. All this is, of course arrant nonsense. The victory of Nazi Germany in the 1936 Olympics—the only time in seven tries that the United States failed to win the Summer Games—did not in the least affect the capacity of the Allied nations to inflict a devastating military and political defeat upon Nazi Germany in 1945.

A REALISTIC PERSPECTIVE

The amateur who performs regularly and exclusively at his sport should no longer be regarded as better than the professional who does the same thing. The 40 to 45 million people who participate in sports in the United States and Canada—in weekend golf, in tennis, in ice skating, in boating, in skiing, in hunting, in hiking, and in hockey—tell us much about the society from which they emerge. But they are participants, not performers; they are not the kind of "amateurs" who turn up in college football or Olympic track meets. Nor do they have any urgent desire to be that kind of amateur. In the society in which these "participating amateurs" thrive, the someone special is the professional athlete—which is one of the reasons why "performing amateurs" covet the prestige of pay.

An important task for the officials of amateur sports is to eliminate the duplicity in which they indulge. They cannot long insist on the absolutes of amateurism in athletics while they themselves hustle multimillion-dollar television contracts, solicit commercial endorsement from advertisers for bulging programs, and do everything to make huge gate attractions of their "amateur" events. They must either give up their own riches or accept neoprofessionalism as a fact of life in the Western countries, just as it is accepted in the state-operated economies, and redefine "amateurism" in these terms.

It is unlikely that this will happen overnight. The pace thus far has been slow. It is much more likely that Brundage will continue his resolute fight against commercialism in amateur sports. But Brundage seems to sense that it is a losing fight. Some time ago, he was lunching with an acquaintance (over an egg-and-bacon sandwich with tomato on the side) and reflecting on how amateurism was being conquered by the crafty apostles of profit. "Well," he said moodily, "bird-watching remains unsullied so far. But sooner or later I suppose they'll find a way to commercialize that, too."

They will—as soon as they manage to put it on television.

Black Africa Saves The Game

by MARION KAPLAN, free-lance writer and photographer, East Africa

ALL PHOTOS BY MISS KAPLAN

"It had been a fruitful day. As the dusk settled over the thick African bush the small band of men, their ragged clothes and hands covered with blood, staggered back to camp laden with elephant tusks and—great luck—two rhinoceros horns. Back at the camp, they joyfully laid their burden on the ugly pile of tusks and skins that already covered the floor of a carefully camouflaged grass-roofed shelter. Outside, one man had lit a fire and was already roasting lumps of meat over the flames. Soon, all the men were gathered around the fire. Blind to the ominous dark shapes slowly circling high above the carcasses they had left behind, they boasted of their day's success. As the meat sizzled, one man glanced up. With a yell, he made a grab for his bow and arrows. He was too late: in an instant every man was pinioned by a burly figure in uniform. Another poaching expedition ended."

A Poacher's Paradise?

This account of poachers trailed and captured by African rangers is imaginary, but hundreds of times over it has been made true. In Africa, poaching exists and will continue to exist on a horrifying scale as long as there is a demand for rhino horns (believed in the Far East to be an aphrodisiac), ivory, such prized skins as leopard and crocodile, and, on a humbler but equally destructive level, game meat. The outlook would be gloomy if it were not for the determined efforts of concerned governments generously helped by external sources that offer equipment, buildings, and funds to combat the menace.

Poachers use a variety of weapons from poison-tipped arrows, spears, vicious snares, and gin traps to sophisticated quick-firing rifles. Ranged against them, armed field forces of disciplined African rangers operate from Land-Rovers, trucks, and, where necessary, boats. On their side increasingly are radios and light aircraft—although their best allies in the continuing contest are still the vultures that gather as signposts wherever poachers make a killing.

So widespread are poaching and dealing in illegal trophies that several African governments are banding together to form what has been dubbed an "animal Interpol," after the abbreviation for the International Criminal Police

Two poachers in Kenya make off with illegal game trophies (upper left). Unaware that their hideout has been observed, they drink and cook meat after a murderous day's work (lower left). One of them pauses outside a concealed cave (center). Meanwhile, the field force has moved up the hill to make the arrest (upper right). Later, handcuffed captives, under guard, await arrival of the police (lower right). The poachers' traps, weapons, and ivory will be used in evidence against them.

Organization, and is aimed, among other things, at curbing the illicit trade. (Licensed hunting safaris, of course, are legal and encouraged; revenues from the costly license fees go toward conservation.) Additionally, a conference on international cooperation in wildlife conservation, the first of its kind, was convened in March 1968 by Perez Olindo, the director of Kenya's national parks. The conference typified the approach of Africa today towards its wildlife. Many Africans, frequently with expert knowledge, are dedicated to the cause of preservation. If only to be practical, they are also well aware of the benefits deriving from tourism.

The African Takes Charge

In the 1950's and early 1960's, when today's African countries were territories seeking independence, the cry was raised among white settlers and international conservationists that wildlife would be sacrificed by independent governments caring nothing about the aesthetic values of their heritage. They have been proved wrong. The dependence of agricultural societies on land for cultivation and cattle raising has inevitably made an impact everywhere, but vast areas of Africa remain wonderlands where creatures, great and small, have a guaranteed future in their natural habitat.

In East Africa, Tanzania had only two national parks at the end of colonial rule. Now it has seven, with an eighth, on the higher slopes of Mount Kilimanjaro, being planned. Kenya has steadily increased its protected areas since independence in 1963 so that it now has 14 national parks—including the first two marine parks created in Africa—five game reserves, and two nature reserves. Uganda has three national parks, 15 game reserves (as opposed to three at independence), and eight sanctuaries.

In Uganda's Murchison Falls National Park, a river patrol ranger displays some of the items confiscated from poachers (left). A patrol boat moves along the river (lower left). The simple but wickedly effective snares used by poachers are examined (right). Ivory seized from poachers is numbered for reference and stacked in the warden's store (below).

The difference between parks, reserves, and sanctuaries, broadly and with exceptions, is that parks are exclusively set aside for the total protection of flora and fauna. Game reserves exclude any other form of land use, but some hunting, under license, is allowed. Sanctuaries are not free from land use but all or some species are protected from hunters.

In a category of its own is Tanzania's unique Ngorongoro Crater Conservation Area, where vast herds of zebras and wildebeests migrate annually from the Serengeti National Park. In 1969 the government announced that it would hand over 80% of the area's 3,200 square miles to a local authority, the Masai Range Development Commission. A lack of qualifying information brought a public furor and emotionally worded protests from international conservationists.

Eventually, however, it became clear that the excised land in whole or part was to remain a "no shooting" area; any unlicensed killing of game was forbidden. While the Masai authorities fiercely defended their ability to live amicably with wild animals, the government, pointing to its widely respected conservation policy, gave a public assurance—clearly emanating from President Julius Nyerere himself—that the animals "will enjoy every natural right they deserve."

East Africa, fast building a reputation as a tourist paradise, is the prime example of sound conservation measures. But elsewhere, despite the pressures of land hunger and political change, reserves are being maintained and new ones established. In West Africa, Ghana is planning to extend the existing Kujani Game Reserve, which stretches westward from the shores of Lake Volta. It also plans to improve its well-developed Mole River Game Reserve in the north and to declare as a game reserve land north of Cape Coast that is already a protected area. Unlike the famed parks and reserves of East Africa, Ghana's game reserves attract few tourists from other countries but rather exist largely to serve the resident population.

Even in war-torn Nigeria, where big game is not plentiful, active measures have been taken to establish game reserves where, the authorities say, "such animals can flourish and be seen." The first of these is Yankari in northeastern Ni-

One animal that Africa is saving is the black species of rhinoceros (left), but in the Victoria Nile it has been necessary to crop 4,000 hippos (lower left) because the riverbanks can no longer support the ones that live there now. A pride of lions takes it easy (below) and some vervet monkeys tend their young (lower right).

In their natural habitat, two giraffes roam freely (left); young orphaned cheetahs live a life free from harm in a spacious paddock (upper right); and a lady elephant shows off her profile (right).

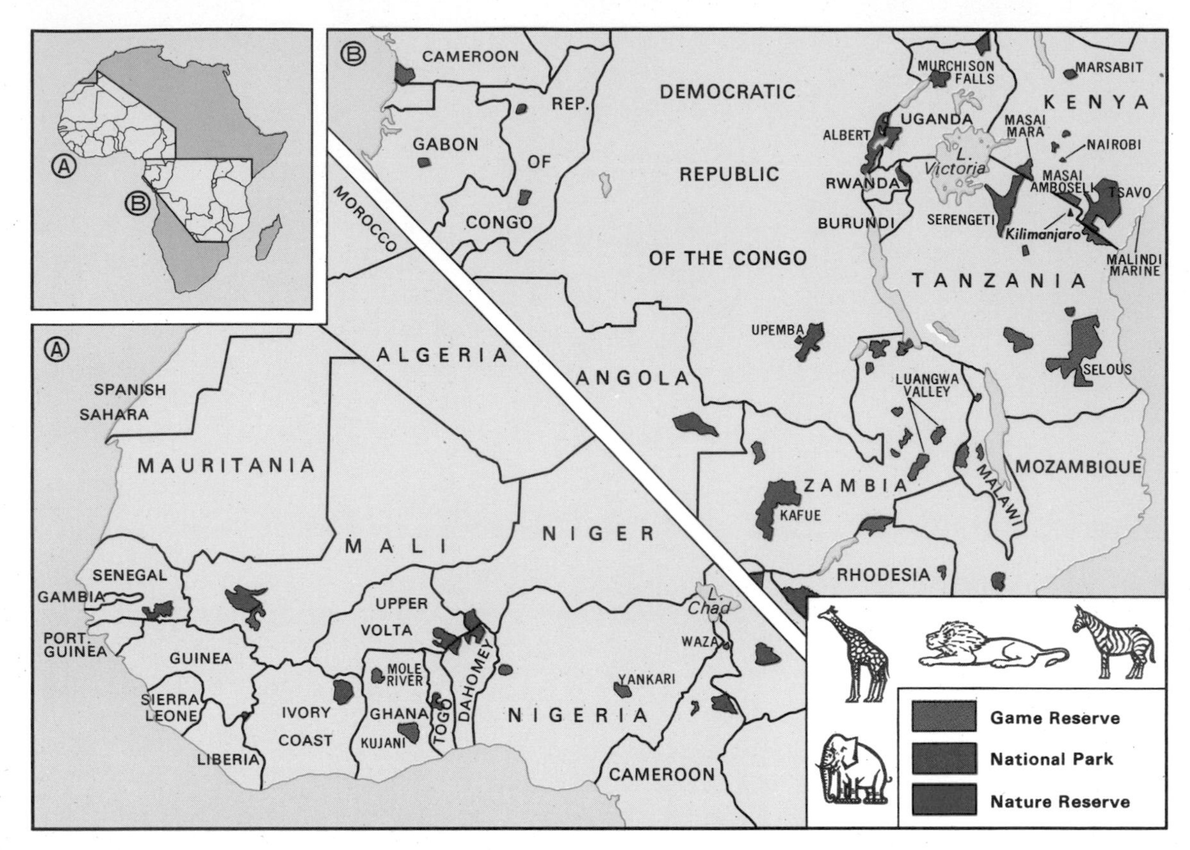

The map (above) shows major national parks and game reserves in the countries mentioned in the article. On the slopes of Mount Kilimanjaro (right), Africa's highest mountain (19,340 feet), the College of African Wildlife Management was built.

geria. The army was called in to help build the roads and bridges, and the game scouts and guides were recruited from the ranks of hunters. Many of the game guards were once soldiers and policemen. (Some countries cleverly employ the skills of former poachers converted to the government side.)

Wild animals still live peaceably around Lake Chad, which is bounded by Nigeria, Chad, Niger, and Cameroon. Niger has printed a map showing districts, mainly in its southern half, inhabited by elephants, rhinos, giraffes, antelopes, and various types of monkeys. Giraffes now exist in western Africa only in limited numbers; most of them are to be found in protected areas in Cameroon, the Central African Republic, Chad, Mali, and Senegal.

Cameroon is one of the West African countries where tourism, if not on the scale of eastern or even central Africa, is a fact of life. In 1970 Cameroon anticipates 36,000 visitors, for whom the chief attraction is the well-administered Waza Game Reserve in the north. There, thousands of giraffes, rare in neighboring lands, form the pride of the park's administrators.

Small Nations Give the Best Example

In Sierra Leone, under a new wildlife conservation act, a number of areas will be constituted as national parks and game reserves and a number of forest reserves given the status of game reserve. The government announced that it would welcome external investment for the development of tourism and the setting up of game reserves. As one of so many African countries that have suffered financial difficulties in the developing process, Sierra Leone has been unable in the past to vote special funds for wildlife conservation. It has, however, paid for the training in Tanzania of a game superintendent, has recruited another superintendent-in-training for further studies, and hopes to vote a modest sum toward conservation very soon.

A signal example of those countries with the enthusiasm for the job but minimal funds to pay for it is The Gambia, a tiny finger of land surrounded, but for its outlet on the Atlantic Ocean, by Senegal. Even Gambia has a nature reserve of 200 acres in which all flora and fauna are safeguarded. Alas, so diminished was Gambia's

wildlife that the original animals had to be donated. Early gifts were two jackal cubs, six porcupines, three royal pythons, two monkeys, and a pair of parrots. Crocodiles were already there —indeed, much of Gambia is river. Gradually the population of the little reserve was built up. Now it includes three chimpanzees, leopards, sun squirrels, red Colobus monkeys and green vervet monkeys, and West African elands, whose local name is *jinki-janko*—and Senegal, which has a big national park of its own, is giving back Gambian species that in the course of time had moved across the borders.

Congo: A Stricken Elephant

Comparing The Gambia with the Democratic Republic of the Congo (Kinshasa) is like comparing a mouse with an elephant. But of the two, for many long years it was the elephant that was stricken and helpless. The Congo contains, as well as other parks, the 2.2-million-acre Albert National Park adjoining Lake Edward. Africa's oldest park, it was created in 1925 by King Albert I of the Belgians. Its purpose when it was set up was primarily to protect the mountain gorilla. Now, the gorilla's numbers have been sadly reduced by the fighting that accompanied the establishment of the independent government and by intrusion on its habitat by human beings.

The Congolese government has made clear its intent to bring order where chaos long existed. In 1968 the Institute of National Parks was set up to replace the Belgian body that disappeared with independence in 1960. While the new authority retains the old and complicated regulations for game protection and hunting control, it may be some time before the government, seated in Kinshasa in the western part of the country, will be able to enforce its laws in the faraway parks near the eastern frontier. After years of depredations by regular and guerrilla troops who shot elephants and other big game for food, trophies, or sport, poaching by Congolese and alien tribesmen continues to be a major problem for the overworked and depleted staffs of the parks.

A Vast Wildlife Laboratory

If in the Congo one army or another has tragically destroyed numberless animals, the story is different elsewhere. To the south in Zambia, the army was ordered into the battle against poachers that were slaughtering two increasingly rare species of antelopes, the red and black lechwe. In Zambia, too, a project under way in 1969 was to turn the Luangwa Valley Game Reserves into a vast "laboratory" thousands of square miles in size. For three years, scientists were to study the habits and movements of wildlife in the valley and make a detailed survey to plan for the eventual control and management of all the game. The object was to see how wildlife could best be conserved—and commercialized. Optimum levels of game populations were to be

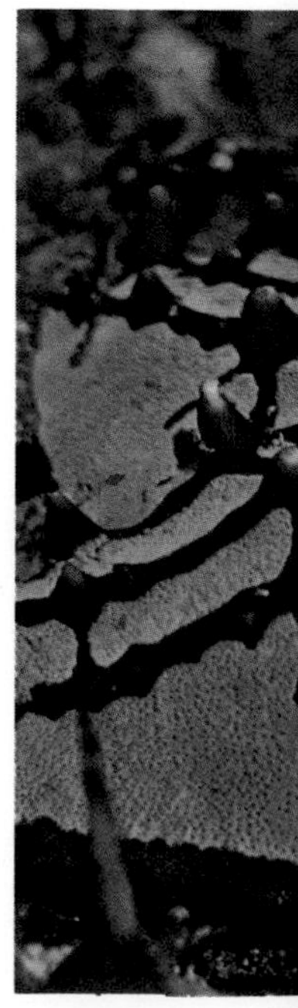

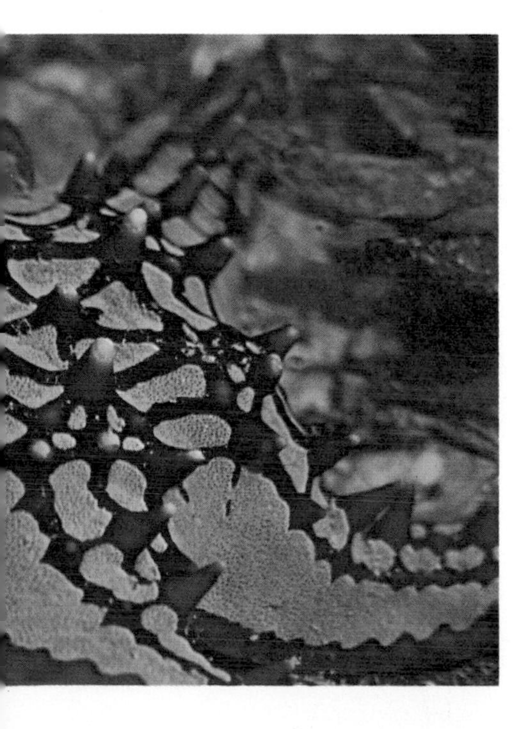

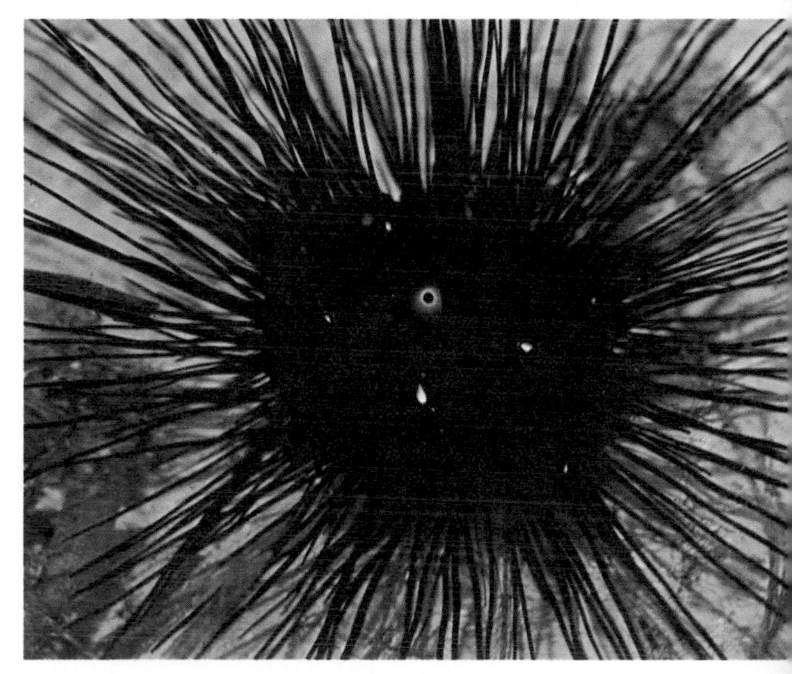

Paraa Safari Lodge (far left) overlooks the Victoria Nile in Uganda's Murchison Falls National Park, and Voi Safari Lodge (upper right) is in the Tsavo National Park in Kenya. Africa's first marine parks, in Kenya, protect the starfish (center) and the spiky sea urchin (above).

In an experimental station (upper left) near Kampala, Uganda, infant crocodiles (lower left) will be cared for until they can survive in the rivers. A young croc is weighed (upper right); its handler wears a tough leather gauntlet (lower right).

determined and numbers over these levels cropped to provide meat and skins.

At first it seems illogical that conservation goes hand in hand with cropping. But, while significant numbers of animals move onto the list of rare species, in certain areas others must be reduced to avoid overcrowding and erosion of the land. Cropping projects are usually undertaken only when the choice is survival or starvation, and then under scientific supervision. But, more and more, game ranching and commercial cropping are coming under study. Indeed, they have many positive effects.

The chief game warden in Uganda, Sylvester Ruhweza, feels that poaching tends to be magnified. People have lived alongside animals since time began—and, as he says, every Ugandan has the right to eat meat. To cope with the traditional view (in the Swahili language the word for meat, *nyama,* is also used for any antelope or herd of small plains game), Uganda has a policy of cropping animals that are overcrowding their habitat and of selling the meat at a modest 7¢ a pound. This practice ensures a cheap supply of protein—and eliminates much poaching.

The "Croc Farm"

But if one problem is on the way to solution, many others exist. Crocodiles, whose numbers were seriously reduced in Uganda by overhunting during the colonial era, are being poached for their valuable skins. In the parks and reserves crocodiles are protected; but, since fishing is also an important industry, the government cannot declare crocodiles totally protected outside the reserves. Therefore, it has begun what, of its nature, must be a long-term experiment with crocodile breeding at a government fisheries station nicknamed the "croc farm."

Crocodiles grow slowly and do not breed until they are about 19 years old. Although a female may lay 50 eggs, the batch may well be devoured by predators—and the tiny crocodiles that emerge from surviving eggs are easy victims for a number of aggressors. At the croc farm not only are crocodile diet, growth, and habits under study, but eggs are safeguarded also and the young are tended until they are big enough to survive in the rivers.

Government ventures and experiments of this nature are becoming quite common. Often they are aided by outside sources or sponsored by foundations or by the United Nations Development Programme. Malawi, for instance, has sought specialists' advice for the improvement of its game reserves, parks, and controlled areas. Less official projects also exist. In Botswana, in southern Africa, not only are there handsome government-controlled reserves but an enterprising tribe has also turned a large tract of tribal land into a preserve known as the Moremi Game Reserve. Its threefold purpose: conserving wildlife, attracting fee-paying tourists, and ensuring constant supplies of meat.

Guarantee for the Future

Africa's determination to ensure a guaranteed future for its wildlife has been amply displayed in a comprehensive document, the African Convention on the Conservation of Nature and Natural Resources, which was presented at the conference in Algiers, Algeria, of the Organization of African Unity (OAU) in September 1968 and signed by representatives of 38 governments. The convention stipulates that contracting states "shall ensure conservation, wise use, and development of faunal resources and their environment, within the framework of land-use planning and of economic and social development." Each state is pledged to adopt or maintain adequate laws on hunting, capture, and fishing. The issue of permits is properly regulated, and prohibited hunting methods are listed in de-

Schoolteachers, as well as schoolchildren, come to the parks in organized groups. Primary teachers gather by the handsome Wildlife Education Centre at the Murchison Falls National Park headquarters (below).

tail, including any likely to cause a mass destruction of wild animals.

The agreement also recognizes the urgent need to provide "special protection to those animal . . . species that are threatened with extinction, or which may become so, and to the habitat necessary to their survival." Two long lists classify species according to the kind of protection they should receive.

Animals in Class A shall be totally protected, and hunting, killing, capture, or collection permitted only if required in the national interest or for scientific purposes. The list covers a wide range of mammals, birds, reptiles, amphibians, and fish, including the chimpanzee, gorilla, cheetah, square-lipped rhino, pygmy hippopotamus, all pelicans, all storks, vultures, the lammergeier eagle, the Cameroon toad, giant tortoises, blind fishes, and the dugong and manatee, from whose strange appearance derive many of the familiar legends about mermaids.

For all animals on the second list, Class B, hunting, killing, capture, or collection is permitted only with "special authorization granted by the competent authority." Among species covered are all monkeys except the common baboon, the caracal lynx, lion, leopard, elephant, black rhinoceros, hippopotamus, giraffe, buffalo, ostrich, and crocodile.

Teaching the Importance of Wildlife

Antipoaching operations, scientific studies, and the care—and extension—of protected land and the animals living on it are only aspects of Africa's conservation efforts. Vital to the whole cause is education; teaching the people the importance of wildlife to their society is an important feature of the policy of many African governments today.

In Tanzania, the national parks have adopted an education program to instill pride in the fact that wildlife is one of the country's finest resources. Organized groups, mostly schoolchildren, who visit the parks are accommodated free of charge in well-designed hostels. Attractively produced literature is given to them, guides supplied, and conducted tours of museums in some of the parks arranged. Organizers estimate that 70% of the adults and children who participate have never before seen anything but a handful of the animals.

Another approach is to bring the parks to the people. A Land-Rover fitted out as a mobile film projection unit travels extensively through the country showing films with a Swahili soundtrack, designed for unsophisticated viewers.

Rangers on early-morning duty in Kenya's Nairobi National Park (upper left) ride bicycles on patrol. In Murchison Falls National Park, Uganda, rangers take an elephant count (center left), one of the most important duties of park staffs. Tourists enjoy the view on the grounds of the Lake Manyara Hotel in Tanzania (upper right), which serves the Lake Manyara National Park. The main attraction of tourists to Murchison Falls is the launch ride up the river (left), which teems with hippopotamuses and a considerable number of crocodiles.

From this effort people in remote villages can glean some idea of the need for conservation. And in cities, small towns, and villages the government puts up posters carrying the conservation message.

A major target in Tanzania's bold campaign is the Masai, a nomadic people whose large herds of cattle have despoiled many a game habitat. Now the Masai are being encouraged to settle down in villages and look to the future. Fortunately, the Masai tradition of proving their manhood by spearing a lion has faded; their reputation, however, as an aloof people reluctant to change a placid (and, to the tourist, picturesque) way of life is often justified. Yet from the Masai tribe have come some of the ablest game conservation officials in such strongholds as Kenya's Masai Amboseli and Masai Mara game reserves and Tanzania's incomparable Ngorongoro Crater Conservation Area—although at least one man admits that he did not plan his career that way.

Solomon ole Saibull, the 34-year-old conservator of Ngorongoro, had looked forward to a career in government. After earning a degree in political science, he was appointed assistant secretary in the Ministry of External Affairs, then transferred temporarily because of a staff shortage to the Ministry of Lands, Forests, and

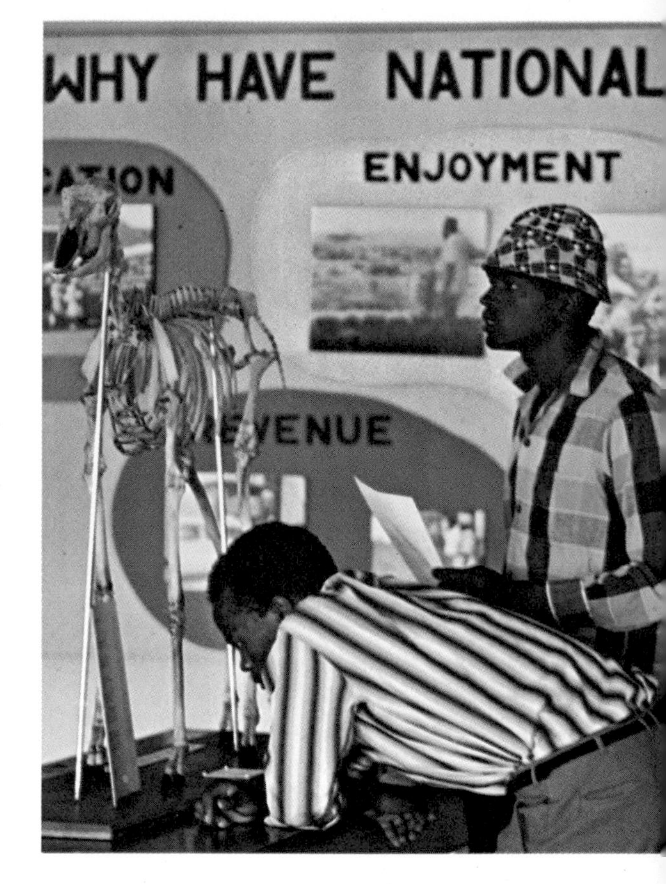

Common cattle (above) have caused more damage to many habitats than almost any wild animal. At Kenyatta College, near Nairobi, Kenya, students look at conservation exhibits (upper left). As part of its education scheme, Kenya's national parks take schoolchildren on tours of the Nairobi National Park (lower left). In Tanzania, schoolchildren look at posters (center) and leaflets (lower center) that tell the conservation message. At Tanzania's African Wildlife Management College students learn to identify animals (below).

The Wild Animals Orphanage at Nairobi, Kenya (upper left), tends motherless and maimed creatures. A ranger applies medicine to an injured heron (above), and a wildebeest is fed (right). A tiny cheetah (top, center) was brought to the orphanage, where it gathers strength. Brutus, a 20-year-old lion, lives out his life in peace (below, center), and Mary, a young chimpanzee, listens to a ranger's watch (upper right). Sylvester Ruhweza, Uganda's chief game warden, holds a young okapi (lower right).

Wildlife. At the point when he was to return to his original post, he was asked to stand in—again temporarily—for the conservator of Ngorongoro, who was going on leave. Now Saibull is an ardent conservationist responsible for one of the world's greatest natural wonders. Yet, in Masai terms, he is still a *moran*—a young warrior who has undergone the considerable, and physically painful, ritual of proving himself worthy to enter his tribe's age group.

In Africa, this is an age of transition when thousands of young men—and women—tactfully compromise with the traditions of their clans and tribes and enter fully into the new world. Another young Masai is John ole Monah, who has completed two years of field work in Tanzania's Serengeti National Park and is taking a diploma course in wildlife management. He says lightly that some of the elders in his village regard him as "lost." To him, however, progress is more important—and friends of his own age are in full agreement.

Wildlife College

The course that John ole Monah is taking is provided by the College of African Wildlife Management at Moshi, Tanzania, on the slopes of Mount Kilimanjaro. Since it was founded in the early 1960's more than 200 Africans have graduated and gone on to work in the field as wardens and game superintendents or to advanced training. A sponsoring agency for the college is the Scientific, Technical, and Research Commission of the OAU. Financial assistance has been provided by external aid sources, but the African governments that send students to the college pay most of the operating expenses. Students take one- or two-year courses covering such diverse subjects as botany, range management, surveying and mapping, vehicle operation and maintenance, taxidermy and museum techniques, administration and wildlife conservation, and law and court procedure. The college is the only institution of its kind in Africa, but plans are under way to set up a similar center in West Africa in Cameroon.

Who will be the students of the future? Many will come from the generation of schoolchildren being taught the values of wildlife for the first time: the children learning from posters in Tanzania, the children in Kenya who are taken on bus tours of the Nairobi National Park, the children in Uganda who are given accommodation at the Wildlife Education Centre in the Murchison Falls National Park and taken in launches to view the teeming animal life and birdlife on the banks of the Victoria Nile.

These children are learning from the men already in the field—rangers who show them what wild animals are like and devoted education officers who teach them how interesting and important wild animals are. Kenya has a wild-animal orphanage at the entrance to the Nairobi park that not only tends orphaned and abandoned creatures but also successfully fulfills its other purpose of showing ordinary people the great variety of their country's animal assets.

Old Problem; New Commitment

The new leaders in an old war—against the rigors of nature, the greed of the poachers, the land hunger of the peasants—are men like

A student at Tanzania's College of African Wildlife Management examines an animal skull (left). Perez Olindo (above) is director of Kenya's national parks.

Solomon ole Saibull, a Masai, acts as the conservator of Ngorongoro Crater Conservation Area, in northern Tanzania. Here, he stands in the Ngorongoro Crater with herds of zebras and wildebeests in the background.

Kenya's director of national parks, Perez Olindo; Tanzania's Solomon ole Saibull; Uganda's Sylvester Ruhweza; and a young Ghanaian named Christopher Manu.

Each man came into wildlife conservation by a different route. Olindo's first ambition was medicine, but even as a boy he was interested in animals. He obtained a bachelor's degree in zoology and wildlife management and, like many of Africa's conservationists, he did his advanced studies at U.S. universities. Married, he has two small children—a little girl called Sable and a baby boy called Bongo, both the names of rare and beautiful antelopes.

Ruhweza studied natural science, physics, and chemistry at Makerere University College, in Kampala, Uganda, and taught for many years before additional studies led him to become the wildlife ministry's first biologist. This in time led to his present position as chief game warden. His responsibilities are to preserve wildlife, cope with the problems of ecology, study the changing pattern of land use, and advise his government. He also chaired the committee that presented the convention on conservation at the OAU conference in Algiers.

Manu first learned about wildlife in his youth when, to pay his school fees and help feed his fatherless family, he had to venture into Ghana's forests to collect kola nuts. He did well enough to continue his studies to degree level on scholarships. When the Ghanaian government chose to send him to Tanzania for the wildlife college's course, he arrived with such impressive qualifications in natural history he was asked to teach.

But these able and enthusiastic young Africans would be powerless without the active support of their governments. With a thousand other priorities in development, education, and health, these governments have also shown that black Africa is concerned about saving the game. Some with greater advantages are facing the challenge with more vigor than others, but across the length and breadth of the continent the conservation movement is under way.

President Nyerere of Tanzania, on the eve of his country's independence, made a specific pledge: "We solemnly declare that we will do everything in our power to make sure that our children's grandchildren will be able to enjoy this rich and precious inheritance. The survival of our wildlife is a matter of grave concern to all of us in Africa. These wild creatures are not only important as a source of wonder and inspiration, but are an integral part of our natural resources and of our future livelihood and well-being."

In Africa today, thousands of young men have shunned the prestige jobs in the civil service, commerce, and the army to devote themselves to wildlife conservation. Serving in the forests, the bush, the vast plains, they are proving to be the unexpected saviors of a unique heritage.

A noted funnyman takes
a serious look at American humor:

What Are We Laughing At?

by STEVE ALLEN
television humorist, author, and composer

We are by now accustomed to the idea that in the fields of science and technology more has been learned in the past 50 years than in all the previous ages of human history and that, of all the scientists who have ever lived, over 80% are active today. Because each new discovery makes others possible, not only is knowledge accumulating in greater supply than ever before, but—what is more startling—the very pace of progress is also constantly accelerating. Predictions of future achievements therefore are risky and will probably prove to have been wide of the mark, most likely far below it.

To a degree the same evolutionary process is discernible in the arts, including humor. Certainly it is true that the sheer volume of humor produced in the last half century—essays, light verse, jokes, cartoons, comedy presented in films, radio, and television—far outweighs everything created during earlier periods of man's history. And, of all the professional humorists and comedians, those alive at the present moment must far outnumber the always thin ranks of funnymen of ages past.

It does not automatically follow in the arts as in the sciences, however, that quantitative progress will also entail qualitative improvement. There are many more painters today than in earlier times, but few if any who put Rembrandt van Rijn, Leonardo da Vinci, or Michelangelo to shame. As to whether today's best comedians surpass the wits of former years it is difficult to say. Comparing Jules Feiffer to Mark Twain, or Bill Cosby to Will Rogers, may be as impossible of resolution as are the endless arguments as to whether John L. Sullivan could have defeated Joe Louis or whether Jack Dempsey was a better fighter than Cassius Clay.

The Phenomenon of Humor

To understand the humor of the 1970's—or, for that matter, the humor of the 16th century—one must, of course, first grasp the phenomenon itself. This is no easy task.

There are simple dictionary definitions of words such as "humor" and "comedy," but they are not truly instructive. Most are incomplete; others are rewordings of things we already sense intuitively. The philosopher Aristotle defined the ridiculous as that which is incongruous but does not represent actual pain or danger. Had there been many vulgar wits in the Athens, Greece, of his day, presumably one would have told Aristotle that incongruity not related to danger is by no means *always* amusing. An all-embracing definition of humor has been attempted by many philosophers but no entirely satisfactory formula has yet been devised. Aristotle's definition is consistent with the theory that much humor is based on a frustrated expectation, but he reported another concept, derived from Plato, which states that the pleasure of laughter grows out of a sense of the misfortune of others and a sudden awareness of self-superiority in that we ourselves are not in the predicament observed. The two theories are obviously mutually exclusive. Laughter, being essentially an emotional response, appears in too many varieties to be adequately encompassed by any one definition.

Another common theory claims that laughter originated in the vindictive shout of triumph to which early man gave vent at the moment of victory over an enemy. In our daily experience we are all familiar with laughter that has an essentially sadistic undercurrent. One of today's most popular comedians, Don Rickles, employs almost no other form of humor; his popularity may, in fact, reveal something about the present mood in the United States. The fact that Rickles offstage is a decent and cordial fellow is, of course, irrelevant to an understanding of his professional style—his barbed humor draws a consistently favorable response from audiences.

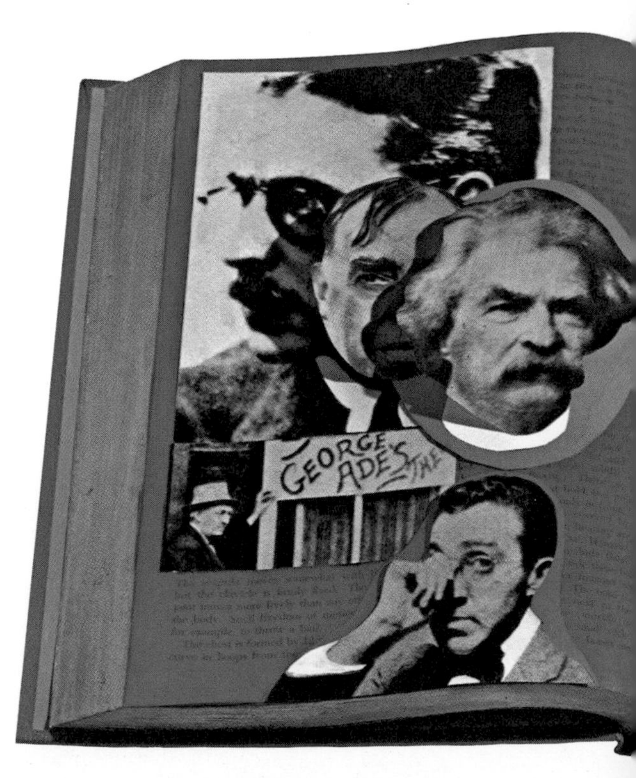

Then, there is another laughter, the innocent laughter of young children. It is the sheer, gleeful, silly, having-a-good-time laughter, to which even sober adults will occasionally succumb.

There is also a familiar theory—which I believe does go far to throw light upon, if not actually explain, the origins of humor—that holds that the funniest individuals, and the most amusing social groups, are those which have known a tragic history. It is difficult to determine how much weight to attribute to the hypothesis since there is apparently no ethnic or tribal group that has not known its share of tragedy. But presumably there is a connection between the tragic theme of Jewish history and the fact that most of our leading humorists, comedians, gag writers, and wits are Jewish. (The list includes Jack Benny, Groucho Marx, Sid Caesar, Milton Berle, Jack Carter, Victor Borge, Jan Murray, Red Buttons, Jack E. Leonard, Jackie Mason, Phil Silvers, Joey Bishop, Lou Holtz, Sam Levenson, Woody Allen, Jerry Lewis, Henry Morgan, Paul Winchell, Phil Foster, Myron Cohen, Ben Blue, Abe Burrows, Irwin Corey, Buddy Hackett, Shecky Green, Alan King, George Burns, Charlie Chaplin, Mel Brooks, Danny Kaye, Jerry Lester, Larry Storch, Bill Dana, Louis Nye, Sid Gould, Dayton Allen, Henny Youngman, Shelley Berman, Mort Sahl, and David Steinberg.)

Another factor explaining Jewish wit and humor is that the Jews have historically been a literate, scholarly people with a respect for the subtleties of language and sophistication of thought. But if these elements explain Jewish humor, how does one account for the recent emergence in the American culture of a vigorous Negro comedy? Tragedy is no stranger to North American blacks, but they have not enjoyed—either in their original African homeland or in their U.S. environment—the benefits of that education which the Jews developed for themselves over the centuries. The apparent paradox evaporates when we consider the differences between Jewish and Negro humor. There is still little highly literate black humor in the United States; rather the vigorous comedy of today's black wits rises up out of the streets and ghettos, at best from the emerging Negro middle class.

The humor of the American Negro is not a new phenomenon, of course; it has merely been hidden underground heretofore, along with black emotional states generally. Largely because of the lack of civilization among whites, Negro comedians of past years were limited to playing Uncle Tom-ish, lazy, smiling, shuffling menials. The humor with which Negroes amused each other had elements of satire, bitterness, sarcasm, and even self-deprecation that were rarely if ever revealed to the white man. But in either form, humor for the American black was an important emotional outlet—as, for that matter, it is for all men. To look purposely for the element of humor in an uncomfortable situation is to make use of an important procedure in emotional control, in the maintenance of one's own mental health. The commonplace observation that we laugh because we are too embarrassed to cry may be amended to include the truth that we sometimes joke and laugh because we do not wish to fight.

Until recently American Negroes had not been permitted to advance to the point of social evolution from which the development of literate, outspoken comedians could be expected of their culture. Restless, reluctant submission to dominant authorities, combined with the inevitable yearning for freedom, can be a powerful mainspring supplying energy to those who have the mysterious comic gift. It is only to be expected, therefore, that so many young Negro comedians are presently emerging in the entertainment world of the United States.

The Demand for More Freedom

To understand the current revolutionary aspect of American comedy we must consider it in relation to the increased demands—on the part of the young, the alienated, the black, and the rebellious—for more "freedom." It is not difficult to see that when the American Negro, in 1970, demands freedom, he has specifics in mind: the freedom to send his children to certain schools, the freedom to move into certain neighborhoods, the freedom to compete for certain jobs, the freedom to vote for candidates truly of his choice. But it is less clear what the word "freedom" means in the mouths of some young radical whites.

As for the youthful Marxists, the puzzle is particularly acute in that, if they had their way, they would lead us into a societal form that even they concede would be much less free than the one we presently enjoy. Of the non-Marxist young, some may wish to be free to smoke marihuana, to be free of the military draft, to be free to grow long hair. One can take time here to observe only that their freedom in these areas is increasingly less restricted. It is against this cultural background that more freedom is being granted to comedians who appeal primarily to the young, and inferentially to American comedians and humorists generally.

As the decade of the 1960's moved to a close, the two television programs best dramatizing the new freedom were The Smothers Brothers Comedy Hour and Rowan and Martin's Laugh-In. Both programs, though well produced and successful, may have been substitutes for those forms of comic entertainment the rebellious young might have devised had they been fully able to dictate their wishes to the television network. As regards Dan Rowan and Dick Martin of Laugh-In, they must have been surprised by their sudden appeal to a youthful audience after many years of success in nightclubs. They had appealed primarily to the Las Vegas (Nev.) habitués who enjoy Danny Thomas, Sammy Davis, Jr., Dean Martin, Frank Sinatra, Buddy Hackett, Milton Berle, and other entertainers whose popularity lies almost entirely with the over-35 crowd. Only within the framework of Laugh-In did Rowan and Martin become attractive to the chronologically or psychologically young, and even here it is possible that the most youthful members of that enjoyable program's viewing audience attached their personal loyalties more to the program's supporting players than to its stars.

As regards the Smothers Brothers, it is odd that they became known as specialists in social satire. Tom and Dick were members of my television show family in 1962, by which time it was apparent that essentially they were not political or social satirists. It would be more nearly correct to say that political and social satire were eventually presented on their series for the Columbia Broadcasting System (CBS). Their personal specialty is the marvelously winning routine they present standing alone on the stage developing humor out of a musical context, with Tom singing his dumb songs and Dick trying to talk some sense into him. Both brothers nevertheless deserve credit for their strong social conscience, a sense that it is proper to employ the power of television to affect society in the ways that their progressive orientation suggests to them that it ought to be affected, and a willingness to use their program as a platform from which to advance modern ideas and attitudes. Consequently their comedy hour was generally of high quality and frequently presented points of view that seemed daring in terms of what television humor generally had been during the preceding 20 years.

The new climate of freedom for television humor brought about two kinds of material formerly presented rarely on the medium: (a) off-color humor and (b) social commentary and satire. The first category grew partly out of the nightclub tradition and partly out of the mysterious unconscious of man, generally self-repressed, but of late given voice because of the new permissiveness. Since presumably no one would urge unlimited freedom for television humorists, the question presents itself as to what forms of restraint would be most appropriate to the new occasion. Anarchism has an appeal

considered as an ideal, but in practice invariably it seems to prove unsuitable for the human race —as it presently behaves or is likely to behave in the immediately foreseeable future. Self-restraint alone, therefore, can scarcely be considered the answer. Those comedians whose primary experience is acquired in nightclubs invariably develop a certain insensitivity to standards of taste appropriate to television, there being enormous differences in the audiences for the two media. This is particularly true for nightclub comedians, whose most dependable response derives from their most vulgar material. Since it is a rare entertainer who will willingly sacrifice the funniest parts of his presentation when working in television, if instructed only by his own conscience, it follows that a degree of censorship must be imposed, either by network officials or—which is preferable—by the production staff of the program involved.

Network officials, in any event, are scarcely a reliable barometer of taste since their own views are affected largely by a given program's ratings. This was first dramatized by Arthur Godfrey, who, during the days of his great radio and television success in the early 1950's, frequently resorted to surprisingly vulgar material but was nevertheless permitted to go his way uninhibited because CBS officials were unwilling to risk the enormous profits his programs brought in. Fifteen years later the Smothers Brothers were generally immune from network interference until their ratings began to falter, after which it became only a question of time as to which of the contending forces would finally prevail.

It is not enough merely to disapprove of vulgarity and obscenity; it is important to understand them. Both forms of communication have a psychological function, whether in an individual or in a society. Where is the most vulgar and obscene humor encountered? It is found precisely in those social contexts characterized by sexual frustration or deprivation: in prisons, military barracks, fraternity houses, boarding schools—wherever people are unable to enjoy free access to company of the opposite sex. What is odd about the present cultural situation, however, is that vulgarity is more common just at the time when freedom of expression is being greatly expanded.

It is possible to detect a difference between the vulgarity a 20-year-old will engage in and that which preoccupies an older man. An obscene joke told by a 45-year-old—assuming the individual's general mental health—may express a momentary outburst against conservative self-repression, but obscenity of the sort exemplified in the tribal-love rock musical 'Hair' seems more a matter of wishing to shock, to challenge the established order. The nudity, sexuality, and vulgarity of such shows are not employed for erotic purposes but rather as gestures of impudent defiance. The question is related to one of the points of origin of formal comedy, in the theater of ancient Athens, when the art grew out of religious exercises celebrating Dionysus, the carefree god of pleasure.

Matters of definition aside, almost all of us are illogical when it comes to humor. Consider the example of the *Reader's Digest,* a conservative, establishment-oriented periodical, which has for many years published off-color jokes about brassieres, girdles, toilets, breasts, and other things, the joking about which would seem inconsistent with the magazine's philosophical orientation.

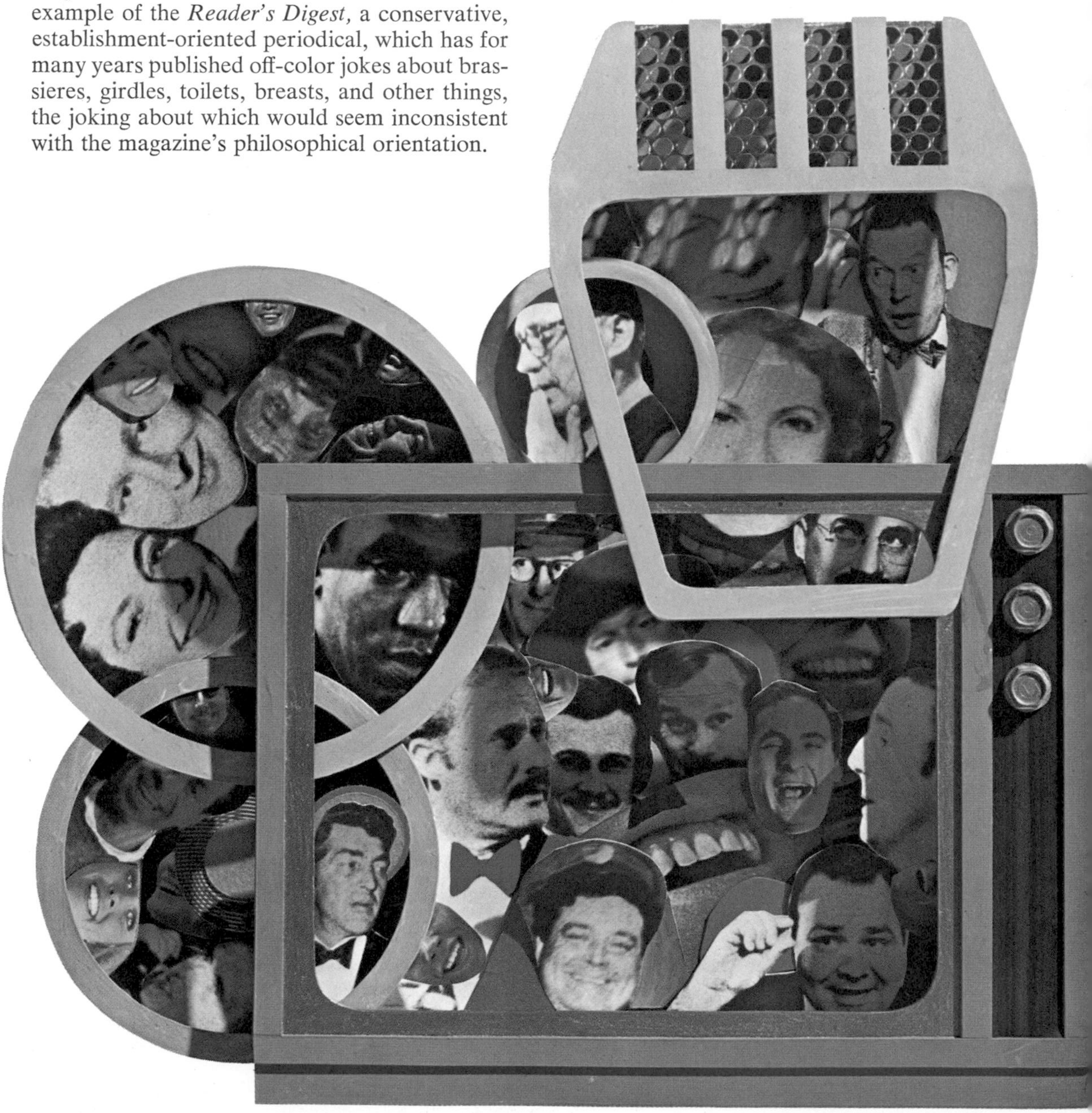

Since there is today a greater receptivity of television audiences to social satire dealing with delicate issues such as the Vietnam conflict, race relations, birth control, abortion, political reaction, the free-enterprise system, and religion, the humorist is in a more secure defensive position when he demands greater freedom than when he asks only to be vulgar. My own view is that the willingness of television audiences to permit the broadcast of the newer jokes and sketches is perhaps less than has generally been assumed. Just because a given program has a high rating does not logically establish that those watching it approve of all they see. Humor has indeed swung gradually to the political left during the past five years, and presumably will continue in the same direction during the 1970's, but it is too early to assess what the ultimate popular response will be. At the moment all that can be said safely is that the audience that is pleased by the liberal tendency is the youthful audience—apparently now in the numerical, if not yet influential, majority—which traditionally has been more progressive or radical than the establishment or the less imaginative middle class.

The Reactionary Response

But a powerful countermovement to the leftward swing of the social pendulum began to make itself felt as the 1960's drew to a close, as the millions of presidential votes cast for George Wallace in 1968 made clear. Out-and-out conservatives, or less principled reactionaries, are probably no more numerous now, relatively speaking, than at any other point during the past quarter century, but of late they are making many converts in the lower middle class, which traditionally had identified itself with the laboring man and the rights of immigrant minorities. The Italian, Polish, Irish, and German crowds who violently attacked nonviolent freedom marchers in Northern cities during the late 1960's added strength to the reactionary groundswell. It is safe to say that recent undisciplined outbreaks by radical representatives of the New Left, Students for a Democratic Society, Black Panthers, and other revolutionary groups aroused far more popular fervor for conservatives than for their own far leftist causes.

If it were possible for the political amalgam of red-neck, reactionary-conservative forces to have its own humor—its own equivalent of a Smothers Brothers Comedy Hour, Laugh-In, or What's It All About, World?—it is probable that the networks would be willing to strike such a balance. The fact is that such a thing is impossible. The American right absolutely loathes the new humor, but its resentment is compounded in that it is incapable, by definition, of putting a counterforce into the field. The reasons are neither specifically American nor political; they are ancient, historic, and psychological. Creative, artistic people—in most historic instances—have generally been found to the left of center of the political spectrum. The eye of the artist, the social critic, the humorist, intuitively perceives certain realities behind political facades some time before they become apparent to the masses. What the artist has to say, therefore—be he composer, dramatist, or poet—will frequently be unpalatable to the powers that be. The overwhelming majority of American entertainers are at the very least affiliated with the Democratic party; their social sympathies incline to the left rather than the right. American conservatives—since there can apparently be no such thing as a right-wing Lenny Bruce, a reactionary Mort Sahl, a Birch Society Woody Allen—must content themselves with the amiable, traditional sort of folk humor they derive from The Beverly Hillbillies, Gomer Pyle, Mayberry RFD, or Green Acres. Such programs are actually *non*political, but at least they do not trespass upon the ancient verities or question middle-class American prejudices.

The heightened interest in popular humor today then is at least partly a matter of serious reactionary response to what many viewers regard as unseemly license on the part of some comedians. Behind much of the present demand for censorship—if not out-and-out banishment of the offenders—is an ignorance concerning the nature of the raw material out of which comedy is constructed. That raw material is tragedy. Consider the content of most jokes, which generally concern how stupid people are, how intoxicated they were last night, how high they got on marihuana, how broke they are, how sexually frustrated, how sinful, how lazy, how cross-eyed, how deaf, how ill, how embarrassed, how trapped by circumstances. It is therefore absurd to assume that there can be such a thing as subject matter totally off limits to the humorist or comedian.

Certain areas are, to a degree, forbidden to the television humorist, but, as the current excesses make clear, this is not the case for American humor generally. Lenny Bruce, Mike Nichols, Elaine May, Mort Sahl, Dick Gregory, Pat Paulsen, the Smothers Brothers, and David Frye, among others, have had much to say that was pithy and penetrating. That they could not say all of it on television is not attributable to a prohibitive government nor to narrow-minded network executives, but simply to the fact that a considerable percentage of the U.S. television audience is made up of small children and others who do not wish to be exposed to humor that will offend or shock. But the unfettered word can still be spoken in nightclubs, coffeehouses, motion-picture and legitimate theaters, college concert halls, and record albums, and written in the medium of print—all proof that we live in a relatively free society. The humorist cannot function fully under dictators like Adolf Hitler, Joseph Stalin, Mao Tse-tung, Fidel Castro, Rafael Trujillo, or Francisco Franco—something that American comedians given to moments of paranoia sometimes neglect to remember or to appreciate.

The New Humor

The primary difference between the humor of the 1970's and that of half a century before is that today's humorous material is largely *performed,* whereas in the old days it was designed to be *read*. In the 1920's the humorist saw himself as continuing the tradition of comic literature, following in the steps of Mark Twain, Artemus Ward, or Josh Billings. He hoped to produce funny books, magazine articles, or short articles, or perhaps write a column for a newspaper. The tradition gave rise to such great humorists as George Ade, Irvin S. Cobb, Stephen Leacock, Robert Benchley, S. J. Perelman, Frank Sullivan, Corey Ford, Don Marquis, Ring Lardner, and James Thurber. It was the mushrooming popularity of radio toward the close of the 1930's that produced a change in the styles of American humor. Young men who discovered within themselves an ability to create jokes and sketches began to dream, not of writing the great American comic novel, but of becoming rich devising—however anonymously—jokes for Eddie Cantor, Jack Benny, Bob Hope, Burns and Allen, and other popular comedians of the period. As a result, the mainstream of American humor flowed out of the realm of literature and into the business of assembly-line jokes. Some of the individual witticisms produced were quite the equal of epigrams conceived by the earlier humorists, but the totality of the new work, because it was mass-produced, was for the most part briefly enjoyed and then discarded like yesterday's newspaper.

Another cultural influence that has produced a change in American humor was the long change from vaudeville—via radio and motion pictures—to television. In the 1920's a fledgling funnyman started in obscure theaters—usually doing something other than comedy to get his foot in the door (juggling, rope twirling, dancing, singing)—and then spent years in relative obscurity perfecting his craft, meanwhile looking forward to becoming a vaudeville headliner or moving to the stage in a legitimate Broadway theater.

Today's young comedians, on the other hand, are relatively handicapped in that, since the

training ground of vaudeville is no more, they are obliged to acquire their early experience in small nightclubs and coffeehouses. They enjoy one enormous advantage that the old-timers never had, however, in that today's young people have grown up in a culture almost constantly brainwashed by mass-produced humor. Literally all of his life, today's 25-year-old comic has known as a constant companion in his home the dominant television comedians and wits: Sid Caesar, Jackie Gleason, Milton Berle, Groucho Marx, George Burns, Lucille Ball, Martha Raye, Jerry Lewis, Red Skelton, Jack Benny, Phil Silvers, Ernie Kovacs, yours truly, and others.

But if television, because of its size and appetite, has created its own supply of young wits and given them opportunity, it has also presented them with the dramatic problem of an accelerated, telescoped professional history. The successful comedian of vaudeville, radio, and motion pictures could generally count on a long career. But a television series can be enormously popular one year and forgotten the next, because networks continue to broadcast only those programs that receive high ratings. Consider the misfortune that befell such gifted and amusing professionals as George Gobel, Red Buttons, Wally Cox, Herb Shriner, Danny Kaye, Fred Allen, Bob Newhart, Ernie Kovacs, and more recently the brilliant Jonathan Winters and Don Rickles as well. Each of these comedians was as funny the day he received the back of television's hand as on the moment he originally appeared on the scene with brass bands and firecrackers. It was the public that changed.

The modern professional comedian must contend with another difficulty which troubles few other professionals, in that every citizen considers himself a lay expert on an art form at which few are, in fact, essentially qualified. Neither brain surgeons, plumbers, television repairmen, nor income-tax experts receive an appreciable amount of critical advice from those outside their fields. We may complain about the prices they charge us, but we do not regard ourselves as qualified to take issue with them. In contrast, we all apparently consider ourselves expert on the subject of comedy.

Lastly, in commenting on the "new humor" one must observe that much of it appears new only to the very young. Older readers and viewers often recognize the sources from which some of the present generation of comedians and writers derive certain of their ideas.

"Sock it to me, baby" was not originated by Laugh-In but was a common phrase in the Negro and music-oriented culture of the 1940's. "Here come de judge" goes back to Negro vaudeville comic Pigmeat Markham in the 1930's. Certain of Laugh-In's comic devices were borrowed from Peter Sellers and Ernie Kovacs. The program's most frequently employed comic construction, the lightning-quick series of cartoonlike sight gags (originally called Crazy Shots), was first introduced to television in 1954 on the National Broadcasting Company's Tonight show—a point Laugh-In's producer George Schlatter cheerfully concedes.

Youth and Tomorrow's Humor

Nevertheless, Laugh-In's creators deserve credit for perceiving that the communications explosion had created a new breed of young Americans whose attention spans were apparently shorter than those of earlier generations reared in more leisurely environments. Although those over 45 could still savor a three-minute story by Danny Thomas, a long, slow "take" by Jack Benny, or a "slow burn" by Jackie Gleason, the new 10-to-20 age group wanted, and could absorb, rapid-fire jokes, loud rock music, and dazzling images—all at once.

One of the still-puzzling questions about the emerging humor of the 1970's concerns the almost complete lack of creative participation in that humor by the hippie or underground, beat, bohemian culture. Reading the underground press, one finds that the funniest contribution is the work of Jules Feiffer, who—though a gifted, progressive, and perceptive humorist—is very much a member of the over-35, button-down-shirt, responsible-citizen category. It is fascinating that the youthful street rebels are almost never purposely, professionally funny. The hippie world has produced some lively journalism, innovative art, freshly vigorous music, and interesting social philosophy, but its contribution to formal, marketable humor is minimal. Perhaps the rest of us require the services of professional humorists because our lives are so essentially serious, if not tragic. It may be that in living a more carefree existence, avoiding rather than coping with troublesome responsibilities, today's more bohemian young people do not have the emotional need for the escape valve that humor apparently represents to a generally more puritanical society. Young comedy writers and comedians are being produced in goodly supply, but those young people who have the true comic gift generally disdain the pot-smoking, long-haired, barefooted way of life.

COLOR FUN, FUNCTION, ILLUSION

Color is really all in your mind

Color may be stimulated by the way things around you radiate or reflect light . . .

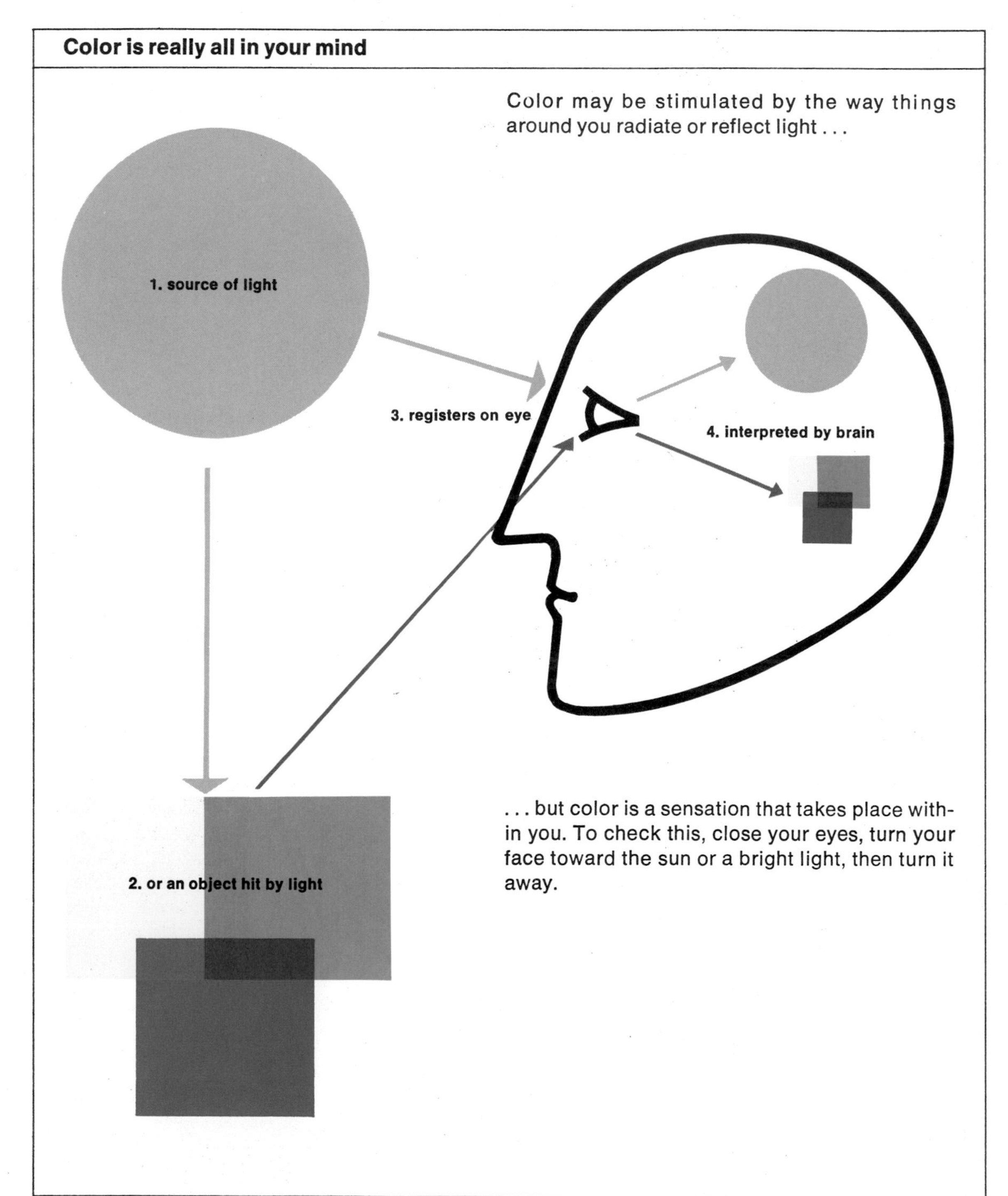

. . . but color is a sensation that takes place within you. To check this, close your eyes, turn your face toward the sun or a bright light, then turn it away.

The Artist Experiments

by MAX KOZLOFF
art editor and critic

Of all the elements of art, color has excited the most controversy. It has mystified painters who were in love with it and annoyed those who did not care to accept its luxuriant, irrational force. Color in a work of art is a decisive agent, though it reveals the strengths of an artist in ways more difficult to describe than do his powers of draftsmanship or composition. To conceive an image

Color can be created in two ways

1. Additive Color Mixture:
Three basic colored light sources interact to produce all other colors. Example: color television

Three basic primary additive colors . . .

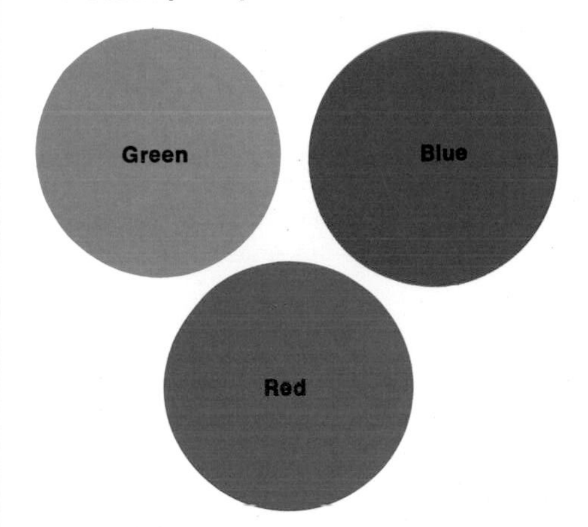

. . . make six major hues and all others (plus white)

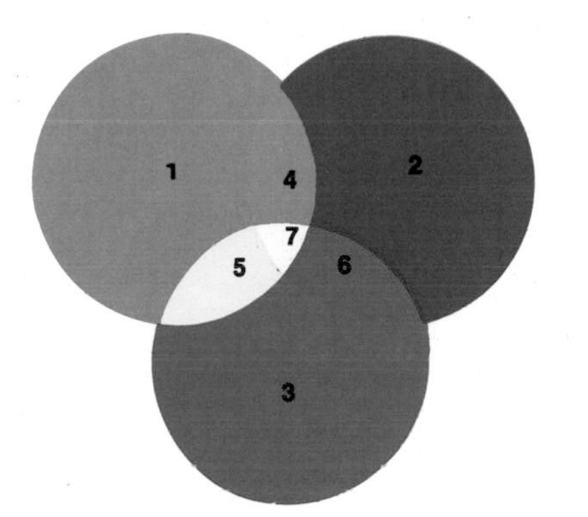

1. Green 2. Blue 3. Red 4. Cyan 5. Yellow 6. Magenta 7. White

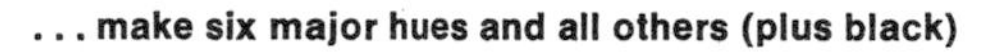

2. Subtractive Color Mixture:
Light interacts with colorant (ink, paint, dye, etc.), which subtracts or absorbs some colors from light. Example: color printing

Three basic primary subtractive colors . . .

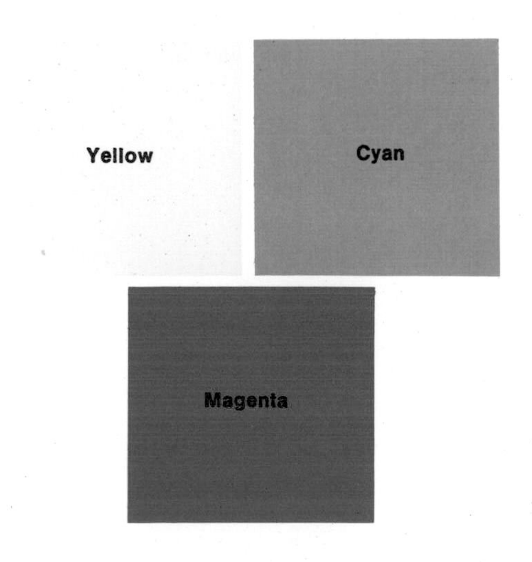

. . . make six major hues and all others (plus black)

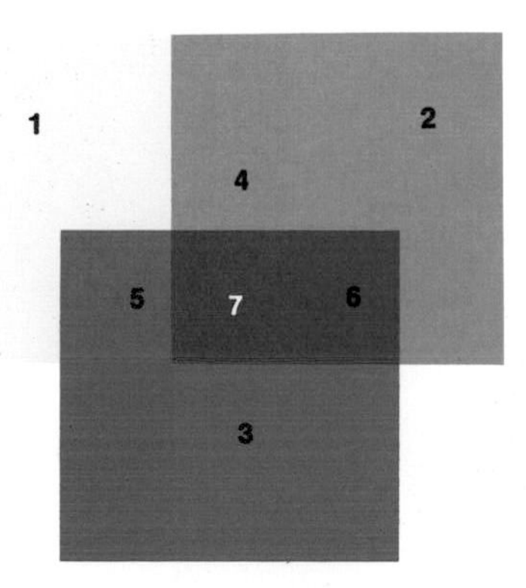

1. Yellow 2. Cyan 3. Magenta 4. Green 5. Red 6. Blue 7. Black

primarily in color is to be absorbed by the sensory, apparent, and emotional qualities of its presence; to outline or place it in space is to be more concerned with the knowledge of what it is or may mean. There exists a whole tradition of writing on art that assigns to drawing the virtues of objectivity, truth, and structure, while considering color to be secondary or cosmetic, even destructive of form. The defenders of the chromatic, however, have worshiped color as the bringer of life and the soul of painting. This conflict has all the aspects of a moral contest.

Insofar as the question of color is predicated on an artist's choice and associated with personal values, morality is not irrelevant—but the problem relates more to the creative intention than to the

Prism photos prove white light is a mixture of colors of the spectrum

The prism bends light of the shorter wavelengths more than light of the longer wavelengths, thus spreading a narrow beam of white light out into the visible spectrum. (The beam extending toward the bottom of the picture is reflected from the surface of the prism without entering it.)

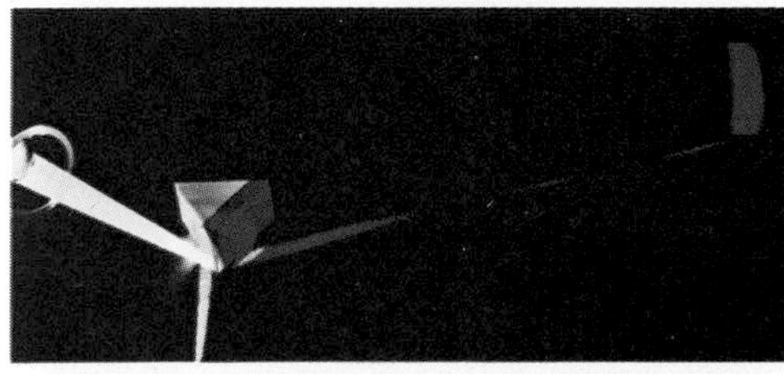

A red filter between prism and screen allows only light of the longer wavelengths to pass.

A green filter passes only the center part of the spectrum, absorbing blue and red light.

A blue filter passes only light of the shorter wavelengths, absorbing green and red light.

These reactions are the basis for color television, as you will see later on.

Prism and spectrum material adapted from Kodak Color Data Book E-74.

effect of the work. Even more, color is by no means entirely separable from drawing, just as drawing may well possess the attributes of hue. One of the major properties of color in art is its capacity to play many different formal roles, just as it is able to cross over the boundaries of objects or envelop them in atmosphere. In one sense, the distinction between color and the other constituents of a painting—including mass, light, space, texture, and volume—is artificial. Can one say of the sky in a landscape by John Constable that it is merely a zone of blue? Or does one speak of the burnished flesh of a Peter Paul Rubens nude solely as a patch of pink? The blue or the pink, once established, is shown to cast reflections everywhere so that the whole world may seem

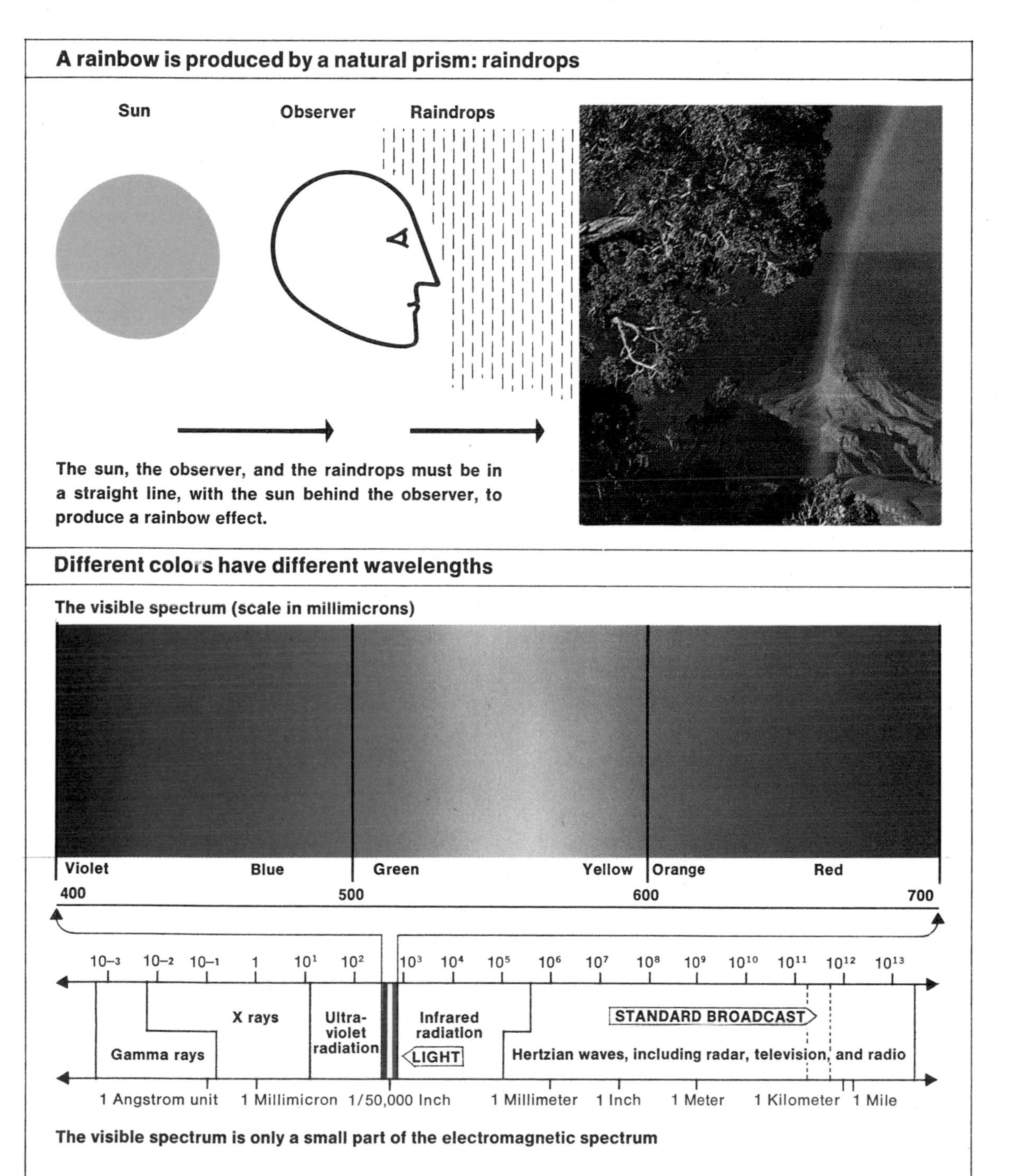

in complicity with one color. And in this world, perceptions have not only an optical but also a thermal point of reference. Théophile Gautier observed:

Drawing is melody, color is harmony. . . . Melody can well subsist independently of harmony . . . but of what prodigious riches of nuances, of what power of effect would one be deprived in suppressing the latter!

This summarizes the orchestral energy of color and indicates to what extent it becomes an imaginative feature of a domain that, no matter how plausible or illusory, exists on a fictional level.

Despite the realism of color, we do not see Gautier's harmony any more than we perceive lines in nature. When we talk of color in art, we are thinking of a chromatic order minted from a dis-

How the eye registers colors

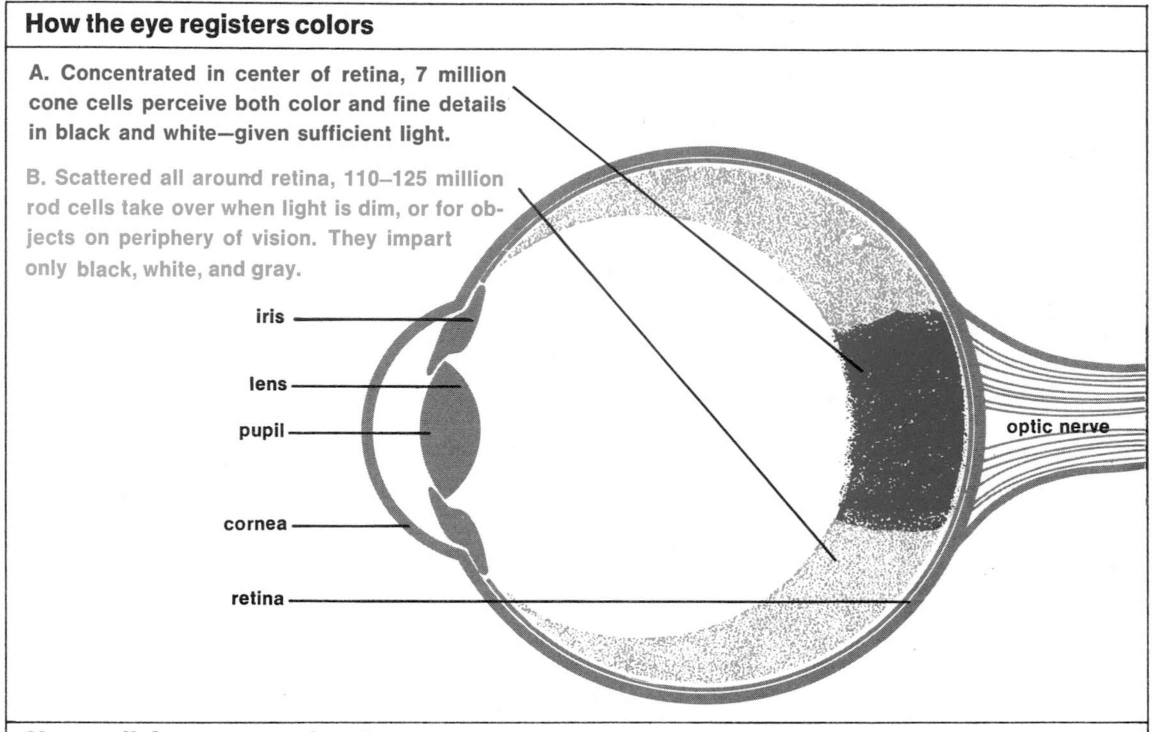
A. Concentrated in center of retina, 7 million cone cells perceive both color and fine details in black and white—given sufficient light.
B. Scattered all around retina, 110–125 million rod cells take over when light is dim, or for objects on periphery of vision. They impart only black, white, and gray.
iris
lens
pupil
cornea
retina
optic nerve

How well do you see colors?

These charts are reproduced through the courtesy of the American Optical Corp. As they are printed here they do not constitute a test for color blindness. They do show the patterns used in color perception tests for red-green color blindness. On the true test, persons with color blindness would have difficulty seeing the circles and triangles.

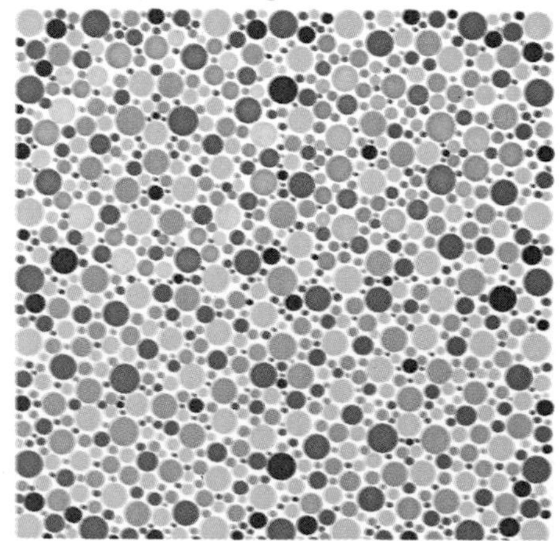

Green triangle in lower left
Green circle in lower right

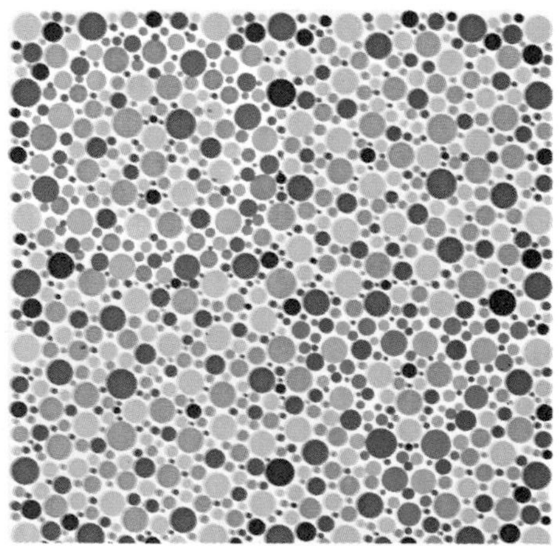

Looked at this way with the page upside down:
Red triangle in upper left
Magenta circle in lower right

tracting chaos. Moreover, the fact that such color is materialized by inert pigments insures its difference from the reflected and variously saturated radiant light waves flooding the world. Textbooks on psychology and optics tell us how we receive and differentiate color stimuli in the light-filled ambience. Their illustrations are schematized in a manner different from art. The scientist's color is a worldless color as far as the viewer of art is concerned. It is not circuited in an imaginative matrix where it is charged with a unique processing, texturing, and density. It is generalized in order to teach certain constants in visual experience. The spectator's color is just as unreal, however, because it is connected with emotional and sensuous factors and has as much to do with a

Color blindness—in man and other species

Normal vision | **Human color blindness**

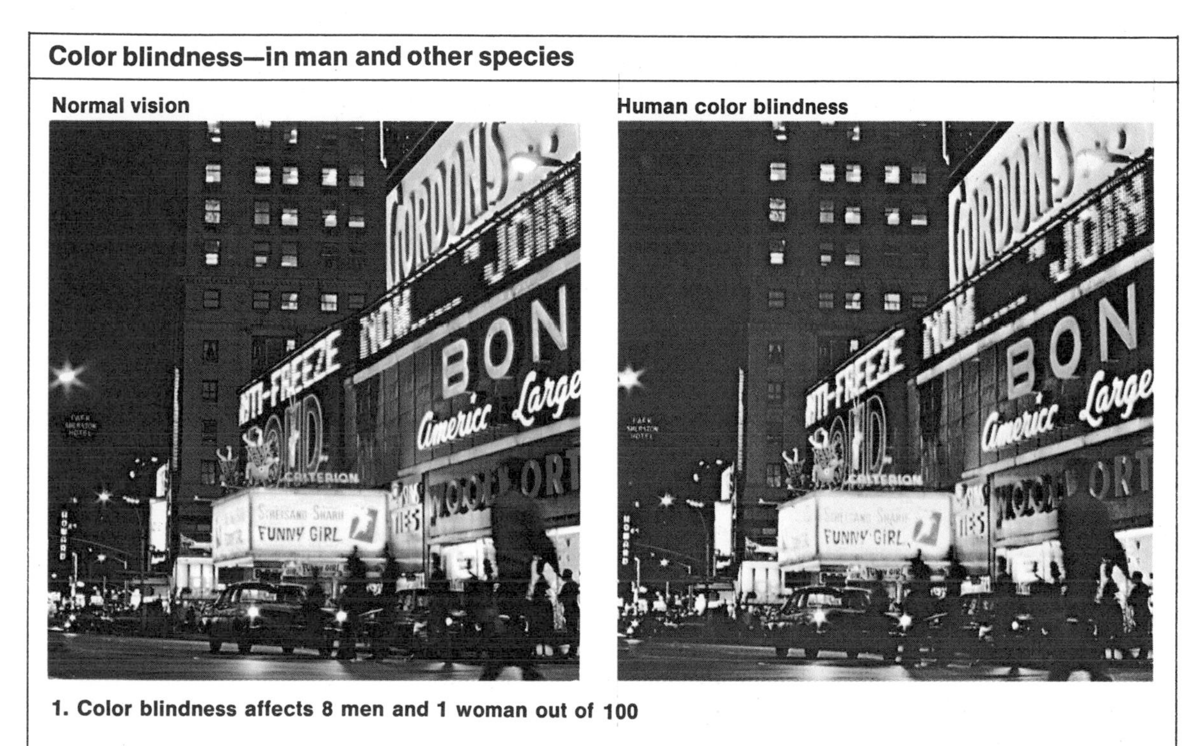

1. Color blindness affects 8 men and 1 woman out of 100

Animal vision

2. Dogs, cats, bulls, horses, and most other animals are color-blind

Insect vision

3. Bees and other insects see ultraviolet light, invisible to man

Color illusions: They make the eyes play tricks

Spots before your eyes

Flickering gray spots appear as you glance at the checkered pattern. Look at one particular gray spot and it disappears. Keep staring to see other effects.

Contrast stripe effect

Colors on a nonuniform background are subject to many unexpected changes.

The blue areas in the pattern are printed with exactly the same color ink. Note how different they look. To observe heightened effects tilt the design or look at it from a distance.

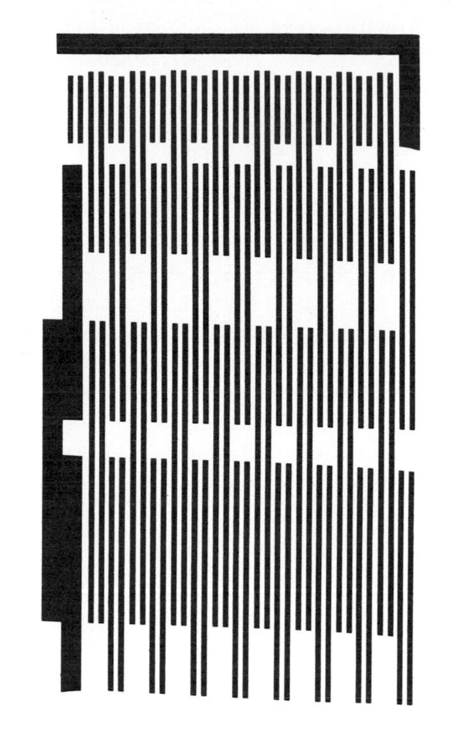

Chromatic black and white

Hold the demonstration an inch or two from your eyes and you will see streaks of different colors next to the black lines.

Spreading effect

Divide the illustration in half by placing your finger or a pencil between the black and white grills. The red behind the black grill will look different from the red behind the white grill.

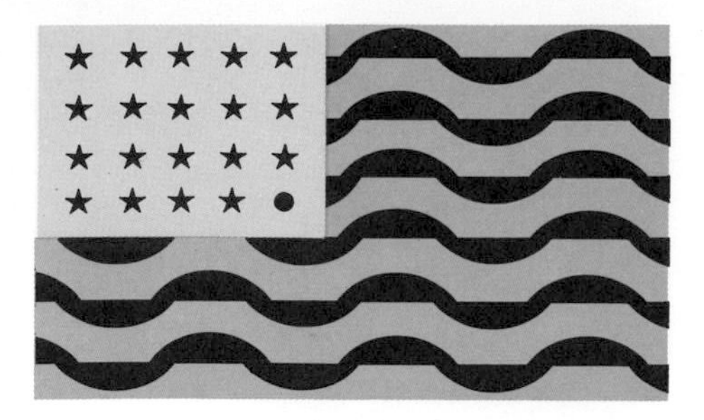

More color illusions

Negative afterimage

Stare at the black dot in the flag for half a minute. Then look at the black dot below it and the American flag will appear. Prolonged staring at the green, black and yellow reduces the sensitivity of the corresponding receptors in the eye. This results in the appearance of the complementary colors red, white and blue in the afterimage when looking at a white surface.

Day and night vision

The red and blue flowers are equally visible but after the eye becomes accustomed to very dim light (in about ten minutes) the red flower disappears and the blue flower looks light gray.

Advancing and receding colors

The red wall at the end of the hall seems closer than the blue wall. Red is an advancing color and blue is a receding color.

Green hearts

Stare for half a minute at the black dot in the green heart, then look at the black dot on the white screen. The pink hearts you may see are the negative afterimage, while the green forms are the reverse afterimage.

Color illusion material adapted with permission from booklet 'The Color Tree' © 1965 by Inmont Corp.

willingness of the spirit as it has to do with an image on the retina.

Artists knew little about color perception until the 19th century. Until then, chromatic vision was an imminence that might rise out of their materials, a means to achieve a poetic unity only imperfectly suggested by nature. Nuances of hue were self-generating, a series of modulations that contributed to the expressive momentum of the picture. In order to model forms in depth, artists depended on schemes of light and dark, with the result that colors were blended into the movement of shadows, those closer to the light source being higher in value. By this method the painter defined the curves or planes of an image, though at some cost to the intensity of his colors because

The psychological effects of color

1. Where you work:

White work spaces with bright lights constrict pupil of the eye, can fatigue eye muscles, cause headaches, eye troubles. Colored walls of softer brightness give greater visual comfort and emotional pleasure.

2. Where you study:

Muted, warm colors provide subtle accents in a generally neutral environment. The subdued color scheme of the library provides a restful but cozy atmosphere, ideal for reading or listening pleasure.

they were weakened into tints or plunged into murk by the patterns of shade. It was Eugène Delacroix who noticed that the shadows of objects were not necessarily gray or black but were composed of distinct hues and that a change of light produced a change of color. It fell to the impressionists to reverse the neutralization of color by tone, livening a palette that became free to concentrate on the luminous sensations within nature. With this priority, they analyzed the interactions of color in light, caring little that the resulting flicker began to dissolve solidity and contour.

Later, the neo-impressionists thought they could achieve more intense harmonies by decomposing the spectrum according to principles formulated by the behavior of real light rays. It was learned, for

3. Where you live:

Teen-ager's bedroom has bright, cheery color contrasts to combat adolescent depressions and provide well-lighted study areas.

4. Where you play:

Psychedelic discotheque uses riotous colors, flashing lights, fluid patterns, and roaring sounds to break down normal sense patterns and propel you into a dream world.

example, that the blendings of pigment or light produced different results. If the artist mixes the three primary pigments—red, yellow, and blue—he attains a muddy gray-brown (almost black); but if he mixes the three primaries of light—red, green, and blue—he attains white. The paintings of Georges Seurat and his followers were attempts to avoid the subtractive, graying effects of mixed pigments by keeping their relatively pure colors separate by means of thousands of tiny points. Although such artists were known as pointillists, they preferred being called divisionists because they segregated the local color of objects, the color of light, and their interactions. From this tempered combustion, the artists hoped to simulate the brilliance of literal, additive lights, supposedly syn-

Color printing

How color is built up as shown in progressive proofs

YELLOW

YELLOW
CYAN

YELLOW
CYAN
MAGENTA

YELLOW
CYAN
MAGENTA
BLACK

thesized by the viewer at a prescribed distance from the canvas. For the reason that paint does not emit light, but rather absorbs certain wavelengths and reflects others, the divisionist theory did not work in practice. Instead of a new kind of illusion, an architectural sense of the relationship between color and light in painting was achieved.

To have objectified color, therefore, was to have moved it away from appearances. Some of the resulting harmonies, however, looked rigid and predictable, and one of the problems of later art was to free chromatic form from the dictates of optical laws. The picture surface became a platform for the imaginative play of hues, as unlimited as the arrangement of notes in music. Many modern artists, however, do not hesitate to make us aware

The final results

Picture seems to be made of continuous tones of color . . .

. . . but magnified blowup of a section shows that the effect is produced by thousands of colored dots

that, before anything else, they are dealing in substances. Opaque and settled, enhanced and orchestrated, hues become compressed images: sensory charges that move toward us, inevitably and potently. Whether inflected with qualities of personal touch, or uniform and flat, they have about them something concrete, a presence similar to dyes. Such color emerges as a new solid that by virtue of its range and saturations can reflect a great deal of concentrated, vibrant light. Such is one outcome of the quest to liberate pure color.

But what of the identification of color with light—that is, with a luminous energy, infinitely more potent than paint and always on the move? To go beyond the impressionists, neo-impressionists, and divisionists, artists had to work against, or deny,

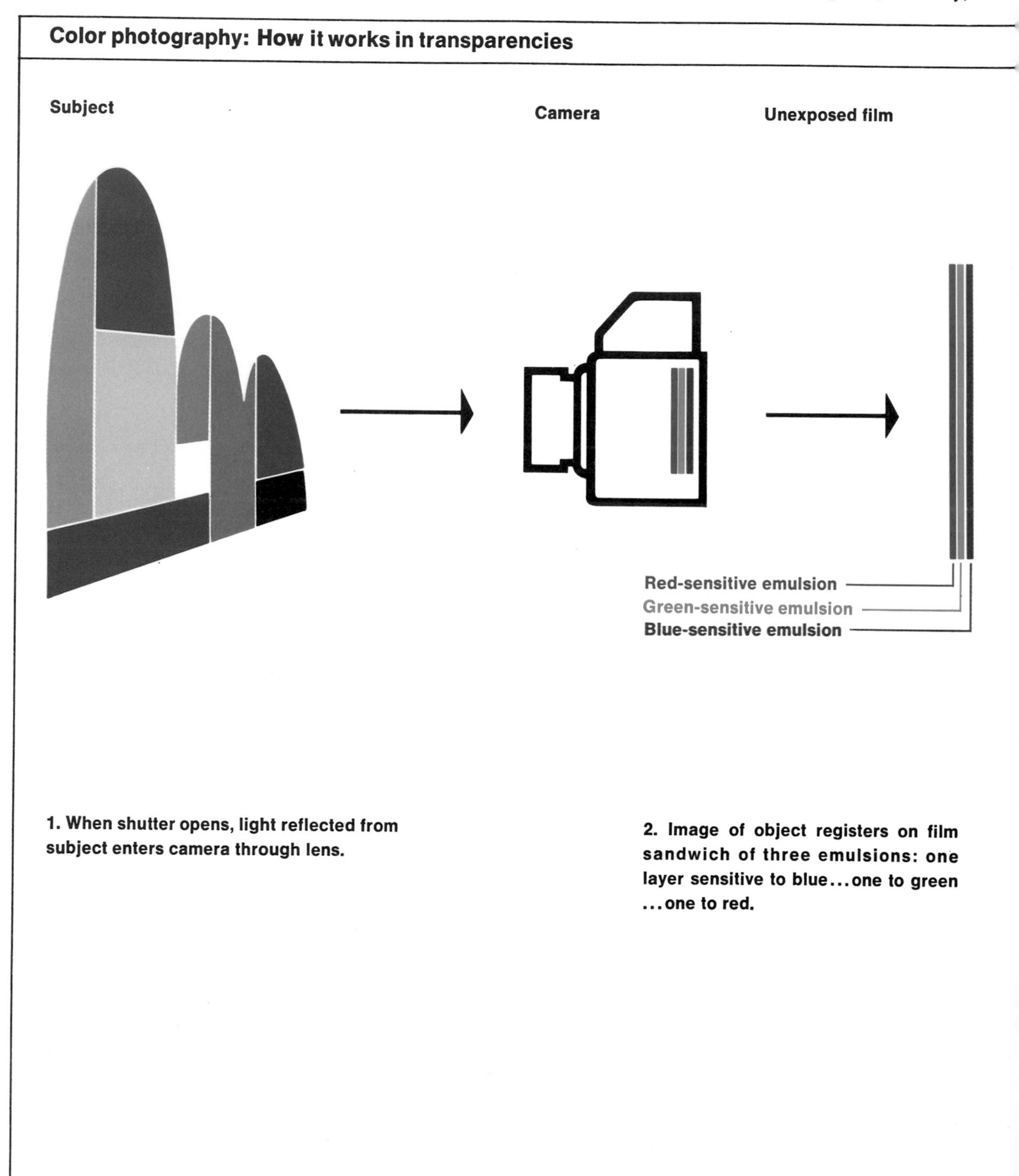
Color photography: How it works in transparencies
Subject
Camera
Unexposed film
Red-sensitive emulsion
Green-sensitive emulsion
Blue-sensitive emulsion
1. When shutter opens, light reflected from subject enters camera through lens.
2. Image of object registers on film sandwich of three emulsions: one layer sensitive to blue...one to green ...one to red.

the tangibility of decorative color. They could not do this literally with pigment, but their purposes set them thinking not of substance but of air, not of the surface as a platform but as a window or screen. Rather than depending on outside lighting, which the painting would shunt back in translated color, they searched to find a method of suggesting that the painting itself is the source of light.

Generally speaking, the most effective way of insinuating light in painting is by employing the white canvas or watercolor paper as the highest value in the composition and causing images to dilate translucently into it. In this sense, happenings on the surface act as a filter for an inner energy that pulses outward. Instead of being a wall upon which color matter is hung, the plane of a

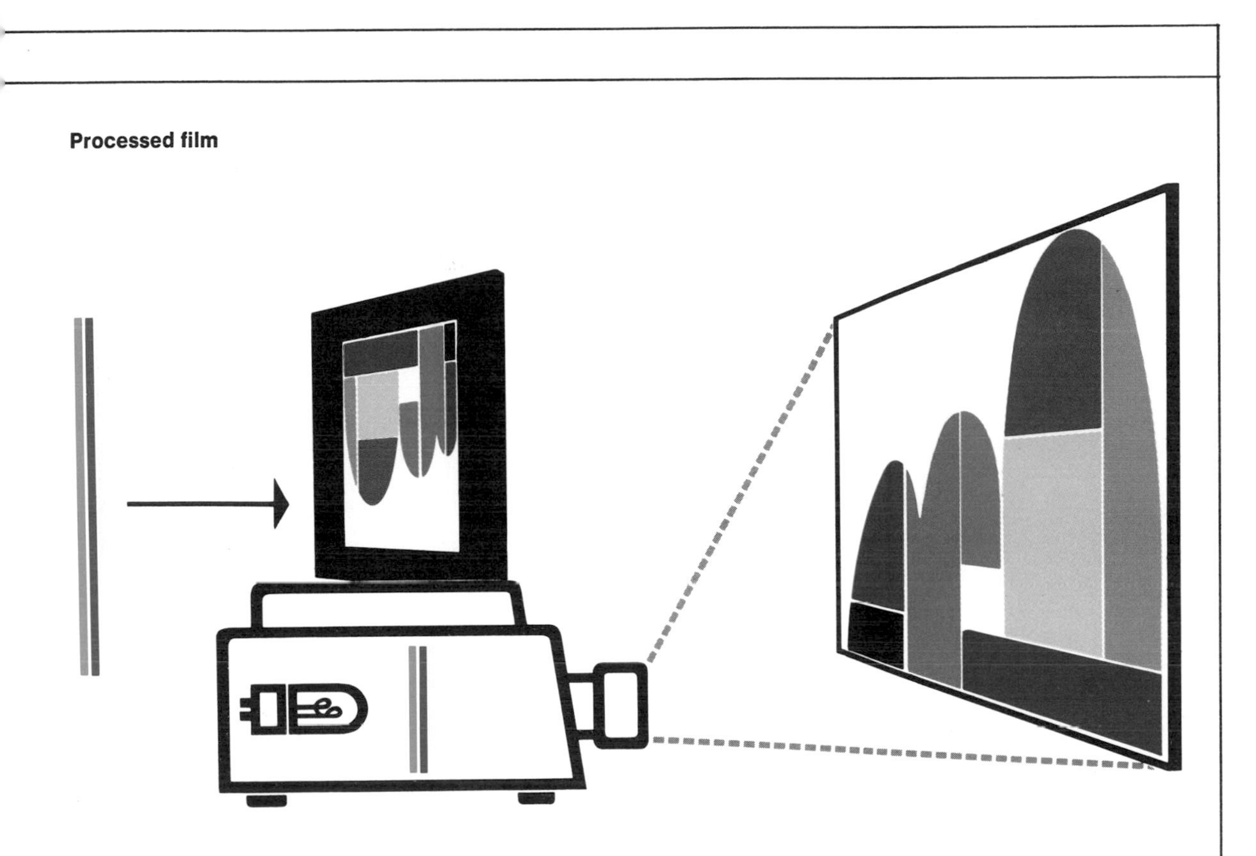

3. In processing, film reverses to subtractive dyes. Blue emulsion becomes yellow dye . . . green becomes magenta . . . red becomes cyan.

4. In projecting processed transparency, dyes subtract from white light of projector beam to produce colors of original object.

light-sensitive colorist dissolves into an amorphous environment, where the paint assumes the identity of steam, haze, or vapor—something, in any event, permeable to the radiance that makes it visible. This mode of seeing had one of its earliest spokesmen in Joseph Turner, whose works seem almost in the process of burning off the material of which they are composed. Light and color were conceived as the ingredients of a spectacle always in the act of creating and destroying itself. With a Pierre Bonnard painting, we become witnesses of an event even more than viewers of an object; and, with a painting by Henri Matisse, there is a different, more oblique expectancy brought about. Bonnard held back the throttle of maximum saturation to conserve the illusion of interior light; Matisse

Color television also takes a picture and projects it

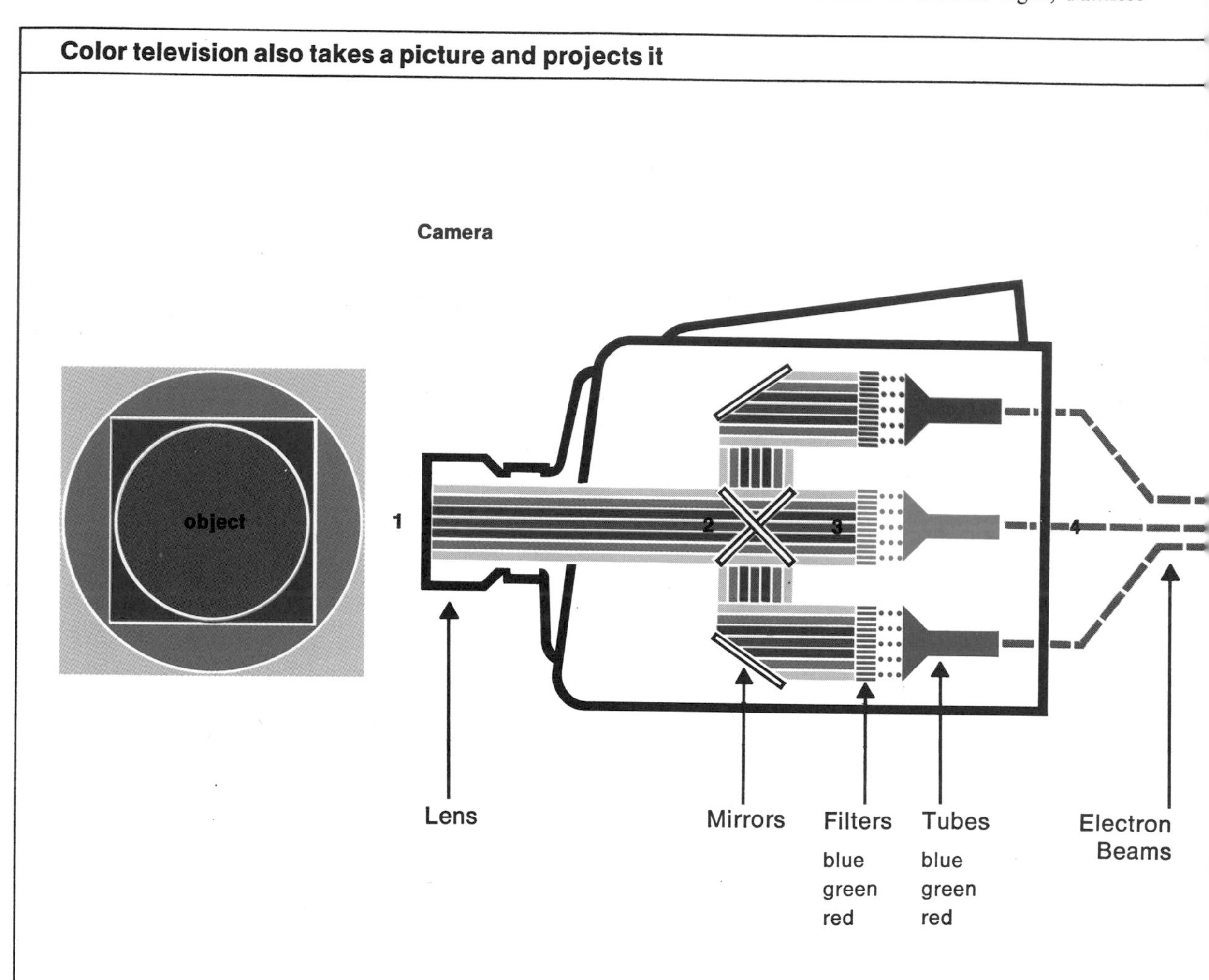

Taking the Picture

1) Color camera lens receives image of subject being televised. 2) Mirrors feed image to three camera tubes. 3) Color filters in front of tubes split image into three additive primary colors, permit light frequencies of only one primary color into each tube. 4) Tubes convert color data into electron beams, with number of electrons proportional to intensity of color of subject being televised.

opened it up to startle the senses. About the latter achievement, Pablo Picasso put it this way:

In Matisse's work, when you find three tones that are put on close to one another—let's say a green, a mauve, and a turquoise—their relationship evokes another color which one might call *the* color. . . . It's not necessary for a color to have a determined form. It's not even desirable. What *is* important is its power of expansion. When it reaches a point a little beyond itself, this force of expansion takes over and you get a kind of neutral zone to which the other color must come as it reaches the end of *its* course. At that moment you can say that color breathes.

Continuing experimentation and discovery with color is one of the major reasons why contemporary art has such widespread fascination.

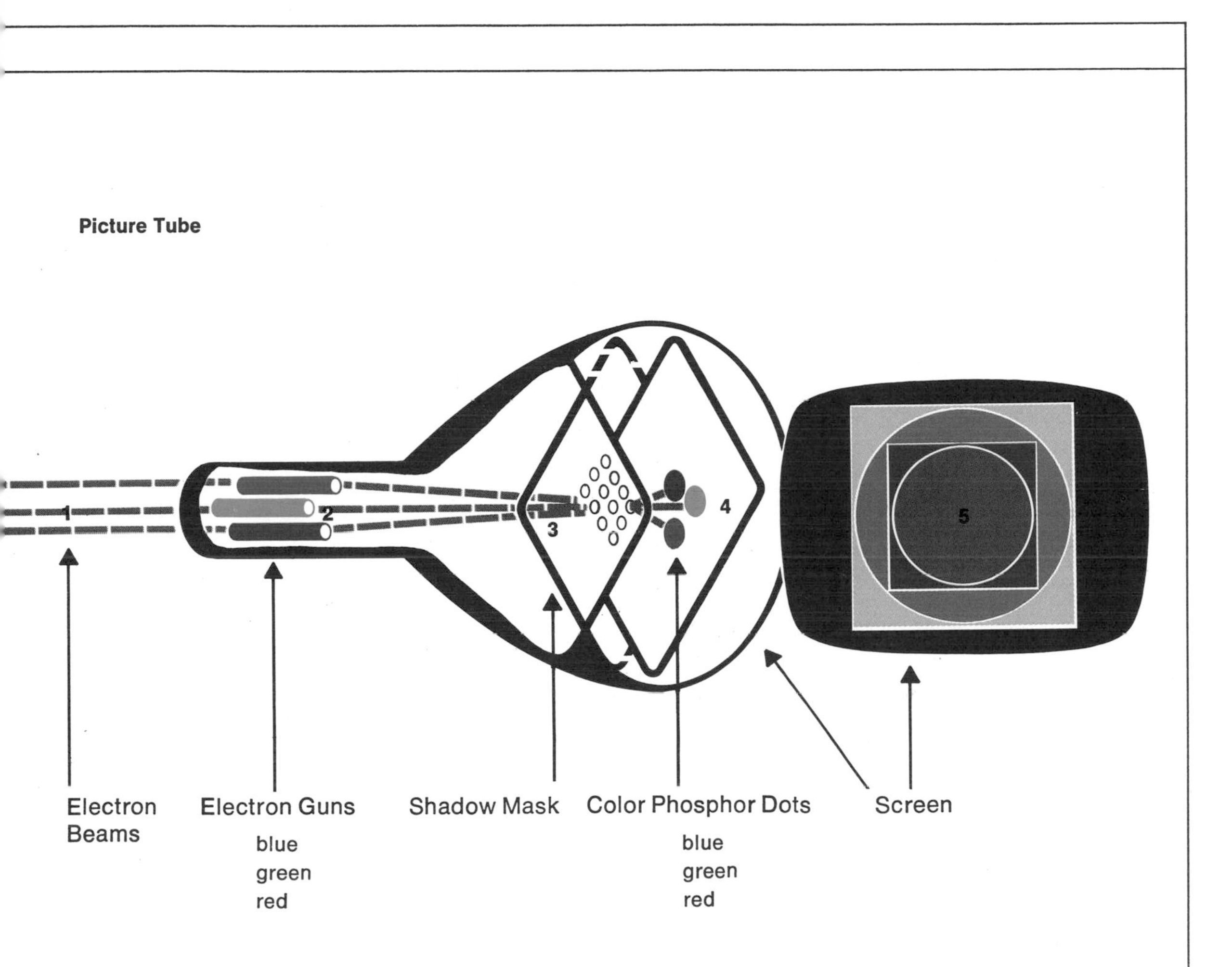

Projecting the Picture

1) At the TV receiver, electron beams originated by TV color camera are processed and sent on to three electron guns inside picture tube. 2) One gun is for each primary color (blue-green-red). Guns fire electron at back of TV screen, which is coated with million blue-green-red phosphor dots. 3) Shadow mask focuses beams so they activate only dots of proper color. 4) Strength of beams causes dots to light up in proportion to intensity of colors entering camera. 5) Eye of viewer mixes light from three color dots into full-color picture like original.

Designed by Graphics Institute, Inc., N.Y.C.

COURTESY, NATIONAL AERONAUTICS AND SPACE ADMINISTRATION

Edwin E. Aldrin, Jr., of Apollo 11 on the moon

PICTORIAL PARADE

Funeral of President Dwight D. Eisenhower

Events of the Year 1969

DON GETSUG FROM RAPHO GUILLUMETTE

Spring flood in the Midwest

Woodstock Music and Art Fair, Bethel, N.Y.

CATHERINE LE ROY FROM BLACK STAR

LOU DE LA TORRE FROM BLACK STAR

People's Park, Berkeley, Calif.

WIDE WORLD

Inauguration of President Richard M. Nixon

Riot in Montreal, Que.

PICTORIAL PARADE

ADVERTISING. In 1969 the advertising industry racked up its ninth consecutive year of increased advertising volume. As the year drew to a close, it was estimated that the gain in ad volume would be at least 7% over that for the preceding year. The total volume of advertising was expected to be around $19.6 billion, as compared to $18.3 billion registered in 1968.

The seven advertising media—televison, magazines, newspapers, radio, business publications, outdoor, and direct mail—anticipated an aggregate of $9.6 billion in national advertising, as compared with the $8.8 billion invested in national advertising during 1968. Newspapers expected a volume of $1.1 billion, up 11.1%; network television, $1.7 billion, up 13.3%; spot television, $1.3 billion, up 18.2%; magazines, $1.24 billion, up 4.2%; business publications, $811.8 million, up 3.9%; network radio, $53 million, up 1%; spot radio, $332 million, the same as the preceding year; outdoor advertising, $168 million, up 8.4%; and direct mail, $2.9 billion, up 7.4%.

COURTESY, AMERICAN MOTORS CORP.

In the "Driving School" series of commercials, the American Motors Corp. Rebel withstands the inept handling of student drivers. The series won a Clio award for excellence.

According to the *Advertising Age* annual report of agency billings for 1968, which was released in 1969, total billings reached $8.9 billion, up from $8.3 billion during 1967. Fifty-six agencies topped the $25-million mark, led by J. Walter Thompson Co. at $638 million. Others of the top ten and their billing statistics were: McCann-Erickson, Inc., $478.5 million; Young & Rubicam, Inc., $472.6 million; Ted Bates & Co., Inc., $334 million; Batten, Barton, Durstine & Osborn, Inc., $319.5 million; Foote, Cone & Belding, Inc., $271.4 million; Leo Burnett Co., Inc., $265.1 million; Doyle Dane Bernbach, Inc., $254.1 million; Grey Advertising, Inc., $207 million; and Ogilvy & Mather, Inc., $205 million.

Profits of advertising agencies showed a modest improvement during the same year, according to statistics released by the American Association of Advertising Agencies. Net profit (after taxes) averaged 3.97% of gross income, up from the 1967 figure of 3.57%. Gross income as a percentage of billing amounted to .76% in 1968, as compared to .69% in 1967.

In 1969 the movement of major agencies into foreign markets was accelerated. Leo Burnett Co. negotiated to acquire the major agency divisions of London (England) Press Exchange, Ltd. Sullivan, Stauffer, Colwell & Bayles, Inc., purchased a minority interest in Lintas, Ltd., a London-based agency. Needham, Harper & Steers, Inc., and its London affiliate, S. H. Benson, Ltd., were working on a joint development of facilities with Havas Conseil of France.

During the year cigarette advertising was once again under fire by both the U.S. Congress and the Federal Trade Commission (FTC). The FTC had been prevented from acting on cigarette health claims until July 1, 1969, under the provisions of the Federal Cigarette Labeling and Advertising Act of 1965. To avert action by the FTC, which gave every indication that it would seek stronger wording of health warnings on cigarette packs and would

Art derived from the cartoon style of the Beatles' movie 'Yellow Submarine' was popular in 1969. This ad uses typical colors and shapes.

COURTESY, IRVING TRUST CO.

Young & Rubicam, Inc., produced the advertising campaign "Give a Damn" for the New York Urban Coalition. The campaign won many major advertising awards in New York City in 1969.

COURTESY, NEW YORK URBAN COALITION

require warnings in cigarette advertising, tobacco manufacturers came up with a proposal in late July. The companies proposed to remove all cigarette advertising from radio and TV by September 1970.

One of the chief concerns expressed by anticigarette forces was how the advertising dollars currently being channeled into radio and television would be distributed when the commercials were removed from the airwaves. An estimated $220 million per year was being spent on commercials, and opponents hoped to keep any substantial portion of that expenditure from being transferred to the other media. However, it was believed that a good percentage of the current expenditures would be diverted into magazines, newspapers, and billboards.

Although radio and television media alone faced an outright embargo of cigarette advertising during the year, some newspapers such as the *Boston Globe* announced that they would no longer accept cigarette advertising. *The New York Times* announced that it would require that all such advertisements be accompanied by health warnings as well as by a disclosure of the actual tar-and-nicotine content.

Awards

During 1969 the television commercial continued to gain recognition as an art form. At the annual American Television and Radio Commercials Festival, held in New York City in May, more than 50 Clio awards were presented for the season's best ads. The awards seemed to put a premium on entertainment value rather than on the selling power of the commercials.

The winner of the most coveted Clio—for the best overall advertising campaign—was the Virginia Slims "You've Come a Long Way, Baby" series. The musical commercials, which were calculated to sell a new cigarette especially designed for women, show how far women have advanced since the days when they had to smoke in secret. Other Clio recipients were the American Motors Corp. "Driving School" series, which demonstrated the durability of the Rebel; the Contac "Cold Diggers" parody of motion-picture musicals of the 1930's; and the New York Urban Coalition series "Give a Damn." (*See also* Magazines; Newspapers. *See in* CE: Advertising.)

AFGHANISTAN.

Domestically, 1969 was a year of quiet administrative and economic progress in Afghanistan. The division of powers between the executive, the legislative, and the judicial branches—laid down in the 1964 constitution—though virtually completed in 1968, entailed much detailed work in its precise application to existing institutions. This was especially true in the judicial field, where the structure and functions of the lower courts, hitherto shaped largely by tradition, were found to need considerable alteration.

In July the government found it necessary to temporarily close primary and secondary schools as well as Kabul University because of student unrest. The second free parliamentary election since King Mohammed Zahir Shah installed a democratic constitution five years before was held in the fall with the conservatives gaining greater control of the government.

In the economic field, the policy of mobilizing local resources—to replace by degrees the massive foreign aid furnished by the United States and the Soviet Union—continued in accordance with Afghan determination to avoid undue dependence on external help. The main obstacle to progress lay in the shortage of capital for investment in the private sector.

In foreign affairs the traditional Afghan determination to preserve complete autonomy, regardless of external aid or of friendly relations with other countries, remained the dominant consideration. India's desire for close relations was shown by a visit from Prime Minister Indira Gandhi and by Indian aid in the restoration of the Bamian antiquities. In May Soviet Premier Aleksei N. Kosygin arrived to attend the country's 50th independence day celebrations. (*See in* CE: Afghanistan.)

AFRICA. The mood of Africa during 1969 ran the gamut from sadness over the continued killing resulting from the Nigerian civil war to elation at the First Pan-African Cultural Festival in July. Contrasts abounded. Several coups d'etat continued the pattern of recent years, but Ghana held national elections three years after the military seized power from Kwame Nkrumah. The Democratic Republic of the Congo (Kinshasa) achieved some measure of economic and tribal stability, but tribalism flared in Kenya. South Africa developed surface-to-air missiles while continuing to ban television. The British were criticized for not doing something more tangible about the white Rhodesian breakaway, but only four African states paid their "liberation dues" for 1968–69 to harass the white-controlled southern states. Cognizant of the winds of change, Spain relinquished control of the small enclave of Ifni to Morocco on June 30, but at the other end of the continent a new political party was formed dedicated to even more extreme *apartheid* in South Africa.

Nigerian Civil War

Despite efforts of the Organization of African Unity, Pope Paul VI, former President Nnamdi Azikiwe, and others to end the war that had begun in July 1967, Nigerian and Biafran positions, both political and military, remained fundamentally the same. Casualties, including civilians, during this period reached approximately 2 million. Secessionist Biafra lost its capital of Umuahia in mid-April but shortly afterward succeeded in taking Owerri by siege from the central government. A severe psychological blow was dealt the Biafrans when Azikiwe (Zik), the hero of Nigerian nationalism, first president of federal Nigeria and an Ibo as well, returned from England in September and said that he would appeal to his fellow tribesmen to give up their secession and join again in a united Nigeria. He insisted that they had no reason to fear genocide at the hands of federal troops. Biafrans reacted coolly to this change of position.

There was no proof, according to an international team that toured Nigerian-held territory, that the several hundred thousand Ibos there were objects of genocide. Biafrans, however, pointed to an air raid on the town of Umuohiagu on February 7, in which 200–300 people were killed and hundreds wounded. France continued to aid Biafra. (*See* Nigeria.)

Coups and Plots

On May 25, young army officers seized power in the Sudan and proclaimed a one-party socialist state with Maj. Gen. Jaafar Mohammed al-Nimeiry heading the revolutionary council. The ousted President Ismail al-Azhari, who had been the Sudan's first premier in 1956, died in August before his interrogation over charges of corruption. One third of the new ministers were avowed Communists. Secession of the three southern provinces, which had been in rebellion for years, would not be tolerated by the new regime; but this did not deter the formation of a new military-led provisional government in the south known as the Anyidi revolutionary government, which pledged to continue the war. On October 28 General Nimeiry took over the premiership from Abubakr Awadallah, who remained in the cabinet.

In a bloodless coup on September 1, Libyan army leaders deposed 79-year-old King Idris I of

Pope Paul VI blesses the altar of the new shrine near Kampala, Uganda. The pope visited Africa July 31–August 2. He was the first pope in modern times to visit the continent. A major purpose of the trip was to lend the dignity and influence of the papacy to the search for peace in the Nigerian civil war.

AFRICAPIX FROM PIP

Mourners paid their respects before Tom Mboya was buried on July 11. Mboya, Kenya's minister of economic affairs, was assassinated on July 5. His fellow Luo tribesmen were grieving and outraged. Political tension in Kenya, at a high level before the killing, reached a fever pitch with Mboya's death.

MOHAMED AMIN FROM KEYSTONE

Libya (who was in Turkey at the time) and proclaimed the Libyan Arab Republic. Colonel Muammar Quaddafi emerged as chairman of the Revolutionary Command Council and Mahmoud Suleiman Al-Maghrabi was named prime minister in charge of forming a new government. A policy of Arab nationalism and socialism was announced for the world's third largest oil-exporting country—though existing agreements were to be honored.

On October 15, Abdirashid Ali Shermarke, who had been president of Somalia since June 1967, was assassinated. Six days later, less than 24 hours after his funeral, an army-inspired national revolutionary council took control of the government, arrested Premier Muhammad Haji Ibrahim Egal, and said it would work to eliminate corruption and institute socialism.

Deaths of Noted Africans

As if symbolizing the end of an era of conflict in the Congo (Kinshasa), two key figures in the early years of independence died. Former President Joseph Kasavubu, who was a rival of the late Patrice Lumumba in 1960–61 and who was deposed in 1965 by Joseph Mobutu, the current president, died on March 24. Moise Tshombe, the man whom Kasavubu had dismissed from the premiership months before he in turn was removed from office, was declared dead in Algeria on June 30.

Kenya's minister of economic affairs, Tom Mboya, 38, was killed on July 5 in downtown Nairobi. (*See* Kenya.) Eduardo Chivambo Mondlane, leader of the anti-Portuguese liberation front (Frelimo) in Mozambique, was killed by a bomb in Dar es Salaam, Tanzania, on February 3.

The Southern Tier; Economic Developments

Whites continued their domination over the southern portion of Africa with comparatively little change. Rhodesia, which had unilaterally broken with Great Britain in November 1965, held a referendum in June that favored a white-dominated republic. In the Republic of South Africa white domination secured further official sanction for its *baasskap* (bosshood) when the new Bureau of State Security received powers over the admission of evidence in court, thus making it practically immune from public control. (*See also* Commonwealth of Nations; South Africa.)

On June 27 the European Economic Community (EEC), or Common Market, agreed to give $900 million in aid over five and one half years to 18 African states, most of them former colonies of France. This continued previous arrangements and, though less than what the Africans requested, would be of great importance to their economies. In another instance of mutual accommodation, the Congo (Kinshasa) and the EEC signed an $18-million agreement on July 13 to begin the financing of a hydroelectric dam on the Inga rapids of the Congo River. And on September 25 the Congo (Kinshasa) and the Belgian mining company Union Minière du Haut-Katanga came to an understanding of their three-year dispute over the seizure of the company's assets. In Zambia, too, an accord was reached in October with two mining companies that had been nationalized in August. The copper companies, worth about $1.2 billion, would receive 49% of the shares. The Zambians wanted the quickest possible "Africanization" of jobs, as did other Africans, but they recognized that for a long time to come they would need outside skills and capital. Neither Niger with its newly found uranium nor Botswana with its recently discovered diamonds could hope to extract the riches by themselves. (*See also* individual countries by name; International Relations; Refugees. *See in* CE: Africa; countries by name.)

AGRICULTURE. Farmers throughout the world brought in an exceptionally fine harvest in 1969. Agricultural production in the United States ranged from satisfactory for some crops to surplus for many others. Farm income generally rose during the year. Livestock raising, moreover, was the most profitable part of the farm economy in 1969. Growing U.S. affluence was at the root of a relentless demand for red meat.

Crop surpluses in much of the world and an eased food crisis that once threatened some areas, especially the Indian subcontinent, caused a reduction in U.S. food exports for the second consecutive year. Sales of U.S. food on the world market totaled $5.74 billion for 1968–69. Until recently sellable U.S. feed grain made up about 50% of the world total. In 1968–69, however, the U.S. share of the world grain trade dropped to 41%.

Farm surpluses were recorded in many nations. It was becoming apparent that agriculture was making such strides in underdeveloped countries that, barring disaster, they would eventually grow an overabundance of food.

KEYSTONE

Early in 1969 the Overseas Tractor Operations of the Ford Motor Co. introduced this new Model 320 planter, which offers 4-, 6- (above), or 8-row capability.

The American Farm Bureau Federation celebrated its 50th anniversary in 1969. Largest of the general U.S. farm groups, the Farm Bureau boasted a membership of 1.8 million families, about 75% of which were actively engaged in farming.

U.S. Crop Production

Farm yield in 1969 was at a record high level. The "all crops" index hit 120 (1957–59=100), an increase of one point over the previous high in 1968. Government diversion programs kept more land out of production. Only 300 million acres were planted in 1969, 6.8 million less than the year before. Of these, about 288.4 million acres were harvested, compared with 293.9 million in 1968 and 300.4 million in 1967.

The wheat harvest totaled 1.467 billion bushels, a drop of 7% from the 1968 yield. However, average wheat yield per acre was at a new high—30.6 bushels. Wheat planting was allowed on only 51.6 million acres in 1969, but of these, only 47.6 million were in production. Diversion payments by the U.S. government apparently encouraged wheat farmers to keep some of their allotted acreage idle. Kansas was the leading producer of winter wheat with 304.1 million bushels. Oklahoma ranked second with 119.2 million bushels. North Dakota grew nearly 90% of the record harvest of durum wheat—104.4 million bushels. Yields of rye reached a new high of 23.7 bushels per acre, 32 million bushels in all. South Dakota led the rye production with 6.7 million bushels.

The corn crop was somewhat smaller in 1969. Even though a record yield of 78.8 bushels per acre was achieved, total production was 4.31 billion bushels, down about 62.5 million bushels from the 1968 yield. Illinois was the top-ranked corn state with 943.3 million bushels. Iowa was next highest with 808.8 million bushels.

Oats production has dwindled since World War II because of unsuccessful competition with other grains. However, the 938.1-million-bushel yield in 1969 was the largest oat crop since 1963. Minnesota led in oat production with 185 million bushels, followed by North Dakota with 140.4 million.

A record yield of sorghum grains, 758 million bushels, was set in 1969. Texas produced 328.6 million bushels of sorghum grains. Next came Kansas with 179 million bushels.

The 1969 cotton crop was substantially smaller than that of the preceding year. Due to a drop in average yield per acre a total of only 10.5 million bales was brought in, about 420,000 bales fewer than in 1968.

Tobacco production rose, even in light of mounting criticism against its use. Total harvest of all types of tobacco was 1.8 billion pounds, up 7% over the 1968 crop. Flue-cured tobacco accounted for 1.1 billion pounds of the total yield.

Aside from sweet corn, melons, and lettuce, the 1969 fresh-vegetable harvest was a disappointment. Vegetables raised for commercial processing also declined, to nearly 25% less than the yield for 1968. However, the potato crop showed improvement in 1969. Total yield was 306 million hundredweight, 33% more than in 1968. The Idaho crop was 66.4 million hundredweight; Maine had 38 million hundredweight. The sweet-potato harvest, mostly in Louisiana, North Carolina, and Virginia, totaled 14.2 million hundredweight.

Fruitgrowers had reason for elation in 1969. The deciduous-fruit harvest, in tonnage, was 11% more than in 1968 and 26% higher than in 1967. A record apple crop of 156.2 million bushels (6.6 billion pounds) was forecast. Abundant harvests were also recorded for other fruits. Peach production was 78.6 million bushels. More than 3.8 million tons of grapes were picked. The pear harvest was 712,500 tons. Only the California plum and prune crop failed to meet 1968 levels.

The 1968–69 citrus-fruit harvest was also excellent. Production of all oranges was 183.8 million boxes; grapefruit, 55 million boxes; lemons, 16.6 million boxes; tangerines, 5.3 million boxes; and limes, 700,000 boxes. The 1969–70 citrus crop was expected to surpass this yield.

Livestock, Dairy, and Poultry Production

Livestock farmers found 1969 to be an opportune year. They increased their livestock production at a time when consumer demand for meat was high. As livestock brought higher prices, raisers' profits rose. Higher prices were in some measure attributable to economic inflation. But consumer demand, relatively low feed costs, and efficient farming were the primary reasons for higher livestock income, according to some experts.

Disgruntled housewives and other consumers felt that high meat prices were caused by excessive profit taking by livestock raisers. A limited meat boycott was in effect during the year. Organizers of it picketed supermarkets and urged meatless weeks, but at year's end the national desire for meat remained unabated.

The annual livestock inventory conducted by the U.S. Department of Agriculture showed that livestock numbers had remained fairly stable for the past five years. At the start of 1969 there were 109.6 million head of cattle and calves in the United States. Numbers of beef cattle, however, continued to rise at the expense of the dairy herd. The general decline in dairy cows did show signs of leveling, prompting estimates that the inventory would stabilize at about 14 million head.

Although larger dairy farms boasted improved management, better stock, and abundant feed and pasture it became clear that the long attrition of the U.S. dairy herd was taking its toll. Milk production into the fourth quarter of 1969 was 80 billion pounds, more than one billion pounds less than the same period a year before. Wisconsin, Minnesota, and New York were again the top dairy states.

BILL COLLINS, "THE GLOBE AND MAIL," TORONTO, ONT.

This contented cow defied 100,000-to-1 odds when she gave birth to live triplets; all three were bull calves.

In Puerto Rico, in order to save labor, more mechanization is planned. This mechanical sugarcane cutter was in use on the Aguirre plantation.

WIDE WORLD

At the beginning of the year there were 57.2 million hogs and pigs on U.S. farms, the highest inventory in five years. It was hoped that the total pig crop of 1969 would exceed the 94.5-million-hog figure of 1968. But by midyear it was evident that hog production would not even match the preceding year's output. By autumn, pork prices were uncommonly high.

Sheep numbers continued to dwindle. There were only 21.1 million head of sheep at the onset of 1969, one million fewer than in 1968. Raisers cited high labor costs, restricted size of operations, and greater profits from cattle raising as reasons for the decline of sheep.

The average consumption of nonpoultry meat for the year ending June 1969 was 182 pounds per person in the United States. Of this, 109 pounds were beef, 3.2 pounds veal, 3.6 pounds lamb or mutton, and slightly more than 66 pounds pork. Within the preceding two decades per-capita consumption of beef and veal rose by 40 pounds, while

AUTHENTICATED NEWS INTERNATIONAL

Bernard L. Pollack of the Rutgers College of Agriculture and Environmental Science sets out a pepper plant in a mulch of plastic film, a method that has provided greatly increased yields.

pork intake remained fairly steady. Each American also ate, on the average, 35 pounds of chicken and eight pounds of turkey, bringing average total meat consumption to 225 pounds per person.

The year began with a reduced inventory of 420.2 million chickens, of which 363.5 million were considered potential layers. Egg production fell short of expectations throughout much of 1969, since there were some 14 million fewer layers than in 1968. The average number of eggs eaten dropped from 323 in 1968 to 320 a year afterward. California was the chief egg-producing state, followed by Georgia and Arkansas.

Broiler output continued to rise. Broiler meat produced in federally inspected poultry-processing plants was 3.7 billion pounds for the first seven months of 1969, an 8% increase over the same period of 1968. Turkey production, about 106.4 million head, only matched the 1968 level.

Farm Income Rises Slightly

Farm assets in the United States as of Jan. 1, 1969, were estimated at $297.9 billion, 5% higher than a year earlier. Individual farmers realized a slight gain in 1969; the net income per farm was $4,841. Although this represented a $300 increase over the 1968 net-income figure, it was still well below the record $5,044 realized by the average farmer in 1966.

Farm real estate continued its upward course in value, reaching a worth of $202.7 billion in 1969. Farmers' equity in their land also increased as a consequence of the rising real-estate values. Commodity Credit Corporation loans to farmers rose to $2.3 billion, a 62% increase within a year.

Canadian Agriculture in 1969

As the rest of the world faced a wheat glut, the Canadian harvest was forecast at 678.1 million bushels, a gain of more than 28 million bushels of wheat over the 1968 yield. Unsellable stocks of the grain added to the problem of a cost-price squeeze that already burdened Canadian farmers. The total wheat acreage in the Prairie Provinces was sharply reduced to 25 million acres, about 15% less than the 1968 figure. In September, 86.2 million bushels of Canadian wheat were sold to China for $135 million.

Although meat prices were generally high due to sharp demand, Canadian livestock numbers dropped in 1969. Hogs also declined, as did turkeys.

The entire Canadian apple crop was 21.8 million bushels, an increase of 1.7 million bushels over 1968 production. British Columbia's fruit crop was hard-hit by the 1968–69 winter, resulting in disappointing harvests of apricots, peaches, grapes, and strawberries.

The problems faced by Canadian farmers received a great deal of government attention. Various short-term proposals to ease the immediate situation were discussed in Canada's House of Commons. In March a government-sponsored conference met to consider the course of agriculture over the next ten years. (*See also* Food. *See in* CE: Agriculture; Farm Life; Farm Machinery.)

AIRCRAFT. International work on the supersonic transport (SST) moved right along in 1969. Prototype models of the Anglo-French Concorde and the Soviet Union's TU-144 were flown at supersonic speeds during the year. However, a big question was whether the United States would proceed with development of its Boeing SST. In September U.S. President Richard M. Nixon quieted fears of SST advocates by announcing that it would indeed be built.

There was some question in 1969 whether the cost of the SST—$1.2 billion for development and $40 million each for purchase—was too exorbitant just to satisfy national pride. Furthermore, the sonic-boom factor presently precluded its use over crowded areas. However, forecasts based on annual increase of air traffic estimated that by 1990 more than 500 SSTs would be absorbed into the international air network.

The Boeing SST will fly at 1,800 mph and carry 300 passengers over a range of 4,000 miles. The

Concorde is to carry about 125 passengers 4,000 miles at 1,400 mph. The TU-144 has a range of about 4,000 miles. Operating at about 1,550 mph, the TU-144 will carry 120 to 160 passengers, depending on final design.

The Concorde and the TU-144 were both expected to be in commercial operation by 1973. Still not off the drawing board, the Boeing SST would not be flight-tested until late 1972 and probably would not go into service until 1978.

Developments in Civil Aviation

In June the largest airplane ever designed for commercial use, the Boeing 747, completed its maiden transoceanic flight, landing at Le Bourget Airport for display at the Paris (France) Air Show. The 747 will carry more than 350 people up to 6,700 miles at a speed of 625 mph. Although it was scheduled for delivery by late 1969, delay in fitting the giant plane with its Pratt & Whitney JT9D engines forced an almost two-month postponement. Pan American World Airways, Inc., the first airline expected to put the jumbo jet into service, had to wait until early 1970 to incorporate it into the New York City-London (England)-Frankfurt (West Germany) route.

The short-range F-28, designed by Fokker (Royal Netherlands Aircraft Factories), made its U.S. debut at Dulles International Airport, Washington, D.C., in September. Carrying from 40 to 65 passengers, it had been called the "right-size corporate jet of the '70's." Powered by two Rolls-Royce turbofan engines, the 500-mph F-28 could operate routinely from low-strength, 4,000-foot runways.

Emphasis rapidly developed on intercity commuter air transportation. During mid-1969 Swearingen Aircraft unveiled its newest commuter airliner, the Metro, at the San Antonio (Tex.) International Airport. The 22-passenger, twin-turboprop Metro could cruise at about 300 mph. It was scheduled for early 1970 delivery.

Russian planners also showed a marked interest in the business-transport field. At the Paris Air Show, Soviet engineers described plans for the YAK-40M. This tourist version of the three-jet YAK-40 was stretched to accommodate 40 passengers, 13 more than the original could hold.

Military Aircraft

The world's largest airplane, the Lockheed C-5A Galaxy of the U.S. Air Force (USAF), was first publicly shown at the U.S. National Air Show at Dulles International Airport in August. By Oc-

KEYSTONE

On March 2, 1969, the Concorde 001 prototype took off on its first flight from the airport at Toulouse, France. The plane, a joint Anglo-French project, was in the air about 25 minutes.

The first of the "jumbo jets," Boeing's new 747, made its maiden flight on Feb. 9, 1969, taking off from the company's plant in Everett, Wash. The flight was scheduled to last for two hours or more but was curtailed after 1 hour and 16 minutes.

These "skycranes" are the first two Sikorsky S-64E commercial helicopters to be used by an oil-drilling company in Alaska.

AFP FROM PICTORIAL PARADE

tober the huge plane began a yearlong series of tests to confirm its cargo- and troop-delivery capability. The C-5A gained some notoriety in 1969 when critics charged that it cost substantially more than planned. Nevertheless, a review board made up of civilian and military members concluded the C-5A was worth the mounting costs.

Twelve years had elapsed since the McDonnell Douglas F-4 Phantom II, the last U.S. fighter plane, became operational. During the intervening years many attempts were made to institute a new fighter but none met requirements or obtained enough support to leave the drawing board. A new fighter, the F-15, was now planned for operation in the mid-1970's. A fixed-wing single-seater capable of Mach 2.5, the F-15 would incorporate a new attack radar system especially designed for air-to-air combat. Three aircraft corporations—Fairchild Hiller, North American Rockwell, and McDonnell Douglas—were competing for the F-15 contract.

The YF-12A, once holder of eight world aircraft records, was to participate in supersonic cruise research studies conducted by the USAF and the National Aeronautics and Space Administration. Under terms of the program the USAF was to provide the two YF-12A's from storage.

The X-15, the rocket aircraft that pioneered the way for space flights, was retired in 1969 and installed in the Smithsonian Institution, Washington, D.C. During its heyday the X-15 reached a record altitude of 354,200 feet and attained a top speed of 4,520 mph.

Helicopters and STOLs

The helicopter has advanced to the point where it is now considered an extension of the airplane. Civil use of helicopters in air ambulance and highway patrol application made gains in 1969. The Fairchild Hiller FH-1100, the civilian version of the U.S. Army's OH-5A, had already proved its worth as a "flying squad car" in New York City. In 1969, therefore, four additional states—New Jersey, Arizona, Louisiana, and California—put the two-litter, two-seater FH-1100 to highway patrol and accident evacuation uses.

The Lockheed Aircraft Corp. suffered a serious setback in its attempts to develop an advanced armed helicopter for the Army. Because of Lockheed's failure to correct design errors in the AH-56A Cheyenne, the Army canceled its order for 375 of the 250-mph armed "choppers."

The rapid growth of air traffic in North America prompted Canadian airline executives to explore the benefits of STOL (short takeoff and landing) transport. De Havilland Aircraft of Canada Ltd. introduced its DHC-7 for "feeder" service. The 48-passenger, four-turboprop STOL was designed to operate from small airfields and "feed" major airlines serving congested metropolitan areas. Capable of taking off within 2,000 feet of a 35-foot barrier, the DHC-7 has a maximum cruising speed of 275 mph at 10,000 feet.

Helio Aircraft Corp. received a Federal Aviation Administration certificate of airworthiness for its Stallion C (controlled)/STOL in 1969. It can take off with a 2,275-pound load in 320 feet. The Stallion cruises at 217 mph and has a range of 640 miles without wing tanks or 1,200 miles with them.

The Boeing Co. was working on a military STOL called the Light Intratheater Transport (LIT) for operation in the 1970's. The LIT featured a tilt-wing configuration. When the wings are vertical the craft functions like a helicopter; when the wings are tilted horizontally the plane achieves forward flight. (*See also* Armed Forces, U.S.: Air Force; Transportation: Airlines. *See in* CE: Air Force, U.S.; Airplane articles.)

ALBANIA. During 1969 Albania received arms and munitions, made in the Soviet Union, from Communist China. This came about as the result of an urgent request from the Albanian government, alarmed by both the presence of the Soviet fleet in the Mediterranean Sea and the occupation of Czechoslovakia by the armies of the Warsaw Pact powers. In September 1968 an Albanian delegation headed by Gen. Beqir Balluku, deputy premier and defense minister, visited Peking, People's Republic of China. The delegation was received by Politburo Chairman Mao Tse-tung of China, and at a banquet given by the Albanian ambassador, China's Premier Chou En-lai declared that the Chinese people were determined to support Albania. An agreement was signed in Peking on Nov. 20, 1968, by Chou and Adil Çarçani, Albania's deputy premier. It provided for substantial Chinese aid to Albania. At Tirana, Albania's capital, Huang Yung-sheng, chief of staff of the Chinese armed forces, assured Albania that it could rely on China and stated that "the Soviet renegade revisionist clique" had sent troops into Bulgaria—an allegation promptly denied by Bulgaria.

In the spring of 1969 the first shipments of military matériel from China arrived at the Albanian ports of Durrës and Vlonë, on the Adriatic Sea. At the same time a strong Chinese military and technical mission reached Albania and began improving roads, railways, and communications. The existing railway lines connecting Durrës with Tirana and Peqin were being extended northward to Shkodër and southeastward to Pogradec on Lake Ohrid. According to some Western press reports, Albania agreed to allow China to construct missile and naval bases on Albanian territory.

On Nov. 8, 1969, shortly before the 25th anniversary of the establishment of the People's Republic of Albania (November 29), the government announced its decision to abolish the individual income tax. The resolution freed agricultural cooperatives in the mountain areas from annual tax and canceled their farm debts incurred as far back as 1966. In addition, prices of consumer goods, medicines, and some agricultural implements were to be cut. (*See in* CE: Albania.)

ALGERIA. President Houari Boumédienne of Algeria continued building up new state structures in 1969. Assemblies were elected in the country's 15 willayas (departments) after the installation of municipal councils two years earlier. The final stage was to be the election of a national assembly and a president of the republic. Efforts to revive the single party, the National Liberation Front, fell short of expectations, and Kaid Ahmed, who had been entrusted with the task at the end of 1967, was quietly removed from office in the summer of 1969. President Boumédienne himself took control of the party, and mass organizations were gradually brought into line with it.

A revolutionary court sitting in the western port of Oran sentenced to death a total of 12 men on conspiracy charges. They included ex-Chief of Staff Tahar Zbiri, who led an abortive rebellion in December 1967, and Belkacem Krim, a former vice-president of the pre-independence Algerian Provisional Government.

Diplomatic relations with the United States, broken over the Middle East issue in June 1967, and with West Germany, in May 1965, remained severed. Algeria's full commitment toward the Palestinian commandos was illustrated by the visits paid to Algiers, the capital, by their leader Yasir Arafat and the political and material aid provided to them.

The most spectacular industrial contract was signed with the U.S.-owned El Paso Natural Gas Co. The agreement called for the annual supply of 10 billion cubic meters of Saharan natural gas for 25 years. The first shipments were expected to reach the United States by 1973. The government also contracted to purchase 28 jet planes from France for use in the Algerian air force. (*See also* Middle East. *See in* CE: Algeria.)

ANIMALS AND WILDLIFE. As though to dramatize the contributions made by animals to space exploration, a 14-pound monkey named Bonny gave its life only a few days before the successful landing of men on the moon in 1969. Bonny's mission was to orbit the earth for 30 days in a study of the physical effects of prolonged space flight. After nine days and 130 orbits, however, Bonny became sluggish, refused to drink water, and had to be brought back to earth. Despite doctors' efforts, Bonny died, probably of internal injuries sustained during reentry of the space capsule in which it had traveled.

Ape "Talks"; Turtle Saves Seaman

An advance in communication between an animal and human beings resulted from a joint research project of the National Science Foundation and the National Institute of Mental Health. Work-

"LONDON DAILY EXPRESS" FROM PICTORIAL PARADE

The identity of this tiny mouselike creature remains a mystery to experts. It was found in West Pakistan and was named *Salpingotus Michaelis*, after its owner, Michael Fitzgibbon of England.

TASS FROM SOVFOTO

In Komsomol'sk, U.S.S.R., a one-year-old bear owned by a taxi driver roams alone and at will along the city's streets. It pays no heed at all to the curious people it meets along the way.

ing with a female chimpanzee named Washoe, psychologists R. Allen Gardner and his wife, Beatrice, taught the animal to understand and use at least 60 signs for words. Sign language, similar to that used by the deaf, was employed because previous experiments using spoken words had not been successful.

Washoe, a wild-born chimpanzee, was nine months old when the training program began. At the end of 22 months, the chimpanzee had learned to communicate 30 signs, including "hurry," "drink," "sorry," "funny," and such combinations as "go out" when starting toward a door and "listen dog" when hearing a dog bark. As the experiment progressed in 1969, the chimpanzee was acquiring new signs at an increasing rate and was beginning to use combinations of signs to form crude sentences.

A giant sea turtle saved the life of Chung Nam Kim, a Korean seaman who was washed off the deck of a freighter in August. When the seaman fell into the Pacific, he was more than 100 miles off the coast of Nicaragua. As he was almost on the point of drowning, he saw the sea turtle and climbed aboard; the turtle cooperated by not diving. Some time later a lookout on the Swedish ship *Citadel* sighted a man's head bobbing in the ocean. After rescue, the seaman commented that he would never again eat turtle soup.

Imports and Ecology

In both the United States and Great Britain, investigations were begun to determine the need for new regulations governing the importation and use of wild or exotic animals. Importation of animals into the United States doubled in the preceding two years (from 75,000 to 150,000), and the number of imported reptiles increased fivefold to about 2 million. Although many of the animals were imported for research purposes, an increasing number were sold as pets. Petshop owners reported rising demand for such offbeat animals as ocelots, monkeys, snakes, iguanas, bats, wolves, coyotes, lions, and tigers. Prices for ocelots were about $300; for tiger cubs, as high as $3,000. Zoologists complained that owners of exotic pets commonly failed to take proper care of their animals, and that most people either tired of them quickly or were forced to dispose of them when they actually became dangerous.

Biologists expressed concern about the increasing number of foreign species being released on ranges and other areas in the United States. The scientists pointed out that imported animals were likely to displace native species, disrupting the natural balance maintained in wilderness areas. In New Mexico, studies were begun on African and Asian game animals to determine their effects upon such native animals as coyotes, cougars, jackrabbits, badgers, and skunks.

An example of an imported species that became a dangerous threat to the freshwater ecology of the subtropical United States in less than two years

Demonstrators at the zoo in Vincennes, France, protest the massacre of baby seals on the shores of Canada.

AGIP FROM PICTORIAL PARADE

COURTESY, NEW MEXICO STATE GAME AND FISH COMMISSION

Gemsbok and ibex graze in the Redrock Game Management Area in New Mexico. These hardy animals thrive and reproduce there. They are not fed, watered, pampered, nor given much protection from predators.

is *Clarias batrachus,* the "walking catfish." It was imported by tropical-fish dealers from Southeast Asia; a few specimens escaped from aquariums into Florida waters. First noticed in 1967 near Boca Raton, considerable numbers of the catfish quickly spread into the canals of adjoining counties and in 1969 were reported migrating southward toward Miami. Biologists of the Florida Game and Fresh Water Fish Commission hoped to eliminate or control the catfish but later conceded that it would remain in Florida as "one of our fish."

Clarias batrachus is light pink in color and has a head like that of a native catfish and the body of a mudfish. At full size it is about two feet long. Because it has a lunglike breathing apparatus, it can live on land for more than 12 hours and for an indefinite period buried under mud. With the aid of its spiny dorsal fins, it can move over the ground at five feet a minute. Tolerant to temperature fluctuations, adaptable to both fresh and brackish water, a prolific breeder, a greedy and omnivorous eater, the "walking catfish" destroyed whole populations of frogs and snails in two Florida counties. Attempts to control its spread by poisoning ponds failed because it could simply climb out and walk away.

Wildlife Conservation; an Elusive "Monster"

In an effort to stop alligator poaching in the Florida Everglades, the National Park Service assigned additional rangers to patrol the feeding grounds of this vanishing species. Secretary of the Interior Walter J. Hickel warned that the alligator was in critical danger of extinction. Fewer than 20,000 were estimated to be left in the United States. Demand for their hides as material for shoes and cases kept prices high enough to encourage poachers in spite of stiff fines and possible prison sentences.

The state of Nevada and the Department of the Interior cooperated to establish in Nevada a 435,000-acre refuge for one of America's last herds of wild horses. During the late winter about 70 of these horses became marooned in mountain snows after fleeing poachers. A group of Nevada helicopter pilots, at their own expense, flew hay to the animals until the horses were able to make their way safely down from the mountains.

The government of Ceylon took steps to save from extinction three species of its native wildlife—the elephant, leopard, and dugong. Other species of wildlife reported in danger in 1969 included the dragon lizards of Komodo in eastern Indonesia, the iguanas of western Mexico, and the lions of India. The American eagle, the peregrine falcon, and the brown pelican were no longer able to reproduce in most areas of the United States. Scientists reported that concentrations of insecticides absorbed from their prey so affected their eggs that the survival of hatching chicks was virtually impossible.

Modern technology was brought into the perennial search for the fabled monster of Scotland's Loch Ness. An American oceanographer obtained permission to penetrate the waters of the loch with a 22-foot-long yellow submarine. As usual, the monster evaded efforts to get a sound-wave fix on it and kept out of range of the underwater cameras. (*See also* Pets; Zoo. *See in* CE: Animals.)

CENTRAL PRESS FROM PICTORIAL PARADE

The 20th anniversary of the North Atlantic Treaty Organization is celebrated in England.

ANNIVERSARIES AND CELEBRATIONS.

The southwesternmost metropolis of the United States—San Diego, Calif.—in 1969 celebrated the 200th anniversary of its establishment as a city. Highlights of the yearlong commemoration included a world trade fair, an international air show, and numerous special events at the city's extensive military facilities.

Three Eastern cities—Philadelphia, Pa.; Boston, Mass.; and Washington, D.C.—competed vigorously for the privilege of being host in 1976 to an international exposition commemorating the 200th anniversary of the Declaration of Independence. The winning city could expect to gain up to $2 billion from exposition visitors, perhaps 100,000 new jobs, and as much as $400 million in new taxable property. Selection of the host city was to be made—probably in 1970—by U.S. President Richard M. Nixon with the advice of a 35-man commission.

Early in June thousands of Allied veterans of World War II returned to the Normandy coast of France for ceremonies marking the 25th anniversary of D-Day—June 6, 1944, when Allied forces began the liberation of Nazi-held Europe. General of the Army Omar N. Bradley, 76, led an official U.S. delegation that included eight generals who had held key World War II commands.

The 100th anniversary of the birth of one of history's least violent men—Mohandas Gandhi—was celebrated in India early in October against a background of violent religious strife. Only a week before, in Gandhi's native state of Gujarat, Hindu-Muslim rioting had claimed an estimated 1,000 to 2,000 lives. Prime Minister Indira Gandhi and other Indian officials took the occasion to urge upon their countrymen a return to Gandhi's principles of nonviolence and Hindu-Muslim peace.

Workers parade on Oct. 1, 1950, the first anniversary of the People's Republic of China.

EASTFOTO

During a military parade celebrating the 150th anniversary of Argentine independence, in Buenos Aires, Argentina, two new AMX-13 army tanks roll by the reviewing stand.

UPI COMPIX

In Communist China in October, relatively subdued celebrations marked the 20th anniversary of the establishment of Communist rule over the world's most populous nation. The most dramatic event was the appearance at a rally in Peking, the capital, of 75-year-old Communist Party Politburo Chairman Mao Tse-tung, who had not appeared in public for more than four months; he had been rumored dead or incapacitated by disease. Lin Piao, vice-chairman and defense minister, also appeared for the first time since May. Speakers urged an end to rivalries for power among political factions; however, Mao did not speak. Foreign representation at the celebrations was slight.

Also in October—on the other side of the Communist world—ceremonies commemorated East

Germany's 20th year of Communism. Some 150,000 Communist youths staged a torchlight parade in East Berlin, and the military display was said to be the largest there since 1965. The Western allies —the United States, Great Britain, and France— who share with Russia the government of Berlin formally protested the military display, terming it a violation of agreements demilitarizing Berlin.

Ceremonies in February commemorated the 50th anniversary of the establishment of the Grand Canyon of the Colorado River as a national park. A new bronze plaque was mounted on the memorial to the explorer John Wesley Powell.

Another 50th anniversary was celebrated by the International Air Transport Association, founded in the Netherlands in 1919. Spokesmen for the organization recounted that, in its first year, international airlines carried some 3,500 passengers; in 1979, they estimated, international airlines would fly some 582 billion passenger miles. (*See also* Fairs and Shows.)

ANTARCTICA. The tenth anniversary of the signing of the Antarctic Treaty was marked in 1969. This treaty set aside national claims to Antarctic land so that the entire continent could be made into a scientific preserve.

Ten nations—the United States, the Soviet Union, Japan, France, Great Britain, Argentina, Chile, South Africa, New Zealand, and Australia—maintained 34 stations in Antarctica during 1969. Belgium and Norway did not have permanent stations but operated summer field parties in cooperation, respectively, with South African and U.S. teams.

Keeping with the spirit of the Antarctic Treaty, international cooperation continued unabated. For example, scientists from the United States, the Soviet Union, France, and Australia planned a sweeping study of Antarctic glaciers. Long-range U.S. aircraft from McMurdo Station airlifted British and Norwegian research parties to remote Antarctic regions.

Most U.S. fieldwork was concentrated in Ellsworth Highland. There, topological and geological surveys were performed in addition to botanical investigations. A new U.S. oceanographic vessel, *Hero,* also engaged in research off the Antarctic Peninsula during the 1968–69 southern summer.

Female scientists were finally allowed to work at U.S. bases in Antarctica. Officials in the past contended that the Navy-run Antarctic bases could not accommodate women, but this did not mollify those who pointed out that Russian women were allowed to conduct research in the Antarctic.

A Japanese team comprised of 11 members completed an arduous round trip to the South Pole in February. They set off on the journey to collect glaciological data. Traveling a total of 3,219 miles, the team made the round trip between Syowa Station and the pole in five months. (*See in* CE: Antarctica; Polar Exploration.)

GAMMA—PIX FROM PUBLIX

WIDE WORLD

The papyrus-reed boat in which the explorer Thor Heyerdahl attempted to sail across the Atlantic was named the *Ra* (top). Students dragged it across the desert to Alexandria, Egypt (above).

ANTHROPOLOGY. In 1969 the Norwegian anthropologist Thor Heyerdahl captured public attention once again. Heyerdahl attempted to prove his theory that ancient Egyptians could have crossed the Atlantic Ocean to Central America in papyrus-reed boats, a theory he based on similarities in ancient Egyptian and Central American cultures such as the intermarriage of royal siblings and the building of pyramids and reed boats. Heyerdahl tested his theory by attempting to sail the *Ra,* a 50-foot-long, 15-ton boat of papyrus reeds constructed like the boats pictured in Egyptian murals, with a six-man international crew, from Morocco to the Yucatán coast of Mexico. Although the boat was abandoned 600 miles from the Yucatán coast, Heyerdahl considered the voyage a success since it had proved the seaworthiness of a reed boat.

With the continued modern development of the Arctic regions, attention focused on the plight of the Eskimo culture, shared by about 80,000 people living in scattered groups around the Arctic Circle. A conference sponsored by the French Foundation of Nordic Studies was held in France in 1969, attended by Eskimos from Greenland, Canada, and Alaska and by specialists in their culture. Although there was general agreement that the Eskimo was more a victim than a beneficiary of modern developments, there was disagreement over the course to take in the future. Some delegates were in favor of preserving the language and the hunting-and-fishing society that are the basis of Eskimo culture. Others felt that assimilation was the solution. (*See in* CE: Anthropology.)

ARCHAEOLOGY. The uneasy political climate in parts of the Near East continued to hamper much fieldwork. Even where work was not hindered, such as in archaeologically rich Italy, Greece, and Turkey, theft ruled out the orderly examination of some sites. An expanding market for antiquities encouraged the looting of sites for their sellable artifacts. A sizable robbery of ancient objects from a museum in Izmir, Turkey, so aroused national anger that all foreign excavation was in jeopardy.

Discoveries in the Eastern Hemisphere

Details of the oldest known man-made shelters were released in 1969. The crude, ancient oval huts were found in a 300,000-year-old campsite in the French Riviera region. At a nearby cave site, only slightly less old, there was evidence of hut-like lean-tos originally built against the sides of the cave.

Two 30,000-year-old burials, of an adult and of a child, were recently uncovered in a cave near Santander, Spain. Archaeologists and anthropologists were delighted with the appearance of the adult remains. Clay had filled in decaying flesh and thus provided a cast of the features of ancient man. Inhabitants of the cave probably had an inkling of an afterlife. Meat bones were found at the feet of the remains, and a trussed deer or goat evidently had been laid over the head, either as food for a postlife journey or as an offering.

ARIEL VALENCIA RAMIREZ

This is a front view of a basalt sculpture of an Aztec goddess. It was unearthed in the excavations for a subway system in Mexico City, Mexico, and dates possibly from the 15th century.

The oldest written monument in Europe is this clay seal, discovered at Karanovo village, near Nova Zagora, Bulgaria. It was estimated that it dates back to the 3d or 4th millennium B.C.

KEYSTONE

Luis W. Alvarez, a Nobel prizewinner, had tried since mid-decade to locate a suspected burial chamber in the pyramid of Khafre, a 4th-dynasty Egyptian pharaoh. Alvarez was relying on cosmic-ray detectors placed beneath the towering structure to reveal any overhead chambers. Results were negative thus far, Alvarez admitted, but he probably would continue the quest.

William F. Albright, a professor at Johns Hopkins University, was made a "worthy" of Jerusalem, Israel, in honor of his half-century-long archaeological studies of the Palestinian region. One of Albright's key accomplishments was the origination of ceramic chronology, a method of dating finds based on identification of surviving pottery.

Archaeological work within gun range of the Jordan River was halted while the dispute between

Israel and the Arab states continued. Israeli officials, however, allowed some research to resume in areas of occupied Jordan. As a consequence, additional clearing took place at the early Bronze Age (about 2750 B.C.) fortifications of Ai. At Shechem, excavations unearthed buildings from three ages—Bronze, Iron, and Roman.

In Lebanon an important early-1st-millennium B.C. site, Tell el Ghassil, continued to yield rich archaeological data. The site, under excavation by workers from the American University of Beirut, contained fire-destroyed temples. Assyrian invaders were thought to have set the blazes.

The important Keban salvage effort in the Turkish region of central Anatolia progressed in 1969. In nearly a dozen projects British, German, and U.S. excavators worked in collaboration with Turkish archaeologists. One of these efforts, directed by Maurits van Loon of the University of Chicago (Ill.), resulted in the uncovering of a sequence of archaeological levels that spanned 5,000 years.

An expedition sponsored by Indiana University and the University of Pennsylvania kept on with its exploration of the Franchthi Cave in Greece, revealing a long sequence of habitation that began when the early occupants were food-gatherers to the time when they became food growers, about 6000 B.C. On the Greek island of Crete archaeologists discovered a complete early Minoan village, which actually appeared to have been a single-building complex.

Work proceeded in Athens, Greece, on excavations of the agora, market area and meeting place of the ancient city. The long-term American archaeological project concentrated on clearing some of the old streets that led into the agora.

University of Hawaii archaeologists reported on the yield from Spirit Cave in Thailand. At the site they found evidence of agriculture dating from as early as 7000 B.C.

Archaeology in the Western Hemisphere

A University of Alberta scientist proposed that early man reached the New World before the waters of Bering Strait covered a Siberia-Alaska land bridge during a thaw in the Wisconsin period of the Ice Age. This thaw, which cut off the link, occurred between 25,000 and 35,000 years ago. It was further theorized that man's migration down an ice-free corridor in Alaska and Canada was halted by coalescing ice masses about 25,000 years ago. All bifacially flaked projectile-point traditions of toolmaking particular to the prehistoric cultures of mid-North America hence would have evolved on the continent and could not have been acquired from Asia. The view was based on evidence that this particular way of making stone tools had not evolved anywhere else in the world when the ice closed off the migration route.

Amateur archaeologists hauling dirt and rock-fill from the base of a "buffalo jump" near Wilsall, Mont., discovered human skeletal remains and a

This drawing of a horse's head, estimated to be 15,000 years old, was found on the wall of a cave in Spain and merited scholarly attention in 1968–69.

"PARIS MATCH" FROM PICTORIAL PARADE

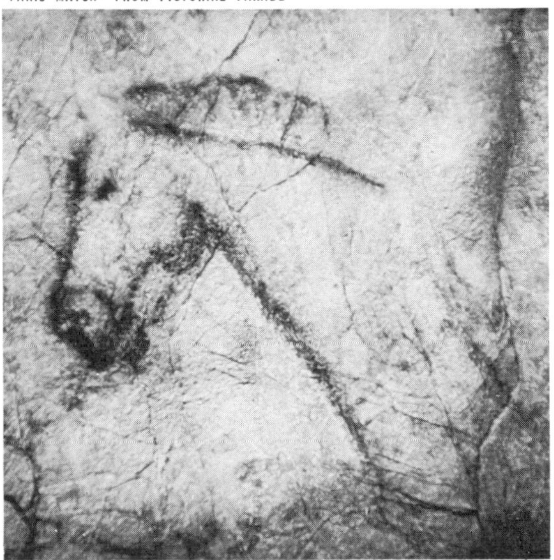

Amulet statuettes that represent Egyptian gods and goddesses, including Isis, Osiris, Ptah, and Imhotep, are part of the archaeological finds from an excavation in Memphis, the capital of the pharaonic Old Kingdom in Egypt.

KEYSTONE

number of Stone Age artifacts presumably associated with the skeleton. The artifacts included five fluted Clovis points and stone fleshing tools.

An early-man site was located on the south shore of Tulare Lake in California's San Joaquin Valley. Artifacts found in the site included a number of stone points resembling those of the Clovis-Folsom tradition of toolmaking. Other chipped stone tools found in the area suggested that the site was of great age.

Inundation was threatening the archaeological site in southeastern Washington where remains of the pre-Indian Marmes man were found. The ancient rock-shelter, the most important archaeological site in the United States, began to flood when a cofferdam, built to stem the waters of nearby Lower Monumental Dam reservoir, sprang a leak. Archaeologists had hoped that protracted excavation of the site would reveal more about the 13,000-year-old man.

Theft was beginning to be a plague of New World archaeological sites. As an example, a stone relief of a Mayan sun-god was smuggled into the United States from an unknown site in Mexico. The smugglers wanted $500,000 for the relief but were thwarted in their attempts to sell it to a New York museum. The U.S. State Department was instrumental in its return to Mexico's National Museum of Anthropology.

Work was under way on deciphering the puzzling Mayan language. Archaeologists thought that Mayan text might offer clues on the disintegration of this impressive civilization, which flourished between A.D. 300 and 900. The rain forests of Mexico's Yucatán Peninsula and of nearby Central America would be probed for Mayan monuments and all ideographs (inscriptions) on them photographed. After compilation of the ideographs, cryptanalysis would be used to try to "break" the language. (*See in* CE: Archaeology.)

ARCHITECTURE. The profession of architecture was saddened in 1969 by the deaths of two of its most brilliant modern pioneers. Walter Adolf Gropius, founder of the famed Bauhaus school of design in Weimar, Germany, and for many years a professor at Harvard University, at Cambridge, Mass., died in July at the age of 86. In August Ludwig Mies van der Rohe died in Chicago, Ill. He was the originator of the understated, refined, steel-and-glass style of architecture, exemplified beautifully in his West Berlin (Germany) National Gallery of 1968. (*See also* Obituaries.)

The influence of these two men, together with that of Le Corbusier, who died in 1965, can be seen in countless 20th-century buildings. Gropius' influence was great as a teacher and as a promoter of the application of good design principles to everyday objects. Mies van der Rohe's philosophy of "less is more" underlay the design of the elegant steel-and-glass skyscrapers that today dominate the skylines of many U.S. cities.

COURTESY, VINCENT G. KLING AND ASSOCIATES

The Monsanto Co. of St. Louis, Mo., built this cafeteria for its employees. It was designed by Vincent G. Kling and Associates and provides facilities for 1,000 people.

WILLIAM J. TOOMEY © "ARCHITECTS' JOURNAL"

This building in Boness, Scotland, is an example of the work of Jack Coia of Glasgow, Scotland, who won the Royal Gold Medal for Architecture for 1969.

Architectural Awards

The American Institute of Architects in 1969 presented 14 honor awards for excellence in design. Award-winning buildings included a private home, museums, a library, housing projects, and public and private office buildings. One award was given for the restoration to its 19th-century opulence of Louis Sullivan's long-unused Auditorium Theatre in Chicago.

The Prestressed Concrete Institute presented 12 awards for outstanding use of that material. The prizes were won by such buildings as an Ohio bank, the Boston (Mass.) City Hall, a university library in New York, a science center in Ontario, and—perhaps not surprisingly—a prestressed-concrete manufacturing plant in Georgia.

Among 12 structures cited for excellence by the National Conference of Religious Architecture was the Roman Catholic Church of the Resurrection in Wallingford, Conn. In Great Britain, the Royal Institute of British Architects awarded its 1969 Royal Gold Medal for Architecture to the 70-year-old Glasgow, Scotland, architect Jack Coia, known chiefly as a designer of Roman Catholic churches.

Expo '70 Architecture

In general, 1969 was not a year of spectacular new buildings, though plans advanced in many nations for structures for Expo '70, to be held at Osaka, Japan. Expo '70 promised to be something of an architectural event. Designs for the main Festival Plaza were completed by the Japanese architects Arata Isozaki and Atsushi Ueda. In charge of overall planning was Prof. Kenzo Tange.

The rectangular Symbol Zone—partly covered by an enormous translucent roof (measuring 364 feet by 964 feet) made of aluminum ball-jointed steel pipes—contains theaters and display halls. Through the building rises the conical Tower of the Sun, inside which is the Tree of Life.

At Expo '70 the ever-present world's fair tower, aptly titled EXPOTower, rises 396 feet and affords a dramatic view of the Kita Settsu mountain range to the northwest. On clear days it also yields a panorama of the industrial city of Osaka ten miles to the southwest.

The U.S. national pavilion at the fair is a $10-million elliptical air-supported plastic dome housing a variety of exhibits. Russia's pavilion resembles a sharp-edged sickle topped by a huge red star. Canada's building features outside walls covered with yard-square mirrors. (*See* Japan Special Report.)

Preserving the Past

Of the year's new buildings a surprisingly large number of new museums merited attention. Mies van der Rohe's West Berlin art gallery was followed by two more new West German museums. Philip Johnson, a U.S. architect, designed the Richard Kaselowsky art gallery at Bielefeld. Two of the three units of the Wilhelm Lehmbruck museum and sculpture gallery in Duisburg were completed; the architect was Manfred Lehmbruck, the son of the sculptor for whom the museum was named.

In Oakland, Calif., a new city museum of unusual design was completed. The three-tiered labyrinth—resembling a Babylonian garden—houses collections in art, natural science, and history. The museum, which opened in the fall, was designed by Kevin Roche.

On the campus of Westminster College in Fulton, Mo.—where Britain's Sir Winston Churchill delivered the speech that added the phrase "iron curtain" to the English language—Christopher Wren's London (England) Church of St. Mary, Adlermanbury, was reconstructed under the supervision of

This is a view from the east, near the Rideau Canal, of Canada's new National Arts Centre in Ottawa, Ont. The building was officially opened in June 1969 when a production of the ballet 'Krannerg' was presented by the National Ballet.

JOHN EVANS PHOTOGRAPHY LTD.

Marshall Sisson of London and Frederick G. Sternberg of St. Louis, Mo. The transplanted structure, badly damaged by bombs in World War II, was to serve as the student chapel. It also houses a Churchill library and museum.

Other Important Buildings

On the campus of the University of Illinois at Urbana-Champaign, the Krannert Center for the Performing Arts (incorporating four theaters) was designed by Max Abramovitz, architect of Philharmonic Hall in Lincoln Center for the Performing Arts, New York City. At Cornell University, Ithaca, N.Y., a new wing was added to the home economics building. Designed by Ulrich Franzen, it was hailed as the first distinguished example of modern architecture on that campus. The reinforced-concrete structure, clad in rust-colored weatherproof brick, houses laboratories and administrative offices. A new faculty club at the University of California's Santa Barbara campus was designed by architects Moore and Turnbull. It was intended to reflect various facets of the Los Angeles, Calif., area—neon lights, freeways, motels, Hollywood, and the Hispanic style.

The new City Hall of Boston was completed. Constructed with cast-in-place and precast concrete columns and cores, the building was designed by the firm of Kallmann, McKinnell, and Knowles, winner of the project in a 1962 competition. The firm of Campbell, Aldrich, and Nulty collaborated in the design. Situated on a brick-paved square, the new building is flanked by the raised podium of the Federal Building and by Faneuil Hall. The architect responsible for the master plan for the Boston Government Center was I. M. Pei.

In San Francisco, Calif., the recently completed Alcoa Building, by the architectural firm of Skidmore, Owings, and Merrill, is a study in structural expressionism. Its facades are sheathed in exposed diagonal seismic bracing. The Marin County Civic Center in nearby San Rafael, the last work of Frank Lloyd Wright, was finally completed, ten years after his death. In Tokyo, Japan, the new 1,000-room Imperial Hotel to replace Wright's demolished 1916 masterpiece was designed by Teitaro Takahashi. (*See also* Building Construction; Cities and Urban Affairs. *See in* CE: Architecture.)

ARCTIC. An oil and mineral boom in the icy wastes of North America's Arctic seemed imminent in 1969. In September the state of Alaska sold leases on 431,104 acres of its North, or Arctic, Slope, all potential oil-bearing land. It collected nearly $1 billion in bonus lease bids for the one third of the Arctic oil field put up for sale. This transaction was the biggest of its kind in U.S. history.

By late 1969 the tanker-icebreaker SS *Manhattan* completed a historic round-trip voyage from New York City to Point Barrow, Alaska, through the treacherous Northwest Passage. The test voyage

PICTORIAL PARADE

The conning tower of the nuclear submarine *Whale* and a crew member are seen at the North Pole. The *Whale* broke through the polar ice cap on April 6, 1969—60 years after Adm. Robert E. Peary reached the pole in 1909.

seemed to assure that the vast mineral resources of Alaska, the Yukon, and the Northwest Territories could be moved economically to world markets. (*See* Ships and Shipping.)

As massive exploitation of resources loomed, the circumpolar nations realized that immediate steps were needed to protect the delicate ecology of the Arctic from industrial pollution. Road-building and pipeline-laying activities in the Arctic oil fields, for example, were viewed by conservationists as environmental hazards. (*See also* Conservation.)

In June a British trans-Arctic team led by 34-year-old Wally Herbert completed probably the longest, loneliest walk in the world. Traveling by dogsled and ice floe from Point Barrow across the North Pole to the Spitsbergen archipelago north of Norway, they made the first journey over the

Members of the four-man British Trans-Arctic Expedition are shown during their nearly 4,000-mile journey, the first successful surface crossing of the Arctic Ocean.

UPI COMPIX

Arctic Ocean on record. The trip was made by dead reckoning over a map distance of 1,800 miles. In reality, however, more than twice this distance was covered because of erratically drifting ice.

A romantic part of Canada's past ended in May when a Royal Canadian Mounted Policeman and his guide, with their dog teams and sleds, returned from an 800-mile spring patrol of the vast northern wilderness, the last ever by dogsled. A growing use of snowmobiles has made this mode of Arctic travel all but extinct. (*See in* CE: Arctic Regions.)

ARGENTINA. The strikes and violent disorders in the large cities of Argentina in May and June 1969 marked the first serious challenge to the three-year-old regime of President Juan Carlos Onganía. The unrest also threatened the monetary stability and orderly economic development fostered by Adalbert Krieger Vasena since his appointment as minister of economy and labor in January 1967. The May disturbances in Córdoba, Rosario, and elsewhere, in which more than 20 people lost their lives, were sparked by comparatively trivial grievances but appeared symptomatic of popular dissatisfaction with the lack of communication between government and community and with some features of economic and social policy, notably the strict wage freeze.

UPI COMPIX

Juan Carlos Onganía, president of Argentina, salutes as he passes a parade reviewing stand. On the president's left is Gen. Gustavo Martinez Zuviria.

President Onganía declared that the regime would not bow to violence and would remain faithful to the aims of the so-called "Argentine Revolution" that it had instituted. A wholesale revision of the administration was undertaken, nevertheless, in June, and many members of the government, including all the ministers, were replaced.

In late June, during protests against the impending state visit of New York's Gov. Nelson A. Rockefeller, time bombs exploded in several U.S.-owned stores in Buenos Aires, the capital, and a call was made for strike action by the militant antigovernment faction of the union movement. In the midst of this unrest the prominent labor leader Augusto T. Vandor was murdered in his office by a group of armed men. The government adopted emergency powers by declaring a state of siege.

Imports rose sharply during the year; their value in the first seven months was more than 50% higher than in the comparable period of 1968. This growth was partly matched by a fairly buoyant export performance. A notable feature of this was the substantial increase in beef shipments, running at 50% above their 1968 level for much of the year. (*See in* CE: Argentina.)

ARMED FORCES, UNITED STATES. Throughout the world, the armed forces of the United States continued in 1969 to guard the interests of the nation and much of the non-Communist world. Units of all services fought in South Vietnam, though a phased withdrawal of U.S. forces from that nation was begun at the direction of U.S. President Richard M. Nixon. (*See* Vietnam.) At home, the Administration and the Congress considered modifications of the draft law and means of reducing the nation's heavy military expenditures. (*See* Defense; Selective Service.)

AIR FORCE

More than 1.2 million U.S. Air Force men and women and civilians manned 220 installations around the world in 1969. The Air Force budget exceeded $25 billion. Air Force personnel strength was reduced during the year by the release of Air Force Reserve and Air National Guard members who had been called to active duty in the wake of North Korea's capture of the U.S. Navy's intelligence vessel USS *Pueblo*. A 50,000-man reduction in force was also announced by the Nixon Administration in September. The Air Force continued to improve the quality of its reserve forces with the aim of providing the United States with a strategic reserve for less money than would be required to maintain a larger regular Air Force.

Strategic forces became increasingly dependent upon missiles as the manned-bomber force continued to be phased down. It was announced late in 1969 that the Air Force's 78 supersonic B-58 bombers would be retired, leaving some 450 B-52's as the manned heavy-bomber force. The Air Force's intercontinental ballistic-missile inventory included 54 Titan II's and 1,000 Minuteman I's and II's. Testing of the advanced Minuteman III continued, and production of its multiple independently targetable reentry vehicle (MIRV) warheads

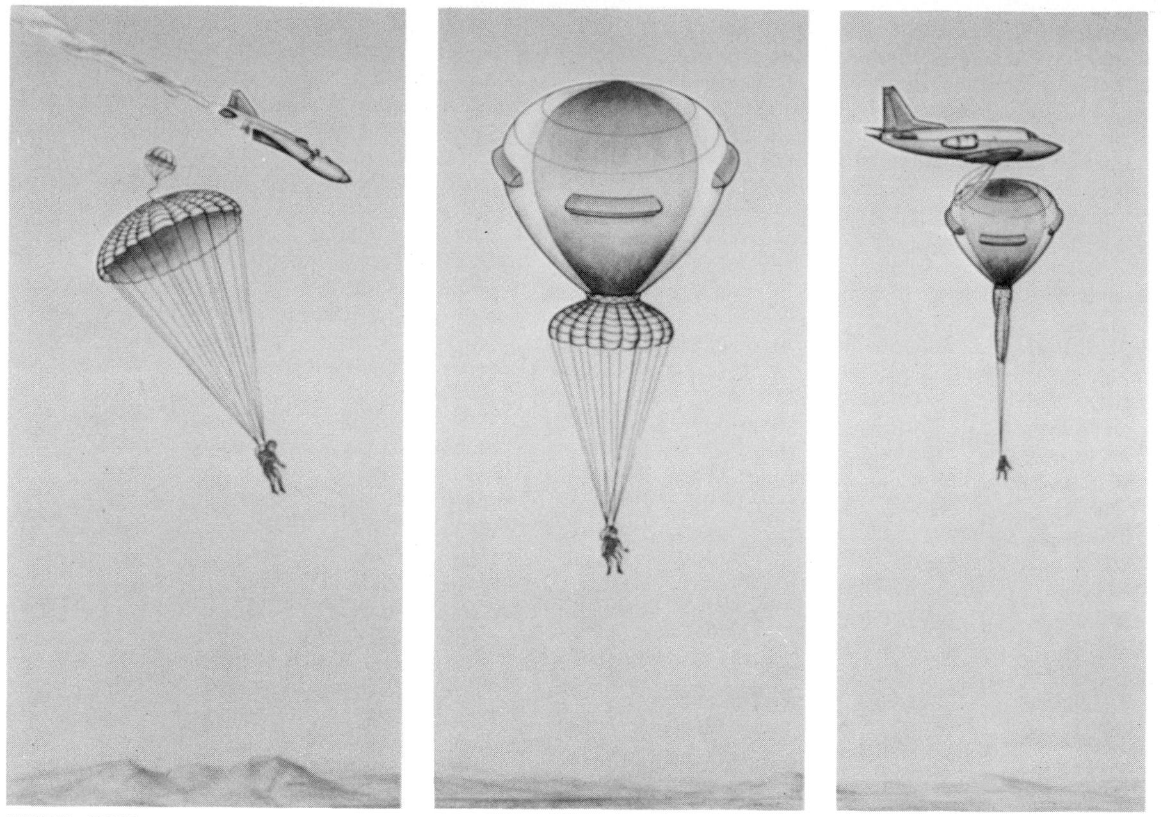

COURTESY, GOODYEAR TIRE & RUBBER CO.

The newly developed Pilot Airborne Recovery Device consists of a parachute (left) and a balloon forced open by air (center). A burner ignites and heats the air in the balloon, which lifts the apparatus upward. Another aircraft (right) makes the recovery.

was ordered. The MIRV will permit a single missile to deliver warheads to several separate targets and also to carry penetration aids to confuse enemy defenses.

While a substantial part of the B-52 force was committed to Vietnamese operations, some 40% of the bombers remained on nuclear alert. The Air Force's tactical, or ground support, units operated largely in Vietnam. Air defense forces included 771 interceptors in 41 squadrons.

Partly as a result of newly efficient management, the Air Force's airlift capacity increased in 1969 though the number of its transports decreased by more than 100 to a total of fewer than 1,500. The latest Air Force transport—the huge Lockheed C-5A—was expected to enter operational service in mid-1970.

Looking to the future, the Air Force in 1969 awarded three contracts for preliminary work on a new air-superiority fighter, the F-15. The plane will be a single-seat, twin-engine craft designed primarily for air-to-air combat. Although the Air Force's Manned Orbiting Laboratory program was canceled, the service continued its unmanned space operations and its close coordination with the National Aeronautics and Space Administration in the exchange of technology, hardware, and experience.

The top command structure of the Air Force changed in 1969. Robert C. Seamans, Jr., replaced Harold Brown as secretary of the Air Force—the service's civilian chief—and Gen. John D. Ryan moved up from his position as vice-chief of staff to replace Gen. John P. McConnell, who had completed four years of service as Air Force chief of staff. (*See in* CE: Air Force, U.S.)

ARMY

Scandals, controversies, and an alleged massacre placed the U.S. Army on the defensive during 1969. In a year of rising dissent against the U.S. involvement in the Vietnam conflict, U.S. soldiers were accused of massacring Vietnamese villagers, and the commander of the U.S. Army Special Forces in Vietnam was implicated in the suspected murder of a Vietnamese civilian. Noncommissioned officers were investigated on charges of embezzling funds from Army service clubs, and the adverse effects of tests of chemical and biological weapons were brought to public attention.

In November, accounts of an alleged massacre of the inhabitants of My Lai 4, one of nine hamlets in the village of Song My, South Vietnam, were made public more than a year after the event occurred. Former soldiers who witnessed and/or participated in the mass murders on March 16, 1968, told how the Vietnamese—old men, women, and children—were herded into groups and shot to death with automatic weapons. The Army had conducted an inquiry into the killings shortly after they occurred but had concluded that nothing was amiss. In 1969 that inquiry was also under investigation.

The 1969 investigation began after Ronald L. Ridenhour, a discharged serviceman, wrote letters describing the atrocity to the U.S. president, the secretary of defense, several congressmen, and other officials. On September 5 First Lieut. William L. Calley, Jr., was charged with the murder of "at least 109 civilians." Staff Sgt. David Mitchell in October was charged with assault with intent to murder 30 Vietnamese noncombatants. Other members of the company that attacked the village in Viet Cong territory were also under investigation, including the company commander, Capt. Ernest L. Medina. He denied issuing orders to massacre civilians and said he saw no massacre at My Lai. At a televised press conference in December, however, U.S. President Richard M. Nixon affirmed that a massacre had in fact occurred. Reports of the number of villagers killed ranged from 109 to 567.

The commander of all the Army Special Forces troops in Vietnam—Col. Robert B. Rheault—and seven other "Green Berets" were arrested in July and later charged with murder and conspiracy to commit murder in the alleged slaying of a Vietnamese man. The Green Berets suspected the man of being a double agent for the Viet Cong. Allegedly,

WIDE WORLD

The commander of the U.S. Army Special Forces in Vietnam, Col. Robert B. Rheault (foreground), was among those accused of conspiring to murder a Vietnamese. Charges against the "Green Berets" were dropped.

after receiving long-awaited instructions from the U.S. Central Intelligence Agency (CIA), the Green Berets injected the agent with morphine, shot him, and dropped his body into the South China Sea. The body was never found. Later the CIA was said to have rescinded its earlier instructions and ordered that the agent be spared.

The charges were dropped after the CIA told the Army that for reasons of national security it would not allow CIA agents to testify at the courts-martial. Colonel Rheault, bitter because he was never given a chance to prove his innocence, retired from the Army on October 31.

A group of sergeants, including William O. Wooldridge, the Army's first sergeant major, were accused of conflict of interest in the course of their duties as custodians of Army service clubs. A Senate subcommittee heard testimony that the custodians had received large kickbacks from entertainers' agents and from food and beverage suppliers. They also allegedly pilfered money from club slot machines. At the hearing Wooldridge and three other former custodians refused to answer questions, invoking the 5th Amendment 114 times. A transcript of the hearings was sent to Pentagon officials, but the Army did not feel there was sufficient evidence to warrant prosecutions.

In May the Army admitted that some 6,000 sheep had died as the result of an accident that happened during nerve-gas tests in Utah in 1968. The Army's policy of shipping poisonous gases through populated areas of the United States also stirred controversy.

In November the National Conference on GI Rights adopted a resolution calling for the organization of a "GI lobby" in Washington, D.C., to protect servicemen's civil rights. Antiwar sentiment among soldiers increased in 1969. (*See also* Defense Special Report; Vietnam. *See in* CE: Army, U.S.)

PEARSON, "KNICKERBOCKER NEWS," FROM BEN ROTH AGENCY

"He must be the sergeant who runs the service club."

COAST GUARD

In 1969—its 179th year—the U.S. Coast Guard continued to promote maritime safety, conduct oceanographic research, and participate in U.S. military activities. Although its budget increased to $585.7 million from the $571 million of 1968, the Coast Guard's personnel declined in number. Uniformed personnel fell from 36,700 to 34,000 and civilian employees from 6,060 to 5,860 as a service-wide modernization program continued.

In the coastal waters of South Vietnam, twenty-four 82-foot Coast Guard cutters and five oceangoing cutters formed part of a naval shield that hindered infiltration from North Vietnam. Two of the original Coast Guard Vietnamese flotilla of twenty-six 82-foot cutters were turned over to the South Vietnamese. Other transfers were to follow as trained South Vietnamese crews

OFFICIAL U.S. COAST GUARD PHOTO

The U.S. Coast Guard acquired the longest-range helicopters ever built. These amphibious helicopters have a cruising speed of 150 mph and a range of 700 miles and can carry up to six passengers.

became available. Elsewhere in the Vietnam theater, the Coast Guard aided in the improvement of port security, the establishment and maintenance of a system of aids to navigation, and the handling of traffic and other problems generated by a heavy increase in shipping.

In U.S. waters, the Coast Guard in 1969 inspected 1,138 foreign vessels, inspected for certification 5,470 vessels, conducted 5,293 dry-dock examinations, and made 6,900 vessel reinspections. Miscellaneous vessel inspections totaled more than 30,000, and 32,332 merchant-vessel plans were reviewed. The number of waterfront workers screened for security was 9,051.

Coast Guard search and rescue units in 1969 responded to 48,108 calls for assistance, answered 19,508 requests for towing, and provided aid to 4,675 persons in peril. Worldwide, the service continued to maintain more than 44,600 aids to navigation for ships and aircraft. Coast Guard icebreakers conducted oceanographic research in the polar regions, and the icebreaker *Northwind* aided the tanker-icebreaker SS *Manhattan* on its traverse of the Northwest Passage from the East coast to the new oil fields in northern Alaska.

The Coast Guard also continued its services to recreational boating. Its Auxiliary, a voluntary organization, was active in 1,011 flotillas. It gave instruction in safe boating to 423,950 persons, examined 161,774 motorboats, patrolled 1,034 regattas, and saved 215 lives. (*See in* CE: Coast Guard, U.S.)

MARINE CORPS

In 1969, as in the four preceding years, the U.S. Marine Corps concentrated its major effort in the Republic of Vietnam. The 78,000 Marines in South Vietnam were members of the III Marine Amphibious Force, made up of the 1st and 3d Marine divisions—reinforced by part of the 5th Marine Division, the 1st Marine Aircraft Wing, and a Force Logistic Command. Two U.S. Army divisions with supporting units were attached to the Marine force of ground, jet, and helicopter units. All operated throughout the five northernmost provinces of South Vietnam. Some Marine units were withdrawn from South Vietnam in the second half of the year as part of a phased disengagement of U.S. forces.

During the year the Marines deactivated several fixed outposts in favor of a more mobile posture, seeking to push Viet Cong and North Vietnamese army units from mountain and jungle bases. Unprecedented amounts of enemy munitions and supplies were captured. Operations involving combined helicopter assault and amphibious landings—a Marine specialty—met repeated success on the heavily populated coastal plain. By August a total of 23 Marines had received the Medal of Honor for heroism in South Vietnam.

The Marine Corps supplemented its combat activities in South Vietnam with a massive civic-action effort. The 100 units of the Combined

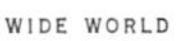

On a hilltop southwest of Da Nang, South Vietnam, U.S. Marines set up a command post and artillery base as part of an operation against North Vietnamese troops thought to be in the area.

WIDE WORLD

Amphibious vehicles carry U.S. Marines ashore at Red Beach, 17 miles south of Da Nang, South Vietnam. These Marines were part of a 4,000-man operation against a Viet Cong stronghold.

UPI COMPIX

Action Program (CAP) joined other Marines and South Vietnamese militia in platoons that worked for and defended rural villages. Most of the CAP Marines were volunteers, many serving a second or third tour in South Vietnam. In 1969 some 13,000 Marines voluntarily extended their tours in the war zone, bringing the total of such volunteers to 36,000 since the beginning of the conflict.

Other Marine civic action in South Vietnam ranged from direct gifts of food and clothing to long-range projects in education, public works, agriculture, and health. In the United States the Marine Corps Reserve, in cooperation with CARE (Cooperative for American Relief Everywhere), continued to seek cash contributions for use in civic action in South Vietnam under a program that had realized donations of more than $750,000 since 1965.

Worldwide, Marine Corps strength in 1969 totaled four active-duty divisions, three aircraft wings, and more than 313,000 men—a number second only to its World War II peak of 475,604. Organized Reserve strength was 48,000 in a fully equipped division/aircraft wing team. Another 90,000 Marines served as a backup force in the Ready Reserve.

In the United States, depots at Parris Island, S.C., and San Diego, Calif., provided eight weeks of boot camp, or basic training, to some 89,000 recruits. During the year, controversy arose over charges that some Marine recruits suffered maltreatment during boot training. Fights between groups of white and black Marines broke out at a number of Marine installations in the United States. In an effort to ease racial tension in the Corps, Gen. Leonard F. Chapman, Jr., commandant, ordered an end to discriminatory practices and opened new avenues of appeal to Marines who felt that they were the victims of racial prejudice.

It was General Chapman's second year as the Marine Corps commandant. In August Sgt. Maj. Joseph W. Dailey became sergeant major of the Marine Corps, the service's top enlisted post. Colonel Jeanette I. Sustad became director of Women Marines, whose numbers totaled some 290 officers and 2,600 enlisted personnel. (*See in* CE: Marine Corps, U.S.)

NAVY

Cuts in the Department of Defense budget required a reduction in U.S. Navy strength in 1969 and early 1970. Some training operations in the United States were curtailed; manpower was to be reduced by about 72,000 to a total of some 700,000; and more than 100 ships were to be decommissioned, reducing the active fleet to about 800.

The ships chosen for deactivation averaged about 25 years old. The average quality of active naval vessels was improved by the commissioning of about 50 new ships and the recommissioning of 10 extensively converted older ships. A major new vessel was the tank-landing ship USS *Newport,* faster and more efficient than its predecessors. Among the decommissioned ships was the world's only active battleship, the USS *New Jersey*.

In Vietnam the Navy continued to provide air and gunfire support for ground forces and to patrol coastal waters, rivers, and canals. By the end of October, in a continuing program to give the South Vietnamese a greater share of combat responsibility, more than 200 of the Navy's small craft had been turned over to U.S.-trained South Vietnamese crews. Ashore, Navy Seabees built airfields and other structures.

Although a Navy Court of Inquiry had recommended court-martial for two officers of the reconnaissance ship USS *Pueblo*—captured by North Korea in January 1968—and nonjudicial punishment for others, in May Secretary of the Navy John H. Chafee announced that no disciplinary action would be taken. North Korea released the 82 survivors of the *Pueblo*'s crew in December 1968. In April 1969, North Korean aircraft shot down an unarmed Navy reconnaissance plane over international waters. Its 31 crewmen were lost. A 29-ship task force was dispatched to patrol the waters off Korea until the crisis cooled.

Fire and explosions aboard the nuclear-fueled aircraft carrier USS *Enterprise* in January killed 27 crewmen and injured 85; another man was missing and presumed dead. The $6-million damage to the ship was repaired by March, and it returned to action. The nuclear submarine USS *Guittaro* sank while undergoing final fitting at Mare Island

AUTHENTICATED NEWS INTERNATIONAL

A model of the U.S. Navy's Deep Submergence Rescue Vehicle is loaded aboard an Air Force C-141 jet transport. The new rescue submarine will be able to reach the scene of a submarine disaster anywhere in the world within 24 hours.

Naval Shipyard in California in May. The submarine was extensively damaged, but no one was injured.

The destroyer USS *Frank E. Evans* was sliced in two by the bow of the Australian aircraft carrier HMAS *Melbourne* during a Southeast Asia Treaty Organization naval exercise in June. The bow of the destroyer sank immediately, carrying 73 men to their deaths. The *Evans'* commanding officer and its officer of the deck at the time of the collision were reprimanded after court-martial.

The Navy's most widely publicized missions in 1969 were its pickups of Apollo astronauts. The USS *Guadalcanal* recovered the Apollo 9 crew in March; the USS *Princeton,* the Apollo 10 crew in May; and the USS *Hornet*—after man's first moon landings—the Apollo 11 crew in July and the Apollo 12 crew in November. Apollo 12, the second moon-landing mission, had an all-Navy crew: Comdr. Charles Conrad, Jr.; Comdr. Richard F. Gordon, Jr.; and Comdr. Alan L. Bean. (*See also* Space Exploration. *See in* CE: Navy, U.S.)

ARMSTRONG, NEIL A. On July 20, 1969, U.S. astronaut Neil A. Armstrong became the first man to step onto the moon. He was accompanied to the lunar surface by astronaut Edwin E. Aldrin, Jr., while astronaut Michael Collins remained in lunar orbit in the command module of the spacecraft Apollo 11. While on the moon, Armstrong and Aldrin set up scientific experiments, gathered rock and soil samples, and took pictures. Their journey, which had begun on July 16, ended on July 24 with a safe recovery in the Pacific Ocean. (*See* Space Exploration.)

Armstrong was born in Wapakoneta, Ohio, on Aug. 5, 1930, the son of Mr. and Mrs. Stephen Armstrong. As a teen-aged youngster Armstrong took flying lessons and in 1946, on his 16th birthday, he received his first pilot's license—before he had obtained an automobile driver's license.

He was a U.S. Navy flier from 1949 to 1952, completing 78 combat missions during the Korean War. In 1955 he received a degree in aeronautical engineering from Purdue University, in Indiana. In January 1956 he married Janet Shearon in Wilmette, Ill. They have two children, Eric and Mark.

Joining the National Advisory Committee on Aeronautics—which later became the National Aeronautics and Space Administration—Armstrong became a skilled research pilot. The record-setting X-15 was among the experimental aircraft he flew.

Armstrong was selected as an astronaut candidate in September 1962. In his first space flight he commanded Gemini 8, the first spacecraft to dock with another in orbit. He was named commander of Apollo 11 in January 1969.

With the words "Houston, Tranquillity Base here. The Eagle has landed," the taciturn Armstrong announced the touchdown of his lunar lander. When, some six hours later, he first stepped onto the lunar surface, he said, "That's one small step for a man, one giant leap for mankind."

Astronaut Neil A. Armstrong, commander of the Apollo 11 lunar-landing mission, was the first man to set foot on the moon. The historic event occurred on July 20.

UPI COMPIX

ASIA. The Vietnam conflict continued to overshadow all other events in Asia in 1969. The level of fighting diminished somewhat, but the attainment of peace remained elusive. At year's end the peace talks in Paris, France, seemed to be at an impasse, with the major parties—the United States and North Vietnam—unyielding in their positions and accusing one another of intransigence. (*See* Vietnam.)

The death in September of North Vietnam's President Ho Chi Minh became an occasion for an exhibition of rivalry between the People's Republic of China and the Soviet Union. In Ho's will, which was read at his funeral, the dead leader had made an impassioned appeal for unity in the world Communist movement. The plea seemed to have some effect on the Soviet Union and China, for they made an attempt to improve relations. Soviet Premier Aleksei N. Kosygin flew to Peking, the Chinese capital, where he met with his Chinese counterpart for talks "in the spirit of the Ho Chi Minh will." In October the Soviet Union and China initiated discussions on their border dispute, which had erupted into armed conflict several times during the year. Besides taking a more flexible stance toward the Soviet Union, the Chinese made cautious efforts to improve their relations with East European Communist countries and with the United States. (*See* China, People's Republic of; Communist Movement; Union of Soviet Socialist Republics.)

Japan continued to assert itself economically, maintaining its position in 1969 as the second largest economic power in the non-Communist world, surpassed only by the United States. One thorny issue between the United States and Japan, that of the future status of Okinawa, was settled during the year. The United States agreed to return Okinawa to Japanese rule, free from nuclear weapons, sometime in 1972. In return, the Japanese gave the United States greater freedom of action to use its bases in Japan not only in defense of the country but also to fulfill U.S. security commitments in the Far East. The successful settlement of the question seemed to strengthen the special Japanese-U.S. relationship and to augur the assumption by Japan of a greater role in Asian and world affairs. (*See* Japan.)

Racial riots in Malaysia between citizens of Malay origin and those of Chinese origin caused the suspension of constitutional government and the imposition of a state of national emergency in the country. The Malaysian situation had an unsettling effect in the rest of Southeast Asia. In India the split in the ruling Congress party of Prime Minister Indira Gandhi threatened the stability of the government. (*See* India; Malaysia.)

Great Power Interests in Asia

In 1969 Great Britain continued to disengage itself progressively from Asia, and the United States announced its intention of doing the same once the Vietnam conflict ended. The Soviet Union, however, exerted efforts during the year to make its presence felt in Asian affairs. Soviet Communist Party General Secretary Leonid I. Brezhnev indicated the extent of the Soviet Union's newfound interest in the region with his proposal in June of "a system of collective security in Asia." Asian governments and outside observers interpreted the Soviet move as an offshoot of Soviet anxiety to contain China. The Chinese denounced the collective-security idea as an example of Soviet aggression and accused several Asian governments of collusion with the Soviet Union.

UPI (UK) LTD.

Wong Chark was released from jail in 1969. He was the last of 13 leftist journalists, imprisoned in Hong Kong in 1967, to be let out. They were arrested during riots inspired by the Communist Chinese.

Initially Soviet activities in Asia seemed confined to trade and cultural programs in Singapore, Hong Kong, and Malaysia. But the campaign to build goodwill was later extended to countries that the Soviet Union had ignored—the Philippines, Thailand, and Indonesia. Soviet naval activity in the Indian Ocean area also increased.

The growing Soviet influence caused some concern in Australia, though other developed countries, including Japan, seemed to take it in stride. Gordon Freeth, Australia's minister for external affairs, won Soviet approval—and much criticism at home—when he said that it was natural for a world power like the Soviet Union to seek to promote its influence in such an important area as the

WIDE WORLD

WIDE WORLD

A U.S. Air Force B-52 jet bomber streaks over an angry crowd of demonstrators outside Kadena Air Force Base, Okinawa. The demonstration protesting the presence of B-52 bombers on Okinawa was called by the labor unions after plans for a general strike were canceled. Okinawan students (bottom) throw rocks at riot police outside the gates of the air base. Ten persons were injured.

Indian Ocean. Australia's minister for defense, Allen Fairhall, was among those who attacked this line, warning that the Soviet Union intended to fill the power vacuum in the Indian Ocean created by Great Britain's decision to withdraw its troops from Asia by 1971.

Britain repeatedly pointed out in 1969 that its planned military withdrawal from Asia would not mean desertion. British political and military spokesmen stressed that Britain would continue to work closely with Australian and New Zealand forces through joint exercises and would continue to train troops in Malaysia and Singapore after 1971 "continuously and on quite a substantial scale." At the five-power Commonwealth defense conference in Australia in June, attended by Britain, Australia, New Zealand, Malaysia, and Singapore, Britain expressed its readiness to tailor its defense approach in the region to suit the needs of the concerned countries. An element of uncertainty, however, was introduced by the British Conservative party's claim that, if returned to power, it would continue to maintain a British presence in the region.

During U.S. President Richard M. Nixon's tour of Asian countries in July, the president announced a new policy of disengagement and of encouraging "Asian solutions to Asian problems." Asian countries were reassured, however, that the United States was not abandoning the area or going back on its commitments. Nixon made it clear that the United States would continue to assert its role as a Pacific power and would honor its commitments but would not expand them. It would give aid and hardware "where it would be meaningful and worthwhile," such as in Thailand, but even there no commitment of ground forces would be extended. Nixon reported that Asian leaders had accepted this policy.

Regional Organizations

Despite President Nixon's pledge of continued U.S. support of the Southeast Asia Treaty Organization (SEATO), this kingpin of previous U.S. security arrangements for the region continued to decline in importance. A naval exercise that SEATO organized in June, intended as a morale booster, turned into a disaster. During the exercise the destroyer USS *Frank E. Evans* collided with the Australian aircraft carrier HMAS *Melbourne* and was cut in two. More than 70 U.S. sailors died, and the exercise was called off.

The nonmilitary regional organizations in Asia managed to survive, if not to flourish. The most ambitious and potentially the most important of the groupings was the Association of Southeast Asian Nations (ASEAN), made up of the Philippines, Indonesia, Singapore, Malaysia, and Thailand. It took some serious knocks in quick succession—the dispute between Malaysia and the Philippines over Sabah, the quarrel between Singapore and Indonesia over Singapore's execution late in 1968 of two Indonesian marines on terrorist charges, and the bitterness that grew between Malaysia and Singapore following Malaysia's racial disturbances. With each crisis the organization seemed about to go under, but apparently its members were anxious to avert a total collapse and managed to sustain it.

Although the quarrels among its members were a serious obstacle to development, ASEAN made serious efforts at economic cooperation. At an ASEAN meeting in May a series of permanent committees were set up: for food, in Indonesia; for air-traffic services and meteorology, in Malaysia; for civil aviation, in Singapore; for shipping, in Thailand; and for commerce and industry, in the Philippines.

The United Nations Economic Commission for Asia and the Far East (ECAFE) received a barrage of criticism from some Asian countries at its 25th session, held in Singapore. The Philippine delegation called for an overhaul of ECAFE, suggesting that it was spread out too thinly to give effective leadership. (*See also* individual Asian countries by name. *See in* CE: Asia; individual Asian countries by name.)

ASTRONOMY. The greatest news of 1969 was the closeup observation of the moon by two Apollo 11 astronauts who walked on its surface on July 20 and who brought back with them about 55 pounds of lunar surface soil. A number of scientists eagerly started a series of physical and chemical analyses on the grayish-black stones and dust, which proved to be free of any living matter. Chemical tests identified a heavy concentration of titanium. Preliminary dating studies fixed the age of the soil at a minimum of 3 billion years.

Early in the year, McDonald Observatory, on Mount Locke, in Texas, reported "absolutely conclusive proof" that the atmosphere of Mars contains water. In July photographs of Mars taken by Mariners 6 and 7 showed a varied terrain: flat plains, cratered areas, valleys, and ridges.

At Harvard Observatory, at Cambridge, Mass., a precise measure of the carbon dioxide in Mars's atmosphere indicated that it is equivalent to a surface layer about 274 feet deep (at standard temperature and pressure). This principal constituent of the Martian atmosphere exerts a pressure of about 0.09 pounds per square inch at the planet's surface; the total atmospheric pressure is perhaps as much as 0.13 pounds per square inch. The total atmospheric pressure at the earth's surface is about 14.7 pounds per square inch.

Also at Harvard, David Morrison found that the temperature at the Martian equator rises from about −135° F. near the time of sunrise to about 80° shortly after local noon. The dark markings on Mars are always slightly hotter than the bright areas. From the rate of heating, Morrison concluded that the average soil particles are about 8 to 16 ten thousandths of an inch in diameter in the light areas and roughly five times larger in the dark ones.

Two Soviet space probes, Veneras 5 and 6, entered the atmosphere of Venus in May. During the descent by parachute, measurements revealed

A giant 107-inch reflector telescope was installed at the McDonald Observatory in Texas. Its size is striking when compared with the doors at the bottom in the picture.
SKY PUBLISHING CORP.

SKY PUBLISHING CORP.

This is the solar eclipse of Sept. 22, 1968, as it looked from Yurgamysh, Siberia, U.S.S.R. The photograph was taken by Colin Hunt, a British amateur astronomer, with a three-inch refracting telescope.

atmospheric pressures at least 25 times greater than that at the earth's surface. Some scientists think that Venus is shrouded in mercury compounds.

Three astronomers at the U.S. Naval Observatory, at Washington, D.C., reevaluated the mass of Pluto, the most distant planet of the solar system. They found that the previous determination of 91% of the earth's mass should be drastically reduced to 18%. The resulting average density of Pluto is 1.4 times that of the earth.

A direct measure of the extremely weak magnetic fields of our galaxy has been made by G. L. Verschuur with the 140-foot radio telescope at the National Radio Astronomy Observatory, at Green Bank, W.Va. He determined that interstellar clouds of the Milky Way have magnetic fields approximately 1/50,000 times as strong as that of the earth. These fields may be important to the study of the evolution and dynamics of our galaxy.

Of major importance was the optical identification of a pulsar, a source of pulsating radio signals. Several teams of investigators found that the fastest-pulsing pulsar known was identical to a faint star near the center of the well-known Crab nebula. The Crab nebula is the remnant of a supernova, a star that suddenly increases in brightness as much as a billion times. The pulsar's light flashed every 33 thousandths of a second, the same rate as the radio signals.

The chemical composition of clouds of gas and dust in interstellar space was found to be unexpectedly complex. By the end of 1969, radio astronomers had detected the presence of ammonia (NH_3) in several clouds near the center of our galaxy, as well as water (H_2O) and formaldehyde (H_2CO) in others.

An experiment by Joseph Weber of the University of Maryland detected what appeared to be gravitational waves from space. Albert Einstein in 1916 predicted such waves to arise from changes in the distribution of mass in the universe. The source of these waves was not yet known, but supernovas could produce the observed effect.

With the dedication of the 107-inch reflector at McDonald Observatory in Texas, the world's third largest optical telescope became operational. Its principal use will be the spectroscopic observation of planetary atmospheres. (*See also* Space Exploration. *See in* CE: Astronomy; Moon.)

AUSTRALIA. Prime Minister John G. Gorton and his Liberal-Country party coalition government weathered an election and an intraparty revolt in 1969. The conservative coalition emerged from the October 25 elections with a greatly reduced majority after a strong challenge from the Labor party. The Labor campaign focused on promises to bring Australia's 8,000 troops home from Vietnam by June 1970 and a pledge to reduce military commitments in Southeast Asia.

When the voting was completed Gorton's government had 66 of 125 seats in the House of Representatives, where previously they had held 79 of 124. Gorton faced more difficulties in November when his Liberal party leadership was threatened by Treasurer William McMahon and by David Fairbairn, minister for national development. After winning a narrow victory Gorton demoted McMahon. Fairbairn resigned. The Gorton government strongly supported U.S. policy in Vietnam and favored retention of combat troops in Malaysia. There was also disagreement in the party over policies on social welfare. A former minister of external affairs, Paul Hasluck, was appointed governor-general of Australia in February.

In April transit and power workers staged a weeklong strike in support of a union official who was jailed for refusal to appear before the Commonwealth Industrial Court. July 4, U.S. Independence Day, touched off demonstrations in Australia's major cities. At Sydney and Melbourne U.S. flags were burned. There were riots on Bougainville over a decision of the Papua-New Guinea government to lease land of the Rorovana people to the Conzinc Rio Tinto of Australia Ltd., a giant mining corporation. The deal was made after Australia, which governs the islands, contracted to supply Japan with 950,000 tons of copper in 15 years from the rich New Guinea mines.

Australia's economic boom continued with a trend toward rising prices and wages. There was no relief in the labor shortage. Building-construction activity remained strong. In August credit regulations were tightened and interest rates were raised. Australia joined the international wheat price-cutting war as the world market was glutted with wheat in 1969. The biggest wheat sale in the history of the country was made when Australia negotiated a contract for sale of 2.5 million tons of wheat to Communist China. Meat sales to the United States amounted to more than 505 million pounds. In November the government announced plans to run its own cargo ships for British-European-North American trade.

The 1969 budget allowed for increases in social services, school aid, and foreign aid. Defense spending was cut 5%. There was a $30-million allotment for rural industry and extensive help for Australia's 45,000 aborigines.

In foreign policy the government announced it would keep troops in Malaysia and Singapore after British withdrawal. Talks on Asian security were slated with the Soviet Union. Troop reduction in Vietnam remained dependent on progress of the war. (*See in* CE: Australia.)

AUSTRALIAN NEWS AND INFORMATION BUREAU

The Australian government in 1969 announced its willingness to relax a 40-year-old embargo on the export of Merino sheep, noted for the fine quality of their wool. A Merino ram can cost as much as $11,400.

AUSTRIA. Tension continued in Austria during 1969, following the 1968 Soviet-led invasion of Czechoslovakia. Austria was the target of new outbursts of Communist propaganda warning that Austria harbored "imperialist centers" that would send spies into Czechoslovakia. The Austrian government denied these accusations and maintained its efforts to promote stability in central Europe.

Leaders of Eastern and Western countries alike visited Austria during the year. Bulgaria's Premier Todor Zhivkov met with Austria's Chancellor Josef Klaus in April. In May Hungary's Premier Jeno Fock arrived in Vienna, the capital, for talks urging Austria's participation in a European security conference proposed by the Warsaw Pact countries. West Germany's Chancellor Kurt Georg Kiesinger on a visit to Austria in March had expressed skepticism of the offer for a conference. Klaus offered Austria's aid to West Germany in dealing with the Communist bloc. Great Britain's Queen Elizabeth II also visited Austria.

Franz Olah, a former president of the Austrian Trades Union Federation, was brought to trial in February on a charge of mismanaging union funds. His defense attorneys attempted to prove that the money—used for financing political projects—came from the U.S. Central Intelligence Agency (CIA). The CIA refused to comment, and Olah was sentenced to one year in prison.

The Austrian People's party suffered losses in the state elections held in Salzburg and Vienna. Austria's Socialist party and Freedom party both showed gains. In Vienna the Communist party lost the seats it had held.

During 1969 Austria's economy continued the upward trend begun in 1968. The growth rate of the gross national product was estimated at 7% for 1969, as compared to 4% for 1968. (*See also* Europe. *See in* CE: Austria.)

AUTOMOBILES. Henry Ford II, chairman of the board of Ford Motor Co., stunned the automobile industry with the announcement on Sept. 12, 1969, that Semon E. (Bunkie) Knudsen "would be leaving" as president of the company. The ouster came 19 months after Ford personally hired Knudsen, who shortly before had resigned as executive vice-president of rival General Motors Corp. (GM), with which he had served for 29 years. Ford gave no reason for the firing other than to say that "things had not worked out." To replace Knudsen, Ford appointed three "presidents" of basic company operating groups, decentralizing management of the firm.

New Cars Introduced

Ford reported that its subcompact Maverick, introduced in April, was the best-selling new car in history. It outsold the popular Mustang during its first six months on the market. Sales for the first four months totaled 124,488. Maverick was the domestic auto industry's first reaction to growing imported-car sales since the first compact cars were brought out in the late 1950's. Ford priced Maverick at $1,995, a figure that many cited as its greatest reason for success. Maverick was built in only one body style, a two-door semifastback sedan, and was offered initially with a six-cylinder engine.

Three other new cars were introduced during the year—American Motors' subcompact Hornet, Dodge's Challenger, and Chevrolet's Monte Carlo. Hornet replaced the Rambler in American's lineup and, like Maverick, listed for under $2,000. Challenger and Monte Carlo were designed to compete in the sporty-compact and personal-luxury markets.

Similar in size to Maverick, Hornet was available in both two- and four-door models; V-8 engine, power brakes, and power steering were optional. Monte Carlo was priced just under $3,000, the least of any car in the personal-luxury field. A close-coupled four-seater, it was built only as a two-door hardtop; a choice of three V-8 engines, ranging from 350 to 454 cubic inches, was offered. Challenger was Dodge's belated entry in the sporty-compact market, which accounts for about 9% of domestic car sales. Its engines ranged from 225 to 440 cubic inches; its base price was $2,674.

The 1970 Models

Other 1970 models, introduced in the fall of 1969, offered few outstanding changes from 1969 models. An exception came in the intermediate-size field, where both GM and Ford made extensive redesign. Ford's Torino and Montego lines offered all-new body styling and a wheelbase one inch longer. GM intermediates also had new sheet metal and incorporated side-impact safety bars similar to those built into the doors of larger GM cars beginning in 1968. Side-impact bars also appeared on Chrysler Corporation's 1970 Barracuda and Challenger.

Intermediate "muscle cars"—equipped with huge engines, high rear-axle ratios, heavy-duty suspensions, and oversized tires—were promoted by all four major U.S. automakers under such names as GTO, 442, State I, SS, GT Cobra, Spoiler, Machine, Road Runner, and R/T. The engine size of these cars—often used for illegal street racing—rose after GM announced that a 400-cubic-inch limit had been lifted. Sizes ranged up to 455 cubic inches.

With the exception of Ford's Lincoln, all standard-sized cars were merely face-lifted for 1970. Lincoln offered an all-new body and switched from unit-body construction, used for ten years, to body-and-frame construction. The change was made primarily to standardize Ford's assembly operations, since all other full-sized Ford cars have body-and-frame construction. An automotive milestone was reached when Cadillac announced that its 1970 Eldorado would have a 500-cubic-inch engine—the largest in the industry and the first production-car engine to reach that displacement.

Sales and Prices

Sales of new cars in 1969 were at a high level but trailed the record set in 1968. An estimated 9,385,000 new cars were sold in 1969, including an estimated 1,050,000 imported cars. The total was second only to 1968, when 9,403,862 cars were sold, and put 1969 in all-time second place by surpassing the 1965 total of 9,313,912. Imported-car sales continued their upward swing, reaching the highest total in history and leading the major U.S.

DODGE NEWS PHOTO

GENERAL MOTORS CORP.

AMERICAN MOTORS

FORD MOTOR CO.

The U.S. automobile industry introduced several new models for 1970 and continued experiments with new types of power. From the top are: the new Dodge Challenger; a mock-up of General Motors' hybrid gasoline-electric-powered commuter car; American Motors' Hornet; and the Ford Maverick. The Citroën Mehari (below) features a plastic body.

CITROËN CARS CORP.

automakers to announce that they would bring out import-sized cars in the near future.

In 1969 GM continued to hold first place in sales, accounting for 47.5% of the U.S. market. Ford solidified its second-place standing with just over 24% of the market—a slight increase over 1968, largely due to high Maverick volume. Chrysler's share slipped more than a full percentage point to 15.5%; American Motors' share of the market was 2.7%. Imports—led by Volkswagen, Toyota, Opel, Datsun, and Fiat—took some 11% of the market despite a dock workers' strike that curtailed deliveries in the first part of the year.

Auto-industry officials predicted that in the 1970 model year intermediate-sized cars would outsell standards for the first time in history. They noted that standard-sized cars had been losing ground in percentage of total sales since the compacts were introduced in the late 1950's, and by 1969 the standard-sized cars were accounting for just over half the market. Intermediates, they pointed out, were gaining in popularity and would have yet more appeal with new styling for 1970. Most standards, on the other hand, were merely face-lifted, a traditional signal of a sales downturn. So, it was predicted, an era would pass.

Detroit raised 1970-model prices an average of $107 to $125 a car, the highest boost in more than a decade. James C. Roche, GM chairman, said the price rises were caused by cost increases, especially in labor and such materials as steel, copper, lead, aluminum, zinc, and nickel. The addition of bias/belted tires to GM cars cost the buyer approximately $29. California's rule that all 1970 cars sold in the state must have evaporative-emission control systems resulted in a $35-a-car extra charge when 1970 GM models were sold in the state.

Product Developments

Safety features—especially the controversial safety air bags—captured wide attention. The air bags, stored in the instrument panel, inflate in head-on collisions to form a cushion that prevents passengers from being thrown forward. Working models were demonstrated during the year, and federal safety officials indicated intent to legislate the bags into regular production within two years. Ford hinted that the air bags would appear on one of its models as early as 1971.

Chrysler equipped its 1970 Barracuda and Challenger with hidden "rollover structures" to protect occupants from crushed car tops. It was the first time that rollbars were designed into U.S. production cars. Lincoln's 1970 Mark III luxury car was the first to have antiskid braking as standard equipment. Bias/belted tires became standard equipment on virtually all 1970 cars.

Warranties and Woes

In a move to reduce administrative costs and make its warranty more understandable to customers, Ford covered its 1970 cars with a flat 12-month warranty on the entire vehicle—except tires, which were covered separately. GM and Chrysler continued their similar warranty plans—5 years or 50,000 miles on the power train, 12 months or 12,000 miles on the complete car.

The industry faced lawsuits concerning pricing, antismog devices, and warranties. The pricing suits contended that the "list" prices of new cars were not the actual (usually lower) prices. The industry replied that the window-sticker prices were required by federal law and were uniform throughout the United States.

The federal government withdrew an antitrust suit in which it had charged that the automakers conspired to delay the introduction of antismog devices after the companies agreed, among other things, to abandon cooperative research on the devices. Among warranty suits was one that called for GM to replace certain light-truck wheels that were known to fail under overload. (*See also* Safety. *See in* CE: Automobile articles.)

AUTO RACING.

During the 1969 season automobile racing continued to gain in popularity. Formula One (Grand Prix) road racing remained the highest form of the sport. Some observers felt, however, that the far greater monetary rewards of various forms of U.S. racing might in the future diminish the acclaim of the Formula One.

Jackie Stewart of Scotland, driving a Ford-powered French Matra—the season's dominant car—won the Formula One world driving championship. Stewart won the Grand Prix races of South Africa, Spain, France, England, Holland, and Italy.

Among the year's technical developments in Formula One racing was the appearance of four-wheel-drive cars. However, the vehicles—tested by several builders—were unable to match the performance of conventional rear-wheel-drive cars.

There was new emphasis on safety along the Formula One circuit. Large airfoils, added to cars to give greater traction to the tremendously wide modern racing tires, were declared dangerous to both drivers and spectators. Beginning with the Monaco Grand Prix, they were banned in their more extreme forms. The Grand Prix Drivers Association inspected the courses over which its members would be required to race and refused to allow competition on the famous Spa circuit in Belgium until it was improved.

Indianapolis; USAC Racing

The 1969 Indianapolis 500 on May 30 brought an end to 23 years of frustration for controversial car owner Andy Granatelli of Illinois. Mario Andretti of Nazareth, Pa., piloted Granatelli's supercharged Ford-Hawk, prepared by Clint Brawner, to victory in the race at a record average speed of 156.867 mph. Dan Gurney of California finished second, Mel Kenyon of Indiana third, and Bobby Unser of New Mexico fourth.

Andretti also won the United States Auto Club

Denis Hulme and Bruce McLaren (numbers 5 and 4), driving winged cars, placed first and second in the Can-Am race at Mont-Tremblant, Que. (right). In the Indianapolis, Ind., 500-mile race (below) Mario Andretti in car number 2 pushes to overtake A. J. Foyt, Jr., in number 6. Andretti won the race.

BELOW: WIDE WORLD. ABOVE: "MONTREAL GAZETTE"

The Young Pilot's International Criterium, held in France, gave youngsters a chance to drive replicas of famous cars in a sample race. At the left is a Renault Alpine; the other car is a model Ferrari.

AFP FROM PICTORIAL PARADE

(USAC) "big car" driving championship, amassing most of his points in a supercharged Ford special. He clinched the title by winning the Trenton 300 on September 21. Roger McCluskey, driving a Plymouth, won USAC's stock-car championship. He, Don White, and A. J. Foyt, Jr., contested the title hotly down to the close of the season.

Other North American Events

Controversy over the safety of a new track gripped the National Association for Stock Car Auto Racing (NASCAR) in 1969. Top-name drivers boycotted the inaugural 500-mile event at the new "fastest superspeedway in the world" at Talladega, Ala. It was contested by a last-minute collection of lesser-known drivers and won by an "unknown," Richard Brickhouse. The number of pit stops made by the competitors appeared to support the top drivers' contention that available tires were unequal to the speeds permitted by the oval with turns banked at 34 degrees.

The NASCAR counterpart of Indianapolis—the Daytona 500—was won by Lee Roy Yarbrough, who in the last lap moved his Ford around Charlie Glotzbach's Dodge. Donnie Allison and A. J. Foyt won third and fourth for Ford, and pole winner Buddy Baker of Dodge was fifth. Yarbrough came back in the Daytona Firecracker 400 to nip Baker by four car lengths.

Bruce McLaren and Denis Hulme of New Zealand completely dominated the premier series of the Sports Car Club of America, the $1-million Canadian-American Challenge Cup race for Group Seven cars (two-seaters of unlimited engine size). They won all 11 races in the series; McLaren captured the individual championship.

Mark Donohue of Media, Pa., and car owner Roger Penske won the Trans-American Sedan crown for Chevrolet Camaro. In the Continental Championship, A class was won by Tony Adamowicz of Wilton, Conn., and Mike Eyerly of Salem, Ore., won in B class.

International Sports-Car Racing

Porsche of Germany won the manufacturer's championship for sports cars, though its product failed to capture the most important endurance race, the 24 hours of Le Mans, France. In that event the Porsches—which led through the first 21 hours—suddenly found their huge entry diminished by crashes and clutch trouble. The winner was a John Wyer Ford GT-40 driven by Jackie Ickx and Jackie Oliver. Hans Hermann and Gerard Larrouse in a Porsche were second. Another GT-40 driven by David Hobbs and Mike Hailwood was third, and a pair of Matras rounded out the top five.

Earlier, Ickx and Oliver had embarrassed Porsche by winning the 12-hour Sebring Grand Prix. Chris Amon and Mario Andretti, in a Ferrari, finished second. Three Porsches followed. In the opening of the sports-car series at Daytona, both the GT-40's and the Porsches succumbed to mechanical failures late in the race. Victory went to Mark Donohue and Chuck Parsons in a Lola-Chevrolet.

In Europe, however, Porsche dominated the season. Late in the year, it introduced a new 4½-liter model, the 917, which helped to assure its capture of the manufacturer's title. (*See in* CE: Automobile Racing and Rallies.)

AWARDS AND PRIZES. Among the Nobel prizes announced in October 1969 was the first Albert Nobel Memorial Prize in Economics, awarded to two European economists who were pioneers in the field of econometrics, "the mathematical expression of economic theory." Ragnar Frisch of Norway and Jan Tinbergen of the Netherlands were the two recipients of the prize, which had been endowed by the national bank of Sweden to commemorate its 300th anniversary. Both men were cited for their work in making the discipline of economics a more precise field of study and analysis by replacing its vague conceptual tools with concrete statistical elements.

Three U.S. scientists whose work involved research into the nature and genetics of viruses were named joint winners of the 1969 Nobel prize in medicine or physiology. They were Max Delbruck, a biology professor at the California Institute of Technology; Alfred D. Hershey, director of genetics research for the Carnegie Institution of Washington (D.C.); and Salvador E. Luria, a professor of microbiology at the Massachusetts Institute of Technology. In accepting the award, Luria and Delbruck both denounced their scientific colleagues who performed biological and chemical warfare work.

Irish expatriate writer Samuel Beckett received the Nobel prize for literature for the body of his writings. Beckett's best-known work was 'Waiting for Godot' (1952), a play that goaded Western theater into an important new direction.

The Nobel prize in physics was won by a U.S. physicist, Murray Gell-Mann, a professor at the California Institute of Technology. He was cited for his "contributions and discoveries concerning the classification of elementary particles and their interactions." Two European chemists shared the prize for chemistry: Derek H. R. Barton, professor of organic chemistry at the Imperial College of Science and Technology, in London, England, and Odd Hassel, professor emeritus at Oslo University, in Norway. The two scientists were honored for their research into the shape—or three-dimensional conformation—of molecules.

The Nobel peace prize was awarded to the International Labor Organization, founded in 1919 and now associated with the United Nations. The organization was cited for its activities before World War II in "reducing social barriers between peoples in an effort to make nations work together in peace" and for its recent work in coping with the problem of unemployment in the world as a means to achieve peace.

Pulitzer Prizes

The Pulitzer prizes for 1969 went to a number of journalists for work that dealt with the Vietnam conflict. William Tuohy of the *Los Angeles Times* won the award in international reporting for his articles on the course of the Vietnam conflict, which he had covered off and on for four years. John Fetterman of the *Louisville Courier-Journal* won in the local-reporting category for an account of the hometown burial of a U.S. soldier killed in Vietnam. Edward T. Adams of the Associated Press received

The Paul Ehrlich prize was awarded to Anne-Marie Staub (right) for her research with typhoid bacteria. *Los Angeles Times* war correspondent William Tuohy (below) won the Pulitzer prize for international reporting.

BELOW: WIDE WORLD. ABOVE: KEYSTONE

the prize in spot news photography for his widely published photo of the summary execution of a Viet Cong prisoner in Saigon, South Vietnam.

Other Pulitzer prizewinners in journalism were the *Los Angeles Times* for its exposé of wrongdoing in local government; Albert L. Delugach and Denny Walsh of the *St. Louis Globe-Democrat* for their series exposing fraud and power abuse in one of the locals of the St. Louis (Mo.) Steamfitters Union; Paul Greenberg of the *Pine Bluff Commercial* for a number of his editorials published in 1968; and John Fischetti of the *Chicago Daily News* for his cartoons in 1968. Robert Cahn of the *Christian Science Monitor* won for his articles on national parks, and Moneta J. Sleet, Jr., of *Ebony* magazine, for his photo of Mrs. Martin Luther King, Jr., and her daughter Bernice at King's funeral.

For the second time in five years Pulitzers were given in all categories of letters and music. In nonfiction the prize was shared by Norman Mailer for 'The Armies of the Night: History as a Novel, the Novel as History', his personal account of the antiwar demonstrations at the Pentagon in 1967, and René Jules Dubos for 'So Human an Animal: How We are Shaped by Surroundings and Events'. N. Scott Momaday, a Kiowa Indian, won the prize in fiction for 'House Made of Dawn'; Howard Sackler won in drama for 'The Great White Hope'; Leonard W. Levy, in history for 'Origins of the Fifth Amendment'; and Benjamin Lawrence Reid, in biography for 'The Man From New York: John Quinn and His Friends', an account of the life of John Quinn. In poetry George Oppen received the award for 'Of Being Numerous', and in music Karel Husa was honored for his composition 'String Quartet No. 3'.

Awards in Literature

The U.S. publishing world's most celebrated prizes, the National Book Awards, were announced in March for work published in 1968. Norman Mailer won in arts and letters with 'The Armies of the Night'. Another of Mailer's books, 'Miami and the Siege of Chicago', had been a candidate in the history and biography category. Polish-born writer Jerzy Kosinski, now living in the United States, won the fiction prize for 'Steps', his second novel, an impressionistic work of autobiographical fragments. The well-known U.S. poet John Berryman received the poetry prize for 'His Toy, His Dream, His Rest'. Robert J. Lifton won in the science category for a psychological study, 'Death in Life: Survivors of Hiroshima'. Winthrop D. Jordan's 'White over Black: American Attitudes Toward the Negro, 1550–1812' received the prize in history and biography. The prizewinning translated work was William Weaver's translation of Italo Calvino's 'Cosmicomics'. In the newly created category for children's literature, Meindert DeJong won for 'Journey from Peppermint Street'.

The prestigious Bollingen Prize in Poetry, a $5,000 award presented every other year by Yale University Library, was shared by two poets, Karl

Leonard Bernstein, U.S. composer and symphony orchestra conductor, accepts the Golden Knight award at Vienna, Austria.

"LONDON DAILY EXPRESS" FROM PICTORIAL PARADE

Shapiro and Berryman. Shapiro was cited for 'Selected Poems', a collection covering 30 years of his work. Berryman was honored again for 'His Toy, His Dream, His Rest'.

Conrad Aiken, known primarily as a poet, was named winner of the National Medal for Literature. The prize, worth $5,000, was the fifth ever to be awarded. A poem written by Senator Eugene McCarthy (D, Minn.) was singled out for the $500 poetry prize of the National Endowment for the Arts. The poem, 'Three Bad Signs', was written by the former presidential candidate during the Indiana presidential primary in 1968.

The winners of the annual Bancroft prizes for the best books in U.S. history and international relations were announced in April. Three authors were honored for works published in 1968: Jordan for 'White over Black'; Rexford Guy Tugwell for 'The Brain Trust'; and N. Gordon Levin, Jr., for 'Woodrow Wilson and World Politics: America's Response to War and Revolution'. Each prize had a cash value of $4,000.

Awards in Science

In January U.S. President Lyndon B. Johnson presented 12 scientists with the 1968 National Medal of Science award, the federal government's highest honor for distinguished achievement in science, engineering, and mathematics. Winners in the biological sciences were H. Albert Barker of the University of California at Berkeley; Bernard B. Brodie of the National Institutes of Health; Detlev W. Bronk of The Rockefeller University; J. L. Lush of Iowa State University; and B. Frederic Skinner of Harvard University. In engineering sciences two men were honored, J. Presper Eckert of Sperry Rand Corp. and Mason N. Newmark of the University of Illinois. Jerzy Neyman of the University of California at Berkeley was the sole recipient in mathematical sciences. In the field of physical sciences the prizewinners were Paul D. Bartlett of Harvard, Herbert Friedman of the Naval Research Laboratory, Lars Onsager of Yale, and Eugene P. Wigner of Princeton University.

"One of the world's foremost developers" of nuclear power and atomic reactors, Walter H. Zinn, received the $25,000 Enrico Fermi Award. Zinn was a member of the group of scientists (headed by the late Fermi) who built the first atomic reactor.

UPI COMPIX

KEYSTONE

UPI COMPIX

UPI COMPIX

UPI COMPIX

The 1969 Nobel prizewinners include: Ragnar Frisch, economics (top left); Samuel Beckett, literature (top right); Jan Tinbergen, economics (center left); Derek Barton, chemistry (above); and Murray Gell-Mann, physics (left).

Seven scientists received the Atoms for Peace Award for their contributions in developing the peaceful uses of atomic energy. The winners were Agae N. Bohr and Ben R. Mottelson of Denmark; Floyd L. Culler, Jr., Henry S. Kaplan, and Anthony L. Turkevich of the United States; Compton A. Rennie of Great Britain; and M. S. Ioffe of the Soviet Union. Each received $15,000. Former U.S. President Dwight D. Eisenhower was honored posthumously with a special honorarium of $50,000 as a tribute to his contribution to furthering the peaceful use of atomic energy.

The $10,000 Albert and Mary Lasker Awards for Medicine were given to two men. George C. Cotzias received the award for his pioneering work in the use of the drug L-DOPA as a treatment for Parkinson's disease. Bruce Merrifield was honored for developing a new automated way to produce proteins in the laboratory. (*See also* Literature; Literature, Children's.)

BANKS. The number of banks in the United States remained almost unchanged in 1969 with the Federal Reserve System reporting a midyear total of 14,173—down six from the 1968 year-end figure. During the same period, however, 542 new branches were established, bringing the total to 20,453 at the end of the second quarter.

Commercial banks held loans totaling $282.3 billion at the end of the third quarter, up more than $30 billion from the same period in 1968. Second-quarter reports on mortgage loans held by commercial banks showed a total of $69.1 billion, an increase of over $7 billion from the preceding year.

The interest rate on such loans rose three times during the year. The prime interest rate—the rate that banks charge their best customers—went up to 7% in January, to 7.5% in March, and to 8.5% in June. In testimony before the Senate Committee on Finance in July, U.S. Secretary of the Treasury David M. Kennedy defended the increases as a necessary measure to curb inflation. Nevertheless, the hike in interest rates contributed to increased net operating earnings for many banks that ranged as high as 21% from July 1, 1968, to June 30, 1969.

A less fortuitous result of inflation, however, was a shrinkage in deposits held by commercial banks. By the end of September deposits were down to $401.7 billion, a drop of $6 billion from the beginning of the year. Funds were thought to have been channeled into institutions that paid higher rates of return than banks were legally able to.

The shrinkage in deposits and the resulting shortage of loanable funds intensified the banking industry's already acute difficulties in providing funds for government-guaranteed educational loans. The ceiling of 7% on the interest rate that the banks were allowed to charge was 1.5% below the prime interest rate in force at the beginning of the academic year.

In October the U.S. Congress passed a bill permitting the Department of Health, Education, and Welfare to pay a "special allowance" of up to 3% above the 7% currently allowed. The subsidy payment was designed to vary with money-market interest-rate conditions and to serve as an incentive to lenders to make money available to college students despite tight money conditions. The amount of the subsidy was to be determined by the secretary of health, education, and welfare each quarter and would be applicable to loans made from August 1969 through July 1971.

The most significant Congressional action in 1969 in the area of banking was the passage by the House of Representatives of a bill to regulate the operations of one-bank holding companies known

WIDE WORLD

An official of the Sumitomo Bank in California demonstrates the bank's instant money dispenser. A coded credit card is inserted, buttons are pushed, and out comes the cash requested.

as "congenerics." As part of a congeneric, the bank is subject to state and local bank regulations but the holding company is free to expand bank activities into other areas and to compete with nonbanking financial institutions.

In an effort to attract young depositors, several metropolitan banks operated "youth clubs" during the year. The clubs, with memberships consisting primarily of young people in their twenties and early thirties, afforded a wide array of social activities as well as special banking services. Social activities sponsored by the clubs ranged from weekend outings in Acapulco, Mexico, to private movie premieres to speed-reading classes. Special banking services included free books of rainbow-colored checks and discounts with local merchants. (*See in* CE: Banks.)

BASEBALL. The New York Mets, traditionally the doormat of the National League (NL), rose in 1969 to become baseball's world champions. The Mets came from behind to win their division's title, swept the NL play-off series, then defeated the Baltimore Orioles of the American League (AL) four games to one in the World Series.

Both the NL and the AL expanded from 10 to 12 teams for the 1969 season. Each league was split into two divisions, Eastern and Western. Manager Gil Hodges and his Mets, who had finished ninth among ten teams in 1968, were held in total disregard by preseason oddsmakers. But between August 14 and October 2 the Mets overcame a $9\frac{1}{2}$-game deficit and pulled 8 games in front of the Chicago Cubs, who had led the Eastern Division for the first 155 days of the season.

In the NL's best-of-five pennant play-off, the Mets wrecked the Western Division champion Atlanta Braves in three straight games, 9–5, 11–6, and 7–4. Meanwhile, Baltimore's Orioles, who had finished 19 games ahead of defending world champion Detroit to win the AL's Eastern Division crown, captured the AL pennant play-off by beating Western Division titlist Minnesota in another three-game sweep, 4–3, 1–0, and 11–2. In the World Series, the Mets required only five games to demolish the heavily favored Orioles. They lost the first, then reeled off four successive triumphs.

Major League Races; World Series

Five of the six teams in the NL's Western Division entered the stretch run with a chance for the title. The Atlanta Braves finished with a rush to outlast San Francisco by three games and Cincinnati by four, while Los Angeles and Houston slumped in the season's closing weeks.

Left in the lurch by the Mets in addition to Chicago in the NL's Eastern Division was St. Louis, the defending league champion. The Cardinals, preseason favorites, faded to fourth, 13 games out. The Mets won 100 games in building their margin of 8 games on the runner-up Cubs and 12 games on third-place Pittsburgh.

Baltimore compiled 109 wins in breezing to the AL's Eastern Division honors by 19 games over the Tigers. In the AL's Western Division, the Minnesota Twins beat out Oakland by nine games.

Baltimore captured the World Series opener in its home park 4–1, behind the six-hit pitching of Mike Cuellar. The Mets won the second game 2–1 on a ninth-inning single by Al Weis.

In the third game, at New York, a lead-off home run by Met center fielder Tommie Agee started the Mets on the road to a 5–0 triumph. A spectacular catch by right fielder Ron Swoboda in the ninth inning saved the Mets from disaster in the fourth game, which they went on to win 2–1 in ten innings; the winning run scored after Oriole outfielders played a pop fly into a double. In the fifth and final game, the Mets overcame a 3–0 deficit to win 5–3 behind the pitching of Jerry Koosman.

In July the NL won its seventh consecutive All-Star game 9–3 in Robert F. Kennedy Memorial Stadium at Washington, D.C. The NL thus increased its lead in the series to 22–17; one game ended in a tie.

Individual Honors

Harmon Killebrew of Minnesota won the AL home-run crown with 49. He was followed by

New York Mets pitcher Gary Gentry sends a pitch to Baltimore Orioles batter Don Buford in the third game of the World Series. The Mets, baseball's long-standing underdogs, became world champions after a dramatic season in which they captured the Eastern Division title in the National League, then the pennant, and finally the World Series from the favored Orioles of the American League.

WIDE WORLD

Washington's Frank Howard (48) and Oakland's Reggie Jackson (47). Killebrew also drove in the most runs, 140. Rod Carew of Minnesota took the batting title with .332 and tied Pete Reiser's major league record by stealing home seven times. Seattle's Tommy Harper led the majors in stolen bases with 73. Detroit's Denny McLain, a 31-game winner in 1968, again paced the AL's pitchers, this time with a 24–9 mark. Other AL 20-game winners were Baltimore's Mike Cuellar (23–11) and Dave McNally (20–7), Minnesota's Jim Perry (20–6) and Dave Boswell (20–12), and New York's Mel Stottlemyre (20–14). Washington's Dick Bosman (14–5) showed the finest earned-run average, 2.19.

Willie McCovey of San Francisco led the NL in home runs with 45; Atlanta's Henry Aaron followed with 44. McCovey also led in runs batted in with 126. Pete Rose of Cincinnati hit .348 to repeat as NL batting champion, while Pittsburgh's Matty Alou paced the majors with 231 hits. The NL had nine 20-game winners, led by the Mets' Tom Seaver (25–7). Others were Atlanta's Phil Niekro (23–13), San Francisco's Juan Marichal (21–11), Chicago's Ferguson Jenkins (21–15) and Bill Hands (20–14), Los Angeles' Bill Singer (20–12) and Claude Osteen (20–15), St. Louis' Bob Gibson (20–13), and Houston's Larry Dierker (20–13). Marichal led in earned-run average with 2.10.

Cub outfielder Billy Williams played in his 896th consecutive game on June 29 to take over the NL record previously held by St. Louis' Stan Musial. Willie Mays of San Francisco hit his 600th home run on September 22, becoming the only player other than Babe Ruth to reach that mark.

Bill Stoneman of the expansion Montreal Expos pitched the first of the year's no-hit games. Jim Maloney of Cincinnati, Don Wilson of Houston, Jim Palmer of Baltimore, Ken Holtzman of the Cubs, and Bob Moose of Pittsburgh also tossed no-hitters.

Steve Carlton of the Cardinals struck out 19 Mets in a nine-inning game to surpass the record of 18 shared by Bob Feller, Sandy Koufax (twice), and Don Wilson. As had several previous strike-out-record pitchers, however, Carlton lost the game—the Mets won 4–3.

Four players entered the National Baseball Hall of Fame in Cooperstown, N.Y., in 1969. They were Stan Musial, Roy Campanella, Waite Hoyt, and Stan Coveleski.

Baseball Notes

Bowie Kuhn, a 42-year-old member of a New York City law firm who had been the NL's attorney, in 1969 became baseball's fifth commissioner. He succeeded retired Air Force Gen. William D. Eckert, whose resignation under pressure had been announced in December 1968. Kuhn found solutions to various baseball problems, including a threatened strike by the Major League Baseball Players Association over a pension dispute. After a 50-year association with baseball, NL president Warren C. Giles retired at season's end. A successor was expected to be named early in 1970.

Baseball made progress in its effort to put more offense into the game. For 1969, the strike zone and the height of the pitcher's mound were reduced. An average of 8.16 runs were scored per game, compared with 6.84 in 1968, and the overall "average batting average" climbed from .237 to .248.

Two of baseball's greatest stars—Yankee slugger Mickey Mantle and Dodger pitcher Don Drysdale—retired in deference to injuries. Mantle's decision, in the spring, ended a career in which he had hit 536 home runs. Drysdale retired in August with a lifetime record of 209–166 and the all-time record for consecutive scoreless innings pitched, $58\frac{2}{3}$. Former star Ted Williams emerged from retirement to manage the Washington Senators to an 86–76 record.

Major league managerial changes were numerous in 1969. Ill health forced the re-retirement of the Chicago White Sox's Al Lopez early in the season; he was replaced by Don Gutteridge. Late in May the California Angels replaced Bill Rigney with Harold (Lefty) Phillips. Philadelphia's Bob Skinner resigned in August; George Myatt finished the season, and the Phillies announced that Frank Lucchesi would run the team in 1970.

In late-season and postseason moves, John McNamara replaced Hank Bauer at Oakland, Danny Murtaugh was named in place of Larry Shepard at Pittsburgh, and Boston hired Eddie Kasko to replace Dick Williams. Cincinnati hired George (Sparky) Anderson after ousting Dave Bristol. Charlie Metro became Kansas City's manager after Joe Gordon resigned. The Minnesota Twins shelved Billy Martin; Bill Rigney replaced him.

Rumors that the Chicago White Sox might leave town because of declining attendance were dispelled late in the season when Arthur C. Allyn sold his controlling interest to his younger brother John, formerly a White Sox vice-president. John announced that the Sox would remain in Chicago.

Amateur Baseball

Arizona State beat Tulsa 10–1 behind Larry Gura's six-hit pitching to win the College World Series in the 20th annual National Collegiate Athletic Association baseball showdown at Omaha, Neb., on June 20. Gura finished the season with a 19–2 record, while his team won 56 and lost 11.

The first team from Nationalist China ever to play in the Little League World Series became the organization's 1969 world champion by blanking Santa Clara, Calif., 5–0 in the final game of the 23d annual tournament at Williamsport, Pa. The Little League—which included more than 7,000 teams in 50 States and 15 foreign countries—marked its 30th anniversary. (*See in* CE: Baseball.)

UPI COMPIX

Retiring baseball star Mickey Mantle takes a last look at uniform 7, the number he wore for 18 years in an outstanding career with the New York Yankees.

BASKETBALL. The University of California at Los Angeles (UCLA), led again by Lew Alcindor, a 7-foot $1\frac{1}{2}$-inch center, won its third consecutive National Collegiate Athletic Association (NCAA) championship. It was the first time a school had ever won three titles in a row. The UCLA Bruins defeated Drake in the semifinals 85–82 and won over Purdue in the final game 92-72.

FINAL 1969 MAJOR LEAGUE STANDINGS

AMERICAN LEAGUE

Team	Won	Lost	Pct.	GB
Eastern Division				
Baltimore	109	53	.673	—
Detroit	90	72	.556	19
Boston	87	75	.537	22
Washington	86	76	.531	23
New York	80	81	.497	$28\frac{1}{2}$
Cleveland	62	99	.385	$46\frac{1}{2}$
Western Division				
Minnesota	97	65	.599	—
Oakland	88	74	.543	9
California	71	91	.438	26
Kansas City	69	93	.426	28
Chicago	68	94	.420	29
Seattle	64	98	.395	33

PLAY-OFFS: Baltimore 3 games, Minnesota 0.

NATIONAL LEAGUE

Team	Won	Lost	Pct.	GB
Eastern Division				
New York	100	62	.617	—
Chicago	92	70	.568	8
Pittsburgh	88	74	.543	12
St. Louis	87	75	.537	13
Philadelphia	63	99	.389	37
Montreal	52	110	.321	48
Western Division				
Atlanta	93	69	.574	—
San Francisco	90	72	.556	3
Cincinnati	89	73	.549	4
Los Angeles	85	77	.525	8
Houston	81	81	.500	12
San Diego	52	110	.321	41

PLAY-OFFS: New York 3 games, Atlanta 0.

WORLD SERIES: New York (NL) 4 games, Baltimore (AL) 1.

In the finals of the National Invitation Tournament (NIT) in New York City, Temple University defeated Boston College 89-76. It was Temple's second NIT crown.

Pete Maravich, a junior from Louisiana State University (LSU), won the NCAA's major division scoring championship for the second year in a row. Playing despite numerous injuries, Maravich totaled 1,148 points in 26 games, a record 44.2 average that broke the 43.8 he had set in the preceding season.

WIDE WORLD

UCLA's Lew Alcindor (left) successfully blocks a backhand shot from Drake's Don Draper at an NCAA semifinal championship game in March. UCLA won 85–82.

Players chosen on the first-team consensus All-America, as published in the Official NCAA Basketball Guide, were Alcindor, UCLA; Spencer Haywood, University of Detroit; Calvin Murphy, Niagara; Maravich, LSU; and Rick Mount, Purdue. The second team consisted of Dan Issel, Kentucky; Mike Maloy, Davidson; Bud Ogden, Santa Clara; Charlie Scott, North Carolina; and Jo-Jo White, Kansas.

Professional Basketball

The Boston Celtics, a traditional power in the National Basketball Association (NBA), set still another precedent in 1969 when they became the first team to finish lower than second during the regular season but then bounced back to win the championship play-offs. It was the 11th NBA title in the last 13 years for the Celtics. Coached by Bill Russell, who also continued as a player, the Celtics barely managed to qualify for the play-offs and finished fourth in the Eastern Division—behind Baltimore, Philadelphia, and New York in that order. Baltimore, which rose from last to first place in one season, was eliminated by New York in the semifinal play-offs. Boston eliminated Philadelphia in the other Eastern semifinal, then beat New York for the divisional title and climaxed its season by defeating the heavily favored Los Angeles Lakers, the Western Division champs. The final series went the full seven games, the Celtics winning the last game 108–106.

Several rookies leaped into immediate prominence during the NBA season. The most outstanding first-year men were Westley Unseld of Baltimore, who won the most-valuable-player and rookie-of-the-year honors, and Elvin Hayes of San Diego, who won the scoring title. NBA attendance was 4,427,297.

The Oakland Oaks, coached by Alex Hannum, won the championship in the rival American Basketball Association. (*See in* CE: Basketball.)

The Los Angeles Lakers' Wilt Chamberlain (left) makes a shot in a Lakers-Boston Celtic game in May. The Celtics scored a 108–106 victory to clinch the NBA championship.

UPI COMPIX

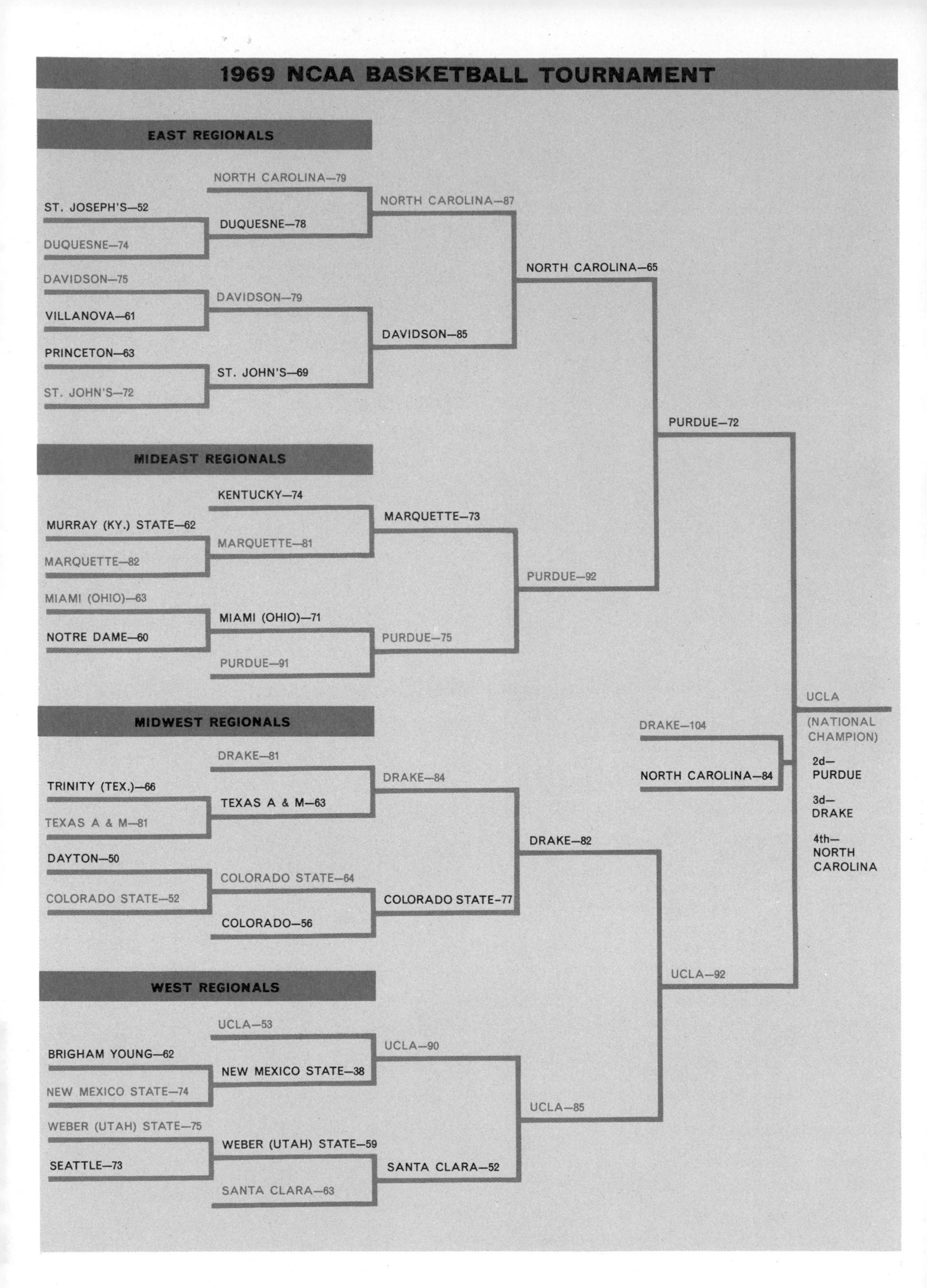

1969 NCAA BASKETBALL TOURNAMENT
EAST REGIONALS
NORTH CAROLINA—79
ST. JOSEPH'S—52
DUQUESNE—78
DUQUESNE—74
NORTH CAROLINA—87
DAVIDSON—75
DAVIDSON—79
VILLANOVA—61
PRINCETON—63
ST. JOHN'S—69
ST. JOHN'S—72
DAVIDSON—85
NORTH CAROLINA—65
MIDEAST REGIONALS
KENTUCKY—74
MURRAY (KY.) STATE—62
MARQUETTE—81
MARQUETTE—82
MARQUETTE—73
MIAMI (OHIO)—63
MIAMI (OHIO)—71
NOTRE DAME—60
PURDUE—91
PURDUE—75
PURDUE—92
PURDUE—72
MIDWEST REGIONALS
DRAKE—81
TRINITY (TEX.)—66
TEXAS A & M—63
TEXAS A & M—81
DRAKE—84
DAYTON—50
COLORADO STATE—64
COLORADO STATE—52
COLORADO—56
COLORADO STATE—77
DRAKE—82
WEST REGIONALS
UCLA—53
BRIGHAM YOUNG—62
NEW MEXICO STATE—38
NEW MEXICO STATE—74
UCLA—90
WEBER (UTAH) STATE—75
WEBER (UTAH) STATE—59
SEATTLE—73
SANTA CLARA—63
SANTA CLARA—52
UCLA—85
UCLA—92
DRAKE—104
NORTH CAROLINA—84
UCLA
(NATIONAL CHAMPION)
2d—PURDUE
3d—DRAKE
4th—NORTH CAROLINA

BELGIUM. As a possible solution to Belgium's language dispute a plan to establish cultural autonomy for the Dutch-speaking Flemish and the French-speaking Walloon communities was proposed by the government in 1969. This called for a revision of the Belgian constitution and resulted in heated political battles.

The government proposed that Belgium's unitary system be abolished and replaced with a federal state. The plan provided for political and economic decentralization as well as for regional autonomy for Flemings and Walloons. The coalition government of Social Christians and Socialists was unable to obtain the necessary two-thirds majority vote in parliament on the revision.

The Party of Liberty and Progress (PLP) found the government's proposals unacceptable and presented their own. The PLP proposals were in turn rejected by the government. The Flemish Nationalist party declared it would not vote for the revision if rules for the protection of minority voting rights were included in the revision. Some factions also favored the establishment of Brussels, the capital, as a third state in the proposed federation. In September Premier Gaston Eyskens asked the opposition groups to work out solutions that could win a two-thirds majority vote in parliament.

In spite of the devaluation of the French franc Belgium's currency remained sound. During the first seven months of 1969 the amount of export trade was 21.5% higher than it had been in the corresponding months of 1968. The cost of living rose by 4%. In April Belgium and the two other Benelux countries (Luxemburg and the Netherlands) agreed to abolish all economic and administrative internal frontier controls by Nov. 1, 1970.

"PARIS MATCH" FROM PICTORIAL PARADE

King Baudouin I and Queen Fabiola of Belgium enjoy a formal occasion during their visit to Finland in 1969. Among the places they toured was Lapland, home of the nomadic Lapps and their herds of reindeer.

In February U.S. President Richard M. Nixon made Brussels the first stop on his European tour. (*See also* Europe. *See in* CE: Belgium.)

BIOLOGY. When the genetic role of deoxyribonucleic acid (DNA) in chromosomes came to light it was only a matter of time before a gene—the segment of DNA responsible for a single genetic trait—would be isolated. That feat was reported in November 1969. A team of Harvard Medical School scientists isolated and took electron micrographs of the gene responsible for lactose sugar metabolism in *Escherichia coli,* a bacterium. The finding presaged "genetic engineering," the correction of genetic disorders by addition of new genes.

Molecular biologists in 1969 concentrated on the ribosome, a tiny cellular structure in which genetic messages are turned into amino-acid sequences of proteins. Each ribosome contains two components—the 50S subunit with ribonucleic acid (RNA) molecules and proteins, and the 30S subunit with proteins only. Segments of RNA attach amino acids to a growing protein chain in a very specific way, thus producing a variety of proteins. However, the roles of the ribosomal proteins were in question. Recent studies showed that one was an enzyme that catalyzed the addition of amino acids to the protein chain.

Enzyme Synthesis

In January 1969 two groups announced that, working independently, they had synthesized an enzyme from its amino-acid components for the first time. The enzyme created was ribonuclease, which helps break down RNA.

Using special electronic equipment, researchers at New York City's Rockefeller University attached the first of 124 amino acids to a polystyrene bead and added the remaining amino acids one at a time. The second team, from the Merck Sharp & Dohme Research Laboratories in Rahway, N.J., constructed fragments of the chain using from 6 to 17 amino acids apiece and then put the fragments together to form a complete chain. In both cases, once the synthesized enzyme was placed in a simple

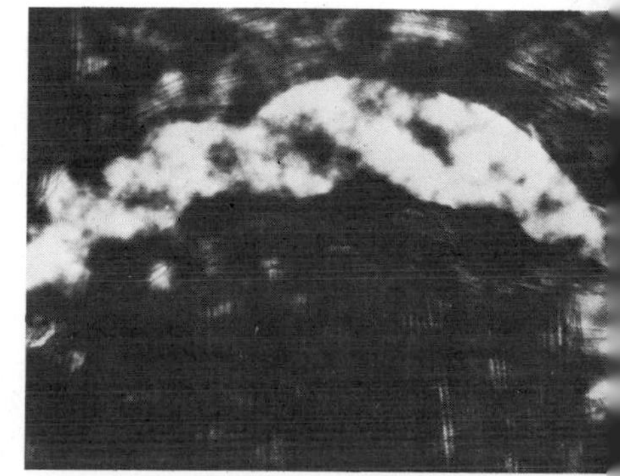

A coiled strand of what is believed to be DNA (deoxyribonucleic acid), the basic genetic material of life, is shown for the first time in a photograph, greatly magnified. Graduate student Jack Griffith developed the photographic technique.

WIDE WORLD

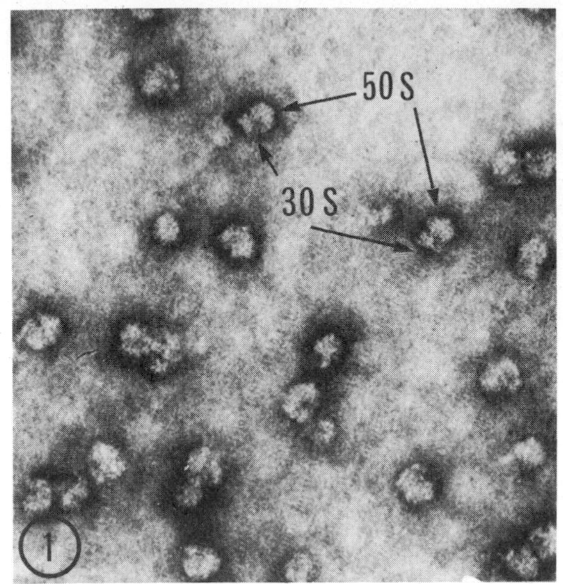

COURTESY, DR. AJIT KUMAR

A greatly magnified photograph shows ribosomes, tiny cellular particles, that have been isolated from a one-celled organism. The arrows indicate the two components of a ribosome, 50S and 30S.

solution it adopted the folded, three-dimensional configuration and the catalytic activity of a natural enzyme.

Developmental Biology

The immediate environment of the cell is important to its development. For tooth formation the epithelial tissue, which covers the developing tooth and later forms the enamel, must lie adjacent to the spongy interior mesenchyme, which will form the pulp. According to a 1969 report the type of tooth that develops was found to be determined by the mesenchyme.

Mesenchyme from molar and incisor tooth germs was interchanged in mouse embryos, and the type of tooth that developed was always the same as the source of the mesenchyme. In addition, cheek mesoderm was able to produce bristles in the epithelium of the sole of the foot and, more remarkably, incisor mesenchyme could produce an incisor when combined with epithelium from the foot.

Environmental Concerns

In 1969 the U.S. Department of Agriculture reported on the effects of defoliation in Vietnam. It was felt that the changes produced were not irreversible but that some recovery might take years. In mangrove forests, for example, repeated defoliation permitted invasion by bamboo plants, which retarded mangrove regeneration.

Every precaution was taken against the eventuality that the earth might be contaminated by material brought back from the moon by U.S. astronauts. Returning astronauts and their lunar samples were quarantined in specially designed laboratories until it was proved that they carried no living organisms. (*See in* CE: Biology.)

BIRTHS. These births to well-known couples attracted public attention in 1969:

To Mario Andretti, racing-car driver and winner of the 1969 Indianapolis 500, and his wife, Dee Ann, on July 13, a daughter.

To Joan Baez, U.S. folk singer, and David Harris, presently in federal prison for refusing induction, on December 2, a son.

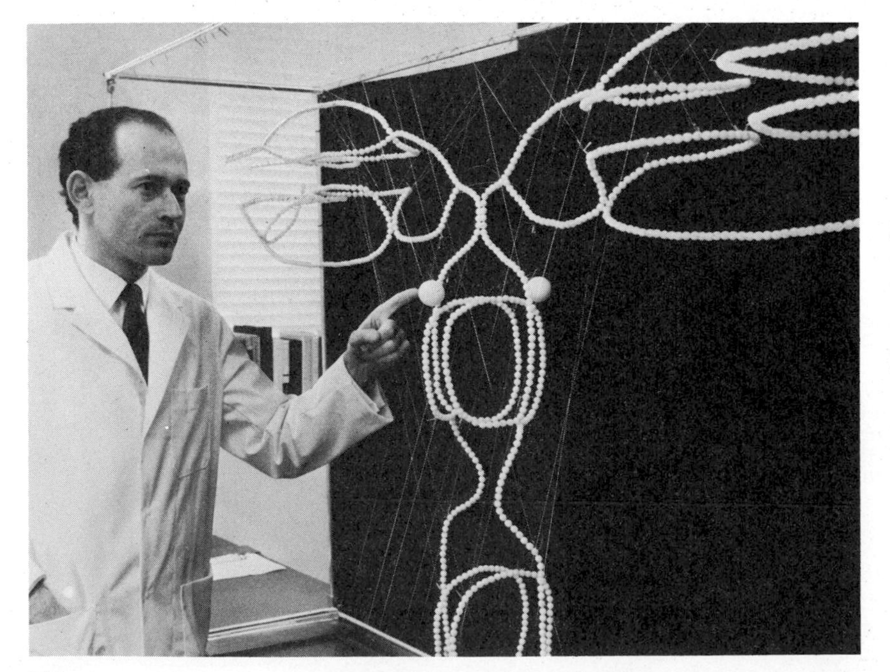

Gerald M. Edelman points to a model of gamma globulin, one of the chemical substances that defend the body against disease. Edelman announced in April that he and his colleagues at The Rockefeller University in New York City had been able to unravel the structure of the complex molecule.

UPI COMPIX

"LONDON DAILY EXPRESS" FROM PICTORIAL PARADE

Denmark's Princess Margrethe, Prince Henrik, and year-old Prince Frederick smile at a new family member, a boy born in June.

"LONDON DAILY EXPRESS" FROM PICTORIAL PARADE

Rolling Stones musician Keith Richards and actress Anita Pallenberg pose with their son.

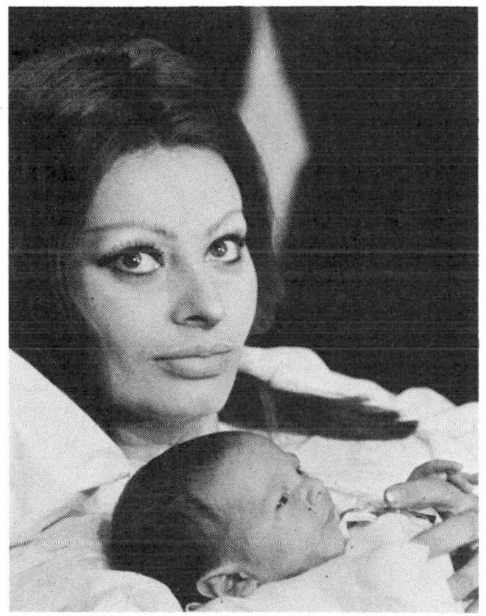

WIDE WORLD

Italian actress Sophia Loren rests with her son, Carlo Ponti, Jr., born Dec. 29, 1968, in Geneva, Switzerland.

To Crown Princess Beatrix of the Netherlands and Prince Claus, on October 11, a son.

To Salvatore (Sonny) Bono and Cheryl (Cher) Bono, popular singing duo, on March 4, a daughter.

To Zoe Caldwell, Australian actress ('The Prime of Miss Jean Brodie'), and Robert Whitehead, producer, on July 6, a son.

To Glen Campbell, popular singer and television personality, and his wife, Lillie, on February 12, a son.

To Eldridge Cleaver, self-exiled leader of the Black Panthers, and Kathleen Cleaver, the Panthers' communications secretary, on July 29, a son.

To King Constantine II of Greece and Queen Anne-Marie, on October 1, a son.

To Sophia Loren, Italian-born actress, and Carlo Ponti, motion-picture film producer, on Dec. 29, 1968, a son.

To Princess Margaretha of Sweden and John K. Ambler, a British businessman, on June 10, a son.

To Princess Margrethe, heiress to the Danish throne, and Prince Henrik, on June 7, a son.

To Paul McCartney, of the singing Beatles, and Linda Eastman McCartney, U.S. photographer, on August 28, a daughter.

To Vanessa Redgrave, British actress ('Blow-Up' and 'Camelot'), and Franco Nero, Italian actor ('Camelot'), on September 15, a son.

To Keith Richards, Rolling Stones musician, and Anita Pallenberg, German actress, in August, a son.

To John D. (Jay) Rockefeller IV, the only Democrat in the famed Rockefeller family and secretary of state of West Virginia, and Sharon Percy Rockefeller, daughter of Senator Charles H. Percy (R, Ill.), on July 6, a son.

BOATS AND BOATING. An estimated $4 million was spent on boating in the United States in 1969, making it the form of recreation with the biggest price tag. Some 44 million Americans went boating, using 9 million pleasure craft.

Preparations continued for a renewal in September 1970 off Newport, R.I., of yachting's premier event—racing for the America's Cup. France and Australia were preparing challengers that would have a "sail-off" to determine which should meet a defending American 12-Meter sloop. Two new 12's—*Heritage,* designed by Charles E. Morgan, Jr., of Florida, and an unnamed boat designed by Olin J. Stephens—were among candidates to represent the United States, which had never lost the cup.

Sailboat racing continued to grow in popularity in 1969. Some important national champions were

"PARIS MATCH" FROM PICTORIAL PARADE

Adventurer Kno Johnston waves to a photographer during the last few hours of his ten-month-long sailing trip around the world. He became the first man to make such a trip alone and nonstop.

James Hunt, winner of the men's Mallory Cup; Jan O'Malley, winner of the women's Adams Cup; and Manton D. Scott, winner of the Sears Cup for junior racers.

Punishing long-distance races drew many entries. The transatlantic Newport-to-Cork (Ireland) run was won by *Kialoa II*, owned by John B. Kilroy of California. The 473-mile Annapolis (Md.)-to-Newport race was won by *American Eagle*, owned by Robert E. Turner III of Georgia. Jon Andron of Los Angeles, Calif., won the race from his hometown to Honolulu, Hawaii, in *Argonaut*, and the Australian-American Challenge Cup was won by Brian Wertheimur of Washington in *Goose*. On the Great Lakes, *Bay Bea*, sailed by Pat Haggerty of Wisconsin, won the Chicago (Ill.)-to-Mackinac Island (Mich.) race. The heat from Port Huron, Mich., to Mackinac was won by *Diavolo*, owned by Peter Stern of Chicago.

Powerboat racing gained moderately in popularity in 1969 as more than 5,000 boats competed in some 600 regattas. *Miss Budweiser* won the unlimited-hydroplane Gold Cup, and Bill Muncey repeated to win the unlimited world championship in *Miss U.S.* (*See also* Sports Champions of 1969. *See in* CE: Boats and Boating; Canoes and Canoeing; Motorboats.)

An enclosed lifeboat, the Brucker Survival Capsule, was put on the market in 1969. The sea rescue craft, which holds 28 persons, is unswampable and self-propelled.

COURTESY, WHITTAKER CORP.

BOLIVIA. In early 1969 the administration of President René Barrientos Ortuño became increasingly unpopular. In January a state of siege was imposed and seven opposition leaders were arrested and exiled to Paraguay following the uncovering of a so-called "subversive plot," said to be financed from Cuba. The crisis provoked resignations by two cabinet members, although the influential minister of the interior, Capt. David Fernández, was later persuaded to return. Both the government and Comibol, the state mining corporation, came under attack from the church over mining conditions; the church claimed that the government had dishonored past agreements. Urban guerrilla incidents led to reports that a major guerrilla insurgency was planned under the leadership of Guido (Inti) Peredo, chief Bolivian lieutenant of the late Ernesto (Che) Guevara of Cuba.

Dissatisfied army officers, especially junior officers intolerant of the role that the U.S. Central Intelligence Agency had allegedly played in Bolivian affairs during Barrientos' administration, urged Gen. Alfredo Ovando Candia, commander in chief of the army, to seize power. To consolidate his position Barrientos went to the Cochabamba region, where, on April 27, a week after the state of siege was lifted, he died in a helicopter crash.

In the absence of Ovando, visiting in Washington, D.C., the deputy army chiefs supported the constitutional successor, civilian Vice-President Luis Adolfo Siles Salinas, whose presidency was endorsed by Ovando on his return. President Siles formed a caretaker government with a number of Ovando nominees in the new cabinet. General Ovando, a declared candidate in the presidential elections due in May 1970, seemed content to wait to succeed to power by constitutional election. But then on September 26 the Siles government was overthrown by a military junta in a bloodless coup, and Ovando took over the presidency. It quickly became evident that the new regime would pursue a strongly nationalistic policy; one of Ovando's first acts was to nullify the agreement under which the U.S.-owned Bolivian Gulf Oil Co. operated.

Bolivians, aware of the nationalization of U.S. oil and copper interests in Peru and Chile respectively, expressed increasing anti-imperialist senti-

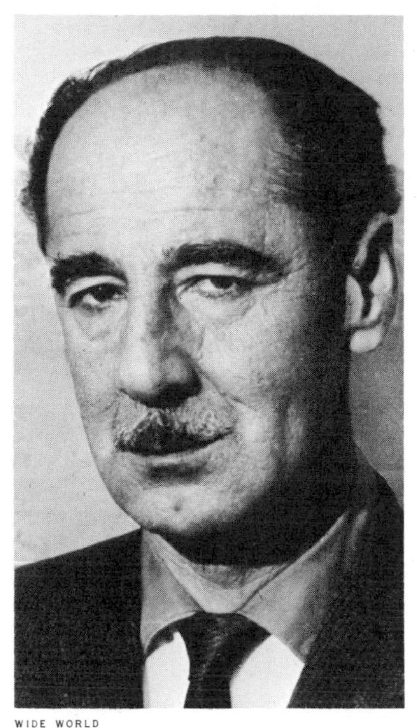

WIDE WORLD

General Alfredo Ovando Candia was named president of the new revolutionary government of Bolivia. He replaced Luis Adolfo Siles Salinas, who was deposed by a military junta.

ments during 1969. Anti-U.S. demonstrations caused the visit on May 31 of U.S. President Richard M. Nixon's special emissary Nelson A. Rockefeller to be curtailed to a three-hour airport meeting with Siles. The Falange Socialista Boliviana attacked Siles for granting the building contract for the Santa Cruz-Yacuiba gas pipeline to a U.S. company. In late August, however, a major change in policy became apparent when Siles secured Senate approval for a bill outlining a new petroleum code, which passed to committee. The aim of the code was to declare all natural-gas reserves the property of the state and thus not included in oil concessions granted to private companies.

In 1969 Bolivia's economy strengthened despite political confusion. Monetary stability was maintained and international reserves increased due to the firm world price of tin. The policy of economic diversification to reduce the nation's dependence on tin continued. Crude-oil exports rose slightly; however, the gradual extinction of oil reserves after 1971 was forecast unless investment in further exploration was forthcoming. Natural gas emerged as a future large earner of foreign exchange, and an agreement was reached to supply gas over the next 20 years to Argentina via the projected Santa Cruz-Yacuiba pipeline, for which a World Bank loan equivalent to $23 million was announced in July. (*See in* CE: Bolivia.)

BOTSWANA. Landlocked, drought-ridden Botswana continued in 1969 to depend on foreign aid for survival. Cattle and animal products, which comprised 90% of the exports, remained the country's economic lifeblood. Reports early in 1969 showed that record prices were paid for the 100,000 head of cattle sold by local producers in 1968. Water shortages continued. Land tenure continued to pose difficulties; there was no written title to serve as security for loans. Despite rains and increased planting the government was compelled to ask for an extension of famine relief under the United Nations World Food Programme for 1969.

Hopes for economic improvement lay in development of the copper, nickel, coal, and kimberlite diamond discoveries. In 1969 an extradition treaty was signed with South Africa to counter infiltration of armed terrorists.

In this election year President Seretse Khama announced the acquisition of 338,600 acres from the South Africa-owned Tati Co. One third of the long-disputed land was donated by the company; the rest was bought by the government for $1.5 million.

In elections on October 18, Khama's ruling Botswana Democratic party was returned to office with 24 of 31 elected seats in the National Assembly. The victory came despite the president's ill health and serious opposition by the newly formed Botswana National Front. (*See in* CE: Botswana.)

BOWLING. The 66th annual American Bowling Congress (ABC) tournament was held in Madison, Wis., with 6,258 teams competing. The Dick Weber Wrist Masters, of Santa Ana, Calif., won the classic (professional) team championship with a six-game score of 6,413. Nelson Burton, Jr., St. Louis, Mo., was the singles titlist with a 732; Don McCune, Munster, Ind., and Jim Stefanich, Joliet, Ill., won the doubles with 1,355; and the all-events crown was taken by Larry Lichstein, Hartford, Conn., who rolled a 2,060 total score.

The ABC's regular division winners were: team, PAC Advertising Co., Lansing, Mich., 3,165; singles, Greg Campbell, St. Louis, 751; doubles, Robert Maschmeyer and Charles Guedel, Indianapolis, Ind., 1,379; and all events, Eddie Jackson, Cincinnati, Ohio, 1,988.

Jim Chestney, Denver, Colo., won the ABC Masters title. At 21, he was the youngest winner.

The winners of the 50th annual Women's International Bowling Congress (WIBC) championships, staged in San Diego, Calif., were: team, Fitzpatrick Chevrolet, Concord, Calif., 2,986; singles, Joan Bender, Denver, 690; doubles, Gloria Bouvia, Portland, Ore., and Judy Cook, Kansas City, Mo., 1,315 (an all-time record); and all events, Helen Duval, Berkeley, Calif., 1,927. Ann Feigel, Tucson, Ariz., won the WIBC Queens title, averaging a record 214 in the finals.

Billy Hardwick, Louisville, Ky., and Dottie Fothergill, North Attleboro, Mass., won the Na-

COURTESY, AMERICAN BOWLING CONGRESS

Jim Chestney raises his 1969 American Bowling Congress Masters trophy high above the lanes where he bowled his way out of a losing streak to become Masters champion.

tional All-Star tournament. Hardwick also won five other tournaments.

Wisconsin State University—La Crosse continued to dominate the collegiate scene. For the third consecutive year the team won the National Association of Intercollegiate Athletics title, going unbeaten in a final field of eight teams. Bob Bush won the singles and shared the doubles with La Crosse teammate Ron Herald. In the Association of College Unions-International championships, Glenn Mueller of La Crosse captured the all-events title with a six-game total of 1,205 and also won the singles with a 618.

Joe Joseph, Lansing, and John O. Martino, Syracuse, N.Y., were named to the ABC Hall of Fame. Honored for meritorious service were R. F. Bensinger and the late Dave Luby, both of Chicago, Ill.

It was announced during the year that the United States would host the seventh world tournament of the Fédération Internationale des Quilleurs in Milwaukee, Wis., in 1971. More than 300 amateurs were expected to participate in the tournament. (*See in* CE: Bowling.)

BOXING. New boxing champions were named in all but the three heaviest divisions in 1969. The continued absence of Cassius Clay (Muhammad Ali), who was banned from the ring in 1967, left Joe Frazier of Philadelphia, Pa., the recognized champion in six states and Jimmy Ellis of Louisville, Ky., the choice of the World Boxing Association (WBA). Frazier disposed of Dave Zyglewicz in one round in April, and two months later he stopped Jerry Quarry in seven rounds. Ellis did not defend his title in 1969.

Bob Foster retained his light-heavyweight crown by knocking out Frankie De Paula in the first round in January and Andy Kendall in four rounds in May. Nino Benvenuti of Italy retained his middleweight title in October by beating Fraser Scott, who was disqualified in the seventh round for butting, and again in November by knocking out Luis Rodriguez in the 11th round.

The welterweight title went to Mexico's José Napoles, who stopped Curtis Cokes in 13 rounds in April, won a return match against Cokes in June, and registered a 15-round decision over Emile Griffith in October. Carlos Cruz of the Dominican Republic lost his lightweight crown to Mando Ramos by an 11th-round knockout in February. Ramos successfully defended his title in October with a sixth-round knockout of Yoshiaki Numata.

Australia's Johnny Famechon defeated José Legra of Spain for the world featherweight crown in January, and he successfully defended it in July with a 15-round decision over Masahiko Harada. Shozo Saijo retained his WBA featherweight title with a 15-round decision over Pedro Gomez in February, followed by a two-round knockout of José

Jerry Quarry (left) throws a right to Joe Frazier during their heavyweight championship fight. Frazier went on to win a brutal victory and retain his title.

WIDE WORLD

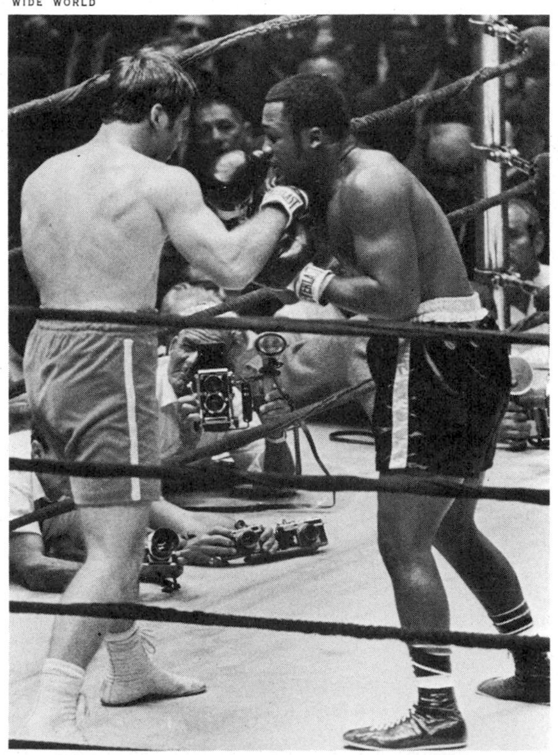

1969 WORLD CHAMPIONSHIP FIGHTS

Division	Boxer*	Date and Place
Flyweight	Efren Torres	February 23
	Chartchai Choinoi †	Mexico City, Mexico
	Hiroyuki Ebihara	March 30
	José Severino	Sapporo, Japan
	Bernabe Villacampo	October 19
	Hiroyuki Ebihara ‡†	Osaka, Japan
Bantamweight	Lionel Rose †	March 8
	Alan Rudkin	Melbourne, Australia
	Ruben Olivares	August 23
	Lionel Rose †	Inglewood, Calif.
	Ruben Olivares †	December 12
	Alan Rudkin	Inglewood, Calif.
Featherweight	Johnny Famechon	January 21
	José Legra	London, England
	Johnny Famechon †	July 28
	Masahiko Harada	Sydney, Australia
	Shozo Saijo †‡	February 9
	Pedro Gomez	Tokyo, Japan
	Shozo Saijo †‡	September 7
	José Pimental	Sapporo, Japan
Lightweight	Mando Ramos	February 18
	Carlos Cruz †	Los Angeles, Calif.
	Mando Ramos †	October 4
	Yoshiaki Numata	Los Angeles, Calif.
Welterweight	José Napoles	April 19
	Curtis Cokes †	Inglewood, Calif.
	José Napoles †	June 29
	Curtis Cokes	Mexico City, Mexico
	José Napoles †	October 17
	Emile Griffith	Inglewood, Calif.
Middleweight	Nino Benvenuti †	October 4
	Fraser Scott	Naples, Italy
	Nino Benvenuti †	November 22
	Luis Rodriguez	Rome, Italy
Light Heavyweight	Bob Foster †	January 22
	Frankie De Paula	New York City
	Bob Foster †	May 24
	Andy Kendall	West Springfield, Mass.
Heavyweight	Joe Frazier †	April 22
	Dave Zyglewicz	Houston, Texas
	Joe Frazier †	June 23
	Jerry Quarry	New York City

* Top name in each pair is winner. † Title defender.
‡ As recognized by World Boxing Association.

Pimental in September. The world bantamweight title was retained by Lionel Rose in a 15-round decision over Alan Rudkin in March and then was lost to Ruben Olivares by a fifth-round knockout in August. Olivares defended his title against Rudkin

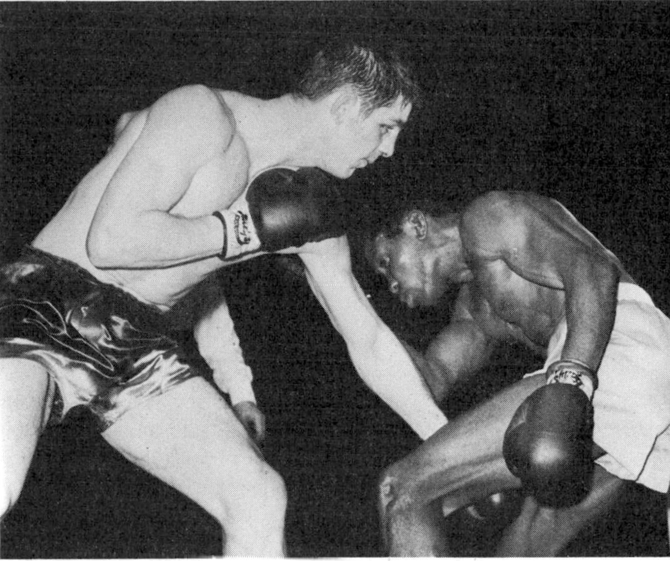

CENTRAL PRESS FROM PICTORIAL PARADE

José Legra (right) avoids a right from his opponent, Johnny Famechon, as he fights to defend his world featherweight crown. Famechon, however, captured the title.

in December. Another Mexican, Efren Torres, captured the flyweight crown from Chartchai Choinoi of Thailand in February, with the WBA version of the title going to Hiroyuki Ebihara in a 15-round decision over José Severino in March. Ebihara lost his title to Bernabe Villacampo in October.

Bob Foster, the light-heavyweight champion, was named Fighter of the Year by the Boxing Writers' Association of New York in February. (*See in* CE: Boxing.)

BRANDT, WILLY. After failing twice in the preceding decade to win leadership of the West German government, Willy Brandt on Oct. 21, 1969, became chancellor—the first Social Democrat to do so since 1930. In the secret balloting at least 27 Free Democrats formed a coalition with the 224 Social Democrats to put them over the 249 majority. (Chancellor Kurt G. Kiesinger's Christian Democrats held 242 seats.) The Bundestag, or lower house of Parliament, elected Brandt by a three-vote majority.

One of Brandt's first acts as chancellor was the revaluation of the German mark. (*See* Money and International Finance.) Although he did not offer diplomatic recognition to East Germany, the new chancellor recognized the existence of two German states, which he said "are not foreign to each other." He pledged continued ties with the United States and proposed meetings with the Soviet Union, Poland, and East Germany. His domestic program included a voting age of 18.

Brandt was mayor of West Berlin from 1957 to 1966. He became chairman of the Social Democratic party in 1964 and was vice-chancellor and foreign minister in the coalition with the Christian Democrats 1966–69. He was born Herbert Frahm on Dec. 18, 1913, at Lübeck. He fled Germany in 1933 and worked in Norway and Sweden as a journalist, returning to Germany in 1947. (*See also* Germany, West.)

BRAZIL. The rule of Artur da Costa e Silva, president of Brazil since 1967, came to an abrupt end in August 1969 when the 66-year-old marshal suffered a paralyzing stroke. The illness struck eight months after the president imposed a rule by decree in the wake of continued political agitation and terrorist activities.

Under Costa e Silva's emergency reign Congress and other legislative bodies had been recessed. There followed a removal of military and civilian officers, suspension of political rights, and annulment of mandates. Elections were suspended and political conventions postponed. A military police committee was created to investigate subversion.

The government meanwhile took certain constructive measures in rural, university, and political reforms. A committee on constitutional changes was appointed. Late in August final drafts of the proposed amendments were submitted to the president and he planned to announce on September 7 that he would reconvene Congress.

Then the crippling illness struck. A military triumvirate assumed rule of the country. Meanwhile, on September 4 a band of terrorists kidnapped U.S. Ambassador C. Burke Elbrick. The veteran diplomat was returned 78 hours later after the government met ransom demands for the release of 15 political prisoners. The government subsequently imposed severe penalties for political crimes, including the sentence of death.

On October 7 the armed forces' high command named an obscure general, Emílio Garrastazú Médici, to become president of Brazil. The 63-year-old commander of the Third Army was the onetime head of Brazil's National Intelligence Service. Before taking office he told Brazilians he hoped to establish democracy and provide a firm basis for further economic and social development in Brazil. The lack of basic freedoms was discussed by New York Gov. Nelson A. Rockefeller on his June visit to Brazil, and in September Brazil's Roman Catholic bishops protested the virtual dictatorship in the country.

Despite political problems the economy prospered. Early 1969 reports showed an increase of 6% in the gross national product for 1968 and increases of 14% in steel production, 13% in electric power, and 41% in automobile production. By the middle of 1969 the country's exchange reserves had climbed to $100 million, and exports were expected to reach $2 billion by the end of the year.

In 1969 a government-controlled iron-ore exporting company signed an agreement with the U.S. Steel Corp. for the development of resources in the Tocantins Valley and the ore district of Minas Gerais. In May the government announced an increase in the national minimum wage and the establishment of a social security program for rural workers. Also begun in 1969 was a reparations program for crimes against Indians committed by the now-defunct Indian Protection Service. Recovery of lands sold illegally to ranchers was started and a hospital for Indians opened in northern Goiás. Plans were laid to upgrade the fishing industry to reach a 2-million-ton catch by 1972. (*See in* CE: Brazil.)

WAITE FROM BEN ROTH AGENCY

"The ambassador will see you now, señor, if you stand in front of the keyhole."

BUILDING CONSTRUCTION. The construction industry became the focal point of national attention several times during 1969. The industry was repeatedly disrupted from inside and out by blacks who objected to labor policies. It was also the object of government interest as it became a prime target for anti-inflationary measures.

In late summer, demonstrations led by black community groups in Chicago, Ill., and Pittsburgh, Pa., interrupted work on a number of unfinished building projects. The protests were directed against building trade unions that control the hiring of construction workers. The blacks charged that the unions deliberately barred them from membership. During the year, blacks held only 2% of the 800,000 highest-paying construction jobs in the nation. They comprised only 7.2% of all building craftsmen. (*See* Employment.)

Costs and wages in the industry came under scrutiny in 1969 as U.S. President Richard M. Nixon indicated great concern over their contribution to the accelerating rate of inflation. The federal government announced a 75% cutback in federal building expenditures and urged state governments to take similar measures. The cutback would primarily affect the construction of post offices, federal office buildings, forest roads, and other reclamation projects. Although construction contracts would be reduced by $1.6 billion during the 1969–70 fiscal year, expenditures would be only $300 million lower, since most fees are not paid until months after contracts are signed.

In September, Nixon announced the formation of a tripartite commission with members from government, unions, and employers, to mediate wage discussions when 2,500 contracts came up for renewal in 1970. The Administration's aim was to avoid strikes while holding wage increases to a sub-inflationary level.

In 1969, as in previous years, building construction was one of the largest industries in the United States. The construction of new buildings, dams, highways, and other immobile structures accounted for approximately 10% of the nation's total output of goods and services.

At the end of the first eight months of 1969 contract placements in the industry totaled over $41 billion, a gain of 11% over the same period in 1968. Nonresidential building was 20% ahead for the period; nonbuilding construction, 8% ahead; and residential building, 6% ahead. In the construction of private dwellings, a decline in contracts for single-family housing had become evident by August. This decline was offset, however, by a strong showing in multiunit dwelling contracts.

Construction costs rose sharply during the first eight months of 1969, maintaining a projected annual increase of 12%. Even compared to the general rate of inflation, cost and labor increases were extremely high during the year. The average weekly earnings of contract construction workers were 10% higher in August 1969 than they were a year earlier.

Partly in response to cost pressures, developers continued to take advantage of savings by erecting large projects whenever possible. The largest single commercial development under way during 1969 was the World Trade Center on the Lower West Side of Manhattan in New York City. The six-building complex was expected to cost $600 million by the time it is completed. Other large-scale projects begun during the year included a $300-million electric generating plant in Tennessee, a $150-million skyscraper plaza in Manhattan, and a $75-million building in Rockefeller Plaza, also in Manhattan. (*See also* Architecture; Housing; Labor Unions. *See in* CE: Building Construction.)

UPI COMPIX

Buildings of the World Trade Center begin to rise on the Lower West Side of Manhattan in New York City. The mammoth construction job was expected to cost $600 million by the time of completion in 1973.

BULGARIA. On Sept. 9, 1969, Bulgaria celebrated the 25th anniversary of its national Communist revolution. At ceremonies in Sofia, the capital, Premier Todor Zhivkov expressed "eternal gratitude" to the Soviet Union for its role in the Bulgarian takeover. General Dobri Dzhurov, Bulgaria's defense minister, took the occasion to criticize revisionists of the left and right, whom he described as helping imperialism. The Communist Chinese delegation walked out of the ceremonies to protest Dzhurov's remarks.

Bulgaria maintained extremely close ties with the Soviet Union. The Soviet press carried a number of articles praising economic progress in Bulgaria, and the Bulgarian press in turn praised Soviet aid. Per-capita income had risen, and industrial production for 1968 was estimated to be 30 times that of 1939. The Soviet Union had granted approximately $3 billion in credits to Bulgaria since the end of World War II.

Relations between Bulgaria and Yugoslavia remained cool, but some overtures were made to restore friendly ties. Bulgaria had refused to recognize Macedonia as a separate republic within Yugoslavia and had contended that all "Macedonians" were actually Bulgarians. Yugoslavia had accused Bulgaria of territorial ambitions involving Macedonia—which is on the border between the two countries. In 1969 Bulgaria's deputy foreign minister said that the dispute should be left to historians. Bulgarian authorities recalled from circulation copies of the "blue book" of history that had discussed Macedonia in a manner that was objectionable to Yugoslavia.

Bulgarian intellectuals were cautioned against Western or revisionist influences. Authorities

KEYSTONE

An impressive military parade highlighted the 25th-anniversary celebration of the birth of the Bulgarian People's Republic.

warned them about the type of "subversion" prevalent in Czechoslovakia before the Soviet-led invasion in late August 1968. (*See also* Communist Movement; Czechoslovakia; Europe. *See in* CE: Bulgaria.)

BURGER, WARREN E. In May 1969 U.S. President Richard M. Nixon nominated Warren Earl Burger to become the 15th chief justice of the United States. The president hoped that Burger would change the speed if not the direction charted for the nation by the U.S. Supreme Court under its 14th chief justice, Earl Warren. Burger thus surprised many with his first major decision after being sworn in as chief justice. He voted, along with the other justices, to bring an end to school segregation "at once."

The new justice went to the Supreme Court from the U.S. Circuit Court of Appeals for the District of Columbia, where he was a frequent dissenter on a progressive bench. His decisions, however, did not label him "liberal" or "conservative." In civil rights cases, for instance, Burger had no trouble matching strides with the Supreme Court. It was his criticism of the Warren court's approach to individual liberties in conflict with the criminal process that brought Burger to the attention of President Nixon. While not quarreling with the outcome of most of the celebrated criminal cases, Burger criticized the Warren court for what he called inadequate concern for the rights of the law-abiding majority.

Warren Earl Burger was sworn in as the 15th chief justice of the United States in June 1969.

WIDE WORLD

Burger attended the University of Minnesota and won his law degree by studying nights at St. Paul College of Law (now the Mitchell College of Law). He practiced law in a private firm until 1953 when he became an assistant attorney general during President Dwight D. Eisenhower's first term. Eisenhower appointed Burger to the District of Columbia circuit in 1956. (*See also* Supreme Court of the United States.)

BURMA. The political and economic situation in Burma remained largely unchanged during 1969. The government claimed major victories over the Burmese Communist guerrillas. General Ne Win, chairman of the Revolutionary Council and prime minister, continued his policy of political and economic isolation. Burma's depressed economy continued to suffer under the weight of an inefficient bureaucracy.

A 33-member advisory board presented Gen. Ne Win with its recommendation for a return to parliamentary government. The advisory board had been established in early December 1968 to advise the general on possible means of improving the government and on drafting a national constitution.

Former Prime Minister U Nu was among the board members. Nu contended that he was still the legal prime minister and recommended that he be restored to power. Nu's recommendation along with all the other proposals presented by the board was rejected by Gen. Ne Win. Nu then left Burma, denouncing the general's regime as fascist and calling for an overthrow of the government.

In March Communist China confirmed reports that the leader of Burma's Communist guerrillas, Thakin Than Tun, had been assassinated in September 1968. He was killed by another Communist guerrilla. This loss and the violent split between the pro-Soviet and pro-Chinese factions of the Burmese Communists weakened the guerrillas' strength. The Burmese army succeeded in stamping out guerrilla activity in lower and middle Burma. The insurgents then concentrated their strength in the north where they could retreat across the Chinese border if necessary.

The government made an effort to stimulate the economy by allowing a limited number of tourists into Burma for up to 72 hours. Visitors were flown in on a chartered jet and taken on a three-day guided tour. (*See in* CE: Burma.)

BURUNDI. Twelve leaders of Burundi's old monarchal regime, overthrown in 1966, faced political trial in December 1968. Six former ministers, including former National Assembly President Thaddée Siryuyumunsi and his deputy Siniremera, received ten-year sentences on charges of writing and distributing an open letter hostile to the government. Other terms ranged up to seven years.

Close relationships were maintained with neighboring states. In January President Michel Micombero received President Léopold S. Senghor of Senegal. In February Burundi applied again for membership in the East African Economic Community. Officials attended the foreign ministers' conference of the East and Central African section of the Economic Commission for Africa and the Lusaka, Zambia, summit conference convened by President Kenneth Kaunda in April. In May Micombero attended the second convention of the People's Revolutionary Movement of the Congo (Kinshasa). Relations with Rwanda were resumed in February. During June the foreign ministers of the Democratic Republic of the Congo (Kinshasa) and Burundi met to consider mutual development problems and the formation of a regional group according to an Organization of African Unity plan. Three commissions were established: political and judicial, social and cultural, and financial and technical.

Financial aid received during the year included $2.8 million for roads, $1 million for the tea industry from the European Development Fund of the European Economic Community, and $4 million from the International Monetary Fund for the tea industry as part of a $12-million development plan that included the building of tea-processing factories. (*See in* CE: Burundi.)

BUSINESS AND INDUSTRY. In 1969 the business community began to feel the effects of government efforts to curb inflation. At the end of the second quarter, economic indicators gave the first signs that business was slowing down in response to Administration policies enacted at the beginning of the year. Nevertheless, prices remained at record levels throughout the year, and by the beginning of August the value of the dollar had dropped 5% from its August 1968 level.

Corporate profits first showed a decline during the second quarter of 1969, falling about 1%. The decrease in profits centered in durable-goods manufacturing and was most marked in the automobile industry and in other transportation-equipment manufacturing industries. A larger rise in unit costs than in unit selling prices was partially responsible for the decline in profits. During the second quarter, labor costs rose 1.5% and nonlabor costs —interest, depreciation charges, and indirect business taxes—advanced 2%. At the same time, selling prices rose only 1%.

Industrial production also began to lag in August, showing a downturn for the first time during the year. Although the decrease was small—only .2% —it marked a decided change from the average increase of .5%, which had prevailed in the first half of the year.

The stock market also suffered through one of the most "bearish" years in recent history. At the beginning of October, the Dow-Jones industrial average stood at 827, considerably below the 1968 high of 969. The market decline was attributed to the increase in interest rates and the likelihood of higher taxes on capital gains.

With lower profits and the falling stock market came a decline in business investment. Early in the year a survey of business investment plans revealed that companies intended to spend some 14% more on new facilities and equipment during 1969 than during 1968. By August, the increase planned for capital spending had been reduced to 11%.

Despite the effect of anti-inflation measures and the anticipated slowdown, the business scene continued to yield dramatic news. In September Ford Motor Co., the nation's third largest industrial corporation, announced the firing of its president of 19 months, Semon E. Knudsen, a former General Motors Corp. executive. Knudsen's firing was thought to have been a result of his power struggle with executive vice-president Lee A. Iacocca. (*See* Automobiles.)

Also in September, Alaska announced the close of the richest land deal in history. A group of oil companies paid almost $1 billion for the rights to drill for oil in the frozen northern slope of the state, following a joint discovery by Atlantic Richfield Co. and Humble Oil & Refining Co. of what may be the largest oil field on the continent. The $1 billion goes into the Alaska state treasury, along with royalties of 12.5% of the value of oil produced, plus severance taxes. (*See* Arctic; Fuel and Power: Petroleum; Ships and Shipping.)

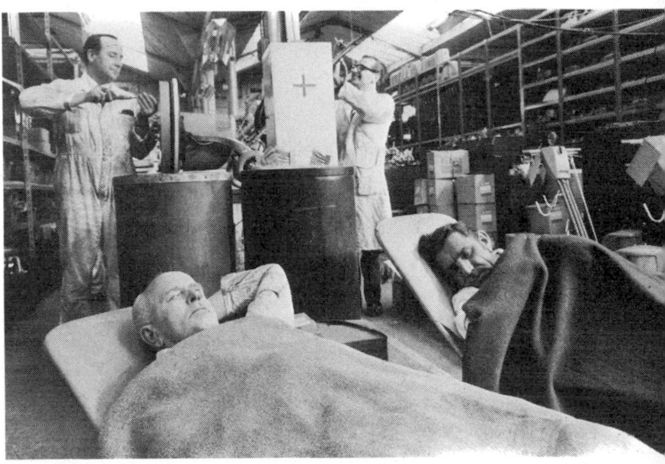

KEYSTONE

Two workers sleep as two others work to keep up round-the-clock production of goods for export at a factory in Great Britain. The efforts were symbolic of the British drive to vastly increase exports.

The Rev. Jesse Jackson uses a police microphone in an attempt to quiet demonstrators at the University of Illinois's Chicago Circle Campus. About 600 were protesting discrimination against blacks by construction trade unions. A series of such demonstrations were held in other cities in late summer.

WIDE WORLD

Although merger announcements for the first nine months of the year were 34% above the first nine months of 1968, there was a drop in the number of blockbuster corporate mergers that had characterized much of the late 1960's. This was partly due to statements from the U.S. Department of Justice that prompted a growing uncertainty over which mergers were legal and which were not. In March Assistant Attorney General Richard W. McLaren stated his belief that conglomerate mergers were injurious to the economy because they tended to reduce competition and increase prices. McLaren also announced plans to extend the interpretation of the Clayton Act in order to challenge most types of conglomerate mergers.

The drop-off in big mergers also reflected depressed stock-market prices of many formerly acquisitive companies. Since many mergers depend on an exchange of stock, an undervalued stock is much weaker in buying power. Another medium of acquisition, debt securities, was brought into a less favorable light after the New York Stock Exchange announced that it was considering delisting some conglomerates because of their methods of borrowing to make acquisitions.

Despite the seeming disenchantment, several important corporate marriages were consummated. Atlantic Richfield Co. acquired Sinclair Oil Corp. in a $3.7-billion transaction that made the combine the fifth largest oil company. Youngstown Sheet & Tube Co. merged with Lykes Corp. Warner-Lambert Pharmaceutical Co. acquired Eversharp, Inc., and Santa Fe Industries, Inc., purchased Dresser Industries, Inc.

Other mergers were executed only after careful manipulation. In a rare agreement with the U.S. Department of Justice, Ling-Temco-Vought, Inc., agreed to divest itself of all Jones & Laughlin Steel Corp. interests if the courts found the merger of the two companies illegal. In doing so, Ling-Temco-Vought agreed to waive its rights to all legal alternatives if it lost its case. In return the conglomerate proceeded with its take-over of the steel company while the case was pending.

A battle for the control of Armour & Co. that had been waging since June 1968 was resolved in September. The Chicago, Ill., meat company had been the object of a war between General Host Corp. and Greyhound Corp. with each corporation trying to purchase a majority of its common stock. Although General Host finally succeeded in acquiring a majority of Armour stock, it was unable to consolidate its holdings in the company and ultimately sold its majority shares to Greyhound.

In 1969 antitrust suits were brought against two of the nation's largest corporations. By April International Business Machines Corp. (IBM) had become the defendant in suits filed by four separate corporations. The corporations, all involved in the data-processing field, charged that IBM violated antitrust laws by restraining competition. U.S. Steel Corp. was charged with violating the Sherman Antitrust Act by forcing its suppliers to purchase its products in return. A consent agreement, in which U.S. Steel agreed "perpetually" to refrain from engaging in such reciprocal agreements, was accepted as a settlement.

Business enterprises operated by racial minority groups made some headway during the year. The Bedford-Stuyvesant Restoration Corp., created to develop businesses, jobs, sound housing, and other urgent necessities for the slum-ridden section of New York City, marked a number of achievements. Among them were the development of a mortgage pool that provided $5 million in low-interest loans, the creation of seven new minority-owned businesses, and the employment of neighborhood labor.

(continued on page 164)

Special Report: The Conglomerate

by Joel Segall, Professor of Finance,
Graduate School of Business, University of Chicago

In the past few years the conglomerate corporation has become the most controversial entity in the business world. It has been deplored because of its tendency to produce economic concentration; applauded for its business efficiency; attacked for its unorthodox financing techniques and accounting procedures; and defended as the embodiment of the creativity and ingenuity of the times. It has been a source of fascination for the financial press, the investment community, and, more recently, the antitrust authorities.

The current preoccupation with conglomerates is not surprising. The firms classified as conglomerates are usually huge and diverse; their financial dealings are complicated and often associated with proxy fights or other public contests for stockholder approval; and their stock prices often vacillate widely and abruptly.

Although the term "conglomerate" became a household word only slightly before "Spiro Agnew" did, its origin dates back to 1940, when the New Deal's Temporary National Economic Committee coined it to describe the diversified corporation. Unlike the vertical merger (the combination of a firm with its supplier or customer) or the horizontal merger (the combination of firms producing similar products), the conglomerate merger involves unrelated businesses. This characteristic kept the antitrust authorities away for two decades and enabled conglomerates to multiply rapidly.

Although the conglomerate has been subject to provisions of the Clayton (Antitrust) Act, amended in 1950 to ban all mergers where the effect "may be substantially to lessen competition or to tend to create a monopoly," it has escaped the fate that has befallen so many vertical and horizontal mergers—simply because its type of combination has made it difficult to prove the threat of monopoly. As a result, the proportion of major conglomerate mergers rose from 50.6% of all mergers in 1951 to 83.9% in 1968. During the same period, the number of vertical mergers declined from 12.3% to 8.9% and horizontal mergers from 37.0% to 7.3%.

Another factor contributing to the popularity of conglomerate mergers is the flexibility of financing. One or more firms may exchange cash or other assets, bonds, stocks, convertible securities, options, warrants, or some combination of these for all or part of the stock assets of one or more other firms. These varied financing techniques make it possible for an acquiring company to record—at least temporarily—dramatic increases in earnings even without operating benefits from the merger. These techniques are available in all mergers, but only in conglomerate mergers have they been employed so masterfully.

"Most closely run conglomerate on Wall Street."

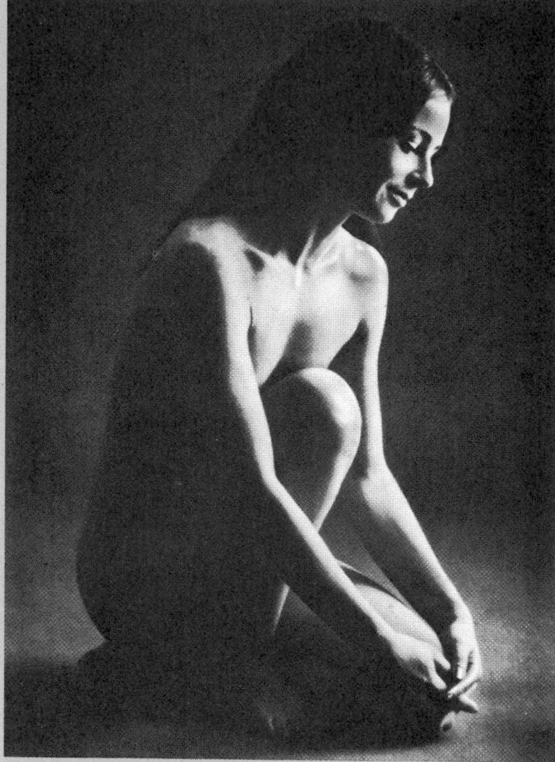

COURTESY, THE SIGNAL COMPANIES

The Signal Companies, a conglomerate, sponsored advertising to win public acceptance of conglomerates in general. The U.S. Congress, the Department of Justice, and the Securities and Exchange Commission were investigating and acting on the concentration of assets in conglomerates during 1969.

Wall Street's fondness for the conglomerate also helped. Prices on conglomerate stocks seemed to rise with the consummation of each new merger. Even in a simple stock-for-stock exchange, an acquiring company with a high price/earnings ratio will immediately increase its earnings per share by acquiring a company with a low price/earnings ratio (as long as the exchange ratio is close to the relative value of the stocks involved). For example, a conglomerate whose stock (1) sells at $40 a share, (2) is earning $1 a share (p/e = 40), and (3) has 6,000 shares outstanding offers to acquire a company with the same number of shares outstanding. The company's stock is currently selling at $10 a share, but it also earns $1 a share (p/e = 10). The conglomerate offers one of its shares for every three of the company's—an attractive offer to the company's stockholders, who stand to make a 33% premium. When the merger is completed, the conglomerate, with 6,000 shares still outstanding as well as 2,000 new shares created to use in the merger, can combine the earnings and restate the price of its shares. By this time, the conglomerate has 8,000 shares outstanding and the earnings of 12,000. Where two of the conglomerate's shares used to earn $2, they now earn $3—a per-share increase of 50¢. The stock, based on the original p/e of 40, rises in value to $60 per share.

The same principle applies when bonds or stock options are used as a means of exchange. Although theoretically the acquisition should not increase the market value of the stock, it often does. For even if the original company wasn't able to sell shares for as much as the conglomerate could—despite the fact that its per-share earnings were the same—the conglomerate, through the acquisition of the first company, endows the company with its own high growth expectation. Thus the company's stock is immediately worth more, and by adding it, so is the conglomerate's.

Accompanying these financial advantages is the conglomerate's appeal to management. Having acquired a reputation as a bastion of new management techniques, the conglomerate is often run by vigorous administrators who are anxious to innovate rather than to resist change. Management functions are also distributed in a manner different from that of the monolithic corporation. The central staff is comparatively small and is involved with general corporate business such as accounting, legal operations, and corporate research. The subsidiaries operate almost independently under the direction of management and technical specialists in the particular fields.

Management also enjoys the advantages of being in many unrelated industries, so that the danger of being manipulated by one market is avoided. This lack of attachment to one particular market can also enable corporate administrators to transfer capital to any promising new market area.

As is inevitable with any boom, the conglomerate boom has begun to cool. The damper was applied in part in Washington, D.C., where members of Congress, the Department of Justice, and the Securities and Exchange Commission (SEC) began to look upon various conglomerate activities with a suspicious eye. In the spring of 1969 the Antitrust Division of the Department of Justice initiated an expansion of the Clayton Act by filing suits against two purely conglomerate mergers. The action was an indication of a change in antitrust philosophy and reflected apprehension that conglomerate mergers will reduce the likelihood of independent entry into the industries involved; that they will increase the incidence of reciprocal buying arrangements; and that they will increase the concentration of ownership of assets.

The first suit was brought against the acquisition of major stock interest in Jones & Laughlin Steel Corp. (J&L) by Ling-Temco-Vought, Inc. (LTV). The Department of Justice alleged that LTV and J&L "considered" entering the same industries; the merger had therefore reduced "potential competition." Another interpretation of the law was invoked in a suit to force International Telephone and Telegraph Corp. (ITT) to divest itself of Canteen Corp. The Department of Justice contended that the combined firm would benefit from "reciprocity" by inducing ITT suppliers to become buyers from Canteen. In the LTV-J&L suit as well, the Department of Justice pointed out that LTV buys many automobiles for its subsidiary National Car Rental System, Inc., and could induce an automobile manufacturer to buy steel from J&L.

Although these conglomerates were attacked by means traditionally employed to break down other forms of mergers, the concern stemmed not so much from the fear that the conglomerate would develop into a monopoly as from the apprehension of its potential size. While antitrust concern over concentration historically involved particular markets and industries, the concentration of assets is now the biggest worry. The most commonly cited statistic on concentration is that the proportion of all manufacturing assets owned by the 200 largest U.S. firms increased from less than 50% in 1948 to 60% by 1969. Conglomerate mergers have undoubtedly played a major role in this increased concentration.

James J. Ling is chairman of the board of LTV—a conglomerate much in the news in 1969.

SHEL HERSHORN FROM BLACK STAR

A Federal Trade Commission (FTC) staff report submitted to the U.S. Congress in November 1969 divulged similar fears, naming conglomerate interdependence as the biggest existing threat to competition. It stated that conglomerates did not try to compete vigorously in markets where other conglomerates existed because of a fear of retaliation in other markets. A report of a task force of economists and lawyers, ordered by former U.S. President Lyndon B. Johnson and released in May 1969, recommended a solution. The report proposed that the acquisition by a conglomerate of a company already among the top four in its industry be prohibited.

The FTC report also attacked the accounting profession for allowing merger-minded companies to use procedures that misled investors and enabled such companies to get more support in the securities market than they warranted. Among these procedures was the practice of "pooling of interests," in which a new acquisition is treated as though it had always been a member of the corporation. Thus, a company acquired in December can have its profits for the entire year incorporated into those of the parent company.

As an aid to investors, the SEC passed a ruling that disallowed the practice of issuing securities-registration reports that were statements for the conglomerate as a whole and did not give the stockholder any indication of the relative contribution of the different product lines. However, investors still continued to be uncertain and often misinformed of the value of the warrants, options, and convertible securities used in acquisitions.

In the wake of such attacks, conglomerate stocks declined sharply after the beginning of 1969. Such giants as Litton Industries, Inc., and LTV dropped in price per share from over $74 to around $34 and from over $97 to around $24 respectively during 1969. The conglomerate's tenuous position on the market was worsened by a warning from Robert W. Haack, president of the New York Stock Exchange, that the exchange might reject listing applications of companies that made acquisitions by debt financing. As stock prices fell, so did the rate of mergers—a result of the decreased values of stocks commonly used in acquisitions.

At the end of 1969, the future of the conglomerate appeared to be considerably less rosy than it had seemed in 1968. The conglomerate faced continued scrutiny by the Department of Justice, the SEC, Congressional committees and subcommittees, and the New York Stock Exchange. It could also expect the investor to view it with greater suspicion.

The conglomerate was still in little danger of disappearing from the business scene. But, as one stock analyst declared, "The big conglomerates won't be the swinging stocks of tomorrow."

Lee A. Iacocca, an executive vice-president of Ford Motor Co., was named the firm's president for North American automotive operations following the ouster of Semon E. Knudsen from Ford's presidency.

J. EDW. BAILEY

(continued from page 160)

In Rochester, N.Y., a corporate venture into black capitalism, Fighton, Inc., was organized by a militant black group with the backing of the Xerox Corp., Rochester Business Opportunities Corp., and the U.S. Department of Labor. The company produces a compact portable vacuum cleaner used to service Xerox machines.

However, on the national level, programs to promote black capitalism seemed to be floundering. By midsummer many of the executive personnel of the Small Business Administration had resigned because of lack of Administration support for their programs. (*See also* Business Special Report; Economy. *See in* CE: Industry, American.)

CAMBODIA. Throughout 1969 Prince Norodom Sihanouk, Cambodia's chief of state, continued his erratic policies toward the Communist powers and the United States alike, in an effort to maintain his country's precarious neutrality. With an end to the Vietnam conflict in sight and faced with a growing threat from Communist insurgents inside Cambodia, Sihanouk became more friendly toward the United States during the year.

One of Cambodia's greatest concerns during 1969 was the number of Viet Cong and North Vietnamese regular army troops within Cambodia's borders. It was estimated that about 30,000 North Vietnamese and Viet Cong troops were based in Cambodia. The greatest concentrations of enemy soldiers were in the sparsely populated province of Ratanakiri in the northeast and in Svay Rieng province in the southeast, near Saigon, South Vietnam. The Khmer Rouge, Cambodian Communist guerrillas, were also concentrated in Ratanakiri and received support from the Viet Cong.

To the Cambodian government the presence of such large numbers of Vietnamese Communist troops posed a threat to Cambodia's independence. The government feared that Cambodia might become a prime target for Communist activities when hostilities were ended in South Vietnam. In June, however, Sihanouk received a written promise that all Vietnamese Communist troops would be withdrawn from Cambodia at the end of the Vietnam conflict. Following this there was an increase in the amount of Communist Chinese supplies flowing through Cambodia to Communist bases in South Vietnam.

Diplomatic relations between Cambodia and the United States were resumed after U.S. President

Cambodian mercenaries relax and enjoy the view as they are carried by helicopter to a site near the Cambodian-Vietnamese border for a raid on Communist troops.

UPI COMPIX

Richard M. Nixon stated that the United States would respect Cambodia's present frontiers. General Lon Nol, a former premier with close U.S. contacts, was once again chosen as Cambodia's premier. In May Cambodia granted full diplomatic recognition to East Germany. West Germany retaliated by recalling its ambassador to Cambodia.

Early in the year Sihanouk began implementing plans for revitalizing Cambodia's stagnant economy. Cambodia reactivated its membership in the Asian Development Bank and applied for membership in the International Monetary Fund. In August the Cambodian riel was devalued by 12.5%. There was also the possibility that U.S. foreign aid to Cambodia might be renewed. (*See in* CE: Cambodia.)

AGIP FROM PICTORIAL PARADE

Cameroon's President Ahmadou Ahidjo (left) conferred with France's Premier Georges Pompidou in Paris, France, during the early part of September.

CAMEROON. The political scene in Cameroon remained stable in 1969. On several occasions during the year, President Ahmadou Ahidjo stressed his hostility to Biafran separatism. In his view, the only solution to the civil war in Nigeria lay in a compromise that would respect Nigeria's integrity while giving a degree of autonomy to its various regions. (*See* Nigeria.)

On July 17, the village of Djoum was attacked by members of the Union of the Cameroon Peoples. Nothing had been heard from this secret movement for a year and a half.

On July 29, at the National Assembly in Yaoundé, the capital, a second economic convention was signed between the European Economic Community (EEC), or Common Market, and the 18 African associated states. The World Bank loaned $7.9 million and France $3.6 million for further development of Cameroon's palm-oil industry. The Export-Import Bank of Washington (D.C.) loaned approximately $3 million for improving the telecommunications network between Yaoundé and Fort-Foureau.

In April the president inaugurated a road from Douala to Tiko and a railway from M'Banga to Kumba. On April 22 a financial convention was signed with the EEC for the second section of the trans-Cameroon railway. (*See in* CE: Cameroon.)

CAMPING. Camping continued to grow in popularity in the United States during 1969, but the traditional practice of roughing it in the outdoors waned in appeal. Less than 30% of the nation's 30 million campers slept in tents and cooked over open fires; the remainder took most—or all—the comforts of home with them in a wide variety of "recreational vehicles."

Roughing It in Style

Recreational vehicles include camping trailers, pickup campers (converted small trucks), travel trailers, and motor homes (similar in appearance to small buses). Their popularity has increased rapidly—approximately 84,000 were built in 1961, but nearly 500,000 in 1969. Of the vehicles produced in 1969, 24% were camping trailers, 31% pickup campers, 41% travel trailers, and 4% motor homes. Their cost ranged up to $30,000.

The evolution of the "mobile luxury" concept of camping made necessary rapid change in campground facilities. Practically all recreational vehicles—except some of the camping trailers—have electric power and lights; gas or electric stoves, ovens, and refrigerators; temperature-control systems; and bathroom facilities including showers and sewage outlets or holding tanks.

In the past, most campgrounds supplied only well-drained campsites, a central water supply, and rudimentary sanitary facilities. Now, public and private campgrounds are having to consider providing water, electric, and sewage outlets for individual campsites. Many are also answering a demand for laundry facilities, recreation halls, hard-surfaced roads, and sewage-dumping stations.

It was estimated that camping contributed more than $1 billion to the U.S. economy in 1969. The automotive, appliance, and furniture industries were among those to profit, and publishers offered an increasing number of campground directories, how-to-do-it books, and camping magazines.

Youth Camps Change

Organized youth camping also continued to grow. In 1969 an estimated 12,000 resident and day camps served some 7 million children. In increasing number, camps changed to meet the demands of modern youth. More professional instructors and coaches, skilled technicians and craftsmen, and doctors and psychologists served on

INDIANA STATE DEPARTMENT OF NATURAL RESOURCES

This Indiana campground is typical of most of the camping facilities utilized in 1969. It provides accommodations for both tents and trailers. Some of the more luxurious campgrounds feature additional amenities, such as movie theaters and gymnasiums.

camp staffs as camps strove to provide "fun with a purpose."

Camp facilities took on a new look as tents gave way to cabins and elaborate dining lodges and as assembly and recreation buildings replaced open "rustic" buildings. Some camps offered gymnasiums and theater buildings. Camps for physically and mentally handicapped children grew in number, and government subsidies made camping available to more and more of the children of the poor. Some 1.35 million disadvantaged children were provided camping experiences in 1969.

The pressure of taxes, insurance costs, capital expenditures, and competition led many camp operators to winterize their facilities so they could be used for six or eight months instead of the customary eight weeks. Many camps rented their facilities to church, school, and family groups in the off-season. Co-ed camps grew in number, and many camps increased the number of campers by shortening camping periods. Some camps recruited counselors from abroad because many U.S. college students, faced with rising educational costs, could no longer afford to work for what camps could afford to pay. (*See in* CE: Camping; Tent.)

NORRIS, "VANCOUVER (B.C.) SUN," FROM BEN ROTH AGENCY

"Terrible news! We have to stay at air-conditioned motels, sleep on soft mattresses, make do with a regular stove and fridge . . ."

CANADA. The government of Canada's Prime Minister Pierre Elliott Trudeau came under strong attack during 1969 from opposition political parties as attempts were made to implement government programs, including a reform of parliamentary procedures. There was also considerable disagreement between the federal and the provincial governments. The conflict between French-speaking Canadians and the government remained unresolved, and new strains were placed on Canada's relations with France. Western nations were greatly concerned over Canada's announced cuts in its troop commitments to the North Atlantic Treaty Organization (NATO). Oil discoveries in Alaska prompted new interest in and concern about Canadian territory in the North and Northwest.

Action in Parliament

The first session of Parliament under the government of Prime Minister Trudeau ended in July with a session of name-calling between Trudeau and the Opposition's Conservative party and New Democratic party leaders. The Opposition called Trudeau a "dictator," and Trudeau in turn said his opponents were "nobodies" who did nothing but talk. The parliamentary friction resulted when the government forced the end of a filibuster blocking a bill aimed at reforming debate rules. The bill would allow a government schedule determining the length of time that a piece of legislation could be debated in Parliament. The bill was finally adopted. After Parliament reconvened in October the government presented an extensive tax-reform program that would restrict expense-account tax deductions and oil-depletion allowances and reduce taxes for persons in lower income brackets.

Two of the most important legislative acts passed by Parliament during the year were the Official Languages Act and an omnibus bill reforming the criminal code. The languages act declared both English and French the official languages of Canada and guaranteed that federal public services, administrative and judiciary, would be offered in both languages. Amendments to the criminal code included legalizing therapeutic abortions, legalizing homosexual acts between consenting adults, and restricting the use of firearms.

PAUL CONKLIN—PIX FROM PUBLIX

Trudeau (left) made a state visit to the United States in March and conferred with U.S. President Richard M. Nixon.

Quebec Revisited

French separatists in the province of Quebec continued to cause problems for the Canadian federal government. After France's President Charles de Gaulle resigned in April the Canadian government hoped for a better understanding with France about the French Canadians living in Quebec. This, however, was not the case.

In October Jean de Lipkowski, France's secretary of state for foreign affairs, paid a visit to Quebec. His visit brought back unpleasant memories of De Gaulle's visit in 1967 when the former French president called for a free Quebec. The Canadian government invited De Lipkowski to visit Ottawa, Ont., the capital of Canada, but De Lipkowski refused. This brought an angry reaction from Prime Minister Trudeau and other officials who felt the federal government had been snubbed.

The French official was visiting Quebec under the provisions of a 1965 agreement between Canada and France, which stated that individual Canadian provinces may have relations with France on matters of culture and education. De Lipkowski further infuriated the federal government by publicly interpreting the agreement and also the Canadian constitution. He contended that the constitution allowed Quebec to have direct relations with France, independent of the Canadian government. Trudeau countered that only Canada could interpret its own basic law and warned that he might denounce the 1965 agreement if such incidents continued.

In reply to the accusations De Lipkowski said that it was not unusual for a French official to visit Quebec without visiting Ottawa. He also stated that Gaullist policies toward Canada remained unchanged under President Georges Pompidou.

Late in October thousands of students staged a mass protest rally at the provincial Parliament buildings in Quebec, Que. The students were protesting a bill that would continue the bilingual system in Quebec's schools. The demonstrators wanted only the French language to be taught.

The city administration of Montreal, Que., charged that many members of the Company of Young Canadians—similar to the U.S. Volunteers in Service to America—were French separatists and had engaged in terrorist activities. They were accused of taking part in the looting and rioting that occurred in Montreal during a 20-hour police strike in October. (*See* Canadian Provinces.)

The Montreal administration called for an investigation and asked that federal funds be withheld from the Company of Young Canadians. Prime Minister Trudeau defended the young volunteers but also ordered an investigation by Parliament.

International Relations

Canada's relationship to NATO was in question during the early part of the year. In January Prime Minister Trudeau said there was a possibility that Canada would withdraw from NATO. After reviewing Canada's foreign policy the government announced in April that Canada would remain a NATO member but would begin in 1970 to reduce Canadian forces in Europe. The West German government was not pleased with the announcement.

The U.S. government tried to dissuade Canada from the plan, but Canadian officials said the troop-withdrawal decision was nonnegotiable. The Canadians planned to withdraw three Air Force Starfighter squadrons and almost half of their troops by 1972. This would leave 5,000 Canadian soldiers in Europe. Canada also announced it would give up its nuclear role in Europe. (*See* Europe.)

The NATO troop reduction was part of Canada's

Buses burn at the Murray Hill Limousine Service garage in Montreal, Que., while firemen and policemen are on strike. Mobs roamed the city throughout the 20-hour strike on October 7 and 8. Troops (below) were called in to restore order during the strike.

ABOVE: "MONTREAL (QUE.) GAZETTE." BELOW: "MONTREAL STAR"

plan to hold defense spending at its 1969 level of about $1.8 billion a year. The Canadians planned to reduce their entire Armed Forces from 98,000 to between 80,000 and 85,000 men over a three-year period.

During the year Canada moved toward establishing diplomatic relations with Communist China. Secret talks began in February between Canadian and Chinese officials in Stockholm, Sweden. Before the talks began, Trudeau stated that Canada would not sever diplomatic relations with the Nationalist Chinese on Taiwan, as the Communist Chinese insisted. During the year, however, the Canadian government reversed its position, saying that Canada would pursue a "one-China" policy—recognizing only Communist China—if an agreement could be reached between Canada and the Communist Chinese. Negotiations were complicated by the Communist Chinese demand that its territorial claim to the island of Taiwan be endorsed by the Canadian government.

The Soviet Union's Foreign Minister Andrei A. Gromyko visited Canada in the fall. Talks between Gromyko and Canadian External Affairs Minister Mitchell Sharp centered on scientific and cultural exchanges and on the problem of the nations to be included in a European security conference. The issues of the 1968 Soviet-led invasion of Czechoslovakia and Canada's possible recognition of Communist China created the only tense moments in the talks. At the end of his visit Gromyko predicted the growth of "good-neighbor" relations between Canada and the Soviet Union. Canada also established diplomatic relations with the Vatican.

The planned U.S. antimissile system touched off a controversy in Canada when it was reported that the United States, in the event of an attack by China or the Soviet Union, would fire antimissile missiles over Canada. Prime Minister Trudeau met with U.S. President Richard M. Nixon at Washington, D.C., in March to discuss the missile problem and North American defense. Following the conference Trudeau affirmed that Canada would pursue policies that were friendly toward, but independent of, the United States. He stated that Canada was extremely sensitive to the strength of the United States and compared Canada's geographical proximity to the United States to "sleeping with an elephant." Canadian-U.S. relations underwent some strain as a result of Canada's new policies toward NATO and toward China.

YARDLEY JONES, "TORONTO (ONT.) TELEGRAM," FROM BEN ROTH AGENCY

"Tell 'em the one about Trudeau denying there's a housing crisis . . ."

At the disarmament conference in Geneva, Switzerland, the Canadian representative proposed a ban, not only on nuclear weapons, but also on all undersea military installations with offensive capabilities. The Canadians did, however, favor limited defensive installations. (*See* Disarmament.)

Way Up North

The discovery of oil deposits in Alaska created new interest in Canada's Arctic territories, with possible repercussions in international politics as well as in the Canadian economy. The economic implications of Prime Minister Trudeau's stated policy on Northern sovereignty were as great as the political ones. The way the oil from the Alaska fields would be transported was of prime concern to the Canadian government. The Canadians hoped that the oil would be piped through Canada to markets in the United States.

Fears for Canada's Northern sovereignty were heightened when Trudeau told the House of Commons during the year that Canada definitely owned the islands in the North American archipelago but that he was not certain about the status of the waters surrounding the islands. The U.S. position was that the Northwest Passage is an international waterway. A major event giving impetus to Canadian fears that U.S. interests would dominate the Northlands was the successful voyage of the huge oil

This 900-seat theater is part of the complex making up the National Arts Centre, which opened in Ottawa, Ont., on May 31. Among the stars to appear there during the summer were Harry Belafonte, Juliette Greco, Duke Ellington, and Count Basie.

CHARLES MITCHELL—CANADIAN PRESS

tanker SS *Manhattan* through the Northwest Passage in 1969. (*See* Ships and Shipping.)

The problem of the pollution of Arctic waters by shipping operations was underscored when a ship and the two barges it was towing were crushed by ice. The barges were carrying 400,000 gallons of oil. Some Canadian officials saw the incident as one more reason why Canada should have control of shipping in the Arctic.

The Canadian government came under renewed pressure during the year from economic nationalist groups to curb the amount of U.S. investments in Canada. The government studied ways to encourage Canadian development of new Arctic oil fields. Telesat, Canada's planned communications satellite, was to send 12 hours of televised programs a day to remote Northern areas by 1972. The government hoped this would aid in attracting more Canadian settlers to the Arctic. (*See also* Canadian Economy; Canadian Provinces; Trudeau. *See in* CE: Canada.)

CABINET

The Cabinet of Canada's Prime Minister Trudeau stayed almost entirely intact throughout 1969. There were a few changes when individual ministries were reorganized as part of Trudeau's plan for government reform. The one important loss from the Cabinet in 1969 was Paul T. Hellyer, minister of transport, who resigned on April 24.

When the new Trudeau Cabinet was formed in 1968 Hellyer was given the responsibility for developing a housing policy while holding the transport portfolio. Hellyer was the chairman of a task force on housing problems that toured Canada for three months and then recommended a series of sweeping changes in the federal government's role in the housing area. When these proposals were not approved after two months' consideration by the Cabinet Hellyer decided to resign.

Perhaps more important than the specific housing issue was Hellyer's feeling toward the Trudeau government's basic theory of federalism. Hellyer charged that the prime minister was letting the power of the federal government slip away in discussions with the Canadian provincial governments about reform of Canada's constitution. He claimed that Trudeau's approach to federalism was "a theory of ten essentially autonomous provinces held together by the string of a fairly weak federal government. . . ." Trudeau replied that his approach was supported by the nation. Hellyer was replaced by Donald Campbell Jamieson.

Opposition leader Robert L. Stanfield disagreed sharply with Prime Minister Trudeau's assertion that Canada had no serious housing shortage.

CHARLES MITCHELL—CANADIAN PRESS

THE CANADIAN CABINET

Members of the Canadian Cabinet at the close of 1969, listed in order of precedence, were these:

Prime Minister. . . Rt. Hon. Pierre Elliott Trudeau
Leader of the Government in the Senate. . . . . Hon. Paul Joseph James Martin
Secretary of State for External Affairs. . . . . Hon. Mitchell Sharp
Solicitor General of Canada. . . . . . Hon. George James McIlraith
Minister of Public Works. . . . . Hon. Arthur Laing
Minister of Manpower and Immigration. . . Hon. Allan Joseph MacEachen
President of the Treasury Board. . . . . Hon. Charles Mills Drury
Minister of Finance and Receiver General. . . . Hon. Edgar John Benson
Minister of National Defense. . Hon. Léo Alphonse Joseph Cadieux
Minister of Industry, Trade, and Commerce. . . . Hon. Jean-Luc Pépin
Minister of Regional Economic Expansion. . . . Hon. Jean Marchand
Minister of Energy, Mines, and Resources. . . . . . Hon. John James Greene
Minister of National Revenue. . Hon. Joseph Julien Jean-Pierre Côté
Minister of Justice and Attorney General of Canada. . Hon. John Napier Turner
Minister of Indian Affairs and Northern Development. . . . . . . Hon. J. J. Jean Chrétien
Minister of Labor. . Hon. Bryce Stuart Mackasey
President of the Queen's Privy Council for Canada. . . . Hon. Donald Stovel Macdonald
Minister of National Health and Welfare. . . . Hon. John Carr Munro
Secretary of State of Canada. . . . . Hon. Gérard Pelletier
Minister of Fisheries and Forestry. . . . . Hon. Jack Davis
Minister of Agriculture . . . . . . Hon. Horace Andrew Olson
Minister of Veterans Affairs. . . . . . . Hon. Jean-Eudes Dubé
Minister of Consumer and Corporate Affairs. . . . . Hon. Stanley Ronald Basford
Minister of Transport. . . . Hon. Donald Campbell Jamieson
Minister of Communications. . . Hon. Eric William Kierans
Minister Without Portfolio. . . . . Hon. Robert Knight Andras
Minister of Supply and Services. . . Hon. James Armstrong Richardson
Ministers Without Portfolio
Hon. Otto Emil Lang
Hon. Herb Gray
Hon. Robert D. G. Stanbury

"THE GLOBE AND MAIL," TORONTO, ONT.

Secretary of State for External Affairs Mitchell Sharp (right) and Gordon Hawkins, director of the Canadian Institute on International Affairs, were among the leaders who met to discuss Canada's Latin American policies.

The new Ministry of Regional Economic Expansion was created during the year to stimulate economic activity in depressed regions and to work for a more uniform level of incomes throughout Canada. The new ministry was headed by Jean Marchand. The former ministries of forestry and of fisheries were combined into one department, as were the ministries of trade and commerce and of industry. A new department of communications was set up under Eric Kierans.

CANADIAN ECONOMY. During 1969 Canada's economy felt the impact of federal and provincial measures designed to curb an increasingly entrenched inflationary trend. Restrictive monetary and fiscal policies were employed to inhibit the growth of disposable income and to hold consumer spending down. However, by year-end the use of these measures had become a source of controversy. The independent Economic Council of Canada warned in its annual report that such strong economic restraints might precipitate a depression. The council placed greater blame on the inflationary pressures generated by the U.S. economy than on those originating in Canada.

Although the nation's gross national product was expected to increase by at least 9% over the 1968 level of $67.4 billion, inflation was expected to hold the real growth rate to 5%. Employment, foreign trade, industrial production, and retail sales began to falter during the second quarter, initiating a downward trend that was expected to continue.

Personal incomes remained buoyant, partly as a result of wage settlements that outpaced productivity gains by a wide margin. However, when employers began to exert firmer resistance to wage increases, a number of strikes were precipitated. British Columbia was plagued by tie-ups in its telephone service, oil refineries, and supermarkets, while long strikes occurred in Ontario's nickel, iron-ore, and steel industries. Average hourly earnings, which were held in check by the government, rose about 7% above their 1968 level.

The extension of the income surtax levied by the federal government siphoned off some of the extra income, allowing disposable income to rise only modestly. Federal taxes were calculated to yield $12 billion during the 1969–70 fiscal year, thus converting the budgetary deficit of 1968 into an anticipated $250-million surplus.

Controls exerted in the public sector were reinforced by tightened monetary policies that drove interest rates skyward. The Bank of Canada reined in the growth of the commercial banking system's assets by raising its discount rate (the rate at which it lends money to other banks) to a record 8% in July. Mortgage rates ranged from 9% to 11.5% but were accepted by borrowers, apparently in the expectation that housing costs would be even higher in the future.

Canada's wheat farmers were among those hardest hit by the shortage of cash in 1969. With $65 million in credit from 1968 still outstanding, the farmers began the autumn harvest with a carryover of 850 million bushels and an anticipated crop of over 675 million bushels. The glutted wheat market, which had forced prices down to cut-rate levels, was expected to result in slow export sales and increasing debt levels for farmers in the Prairie Provinces.

Reduced wheat sales were an important factor in suppressing the growth of total exports. Canada's projected export growth, however, was still at 10%, due to the exceptional sale of motor vehicles and parts, lumber, wood pulp, and crude petroleum. The United States was Canada's best customer in 1969, accounting for most of the export increases and about 70% of the total foreign sales.

At the end of the second quarter, Canada showed a scant $5-million foreign-trade deficit. The balance of trade was down sharply from a $300-million surplus during the same period in 1968, when tourism and trade were at record highs. Capital inflows from the United States helped offset the deficit somewhat, and the Canadian dollar held up strongly on international exchange markets. (*See also* Canada; Canadian Provinces.)

CANADIAN PROVINCES. Marked differences of interest among the provinces became increasingly apparent as Canada pursued its constitutional reform in 1969. New constitutional powers demanded by Quebec and Ontario would be of little use to the smaller, relatively poor provinces of the Atlantic region. At a closed conference of government leaders early in the year, premiers of

"TORONTO (ONT.) STAR"

Indian militants from St. Regis reserve near Cornwall, Ont., picket in Toronto, Ont., after walking out of a January meeting between Indian groups and Canada's federal government.

these "have-not" provinces spoke out against reforms that would sap the strength of the federal government to control the Canadian economy and to redistribute income.

An example of the difficulties came into focus in the debate over federal spending power and its use in launching a countrywide program of prepaid medical care. The medicare programs, though constitutionally outside federal jurisdiction, in practice must meet federal standards imposed when the provinces accept federal money—which pays about half the cost. When the federal government launched its medicare program in 1969, some provinces objected that they were being taxed whether or not they implemented the program. However, by the end of the year most provinces had joined or expected to participate in the plan. Although New Brunswick voted to accept the program, it had neither the funds nor the facilities to put medicare into action.

While the federal government was firmly committed to the medical insurance, Prime Minister Pierre Elliott Trudeau promised there would be no more "medicares," and the provinces were given a modified veto over future initiatives of this kind. The federal government, on its part, gave ground to the provinces on some major constitutional issues. Some progress was made in federal-provincial harmony when there was a general agreement to promote French-English bilingualism in the public service.

Quebec

Conditions in predominantly French-speaking Quebec demonstrated the cultural aspects of Canada's constitutional problems. Traditionally Quebec has been scrupulously fair to its English-speaking minorities. In 1969, Italian immigrant families in the St. Léonard section of Montreal fought with French-speaking residents over a decision to deny English to the immigrants' children.

Meanwhile, there was growing political and popular support of Quebec nationalism and continued fear that the province would eventually separate from Canada. During the year the province signed an agreement with France for a satellite study project and another with Gabon for a small exchange of teachers.

On the other hand, René Lévesque, the political leader for the separatists, made no attempt to test his party's strength in by-elections for provincial legislative seats. Jean-Jacques Bertrand, head of the Union Nationale party, reinforced his position by defeating separatist-inclined Jean-Guy Cardinal in a June leadership election.

In October the Canadian army was called to Montreal when looting, rioting, and burning occurred during a 20-hour strike by city policemen and firemen. The men, who were striking for higher pay, returned to work after the provincial legislature ordered them back under threat of fines and imprisonment. There were 3,700 policemen and 2,400 firemen in the city. In other legislative action divorce was legalized, and Indians in Quebec were given provincial voting rights for the first time in 1969.

Ontario

Ontario continued to lead Canada in new industry, new jobs, and population growth. Inflation was a major problem to the province, spurred by a 15.5% capital-investment growth at a time of almost full employment. The government cut its usual budget increase of 20% to 7.5% for the fiscal year and levied tax increases on industry.

Toronto suffered a near crisis in housing as the average cost of homes rose from $26,000 to $30,000 in a little over a year. In September Ontario opened the $30-million Science Center in Toronto.

Atlantic Provinces

The creation of a new federal department of regional economic expansion brought hope of correcting the chronic income and employment lags in the Atlantic Provinces in 1969. Under a plan to consolidate and coordinate development in the Atlantic region, eastern Quebec, and part of Manitoba, grants of up to $12 million were made available to industries being established in slow-growth areas.

Tax increases brought bitter protests in New Brunswick. Premier Louis J. Robichaud was burned in effigy at a demonstration in the university town of Sackville. The budget put a 10% surtax on incomes, increased sales taxes from 6% to 8%, and boosted the gasoline, cigarette, and alcoholic-beverage taxes. In spite of these measures the provincial debt rose to almost $400,000.

Nova Scotia surged ahead of its neighbors. A French tire company announced plans for two plants in the province. In the Canso Strait area a $250-million development was under way incorporating construction or expansion of electronics and pulp-mill facilities, a thermal plant, a heavy-water plant, oil refining, a deepwater port, and a petrochemical industry. At Canso itself plans were under way to build the world's first commercial plant to produce high-purity fish protein.

Political and financial problems plagued Newfoundland in 1969. Premier Joseph Smallwood, who in 1968 announced his resignation for 1969, changed his mind during the year and late in 1969 was contesting the leadership convention originally set up to pick his successor. Per-capita debt in the province rose to $1,297, the highest in Canada, and the government found it difficult to meet capital requirements. A $25-million bond issue attempted in the United States had to be withdrawn.

Prince Edward Island signed a joint 15-year plan with the federal government in 1969. It called for $725 million to be spent to aid agriculture, extend

"It is my duty to inform you that anything you say may be used against you.
Il est de mon devoir de vous informer que tout ce que vous dites pourrait être . . ."

credit to business, develop tourism, and improve provincial administration.

Prairie Provinces

A world wheat glut posed critical problems for the agricultural communities in Manitoba, Saskatchewan, and Alberta. Exports fell and sales were made at cut-rate prices. Farmers, left short of cash, cut purchases of farm equipment and consumer goods. Hardest hit was Saskatchewan, which normally produces nearly two thirds of the nation's wheat crop. Bankruptcies in retail stores increased, and some hotels were in financial difficulty. In addition, mining operations in both potash and uranium were reduced due to a world surplus of these metals.

Manitoba acquired the first Socialist head of government in North America since 1946, when the New Democratic party (NDP) scored a decisive victory over the incumbent Progressive Conservatives. Ed Schreyer became the new premier after the NDP won 28 of 57 seats in the provincial legislature in a June election. Schreyer's platform included an 88% cut in medicare premiums financed by sharp income-tax increases, a reduction of the voting age from 21 to 18, and a consumer protection program. The NDP leader promised to keep socialism out of big business and took the key portfolios of dominion-provincial relations and of industry and commerce into his own cabinet.

In September the only commercial tantalum mine and mill in North America was opened at Bernic Lake. The province also obtained a license to dam and divert the Churchill River.

After directing Alberta's affairs for 25 years, E. C. Manning retired in December 1968 as premier of the province's Social Credit government. He was succeeded by Harry Strom, who inherited a

CHARLES MITCHELL—CANADIAN PRESS

Alex Campbell, premier of Prince Edward Island, talks with reporters as he arrives for the federal-provincial conference in Ottawa, Ont., in June. He expressed confidence in the talks.

government and provincial economy as strong as any in Canada. Alberta's wheat acreage is only one third that of the Saskatchewan acreage, with farming typically split between grains and livestock. One quarter of the province's revenues comes from the sale of petroleum and natural-gas leases and reservations. In 1969, coal producers landed new long-term contracts for sales to Japan, and work began on several pulp mills. An agreement was made with Calgary Power Ltd. for the construction of a $30-million dam in the North Saskatchewan River. Work was to begin in 1970.

British Columbia

In an August election W. A. C. Bennett, Social Credit premier, scored his seventh consecutive triumph in the face of predictions that the NDP, led by Tom Berger, would bring down his aging government. Bennett captured 39 of 55 seats, while Berger was defeated in his own district and resigned the party leadership.

Recoveries in the pulp and paper industries and increased shipments of copper and zinc boosted British Columbia's economy in 1969. At one time labor troubles in the telephone service, oil refineries, and supermarkets left 10,500 persons out of work.

Bennett pursued a tougher line than any other premier with escalating university costs and faced another year of extreme discontent at the University of British Columbia, at Vancouver, and at Simon Fraser University, at Burnaby. At Simon Fraser, the problem of strict limits on government grants was coupled with internal strife as some faculty members lined up with extremist students to demand influence in university decisions.

Northwest Territories

A record $40-million budget was set forth by Northwest Territories in 1969. Most of the money was allocated for education, public works, and certain public welfare programs shared with the federal government.

Provisions were made for setting up the 1970 Arctic Winter Games to be held as part of the Territories' 100th anniversary. The Territories were established on July 15, 1870.

Yukon Territory

The Yukon Territory, in its opening legislative session in 1969, predicted continued economic improvement due to the vast new Alaskan oil explorations. (*See* Arctic; Ships and Shipping.)

In April the Territory created a new municipal-affairs department. In 1969 for the first time television coverage of certain territorial proceedings was permitted. (*See also* Canada; Canadian Economy; Trudeau.)

CANADIAN PRESS

A boatload of children is pulled across the swollen Qu'Appelle River in Saskatchewan after spring rains and thawing created flood conditions in the province in April.

CARTOONS. Did situations in newspaper cartoon strips depict plausible events? Not usually, said young panelists at an October 1969 meeting of the Newspaper Comics Council, Inc., in New York City. Numerous examples of a generation gap in newspaper comics were cited. One charge was against stereotyped treatment of establishment figures, such as doctors, policemen, and the military. Their actions were unswervingly correct. Also, in the view of the teen-aged critics, the clean-cut, college-hero type in the cartoons was always treated favorably, while the hippie was shown in a scornful way. Cartoonists in the panel said they were not political analysts but creators of escapist fare, designed to give readers short relief from real problems. Although the relevance of comics was in

OLIPHANT, COURTESY OF LOS ANGELES TIMES SYNDICATE

dispute, surveys showed that 80% of U.S. teen-agers read them.

Judging from the number of cartoons hanging in the White House study, it seemed that U.S. President Richard M. Nixon had a liking for them. Members of the American Association of American Editorial Cartoonists noted the prominent display of political caricatures in Nixon's office in an October visit, when they presented him with a leather-bound volume of original cartoons.

Several newspapers were curious to see how the public would respond to a cartoon contest. After asking readers to sketch "Mungs"—cartoon creatures improvised from triangles—the *Long Island Press* received 105,000 cartoons within two weeks. The *Chicago Daily News* initiated the contest when "Mungs" were discovered at the Great Lakes Naval Training Center, near Chicago, Ill. The overwhelming response to the contests brought to light a hitherto undiscovered pool of secret cartoonists.

A new cartoon called "Versus" appeared in some King Features Syndicate newspapers late in the year. Drawn by New York City advertising man Jack Wohl, "Versus" featured an "Everyman" figure called Arthur, who battled for survival in a seemingly hostile world. (*See* Newspapers.)

LE PELLEY IN "THE CHRISTIAN SCIENCE MONITOR" © TCSPS

"My parents tell me you're beautiful."

BUCK BROWN, COURTESY OF "TUESDAY" MAGAZINE

"Say, baby, what's happening?"

The American Stock Exchange commissioned a 24-page cartoon book to tell the story of stocks and bonds. It hoped the book would make potential stock buyers of youthful readers.

Saturday-morning cartoons on television had a large audience in 1969. Because of the size, advertisers were spending about $50 million to reach the tots-to-teen-agers who watched TV funnies.

CENTRAL AFRICAN REPUBLIC. In 1969 an attempted coup d'etat, the second in the history of President Jean-Bedel Bokassa's Central African Republic government, was thwarted, and the minister of health was executed for his role in the coup. Shot by a firing squad on April 12 was Lieut. Col. Alexandre Banza, a minister since Bokassa's military takeover in 1966. Banza was also charged with plotting the president's assassination. In February Bokassa reorganized his cabinet, adding two ministries of state and two secretaries of state. The president retained the portfolios of defense, information, and the interior.

The republic signed its first trade agreement with Sudan in 1969. Foreign loans were received for a road project, for the construction of the Nola river port, and for the development of a wood-transport fleet on the Sangha River. A fish farm was opened at Ouandjia and a cotton ginnery at Bambari. Construction was begun on a uranium-processing plant for the development of deposits in the Bakouma region. (*See in* CE: Central African Republic.)

CEYLON. In 1969 Ceylon completed 21 years of independence with an improving record of political stability, a greater degree of national unity, and an encouraging economic situation. Prime Minister Dudley Senanayake said it was Ceylon's good fortune that freedom had been preserved intact. However, no democratic system was safe, he said, without economic stability, and this was possible only with proper development. In Ceylon, where 70% of the people worked on the land, agricultural development had to come first, and the prime minister drew attention to the outstanding success of the national campaign for increased production of homegrown food.

In fact, economic growth in 1968 reached the high rate of 8.3%, compared with 4.2% the preceding year. The increase in rice production, in particular, was impressive, and in 1969 the harvest was expected to yield 71 million bushels. The finance minister, U. B. Wanninayake, also drew attention to the steady increase in the output of the new industrial corporations, which rose from a value of $11.8 million in 1965 to $44 million in 1968. Private industrial production had also gone ahead and the growth of investment in construction reached a rate of 27% for 1968.

Ceylon's largest hydroelectric power station, with a capacity of 75 megawatts, required to meet the increased demand for electricity for industrial expansion, was opened at Polpitiya in May. The country's first oil refinery went into production in July. (*See in* CE: Ceylon.)

CHAD. President François Tombalbaye, re-elected for a second seven-year term on June 15, 1969, continued to confront the growing Arab guerrilla threat to his French-backed regime. In April he felt compelled to invoke his country's defense pact with France, calling for significant administrative and military aid when the rebellion became too difficult for his 4,000- to 5,000-strong army to handle.

In 1969 Chad's President François Tombalbaye once again called upon France to send troops to aid in coping with the growing Arab guerrilla threat to his regime.

KEYSTONE

The April troop reinforcements were sent by plane from Corsica to Fort-Lamy, the capital, where 800 men of the French Overseas Intervention Force were already based. The French soldiers, who in the beginning gave simple logistic assistance, became directly engaged in the maintenance of order in several districts, notably Borkou, Ennedi, Tibesti, Ouaddai, and Salamat.

By the end of the year more than 800 men of the French Foreign Legion (the 2d Overseas Parachute Regiment) were garrisoned at Fort-Lamy, Mongo, Fort-Archambault, and Abéché. In September Brig. Gen. Edouard Cortadellas replaced Brig. Gen. Michel Arnaud as special military representative of France in the service of President Tombalbaye, with orders to crush the rebels by April 1970. (*See also* Feature Article: "Africa Saves the Game"; Africa. *See in* CE: Chad.)

CHEMISTRY. A new form of an old and commonplace substance—water—captured the attention of chemists in 1969. The substance, variously called orthowater, anomalous water, polywater, and superwater, differs radically from ordinary water. Identification of the substance was announced in the mid-1960's by Boris Deryagin of the U.S.S.R. Academy of Sciences.

Properties and Preparation

Polywater—which will mix with ordinary water to some degree—has a freezing range below $-10°$ C., a density of up to 1.4 grams per milliliter, a viscosity several times that of ordinary water, and a refractive index of 1.44 (compared with ordinary water's 1.33). Using Deryagin's method of preparation (condensing the substance from ordinary water in capillaries one to ten microns in diameter) Western scientists have repeated and confirmed some of his observations. No one has been able, however, to make polywater in more than milligram quantities.

Some major U.S. investigators—Ellis R. Lippincott and Gerald L. Cessac of the University of Maryland and Robert R. Stromberg and Warren H. Grant of the National Bureau of Standards—believe that the polywater molecule may be a polymer of three-center O-H-O units, including 12-membered rings of alternating oxygen and hydrogen atoms. One reason for this suggested structure is the spectrochemical similarity between concentrated polywater and bifluoride ions.

If polywater could be made—or found in nature—in large amounts, scientists envisioned several possible uses. It might serve as a high-temperature lubricant, as feed water for steam engines, or as a control fluid in nuclear reactors.

Insulin Structure Revealed

Scientists at England's Oxford University, led by Nobel laureate Dorothy C. Hodgkin and Guy Dodson, determined the structure of the hormone insulin, used in the treatment of diabetes. Their results showed that insulin, the first protein hormone to be resolved, is a complex, multicomponent molecule. It contains two amino-acid chains (A and B). Chain A has 21 amino acids; chain B, 30. The chains are built up by several bonding means to form a hexameric (six-part) molecule. The molecule is a roughly triangular ring of three tilted, football-like dimers around two zinc atoms in the core.

The insulin taken by diabetics makes up for missing natural insulin, which controls the glucose level in the blood. Exactly how this control is effected is not known, but the mechanism is probably related to the molecule's spatial arrangement. Thus the determination of insulin's configuration—made with the aid of tens of thousands of X-ray measurements—represents a major advance in the long-term effort to understand diabetes.

A technician, clad in protective garb, checks over a batch of the first vaccine produced for immunization against German measles. The vaccine, developed by a U.S. drug firm, became available in 1969.

WIDE WORLD

Elsewhere in Chemistry

Gerald M. Edelman and co-workers at The Rockefeller University in New York City discovered the structure of gamma globulin, a protein antibody that defends the body against disease. The molecule was found to consist of 19,996 atoms in 1,320 amino-acid units.

Two independent teams of chemists in 1969 achieved the first total synthesis of an enzyme (*see* Biology). Scientists throughout the world eagerly awaited the results of analysis of lunar material gathered by Apollo astronauts (*see* Space Exploration). (*See in* CE: Chemistry.)

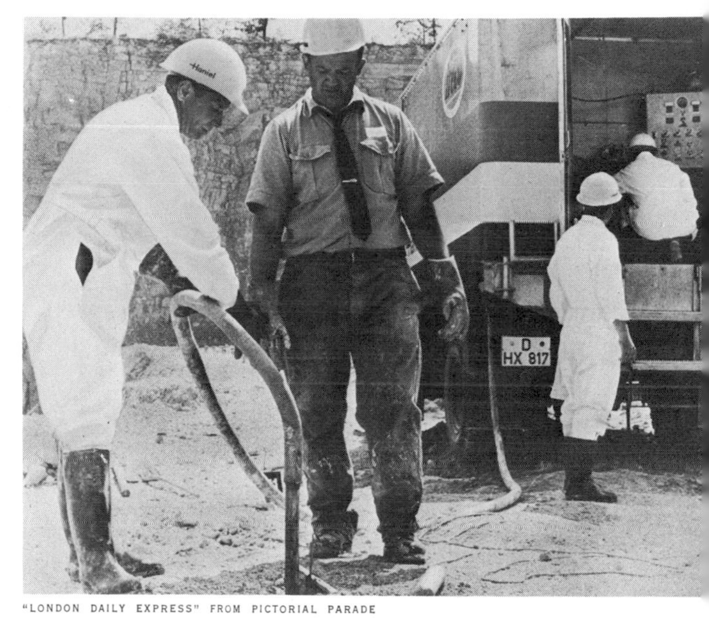

"LONDON DAILY EXPRESS" FROM PICTORIAL PARADE

Engineers demonstrate a newly developed explosive, a gelatinous liquid. The explosive can be safely transported by truck and then quickly drained from the vehicle by hose into blasting holes.

CHESS. Two world chess crowns were at stake in 1969. The world championship among male chess devotees was taken by Boris Spassky, who defeated Tigran Petrosian, the reigning champion. By June 17 Spassky had amassed the $12\frac{1}{2}$ points necessary to unseat Petrosian. The match between the two Russians, which began in April, was played at a theater in Moscow, U.S.S.R. In August Nona Gaprindashvili kept her title as women's world chess champion by defeating Alla Kushnir, a fellow Russian. Miss Gaprindashvili showed great stamina under her opponent's attacks while amassing the eight points needed to retain the championship.

International chess tournaments of 1969 included a January event at Beverwijk, Netherlands, which ended in a tie between Mikhail Botvinnik, a former world champion, and Evfim Geller; the an-

CENTRAL PRESS FROM PICTORIAL PARADE

Vasili Smyslov of the U.S.S.R. (right) contemplates a move in his game with Jan Smejkal of Czechoslovakia during the Hastings (England) Christmas Congress in 1968. Smyslov won the tournament.

nual event at Málaga, Spain, which also ended in a tie between Pal Benko of the United States and Boris Ivkov of Yugoslavia; and the second Adolf Anderssen Memorial Tournament at Büsum, West Germany, won by Bent Larsen, the grand master from Denmark. Veteran U.S. grand master Sammy Reshevsky scored an outstanding win at Natanya, Israel, where he triumphed over the closest contender by two points.

The U.S. Open Chess Championship, held at Lincoln, Neb., in August, was won again by Benko. The rapid competition, or ten-second move, segment of this event was won by Robert Byrne of Indianapolis, Ind. The quick-move segment was termed the U.S. National Chess Tournament. Also in August, a record 129 youths participated in the U.S. Junior Open Chess Tournament, at Boston, Mass. Larry Day of Ottawa, Ont., beat the field in the hard-fought tourney without suffering one loss.

In the U.S. Armed Forces chess championship, a team of soldiers took the prize for the Army for the third consecutive year. The event was played in Washington, D.C. (*See in* CE: Chess.)

CHILE. For the first time in nearly four decades, a mutiny occurred in Chile's army in 1969. In October two regiments rebelled, allegedly in protest against low pay and inadequate equipment. Although the rebels claimed no political objectives, President Eduardo Frei Montalva claimed that the 24-hour revolt was, in fact, an attempted coup. Fourteen persons were wounded in an exchange of gunfire at Santiago, the capital, and in the end the army demands for the resignation of the defense minister and the army commander in chief were met.

Although Frei cannot succeed himself, the Christian Democrats, in power since 1964, faced a presidential election in 1970. Parliamentary elections in March brought the conservative National party from near oblivion to second place. The splitting of Chile's traditional political parties was virtually completed shortly afterward when both the Christian Democrats and the Radicals split, forming new left-leaning organizations.

Rains in May broke a 24-month drought, the longest and most severe in Chile's history. Inflation continued to threaten the economy; the rate of inflation accelerated beyond the 30% registered for 1968. Economic growth continued at about 4.5% and the balance of payments improved, due mainly to record prices for copper on the London (England) Metal Exchange. Two Anaconda Co. subsidiaries were bought.

A national television network was inaugurated in September. In 1969, with aid from France, work was begun on the first phase of a $300-million subway system in Santiago. (*See in* CE: Chile.)

A blast loosens ore in an open-pit copper mine, owned by U.S. mining interests, in Chuquicamata, Chile. In 1969 the Chilean government made major purchases of stock in a number of foreign-owned copper mines in order to "Chileanize" them.

COURTESY, THE ANACONDA CO.

CHINA, PEOPLE'S REPUBLIC OF.

The most significant internal event of 1969 in Communist China was the convocation in April of the long-postponed Ninth Congress of the Chinese Communist Party. The congress consummated the protracted "cultural revolution," directed against traditional and bureaucratic ideas and tendencies, bourgeois individualism, factionalism, and internal and external revisionism, as well as political opponents of Communist Party Politburo Chairman Mao Tse-tung. By consecrating a purge of the so-called revisionists who had "followed the capitalist road," the congress proclaimed the victory of Maoism and acclaimed Mao and Lin Piao, the vice-chairman and defense minister, as the supreme leaders. Nevertheless, the congress failed to solve the problem of internal struggle, as factionalism continued to hold up party rebuilding at the provincial level and factional fighting was reported in a number of provinces.

Toward the latter part of the year there was a notable reduction of Mao's personality cult in the official press, which began to emphasize the collective unity of the country's top leadership. This seemed to reflect a shifting or realignment of political forces, with Premier Chou En-lai taking a prominent role in public and foreign affairs. While Chinese propaganda continued with a policy that was equally antagonistic to the United States, capitalism, and Soviet revisionism, the government took a more flexible and pragmatic attitude in the conduct of foreign relations and agreed in early October to hold talks with the Soviet Union on the Chinese-Soviet border disputes, which had led to open hostilities.

Domestic Affairs

The main tasks of the Ninth Congress, which lasted from April 1 to 24, mostly in closed sessions, were to adopt a draft constitution, approve Lin's political report, and elect a new Central Committee. The congress was attended by 1,512 delegates (1,022 were at the Eighth Congress in 1956)—selected by consultation with the revolutionary committees and not by election of provincial and local party congresses as was done previously. The composition of the delegates to the congress reflected the composition and influence of the revolutionary committees of the 29 administrative areas.

The draft constitution was adopted without significant amendments. Lin's political report made at the opening meeting was not approved until April 14. The report proclaimed Mao's thought on an equal status with Marxism-Leninism as the basis for all the actions of the people of China, laid down the guidelines on foreign policy in broad terms, and emphasized the importance of unity under the guidance of Mao's thought in aiming toward the realization of world Communism by revolution.

At the first session of the new Central Committee on April 28, a 21-member Politburo and a Standing Committee of five members were elected.

AFP FROM PICTORIAL PARADE

Against a background of exploding fireworks, men and women of the Chinese army enthusiastically wave their little red books of 'Quotations from Chairman Mao Tse-tung' during a celebration of May Day, the Communist International Labor Day, in Peking, People's Republic of China.

AFP FROM PICTORIAL PARADE

A Chinese frontier guard addresses an anti-Soviet meeting held on Chenpao (or Damanskiy) Island in the Ussuri River, part of the disputed territory claimed by both China and the Soviet Union. The island was the scene of a fierce four-hour battle between Chinese and Soviet troops in March.

Chairman Mao and Lin, his designated successor, headed the list of names of the Standing Committee. The other three members were Chen Po-ta, Chou En-lai, and Kang Sheng.

The disappearance of the 75-year-old Chairman Mao from public view from May 19 to October 1 had caused a great deal of speculation and rumors about his health and capability. On October 1 Mao's appearance at T'ien-an Men Square in Peking, the capital, to preside over ceremonies marking the 20th anniversary of Communist rule in China attracted great attention, but Mao made no speech to mark the occasion. Compared with the 10th-anniversary celebration in 1959, the 20th-anniversary celebration appeared to be a muted affair. However, China heralded the occasion by setting off its first underground nuclear explosion on September 23 and its fourth three-megaton hydrogen bomb in the atmosphere in the Lop Nor area on September 29.

In the economic field, up-to-date statistics remained unavailable. The 1968 agricultural output was below the bumper-crop year of 1967. Grain production in 1967 was estimated at 190 million tons and that of 1968 at slightly less. In September 1969, official publications boasted that the year's wheat and barley harvest had been abundant and that as a result of the discovery of new deposits and the development of refining and production facilities, China was self-sufficient in oil.

Foreign Relations

The guidelines of foreign policy adopted by the Ninth Party Congress pointed in the following directions: the promotion of good relations among socialist countries friendly to China; the support of revolutionary movements of oppressed peoples; opposition to capitalist and "social" imperialism; and coexistence with friendly nonsocialist countries. In the implementation of these directives there was a definite change of attitude and style as evidenced by the restoring of diplomatic relations with nearly 20 countries by reappointment of Chinese ambassadors (all but one—in the United Arab Republic, or Egypt—of some 50 ambassadors were recalled during the cultural revolution); by the lifting of restrictions on travel of foreign diplomats in China; and by the releasing of British and other foreign correspondents under detention during the cultural revolution.

With the end of U.S. bombing of North Vietnam, China in 1969 withdrew a major portion of its worker-troops stationed in North Vietnam to maintain the railway link between the two countries. After the death of North Vietnam's President Ho Chi Minh and following the visit of that country's Premier Pham Van Dong to Peking in October, China reaffirmed its friendship with North Vietnam. China recognized the Viet Cong's new provisional revolutionary government in June and continued to give publicity to liberation struggles in Laos and Thailand.

On Nov. 26, 1968, China had made a surprise suggestion that the Sino-American ambassadorial talks be resumed in Warsaw, Poland, in February 1969 after the inauguration of U.S. President Richard M. Nixon. In January Liao Ho-shu, chief of the Chinese diplomatic mission at The Hague, Netherlands, defected to the United States. In a protest statement on February 6, which was delivered to the U.S. ambassador in Warsaw, China charged the U.S. government in collusion with the Netherlands government with engineering Liao's defection. On February 18 China canceled the ambassadorial talks scheduled for February 20. By December, however, the political climate had improved, and it appeared that the ambassadorial talks would be resumed in the near future.

While the Nixon Administration proposed no change of U.S. policy on the admission of China to the United Nations or on the defense of Taiwan, it gave indication that it was abandoning the old "cold war" policy of containment and isolation of China. In August U.S. regulations on travel to China were eased and American citizens abroad were permitted to buy up to $100 in Chinese products. In December the Nixon Administration further relaxed trade regulations with such measures as lifting the $100 ceiling and ending a ban on commercial transactions with China by foreign subsidiaries of U.S. companies. On various occasions Secretary of State William P. Rogers reiterated the willingness of the United States to ease international tensions and to improve relations with the Chinese government. In order to alleviate its own fear of two-front encirclement, China appeared to show interest in the U.S. overtures. (*See* Feature Article: "China and the United States: Distorted Images.")

Sino-Soviet Border Conflict

On March 2 fighting broke out at Chenpao (or Damanskiy) Island, an uninhabited islet on the Ussuri River that makes up a large portion of the Manchurian border between China and the Soviet Union; and each country charged the other with aggression. Mutually antagonistic demonstrations spread in both countries. The Soviet Embassy in Peking was reported under siege, and on March 7 in Moscow demonstrators smashed numerous windows of the Chinese Embassy. On March 15 a second major clash occurred at Chenpao Island, with casualties again on both sides. Following the Soviet Union's repeated suggestions for reopening border talks, China on May 12 accepted the Soviet proposal for a meeting of the joint Commission for Navigation on Boundary Rivers, which met in Khabarovsk, U.S.S.R., on June 18. It was not until August 8 that navigation talks were concluded with the signing of a protocol to improve the shipping situation on border rivers.

In May, incidents occurred on the border separating the Kazakh S.S.R. and Sinkiang-Uigur Autonomous Region, where a major oil field and Chinese nuclear installations are located. On June 10, Chinese and Soviet troops clashed at the Dzungarian Gates on the Sinkiang border. China charged that Soviet forces had intruded into Sinkiang, and the Soviet Union contended that its frontier guards had fired in self-defense.

On August 13 a new and bloody clash between Chinese and Soviet troops broke out on their central Asian border. China and the Soviet Union continued to trade charges and denunciations. The Chinese protest of August 19 claimed 429 border violations in June and July by the Soviet Union. In reply on September 10 the Soviets charged China with 488 deliberate frontier violations between June

Communist Party Politburo Chairman Mao Tse-tung (left) casts his vote for a new Central Committee during the Ninth Congress of the Chinese Communist Party, held in 1969. Waiting to cast their votes in hierarchic order are (left to right) Lin Piao, Chou En-lai, Chen Po-ta, Kang Sheng, and Chiang Ching (Mao's wife)—all leaders in the innermost policy-making circle around Chairman Mao.

AFP FROM PICTORIAL PARADE

and mid-August. It was believed that the final testament of Ho Chi Minh, calling for Communist unity, might have contributed to the dramatic 11th-hour meeting between Premiers Aleksei N. Kosygin and Chou En-lai to smooth the differences between their two countries.

On September 4 Chou flew to Hanoi, North Vietnam, to offer condolences on the death of President Ho but returned to Peking before Kosygin's arrival in Hanoi for the same purpose. However, on his way home from Ho's funeral, Kosygin made a special and unexpected stop in Peking on September 11 and held a long conference with Chou at the Peking airport. The press speculated that Kosygin had concretely proposed that the border issues be negotiated at the deputy-ministerial level and that each side drop its campaigns against the other and resume full Sino-Soviet diplomatic and economic relations. Subsequently, tensions between China and the Soviet Union were significantly eased, and on October 7 the Chinese government officially confirmed that China and the Soviet Union had agreed to hold talks in Peking. On October 18 the Soviet delegation of 30 persons, led by First Deputy Foreign Minister Vasili V. Kuznetsov, who served as the Soviet ambassador to China from 1953 to 1955, arrived in the Chinese capital. Chiao Kuan-hua, a deputy foreign minister and a right-hand aide to Chou, headed the Chinese delegation, and formal negotiations began on October 20.

In its statement of October 7 on negotiation of border issues, China accepted Sino-Soviet boundary treaties "imposed on China by czarist Russian imperialism" as the basis for an overall settlement of the boundary question and proposed that, in order to maintain the status quo of the border and avert armed conflicts, the armed forces of both sides should withdraw from all the disputed areas along the Sino-Soviet border. Furthermore, the Chinese statement, while recognizing the existence of an ideological gap and the "irreconcilable differences of principle between China and the Soviet Union," stressed that normal state relations between the two countries should be maintained. By mid-November there were still no official reports on the progress of the negotiations in Peking. (*See also* Communist Movement; International Relations; Union of Soviet Socialist Republics. *See in* CE: China, People's Republic of.)

CITIES AND URBAN AFFAIRS.

Contrasting with triumph in outer space, the cramped and explosive situation in cities throughout the United States showed in detail man's failure to deal with earthbound problems. Although in 1969 inner-city riots had decreased about 50% in number and severity from the 1968 total, the underlying causes of such disturbances were still very much in evidence. While travel to the moon became a reality, efficient garbage removal and effective air-pollution control appeared to be far in the future.

A follow-up study was made on the 1968 report of the President's National Advisory Commission on Civil Disorders that was headed by Otto Kerner, then governor of Illinois. The follow-up report, entitled 'One Year Later', was released in February 1969 and stated that most of the recommendations made in the "Kerner report" had not been put into effect. The conclusion drawn in 'One Year Later' was that the United States was one year closer to being split into two societies, one black and one white. The follow-up report also pointed out that since 1966 there had been a sharp increase in the number of whites leaving the cities and a slowing of the black migration from the rural South to Northern and Western cities. Ghettos had increased in area, and slums had sprung up in the suburbs. The report did state, however, that some improvements had been made, notably in better police techniques for controlling riots and in the hiring of hard-core unemployed persons.

COURTESY, CITY OF BOSTON

The street signs, part of an experimental information system in Boston, Mass., indicate to the passerby the intersection, the address numbers on the street, and the next major cross street.

Small-Town Troubles

Based on the relatively quiet urban situation in 1969, many U.S. officials believed the era of the big-city riot was over. There was a decrease in the number of disturbances involving large groups of people, but there was a marked increase in the number of incidents involving small bands of militants and the police. Teenage street gangs were a major cause for concern. The mainstream of urban violence shifted from major U.S. cities to smaller cities and towns. There were riots in such places as Kokomo, Ind.; Santa Ana, Calif.; and Middletown, Conn.

Most of the racial violence that occurred in cities during the year was sparked by disputes between minority groups and the police. In October three days of violence in Las Vegas, Nev., followed an incident between two black policemen and a black taxi driver. During the summer a Negro girl in Omaha, Neb., was shot and killed by a white policeman investigating a burglary. This resulted in several days of rioting in the city's ghetto. Similar violence erupted in Harrisburg, Pa., after a Negro woman was arrested for disorderly conduct.

In September rioting broke out on a large scale in the Puerto Rican section of Hartford, Conn., when youths pelted a fire station with rocks and bottles. Also in September there were disturbances in Camden, N.J., and Fort Lauderdale, Fla.

Severe racial trouble occurred in Cairo, Ill. Cairo's black citizens demanded more jobs and the disbanding of a white vigilante group known as the "White Hats." The vigilantes were armed and patrolled the streets in radio-equipped cars. Sniping incidents, fire bombings, and actual gun battles occurred in Cairo throughout the year. (*See also* Race Relations.)

Build, Don't Burn

Among the reasons offered for the comparatively quiet summer of 1969 were that police in major cities had become more efficient in dealing with the first signs of a disturbance and also that Negroes in the inner cities had developed a greater sense of community. Some observers felt that this sense of community among blacks, coupled with a growing white backlash, could result in a greater polarization of the two races. Nevertheless, the sentiment of most urban Negroes during 1969 was more toward building than toward burning.

The frustration and general discontent that underlay the great riots of previous years crystallized into specific goals and demands. Negroes concentrated on winning greater local control of schools, better job opportunities, and ownership of businesses. (*See also* Colleges and Universities.)

The slogan "Build, baby, build" symbolized attempts by Negroes to gain jobs in the construction industry. In Chicago, Ill.; Pittsburgh, Pa.; and Seattle, Wash., there were angry demonstrations

(*continued on page 186*)

A sign invites residents of a neighborhood in Chicago, Ill., to join in the cleanup of a vacant lot and build a "people's park" rather than allow the area, cleared of old buildings by Chicago's Department of Urban Renewal, to be used for an expensive private tennis club.

WIDE WORLD

Special Report: The Trash Crisis

by Gladwin Hill, National Correspondent,
Environment and Conservation, *The New York Times*

Just as much of our air in recent years has become supersaturated with contaminants, and waterways overloaded with pollutants, so have communities throughout the United States and elsewhere suddenly been confronted with "the third pollution." It is an increasingly formidable cascade of solid waste.

Solid waste includes garbage and other trash from homes, commercial refuse, industrial scrap, the rubbish from construction and demolition, agricultural wastes, and mining debris. Altogether, the total in the United States, according to the federal Bureau of Solid Waste Management, is 3.5 billion tons a year—17 tons for every person in the country.

Fortunately, the bulk of this vast mass of refuse —2 billion tons of agricultural wastes and one billion tons of mining debris—is widely dispersed outside cities. But that leaves some 350 million tons a year of urban wastes—more than a ton per person, roughly ten pounds per person per day.

It is axiomatic that material that goes into a community must eventually be removed or the community will be overwhelmed by debris. However, that axiom has been widely ignored until recently. Since prehistoric times, refuse traditionally has been disposed of by dumping it on the outskirts of communities, with the occasional supplement of burning.

New technology is needed to cope with the massive quantities of solid waste that plague U.S. cities. One recently developed process is that of compacting. The chunk below was once equal to a full can of garbage. The waste was compressed to $\frac{1}{20}$ of its original volume.
COURTESY, UNION CAMP CORP.

Suddenly this traditional system has become uncomfortably inadequate. Population in most communities has soared. The per-capita generation of refuse is twice what it was in the 1920's and is expected to double again within the next 20 years.

A significant part of the waste volume comes from packaged commodities, particularly prepared foods: packaging and containers now account for nearly 15% of the national waste load. Ubiquitous roadside litter is a distasteful witness to the annual use of, among other things, 60 billion cans and 30 billion bottles.

Meanwhile, affluence has virtually eliminated the old-time salvaging and reuse of materials. Junk men no longer course the streets crying, "Old rags! Bottles!" as they did in the early years of the century. The changed economics are reflected most conspicuously in the rash of derelict automobiles littering the countryside and city streets. Repair costs have risen so, and scrap metal values dropped, that people are just abandoning cars that might once have gone to salvage. Cities like New York, N.Y.; Philadelphia, Pa.; and Chicago, Ill., have to cope with as many as 30,000 abandoned cars a year—with removal costing up to $30 a car.

Room for disposing of refuse has dwindled literally to the vanishing point in many places. Expanding communities have impinged until the old "outskirts" are no longer there. Real estate is too valuable to be used for dumps, and the mounting problem of air pollution has made the old practice of casual burning intolerable. Los Angeles, Calif., where the smog problem first became acute, outlawed backyard incinerators, and even closed down its municipal incinerators, more than a decade ago.

The solid waste crisis in the United States is essentially economic—a sudden convergence, in mathematical terms, of three curves representing growing waste volume, scarcity of urban land, and rising haulage costs. A year's refuse from 10,000 people is enough to cover an acre of land seven feet deep.

There are only two things that can be done, ultimately, with refuse: burn it or bury it, either on land or in the ocean. Since even scientific burning leaves a residue of up to 30% of the original volume, there will always be material to be buried. The vast reaches of the ocean are a tempting repository, but they have two limitations: the ecological consequences of large-scale infusion of such substances into the ocean are not yet known,

Abandoned automobiles litter a deserted area under a bridge in New York City. Large U.S. cities have to cope with as many as 30,000 junked cars a year. Removal costs are as high as $30 a car.

UPI COMPIX

and the ocean would obviously be useful as a disposal area chiefly to coastal communities.

The growing problem of waste impelled the U.S. Congress in 1965 to pass the Solid Wastes Disposal Act. The law created the Bureau of Solid Waste Management in the U.S. Public Health Service and provided for both research financing and grants to states for waste management planning. Little information about the national waste picture was available. The bureau's first task was to mount a comprehensive survey. It was not scheduled to be completed until 1971.

Waste handling in 1969 cost the United States about $4.5 billion—over $20 per capita, a community expenditure exceeded only by outlays for education and highway construction. New York City, for instance, had 14,000 personnel in its Department of Sanitation, which is concerned largely with refuse removal. Its payroll was approximately $2 million a week; its annual budget reached more than $130 million.

About 80% of the collected waste in the United States, by weight, goes to dumps; about 15% is incinerated; only about 3% is salvaged. In 1969 there were about 12,000 dumps in the country and 300 community incinerators. A federal survey classified 94% of the dumps, and at least 70% of the incinerators, as "unacceptable" in terms of good sanitation.

The prospects seemed nil for diminishing waste volume at the source to a degree that would appreciably alleviate the problem. Someone said that "everything man touches eventually becomes waste." The nation's consumption of commodities is going to increase inexorably, and with it the amount of refuse.

The U.S. position in relation to the solid waste problem, at the close of 1969, could be summarized as one of dawning awareness, extensive research, and initial moves toward improvement. In addition to the national outlay of $4.5 billion a year for waste handling, the Bureau of Solid Waste Management estimated that expenditure of $835 million a year for five years would be needed to bring collection systems up to par, to improve and develop dump sites, and to replace inadequate incinerators.

A 1969 report of the California Department of Health said: "With but a few notable exceptions, solid waste management practices are unrealistic and clearly inadequate. The five basic deficiencies of the current systems are fragmented authority and lack of cooperation, inadequate planning, inadequate standards, poorly developed technology, and inadequate financing."

The ultimate resolution of these deficiencies, federal experts felt, would require, along with advanced technology, abandonment of the prevailing community-by-community pattern of waste disposal in favor of regional collaboration.

Boy Scouts load bags of discarded aluminum cans to be redeemed for half a cent each at a Reynolds Metals Co. scrap-aluminum plant. The company is sponsoring the experimental antilitter program.

COURTESY, REYNOLDS METALS CO.

(*continued from page 183*)
by militant blacks and by white construction workers alike. The Negroes charged that there was discrimination in the hiring practices of the construction industry and in the labor unions. (*See* Building Construction; Employment.)

Making Change

One of U.S. President Richard M. Nixon's first official acts after taking office in 1969 was to set up the Council for Urban Affairs and name Daniel Patrick Moynihan, a liberal Democrat, as its head. The purpose of the council was to aid in developing a national urban policy and to study existing poverty and urban programs, minority business enterprises, crime, and mass transportation.

Floyd H. Hyde, the mayor of Fresno, Calif., was appointed head of the model-cities program. The Nixon Administration indicated that model cities would have a high priority on its list of programs. In the fall, however, the Administration cut $215 million from the model-cities budget.

A shortage of money was the greatest problem facing urban improvement programs during the year. The mayors of ten major U.S. cities were in disagreement with Vice-President Spiro T. Agnew over the Nixon Administration's revenue-sharing plan. Agnew favored distributing federal funds to state governments that would in turn allot money to the cities. The mayors protested that many state legislatures were dominated by rural interests and feared that the cities would not receive sufficient funds. (*See* State Governments.)

Along with the revenue-sharing plan the Administration proposed a plan for simplifying the task of enrolling in federal job-training programs, a reform of the welfare system, and federal aid for public transportation. Many U.S. mayors felt the proposed funds were inadequate.

In May, George Romney, secretary of housing and urban development, announced a plan for increasing production of low-cost housing. Operation Breakthrough, as the plan was called, emphasized cooperation between local officials, labor unions, and construction companies in building inexpensive, prefabricated homes. (*See* Housing.)

The first project reflecting President Nixon's policy for black capitalism was announced in February. The federal government granted more than $7 million in loans for an industrial park in the Watts section of Los Angeles, Calif.

New emphasis was placed on city beautification during the year. The Department of Transportation commissioned a study for coordinating "street furniture"—lampposts, trash bins, street signs, telephone booths—in U.S. cities. The report, made in June, recommended that an intercity advisory team be set up to develop unified designs.

Police and firemen staged strikes and work slowdowns in several cities, demanding higher wages and better working conditions. In Gary, Ind., Mayor Richard G. Hatcher forced striking firemen to return to work by ordering arrests, suspensions, and demotions of those who refused to return to their jobs. (*See* Police.)

Politics and Pollution

Mayoral elections were held in many U.S. cities in 1969. The issue of "law and order" that had been so prominent during the 1968 presidential campaign was evident in many of the 1969 local campaigns. (*See* Political Parties.)

In Los Angeles incumbent Mayor Samuel W. Yorty won a third term by defeating Thomas Bradley, a black city councilman. In his campaign speeches Yorty warned that Bradley, if elected, would turn the city over to black militants and that many police officers would resign. Yorty

Youngsters play with a nylon "moonscape" stretched over a vest-pocket park in an East Harlem neighborhood in New York City. The simulated moonscape, made from a large piece of cloth, has holes for "craters" and raised sections for "mountains." At one end of the park is a brightly colored cardboard spacecraft. The cloth for the moonscape was donated to the city by its manufacturer, West Point-Pepperell, Inc.

"THE NEW YORK TIMES" FROM WIDE WORLD

was widely criticized for his campaign tactics.

A Minneapolis, Minn., detective, Charles Stenvig, won that city's mayoral election by conducting a campaign based on law and order, pledging to "take the handcuffs off the police." Crime was the greatest concern of voters in Detroit, Mich., where Wayne County Sheriff Roman S. Gribbs defeated County Auditor Richard H. Austin, a Negro, in the November mayoral election.

Sam H. Massell, Jr., was elected the first Jewish mayor of Atlanta, Ga., in October. Maynard Jackson, a Negro, was elected vice-mayor of Atlanta. Charles Evers, a Negro civil rights leader, became the mayor of Fayette, Miss. Negro Mayor Carl B. Stokes was reelected in Cleveland, Ohio.

Voters in the largest U.S. city, New York, reelected Mayor John V. Lindsay in November. Lindsay was opposed by City Controller Mario Procaccino and New York State Sen. John J. Marchi. (*See* Lindsay.)

An experiment in garbage disposal was undertaken in Boston, Mass., during the year. In the inner-city areas, studies were made on new types of home incinerators, individual garbage compactors, and a system of pneumatic tubes that removed garbage directly to disposal areas. (*See* Cities and Urban Affairs Special Report.)

In October a study of local efforts for pollution control revealed that of all U.S. cities only Los Angeles had an effective antipollution program. In 1969 Los Angeles budgeted $4.6 million for pollution control. Only $47 million was allotted by all the state and local governments in the United States for such programs. (*See also* Crime; Education; United States. *See in* CE: City; Municipal Government.)

COIN COLLECTING. Late in 1969 the standard 1970 edition of 'A Guide Book of United States Coins' reported that the U.S. coin market remained strong during the year as prices continued to climb. Common-date gold coins, commemorative coins, proof sets, and type sets in choice condition were in greatest demand.

Actions of the U.S. Treasury Department opened opportunities for U.S. collectors of gold coins. Under new rules announced by the department, gold coins minted before 1934 may be imported into the United States without a license, and gold pieces dated from 1934 to 1960, "if of sufficient numismatic interest," may be imported under license. Gold coins issued by the Bahamas, Bhutan, Tonga, and other governments were being reproduced on postage stamps for collectors unable to obtain the actual coins.

The melting of U.S. silver coins for their silver content was authorized. Under a plan recommended by the Joint Commission on the Coinage in 1968, it was announced that 2.9 million rare silver dollars held in U.S. Treasury vaults would be sold.

In 1969 the U.S. Congress considered legislation authorizing the striking of silverless half-dollars and of a dollar coin bearing the likeness of former President Dwight D. Eisenhower. Both houses approved the Eisenhower dollar in principle. The Senate, however, voted for a 40%-silver coin and for continuance of the 40%-silver half-dollar, while the House of Representatives favored silverless copper-and-nickel coins.

The new U.S. Mint at Philadelphia, Pa., was officially opened on August 14. Built at a cost of $39.4 million, it can produce 10,000 coins per minute. The opening of this fourth mint to be constructed in Philadelphia—the first was built in 1792—was memorialized in a bronze medal. Another new mint was that of Guatemala, with a production capacity of up to 300,000 coins per day.

U.S. mints struck a number of coins for foreign governments in the year. Among them were Can-

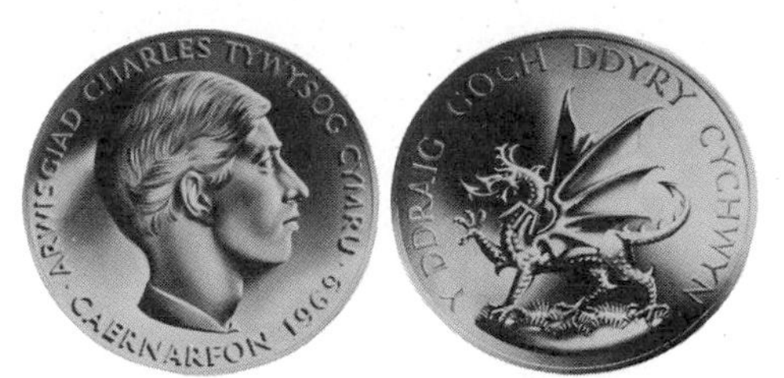

"LONDON DAILY EXPRESS" FROM PICTORIAL PARADE

To mark the investiture of Prince Charles as prince of Wales, the British mint issued a medal (above) with his portrait and the dragon, symbol of Wales.

The 1970 Canadian dollar (right) will depict the prairie crocus, Manitoba's floral emblem, to commemorate the centennial of the province's entry into the Canadian confederation.

AUTHENTICATED NEWS INTERNATIONAL

West Germany's mint issued a special coin honoring the XX Olympic Games, which were to be held in Munich in 1972.

ada, 10¢; Costa Rica, 1 colón, 50 centimos, and 5 centimos; El Salvador, 10 centavos and 1 centavo; Liberia, 25¢; Panama, 5 centesimos and proof coins and sets of 50, 25, 5, and 1 centesimos; and the Philippines, 50, 25, 10, 5, and 1 centavos.

Among new currency issues were Fiji bank notes in 20-, 10-, 2-, 1-, and .5-dollar denominations. Malawi's decimal currency was to be introduced in March 1971; the new unit, the kwacha, is divided into 100 tambolas. The new Argentine peso—to be released by Jan. 1, 1970—is equivalent to 100 of the existing *pesos monedas nacionales*. The Argentine bills will be in denominations of 100, 50, 20, 10, 5, and 1 pesos, with coins of 50, 20, 10, 5, 2, and 1 centavos. Jamaica adopted the dollar-decimal system of currency in September; the new dollar was worth ten shillings sterling, or $1.20, of the currency. Old-type Italian large-size 10,000-, 5,000-, and 1,000-lire notes ceased to be legal tender on June 30.

Although the United States maintained its policy of producing no commemorative coins, other nations continued to issue commemoratives of interest to collectors. A number of the coins—struck at the suggestion of the Food and Agriculture Organization of the United Nations—illustrated world progress in agriculture and food production. Among them were Uganda, five shillings (copper-nickel); Vatican City, eight denominations in aluminum, bronze, Ackmonital, and silver; and South Vietnam, 20 dong (nickel-clad steel). (*See also* Stamps. *See in* CE: Mint, U.S.; Money.)

COLLEGES AND UNIVERSITIES. Violence and student protest continued at the world's colleges and universities in 1969. In April there was police action at Harvard University, at Cambridge, Mass. This institution had long been thought of as a model of liberal attitudes, with its cultivation of good relations between students and senior staff. It had been among the first to deny academic credits for membership in the Reserve Officers Training Corps (ROTC), and its president, Nathan N. Pusey, had been a noted opponent of McCarthyism in the 1950's. Even so, demonstrators led by the militant Students for a Democratic Society (SDS) occupied the University Hall, demanding, among other things, an end to ROTC on campus as well as a reduction of rents in university-owned buildings. A force of 400 policemen cleared the hall, and nearly 200 arrests were made. As had happened elsewhere, the police intervention embittered some of the moderate students, though President Pusey declared that it had been necessary in the face of direct defiance of authority; and subsequently there was a strike of students in protest.

Programs in ROTC were also the targets of campus radicals at many other schools, including Yale University, at New Haven, Conn.; Stanford University, at Palo Alto, Calif.; Tulane University, at New Orleans, La.; and the University of Wisconsin, at Madison, Wis. The corps was established by the National Defense Act of 1916 and became a part of the academic program at 191 colleges and universities by 1919.

WIDE WORLD

Wooden crosses mark the campus of Harvard University in Cambridge, Mass., as part of a protest by university students against the Vietnam conflict.

In November demonstrations occurred at the Massachusetts Institute of Technology (MIT), in Cambridge; student demonstrators, some carrying Viet Cong flags, protested that school's work in weapon development for the U.S. military. The main object of the protesters' anger was the Instrumentation Laboratory, site of many notable scientific achievements.

While military affairs had been among the items of protest at Harvard and at MIT, observers elsewhere noted a swing from the Vietnam conflict to racism as the main issue in U.S. student disturbances. Racial troubles erupted at many campuses, with demands, in particular, for courses in black studies and for exclusively Negro facilities. In April black students brought rifles onto the campus at Cornell University, in Ithaca, N.Y., in an attempt to gain their objectives. Later in the year there was a dispute over the dismissal of Angela Davis, a black woman philosophy professor at the University of California, Los Angeles campus (UCLA), on the grounds that she was a member of the Communist party.

More courses in black studies were offered in U.S. institutions of higher learning in 1969, and Harvard announced in the fall that it had added 15 courses in that area to the curriculum. Black studies at Stanford, however, dwindled because of a lack of support.

The U.S. student troubles provoked much comment. In his annual report in July J. Edgar Hoover, director of the Federal Bureau of Investigation (FBI), noted that 225 of the country's institutions of higher learning had been "disrupted" in the preceding 12 months through sit-ins or violent and sometimes destructive disorders. On the subject of campus unrest he said, "Never before in our history has there been such a strong revolutionary Marxist movement of young people so eager to tear down established authority, while it is the immediate goal of the 'New Left' to gain complete control of our educational system. It is apparent that it hopes to lead a revolution ultimately designed to overthrow our system of government."

Hoover's report reflected much hardening of opinion against student disturbances. An opinion poll in California in the spring showed that 72% of that state's citizens were strongly in favor of expulsion for all students who challenged and defied the authorities. The poll also suggested that the biggest factor in the increasing popularity of California's Gov. Ronald Reagan was his firm handling of student riots. In February the governor had

ROBERT H. NEFF

Garbed as "war victims," members of SDS at the University of Connecticut, at Storrs, demonstrate against ROTC courses on campus and U.S. involvement in Vietnam.

WIDE WORLD

At an experimental "Coeducation Week" in February at Princeton University, Princeton, N.J., a visitor changes the sign on the bathroom door to suit the occasion. Princeton became coeducational in the fall.

declared a "state of extreme emergency" in and around the University of California, Berkeley, after student violence. He said that he would propose legislation to make it a criminal offense for anyone suspended from a state educational institution to enter it or any other without permission.

By contrast, a committee of inquiry into the troubles at Cornell criticized the university authorities for allowing lax discipline during the preceding two or three years. Concerning the tension between black and white students that led to some black students' arming themselves, the committee said that secrecy over a program for Negroes who were culturally disadvantaged led to misunderstanding and resentment.

U.S. President Richard M. Nixon made a number of statements about campus problems during the year. In a presidential statement on student unrest published in March, he condemned violence and intimidation, drew attention to the dangers to intellectual freedom, and declared that when the actions or judgments of the university community were influenced by violence or threats the community ceased to be a university. At the same time he deplored the depersonalization of education and called for more experiments in the university curriculum and more student involvement in the decision-making process.

A month later in an address to the U.S. Chamber of Commerce President Nixon strongly condemned student revolutionaries and said that the universities should have the backbone to stand up against them. In June in an address at General Beadle State College at Madison, S.D., he sharply attacked permissive college administrators and professors who surrendered to extremists or supported them.

Also in June the President's National Commis-

Students from the University of Chicago (Ill.) stand in a window of the school's administration building. They took over the building to protest a faculty decision not to rehire Marlene Dixon, an assistant professor of sociology. The Dixon case opened up a new area of campus conflict over the question of whether students were to be given any voice in the hiring and firing of faculty.

UPI COMPIX

sion on the Causes and Prevention of Violence urged universities to develop plans for dealing rapidly and effectively with student demonstrations. The commission, under the chairmanship of Milton S. Eisenhower, president of Johns Hopkins University, Baltimore, Md., said that while scholarly examination and decision were admirable qualities for the process of education they could be a prescription for disaster in dealing with disturbances. The commission felt that there was no need for special laws to withhold grants from militant students but that the civil courts should have stronger powers of injunction against the students. At the same time the commission expressed itself as disturbed at some public reactions. People who wanted to punish the colleges by cutting off funds could unwittingly be helping the radical student minority. (*See also* Education. *See in* CE: Universities and Colleges.)

COLOMBIA. Economic and political progress continued in Colombia in 1969 under constitutional reforms of the preceding year. The present constitution provides for government by a simple majority with the stipulation that the head of state may rule for a limited time in cases of emergency.

Under the National Front arrangement Liberal President Carlos Lleras Restrepo would be succeeded by a Conservative party president in 1970. Favored for the post was Misael Pastrana Borrero, Colombia's ambassador to the United States.

Colombia's gross national product was expected to rise 6.5% in 1969, compared to a growth rate of 6% in 1968. Continued emphasis on diversification raised the value of minor exports by nearly $35 million in the first half of 1969.

Loans granted to the country in 1969 included $328 million from the Consultative Group for Colombia, $60 million from the U.S. Agency for International Development, and $33.25-million standby credit from the International Monetary Fund.

At the capital, Bogotá, in May Colombia signed the Andean Common Market pact with Bolivia, Chile, Ecuador, and Peru. In September Colombia and Panama announced agreement on a new Colombia-Panama border route for a sea-level canal to supplement the Panama Canal. The proposal was submitted to the Atlantic-Pacific Interoceanic Canal Study Commission. (*See also* Latin America. *See in* CE: Colombia.)

COMMONWEALTH OF NATIONS. From the once-mighty United Kingdom of Great Britain and Northern Ireland to the tiny island of Anguilla, violence and bloodshed, crisis and protest plagued several member countries in the Commonwealth of Nations during 1969. Foremost among Commonwealth trouble spots was Northern Ireland, where religious animosity exploded into rioting during the year. The 1969 Commonwealth Prime Ministers' Conference took up the troublesome topics but failed to reach agreement on many vital points.

Old Woes and Other Stories

The centuries-old conflict between Northern Ireland's Protestant and Roman Catholic religious groups once again flared into violence in 1969. Belfast and Londonderry, two cities in Northern Ireland, were the scenes of the worst rioting. Northern Ireland's Catholic minority continued to press their demands for equal rights with the Protestant majority. Extremist Protestants feared that the Catholics were trying to bring about a united Ireland (Northern Ireland and the Republic of Ireland) in which Catholicism would be the religion of the majority of Irishmen.

In August Northern Ireland's Prime Minister James Chichester-Clark sent for British troops.

When the troops arrived, the rioting temporarily ended but broke out again in September and October. Under pressure from Great Britain the government of Northern Ireland proposed sweeping reforms in housing, employment, and voting practices. These reforms were violently opposed by many Protestants. (*See* Great Britain and Northern Ireland, United Kingdom of.)

One of Great Britain's most sensitive problems abroad during the year was the island of Anguilla. A British official, sent to Anguilla in March with a proposal for installing a British commissioner while the Anguillans worked out their internal affairs, claimed he was driven from the island by "gangster types." The Anguillans denied that the government was run by gangsters and invited the United Nations to investigate the charges.

Nevertheless, on March 19, British paratroopers seized Anguilla, and British officials took over the government. Anguillans staged demonstrations to protest the move. Ronald Webster, Anguilla's self-proclaimed president, asked for a referendum so that the Anguillans could decide for themselves whether they wanted independence, association with Great Britain, or a return to the alliance with Nevis and St. Kitts. The British commissioner indicated that this would not be possible for several years. On March 30 the Anguillans, represented by Webster, signed a truce with Great Britain pledging constructive cooperation between Anguilla and the British government. (*See also* West Indies.)

Efforts to bring about peace in Nigeria failed again in 1969. Great Britain's Prime Minister Harold Wilson visited Nigeria in March, but the Nigerian federal government discouraged any British overtures for an end to the civil war. Great Britain continued to support Nigeria's federal government with shipments of arms and ammunition. The Organization for African Unity (OAU) proposed a cease-fire and the opening of peace negotiations and supported the concept of "one Nigeria." The Biafrans could not accept the principle of a united Nigeria and so rejected the OAU proposals.

Four for Show

Commonwealth nations in the Far East worked rapidly toward establishing a suitable defense system to take the place of the British forces that were to be withdrawn by the end of 1971. Australia, Singapore, Malaysia, and New Zealand made plans for combining their military and naval strength to present a common front for defense.

The four Pacific nations began adding to their military forces. Singapore began drafting all eligible men and women up to age 25. Malaysia planned to add three battalions to its army and to recruit 7,000 additional men for paramilitary training. Australia contributed ten jet fighter planes

Seated around the table, the prime ministers of the 28 member countries of the Commonwealth of Nations begin deliberations at their 1969 conference in London, England. The weeklong conference was dominated by disputes over Britain's policy toward Rhodesia's white minority regime and by Britain's new immigration policy.

FOX PHOTOS FROM PICTORIAL PARADE

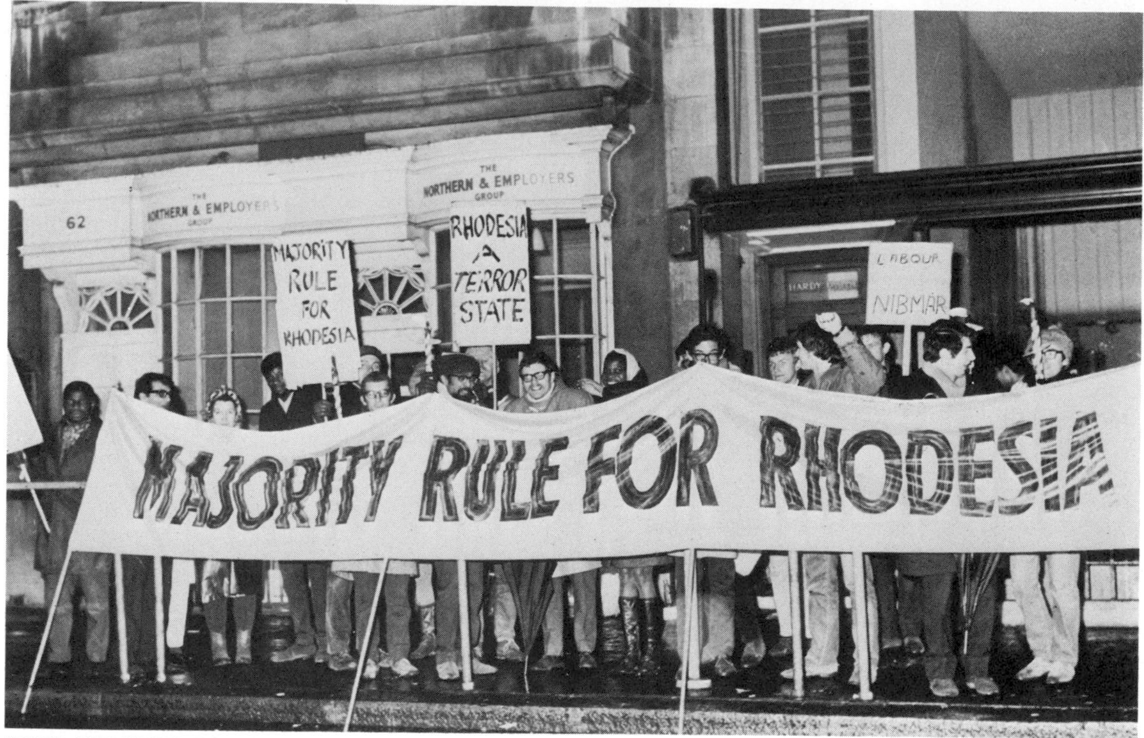

"LONDON DAILY EXPRESS" FROM PICTORIAL PARADE

In January members of the Anti-Apartheid League and sympathizers lined the pavement outside Marlborough House in London, England, during the Commonwealth Prime Ministers' Conference. The demonstrators demanded that Rhodesia's black majority be permitted to rule the nation.

to Malaysia's air force. Both Australia and New Zealand planned to station troops in Malaysia and Singapore.

Agreeable Disagreement

The Commonwealth Prime Ministers' Conference met for the first time since 1966, at London, England, in January. Although there was considerable disagreement among member nations the discussions were polite and no one walked out.

One of the problems discussed was Rhodesia's illegal white-minority government. President Kenneth Kaunda of Zambia held that Great Britain should use military force to overthrow the Rhodesian regime. Most African Commonwealth nations favored stronger economic sanctions against Rhodesia. The British government refused to guarantee that it would not grant independence to Rhodesia before black African rule had been established. The conference failed to produce a positive resolution on the Rhodesian question.

No progress was made at the conference on the problem of the forced Asian migration from Africa. Kenya, Tanzania, Uganda, and Zambia—the nations that created the situation by forcing Asian aliens to emigrate—boycotted talks on the migration problem. The British government remained firm in its refusal to allow the Asians into England even though they were British citizens and held British passports.

The presidents and prime ministers did agree, however, that Communist China should be allowed to participate in world peace efforts. (*See also* Africa; individual countries by name.)

COMMUNIST MOVEMENT. The international Communist movement suffered in 1969 when border disputes, complicated by ideological differences, resulted in military as well as political clashes between Communist China and the Soviet Union. In spite of the wide split in the Communist world the Soviet Union went ahead with its planned world Communist conference, which was held in June. The Soviet Union worked hard during the year to repair the dissension among Communist factions all over the world caused by the 1968 Soviet-led invasion of Czechoslovakia.

Making Waves

The Ussuri River, which divides the northeasternmost part of China from the Soviet Union, on March 2 was the scene of the year's first armed confrontation between Chinese and Soviet troops. The conflict centered around Chenpao (or Damanskiy) Island, territory claimed by the Chinese and Soviets alike. Each nation accused the other of instigating the incident, and both tried to gain the utmost benefit in propaganda.

When the four-hour battle ended, 31 Russian border guards and an unknown number of Chinese had been killed. The Soviet Union charged that retreating Chinese troops had killed wounded Russians and had mutilated the bodies of the dead.

Both nations organized massive protests. Crowds estimated at up to one million persons stormed the Soviet Embassy in Peking, the Chinese capital. About 50,000 Russians marched in one day on the Chinese Embassy in Moscow, U.S.S.R. China accused the Soviet Union's "revisionist renegade clique" of pursuing a "social-imperialist policy." The Russians decried China's "adventuristic policies" and said the border incident was provoked to divert attention from the economic and political failures of the government of China's Communist Party Politburo Chairman Mao Tse-tung.

Several other shooting incidents occurred on the Ussuri and Amur rivers later in the year. The continuing incidents and their accompanying propaganda were an ominous backdrop to the Soviet military buildup along the Soviet-Chinese border.

The Ninth Congress of the Chinese Communist Party was held at Peking in April. Soviet leaders stated that the congress was not a meeting of the Communist party, since the true party had been destroyed by the cultural revolution. It was, the Soviets said, the first congress of a new organization separate from the world Communist movement. (*See* China, People's Republic of.)

In September the Soviet Union's Premier Aleksei N. Kosygin met with China's Premier Chou En-lai at Peking. The meeting produced no positive results. In October, however, the Chinese and Soviets alike expressed interest in opening negotiations to resolve the border dispute. The Italian and Japanese Communist parties called on China and the Soviet Union to settle their ideological as well as their national differences.

No. 1—Or Trying Harder?

While the quarrel with China went on, Soviet leaders anxiously awaited the world Communist conference, which they hoped would pass a resounding condemnation of, or even excommunicate, the Chinese Communist party. The Soviet Union wished to emerge from the conference confirmed as the leader of a united international Communist movement. The conference, however, produced something less than a show of solidarity with the Soviet Union by the leaders of the other Communist countries.

During one of the year's border clashes between the Soviet Union and Communist China, a Soviet border guard fires on a Chinese position while another talks by telephone with his unit's commander.

"LONDON DAILY EXPRESS" FROM PICTORIAL PARADE

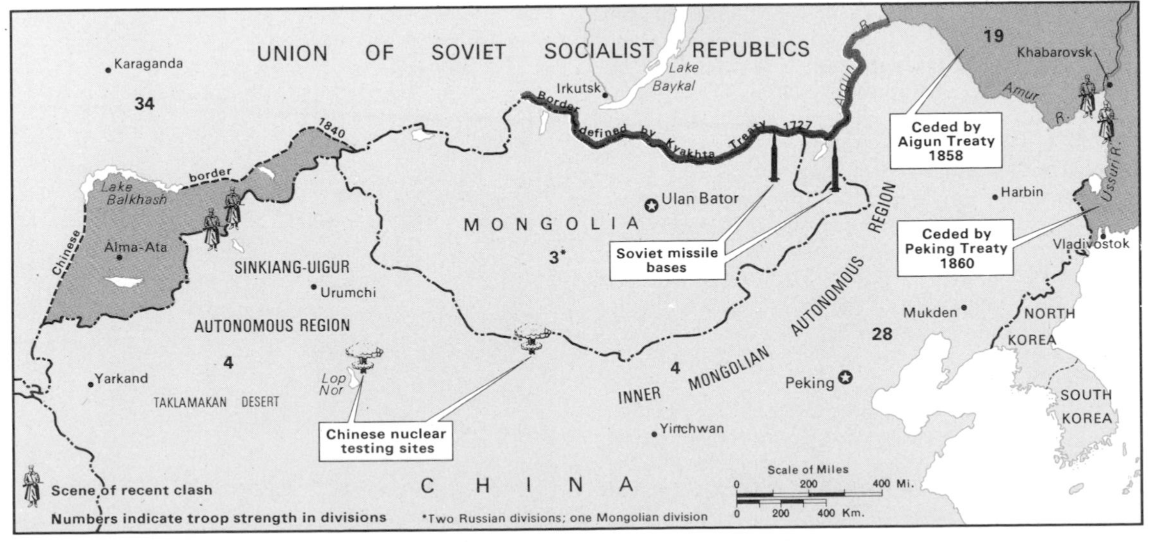

On June 5, leaders of 75 national Communist parties gathered in Moscow for the opening of the Conference of Communist and Workers' Parties. Conspicuously absent from the conference were party representatives from Albania, China, Japan, North Korea, North Vietnam, and Yugoslavia. The Cuban party sent an observer.

At the conference the Soviet Union's aims were directed toward the problems posed by China and Czechoslovakia. Soviet Communist Party General Secretary Leonid I. Brezhnev vaguely but ominously called for a collective security system in Asia. Most of the speeches contained denunciations of China's "Maoist clique." The Soviets also defended their policy of "limited sovereignty"—the right to intervene in another country's affairs if it appeared that Communism in the country was in danger. This was the justification used for the 1968 invasion of Czechoslovakia.

Criticism of the Czechoslovak invasion was voiced by the Australians, Italians, and Romanians. The strongest anti-Soviet criticism came from the Italian delegate and from Romania's Communist Party First Secretary Nicolae Ceausescu. Both men denounced the verbal attacks on China and opposed Brezhnev's doctrine of limited sovereignty. Czechoslovak Communist Party First Secretary Gustav Husak defended the 1968 military intervention by saying the leadership in Czechoslovakia had been naïve.

Another reflection of dissent in the world Communist movement was the principal document of the conference containing resolutions to be endorsed by the attending Communist parties. Work began on the document in February 1968 but was interrupted by the tumult surrounding the invasion of Czechoslovakia. Before the document reached its final form some 300 amendments had been suggested, of which about 100 were adopted.

In its final form the document was a set of platitudes that offended almost no one. Points emphasized were support for North Vietnam, reaffirmation of the struggle against imperialism, and support for national sovereignty as well as for the doctrine of limited sovereignty. It contained no mention of either Communist China or the invasion of Czechoslovakia. The document did, however, state that there was no leading center for the international Communist movement.

Nevertheless the document did not receive unanimous approval, since 14 Communist parties either refused to sign or signed with reservations. In spite of this refusal to show a united pro-Soviet stand, the Russians said they were satisfied with the results of the conference.

Europe and Asia

During the year Alexander Dubcek, former first secretary of Czechoslovakia's Communist party, rapidly fell from power in both the party and the government. The new Czechoslovak government that was eased in conformed to Soviet policy.

Under Soviet pressure all Warsaw Pact nations, with the exception of Romania, boycotted the Yugoslav Communist Party Congress in March. At Romania's party congress in August the Soviet delegate indirectly criticized U.S. President Richard M. Nixon's 1969 visit to Romania.

Following the death of North Vietnam's President Ho Chi Minh in September, Soviet and Chinese delegates were sent to North Vietnam in hopes of winning the favor of the new leadership. China and North Vietnam appeared to have developed closer ties during the year. (*See also* Feature Article: "China and the United States: Distorted Images"; individual countries by name. *See in* CE: Communism.)

COMPUTERS. In 1969 the International Business Machines Corp. (IBM) added two new computers to its line. Designed for small businesses that previously found computers uneconomic, the System 3 was the smallest computer yet produced by IBM for commercial application. It was the first IBM computer to be completely self-contained, requiring no cable connections between components. It employed a new type of punched card, one third the size of the standard card yet capable of recording 20% more information.

At the other extreme was the System 360 model 195—IBM's most powerful computer to date. Offering great computing speed, it incorporated an extremely rapid-access buffer memory made of solid-state electronic elements and had several arithmetic units, permitting it to execute a number of different instructions simultaneously. Control Data Corp. brought out its 7600 computer.

During the year IBM faced a number of antitrust lawsuits, variously contending that its selling

In 1969 five high schools in the Boston, Mass., area continued Project LOCAL (Laboratory Program for Computer-Assisted Learning). The schools cut per-pupil computer costs 75% by buying their own computers instead of renting time.

AUTHENTICATED NEWS INTERNATIONAL

President Joseph Mobutu remained firmly in control of the Democratic Republic of the Congo (Kinshasa) in 1969. Here, he is welcomed by citizens during a visit in March to his nation's Bandundu Province.

AFP FROM PICTORIAL PARADE

methods were unfair to its competitors: that it sold products and services as a package rather than separately; that it took unfair advantage of program-writing companies by providing computer programs for its customers; and that it monopolized the computer business simply by being very large. Partly as a counter to some of the suits, IBM said it would begin to charge its customers for certain services, including some programs. Other computer manufacturers began to review their own policies in the wake of IBM's announcement.

A new firm, Viatron Computer Systems Corp., was scheduled to make the first deliveries in 1969 of a microprocessor system. It said the rental for a complete installation would be perhaps $40 a month—a very low price based on plans to make and rent large numbers of machines embodying the latest in electronics technology. (*See also* Electronics. *See in* CE: Computers.)

CONGO, DEMOCRATIC REPUBLIC OF THE (Kinshasa).

The turbulent years that followed the Congo's achievement of independence faded further into the past in 1969 with the deaths of two early leaders, the visit of a high-ranking Belgian economic mission, and growing stability in the economy. Joseph Kasavubu, the Congo's first president, died in March. In June Moise Tshombe, leader of secessionist Katanga Province and later premier, died in captivity in Algeria.

The warm welcome given in March to a large Belgian economic mission, led by Prince Albert, marked the end of hostile Congolese-Belgian relations. In September the Congo agreed to pay compensation to Union Minière du Haut-Katanga for assets of the Belgian company seized by the Congo in 1966.

As a result of monetary reforms begun in 1967, a reduction in government spending, and high prices obtained for copper, the Congo's economy in 1969 achieved unprecedented stability. Although economic development plans were incomplete, the channeling of Congo River waters into the Deuren Valley was begun as part of a hydroelectric project to provide new power resources.

President Joseph Mobutu remained in firm control of the country. Student demonstrations were put down by soldiers in June, and French and Bulgarian diplomats were expelled from the Congo for aiding escaping students. Strict government control was imposed on high schools and on Lovanium Catholic University, which had been closed by unrest. In August Mobutu reorganized his cabinet.

In foreign affairs, attempts were made through an African economic organization to revive relations—broken off in 1968—between the two Congo nations. Early in the year, after Mobutu's charge that the Central African Republic was responsible for the murder of several Congolese citizens, the republic suspended relations with the Congo. (*See in* CE: Congo, Democratic Republic of the.)

CONGO, REPUBLIC OF (Brazzaville).

Early in 1969 Maj. Alfred Raoul, who had been interim president of the Republic of Congo since September 1968, was replaced as chief of state by Maj. Marien Ngouabi. The new president was the head of the army and the National Council of the Revolution. Raoul remained the prime minister.

In February Congolese leaders decreed the establishment of a Revolutionary Court of Justice in Brazzaville and arrested a number of politicians and officers in a government purge. Political trials resulted in severe sentences for both Congolese and foreigners, including supporters of former President Fubert Youlou, who was in exile.

In December the government changed the country's name to the Popular Republic of the Congo and adopted both a new national anthem, the 'Internationale', and a new red flag that included a hammer-and-sickle motif. (*See in* CE: Congo, Republic of.)

CONGRESS, UNITED STATES. The 91st Congress convened on Jan. 3, 1969, with Democrats in control of both the House of Representatives and the Senate but with a Republican president about to be inaugurated. In the House the Democrats held 243 seats, the Republicans 192. During 1969 the Republicans lost two seats to the Democrats. The Democrats controlled the Senate 57 to 43. (*See* Political Parties.)

As Congress convened, Speaker of the House John W. McCormack (D, Mass.) easily defeated a challenge to his leadership by Representative Morris Udall (D, Ariz.). In the Senate, Mike Mansfield (D, Mont.) remained as majority leader, but Senator Edward M. Kennedy (D, Mass.) unseated Senator Russell B. Long (D, La.) as assistant majority leader. Senator Hugh Scott (R, Pa.), a moderate, was elected assistant minority leader over conservative Roman L. Hruska (R, Neb.). After the death of Senate minority leader Everett M. Dirksen (R, Ill.) in September, Scott was elected to succeed him. Robert P. Griffin (R, Mich.), another moderate from an industrial state, was elected to succeed Scott as assistant.

The House voted to seat the controversial Negro legislator Adam Clayton Powell (D, N.Y.) but charged him $25,000 for alleged misuse of travel and payroll funds. They also voted to strip him of the seniority that earlier had made him chairman of the House Education and Labor Committee. In June the Supreme Court ruled that the House had acted improperly by excluding Powell from the 90th Congress.

Two other controversial members of Congress in 1969 were Senator Kennedy and Speaker of the House McCormack. In July a car that Kennedy was driving plunged off a bridge, killing the passenger, Mary Jo Kopechne. Kennedy failed to report the accident immediately to the police. Because of the scandal that surrounded the accident Kennedy considered resigning from his seat in the Senate.

Martin Swieg, a longtime friend of McCormack, was suspended from his post as top aide to the speaker of the House after he was accused along with Nathan M. Voloshen of using the office of the speaker improperly to influence government agencies, courts, and parole boards. McCormack denied any knowledge of the "influence-peddling" operation.

Congress doubled the president's salary to $200,000 a year and allowed the action of a presidential commission for increasing the pay of congressmen by $12,500 a year to stand, unless the move was reversed in 1969. In effect, the Congress gave tacit approval to its own pay increase.

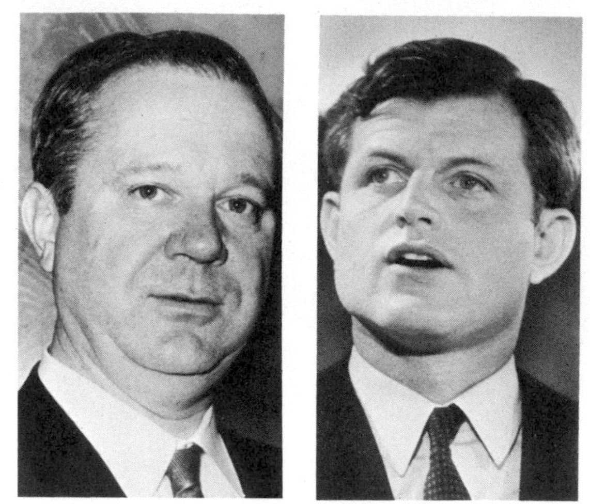

WIDE WORLD

In a heated contest for Senate Democratic whip, Senator Edward M. Kennedy of Massachusetts (right) defeated his senior rival, Senator Russell B. Long of Louisiana, in January.

Nixon's Victories and Defeat

After months of controversy, U.S. President Richard M. Nixon scored a major legislative victory on August 6 when the Senate voted to allow funds for deploying an antiballistic missile system. On May 21, the Senate confirmed the nomination of Warren Earl Burger, a federal appeals judge, to be U.S. chief justice. He succeeded Earl Warren, who retired.

But later in the session, a nomination to the Supreme Court brought the Nixon Administration its most stunning defeat. The Senate rejected the nomination of Federal Judge Clement F. Haynsworth, Jr., of South Carolina, also an appeals judge, despite an intensive Administration campaign on his behalf. He was the first Supreme Court nominee to be rejected since 1930. The 55–45 vote was a result of opposition by labor and civil rights groups and of disclosure of Haynsworth's participation in cases in which it was alleged he had a financial interest.

One Administration triumph was a one-sentence measure of great significance for young people. It repealed a section of the 1967 selective service law that barred a draft lottery. This cleared the way for a lottery for 19-year-olds based on birth dates and on alphabetical listings within each birth-date group. It was designed to reduce vulnerability to the draft to one year for most 19-year-olds. Those with deferments, however, would retain their draft-call order in the lottery when their deferments lapsed. The first lottery, for men to be inducted in 1970, was held on December 1; for the first year only it included men 19 to 25. (*See* Selective Service.)

Foreign Policy

A treaty to halt the spread of nuclear weapons was approved by the Senate on March 13. It prohibited nuclear powers from helping other states to develop such weapons and prohibited them from giving the weapons to nonnuclear powers.

Several actions during the session tended to assert the legislative role in making foreign policy. The Senate on June 25 adopted a so-called "national commitments" resolution, calling on the president not to commit troops or funds to other nations without the express approval of Congress. Late in the session, Congress inserted in the military-appropriations bill a provision barring use of the funds to introduce U.S. ground troops into Laos or Thailand.

Congress slashed the foreign-aid authorization bill for fiscal 1970 to just under $2 billion, the smallest sum since the aid program began. The actual appropriations bill also had difficulty. The Senate rejected a House version of the bill because of its insertion of an appropriation, not requested by the Administration, for jet planes for Taiwan. At year's end the bill was still being debated.

Earlier, on December 2, the House approved an Administration-backed resolution calling for a "just peace" in Vietnam. In effect it called for free, supervised elections in South Vietnam and appealed to North Vietnam to abide by the results. The passage was hailed as a victory for the president.

One of the strongest stands by the Senate for a foreign-policy role was a resolution calling on President Nixon not to make a final agreement on return of the island of Okinawa to Japan without first obtaining Senate consent. In November, however, the House voted against requiring such consent from Congress.

Congress and Vietnam

Congressional critics of the U.S. involvement in Vietnam became more outspoken in 1969. The antimilitary feelings of an increasing number of senators and representatives resulted in pressure to cut down on defense spending. In June the Joint Subcommittee on Economy in Government opened hearings on the size of the proposed defense budget. One topic discussed was the $1.5-billion overrun on the cost estimates for the C-5A super-transport plane. In August the Senate attempted to gain effective control over spending on major military projects by voting in favor of having such projects subject to investigation by the General Accounting Office.

The Department of Defense, anticipating new restrictions on spending, ordered reductions of $3 billion in military expenditures. The military budget was revised downward by $2.2 billion by the Administration in April. In December the House Appropriations Committee cut an additional $5.3 billion from the proposed $75.2-billion budget. (*See* Defense Special Report.)

Retired Maj. Gen. Carl C. Turner (left) and Chicago, Ill., police Lieut. Paul T. Duellman (right) testified in October at a Senate investigation of charges that the general had obtained for his personal collection guns the Chicago police had confiscated from lawbreakers.

WIDE WORLD

UPI COMPIX

William H. Stewart, U.S. surgeon general, appeared in April before the House Committee on Commerce to ask Congress to strengthen the required health warning on cigarette packages and to require that the warning appear in cigarette advertising.

An investigation into the alleged massacre of civilians in a South Vietnamese village was opened by the Armed Services Committee in November. A special investigating committee headed by Representative L. Mendel Rivers (D, S.C.) heard testimony from participants in the alleged massacre and from the secretary of the Army. (*See* Armed Forces, U.S.: Army.)

Tax Reform

The action of Congress during 1969 affecting most Americans was income-tax reform. Fairly early in the session, the legislators passed a measure extending the income-tax surcharge through 1969. Then they tackled the first thorough reform of the entire federal income-tax system since its adoption in 1913.

Under the bill that was passed in the last days of the session the surcharge for the first six months of 1970 was set at 5%. The personal exemption that could be deducted for a taxpayer and his dependents was increased to $650 a person for income earned after July 1, 1970, and through 1971; to $700 in 1972; and to $750 in 1973.

The standard deduction for taxpayers who do not itemize expenses was also increased from 10% with a maximum of $1,000 to a new rate of 13% with a maximum of $1,300 in 1970; to 14% with a maximum of $1,500 in 1971, and to 15% with a maximum of $2,000 in 1972. Social security benefits were increased by 15% effective on Jan. 1, 1970; a provision for a minimum $100 benefit for a single person and $150 for a couple was killed. The new tax bill provided that in no circumstances would an unmarried taxpayer have to pay over 20% more than the amount he would be charged if he were married.

Previously tax-exempt foundations were required to pay out 6% of their assets annually and would be taxed a flat 4% of their income. The 7% investment-tax credit was repealed, effective on April 18, 1969. Oil and gas depletion allowances, previously 27.5%, were reduced to 22%, as were rates for other minerals with depletion allowances above 22%. Depletion allowances of 15% were reduced to 14%.

A special tax of 10% was levied on some types of tax-exempt income above $30,000 to collect some revenue from very rich citizens who escape taxation through special provisions of the law. While there was no general reduction in percentage rates of taxation, the top rate of 70% for married men with earned income of $52,000 after deductions was to be reduced to 60% in 1971 and 50% in 1972. Income from investments would continue to be taxed at 70% in these cases.

Unfinished Business

Measures left by the 91st Congress when it recessed just before Christmas 1969 were carried over to the second session, which began in January 1970. One of the major items was a civil rights bill that would extend voting-rights legislation to all 50 states and thus lessen pressure on Southern states originally affected. The bill passed the House but not the Senate.

Senator Edward W. Brooke (R, Mass.) listens intently during a committee hearing. In 1969 Brooke—the only Negro in the Senate—opposed deployment of an ABM (antiballistic missile) system, Job Corps cutbacks, and testing of multiple warheads for missiles.

UPI COMPIX

The appropriation for the Department of Health, Education, and Welfare was postponed in the Senate after the president threatened to veto the bill, which provided $1.1 billion more than had been requested. Also deferred to the next session was Senate action on a House-passed constitutional amendment to abolish the electoral college and provide for popular election of presidents.

Congress failed to take final action on a number of proposals by the Administration. These included revision of the welfare system, reorganization of the Post Office, and sharing tax revenue with the states. (*See also* Disarmament; Supreme Court of the U.S. *See in* CE: Congress of the United States.)

MEMBERS OF THE CONGRESS OF THE UNITED STATES

1st Session, 91st Congress

THE SENATE

President of the Senate: Spiro T. Agnew

State	Senator	Current Service Began	Current Term Expires
Ala.	John Sparkman (D)	1947	1973
	James B. Allen (D)	1969	1975
Alaska	Ted Stevens* (R)	1969	1973
	Mike Gravel (D)	1969	1975
Ariz.	Paul J. Fannin (R)	1965	1971
	Barry M. Goldwater (R)	1969	1975
Ark.	John L. McClellan (D)	1943	1973
	J. W. Fulbright (D)	1945	1975
Calif.	George Murphy (R)	1965	1971
	Alan Cranston (D)	1969	1975
Colo.	Gordon Allott (R)	1955	1973
	Peter H. Dominick (R)	1963	1975
Conn.	Thomas J. Dodd (D)	1959	1971
	Abraham Ribicoff (D)	1963	1975
Del.	John J. Williams (R)	1947	1971
	J. Caleb Boggs (R)	1961	1973
Fla.	Spessard L. Holland (D)	1946	1971
	Edward J. Gurney (R)	1969	1975
Ga.	Richard B. Russell (D)	1933	1973
	Herman E. Talmadge (D)	1957	1975
Hawaii	Hiram L. Fong (R)	1959	1971
	Daniel K. Inouye (D)	1963	1975
Idaho	Frank Church (D)	1957	1975
	Len B. Jordan (R)	1962	1973
Ill.	Charles H. Percy (R)	1967	1973
	Ralph T. Smith† (R)	1969	1971
Ind.	Vance Hartke (D)	1959	1971
	Birch E. Bayh (D)	1963	1975
Iowa	Jack Miller (R)	1961	1973
	Harold E. Hughes (D)	1969	1975
Kan.	James B. Pearson (R)	1962	1973
	Robert Dole (R)	1969	1975
Ky.	John Sherman Cooper (R)	1957	1973
	Marlow W. Cook (R)	1969	1975
La.	Allen J. Ellender (D)	1937	1973
	Russell B. Long (D)	1948	1975
Maine	Margaret Chase Smith (R)	1949	1973
	Edmund S. Muskie (D)	1959	1971
Md.	Joseph D. Tydings (D)	1965	1971
	Charles McC. Mathias, Jr. (R)	1969	1975
Mass.	Edward M. Kennedy (D)	1962	1971
	Edward W. Brooke (R)	1967	1973
Mich.	Philip A. Hart (D)	1959	1971
	Robert P. Griffin (R)	1966	1973
Minn.	Eugene J. McCarthy (D)	1959	1971
	Walter F. Mondale (D)	1964	1973
Miss.	James O. Eastland (D)	1943	1973
	John C. Stennis (D)	1947	1971
Mo.	Stuart Symington (D)	1953	1971
	Thomas F. Eagleton (D)	1969	1975

* Appointed to fill the unexpired term of the late E. L. Bartlett (D).
† Appointed as interim successor to the late Everett M. Dirksen (R) until November 1970 election.

State	Senator	Current Service Began	Current Term Expires
Mont.	Mike Mansfield (D)	1953	1971
	Lee Metcalf (D)	1961	1973
Neb.	Roman L. Hruska (R)	1955	1971
	Carl T. Curtis (R)	1955	1973
Nev.	Alan Bible (D)	1954	1975
	Howard W. Cannon (D)	1959	1971
N.H.	Norris Cotton (R)	1955	1975
	Thomas J. McIntyre (D)	1963	1973
N.J.	Clifford P. Case (R)	1955	1973
	Harrison A. Williams, Jr. (D)	1959	1971
N.M.	Clinton P. Anderson (D)	1949	1973
	Joseph M. Montoya (D)	1965	1971
N.Y.	Jacob K. Javits (R)	1957	1975
	Charles E. Goodell‡ (R)	1968	1971
N.C.	Sam J. Ervin, Jr. (D)	1954	1975
	B. Everett Jordan (D)	1958	1973
N.D.	Milton R. Young (R)	1945	1975
	Quentin N. Burdick (D)	1960	1971
Ohio	Stephen M. Young (D)	1959	1971
	William B. Saxbe (R)	1969	1975
Okla.	Fred R. Harris (D)	1964	1973
	Henry Bellmon (R)	1969	1975
Ore.	Mark O. Hatfield (R)	1967	1973
	Robert W. Packwood (R)	1969	1975
Pa.	Hugh Scott (R)	1959	1971
	Richard S. Schweiker (R)	1969	1975
R.I.	John O. Pastore (D)	1950	1971
	Claiborne Pell (D)	1961	1973
S.C.	Strom Thurmond (R)	1955	1973
	Ernest F. Hollings (D)	1966	1975
S.D.	Karl E. Mundt (R)	1949	1973
	George McGovern (D)	1963	1975
Tenn.	Albert Gore (D)	1953	1971
	Howard H. Baker, Jr. (R)	1967	1973
Tex.	Ralph Yarborough (D)	1957	1971
	John G. Tower (R)	1961	1973
Utah	Wallace F. Bennett (R)	1951	1975
	Frank E. Moss (D)	1959	1971
Vt.	George D. Aiken (R)	1941	1975
	Winston L. Prouty (R)	1959	1971
Va.	Harry F. Byrd, Jr. (D)	1965	1971
	William B. Spong, Jr. (D)	1967	1973
Wash.	Warren G. Magnuson (D)	1944	1975
	Henry M. Jackson (D)	1953	1971
W.Va.	Jennings Randolph (D)	1959	1973
	Robert C. Byrd (D)	1959	1971
Wis.	William Proxmire (D)	1957	1971
	Gaylord Nelson (D)	1963	1975
Wyo.	Gale W. McGee (D)	1959	1971
	Clifford P. Hansen (R)	1967	1973

‡ Appointed to fill the unexpired term of the late Robert F. Kennedy (D).

THE HOUSE OF REPRESENTATIVES *

Speaker of the House: John W. McCormack

Alabama
Jack Edwards, 1 (R)
William L. Dickinson, 2 (R)
George Andrews, 3 (D)
Bill Nichols, 4 (D)
Walter Flowers, 5 (D)
John Buchanan, 6 (R)
Tom Bevill, 7 (D)
Robert E. Jones, 8 (D)
Alaska
Howard W. Pollock (R)
Arizona
John J. Rhodes, 1 (R)
Morris K. Udall, 2 (D)
Sam Steiger, 3 (R)
Arkansas
Bill Alexander, 1 (D)
Wilbur D. Mills, 2 (D)
John Paul Hammerschmidt, 3 (R)
David Pryor, 4 (D)
California
Don H. Clausen, 1 (R)
Harold T. Johnson, 2 (D)
John E. Moss, 3 (D)
Robert L. Leggett, 4 (D)
Phillip Burton, 5 (D)
William S. Mailliard, 6 (R)
Jeffery Cohelan, 7 (D)
George P. Miller, 8 (D)
Don Edwards, 9 (D)
Charles S. Gubser, 10 (R)
Paul N. McCloskey, Jr., 11 (R)
Burt L. Talcott, 12 (R)
Charles M. Teague, 13 (R)
Jerome R. Waldie, 14 (D)
John J. McFall, 15 (D)
B. F. Sisk, 16 (D)
Glenn M. Anderson, 17 (D)
Robert B. Mathias, 18 (R)
Chet Holifield, 19 (D)
H. Allen Smith, 20 (R)
Augustus F. Hawkins, 21 (D)
James C. Corman, 22 (D)
Del Clawson, 23 (R)
Glenard P. Lipscomb, 24 (R)
Charles E. Wiggins, 25 (R)
Thomas M. Rees, 26 (D)
Barry M. Goldwater, Jr.†, 27 (R)
Alphonzo Bell, 28 (R)
George E. Brown, Jr., 29 (D)
Edward R. Roybal, 30 (D)
Charles H. Wilson, 31 (D)
Craig Hosmer, 32 (R)
Jerry L. Pettis, 33 (R)
Richard T. Hanna, 34 (D)
James B. Utt, 35 (R)
Bob Wilson, 36 (R)
Lionel Van Deerlin, 37 (D)
John V. Tunney, 38 (D)
Colorado
Byron G. Rogers, 1 (D)
Donald G. Brotzman, 2 (R)
Frank E. Evans, 3 (D)
Wayne N. Aspinall, 4 (D)
Connecticut
Emilio Q. Daddario, 1 (D)
William L. St. Onge, 2 (D)
Robert N. Giaimo, 3 (D)
Lowell P. Weicker, Jr., 4 (R)
John S. Monagan, 5 (D)
Thomas J. Meskill, 6 (R)
Delaware
William V. Roth, Jr. (R)
Florida
Robert L. F. Sikes, 1 (D)
Don Fuqua, 2 (D)
Charles E. Bennett, 3 (D)
Bill Chappell, Jr., 4 (D)
Louis Frey, Jr., 5 (R)
Sam Gibbons, 6 (D)
James A. Haley, 7 (D)
William C. Cramer, 8 (R)
Paul G. Rogers, 9 (D)
J. Herbert Burke, 10 (R)
Claude Pepper, 11 (D)
Dante B. Fascell, 12 (D)
Georgia
G. Elliott Hagan, 1 (D)
Maston O'Neal, 2 (D)
Jack Brinkley, 3 (D)
Benjamin B. Blackburn, 4 (R)
Fletcher Thompson, 5 (R)
John J. Flynt, Jr., 6 (D)
John W. Davis, 7 (D)
W. S. Stuckey, 8 (D)
Phil M. Landrum, 9 (D)
Robert G. Stephens, Jr., 10 (D)
Hawaii
Spark M. Matsunaga (D)
Patsy T. Mink (D)
Idaho
James A. McClure, 1 (R)
Orval Hansen, 2 (R)
Illinois
William L. Dawson, 1 (D)
Abner J. Mikva, 2 (D)
William T. Murphy, 3 (D)
Edward J. Derwinski, 4 (R)
John C. Kluczynski, 5 (D)
‡ 6

GRAHAM, "ARKANSAS GAZETTE," FROM BEN ROTH AGENCY

"Right! The Fortas thing was different—he was a liberal!"

* Numbers after names indicate Congressional districts; where no number is given, congressman is elected at large.
† Elected in April 1969 to fill unexpired term of Ed Reinecke (R).
‡ Vacancy caused by death of Daniel J. Ronan (D), Aug. 13, 1969.

Frank Annunzio, 7 (D)
Dan Rostenkowski, 8 (D)
Sidney R. Yates, 9 (D)
Harold R. Collier, 10 (R)
Roman C. Pucinski, 11 (D)
Robert McClory, 12 (R)
Philip M. Crane†, 13 (R)
John N. Erlenborn, 14 (R)
Charlotte T. Reid, 15 (R)
John B. Anderson, 16 (R)
Leslie C. Arends, 17 (R)
Robert H. Michel, 18 (R)
Tom Railsback, 19 (R)
Paul Findley, 20 (R)
Kenneth J. Gray, 21 (D)
William L. Springer, 22 (R)
George E. Shipley, 23 (D)
Melvin Price, 24 (D)

Indiana

Ray J. Madden, 1 (D)
Earl F. Landgrebe, 2 (R)
John Brademas, 3 (D)
E. Ross Adair, 4 (R)
Richard L. Roudebush, 5 (R)
William G. Bray, 6 (R)
John T. Myers, 7 (R)
Roger H. Zion, 8 (R)
Lee H. Hamilton, 9 (D)
David W. Dennis, 10 (R)
Andrew Jacobs, Jr., 11 (D)

Iowa

Fred Schwengel, 1 (R)
John C. Culver, 2 (D)
H. R. Gross, 3 (R)
John Kyl, 4 (R)
Neal Smith, 5 (D)
Wiley Mayne, 6 (R)
William J. Scherle, 7 (R)

Kansas

Keith G. Sebelius, 1 (R)
Chester L. Mize, 2 (R)
Larry Winn, Jr., 3 (R)
Garner E. Shriver, 4 (R)
Joe Skubitz, 5 (R)

Kentucky

Frank A. Stubblefield, 1 (D)
William H. Natcher, 2 (D)
William O. Cowger, 3 (R)
M. G. (Gene) Snyder, 4 (R)
Tim Lee Carter, 5 (R)
John C. Watts, 6 (D)
Carl D. Perkins, 7 (D)

Louisiana

F. Edward Hébert, 1 (D)
Hale Boggs, 2 (D)
Patrick T. Caffery, 3 (D)
Joe D. Waggoner, Jr., 4 (D)
Otto E. Passman, 5 (D)
John R. Rarick, 6 (D)
Edwin W. Edwards, 7 (D)
Speedy O. Long, 8 (D)

Maine

Peter N. Kyros, 1 (D)
William D. Hathaway, 2 (D)

Maryland

Rogers C. B. Morton, 1 (R)
Clarence D. Long, 2 (D)
Edward A. Garmatz, 3 (D)
George H. Fallon, 4 (D)
Lawrence J. Hogan, 5 (R)
J. Glenn Beall, Jr., 6 (R)
Samuel N. Friedel, 7 (D)
Gilbert Gude, 8 (R)

Massachusetts

Silvio O. Conte, 1 (R)
Edward P. Boland, 2 (D)
Philip J. Philbin, 3 (D)
Harold D. Donohue, 4 (D)
F. Bradford Morse, 5 (R)
Michael Harrington‡, (D)
Torbert H. Macdonald, 7 (D)
Thomas P. O'Neill, Jr., 8 (D)
John W. McCormack, 9 (D)
Margaret M. Heckler, 10 (R)
James A. Burke, 11 (D)
Hastings Keith, 12 (R)

Michigan

John Conyers, Jr., 1 (D)
Marvin L. Esch, 2 (R)
Garry Brown, 3 (R)
Edward Hutchinson, 4 (R)
Gerald R. Ford, 5 (R)
Charles E. Chamberlain, 6 (R)
Donald W. Riegle, Jr., 7 (R)
James Harvey, 8 (R)
Guy Vander Jagt, 9 (R)
Elford A. Cederberg, 10 (R)
Philip E. Ruppe, 11 (R)
James G. O'Hara, 12 (D)
Charles C. Diggs, Jr., 13 (D)
Lucien N. Nedzi, 14 (D)
William D. Ford, 15 (D)
John D. Dingell, 16 (D)
Martha W. Griffiths, 17 (D)
William S. Broomfield, 18 (R)
Jack H. McDonald, 19 (R)

Minnesota

Albert H. Quie, 1 (R)
Ancher Nelsen, 2 (R)
Clark MacGregor, 3 (R)
Joseph E. Karth, 4 (D)
Donald M. Fraser, 5 (D)
John M. Zwach, 6 (R)
Odin Langen, 7 (R)
John A. Blatnik, 8 (D)

Mississippi

Thomas G. Abernethy, 1 (D)
Jamie L. Whitten, 2 (D)
Charles H. Griffin, 3 (D)
G. V. (Sonny) Montgomery, 4 (D)
William M. Colmer, 5 (D)

Missouri

William Clay, 1 (D)
James W. Symington, 2 (D)
Leonor K. Sullivan, 3 (D)
William J. Randall, 4 (D)
Richard Bolling, 5 (D)
W. R. Hull, Jr., 6 (D)
Durward G. Hall, 7 (R)
Richard H. Ichord, 8 (D)
William L. Hungate, 9 (D)
Bill D. Burlison, 10 (D)

Montana

Arnold Olsen, 1 (D)
John Melcher§, 2 (D)

Nebraska

Robert V. Denney, 1 (R)
Glenn Cunningham, 2 (R)
Dave Martin, 3 (R)

Nevada

Walter S. Baring (D)

New Hampshire

Louis C. Wyman, 1 (R)
James C. Cleveland, 2 (R)

New Jersey

John E. Hunt, 1 (R)
Charles W. Sandman, Jr., 2 (R)
James J. Howard, 3 (D)
Frank Thompson, Jr., 4 (D)
Peter H. B. Frelinghuysen, 5 (R)
William T. Cahill◆, 6 (R)
William B. Widnall, 7 (R)
Robert A. Roe¶, 8 (D)
Henry Helstoski, 9 (D)
Peter W. Rodino, Jr., 10 (D)
Joseph G. Minish, 11 (D)
Florence P. Dwyer, 12 (R)
Cornelius E. Gallagher, 13 (D)
Dominick V. Daniels, 14 (D)
Edward J. Patten, 15 (D)

New Mexico

Manuel Lujan, Jr., 1 (R)
Ed Foreman, 2 (R)

New York

Otis G. Pike, 1 (D)
James R. Grover, Jr., 2 (R)
Lester L. Wolff, 3 (D)
John W. Wydler, 4 (R)
Allard K. Lowenstein, 5 (D)
Seymour Halpern, 6 (R)
Joseph P. Addabbo, 7 (D)
Benjamin S. Rosenthal, 8 (D)
James J. Delaney, 9 (D)
Emanuel Celler, 10 (D)
Frank J. Brasco, 11 (D)
Shirley Chisholm, 12 (D)
Bertram L. Podell, 13 (D)
John J. Rooney, 14 (D)
Hugh L. Carey, 15 (D)
John M. Murphy, 16 (D)
Edward I. Koch, 17 (D)
Adam Clayton Powell, 18 (D)
Leonard Farbstein, 19 (D)
William F. Ryan, 20 (D)
James H. Scheuer, 21 (D)
Jacob H. Gilbert, 22 (D)
Jonathan B. Bingham, 23 (D)
Mario Biaggi, 24 (D)
Richard L. Ottinger, 25 (D)
Ogden R. Reid, 26 (R)
Martin B. McKneally, 27 (R)
Hamilton Fish, Jr., 28 (R)
Daniel E. Button, 29 (R)
Carleton J. King, 30 (R)
Robert C. McEwen, 31 (R)
Alexander Pirnie, 32 (R)
Howard W. Robison, 33 (R)
James M. Hanley, 34 (D)
Samuel S. Stratton, 35 (D)
Frank Horton, 36 (R)
Barber B. Conable, Jr., 37 (R)
James F. Hastings, 38 (R)
Richard D. McCarthy, 39 (D)
Henry P. Smith III, 40 (R)
Thaddeus J. Dulski, 41 (D)

North Carolina

Walter B. Jones, 1 (D)
L. H. Fountain, 2 (D)
David N. Henderson, 3 (D)
Nick Galifianakis, 4 (D)
Wilmer (Vinegar Bend) Mizell, 5 (R)
Richardson Preyer, 6 (D)

† Elected in November 1969 to fill unexpired term of Donald Rumsfeld (R).
‡ Elected in September 1969 to fill unexpired term of the late William H. Bates (R).
§ Elected in June 1969 to fill unexpired term of James F. Battin (R).
◆ Resigned after elected governor of New Jersey in November 1969.
¶ Elected in November 1969 to fill unexpired term of Charles S. Joelson (D).

Alton Lennon, 7 (D)
Earl B. Ruth, 8 (R)
Charles Raper Jonas, 9 (R)
James T. Broyhill, 10 (R)
Roy A. Taylor, 11 (D)

North Dakota

Mark Andrews, 1 (R)
Thomas S. Kleppe, 2 (R)

Ohio

Robert Taft, Jr., 1 (R)
Donald D. Clancy, 2 (R)
Charles W. Whalen, Jr., 3 (R)
William M. McCulloch, 4 (R)
Delbert L. Latta, 5 (R)
William H. Harsha, 6 (R)
Clarence J. Brown, 7 (R)
Jackson E. Betts, 8 (R)
Thomas L. Ashley, 9 (D)
Clarence E. Miller, 10 (R)
J. William Stanton, 11 (R)
Samuel L. Devine, 12 (R)
Charles A. Mosher, 13 (R)
William H. Ayres, 14 (R)
Chalmers P. Wylie, 15 (R)
Frank T. Bow, 16 (R)
John M. Ashbrook, 17 (R)
Wayne L. Hays, 18 (D)
Michael J. Kirwan, 19 (D)
Michael A. Feighan, 20 (D)
Louis Stokes, 21 (D)
Charles A. Vanik, 22 (D)
William E. Minshall, 23 (R)
Donald E. Lukens, 24 (R)

Oklahoma

Page Belcher, 1 (R)
Ed Edmondson, 2 (D)
Carl Albert, 3 (D)
Tom Steed, 4 (D)
John Jarman, 5 (D)
John N. Happy Camp, 6 (R)

Oregon

Wendell Wyatt, 1 (R)
Al Ullman, 2 (D)
Edith Green, 3 (D)
John Dellenback, 4 (R)

Pennsylvania

William A. Barrett, 1 (D)
Robert N. C. Nix, 2 (D)
James A. Byrne, 3 (D)
Joshua Eilberg, 4 (D)
William J. Green, 5 (D)
Gus Yatron, 6 (D)
Lawrence G. Williams, 7 (R)
Edward G. Biester, Jr., 8 (R)
G. Robert Watkins, 9 (R)
Joseph M. McDade, 10 (R)
Daniel J. Flood, 11 (D)
J. Irving Whalley, 12 (R)
R. Lawrence Coughlin, 13 (R)
William S. Moorhead, 14 (D)
Fred B. Rooney, 15 (D)
Edwin D. Eshleman, 16 (R)
Herman T. Schneebeli, 17 (R)
Robert J. Corbett, 18 (R)
George A. Goodling, 19 (R)
Joseph M. Gaydos, 20 (D)
John H. Dent, 21 (D)
John P. Saylor, 22 (R)
Albert W. Johnson, 23 (R)
Joseph P. Vigorito, 24 (D)
Frank M. Clark, 25 (D)
Thomas E. Morgan, 26 (D)
James G. Fulton, 27 (R)

Rhode Island

Fernand J. St. Germain, 1 (D)
Robert O. Tiernan, 2 (D)

South Carolina

L. Mendel Rivers, 1 (D)
Albert W. Watson, 2 (R)
Wm. Jennings Bryan Dorn, 3 (D)
James R. Mann, 4 (D)
Tom S. Gettys, 5 (D)
John L. McMillan, 6 (D)

South Dakota

Ben Reifel, 1 (R)
E. Y. Berry, 2 (R)

Tennessee

James H. Quillen, 1 (R)
John J. Duncan, 2 (R)
W. E. Brock, 3 (R)
Joe L. Evins, 4 (D)
Richard Fulton, 5 (D)
William R. Anderson, 6 (D)
Ray Blanton, 7 (D)
Ed Jones†, 8 (D)
Dan Kuykendall, 9 (R)

Texas

Wright Patman, 1 (D)
John Dowdy, 2 (D)
James M. Collins, 3 (R)
Ray Roberts, 4 (D)
Earle Cabell, 5 (D)
Olin E. Teague, 6 (D)
George Bush, 7 (R)
Bob Eckhardt, 8 (D)
Jack Brooks, 9 (D)
J. J. Pickle, 10 (D)
W. R. Poage, 11 (D)
Jim Wright, 12 (D)
Graham Purcell, 13 (D)
John Young, 14 (D)
Eligio de la Garza, 15 (D)
Richard White, 16 (D)
Omar Burleson, 17 (D)
Robert Price, 18 (R)
George H. Mahon, 19 (D)
Henry B. Gonzalez, 20 (D)
O. C. Fisher, 21 (D)
Bob Casey, 22 (D)
Abraham Kazen, Jr., 23 (D)

Utah

Laurence J. Burton, 1 (R)
Sherman P. Lloyd, 2 (R)

Vermont

Robert T. Stafford (R)

Virginia

Thomas N. Downing, 1 (D)
G. William Whitehurst, 2 (R)
David E. Satterfield III, 3 (D)
Watkins M. Abbitt, 4 (D)
W. C. (Dan) Daniel, 5 (D)
Richard H. Poff, 6 (R)
John O. Marsh, Jr., 7 (D)
William Lloyd Scott, 8 (R)
William C. Wampler, 9 (R)
Joel T. Broyhill, 10 (R)

Washington

Thomas M. Pelly, 1 (R)
Lloyd Meeds, 2 (D)
Julia Butler Hansen, 3 (D)
Catherine May, 4 (R)
Thomas S. Foley, 5 (D)
Floyd V. Hicks, 6 (D)
Brock Adams, 7 (D)

West Virginia

Robert H. Mollohan, 1 (D)
Harley O. Staggers, 2 (D)
John M. Slack, 3 (D)
Ken Hechler, 4 (D)
James Kee, 5 (D)

Wisconsin

Henry C. Schadeberg, 1 (R)
Robert W. Kastenmeier, 2 (D)
Vernon W. Thomson, 3 (R)
Clement J. Zablocki, 4 (D)
Henry S. Reuss, 5 (D)
William A. Steiger, 6 (R)
David R. Obey‡, 7 (D)
John W. Byrnes, 8 (R)
Glenn R. Davis, 9 (R)
Alvin E. O'Konski, 10 (R)

Wyoming

John Wold (R)

"—It's my tax reform-reform bill—"

GRAHAM, "ARKANSAS GAZETTE," FROM BEN ROTH AGENCY

† Elected in March 1969 to fill unexpired term of the late Robert A. Everett (D).
‡ Elected in April 1969 to fill unexpired term of Melvin R. Laird (R).

CONSERVATION. Man continued in 1969 to poison his surroundings as a consequence of the technology that has given him great material gains. A gloomy report on human environment issued by the United Nations (UN) in June said, "It is becoming apparent that if current trends continue, the future of life on earth could be endangered." It was forecast that the earth could begin to become uninhabitable by as early as 1990.

UPI COMPIX

Oil from a leaking offshore well near Santa Barbara fouled southern California beaches early in 1969. New regulations were designed to prevent a recurrence.

Efforts to Stem Environmental Pollution

In March the UN began planning for an international conference on environmental pollution in 1972. Worldwide base stations for pollution study were preliminarily proposed. These stations would conduct continuing tests of air, water, soil, and plant and animal life. Results would be coordinated in central stations for evaluation and response.

Senator Edmund S. Muskie (D, Me.) worked unsuccessfully to establish a select Senate committee on technology and the human environment. Scientists testifying before the Senate Subcommittee on Intergovernmental Affairs, headed by Muskie, endorsed the idea of a new committee and sounded dire warnings about the future of man's environment if technology is not controlled.

Pesticidal use of DDT and other chlorinated hydrocarbons came under mounting attack. Sweden banned all applications of DDT for two years; some Australian states outlawed it indefinitely. In July the U.S. Department of Agriculture temporarily halted use of DDT and eight other pesticides.

Nitrogen fertilizers were blamed for raising the nitrate content of food plants and groundwater to levels surpassing the safety limits established by the U.S. Public Health Service. Through drainage the excess nitrogen was also responsible for premature aging of streams and lakes by aiding alga growth. Unchecked growth of algae consumed the oxygen needed by fish and other aquatic life.

Water Pollution Makes Headlines

Pacific coastal waters from Alaska to California were plagued by damaging oil slicks in 1969. The most disastrous took place in the Santa Barbara Channel along the coast of southern California. There, an offshore oil well sprang an undersea leak that spread some 200,000 gallons of crude oil along 30 miles of gleaming beach. Thousands of cormorants, ducks, gulls, sandpipers, and loons died from oil poisoning. Ecological damage to shellfish, plankton, seals, and whales was expected to be severe. The disaster prompted U.S. Secretary of the Interior Walter J. Hickel to temporarily halt drilling on federal offshore leases in the channel. By April, however, drilling was resumed on some of the Santa Barbara leases because operations allegedly could be done with "minimum hazard."

In other mishaps, a disabled oil tanker spread several thousand barrels of petroleum over 180

Engineers in 1969 virtually stopped the flow of water over the American Falls at Niagara, N.Y., while they studied means of reinforcing the rock to prevent further erosion of the falls.

CANADIAN PRESS

square miles of ocean southwest of Anchorage, Alaska. In Humboldt Bay, near Eureka, Calif., a broken hose caused some 60,000 gallons of diesel fuel to flow into the sea. The oil leak caused the death of 5,000 waterfowl, mostly ducks.

Communities threatened by offshore oil leaks were generally powerless in containing the oil spread. To combat beach pollution the Federal Water Pollution Control Administration's "Project Bubble" began during the year. In an initial experiment, perforated underwater pipes were laid in the water near test beaches. Then, air pumped from powerful compressors formed thick barriers of bubbles capable of blocking flows of oil, floating debris, garbage, and dissolved sewage.

A proposed pipeline to carry heated oil from Alaska's North Slope to the Gulf of Alaska upset many conservationists. Ecologists warned that industrial intrusion into this wilderness would create difficult problems in protecting natural resources and wildlife. A ground-level pipeline, for example, might block the migration paths of the caribou that traverse the area. Another concern surrounded the possible damage the pipeline, which would carry oil at 180° F., might impose on the frozen tundra supporting the region's wildlife. Secretary Hickel promised that the Department of the Interior would hold public hearings to consider all views on the proposed pipeline. (*See* Fuel and Power: Petroleum.)

Water Pollution Continues

Disastrous pollution of the Rhine River, one of Europe's major waterways, occurred in June. An undetermined amount of endosulfan, a chlorinated sulfate insecticide, somehow entered the river and poisoned its German and Dutch portions. Endosulfan, deadlier than DDT, wiped out virtually all the fish in the north Rhine, killed many waterfowl, and alarmed cities that relied on Rhine water for drinking. So destructive was the poison that live trout placed in the Rhine for testing purposes died within seven minutes.

Pollutants affected two U.S. rivers that were undergoing cleanup efforts. An earthen wall broke north of Pittsburgh, Pa., releasing several thousand gallons of slimy oil wastes into the Allegheny River. The 15-mile-long sludge killed more than a million fish before it reached the Ohio River. In addition to oil wastes the river system was increasingly contaminated with raw sewage, iron oxide, sulfuric acid, and other industrial wastes. The rising pollution pointed up the weak enforcement powers of the Ohio River Valley Water Sanitation Commission, which since 1949 had spent a billion dollars trying to rid pollution from the waterway.

Federal and provincial agencies in Canada began an unprecedented cooperative program of water-pollution control in 1969. The 35,000 square miles of Canadian industrial area bordering the United States was the target of initial efforts. Canadian authorities formerly blamed much of the area's pollution problem on U.S. sources. However, a recent survey showed that 90% of Quebec province's untreated sewage was being emptied into lakes and rivers, factories and paper mills were dumping excessive chemicals and wood wastes into the Ottawa River, and lower Ontario's industrial complex was

Near Koblenz, West Germany, in June 1969, workmen in a rowboat collect dead fish from the Rhine River. Masses of fish were killed by endosulfan, a chlorinated sulfate insecticide. Authorities discouraged drinking Rhine water or swimming in the river.

DPA FROM PICTORIAL PARADE

in fact a major polluter of Lakes Huron, Erie, and Ontario.

In the Soviet Union, conservationists triumphed in efforts to save Lake Baykal, one of the world's largest bodies of fresh water, from industrial pollution. The Soviet government declared the lake and its drainage area a protected zone.

Drive Against Air Pollution

A coordinated attack by city, state, and federal governments was waged against the nation's dirty air in 1969. The National Air Pollution Control Administration issued guidelines indicating the minimum levels at which certain air pollutants are harmful to health. These pollutants, harmful in specified amounts, were "particulate matter," including dust and smoke, and the sulfur oxides, which result from the burning of coal and oil containing large percentages of sulfur.

Studies began on nationwide criteria for measuring dangerous levels of carbon monoxide, oxidants, nitrogen oxides, and other automobile-caused contaminants. Some states even introduced regulations to control automobile exhaust fumes. There was also increasing interest in the development of an electric or steam car as an alternative to the present gasoline-engine automobile.

Conservationists Say "No" to Wilderness Resort; Other Conservation Events of 1969

Strong opposition was voiced when the U.S. Forest Service allowed private interests to develop a resort in California's Sequoia National Forest. Conservationists feared that a highway and high-voltage power line needed to service the resort would upset the ecology of the forest. Furthermore, it was surmised that the area would experience the same blight from overuse befalling Yosemite National Park. The resort plan was temporarily stymied by a court injunction calling for additional hearings on the land-use proposal.

On his last day in office, former U.S. President Lyndon B. Johnson proclaimed part of the Colorado River area off limits to further commercial intrusion. The proclamation added some 50,000 acres to the Arches National Monument and 215,000 acres to the Capitol Reef National Monument. It also created a new national monument—Marble Canyon—eventually to be included in Grand Canyon National Park. Although mining and livestock interests objected, Congress was loath to revoke any president's conservation proclamation.

As a first step toward development of the new National Wild and Scenic Rivers System, the National Park Service became responsible for 134 islands in Wisconsin's St. Croix River. Also, the federal government and the state of Florida opposed construction of an airport near Miami that would endanger Everglades National Park, a unique ecosystem often threatened in recent years, especially with water deprivation. The U.S. Soil Conservation Service made the encouraging dis-

BARRY GINBUTT, "LONDON TELEGRAPH," FROM BEN ROTH AGENCY

closure that wind erosion on the Great Plains was at its lowest in 35 years.

Removed from the Department of the Interior's extinct list were three birds—the Molokai creeper, the Maui Nukupuu, and the Puerto Rican plain pigeon. Small groups of the birds were recently sighted. However, they were transferred to the agency's list of rare and endangered species. The peregrine falcon, possibly falling victim to pesticides, was also placed on the endangered list. In 1966 the first such list contained 78 endangered species. In 1969, about 90 species were considered to be in jeopardy. (*See* Feature Article: "Black Africa Saves the Game.")

Conservationists from several countries tried to halt devastation of the famed Great Barrier Reef off Australia. Starfish called the "crown of thorns" were blamed for wiping out the coral that have kept the reef and other coral islands of the Pacific Ocean constantly rebuilt. Decline of triton shellfish, natural predators of the crown of thorns, was thought the explanation for overabundance of the starfish. (*See also* Animals and Wildlife; Fish and Fisheries; National Park Service. *See in* CE: Conservation.)

CONSUMER PROTECTION. Thirty-three states had established consumer-affairs offices by Nov. 1, 1969. Members of the U.S. Congress evinced increasing interest in the problems of the consumer and introduced more than 100 bills relating to consumer problems.

Bess Myerson Grant, a former Miss America, was sworn in as New York City's commissioner of consumer affairs in March. A controversial order requiring unit pricing of a variety of food packages was issued by Mrs. Grant's department in September. By Nov. 20, 1969, food retailers were required to state the price per pound, ounce, or other unit for many items—easily enabling the consumer to see the comparative prices of various packages.

Other Measures to Aid the Consumer

A class-suit action may be filed by an organization on behalf of an entire group of consumers. One consumer who feels wronged may be unwilling to sue, thinking that the amount of money involved may be too small to justify the expenses of a lawsuit. When an organization, public or private, brings suit, then all of the consumers affected may achieve redress. For example, in a class-suit action the Supreme Court of the United States ruled invalid a Wisconsin law that allowed creditors to garnishee wages without first proving in court that a valid debt existed.

Proponents of the class-suit action were alarmed by one provision of U.S. President Richard M. Nixon's consumer message, issued on October 30. Nixon said that he would ask Congress to restrict consumer-damage suits against businesses in federal courts—only after the U.S. attorney general had proved the case in court could individuals seek redress. Mrs. Grant asked, on the one hand, why consumers had to wait for government action or, on the other hand, why government proof was not sufficient to initiate redress to individuals.

Other provisions of President Nixon's consumer message proved more popular with consumer advocates. One was a request for a division of consumer protection to be established in the Department of Justice. Another was a request for increased authority for the Federal Trade Commission (FTC), including the initiative to seek preliminary injunctions in federal courts against deceptive practices. In September a group of renowned economists and lawyers had issued a report calling for sweeping changes in the FTC, or its abolition; the report charged that the FTC spent its time on "trivial matters" when it should have been concentrating on protecting the poor and the uneducated against retail abuses.

Another aid to consumers was the new "truth in lending" law, effective July 1, 1969. The law does not regulate rates of interest or terms of credit, but it does require a conspicuous disclosure of true annual rates of interest, finance charges, or service charges. (For example, a retailer who fixes the typical service charge of 1.5% per month must now state that this amounts to 18% per year.) The new law also provides that if any credit terms are disclosed in an advertisement, then all terms must be disclosed—such as the interest rate and the monthly payment.

NORRIS, "VANCOUVER (B.C.) SUN," FROM BEN ROTH AGENCY

". . . Now, you say these essential safety features will add about $150 to the price?"

The effects of cyclamates in low-calorie foods and monosodium glutamate (MSG) in baby food were deemed potentially harmful. The Food and Drug Administration took action to protect consumers. (*See* Drugs; Food; Home Economics.)

Other Consumer Advocates in the News

Ralph Nader continued to battle for the consumer. He was the first to issue warnings against MSG in baby food, and he made repeated public warnings about the dangers of DDT. (*See* Insects and Pesticides.) He also called for a Congressional investigation of airline safety standards.

President Nixon appointed Virginia H. Knauer of Philadelphia, Pa., his special assistant for consumer affairs in April. Earlier in the year he had appointed Willie Mae Rogers; she resigned after a few days because of conflict-of-interest charges involving her job with the Good Housekeeping Institute. (*See also* Economy; Toys and Games.)

COOPERATIVES. Five cooperatives ranked among the top 500 businesses in the United States in 1969, according to an annual survey of industrial firms by *Fortune* magazine. Agway of Syracuse, N.Y., a farm supply cooperative, was judged the largest cooperative in the nation on the basis of its volume. Farmland Industries of Kansas City, Mo., attained the largest net income of the cooperatives on the list. Other high-ranking cooperatives included Land O' Lakes, a dairy cooperative; Cotton Producers Association of Atlanta, Ga., a farm marketing cooperative; and Farmers Union Central Exchange, a farm supply and marketing cooperative.

Many cooperatives continued to pledge aid or assistance to persons in the United States and abroad. The Cooperative for American Relief Everywhere, Inc. (CARE), received donations of $12,252,404, which made possible distribution of aid valued at $79,956,809, including the value of U.S. commodity donations.

Many Negro leaders exploited the potentials of cooperative unions to aid in achieving black economic goals. For example, the Harlem Consumers Cooperative, Inc., supermarket in New York City, built in 1968 with $5 shares bought by the people of Harlem, averaged $39,000 worth of business a week—exceeding the original goal.

There were about 700 cooperative housing programs providing shelter for 200,000 families in 1969, and many more programs were in various stages of planning. The cooperatives ranged in size from Co-op City in New York City with 15,372 units—which makes it equivalent in size to the tenth largest city in New York State—to apartment buildings with a dozen or fewer units. On the West coast, the Mutual Ownership Development Foundation (MODF) was the primary developer of housing cooperatives. In Oakland, Calif., MODF embarked on a rehabilitation of a run-down 72-unit housing development for cooperative ownership. The cost was expected to be about two thirds that of comparable rental units in the city. (*See in* CE: Co-operative Societies.)

COSMETICS. In 1969 the trend toward a healthier, more natural look in makeup continued. The year's contribution from the cosmetic industry came in the form of the "discovery" of soap and water as a cleansing agent. Although at first this seemed to be a boon to the woman who had been using high-priced cleansing creams, the new scrub soaps proved to be even more expensive. One U.S. firm offered a 6-ounce cake of facial soap at a price of $7.50.

The face did lose some of the industry's attention, however, as a new concentration was given to "below the neck" beauty. Newly marketed products included a body night cream, a leg-conditioning lotion, and a cleansing gel.

Actress Zsa Zsa Gabor entered the beauty business during the year, advising women, "Never put anything on your skin that isn't good enough to eat." The products developed by her company, Zsa Zsa Ltd., have edible bases. Among them were an herb-scented formula and an almond cleansing oil.

Another newcomer to the industry was Blanche Calloway, sister of the entertainer Cab Calloway. Miss Calloway's firm, Afram House of Miami (Fla.), offers its line through the mail and in department-store boutiques. Afram cosmetics are especially created for the black woman's skin color and texture. They differ from those used by white women in that the cosmetics for black women are water-based rather than oil-based, in order to accommodate the natural oils in the black woman's

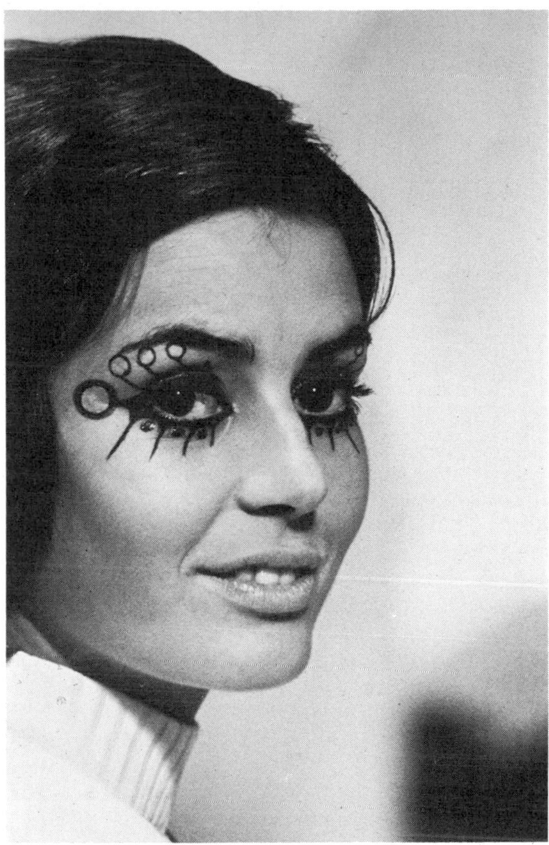

LIAISON AGENCY

AGIP FROM PICTORIAL PARADE

Although the "painted look" was generally viewed with disfavor in 1969, this Paris, France, model (top) sported flamboyant eye makeup. Artificial "naturalness" (bottom) was displayed by a girl who overcame with makeup her lack of freckles.

skin. The Afram line includes a foundation cream, a lime facial mask, lipstick, powder, eyeshadow, and a water-free hair-set spray.

During 1969 some 22 cosmetics firms received adverse pubilicity when the U.S. Food and Drug Administration revealed that each one had failed to make adequate bacteriological tests of the raw materials used as well as the finished products. As a result a number of products, primarily baby and hand lotions, were labeled "significantly contaminated" and recalled from the market.

COSTA RICA. Despite altercations with its partners in the Central American Common Market, Costa Rica maintained a healthy economy in 1969. Repeated disagreements with the other nations stemmed largely from the Legislative Assembly's refusal to ratify the Protocol of San José signed by the other four countries in 1968. The pact was also a main source of conflict between President José Joaquín Trejos Fernández of the National Unification party and the National Liberationist-dominated assembly.

Provisions of the disputed agreement included a five-year imposition of a 30% surcharge on imports of nonessential goods from outside Central America and an emergency sales tax of 10% to 20% on semiluxury and luxury products made in Central America. Another point of contention with market partners was Costa Rica's refusal to import cheap rice from El Salvador in face of heavy surpluses of more expensive Costa Rican rice.

Growth in manufacturing output and large increases in the banana crop for export helped the economic picture in 1969. Costa Rica recorded a 10.2% growth rate in 1968, probably the largest in Latin America.

In 1969 the World Bank granted Costa Rica an $18.5-million loan for the expansion of power and telecommunications. Two foreign finance companies were established, and plans progressed for the $71-million bauxite-mining and -processing facilities to be established by Aluminum Co. of America (Alcoa). (*See in* CE: Costa Rica.)

CRIME. Serious crimes in the United States in 1968 totaled almost 4.5 million, an increase of 17% over 1967, according to the Uniform Crime Reports published by the Federal Bureau of Investigation (FBI). From 1960 to 1968 daytime burglaries of residences rose 247%. A study of offenders released in 1963 revealed that 63% were rearrested within five years and 43% within one year.

During the first six months of 1969 serious crimes in the United States increased 9% over the same period in 1968. Violent crimes rose 13%, with robbery up 17%, forcible rape 15%, aggravated assault 10%, and murder 8%. Large cities of 250,000 and above in population had an increase of 8% in serious crime during the first six months of 1969. The rise in the suburbs was 11%; in rural areas, 8%.

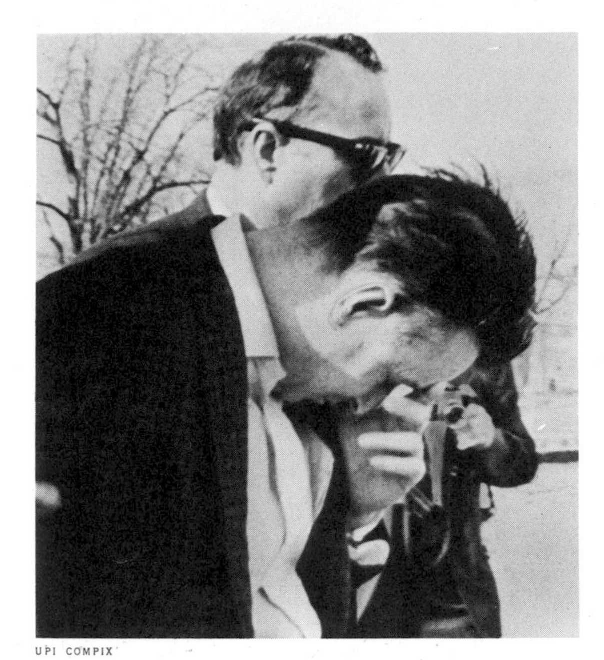

UPI COMPIX

James Earl Ray holds his hand to his face as he is led into the Tennessee State Prison to begin serving a 99-year sentence for the 1968 murder of the Rev. Martin Luther King, Jr., the leader of the nonviolent black civil rights movement.

For the first time since the Federal Bureau of Prisons began keeping records of civil executions in 1930, there were no persons executed in the United States in 1968. From 1930 to 1968 there were 3,859 persons executed, with a high of 199 in 1935. As of Dec. 31, 1968, there were 479 persons under sentence of death as compared with 435 on the same date the preceding year.

Terror gripped eastern Michigan as a result of a series of murders of young women, all following a similar pattern. On March 21, 1969, the body of Jane Louise Mixer, 23, a first-year law student at the University of Michigan in Ann Arbor, was found in a cemetery. Four days later the unclothed body of 16-year-old Marilyn Skelton was found near a lovers' lane section of Ann Arbor. She had been sexually assaulted, beaten, and strangled with a belt. Her murder was the fourth within a 15-mile triangle during a 21-month period and the second in four days.

A University of Michigan graduate student, Margaret Phillips, was engaged in research work on the slayings in the area. When a convicted rapist, Ernest R. Bishop, Jr., was paroled on Dec. 27, 1968, and placed under the supervision of a former University of Michigan sociology professor, Tom Mayer, Miss Phillips was asked to aid in the exconvict's rehabilitation program. The girl was later found murdered and on July 7, 1969, Bishop was arrested and charged with murder.

Karen Sue Beineman, an 18-year-old freshman at Eastern Michigan University in Ypsilanti, left her

PICTORIAL PARADE

A sign on a Washington, D.C., bus indicates that the driver has no cash on hand. Bus companies in several major U.S. cities switched to exact-fare systems in order to eliminate the threat of robbery.

dormitory after lunch on July 23. She was last seen riding with a motorcyclist. Her body was found in a wooded ravine on the outskirts of nearby Ann Arbor on July 26. A 22-year-old college senior, John Norman Collins, a motorcycle enthusiast, was arrested on August 1 and charged with the murder of Miss Beineman. She was the fourth young woman to be murdered in the area since March and the seventh within a two-year period.

The bodies of five slain persons, including the motion-picture and television actress Sharon Tate, were discovered in a plush Bel Air home in Los Angeles, Calif., on August 9. In the house, officers found some hashish and methedrine. The home had been rented by the actress' husband, Roman Polanski, who was in Europe directing a movie. On December 8 a Los Angeles grand jury indicted Charles Manson, leader of a nomadic group of young people, and four others for the murders.

Following a trial lasting almost four months, a jury in Los Angeles, Calif., on April 23, returned a death-penalty verdict against Sirhan Bishara Sirhan, a 25-year-old Jerusalem-born Jordanian, for the assassination of Senator Robert F. Kennedy (D, N.Y.). On May 21 Judge Herbert V. Walker ordered death in the gas chamber for Sirhan.

On March 10 James Earl Ray, a 41-year-old escaped convict from the Missouri State Penitentiary, entered a plea of guilty in Memphis, Tenn., to the assassination on April 4, 1968, of the Rev. Martin Luther King, Jr., noted Negro civil rights leader. Judge W. Preston Battle, Jr., sentenced Ray to 99 years in prison. On March 11 Ray was taken from Memphis to the state prison in Nashville, Tenn., to serve his sentence.

The long-awaited trial in New Orleans, La., of Clay L. Shaw, a retired New Orleans businessman, accused of conspiring with Lee Harvey Oswald to assassinate the late President John F. Kennedy in Dallas, Tex., on Nov. 22, 1963, ended on March 1. The jury deliberated only 50 minutes and on the first ballot unanimously acquitted Shaw.

Numerous airplanes were hijacked again in 1969. Most of the hijackings occurred in the Eastern part of the United States, and the planes were forced to fly to Cuba. On June 17 the longest U.S. hijacking as of that date occurred when a Trans World Airlines (TWA) jet carrying 87 persons was seized as it was in flight from Oakland, Calif., to New York City and forced to fly to Havana. The hijacking

Police and FBI agents swarm around the TWA plane hijacked by Raffaele Minichiello just after it landed at John F. Kennedy International Airport in New York City on November 1. The plane took off again, landing finally in Rome, Italy. The hijacking was the longest to date.

"THE NEW YORK TIMES"

was the 28th in 1969. This record was broken, however, on October 31, when a TWA jet en route from Los Angeles to San Francisco, Calif., was hijacked to Rome, Italy. Several stops were made for refueling during the 6,900-mile trip. Italian police arrested Raffaele Minichiello, a lance corporal in the U.S. Marine Corps, for the crime. (*See also* Transportation: Airlines.)

The alarming rise in robberies on public transportation systems created major crime problems in most major U.S. cities. During the first eight months of 1969 there were 356 bus robberies in New York City as compared with 244 in 1968, 97 in 1967, and 59 in 1966. In Chicago, Ill., there were 57 bus robberies in the month of December 1968 as compared with 28 in December 1967. Following the murder of a bus driver in Washington, D.C., a plan was adopted there on June 1, 1968, to install an exact-fare system, which eliminates the need for the driver to carry money or make change. By August 1969 the exact-fare system had spread to 34 other cities and resulted in a marked decrease in robberies. (*See also* Law; Police; Prisons. *See in* CE: Prisons and Punishments.)

CUBA. Relations between Cuba and the Soviet Union showed marked improvement during 1969. This was attributed in part to Cuba's decision to concentrate on economic development rather than on openly instigating violent revolution in other Latin American nations. Also, it was revealed that a secret agreement had been made between Cuba and the Soviet Union. Cuba's standard of living continued to fall during the year, and further rationing was imposed on the people.

"Our Friends the Russians"

In a January speech Cuba's Premier Fidel Castro praised Soviet-Cuban ties, and soon thereafter the Cuban government signed a new trade agreement with the Soviet Union. In July a squadron of Soviet warships paid a weeklong visit to Cuba. Castro stated that Cuba's ports would always be open to ships of the Soviet Union. This abrupt change of attitude was explained by a Cuban defector to the United States.

Two Cuban officials defected to the United States in 1969: one was an intelligence officer, the other a diplomat. Both said their defection was motivated

Cuban students march in a massive parade in Havana on Jan. 2, 1969, commemorating the tenth anniversary of the Cuban revolution. The poster on the building honors two dead heroes of the revolution, Ernesto (Che) Guevara (left) and Camilo Cienfuegos.

CAMERA PRESS—PIX FROM PUBLIX

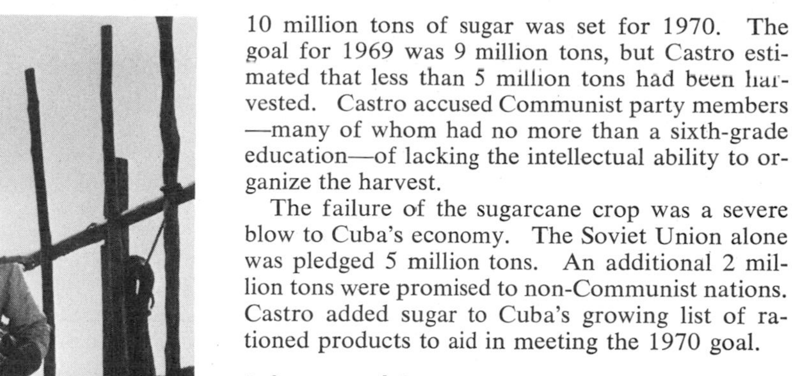

HOWARD HARRISON FROM NANCY PALMER AGENCY

Agricultural workers are seen at the task of bringing in Cuba's sugarcane harvest. The goal for 1969 for production of this important crop was set at 10 million tons.

by disillusionment with the extent of Soviet domination over Cuba. The intelligence officer, who defected in March, told of a secret Cuban agreement with the Soviet Union made in 1968. The Soviets agreed to continue their economic aid and increase their technical aid. In return Cuba agreed to curtail its criticism of the Soviet Union. (*See* Intelligence Operations.)

A Return to the Soil

In 1969 Cuba appeared to place more emphasis on improving its own economy than in inciting other Latin American revolutions. Castro, however, pledged Cuban support for any "true revolution" in Latin America. Another Cuban official stated that Cuba would remain an ideological base for Latin American revolutions.

The new economic emphasis in 1969 was on agriculture rather than on industrialization. A goal of 10 million tons of sugar was set for 1970. The goal for 1969 was 9 million tons, but Castro estimated that less than 5 million tons had been harvested. Castro accused Communist party members—many of whom had no more than a sixth-grade education—of lacking the intellectual ability to organize the harvest.

The failure of the sugarcane crop was a severe blow to Cuba's economy. The Soviet Union alone was pledged 5 million tons. An additional 2 million tons were promised to non-Communist nations. Castro added sugar to Cuba's growing list of rationed products to aid in meeting the 1970 goal.

Refugees and Runaways

In January an estimated 150 Cubans attempted a daring escape from Cuba by entering the U.S. naval base at Guantánamo Bay. The Cubans used a truck to approach the base and then, armed with only one pistol, fought their way past Cuban sentries and over barbed-wire fences. Only 88 of the escapees reached safety inside the base. The others were killed or captured by Cuban soldiers.

On September 19 the Cuban government announced the enactment of an antihijacking law that provided for the extradition of airplane or boat hijackers who were not genuine political refugees. The Cubans claimed the right to decide if the hijacker was a political refugee or a common transgressor. Most of the planes hijacked in 1969 belonged to U.S. companies. (*See in* CE: Cuba.)

CYPRUS. The situation on Cyprus was peaceful during 1969. The United Nations (UN) peacekeeping force continued to watch over the island. In June the UN Security Council extended the mandate for keeping the 3,480 men on Cyprus for another six months.

Little progress was made in the negotiations between the Greek Cypriots and the Turkish Cypriots during the year. The Greek Cypriots felt that the Turkish Cypriots still wanted a system that would amount to a virtual separation of the two communities. The Greek Cypriots wanted to avoid even a semipartition of the island.

Both sides wanted autonomous control set up in the Turkish and the Greek communities. Disagreement arose in the discussions over the extent of autonomous control in the Turkish community. The Turkish Cypriots wanted their areas to be completely under the rule of Turkish Cypriot councils with control over the police, public services, and taxation. The Greek Cypriots wanted the areas with a predominantly Turkish population to have just a majority of Turkish Cypriot officials in charge of the local government.

Two subcommittees were created during the year to examine the problem of reemploying Turkish Cypriots in the island's public services and to consider a new law that would allow Greek and Turkish Cypriots to vote in a common electoral roll. (*See in* CE: Cyprus.)

CZECHOSLOVAKIA. The last vestiges of the liberal reform in Czechoslovakia were wiped out in 1969. Former Communist Party First Secretary Alexander Dubcek was relegated to an obscure diplomatic post. Liberal supporters of Dubcek were removed from the Central Committee, and the government gradually came under the control of pro-Soviet administrators. Resistance to the Soviet occupation by the Czechoslovak people, however, continued throughout the year in isolated incidents.

The Fall of Dubcek

On April 17 Dubcek was replaced by Gustav Husak as Communist party leader. Dubcek had led the liberal reforms before the 1968 Soviet-led invasion of Czechoslovakia. Dubcek remained temporarily in the Czechoslovak Presidium.

In the purge that followed Dubcek's removal, Josef Smrkovsky and other liberals were also ousted from their posts, reducing the Presidium from 21 to 11 members. Earlier in the year Smrkovsky had urged his supporters not to stage a strike in the event of his removal from power. He cited the desire of the Slovak Socialist Republic, one of two states in the new federal government, to install a Slovak chairman. Smrkovsky was, however, a symbol of the liberal movement, and his removal was favored by the Soviet Union.

Dubcek was later named chairman of the Federal Assembly. Although Husak pledged to carry on the reforms begun by Dubcek, he warned that resistance by "counter-revolutionary" forces would not be tolerated.

As the Soviet Union succeeded in having the liberal government replaced, attacks on Dubcek increased and a general purge followed. Communist "hard-liners" accused Dubcek of treason, charging that he had advance knowledge of the 1968 Soviet-led invasion. In September Dubcek was removed from the Presidium, and in October he was replaced as chairman of the Federal Assembly by Dalibor Hanes. Dubcek was allowed to remain in the Central Committee, but 29 other liberals were removed.

As part of the antiliberal purge the cabinet resigned. Oldrich Cernik was retained as premier and asked to form a new cabinet. Cernik, a former supporter of Dubcek, in 1969 became a critic of the liberal leader. Dubcek's final fall from power came in December when he was appointed to the relatively obscure post of ambassador to Turkey.

Return to Hard Line

The Control and Audit Commission of the Czechoslovak Communist party said in September that the "right-wing opportunists" who had supported the attempts at liberalization would be disciplined. It said that the authors of the liberal document entitled "2,000 Words" would also be punished. Earlier in the year the more liberal Presidium members had warned the Czechoslovaks not to stage demonstrations for fear that Soviet troops would once again invade the country in force. Also faced with warnings that another Soviet invasion might ensue if anti-Soviet attacks by the press continued, Czechoslovak journalists were "persuaded" to impose voluntary restrictions on the press and on broadcasting media.

As another example of the new pro-Soviet poli-

In Prague, Jan Palach's funeral services were attended by 500,000 people. To protest the Soviet Union's occupation of Czechoslovakia, Palach set himself on fire at the statue in Wenceslaus Square.

GAMMA—PIX FROM PUBLIX

Huge demonstrations occurred in Prague on the night of the first anniversary of the Soviet-led invasion of Czechoslovakia. Here youths shout and shake their fists at the troops.

GAMMA—PIX FROM PUBLIX

cies Husak refused to allow any discussion of the 1968 invasion at the world Communist conference held in Moscow in June. During another visit to Moscow in October Husak condoned the 1968 Soviet-led invasion as a brotherly act.

There were protests by Czechoslovak students and workers against the Soviet pressure to halt the reforms. The most extreme protest was staged in January by one student, Jan Palach. Palach poured gasoline over his body and set himself on fire in Wenceslaus Square in Prague, the capital of Czechoslovakia. Before he died Palach stated that his self-immolation was a protest against the Soviet occupation of Czechoslovakia.

The suicide touched off international expressions of sympathy, and liberal Czechoslovak leaders, including Dubcek and President Ludvik Svoboda, sent a telegram to the boy's mother. Palach was given a hero's funeral, and an estimated 35,000 persons filed past his bier. Contrary to government fears, no outbreak of violence accompanied the funeral.

An ice-hockey game between Czechoslovak and Soviet teams touched off violence in March. After the game, which the Czechoslovak team won, Soviet army barracks were damaged by rioting Czechoslovaks, and the Soviet airline office in Prague was ransacked. After the hockey-game riot strict censorship was reimposed on the press.

The first anniversary of the 1968 invasion was celebrated in August with demonstrations and street fighting. Armored vehicles and Czechoslovak troops moved into Prague to quell the disturbance. Two persons were reported killed and more than 1,300 were arrested. In the yearlong struggle between conservatives and liberals more then 600,000 Communist party members were reported to have resigned.

During the year Col. Emil Zatopek, a long-distance runner and the winner of three gold medals at the 1952 Olympic Games, was expelled from the Czechoslovak army, presumably for supporting democratic reform. The official reason given for his dismissal was that he had violated "legal norms" and had given information about Czechoslovak officials to West European journalists. In November Zatopek resigned from the Czechoslovak Olympic Committee.

Czechoslovak citizens confront the occupation troops. At least two people were killed during the demonstrations.

GAMMA—PIX FROM PUBLIX

In 1968, under Dubcek, an investigation was begun into the death of Czechoslovakia's last non-Communist foreign minister, Jan G. Masaryk. Masaryk had died mysteriously in 1948, and there were suspicions that he had been murdered by Communist agents. Until 1968 the cause of his death had officially been regarded as suicide. In 1969 the Czechoslovak attorney general, under the new hard-line government, issued a report saying that the possibility of murder had been excluded. The report suggested instead that Masaryk may have fallen accidentally from a window ledge to his death. (*See also* Communist Movement. *See in* CE: Czechoslovakia.)

DAHOMEY. Poverty and political instability continued to plague Dahomey in 1969. President Emile Derlin Zinsou, unable to obtain aid from France in January, made an effort to cut Dahomey's annual $32-million budget. The civil service payroll, which consumes about two thirds of the budget, was somewhat reduced. As a result the civil servants became openly hostile toward Zinsou.

Other groups in opposition to the president were unions, the army, and students. Zinsou's regime was in constant danger of being overthrown. In May, 22 persons were arrested for plotting to overthrow the government. In July a group of army officers were charged with plotting to assassinate the chief of staff. Teachers, students, and postal and railway workers staged strikes. In December Zinsou's government was finally toppled by a group of military men, apparently headed by Lieut. Col. Maurice Kouandete, who took over the reins of power.

Dahomey's main hope for economic development appeared to rest on the discovery of oil in offshore waters. Two successful test wells were drilled early in the year. (*See also* Africa. *See in* CE: Dahomey.)

DANCE. In 1969 New York City continued to be the center of dance in the United States, and that city saw more dance than ever before. The primary increase was in modern-dance performances, while black choreographers and dancers were given increasing attention. Once again, foreign and regional companies offered resident New York ballet companies some competition.

January saw the beginning of a month-long season of the Theater 1969 Dance Repertory on Broadway. Featured were modern-dance and ballet troupes under the direction of Merce Cunningham, José Limón, and Alvin Ailey, each of which held the stage for a week. The fourth week was shared by four avant-gardist troupes directed by Twyla Tharp, Meredith Monk, Yvonne Rainer, and Don Redlich. The repertory was financed by a grant from the Ford Foundation.

The Alvin Ailey American Dance Theater gained special recognition and critical acclaim. The company, composed of ten black and three white dancers, presented works that were founded in Negro life and set to Negro-created music. Among the works presented were 'The Black Belt' and 'The Road of the Phoebe Snow', with music by Duke Ellington. Both were created by Talley Beatty, a black choreographer.

Other black choreographers held classes at a symposium cosponsored by the Harlem Cultural Council and Barnard College in March. The symposium was the first of three dance events financed by Columbia University's urban center and involved Barnard College and the black artistic community.

In June the Stuttgart Ballet from the Württemberg State Theater in Stuttgart, West Germany, opened to an unprecedented reception in New York City. The company, which was virtually unknown in the United States before its Metropolitan Opera House engagement, returned in the fall for a coast-to-coast tour. Under the direction of South African-born John Cranko, it performed a repertoire of three evening length ballets while on tour: Cranko's 'Romeo and Juliet', to the Sergei Prokofiev score; 'The Taming of the Shrew', with a special score by Kurt-Heinz Stolze; and 'Eugene Onegin',

Egon Madsen played the part of the Joker in 'Jeu de Cartes', performed by the Stuttgart (Germany) Ballet in 1969.
HANNES KILIAN

MARTHA SWOPE

John Clifford and Linda Merrill perform in Clifford's new work for the New York City Ballet, 'Prelude, Fugue, and Riffs'. The score was written by Leonard Bernstein.

based on the Aleksander Pushkin tale and the Peter Ilich Tchaikovsky score. In New York, these dances were augmented by the romantic ballet classic 'Giselle'. Principal dancers Richard Cragun and Marcia Haydée received wide acclaim.

The Royal Ballet from the Royal Opera House at Covent Garden in London, England, returned to the United States for an engagement at the Metropolitan Opera House followed by a long transcontinental tour. It was not only the company's 20th anniversary of its American debut but also the 50th birthday celebration of Dame Margot Fonteyn, who heads the troupe as prima ballerina. Dame Margot once again danced the dual role of Odette-Odile in 'Swan Lake' and, as she had done 20 years earlier, played the role of the 16-year-old Princess Aurora in 'The Sleeping Beauty'. She was also seen with Rudolf Nureyev in 'Pelléas and Mélisande', a new ballet created especially for them by Roland Petit.

In 1969 a new dance group, the American Ballet Company, was founded under the direction of 26-year-old Eliot Feld, formerly a principal dancer and a choreographer for the American Ballet Theatre. The company was brought into being with the help of grants and of its resident status at the Brooklyn (N.Y.) Academy of Music. The $350,000 Rockefeller Foundation grant, awarded to the academy in the fall of 1969, benefited the Feld group, two modern-dance companies, and other

In 1969 the Royal Ballet company of London, England, staged Roland Petit's 'Peleas and Melisande'. Margot Fonteyn and Rudolf Nureyev starred.

ZOE DOMINIC

academy enterprises. The American Ballet Company debuted at the Festival of Two Worlds in Spoleto, Italy, and in the United States at a two-week engagement at the Brooklyn Academy.

The American Ballet Theatre was also seen at the Brooklyn Academy of Music early in 1969, ending a two-week season that began in December 1968. Its repertoire included 'Swan Lake', 'Coppélia', 'Les Noces', and 'Gala Performance', as well as two premieres, Michael Smuin's 'The Eternal Idol' and Dennis Nahat's 'Brahms Quintet'. The company traveled to Spain to make a movie of its production of 'Giselle', scheduled for release in 1970.

The New York City Ballet, directed by George Balanchine and Lincoln Kirstein, continued as resident ballet company at the Lincoln Center for the Performing Arts. In 1969 the company's new presentations included Jacques d'Amboise's 'Tchaikovsky Suite'; John Clifford's 'Fantasies', with music by Ralph Vaughan Williams; and Jerome Robbins' 'Dances at a Gathering', to piano music by Frédéric Chopin. Robbins' ballet, his first in many years, was largely classic in form, marking a departure from his characteristically modern style of choreography.

The City Center Joffrey Ballet, in its fourth year of residence at New York City Center, included two 19th-century Danish ballets, August Bournonville's 'Konservatoriet' and 'William Tell Variations', in its repertoire. Other new works were 'Animus', to music of Jacob Druckman, and 'The Poppet', both dances by the company's choreographer, Gerald Arpino. A widely acclaimed Joffrey effort was the production of Léonide Massine's 'The Three-Cornered Hat', a ballet dating back to the Diaghilev era, with music by Manuel de Falla and scenery and costumes by Pablo Picasso. Massine himself directed the revival.

The Harkness Ballet enjoyed an extensive season in Europe and two New York engagements. During the year Lawrence Rhodes, one of the company's principal male dancers and its director, was joined by codirector Benjamin Harkarvy, who was previously with the Netherlands Dance Theater.

Among Europe's major events of 1969 was the Soviet Union's First International Ballet competition, which was held in Moscow. Icelandic-born Helgi Tomasson, a male principal of the Harkness Ballet, received a silver medal. Also during the year the Royal Swedish Ballet featured the first European production of 'Les Noces'. Three Americans—George Balanchine, Norman Walker, and Bill Evans—were invited to stage ballets by the Berlin Opera Ballet. (*See in* CE: Ballet; Dance.)

DEFENSE. Military policies were the subject of increasingly intense controversy in the United States during 1969. Major points of contention included U.S. involvement in the Vietnam conflict; the military draft; the development and deployment of new weapons systems; and defense spending and procurement policies.

Vietnam and the Draft

While the Vietnam peace talks in Paris, France, remained fruitless, U.S. President Richard M. Nixon announced in the year a program for U.S. disengagement in Vietnam. Described as "Vietnamization" of the conflict, the program involved phased withdrawal of U.S. forces from Vietnam as South Vietnamese forces became able to assume increased combat responsibility. (*See* Vietnam.)

In the United States, sharp controversy continued over U.S. participation in the war. President Nixon said in November that a majority of Americans approved his plan of gradual withdrawal. A growing minority continued to demand immediate and unconditional U.S. withdrawal from Vietnam, while some strident voices clamored for military victory over North Vietnam and the Viet Cong.

President Nixon moved also to lessen criticism of the draft—which was particularly unpopular among the young men who were subject to it. Late in the year Congress amended a 1967 law, to permit the implementation of President Nixon's plan to conduct the draft by lottery. It was expected that Congress would consider further draft reforms in 1970. (*See* Selective Service.)

Weapons and Arms Control

Weapons systems also aroused disagreement in the year, both in Congress and among the U.S. public. Principally at issue were the development of an ABM (antiballistic missile) system and of MIRV (multiple independently targetable reentry vehicle) warheads for ballistic missiles.

After extended and acrimonious debate, the U.S. Congress late in the year approved initial deployment of the limited Safeguard ABM system evolved by the Nixon Administration from the similar but more extensive Sentinel ABM system proposed by the Administration of former President Lyndon B. Johnson. The first Safeguard installations—one to be in service in 1973—are intended to protect

F. BEHRENDT, FROM BEN ROTH AGENCY

"You too, Richard?"

In April the White House was picketed by physicists who said they were protesting the plan to install an antiballistic missile system in the United States.

WIDE WORLD

Minuteman missile sites in Montana and North Dakota. The system employs sophisticated radars and two types of interceptor missiles. One, the Spartan, is designed to disable incoming warheads at long range—some 400 miles. The second, the Sprint, is meant to operate at shorter range.

Foes of the ABM system argued that it was too costly, that it was probably ineffective, and that it might provoke a new round in the arms race between the United States and the Soviet Union. Proponents held that it was necessary to the nation's security and pointed out that the Soviet Union had already deployed an ABM system thought to be similar. There was general agreement that the ABM system would offer little protection against an attack by the Soviet Union but that it might be an adequate shield against the limited ballistic-missile attack that Communist China was expected to be able to mount in the mid-1970's.

Development of the MIRV warheads in the United States also continued despite opposition. The system would permit a single Minuteman or Poseidon missile to deliver several nuclear warheads to widely separated targets and to carry penetration aids to confuse enemy defenses. Opponents of MIRV development held that it would intensify the arms race and pointed to high cost. Proponents insisted that it was essential to maintain nuclear parity with the Soviet Union.

Weapons-development foes apparently won a round in November, when President Nixon announced that he had directed the Department of Defense to stop development and production of biological-warfare agents and to destroy existing stocks of such materials. The President said that future U.S. biological-warfare research would be confined to the development of defensive measures. He also renounced "first use" of lethal or incapacitating chemical agents. The use of riot-control agents such as tear gas would be continued under closer restriction.

Hopes for a halt in the global arms race were raised as the United States and the Soviet Union, the two major nuclear powers, finally initiated preliminary strategic-arms-limitation talks (SALT) in November in Helsinki, Finland. An atmosphere of cordiality prevailed during the five weeks of discussions. The concluding agreement provided for substantive talks to begin in April 1970 in Vienna, Austria.

Spending and Procurement

Reductions in U.S. military expenditures were planned as a result of the need to combat monetary inflation and of widespread opinion that a greater proportion of federal revenues should be spent on efforts to solve internal social problems. Late in the year it was estimated that, in fiscal 1971, U.S. defense spending might be cut to $70 billion—$7 billion below the figure for the preceding year. For fiscal 1970, the Nixon Administration had reduced by some $4 billion the $81-billion spending plan prepared by the previous Administration.

By mid-1970, the spending cuts announced in 1969 were expected to reduce military manpower by more than 200,000, the Department of Defense civilian staff by nearly 70,000, and the defense-industry work force by more than 200,000. Some 100 naval vessels and more than 200 Air Force planes were to be retired; units of all services were to be eliminated; and such programs as the Air Force's Manned Orbiting Laboratory and development of the Army's Cheyenne helicopter were canceled. Reductions were also ordered in the number of U.S. troops and bases overseas.

Apparently feeling that the United States could no longer be "the world's policeman," the Nixon Administration announced that succeeding years would see further reductions in U.S. military expenditures. Global military capabilities—and commitments—were to be reduced, though sufficient

(continued on page 221)

Special Report: Military Values Revisited

by Robert G. Sherrill, Washington (D.C.) Correspondent, *The Nation* Magazine

At least outwardly, the ambitions of the military and of its friends in industry appeared to be under more relentless criticism in 1969 than at any time since the mid-1930's, when "merchants of death" was the popular term for munitions manufacturers and when 71% of the people interviewed in a Gallup Poll thought it had been a mistake to fight in World War I. By mid-1969 pollsters found that a majority of people believed the United States was spending too much on arms and that it had been a mistake to get into the Vietnam conflict. This was not a return to the isolationism of the 1930's; there was no evidence that Americans were fed up with foreigners—only that they were disenchanted with the military and with U.S. foreign policy.

Something had developed between the cocky years of U.S. President John F. Kennedy and the first cautious year of President Richard M. Nixon: this was a military-bureaucratic-industrial combine, over which the U.S. Congress seemed to have little control but against which the public had begun to react. The remarkable feature of this opposition was that it represented such a diverse cross section of the public—radical students, liberal professors, liberal and conservative economists and congressmen (the latter mainly for reasons of economy), apolitical soldiers, and nonpolitical federal courts.

The tide of promilitarism, which had risen since President Kennedy's sharp increase in the 1961 Pentagon budget, receded far enough to leave the admirals and the generals vulnerable to attack. A great part of the trouble came from the growing alienation between a hip citizenry that could handle sophisticated dialogue and a military hierarchy that bored people with tired old arguments.

One sign of changing attitudes was the downfall of popular idols. The storied Special Forces—the "Green Berets" who had been revitalized and given rare autonomy by Kennedy—were spoken of even in the daily press as assassins and torturers. And nothing sounded more antiquated by 1969 than some of the Kennedy-era boasting of Pentagon efficiency, quoted with sarcasm in the newspapers.

Symbolic of the year was public reaction to the U.S. Navy's inquiry into the conduct of Comdr. Lloyd M. Bucher and his crew, who had been im-

Checkpoint

RENAULT, "OPEN FORUM," FROM BEN ROTH AGENCY

Released crewmen of the USS *Pueblo* cross the "Bridge of No Return," which runs between North and South Korea, after being freed by the North Koreans in December 1968. The decision of *Pueblo* Cmdr. Lloyd M. Bucher not to risk his life and the lives of his men when they were captured was applauded by the U.S. public.

WIDE WORLD

prisoned in North Korea after their poorly equipped intelligence ship, the USS *Pueblo,* was captured off North Korea in January 1968. When the North Koreans demanded Bucher confess that the *Pueblo* had been spying, he played it square and safe and signed the confession without extended duress. He saw no reason to risk his life and those of his men—that was the stuff of a different era, when military men gave greater weight to heroics. Bucher's conduct appealed at this moment in history to both sides of America: to the squares because they were fed up with the U.S. refusal to go all out against the Communists and saw no reason for the *Pueblo* crew to pay a price the top brass would not pay, and to the sophisticated Left because Bucher had lived for the moment in order to live at all and had thrown over establishment and storybook values, as well as Naval tradition. Bucher's action was applauded by the public as both wise and heroic.

More devastating to the military establishment because of its unexpectedness was criticism from its old friends on the House Armed Services Committee (HASC). In a slashing attack on the Department of Defense a subcommittee of the HASC cited the *Pueblo's* capture and the later downing of a reconnaissance plane by North Korea as evidence of "serious deficiencies" requiring a "complete review of our military-civilian command structure and its capability to cope with emergency situations." It blamed the *Pueblo's* capture on the Pentagon for failing to properly interpret warning signs from North Korea and—perhaps most startling—recommended that the military Code of Conduct be changed to "provide some latitude" so that captured U.S. servicemen could give more information than their identity and so avoid excessively rough treatment.

Dissent in the Ranks and the Classroom

For the first time in history there was enough organized opposition within the ranks of the armed forces to make headlines. It had been building for several years and ranged from soldiers who wanted to reform the U.S. Army to those who thought a conscript army should be abolished altogether. Two dozen or more underground GI newspapers, published both on and off bases, reflected the concern of thousands of young men whose lives had been interrupted to fight a war. There were also individual protests by junior officers and enlisted men, who picketed or circulated petitions against the war and the military itself.

Perhaps not as significant, but more serious to the Pentagon, were rebellions that broke out on various bases: at Fort Jackson, S.C., where some 100 men objected when officers attempted to suppress their political bull session; at the Fort Ord, Calif., and Fort Dix, N.J., stockades, where hundreds rioted to protest living conditions; and at the Presidio stockade at San Francisco, Calif., where 27 prisoners staged a sit-down in what the Army insisted was a mutiny. Out of this turmoil developed several court cases that stand an excellent chance of extending the Bill of Rights, especially freedom of speech, to the men in uniform.

These legal attacks on the constitutionality of the Uniform Code of Military Justice were successful in attracting public attention and in shaking the Pentagon. The federal courts set several historic curbs on the military. The U.S. Supreme Court ruled that the military cannot court-martial men for activities conducted off base, off duty, and out of uniform. Of less importance but equally symbolic was a decision forbidding the court-martialing of U.S. civilians working in war zones.

On college campuses elements of the student body and the faculty continued to demonstrate against the draft, against the Reserve Officers Training Corps (ROTC), and against permitting war-production companies to use on-campus facilities for recruiting employees. There were some measurable effects: the Pentagon promised to withdraw ROTC training at Harvard University and

Military policemen escort from a courtroom 24 soldiers accused of mutiny for taking part in a sit-down at the Presidio stockade in San Francisco, Calif. The soldiers' trial ended with 22 of the defendants convicted of mutiny and two others found guilty of lesser charges. Three soldiers who participated in the sit-down had escaped before the trial.

UPI COMPIX

Dartmouth College at the end of the 1969–70 school year, and ROTC programs at other Ivy League schools may also be affected.

The most important development, however, was in campus laboratories, which the Pentagon has depended upon for much of its research. On one day of simultaneous protest, students and professors at campuses from Cambridge, Mass., to Berkeley, Calif., held rallies and strikes at which laboratory service to the military-industrial complex was deplored. Over the past few years some professors had refused further work on Pentagon contracts, and others threatened refusal. Massachusetts Institute of Technology and Stanford University, major Pentagon contractors, cut back on secret research for defense.

The Critical Congress

In Congress, critical analyses of the defense budget expanded dramatically. When the chairmen of the Armed Services and Appropriations committees in the House, L. Mendel Rivers and George H. Mahon, engaged in a public quarrel over military spending, the event was unprecedented. Mahon, usually a promilitarist, demanded a cut in the arms budget because military mistakes had led to a lack of confidence.

The proposal for the antiballistic missile (ABM) Safeguard system passed the Senate by the narrowest margin. But the debate over ABM was only a prelude to the extended controversy over the $20-billion military procurement authorization bill, on which so much time was spent that the Congressional timetable for other programs fell behind.

The Juggernaut Rolls On

Yet when all was done, could it truly be said that 1969 was a watershed year, after which the militarists' hold on the national budget and the federal commitment would inevitably decline? Not at all. Nothing occurred that could be seen as the beginning of a trend away from what the *Washington Post* termed a "warfare state." The opposition was noteworthy not because it was large but because it occurred on several levels of society, after years in which the only opposition to the Pentagon had come from "peacenik" organizations easily identified and dismissed by the establishment.

The assault on the arms budget did shake from the industry the admission that only about $20 billion of the $80-billion budget actually went toward arms-production costs; the remainder went into overhead, including pork barrel. However, the challenge to the defense industry resulted in few reforms. The General Accounting Office, now empowered to keep a closer watch on defense contracts, stated that it would continue to report on Pentagon spending "in constructive terms rather than in terms of the deficiencies being reported."

As for the revolt against secret research on campuses, Foster and Lee DuBridge, Nixon's science adviser, assured Congress and the scientists that the amount of such research had dropped from 8% to 4% in the last few years and that they hoped to reduce it to zero. Yet 75% of all university research continued to be supported by the government—most of it by the Pentagon.

The Pentagon's reaction to the Supreme Court's decisions on military justice was to send out a directive to field commanders to disregard the court and proceed with justice as usual. Obviously the military meant to fight it out with the court on a case-by-case basis, which could hold off any practical effect of the court's decisions for years. While the revolt against college ROTC drew headlines, statistically it was not impressive: only about 3% of the 497 ROTC units in the nation experienced any trouble.

In spite of the protests, America was still carrying the deep intaglio of the military: defense spending at the rate of $1,000 per taxpayer a year; a military budget that buys 15% of all finished industrial products; and a defense industry that employs 38% of all physicists. It still appeared to be an America that was, in the Biblical phrase, "a nation of fierce countenance."

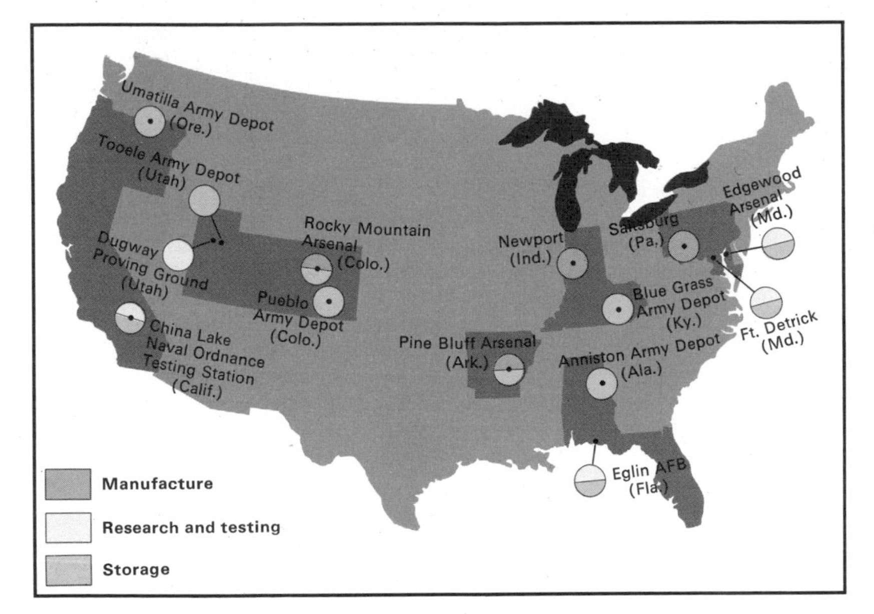

The map shows the major chemical and biological warfare facilities in the United States and indicates the primary activity performed at each facility.

(*continued from page 217*)
nuclear and conventional strength would be retained to deter attack on the United States.

Partly as a result of opposition to the Vietnam conflict, Department of Defense budget requests—and purchasing practices—came under sharp Congressional scrutiny in 1969. Investigations revealed that the costs of the Air Force's fleet of huge C-5A transport planes had risen nearly $2 billion above the initial estimate, and the Air Force announced that it would order only 81 of the planes instead of the planned 120. Another investigation revealed that the Army had spent more than $1 billion on its so-far-unsatisfactory armed tanks—the Sheridan and MBT-70 (main battle tank)—and accompanying Shillelagh missile system. (*See also* Armed Forces, U.S.; Congress, U.S.)

DENMARK. Inflation, unemployment, and a considerable deficit in the balance of payments persisted in Denmark in 1969. Agricultural exports met with many obstacles, especially from central European markets. Although they were displaced by industrial exports as the most important source of foreign currency, agricultural exports remained a vital part of the economy.

Following complaints from industrial management that costs were outstripping artificially controlled prices, the remaining restrictions in the "prices and profits freeze" system were abolished. These restrictions were replaced by rules of arbitration. Under the new setup the monopoly commission was empowered to dictate a price freeze for 40 days. During that time disputing companies could negotiate price rises with authorities, thus allowing some measure of control over inflationary wage-price spirals. A strike by 40,000 agricultural workers in May was halted after an emergency session of the Folketing.

The value-added tax remained at 12.5% in 1969. A pay-as-you-earn tax system was scheduled to start on Jan. 1, 1970. The crises over the French franc and the West German mark led to considerable outflow of Danish currency. (*See* Money and International Finance.) During the first half of 1969 the outflow exceeded $66.75 million, compared to less than $7 million for 1968. The bank rate was raised to 9% (a European record), interest on some mortgages reached 11%, and the stock market fell. To halt the reserve drain the Folketing increased certain transportation and communications charges. However, by autumn Denmark had only enough foreign reserves to cover a month's imports.

In 1969 Danish commercial interests approved joining the European Economic Community, or Common Market, in the event of Great Britain's entry. Otherwise the proposed Scandinavian customs union, the Nordek plan, was favored. Following the removal of a ban on pornography, a sex fair opened in Copenhagen, the capital, in October and drew large crowds. (*See in* CE: Denmark.)

DENTISTRY. Dental scientists persisted in their goal of eradicating caries (tooth cavities) and periodontal (gum) diseases. For example, workers at the Eastman Dental Center in Rochester, N.Y., found that application of a plastic coating to children's tooth surfaces reduced decay.

The use of laser beams to prevent the onset of caries was a research project at the University of California at Los Angeles. Preliminary findings suggested that the laser beam fuses decayed enamel, thus inhibiting further decay.

At the 110th annual session of the American Dental Association, in New York City in October, studies of periodontal disease were heard. One report blamed biting pressures as a cause of gum inflammation. Another predicted mass vaccination would someday prevent gum disorders. Dental scientists were becoming convinced that periodontal diseases stem in part from mouth bacteria.

The promises of tooth transplantation continued to intrigue dentists. Root resorption by the mouth's bony supporting structures was the chief cause of transplant loss. Researchers in 1969 were experimenting with fluoride in hopes that it would prevent the troublesome resorption. Also, workers at Brown University, Providence, R.I., reported successful plastic-tooth implantation in monkeys and baboons. However, the plastic implants had yet to be tested in humans.

Since the first fluoridation effort in 1945, more than 4,000 U.S. communities have fluoridated their water as a public health measure for the prevention of caries. In 1969 these locales served some 73 million people. An additional 8 million people lived in the 2,600 communities where enough fluoride to prevent decay occurs naturally in the water. In addition, more than 40 nations have fluoridation programs as a consequence of satisfaction with U.S. scientific studies on the value and safety of the measure. (*See in* CE: Dentistry.)

DISARMAMENT. There was hope in 1969 that talks would begin shortly on general limitation of all strategic arms, nuclear and nonnuclear alike. The United States even dropped its once-firm demand for inspection rights over Soviet nuclear installations. But aside from a joint U.S.-Soviet draft treaty submitted to the United Nations (UN) to bar fixed nuclear weapons from much of the ocean floor, little was done to curtail what UN Secretary-General U Thant called the "mad momentum of the arms race."

SALT in the Kettle

Strategic-arms-limitation talks (SALT) between the United States and the Soviet Union were started late in the year. Russian interest in SALT waned somewhat after the 1968 Soviet-led invasion of Czechoslovakia. However, early in 1969, Soviet officials offered to "start a serious exchange of views" with the United States on SALT.

United States President Richard M. Nixon, newly installed in office, replied that he favored SALT in principle. Observers noted that the Nixon Administration would first have to make defense studies, consult with allies, and determine the progress of peace in the Middle East before the talks could take place.

In the midst of disarmament hopes President Nixon in March decided to proceed with the controversial Safeguard ABM (antiballistic missile) program. Opponents felt that building the ABM in the face of proposed strategic arms talks would be an error, since the ABM was viewed by critics as a stimulant to the arms race.

On July 5, Nixon named a U.S. delegation to SALT. It was headed by Gerard C. Smith, who replaced William C. Foster as director of the Arms Control and Disarmament Agency. Nixon called for July 31 as the target date for disarmament talks. This deadline was not met, but by mid-November U.S.-Russian disarmament talks were under way. The parley was being held in Helsinki, Finland.

Disarmament Talks at Geneva

In March the Eighteen-Nation Committee on Disarmament met again at Geneva, Switzerland. France, one of the charter members of the conference, continued its long-standing boycott. Three major developments occurred at the 1969 Geneva meeting. First, the membership was raised to 26 nations. Realizing the long-felt need to expand the disarmament forum, the U.S. and Soviet cochairmen agreed, with committee approval, to admit Argentina, Hungary, Japan, Mongolia, Morocco, the Netherlands, Pakistan, and Yugoslavia. The committee name was changed to the Conference of the Committee on Disarmament (CCD).

Another CCD concern was an intensive but inconclusive debate on the problem of chemical and biological warfare (CBW). Harking to the 1925 Geneva Protocol, the UN desired all nations to halt development, production, and stockpiling of CBW. In November President Nixon renounced the use of biological weapons and pledged that the United States would not strike first with chemical weapons. (*See* Defense.)

A third Geneva development in 1969 was the joint U.S.-Russian draft treaty to exclude the seabeds, except areas within a 12-mile continental limit, from the emplacement of nuclear weapons. However, since the draft treaty excluded nuclear-missile-carrying submarines it was likened by critics to a law that "forbids the robbing of banks except when it's done by armed holdup." Others thought the treaty would stem the arms race in some measure. (*See also* Nuclear Energy.)

DISASTERS OF 1969. Among the catastrophes that occurred around the world in 1969 were:

Air Disasters

Jan. 5 Gatwick, England. Afghan 727 commercial airliner, landing in dense fog, misses runway and rams into house; 50 persons, including 2 in the house, die; 13 are injured.

March 16 Maracaibo, Venezuela. Venezuelan DC-9 jet airliner crashes and explodes at takeoff, plunging into a residential area; 84 people aboard the jet and at least 71 on the ground are killed.

March 20 Aswan, United Arab Republic (UAR). UAR Ilyushin-18 cracks up; 87 persons perish; 14 survive.

April 3 Near Cracow, Poland. Polish AN-24 plunges to the ground, killing all 51 persons aboard.

June 4 Near Monterrey, Mexico. Mexican 727 jet rams into a mountainside during a rainstorm; all 79 persons aboard perish.

Sept. 9 Shelbyville, Ind. Twin-engine DC-9 is sliced in two by a small Piper Cherokee flown by a student pilot; the two aircraft plummet into a field, killing all 82 persons aboard the DC-9 and the one man in the small plane.

Fires and Explosions

Jan. 15 Victoria State, Australia. Weeklong bush fires fanned by strong winds rage through thousands of acres of forest and range land; 17 persons die; 200 homes are destroyed.

Feb. 7 Koriyama, Japan. Fire engulfs a resort hotel and spreads through an amusement center, killing 30 persons.

Dec. 2 Notre Dame du Lac, Que. A wooden home for the aged and infirm is ravished by a fire that kills 38 of the elderly pensioners; 29 persons survive.

Marine Disasters

Jan. 14 Pearl Harbor, Hawaii. Nuclear aircraft carrier USS *Enterprise* is swept by fire and explosions; 27 men die and 85 others are injured.

June 2 South China Sea. Navy destroyer USS *Frank E. Evans,* on maneuvers with about 40 other warships, is sliced in two by the Australian aircraft carrier HMAS *Melbourne;* when the sheared-off portion of the *Evans* sinks, 73 persons go down and are presumed dead; 200 others are rescued.

June 21 Beira, Mozambique. A barge transporting 150 Portuguese troops and their vehicles, en route to reinforce a garrison beleaguered by guerrillas, sinks and drowns 108 of the men.

Mine Disasters

March 31 Barroteran, Mexico. Deadly gases prevent rescuers from reaching coal miners trapped 800 feet underground by explosions that ripped through the mine; at least 180 miners are given up for dead.

Nov. 7 Buffelsfontein, South Africa. A dynamite explosion in a gold mine buries a blasting team 1½ miles beneath the surface, killing 64 members of the crew and injuring 14 others.

Natural Disasters

Jan. 27 Southern California. Nine days of torrential rains end, leaving the area a sea of mud and

"THE TIMES", LONDON, FROM PICTORIAL PARADE

Fifty people were found dead in the wreckage of an Ariana Afghan Airways jet that crashed in dense fog near the Gatwick (England) Airport on January 5.

On January 23 a tornado ripped through Hazlehurst, Miss. President Richard M. Nixon was asked by Mississippi's Gov. John Bell Williams to declare that section of the state a disaster area.

UPI COMPIX

debris with a death toll of at least 100 persons; more than 9,000 homes are damaged or destroyed; property loss is estimated at $60 million.

Feb. 9–10 Northeastern United States. Two-day storm dumps 15 inches of snow along the Eastern seaboard, causing a total of 166 deaths.

March 17 Alagoas State, Brazil. A flash flood, sweeping through a drought-stricken area of northeastern Brazil, kills a reported 200 persons and leaves 5,000 others homeless.

April 16 East Pakistan. A 90-mph tornado strikes the region, hitting the cities of Dacca and Comilla most heavily; at least 531 persons are dead and more than 4,000 others are injured.

May 17–21 Southern India. Windstorms and tidal waves strike villages along the Bay of Bengal and kill 300–500 persons in the city of Vijayavada; 20,000 others are homeless.

Aug. 17–20 Gulf of Mexico. Mississippi, Louisiana, and Alabama are ravished by Hurricane Camille, spawned off Cuba on August 15 and finally dissipating off the Virginia coast; at least 400 persons are presumed dead; damage is estimated at $1 billion.

DPA FROM PICTORIAL PARADE

At least a dozen persons died when a railroad car containing grenades exploded in the Hanover-Linden railway station in West Germany in June. Workers clear away debris from the disaster.

Sept. 14 South Korea. Southern coastline is heavily battered by the most severe rainstorms in 60 years; most of the 475 death toll is caused by flooding; 407 persons are injured, 78 are missing, and property damage is about $61 million.

Sept. 28 Taiwan. Typhoon Elsie rages across the island, killing 102 persons and leaving 24 missing and 227 injured; crops are heavily damaged.

Sept. 28–Oct. 8 Tunisia. After five years of drought the country is deluged by ten days of torrential rain and flooding, with half of the land under mud and water; 500 persons are listed as dead; 50,000 homes are destroyed, as are highways, railroads, bridges, and whole villages.

Railroad Disasters

June 21 Near Benares, India. A train jumps the tracks as it passes over a bridge across a river; 69 persons perish; at least 150 are injured.

July 15 Near Cuttack, India. A train is halted by a passenger who pulls the emergency switch to get off where there is no stop; while halted the train is rammed from the rear by a speeding freight; 81 and possibly as many as 100 persons perish; more than 150 others are injured.

Traffic Accidents

Jan. 15 Tuzla, Turkey. Bus topples off a bridge, bringing death to 22 riders; 14 are injured.

March 17 Near Fresno, Calif. Bus accident causes 30 deaths; 19 persons are injured.

June 21 Central Syria. Truck transporting 35 girls to harvest fields overturns, killing 25.

July 15 Dinant, Belgium. Dutch vacationists are dumped into the Meuse River when their tour bus leaves the road because of faulty brakes; 21 passengers die, 4 others who swim ashore survive.

Dec. 12 Bulawayo, Rhodesia. A bus flips off a bridge and falls 100 feet into a river; 21 persons perish; many others are missing and are presumed to have drowned.

Miscellaneous Disasters

June 15 San Rafael, Spain. An opening-day celebration by 500 patrons of a new restaurant turns to horror as a second-story floor begins to sag, the walls quickly crumble, and the roof falls down, crushing to death at least 57 persons and injuring another 140.

Nov. 8–9 Rio de Janeiro, Brazil. A hot, sunny weekend combined with rough seas off the beaches causes 35 deaths by drowning; 440 other persons require treatment for dehydration.

Nov. 29 Guadalajara, Mexico. The roof of a church collapses upon 200 worshipers, killing at least 19 persons.

DOMINICAN REPUBLIC.

During 1969 politicians in the Dominican Republic were looking ahead to the presidential election scheduled for 1970. President Joaquín Balaguer caused apprehension among his political rivals when he announced that he might run for reelection. Balaguer expected to draw his support from the middle class and the business community. Among those who opposed the president was ex-president Juan D. Bosch of the leftist Dominican Revolutionary party. Even the incumbent vice-president announced he would oppose the president, thus dividing loyalties in Balaguer's Reformist party. There was widespread fear that attempted coups and accompanying bloodshed would be a prelude to the election.

Three persons were killed during the disturbances that surrounded the visit of New York's

AMEX—PIX FROM PUBLIX

AMEX—PIX FROM PUBLIX

Governor Rockefeller (top, in center) arrives at the airport in Santo Domingo, Dominican Republic. The writing on the wall (bottom) says in Spanish, "Get out Rockefeller assassin."

Gov. Nelson A. Rockefeller to the Dominican Republic in July. Dominican officials said the three were accidentally shot by nervous soldiers.

Economic gains were made during the year, particularly in agriculture and tourism. The sugarcane harvest in 1969 was estimated at a record one million tons. Construction began on expanded irrigation systems. Highway construction and city beautification programs were undertaken to encourage tourist trade. In May a modern international airport was opened near Santo Domingo, the capital. (*See in* CE: Dominican Republic.)

DRUGS. Is marihuana the inescapable precursor of "hard" narcotic use, or is it merely a mild intoxicant, as tolerable as small amounts of alcohol? The U.S. Treasury and Justice departments held the hard view as they engaged in Operation Intercept, an attempt to curtail marihuana traffic from Mexico. However, a growing number of scientists were voicing the latter view. According to an official of the National Institute of Mental Health, in testimony to a group from the U.S. Senate Committee on the Judiciary, the legal penalties imposed on marihuana use were probably more harmful to the user than the drug itself. Marihuana use, a felony under U.S. narcotics laws, could result in up to ten years' imprisonment on conviction. Most scientists agreed that in-depth research on the effects of marihuana was woefully lacking. This study, they said, had to be conducted before a dispassionate evaluation could be made.

In October, John E. Ingersoll, director of the Bureau of Narcotics and Dangerous Drugs, testified before the Senate group that the Administration of U.S. President Richard M. Nixon would not oppose an easing of the drug laws. The Administration even suggested that heroin use be dropped to a misdemeanor.

The United Nations (UN) International Commission on Narcotic Drugs consented early in the year to devise a way in which psychotropic drugs, such as amphetamine (Benzedrine), dexamphetamine (Dexedrine), and methamphetamine ("speed"), would be put under the same worldwide control as the narcotics. A Swedish health official made the initial plea for UN action because a growing number of young Swedes were experimenting with the often harmful drugs.

FDA Continues Its Drug Crackdown

The list of drugs considered ineffective by the U.S. Food and Drug Administration (FDA) grew in 1969. In April the FDA decertified 78 more antibiotic combination drugs. In the opinion of the FDA they contained ingredients that were unnecessary in treating a prescribed ailment. Herbert L. Ley, Jr., FDA commissioner, judged that these fixed antibiotic combinations were exposing patients to an undue hazard. Only one or another of the antibiotics, he said, was actually needed to overcome the malady for which the combination was prescribed.

In September the FDA removed eight additional drugs from the market. These drugs, used as diuretics to remove excess fluids from the body, featured fixed combinations of thiazide and potassium. Since some of the potassium needed for healthy cardiovascular function was often eliminated from the body when diuretics were used, the combination drugs were devised to reintroduce adequate amounts of the chemical into the body. The FDA, however, armed with findings of a National Academy of Sciences-National Research Council panel, said the drugs were ineffective.

KEYSTONE

Drug addiction is a problem in many parts of the world. This dramatic poster, widely circulated in Switzerland, warns young people that drugs can destroy beauty and health.

In October the FDA shocked many users of low-calorie soft drinks when it denounced the cyclamate sweeteners used in most diet drinks. Effective Jan. 1, 1970, all soft drinks containing cyclamates were banned from the market. Tests had revealed that experimental mice developed cancer when given large doses of cyclamates. Also, the FDA was reconsidering the safety of other commonly used food additives. (*See also* Food.)

Drug Evaluation in Question

The reliability of the testing of drug-efficacy came under a cloud in 1969. The FDA learned that some new drugs had undergone questionable trials in humans. An FDA official admitted that the person responsible for running a number of evaluation tests—a physician associated with some Southern prison hospitals—did not maintain proper scrutiny over all facets of his drug testing. Nevertheless, data from these evaluations were used to bolster sales of the drugs in question. By year's end the U.S. government was investigating the evaluation program to uncover any fraud.

The backlog of new-drug applications that the FDA had nearly disposed of again took on alarming proportions. Commissioner Ley said the drug applications were not being quickly acted upon because of inadequate manpower. During prior years the FDA was able to expedite new-drug applications by borrowing physicians from the Public Health Service. However, in mid-1968 the FDA lost their services as a result of Congressional disfavor. Congress did not believe this was a proper

Young people are counseled on the dangers and problems of drug addiction through the Encounter program in the Greenwich Village area of New York City. Encounter provides group therapy at no cost to "pre-addicts" who have experimented with drugs.

"THE NEW YORK TIMES" FROM WIDE WORLD

way for physicians to satisfy government service obligations.

New Studies; New Drugs

Recent research was increasingly aimed at determining the action of drugs on cells and subcellular structures. The result was a new scientific activity called molecular pharmacology. Molecular pharmacologists hoped to discover new drugs by observing cellular chemical action rather than by relying on classical methods of drug screening that centered on organs or on entire animals.

Two new antituberculosis agents were made available in 1969. Ethambutol hydrochloride, a synthetic drug, was one. Rifamycin, an antibiotic, was another. They were developed for combination use with previously established antituberculosis drugs. Therapy using a drug combination had the advantage of delaying bacterial resistance. A one-component drug would be rendered ineffective if the bacteria rapidly developed resistance.

Gentamycin, a new antibiotic, appeared to be effective against gram-negative bacteria, including the pseudomonades that caused serious infections in the urinary tract. Since the pseudomonades were also a dangerous threat in burns, Gentamycin in topical application seemed to offer valuable protection against this kind of infection.

Pentazocine, a powerful pain-reliever introduced in recent years, was under attack. When first released, the analgesic was thought to be free of the morphine group's addictive properties. New evidence, though, indicated that pentazocine might not be so harmless. (*See also* Chemistry; Medicine. *See in* CE: Drugs.)

EARTH SCIENCES.

An exciting new dimension was added to the earth sciences in 1969 with the return of the Apollo 11 moon mission with its load of lunar rocks. Then, seismic equipment left on the moon by Apollo 12 astronauts sent back data that left seismologists baffled. Some suggested "the book had to be thrown away" since explanations based on terrestrial dynamics were inadequate and incomplete.

The Moon Rocks

The rocks brought back by Apollo 11 astronauts were picked up in the Sea of Tranquillity, the site of man's first landing on the moon. The lunar-landing surface consisted of fragmentary debris ranging in size from dust particles to chunks about 2 feet wide. Most of the rock fragments had rounded or subrounded upper surfaces, suggesting that some type of erosion was active on the lunar surface. Some of the rock samples showed differential erosion; that is, resistant portions of the rock were left in raised relief to more worn sections. Since there was no evidence that the moon ever had surface waters, geologists speculated that small particle bombardment of the moon's surface could have caused this differential erosion.

Most moon rocks with rounded surfaces were also deeply pitted with tiny holes. Many of the pits were lined with glass. It was apparent that they had been produced by objects that hit the moon's exposed surface, probably small particles.

Mineralogy of the Moon Rocks

The rock samples returned from the moon were broken down into two major groups—crystalline rock and breccia. The crystalline rocks were of igneous origin, once lavas or near-surface molten materials and thus volcanic. The presence of volcanic rocks did not necessarily mean that they were formed in the same manner as those generated by volcanoes on earth. The moon's once-fluid material could have been melted by some unknown kind of impact mechanism that generated great heat.

Lunar breccias were mixtures of differing rock fragments. They were gray to dark gray in color, interspersed with flecks of white, light gray, and brownish gray. Most of the breccias were fine-grained, containing tiny, angular fragments of rocks, minerals, and glass.

Moon rocks were significantly higher in titanium and zirconium content than their earth counterparts. No evidence of living matter had yet been found in the samples. An interesting find showed that the moon's surface has been remarkably stable for eons. The presence of nuclides in the rocks under study indicated that these rocks had lain within three feet of the lunar surface for at least 100 million years. Cosmic rays striking the moon surface produced the nuclides.

Potassium-argon measurements indicated that the moon's igneous rocks crystallized 3 to 4 billion years ago. If these dates prove accurate, then some of the lunar rocks may be older than the oldest rocks yet found on earth, raising new speculation on the moon's original relationship with the earth.

Moon Shocks Puzzle Scientists

The moon's first seismic station sent initial data to earth by recording the footsteps of the Apollo 11 landing team on July 21. The seismometer system consisted of four seismometers and two radioisotope heaters fueled with plutonium 238 to protect the unit against the bitter lunar cold. Although the unit operated for only a few weeks, it transmitted signals from several disturbances on the moon's surface. Whether the shocks were caused by moonquakes, volcanic action, or meteorite impact was not yet known.

Still more confounding was the aftermath of the crash of Apollo 12's lunar module, Intrepid. After its occupants transferred into the command module, the lunar module was deliberately crashed into the moon to test the seismometer system left by Apollo 12 members. At first, weak seismic signals were picked up at one-second intervals. The signals grew in intensity for 15 minutes and then

WIDE WORLD

An aerial photograph of the Colorado River delta was made by the U.S. Geological Survey of the Department of the Interior.

slacked off 20 minutes after the crash. As late as 30 minutes after impact the seismometers were still detecting reverberations, an event unheard of on earth for an impact so close to a recording unit. If the approximate location of the crash site was correct—about 45 miles from the Ocean of Storms landing site—scientists thought a major but unexplainable discovery had taken place. One theory was that the impact might have set off a series of structural collapses in the moon crust.

Seismic Events of Earth Origin

The first documented case of an earthquake on one crustal fault affecting movements on other faults was reported in 1969. The initial shock took place at Borrego Mountain in southern California early in 1968. The shock had a Richter Magnitude Scale grade of 6.5, the area's severest jolt in 15 years. Recent studies at the California Institute of Technology revealed that the shock triggered small displacements on other faults in or near California's Imperial Valley. The faults were all within 50 miles of the Borrego Mountain shock's epicenter. Seismologists said that even though an earthquake might be centered on some distant fault, damage to structures on or near other fault systems must now be considered possible.

Dire forecasts that a disastrous earthquake would rock the San Francisco, Calif., area early in 1969 came from a number of supposedly occult sources. Although the "predicted" event did not occur, scientists were nevertheless concerned about possible quake-caused tragedies in the heavily populated area. The San Andreas Fault lies nearby. Los Angeles, Calif., was also located in a highly seismic area. In an attempt to study the stability of the city's structures, Los Angeles officials programmed an IBM-360 computer to see how existing buildings might react to strong seismic forces. Data on the natural sway of the buildings under study were fed into the computer. Thus if a quake were to occur in the Los Angeles area the computer would register changes in the sway measurements, indicating whether structural damage had weakened the buildings even if no damage was immediately visible after the quake.

More on Continental Drift

Earth scientists assembled in Madrid, Spain, on September 1–12, for the International Union of Geodesy and Geophysics meetings. Under discussion was the increasingly popular hypothesis of sea-floor spreading as the cause of continental drift. (*See* Oceanography.) Modern theories of global tectonics (folding and faulting) were based on the slow slippage of hypothetical plates of earth surface over long periods of time. These crustal plates were usually associated with the mid-ocean ridges from which the sea floors are thought to emanate.

The continental-drift theory received important support in 1969 from studies of South American and African regions thought to have once bordered one another. Geographers believe both continents were combined with India, Australia, and Antarctica in a vast protocontinent called Gondwanaland. The regions under scrutiny—the Sergipe Basin in Brazil and the Gabon Basin in Africa—showed amazing geological similarities, as would be expected if they were once adjacent regions. Examination of the lower rock strata of the areas revealed a number of similar fossils until a stratum of salt-water incursion was reached (probably signaling the formation of the Atlantic Ocean). Then the geological development of the two regions diverged. (*See in* CE: Earth; Moon; Geology; Maps.)

ECONOMY. At the close of 1969 the condition of the U.S. economy was difficult to assess, since its major indicators seemed to be pointing in different directions. The unemployment rate was at a high point, a condition that usually indicates a deflationary trend. In the same vein, industrial production was slowing down and construction starts were off markedly from the previous year. Inflation, however, continued unabated with accelerating increases in prices and in the growth rate of the gross national product (GNP).

Although the year's indicators had failed to draw any definite picture of the nation's economic status, it was generally believed that a downturn was under way. In a speech to the nation in mid-October U.S. President Richard M. Nixon averred that his Administration was determined to stop inflation even though the country might experience some "slowing pains" in the process. The president asked the cooperation of consumers, business, labor, and legislators in cooling the economy.

Despite such attempts to brake inflation, the GNP rose at an accelerated rate. At the end of the third quarter, it stood at $942.3 billion, an increase of over 8% from the same period in 1968. Inflation held the "real" increase in the GNP down to 2% during the quarter. The rate was about the same as that for the second quarter, but far below the real-growth figures for the GNP that were reported during 1968.

Nevertheless, spending in all sectors did seem to reach a plateau, or at least to grow at a slower rate. The federal government's expenditures for goods and services declined in the first and second quarters, only to rise $2.7 billion to an annual rate of $103.3 billion in the third quarter. The third-quarter increase was largely due to pay raises received by government employees. Spending for defense dropped in the first half of the year, but the rate increased during the third quarter. The rate of defense spending was severely cramped by the combined effects of the leveling-out of the U.S. commitment in Vietnam and the Nixon Administration's pledge to reduce the size of the Pentagon budget in general.

Capital spending by business and industry also increased at a slower rate in 1969. At the end of the year capital outlays were an estimated 10.5% over those of 1968. Spending in the business sector was down from a projected 14% increase forecast in February.

Consumer spending, which had failed to respond to such inhibitory measures as the income-tax surcharge and increased interest rates in 1968, began to slow down in 1969. Retail sales responded only sluggishly to the substantial increases in personal income. Consumer hard-goods sales were down in the third quarter, and there were indications that the sale of new cars was not proceeding as rapidly as expected at the close of the year.

After rising throughout the first half of the year, the rate of industrial production began to head downward in June and fell .3% in August. The downward shift reflected a general trend in industries ranging from heavy machinery to apparel manufacture. At the same time, inventories continued to increase, indicating a slackening in demand.

Another economic indicator, the rate of new construction, peaked at the beginning of the year and remained fairly steady for the duration of 1969.

WIDE WORLD

Secretary of the Treasury David M. Kennedy (left) and Robert P. Mayo, director of the Bureau of the Budget, give Administration views on the economy to the U.S. Congress.

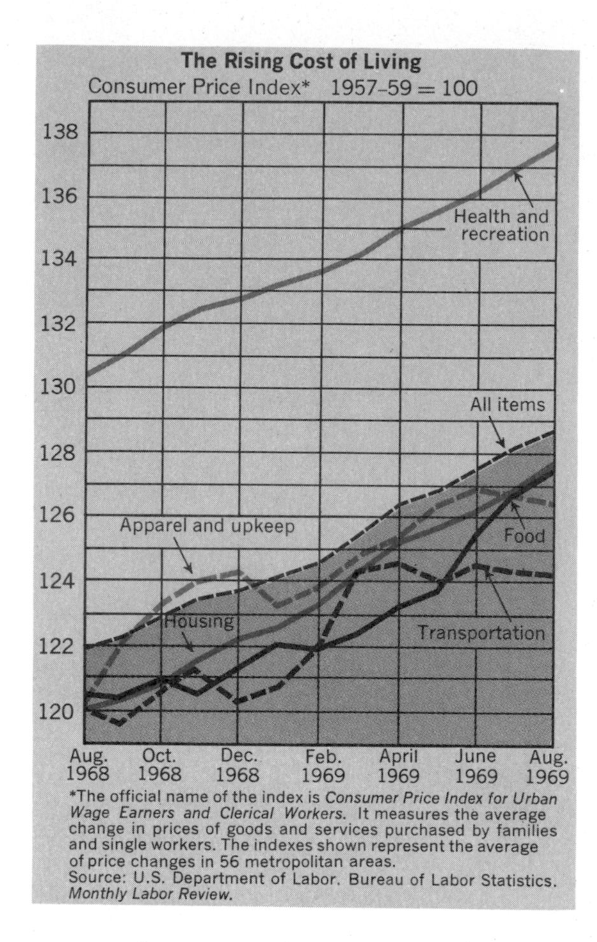

*The official name of the index is *Consumer Price Index for Urban Wage Earners and Clerical Workers.* It measures the average change in prices of goods and services purchased by families and single workers. The indexes shown represent the average of price changes in 56 metropolitan areas.
Source: U.S. Department of Labor. Bureau of Labor Statistics. *Monthly Labor Review.*

The failure of construction to advance was attributed to the tightening of credit and increased interest rates.

Personal Income

The Department of Commerce reported that personal income in the United States was at a record seasonally adjusted $759.8 billion at the end of the third quarter. For the same period in 1968, the figure was $694.3 billion. During the first nine months of 1969, personal income averaged 9% ahead of personal income during 1968.

Of these figures, salaries and wages comprised $519.1 billion; other labor, $26.6 billion; proprietary income, $50.5 billion; farm revenues, $16.8 billion; rent, $21.7 billion; dividends, $25.1 billion; and interest, $60.2 billion. The remainder of the total personal income arose from transfer payments (government benefits such as social security).

By October the increase in personal income had begun to slow down. The month's advance of $2.4 billion followed a gain of $3.2 billion in September. Wages and salaries had been rising at twice the October rate from January through August.

The Cost of Living

The U.S. Department of Labor's Bureau of Labor Statistics reported that the Consumer Price Index had risen to 129.3 at the end of the third quarter, indicating that the cost of living had risen 29.3% since the base period of 1957–59. The cost of living rose rapidly in the first and second quarters of 1969 but decelerated somewhat in the third quarter. However, the 4.5% climb during the first nine months of the year was appreciably higher than the 3.4% increase registered during the same period of 1968.

In September the purchasing power of the dollar was $.774 compared to that of the 1957–59 dollar. Comparing 1969 dollars to 1939 dollars, the value had diminished to $.375 at the beginning of October.

The cost of living increased by a projected 6% in 1969. The figure marked the largest annual increase since 1951, when it increased 8%. However, some items were priced below the 1957–59 average. These included such food products as ice cream, bananas, eggs, and regular coffee. Costs of medical care and home ownership showed the largest increases for the first three quarters of 1969. Medical costs were 57% above the 1957–59 average and .8% above those that prevailed at the end of August. (For chart, *see* Medicine.)

Consumer Credit

Total consumer credit outstanding at the end of September was $118 billion, compared to $108 billion at the end of September 1968. The latest monthly increase was almost $700 million.

Automobile loans totaled $36.3 billion for the same period, an increase of almost $3 billion from the preceding year. Personal loans stood at $29.2 billion and were also up about $3 billion from the same period in 1968.

Home repair and modernization loans totaled $4 billion at the end of the third quarter, making a modest gain of more than $200 million for the nine-month period. Charge-account credit totaled $7 billion, up $455 million for the year.

NORRIS, "VANCOUVER (B.C.) SUN," FROM BEN ROTH AGENCY

"Not while I'm paying 11% you don't . . ."

Taxes

On December 30 President Nixon signed into law a tax bill that made a number of changes in existing income-tax regulations. Among the scores of reform provisions incorporated into the new law were the imposition of increased taxes on capital gains realized by the wealthy, new restrictions on unlimited charitable deductions, an increase in taxes imposed on banks and other financial institutions, and the creation of a new "minimum tax" that would be applied at a flat rate of 10% to some individual and corporate income that was not previously subject to taxation.

Other reforms were aimed at aiding low- and middle-income individuals. One was the creation of a special tax-free low-income allowance which would exempt 9 million persons from the tax rolls. Another provided for an increase in the personal exemption from $600 to $750 by 1973. Also included were new and lower tax rates for single persons and the reduction of the top rate on "earned income" (salaries, professional fees, and commissions) from 70% to 50%.

The income-tax surcharge, a 10% tax on the personal income tax, remained in force throughout the year. It was proposed that the surcharge be extended, but at a reduced rate of 5% during the first half of 1970.

Monetary Policy

President Nixon gave an indication of his Administration's future monetary policies when he appointed Arthur F. Burns to succeed William McChesney Martin, Jr., as chairman of the Federal Reserve System's Board of Governors in October. The Board of Governors determines the going national interest rates by deciding the interest rates on loans to member banks. Commercial banks then raise or lower their rates accordingly. The board also sets the expansion rate for the national money supply.

As chairman, Burns was appointed to a 14-year term that was to begin in 1970. Unlike his predecessor, Burns, who was previously chairman of the Council of Economic Advisers for the Dwight D. Eisenhower Administration and one of Nixon's chief advisers, is an economist rather than a banker. Instead of "fine tuning" monetary policy to respond to subtle or momentary changes in the economy, Burns was expected to adopt and adhere to long-range policies. (*See also* Business and Industry; Money and International Finance.)

ECUADOR. Student violence, a struggling economy, and a potential for political upheaval beset Ecuador during 1969. Ecuador's President José María Velasco Ibarra met the nation's crises by simply giving in to his opposition. In March a new agreement on drilling rights was reached between two U.S. oil companies and the Ecuadorian government.

Velasco, who in his five terms as president had been ousted three times by military coups, improved his relations with the police and armed forces in 1969 by increasing their pay. In the spring Ecuador's university students voiced their demands for easier examinations, more qualified teachers, and an end to entrance examinations. There were serious student-led disorders in several cities. Finally, Velasco granted their demands. Some students then protested against the lowering of educational standards.

AMEX—PIX FROM PUBLIX

Troops, with bayonets at the ready, patrol the streets of Quito, Ecuador, to disperse demonstrators protesting the visit of New York's Gov. Nelson A. Rockefeller in May 1969.

During the year Velasco undertook a program of public spending that gained popular support but reduced the nation's foreign-exchange reserves to about a million dollars. The economy was already beset by a drop in banana, coffee, and cacao exports. The importers, Velasco's foremost opponents, then readily complied with rigid government controls. A deposit of $2,500 was required for every $1,000 worth of imported goods. By September Ecuador's foreign-exchange reserves had risen to more than $30 million.

Another important aid to the economy was the government's new oil-rights agreement with Texaco, Inc., and Gulf Oil Co. The oil companies increased the government's royalties from 6% to 11% and agreed to pay more in surface taxes.

Ecuador continued to seize U.S. fishing boats inside the 200-mile territorial limit claimed by Ecuador, Peru, and Chile. Talks were held with the United States in an effort to resolve the dispute over fishing rights. (*See in* CE: Ecuador.)

EDUCATION. The rumblings of student power, so much a feature of education in recent years, continued to be heard throughout 1969, and in the United States and elsewhere they could be detected in the secondary schools as well as in the universities as militant associations of adolescent pupils began more and more to follow the college undergraduates. (*See* Colleges and Universities.) At the same time, 1969 was a year of recriminations as a number of educators and others examined and reported on specific instances of student unrest. The earlier mood of acknowledging faults and seeking reforms was overtaken by a new tendency to apportion blame.

From the point of view of history, however, the most important fact of education in 1969 went almost unnoticed and certainly undiscussed. It had nothing to do with student power; it was the revelation that, in spite of the drive for literacy, the number of illiterates in the world was increasing. This fact emerged in a report published on the occasion of International Literacy Day (September 8) by the United Nations Educational, Scientific, and Cultural Organization. The report, covering 92 member nations, showed that, though the actual percentage of illiteracy in the world was being reduced by current literacy campaigns, the increase in world population was outstripping the campaigns. Survey results suggested that out of a world population of 2.34 billion adults in 1970 some 810 million would be illiterate if the previous rate of reduction were maintained; this would be an increase of 70 million over the figures for 1960.

CHESTER SHEARD, CHICAGO COMMITTEE ON URBAN OPPORTUNITY

These preschool children are engrossed in looking at picture books in their Project Head Start class in Chicago, Ill.

The increase of student unrest at the junior and senior high school levels in the United States continued to worry educators and government officials alike. No section of the nation was left untouched

Ray Griggby (right) of the Black Panther party "tells it like it is" to a group of white students at the Columbia Grammar School in New York City. The school's Black Students Society organized a one-day program of black culture for their white fellow students.

"THE NEW YORK TIMES"

More than 200 striking teachers in New Orleans, La., took part in demonstrations at the Orleans Parish School Board in April; 14 persons were arrested, including a union official. Some teachers pound on the side of a police car taking away the union official.

WIDE WORLD

by the active protests of students in 1969, and administrators everywhere voiced the opinion that the problem would undoubtedly grow worse in 1970. The student disorders included strikes, demonstrations, sit-ins, and violent disruptions. In the larger city schools, racial conflicts were blamed for much of the trouble, and police patrols became commonplace.

Teachers Press Their Demands

It was not, of course, pupils alone who were concerned about strikes during 1969. Once more the year was marked by much dissatisfaction among teachers in many countries over such matters as pay and status, with the dissatisfaction crystallizing into one form or another of disruptive action.

In the United States, where there were a rash of teacher strikes, the unions took a more active part than ever before in attempting to secure further benefits for their ever-growing membership. Teachers said they wanted not only more pay and a lighter work load but also more control over school policies. The National Education Association reported teacher strikes in Illinois, Indiana, Massachusetts, New Hampshire, Ohio, Pennsylvania, Tennessee, and Utah. The rival union, the American Federation of Teachers, added Connecticut, Minnesota, New York, Rhode Island, and Wisconsin to the list of states where teachers in one or more communities had walked out on their jobs.

New York City began the 1969–70 school year with a record number of 1,149,475 pupils on the roll, an increase of 27,500 over the preceding year. With a new contract for teachers, which gave them the nation's highest average salary for their profession, pay was not a source of trouble. It was reported that the staffing situation was better than it had been for 20 years. However, reductions in welfare benefits, such as clothing allowances for poor pupils, were a cause of much dissatisfaction.

Desegregation

In the United States generally, however, the burning issue in 1969 was once more racial desegregation. In July, for instance, Georgia's Gov. Lester G. Maddox was planning to close state schools rather than accept government proposals for desegregation. School desegregation, he declared, was part of a Communist plot to overthrow the nation. He called for a massive school boycott by white children and proposed that Sunday-school rooms be turned into private schools, which would not be subject to the desegregation plans. He also declared that he did not mind if the federal government took away its annual aid for that state's education. At least Georgia, he maintained, would then be able to run its own schools. On August 1 a lawsuit was filed against Georgia by the Department of Justice. It demanded that officials end all racially dual public-school systems there.

At the same time George C. Wallace, the former governor of Alabama, was making repeated speeches to enthusiastic all-white audiences in which he urged them to use civil disobedience to regain freedom of choice in their children's schooling. He urged that parents take their children wherever they chose, regardless of what the courts said, and stay there until they got what they wanted.

Even where desegregation itself was not opposed, the year emphasized some practical difficulties. In Charlotte, N.C., the board of education proposed to close all-Negro schools in the city and to convey the 4,200 Negro pupils by bus to white schools in the suburbs. Negroes mounted a vigorous campaign against this. A spokesman asked, "Why should the black students forget school tradition, mascots, honor programs, athletic prominence, school pride, and self-pride, with no assurance that they will receive anything in return?" White parents had been equally incensed at an earlier sug-

Young children attend the Montessori school in Santiago Atitlán, Guatemala. The school was founded in 1967 by the Rev. Tomas Stafford of the Oklahoma Mission in Guatemala.
RICHARD BELLAK

gestion that white children be transported to black schools.

The position of the Administration of U.S. President Richard M. Nixon seemed ambivalent, and in September the independent, fact-finding U.S. Commission on Civil Rights accused the Administration of slowing the pace of school desegregation. This censure was touched off by a decision by Robert H. Finch, secretary of health, education, and welfare, to postpone the carrying out of desegregation plans for 33 recalcitrant school districts in Mississippi. His decision was overruled by the U.S. Supreme Court when that body ruled unanimously that it was "no longer constitutionally permissible" to go on employing the old deliberate-speed formula. The court went on to state, "The obligation of every school district is to terminate dual school systems at once and to operate now and hereafter only unitary schools."

The Teaching of Evolution and Sex

At the end of 1968 the U.S. Supreme Court struck out the so-called Arkansas "monkey law," which had banned the teaching of the Darwinian theory of evolution in that state's schools. The court held that the law in Arkansas was contrary to the U.S. Constitution, which guarantees religious freedom and makes the guarantee binding on the states. The Supreme Court decision left only Mississippi with an antievolution law on its books. The whole matter, however, echoed the historic trial at Dayton, Tenn., in 1925 when a local teacher was prosecuted for teaching Darwinism and was defended by lawyer Clarence S. Darrow.

The controversy concerning the teaching of sex education in the U.S. public schools grew warmer in 1969. Citizens across the nation debated the issues, and disputes set neighbor against neighbor. It was estimated in the fall that 15 states were considering legislation to ban sex instruction in schools. Louisiana had already done so and New York had banned the use of state funds for that purpose. Parent groups such as POSSE (Parents Opposed to Sex and Sensitivity Education) and MOMS (Mothers for Moral Stability) became common. These critics felt that sex instruction encouraged lax behavior, and some also felt that it was part of a Communist plot to demoralize the nation. According to a Gallup Poll taken during the year, 71% of the U.S. adult population approved of the teaching of some courses in sex education.

By contrast, the Mexican government recommended in 1969 that sex instruction be given in schools; and the British Broadcasting Corp. announced plans to give sex instruction for eight- and nine-year-olds on both radio and television in 1970. Education in France was also giving a new emphasis to the healthy body. Announcing plans in September to make physical education part of the curriculum of the lycée, the ministry declared that it was as fundamental to human culture as intellectual and cultural study. Activities to be encouraged included wrestling, boxing, judo, and fencing as well as swimming and tennis. (*See also* Families; Supreme Court of the United States. *See in* CE: Education.)

ELECTRONICS. A significant development in avionics (aviation electronics) in 1969 was the U.S. Federal Aviation Administration's approval of area navigation systems. The systems permit an airplane pilot to fly directly toward his destination over long distances, informing him en route of his position. Under the previous navigation system, airliners flew zigzag courses, from one radio beacon to another.

Consumer Electronics

An expensive and sophisticated television receiver was scheduled to become available in 1969. It had an electronic switching system—employing computer-type digital circuits—that permitted the tuning in of any channel from 2 to 13 in no more than two seconds.

The field sequential system—one of the oldest concepts in color television—was used in the television cameras carried in Apollo spacecraft. The cameras transmit three different pictures—one red, one green, and one blue—one after the other. On earth, signals from the Apollo cameras were instantly converted to ordinary signals combining all three colors for transmission by commercial stations. The field sequential system was chosen for the Apollo cameras because it requires less complex equipment. The three-at-once system, used for everyday television, produces a better picture.

Electronic devices—such as voltage regulators and nonskid computers—began to appear on automobiles in 1969 as electronic circuits were developed that could withstand the inevitable exposure to dampness, dirt, heat, and vibration. A voltage regulator controls the output of a car's generator; ordinary ones are mechanical, not electronic. A nonskid computer prevents a car's wheels from locking by producing a very rapid on-off, on-off brake action—the safest way to stop a car on wet or icy roads without skidding.

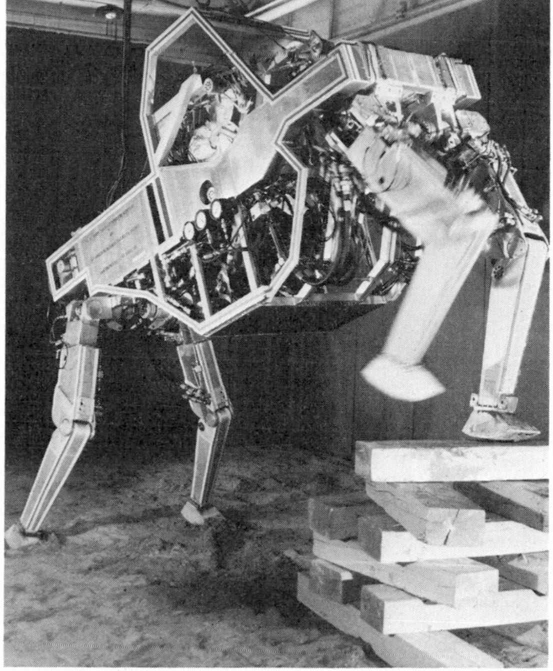

UPI COMPIX

An advanced electronic control system enables this four-legged machine to perform intricate tasks of handling materials under trying conditions. The machine was designed by the General Electric Co. under a U.S. Army contract. This is a research prototype.

Industrial Electronics; New Technology

The year 1969 witnessed an explosive growth in minicomputers—small computers, usually selling for less than $10,000, often rather slow or specialized in function but by no means limited in capability. Many were purchased to control manufacturing processes or to govern machines.

Large-scale integrated circuits—until recently known only in laboratories—began to appear on the market in 1969. A Japanese firm, for instance, produced a rather complicated desk calculator no larger than this book, yet possessing all the capabilities of older calculators that occupied almost half of an ordinary desk top.

A new storage device for computers was announced by Bell Telephone Laboratories. Magnetic bubbles can be formed by an external magnetic field in a material called orthoferrite. Controlled changes in the field can make the bubbles move around; the presence or absence of a bubble in a particular place represents a "bit" of information.

A new kind of display screen, called a plasma display panel, became a practical reality in 1969. It is similar in appearance to a television screen, though it can show only letters, numbers, and a few special kinds of diagrams, not pictures. It costs less than a television set and is flat, whereas a television screen is really the front of a cone-shaped tube. Information made to appear on the screen stays there until removed; on a television screen, the information would have to be traced out over and over again. (*See also* Computers. *See in* CE: Electrons and Electronics.)

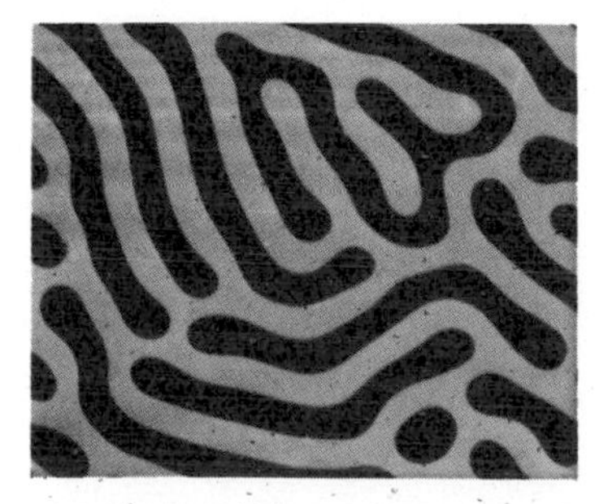

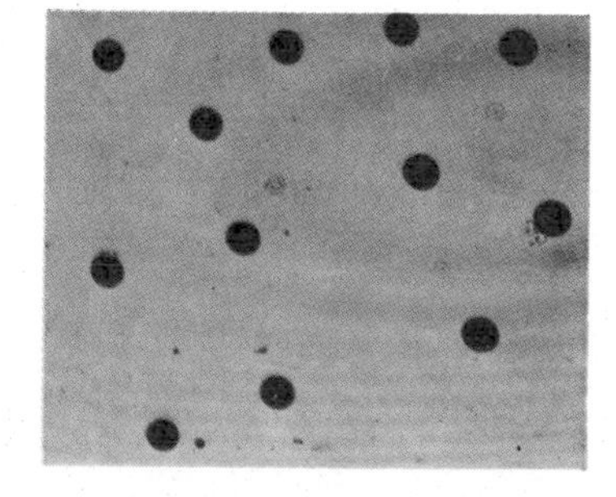

Bubbles (right) are formed from a magnetic field applied to a sheet of terbium orthoferrite (left). A storage device for computers is based on these bubbles, which are seen here greatly enlarged.

BELL TELEPHONE LABORATORIES

EL SALVADOR. An undeclared war broke out in July 1969 between small, densely populated El Salvador and its larger neighbor Honduras. The immediate cause of the conflict was a soccer game. Hostility between the two countries had, however, existed for some time over border demarcations and over El Salvador's concern about its citizens living in Honduras.

Rioting broke out in June following a series of soccer games between teams from El Salvador and Honduras. The Salvadoran team won, and the Hondurans charged foul play. Soon afterward, diplomatic relations between the two countries were severed. The Honduran government expelled 14,000 Salvadorans from Honduras. Salvadorans charged that genocide and other atrocities were committed against their countrymen.

The Fighting Escalates

On July 14 the fighting broke out in earnest. Salvadoran troops crossed into Honduras. El Salvador's air force—consisting of World War II surplus planes and small private planes—engaged in ineffectual bombing missions. Salvadoran ground forces penetrated 25 miles into Honduras along the Pan American Highway. After five days of fighting, during which about 2,000 persons were killed, the Organization of American States (OAS) arranged an uneasy cease-fire.

El Salvador, however, refused to withdraw its troops from Honduras, in compliance with OAS demands, when the ruling class of landowners in El Salvador (known as the "14 families") pressured the president, Col. Fidel Sánchez Hernández, to keep his troops in Honduras. They feared that social and economic upheaval along with demands for land reform would result if the 300,000 Salvadorans in Honduras fled back to El Salvador.

Settling the War

Sánchez maintained his position and stated that the troops would not be withdrawn unless the OAS could guarantee that Salvadorans in Honduras would be protected and their homes and property returned. In addition he demanded that certain Hondurans be tried before an international court for their alleged "war crimes." The OAS threatened to impose crippling economic sanctions on El Salvador, and Sánchez withdrew his troops.

Although the war was short-lived, it had far-reaching effects on El Salvador's economy. Money for much-needed social and economic reforms was diverted to the military budget. The activities of the Central American Common Market came to a halt. Trading between El Salvador and Honduras was ended, and Honduras closed its section of the Pan American Highway to all transport vehicles from El Salvador. Problems created by the thousands of refugees returning to El Salvador from Honduras, however, stimulated efforts for land reform. (*See also* Honduras; Latin America. *See in* CE: Salvador, El; Central America.)

EMPLOYMENT. The biggest employment news of 1969 broke in October when the U.S. Department of Labor's Bureau of Labor Statistics reported that the unemployment rate for the month of September had risen to 4%. At 3 million, the number of unemployed marked an increase of .5% from the month of August and was the highest monthly rise since October 1960.

The sudden increase in the jobless rate took most government officials and observers by surprise. Although the unemployment rate had been rising since the first quarter of the year, it had been expected to decline by September. During that month employment usually rises as many of the teen-age unemployed return to school and as the production of new models of automobiles creates more jobs.

WIDE WORLD

The Rev. James Groppi, a Roman Catholic priest, leads a demonstration against the Allen-Bradley Co. of Milwaukee, Wis., in August 1969. The protest involved charges of discriminatory hiring practices.

Demographically, the unemployment was even more of a surprise. As in most years, the principal victims of the new joblessness were young blue-collar workers looking for steady employment and teen-agers seeking part-time jobs. However, the newly unemployed were primarily white rather than black. While the white unemployment rate climbed from 3.2% to 3.6%, the rate for Negroes remained unchanged at 6.8%.

Reactions to the announcement of the new unemployment statistics were mixed. David M. Kennedy, U.S. secretary of the treasury, first declared that the figure was "acceptable" to the Administration of President Richard M. Nixon and compatible with Administration measures to curb inflation. He later modified his remarks with a statement that any amount of unemployment is undesirable. Administration critics charged that government economics policies were putting people out of work without bringing inflation to a halt.

Throughout the year, however, both private and public agencies and organizations made efforts to increase the rate of employment. Most programs undertaken were designed to find jobs for the hard-core unemployed, a group comprised primarily of members of minority groups with poor education. By September, one private group, the National Alliance of Businessmen (NAB), was able to report unanticipated success. In the program initiated at the beginning of 1968, NAB had placed more than 225,000 men and women from urban slums and rural poverty pockets and was able to boast a 54% job-retention rate—equivalent to that for the nation's white- and blue-collar workers as a whole.

Also in September, Arthur A. Fletcher, undersecretary of labor, announced that the Nixon Administration had decided to require contractors on federally financed projects to make specific commitments to hire nonwhites. Previously the government had required contractors to sign a nondiscrimination contract but had left open the number of minority workers that were to be hired. The announcement came in the wake of demonstrations by blacks who were protesting discriminatory union policies. (*See* Building Construction; Business and Industry.)

During the year President Nixon presented Congress with two programs designed to aid the unemployed and to alleviate unemployment. In July he announced a plan to expand the existing system of unemployment compensation and to increase benefits. The plan called for the addition of 4.8 million low-income workers to the unemployment insurance system. It was also designed to influence individual states to improve their benefits so that 80% of all workers covered would receive at least

UPI COMPIX

Racial tensions plagued Cairo, Ill., in 1969. Black youths picket stores that allegedly discriminate in their hiring practices. The picket signs urge black consumers not to buy where they cannot work.

half of their wages when they are unemployed. The expanded coverage would affect more than 25% of the 17 million workers—primarily farm workers, employees of nonprofit organizations, and domestic servants—who had been previously excluded.

In August President Nixon proposed the adoption of a manpower training act that would make jobs and training available through state employment agencies rather than through federal programs. The act would have the effect of decentralizing the Manpower Development and Training Act of 1962 by apportioning most of the funds to

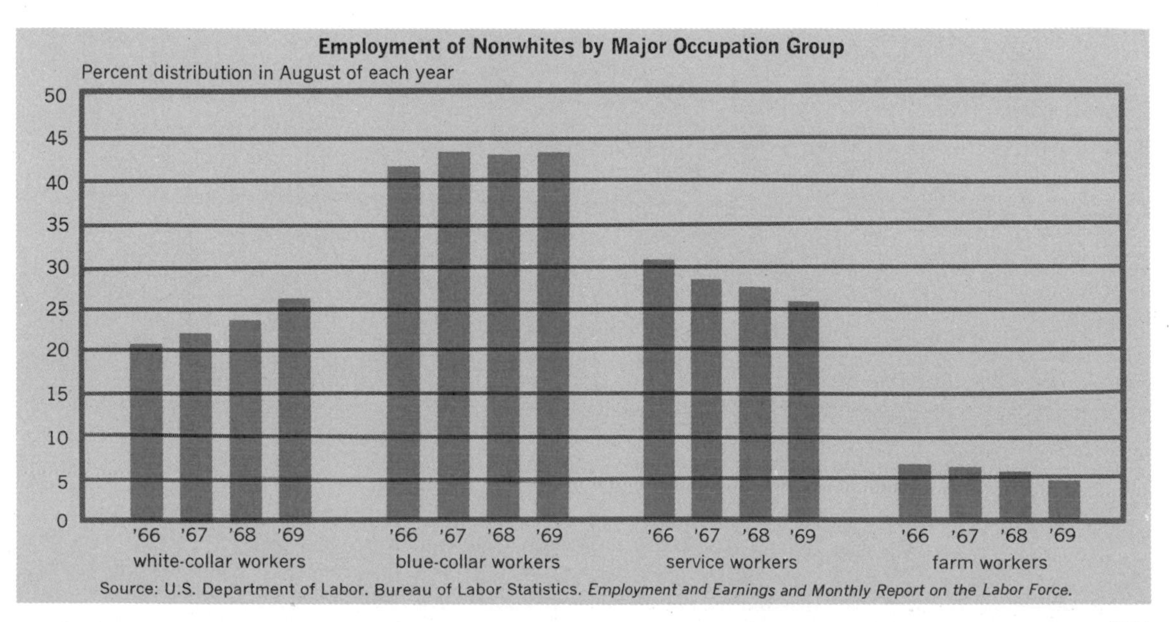

Source: U.S. Department of Labor. Bureau of Labor Statistics. *Employment and Earnings and Monthly Report on the Labor Force.*

local authorities. The basic allowance to a trainee in one of the programs would be based on the average weekly wage in his state and would begin at 40% of that wage in 1971 and rise to 50% by 1973. (*See also* Labor Unions.)

ENGINEERING PROJECTS. New construction techniques were widely exploited in the major engineering projects of 1969. Throughout the world, work progressed on bridges, roads, and tunnels to meet burgeoning transportation demands and on dams to meet mounting needs for power, water, and food control.

BRIDGES

The use of prefabricated cable strands in the construction of suspension bridges, common in Europe, was introduced to the United States in the Newport Bridge, completed in June 1969. The Narragansett Bay crossing between Newport and Jamestown, R.I., is the first major suspension bridge with prefabricated parallel-wire cable strands. The cables are protected by glass-reinforced acrylic resin. These cables afforded considerable savings in construction time and money, as well as improved protection against corrosion. Ordinarily, parallel-wire bridge strands are spun one or two (and recently four) wires at a time.

In 1969 a lower level was added to the Verrazano-Narrows Bridge, linking Brooklyn and Staten Island in New York City, increasing its capacity to 48 million vehicles a year. During the year three projects arose to challenge the Verrazano's 4,260-foot-long suspension-bridge center-span record: Great Britain's Humber Bridge, near Hull, England, with a central span of 4,580-feet; Japan's Kobi Bridge, with a central span of 4,996 feet; and Italy's Strait of Messina Bridge, with a central span of about 5,580 feet. While the Humber Bridge was approved for construction by the British government, the latter two were still in the proposal stages.

The Baton Rouge, La., cantilever bridge over the Mississippi River, with a main span of 1,233 feet, was completed in 1969. Work began on a cantilever-truss bridge over the Delaware River between Chester, Pa., and Bridgeport, N.J. It was to have a central span of 1,643 feet between outer spans of 823 feet, making it the third longest cantilever-span bridge in the world. The Fremont Bridge over the Willamette River near Portland, Ore., was to be the world's longest tied-arch bridge. The 2,152-foot-long bridge, spanning 1,255 feet, was scheduled to open by late 1971. (*See in* CE: Bridge.)

DAMS

A number of major dams were completed in the United States during 1969. The Amistad earth-fill-and-concrete gravity dam, which straddles the Rio Grande between Del Rio, Tex., and Ciudad Acuña, Mexico, was dedicated in September. The Mossyrock, Wash., arch dam on the Cowlitz River—605 feet high and 1.3 million cubic yards in volume—was completed in May. In July the New Bullards Bar double-curvature arch dam on the North Yuba River near Marysville, Calif., was completed; it became the nation's fourth highest at 635 feet. In October officials of Texas and Louisi-

The Canadian National Railway builds a new Second Narrows bridge next to the old one. Tugboats position a 503-foot-long lift span they had moved into Burrard Inlet at Vancouver, B.C., in January 1969.

CANADIAN PRESS

ana joined in dedicating the multipurpose Toledo Bend Dam on the Sabine River between the two states. The rolled-earth-fill dam created the 14th largest man-made lake in the United States.

Construction continued on the Dworshak concrete gravity dam on the Clearwater River near Orofino, Idaho. Scheduled for completion in 1972, the Dworshak was to be the highest (717 feet) concrete gravity dam in the United States; its crest length is 3,287 feet and its volume 6.7 million cubic yards. Advanced construction methods employed on this dam included radio-controlled high-speed cableways for rapid placement of concrete; a new system of self-raising forms; installation of an underground rock-crushing plant; and an electronically controlled aggregate complex.

Also under construction were the 385-foot-high Jocassee Dam, of compacted rock fill with clay core, on the Keowee River in northwestern South Carolina; the New Don Pedro rock-fill dam, 585 feet high, on the Tuolumne River near La Grange, Calif., and the 420-foot-high Libby concrete gravity dam on the Kootenai River near Libby, Mont. In this last dam, due for completion in 1972, six gantry cranes placed the concrete, working from a 2,000-foot-long steel trestle.

In Canada the 600-foot-high W. A. C. Bennett Dam on the Peace River in British Columbia was completed late in 1968. The 790-foot-high Mica earth-and-rock-fill dam on the Columbia River near Revelstoke, B.C., was under construction. The Mica project, scheduled to be completed in 1973, involved the placing of 42.2 million cubic yards of fill by a fleet of 120-ton tractor-trailer bottom dumps. (*See in* CE: Dam.)

ROADS

Important new projects in highway engineering were completed in nations throughout the world during 1969. As the year advanced, two general trends in highway-building policies became evident.

The governments of the developing countries tended more and more to consider transportation in the context of their overall plans for economic and social development. This led them to concentrate effort upon the development of networks of secondary roads so that agricultural products and other goods might be delivered more quickly and easily to domestic and foreign markets. In nations that already had highly developed road systems, there was increased concentration upon urban transport problems. This led to the building of more urban highways.

In the United States, changes in federal highway-construction policies that had been effected under the Administration of President Lyndon B. Johnson remained largely in effect after President Richard M. Nixon took office in January. The reforms were intended to promote more representative public hearings on proposed highways, more equitable payments to persons whose property is acquired for highways, and higher standards for housing built

COURTESY, ALASKA HIGHWAY DEPARTMENT

A 470-mile-long road was built through Anaktuvuk Pass in Alaska to provide access to the Arctic Slope oil fields. However, in the spring melting ice floods the road.

to replace that which is demolished to make way for roads. It was claimed, however, that under the new Administration the relative costs of alternative proposals for highway construction would receive more attention than they had in the recent past.

Independent observers concluded that the federal highway beautification program, begun in 1965, had fallen far short of its goals. Roadside billboards and junkyards remained abundant in all but a few areas of the nation. The relative ineffectiveness of the program was laid to a combination of governmental inaction—at both the federal and state levels—and public apathy.

In 1969 U.S. Secretary of Transportation John A. Volpe announced that 27,975 miles of the 42,-500-mile-long network of Interstate and Defense Highways were open to traffic. Another 5,050 miles were under construction. (*See in* CE: Roads and Streets.)

TUNNELS

In 1969 there was substantial activity in the study of tunneling problems and potentialities. A 1968 conference at the University of Minnesota had drawn attention to the limitations of current tunneling techniques and recommended studies that might forecast technological requirements. At a meeting later in the year at Sacramento (Calif.) State College, it was emphasized that if research could lead to greater efficiency, the possibilities for tunneling were enormous. The two meetings led to the laying of plans in 1969 for a June 1970 meeting in Washington, D.C. It was hoped that the 1970 meeting would define those public policies needed to accelerate the development of tunneling technology.

During the year new tunneling machines continued to improve rates of advance. An 866,000-pound-thrust "mole," guided by a laser beam, bored a 12-foot-diameter tunnel through 3.9 miles of the

River Mountains near Las Vegas, Nev., in nine months as the U.S. Bureau of Reclamation's Southern Nevada Water Project advanced. Three British-built soft-tunneling shields of unique design, weighing 240 tons apiece, were employed in advancing one of the longest tunnels under construction during the year. The tunnel, a 20-foot-diameter sewer under Mexico City, Mexico, would ultimately extend 70 miles through mud and rock to discharge into a mountain lake. (*See in* CE: Tunnels.)

EQUATORIAL GUINEA. After speeches by President Francisco Macías Nguma demanding economic independence and a reduction of the number of Spanish flags flown on the Spanish Embassy in Equatorial Guinea, incidents took place in Bata, the capital, in February 1969 that led to the death of a Spanish civilian. The Spanish ambassador, Juan Durán Loriga, called out the 260-strong civil guard left behind by Spain as a temporary measure following independence. On February 28 Macías complained to Spain's Generalissimo Francisco Franco that the ambassador and the consul-general had been plotting against his government and using the civil guard as their instrument. On the same day he also wrote to the secretary-general of the United Nations, U Thant, asking him to send a peace-keeping force to counter Spanish aggression.

The Spanish government then advised Spanish civilians in Equatorial Guinea to seek the protection of the Spanish Consulate-General; by April 5 the majority had left the country. It was reported that there had been an unsuccessful attempt to overthrow the government and shortly afterwards several leaders of the abortive coup were reported dead. Macías then assumed dictatorial powers.

ETHIOPIA. A number of cabinet changes took place in 1969. The long-time minister of finance, Ato Yilma Deressa, was transferred to the Ministry of Commerce, Industry, and Tourism and was replaced by Ato Mamno Tadessa, previously minister of justice. The minister of education, Ato Akale Worq Habte Wold, was replaced by Ato Seifu Mahatme Selassie, who had been with the Ministry of Public Works. Ato Akale Worq was appointed minister of justice. In a structural change, the previous Ministry of Planning and National Development was incorporated as a commission in the prime minister's office and the vice-minister, Ato Belai, was appointed the first chief commissioner. Parliamentary elections, held every four years, to the fourth session of the lower chamber also occurred in 1969.

In the economic sphere, Ethiopia still faced difficulties in the export trade, partly caused by the closure of the Suez Canal in 1967, and was seeking ways to diversify agriculture away from the concentration on coffee cultivation in the south. Discussions took place with the World Bank for the development of a large area in the north, suitable for dry farming, stretching from Umm Hajar, on the Takkaze (Setit) River southward along the border of Sudan. In September, a $10-million agreement was signed with the U.S. Agency for International Development for the improvement of airport facilities at Addis Ababa, the capital, and Asmara.

The education system was again considerably disrupted by student unrest. In September, at the beginning of the Ethiopian New Year, Emperor Haile Selassie I declared an amnesty for all students who had been imprisoned or suspended from schools and universities. (*See in* CE: Ethiopia.)

EUROPE. Major and political shifts occurred in Europe during 1969. With the resignation of Charles de Gaulle as president of France, hopes were raised for real progress toward an economically and politically unified Europe. There were also some indications that the tension between Eastern and Western Europe might be eased when the Warsaw Pact nations made a proposal for a European security conference and when the West German government and the Soviet Union moved toward talks on renouncing threats and use of force. The military regime in Greece continued to be an embarrassment to Western allies.

The Common Market

There were important developments within the European Economic Community (EEC), or Common Market, during the year. When France's President De Gaulle resigned in April, Great Britain's dream of entry into the Common Market was revived. The entry of Great Britain into the Common Market was a prerequisite for unity in Western Europe.

Under the new president, Georges Pompidou, France's attitude toward British entry into the Common Market changed. In June the new French premier, Jacques Chaban-Delmas, announced that France was willing to cooperate with its European partners toward creating a unified Europe. In July Pompidou told Willy Brandt, then foreign minister of West Germany, that the Common Market could be enlarged. The French government warned, however, that British entry could not be considered until the Common Market had stabilized its agricultural policy.

On December 1, a summit conference of all the leaders of the Common Market countries was held at The Hague, Netherlands. In his opening remarks, Pompidou returned to the old Gaullist position against British entry, suggesting that Great Britain would weaken the economic organization.

West Germany's new chancellor, Willy Brandt, opposed the French viewpoint and called for definite arrangements for Britain's entry into the Common Market. Finally a compromise was reached, and the French agreed to allow negotiations with the British to begin by July 1970. In return France was promised a favorable agricultural agreement.

DOMINIQUE BERRETLY FROM RAPHO GUILLUMETTE

KEYSTONE

Charles de Gaulle (left) visits Brittany, France, in February. On April 28 he resigned as president of France. The new president, Georges Pompidou, is inaugurated in the Élysée Palace (above) in Paris.

Negotiations with Norway, Denmark, and Ireland were also part of the agreement with France.

The results of the summit conference showed that a definite changeover of power had occurred among EEC nations. The French, without the leadership of De Gaulle, backed down from their previous position, and Brandt emerged as the new leader in Western Europe. Britain's Prime Minister Harold Wilson expressed hope that Britain would be a member by 1973. Meanwhile the British public had lost their enthusiasm for EEC membership. The press warned that higher food prices would result, in exchange for long-range economic gains.

While discussions about enlarging the EEC were in progress the European Free Trade Association (EFTA) announced that entry of any of its member nations—Great Britain, Austria, Denmark, Finland, Norway, Portugal, Sweden, or Switzerland—into the EEC must not result in tariff barriers between other EFTA nations remaining outside the EEC.

Two important currency changes affected the Common Market during 1969. In August the French franc was devalued 12.5%. In October the West German mark was revalued. Following the devaluation of the franc the EEC suspended uniform farm-price supports. Levies were imposed on French agricultural imports and exports to offset the effects of the devaluation on foreign agricultural products. The move was designed to hold the prices of French agricultural products at their predevaluation level through the 1969–70 harvest year and to protect the French economy from inflationary forces.

If French farm prices had been allowed to rise, additional surpluses would have resulted, and the EEC was already plagued by heavy surpluses. The Netherlands opposed the suspension of the joint farm program. The suspension, however, was helpful to Great Britain's bid for entry, since it both set a precedent of making exceptions for EEC members and weakened France's demand that the EEC farm policy be worked out before new members were considered.

The joint farm-price policy was also suspended for West Germany after the revaluation of the mark to combat the falling prices of West German agricultural products. The revaluation of the mark produced a favorable effect on France's balance of trade. West German products became more expensive in France, and French products were less expensive in West Germany.

In November the EEC decided to negotiate its first trade agreement with Japan. Also in November the EEC agreed to cooperate with Great Britain on the development of advanced industries such as data processing and telecommunications.

Bridge Building

There was a marked improvement in East-West relations late in the year. While the United States and the Soviet Union prepared to hold talks on arms limitation, the Warsaw Pact nations on October 31 invited the nations of Western Europe to participate in a European security conference sometime in 1970, with the purpose of reducing tensions in central Europe. The Warsaw Pact proposal was

KEYSTONE

Great Britain's Prince Charles kneels before his mother, Queen Elizabeth II, during his investiture as prince of Wales. The ceremony took place on July 1 at Caernarvon Castle in Wales.

a major topic at the meeting of foreign, defense, and finance ministers of the North Atlantic Treaty Organization (NATO) in December at Brussels, Belgium.

The nations of Western Europe were particularly interested in "building bridges" with the East since the United States was preoccupied with Vietnam and domestic difficulties, and they feared the U.S. presence in Europe might be weakened. Also, Canada had announced earlier in the year that it would withdraw about half of the Canadian troops committed to NATO. The United States was skeptical of the Warsaw Pact offer, citing the 1968 invasion of Czechoslovakia as an example of setbacks to East-West conciliatory moves already in progress.

At the December meeting the NATO members finally agreed to test the sincerity of the Warsaw Pact by asking them to prove that their proposed security conference would take up the major issue of balanced troop reductions in Europe. The NATO ministers indicated a willingness to participate in a European security conference but insisted that careful preparations be made for such a conference. They also insisted that the United States and Canada be present at the talks.

While the NATO meeting was in progress, leaders of the Warsaw Pact nations also met at Moscow, U.S.S.R. The Warsaw Pact leaders affirmed the original conference proposal calling for new security arrangements in Europe, an expansion of East-West trade, and greater scientific and technological exchange. They also indicated that they would have no objections to having the United States and Canada join in the conference.

During the year steps were also taken to strengthen NATO defenses. New political guidelines for fast communications in a situation possibly calling for the use of short-range nuclear weapons were approved for the defense of Western Europe. The leaders of NATO nations felt that anticipated reductions in ground forces would make a nuclear response in the event of an attack highly probable, and so rapid communications and consultations between nations would be necessary.

In January NATO ministers approved the concept of an allied naval fleet for the Mediterranean Sea. The proposed Mediterranean fleet would be similar to NATO's Atlantic fleet. The new naval plan was in response to the buildup of Soviet naval strength in the Mediterranean.

Brandt and the Russians

A radical change in West Germany's relations with the East began to take shape after Willy Brandt succeeded Kurt G. Kiesinger as West Germany's chancellor. Brandt announced his intention of pursuing a good-neighbor policy toward the Soviet Union and Eastern Europe. (*See* Brandt; Germany, West.)

Brandt offered to begin talks with the Russians on renouncing the threat and use of force. He also agreed to recognize the "existence of two states in a single Germany." Brandt did not, however, agree to grant diplomatic recognition to East Germany. The Soviet Union and most East European nations reacted favorably to Brandt's declaration. The East German government continued to insist on full diplomatic recognition from West Germany, but other Warsaw Pact nations were not as insistent on that point as in the past.

The Soviet Union agreed to begin negotiations with West Germany on a renunciation-of-force agreement. At a Warsaw Pact meeting in December the Russians appeared willing to allow other East European nations to begin separate negotiations with West Germany. Poland resumed talks on expansion of trade with West Germany, and Hungary made plans for negotiating a trade agreement. The stability of West Germany's economy and the Communist Chinese threat were thought to be major factors in the Warsaw Pact nations' desire for a more secure situation in central Europe. (*See* International Relations.)

The Trouble with Greece

The military regime in Greece came under increasing criticism from Western allies in 1969. In October the NATO Political Committee charged that Greece was a police state and urged NATO members to apply pressure on the military government for a return to democracy.

In November the European Commission on Human Rights completed a two-year investigation of the situation in Greece and concluded that political prisoners were being tortured and that basic human rights were denied the Greek people by the military regime. The report also stated that there was not and had never been a threat of Communist takeover in Greece. The Greek government denounced the report as "shocking and deplorable."

The 18-nation Council of Europe met in December and planned to suspend Greece from the organization until democratic rule was restored in Greece. Before the council could vote on the expulsion, however, Greece's foreign minister announced the withdrawal of Greece from the Council of Europe. (*See also* individual countries by name. *See in* CE: Europe.)

CLAUDE GAZUIT FROM RAPHO GUILLUMETTE

This solar furnace near Font-Romeu, France, is used to study the purification of metals at very high temperatures. Temperatures produced are almost as hot as the sun.

Strikes and student demonstrations, which had become commonplace in most major European cities in recent years, affected Rome and other Italian cities in 1969. This demonstration against police brutality was characteristic of the many that disrupted Rome.

MARC GARANGER FROM RAPHO GUILLUMETTE

FADS OF 1969. Hair—the more the better—was increasingly popular in 1969, especially among the younger generation. Many men sported longer hair, longer sideburns, and even beards. For those who could not grow their own, who were not allowed to wear the newer styles on the job, or who just wanted a change of color, many different types of hair-pieces (even mustaches) were available on the market. In 1969 women could buy full wigs of synthetic material for approximately $25. The wig industry was expected to gross $500 million in sales for 1969—a fantastic growth since 1960 when sales were around $10 million.

A transit labor dispute in New York City in 1969 involved beards, mustaches, and sideburns for men. A 1963 transit-authority regulation stipulated that bus drivers and other operating personnel "must be clean-shaven while on duty." Nine employees fought to have their case referred to arbitrator Theodore W. Kheel, who ruled that facial hair was acceptable if it was "neatly trimmed." In announcing his ruling, Kheel made reference to distinguished historical personalities who were bearded, including Aristotle, Plato, Jesus Christ, Moses, and U.S. President Abraham Lincoln.

Is It Fashionable?

As usual, fashion commentators competed in predicting which trends would last and which would be brief fads. Designers' signatures or initials on scarves and other items of apparel were extremely popular in 1969. For example, French designer Yves Saint Laurent started by splashing his initials on scarves and then went on to spread his famed "YSL" on jewelry; he branched into interior design with initialed towels and sheets.

Wooden clogs enjoyed a burst of popularity. The heavy, chunky shoes—imported from Sweden—required a breaking-in period for U.S. women, whose feet were used to conventional shoes.

Maxi-coats swept the fashion world for women in the fall and winter. However, the mini length

The books, chart, and plaques in this store window reflect a major fad of 1969—astrology. Cups, stationery, and clothes with zodiacal designs were popular. Even computers were casting horoscopes.

JAN A. WESSELS

ARTHUR SCHATZ, "LIFE" MAGAZINE © TIME INC.

PAUL FENTON FROM NANCY PALMER AGENCY

"Wear your own thing" was the spirit of 1969. These girls are wearing colorful tights by Italian designer Emilio Pucci (top). The maxi-coat was popular in the fall, and big sunglasses were "in" all year (above).

was still popular with most young women for skirts and dresses. A minidress or tunic was often worn over pants. (*See* Fashion.)

Men's clothes were increasingly available in bright new colors, patterns, textures, and styles. The "unisex" boutique continued to attract young customers especially. (*See* Fashion Special Report.)

Astrology for Everyone

In 1968–69 astrology grew from a small cult to a big pastime. Americans of many backgrounds evinced new interest in their horoscopes.

Merchants offered a wide variety of related products—including stationery with zodiac symbols and cookbooks, jewelry, and posters with astrological themes. (*See* Psychology Special Report.)

FAIRS AND SHOWS. Virtually all the world's major fairs and shows closed the 1969 season with substantial increases in attendance and gross revenue. More than a billion people flocked to an estimated 14,500 indoor and outdoor events during the year. The gains were stimulated by generally rising economic activity and by the continuing increase in people's leisure time.

Smaller fairs—those with attendance under 200,000—slipped marginally. They found it difficult to compete with the expanded facilities and top-talent entertainment offered by larger fairs, and they suffered a decline in their ability to meet mounting costs of operation. Some industry spokesmen in North America were predicting the ultimate disappearance of traditional county and district fairs in the United States and Canada because of their inability to compete in bidding for popular attractions and the lack of year-round use of their facilities to augment their income. State and provincial fairs in 1969 recorded gains of up to 22%, while most county and district fairs showed no gains unless admission prices were raised.

Show Popularity Rises

More than 113 million people—3 million more than in 1968—visited nearly 3,200 fairs in the United States and an estimated 800 in Canada in 1969. Attendance at arenas, amusement parks, stadiums, and fairs totaled one billion, including multiple visits. In the United States and Canada, visitors to such amusement places spent more than $1 billion on food and drink alone.

North American fairs spent more than $22 million on big-name stars ranging from Roy Rogers and Dale Evans to Bob Hope. Most fairs increased admission prices but offered free grandstand shows. Admission prices were also generally higher elsewhere in the world, except in South America and Asia, where prices remained uniformly low.

Carnivals, rodeos, circuses, and livestock and horse shows also increased in popularity during the year. More than 90% of the fairs in the United States and Canada booked carnival shows in 1969. Rodeos nearly doubled in number as they became increasingly popular at livestock shows and fairs. Circuses around the world were more popular than ever. The 1969 season spawned an estimated 125 new circus units, bringing the number of circuses

At the U.S. national championship Arabian horse show, costume as well as performance counts. The judging is based 75% on performance and 25% on costume. Rajag, a 13-year-old horse, and his owner, Karolyn Kime, pose after winning the 1969 U.S. national grand championship in the native-costume division.

COURTESY, ROGERS, COWAN AND BRENNER, INC.

touring the world to more than 400. Fifty-six units operated on the North American continent.

Amusement and theme parks continued to increase in number in North America and Europe. At year-end their total was estimated to exceed 16,500. Worldwide, more than 2 billion people visited such parks in 1969, while an additional 1.4 billion visited the world's community parks, zoos, and aquariums. Overall attendance was the highest in history.

Trade and World's Fairs

Spurred by the vigorous pace of economic activity, the world's great commercial fairs boomed in 1969. Attendance by foreign buyers reached an all-time high, and more than 80% of the world's 800 international trade fairs reported substantial increases in demand for exhibit space. Billions of dollars were exchanged at these events as demand for goods and services of foreign origin continued to mount. West Germany remained the world's key trade-fair center; Cologne was host to more trade fairs than any other city. The traditionally popular automobile shows in Paris, France; New York City; Chicago, Ill.; Turin, Italy; and London, England, also continued to grow.

Appropriations for the construction of new exhibit, convention, meeting, and hotel complexes throughout the world soared to new heights during the year, with more than $100 billion committed. Cities, states, counties, provinces, and districts joined in massive efforts to attract more business dollars to regional and local coffers.

The frequency of world's fairs in recent years has made their development and promotion exceedingly more difficult. Such was the case in 1969 with Expo '70, Asia's first universal exhibition, scheduled to run March 15 through Sept. 13, 1970, near Osaka, Japan.

More than 200 buildings—most of avant-garde architecture—were rising from an 815-acre former bamboo grove and rice paddy. More than 75 nations planned to participate in Expo '70. Advance ticket sales, however, were far from encouraging. Fewer than a million advance tickets were sold during a peak promotional effort. Fair officials were also concerned by a shortage of hotel facilities. (*See* Japan Special Report. *See also* Anniversaries and Celebrations; Photography Exhibitions. *See in* CE: Fairs and Expositions.)

FAMILIES. Statistics made available in 1969 revealed there were 50 million families in the United States in 1967. A family is a living arrangement with at least two related persons, distinguished from a household, which need not contain relatives. The average U.S. family had 3.7 persons, but the number will undoubtedly dwindle because in 1968 the nation experienced its lowest birthrate ever—17.4 births per 1,000.

Figures indicated that the U.S. family continued to flourish as an institution. In 1968, 2.1 million marriages were recorded, exceeded only during the postwar marriage boom of 1946. The formation of new families was growing at a rate faster than that of the general U.S. population.

Divorces on the Rise

Since 1960 the U.S. divorce rate has edged upward. In 1968, 600,000 marriages were dissolved, about one for every three new marriages. Again, the total was topped only by divorces in 1946. Statistics also showed that the annual remarriage rate for men, between 1960 and 1966, increased from 168 to 211 nuptials per 1,000 divorced men. For women, the rate rose from 122 to 130 per 1,000 divorcées. The Population Reference Bureau, based in Washington, D.C., concluded that divorce rates were not threatening the stability of the U.S. family per se but were an indication that "American couples have become increasingly disinclined to suffer marriages that are unhappy."

A new phenomenon—the "reconstituted" family—was becoming prominent. Reconstituted families included the children of a divorced but remarried person and those of the new mate. They were generally considered unnatural family units because of the difficulty of effective child discipline. Aware of these pitfalls, marriage counselors were cautioning couples against divorce.

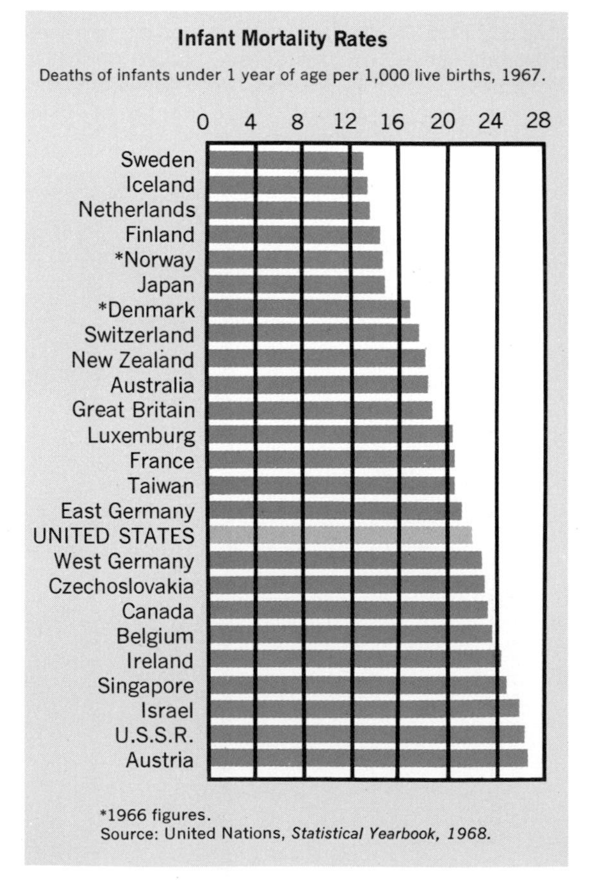

ABOVE AND BELOW: EVE ARNOLD FROM MAGNUM

Communal living gained an increasing number of devotees among full-time dropouts and weekday "straights" who adopted it as a weekend life-style. Members of such communities shared possessions as well as chores ranging from house building to child rearing. Living quarters varied from the comparatively elaborate geodesic dome at Drop City, Colo. (top), to the simple adobe house under construction (above).

Potshots at Sex Education

Sex education was a subject of spirited dispute in 1969. In the opinion of opponents, the teaching of sex was the duty solely of the family. Advocates held that many parents had neither the knowledge nor the inclination to teach their children about sex and reproduction and thus abdicated that duty to the nation's educators.

By the end of 1969 more than half of the state legislatures throughout the nation either had debated the issue of sex education or intended to do so shortly. Private citizens opposed to such teaching usually vented their views through groups such as Sanity of Sex (SOS), Parents Against Universal Sex Education (PAUSE), and the Movement to Restore Decency (MOTOREDE).

One of the most eminent groups arguing the need for sex education was the Sex Information and Education Council of the United States, Inc. (SIECUS). Under the direction of physician Mary S. Calderone, SIECUS sponsored no sex education program of its own but advised communities on how to establish their own programs. Officials of SIECUS said that independent surveys indicated the majority of U.S. parents favored this teaching.

Recent Views on Abortion

A Gallup Poll in November found that 40% of the U.S. adult population would not object to laws permitting voluntary abortion during the first three months of pregnancy. A move was made in many states to revise present abortion legislation, which in most states permitted termination of a pregnancy only when the mother's life was endangered or when there was a likelihood that the child would be born deformed.

A position that was attracting many adherents was the view that abortion should be a matter resolved between physician and patient and should not be subject to criminal law. Maryland, which enacted a liberal abortion law in 1968, allows abortion for any reason, as long as it is performed in an approved hospital.

Militant Women

Feminists were protesting with a vigor that harked to the days of suffragette activity in the early 20th century. Present advocates of women's rights ranged in philosophy from the moderate National Organization for Women (NOW) to the radical Women's International Terrorist Conspiracy from Hell (WITCH).

A keynote of the new feminism was a reevaluation of the woman's role in the family. Some likened it to a form of slavery. Members of NOW also urged such steps as an end to sex discrimination in jobs and salaries and a repeal of abortion laws. One of their major goals was the development of more child-care facilities for working mothers. WITCHes were described as guerrillas fighting against oppression of women. Some publicly shed their bras to symbolize their liberation. (*See also* Population. *See in* CE: Family.)

FASHION.

The accent on fashion in 1969 was again on extreme youth, with older women continuing to despair that there was nothing for them in the stores. In the fall, however, an era of casual, quiet, more classic dressing was felt to be on the way in. "Country-into-town tweeds, unobtrusive colors, well-bred accessories" were reported from Paris, France, by the British newspaper *The Guardian*. The Paris-based International Fashion Office (a branch of the International Wool Secretariat) seemed to be of much the same opinion. In a listing of out-of-date styles, they censured "sensation-seeking and gimmicky garments." Also on their list as out of fashion in 1969 were the classic suit, the coordinated dress-and-coat ensemble, and the "real" cocktail dress.

The Pantsuit; Hemline Controversies

The most significant fashion trend to emerge during the year was the acceptance of pants outfits as rational everyday wear for every occasion. No longer were there echoes in the press of trousered young women's being turned away from elegant restaurants. The acceptability of the pantsuit and its derivatives did not mean, however, that pants were as yet in the majority. The skirted leg was still the norm, despite mounting pressures from trend-setting sources.

Leading Paris couturier Yves Saint Laurent, from whose influence the vogue for pants could be said to have stemmed, continued to promote trousers in his spring and fall collections. The fashion editor of the British *Daily Telegraph* reported a pants trend in London, England: "This autumn British fashion is moving resolutely into pants." From San Francisco, Calif., "one of the great suit cities of the world," the *Christian Science Monitor* reported that "pants and suits are synonymous this year. Combined, they are an answer to the hemline controversy."

The hemline controversy—whether to wear a mini, midi, or maxi length—remained unresolved during the year. Younger girls in particular were reluctant to abandon their miniskirts for longer lengths. Pants, however, did encroach upon the position of the mini. A popular compromise style was a dress or tunic with pants added.

The men—at least the Paris-based avant-garde designer Ruben Torres—seemed to be fighting back. Speaking of his new skintight pants and of the "uplift-aerodynamic" underpants designed to

In the fall young women wore slinky, layered knits. This ensemble features a sleeveless pullover and a striped cardigan sweater with matching pants.

A patchwork of vibrant colors outlined in silver and gold was created by Giorgio di Sant' Angelo (above, left). Bright scarves accented gray costumes—a favored daytime look (above). Shoes in 1969 were chunky and came in bold colors (right).

go under them, he said, "My designs are strictly masculine—it means that no woman will be able to wear our trousers."

At issue with this defensive attitude, Paris couturier Jacques Esterel stated that "identification of the sexes in terms of clothes will become a thing of the past." He designed identical tunic and pants outfits for father, mother, and child. "Unisex" clothes did become a minor fad in London, with the psychological implications of such clothes being eagerly discussed.

The advent of flaring pants on the fashion scene opened up the way for the long, swirling maxi-coats that were the talk of the fall collections in Paris and London as well as in New York City; Madrid, Spain; and Rome, Italy. Controversial as the new trend appeared at the time, many leading designers were prepared to take it seriously and the battle of the maxi length—pro and con—raged through the fall. Most designers and buyers, however, opted for a safe approach by regarding the maxi as simply an extra outfit rather than as an indication that the general hemline was going down. The major international buyers in Paris, in fact, settled for the maxi-coat over a miniskirt.

The Overall Look—Long, Flat, and Clinging

Proportion was the key to the long, flat, clinging look that was typical of fashion throughout the year. Reporting on the French ready-to-wear collection, the International Fashion Office said that the tunic look was the most characteristic. The top of the silhouette continued to lengthen, contrasting with ultrashort skirts or with pants.

The most significant coat silhouette was the redingote featuring a double-breasted cut and buttoning high under wide lapels. Other acceptable coat shapes were those that fastened on the side, the perennial trench coat, and a wrapover bathrobe style.

The trend in knitwear was toward lanky, hugging effects directly inspired by Saint Laurent's vests and tunics. The long, long vest or sweater paired with pants was reported important everywhere. Ribbed knitwear was featured prominently in the fall Paris showings.

The "Underall" Look—Little or Nothing

In contrast to the overall covered-up look—long sleeves, high necklines, long skirts, and pants—was the see-through look, popular for evening. The waist-deep V neckline revealing a no-bra bosom was accepted evening wear.

Designers of underwear lost no time in coming to terms with the no-bra cult and with the typically lean, clinging, unstructured style of clothes. In the summer Formfit Rogers, a major underwear company, started an "instant dressing" campaign (*continued on page 253*)

Special Report: The Peacock Revolution

by Antony King Deacon, Menswear Editor, *The Times* of London, England

AUTHENTICATED NEWS INTERNATIONAL

Shirt collars were higher and ties were wider in 1969. In the fall strong plaids appeared in sportsuits. This suit has wide lapels and buttoned pockets.

What might be called the Peacock Revolution began in Carnaby Street, an insignificant back street in the West End of London, England, when in 1957 John Stephen, a young shop assistant from Glasgow, Scotland, opened a boutique there. But the influences that led Carnaby Street to become a synonym for far-out male fashions and one of London's major tourist attractions, and that caused the conservative menswear industry to reorient itself during the 1960's, could be traced back to the end of World War II.

During the years immediately following the war, Great Britain was suffering the deprivations and moral staleness characteristic of a nation's postwar life. Food and clothing were still rationed, and drabness was everywhere, exemplified by the pervasive "demob suit" issued free to all members of the armed forces upon their discharge. As the 1950's progressed and rationing ended, young men began to experiment with their clothes. The first really cohesive fashion was that set by the Teddy boys. They wore very long jackets, often with velvet collars and lapels, which hung in a straight line from the shoulder to a point about two inches above the knee. Colors were usually dark shades of blue, wine, gray, and brown. Matching trousers—"drainpipes" or "stovepipes"—were cut very tight from top to bottom. Shoes were either long and pointed Italian style or thick, crepe-soled suedes.

The British Teddy boys were superseded in the mid-1950's by the Rockers, who wore leather jackets studded with anything that would glitter and sparkle, or festooned with small plastic dolls and other trinkets. They would sand their jeans to make them look worn and old.

About 1958 there began an anti-Rocker movement toward tidiness and toward smart rather than colorful or showy clothes: well-cut two-piece suits without cuffs, pastel-colored shirts, and slip-on shoes with rounder toes than had been worn previously. The followers of this new fashion were called Mods. Hostilities between the Mods and the Rockers developed into fights at some resorts.

It was the Mods who were the first customers of Carnaby Street. Great Britain had become more affluent, and young men were earning higher wages and were able to spend considerably more money on their clothes than British youth had ever done. The Mods were interested in dress from a studied carefulness, from a need to be tidy and respectable, and from an urge to be fashionable. They wanted their clothes to be entirely different from those worn by their elders.

Carnaby Street supplied this difference. Suddenly the brightest and the craziest clothes were the best. Carnaby Street wooed a large number of seamstresses and other outworkers from the Savile Row trade, and the small boutiques made and sold "one-off" garments straight from the sewing machines. The prices were high and the turnover enormous. In a matter of 18 months practically the whole street was taken over by menswear retailers of an entirely new and revolutionary brand.

It was not until the early 1960's that the general menswear industry overcame its initial skepticism toward Carnaby Street, but when it received the message of sartorial revolution it exploded into a frenzy of activity. Soon long-established stores that had previously cultivated an image of staid conservatism—like Harrod's of London—were jumping on the bandwagon.

To supply the growing demand from an ever-widening public, the general menswear industry, large manufacturing companies, and chain stores began to experiment with high fashion for men. And as the merchandise became more readily available, retailers in the provinces and abroad began to buy Carnaby-type clothing such as cheap mohair and worsted suits, bright, colorful shirts with large collars, wide "kipper" ties, and gaudy accessories. At one time the exports to the United States of high-fashion clothes far exceeded the total of any other type of garment export to that market.

Soon every town in Great Britain had at least one men's boutique where young men—and women—could buy clothes to emulate what they saw in press photographs and on television of stars such as the Beatles and the Rolling Stones. For it was certainly one of the most important single factors in the Peacock Revolution that pop stars wore outlandish and overstated fashions. (*See* Popular Music Special Report.)

Suddenly two things happened that radically changed the course of the revolution. First, King's Road, Chelsea, which had long been known as the artists' quarter of London, became the new important area for men's and women's fashions. Small shops with names like Granny Takes a Trip and Hung on You opened and were immediately followed by branches of Carnaby Street shops and other firms. Simultaneously, the use of drugs became more common, and with it a frenzy of sartorial activity. Boys and girls were "blowing their minds," and they wanted clothes that reflected their total war with society, that had nothing to do with whatever had happened before, and that must, in fact, be as uninhibited as their minds. And as a large proportion of the drugs and the drug philosophy came from the East, so the clothes sold were of Eastern influence—for example, long, flowing caftans and wild *chukhas* (silk squares).

It took about 18 months for the Eastern influence to reach the large-scale manufacturers, and when it did there was a period of Nehru jackets for day suits, even raincoats with Nehru-type collars, and, after Lord Snowdon and other prominent men had been seen wearing them, turtleneck shirts that went under the new jackets.

The other major occurrence was the emergence of the designer. Until only recently the designer

KEYSTONE

SYNDICATION INTERNATIONAL

The fur-trimmed midi-coat (above) and the belted paisley tunic and pants (left, below) reflected the marked influence of recent women's styles on designs for men.

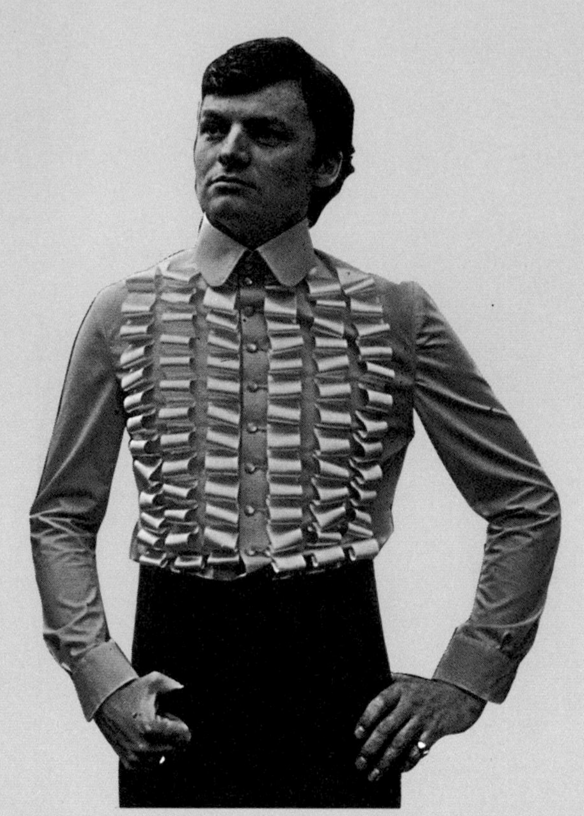

KEYSTONE

Ruffles, ribbon, and lace were no longer reserved for the ladies as men's fashions took on Edwardian frills. This cotton evening shirt trimmed with satin ribbon was typical of the look.

was someone sitting in a back room of the factory who helped make the coffee when he was not working out a sleeve length or the shape of a lapel. Now everyone was interested in who had designed the new merchandise.

Outside Great Britain, the Carnaby Street type of merchandise was soon to become outdated and not suitable for discerning and affluent young people. In the United States, the designer cult—which had always been stronger there than in Great Britain in the womenswear field—grew rapidly for menswear, and men such as Oleg Cassini, Bill Blass, and John Weitz began to design clothes under license to large manufacturers.

The U.S. newspaper and television media did much to publicize and promote these new male fashions. When a number of professional athletes took to wearing them, following many entertainers who had already done so, more adult interest was stirred up. Boutiques opened all over the United States, and sales skyrocketed. Towards the end of 1968, Edwardian outfits largely replaced the Nehru suits and jackets. Early in 1969 Christian Dior—New York announced that for the first time it would produce suits, sports coats, topcoats, and trousers for the fall season.

In Italy the well-known tailors and women's designers such as Valentino, Datti, Litrico, Bruno Piattelli, Patrick de Barentzen, and Carlo Pallazzi all began to sell their names to large clothing manufacturers in order to make their designs available to a mass public. Paris, France, also took up the flag of male fashions with men like Pierre Cardin, Gilbert Feruch, Ted Lapidus, and Jacques Esterel.

At the end of the 1960's, fashion in the sense of the "color of the season" or the "line of the season" ceased to exist, and men and women were wearing anything they felt suited them, borrowing freely from the opposite sex. The "unisex" look arrived (advertised by Harrod's Way In boutique as "one-sex clothes in two-sex sizes") and emphasized the trend toward a merging of the sexes in the wearing of jewelry by men (in the form of pendants and rings), in the use of handbags that made up for the lack of pocket space in close-fitting garments, and in the vast consumption by men of cosmetic preparations—mainly deodorants and after shaves, but soon to include the full range of makeup such as eyeliner and face powder.

The "Afro" look, which continued to gain popularity with blacks, is emphasized in the style of this loose shirt, or dashiki.

CHESTER SHEARD

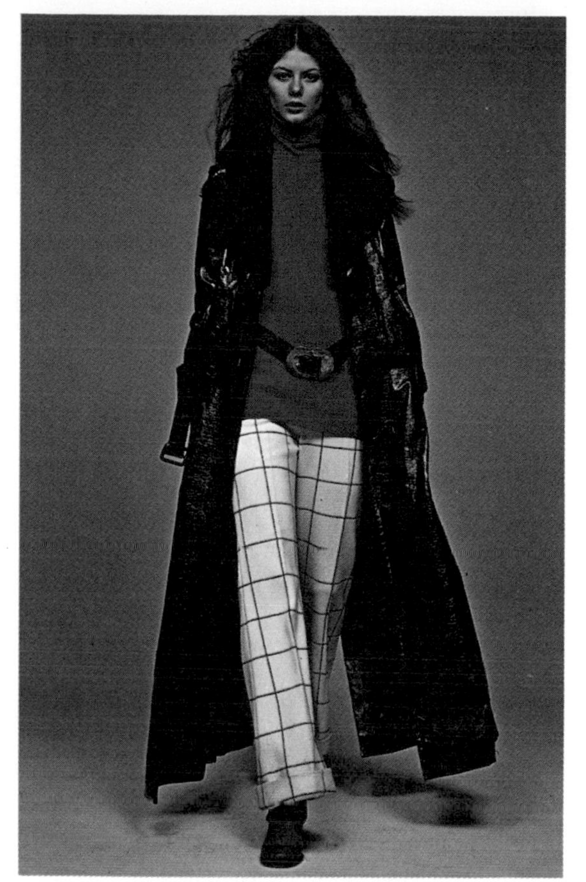
"GLAMOUR" MAGAZINE © 1969 CONDÉ NAST PUBLICATIONS, INC.

The "total" look is shown: a black, fur-trimmed maxi-coat; belted sweater; bold-plaid pants; and (of course) boots.

(*continued from page 249*)
with a "bra-dress," in one form, a tricot and spandex bodysuit sewn into the shell of a polyester tricot dress. The bra-dress was widely hailed as the year's bright notion. Sleepwear also was streamlined to a minimum, but there was a renewed interest in ultrafeminine, full-length nightgowns.

Accessories

Plain, colored stockings and tights were worn by the fashion-conscious for all but formal occasions. Shoe styles remained chunky looking, but in the fall a more pointed toe, designed to go with the maxi length, made its appearance. Heeled ankle boots were also introduced for maxi lengths.

Teen-agers and younger women took a renewed interest in hats. The small, neat, bonneted or helmeted head was the general trend, with the knitted beret, matched with a long scarf, a favorite winter shape. This small, neat look was introduced to give the illusion of a longer body. In the final analysis, it was this illusion of length that was the aim of everything of fashion in 1969. (*See also* Fads of 1969; Fashion Special Report. *See in* CE: Fashion; Dress.)

FINLAND. In 1969 Finland was officially welcomed as the 22d member of the Organization for Economic Cooperation and Development (OECD). Meanwhile, the country continued its upward economic trend. The balance of payments improved, unemployment decreased, and industrial activity expanded. The 1968–69 labor-market stabilization program was renewed through 1970 in order to control prices and wages. Reports released early in 1969 showed a foreign-trade surplus for 1968, the first in ten years, following the 1967 devaluation of the markka.

Great Britain remained Finland's foremost trading partner in 1969, followed by Sweden, the Soviet Union, West Germany, and the United States. The determination of Great Britain to enter the European Economic Community (EEC) posed a possible economic threat. Should Britain join the EEC, Norway and Denmark were expected to follow suit, thus putting a sizable part of Finland's foreign trade behind the EEC tariff wall. Finland's neutrality precludes entry into the EEC, a Western organization.

In 1969 Finland arranged to buy its first nuclear power plant under a Soviet trade agreement effective from 1971 to 1975. The diplomatic highlights of the year were President Urho K. Kekkonen's state visits to Romania and Hungary, the first in the history of Finland.

Finland's Communist party made political headlines in 1969 when it rejected Soviet policies for the first time, causing a split in the party at the Finnish congress. Liberal Communists under Aarne Saarinen won a decisive victory over the Stalinist faction. Stalinist Ville Pessi, 67, party secretary since 1945, resigned, and the two groups announced that they would nominate separate candidates for the 1970 general elections. This forecast the weakening of the Communist-affiliated Finnish People's Democratic League, the third largest party in the Diet, with 41 of the 200 seats. (*See in* CE: Finland.)

FISH AND FISHERIES. The U.S. Department of the Interior's Bureau of Commercial Fisheries (BCF) played a leading role as fisheries research assumed new dimensions in 1969. "Spacecraft oceanography" became a familiar term as photographs and data from manned and unmanned spacecraft offered exciting possibilities for exploring weather and the wealth of the oceans.

In Project Tektite I—a cooperative venture of the National Aeronautics and Space Administration, the U.S. Navy, BCF, other Department of the Interior bureaus, and industry—four diver-scientists conducted biological and geological studies for 60 consecutive days from a habitat at a depth of 50 feet in Great Lameshur Bay off St. John island in the Virgin Islands. This and similar experiments are expected to provide both physiological data and a fuller understanding of commercially useful maritime species.

The total U.S. fish catch in 1969 was expected to approximate the 4.1 billion pounds reported in 1968 and 1967. Imports therefore supplied the bulk of the estimated 17 billion pounds of fishery products consumed in the United States.

Fishermen on the Gulf of Mexico and in New England felt the impact of resource disasters. Hurricane Camille damaged shrimp and menhaden processing facilities and oyster beds in the Gulf, and in New England poor spawning combined with heavy catching of immature fish to produce a continuing decline in the haddock catch. Cape Cod, Mass., lobstermen complained that poachers were threatening their livelihood. The International Commission for the Conservation of Atlantic Tunas was established to regulate commercial tuna fishing in the Atlantic Ocean. In cooperation with industry, state agencies, and other groups, the BCF began to lay the foundation for a joint master plan for U.S. commercial fisheries. (*See in* CE: Fish.)

FISHING AND HUNTING.

Sport fishing became a truly big business in fiscal 1969. The American Fishing Tackle Manufacturers Association announced that tackle sales had exceeded the $500-million mark for the first year in history.

Ice fishing was a rapidly growing sport in the United States in 1969. More and more fishermen were braving the cold to bore holes in the ice and either spear fish or catch them on a hook and line.

JIM STANFIELD FROM BLACK STAR

Fishermen discovered in the summer of 1969 that the Gulf coast waters beyond the Mississippi Delta may be a vast new angler's paradise. Fishing cruisers operated there in large numbers for the first time and found important big-game fish in abundance. Among the varieties of fish taken were Atlantic sailfish, tuna, wahoo, amberjack, dolphin, and even blue marlin.

Great Lakes fishermen—learning more about the habits of the recently introduced coho and Chinook salmon—took more in 1969 than in 1968, though the salmon fishing was not so good as in 1967, the first full season. The big fish were first introduced to the Great Lakes by the Michigan Department of Conservation in 1966 and have thrived. Record spawning runs of Chinook salmon occurred on Oregon's Rogue and Umpqua rivers.

Waterfowl hunters were cheered in 1969 by the appearance of ducks in greater numbers than had been seen in recent years. Most species, with the possible exception of the canvasbacks, appeared to have found good nesting and to have multiplied satisfactorily.

Most states also reported unusually large numbers of whitetails. Thanks to sound game-management practices, a number of prime deer states—including Pennsylvania, West Virginia, Texas, California, Michigan, Wisconsin, and Montana—were able to report sizable deer populations.

In Ontario, Manitoba, and Saskatchewan, moose were reported more abundant than ever before. Saskatchewan alone anticipated that more than 7,000 moose would be taken—most by U.S. hunters. (*See in* CE: Fishing; Hunting.)

FLOWERS AND GARDENS.

Progress in two programs to develop better shade trees for city streets and gardens was reported in 1969 by the U.S. Department of Agriculture (USDA). The experiments were conducted by the USDA's National Arboretum in conjunction with the USDA Agricultural Research Service.

The major species of trees now planted in cities —oaks, elms, maples, and sycamores—have been seriously weakened by air pollution, soil compaction, and salt in the soil, a result of the heavy use of salt for deicing roads. The trees' vitality has been so reduced that they are very susceptible to the attacks of insects and diseases.

One program is designed to provide better trees for planting within 10 to 20 years. It is hoped that the trees will have attractive form; good growth rates; tolerance for air pollution, soil compaction, and salt; and resistance to soil-borne diseases. The other project is a long-range breeding program intended to provide trees more adaptable to the urban environment.

Awards and New Varieties

A rich deep-pink hybrid tea rose, called First Prize, was the All-America award winner for 1970. The underside of its petals is almost a light red,

LEFT, RIGHT, AND CENTER: COURTESY, ALL-AMERICA SELECTIONS

These Small Fry cherry tomatoes won the only silver medal in the All-America selections for 1970 (above, left). The snapdragon Madame Butterfly (above, center) was considered the novelty of the year. Waltham Butternut winter squash (above, right), was an All-America vegetable selection. The W. Atlee Burpee Co. developed the Senator Dirksen variety of marigold (right).

while the upper side is pink, providing a striking bicolor effect.

Seven new vegetables were given 1969 All-America awards. Green Comet F1 hybrid broccoli received a gold medal; Stonehead F1 hybrid cabbage, a silver medal; and Harvest Queen F1 hybrid cabbage, Tokyo Cross F1 hybrid turnip, Snow King F1 hybrid cauliflower, St. Pat Scallop F1 hybrid squash, and Kindred winter squash received bronze medals.

Mrs. Lyndon B. Johnson gave permission for a vivid coral-red hybrid tea rose developed by Eldon C. Curtis of Dallas, Tex., to be named the Lady Bird Johnson rose. The National Arboretum in 1969 released eight hybrid magnolias, four hybrid hollies, eight viburnums, four Lagerstroemia (crape myrtles), one pyracantha, and one China rose (*Hibiscus rosa-sinensis*) to commercial nurserymen for propagation. The arboretum furnishes commercial nurseries with propagating stock of new plants it has developed, tested, and found worthy of introduction.

Two new apple varieties, Jonagold and Spijon, were released by the New York State Agricultural Experiment Station. They resulted from crosses made a quarter century ago. Jonagold retained excellent eating quality and attractive color after six months' storage, and Spijon still had good eating quality and color after three months' storage at 35° F. A new purple raspberry, Amethyst, was introduced by Iowa State University. A cross between Robertson and Cuthbert, it bears shiny

COURTESY, BURPEE SEEDS

berries that are sweeter than most red varieties but less sweet than black types.

Plant Research

Strips of aluminum foil spread on the ground more than doubled vegetable yields and improved the quality of gladiolus flowers during tests at the USDA's Agricultural Research Center at Beltsville, Md. The foil reflects ultraviolet radiation, causing disease-bearing flying insects to avoid the flowers.

Studies at the Florida Agricultural Experiment Station showed that a holding solution of quinoline salts (8-hydroxyquinoline citrate) and sucrose could double the vase life and improve the quality of fresh-cut gladiolus. Scientists believe the salts kill stem-clogging bacteria, allowing the flowers to absorb more water through vessels in their stems.

Studies at the Florida Citrus Experiment Station resulted in a recommendation that dwarf citrus trees be substituted for standards in orchards and gardens. The station said the change was made necessary by rising labor costs and a scarcity of hand labor that produced a need for mechanized harvesting. A mechanical harvesting machine for raspberries was developed in Canada. A shaker vibrates bent raspberry canes to detach the fruit, which falls on a catching belt. Only mature berries detach, the immature ones remaining on the canes for later harvesting.

Studies in the white-pine plantations in the Blue Rock State Forest east of Columbus, Ohio, indicated that air pollution is strangling the eastern white pine, a fine ornamental tree and an important source of lumber in the Northeast and parts of the Midwest. Affected trees were dwarfed and died early. Scientists hoped to develop white pines more resistant to pollution.

Scientists at the Beltsville research center discovered that the red and violet or bluish colors of day lilies are caused by water-soluble pigments known as anthocyanins. They hoped that, with this knowledge, plant breeders could develop day lilies with redder reds and bluer blues.

The results of an eight-year experiment at Michigan State University indicated that the productivity of fatigued soil could be improved by deep (20 inches) plowing. (*See also* Agriculture; Conservation; Forest Products. *See in* CE: Flower, Fruit, Garden, and Plant articles.)

CHESTER SHEARD

A woman cries out against hunger during a demonstration at the Civic Center Plaza in Chicago, Ill. Hunger continued to be a problem among the rural and urban poor alike in the United States during 1969.

FOOD. Overabundant food yields were again recorded by the world's developed nations. Forecasts of even greater food production in the 1970's encouraged hopes that the war on hunger would be won. Nonetheless, in 1969 many of the world's 3.42 billion people lived on inadequate diets.

Most often the people in underdeveloped lands were in need of more protein in their diets. A grain that promised to fill this need was high-lysine corn. Each kernel provided twice the lysine and certain other amino acids found in regular corn.

The "green revolution" of recent years, especially in the Far East, has in great part been due to the development of new varieties of wheat and rice.

The famous open-air market les Halles was moved from Paris, France, to a town outside the city in 1969. This was the scene on the last night before closing as merchants prepared to move their produce out of the area.

SIMONET BUIGHÉ FROM RAPHO GUILLUMETTE

Research on these grains was performed mainly at the International Maize and Wheat Improvement Center in Mexico and the International Rice Research Institute in the Philippines. Two new centers—in Colombia and in Nigeria—planned to attempt similar advances in tropical-food research.

Hunger in the United States

Americans spent more than $105.5 billion, or 17% of disposable income, on food in 1969. Of this record amount, some $20.7 billion was spent on dining away from home. Though these figures tended to confirm a rising level of U.S. affluence, an estimated 25 million poor lived in the nation. The Senate Select Committee on Nutrition and Human Needs, headed by Senator George S. McGovern (D, S.D.), probed the extent of U.S. poverty and hunger.

Early in the year the U.S. Public Health Service testified before the McGovern committee that preliminary data of a nutritional survey revealed some alarming facts. The survey of low-income families in four states showed that 34% of the preschool children examined were seriously anemic and 33% of them had vitamin A deficiency. Some of the tots examined had kwashiorkor (a protein deficiency), scurvy, beriberi, or rickets—diseases usually linked with famine conditions in poorer areas of the world.

Addressing Congress, U.S. President Richard M. Nixon said hunger and malnutrition in the United States were "embarrassing and intolerable." The Nixon Administration hoped to extend the Food Stamp Program by $1 billion, provide free food stamps to persons in the lowest income brackets, and offer stamps to other eligible persons at a cost no greater than 30% of their income.

In September Nixon Administration officials testified before the McGovern committee to urge transfer of the Food Stamp Program from the U.S. Department of Agriculture, where interests tended to be farmer-oriented, to the U.S. Department of Health, Education, and Welfare (HEW), traditionally associated with poverty programs. Robert H. Finch, HEW secretary, said the transfer, a few years off, would fit plans to administer the welfare and food stamp programs jointly.

Mounting Cost of Food Provokes Consumer Action

The Consumer Price Index for U.S. food (1957–59 = 100) exceeded 127 in August. Discontent among consumers rose at almost the same rate as retail food prices. Mrs. Mickey De Lorenzo, a New York housewife, organized a meat boycott in August that had spread to four other Eastern states by late in the year.

Food-buying clubs found favor in some areas in 1969. Comprised of a dozen to several hundred families, the buying clubs were popular because they took advantage of lower wholesale prices from volume food buying. (*See also* Agriculture; Consumer Protection. *See in* CE: Food articles.)

FOOTBALL.

In January 1970, as in January 1969, a gimpy-kneed quarterback led an underdog American Football League (AFL) team to football's world championship. Before 80,897 spectators in New Orleans, La., on January 11 Len Dawson guided the Kansas City Chiefs to a convincing 23–7 Super Bowl conquest of the Minnesota Vikings, champions of the National Football League (NFL) and 13-point pregame favorites.

Roads to New Orleans

A two-level play-off system, designed to generate additional television revenue, had permitted Kansas City to win the AFL crown. Both the first- and second-place teams in each AFL division were given play-off berths. The Chiefs (11–3) had finished second to the Oakland Raiders (12–1–1) in the Western Division. In the Eastern Division the New York Jets (10–4), defending world champions, were trailed by the Houston Oilers (6–6–2). In the first play-off round, Kansas City eliminated New York 27–24, while Oakland annihilated Houston 56–7. In the title game Kansas City—which had twice lost to Oakland in regular-season play—upset the Raiders 17–7.

Minnesota—the first expansion team to win the NFL title—had reached the Super Bowl by capturing the Central Division crown with a 12–2 record, defeating the Coastal Division champion Los Angeles Rams (11–3) 23–20 for the Western Conference title, then crushing the Eastern

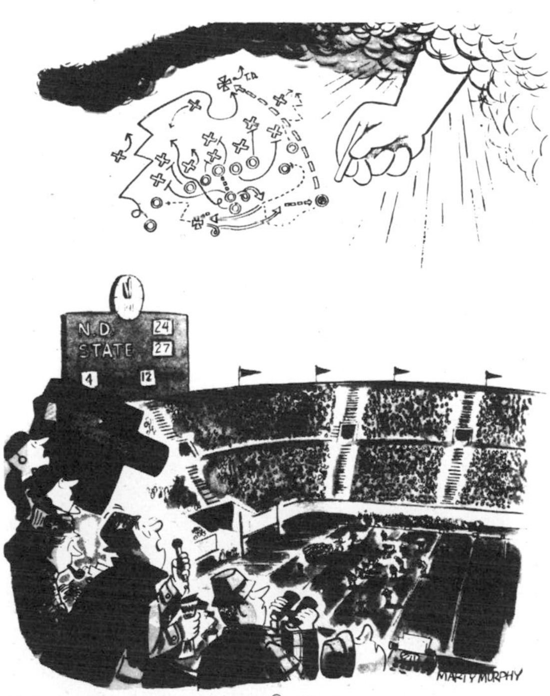

"Well, fans, Notre Dame will have to come up with *some* kind of miraculous play to pull *this* game out and . . . and . . . and . . ."

Conference champion Cleveland Browns 27–7. Cleveland (10–3–1) had won in the Century Division, then mauled the Capitol Division victors, the Dallas Cowboys (11–2–1), 38–14 to win the Eastern title.

Both major professional leagues enjoyed big seasons at the gate in 1969. In the NFL, regular-season attendance topped the 6-million mark for the third year in a row with 6,292,243 paid admissions. AFL paid attendance totaled 2,988,069, also a record.

The NFL and the AFL completed their merger plans in May. Three NFL clubs—Baltimore, Cleveland, and Pittsburgh—were to switch to the AFL in 1970, balancing the leagues (to be called "conferences") at 13 teams each. All 26 major teams share equally in television revenue.

Star Pro Performers

Los Angeles quarterback Roman Gabriel, who threw 24 touchdown passes during the season, was named the NFL's most valuable player. Calvin Hill, Dallas running back, won NFL rookie-of-the-year honors. Making a remarkable recovery from a 1968 knee injury, Gale Sayers of the Chicago Bears won the NFL rushing title, gaining 1,032 yards from scrimmage. Minnesota place-kicker Fred Cox took the league scoring title with 121 points, and Sonny Jurgensen of the Washington Redskins was the NFL's leading passer.

Daryle Lamonica of Oakland, whose 39 regular-season touchdown passes led both leagues, was the AFL's most valuable player. AFL rookie-of-the-year honors went to Cincinnati Bengals quarterback Greg Cook, who also was the league's leading passer. Dick Post of the San Diego Chargers led AFL rushers with 873 yards, and kicker Jim Turner of New York took the scoring crown with 129 points.

Five former players were named to the Pro Football Hall of Fame, in Canton, Ohio. They were Albert (Turk) Edwards, Washington tackle from 1932 to 1940; tackle Leo Nomellini, who played 174 consecutive games for San Francisco; Earl (Greasy) Neale, who coached Philadelphia to the NFL title in 1948; Ernie Stautner, a defensive tackle who starred for Pittsburgh; and Joe (Jet) Perry, the number-two ground gainer in professional football history.

University of Texas halfback Ted Koy scores a touchdown against Notre Dame in the Cotton Bowl game, played on New Year's Day 1970 in Dallas, Tex. The Longhorns beat the Irish 21–17.

WIDE WORLD

College Football

In the popular polls, the Buckeyes of Ohio State University, a traditional football power, were rated best in the nation through most of the 1969 football season. The Buckeyes' stock plummeted, however, when in the season's final game—played before 103,588 spectators, the largest crowd ever to see a regular-season college game—they bowed to Michigan's Wolverines 24–12. Michigan's victory gave it a tie with Ohio State for the Big Ten championship and qualified it for a trip to the Rose Bowl.

The undefeated Longhorns of Texas, which assumed top billing in the polls after Ohio State's fall, maintained their number-one ranking through season's end. In their final game, the Longhorns came from behind to defeat Arkansas 15–14.

In the final Associated Press ratings—compiled after the bowl games—Texas remained number one. Penn State was ranked second, and others in the top ten were, in order, the University of Southern California (USC), Ohio State, Notre Dame, Missouri, Arkansas, Mississippi, Michigan, and Louisiana State. Texas and Penn State topped the United Press International poll too.

On New Year's Day 1970 the major bowl games produced several million bleary-eyed televiewers and a trio of minor upsets. In the Rose Bowl, USC overcame favored Michigan 10–3, before a crowd of 103,878—the largest in bowl-game history. In the Sugar Bowl, Mississippi outdid favored Arkansas 27–22, and in the Orange Bowl, Penn State surprised Missouri 10–3.

Notre Dame bowed to top-ranked Texas 21–17 in the Cotton Bowl. It was the first postseason appearance of the Fighting Irish since their 1925 Rose Bowl victory over Stanford.

In the East, Penn State won the Lambert Trophy —symbol of Eastern supremacy—for a third consecutive year, tying the record set by the legendary Army teams of the mid-1940's. Penn State extended its unbeaten streak to 30 games with an 11–0 season. Wesleyan and Delaware shared the Lambert Cup for excellence in Division II of Eastern

Wendell Hayes scores Kansas City's first touchdown in the Chiefs' 17–7 win over Oakland for the American Football League championship, played on Jan. 4, 1970. The Chiefs went on to win the Super Bowl.

WIDE WORLD

football. Yale, Princeton, and Dartmouth, with identical 6–1 records, tied for the Ivy League title. In their traditional game, Yale nipped Harvard 7–0. Army and Navy, no longer national powers, had mediocre seasons. Navy lost 9 and won 1, while Army had a 4–5–1 record that included a 27–0 conquest of Navy. Massachusetts won the Yankee League title.

In the Midwest, Ohio State and Michigan shared the Big Ten title with identical 6–1 records. Purdue was third in the conference with a 5–2 record; Minnesota, at 4–3, was fourth. Notre Dame finished with an 8–1–1 mark, then changed its long-standing "no postseason games" policy and accepted a bid to the Cotton Bowl. Missouri and Nebraska shared the Big Eight crown.

In the Far West, USC came from behind in the final minutes to edge its traditional rival, the University of California, at Los Angeles (UCLA), 14–12 and to capture the Pacific Eight title and a Rose Bowl invitation. Stanford and UCLA tied for second with 5–1–1 records.

In the South, Tennessee and Louisiana State led the Southeastern Conference, though they were not overpowering teams. South Carolina won the Atlantic Coast Conference title; and Davidson and Richmond shared the Southern Conference crown. In the Southwest, Texas preserved its title, its number-one poll ranking, and its Cotton Bowl invitation with its 15–14 victory over Arkansas.

Because there were no significant rule changes, football statistics—after years of fluctuation—showed a remarkable stability from 1968 to 1969. The average number of offensive plays per game (for both teams combined) in 1969 was 149.8, compared with 150.1 for the previous season. Average total yardage (running and passing, both teams) was 657.7, compared with 657.0 for 1968. There was also a microscopic change in total per-game passing yardage, which dropped from 315.4 in 1968 to 314.1 in 1969.

The field goal continued to gain in importance in college football. A total of 669—18% more than in 1968—were kicked in 1,402 attempts in major-college games in 1969.

Attendance increased for the 16th consecutive year, reaching a record 27,626,160 for the 2,820 games played by the 615 major college teams. The figure does not include attendance at postseason bowl or all-star games. Ohio State, which had won 22 consecutive games before its loss to Michigan, took the national attendance title with 431,175 for its five home games.

Outstanding Collegians

Steve Owens, a running back from Oklahoma—who broke the Big Eight rushing record and accumulated a three-year "career" total of 3,867 yards—won the coveted Heisman Memorial Trophy, awarded annually to the nation's outstanding college player. Purdue quarterback Mike Phipps was second in the voting, and Ohio State quarterback Rex Kern was third.

Dennis Shaw, San Diego State's quarterback, put more points on the scoreboard than any previous collegian. Shaw, running and passing, was responsible for 270 points in the Aztecs' ten regular-season games. Ranked as a major college for the first time, San Diego State compiled a flawless 11–0 record.

North Texas State quarterback Steve Ramsey set four principal records for a three-year career, including a new mark for most yards—6,568—total offense. Wyoming's Bob Jacobs booted 18 field goals to set a new individual one-season mark. Al Limahelu of San Diego State made 59 of 60 extra-point attempts, both records. (*See in* CE: Football.)

GAMMA—PIX FROM PUBLIX

Young Vietnamese girls gave flowers and gifts to departing U.S. troops during South Vietnamese government ceremonies honoring the soldiers for their help. The United States began to disengage itself from the conflict by withdrawing troops.

FOREIGN POLICY, UNITED STATES. Problems abroad continued to be of paramount concern to the United States in 1969. The most pressing issue was the Vietnam conflict, which remained unresolved at year's end. United States President Richard M. Nixon, however, was credited with having successfully reversed the general trend of further U.S. involvement in Vietnam, though his critics felt that his policies had made little discernible progress in actually extricating the United States from the conflict.

Other major problems faced by Nixon included the strengthening and development of East-West détente, particularly through arms control, and the enunciation of a new U.S. policy of "disengagement" in European, Asian, and Latin American affairs. Nixon also had to deal with a Congress increasingly hostile to supporting a huge defense establishment and providing foreign aid, as well as anxious to reassert itself in the process of making U.S. foreign policy. (*See* Defense Special Report.)

Vietnam

President Nixon's policy with regard to Vietnam was to seek a negotiated settlement in the peace talks in Paris, France, and to promote "Vietnamization" of the conflict by withdrawing some U.S. troops and attempting to turn over the burden of fighting to South Vietnamese troops. He gave substance to his policies by appointing the veteran diplomat Henry Cabot Lodge as chief U.S. negotiator at the peace talks and also by ordering the withdrawal of 25,000 troops by the end of August and another 35,000 by mid-December.

Although much of the nation was content to let the president handle the conflict in his own way, by fall a substantial number had become disillusioned with the efficacy of the Nixon approach since there was little, if any, visible progress toward ending the conflict. To emphasize their desire for "peace now," many participated in massive antiwar demonstrations. Nixon's reply to the demonstrators was that he would not allow U.S. foreign policy to be made "in the street." In a major speech on Vietnam in November, Nixon appealed

A U.S. passenger jet stands in a Syrian airport, its nose blown off by a bomb that exploded after the plane landed. The jet had been hijacked by Arab guerrillas.

CAMERA PRESS—PIX FROM PUBLIX

to the "silent majority" of Americans for support for his approach.

His plea for more time in which to make his policies effective seemed to work. Protest demonstrations decreased, and polls conducted after the president's speech indicated that the majority of those interviewed supported him.

Shortly after Nixon delivered his address, the Paris peace talks came to a virtual halt. Lodge resigned from his post, claiming that the Communist negotiators had "flatly refused to reciprocate in any kind of meaningful way" to U.S. initiatives. Philip C. Habib was named *acting* chief U.S. negotiator. The fact that Habib was not given Lodge's status seemed to indicate that the Nixon Administration was turning away from negotiation as a method of achieving peace and instead was emphasizing Vietnamization. In December an announcement was made of a planned withdrawal of 50,000 U.S. troops to be completed by April 1970. (*See also* Vietnam.)

"Disengagement" and a Cautious Approach

President Nixon emphasized two significant themes of a new U.S. foreign policy during the year. These were the gradual reduction and "disengagement" of the U.S. presence in such areas as Asia, Europe, and Latin America and the encouragement in these areas of less reliance on U.S. leadership and of more regional initiative in solving regional problems.

In his first overseas journey as president, Nixon visited five West European nations in late February and March. In particular, the president sought to indicate that in the future the United States would encourage European initiative in solving European problems. (*See also* Europe.)

In July and August Nixon visited various Asian countries where he also stressed the theme of gradual U.S. disengagement from the region and of encouraging "Asian solutions to Asian problems." He said that, though the United States would continue to assert its role as a Pacific power and would honor its commitments, it would not expand them. (*See also* Asia.)

"Increasing Aid to Underdeveloped Countries . . . "

BEHRENDT, "ALGEMEEN HANDLESBLAD," AMSTERDAM, NETHERLANDS, FROM BEN ROTH AGENCY

In the president's first policy statement on U.S.-Latin American relations, delivered on October 31, he called for a "more mature" partnership of Western Hemisphere countries. He indicated that social and economic progress in Latin America should in the future depend less on U.S. leadership and more on Latin America—again the themes of a reduction in U.S. presence and of regional self-help. (*See also* Latin America.)

Nixon was regarded as low-keyed and cautious in his overall approach in foreign policy. He seemed to emphasize the principle of pragmatism. His cautious approach was exemplified in his handling of the expropriation of U.S.-owned companies in Peru and Bolivia and of the shooting down of a U.S. reconnaissance plane by North Korea. In these instances restraint and diplomacy were the key U.S. responses rather than retaliation.

Arms Control

Despite deep Congressional and public controversy, the Nixon Administration obtained Congressional approval of its Safeguard ABM (antiballistic missile) program, which it argued was necessary in view of the Soviet multiple-target missile. The ABM was viewed by critics as another escalation of the arms race.

In November, however, a positive step was taken toward arms control when the United States and the Soviet Union opened preliminary talks on strategic-arms limitation. After five weeks of what was termed "useful" discussion, both sides agreed to open formal negotiations in April 1970.

Also in November, Nixon signed the nuclear nonproliferation treaty, eight months after Senate ratification. The United States thus became the 23d nation to ratify the treaty; 43 ratifications were required before the treaty could take effect. (*See* Defense; Disarmament.)

The thorny issue of the return of Okinawa to Japan was also settled through the negotiative process.

Nixon did not seem to hesitate in discarding, when necessary, what he felt were outmoded cold-war policies such as the isolation and containment of Communism. Several tentative gestures toward the improvement of relations with the People's Republic of China were in fact made in 1969. A travel ban was lifted to allow U.S. scholars and journalists to visit China, and the long-standing U.S. trade embargo was also relaxed. Nixon also made a visit to Romania, the first journey by a U.S. president to a Communist nation in nearly 25 years. (*See* China, People's Republic of; Romania. *See also* Feature Article: "China and the United States: Distorted Images.")

Congress and Foreign Policy

Besides initially balking at President Nixon's ABM program and defense budget, Congress cut his $2.7-billion foreign-aid bill to $1.97 billion. The bill, signed on December 31, was the lowest figure authorized since the aid program began.

Congress also expressed its desire to reassert its constitutional prerogatives in the making of foreign policy in a number of key issues. The most important was the Senate "national commitments" resolution, which called on the president not to commit troops or funds to other nations without express approval by Congress. These assertive moves in foreign policy were perhaps the most significant Congressional actions in 1969 and may have presaged a trend. (*See also* Congress, U.S.)

FOREST PRODUCTS. Figures for 1967 from 180 countries, released in 1969 by the Food and Agriculture Organization of the United Nations, indicated a continuing rise in the value of the world's output of forest products. In constant 1960 U.S. dollars, 1967's output totaled $43.1 billion, compared with $33.9 billion in 1960 and $23.9 billion in 1950. Of the total, wood-pulp products (paper and paperboard) represented $17.8 billion; lumber, $15 billion; panel products (plywood, etc.), $4.9 billion; and other wood products, $5.4 billion. The Soviet Union led in lumber production with more than 46 billion board feet; the United States followed with nearly 35 billion board feet. Canada's production exceeded 10 billion board feet.

According to preliminary estimates by the National Forest Products Association, U.S. lumber production exceeded 37 billion board feet in 1968. The post-World War II high of 38.9 billion board feet was reached in 1950. U.S. lumber imports—totaling more than 6 billion board feet—exceeded exports by more than 5 to 1. Wholesale lumber prices rose 27% during 1968 but by August 1969 had fallen back nearly 8%.

Prices had risen and temporary shortages developed early in 1969 under heavy demand for lumber for housing construction. Later, a slackening in construction reduced demand and prices. The lumber industry, however, continued to press for increased commercial use of U.S. national forests, as its own forests—cut heavily in past years—now contain mostly young, immature timber, and private forest lands in farm and other nonindustrial ownerships produce little usable timber. (*See in* CE: Lumber; Paper; Plywood; Wood.)

Scientists grew a tree from callus tissue culture. Tiny shoots (left) grew from the culture in a few weeks. After seven months one shoot (right) had become a small tree.

COURTESY, PHOTOGRAPHIC DEPARTMENT, THE INSTITUTE OF PAPER CHEMISTRY

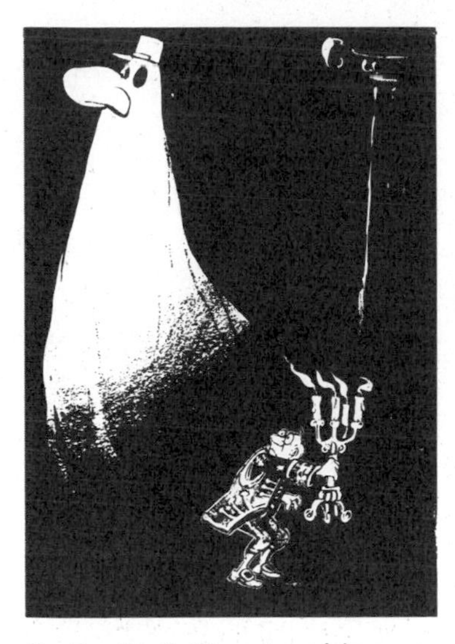

BELOW: KEYSTONE; LEFT: HORST, "COLOGNE EXPRESS," GERMANY; FAR LEFT: UPI COMPIX

De Gaulle (left) resigned in April. In June Pompidou (right) was elected to succeed him. The cartoon "Midnight in the Elysée" shows De Gaulle's spirit lingering on in the new government.

FRANCE. A long chapter of French political history ended quietly in 1969 with the resignation of President Charles de Gaulle. The aging leader's retirement came on April 28 in a move that one U.S. newspaper termed "political suicide." De Gaulle lost his last political gamble in a bid for constitutional changes that would have relegated the Senate to consultative duties only, created 22 new regions, and transferred some centuries-old central-government powers to the provinces.

The questions were combined for a single "yes" or "no" vote and De Gaulle staked his presidency on the outcome. When the voting was over, 52.41% of the people (12,007,102 votes) had said "no" to the president's proposals and, therefore, "yes" to his resignation.

De Gaulle in Retrospect

The end came abruptly and without the disorders he had predicted. Signs of waning power first appeared in 1965 when he failed to win the presidency on the first ballot. In 1968, while De Gaulle was in Tehran, Iran, France came to the brink of revolution. A general strike paralyzed the nation and rioting students took over the streets of Paris. There was growing discontent over inadequate schools and housing, the high cost of living, and low wages.

During his rule, however, De Gaulle did restore political stability to a chaotic country. When he was recalled from retirement (after quitting in 1946 as head of the postwar coalition government) in 1958 to settle the war in Algeria, France had installed nine governments in five years. The charter of the Fifth Republic, created in 1959, provided broad presidential powers and weakened the role of the National Assembly and the Senate. Under De Gaulle France became a nuclear power. The French franc was a strong currency for many years. On the international scene France was heard and often heeded. Over the years it was De Gaulle who blocked Great Britain's entry into the European Economic Community (EEC), or Common Market, opposed U.S. policy in Southeast Asia and U.S. investments in Europe, withdrew from the North Atlantic Treaty Organization's military bloc, put an embargo on arms to Israel in 1969, encouraged Quebec province to separate from Canada, recognized Communist China, and wooed the Soviet Union.

Pompidou, the People's Choice

Two months after the referendum the French people chose Georges Pompidou, a De Gaulle associate since the days of coalition rule, to head the government. Pompidou, who had served as premier from 1962 to 1968, was abruptly dismissed after the 1968 civil disorders. De Gaulle asked for his resignation allegedly because the premier, popularly credited with restoring order, had become too much of a rival. (*See also* Pompidou.)

The presidential campaign was hectic. On the first vote the score was Pompidou 44.46%; Alain Poher (Centrists) 23.30%; Jacques Duclos (Communists) 21.27%; and Gaston Defferre (Socialists) 5.01%. On the second ballot Pompidou polled 11,064,371 votes for 58.21% of the total against Poher's 7,943,118, or 41.78%.

The new president chose Jacques Chaban-Delmas, longtime president of the National Assembly, as his premier. He enlarged the Government, or cabinet, from 31 to 39 members, 20 of whom were secretaries of state. The old Ministry of Information was abolished, and French radio and television began a new era of freedom of the press.

The Long Arm of Devaluation

Pompidou's first major departure from Gaullist policy was the devaluation of the franc from 20.255¢ to 18.004¢, a measure bitterly opposed by De Gaulle. The monetary move was designed to halt inflation (intensified by wage raises with which De Gaulle quieted striking workers in 1968), to bring more foreign dollars into the country, and to increase export sales. Devaluation cheapened French goods on the world market and gave tourists more for their money, but at the same time it gave the French less buying power. Food prices rose because France was committed to maintaining EEC practices in agriculture.

Additional economic measures included attempts to stabilize the budget, to coordinate production and internal demand, and to achieve a balance of payments by 1970. Five guidelines were set to achieve these goals, including reduction of state expenditures, lessening of tension in industry, encouragement of individual savings, substitution of exports for internal demand, and spreading the "burden of sacrifice" by protection of the weak. Budget plans called for a 6% rise in public spending with a 9% growth in production. The Bank of France increased its discount rate from 7% to 8%. A price freeze was invoked in early August. By September dissatisfaction with economic adjustments had increased unrest. The small- and medium-business revolt spread, resulting in sporadic strikes; a six-day railway stoppage reduced service by 80%. Subsequently there were some increases in wage rates to low-income groups and government employees, as well as increases in old-age pensions and family allowances. Late in August the government obtained a $2.5-billion outside fund to protect the franc against speculation.

Changes, Domestic and Foreign

For Parisians the most obvious change in 1969 was physical. The Council of Paris decided to move the Halles, the sprawling marketplace of Paris. The colorful 70-acre plot, where for eight centuries Frenchmen bought flowers and food, lavender, lace, and leather, got a new 1,400-acre home in the suburbs. The gathering place was gone from the heart of the city. Only the little bistros remained, unable to afford the move.

Mergers of major companies made industrial headlines in 1969. Premier Chaban-Delmas denounced France as an "archaic" society and demanded sweeping economic and social changes.

A major change in foreign policy was widely anticipated—the removal of France's political veto to Britain's entry into the EEC. Still remaining was the adjustment of agricultural policy. An EEC meeting scheduled for November was postponed until December 1; the delay permitted the foreign ministers of France and West Germany to meet on areas of contention and resulted in eased tensions regarding agricultural policy and British membership. (*See also* Europe.)

France was expected to attend the next meeting of the Western European Union; relations with the union were all but broken earlier in the year by De Gaulle because of discussion of British membership in the EEC. (*See in* CE: France.)

FUEL AND POWER.

Demand for fuels and the power they provide continued to increase throughout the world in 1969. The search for new reserves of fuels was intensified.

Exploration of the huge oil field on the Arctic Slope of Alaska—between the Brooks Range and the Arctic Ocean—provided perhaps the year's most exciting news. Oil firms which had, amid great secrecy, been drilling test wells in the field—discovered in 1968—paid the state of Alaska nearly $1 billion in 1969 for leases on the 450,000 acres of land. It was the largest lease sale of state or federal lands in history. Meanwhile, plans advanced for transporting the oil to U.S. markets. An application was made for permission to construct a pipeline 48 inches thick over the 800 miles from Prudhoe Bay on the north coast to the port of Valdez on the south coast. The SS *Manhattan,* a 115,000-ton tanker equipped with an ice-breaking bow, tested the feasibility of reaching the new field by ship, through the Northwest Passage from the East coast of the United States.

The coal industry continued to develop more efficient methods of mining and transporting its product. Construction was begun during the year on two experimental plants for the production of synthetic fuels—crude oil, gas, and solid fuel—from coal. A previously constructed conversion plant successfully completed its first test run, producing synthetic crude oil from coal in a continuous process.

Demand for electricity—particularly in the United States—again reached a new peak in 1969. The long-term trend toward higher voltages in power transmission continued with the placing in service, between Kentucky and Ohio in October, of the first 765,000-volt line.

The young liquefied-natural-gas industry continued to grow throughout the world. In the United States utility firms on both coasts announced plans for the use of the product in the engines of their car and truck fleets. Near Grand Valley, Colo., the use of an underground nuclear explosion to release commercial quantities of gas from otherwise impermeable rock was apparently successful.

COAL

In 1968—the latest year for which figures were available—a brief halt in the expansion of the world's coal production came to an end. Production of hard coal rose by 2.2% to some 2.26 billion tons. Although this figure was below the record set in 1966, combined with the lignite output in 1968 of nearly 910 million tons, it made 1968 a record year for total coal production.

Coal remained the most important of the world's fuels. An international survey of the world's workable reserves of fossil fuels revealed in 1968 that coal accounted for 88% of the total, petroleum 3%, oil shale 6%, and natural gas 3%.

In the United States, a 6.5% increase in demand from power stations led the coal industry to expect its highest sales level in 20 years. It was thought likely that the expected consumption of 568 million tons (including 51 million tons for export) would exceed production, which decreased slightly—due largely to a miners' strike in October 1968. The industry continued work on an expansion program, begun in 1968, involving the opening of 75 new collieries that would add 90 million tons to its annual capacity in five years.

Canadian coal production in the first quarter of 1969 increased by 1% over the comparable period of 1968. In 1968, production had fallen by .5 million tons from the 1967 figure to a total of 7.95 million tons. (*See in* CE: Coal.)

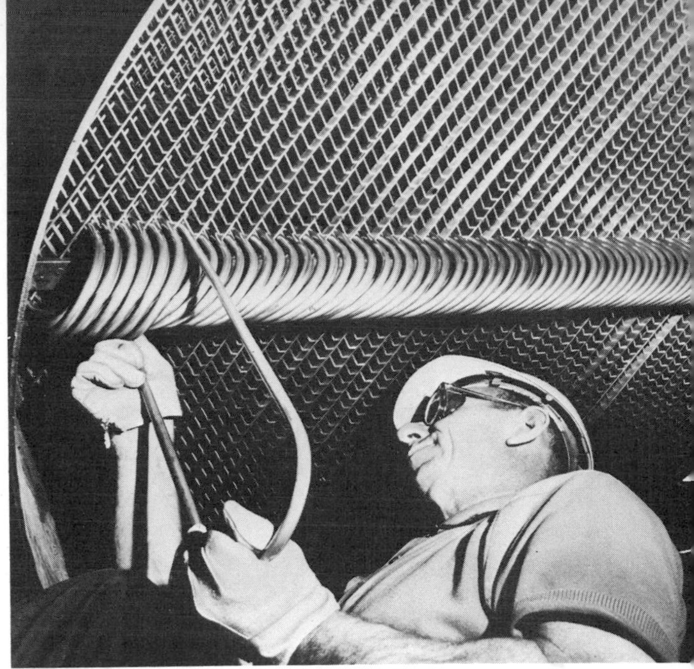

CANADIAN PRESS

A workman fits tubing into a nuclear heat exchanger being built for a nuclear power plant under construction in 1969 in Pickering, Ont.

ELECTRICITY

Worldwide demand for electric power, which had increased by 8.4% in 1968, continued to grow at a similar rate in 1969. In the United States, consumption increased by 9% in the first six months of the year.

Nuclear power plants suffered a decline in popularity in the United States; not until April was the year's first order for a nuclear power station placed. Reasons for the slowdown included drops in the prices of competing sources of power, difficulties encountered in perfecting high-capacity installations, slowness in the manufacture of equipment, and a rise in construction costs—which had doubled in the five years preceding 1969—attributable largely to a shortage of specialized labor.

Great Britain continued to lead the way in nuclear power, with more than 44% of the world's installed capacity; the United States remained second with some 26%. The number of power reactors in the world was expected to reach 105—in 15 countries—by the beginning of 1970. By 1975, it was expected that more than 280 power reactors would be in service in 21 countries.

Thermoelectric (steam) power plants continued to account for most of the world's production of

California's new San Luis Dam forms a giant reservoir (background) that holds more than 2 million acre-feet of water for irrigation and hydroelectric power. The San Luis complex is part of one of the world's largest water-development projects.

AUTHENTICATED NEWS INTERNATIONAL

electricity. In 1969 their construction was encouraged by declines in the prices of fossil fuels, notably fuel oil.

The rate of construction of hydroelectric power plants continued to decrease in the world's industrial nations, most of which had already exhausted the possibilities of their most promising waterfalls. Many were turning attention to pumped-storage power stations, in which water is pumped into reservoirs during periods of low demand for electricity, then is used to run generators during periods of high demand. In the developing nations, however—notably those of Africa and South America—the exploitation of hydroelectric resources advanced. (*See also* Nuclear Energy. *See in* CE: Electric Power.)

GAS

In March 1969 the annual report on oil and gas reserves of the United States, compiled by committees of the oil and gas industries, revealed that in 1968—for the first time since reserve statistics began to be collected in 1946—consumption of natural gas (19.4 trillion cubic feet) exceeded reserve additions during the year (13.8 trillion cubic feet). As a result, proved U.S. gas reserves declined from an estimated 292.9 trillion cubic feet to 287.3 trillion cubic feet.

The reserve report added fuel to the controversy over the policies of the Federal Power Commission (FPC) in its regulation of the field prices of natural gas that had developed in 1968. The gas-producing and pipeline industries contended that the ceiling prices—set by the FPC in a series of cases extending back to 1960—were too low to encourage the necessary exploration and development of new gas reserves. Supporters of the FPC's policies held that the prices were adequate and that the decline in the nation's gas reserves was only temporary.

The U.S. gas industry, which served 39.9 million customers in 1969, expected to add 6.6 million new customers by 1975. The industry's plant investment in 1969 was slightly more than $3 billion, a fraction higher than in 1968. Gross revenues were expected to exceed $9 billion, up from $8.8 billion in 1968 and $8.3 billion in 1967.

Canada's natural-gas industry reported that its 1968 sales totaled 766 billion cubic feet, 9.7% above the 698 billion cubic feet sold in 1967. Exports to the United States amounted to 604 billion cubic feet, a jump of 17.7% from the 513 billion cubic feet exported a year earlier. Imports in 1968 increased to 80 billion cubic feet, up from the 70 billion cubic feet of 1967. (*See in* CE: Gas, Manufactured; Gas, Natural.)

PETROLEUM

The petroleum industry, on a worldwide basis, in 1969 had another good, but not outstanding, year. International oil companies, however, were affected by continued tension in the Middle East and by a slimming of profit margins as many foreign countries demanded—and got—higher bounties for exploration and production privileges.

The U.S. petroleum industry enjoyed another successful and profitable year despite spiraling inflation and political attacks. Operations moved to record levels in the first half of 1969, easing somewhat in the second. Demand for oil during the first six months averaged 14.09 million barrels per day. Total demand for the year was expected to average about 13.87 million barrels per day for a 4.2% increase over 1968. Although domestic production suffered slightly because of increased imports, it was expected to average 9.24 million barrels a day, up 1.5% from 1968.

The total proved and probable crude-oil reserves of the world increased by 2.7%, from an estimated 495.95 billion barrels at the end of 1967 to 509.88 billion barrels in 1968. The gain was largely accounted for by discoveries in Latin America and Alaska. Estimates of the total oil reserves of Alaska's Arctic Slope ranged from 5 billion to 100 billion barrels.

In January a drilling mishap in the Santa Barbara Channel off southern California resulted in the re-

A drilling crew in Alaska swings a new "head" into position to fit it over a drill pipe. The men are drilling through frozen earth to reach oil in what has been called North America's richest strike.

"LONDON DAILY EXPRESS" FROM PICTORIAL PARADE

A small, 23-foot-long submarine, hoisted onto the back of a larger boat, is readied for a trip to the depths of the Gulf of Mexico on a geological research and exploration mission for the Humble Oil and Refining Co. The submarine is part of a vast new array of specialized equipment developed for oil exploration.

AUTHENTICATED NEWS INTERNATIONAL

lease of an estimated 21,000 gallons of crude oil a day. Large stretches of beaches on both the mainland and nearby islands were contaminated. A massive effort extending over several months finally brought the sea-floor leak under control and cleaned up the beaches. All offshore drilling in the area was temporarily halted, then resumed under strict new federal regulations designed to minimize the chance of a recurrence. (*See in* CE: Fuel; Petroleum articles.)

FURS. Economic conditions—including tight money, expensive credit, and a soft stock market—combined in 1969 to produce a trying year for the U.S. fur industry. People had less money to spend for luxury items, and high interest rates forced many stores to channel their investments into merchandise that would turn over faster than furs. Industry sources estimated that retail fur sales declined perhaps 10% from the 1968 figure of some $400 million.

Heightened interest in relatively inexpensive "fun furs," or "young furs," afforded some measure of relief, though it did not fully compensate for the slowing of high-ticket sales. Purchased mostly by the young and young-thinking, fun-fur garments were made of such skins as rabbit, lamb, raccoon, fox, calf, bobcat, bassarisk, and muskrat. Assembled furs, crafted from paws, tails, and other discards sewn together in interesting patterns, were also popular. Furs for men continued to win increased acceptance.

The bulk of 1969's decline in fur sales came in mink, which in past years had accounted for more than two thirds of the industry's dollar volume. Fashion houses whose customers were wealthy enough to withstand a stock market decline enjoyed normal business; those that catered to less affluent customers suffered. Mink-pelt prices, like those of other skins, were generally higher than in 1968, though production dropped. U.S. mink production was about 5.5 million skins, down well over

Among the imaginative "fun fur" garments created in 1969 were these two by French designer Chombert—a black monkey-skin dress (left) and a four-color patterned coat.

AFP FROM PICTORIAL PARADE

a million from the 1968 figure, while mink imports totaled about 3.3 million pelts as against 4.1 million in 1968. The number of mink ranches in the United States also continued to decline.

Toward year-end, motivated by the poor season, leading segments of the U.S. fur industry banded together into the American Fur Trade Council. It was intended to aid in solving the industry's major problems. (*See also* Fashion. *See in* CE: Furs.)

GABON. Following the February 1969 legislative elections, in which the Gabonese Democratic party—the only one authorized—gained a nearly unanimous majority, President Albert B. Bongo issued a set of decrees providing for military intervention in the civil administration, and he named three officers to ministerial posts. The decrees also reestablished Bongo's direct control over all information media. In March an amnesty was granted to political prisoners who had participated in the attempted coup d'etat of February 1964.

France agreed to help finance the construction of a railway that would connect the iron deposits of the Mekambo region with the new deepwater port of Owendo. The French government also gave financial aid for the building of the Kinguele hydroelectric dam.

Gabon, which had recognized secessionist Biafra, was disturbed by the attempted coup d'etat in March in Equatorial Guinea. That country's leaders had cooperated with the Nigerian federal authorities. (*See also* Nigeria. *See in* CE: Gabon.)

GAMBIA. In spite of poor rainfall the production of Gambia's basic crop, peanuts, rose 3% in 1968–69, to a total of 120,000 tons. The estimated budget for 1969 was $7.6 million, an increase of 15% over the budget for the preceding fiscal year.

At the 1968 meeting of the International Monetary Fund and the International Bank for Reconstruction and Development, or World Bank, Gambia reported that the terms of its trade had deteriorated over the past 15 years. Gambia asked the World Bank for aid to develop the port at Bathurst, the capital. The United States granted the Senegalese-Gambian committee a $40,000 loan to obtain advice by three U.S. experts on communications between the two African countries. Smuggling between Senegal and Gambia increased.

In August Prime Minister Dawda Jawara announced that a draft constitution had been prepared. When it was accepted, Gambia would be proclaimed a republic within the Commonwealth of Nations, probably in April 1970. (*See in* CE: Gambia.)

GERMANY, EAST. History was made on both sides of the Berlin wall in 1969 when Willy Brandt, the new West German chancellor and a Socialist, referred to the German Democratic Republic, or East Germany, by name and acknowledged its existence as a separate state. (*See also* Germany, West.)

PEPPE OLSSON FROM NANCY PALMER AGENCY

East German border guards temporarily close an access route to West Berlin. The blockade was part of the East German protest against the holding of a West German presidential election in the city.

The East Germans celebrated their 20th anniversary on Oct. 6, 1969. Most Communist countries sent representatives. In East Berlin, the capital, a huge military torchlight parade was held. Walter Ulbricht, the 76-year-old first secretary of the Communist party, in his anniversary speech extended an offer of "good neighborly relations on the basis of equality of rights and peaceful coexistence." In another speech Leonid I. Brezhnev, general secretary of the Soviet Communist party, hailed the defeat of the National Democratic party in the West German elections.

East Germany's 20th year was one of gain in international recognition, with Southern Yemen, Sudan, Cambodia, Syria, and Iraq establishing diplomatic relations with the East German government. Although the number of refugees escaping the country declined, barriers were strengthened along the West German boundary and stricter regulations were enforced to stop sea escapes along the Baltic coast.

Trade between the Soviet Union and East Germany was expected to increase by 7% in 1970, according to a protocol signed in East Berlin on October 2. In the first half of 1969 trade between East and West Germany rose 26% over the same period for 1968, making West Germany a strong rival for replacing Czechoslovakia as East Germany's second-ranking trade partner. At the Leipzig trade fair in September West Germany had 560 exhibits. Total exhibits numbered 1,800 from 55 countries, and 165,000 visitors attended.

The 1969 budget called for defense spending totaling about 8.6% of the total state expenditure. Soviet and East German armies were to cooperate on army education under a pact signed in East Berlin on January 29. On January 16, Polish and East German officials discussed army youth education. In October a new color-television system was installed in East Germany. (*See in* CE: Germany, East.)

UPI COMPIX

In West Germany, youths demonstrate against the NPD, an extreme right-wing party, during the country's parliamentary election. NPD polled less than 5% of the vote and thus did not gain parliamentary representation.

GERMANY, WEST. In one of the closest elections in West German history, voters in 1969 put a Socialist into the chancellor's office for the first time since 1930. The election brought to an end the 20-year rule of the Christian Democratic Union (CDU), which was forced out of power despite emerging with the most votes. The Social Democratic party (SPD), partners since late 1966 in the grand coalition CDU government, aligned with the Free Democratic party (FDP). On October 21 the Bundestag elected SPD leader Willy Brandt chancellor of West Germany by a three-vote margin. (*See also* Brandt.)

Chancellor Kurt Georg Kiesinger's CDU (with its Bavarian branch, the Christian Social Union) won 46.15% of the votes with 242 parliamentary seats. The SPD took 42.7% and 224 seats. Third place went to the FDP with 5.8% and 30 seats. The extreme right-wing National Democratic party polled 4.3%—.7% below the requirement for representation. The FDP's poor showing was attributed to leader Walter Scheel's open courting of the Socialists—too far to the left for many of the party faithful. The SPD-FDP alliance produced 254 seats, giving the coalition a slender 12-seat majority. Scheel was installed as vice-chancellor and foreign minister.

A week later, in a government policy statement, Brandt broke West German tradition by referring to East Germany as a separate state. Although he emphasized that his country would not grant official recognition to East Germany, the new chancellor offered cooperation—by treaty if necessary. The new chancellor also said that a date would be suggested for negotiations with the Soviet Union on exchanging nonaggression declarations and that the Polish offer to open talks aimed at reconciliation would be accepted. Brandt reaffirmed loyalty to

Government workers in West Berlin erect a huge sign facing the Berlin wall to mark the spot where a refugee, attempting to escape to the West, was shot to death by East Berlin border guards. The sign says, "Soldier, you remain alone with your guilt!"

DPA FROM PICTORIAL PARADE

ROSEN, "ALBANY (N.Y.) TIMES-UNION"

"WAS IST LOS?" ("What is this?")

the North Atlantic Treaty Organization and declared that his country would sign the nuclear nonproliferation treaty when some clarifications were made. He also endorsed enlargement of the European Economic Community (EEC), or Common Market, backing British entry as well as admission of certain other nations. (*See also* Europe.)

West Germany's efforts to prevent recognition of East Germany by uncommitted countries got a setback in 1969 when five nations established diplomatic relations with the East. The West German ambassador was withdrawn from Cambodia, the only country with which West Germany had ties. (*See also* Germany, East.)

A new Berlin crisis threatened in 1969 when the Bonn government chose West Berlin as the election site. The Soviet Union and East Germany claimed this was a violation of the city's four-power status. However, for all their protests the Communists contented themselves with staging military maneuvers in the area and restricting delegates' travel.

A distinct departure from CDU policy came on October 24 when Economics Minister Karl Schiller announced the revaluation of the German mark from the old parity of 25¢ (U.S. money) to 27.3224¢. One of the last acts of the previous coalition government had been to permit the mark to float on the international market, rising in value to meet the demands on the free market. Revaluation, bitterly opposed by Kiesinger, had been one of the major controversies in the federal election.

Revaluation was aimed at eventual reduction of West Germany's enormous trade surplus and at speeding the outflow of foreign speculative capital that poured into the country in anticipation of the move. By boosting prices of German goods on the world market, revaluation helped equalize competition suffered by West Germany's trading partners as a result of the huge German export trade. Imports will be less costly and more profitable for these countries.

The monetary move was expected to channel export resources into regional development, welfare programs, and consumer spending. West German farmers were to receive a special subsidy to alleviate effects of the flood of cheaper foodstuffs from other EEC countries. In September the German Central Bank raised its discount rate from 5% to 6%. (*See* Money and International Finance.)

The Federal Republic's first Socialist president, Gustav Heinemann, was sworn in at Bonn, the capital, on July 1. Toward the end of the year Kiesinger was reelected head of the CDU.

In June the government abolished the statute of limitations for genocide and extended that for murder from 20 to 30 years. The extension was needed for Nazi war criminals but applies generally to all murders. The existing statute was to expire on Dec. 31, 1969.

In June the government announced plans for the biggest European road expansion in history, 3,437 miles of four-lane autobahn. The $23.25-billion program to be completed in 1985 would more than double West Germany's lagging 2,479-mile highway network. (*See in* CE: Germany, West.)

GHANA. The long discussions about a return to civilian rule in Ghana were interrupted on April 2, 1969, when Lieut. Gen. Joseph A. Ankrah resigned as chairman of the National Liberation Council (NLC) and was replaced by Brig. Akwasi A. Afrifa. Ankrah admitted complicity in a fund-raising campaign aimed at supporting his own candidacy for president and was alleged to have accepted money from foreign companies. Afrifa, who had been one of the leaders of the 1966 coup that ousted President Kwame Nkrumah (still exiled in Guinea), had done much as commissioner of finance to restore Ghana's credit and to control government spending.

In January the constituent assembly met to discuss the drafting of a new constitution, in accordance with the report of the 1968 constitutional commission. The proposed constitution provided for a division of executive power between the prime minister and the president, who was to be indirectly elected, be over the age of 50, and serve for only one term of eight years.

The election took place on August 29, in time to allow three weeks for the promised transfer to civilian government by October 1. The voting resulted in a landslide victory for the Progress party led by Kofi A. Busia, a sociology professor, with 105 of the 140 seats in the National Assembly.

The new government took office under a three-man presidential commission, formed of remaining members of the disbanded NLC—including Afrifa, who had resigned from the army. There were accusations of election rigging by the defeated National Alliance of Liberals, and tribal trouble was evidenced in Yendi, where 18 persons were shot and killed in rioting over the choice of a new Dagoma chief. One of the major economic problems of the new regime was to find ways and means to revitalize Ghana's slumping cocoa industry. (*See in* CE: Ghana.)

GOLF. First-time winners in the three major U.S. tournaments and a brilliant individual performance by Great Britain's Tony Jacklin made golf headlines in 1969. Towering George Archer, a Californian, won the Masters with a 281 at Augusta, Ga., in mid-April, edging Tom Weiskopf, Billy Casper (the leading money winner in 1968), and Canadian George Knudson by a single stroke. Archer's feat was duplicated by Orville Moody, an ex-Army sergeant, at the U.S. Open in Houston, Tex., in mid-June, with Al Geiberger, Deane Beman, and Bob Rosburg bracketed as runners-up. In mid-August Ray Floyd of Chicago, Ill., took the Professional Golfers' Association of America (PGA) crown at Dayton, Ohio, with a 276, a stroke ahead of South Africa's Gary Player, in a tournament highlighted by the arrest of a number of poverty demonstrators. In rounding out his remarkable season, the 25-year-old Jacklin not only won the British Open by two strokes but also sparked his team to a surprising tie with the U.S. squad by winning four and halving two of his six matches in the Ryder Cup classic. Although held to a draw, the U.S. team managed to retain the trophy.

Tommy Aaron tees off at the tenth hole of the Canadian Open golf championship in Montreal, Que. Aaron won the title, his first in nearly a decade.

KIRK BROWN FOR CANADIAN PRESS

WIDE WORLD

George Archer blasts out of a sand trap on the second hole during the Masters tournament in Augusta, Ga. He went on to win the event by a single stroke.

Winners of other tournaments were George Archer in the Bing Crosby Pro-Am; Billy Casper in the Bob Hope Desert Classic, Western Open, and Alcan; Ray Floyd in the American Golf Classic; Orville Moody in the World Series of Golf at Akron, Ohio; Tommy Aaron in the Canadian Open; and Lee Trevino and the U.S. team in the World Cup Golf Tournament at Singapore. Gary Player won the Australian Open and the Tournament of Champions at Rancho la Costa, Calif., and Frank Beard took the Westchester (N.Y.) Golf Classic, the game's richest competition. Top money winner in professional golf for the year 1969 was Frank Beard, who amassed a total of approximately $174,916.

In amateur play, the U.S. Walker Cup team was forced to the limit to turn back the British invaders in Milwaukee, Wis., in August by a 10–8 score. Steve Melnyk, a University of Florida student from Brunswick, Ga., easily outdistanced the field to win the U.S. National Amateur tournament with a 286 at Oakmont, Pa., late in August. The National Collegiate Athletic Association tournament, played in June at Colorado Springs, Colo., was won by Bob Clark of California State College at Los Angeles with a 298. Michael Bonallack retained the British Amateur title that he captured in 1968.

Catherine Lacoste of France, U.S. Women's Open champion in 1967, swept the amateur championships of Great Britain, Spain, and the United States (the latter at Irving, Tex., in August). She thus became the first foreign player to capture the U.S. amateur title in 33 years. Donna Caponi won the U.S. Women's Open at Pensacola, Fla., in June with a 294; and Betsy Rawls took the Women's PGA title at Kiamesha Lake, N.Y., in July with a 293 for a purse of $5,250.

Late in January Joseph C. Dey, Jr., executive director of the U.S. Golf Association since 1934, was named the first commissioner of professional golf. During the year the United States Golf Association announced that the new continuous putting rule would cease to operate after Jan. 1, 1970. In October Charles Walter Hagen, father of modern professional golf and one of its most colorful stars, died of cancer at the age of 76. Hagen won the U.S. Open at the age of 21, took the British Open in 1922, 1924, 1928, and 1929, and also annexed the Western Open in 1916, 1921, 1926, and 1927. (*See in* CE: Golf.)

GREAT BRITAIN AND NORTHERN IRELAND, UNITED KINGDOM OF. As 1969 came to a close Great Britain appeared to be winning its long fight to regain a measure of power in Europe. The most dramatic development was a turnabout in the uphill climb against the balance-of-payments deficit. The door to the European Economic Community (EEC), or Common Market, closed against the British by French veto since 1962, was reopened by the resignation of France's President Charles de Gaulle and increased pressure for a European unity that would include Great Britain.

It was also the year of tragic political-religious turmoil in Northern Ireland. The year ended with a flu epidemic that killed hundreds.

Closing the Trade Gap

The payments deficit, a source of British and international concern for more than a decade, began to clear early in the year. The improvement—hoped for since the devaluation of the pound in 1967—showed up in January when deficits dropped to $24 million from $132 million in December 1968. When added to the customary surplus in invisible earning—including dividends, insurance premiums, overseas investments, tourism, and shipping charges—the deficit was overcome. When accounts were tallied for the first half of the year the British Treasury reported a surplus of $115 million. In the July–September quarter the surplus rose to $513.6 million. As the year ended, Chancellor of the Exchequer Roy Jenkins predicted a $720-million surplus for 1969. Economic growth for 1969–70 was estimated at 3.5%. The budget allowed less than 6% of the gross national product for defense.

BIPPA

Caernarvon Castle in Wales was the scene of the investiture of Prince Charles as prince of Wales. Charles stands with his mother, Queen Elizabeth II.

"THE TIMES," LONDON, FROM PICTORIAL PARADE

Factors in the brightening of the British economic fortunes included a boom in trade abroad and stringent deflationary controls at home. In February bank rates were raised to 8%, and taxes were increased in April to curb spending. The devaluation of the pound from $2.80 to $2.40 in 1967 brought down prices of British exports and increased the costs of foreign goods, discouraging import buying at home. The continued favorable economic climate brought hope that there could be some lessening of restrictive measures—for example, a cut in taxes or the easing of credits—before the expected elections in 1971. Any of these might improve the chances of Wilson's Labor party, which had borne the brunt of widespread discontent over the severe austerity policies.

Closer to the Common Market

In December, EEC members met at The Hague, the Netherlands, to ponder the perennial question of British entry, this time without the shadow of De Gaulle to cloud the issue. Georges Pompidou, successor to De Gaulle, had previously removed so-called "political" objections to British membership. As talks progressed, France issued a declaration that it would enter into negotiations with Britain no later than mid-1970. Formidable problems remained to be ironed out by the EEC partners, chiefly in the area of agricultural policy, under which French farmers are the chief beneficiaries of support prices. (*See* Europe.)

In a Cabinet reorganization in October, designed to meet the pressing problems of the 1970's, Wilson appointed George Thomson, a Scotsman and former minister without portfolio, as a deputy foreign secretary charged with the task of negotiating British entry into the EEC. The Ministry of Technology was enlarged to include responsibility for the Ministry of Power, much of the work of the abolished Department of Economic Affairs, and the industrial concerns of the Board of Trade. A new department of local government, transport, and regional planning was to deal with the growing menace of environmental pollution. The reshuffle reduced the number of Cabinet ministers from 23 to 21.

Politics and Labor

Prime Minister Harold Wilson's Labor government, traditionally union-backed, suffered loss of support within the party over attempts to bring some semblance of control to the wildcat strikes that had repeatedly hobbled the economy throughout the year. (British law provides almost no control over labor activity.) In December, the prime minister, whose popularity poll rating had climbed slowly from a July low, suffered a crushing defeat as members of his party in Parliament reduced his majority from 60 to 28 in a vote on union reform.

The Labor party won six of eight by-elections during the year but suffered percentage losses ranging from 10.5% to 18%. In local elections the

KEYSTONE

On Jan. 11, 1969, demonstrators outside Australia House, in London, England, protested fighting by Australians in the Vietnam conflict.

Labor party retained control of only 28 of 342 English and Welsh boroughs. Two by-elections produced startling results. In June Birmingham elected its first Liberal candidate since 1885. In April Bernadette Devlin, a 21-year-old student and leader in the Ulster civil rights movement for Catholics, was elected to the British Parliament. A fiery speaker, the girl from Bogside later made headlines when she took part in street fighting in Londonderry and visited the United States and the United Nations to plead for support and financial aid for both Catholics and Protestants displaced in the civil disruption there.

Bigotry and Blood in Ireland

Death and destruction rocked the streets of Northern Ireland as age-old Catholic-Protestant prejudice—compounded by political and economic unrest—swelled into mayhem. In Belfast and in Londonderry fire bombs flared, homes fell, and barricades went up. Policemen, soldiers, and civilians were killed and injured in a fight that pitted Protestants (a two-thirds majority) against Roman Catholics in the six Crown counties of Northern Ireland.

GAMMA—PIX FROM PUBLIX

ABOVE AND BELOW: "LONDON DAILY EXPRESS" FROM PICTORIAL PARADE

Fighting between Protestants and Catholics raged in Northern Ireland in 1969. Belfast (above) looks like a bombed city after one night's rioting. Bernadette Devlin, a militant young member of Parliament, uses a bullhorn to speak from the barricades (above, right). A police riot truck burns in Newry (right). Northern Ireland's Catholic population is shown on the map below.

The Catholics, traditionally the poorest of the poor in this low-income corner of the United Kingdom, rose under Miss Devlin to demand an end to social ills and to discrimination under the rule of the conservative Unionists. The Protestant party has ruled the land since southern Ireland became a republic in 1921. Protestants, long fearful of the role of the Roman Catholic church (predominant in the Irish Republic), fought against reforms aimed at equal rights for Catholics. The Catholics pressed for instant relief from oppression. In the end, Capt. Terence O'Neill, the prime minister, was reelected by a narrow margin in February, only to resign in late April for lack of support for his proposed reforms. The Unionists appointed an inquiry board that found discrimination in several areas: 1) gerrymandering to keep down influence in predominantly Catholic areas, 2) franchise limitations that excluded Catholics, 3) job discrimination, 4) pro-Protestant civil appointments, and 5) assignment of public housing on a basis that reflected bias.

In October Maj. James Chichester-Clark, successor to O'Neill, and Britain's Home Secretary James Callaghan announced a program of social, economic, and political reforms. The announcement engendered new violence from the Protestant sector. British troops, called at the height of the riots in August, continued to maintain an uneasy vigil. In the autumn a Protestant extremist, the Rev. Ian Paisley, paid a visit to the United States

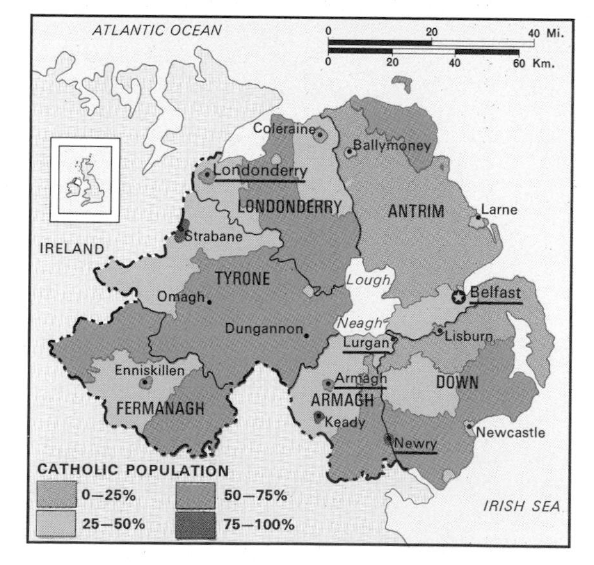

on behalf of his faction. In December Miss Devlin was sentenced to six months in prison for her part in the street fighting. She was released on bond for appeal set for February 1970.

Sunset on the Empire

Time turned back to the 13th century in July when, at the ancient Caernarvon Castle, Caernarvon, Wales, Charles Philip Arthur George, heir to the British throne, was crowned 21st prince of Wales. In an hourlong, two-language investiture ceremony, he pledged allegiance to his mother, Queen Elizabeth II, before a crowd of 4,000. Afterward, Welshmen cheered as he greeted them from a castle balcony. But behind the pomp and ceremony there was a growing demand for home rule in Wales. Once again a bill on home rule died in the House of Commons, but the Welsh continued to plan.

The Scottish Nationalist party showed soaring membership figures (from 2,000 to 128,000 in ten years) while a 1969 newspaper poll showed that 88% of the Scotsmen who took part favored a self-government referendum.

The people of Gibraltar, whose new constitution confirms their ties with Britain, felt the iron hand of Spanish retaliation in 1969. The border post and the Algeciras, Spain, ferry were closed, cutting off the Spanish labor supply from "the Rock." Telephone links were cut and Spanish warships roamed the harbor. A ray of hope for settlement came with a reshuffle of Spain's cabinet in October, followed by some signs of relenting.

Wilson made a futile trip to Africa in March in hopes of bringing about a settlement of the Nigerian civil war. The leader of rebel Biafra, Lieut. Col. C. Odumegwu Ojukwu, refused to meet with him. Political dissension over British arms shipment to Nigeria and alleged indifference to Biafran relief continued. The last Union Jack (British flag) was lowered in rebel Rhodesia in July.

Parliament and Policy

The voting age was lowered from 21 to 18, making some 6 million voters under 25 (one fifth of the electorate) eligible for the next election. Capital punishment for murder was abolished after a 40-year drive, over opposition by the Conservatives. The legislation did not affect other capital crimes and could be reversed, should the Conservatives come to power. The traditional grounds for divorce—desertion, adultery, cruelty, and sodomy—were scrapped in 1969 for a single test: "the irretrievable breakdown of marriage." There were widespread social security reforms basing benefits on earnings.

The queen's message of policy to Parliament in October outlined a proposal that would revise the educational system to combine vocational and college curricula, doing away with tests that determined the educational future of British children at age 11. Another major proposal called for stiffening of penalties for illegal drug peddling and manufacture and a crackdown on physicians who over-prescribe amphetamines and barbiturates. The proposal would not affect the current practice of providing heroin and cocaine free at special clinics for known addicts. (*See also* Wilson. *See in* CE: Great Britain and Northern Ireland, United Kingdom of.)

GREECE. Martial law became a way of life in Greece in 1969 as Premier George Papadopoulos' government continued to pay only lip service to democracy. The constitutional guarantees of civil and political liberties remained suspended for the most part. Terrorist activities erupted from time to time, and continuing political arrests created a climate of fear. In May the Council of Europe warned the Greeks that their disregard for civil rights could lead to expulsion; on December 12 Greece resigned from the council to avoid expulsion.

In a major violation of the 1968 constitution, the regime reversed a supreme-court decision that had invalidated the firing of 21 of 30 senior judges dismissed in May 1968. As a consequence of the reversal the chief justice and nine other justices were fired. Three lawyers who had defended the appeal of the 21 ousted judges were deported from Athens, the capital.

A number of institutional reforms aimed at strengthening the central government were put into

Some of Greece's 2,500 political prisoners are confined to Averof Prison in Athens. These inmates demonstrate on the roof for better treatment.

CAMERA PRESS

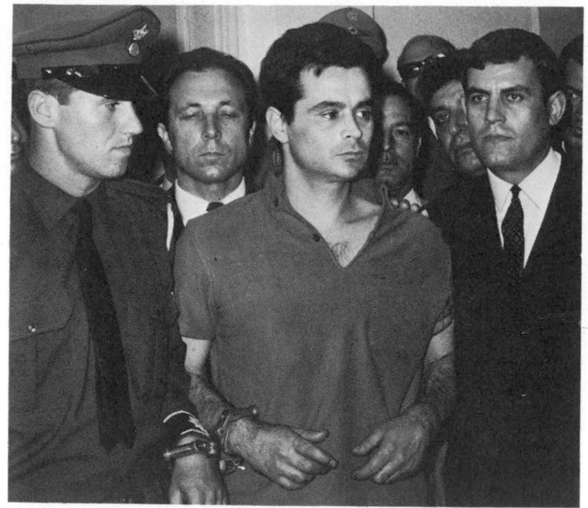

CAMERA PRESS—PIX FROM PUBLIX

Alexandros Panaghoulis (center), who was given a life term in 1968 for trying to kill Greece's Premier George Papadopoulos, was recaptured three days after he escaped from prison on June 6, 1969.

effect in 1969. In February the Greek Orthodox church was given a charter granting it some measure of autonomy under the new General Church Assembly. However, the charter transferred all assembly power to the regime for three years. Labor legislation was passed to eliminate professional trade-union officials. In May retired army generals were appointed government commissioners to all Greek universities. In July another army general was appointed ombudsman with special authority to probe into the private lives of civil servants. Generals were also nominated as Greek ambassadors to Great Britain and France. Student protests were barred.

As the year ended, many opponents of the regime pinned their hopes on the leadership of former Premier Constantine Caramanlis. From self-exile in Paris, France, Caramanlis—the founder of the National Radical Union party—called upon the Greek armed forces to overthrow the leaders of the 1967 military coup. He offered to undertake leadership of an interim government that would restore democracy to Greece. In Athens there was speculation that the former premier had either the backing of officers loyal to the exiled King Constantine II or a go-ahead from the United States.

The prolonged suspension of democracy in the country worsened foreign relations not only with Western European countries but also with the United States. The U.S. ambassador's post in Athens was left vacant, and shipments of military equipment to Greece dwindled.

The Greek economy, for the third year of the military rule, suffered serious lack of foreign investment. This, combined with lavish credits granted in previous years to combat domestic recession, posed a balance-of-payments problem. That deficit was expected to reach some $300 million in 1969. To ease the difficulty the government obtained high-interest loans from abroad and imposed equalization levies and time-consuming controls on import invoices. Figures released at the start of 1969 showed that imports reached $1.25 billion in 1968, while exports rose by only $12 million. Tourism declined. The foreign debt was expected to rise by $83 million in 1969 from the 1968 figure of $428 million.

One encouraging area of economic growth came in increased shipping remittances. Another source of foreign income on the increase was in money sent home by emigrants. (Emigration rose by 8,000 in 1968 when 51,000 Greeks left.)

Meanwhile King Constantine was publicly denounced by the regime for failure to discourage known conspiracy, and the censored press warned Constantine that his throne was in danger. The statements followed a wave of arrests of right-wing military officers. Meanwhile the king remained in exile in Rome, Italy, where in 1969 his wife gave birth to their third child and second son. (*See also* Births; Europe. *See in* CE: Greece.)

GUATEMALA. In 1969 Guatemala continued to make progress toward political normalcy and an improvement in its economy, both trends that had begun in the latter half of 1968. Even the development of a bitter campaign for the presidential elections, which were scheduled for March 1970, did not lead to a renewal of the terrorist activity that in recent years had kept the country on the brink of civil war.

Guatemala's economic affairs, however, were somewhat clouded as a result of two outside forces

RICHARD BELLAK

At Bananera, Guatemala, workers are busy trimming banana plant roots at a United Fruit Co. plant. New banana plants are grown from the rootstock.

—war and weather. The war between El Salvador and Honduras in July had a disruptive effect on Guatemala's economy and the development of the Central American Common Market to which Guatemala, El Salvador, Honduras, Costa Rica, and Nicaragua belonged. The severe storms in September and early October also affected the country's economy.

Political events of the year focused on the upcoming presidential elections and the activities of the country's three major political parties. Early in 1969 the right-wing National Liberation Movement (MLN) selected Col. Carlos Arana Osorio as its candidate. Later the ruling Revolutionary party chose the minister of finance, Mario Fuentes Pieruccini, as its candidate. The Christian Democratic party nominated its first presidential candidate, Jorge Lucas Caballero.

The limited violence that did break out centered around the campaign of Colonel Arana. In June left-wing elements were accused of having assassinated several leaders of Arana's party, the MLN. In turn, the MLN was accused of the attempted assassination of Irma Flaquer, a journalist and secretary to the wife of Guatemala's President Julio César Méndez Montenegro. In October the Institutional Democratic party, another right-wing party, joined in support of Colonel Arana, thus placing him in a strong position as a presidential aspirant. Although the extremist left-wing terrorist group known as the Revolutionary Armed Forces issued a statement condemning Colonel Arana to death, terrorist activity was considerably subdued. There was relative political calm in the country as indicated by the fact that the national "state of alarm," imposed at the time of the assassination of the U.S. ambassador in August 1968 and lifted later that year, had not been reinstituted since then.

Business and government activities continued to expand favorably. The government restraints on imports limited them to their 1968 level. In contrast, income from exports appeared to have increased during 1969 by nearly 25%. These trends contributed significantly to an improvement in the country's balance of payments. A program of federal government austerity and improved export earnings provided the basis for the economic stability and moderate economic gains achieved during the year. Continuing economic expansion in 1970, particularly in light industry, depended on the maintenance of Central American Common Market trade. It remained to be seen how the El Salvador-Honduras conflict would affect the growth of the common market. (*See in* CE: Guatemala.)

GUINEA. Reports of conspiracies and plots against the life of President Sékou Touré created a tense atmosphere in Guinea during 1969. In January, following the discovery of the first conspiracy of the year, "counterrevolutionary" demonstrations took place in Conakry, the capital.

In March another plot was uncovered, involving the army and two members of Touré's cabinet. The secretary for civil service, Col. Kaman Diaby, and the secretary for rural economy, Fodeba Keita, along with ten other alleged conspirators were sentenced to death. There was a purge of the army, and many civilians were also arrested. Touré accused France of aiding the conspirators.

A physical attack was made on Touré in June as he rode into Conakry in a motorcade with Zambia's President Kenneth Kaunda and Kwame Nkrumah, the former president of Ghana. The attacker, a young Guinean, was seized by an onlooking crowd and lynched. (*See in* CE: Guinea.)

GUYANA. Continuing border disputes pressured the Guyanese government in 1969. In January the Guyanese put down a rebellion led by ranchers in the Rupununi region, part of the vast area claimed by Venezuela. The Venezuelans denied charges that they financed the uprising.

In August Guyanese troops clashed with Surinam forces on the southeast border. Surinam has laid claim to 6,000 square miles of Guyanese territory, while Venezuela has long pressed for possession of 50,000 of Guyana's 83,000 square miles.

Domestic problems lessened for Prime Minister Forbes Burnham's government. There was no return to racial strife, and the economic picture improved. The government at Georgetown, the capital, announced a $10-million developmental loan from Great Britain. In November the governor-general, Sir David Rose, died in an accident in England. He had gone to resign before Guyana became a republic in 1970. (*See in* CE: Guyana.)

COURTESY, GUYANA MINISTRY OF WORKS AND HYDRAULICS

This is a new seawall under construction in 1969 at Kitty, Demerara, Guyana. The country was in the process of building 17,000 feet of seawall along its 230-mile-long coastline.

HAITI. Political turmoil, economic problems, and the illness of the president plagued the government of the poverty-stricken Republic of Haiti in 1969. In February two underground opposition factions, the Haitian Party of Popular Accord and the National Liberation People's party, formed a disciplined guerrilla group, the United Party of Haitian Communists. Terrorist activities, including attacks on villages and bombing in the capital, Port-au-Prince, were aimed at the dictatorship of President François Duvalier. The organization claimed to have the support of a progressive Catholic group, Haiti Progress.

CAMERA PRESS—PIX FROM PUBLIX

Duvalier (second from left) and his wife are surrounded by the Tonton Macoute, Haiti's secret police, at the opening of a Red Cross building in Port-au-Prince.

In April the government passed a law making "Communist activities" a crime against national security to be tried by military court with the possibility of the death sentence. In August nine Roman Catholic priests were deported on charges of conspiring to overthrow the government. Internal dissension meanwhile weakened the traditional anti-Duvalier groups.

President Duvalier, 62, suffered a severe heart attack in May. He appeared publicly, however, during New York Gov. Nelson A. Rockefeller's July visit.

On the economic side the Inter-American Development Bank reported that Haitian per-capita income fell to $25 during the year. A loan of $1.5 million from the International Monetary Fund helped to alleviate Haiti's balance-of-payments problem. (*See in* CE: Haiti.)

HEADS OF GOVERNMENT

Although not all of those listed were official heads of state, they controlled the government as of Dec. 31, 1969.

COUNTRY	LEADER
Afghanistan	Mohammed Zahir Shah
Albania	Communist Party First Secretary Enver Hoxha
Algeria	President Houari Boumédienne
Argentina	President Juan Carlos Onganía
Australia	Prime Minister John G. Gorton
Austria	President Franz Jonas
Barbados	Prime Minister Errol W. Barrow
Belgium	Premier Gaston Eyskens
Bolivia	Gen. Alfredo Ovando Candia
Botswana	President Seretse Khama
Brazil	Gen. Emílio Garrastazú Médici
Bulgaria	Premier Todor Zhivkov
Burma	Gen. Ne Win
Burundi	President Michel Micombero
Cambodia	Prince Norodom Sihanouk
Cameroon	President Ahmadou Ahidjo
Canada	Prime Minister Pierre Elliott Trudeau
Central African Rep.	President Jean-Bedel Bokassa
Ceylon	Prime Minister Dudley Senanayake
Chad	President François Tombalbaye
Chile	President Eduardo Frei Montalva
China	Politburo Chairman Mao Tse-tung
China, Rep. of	President Chiang Kai-shek
Colombia	President Carlos Lleras Restrepo
Congo, Dem. Rep. of the	President Joseph Mobutu
Congo, Rep. of	Maj. Marien Ngouabi
Costa Rica	President José Joaquín Trejos Fernández
Cuba	Premier Fidel Castro
Cyprus	President Archbishop Makarios
Czechoslovakia	Communist Party First Secretary Gustav Husak
Dahomey	Lieut. Col. Maurice Kouandete
Denmark	Premier Hilmar Baunsgaard
Dominican Rep.	President Joaquín Balaguer
Ecuador	President José María Velasco Ibarra
El Salvador	Col. Fidel Sánchez Hernández
Equatorial Guinea	President Francisco Macías Nguma
Ethiopia	Emperor Haile Selassie I
Finland	Prime Minister Mauno Koivisto
France	President Georges Pompidou
Gabon	President Albert B. Bongo

EDUARDO FREI MONTALVA

LISL STEINER FROM KEYSTONE

Gambia .... Prime Minister Dawda Jawara
Germany, East . Communist Party First Secretary Walter Ulbricht
Germany, West . Chancellor Willy Brandt
Ghana .... Prime Minister Kofia A. Busia
Great Britain .. Prime Minister Harold Wilson
Greece .... Premier George Papadopoulos
Guatemala ..... President Julio César Méndez Montenegro
Guinea .... President Sékou Touré
Guyana .... Prime Minister Forbes Burnham
Haiti .... President François Duvalier
Honduras ...... President Osvaldo López Arellano
Hungary ...... Communist Party First Secretary Janos Kadar
Iceland .... Premier Bjarni Benediktsson
India .... Prime Minister Indira Gandhi
Indonesia ...... President Suharto
Iran .... Shah Mohammed Reza Pahlavi
Iraq .... President Ahmed Hassan al-Bakr
Ireland .... Prime Minister John Mary Lynch
Israel .... Prime Minister Golda Meir
Italy .... Premier Mariano Rumor
Ivory Coast .... President Félix Houphouët-Boigny
Jamaica .... Prime Minister Hugh L. Shearer
Japan .... Premier Eisaku Sato
Jordan .... King Hussein I
Kenya .... President Jomo Kenyatta
Korea, North .. Premier Kim Il Sung
Korea, South .. President Chung Hee Park
Kuwait .... Sheikh Sabah al-Salim al-Sabah
Laos .... Premier Souvanna Phouma
Lebanon .... President Charles Helou
Lesotho .... Prime Minister Leabua Jonathan
Liberia .... President William V. S. Tubman
Libya .... Revolutionary Command Council leader Col. Muammar Quaddafi
Luxemburg .... Premier Pierre Werner
Malagasy Rep. .. President Philibert Tsiranana
Malawi .... President H. Kamuzu Banda
Malaysia ...... Prime Minister Tunku Abdul Rahman
Maldives, Rep. of ...... President Ibrahim Nassir
Mali .... Lieut. Moussa Traore
Malta .... Prime Minister George Borg Olivier
Mauritania .... President Mokhtar Ould Daddah
Mauritius ...... Prime Minister Seewoosagur Ramgoolam
Mexico .... President Gustavo Díaz Ordaz
Monaco .... Prince Rainier III
Mongolia ...... Premier Yumzhagiyin Tsedenbal
Morocco ...... King Hassan II
Nauru .... President Hammer de Roburt
Nepal .... King Mahendra
Netherlands .... Premier Piet J. S. de Jong
New Zealand ... Prime Minister Keith J. Holyoake
Nicaragua ..... President Anastasio Somoza Debayle

DPA FROM PICTORIAL PARADE
WILLY BRANDT

KEYSTONE
AGHA MOHAMMED YAHYA KHAN

GOLDA MEIR
DAVID RUBINGER FROM PICTORIAL PARADE

MOHAMED AMIN FROM KEYSTONE
JULIUS K. NYERERE, KENNETH KAUNDA, JOMO KENYATTA

WIDE WORLD

RAFAEL CALDERA RODRIGUEZ

AUTHENTICATED NEWS INTERNATIONAL

NICOLAE CEAUSESCU

Niger	President Hamani Diori
Nigeria	Maj. Gen. Yakubu Gowon
Norway	Premier Per Borten
Pakistan	President Agha Mohammed Yahya Khan
Panama	Brig. Gen. Omar Torrijos Herrera
Paraguay	President Alfredo Stroessner
Peru	Gen. Juan Velasco Alvarado
Philippines	President Ferdinand E. Marcos
Poland	Communist Party First Secretary Wladyslaw Gomulka
Portugal	Premier Marcello José das Neves Alves Caetano
Rhodesia	Prime Minister Ian D. Smith
Romania	Communist Party First Secretary Nicolae Ceausescu
Rwanda	President Gregoire Kayibanda
Saudi Arabia	King Faisal
Senegal	President Léopold S. Senghor
Sierra Leone	Prime Minister Siaka Probyn Stevens
Singapore	Prime Minister Lee Kuan Yew
Somalia	Gen. Muhammad Siyad
South Africa	Prime Minister Balthazar J. Vorster
Southern Yemen	Presidential Council Chairman Salem Ali Rubaya
Spain	Generalissimo Francisco Franco
Sudan	Maj. Gen. Jaafar Mohammed al-Nimeiry
Swaziland	Prime Minister Prince Makhosini Dlamini
Sweden	Prime Minister Olof Palme
Switzerland	President Hans-Peter Tschudi
Syria	Premier Nureddin al-Attassi
Tanzania	President Julius K. Nyerere
Thailand	Premier Thanom Kittikachorn
Togo	President Étienne Eyadema
Trinidad-Tobago	Prime Minister Eric Williams
Tunisia	President Habib Bourguiba
Turkey	Prime Minister Suleyman Demirel
Uganda	President Milton Obote
Union of Soviet Socialist Reps.	Communist Party General Secretary Leonid I. Brezhnev
United Arab Rep.	President Gamal Abdel Nasser
United States	President Richard M. Nixon
Upper Volta	President Sangoulé Lamizana
Uruguay	President Jorge Pacheco Areco
Venezuela	President Rafael Caldera Rodriguez
Vietnam, North	Premier Pham Van Dong
Vietnam, South	President Nguyen Van Thieu
Yemen	President Abdul Rahman al-Iryani
Yugoslavia	President Tito
Zambia	President Kenneth Kaunda

HOBBIES. The successful landing on the moon by the U.S. astronauts in 1969 greatly influenced the development of space toys and hobbies, especially model rocketry. The total retail volume for 1969 was between $5 million and $7 million received from an estimated 3 to 5 million rocket hobbyists in the United States.

Model-rocket building came into being as a hobby partly as a result of accidents caused by homemade rockets. Both the Hobby Industry Association of America and the National Association of Rocketry (NAR) promoted the safe and educational use of rocketry as a hobby and claimed that in some 10 million launchings since 1962 there have been no serious injuries.

To protect rocketeers, California and New Jersey began licensing wholesale and retail dealers. The NAR developed a safety code with three key points: rockets must be ignited electrically and not by lighted fuse; rockets must not be launched ballistically and the angle of ascent must never deviate more than 30 degrees from vertical; and children under 14 must have an experienced adult to supervise activities.

The first world championship in model rocketry was planned for 1970 in Vršac, Yugoslavia, under the auspices of the Aeromodelling Committee of the Fédération Aéronautique Internationale.

Road racing and slot-car racing declined in popularity in 1969 although smaller HO-scale model cars were still popular. Plastic model kits of automobiles, boats, and planes were larger and were of a much better quality in 1969. They were described by one trade magazine as "the dominant category in the hobby field."

One of man's oldest inventions, the potter's wheel, dating back more than 2,000 years, became available in kit form for $67.50. The assembler must cast his own 140-pound concrete kick-wheel in a mold furnished with the kit. (*See in* CE: Hobbies.)

HOME ECONOMICS. The ingredients used in prepared and packaged foods became a prime concern to homemakers in the United States during 1969. In October, U.S. Secretary of Health, Education, and Welfare Robert H. Finch announced a ban on cyclamate sweeteners after research had shown that cyclamates produced cancer and congenital deformities in rats and mice. The artificial sweeteners had been used in a wide variety of dietetic and low-calorie foods, all of which were ordered off grocery shelves by Feb. 1, 1970. (*See* Drugs; Food.)

Another food additive, monosodium glutamate, came under fire in October when it was discovered that the substance had contributed to brain damage in mice. Three manufacturers of baby foods in which monosodium glutamate was used as a flavor enhancer immediately suspended its use.

The outlook in the field of household appliances, however, was much brighter. Making use of the most sophisticated materials and processes of modern technology, prototypes of new appliances introduced during the year foresaw an era of increased convenience with reduced noise and maintenance. Among them were a laser-beam can opener and a self-cleaning ultrasonic blender.

A new concept in appliances was presented during the year in a competition in kitchen design sponsored by the Birds Eye Co. The prizewinning design featured a home freezer, two gas rings, two electric warming plates, a microwave oven, and a sink and dishwasher—all incorporated into a single cylindrical unit. The unit can be rotated for use by a seated housewife.

Another kitchen convenience, a minicomputer, became available in October. The computer, which sold for $10,600, is capable of producing scientifically planned menus and household budgets and of balancing checkbooks. (*See also* Interior Decoration. *See in* CE: Home Economics and Management.)

HONDURAS. A series of soccer games in 1969 became the spark that drew Honduras into armed conflict with the neighboring country of El Salvador. Relations between the two nations had been strained because of a border dispute. Also, about 300,000 citizens of overcrowded El Salvador were living in Honduras, and there were rumors that these expatriate Salvadorans were being mistreated by the Hondurans.

In this tense atmosphere a three-game soccer play-off, part of the World Cup soccer competition, was held in June between Honduran and Salvadoran national teams. The first game in the series was won by Honduras, and the situation between the two nations worsened. The second game, held in San Salvador, El Salvador's capital, was won by El Salvador. Rioting broke out in Honduras, and the two nations severed diplomatic relations. Following the third game, which was played in Mexico City, Mexico, and won by El Salvador, Honduras sent a military plane over Salvadoran territory as a show of force. The government of El Salvador then decided to launch a "preventive" war against Honduras.

The fighting broke out on July 14 when Salvadoran troops crossed over into Honduras. Both nations conducted air raids against each other, but the raids were largely ineffectual. The Honduran air force, consisting of old World War II planes and converted cargo planes, did succeed in inflicting some damage on an oil refinery at Acajutla, El Salvador.

Some of the worst fighting took place inside Honduran territory at Nueva Ocotepeque as Salvadoran troops advanced on and captured the town. Thousands of civilians fled into Guatemala, and during the battle hundreds of civilians were killed. At various points along the El Salvador-Honduras border Salvadoran troops penetrated as far as 45 miles inside Honduras.

The Organization of American States (OAS) arranged a cease-fire on July 18 and presented a peace proposal that included a withdrawal of Salvadoran troops from Honduran territory. Although the government of El Salvador was reluctant to accept the terms of the OAS proposal, Salvadoran troops were withdrawn from Honduras by the end of July. The OAS had threatened to impose severe economic sanctions on El Salvador if the troops were not withdrawn.

The five-day war was damaging to the economy of Honduras. Trade between El Salvador and Honduras was broken off altogether, and the section of the Pan American Highway leading from El Salvador to Honduras was closed to all commercial Salvadoran vehicles. The Central American Common Market, of which Honduras is a member, ceased to function in any effectual way. (*See also* El Salvador. *See in* CE: Honduras.)

Honduran army troops, carrying bazookas and recoilless rifles, prepare to leave on July 17 for Nueva Ocotepeque, Honduras, which was under fire by El Salvador.

UPI COMPIX

HOSPITALS. Throughout the United States, hospitals in 1969 took bold steps to relate more directly to their communities and bring medical care to those who lacked it. Stepping away from the traditional practice of waiting for patients to come to them, more and more hospitals went to their patients—operating health centers in convenient neighborhood locations, using mobile units, bringing home care to shut-ins, and providing health-related social services.

Both hospital utilization and expense increased. Statistics gathered from the 7,137 registered hospitals in the United States showed that they provided more health-care services during the reporting year ending Sept. 30, 1968, than ever before. The hospitals expended a record $19 billion in delivering services to both inpatients and outpatients. Hospital inpatient admissions increased to 29.8

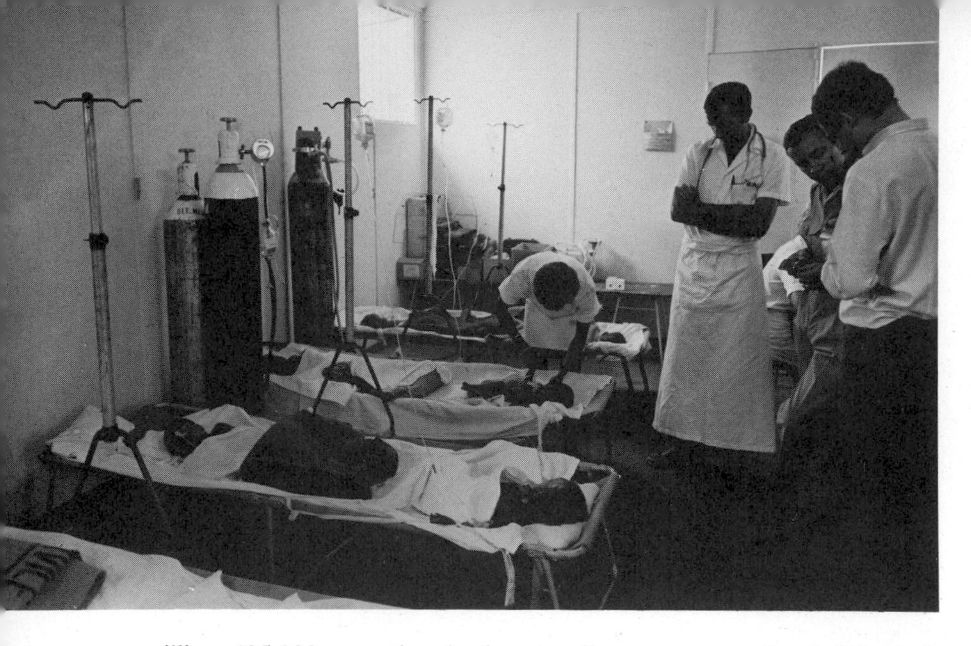

At a French military hospital in Libreville, Gabon, children flown in from Biafra are being treated for malnutrition and other diseases.

GAMMA—PIX FROM PUBLIX

million, 405,000 more than in the preceding year. The figure represented one admission for every seven citizens—and an expenditure equal to $95 for each resident of the United States. Outpatient visits also reached a new high of 156,138,641, up from the 148,299,113 outpatient visits of the preceding year.

Utilization of community hospitals continued to increase through the first half of 1969. While admissions of patients under age 65 remained constant in number, admissions of medicare patients increased by 6.7%. The average length of stay for medicare patients was 13.1 days, down slightly from the average stay of 13.4 days noted for the first half of 1968.

The American Hospital Association (AHA) reported that in the six years 1963–68 the number of U.S. community (nonfederal, short-term general, and special) hospitals increased by 2% to 5,820, while the number of beds in such hospitals grew by 16%. Community-hospital admissions grew by 8% in the period, while days of inpatient care increased 19%, indicating a lengthening of the average hospital stay. The volume of outpatient services increased by a third. Overall, expenses jumped 88%, from $7.5 billion to just over $14 billion. The cost increase reflected the increasing range of services available in community hospitals, the increasing use of those services, a 34% rise in employment (from 1.28 million to 1.72 million), and increases in the salaries of hospital personnel. (*See also* Medicine; Nursing; Social Services. *See in* CE: Hospitals.)

HOTELS AND MOTELS.

In 1969 there was a continuation, and even some acceleration, in the expansion of the lodging industry in the United States and abroad. Probably the most ambitious expansion program announced during the year was that of Sheraton Hotels, which planned an $85-million building effort that would increase its 1969 total of 162 hotels and motels in 14 countries to 746 properties in 38 nations over the following three to four years.

One lodging-industry expert predicted that if all the proposed hotel-motel projects that had been planned recently were completed there would be a nearly 100% growth in facilities in the next five years. The same expert cautioned that, if this rash of new construction were to take place, it could result in economic hardship for hotels and motels in areas with little potential for expansion.

Another situation that concerns the lodging industry is the extreme shortage of qualified execu-

The Landmark Hotel in Las Vegas, Nev., was opened on July 1. It is owned by Howard Hughes and has a superstructure three stories high that resembles a flying saucer.

COURTESY, LANDMARK HOTEL

DPA FROM PICTORIAL PARADE

This building in Hamburg, West Germany, was constructed in record-breaking time. The first occupants moved in five days after the foundation stone was laid on June 13.

"TORONTO (ONT.) STAR"

On October 5, in Toronto, Ont., members of the Ontario Tenants Association assemble prior to a demonstration against "unscrupulous" landlords.

tives, as well as competent help at all levels. The hotel-motel employment figure, nearly 700,000 in 1969, increased by only about 6% over 1968.

Among the most unusual and largest hotels opened in the United States were the 500-room Hilton Palacio Del Rio in San Antonio, Tex., and the 715-room Washington Plaza Hotel in Seattle, Wash. The Palacio Del Rio hotel was built using a special construction method employed at Expo 67 in Montreal, Que.

Also opened in 1969 was the $60-million Las Vegas (Nev.) International Hotel. Billed as the world's largest resort hotel, it has 1,519 bedrooms and suites and 75,000 square feet of convention and meeting facilities.

HOUSING. In 1969 housing was characterized as the "sick man" of the U.S. economy. During the year housing "starts" (beginning construction of nonfarm dwelling units) were projected to total only 1.4 million to 1.5 million. For the second and third quarters of the year, home construction was 14% below the preceding two quarters and 4% below the rate for the same period in 1968.

The decline in housing starts, which exacerbated the already serious housing crisis, was attributed to a combination of factors—high interest rates that lessened the availability of mortgage money, rising property prices, and an increasing shortage of lumber. At the beginning of the year, land prices were already 300% above their 1950 level and plywood was selling for twice as much as at the start of 1968. By the end of 1969, mortgage rates had risen to a record high of 8.12% for new homes and 8.13% for used homes.

The federal government adopted a number of programs to alleviate the housing shortage for the low- and middle-income classes. Setting a ten-year goal of 26 million new housing units, the Administration urged the formation of a working partnership among government agencies, industry, and labor. To implement this program, the federal government offered aid to local governments.

One key to solving the housing crisis that was cited often during the year was the use of mass-produced modules in constructing public and private housing. The prefabricated room units were factory-produced and transported to the building site, where they were stacked together and provided with exterior finishing. Construction time was drastically reduced—a two-story home could be set up in two to three days and a 110-unit apartment building in seven months. The mass-produced dwellings, which were being tested in Detroit, Mich., were slated for construction in 8 to 12 cities under Operation Breakthrough, a Department of Housing and Urban Development project formulated in 1969.

Early in the year a fair-housing law went into effect, placing under the Civil Rights Act of 1968 virtually all multifamily apartment buildings and all homes sold by housing developers. The new law banned discrimination in sales and rentals, advertising practices, and allocations of loans.

In December Congress passed a $4.8-billion compromise housing bill essentially providing for a one-year extension of current programs of the Housing and Urban Development Act of 1968. The bill included new provisions increasing rent subsidies for residents of public housing, raising ceilings on construction costs allowed per room in public housing, and requiring that any slum dwellings razed had to be replaced on a one-to-one basis with new low-income homes. (*See also* Building Construction. *See in* CE: Housing.)

HUNGARY. In a broadcast to the Hungarian people on Jan. 1, 1969, Premier Jeno Fock described 1968 as "a successful year" with regard to national unity. Nevertheless, three groups of dissidents were singled out for attention: those not interested in building socialism, the passive adversaries, and the active troublemakers.

Janos Kadar, the Communist party first secretary, stayed in Moscow, U.S.S.R., for five days in February. The visit was termed unofficial, but it was believed that he discussed with Soviet leaders the coming meeting of the Warsaw Pact powers on European security at Budapest, the capital of Hungary. The meeting took place on March 17 and produced an appeal to all European countries to assist in the convocation of a European conference to discuss security and peaceful cooperation. On May 27 Fock arrived in Vienna, Austria, to confer with Austria's Chancellor Josef Klaus and Foreign Minister Kurt Waldheim on the proposed conference.

Under the terms of a new agreement concluded between Hungary and the Vatican on January 23—the first since Sept. 15, 1964—ten new bishops, archbishops, and apostolic administrators of Hungary's Roman Catholic hierarchy took the oath on the constitution before Pal Losonczi, chairman of the Presidential Council. Two new archbishops, Jozsef Ijjas and Pal Brezanoczy, and five new bishops were invested in leading sees.

On March 21, the 50th anniversary of the first Hungarian Communist revolution was celebrated as a holiday. Bela Kun's widow and other veterans of the 133-day Soviet republic took part at a rally in the central hall of the Parliament Building.

In June Premier Fock opened southwest of Budapest a twin industrial plant of major importance to the country's power industry: the 3.5-million-ton-a-year Danube Oil Refinery and the 615-megawatt Danube Power Station. The refinery would supply about 60% of the national demand for oil products.

In April a consortium of eight Western banks, headed by the Bank of London and South America, Ltd., signed an agreement with the National Bank of Hungary for a $15-million loan to the state-owned Hungarian Aluminum Corp. Hungary would use this money to build its own aluminum-processing plant and thus eliminate its dependence on Poland and the Soviet Union for the finishing of its alumina. (*See in* CE: Hungary.)

ICE HOCKEY. The Montreal Canadiens annexed their fourth Stanley Cup in five seasons in 1969—their 15th in the 53-year history of the National Hockey League (NHL). In their sweep through 14 play-off games, the Canadiens dropped but two contests, both to the Boston Bruins in the tense six-game final in the Eastern Division of the NHL. They had previously eliminated the New York Rangers in a four-game semifinal.

In the finals against the St. Louis Blues, Montreal outclassed the Western Division champions 3–1, 3–1, 4–0, and 2–1. It was the second consecu-

Ted Harris of the Montreal Canadiens fails to stop a puck before it goes into the net in a Stanley Cup finals game with the St. Louis Blues. Montreal won the series 4–0.

"MONTREAL (QUE.) STAR"

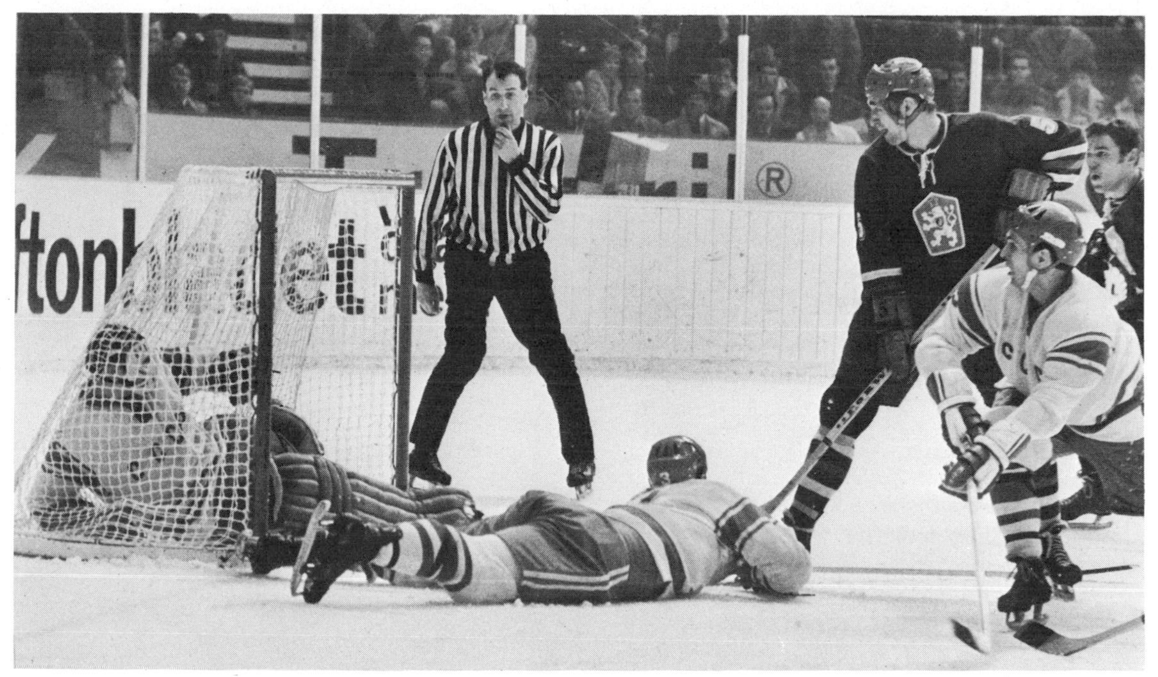

SVENSKT PRESSFOTO FROM KEYSTONE

The action heats up in a game between the Czechoslovak (in dark jerseys) and the Soviet amateur ice hockey teams. The Russians won the world and European titles at Stockholm, Sweden, in March 1969, despite losing both of their contests with the Czechoslovaks.

tive season that the Canadiens had downed the Blues in four successive games. Before their humiliating defeat, the Blues eliminated the Philadelphia Flyers and the Los Angeles Kings in eight straight play-off victories.

Other Pro News

Outstanding player of the Stanley Cup clashes and winner of the Conn Smythe Trophy was Serge Savard, Montreal's rangy second-year defenseman. Dominating individual awards during the season was Phil Esposito, Boston center, who received the Hart Trophy as the league's most valuable player and the Art Ross Trophy as the leading scorer with a record 126 points. Bobby Orr, Esposito's teammate, won the James Norris Memorial Trophy for the second straight year as the league's outstanding defenseman; Alex Delvecchio, 18-year veteran of the Detroit Red Wings, the Lady Byng Trophy for sportsmanship for the third time; and Danny Grant, 23-year-old left wing for the Minnesota North Stars, the Calder Memorial Trophy for Rookie of the Year. The Vezina Trophy for goalkeepers allowing the fewest goals was shared by Glenn Hall and Jacques Plante, both of the St. Louis Blues.

Named to the all-star first team were Toronto's Tim Horton and Boston's Orr, defense; Esposito, center; Bobby Hull, Chicago, and Gordie Howe, Detroit, wings; and Hall, goalie.

Off the ice, the NHL governors voted to expand the league from 12 to 14 members by 1970–71. First in line with $6 million for a franchise and 20 players were Vancouver, B.C.; Buffalo, N.Y.; and Baltimore, Md.

In other professional play, the Hershey Bears won the Calder Cup as champions of the American Hockey League, topping the Quebec Aces, four games to one. The Vancouver Canucks dominated the Western League play-offs, outclassing the Seattle Totems and the Portland Buckaroos in eight play-off games. The Dallas Black Hawks beat the Oklahoma City Blazers for the Central Professional League championship in five games.

Amateur Ice Hockey

The U.S.S.R. won the world and European amateur titles at Stockholm, Sweden, March 15–30, for the seventh straight year, but were closely pressed by runner-up Sweden and third-place Czechoslovakia, who tied the Russians on points. Canada, Finland, and the United States trailed far behind. In July a Canadian proposal to open the senior competition to professionals was rejected by the International Ice Hockey Federation, but it was agreed to permit a maximum of nine professionals on each amateur team for a limited trial period.

The third annual junior world championship at Garmisch, West Germany, Dec. 27, 1968–Jan. 3, 1969, was also captured by Russia, followed by Czechoslovakia, Sweden, Finland, West Germany, and Poland. The National Collegiate Athletic Association championship, played at Colorado Springs, Colo., was won by the University of Denver. (*See in* CE: Ice Hockey.)

ICELAND. By 1969 almost 40% of Iceland's trade was with countries of the European Free Trade Association (EFTA). Iceland tabled a formal application for membership in EFTA on Jan. 24, 1969, and laid down three conditions: the establishment of free trade in fish; a ten-year period in which to lower its tariffs; and permission to continue importing Soviet oil and gasoline.

In September Sweden, Norway, Denmark, and Finland agreed to set up a fund to help Iceland diversify its industries, which were almost entirely dependent on fish. Hopes centered on the export of meat, wool, and hides and on making far greater use of the country's natural resources for hydroelectric and geothermal power.

The further harnessing of the Thjorsa River was planned in conjunction with expansion of the aluminum industry and the building of a seawater plant designed to produce salt and other minerals. The Althing (parliament) passed a law that permitted mink farming, banned since the 1950's. (*See in* CE: Iceland.)

The 1969 women's world figure-skating championship was won by Gabriele Seyfert of East Germany.

AGIP FROM PICTORIAL PARADE

ICE SKATING. The world ice dance and figure-skating championships were held at the Broadmoor World Arena, Colorado Springs, Colo., Feb. 25–March 1, 1969, for the fourth time in 12 years, with 95 skaters from 14 nations competing in the four events. The competition was marred by practice accidents—Karen Magnussen, the Canadian champion, fractured a leg, and Hana Maskova, the Czechoslovak women's champion, suffered a bad back strain.

Tim Wood, the first U.S. victor in ten years, emerged as the new men's figure-skating champion, defeating Ondrej Nepela of Czechoslovakia by a comfortable margin. Patrick Pera of France finished third. Wood's clear superiority both in free and figure-skating gained three sixes for artistic impression.

Gabriele Seyfert of East Germany captured the women's title with a brilliant free-style performance, after she had trailed in the figures behind Beatrix Schuba, the Austrian runner-up. Suzy Almassy of Hungary finished a close third.

Tim Wood captured the men's world figure-skating championship in 1969. He was the first U.S. winner in ten years.

WIDE WORLD

Oleg and Ludmila Protopopov of the Soviet Union lost their pairs skating crowns to their compatriots Alek Ulanov and Irina Rodnina, who sparkled with superbly timed flying camels and a skillful double twist lift. The Protopopovs, former champions, could finish no better than third, fractionally behind Alek Mishin and Tamara Moskvina, in a Soviet grand slam.

The ice-dancing championship went to Great Britain's Bernard Ford and Diane Towler for the fourth consecutive year. Alek Gorshkov and Ludmila Pakhomova of the Soviet Union edged James Sladky and Judy Schwomeyer of the United States for second-place honors.

In the North American championships, held at Oakland, Calif., in February, Wood far outclassed Jay Humphry of Vancouver, B.C., for the men's figure-skating crown; Janet Lynn of Rockford, Ill., took the women's title; and Cynthia and Ronald Kauffman of Seattle, Wash., successfully defended their pairs title. Earlier in the month Miss Lynn had captured the U.S. women's figure-skating title and the Kauffmans the senior pairs championship in Seattle.

The outstanding male skater and overall world champion in speed skating at Deventer, Netherlands, in February, was Dag Fornæss of Norway, though he failed to finish first in any of the four distances. During the season Kees Verkerk of the Netherlands won both the 1,500- and 5,000-meter events, and his compatriot Jan Bols, the 10,000-meter. The 500-meter sprint was won by Keiichi Suzuki of Japan, pointing up his country's clearly growing strength in the sport.

Lasma Kauniste of the Soviet Union captured the women's world overall speed title at Grenoble, France, in February and was the winner of the 1,000-meter event. Kirsti Biermann of Norway took the 500-meter race and two Dutch racers, Stien Kaiser and Ans Schut, the 1,500- and 3,000-meter.

New records were set or equaled for every world championship distance in speed skating in 1969. New standards were clocked by Verkerk for the 1,500-, 5,000-, and 10,000-meter and by Fornæss in the 3,000-meter. Suzuki equaled the best 500-meter time, set by Erhard Keller of West Germany in 1968. Miss Schut lowered the women's 1,500- and 3,000-meter marks, and new figures were also established by Ruth Schleiermacher of East Germany in the 500-meter and Elly van de Brom of the Netherlands in the 1,000-meter. (*See in* CE: Skates and Skating.)

IMMIGRATION AND CITIZENSHIP. In the United States, the year 1969 was one of review and evaluation of immigration laws in effect since July 1, 1968, following a two-year transition period from the former system. The laws, enacted in 1965, were the first major revision of the U.S. statutes since 1924. They wiped out the old system based on the national origin of the U.S. population

"THE TIMES," LONDON, FROM PICTORIAL PARADE

In Southall, England, the Pathway Further Education Centre helps young immigrants acquire skills in English studies and mathematics. These students are using the language laboratory.

in 1920, a system that favored northern and western Europe where the first waves of U.S. immigrants came from. The 1965 act instituted instead a system of "preferences" designed to reunite U.S. citizens and permanent residents with families abroad and to encourage applicants with needed skills. It also placed a limit of 170,000—not counting spouses, parents, and children of citizens—on entries from outside the Western Hemisphere and for the first time imposed a ceiling of 120,000 on entries born in the Western Hemisphere.

In its 1968 annual report the U.S. Department of State's visa office said the purposes of the 1965 act "have been well served by the legislation." It added, "No longer does a natural advantage or disadvantage accrue from birth in a specific area." However, the report further noted that radical shifts in the pattern of immigration and unexpected backlogs in certain "preference" categories had occurred. Many of the former primary countries of origin no longer supplied large numbers of immigrants to the United States because most U.S. residents from these nations no longer had close relatives overseas. Instead, countries with recent entries who still had relatives in the country of origin became an increasing source of new arrivals. The other obvious difference between the old and new systems was the reduction in the number of immigrants, down from preceding years because of the imposition of limitations. Hardest hit were Western Hemisphere entries, a development that was criticized and reviewed in the United States.

This shifting pattern of origin for immigrants to the United States, which had already manifested itself during the transition period, solidified in fiscal 1969. The countries of northern and western Eur-

LOLA ALVAREZ BRAVO

Mexican author Carlos Fuentes wanted to spend a few hours in Puerto Rico. The leftist writer was considered "undesirable" by U.S. immigration officials, who denied him entrance and thus set off an ideological storm.

ope declined in the ranking and gave way to other countries in southern Europe and Asia. The shift was apparent in the ranking of the top ten non-Western countries of origin in fiscal 1969. Italy ranked first with 24,465 visas issued, followed by the Philippines with 23,335, Nationalist China with 21,811, Greece with 19,448, Portugal with 17,567, Great Britain with 10,994, Yugoslavia with 9,469, West Germany with 8,695, India with 6,823, and Korea with 6,469. This compared with fiscal 1968 rankings of Great Britain with 35,200, Italy with 23,267, West Germany with 17,799, the Philippines with 16,390, Nationalist China with 12,424, Greece with 12,202, Portugal with 11,954, Poland with 6,234, Yugoslavia with 5,897, and India with 4,326.

The break of the past two years with the old system can be seen by comparing the figures of those years to the ranking in fiscal 1965, when the order was: Great Britain, West Germany, Italy, Poland, Ireland, France, the Netherlands, Japan, the Soviet Union, and Nationalist China. Five of these top contributors to the U.S. population dropped from the listing of the top ten after the change in 1965 to the new system.

In 1969 the U.S. Congress also began a review of the new laws and a consideration of legislation to correct what were deemed undesirable or troublesome results. In the first step of this Congressional process, a subcommittee of the House of Representatives held hearings on certain problem areas and considered remedial legislation.

INDIA. In 1969 there were dramatic political developments in India. The president died. A deputy prime minister resigned. Major banks were nationalized. A power struggle divided the Indian National Congress party. Anti-Congress alliances were in difficulty in many states and more than one ministry fell. Elections in five states in February did not provide much support for the troubled party. On October 2 the centenary of the birth of Mahatma Gandhi was celebrated.

Domestic Affairs

Despite the radical faction's attack on the deputy prime minister, Morarji Desai, an outward semblance of unity was maintained at the party's annual session at Faridabad in April. The sudden death of the president of the republic, Zakir Husain, on May 3 set off a series of events that shook both Congress and the country.

The election of a new president became the focal point of conflict between the prime minister, Indira Gandhi, and the conservatives in the Congress, generally referred to as "the Syndicate." A confrontation took place in July at Bangalore, where the All-India Congress Committee met. Mrs. Gandhi's radical economic program was unanimously adopted, but the conservatives, holding the levers of the party machine, struck back by getting the Congress parliamentary board to adopt Neelam Sanjiva Reddy, speaker of the Lok Sabha (House of the People), as the official party candidate for the presidency against Mrs. Gandhi's wishes. V. V. Giri, vice-president, who had been sworn in as acting president, announced his decision to contest the election as an independent candidate.

Returning from Bangalore, Mrs. Gandhi divested Morarji Desai, one of the leaders of the Syndicate, of the finance office on the ground that she, Mrs. Gandhi, should assume direct responsibility for implementing the economic program; Desai resigned. In spite of efforts by several party leaders to bring about a reconciliation, the resignation was accepted on July 19 and the government issued on the same day an ordinance nationalizing 14 leading banks. This move assured Mrs. Gandhi of the support of the left wing of her party as well as the leftist opposition groups.

Although the voting was confined to an electoral college consisting of members of parliament and state assemblies, the presidential election generated high popular excitement and there was an obvious polarization of left and right. Voting took place on August 16, with Giri securing 420,077 votes—against Reddy's 405,427—to become president. Later in the month Gopal S. Pathak, governor of Mysore and the unanimously chosen Congress candidate, was elected vice-president.

The defeat of the official Congress candidate led to demands from the organizational wing that the prime minister and her associates be arraigned for defiance of the party mandate, but a resolution of unity was adopted by the Congress working com-

RAGUBIR SINGH FROM NANCY PALMER AGENCY

Indira Gandhi, prime minister of India, is accompanied by V. V. Giri (bareheaded), the new president of India. Giri's election was a triumph for Mrs. Gandhi because she waged a vigorous campaign for him.

mittee on August 25. The truce was short-lived. The prime minister's group by then had the support of Y. B. Chavan, the home minister, and a move was begun by that group to summon the All-India Congress Committee to elect a new president of the party.

Mrs. Gandhi set up her own committee, while the official committee met to censure her action, accusing her of being a potential dictator. On November 12, in what some observers felt to be probably the most historic political event since independence, Mrs. Gandhi was expelled from the party by the organizational members, comprising 11 of the 21 members of the working committee. Congress leaders directed Congress members of parliament to take immediate steps to elect a new leader. The prime minister announced that she did not recognize the official ruling. In spite of bitter clashes in parliament between the two factions, Mrs. Gandhi retained the support of a majority of Congress members of parliament and her position was secure at least for the time being.

Midterm elections took place in February in four states that had been under presidential rule. In West Bengal a united front of non-Congress parties trounced the Congress and formed a ministry dominated by the Communist party. In Bihar the Congress party formed a coalition government that was voted out in June after 115 days. After a short-lived non-Congress government, the state again came under presidential rule in July. In Uttar Pradesh the Congress won 208 seats in a house of 425 and assumed office. In the Punjab, the Akali Dal and Jan Sangh combined to form a coalition cabinet. In the Nagaland elections, the Naga Nationalist Organization was again victorious. In October a Communist-led government was sworn in for Kerala.

There was turmoil in Andhra Pradesh state in the first half of the year because of a demand by people of the Telengana region for separate statehood. A plan was announced by Mrs. Gandhi to remove the economic and administrative grievances of the agitators. In Gujarat state there was widespread religious rioting in September in which the death toll was placed officially at 431.

A group of Tibetans living in India show their displeasure with Maoist policies in China by demonstrating at the gates of the Chinese Embassy in New Delhi, the capital.

"LONDON DAILY EXPRESS" FROM PICTORIAL PARADE

The Economy

The economic situation showed steady improvement. Food prices in October 1969 were 4.2% lower than in October 1968. However, industrial raw materials were scarcer, leading to a rise in the index of wholesale prices to 173.2 on Oct. 4, 1969, from 171.6 on Oct. 5, 1968. The National Institute of Applied Economic Research in a midyear assessment placed the agricultural growth rate in 1969–70 at between 5% and 6% and the industrial growth rate at 7%. In 1968–69, exports were 12.9% higher than in the preceding year. The government's budget for 1969–70 placed income at $4.7 billion, including $133 million through revised taxation, and expenditures at $3.4 billion. Together with the capital budget, the total allocation for development programs was $2.3 billion, including deficit financing of $333 million.

The fourth five-year plan was launched on April 1. Its draft, as adopted by the National Development Council and presented to parliament on April 21, envisaged a public expenditure on development of $19.1 billion and a private investment of $13.3 billion over a five-year period.

In 1969 the state of Madras, at the southern tip of India, experienced one of the most arid periods of its history. Farmers in critical need of water were forced to dig deeper into existing wells.

UPI COMPIX

A major structural change in the economy was effected by bringing the 14 banks under public ownership. Nationalization was effected to remove control by a few, prevent the use of bank credit for speculation, and provide more credit. The take-over was made on July 19 through an ordinance confirmed by an act of parliament. However, its constitutionality was questioned and the issue was still before the Supreme Court in November.

In February 1969 the first nuclear power station in India became operational at Tarapore in Maharashtra state. Work on the satellite tracking station near Poona was drawing toward completion.

Foreign Affairs

In February Mrs. Gandhi gave the portfolio of external affairs to Dinesh Singh, formerly minister of commerce. In July India and Pakistan settled their dispute over the Rann of Kutch, signing maps to show the border as fixed by the 1968 international tribunal. The government's decision to seek admission to the conference of Islamic powers at Rabat, Morocco, in August, led to adverse reaction in the country; the India delegation was heard and later excluded. The Soviet Union's decision to offer military equipment to Pakistan caused dismay, and India offered a cool reception to the Soviet Union's proposals for Asian collective security.

Among important visitors to India in 1969 was U.S. President Richard M. Nixon, with whom Mrs. Gandhi raised the question of U.S. arms supplies to Pakistan. Other visitors during 1969 were Soviet Premier Aleksei N. Kosygin, the shah of Iran, the presidents of Romania and Hungary, and the prime ministers of Bulgaria and New Zealand. Mrs. Gandhi attended the Commonwealth Prime Ministers' Conference in London, England, in January and also visited Burma, Afghanistan, Japan, and Indonesia. (*See also* Asia; Pakistan. *See in* CE: India.)

INDIANS, AMERICAN. On Nov. 9, 1969, a group of 14 American Indians landed on Alcatraz Island in San Francisco Bay on the coast of California. They offered to buy the island from the federal government for the sum of "$24 in glass beads and red cloth, a precedent set by the white man's purchase of a similar island (Manhattan) 300 years ago." The group left peacefully after scouting the island and its facilities for 19 hours. The Alcatraz incident more than any other in 1969 symbolized the growing militancy among American Indians.

A larger band of Indians returned on November 28 and took over the abandoned prison. The Indians held the island for the remainder of the year. They intended to build an Indian cultural and educational center on the island. The Indians' claim to Alcatraz was based on an old Sioux treaty giving them the right to unused federal lands.

The new militant tone was also noticeable at the

UPI COMPIX

A group of Indians took over a building on Alcatraz island, a former federal prison site, to stake their claim on the land. Indian groups hoped to establish an American Indian cultural center there.

annual convention of the National Congress of American Indians held at Albuquerque, N.M., in October. Vice-President Spiro T. Agnew, Senator Edward M. Kennedy (D, Mass.), and Secretary of the Interior Walter J. Hickel spoke at the convention. Agnew and Kennedy, who called for a policy of self-determination for the Indians, were politely received. Some Indians were suspicious of the speeches, however.

The Indians were not so polite to Hickel. Earlier he had indicated that Indians were too dependent on the reservation system, and the Indians feared the Administration would revert to the disastrous "termination" policy of the 1950's. Hickel assured the Indians that their lands would remain under federal trusteeship.

In November a Senate subcommittee completed its report on Indian education and found that the federal government had failed to provide adequate educational opportunities for Indian children. The report was highly critical of the Bureau of Indian Affairs and offered 60 recommendations for improving educational programs for Indians. More participation by Indians in running the programs was urged. The report also stated that 90% of Indian housing was atrocious and beyond repair; that health conditions were the worst in the nation; and that the Indian unemployment rate was 40%.

The discovery of oil in the Arctic wastelands prompted the U.S. Congress in 1969 to try to settle the land claims of Alaska's Indians, Eskimos, and Aleuts. The claims had been outstanding for 102 years. The Alaskan Federation of Natives asked for $500 million, 40 million acres of land, and a perpetual 2% royalty on all oil produced. Hickel proposed that the natives be given the $500 million and the suggested acreage. A bill introduced in Congress called for a settlement of $100 million, 47 million acres, a percentage of federal and state mineral revenues for ten years up to $1 billion, and a statewide management corporation to administer these assets for the next ten years. During the year a tribe of Alaskan Indians filed a $1-billion suit against eight oil companies for removing gas and oil from the Cook Inlet area without first consulting the natives.

Louis R. Bruce, an Indian from Richfield Springs, N.Y., was appointed commissioner of Indian affairs. He replaced Robert L. Bennett. (*See also* Arctic. *See in* CE: Indians, American.)

UPI COMPIX

Eugene Francis (center), a leader of the Passamaquoddy Indian nation, was among those ousted from a highway in Maine where a protest roadblock was set up to raise funds needed for milk and medicine.

INDONESIA. With the formal acquisition of the territory of West Irian in 1969, the Republic of Indonesia for the first time stretched "from We Sabang (in Sumatra) to Merauke (in West Irian)," thus fulfilling the long-standing goal of the Indonesian nationalist movement. With West Irian, all the territories that were once part of the Netherlands East Indies empire were now Indonesian.

The formal acquisition climaxed a 20-year campaign by the Indonesian government for the territory—160,618 square miles of jungle and mountains, inhabited by fewer than one million people living in scattered tribal units. Under the terms of a 1949 agreement, providing for the trans-

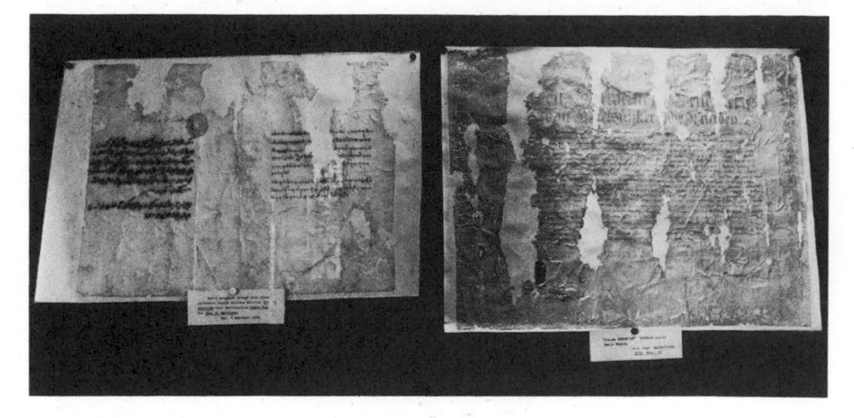

Humidity and insect attack were destroying priceless documents in Djakarta's National Archives Institute. Some of the papers dated from the early 1600's, when the islands of modern Indonesia first came under Dutch authority as the Netherlands Indies.
UPI COMPIX

fer of sovereignty from the Netherlands to Indonesia, both countries agreed to the exclusion of West Irian pending negotiations.

After years of unsuccessful negotiations within and without the United Nations (UN), Indonesia attacked the disputed territory in 1962. The Dutch then agreed to a UN-sponsored accord. It stipulated that by 1969 the Papuans of West Irian would be permitted an "act of free choice" to decide their status. In 1963 Indonesia took over the administration of the disputed territory pending a UN-sponsored plebiscite to decide the issue.

Indonesian administration of the territory was pockmarked by armed disturbances. The most serious occurred in April and May 1969 and were promoted by the Free Papua Movement, which sought independence for the territory. The UN representative in West Irian held that the "act of free choice" should be conducted on a "one man, one vote" basis. Indonesia rejected this on the grounds that the politically unsophisticated Papuans did not comprehend the meaning of regular balloting. Instead, Indonesia used the process of *musjawarah,* a traditional method of consultation, to select 1,025 delegates to vote on behalf of the people of the territory. The delegates voted unanimously that West Irian should remain with Indonesia.

The unanimity of the vote confirmed the suspicions of many of Indonesia's critics, who felt that the whole performance was a farce. The options, however, were limited. An independent West Irian was widely considered a politically unrealistic solution, and the UN lacked the financial resources and the interest to assume the role of guardian through some trusteeship format.

Rebuilding the Economy

Despite the historic significance of the acquisition of West Irian, Indonesia in 1969 was preoccupied more with rebuilding the country's shattered economy and restoring a constitutional democracy in the aftermath of the disastrous era of President Sukarno. During the year the economy continued to improve, but the pace of recovery slackened. The government concentrated on its economic stabilization and rehabilitation program, in particular attaining success in controlling inflation. A bumper crop of rice, the basic Indonesian foodstuff, was harvested. The country's balance of payments improved, primarily as a result of increased oil exports.

Against this background, President Suharto's government unfolded its new five-year development plan in March. The plan called for an investment of $4 billion by the government and upwards of $600 million by private foreign enterprise. A primary objective of the plan was to make Indonesia self-sufficient in food. The plan's success depended in part on foreign aid, especially from Japan and the United States. It also hinged on the

Djakarta had been quiet since the removal of Sukarno from the presidency in 1967. Nevertheless, armed troops could still be seen patrolling the capital's streets.
UPI COMPIX

ability of the Suharto government to combat corruption and smuggling and to trim the oversize and inefficient bureaucracy. In July the Indonesians were heartened when U.S. President Richard M. Nixon, in the course of his Asian journey, visited Indonesia and had words of praise for the plan.

Creating a New Political System

In contrast to the overall economic improvement, less progress was achieved in the creation of a new political system. President Suharto had pledged to restore representative government and civil liberties when he formally succeeded President Sukarno in 1968. Suharto moved in this direction, allowing the country for the first time in years to have a popular, critical press. Suharto also supported the plan of the Provisional People's Consultative Congress (MPRS), the country's highest constitutional body, to schedule general elections by 1971. The MPRS, however, struggled endlessly to reach agreement on three election bills setting up the ground rules of the election, the organization of the political system, and the role of political parties and mass organizations.

It was felt that the delay in adopting the bills might lead to a postponement of the election and thus give rise to political tension. In 1969 some student groups passed resolutions demanding that elections be held on schedule, an indication of the pressures ahead for the government.

Another political issue was the question of the fate of some 70,000 or more Communists held in detention as a result of the abortive 1965 coup in which Sukarno and the Indonesian Communist party were implicated. In the aftermath of the coup, thousands of Communists were killed and others rounded up. In 1969 the government began resettling some detained Communists on the underdeveloped island of Buru. But there were also reports of a new massacre of Communists in central Java where the underground Communist party had apparently sought to regroup itself. The government vigorously denied these reports. (*See in* CE: Indonesia, Republic of.)

INSECTS AND PESTICIDES.

The question of whether pesticide residues pose a threat to man's health remained a hotly debated issue in 1969. Following a conclave of world pesticide experts in March, the government of Sweden imposed a two-year ban on the use of the controversial insecticide DDT. It also banned use of the insecticides aldrin and dieldrin.

On April 21 a commission was appointed by Robert H. Finch, secretary of the U.S. Department of Health, Education, and Welfare, to investigate the possibility of such a threat. Emil Mrak, a food chemist, was named to head the commission.

Finch pointed out that a residue of DDT, "which has been used in great quantities since the early 1940's, persists in the environment. . . . Food and Drug Administration studies show that Americans have an average of 12 parts per million of DDT in the fatty tissues of their bodies." He added, however, that there was no proof that this had had an adverse effect on man.

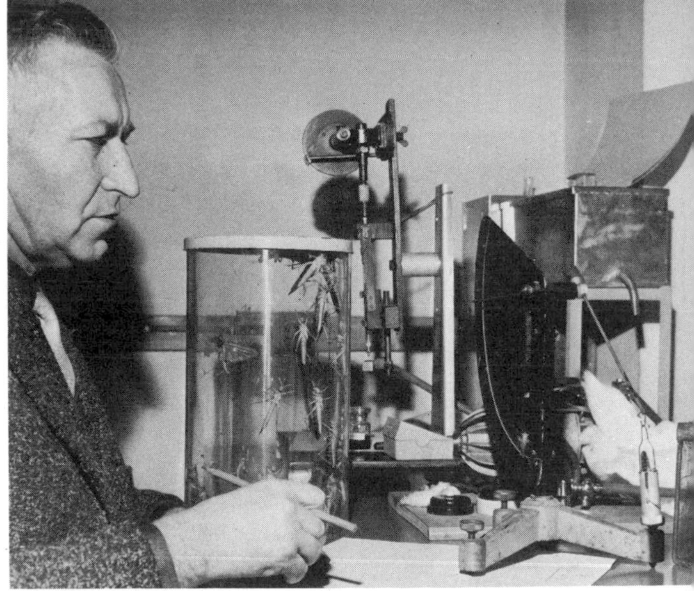

KEYSTONE

An international effort has been under way to check the locust, a prime destroyer of crops. A scientist weighs one of the insects before injecting it with an insecticide.

In California the mosquito problem was becoming worse in 1969, noted E. Gorton Linsley, a scientist at the University of California at Berkeley. He pointed out that this was due to the steady increase in California's population, expanded mosquito breeding areas, and a greater genetic resistance in succeeding generations of mosquitoes to insecticides—many of which contained DDT.

Man appeared to be winning—at least temporarily—his age-old war against the locust, an insect that has devoured billions of tons of man's food crops. A worldwide network of locust-observing stations, under United Nations (UN) sponsorship, had failed to see a single swarm of the insects. Officials at the UN said that what appeared to be a "total recession" of the insect could be traced to a cold winter and late monsoon in 1961, "internal biological control," and the UN's own eradication program, which includes the use of insecticides. (*See also* Conservation. *See in* CE: Insecticides; Insects.)

INSURANCE.

The life and health insurance businesses continued to set new records for the number of persons covered and amount of benefits paid in 1969. More than 132 million persons in the United States owned policies amounting to a record $1.29 trillion of life insurance protection. This was an increase of $107 billion of coverage over 1968. The average amount of life insurance owned by a family in the United States increased by $600 to $19,500. Life insurance benefit payments increased to $15.5 billion, about 8% more than in 1968; of this amount, benefits to living policyholders were $8.75 billion. New life insurance bought during 1969 amounted to $155 billion, an increase of $5.5 billion over the figure for the preceding year, and assets of the nearly 1,800 life insurance companies in the nation rose $11 billion to a record $200 billion.

The number of people protected by some form of private health insurance in the United States was 175 million at the end of 1968. Benefits, including payments under disability policies, totaled nearly $12.2 billion during fiscal 1968. Insurance companies paid $6.7 billion, while the remaining $5.5 billion came from Blue Shield, Blue Cross, and other plans.

All forms of health insurance showed increases in the number of persons covered. The new coverage totals were 175 million for hospital expenses, 160 million for surgical expenses, 135 million for regular medical expenses, 75 million for major medical expenses, and 69 million for disability income. Benefit payments in these categories were $7.6 billion (hospital expense), $4 billion (surgical and medical expense), and $1.6 billion (disability income).

Greater affluence and a higher level of education among young persons 20 to 34 years of age—the prime group buying insurance protection—contributed to the record holdings in life and health insurance. Other factors were a growing economy, more marriages with subsequent increase in the number of children, and rising medical costs.

A pledge in 1967 by the life insurance business to invest $1 billion to improve the living conditions of people in blighted urban areas was virtually completed in 1969 and was followed in April by a decision to invest another billion dollars. Since the original pledge in September 1967, more than $900 million of the first $1 billion was committed or disbursed to help families with low and moderate incomes. The money financed projects in 227 U.S. cities, including more than $680 million for the construction or rehabilitation of 63,000 housing units and approximately $220 million to build commercial, industrial, and medical facilities that helped create 30,000 new jobs.

In the Housing and Urban Development Act of 1968, the U.S. Congress set up an advisory board to assist state governments in establishing a fair access to insurance requirements (FAIR) program. The FAIR program was designed to provide moderate-cost insurance coverage in riot-torn areas. However, FAIR was not adopted by 18 states and was nonoperative in many of the 32 states that did adopt it. Despite provisions in the act that the federal government would absorb a large percentage of riot losses, the insurance industry was generally opposed to the program. (*See in* CE: Insurance.)

INTELLIGENCE OPERATIONS. In 1969 the usual sporadic crop of arrests for espionage and counterespionage were made. The year was notable for the agreement between Great Britain and the Soviet Union to exchange Soviet spies Helen and Peter Kroger for the British lecturer Gerald Brooke. In one of the year's most curious spy cases Hannsheinz Porst, West German millionaire and East German spy, received a mild sentence for his espionage activities.

Morris Cohen, alias Peter Kroger, and Lola Petka, alias Helen Kroger, both members of the U.S. Communist party since the mid-1930's, began work with the Soviet spy network operating in the United States under Rudolf Abel. They vanished from New York City in 1950 within hours of the arrest of David Greenglass, who had been detained on charges of stealing atomic secrets and who had denounced his sister Ethel and her husband, Julius Rosenberg. The Krogers reappeared under that name in London, England, in December 1955 with forged New Zealand passports, and started another spy ring with Konon Trofimovich Molody, alias Gordon Lonsdale. The main task of this ring was to obtain secret information about ships of the British Royal Navy and particularly about the Admiralty Underwater Detection Establishment at Portland, Dorset. The three spies, with their two

Convicted spies Helen and Peter Kroger were released from a British prison and flown to Poland. They were exchanged for Gerald Brooke, whom the Soviets were holding as a British spy.

UPI (UK) LTD.

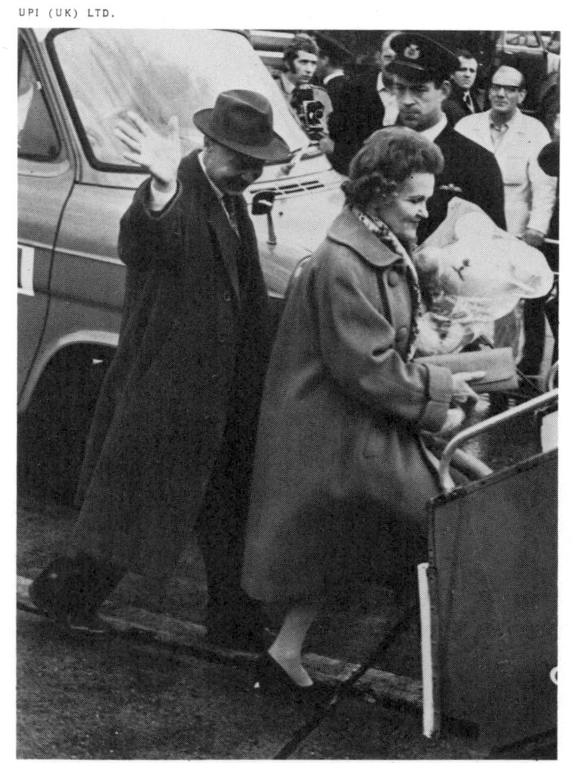

UPI COMPIX

A Soviet factory ship with a fishing trawler alongside was kept under surveillance by a U.S. Coast Guard plane off the Virginia coast in February. Soviet trawlers were found within the 12-mile territorial limit set by the United States and warned to sail clear of the line.

English aides Harry Houghton and Elizabeth Gee, were arrested on Jan. 7, 1961. On March 22, Lonsdale was sentenced to 25 years' imprisonment and the Krogers to 20 years each.

The Soviet State Committee on Security (KGB or Komitet Gosudarstvennoi Bezopasnosti) had arrested Gerald Brooke in Moscow, U.S.S.R., on April 25, 1965. Brooke, a London lecturer, had acted as a courier for an anti-Soviet émigré group, the People's Labor Alliance (Narodno-Trudovoi Soyuz), carrying coded instructions for receiving radio signals concealed in a postcard album and a dressing case. He was sentenced on July 23, 1965, to a year in jail and four years' detention in a labor colony because of anti-Soviet activities.

Almost immediately after the trial, feelers were put out from Moscow about the possibility of swapping Brooke for the Krogers. The British government showed no interest until more sinister hints were dropped that Brooke could be tried again on new charges and be sentenced to another 10 or 15 years. This time the British government opened discussions with the Soviet Union, and it was agreed to release the Krogers for Brooke. On July 24, 1969, Brooke returned to London. On October 24 the Krogers left London by air for Warsaw, Poland, under the pretense of being Polish citizens supposedly going to a home in Lublin.

West German, U.S. Events

Hannsheinz Porst, 46, a millionaire from Nuremberg, West Germany, whose photo-supply shops were on almost every main street in West Germany, agreed in 1953 to work for the East German security service. Two years later he secretly joined the East German Socialist Unity (Communist) party and, more openly, the West German Free Democratic party (FDP). Porst became friendly with Erich Mende, then leader of the FDP and vice-chancellor of the West German coalition government. Arrested in October 1967, he was released on bail. At his trial, beginning in May 1969 before the West German federal court at Karlsruhe, the prosecution uncovered Porst's relations with the East German Ministry of State Security, to whom he had passed confidential political information. On July 8 Porst was fined and sentenced to two years and nine months in prison.

On May 6, 1969, U.S. Secretary of the Navy John H. Chafee announced that there would be "no disciplinary action" taken against the crew of the reconnaissance ship USS *Pueblo*—including Comdr. Lloyd M. Bucher, who had been recommended for a general court-martial by a Navy court of inquiry. The *Pueblo* was captured in the Sea of Japan by North Koreans on Jan. 23, 1968. In a similar development, the U.S. Army on September 29 dropped proceedings against six Special Forces soldiers ("Green Berets") who had been charged with the alleged murder of a Vietnamese double agent in June. (*See* Armed Forces, U.S.; Defense; United States.)

INTERIOR DECORATION. In 1969, though traditional styles still commanded the greatest share of the home-furnishings market, contemporary furniture designs made the strongest impact on interior decoration. Italian designers, who had exerted a prominent influence for the last few years, came to dominate the scene. In the United States, decorators and designers indicated a preference for combinations of traditional and contemporary treatments for interiors. On the international level, a great deal of attention was given to the design and development of modular furniture units.

Among the Italian designers whose furnishings, lamps, and fabrics were widely heralded during the year were Joe Colombo, Gae Aulenti, Gina

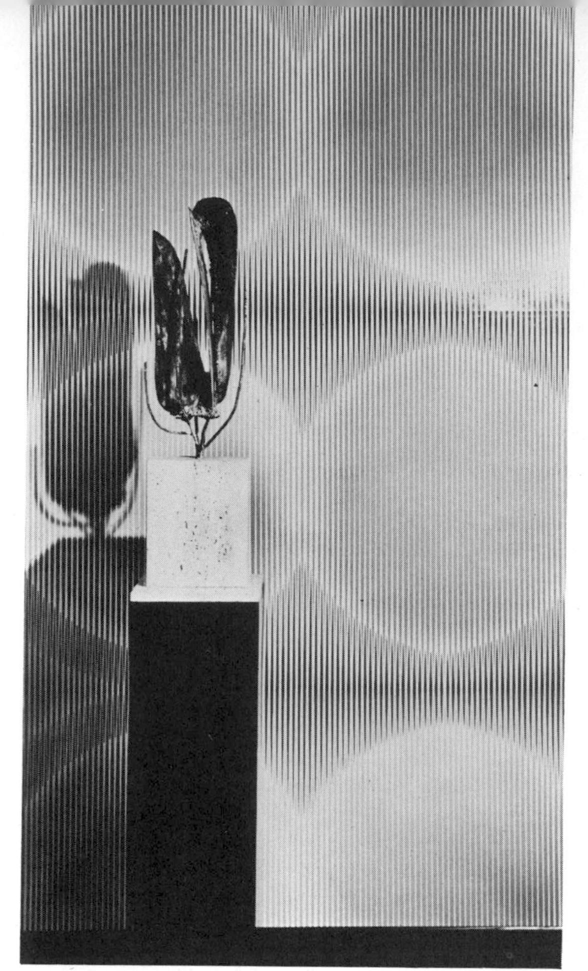

COURTESY, AMERICAN INSTITUTE OF INTERIOR DESIGN

The American Institute of Interior Designers staged its 24th Annual International Design Awards program in 1969. One of the award winners was this wallpaper with a linear design that gives the illusion of movement.

Sarfatti, Elio Martinelli, Marco Zanuso, Cesare Leonardi, Franca Stage, and Giuseppe Raimondi. Unlike the Scandinavians, whose designs were popular throughout the 1950's and early 1960's, the Italian designers did not rely heavily on wood for form. Instead they employed plastics, malleable metals, foam rubber, and structural fiber glass for shape.

Giuseppe Raimondi made wide use of polyurethane foam to produce bouncy, comfortable chairs and ottomans. One of Raimondi's most popular designs was a lounge chair carved from a single block of expanded polyurethane and covered with vinyl. Although amazingly light, the chair resists such harsh treatment as bouncing and shoving. Another Raimondi design is a flower-shaped dining table executed in wood padded with polyurethane and covered with vinyl. The accompanying chairs have rounded backs that conform to the petallike rim of the table.

Another Italian designer, Cini Boeri, developed a "nocturnal" room with walls of shiny navy patent leather, painted fold-up movable storage cases in a brighter blue, and accent pieces of brown and beige. A projector flashes a continual stream of cosmic images on the walls and ceiling.

The Italian furniture company Gavina introduced a wall of slipcovered plastic foam that separates like a jigsaw puzzle to form four chairs and an ottoman. Designed by Roberto Matta Echaurren, the furniture was carved from a single block of foam which can be reassembled for shipment.

One of the year's major innovations was the development of a modular concept in which several pieces of furniture were functionally or physically combined. American and European designers alike employed the idea to create living units, bedroom ensembles, and office furniture.

New York designer Kenneth Isaacs was responsible for possibly the most ambitious module. His jungle-gymlike structure incorporates a bed, living area, closet, bookshelves, dining table, and fireplace into an eight-foot cube capable of fitting into a small living room. Created in response to a demand for simpler furnishings in the home, the structure can be dismantled and moved easily. A similar concept was developed in Isaacs' "Super-Bed." The width of a king-size bed, the unit is composed of a chest of five large drawers, a desk, bookshelves, and a ladder for reaching the upper level.

A similar bed for children was designed by Giorgio Bersano. The bed sits on top of two storage units that open in a variety of ways to reveal hanging space and bins in which to store clothes or toys. A large play table at the back of the structure and a pull-down desk supported by a storage cylinder complete the structure, which sold for $2,000.

For even smaller children, a nursery complex that comes equipped with a small bed mounted on a chest of drawers was introduced. An extensor table is available for use in changing the baby or converting the unit into a full-size bed. A crib railing can also be removed and converted into a playpen.

The modular unit was adapted for office use by Italian designers Bob Noorda and Franco Mirenzi. In their Modulo 3 group, the designers presented a table that could be used as a desk top and typewriter stand with cabinets that fit under the desk.

Not all of the furnishings and designs introduced in 1969 emphasized space-saving practicality and simplicity. New York decorator Elaine Eisen presented rooms that projected a new romanticism by incorporating brilliant colors, huge patterns, and traditional shapes into furnishings with a few contemporary accents. Fabrics that covered walls, windows, and upholstery came in color combinations of red with yellow or plum with peach and featured designs that varied from wildlife to patchwork quilt patterns to plaids.

A New York designer, Shelley Mowell, reversed the idea and developed rooms that were primarily modern but featured one baroque or rococo piece of furniture. In one room, Mowell showed a gilded Siamese bed topped with a stark bull's-eye-patterned spread. The walls were papered in a

There's no need to worry about crayon marks on this plastic furniture made in West Germany. Children's furniture of this type is comfortable, washable, and nearly indestructible.

BRUDER BELTZIG DESIGN

geometric print, and other furnishings were a modern mix of Italian, Scandinavian, and American designs.

Late in the year a New York City department store opened a shop dealing exclusively in Plexiglas furniture and accent pieces. The pieces were intended to serve as accents in traditional or contemporary rooms rather than to comprise part of a setting furnished entirely in Plexiglas. The furnishings ranged from austere to romantic.

The leather-covered "Sacco" chair from Italy conforms to the user's body. A person can sit upright, lounge casually, or even lie down on the sacklike chair.

COURTESY, GIMBEL BROTHERS, INC.

In contrast to boldly contemporary Italian designs, furniture from other countries tended to be more mannered and stylized. Scandinavian modern designs, which had fallen from favor after poor and indifferent copies invaded the market, made a moderate comeback. The new designs were often executed in pale woods, particularly scrubbed pine and ash. Unlike the styles of earlier years, the new Scandinavian furniture was meant to be juxtaposed with other types of contemporary furniture as well as with antiques.

The Oriental influence was also on the rise during 1969, particularly on the West coast. One manufacturer introduced a line that employed cherry veneers and pecan solid woods and, though highly contemporary in design, was reminiscent of Chinese antiques. One model that was especially popular was the campaign chest, or Officer's Chest, that had originally been imported from the Orient by the British in the 18th century. The current versions of the chest followed the traditional rectangular shape but came in various heights and widths for adaptation as dressers, coffee tables, and storage units. (*See in* CE: Interior Decoration.)

INTERNATIONAL RELATIONS. Despite the persistence of such major world problems as the arms race, the Vietnam conflict, the Middle East crisis, and the Sino-Soviet dispute, tensions in international relations abated somewhat in 1969. At year's end the international mood was one of optimism. There were hopeful signs that an "era of confrontation" was being replaced with one of "negotiation."

Arms Limitation

The world's two major powers, the United States

ISRAEL SUN LTD.—PIX FROM PUBLIX

Al Aksa Mosque in Israeli-held Jerusalem was gutted by fire in 1969. The mosque was revered by Muslims, and some Arab leaders called for war against Israel. An Australian Christian was arrested by Israeli authorities for setting the fire.

and the Soviet Union, continued to arm in 1969. The United States launched an ABM (antiballistic missile) program as an answer to the Soviet multiple-target missile threat. The danger and cost of the arms race, however, led to a growing demand in the United States for a reduction of military expenditures. It was apparent also that the Soviet Union confronted similar problems of a heavy military budget and a military-industrial complex.

With these factors underlining the urgent need for ending the arms race, the United States and the Soviet Union finally began preliminary strategic-arms-limitation talks (SALT) in November and December. These discussions concluded with agreement for more substantive talks in April 1970.

Vietnam

Most of the world outside the U.S. sphere of influence continued to criticize the United States for its role in the Vietnam conflict. The U.S. public itself seemed disillusioned with the conflict and anxious for its dissolution. In response U.S. President Richard M. Nixon pursued a policy of "Vietnamization," withdrawing some U.S. troops and attempting to shift the burden of the fighting to South Vietnamese forces. Hope for a negotiated peace dimmed as the peace talks in Paris, France, remained unproductive and stalemated at year's end.

The death in September of North Vietnam's President Ho Chi Minh led to the possibility of a split between pro-Soviet and pro-Chinese factions among the leadership in North Vietnam. Aid continued to flow to North Vietnam from both the People's Republic of China and the Soviet Union, a reflection of their rivalry for leadership of the Communist world. (*See* Vietnam.)

Latin America

In 1969 Latin America was the scene of extensive nationalist and leftist agitation. The general pattern was military dictatorship, in some cases to check Communism but in others to meet demands for welfare measures for the poverty-stricken masses.

Nationalist rejection of U.S. influence was widespread. It was evident that the United States could not exercise hegemony in the Western Hemisphere as it had in the past. (*See* Latin America.)

Asia

The People's Republic of China exploded more nuclear weapons in 1969; informed opinion held that such weapons could reach any city in Asia. China's uncompromising militancy caused uneasiness in many quarters, particularly in the Soviet Union. Armed clashes occurred during the year on the Sino-Soviet border. The initiation of meetings between Soviet and Chinese leaders, however, suggested that the two Communist powers were aware of the danger of allowing their differences

The dispute between Spain and Great Britain over Gibraltar was reaching a climax. Spain closed the land border early in 1969 and later canceled the sea ferry to the rock. These citizens of Gibraltar show their preference for continued British rule.

UPI (UK) LTD.

to mushroom into war. (*See* China, People's Republic of; Communist Movement; Union of Soviet Socialist Republics.)

Some observers felt there were indications that the United States was softening its attitude toward China. The United States relaxed its long-standing trade and travel bans concerning China.

Japan's vast economic strength, which ranked behind only the United States and the Soviet Union, put it in a position to assume a greater role in Asian and world affairs. The United States, desirous of maintaining Japan's friendly stance, agreed to meet the Japanese demand for the return of Okinawa, free of U.S. nuclear weapons, in 1972. (*See* Asia; Japan.)

The Middle East and Africa

The Arab-Israeli conflict continued with almost daily skirmishes that constantly threatened to erupt into another full-scale war. Israel purchased U.S. planes, and Soviet arms flowed into the Arab states. Arab guerrillas placed great pressure upon Arab governments to take action against Israel. The collapse of the Arab summit conference in December, however, illustrated the lack of Arab solidarity on the issue. The "big four" powers (Great Britain, France, the Soviet Union, and the United States) discussed a settlement for the Middle East, but both Arabs and Israelis announced that they would not accept dictation from the great powers. (*See* Middle East.)

Attempts to end the civil war in Nigeria between the federal government and the breakaway state of Biafra failed to come to fruition in 1969. Arms flowed to both sides, perpetuating the struggle. (*See* Africa.)

Europe

The Soviet Union's hard-line approach to East European Communist nations in 1969 generally reflected Soviet fear of the development of more liberalization movements such as that which had occurred in Czechoslovakia in 1968. Soviet Communist Party General Secretary Leonid I. Brezhnev theoretically justified the 1968 Soviet-led invasion of Czechoslovakia with the enunciation of a doctrine of "limited sovereignty" for Communist states. The doctrine was viewed as a possible threat to such mavericks in the Soviet orbit as Albania and Yugoslavia. It also created uneasiness among the neutral states, and the United States issued a warning against intervention in countries like Austria.

In the latter half of 1969, however, there was a growing wave of optimism in Europe. The long-quiescent situation seemed at last to be on the verge of change. The fall of France's President Charles de Gaulle created a more favorable climate for the pursuit of West European political and economic unity. The accession to power of Willy Brandt as chancellor of West Germany also seemed to signal the beginning of a "political thaw" in the European post-World War II situation. Brandt expressed a willingness to engage in dialogue over major issues with East Germany, other Communist nations of East Europe, and the Soviet Union. The favorable response of the North Atlantic Treaty Organization to the Warsaw Pact invitation to hold talks to reduce general tension in Europe was further indication of the new spirit of negotiation. (*See* Europe. *See in* CE: International Relations.)

CENTRAL PRESS FROM PICTORIAL PARADE

Here is bad news for payroll bandits. An inventor demonstrates a 100-square-yard net of fine nylon ejected from a special pistol. The device is effective up to 25 feet.

INVENTIONS AND PATENTS. Some 67,000 patents would be issued by the end of fiscal 1970, by U.S. Patent Office estimates. In order to handle more efficiently the 233,000 patent applications that were pending, a reorganization of the Patent Office was begun in November 1969.

The Patent Office reversed its attitude on the patentability of computer instructions, or "software," during the year. Backpedaling from its formerly negative view toward computer-software patent applications, the agency decided to consider them on the basis of merit and innovation.

A December patent was issued for a television channel-splitting system, called DuoVision, that permitted simultaneous broadcasts of two programs on the same channel—one a conventional

TV show and the other a pay-TV program. If the pay-TV program was desired as a substitute for regular programming, a viewer could switch on a special adapter hooked to his TV set. Another invention allowed tape replay of TV programs through home sets. Called Electronic Video Recording, or EVR, the Columbia Broadcasting System replay scheme employed cartridge film that recorded the desired TV program.

To simulate expensive woods used in cabinetry, General Electric Co. developed a high-impact polystyrene and foamed polyurethane plastic called Acoustaform. It could also be formed to resemble marble, slate, or other furniture materials.

A number of patents for electronic devices were issued in 1969. They included patents for a sonic-boom simulator for high-speed aircraft research, an oculometer that enabled guns aboard military aircraft to be aimed by movements of the pilot's eyes, and a wristwatch that was powered by solar energy. An infant's pacifier containing a magnet received a 1969 patent. It could remove small metal objects that found their way into a baby's mouth. (*See in* CE: Inventions; Patent.)

Iranian students seized their Embassy in Rome, Italy, to protest the jailing of 14 intellectuals in Iran on charges of being Communists. The poster condemns Shah Mohammed Reza Pahlavi.

UPI COMPIX

IRAN. Economic strength, social and educational reforms, and stable relations with the neighboring Soviet Union enabled Iran to liberalize its policies toward former opponents of the regime in 1969. Some of these, including Communists, were released from prison to take up posts in the government and in private institutions. The regime also began to allow "responsible criticism" in the press.

The economic growth rate, under Iran's fourth five-year plan, exceeded 10%. Projects being carried out under the plan included the building of Iran's first steel mill at Ahwaz and development programs in each province.

Iran's main concerns in foreign affairs were regional. Throughout 1969 Iran, Turkey, and Pakistan, partners in the alliance of Regional Cooperation for Development (RCD), expanded cooperative efforts in banking, postal services, shipping, communications, cultural exchanges, and tourism. An agreement to set up a form of common market was accepted in principle. Iran took steps toward economic cooperation with India and made plans with Turkey to build a pipeline from Irani oil fields to the Turkish port of Alexandretta.

A serious dispute with Iraq arose over navigational rights on the Shatt-al-'Arab after Iraqi patrols challenged Irani fishermen early in 1969. Iran retaliated by denouncing and defying a 1937 treaty that fixed the Irani-Iraqi border on Iran's shore and required all ships to fly Iraqi flags and have Iraqi pilots. Iran called for a new treaty to locate the border along the river's median line. Subsequently, thousands of Iranians living in Iraq were expelled, and clashes occurred on the border.

In March Shah Mohammed Reza Pahlavi announced his refusal to recognize the federation of Persian Gulf emirates as long as Bahrein was a member. However, he also renounced the use of force to assert Iran's claim on the island of Bahrein. (*See in* CE: Iran.)

IRAQ. When Iraq's Ba'athist regime marked the end of its first year in power in July 1969, it was proving to be among the most radical of Arab governments. In anniversary speeches President Ahmed Hassan al-Bakr announced the abandonment of Iraq's nonalignment policies and declared his intention of purging Iraq of Western "imperialist" influences. During the year many prominent Iraqis were arrested as spies, and at least 51 Iraqis accused of spying for Israel or the United States were executed—Jews and Arabs alike. International protests against the executions failed to deter the regime.

Ba'athist measures were imposed on the nation by government decree during 1969. Compensation for expropriated land was halted; military conscription was extended from 18 to 23 months, beginning at age 19; and civil servants were forbidden to marry foreigners or to have secretaries.

In March Iraq's Kurdish tribesmen broke a three-year cease-fire with the army on the grounds

LIAISON AGENCY

The General Federation of Iraqi Women called for a female protest in Baghdad of the "Zionist occupation of Arab Palestine." This young woman made her feelings well known during the demonstration in June.

that the government had failed to fulfill a 1966 agreement for Kurdish self-government. Although the regime promised in May to issue a law providing for Kurdish autonomy, the insurgents threatened to disrupt Iraq's vital oil industry.

A considerable blow to Western oil interests fell when Iraq obtained Soviet loans and assistance to develop the rich North Rumaila oil fields. Other agreements provided for Soviet aid in developing deposits of iron ore and natural gas and in building a dam on the Euphrates River. Iraq also obtained development loans from Poland and East Germany. Late in April Iraq became the first Arab nation to recognize East Germany.

Although Iraq's relations with the leftist Ba'athist regime in Syria were cool, the two countries signed a defense pact in July. Relations with Iran were severely strained by a dispute over navigational rights in the Shatt-al-'Arab. (*See also* Iran. *See in* CE: Iraq.)

IRELAND. The Dail Eireann, the Irish house of representatives, which celebrated its 50th anniversary in January 1969, was dissolved May 1. The first general election since Prime Minister John Mary Lynch came into power in 1966 was called for June 18. The Fianna Fail, the ruling party for 12 years, was returned to office after unsuccessful efforts by the Fine Gael and Labor parties to form a winning coalition. The final count of votes gave Fianna Fail 75 seats for a gain of one; Fine Gael, 50 seats for a gain of four; the Labor party with 18 remained the same; and the Independent party with one lost two seats. The previous Dail had, in addition, three vacant seats. Frank Aiken, the last representative of the old civil-war tradition, left the cabinet.

The old question of a united Ireland was raised by Prime Minister Lynch in 1969 following the bloody civil rights strife in Northern Ireland. (*See* Great Britain.) However, experts agreed that such a move was far in the future. A request by the Irish government for United Nations intervention went unheeded. Army reserves were called up and field hospitals opened. In northeast Ireland a refugee center was opened for Catholics fleeing their homes in Northern Ireland. In Dublin, the capital of Ireland, there were demonstrations supporting the Catholic minority of Northern Ireland.

A strike of 3,000 maintenance workers from January to March brought large sections of industry to a halt, causing a food shortage and seriously reducing exports. Both maintenance and building-construction workers got a 20% wage increase. Prices rose more than 8% during the year. The budget, however, allowed for a strong social welfare program and benefits for low-income workers. In March, Lynch and other officials announced they were taking a 15% pay cut to emphasize Ireland's economic difficulties. (*See in* CE: Ireland.)

ISRAEL. The year 1969 was one of considerable adjustment and change in Israel. The escalation of the Arab war of attrition against Israel resulted in new Israeli retaliatory policies and in international efforts to mediate the dispute. In political events, a new prime minister came to power, and a regrouping of political parties produced clearer alignments in elections. The nation's economic base was altered by new industries.

As the year began, Israel reaped international repercussions for raiding the Beirut, Lebanon, airport in retaliation for an Arab attack on an El Al airliner in Greece late in 1968: the United Nations (UN) Security Council condemned Israel's action, and France's President Charles de Gaulle clamped a total embargo on war goods ordered by Israel from France. As tensions built in the Middle East, Arabs attacked a second El Al plane in Zürich, Switzerland, on February 18. Israel refrained from direct reprisals but warned the Arabs and appealed for international curbs on Arab terrorism.

On April 3—at the instigation of the French government—France, the United States, Great Britain, and the Soviet Union began talks aimed at resolving the Arab-Israeli conflict. At year's end, however, the "big four" had not yet found a satisfactory peace formula.

A week after the Zürich incident Israel's Prime Minister Levi Eshkol died of a heart attack. To prevent intraparty power struggles from dividing the nation at a time of crisis, the ruling Labor party selected a compromise candidate, Golda Meir, as prime minister. Mrs. Meir's assumption of office, on March 17, was reflected in the sharpened tones of Israeli policy pronouncements. Mrs. Meir rejected mediation of the Middle Eastern situation by the big four powers, insisting that only direct

ROSEN, "ALBANY TIMES-UNION," N.Y., FROM BEN ROTH AGENCY

"I keep telling him, Gamal, take the chicken soup, it's more nourishing!"

Arab-Israeli talks and signed peace treaties could replace the current cease-fire arrangements. She also called for an end of Arab boycotts and blockades and a disavowal of Arab guerrillas by Arab governments. She dismissed as "not genuine" a Jordanian peace plan presented in Washington, D.C., since the plan differed from Jordanian and Egyptian positions stated to the UN mediator, Gunnar V. Jarring.

Border Clashes and Guerrilla Warfare

In March the United Arab Republic (UAR), or Egypt, began almost daily artillery attacks on Israeli positions along the Suez Canal cease-fire line. Because the Israeli fortifications were strengthened over the winter, the Israelis were able to hold their positions with only a tenth of the force opposing them. In April and again in July UN Secretary-General U Thant warned that a state of open warfare prevailed along the canal and that UN observers at the canal had come increasingly under fire, particularly from the Egyptians. During the spring Israel was also engaged in air duels with Syria and ground fighting with Jordan and with Jordanian-based guerrillas.

By midsummer both the Israelis and the Arabs had greatly hardened their military positions. Faced by renewed Egyptian attacks along the Suez front, a buildup of Syrian forces on the northeastern front, and frequent clashes with regular and guerrilla forces on the Jordanian front, Israel resorted to new tactics—carrying the war to the enemy. Israeli commandos and aircraft struck at targets deep within enemy territory, no longer limiting their action to border areas. In the fall, when Arab guerrillas began operations against Israel from Lebanon, the reprisals were very harsh.

Israel also had to combat growing guerrilla activities within its borders. Terrorists struck at Elath, Haifa, Jerusalem, and Nablus and attacked Israeli patrols and settlements. By November the increase in terrorist activity had forced Israel to raise the maximum age for military reservists from 49 to 55 and to tighten internal security. To force Arabs in occupied areas to cooperate in uncovering terrorists, Israeli authorities instigated a policy of blowing up the homes of Arabs suspected of having knowledge of terrorist acts. Previously the practice had been limited to the homes of those known to be involved in subversion.

The Occupation

Although Arab guerrilla organizations failed to provoke revolts by Arabs in Israeli-occupied areas, they did weaken Arab-Israeli relations by creating friction. Anti-Israeli demonstrations occurred in the Gaza Strip and the West Bank. The Allenby

Many youths, such as this young rock group, took part in Israel's 21st-anniversary celebrations. The festivities, held in Jerusalem, avoided military themes because of Middle East unrest.

GAMMA—PIX FROM PUBLIX

An Israeli soldier views debris left when a bomb exploded in a crowded supermarket in Jerusalem. Planted by Arab terrorists, the bomb killed two and injured nine shoppers making their pre-Sabbath purchases.
KEYSTONE

and Damiya bridges between Israel and Jordan remained open for Arab travelers, though Israeli border inspections for hidden explosives were rigorous.

In Jerusalem the Israeli occupation authority, under the direction of the Ministry for Religious Affairs, completed the eviction of Arabs from homes at the Wailing Wall and began to raze the structures to create a plaza in front of the wall. In July Israel's national police headquarters was moved from Tel Aviv-Jaffa to the former Arab sector of the city. A fire set by an Australian Christian fanatic damaged the sacred Al Aksa Mosque and brought fresh condemnations of Israel by Arab nations. To offset the Islamic reaction, Israel staged an elaborate public trial for the defendant, Denis Michael Rohan.

Other Developments

The strong government of Mrs. Meir and the external pressures on the country helped create political solidarity by the time general elections were held on October 28. The Mapai, Achdut Ha'avoda, and Rafi parties consolidated as the Israel Labor party, with which the leftist Mapam party was electorally aligned. As a result, the election was essentially a contest between Labor, the right-wing conservative Gahal party, and the religious bloc.

Although the Labor party won 56 of the 120 Knesset (parliament) seats, it failed to obtain a majority and Mrs. Meir was compelled to form a new coalition government. The voting results indicated a slight shift to the right in national attitudes. Groups representing extremist policies—calling for either a peace settlement by surrender of all occupied territories or for retention of all occupied lands—failed to obtain seats in the Knesset. An impressive number of Arabs in Jerusalem and the West Bank region turned out to vote in spite of threats from Arab guerrillas and Jordan.

In December an incident occurred that strained Israeli-French relations. Five gunboats—originally built in France for Israel but placed under embargo—left France under mysterious circumstances and were sailed to Israel.

Israel's economy in 1969 felt the effects of successful new aircraft and electronics industries, established to offset French arms embargos imposed since the 1967 Arab-Israeli war. Expenditures for the new industries produced a payments deficit of $800 million in 1969 and reduced Israel's foreign-currency reserves to $500 million; the reserves had been $1 billion in August 1967. Nonetheless, Israel's gross national product increased by 25% in two years, and there was full employment. (*See also* Middle East. *See in* CE: Israel.)

ITALY. In August 1969 Italy installed its 30th postwar government, the second under the leadership of Mariano Rumor. The one-party Christian Democrat minority government was formed after a monthlong political crisis. Rumor's first government—a center-left coalition—was sworn in Dec. 13, 1968. It toppled in July after a schism in the Socialist faction of the cabinet. The Socialists, the Christian Democrats' major partner in the

Traffic clogs Rome's Piazza del Popolo during a transit workers' strike for higher wages in January. Italy was hampered by much labor unrest in 1969.
UPI COMPIX

coalition, split over ties with the Communists. The break occurred despite last-minute intervention by Pietro Nenni, the 78-year-old Socialist foreign minister. Subsequently three Socialist ministers resigned.

President Giuseppe Saragat named Rumor acting premier and requested that he form a cabinet. When the new government took over, Nenni was replaced by Aldo Moro as foreign minister.

The new government, formed August 5, expressed unconditional faith in the center-left policy and could therefore count on the external support of the Socialist and United Socialist parties and on the voting absenteeism of the Republican party. However, the minority government was clearly destined to feel every rocking of the Italian political boat. This was proved later in the year when workers' unrest, especially in the northern industrial cities, showed the government's inability to deal effectively with disorder. The country was repeatedly paralyzed by strikes and random 24- and 48-hour stoppages.

Unrest Grips the Country

The political upheaval came at a time of great unrest throughout the land. During the year 60 major industrial contracts involving 5 million workers were up for renewal. In January there was a student revolt in Milan and in February and March agitation at the University of Rome. On February 3 hundreds of farm workers blocked railway service between Naples and Rome, the capital. The workers were protesting a drop in the price for citrus fruit. Two days later, three unions announced a general one-day strike for increased pensions. On February 12, millions struck to protest a government-backed system of lower pay scales for underdeveloped areas. In April there were prison riots at Bari in the south and at Milan and Turin in the north. Two died in Battipaglia, a little agricultural town southeast of Salerno; there were also 200 injuries during the demonstrations that were staged in protest of general economic conditions.

In May a public-service strike crippled the nation. September saw peaceful demonstrations by 55,000 metalworkers and rubber workers at Milan and Turin. That same month violence erupted at Caserta—this time over the ruling on the status of a soccer team. On October 28, strikes and demonstrations marked the anniversary of the eve of Benito Mussolini's rise to power. In November there were strikes in Bari and Milan and sit-ins in Naples and Bologna. On November 8 the country's 900,000 construction workers won a first victory in the labor strikes with a 12% pay raise and a shorter workweek. A nationwide strike for low-rent housing occurred on November 19.

Government Activity

On April 30 parliament almost unanimously voted in favor of a new law granting pensions to certain categories of people who had not benefited previously and in favor of improving the existing pay scales. In June bills were introduced into parliament. One dealt with review and reform of taxation. A second granted greater powers to industrial unions and outlawed discrimination against workers for political or religious activities.

The major cultural activity of the year was the start of work on a new complete dictionary of the Italian language. In charge of the massive task was the Accademia della Crusca, which has dealt with the Italian language since 1582. The work was being carried out with the aid of a computer. Publication date was set for the end of the century.

At the request of the United Nations Educational, Scientific, and Cultural Organization, the Italian government considered a plan to save the sinking island city of Venice; experts predicted that Venice could be completely underwater in another 70 years if settling of the subsoil continued along with rising tides. Air pollution from mainland factories, meanwhile, was eroding the limestone buildings and attacking the sculptures and paintings in the historic city.

Italy's transportation system got a boost on two fronts in 1969. More than 500 miles of road construction was completed to fill gaps in the 3,665-mile *autostrada* plan. The gigantic highway project, which stretches from the Alps to the southwest portion of the mainland, was expected to be completed by 1973. In 1969, central guard rails were also added to the four- and six-lane highway. The most ambitious part of the undertaking was begun as plans went on the drawing board for the world's longest suspension bridge. The $500-million structure will cross the Strait of Sicily. Italy's outmoded railway system was scheduled for a $2.4-billion overhaul to be completed by 1972.

Economics and Foreign Relations

The most serious effect of Italy's labor unrest was the outflow of capital. Because of this outflow the balance of payments showed a deficit of $854.6 million in the first seven months of the year as against a $175.3-million surplus for the same period in 1968. On the other hand, the export deficit was down and industrial production increased 7.7% for the first half of the year as compared to the first half of 1968. A budget deficit of nearly $3 million was forecast for 1969. The automobile industry remained healthy, upping its production by 70,000 cars and increasing its labor force by almost 10,000 workers.

The most serious international situation came when 10 Italian oilmen were killed and 14 taken prisoner and sentenced to death by the Biafran rebels during the Nigerian civil war. Intervention by Italy, the Vatican, and five other countries saved the doomed men and eventually they were released. Two months later Italy made plans to resume shipments of relief supplies to Biafra. Italy supported the entry of Great Britain and the northern European countries into the European Economic Community, or Common Market. (*See also* Europe. *See in* CE: Italy.)

IVORY COAST. In 1969 the Ivory Coast experienced student protests, which in turn affected its relations with the Soviet Union. Troops were brought in during May to evict militant students from the University of Abidjan, where there had been a week-long strike. The government decided that henceforth the student movement would be integrated into the Democratic Party of the Ivory Coast. This meant that financial grants would be given to only those students who showed themselves willing to cooperate with government (party) policy. Disputes on the matter continued throughout the year between the new, officially recognized Movement of Pupils and Students of the Ivory Coast and the "disbanded" but still active National Union of Students.

Also in May, the government suspended all diplomatic relations with the Soviet Union. The Ivory Coast claimed that it had evidence of Soviet involvement in student strikes; the Soviet Union, however, called the evidence false.

A regional development commission was established to plan for economic development in the 1970's. In January the country's second palm-oil plant began production at Toumangouie. (*See in* CE: Ivory Coast.)

AFP FROM PICTORIAL PARADE

The Hôtel Ivoire, the largest and most modern hotel in western Africa, was completed at Abidjan, Ivory Coast, in 1969. The tower on the left is 31 stories high.

JAMAICA. Cooperation on both a regional and an international level increased in Jamaica in 1969. Industry, commerce, and government benefited from participation in the Caribbean Free Trade Area. During the year Jamaica became the 24th member of the Organization of American States.

Prime Minister Hugh L. Shearer visited a number of European Economic Community (EEC) countries with a view to protecting Jamaica's special interests if Great Britain joined the EEC. He also sought, by state visits, to promote close collaboration with some African nations. Jamaica was represented as an observer at the 1969 meeting of nonaligned nations in Belgrade, Yugoslavia.

New York's Gov. Nelson A. Rockefeller during a visit to Jamaica reportedly discussed the possibility of U.S. aid to the country for urban renewal. With the aid of a $12.5-million loan from the World Bank, 50 junior high schools were scheduled to be built in Jamaica in 1969. The chief obstacle to the ambitious education program was a shortage of teachers. Current government efforts to improve the economy included an expense budget of $240 million and a $12.4-million line of credit with U.S. and British banks to finance medium-term credit for capital goods.

In September the country mourned the death of Norman Manley, who had retired earlier in the year as head of the People's National party. On his retirement his son Michael had been elected to succeed him. (*See in* CE: Jamaica.)

JAPAN. During 1969 Japan maintained its position as the second largest economic power in the non-Communist world, with only the United States surpassing it in total production of goods and services. Japanese government statistics for fiscal 1968 (April 1968 through March 1969) indicated that for that period the Japanese economy had achieved a real growth rate of 14%, the second highest annual rate on record. A continuation of the high economic growth rates into 1970 was forecast by Japanese economists.

Maintaining a climate favorable to such economic growth was a major government consideration. One key incident was the merger between two giant Japanese firms, Yawata Iron and Steel Co. and Fuji Iron and Steel Co. In May the government federal trade commission rejected the proposed merger, expressing fears that "substantial restraints on competition" would result. Later in the year, however, the merger was approved. The new company formed would be the world's second largest steel company. The government expected a wave of merger proposals to follow.

Japan's Premier Eisaku Sato's ruling Liberal-Democratic party (LDP) suffered some decline in national popularity ratings but made a strong comeback in Tokyo Metropolitan Assembly elections in July. In the LDP-dominated Diet (parliament) deliberations during 1969 centered on the question of Okinawa's reversion from U.S. to Japanese control, the security treaty defining U.S.-Japanese relations (due for review in 1970), rising commodity prices, and university disputes.

Student Unrest

By mid-1969, when Sato's cabinet decided to take stern action to deal with university problems, disorders had taken place at some 100 universities. Symbolic of the widespread unrest was the situation at prestigious Tokyo University. In January radical students barricaded in an auditorium withstood a siege by riot police, who used pressurized water cannon and helicopters to drop tear gas. The students hurled Molotov cocktails, acid bottles, and rocks. During the clearing of one Tokyo University campus, 370 students were arrested and 35 persons were injured. A new president was elected in April who promptly set about reordering the university decision-making process.

In an effort to restore order in the universities, the LDP forced a "university normalization" bill through the Diet that called for stiff penalties for students, staff, and faculty who attempted to hinder university "normalization." A general uproar of protest ensued over the ramrod tactics of the LDP, who were accused of trampling on the constitution. Opposition parties boycotted further legislative proceedings.

Besides expressing discontent with the way universities were run, students protested various political issues. In April students in Tokyo, the capital, marked the 17th anniversary of the U.S. occupation of Okinawa by virtually bringing to a halt all passenger train service. In October violence broke out in nearly 100 Japanese towns as

In 1969 the new four-lane Tomei Expressway was opened to traffic. It is 335 miles long and connects Japan's ancient capital of Kyoto with the industrial center of Nagoya.

UPI COMPIX

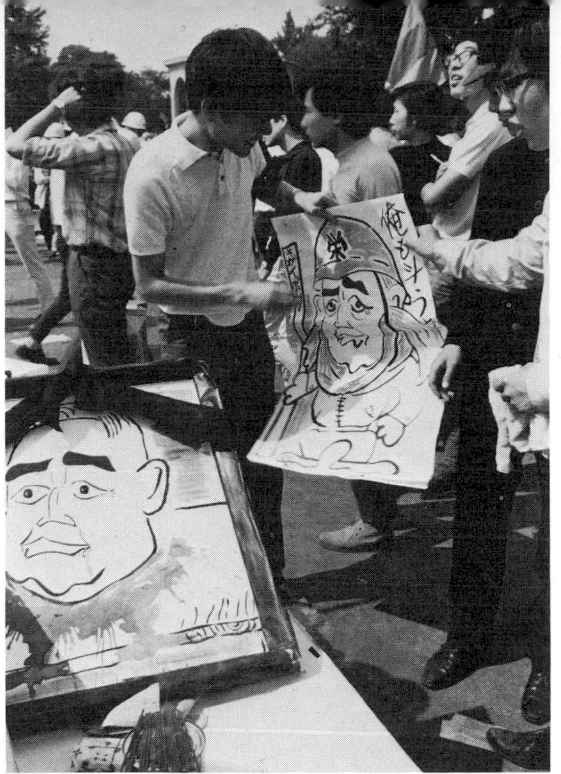

ORION PRESS—PIX FROM PUBLIX

More than 25,000 persons demonstrated in Tokyo on June 15, 1969, to protest the Vietnam conflict and the 1960 Japan-U.S. security treaty. Caricatures of Premier Eisaku Sato (above) are displayed.

radical student groups marked an "international antiwar day" by such tactics as tossing gasoline bombs and smashing windows.

Foreign Affairs

Whereas 1969 was a year of unprecedented economic growth for Japan, the year 1970 loomed as one in which foreign affairs would predominate. On the scheduled agenda were external hard bargaining, mainly with the United States, and a new Japanese-initiated security policy.

The most important issue between Japan and the United States was that of the future status of Okinawa. Chobyo Yara, Okinawa's first popularly elected executive, had appealed for "an immediate, unconditional, and total reversion of Okinawa" to Japan. Events in Okinawa underlined the seriousness of the reversion issue. In February some 30,000 people participated in a protest against the stationing of U.S. B-52 planes on the island. In June the 20,000-member Okinawa Military Employees Union staged a strike in defiance of an American military ordinance prohibiting striking. Carrying guns with fixed bayonets, U.S. military policemen forcibly removed some pickets, with the result that a member of the island's legislature was slightly injured. Sharp protests were heard on the floor of the Diet in Tokyo. Another public outcry occurred in July after the revelation that the United States was storing deadly nerve gas on Okinawa. The United States later announced that all chemical weapons would be removed.

Premier Sato was under pressure to achieve an agreement on the reversion issue not only from Okinawans but also from Japanese who demanded the return of Okinawa by 1972 at the latest and the same restrictions, including nonnuclear status, for U.S. bases on Okinawa as for the main islands. On the eve of Sato's departure for negotiations with the United States in November, thousands of radical students demonstrated against his visit.

In the November accord reached between Premier Sato and President Nixon, the United States formally agreed to return Okinawa to Japanese rule during 1972. Nuclear weapons were to be removed from the island, but the United States received the right to reintroduce such weapons in an emergency if Japan consented. Japan granted greater freedom of action to U.S. forces stationed in the country to fulfill U.S. security commitments in the Far East. Although the accord was criticized in Japan, Sato's party achieved a major victory in the December national elections. (*See in* CE: Japan.)

Yakuda Hall was the last building to be cleared during riots at Tokyo University in January 1969. Radical students had fought police with Molotov cocktails, acid bottles, and rocks.

ORION PRESS—PIX FROM PUBLIX

Japan

Special Report: Expo '70

by David K. Willis, Tokyo (Japan) Bureau, *Christian Science Monitor*

Expo '70 (officially, the Japan World Exposition), the first world's fair to be held in Asia, was scheduled to open its gates on March 15, 1970, and to close, six months later, on September 13. It was expected to draw some 67 million visitors, including 1.2 million from abroad, to its bowl-shaped location in the Senri Hills on the outskirts of Osaka, Japan's second largest city. More than 75 nations planned to take part, as well as the United Nations; the European Economic Community, or Common Market; the Organization for Economic Cooperation and Development; the Asian Development Bank; the U.S. states of Hawaii, Alaska, and Washington; the Canadian provinces of Quebec, Ontario, and British Columbia; the city of San Francisco, Calif.; several U.S. corporations; and more than 20 Japanese companies. The central theme is "Progress and Harmony for Mankind."

Expo '70 is the largest of its kind to date. The Universal and International Exhibition of 1967, or Expo 67, held in Montreal, Que., was host to 51 nations; the New York World's Fair in 1964–65 attracted 46. Japan first participated in a world's fair in Vienna, Austria, in 1873, five years after the Meiji Restoration. Tokyo was to be the host to the 1940 exposition, and one million books of tickets were sold before the outbreak of World War II forced cancellation of the exposition. Expo '70 is the biggest event in Japan since the 1964 Olympic Games in Tokyo. Organizers spent more than $2 billion on preparing the site, which two years before was an expanse of rice fields and bamboo, and on construction of new roads and a new subway line from downtown Osaka.

Osaka (and nearby Kyoto, Kobe, and Nagoya) is in the oldest settled area of Japan. It is now forming the backdrop for an international display of architectural and technological wizardry. The official Expo '70 architect, Prof. Kenzo Tange of Tokyo University, hoped that his overall design would provide new concepts for city planning of the future. Contrast is strikingly evident in the pavilion of the Furukawa group of industries of Japan. The building itself is a 258-foot-high iron replica of an ornate, seven-roofed pagoda that once stood beside the Todaiji Temple at Nara, 1,000 years ago. But inside is a "Computopia"—computers composing and arranging music.

This is what Japan's Expo '70 site looked like when its many buildings were under construction in August 1969. Kenzo Tange of Tokyo University, the official architect, hoped that the overall design would provide new ideas for city planning.

COURTESY, EXPO '70

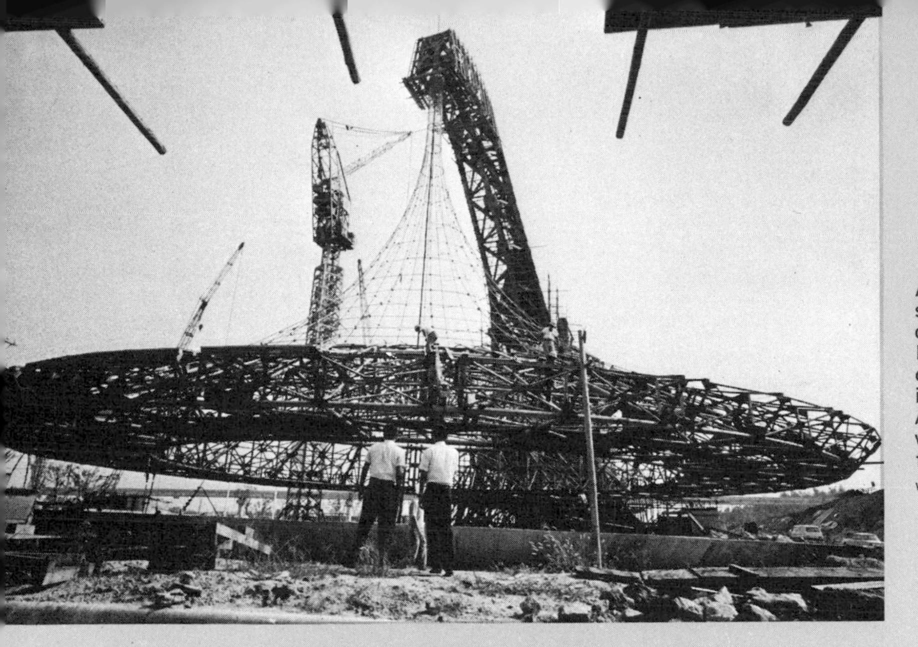

Australia's pavilion is shown under construction at the Expo '70 site. The giant cantilever culminates in a "skyhook" (shown). A giant circular roof was to be suspended from the skyhook.

WIDE WORLD

Visitors enter the 815-acre grounds through five gates, with the main gate in the center of the site. It is a 25-minute subway ride from the Osaka terminal of the New Tokaido Line, whose famous "bullet" trains cover the 350 miles from Tokyo in a fraction more than three hours.

There are about 100 pavilions of every imaginable size and shape on sites arranged to radiate from a central core, like the branches of a tree. The core is the rectangular Symbol Zone, 492 feet wide and more than a half mile long, partly covered by a gigantic translucent Grand Roof made of steel pipes and covered by polyester film. The roof is 115 feet above the ground, 364 feet wide, 964 feet long, and 33 feet deep. Exhibitions inside it bring its weight to about 5,000 tons. Underneath is the Festival Plaza, for official ceremonies and national-day exhibitions; the audience capacity is about 50,000.

Also under the roof is Theme Hall. Visitors climb from underground exhibits on man's past to a presentation of man's future inside the roof itself. They ascend inside the 198-foot Tower of the Sun, designed in primitive style by painter Taro Okamoto. Other, smaller towers are dedicated to "Youth" and "Motherhood."

A long escalator leads back down to the plaza, which also contains Expo Hall, where 1,500 people may watch the Ed Sullivan television show and a Canadian musical, 'Ann of Green Gables'. In the Expo Fine Arts Gallery, 490 works, tracing the development of Oriental art, were scheduled to be shown; and about 260 items were gathered from other countries, including Pablo Picasso's 'Three Musicians' from the Philadelphia (Pa.) Museum of Art and 'The Age of Innocence', by Sir Joshua Reynolds, from the Tate Gallery, London, England.

A welcome diversion is a 64-acre Japanese garden, divided into three sections—traditional (A.D. 700–1000); Edo Era (1600–1800); and futuristic. At the other end of the grounds is Expoland, an amusement park covering 41 acres and featuring such items as a jet-powered roller coaster called "Daidarasaurus" and the "Glass Castle."

The United States is expected to display pieces of the moon as well as other space, industrial, and consumer exhibits inside a $10-million pavilion that resembles a huge upside-down plate. Camphor trees and lawns surround an elliptical frame covered by the largest, lightest translucent plastic dome ever built, weighing only 1.5 pounds per square foot.

The Soviet Union built the tallest pavilion, its high point being 224 feet from the ground and surmounted by a four-ton hammer-and-sickle emblem. The roof line of the semicircular building slopes sharply downwards, and the front panels are painted red. The effect, from the front, is of an unfurling Soviet flag.

The largest and the most expensive pavilion belongs to Japan. It consists of five circular buildings arranged in cherry-blossom shape, housing exhibits of Japan's past, present, and future.

Canada calls its pavilion the "Palace of Mirrors." It looks like a decapitated pyramid. Four trapezoid walls, built of a new plywood called "glulam" (glue-laminated timber), lean inward at 45-degree angles; the outside walls are sheathed in mirrors.

Australia has suspended a circular roof from a curving 120-foot-high steel "skyhook." South Korea has an open, steel-pipe roof perched on 18 columns, each 100 feet tall. Great Britain has hung a huge canopy from four twin masts over an open-air concourse.

Plans called for about 145 restaurants at Expo '70, 5 of which were to offer 20-minute gondola rides to a height of 100 feet during meals. Unprecedented is the 2.4 miles of moving sidewalk, 15 feet from the ground and encased in a transparent plastic tube. The sidewalks carry about 9,000 people an hour, at walking pace, free of charge. Six monorail trains circle the grounds every 2.7 minutes, remote-controlled by computers. The ride takes 15 minutes; each train carries 540 passengers. (*See also* Fairs and Shows.)

JORDAN. With Jordan's West Bank region—including much of its best agricultural land—remaining under Israeli occupation in 1969, the nation's economy continued to depend in part on subsidies from Saudi Arabia, Kuwait, and Libya. In the irrigated areas of the East Bank region, however, agricultural production rose significantly in spite of frequent Israeli attacks throughout the year. Israeli sabotage of irrigation canals was easily repaired.

Israeli retaliatory attacks against Arab guerrillas operating from Jordan occurred almost weekly, but their effectiveness was limited due to the lack of substantial installations on guerrilla bases. An Israeli-backed sabotage network uncovered in July had been aimed at furthering tensions between the Jordanian authorities and the autonomous Palestinian guerrilla organizations. In October the government claimed that a plot by right-wing Muslim extremists to overthrow the regime had been foiled.

At a meeting in Amman, the capital, in February King Hussein I established cordial relations with Yasir Arafat, a leader of the most important guerrilla organization. Arafat had announced earlier that the 3,000-man Palestinian Liberation Army would move from the United Arab Republic (UAR) to Jordan, but discussion of the subject was postponed, apparently because Hussein hoped that mediatory efforts by the United States, Great Britain, France, and the Soviet Union would lead to a political solution to Arab-Israeli problems. When Arab guerrillas attacked the Israeli port of Elath in April, the Jordanian government had those responsible arrested.

Tensions continued between Israel and its Arab neighbors in 1969. Here Arab commandos training in Jordan are being lectured on the art of using and planting mines.

UPI COMPIX

The attack on Elath occurred while Hussein was visiting the United States, where he hoped to find the new Administration of U.S. President Richard M. Nixon sympathetic to the Arab cause. He outlined a six-point peace plan for the Middle East, which was hailed in the United States but was rejected by Israel.

When talks by the big powers showed no signs of progress, Hussein reinstated a proguerrilla prime minister who had been dismissed in March and increased cooperation between the guerrillas and the Jordanian army. Military coordination with neighboring Arab states was attempted; some Syrian forces moved into Jordan to supplement Iraqi troops already stationed there. Jordan's foreign policy was closely aligned with that of the UAR during 1969. (*See also* Israel; Middle East. *See in* CE: Jordan.)

KENYA. Kenya's Trade Licensing Act, which barred non-Kenyans from trading in a large number of basic commodities and from operating transportation companies, came into force on Jan. 1, 1969. Widespread concern about the likely effects of the act upon the Asian population was in no way allayed by the announcement of the minister of commerce and industry, Mwai Kibaki, that during the first six months of 1969 the government intended to refuse licenses to more than 3,000 Asian traders who were already in business in Kenya.

The Kenya government, with other East African governments, asked Great Britain to make it clear that the problem of Asians with British passports was distinct from that of British immigration policy in general, and that Great Britain accepted full responsibility for those Asians who wished to leave East Africa. As the provisions of the act began to be more fully felt in April, it was noted that about 40% of Asians seeking to leave Kenya wished to go to India rather than to Great Britain, in contrast with only 20% in 1968.

On January 27 President Jomo Kenyatta ordered the University College in Nairobi, the capital, to be closed. The students had boycotted lectures to protest the government's refusal to permit Oginga Odinga, leader of the opposition Kenya People's Union (KPU), to address them.

On July 5 Tom Mboya, minister of economic planning and development, was shot and killed in Nairobi. (*See* Obituaries.) There were immediate fears of conflict since many Luo tribesmen suspected the politically powerful Kikuyu tribe of being responsible for Mboya's death. Vice-President and Minister of Home Affairs Daniel Arap Moi declared that in his view the assassination was politically motivated and, though he refused to state who he thought was responsible, his statement that Western nations were not implicated led some to think that he suspected supporters of the Communist Chinese. On July 21, however, a Kikuyu,

MOHAMED AMIN FROM KEYSTONE

Nahashon Isaac Njenga Njoroge, convicted of slaying Tom Mboya in Nairobi, Kenya, on July 5, 1969, is escorted to a courtroom under heavy guard on August 18. Njoroge was sentenced to hang.

Nahashon Isaac Njenga Njoroge, was charged with the murder and in September was found guilty and sentenced to death. No evidence was forthcoming concerning accomplices, and no clear motive for the crime was discovered.

In the National Assembly in August, Odinga called upon the government to deny or confirm that Kikuyu oath-taking ceremonies had taken place in President Kenyatta's house. Rumors of the revival of oath taking had circulated in Nairobi since Mboya's death. The oaths were said to demand loyalty to the president and to the Kenya African National Union. Christian church leaders took up the campaign against secret oath taking and were joined in mid-September by a group of Kamba tribe members of Parliament who issued a statement in which they urged the government to intervene to prevent the forcible administration of oaths.

In October President Kenyatta was the subject of violent demonstrations in Kisumu, the home of Odinga, during which 11 people were killed. With other opposition leaders, Odinga was placed under house arrest, and on October 30 the government banned the KPU, accusing the party of sedition and the fomenting of intertribal strife. In the December parliamentary elections, two of every three incumbents, including five of President Kenyatta's cabinet ministers, were defeated; 600 candidates competed for 158 assembly seats. (*See* Africa. *See also* Feature Article: "Black Africa Saves the Game." *See in* CE: Kenya.)

KISSINGER, HENRY A. The principal adviser on foreign policy to U.S. President Richard M. Nixon, at least in 1969, was Henry A. Kissinger, on leave from Harvard University. A consultant to the last three presidents, Kissinger was named by Nixon in December 1968 as assistant for national security affairs.

Kissinger was instrumental in Nixon's shift from the concept of nuclear "superiority" to that of nuclear "sufficiency." He was the chief planner of the president's trip to Europe in February. He was a central figure in the Administration's effort to reach a negotiated settlement of the Vietnam conflict. Finally, he played a vital role in the presidential decision-making process on the Safeguard ABM (antiballistic missile) system.

Kissinger proved literally to be the president's right-hand man on foreign affairs in 1969. He accompanied Nixon to Europe in February, to Midway Islands in June for a meeting with South Vietnam's President Nguyen Van Thieu, and to Thailand, India, Pakistan, Romania, and Great Britain in late July and early August.

Born in Fürth, Germany, on May 27, 1923, Kissinger immigrated to the United States in 1938 to escape the Nazis. During World War II, he served with the 84th Infantry Division and with the 970th Counterintelligence Corps. At Harvard, he received a doctorate in 1954. (*See also* Foreign Policy, U.S.; Nixon.)

Henry A. Kissinger was named U.S. President Richard M. Nixon's White House adviser on national security affairs.

PICTORIAL PARADE

KOREA. Political turmoil at home and Communist threats from the North kept South Korea on tenterhooks for most of 1969. In February, South Korea's President Chung Hee Park reorganized his cabinet, creating three new ministries and a new portfolio called the Unification Research Board.

The storm broke, however, when Park asked the ruling Democratic Republican party to push through a constitutional amendment that would enable him to seek a third term. (Park himself had limited the presidential tenure to two terms shortly after taking office in 1961.) The proposal was followed by a series of student riots and disruption of the Assembly, where opposition members went on

CAMERA PRESS—PIX FROM PUBLIX

ORION PRESS—PIX FROM PUBLIX

North Korean navy patrol boats are seen on duty in North Korean waters (top). One of the South Korean marines guarding the frontier is shown above. The Han River and North Korea can be seen in the background.

strike. In July Park said he would order a referendum and resign if his proposal was rejected. After a long hassle in the Assembly the measure was put to referendum on October 18 and approved by a vote of 65.1%.

Relations with North Korea also caused disturbances. In July the U.S. Central Intelligence Agency claimed that a Viet Cong-style National Unification Front was being organized by North Korean agents. Two agents were executed in Seoul, the South Korean capital. In September it was announced that a 12-man spy ring had been smashed.

President Park, on a visit to the United States in August, warned U.S. President Richard M. Nixon that North Korea was preparing for another war and cautioned against moderating the U.S. anti-Communist defense policy. He offered the use of Cheju island as a new naval or air base for United States military forces in the Far East.

Nixon renewed the U.S. pledge for support of Korea. It was reported that military aid would continue at about $160 million a year. In October U.S. State Department officials acknowledged that long-range reduction or removal of 55,000 U.S. troops in Korea was under consideration.

South Korean economic growth was a bright spot in a troubled year. The rate was expected to increase 15% in 1969 as against 13.1% in 1968, though a slowdown was forecast for 1970. At Ulsan, a $6-billion, five-year industrial expansion plan was under way. In October the government announced the building of a steel-and-iron mill. The plant will have an annual capacity of more than a billion tons and is expected to save $41 million in imports a year. After reciprocal trade with Canada increased 800% over a four-year period South Korea opened a trade commission office at Vancouver, B.C.

Developments in North Korea

North Korea's relations with the United States deteriorated in 1969. On April 15 a crew of 31 Americans died when their EC-121 reconnaissance plane was shot down by North Koreans in the Sea of Japan. The Navy plane, on an intelligence mission, carried six tons of electronic equipment. Flights were continued with jet protection. On August 17 an unarmed U.S. helicopter on a training flight was shot down over North Korean territory. The fate of the three-man crew was never disclosed by the North Korean government.

In spite of a visit by Soviet President Nikolai V. Podgorny to P'yŏngyang, the North Korean capital, Premier Kim Il Sung declined to send a North Korean delegation to the Soviet Union for the June conference of Communist parties. (*See* Communist Movement.) In December 1968 and in March 1969 North Korean border troops clashed with the Chinese.

The economic picture in North Korea was not encouraging. In March Kim criticized the economic system for its failure to produce enough of the basic necessities of life. Increases of 11% in agriculture and 13% in industry were reported for 1968 as against 16% and 17% for the preceding year. A large share of the 1969 budget was said to be allocated for defense. (*See also* Asia; Vietnam. *See in* CE: Korea.)

KUWAIT. Arab affairs and the oil industry continued to dominate events in Kuwait in 1969. As one of the wealthiest Arab nations, Kuwait once again contributed heavy financial support to Jordan and the United Arab Republic, or Egypt, to offset revenues lost as a result of the Arab-Israeli war of 1967. In addition, Kuwait made substantial loans to Syria, Yemen, and Lebanon through the Kuwait Arab Economic Development fund. In spite of these expenditures the Kuwait budget showed a large surplus, due to a continuing increase in oil revenues.

Early in the year the Kuwait government became alarmed at the sharp increase in the number of Arabs who had immigrated to Kuwait since the 1967 war. The non-Kuwaiti Arab population was estimated at 250,000, many of whom were unemployed. In March the government imposed new entry restrictions.

Of considerable concern to Kuwait's government was the Arab nationalist coup in Libya in September, in which one of the few remaining pro-Western regimes in the Arab world was overthrown. Kuwait was associated with Libya and Saudi Arabia in the Organization of Arab Petroleum Exporting Countries. (*See also* Libya.)

Negotiations between internationally owned oil companies and Iran, under which Iran's oil production might be increased, also caused concern to Kuwait. Kuwait warned the firms that, if the increase were made at the expense of the Kuwaiti oil industry, Kuwait's concessions to the firms would be reviewed. (*See in* CE: Kuwait.)

LABOR UNIONS.

For organized labor in the United States, 1969 was a relatively quiet year. As in the past, the most prominent difficulties stemmed from wage settlements, race relations, and labor union activities.

One reason for the comparative calm during 1969 was that most of the collective-bargaining contracts were not subject to renewal until 1970 or later. Contracts were still in effect throughout the year in such traditionally strike-ridden industries as steel, automobiles, telephones, aerospace, rubber, soft coal, and trucking. One notable exception was the construction industry, in which 1,500 contracts came up for renewal during the year. To mediate wage negotiations in the industry, U.S. President Richard M. Nixon appointed a tripartite commission with the dual purpose of preventing unnecessary work stoppages and attempting to hold down wage settlements to a subinflationary level. (*See also* Building Construction.)

Collective Bargaining

Statistics released early in 1969 showed that settlements under collective bargaining averaged a 6.6% increase in 1968. Wage increases alone averaged 5.6% in 1968. Most of the contracts signed during the year were for two or three years,

ABOVE AND LEFT: WIDE WORLD

Demonstrators in Pittsburgh, Pa. (above), on Sept. 15, 1969, protest the absence of blacks on local construction jobs. In Chicago, Ill., on September 25, some angry white construction workers climb the Picasso sculpture (left) in the Civic Center Plaza.

WIDE WORLD

In June 1969, strike-breaking electronics workers in Philadelphia, Pa., wear paper sacks to conceal their identities as they cross picket lines. Union workers went out on strike in March, demanding higher wages.

with deferred pay increases at intervals. Such deferred wage increases met with the criticism of U.S. Secretary of Labor George P. Shultz, who charged that they were helping kindle inflation.

However, wage increases in 1969 seemed to be pushing even higher. Figures released by the Bureau of Labor Statistics of the U.S. Department of Labor indicated that in the first nine months of the year wage and benefit settlements increased a median 8.1% compared with 6.6% in 1968.

Major strikes in 1968 cost more than 49 million man-days of work in plants, offices, and schools. During the first nine months of 1969, strikes accounted for about 27 million man-days of work, a little less than in the same period in 1968.

Strikes and Settlements

The biggest strike of the year began in October when electrical unions struck the General Electric Co. (GE). The issue was a new contract, but the unions were also united in an attack on GE's traditional bargaining policy of "boulwarism." This policy, so named for a former GE vice-president, Lemuel R. Boulware, involved management initiative, a "fair" offer, and company resistance to changes not warranted by new information. Unions called it a "take it or leave it" policy and prepared to make the strike their greatest attempt ever to upset it.

In January the Wire Service Guild struck the Associated Press throughout the nation for higher wages, improved fringe benefits, and a modified union shop. In the settlement, the guild realized most of its demands except for the modified union shop.

February saw the end of an eight-week strike by the International Longshoremen's Association against the New York Shipping Association. In a settlement the union obtained wage increases of $1.60 an hour, better fringe benefits, and a safeguard against loss of work resulting from the increased use of packing containers.

In October, President Nixon ordered a 60-day cooling-off period in a dispute between seven railroad lines and four shop-craft unions. The threat of a union strike elicited a counterchallenge by the railways, which threatened to halt service completely. Nixon then invoked the Railway Labor Act of 1926, as amended in 1934, to obtain the cooling-off period. In December the railroads and the unions settled on a contract providing an 11% raise for 1969 and a tentative 7% raise for 1970.

Business Unions

In 1969 Joseph Lane Kirkland replaced William F. Schnitzler as secretary-treasurer of the American Federation of Labor-Congress of Industrial Relations (AFL-CIO). Kirkland was appointed by the federation council upon Schnitzler's retirement. The appointment, upon the recommendation of President George L. Meany, stirred speculation that Kirkland might be next in line for the organization presidency.

Both Meany and Kirkland won reelection at the AFL-CIO convention in October. At the same time, the federation increased the size of its executive council and broadened its coverage into expanding areas of unionism.

In February, Meany announced the withdrawal of the AFL-CIO from the International Confederation of Free Trade Unions, an organization which the U.S. labor movement had helped to establish. The organization, upon its establishment in 1949, was directed at opposing the Communist influence in trade unions. Meany charged that the confederation had recently been making efforts at rapprochement with the Soviet Union. The AFL-CIO had been the largest contributor to the confederation, paying annual dues of $360,000.

In 1969 the International Brotherhood of Teamsters (IBT) continued to be barred from the AFL-CIO because of its refusal to answer federation charges that it had once been or continued to be internally corrupt. However, the IBT continued to outperform the AFL-CIO in increasing membership, reporting in 1969 more than 2 million members, the largest membership of any trade union. The independent United Auto Workers, headed by Walter P. Reuther, was second largest with a membership of about 1.4 million.

The United Mine Workers of America was torn by a bitter fight for its presidency in 1969 between the incumbent W. A. (Tony) Boyle and challenger Joseph A. Yablonski, who accused Boyle of misuse of union funds and dishonest election practices.

The U.S. Department of Labor was investigating the charges. In the December election Boyle claimed victory, but Yablonski said he would fight the matter in court.

Labor and Race Relations

Dissatisfaction on the part of minority groups with union policies developed into labor's greatest problem during 1969. The impetus of minority attacks from blacks came in the building trades. Although the building trades provide some of the best opportunities for the poorly educated to earn high wages, they remained under the control of unions that have repeatedly refused to admit blacks. Strikes and demonstrations that broke out in Chicago, Ill.; Pittsburgh, Pa.; and Seattle, Wash., during late summer and early fall were cited as merely symptomatic of widespread discontent.

In September, William H. Brown III, chairman of the Equal Employment Opportunity Commission, attributed the unrest to a general lack of real employment opportunities. The commission, which administers Title VII of the Civil Rights Act of 1964 prohibiting discrimination in employment, investigates cases of violation. Brown announced that the commission had undertaken a program to accelerate investigations and conciliations by adding more manpower and by restructuring its schedule to permit faster action on cases.

According to government statistics released in September, job openings for Negroes in occupations controlled by labor unions were widening. Federal figures showed that in 1969 Negroes comprised 4% of all building-trade employees and that total minority representation in those trades was 7.2%. The figures were approximately the same for the metal trades, manufacturing, public utilities, mining, transportation, commerce, and service industries. In the construction trades the 7.2% marked an increase of more than 5% since the industry was first pressured by the government and civil rights groups two years before.

Another federal government project—the JOBS (Job Opportunities in the Business Sector) program—showed a definite lag during the year. The program, which subsidized businessmen who hire hard-core unemployables, had produced only about a fourth of the jobs hoped for by the end of the third quarter. Late in September, only 26,000 of those employed through the program were still on the job. Funds were set up and available for the employment of 100,000 trainees.

Farm Labor

During 1969 the United Farmworkers Organizing Committee began its fourth year of a strike and boycott against growers of table grapes who continued to refuse to negotiate contracts with the union. In addition to the problem of wages, the use of pesticides in the fields also became an issue between farm workers and growers. The union charged that many of the workers suffered ill effects from contact with the pesticides used on the grapes. The workers complained of symptoms ranging from stomach cramps to loss of vision. (*See also* Agriculture; Conservation.)

An Administration proposal for bringing workers on large farms under new federal collective-bargaining legislation also proved to be unpalatable to farm workers. Labor objected to the proposed legislation on the grounds that it provided for a 30-day cooling-off period for fact finding, mediation, and contract recommendations at the request of the grower. By giving the employer the option of setting the 30-day period, the workers would be prevented effectively from striking during peak season and would therefore be robbed of their strongest economic weapon. (*See also* Business and Industry; Economy; Employment. *See in* CE: Labor.)

On Jan. 17, 1969, loaded freighters remain at anchor in New York City's harbor awaiting the end of an International Longshoremen's Association strike.

UPI COMPIX

LAIRD, MELVIN R. Thrust into a post that he originally did not want and for which he was not U.S. President Richard M. Nixon's first choice, Melvin R. Laird left the House of Representatives to become the secretary of defense in 1969, a year marked by skepticism and criticism of all defense matters. (*See* Defense; Defense Special Report.)

Challenges to the military reached a fever pitch in 1969, fueled by the Vietnam conflict, military spending, and incidents such as the USS *Pueblo* case. Laird dealt with such issues in a cool, hard style and, as a result, became as much a target for criticism as the programs he defended.

The reoriented Safeguard antiballistic missile (ABM) system was the first program Laird had to sell to Congress. Laird defended the system as imperative in the face of mounting Soviet offensive capability. His statements were strongly attacked and the controversial ABM passed the Senate by only the narrowest of margins. In the last half of the year, Laird became the chief defender of the U.S. Vietnam policy. He was reportedly one of the main architects of the Nixon Administration's "Vietnamization" policy. (*See* Vietnam.)

On Jan. 30, 1969, Melvin R. Laird holds his first news conference as the U.S. secretary of defense.
PICTORIAL PARADE

Laird inaugurated and expanded major arms programs, but he was also forced to heed the growing clamor to cut defense spending. He maintained civilian control over the military but restored the Joint Chiefs of Staff to their former influence in policy decisions. In October Laird indicated that he would serve as defense secretary only through the four years of the existing Administration.

Reared in Wisconsin, Laird graduated from Carleton College in Northfield, Minn. He served with the U.S. Navy during World War II. In 1946 he was elected to the Wisconsin senate, where he stayed until his election to Congress in 1953. In Congress Laird became an expert on health, education, welfare, and defense matters.

LANDMARKS AND MONUMENTS. During 1969 increasing emphasis was placed on preserving and restoring historic landmarks, both in the United States and abroad. Promoted by international, national, and local organizations, restoration programs encompassed entire areas of cities as well as individual works of art and architecture.

WIDE WORLD
The Brookline, Mass., birthplace of the late U.S. President John F. Kennedy was made a national historic site on May 29, 1969. Mrs. Joseph P. Kennedy, Sr., is shown with Undersecretary of the Interior Russell Train.

In New Orleans, La., local preservationists aided by the Advisory Council on Historic Preservation won a long battle against the construction of an expressway on the border of the historic French Quarter, or Vieux Carré ("Old Square"), section of the city. Federal funds were denied the highway project after U.S. Secretary of Transportation John A. Volpe accepted the council's recommendation against construction of a highway there.

It was announced that Boston, Mass., would benefit from a $10-million plan to restore the Faneuil Hall market district. Plans were also made known to retain the old city hall building despite the recent relocation of city administration offices.

A redevelopment project allowing for the construction of new buildings as well as the restoration of an existing area was announced for St. Louis, Mo. The riverfront region, called Laclede's Landing, houses the last group of buildings from the 1865–75 era when St. Louis was known as the Gateway to the West. The new structures planned for this area will conform to the character and scale of the existing buildings.

The birthplace of the late U.S. President John F. Kennedy became a national historic site in May. The gray, green-shuttered frame house in Brookline, Mass., was dedicated by Mrs. Joseph P. Kennedy, Sr., on the 52d anniversary of her son's birth.

On the international level several efforts were made throughout the year to implement a resolution adopted by the United Nations Educational, Scientific, and Cultural Organization (UNESCO) in 1968. The resolution urged member nations to protect monuments and cultural properties in their historic surroundings and to arrange for the transfer of threatened properties if it should become impossible to preserve them in place.

One of the most important international projects for the conservation of historic buildings was centered about Venice, Italy. Close cooperation between UNESCO and the Italian government produced a series of immediate and long-range plans for preserving the city's architecture and its valuable works of art. Among legislative measures considered for adoption were those to update old buildings to meet modern health standards and to prevent further pollution of the canal system.

A UNESCO grant was awarded for a study of the problems involved in preserving the ancient shrines, temples, and palaces of Kyoto, Japan. Once the capital of Japan, Kyoto boasts a rich cultural heritage that caused it to be spared from bombing during World War II. However, in recent years urban development and industrialization have threatened many of the monuments in the older section of the city.

Italy's ancient city of Venice continued in 1969 to suffer greatly from gradual inundation and disastrous floods. The city and UNESCO worked to preserve old buildings. This palace on the Grand Canal is sagging and decaying.

GAMMA—PIX FROM PUBLIX

International cooperation was responsible for the preservation of the Church of St. Mary, Aldermanbury, designed by Christopher Wren and erected in London, England, in 1667. The church was moved to Westminster College in Fulton, Mo.,

"THE NEW YORK TIMES"

Connemara, the last home of poet Carl Sandburg, at Flat Rock, N.C., was acquired by the National Park Service on July 1, 1969. The home will be administered as a landmark.

the site of Winston Churchill's 1946 address in which he coined the phrase "iron curtain."

In the Netherlands, a 20-year program budgeting $8.5 million for the restoration of Delfshaven, the port from which Pilgrims set sail to join the *Mayflower* expedition in 1620, was readied during the year. The small port, part of the city of Rotterdam, was the only section of that city not razed by bombs in the 1940's. The Kakkendraggershuis (the ancient headquarters of the stevedores' guild) had been previously restored, as had the neighboring Kraahuis where skilled craftsmen, working with original molds, produce pewterware. The Pelgrimvaderskerk ("church of the Pilgrim Fathers"), where religious exiles worshiped before going to America, was restored to its earlier appearance.

In France, the most significant planning decision of the year determined the fate of the Halles in Paris. This market area, which had remained much the same for eight centuries, had long been inadequate for the city and the outlying area. The plan adopted by the city council of Paris would update the marketplace while retaining the existing atmosphere of its surroundings. All of the market buildings would be razed except one, which was to be restored and used for recreational activities. Monuments such as the St. Eustache Church that had previously been obscured were to be set off by gardens. Other historically interesting buildings were planned for renovation and adaptation as housing. (*See also* National Park Service.)

LAOS. The conflict in Laos between government forces and Communist guerrillas gathered momentum in 1969. The Royal Laotian Army and other anti-Communist forces were given considerable support by the U.S. Army Special Forces, the Air Force, and the Central Intelligence Agency (CIA). This escalation of the Laotian conflict and the nature of the U.S. role in fighting North Vietnamese troops and Pathet Lao guerrillas prompted a U.S. Senate subcommittee investigation during the year. Because the U.S. bombing of North Vietnam had been halted by 1969, there were more U.S. planes available to fly missions in Laos, and the number of air raids on Communist strongholds increased during the year. The Laotian government officially denied the U.S. involvement.

Anti-Communist forces in Laos won a major military victory in the late summer by pushing Communist forces from positions on the Plaine des Jarres in north-central Laos. The Communists had controlled most of the area for about five years. Earlier in the year North Vietnamese and Pathet Lao troops had made substantial advances into government-controlled territory beyond the Plaine des Jarres.

The Plaine des Jarres was taken from the Communists by a clandestine army composed of 40,000 Meo tribesmen and commanded by Maj. Gen. Vang Pao. The secret army was believed to be supported largely by the CIA. Heavy U.S. air support was given to General Pao's troops. It was unofficially estimated that about 300 bombing missions a day were flown against the Communist positions. The military victory won with the support of the U.S. Air Force prompted the investigation by a subcommittee of the Senate Committee on Foreign Relations. The Subcommittee on Near Eastern and South Asian Affairs, headed by Senator Stuart Symington (D, Mo.), met in secret session in October to discuss the extent of U.S. involvement.

Laos' Premier Souvanna Phouma visited the United States early in October to meet with U.S. President Richard M. Nixon. Their meeting was private, and few details were disclosed. The premier, however, said he was confident that the U.S. government would support the defense of Laos.

During the year there were an estimated 45,000 North Vietnamese troops and 20,000 Communist Chinese troops in Laos. The Chinese troops were reported to have been building roads in the north. (*See also* Vietnam. *See in* CE: Laos.)

LATIN AMERICA. Although there were improvements in relations among Latin American republics in 1969, relations between Latin America and the United States were strained. The year's major developments were the clarification of Latin American grievances over trade and assistance in the "Consensus of Viña del Mar" report and the enunciation of a new U.S. approach to Latin American problems by the new U.S. president, Richard M. Nixon.

Relations with the United States

At the Latin American Special Economic Coordinating Committee meeting in Viña del Mar, Chile, Latin American countries discussed a variety of common problems. Among them was the failure of the Alliance for Progress and of the whole principle of bilateral official aid, primarily because of bureaucratic restrictions on the way the aid funds were used and the fact that the aid funds were in reality loans that had to be repaid. It was claimed that in 1968 about 75% of Alliance for Progress funds were used to repay earlier loan maturities. Trade barriers preventing access of Latin American industrial products to the United States and other rich markets were also discussed. The conclusions of the meeting were incorporated into a report called the "Consensus of Viña del Mar," in which Latin American countries adopted a common position on their most critical problems. Chile's foreign minister presented the report to President Nixon in June. The report was also adopted as a basic document for the June meeting of the Organization of American States (OAS) in Trinidad, where agreement was reached on methods for negotiating points contained in the report. Colombia's President Carlos Lleras Restrepo personally urged Nixon to take action on the report.

President Nixon showed considerable caution in his dealings with Latin America and waited almost a full year after taking office before announcing his general policy for the region. In February Nixon announced that he had asked New York's Gov. Nelson A. Rockefeller, a Republican, to lead a fact-finding mission to Latin America. A number of Latin American governments declined to receive Rockefeller, but the mission did visit 20 countries in the spring and early summer. Almost everywhere they were greeted with violent demonstrations of hostility. It was never clear whether these expressions of antagonism were directed against Nixon, or Rockefeller, or the United States, or were merely further evidence of the increasing frustration felt in Latin America at inadequate economic growth.

The Rockefeller report was submitted to the president in August but was not disclosed in full until November. The report described the social and economic crisis facing Latin America and said that the United States had to take measures to alleviate the deteriorating situation in the region or face the prospective developments of further revolutionary or anti-U.S. trends. The report's 83 urgent and far-reaching recommendations primarily involved increasing U.S. trade with and aid to the region.

In President Nixon's speech on Latin American policy, given on October 31, he emphasized that he would reduce the U.S. leadership role played in Latin American affairs and that, though the United States would aid Latin America in a new kind of equal partnership, the region itself should shoulder the main responsibility of solving its problems. Although Nixon indicated that his approach was "substantially shaped" by Rockefeller's report, his proposals to implement the new policy were less explicit and more modest than Rockefeller's. The Latin American reaction to Nixon's speech was mixed, but there was general disappointment with its limitations.

Nixon's generally low-key approach was exemplified in his handling of the sensitive problem of expropriation. Through restraint and diplomacy the United States managed to avoid a breakdown in relations with Peru and Bolivia over their expropri-

CAMERA PRESS—PIX FROM PUBLIX

Cuba's Premier Fidel Castro addresses his people from the Plaza de la Revolución in Havana. The huge statue behind him is of José Martí, a Cuban revolutionary who led a rebellion against the Spaniards in the 19th century.

The Red Cross was forced to employ all means of transportation, including trucks and jeeps, on July 29, 1969, to transfer thousands of displaced persons in Honduras and El Salvador during the war between those countries.

"LONDON DAILY EXPRESS" FROM PICTORIAL PARADE

ation of U.S.-owned companies. (*See* Bolivia; Peru.)

Regional Economic Integration

The Latin American Free Trade Association (LAFTA) held its eighth annual meeting at the end of 1968. Its inability to reach agreement on tariff concessions for such important products as wheat and oil meant that its timetable for complete trade liberalization had to be abandoned. The overall plan to create a Latin American common market to include LAFTA and the Central American Common Market thus appeared unattainable in the near future. However, LAFTA planned meetings to reconsider the whole concept and to formulate new proposals.

Because LAFTA proved to be a difficult association to make cohesive, hopes were raised for more effective forms of economic integration in less unwieldy subregional groups. The Andean Common Market—Bolivia, Chile, Colombia, Ecuador, Peru, and Venezuela—which was first conceived in 1967, finally achieved realization in a treaty in May, though Venezuela did not sign it. The Río de la Plata Basin group, consisting of Argentina, Bolivia, Brazil, Paraguay, and Uruguay—all countries with territory in the Paraná-Paraguay river system—achieved formal existence in a treaty signed in April. The original plan for the joint exploration and development of the area's resources was expanded to include economic integration.

The Central American Common Market, which had been very successful in increasing trade for its members—Costa Rica, El Salvador, Guatemala, Honduras, and Nicaragua—made some technical progress. Politically, however, it was in danger of disintegrating, mainly because of the war that broke out between El Salvador and Honduras. (*See* El Salvador; Honduras.) There was also hesitant progress in the development of the Caribbean Free Trade Area, which included former British territories in the Caribbean.

Cuba

Cuba's Premier Fidel Castro seemed to have ended his attempt to export the Cuban revolution to the South American continent and seemed disposed to renew relations with any country willing to repudiate the 1962 decision of the OAS to ostracize Cuba. Chile and Venezuela expressed the view that the ostracism of Cuba was irrelevant and should be ended.

Organization of American States

During 1969 the OAS was called upon to keep the peace in Central America. In late June the governments of El Salvador and Honduras requested assistance in investigating alleged violations of the rights of about 300,000 Salvadorans who had migrated to Honduras. While the OAS was investigating this charge, fighting broke out between the two countries. The Council of the Organization voted unanimously to take action. Forces from OAS member nations helped implement a cease-fire and maintain peace.

WIDE WORLD

The convictions of (from left) Mitchell Goodman, pediatrician Benjamin M. Spock, Michael Ferber, and the Rev. William Sloane Coffin, Jr., on charges of conspiring to counsel young men to avoid the draft were reversed in July by the U.S. First Circuit Court of Appeals.

The OAS also provided a major forum for reshaping U.S. and Latin American relations during the year. Jamaica became the organization's 24th member in 1969. (*See also* articles on individual countries. *See in* CE: Articles on individual countries; Latin America; South America.)

LAW. Campus disorder was an important subject for legislative concern in 1969. Many state legislatures devoted considerable time to formulating legal curbs on college student protest. In Illinois, for example, a number of laws were passed to limit severely, and in some cases to eliminate, student protest. Scholarships will be taken away from students acting in a manner judged "disruptive"; criminal penalties could also be applied. Other states, including Minnesota and California, have passed similar laws.

In September eight defendants who called themselves "the Conspiracy" went on trial in Chicago, Ill. They were accused of crossing state lines with intent to conspire in inciting a riot at the 1968 Democratic National Convention. (*See* United States.)

Controversial New Attorney General

John N. Mitchell, who took office as attorney general in the new Administration of U.S. President Richard M. Nixon, proved to be very controversial in his first year in the Cabinet. In June the Department of Justice, headed by Mitchell, asserted in court its right to wiretapping and other electronic eavesdropping, without any restrictions or limitations imposed by the judiciary or by the U.S. Congress. This "right" allegedly extended to the activities not only of organized crime but also of anyone the department considered a possible subversive. A number of judges and lawyers, including conservatives, became alarmed at the prospect of such sweeping powers.

In July Mitchell made a statement that seemed aimed at calming fears of invasion of privacy. He said that the number of wiretaps by federal agencies had actually decreased during the first six months of the Nixon Administration. It was the Crime Control and Safe Streets Act of 1968 that had eased restrictions on wiretapping.

Also controversial was Mitchell's proposal for preventive detention. A criminal suspect could be jailed without bail for up to 60 days if a judge thought him likely to commit a crime again before the trial. Preventive detention seemed to run counter to the rule of law that presumes innocence until a man is proved guilty. The provision was part of a crime bill for Washington, D.C., but Mitchell recommended it to the states and cities as well. Senator Samuel J. Ervin, Jr. (D, N.C.), usually considered a conservative, called preventive detention unconstitutional.

Approximately half of the attorneys in the civil rights section of the Department of Justice publicly protested a slowdown in enforcement of the school desegregation laws. (*See* Education; Race Relations.) Jerris Leonard, assistant attorney general and chief of the civil rights section, had asked a federal judge to delay integration for 33 Mississippi school districts. In October, however, the Supreme Court ruled that desegregation should be implemented "at once." It remained to be seen how quickly the ruling would be enforced. (*See also* Supreme Court of the U.S.)

Legal Help for the Disadvantaged

Much remains to be done in the area of providing legal services to the poor. A study of 238 sample cases in Cook County, Ill., showed that approximately 55% of the defendants were designated indigent by the court and that their cases were handled by public defenders. Edward Bennett Williams, a noted criminal attorney, charged that the public-defender system has a strong tendency to settle human problems on a mass-production basis.

An organization called Poverty Lawyers for Effective Advocacy Inc. (PLEA) was formed in 1969 by 83 government-paid attorneys. The purpose of PLEA is to resist pressures against their defense of their clients. The PLEA bylaws noted that the lawyers were brought into "constant conflict with certain powerful vested interests—slum lords, growers, and businessmen whose wealth depends, in varying degrees, upon exploitation of the poor—and the unresponsive bureaucracies of government institutions."

LEBANON. Lebanon's quasi neutrality in Middle Eastern affairs and the political balance between its Christian and Arab Muslim peoples were threatened in 1969 as Arab guerrillas sought to operate against Israel from Lebanese soil. Although many Lebanese favored a more active stand against Israel, the Christians and many Muslims feared Israeli reprisals and the possible seizure of southern Lebanon by Israel. Against this background the year's events were played out.

The Lebanese government fell in January, as a result of an Israeli attack at Beirut, Lebanon's capital, in December 1968. Guerrilla sympathizers demonstrated for an end to the ban on guerrilla activities in Lebanon and for firmer defense policies. A new government was formed by Rashid

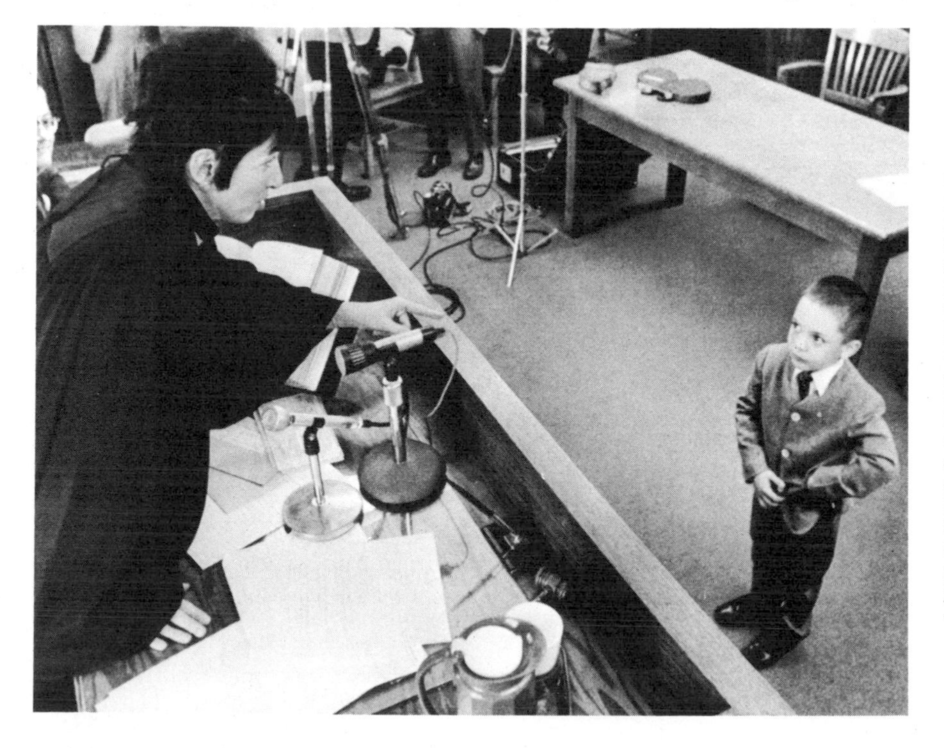

Little Leigh G. Barron, age five, in court for a jaywalking ticket, receives a lecture on traffic safety from a traffic judge in Denver, Colo. Leigh had suffered a broken collarbone and a dislocated hip after he ran into the side of a moving auto while chasing a friend across the street. Before Leigh went to the hospital, a policeman issued him a ticket for jaywalking.
UPI COMPIX

UPI (UK) LTD.

A Lebanese woman, aided by children, works to fill sandbags in the city of Tripoli, the scene of a heavy attack by Arab guerrillas in October.

Karami in spite of feuding leftist Arab and rightist Christian factions.

Late in April, as guerrillas in southern Lebanon strengthened their forces and Lebanese police tried to contain them, clashes erupted and the army was called in to relieve the police. Proguerrilla demonstrations were severely repressed. Criticism of the repression and the inability of government factions to unite on a policy toward the guerrillas led Karami to resign. To avoid a complete breakdown in government, however, he remained as a caretaker premier. The guerrillas were recognized on the understanding that they would avoid populated areas and would not attack Israel.

A more serious crisis arose in October when Lebanese forces attempted to prevent the expansion of the guerrillas in southern Lebanon. In retaliation for the crackdown, Syrian-backed Arab militants invaded eastern Lebanon, attacked towns, and captured Lebanese officials. Riots flared throughout Lebanon, Palestinians clashed with police in refugee camps, and Arab militants seized control of Tripoli, in Lebanon, and the northern coast.

Although the army regained control in many areas, the guerrillas' strong offensive forced the government to face their demand for freedom of action. In November, through the mediation of President Gamal Abdel Nasser of the United Arab Republic, Lebanese and guerrilla leaders reached a secret agreement.

In December caretaker Premier Karami obtained parliamentary approval for the new government he had formed. Thus the country's longest political crisis—214 days—finally ended. (*See also* Middle East. *See in* CE: Lebanon.)

LESOTHO. In 1969 progress was made in all sectors of Lesotho's economy. Agriculture still accounted for more than 70% of Lesotho's gross domestic product, followed by small industry development in the west and diamond exploitation in the Maluti Mountains. In spite of continuing drought—which necessitated some famine relief—record wheat, wool, and cattle exports were achieved in 1968; and irrigation and conservation schemes progressed despite traditional land-tenure problems. Farmers from Taiwan demonstrated diverse vegetable growing and in August Prime Minister Leabua Jonathan visited Taiwan and signed a cooperative agricultural agreement.

The Lesotho National Development Corp. continued to promote small industries. South Africa maintained a supply of technical and practical aid and remained Lesotho's main source of revenue. About 60,000 Basuto working in South Africa earned more than $7 million in 1969. In an effort to increase savings the National Development Bank was established. (*See in* CE: Lesotho.)

Angie Brooks, 15-year veteran diplomat from Liberia, takes over the gavel as the newly chosen president of the United Nations General Assembly. She is the third African and the second woman ever to hold the post.

UPI COMPIX

LIBERIA. A national celebration in January 1969 marked William V. S. Tubman's 25th anniversary as president of Liberia. In a silver jubilee gesture, Tubman announced amnesty to all political prisoners except those already convicted.

In spite of encouraging economic growth in 1969, Liberia's foreign debt of $250 million continued to absorb nearly one third of the budget. Sales of rubber and iron ore, Liberia's two greatest earners of foreign exchange, were expected to reach new highs in 1969. Suspension of the $10,000 deposit required of foreign firms increased business confidence. A second iron-ore pelletizing plant and a $6-million tire plant were planned. Logging and sawmill operations got under way.

Liberia maintained its position as the world's biggest shipper with 27 million tons. Because of cheap registration and labor, some 1,700 ships, mostly American and Greek, sail under the Liberian flag. (*See in* CE: Liberia.)

LIBRARIES. Characteristic of the year 1969, libraries of all types were involved in questionings, confusion, and conflict. During the year a number of public-library trustees went to Washington, D.C., to try to reverse the trend of cuts in library programs in the budget of the Department of Health, Education, and Welfare. Their efforts seemed influential; Congress restored appropriations to the 1968 level. School libraries also felt the budgetary squeeze in 1969.

Librarianship as a career attracted more individuals than ever before. Published statistics revealed that 4,625 graduates received fifth-year professional degrees—595 more than in the preceding year.

Destruction of library property remained a serious headache in 1969. Over the weekend of February 15, vandals broke into the University of Illinois Library at Urbana and removed approximately 16,000 catalog cards. The cards were then either torn up or burned. Damage was placed at $50,000.

During the summer New York City's public library obtained an extensive collection of Sean O'Casey's literary papers. Among the items acquired were 25 manuscript notebooks used by the great Irish playwright, who died in 1964; more than two dozen packages of typescripts; many edited pages and galley proofs; and the manuscript of 'The Harvest Festival', a three-act play turned down by the famous Abbey Theatre of Dublin, Ireland, in 1919 and never published or produced.

Lloyd Alexander reads from his Newbery award-winning book 'The High King' at the Philadelphia (Pa.) Free Library's "Summer Read-In," a ten-week program for young schoolchildren.

JULES SCHICK FOR THE PHILADELPHIA FREE LIBRARY

JOHN LITTLEWOOD FOR THE "CHRISTIAN SCIENCE MONITOR"

Charles Blockson sits surrounded by books from his vast collection on Afro-American history. Part of the collection was displayed by the Freedoms Foundation, Inc., in honor of American Negro History Week.

The American Library Association (ALA) was especially active during 1969, both at home and abroad. In conjunction with the U.S. Agency for International Development, surveys of the need for books and libraries were made in Asia and Latin America. The ALA administered grants from the Ford Foundation to assist the libraries of the University of Algiers, in Algeria, and the University of Brasília, in Brazil. A committee for liaison with Japanese librarians was responsible for U.S. participation in a conference in May in Japan on the role of libraries in higher education and research. The 'Foreign Service Directory of American Librarians' was published.

The Children's Service Division of the ALA published '1968 Children's Books of International Interest', which had been prepared for distribution at the International Federation of Library Associations' (IFLA) annual session at Copenhagen, Denmark, in August, and sponsored the program "Library Service to Children in Other Countries" at the 1969 ALA annual conference. Ten Asian students attended U.S. library schools under an Asia Foundation Grant, and 13 Asian librarians in their home countries were awarded ALA membership.

At the IFLA's annual meeting the main theme was "Library Education and Research in Librarianship." About 400 persons from 38 countries participated. At the session Sir Frank Francis, formerly director of the British Museum, completed his two terms as president (1963–69) and his place was taken by H. Liebaers of Brussels, Belgium, for 1969–72; R. Malek of Prague, Czechoslovakia, was elected as one of the six vice-presidents.

During 1968–69, the United Nations Educational, Scientific, and Cultural Organization (UNESCO) promoted research in the field of libraries by means of contracts signed with IFLA and the International Federation for Documentation for studies on the national planning of library services, the standardization of bibliographical data in catalog entries, a ten-year trilingual supplement to the Universal Decimal Classification, an audio-visual course in librarianship in Spanish and French, and manuals on library legislation and library statistics. The development of library services was promoted by the establishment of a pilot project in school library service in Honduras to serve as a model for Latin America, a pilot project on public and school libraries in Ceylon, and by continued support for training courses at Makerere University College, in Kampala, Uganda, and elsewhere. Library experts were also sent by UNESCO to 17 other countries. (*See in* CE: Libraries.)

LIBYA. In a bloodless coup on Sept. 1, 1969, Libya's monarchy was overthrown by young military officers who proclaimed a republic and established the Revolutionary Command Council (RCC) to govern the country. The coup was staged while King Idris I was vacationing in Turkey and was timed to prevent another coup planned by powerful interests against Crown Prince Hassan al Reda, for whom the king intended to abdicate. Although Hassan al Reda supported the RCC coup and renounced his right to the throne, the RCC declared that he and other royalist officials would be tried for treason and corruption. The king's cabinet and hundreds of officials and political leaders were jailed.

The new regime, which was popularly received throughout Libya, identified itself with Arab nationalism and immediately gave financial aid to the Palestinian guerrilla organization *al Fatah*. Under an "Arabization" program, public notices and signs not in Arabic were destroyed and English ceased to be taught in schools.

Libya's foreign-owned oil industry was not directly affected by the coup, but the RCC promised a more equitable distribution of oil revenues within Libya. It also announced that the U.S. and British air bases in Libya would be closed when current agreements expired. The RCC appointed a largely civilian cabinet and proclaimed a foreign policy of nonalignment. The United States recognized the regime in September. (*See in* CE: Libya.)

"THE TIMES," LONDON, FROM PICTORIAL PARADE

KEYSTONE

Libya's King Idris I (left) was ousted in a military coup in 1969. The coup was timed to prevent another coup planned against Crown Prince Hassan al Reda (above), the king's designated successor.

UPI COMPIX

New York City's Mayor Lindsay flashes a happy grin after winning reelection.

LINDSAY, JOHN V. In an amazing comeback performance, John Lindsay overwhelmed the candidates of the two major political parties to win reelection in November to a second four-year term as mayor of New York City. He had been virtually counted out when he failed to win the Republican nomination in the primary. At that time not only his Republican opponent, John J. Marchi, ran ahead of him, but also three candidates in the Democratic primary together more than doubled the votes cast for him. Lindsay refused to concede defeat, however, and began a strenuous campaign as a candidate of the Liberal party and the newly organized Independent party for what he called "the second hardest job in America." The heated contest cut firmly across party lines with Lindsay managing to win the endorsement of prominent members of both the Democratic and Republican parties. His appeal was mainly to two groups, the city's intellectuals and its poor. The candidates of both the Democratic and Republican parties pitched their campaigns to the conservative middle class. In the outcome, the victorious Lindsay captured more than 160,000 votes over his nearest opponent, Democrat Mario A. Procaccino. His victory greatly enhanced his stature as a national figure.

Lindsay was born in New York City. He graduated from Yale University in 1944, served in the U.S. Navy, and graduated from Yale Law School in 1948. His political career began in 1958 when he defeated the Republican organization candidate in the 17th Congressional district in New York City and won election to the U.S. House of Representatives. Lindsay served in the House until his election as mayor in 1965.

LITERATURE. A few years ago when U.S. publishing firms began to amalgamate and offer stocks, certain predictions were made about the publishing industry. One was that the overwhelming bias of U.S. readers for nonfiction would be even more gratified by an industry that now had to show stockholders the quarterly dividends of quick gains, rather than the production costs of slow starters. A second was that topicality and sensationalism would be even greater factors in the selection of what would be published. In the absence of sound consumer analyses, therefore, one year's best sellers would provide the guide to what would sell in succeeding years, and except for a number of gambles yearly, one year's books would read very much like another's.

It is difficult to tell how accurate these predictions have been. Certainly there have been a number of books published to take advantage of topicality, and certainly a number of best sellers have seemed to be no more than recent or sensational versions of other best sellers. In addition, the surging interest in the book-publishing world in 1969 for editors with experience in political and social issues as well as in contemporary fiction—the two areas of keenest competition in the race for best sellers—gives indication of such a direction. Yet, annually a number of books do get published that do not fit these predictions.

Nonfiction Highlights

Included in the year's nonfiction titles were a number of books that played upon the interest generated by student rebellions: Susan Sontag's 'Styles of Radical Will', Abbie Hoffman's 'Revolution for the Hell of It', James Simon Kunen's 'The Strawberry Statement—Notes of a College Revolutionary', Stephen Spender's 'The Year of the Young Rebels', and 'Up Against the Ivy Wall', written by Jerry L. Avorn and members of the *Columbia* (University) *Daily Spectator*. Books of a similar nature included Joseph Wechsberg's 'The Voices', an account of the invasion of Czechoslovakia in 1968, Peter Yessne's 'Quotations from Mayor Daley', Jessica Mitford's 'The Trial of Dr. Spock', Fidel Castro's 'History Will Absolve Me', and two new books on Ernesto (Che) Guevara, 'The Great Rebel: Che Guevara in Bolivia', by Luis J. González and G. A. Sánchez Salazar, and 'Che Guevara on Revolution: a Documentary Overview', edited by Jay Mallin.

The growing interest in black culture and black identity produced H. Rap Brown's 'Die, Nigger, Die', Julius Lester's 'Revolutionary Notes', Dan McCall's 'The Example of Richard Wright', John Hendrik Clarke's 'Malcolm X: the Man and His Time', August Meier's and E. M. Rudwick's 'The Making of Black America', and Robert Scheer's edition of Eldridge Cleaver's 'Post-Prison Writings and Speeches'.

Two rather controversial books on the Administration of former U.S. President Lyndon B. Johnson appeared: Noam Chomsky's 'American Power and the New Mandarins' and Eric F. Goldman's 'The Tragedy of Lyndon Johnson'. Theodore H. White, whose analyses of presidential races in 1960 and 1964 are standards, wrote what many critics believed to be his best, 'The Making of the President 1968'. Novelist James A. Michener added his views in 'Presidential Lottery', and Senator Eugene J. McCarthy, a candidate for the Democratic party's nomination and one of the leading actors on the scene, supplies an account of his escapades, from the New Hampshire primary to the Democratic National Convention and beyond, in 'The Year of the People'. Coretta Scott King told her story in 'My Life With Martin Luther King, Jr.', and Jack Newfield wrote 'Robert Kennedy: a Memoir'.

The year's supply of nontopical nonfiction books was headed by John Gross's 'The Rise and Fall of the Man of Letters', John Unterecker's 'Voyager: a Life of Hart Crane', Carlos Baker's 'Ernest Hemingway, a Life Story', Ilya Ilyich Schneider's 'Isadora Duncan: the Russian Years', and Stanley Weintraub's 'Shaw: an Autobiography, 1856–1898', put together out of George Bernard Shaw's autobiographical statements. Leon Edel published the fourth and penultimate volume of his biography of Henry James, and Alexander Kendrick brought out 'Prime Time: the Life of Edward R. Murrow'.

The personal essay returned with Wallace Stegner's 'The Sound of Mountain Water', Anne Moody's 'Coming of Age in Mississippi', and MacKinlay Kantor's 'Missouri Bittersweet'. Jane Kramer published 'Allen Ginsberg in America', Richard Burgin added 'Conversations With Jorge Luis Borges'; Graham Greene issued his 'Collected Essays', written over four decades and relating mainly to literature; and Benjamin DeMott supplied 'Supergrow: Essays and Reports on Imagination in America'.

Outstanding history volumes included Harrison E. Salisbury's 'The 900 Days: the Siege of Leningrad', Bruce Catton's 'Grant Takes Command', Dan T. Carter's 'Scottsboro; a tragedy of the American South', John Womack, Jr.'s 'Zapata and the Mexican Revolution', and Herbert B. Ehrmann's review of the Sacco-Vanzetti trial, 'The Case That Will Not Die'. The year also introduced readers to 'The Peter Principle' by Laurence J. Peter and Raymond Hull. Their thesis was that every employee tends to rise to his level of incompetence.

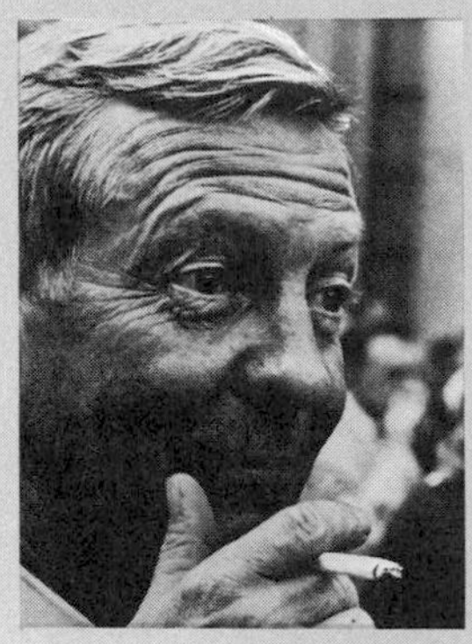

HAROLD STRAUSS—COURTESY, ALFRED A. KNOPF, INC.

JOHN CHEEVER

JUDY FEIFFER—COURTESY, RANDOM HOUSE

PHILIP ROTH

Fiction and Poetry

In fiction, Philip Roth took the stereotypes of the Jewish mother and the Jewish novel and zoomed overnight to the top of the best-seller list with 'Portnoy's Complaint', which remained America's favorite reading until replaced by Jacqueline Susann's newest concoction, 'The Love Machine'. This successor to her record-selling 'Valley of the Dolls', while less a roman à clef, uses the same ingredients of sex, schmaltz, and show business. However, despite the author's extensive personal appearance tour, the book was not able to generate the same sales as her previous work and it was succeeded in turn by Mario Puzo's 'The Godfather', a novel concerning the Mafia. Michael Crichton's 'The Andromeda Strain' dealt with contamination from outer space. Budd Schulberg's first major novel in a decade, 'Sanctuary V', chose as its setting a neutral embassy during a revolution in a Caribbean republic. George MacDonald Fraser's first novel, 'Flashman: From the Flashman Papers 1839–1842', was consistently reviewed as memoir or autobiography by historians who wanted to make it a basis for their understanding of the mid-Victorian Age.

Other noteworthy novels published in 1969 included Vladimir Nabokov's 'Ada, or Ardor: a Family Chronicle'; Jessamyn West's 'Except for Me and Thee', a companion to 'The Friendly Persua-

BOB PETERSON

JOHN BERRYMAN

ABBIE HOFFMAN

UPI COMPIX

PHIL MAC MULLAN

ROBERT LOWELL

JACQUELINE SUSANN

UPI COMPIX

sion'; Evan S. Connell's 'Mr. Bridge', a companion piece to his 'Mrs. Bridge'; Bernard Malamud's 'Pictures of Fidelman: an Exhibition', a picaresque novel, three of whose six episodes had appeared as short stories in 'The Magic Barrel' and 'Idiots First'; Davis Grubb's 'Fools' Parade'; Joyce Carol Oates's 'Them'; John Cheever's 'Bullet Park'; Kurt Vonnegut, Jr.'s 'Slaughterhouse-Five or The Children's Crusade'; and Leonard Gardner's first novel, 'Fat City'.

Among the significant English contributions to U.S. fiction reading were 'Bruno's Dream', by Iris Murdoch; 'The Military Philosophers', by Anthony Powell; 'The Four-Gated City', by Doris Lessing; 'I Want It Now', by Kingsley Amis; and 'The House on the Strand', by Daphne Du Maurier.

In the field of the short story, where quick sales have never been a consideration, the year saw the publication of 'The Collected Stories' of Jean Stafford; 'Nude Croquet', the collected stories of Leslie A. Fiedler; the posthumous 'A Set of Variations', by Frank O'Connor; James T. Farrell's 43d book, 'Childhood Is Not Forever', a collection of 16 stories, many written in the 1950's; and John O'Hara's 'The O'Hara Generation', 22 stories from previous collections. An edition of 'Seventeen Lost Stories by W. Somerset Maugham', compiled by Craig V. Showalter, also appeared.

American poetry had another good year. 'The Complete Poems' of Elizabeth Bishop appeared. New versions of John Crowe Ransom's 'Selected Poems' were also published, as were Robert Lowell's 'Notebook 1967–68', Richard Wilbur's 'Walking to Sleep', and another volume of Charles Olson's 'Maximus Poems'. Collections by younger poets included Robert Creeley's 'Pieces', LeRoi Jones's 'Black Magic Poetry 1961–1967', John Logan's 'The Zigzag Walk', Anne Sexton's 'Love Poems', X. J. Kennedy's 'Growing into Love', Lucien Stryk's 'The Pit and Other Poems', Allen Planz's 'A Night for Rioting', and David Steingass' 'Body Compass'. The 'Selected Letters of e. e. cummings' was also brought out.

Unrest in the Soviet Union

Meanwhile, in the Soviet Union, where sales are not a consideration for publication, intellectuals continued to be haunted by the convictions of Andrei D. Sinyavsky and Yuli M. Daniel in 1966, as well as the ideological disputes that a lessening of governmental censorship on literature was bound to make apparent. Sinyavsky and Daniel figured in the February trial of Ilya Burmistrovich, a mathematician. Burmistrovich was arrested in the spring of 1968 as he left the house of a typist carrying carbon copies of works by the two writers. He was suspected of being one of the major figures in the clandestine publishing of works officially deemed not suitable. His conviction meted him three years in prison. Similarly, the two writers figured in the arrest of Ivan A. Yakhimovich, a collective-farm chairman, who lost his job. Yakhimovich had protested the trial of the two. At Potma, the secret prison camp 250 miles east of Moscow where Daniel is a prisoner, it was variously reported that he and several other inmates had begun a hunger strike to gain the status of political prisoners, that he and five others had written a letter to the Supreme Soviet asking it to do something about prison camp conditions, and that he was going deaf. This last report was contained in 'My Testimony', an account of Soviet prison brutality written by Anatoli T. Marchenko.

Anatoli P. Kuznetsov, author of the controversial novel 'Babi Yar', found asylum in England during the summer and renounced all his previous work, claiming that it was ruined by political censorship. He planned to write under the name A. Anatol.

Nobel prizewinner Mikhail A. Sholokhov ran into trouble with the publication of his new novel 'They Fought for Their Country'. Soviet authorities were reported to have three main objections to the work: it was critical of Stalin's political and military leadership; it was too emphatic in describing the Soviet army's retreat before the German invaders in 1941 and 1942; and it contained uncomplimentary descriptions of life in Soviet prison camps during and after World War II.

Perhaps no book in the Soviet Union went so far to rehabilitate the reputation of Stalin as did Marshal Georgi K. Zhukov's memoirs. The Soviet Union's military commander in World War II portrays Stalin as an alert military strategist who was ready to listen to another person's argument. The work represents the fullest and most favorable account of Stalin to appear in the Soviet Union since 1956, when former Premier Nikita S. Khrushchev opened his anti-Stalin campaign. The book, portions of which were printed by Harper & Row to force the Soviet Union into joining international copyright agreements, was scheduled to appear in the West in 1970.

A newly discovered fragment of a play trilogy projected by the late Boris Pasternak was also published in 1969, first in Italy and later in the United States. The 20,000-word draft of the first part and a segment of the second part of the trilogy was entitled 'The Blind Beauty'. It agrees exactly with the description of the work given to the U.S. writer Olga Carlisle in a 1960 interview with the poet. He described the work then as a trilogy devoted to the abolition of serfdom and laid in 1840, 1860, and 1880 on an estate in the Russian countryside and in St. Petersburg.

Developments in Other Countries

In France, the posthumous 'Rigodon' by Louis Ferdinand Céline provoked excitement and a great deal of controversy. Famous for his novels of the 1930's, 'Journey to the End of Night' and 'Death on the Installment Plan', Céline began to lose favor because of his pro-Nazi sentiments in the late 1930's and early 1940's. Finished in 1961, the work completes the journey through a collapsed Nazi Germany begun with 'D'un Château L'Autre' and 'Nord' and reflects in part his own sympathies with fascism and the French Vichy government. The book affirms, with its vivid descriptions of both Nazi persecution and Allied destruction and its prophecy of the fall of European civilization to the Chinese and Africans, André Gide's description of him as a writer of hallucination rather than of reality. At the same time, in a lighter vein, 34-year-old Michel Bernard was establishing a reputation in erotic literature with the publication of 'Les Courtisanes' and 'La Négresse Muette'.

Greece's army-backed regime ordered Greek newspapers to devote a page a week for the next two and a half years to the printing of modern Greek literature. This new "State Anthology of Modern Greek Letters," selected on literary merit without political or ideological discrimination, included nine self-confessed Communists, nine leftists, and two antimilitarists. It was protested by 18 writers, including 8 literary award winners, who described themselves as "postwar Athenian writers." They charged the government with being "illiberal and oppressive" and complained that their works were being reprinted without their approval to give a false impression at home and abroad of intellectual freedom.

In West Germany, Saul Friedländer's 'Kurt Gerstein: the Ambiguity of Good' and Hans Adolph Jacobsen's 'Nationalsozialistische Aussenpolitik: 1933–1938' seemed to generate the most critical interest. And in Italy Elsa Morante, the talented former wife of novelist Alberto Moravia, surprised readers with her delightful 'Il mondo salvato dai ragazzini'. (*See* Awards and Prizes.)

LITERATURE, CANADIAN. Canadian poetry had a good year in 1969. Phyllis Gotlieb published a new book of verse, 'Ordinary, Moving', as did Tom Marshall with 'The Silence of Fire'. The prolific Irving Layton wrote 'The Whole Bloody Bird', a volume that contained a potpourri of prose observations and a collection of pithy aphorisms, as well as verse. Ralph Barker Gustafson published 'Ixion's Wheel', and Raymond Souster was represented with 'So Far So Good'. The poems in Alden A. Nowlan's 'The Mysterious Naked Man' relied on the poet's experiences and were characterized by a leisurely, conversational pace. Gwendolyn MacEwen explored the world of dreams and nightmares in 'The Shadow Maker'. George Bowering produced 'The Gangs of Kosmos' and 'Rocky Mountain Foot', the latter about Alberta.

There was an abundant supply of fiction in 1969. One of the better books was Margaret Atwood's 'The Edible Woman', which showed what can happen when a consumer identifies herself with the things consumed. Phyllis Gotlieb wrote 'Why Should I Have All the Grief?', in which the central character nightly relives the horrors of Auschwitz, in Poland, and other frightening experiences. Margaret Laurence's 'The Fire Dwellers' is concerned with the verbal exchanges between a husband and his wife in lower-middle-class Vancouver, B.C. David Helwig added to a growing reputation as a story writer with 'The Streets of Summer', and Ray Smith brought out a collection of short stories called 'Cape Breton Is the Thought-Control Centre of Canada'. Other fiction of note included 'The House of Hate', by Percy Janes and 'The Lonely Ones', by James Bacque.

Among the leading nonfiction books in 1969 were George M. Grant's 'Technology and Empire: Perspectives on North America' and Tim Reid's 'Student Power and the Campus'. Patrick Watson's 'Conspirators in Silence' is an account of the Canadian school system, mass media, and political life, and Ramsay Cook's 'French-Canadian Nationalism', a collection of 25 essays that deal with the current dissent in French Canada.

Two books on the Canadian Indian appeared: 'Without Reserve' by Sheila Burnford, about the Cree and Ojibwa of northern Ontario, and 'Potlatch', by George C. Clutesi, about the Indians of British Columbia. The author of the second book was himself a Vancouver Island Indian.

The year was a notable one for the production of children's books. A few of the better ones were 'The Mountain Goats of Temlaham' and 'How Summer Came to Canada', by William Toye; 'The Blind Boy and the Loon', by Ramona Maker; 'A Walk Out of the World', by Ruth Nichols; and 'The Last Voyage of the Unicorn', by Delbert A. Young.

Significant novels in the French language included 'La fille de Christophe Colomb', by Réjean Ducharge; 'Les Voyageurs sacrés' and 'Vivre! Vivre!' by Marie-Claire Blais; 'Le Ciel de Québec' by Jacques Ferron; and 'Tayaout' by Yves Thériault. Poetry was represented by: 'Les Seins gorgés', by Gemma Tremblay; 'Saison pour la continuelle', by Jean-Guy Pilon; 'Soleil de Bivouac', by Pierre Chatillon; 'Sens unique', by André Saint-Germain; and 'Poèmes pour durer', by André Major.

In the literary-essay field, Jacques Brunet published 'Albert Laberge, sa vie, son oeuvre', and Raymond Joly brought out 'Deux études sur la préhistoire du surréalisme'. Among histories, Antoine Champagne's 'Les La Vérendryes et le Poste de l'Ouest' was noteworthy. (*See also* Literature. *See in* CE: Canadian Literature.)

LITERATURE, CHILDREN'S. Books for young people in 1969 reflected a wide range of current national and international concerns. They included Alvin Schwartz's 'University', which dealt with the issues underlying student unrest on college campuses; Joanne Friedlander's and Jean Neal's 'Stock Market ABC', for young investors; and Arnold Shaw's 'The Rock Revolution', a history of the rock 'n' roll movement in music.

Books about minority groups and the civil rights struggle continued to appear. Among the best

Among the best books about black people for young readers was 18-year-old John Steptoe's poignant story 'Stevie', written in ghetto English with illustrations by the author.

books about black people were John Steptoe's moving story 'Stevie' and Tom Cohen's 'Three Who Dared'. Problems facing Puerto Ricans were examined in 'Puerto Ricans; From Island to Mainland', by Arlene Kurtis; and the plight of American Indians caught between cultures was treated in 'Our Cup Is Broken', by Florence Crannell Means.

American history was also a popular subject. 'Tom Paine, Revolutionary', by Olivia Coolidge, was an excellent biography; 'Home and Child Life in Colonial Days', by Alice Morse Earle, vividly told of the early settlers' life from a child's viewpoint. The role of France in early America was well presented in 'The American Revolution: the French Allies', by Robin McKown.

Science and Sex Education

Another continuing trend was the profusion of science books for young people of all ages. Prominent among them were Nancy Rosenberg's and R. K. Snyderman's 'New Parts for People', a survey of organ transplants; Robert Gray's 'The Great Apes', relating observations in the field; and Denise Royal's 'The Story of J. Robert Oppenheimer', a biography that also tells the story of the atomic bomb's development with unusual clarity. Texts and photographs were exceptionally well coordinated in Carla Stevens' 'The Birth of Sunset's Kittens' and in Geraldine Lux Flanagan's 'Window into an Egg', which recorded in detail a chick's gestation.

Notable among books on sex education were 'A Baby Starts to Grow', by Paul Showers, and, for older children, 'The Human Story', by Sadie Hofstein. One series of books included 'Families Live Together', 'How New Life Begins', and 'The World of Living Things', by Esther Meeks and Elizabeth Bagwell, and 'Living Things and Their Young', 'How We Are Born', and 'Man and Woman', by Julian May. Kathleen Elgin's 'The Human Body: The Female Reproductive System' and 'The Human Body: The Male Reproductive System' present factual discussions in scientific terminology. 'Girls and Sex', by Wardell Pomeroy, is unusually frank and comprehensive.

Fiction, Poetry, Fantasy, and Humor

Much of the best fiction had foreign settings. Kitty Barne's 'Barbie' was set in England; Yoshiko Uchida's 'Hisako's Mysteries', in Japan; Mary Stolz's 'The Dragons of the Queen', in Mexico; and Joseph Krumgold's 'The Most Terrible Turk', in modern Turkey. Also outstanding were two stories about World War II—Colette Vivier's 'The House of the Four Winds', about the Parisian resistance, and Elliott Arnold's 'A Kind of Secret Weapon', set in Denmark.

Growing understanding—both of the self and of others—is memorably treated in 'A Girl Called Al', by Constance C. Greene; 'Portrait of Ivan', by Paula Fox; and 'Thy Friend, Obadiah', Brinton Turkle's tale of a Quaker boy. 'The Cay', by

Meindert DeJong won the National Book Award for children's literature with 'Journey from Peppermint Street'.
MARVIN LANNINGA

Theodore Taylor, is a powerful story about a blind boy and an old Negro man marooned on an island.

Among the year's distinguished anthologies of poetry were 'Some Haystacks Don't Even Have Any Needle', compiled by Stephen Dunning and others; 'A Book of Nature Poems', edited by William Cole; June Jordan's 'Who Look at Me'; and 'Come Along!', by Rebecca Caudill.

Notable tales of fantasy were Margaret Mahy's 'A Lion in the Meadow'; Mary Knight's 'The Fox That Wanted Nine Golden Tails'; Ursula Moray Williams' 'The Toymaker's Daughter'; and, for older children, Peter Dickinson's 'The Weathermonger'. Humor dominates 'Archimedes Takes a Bath', by Joan Lexau; 'Contrary Jenkins', by Rebecca Caudill and James Ayars; 'Ghost in a Four-Room Apartment', by Ellen Raskin; and 'Porko von Popbutton', by William Pène du Bois. William Steig's 'Sylvester and the Magic Pebble' is a nonsense story for picture-book readers.

Awards

In 1969, for the first time, a National Book Award was made for a children's book. The winner was Meindert DeJong, for 'Journey from Peppermint Street'. The Caldecott Medal was won by Uri Shulevitz for his illustrations in 'The Fool of the World and the Flying Ship'. Lloyd Alexander was given the John Newbery Medal for 'The High King'.

Great Britain's Library Association awarded the Kate Greenaway Medal to Pauline Baynes for her ilustrations in 'A Dictionary of Chivalry', and the Carnegie Medal for literary merit went to Rosemary Harris for 'The Moon in the Cloud'. The Canadian Library Association's award for distinguished writing went to Kay Hill for 'And Tomorrow the Stars', a biography of John Cabot. (*See also* Literature. *See in* CE: Literature, Children's; Literary Awards.)

LUXEMBURG.

Pierre Werner of the Christian Socialist party again took the office of prime minister of Luxemburg under the Christian Socialist-Liberal coalition formed early in 1969. In the new government the Christian Socialists held four cabinet posts and the Liberals held three. Eugène Schaus, a Liberal, was deputy prime minister.

The old Christian Socialist-Socialist coalition was dissolved in October 1968 after a disagreement involving Socialist trade union demands for wage increases and welfare benefits. After elections Grand Duke Jean asked Werner to join his party with the Liberals. In the elections the Christian Socialists went from 22 to 21 parliamentary seats; the Socialists from 21 to 18; the Liberals from 6 to 11; and the Communists from 5 to 6. The one splinter group lost its representation.

The new government's policies included measures to stimulate the economy through new employment facilities and new industries, restrictions on state debts, and worker participation in state-controlled enterprises. The 1968 estimated gross national product, second largest among states in the European Economic Community, or Common Market, rose to $766 million. Per-capita income increased to $2,280—up $100—and the growth rate reached 4% in 1968.

The Benelux economic union (Belgium, Netherlands, Luxemburg) agreed in 1969 to abolish virtually all border controls by November 1970. Excise taxes, methods of collection, public administration, and judicial practices were to be closely coordinated. The governments also were to bring into line their short- and medium-term economic policies as well as social, transport, tourist, and industrial policies. (*See in* CE: Luxemburg.)

MAGAZINES.

Predicting that "the next decade will be a time of magazine resurgence," the chairman of Time Inc. set the tone for magazines in 1969. With few exceptions, optimism reigned. Publishers forecast a 6% revenue increase for the year and noted a 73% revenue gain over the preceding ten years. Odds for success seemed increasingly assured, particularly for the editor who geared his publication to a small, involved readership.

The few remaining champions of mass magazines suffered a severe setback with the death of the 148-year-old *Saturday Evening Post* in February. Failure to find a loyal audience, coupled with rising costs and loss of advertising, proved an irresolvable problem. The end of one of the most honored names in magazines haunted other general, mass-appeal publications. Either slipping or showing unspectacular revenue gains, *Life, Time, Look, McCall's, Ladies' Home Journal,* and *Good Housekeeping* searched for different approaches.

In May, *Life* appointed a new managing editor, Ralph A. Graves, and began to stress personalized journalism, social issues, and even antiestablishment exposés. Losing ground to *Newsweek, Time* named a new top command in August, reversed

"THE SATURDAY EVENING POST"

WIDE WORLD

The Feb. 8, 1969, edition of *The Saturday Evening Post* (above) was its last issue. *The Post* ceased to be profitable despite attempts by its editor, William A. Emerson, Jr. (right), and its president, Martin S. Ackerman, to make the magazine attractive to a more sophisticated audience.

itself on the Vietnam conflict, curbed the notorious "Timestyle," and tried to shake its relatively conservative image. In its September 23 issue *Look* accused the mayor of San Francisco, Calif., Joseph L. Alioto, of Mafia involvement and gained national publicity when he denied the charges and sued the magazine for $12.5 million. *McCall's* made Shana Alexander its first female editor in 48 years. *This Week,* a Sunday newspaper supplement, decided that its November 2 issue would be the last.

A writer for *Mediascope* observed in the May issue that economic control of the periodical press by advertisers not only could kill a magazine but also could threaten freedom of the press. Claiming that 90% of the gross income of larger magazines came from advertising, he asserted that the editorial staff had lost control of editorial content.

At the 50th-anniversary meeting of the Magazine Publishers Association, warnings were sounded that readers' social and political attitudes were as important as, if not more so than, technological and advertising matters. The success of revised or new magazines such as *Psychology Today, Redbook, Field and Stream,* and *Rotarian* emphasized the need to satisfy readers first, advertisers second. (*See also* Newspapers. *See in* CE: Magazines.)

MALAGASY REPUBLIC. The most important investment contract ever made in the Malagasy Republic was canceled in 1969. In September the government ended a 1967 agreement with a French financial consortium headed by Jacques Mimran. The agreement had granted the firm a number of commercial monopolies in return for development of timber resources in the northeastern section of the country.

The cancellation followed the publication of a tract called "Ten Years of the Malagasy Republic," which laid serious charges against the regime of President Philibert Tsiranana and criticized the Mimran investments. Several arrests were made after the tract was published.

In July the president discussed private and government investments with the premier of France and in April held talks on African policy with the president of Malawi. (*See also* Africa. *See in* CE: Malagasy Republic.)

MALAWI. During 1969 Malawi remained isolated in sentiment from other black African nations. President H. Kamuzu Banda was openly in disagreement with the nationalist opinions of other black African leaders. In April a manifesto condemning the white-minority regimes in southern Africa was adopted at the annual conference of eastern and central African leaders. Malawi, however, would not support the manifesto.

On July 8 President Banda announced plans for road improvements and a new railroad to link Malawi with Rhodesia and Mozambique. South Africa contributed $11 million toward financing the railroad.

The ruling Congress party on September 6 passed a resolution asking all U.S. Peace Corps volunteers to leave Malawi within 18 months. In the resolution the volunteers were accused of bad conduct, which the government felt had an adverse effect on Malawian children. (*See also* Peace Corps. *See in* CE: Malawi.)

UPI COMPIX

Malaysia's Prime Minister Tunku Abdul Rahman (right) talks to newsmen after a week of racial violence between Chinese and Malay citizens. He announced various measures to deal with the crisis.

MALAYSIA. On May 13, 1969, Malaysia was shaken by unprecedented racial disturbances. Official figures gave the number killed as 196, including 123 Chinese, 22 Malays, and 12 Indians. Another 439 were injured and six months later 39 people were still missing. Suspension of constitutional government followed the proclamation of a state of emergency throughout the country. A national operations council with near-dictatorial powers was set up with the deputy prime minister, Tun Abdul Razak bin Hussein, as director of operations. A caretaker cabinet was also set up.

The racial violence followed the general election in which the Alliance party, made up of a coalition of the United Malays National Organization, the Malaysian Chinese Association, and the Malaysian Indian Congress, fared badly in contrast to their landslide victory in 1964. The party won 66 parliamentary seats and 10 seats in Sabah state on election day, giving it a simple majority in the 144-member House of Representatives. Because of the declaration of emergency the remaining elections were suspended leaving 24 seats in Sarawak state, 6 in Sabah, and one in Malacca state still to be decided.

The Communist threat continued throughout the year, and Malaysia decided to raise another nine battalions. In November 1968 the government published a white paper called "The Path of Violence to Absolute Power," which described the threat posed by the Malaysian Communist party and its United Front to the security and public order of the country. This coincided with the arrest of 116 Communist militants in a surprise sweep throughout Malaysia. The white paper quoted extensively from captured Communist documents to show that the Communist United Front had abandoned the parliamentary struggle and that the Malaysian Communist party intended to return to its armed struggle. (*See in* CE: Malaysia.)

MALDIVES, REPUBLIC OF. The United Nations reported in April 1969 that its smallest member, the Maldive Islands, had changed its name to Republic of Maldives. It became a republic Nov. 11, 1968, with Ibrahim Nasir as president.

Although the economy, based on fishing and farming, continued largely at a subsistence level, trade improved. Early 1969 reports showed a favorable balance of trade for 1968.

Great Britain continued to develop Gan Island as a Royal Air Force staging post and military communications center. There were about 560 troops and 40 civilians on the island. Flights between Singapore and Great Britain handled an average of 7,000 passengers and one million pounds of cargo

Malaysians in the capital city of Kuala Lumpur line up to buy food supplies. Many families had been unable to move outdoors since the fighting began.

UPI COMPIX

a month. The island was also in use for meteorological purposes and as a ground station for the Skynet satellite communications system, which was in the final stages of development in 1969. (*See in* CE: Maldive Islands.)

MALI. Three ministerial reshuffles and an abortive coup d'etat on August 12 were evidence of the instability that persisted in Mali throughout 1969. Those responsible for the conspiracy uncovered by the military junta were political friends of the former president, Modibo Keita, who was under detention awaiting trial.

During September the divisions within Mali's new leadership were brought into the open. In the first place, Capt. Yoro Diakité, then president of the military-controlled National Liberation Committee, expelled Jean-Marie Koné, minister of state for foreign affairs, from the government. Some days later, deciding to put an end to a two-headed regime, Lieut. Moussa Traore in turn ousted Captain Diakité, who was allowed to remain in the cabinet as minister of transport, telecommunications, and tourism.

In June Mauritania and Mali held boundary discussions. (*See in* CE: Mali.)

MALTA. Expanded tourism and an unprecedented building boom contributed to continued prosperity as Malta entered its third five-year plan in 1969. The upsurge in the construction industry was due largely to an influx of new residents, mostly British, who were attracted by income tax advantages and the fine climate. Rising employment and a rising standard of living continued.

The 1969–70 budget called for an investment program of some $32 million, about half to come from loans and grants from Great Britain. The funds were withheld pending negotiations on the distribution of the loans and grants. A 225-acre industrial complex was started in Malta in 1969. The government approved a development plan for Gozo island.

Prince Charles of Great Britain visited in November. He opened a new campus as the University of Malta celebrated its 200th anniversary. (*See in* CE: Malta.)

MARRIAGES. Famous individuals who were married in 1969 included the following:

The Aga Khan IV, Prince Karim, 31, spiritual leader of the world's 15 million Ismaili Muslims, to Sarah Croker Poole, 29; October 21, in a civil ceremony in Paris, France, followed by a Muslim religious ceremony a week later.

Leslie Caron, 37, French actress ('Gigi', 'The L-Shaped Room'), to Michael Laughlin, 29, U.S. movie producer ('Joanna'); January 1, in Jamaica.

Josephine Chaplin, 20, daughter of famed U.S. expatriate comedian Charlie Chaplin, to Nicolas Sistovaris, 31, Greek businessman; June 21, in Corsier-Sur-Vevey, Switzerland.

KEYSTONE

CENTRAL PRESS FROM PICTORIAL PARADE

Beatle John Lennon and his bride, Yoko Ono (top), hold a press conference during their honeymoon "love-in" for peace. Another Beatle, Paul McCartney, and his American bride, Linda Eastman (above), fight crowds after their wedding ceremony.

Leo Durocher, 62, manager of the Chicago Cubs baseball team, to Lynne Walker Goldblatt, 40; June 19, in Chicago, Ill.

Orval E. Faubus, 59, former Democratic governor of Arkansas, to Elizabeth Westmoreland, 30; March 22, in Little Rock, Ark.

Major Gen. Yakubu Gowon, 34, head of Nigeria's military regime, to Victoria Zakari, 23; April 19, during the civil war with secessionist Biafra, in Lagos, Nigeria.

WIDE WORLD

UPI COMPIX

Among the year's marriages in the world of sports were those of (top) retired baseball pitcher Sandy Koufax and Anne Heath Widmark and (above) the manager of the Chicago Cubs baseball team, Leo Durocher, and Lynne Walker Goldblatt.

"LONDON DAILY EXPRESS" FROM PICTORIAL PARADE

Screen star Audrey Hepburn and Italian psychiatrist Andrea Dotti smile happily after their wedding.

Arlo Guthrie, 22, son of U.S. folk singer Woody Guthrie and a singer and composer in his own right ('Alice's Restaurant'), to Jackie Hyde, 24; October 9, in Washington, Mass.

Audrey Hepburn, 39, screen star, to Andrea Dotti, 30, Italian psychiatrist; January 18, in Morges, Switzerland.

Dame Zara Holt, 54, widow of Australia's Prime Minister Harold E. Holt, to Jeffrey Bate, 62, member of Australia's House of Representatives; February 19, in Melbourne, Australia.

Herbert Buckingham Khaury (Tiny Tim), falsetto-voiced singer and television personality, 37(?), to Victoria May Budinger (Miss Vicki), 17; December 17, in a televised ceremony watched by some 20 million U.S. viewers.

Sandy Koufax, 33, retired baseball star, now television sportscaster, to Anne Heath Widmark, 23, daughter of actor Richard Widmark; January 1, in West Hollywood, Calif.

John Lennon, 28, of the Beatles, to Yoko Ono, 36, Japanese artist; March 20, in Gibraltar.

Marie McDonald McLaughlin Lawrie ("Lulu"), 20, British popular singer, to Maurice Gibb, 19, member of the Bee Gees singing group; February 18, in Gerrard's Cross, England.

Paul McCartney, 26, of the Beatles, to Linda Eastman, 27; March 12, in London, England.

Major Gen. Yakubu Gowon, head of Nigeria's military regime, and his bride, the former Victoria Zakari, pose after their marriage at Christ Church Cathedral in Lagos.

UPI COMPIX

Sir William David Ormsby-Gore, Lord Harlech, former British ambassador to the United States, 51, to Pamela T. Colin, 33, previously London editor of *Vogue* magazine; December 11, in London, England.

Adam Clayton Powell III, 22, television news producer and son of Representative Adam Clayton Powell, Jr., (D, N.Y.), to Beryl Gillespie Slocum,

UPI COMPIX

The year's happy couples included (above) Herbert Khaury (Tiny Tim) and "Miss Vicki" and (below) Marie McDonald McLaughlin Lawrie ("Lulu") and Maurice Gibb.

FOX PHOTOS LTD. FROM PICTORIAL PARADE

26, novelist and poet; May 30, in Washington, D.C.

The Most Rev. James P. Shannon, 48, previously Roman Catholic Auxiliary Bishop of the Archdiocese of St. Paul-Minneapolis, Minn., to Ruth Wilkinson, 50; August 2, in Endicott, N.Y.

Natalie Wood, 30, screen star, to Richard Gregson, 39, British agent and producer; May 30, in Los Angeles, Calif.

UPI (UK) LTD.

The Aga Khan IV, Prince Karim, and Sarah Croker Poole sit silently with downcast eyes as tradition requires during their Muslim wedding ceremony on October 28.

MATHEMATICS. In 1969 'The Mathematical Sciences: a Collection of Essays' was published under the auspices of the Committee on Support of Research in the Mathematical Sciences (COSRIMS) of the National Academy of Sciences-National Research Council. The volume was edited by COSRIMS in collaboration with George A. W. Boehm. This work followed 'The Mathematical Sciences: a Report', published by COSRIMS in November 1968.

The purpose of the collection was to help provide clear, accurate information and ideas about mathematics for the intelligent layman. One essay, for example, provides a nontechnical explanation of current mathematical ideas about the nature of infinity.

One book reviewer called the collection of essays "probably the best book on higher mathematics ever written." He recommended the book especially to Congressmen and other public officials who have the power to allocate funds for research and education in mathematics.

Despite some signs of a leveling in the growth of mathematics, the problem of keeping informed remained a serious one for mathematicians. There was widespread feeling that new methods of communication were needed to help mathematicians keep up with the latest developments. The American Mathematical Society launched the experimental Mathematical Offprint Service. Subscribers placed a standing order for reprints in fields that interested them. By a scheme intended ultimately to be automatic, journals were scanned and orders filled. Some subscribers received reprints even before the journal was published.

Children's Attitudes Toward Mathematics

A study published in 1969 discussed children's attitudes, ideas, and feelings about the study of mathematics in school. The University of Minnesota at Duluth polled 497 children in grades three through six. The teachers of these children were selected through the university's Experienced Teacher Fellowship Program in science and mathematics for elementary teachers.

When asked to name the source of most of their ideas about science and math, 41% of the children selected their textbooks; 42%, their teachers; and 17%, class discussion. Some 37% of the children agreed that they needed more practice in mathematics.

On the crucial question of liking math, 78.8% said they did and only 21.2% said they did not. (To preserve anonymity the children had not been asked to sign their names to the questionnaire.) Only 55.5% said they usually knew why they did math problems in a certain way. Fully 42.3% thought their teachers did not care if they knew the "why" as long as they could work the problem correctly. (*See in* CE: Mathematics.)

MAURITANIA.

The Islamic Summit Conference held in Rabat, Morocco, in September 1969 was an important event for Mauritania. Nine years after its proclamation of independence and its entry into the United Nations Mauritania finally made a significant appearance on the international scene. A normalization of relations between Mauritania and Morocco was in progress during the year.

On June 27 an agreement was signed with the European Investment Bank for a loan of $2.75 million for enlarging the wharf installations at Nouakchott, the capital. A trade agreement with the Republic of Congo (Brazzaville) was signed in September.

President William V. S. Tubman of Liberia visited Mauritania in March and signed a treaty of cooperation and a cultural agreement providing for student exchanges. Mauritania and Mali held discussions in June to settle the delineation of their common boundary, which had been a source of conflict between them. (*See in* CE: Mauritania.)

MAURITIUS.

The premier of Mauritius, Sir Seewoosagur Ramgoolam, remained in power in 1969 despite the resignation of five cabinet ministers. The move, announced on March 12, the first anniversary of Mauritius' independence, threatened for a time to break up the ruling party.

Economic problems persisted. The population was increasing at 3% a year, while unemployment rose and emigration diminished.

The possibility of British entry into the European Economic Community, or Common Market, posed a threat of loss of stable markets. (Great Britain in 1969 bought 75% of the nation's sugar crop, which comprises 95% of Mauritius' exports.) This threat, plus agitation for nationalization, spurred efforts to diversify the economy. Tea, tobacco, rice, potatoes, vegetables, and tourism were explored for possible expansion. Through British assistance fisheries and secondary industries were also developed. (*See in* CE: Mauritius.)

MEDICINE.

New disease-preventing vaccines, automated devices to replace limbs or help in medical diagnosis, and the rising role of genetics in medical research were some of the highlights of medicine in 1969. Also, strides were made toward inception of national health insurance in the United States. This was a policy of other industrial nations but had long been unpopular with the U.S. health establishment.

More Vaccines Available

A German measles (rubella) vaccine was licensed for public use in June. By year's end some 8 million schoolchildren had received the vaccine.

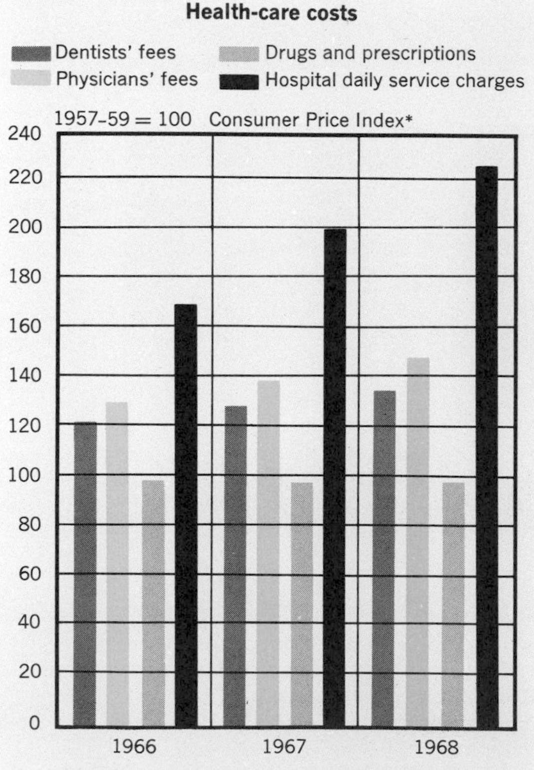

*Measures relative price change in overall consumer prices; does not represent dollars.
Source: Department of Labor. Bureau of Labor Statistics. *Price Indexes for Selected Items and Groups, Annual Averages.*

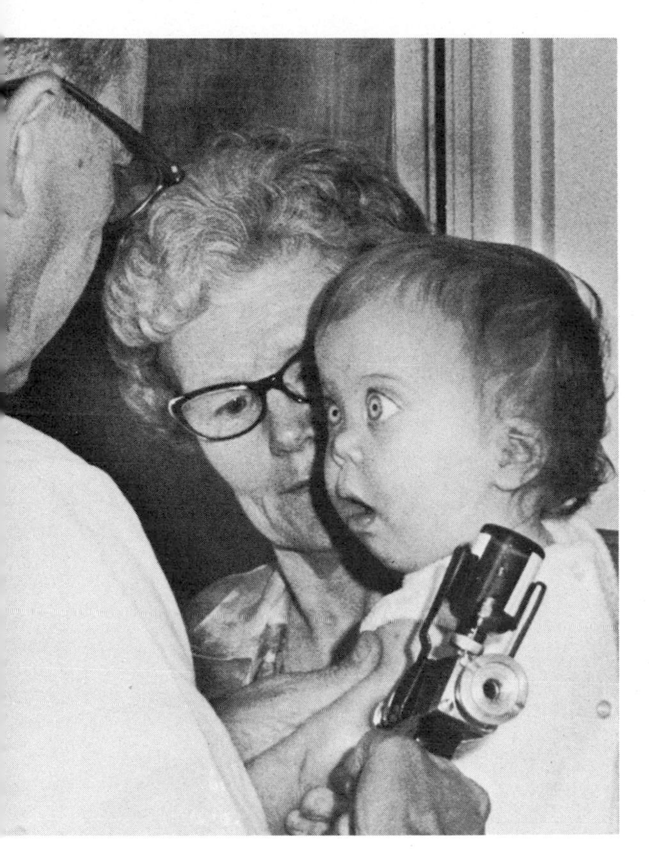

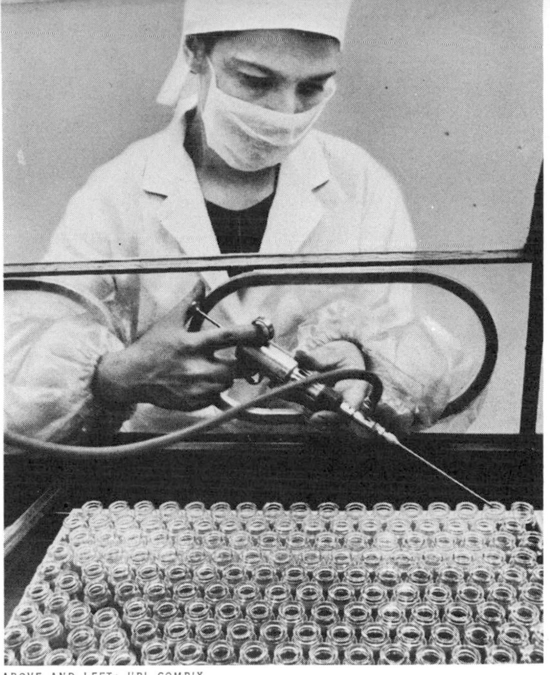

ABOVE AND LEFT: UPI COMPIX

Vials of "Cendehill," a new rubella (German measles) vaccine, are filled at a factory near Brussels, Belgium (above). The vaccine, grown in primary rabbit kidney tissue, was first licensed for use by health authorities in Switzerland. Although she obviously does not approve of the idea, a wide-eyed young lady (left) receives an injection of measles vaccine. She was one of the children who were given the vaccine at a clinic conducted by the Milford (Conn.) Department of Health.

By late 1970 an estimated 20 million children would be protected against the disease. The vaccine was actually more important to the unborn. Although the rubella virus caused only a mild ailment in children, it could be quite injurious to fetuses in the first three months of their development, damaging eyes, ears, and hearts. During the 1964–65 rubella epidemic an estimated 20,000 children were born with virus-caused defects. In addition, some 30,000 fetal deaths were attributed to the virus.

An anticholera vaccine under development at Johns Hopkins University, Baltimore, Md., was more effective in tests than any in present use. Cholera was still a disease to cope with, since it killed thousands of Asians each year.

Other potentially valuable vaccines on trial in 1969 included those against spinal meningitis, snakebite, and syphilis. A vaccine was also being prepared to fight infection by pseudomonas bacteria, a prime killer of burn victims.

A "tailor-made" vaccine against Hong Kong flu, an unexpected influenza variant that struck the United States in 1968 and early 1969, was available in massive amounts by the start of the year. The epidemic reached its peak during the week ending January 11, when 1,151 deaths attributed to the disease occurred in major U.S. cities.

Medical Engineering

The first encouraging signs of developing artificial sight for the totally blind through "skin sensing" were reported in 1969. Biophysicists constructed a "tactile television" device that enabled a blind person with a portable TV camera to sense the outline of large letters and objects on the skin of the back. Visual images received by the TV camera were changed into electrical impulses that activated numerous vibrators in a backpack worn by the blind subject. The vibrators, in effect, traced out the TV image on the back of the subject.

A Dartmouth Medical School scientist programmed a computer to act like a lung, manifesting all the variations of breathing exhibited during different disorders. Thus, if a physician wanted to know what a patient's abnormal breathing signaled, he would need only to consult with the computer.

Bioengineers developed other clinically useful automated devices. One was an artificial hand controlled by the patient by means of nerve impulses. It could be fitted only hours after amputation. Another was a system of electronic sensors that could monitor fetal heart rate and other functions. When in hospital use these sensors were predicted to reduce the need for cesarean birth by 75%.

Leprosy patients and some diabetics often felt neither touch nor pain because their tactile tissue was destroyed. As a result they frequently put too much pressure on parts of their bodies, such as the hands and feet, and damaged those areas. Workers at the Southwest Research Institute, San Antonio,

Tex., devised a special dye-filled fabric capable of showing which body parts were subjected to damaging pressure. For example, if excessive pressure was used in grasping tools, special gloves with tiny dye-containing capsules in the fabric would indicate this by turning red.

Medical Costs Up

During 1968 total health-care costs in the United States were $45.9 billion. Medical costs, in fact, had risen at a rate twice that of the general cost of living. Much of the money went for health-worker salaries, hospital-care costs, and physicians' fees.

The Committee for National Health Insurance (CNHI), a private group of labor union, health, and civil rights leaders, proposed a national system of compulsory health insurance. The insurance scheme, similar to medicare in scope, would be financed by employers and employees as well as by public and private contributions. According to the plan espoused by the CNHI, patients could choose their own physicians.

Lightweight, yet sturdy and rigid, the Greene Rescue and Transport Splint was produced by Allendon Industries for use in removing injured persons from hard-to-reach locations.

COURTESY, ALLENDON INDUSTRIES

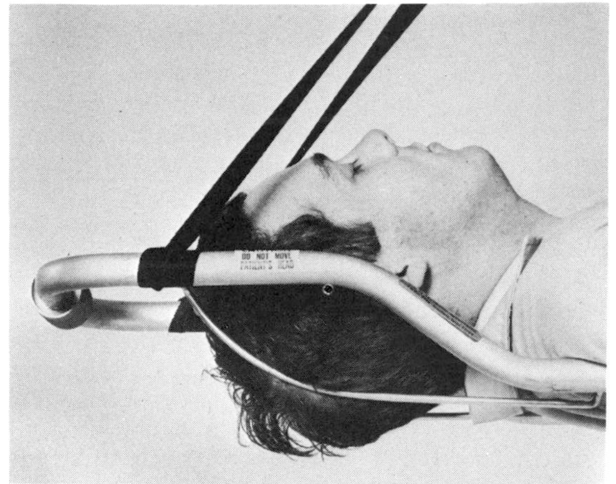

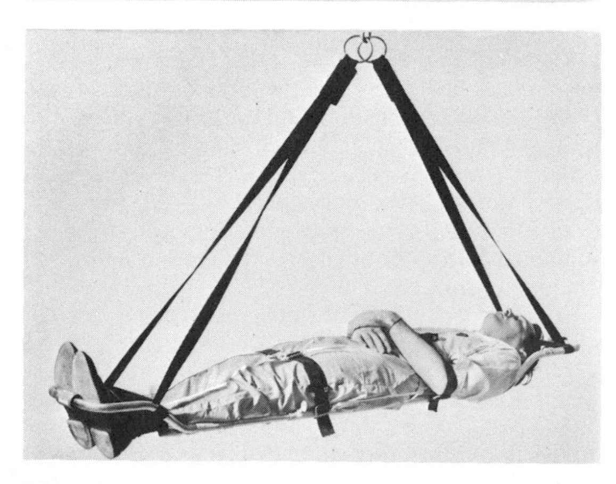

UPI COMPIX

Protesting American Medical Association policies, Richard Kunnes, a New York psychiatrist, remains seated as delegates sing the national anthem at the opening of the organization's national convention.

Diabetes Research Intensified

Recent diabetes research uncovered some enlightening facets of the disease. In one set of experiments, mice injected with a virus of the poliomyelitis group developed abnormalities of sugar metabolism, as in diabetes mellitus. Doctors had long known that diabetes sometimes followed a case of mumps when the mumps virus attacked the pancreas. New clinical evidence suggested that one of the Coxsackie group of viruses might somehow be responsible for diabetes.

Other factors continued to be noted in diabetes. Statistics showed that one in three of the poor had diabetes while only one in eight of those earning more than $10,000 a year contracted the disease. These figures supported previous theories that a diet containing excessive carbohydrates was sometimes responsible for diabetes.

Culminating thirty years of work, Nobel laureate Dorothy C. Hodgkin and her English colleagues at Oxford University used X-ray crystallography to determine the double-chained structure of insulin. Insulin became the first hormone whose shape was definitely known. The feat opened the way for studies on how insulin worked in the body, necessary for a complete understanding of diabetes. (*See* Chemistry.)

Concern for the Unborn

Birth defects through genetic disorders had become one of the leading causes of infant death or disability. Scientists who studied birth defects were giving special attention to early discovery of faulty fetal development. One technique for locating prebirth defects was called amniography. This process entailed X-raying a pregnant woman to procure pictures of the amniotic fluid in the womb and of the condition of the placenta, or "afterbirth." Another method of prenatal diagnosis was called amniocentesis. It involved taking a small amount of amniotic fluid by hypodermic needle. Then, fetal cells awash in the fluid could be analyzed for chromosome disorder or for the presence of a harmful virus, such as the rubella virus.

Geneticists were hopeful that sophisticated techniques of fetal examination would eventually serve as a basis for terminating pregnancies when irreversible disorders were discovered. In the meantime, there were many legal restrictions against abortion that precluded such procedures. Also, "genetic engineering" would hopefully correct fetal disorders once discovered by altering the biochemical makeup of the aberrant cells.

Medicine had help for the elderly as well as for the very young in 1969. For the aged it was found that oxygen therapy could temporarily subdue the effects of senility. The mental disintegration characterizing senility was generally blamed on the inability of atherosclerosis-narrowed blood vessels to supply the brain with sufficient oxygen. By saturating the aging patient with oxygen in a high-pressure chamber, many of the symptoms of senility could be relieved.

Nutrition and Other Medical Concerns

Starvation as a treatment for obesity came under criticism in 1969. Reports of sudden deaths of patients undergoing total starvation were noted. It appeared that loss of body protein damaged muscle fibers, particularly those of the heart. Total starvation seemed to offer no substantial advantage over 300- to 500-calorie diets as a treatment for overweight.

A physician feeling discomfort after a Chinese meal apparently stumbled upon a new disorder, the "Chinese restaurant syndrome." The disorder was marked by short-lived sensations in the neck and chest, tightness of the facial muscles, and a feeling of faintness. The culprit appeared to be monosodium glutamate (MSG), a food additive. As little as three grams of MSG could make some persons ill. No serious or lasting effects were reported, however.

Rumors of oral contraceptives' causing cancer of the cervix received some public credence. However, a 1969 report indicated that no direct relationship between the "pill" and cancer had been found, though "precancerous" changes in the uterus were found in some users of oral contraceptives.

For the first time since 1948 a new medical specialty was recognized. Called "family medicine," the specialty would train supergeneral practitioners, schooled in psychology, sociology, and other behavioral sciences. Family medicine was established to induce young physicians into general practice, on the wane in city and country.

CANCER

An estimated 325,000 persons in the United States died of cancer in 1969. Only heart disease killed more. Lung cancer was the major type of cancer death, resulting in about 59,000 annual fatalities. The American Cancer Society pointed out that, of all types of cancer, lung cancer seemed the most easily prevented. Many cases of lung cancer were attributed to cigarette smoking.

Dr. Nicholas R. Di Luzio (below) and his associates at Tulane University School of Medicine, in New Orleans, La., formed one of many teams that sought improved means of combating the body's tendency to reject transplanted tissues.

DENIS CIPNIC

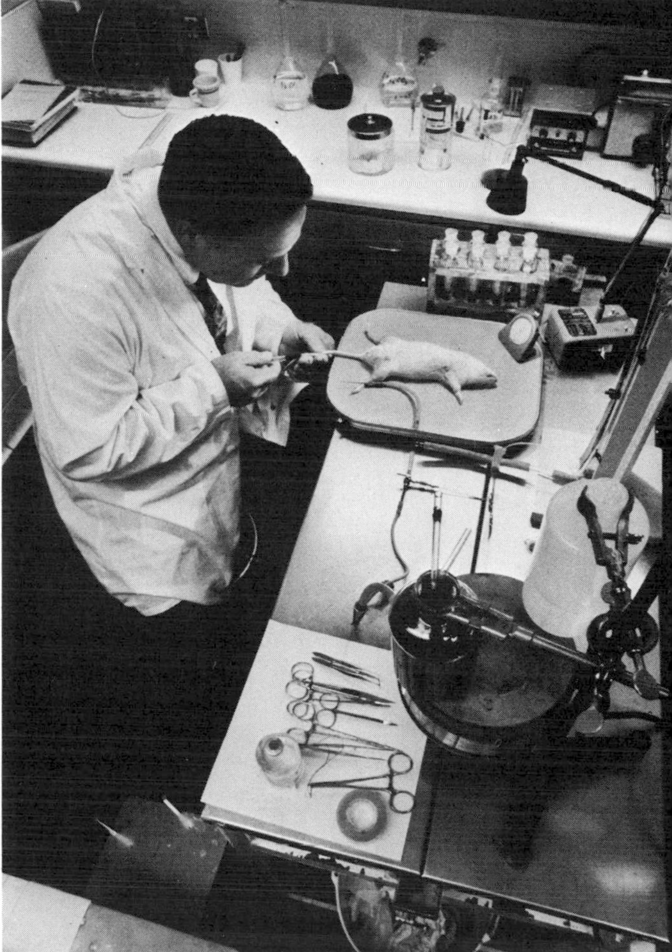

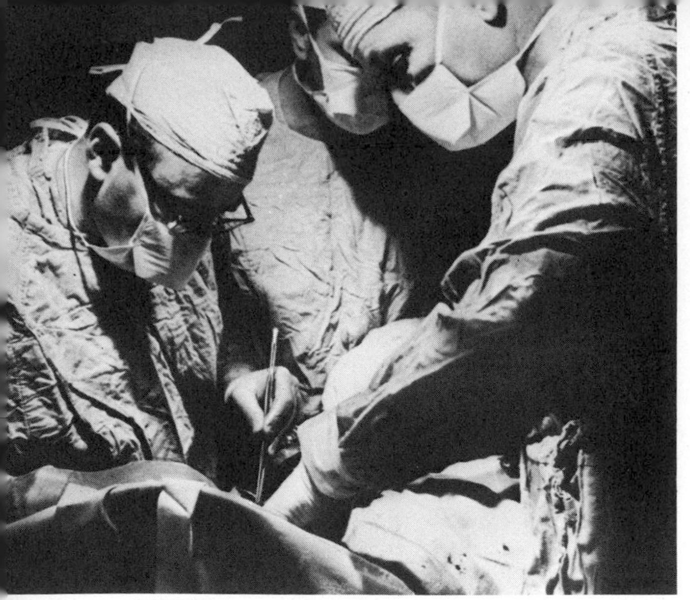

WIDE WORLD

Haskell Karp, 47, of Skokie, Ill., became the first human being to have his heart totally replaced by a mechanical device. The operation (above) is performed in St. Luke's Episcopal Hospital in Houston, Tex., by Dr. Denton A. Cooley (right) and Dr. Domingo Liotta (left). Karp was given the artificial heart (below) until a suitable heart-transplant donor was found. He later died.

UPI COMPIX

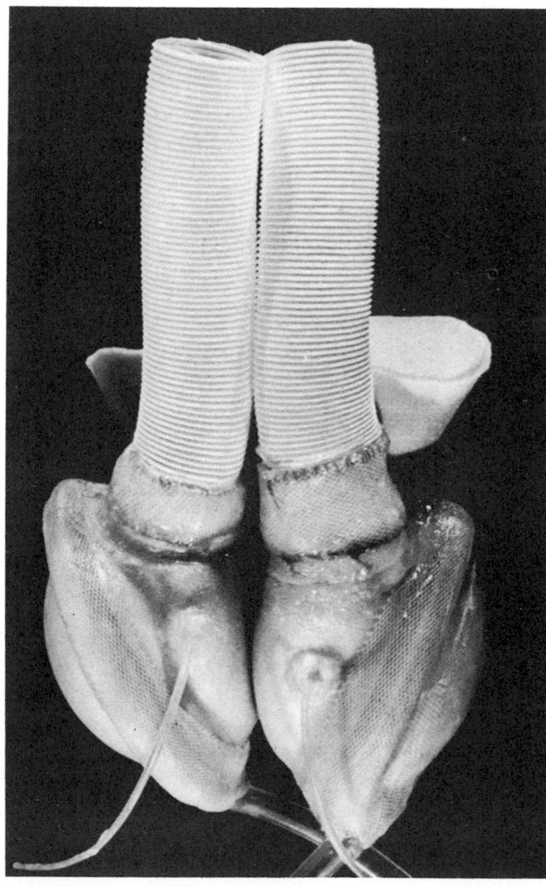

Views About Cancer Cells

Cancer researchers were certain that a real understanding of the disease was within short reach. Knowledge of the causes of cancer would ensure successful treatment.

Curiously, a fresh insight about cancer came from the laboratories of the National Aeronautics and Space Administration (NASA). Clarence D. Cone, Jr., a molecular biophysicist with NASA, learned that cancer cells in mice connect with each other through thin canals called *cytopons* ("cell bridges"). Cellular materials could thus pass between cancer cells through the cytopons. Also, when a "critical mass" or certain number of linked cancer cells were present, they would simultaneously divide, much like an atomic chain reaction. Division was thought to be under electrical control because just prior to cell division an increase in electrical voltage was measured in some of the cancer cells. Scientists at NASA were confident that the voltage changes were transmitted to the other cancer cells in the linked system and were probably responsible for triggering mass division. This view was markedly different from the conventional theory that blamed tumor growth on individual cancer cells that divided chaotically, not in the controlled way implied in the new theory.

Another view of cancer-cell proliferation came from work done in organ-transplant surgery. When drugs to suppress rejection of foreign tissue were given to kidney-transplant patients, an increased incidence of cancer cases was noted among them. Researchers concluded that perhaps cancer formed when the body's natural system of immunological defenses failed to recognize the cancer cells as intruders.

HEART

Philip Blaiberg, a South African dentist, was the longest surviving heart-transplant recipient until his death on August 17. He had survived 19 months and 15 days before his body massively rejected the new heart. The first known human use of an entirely mechanical heart occurred in Houston Tex., early in April. Denton A. Cooley implanted the artificial pump in a 47-year-old man and waited 63 hours for a donation of a human heart. However, the patient died soon after he received the new heart.

Coronary Heart Disease

Many scientists agreed that atherosclerosis (hardening) of the small blood vessels that feed the heart was caused by a number of factors. Those most clearly implicated were increased levels of blood cholesterol, high blood pressure, diabetes, and cigarette usage.

Advocates of exercise for the prevention of heart disease seemed to be developing a following in 1969. Although most scientists agreed that exercise was a good thing, they were unable to discover whether exercise actually prevented or lessened heart disorder.

Alcohol and the Heart

Interest in correlating alcohol consumption with heart disease rose in 1969. It had already been known that thiamine (vitamin B_1) deficiency in chronic alcoholics produced a type of heart-muscle weakness. But some alcoholics getting sufficient thiamine exhibited another form of the muscle weakness. It was concluded that alcohol itself might act as a poison on the heart, resulting in damage to the heart tissue.

When detected early enough, alcoholic damage to the heart was considered curable as soon as alcohol use was stopped. No treatment was thought satisfactory, however, in advanced forms of the disorder.

PUBLIC HEALTH

Environmental pollution was a prime target of public health agencies during the year. There was heightened concern over the effects of industry on man and his surroundings. Federal legislation, for example, was strengthened to protect miners from the lung-damaging influence of coal and asbestos. Similar legislation was under consideration for cotton-mill workers subjected to airborne fiber particles that cause byssinosis, another lung disorder.

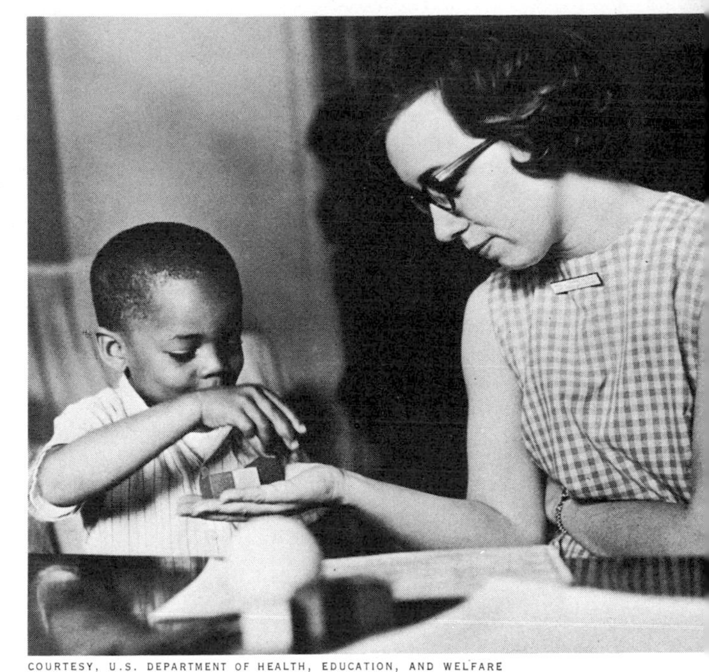

COURTESY, U.S. DEPARTMENT OF HEALTH, EDUCATION, AND WELFARE

A five-year-old participant happily completes one phase of a test administered in conjunction with the Comprehensive Health Care Program conducted by Children's Hospital in Washington, D.C.

New York City in 1969 conducted tests to determine how much carbon monoxide was being absorbed into its inhabitants' bloodstreams. The young man below is among the first to be checked.

WIDE WORLD

The U.S. Public Health Service (USPHS) said that cigarette usage, a form of self-pollution, was on a slow decline. The average smoker consumed 4,213 cigarettes in 1968, the latest year for available figures, compared with 4,292 cigarettes in 1967.

The USPHS announced that its campaign to eradicate measles (rubeola) ran into a snag in the year. Vaccination programs lagged, especially in ghetto areas. As a result, about 25,000 measles cases were forecast for 1969.

VD Still a Problem

Venereal disease (VD) incidence was assuming epidemic proportions. A survey of 134,633 physicians showed that VD cases continued to increase. It was further disclosed that physicians often protected patients from embarrassment by not reporting their cases to public health officials.

The study, instigated by the American Social Health Association, estimated that 1.7 million new VD cases had occurred in 1968, when the survey was undertaken. Gonorrhea was the most rampant, with an estimated 1.5 million cases. Incidence of the more severe syphilis, however, was on the decline.

Poor Health Traced to Environment

The American Public Health Association (APHA) blamed flaws in the quality of U.S. life for the unhealthy living conditions of many minority groups. Public health workers were admonished by the APHA to help eradicate the surroundings that bred poor health, particularly slums and rural poverty areas. The APHA said it was nearly impossible to expect improved medical treatment for the poor when they were merely treated for their ailments and sent back to unhealthful surroundings.

Malnutrition was in evidence in 1969. A U.S. survey found that hunger was a problem of the ghetto and rural backwater; also, malnutrition was present in the middle-class suburb because of poor eating habits. A public health official estimated that 10 million U.S. citizens suffered from improper nutrition. (*See also* Food.)

SURGERY

Although the pace of heart transplantation slackened considerably, other forms of transplant surgery made strides in 1969. In February, Belgian surgeons performed the world's first larynx transplantation on a recipient suffering from throat cancer. Soon after the operation, the 62-year-old recipient was able to speak with his new vocal cords.

Other Transplants

The first successful bone-marrow transplants were made in the United States in 1969. Bone marrow produces the blood cells that make antibodies. The surgical feat was considered an essential step toward the new field of "cellular engineering" against a wide range of genetic disorders, including a total lack of antibodies that battle infections.

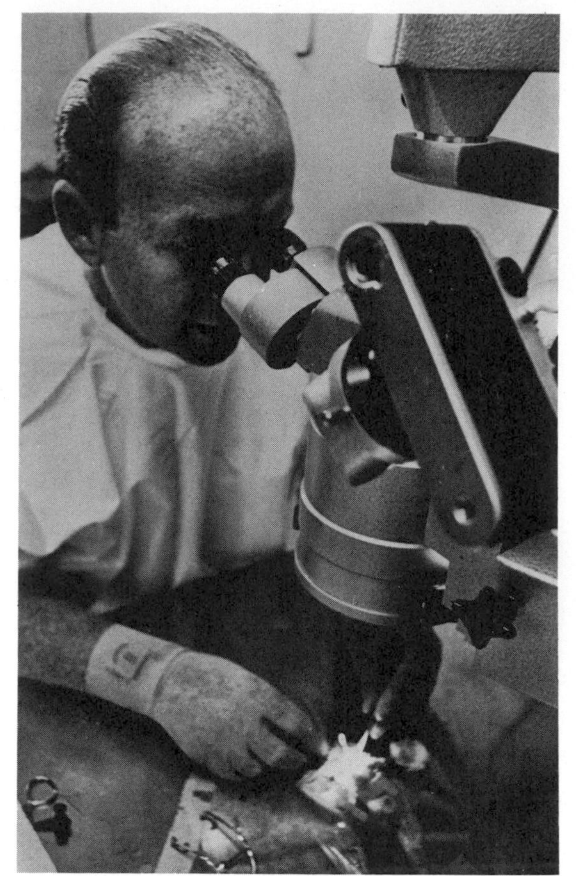

"LONDON DAILY EXPRESS" FROM PICTORIAL PARADE

Dr. E. R. Owen, an Australian surgeon, became the first to perform kidney transplants upon mice. The technique may lead to greater savings in testing methods of preventing the rejection of transplanted tissue.

This tentlike plastic device, inserted through the jugular vein and passed through the heart to lower veins, in 1969 was employed to prevent blood clots (emboli) from reaching the heart, lungs, and brain.

JAY SPENCER, "MIAMI (FLA.) NEWS HERALD"

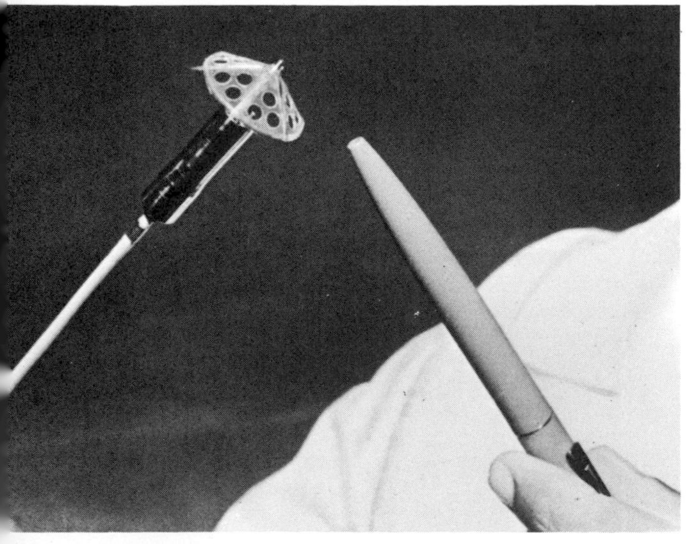

Surgeons were evaluating pancreas transplantation as a remedy for the most serious type of diabetes, which developed in juveniles. When a malfunctioning pancreas caused diabetes mellitus in a youthful patient, insulin therapy was usually ineffective. Although long-term survival results were not yet recorded, more than a dozen pancreas-transplant operations had been achieved.

"Umbrella" in the Vena Cava

Pulmonary embolism, the accumulation of tiny clots in blood vessels of the lungs, was a leading cause of U.S. hospital deaths. Clots would form in the legs of inactive, supine patients and travel to the lungs, where they would block blood vessels and cause increased blood pressure. Rapidly rising blood pressure in many cases then results in fatal heart stoppage.

To counter this tendency, Kazi Mobin-Uddin, of Miami, Fla., devised a "vena caval umbrella." The umbrella was a perforated plastic-like cone enclosed in a steel capsule attached to a plastic catheter. Through a neck incision, the device was inserted into the right internal jugular vein and forced downward into the large vena cava until it rested below the kidneys. Then a wire manipulated by the surgeon forced the umbrella from its enclosure. As large clots eventually sealed off the vena cava, blood from the legs was shunted around it through smaller veins. Any clots passing into these vessels were considered too small to cause pulmonary embolism. (*See also* Dentistry; Hospitals; Nursing. *See in* CE: Diseases, Infectious; Diseases, Non-infectious; Medicine; Surgery.)

MEIR, GOLDA. On March 17, 1969, Golda Meir took the oath of office as Israel's fourth prime minister. Long one of Israel's most powerful and experienced politicians, Mrs. Meir had been called from retirement by the Labor party to be its candidate to succeed Levi Eshkol, who died in February. As the candidate of the strongest party in the *Knesset* (parliament), Mrs. Meir automatically became prime minister.

On assuming office, Mrs. Meir retained the wartime coalition cabinet and continued to demand direct talks with the Arabs on a settlement of the Arab-Israeli war of 1967. Under her decisive leadership Israel's domestic political feuding was suspended. In international affairs she adamantly maintained Israel's independent position and refused to accept any solution to Middle Eastern problems imposed by international powers. Although at first considered an interim prime minister, she and her government were returned to power in general elections in October.

Golda Meir in March succeeded the late Levi Eshkol as Israel's prime minister.

PICTORIAL PARADE

Mrs. Meir was born in Kiev in czarist Russia on May 3, 1898. In 1906 her family emigrated to Milwaukee, Wis., where she grew up, and which she revisited in October 1969. As a Zionist pioneer she went to Palestine in 1921; there she rose to prominence in the labor movement. Later she became Israel's first ambassador to the Soviet Union (1948–49), minister of labor (1949–56), minister of foreign affairs (1956–66), and secretary-general of the Labor party (1966–68). (*See also* Israel; Middle East.)

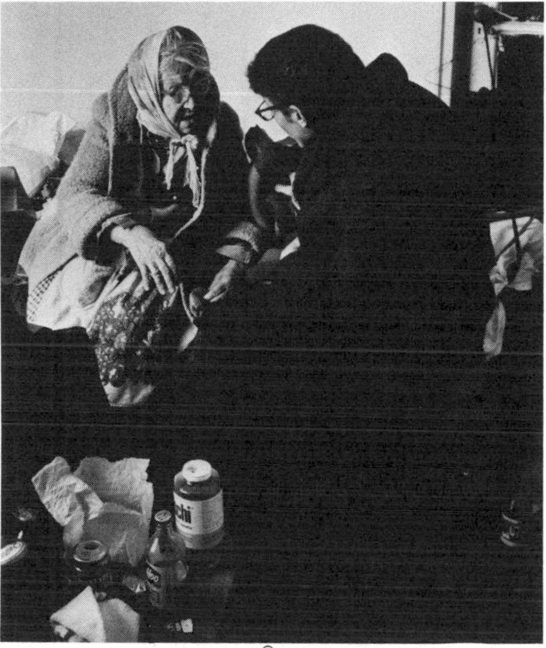

LEONARD MCCOMBE, "LIFE" MAGAZINE © TIME INC.

Seeking to prevent needless commitments to mental hospitals, specialists from Gouverneur Hospital in New York City gave elderly, needy patients psychiatric care in the patients' homes.

MENTAL HEALTH. Community mental health centers continued in 1969 to upgrade the treatment of mental disorders. As a first step, the U.S. Congress had passed the Mental Retardation Facilities and Community Mental Health Centers Construction Act of 1963 to begin abating retardation and mental illness on a national scale.

Ill-Staffed, Crowded Wards on the Wane

In the past, persons who sought mental aid were confined to large, overcrowded hospitals, usually far from their homes and families. However, under the auspices of the National Institute of Mental Health, local centers began to maintain professional staffs capable of treating mentally ill or emotionally disturbed patients in their own communities, and often on an outpatient basis.

By June 30, 1969, a total of 376 community mental-health centers were scheduled for operation. Of these, some 185 centers were already dispensing aid. When the entire program is in operation the centers would serve about 26 percent—approximately 53 million persons in 1969—of the U.S. population.

A Drug to Help the Mind; Some Dissent

Two French scientists received a U.S. patent in 1969 for Cognitum, a drug purported to enhance mental performance, especially among the elderly. Overworked persons were said to get relief from mental fatigue and gain improved memories after daily doses of the drug.

Prednisone, a drug with life-saving attributes for organ-transplant recipients, might not be without drawbacks. Administered to prevent tissue rejection, Prednisone was believed responsible for psychotic reactions in several heart-transplant recipients after they received the drug.

At a meeting of the American Psychiatric Association in May, a group of black psychiatrists decried racism as the "major mental-health problem" in the United States. Among other items, they called for desegregation of all mental-health facilities. (*See also* Psychology.)

METALS. Throughout the world, demand for metals continued to increase in 1969. In particular, the year witnessed a boom in the steel market virtually unprecedented since the years immediately after World War II.

World production of crude steel rose in 1969 to 565 million tons, up 6.9% from the total for 1968. The 6.9% represented a small increase in the rate of production growth, which had been 6.7% in 1968. The market growth—shared by all major steel-making countries—was attributed in part to simultaneous growth in their domestic economies.

In the United States, steel production in 1969 was expected to reach a record 137 million tons, some 7% above the 1968 figure. Domestic steel consumption, however, was expected to fall below the 107.7 million tons of 1968. Spokesmen for the steel industry anticipated that both production and consumption would decline in 1970 under the pressures of tight money and higher taxes.

Steel exports by the United States were greater than they had been since the early 1950's. Imports, on the other hand, declined, falling to 6.6 million tons in the first half as compared with 8.2 million tons in the first half of 1968. Steel companies increased prices at the end of July.

Prices of gold and silver, among other metals, reacted to speculation, tending downward—though silver gained strength toward year-end. Copper rose to high price levels in a fragmented world market, but demand remained strong and there was little apparent substitution of other metals for copper. Nickel prices soared because a strike in Canada cut back mine and plant production. Antimony prices moved sharply upward when the supply from Communist China essentially stopped. Lead, zinc, and aluminum prices rose incrementally in an orderly market. (*See also* Mines and Mining. *See in* CE: Metals; articles on individual metals.)

MEXICO. In contrast with events of the preceding year—a colorful Olympic pageant and violent student unrest—Mexicans experienced a fairly quiet 1969. Although presidential elections would not occur until July 1970, interest was high in much of 1969 over who the ruling Institutional Revolutionary party (PRI) would field as its candidate.

Selection as the PRI candidate was tantamount to being elected because opposition-party threats were sparse. President Gustavo Díaz Ordaz chose his intended successor, as custom deigned, after consulting with former presidents, high-ranking party members, and other influential persons.

By the time the PRI met in national convention in November the guessing was over. Luis Echeverría Alvarez, Mexico's secretary of government, was selected to bear the party's banner.

Ordinarily, once the PRI candidate was designated, interest in the presidential elections waned. But two thirds of the Mexican population, estimated at 47.3 million at the start of 1969, were under the age of 24. If the 1968 disorders were any indication, Mexico's youth was becoming disenchanted with the PRI.

Early in 1969 President Díaz Ordaz proposed lowering the voting age from 21 to 18. Whether the Mexican Congress would consider the legislation before the 1970 balloting was questionable. Analysts thought the lowered voting age would probably have little effect on PRI power, even in light of student unhappiness. Some in the PRI, however, feared the 1970 polls would show that older voters too were losing faith in the party.

Mexican Prosperity Unabated

Worries that unemployment would follow the construction boom of 1968 and that heightened political tension might inhibit economic growth proved groundless. The Mexican peso remained firm as ever 15 years after its last devaluation. The gross national product continued its annual growth —7.1% at the beginning of 1969.

Consumer prices remained fairly stable, thus augmenting the per-capita annual income of $564. Manufacturing was again the economic leader, but agricultural production made some impressive gains. A trade deficit caused by rising imports was absorbed in part by tourist spending and foreign investment.

Encouragement for Mexican employment was noted in two significant announcements. A refinery pipeline would be laid from a substantial oil field discovered in the state of Tamaulipas, about 20 miles from the mouth of the Pánuco River. Also, a major steel plant would be opened in Michoacán to process that state's iron-ore deposits.

Mexico City, the capital, celebrated the opening of a portion of its first subway on September 4. The new subway, constructed with French financial and technical aid, was dug by laborers idled after the 1968 building boom. The underground line was expected to lessen some of the city's chronic transportation problems. Archaeologists had a literal field day in the subway diggings because Mexico City rested over ancient Aztec ruins.

In September also, the Mexican government helped in Operation Intercept, an attempt to halt the smuggling of marihuana and other drugs over the U.S.-Mexico border. (*See* Drugs.) However, the essentially U.S. operation hampered tourism and some normal trade in the border regions of Mexico. (*See in* CE: Mexico.)

MIDDLE EAST. Rising tensions and escalating armed clashes between the Arab states and Israel, as well as the struggle between conservative and progressive forces in the Arab world, dominated events in the Middle East in 1969. Soviet influence and aid continued to play an important part in many Arab nations, while Arab anti-U.S. sentiment increased as it became apparent that the new Administration of U.S. President Richard M. Nixon continued to support Israel. The Palestinian guerrilla movement assumed an increasingly important role in Arab politics.

"LONDON DAILY EXPRESS" FROM PICTORIAL PARADE

In Arab nations of the Middle East, sympathizers with the anti-Israel terrorist organization *al Fatah* affixed one of these stickers near the official postage stamp when they mailed a letter.

The Search for Peace

Throughout 1969 both Israel and the Arab states clung to the basic positions they had held since

Bayonets fixed, young Jordanians engage in a practice attack at an *al Fatah* training camp near Amman in March 1969. During the year Israel continued to react sharply to terrorist attacks upon its border regions. Prospects for peace in the Middle East remained dim.

BLACK STAR

Protesting the August execution in Baghdad, Iraq, of 15 Iraqi citizens —including Arabs and Jews —accused of spying, Rabbi Gilbert Klapperman leads some 50 persons in prayer outside the Iraqi mission to the United Nations in New York City.

WIDE WORLD

the 1967 war. Israel insisted on direct negotiations with the Arabs to work out a signed peace treaty and secure borders before withdrawing its forces from occupied Arab land. The Israelis indicated their willingness to negotiate the return of all Arab territories except the Golan Heights of Syria and occupied Jerusalem. The Arabs insisted on an Israeli withdrawal before negotiations and continued to resist direct talks.

Early in the year, with tensions high in the Middle East as a result of Arab guerrilla actions and severe Israeli reprisals, the French proposed that the United States, the Soviet Union, Great Britain, and France hold talks to find a basis for peace in the Middle East. Although the "big four" powers declared they would not attempt to impose a settlement, Israel rejected a four-power solution on the grounds that lasting peace would be achieved only through direct Arab-Israeli talks.

Arab guerrillas were thought responsible for the explosion that burst a 12-inch oil pipeline at the entrance to the harbor at Haifa, Israel. The line carries fuel for ships and port facilities.

ISRAEL SUN LTD.—PIX FROM PUBLIX

The four-power talks began in the spring but recessed in July without having made progress. Bilateral talks between the United States and the Soviet Union continued. Details of the U.S. and Soviet peace plans revealed in October showed agreement on an Israeli withdrawal from occupied lands; on Arab recognition of and coexistence with Israel; and on the obligation of the United Arab Republic (UAR), or Egypt, to open the Suez Canal to shipping of all nations. The Soviets also proposed a United Nations peace-keeping force controlled by a four-power commission; the United States proposed demilitarization of Israeli-occupied Arab lands. The two powers were unable to agree on the form of either the peace talks or the peace agreement; on the obligations of Israel toward Arab refugees and of the UAR to open the Strait of Tiran; and on the negotiation of secure frontiers.

After the four-power talks had resumed late in the year, U.S. Secretary of State William P. Rogers made public some secret U.S. peace proposals that entailed some concessions to the Arabs. These included a total withdrawal by Israeli occupation forces in exchange for an Arab guarantee of nonbelligerence and, specifically, Israel's withdrawal to the Sinai border of 1967. Israel rejected the proposals as appeasement of the Arabs; Israel's Prime Minister Golda Meir stated that they indicated an erosion of U.S. support for Israel and ignored the need for negotiating secure borders. The UAR's president, Gamal Abdel Nasser, denounced the proposals on the grounds that they aimed at splitting the Arab world.

Military and Guerrilla Developments

Beginning with a series of UAR attacks on Israeli positions across the Suez Canal in March, the tempo of fighting in the Middle East increased throughout the year. By September UAR and Israeli air and ground forces were in frequent action on the Sinai front, and Israel had begun almost daily raids along the length of the Canal and the UAR's Red Sea coast. Israeli retaliatory raids on Jordan were frequent and included for the first time such targets as irrigation canals. General quiet along the Israeli-Syrian border was occasionally interrupted by air and artillery duels.

During the year Israel's long-quiet border with Lebanon threatened to become an active front as Arab guerrillas established bases in southern Lebanon. Lebanese army attempts to suppress the guerrillas resulted in armed clashes, brought down the Lebanese government, and divided the nation. Through the mediation of UAR President Nasser the guerrillas won the right to operate in Lebanon and to maintain a supply route from Syria.

At a meeting of Palestinian nationalists in February *al Fatah,* a leading commando group, won control of the Palestine Liberation Organization (PLO), under which most Palestinian factions were united. Yasir Arafat, the head of *al Fatah,* became chairman of the PLO Executive Committee and emerged as a powerful guerrilla leader. The PLO rejected international mediation efforts as well as attempts by Arab governments to find a political solution to Arab-Israeli problems. The aim of the PLO was the elimination of Israel and the establishment of a Palestinian state that would include both Jews and Arabs. Late in 1969 the Soviet Union granted official recognition to the PLO. Arab terrorists claimed credit for numerous bomb explosions in Israel and for several attacks in Europe on planes and terminals of the Israeli airline El Al.

JUHL FROM BEN ROTH AGENCY

"He fired first!"

Arab Affairs

As a result of a fire in the sacred Al Aksa Mosque in Israeli-held Jerusalem, an Islamic summit conference met in Morocco in September. Although Israel's arrest of an arsonist cooled Arab calls for a Muslim holy war against Israel, the conferees unanimously supported a resolution backing the Palestinian nationalists. Arab militants were unable to persuade non-Arab Muslim nations to break off relations with Israel. (*See also* International Relations; United Nations.)

The Islamic meeting was held at the instigation of King Faisal of Saudi Arabia, a conservative monarch who resisted the call of progressive Arabs for an Arab summit meeting to discuss united action against Israel. Nonetheless, the king attended an Arab League summit conference in Morocco in December. At the meeting the PLO, represented by Arafat, was accorded full status by Arab governments for the first time. The conferees discussed the potential role of each Arab nation in the event of war with Israel. The meeting broke up without achieving unanimity.

The seizure of the governments of Libya and Sudan by revolutionary forces in 1969 added strength to the Arab militant bloc. At the request of the new Libyan regime, the United States agreed to close down the Wheelus Air Force Base near Tripoli, one of Libya's two capitals.

In October the rulers of nine sheikhdoms in the Persian Gulf area established the Federation of Gulf Emirates. The purpose of the union was to safeguard their territories from revolutionaries and the ambitions of foreign powers when British protection was withdrawn in 1970. The nine states—Sharja, Ras al Khaima, Fujaira, Bahrein, Ajman, Dubai, Abu Dhabi, Qatar, and Umm al Qaiwain—designated Abu Dhabi as a provisional capital. (*See also* Israel; Jordan; Lebanon; Libya; Morocco; Saudi Arabia; Sudan; Syria; United Arab Republic.)

MINES AND MINING.

Metals appeared to lead the way as the upward trend in U.S. and world mineral production continued in 1969. The dollar value of mine output, however, increased more than did volume because of higher mineral prices. Despite the record mine output during the year, there was also increased reclamation of scrap materials to supply the buoyant market.

The rising demand for minerals stimulated intensive worldwide search for new mines and spurred the development of additional productive capacity. Paralleling the increase in mining activity was a widespread growth in public concern for current and potential environmental damage from mining and mineral processing and for the health and safety of miners.

Early in the year the Bureau of Mines of the U.S. Department of the Interior published for study the first draft of the proposed Federal Coal Mine

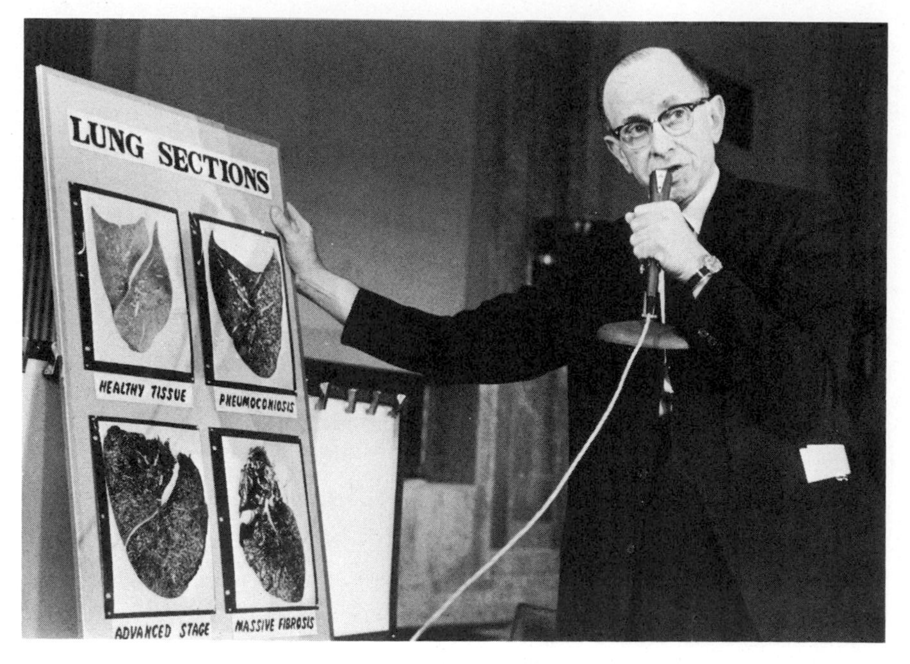

Before U.S. Senate subcommittee hearings on proposed federal mine health and safety legislation, Joel Goldman of the United Mine Workers discusses the effects of coal dust upon miners' lungs.

UPI COMPIX

Health and Safety Act for metal and nonmetal mines. Late in the year the U.S. Senate passed and forwarded to the House of Representatives a bill that raised safety standards in coal mines. It was intended to reduce the risk of underground explosions and the incidence of lung diseases among miners.

Though demand was high, the mineral market was irregular. Because of abundant supply, many mineral prices were soft despite monetary inflation. In the United States, defense requirements helped to firm markets, particularly for metals.

The mining industry was affected by a number of developments in the year. Numerous small work stoppages restricted output, and a major nickel-industry strike in Canada caused a critical shortage of that metal. Uncertainty about the future was generated by the growing tendency of some African and Latin American countries to nationalize foreign-owned industries. The U.S. mining industry also viewed with disfavor those aspects of proposed federal tax reforms that would reduce depletion allowances for most minerals.

Technological Developments

The availability of superior materials, better equipment design, improved controls, and more attention to total mining systems were once again the principal factors in advancing mining technology. The superior materials included such diverse items as high-strength steels to lighten mobile equipment, stronger tires that gave longer life and reduced shutdowns, and harder and stronger cutting materials to speed drilling and boring.

Much of the improvement in equipment design stemmed from on-the-job experience with equipment already in use. Similarly, mining systems designs were improved as engineers' growing acquaintance with modern mechanized equipment enabled them to take better advantage of its capabilities. Sophisticated electronic and hydraulic controls helped improve the performance of machines and reduce direct labor costs.

The continuing increase in the size of mining equipment was highlighted in 1969 by the "Big Muskie," the world's largest dragline, which was placed in operation for stripping overburden at an Ohio coal mine. The 13,000-ton, $20-million machine—490 feet long and 220 feet high—can scoop up 325 tons of earth and rock at one bite.

The transportation of mine products received wide attention. Trucks of a size up to 200 tons were in use; electrically driven wheels gained favor. Belt conveyors, transportation modules, and hydraulic pipelines were major subjects of research and development. (*See also* Fuel and Power; Metals. *See in* CE: Mines and Mining.)

MONACO. The modernization of Monaco's famed Monte Carlo Casino continued in 1969 as the U.S.-trained director Wilford Groote introduced new purchasing and accounting methods and replaced outdated equipment. Reorganization of the *Société des Bains de Mer* (Sea Bathing Society, or SBM), the holding company that controls most of Monaco's gambling and hotel interests, brought protests and resignations from some key personnel. However, most of the 2,000 employees adapted well to the new situation.

While the Americanization of Monaco's unique facilities was bemoaned by some, the program was mainly a success. The SBM, which lost $18 million in the 1966–67 tourist season, operated at a profit during 1969. Many U.S. organizations selected

Monaco as a convention site during the year. In the summer about 75% of the guests registered at the famed Hôtel de Paris were Americans. To counteract charges of over-Americanization, a campaign was put on to promote Monte Carlo in Italy.

In April Prince Rainier III appointed François-Didier Gregh minister of state. Gregh, who entered the civil service in 1930 as finance inspector, has also been a director of the International Bank for Reconstruction and Development, or World Bank, in Washington, D.C.

In October 1969 Spain, Italy, France, and Monaco began a joint study of the Mediterranean Sea in Monaco. Cooperating agencies in the project were the United Nations Educational, Scientific, and Cultural Organization and the Food and Agriculture Organization of the United Nations. Prince Rainier served as president of the scientific study commission. (*See in* CE: Monte Carlo.)

MONEY AND INTERNATIONAL FINANCE. The international monetary and financial climate was relatively calm during 1969—at least in comparison to the turbulence of the preceding two years. Although the year witnessed one crisis, a subsequent adjustment in the values of the French franc and the West German mark did much to alleviate the tension that had prevailed since the devaluation of the British pound in 1967. A decisive change in the functioning of the international monetary system was also initiated during the year with the approved adoption of "Special Drawing Rights" (SDRs) by the member nations of the International Monetary Fund (IMF).

The year's currency crisis was precipitated in May by the defeat of France's President Charles de Gaulle in a national referendum. De Gaulle's consequent resignation touched off expectations of a devaluation of the franc, which resulted in widespread exchange of the weakening francs for stronger marks. Although speculative buying had leveled off somewhat by the beginning of June, the crisis was not resolved until the announcement of the devaluation of the franc in August.

France's devaluation of the franc caught the world by surprise. Although it had been expected for over a year, the announcement came at a time of comparative quiet. The French government had been under pressure to reduce the parity of the franc in terms of other currencies ever since labor strikes brought about disproportionately high wage increases in June 1968. Thus, when the devaluation finally came, it was accompanied by an admission from France's new President Georges Pompidou that the value of the franc had been "out of line" with the values of the other major currencies for some time.

The devaluation had the effect of lowering the worth of the franc by 11.1% to foreigners buying francs or by 12.5% to Frenchmen buying other currencies. The franc, which was formerly 20.255¢, was lowered to 18.004¢.

At the onset of the devaluation France appeared to be in a fairly strong financial position, with treasury reserves standing at $3.6 billion in gold and dollars. However, since the government had taken out $2.4 billion in foreign credit to back the franc during the period following July 1968, its uncommitted reserves amounted to only $1 billion. France did have $2.6 billion in credit still available, however.

To avoid sudden domestic inflationary activity that would nullify the effects of the devaluation, the French government ordered an immediate price freeze on all commodities until September 15. This was followed by a package of deflationary measures that were widely criticized as insufficient. The existing commitment to reduce the budget deficit and the tight squeeze on credit was supplemented by a number of new incentives for higher saving, for an acceleration of corporation tax payments, and for cuts in government spending. These measures were augmented by a 1% increase in the discount rate, which was intended to prevent the French treasury reserves from dwindling.

The speculative selling of the franc that followed the devaluation gave rise to fears that French treasury reserves and credit might be quickly depleted. In October, however, the pressure on the franc was relieved by the announcement that the West German government had agreed to the temporary suspension of the fixed parity that had allowed the value of the mark to range only 1% above or below its official pegged value of 25¢. The announcement came on the heels of a general election that had failed to produce a decisive majority for either po-

PEARSON, "KNICKERBOCKER NEWS," ALBANY, N.Y., FROM BEN ROTH AGENCY

"We've made a terrible mistake. Their foreign aid senator is at our other hotel!"

litical party. The two days prior to the election had witnessed so great a deluge of foreign currencies into West Germany that the nation was forced to close its money markets temporarily. The glut of foreign currencies in exchange for marks resulted from a general belief that a new government would be forced to revalue its currency. The act of freeing the mark and allowing its value to be determined on the international market was a *de facto* revaluation, but it shifted the responsibility of setting the value of the mark from West German officials to international financial speculators.

After three weeks of "floating," the value of the mark was officially established at 27.3224¢—a revaluation of 9.3%. The revaluation was generally unpopular in West Germany because, by making the mark worth more in foreign currencies, it increased the price of German exports, rendering them less competitive abroad. The effects of the revaluation were mitigated slightly, however, by a revocation of the 4% export tax previously imposed.

In 1969 the U.S. Department of the Treasury replaced its old seal (top) with a modernized version (bottom). The new seal now appears on U.S. currency.

COURTESY, U.S. DEPARTMENT OF THE TREASURY

International Monetary Fund Approves "Paper Gold"

The biggest news in the international monetary scene came in October at a meeting of the member nations of the International Monetary Fund with the announcement of the adoption of SDRs, beginning in January 1970. Under the new system, each member nation is allocated a certain amount of credit depending on its productive capacity and the strength of its economy. From this balance, the nation can exercise its special drawing rights in lieu of obtaining a loan. The SDRs are also referred to as "paper gold" because, after the agreement went into effect, each signatory nation was required to accept SDRs as currency.

Initially, the plan was for the IMF to create $9.5 billion in SDRs over the next three years. The amount would be added to world reserves of gold, dollars, and pounds—which were at the $74 billion level near year-end. The new paper gold will not take the form of currency but will be handled as bookkeeping entries.

The proposal to create SDRs had been debated for five years. When put into work it would add greater flexibility to the gold standard upon which the international monetary system is based. It has

Trading was hectic on the floor of the Paris bourse on August 11, the day of its first session after France devalued the franc on August 8. Buyers were eager to convert their newly devalued francs into stocks.

KEYSTONE

been hailed as an appropriate solution to the chronic shortage in the supply of gold, which is in part dependent on the amount of metal that is mined.

At the same meeting, officials of the IMF also agreed to initiate a study of two other methods of making exchange rates more flexible. One plan would allow currencies to fluctuate more than 1% above or below their official values, thus creating a greater leeway for a determination of value by the market. This method weathered a test when the IMF suspended the 1% boundaries on the mark.

The second proposal, the "crawling peg," would allow for frequent but small revaluations of a currency. This procedure has been common among Latin American nations for several years.

Eurodollars and Eurobond Markets Active

Two factors had a dominant influence on the market for Eurodollars (dollars held in banks outside the United States) in the first three quarters of the year. The first was the heavy borrowing demand from U.S. banks, and the second was the repeated speculation in favor of the mark.

During the first quarter the borrowing of Eurodollars exceeded the entire growth of $2.7 billion that was achieved by the market in 1968. Rates rose sharply in response to the rapid expansion and were up to 8.56% in London, England, by April. Immediately following, throughout April and May, the massive exchange of francs for marks led to the accelerated borrowing of Eurodollars. An abnormally high interest rate of 12% was reached in June. Interest subsequently wavered between 10% and 12% until the announcement of West Germany's revaluation.

The rapid expansion of the Eurodollar markets became a cause for alarm to the Board of Governors of the U.S. Federal Reserve System, who viewed it as having a potentially distorting effect on credit flows in the United States and abroad. They ruled that borrowings of member banks from overseas branches, in excess of borrowings during the first four weeks of May 1969, would be subject to a 10% reserve requirement.

With interest rates at a high level, the volume of new issues in Eurobond markets was somewhat reduced. The amounts involved in the first two quarters were $992 million and $962 million, as compared to $1.233 billion and $1.180 billion in the last two quarters of 1968. The restrictions on the activities of Italian banks in international capital markets, the introduction of waiting lists for new issues in West Germany, and the postponement of issues in the hope of lower rates in the future were the major factors behind the reduction. The calls in the market by private U.S. firms were substantially lower both in absolute terms and as a proportion of the total, sharply reversing the trend toward the greater use of the convertible bond that seemed to have been initiated in 1968. (*See also* Economy; World Trade. *See in* CE: Money.)

MONGOLIAN PEOPLE'S REPUBLIC.

Soviet troops and arms buildup in Mongolia increased substantially in 1969. Premier Yumzhagiyin Tsedenbal, in his 18th year in office, pledged continued friendship with the Soviet Union as tensions between the two Communist giants—the Soviet Union and the People's Republic of China—rose. Tsedenbal voiced fears in an interview in May that Communist China would attempt to annex Mongolia by force.

Most of Mongolia's income continued to be derived from livestock raising. Severe winters in 1967 and 1968, however, cut the national herd to an estimated 18 to 19 million head. Some 4 million cattle were lost in the unusually harsh cold of the Mongolian steppes.

Industrial output, nonexistent until recently, rose as the 1966–70 Mongolian economic plan neared an end. In November an East German delegation arrived in Ulan Bator, the capital, for economic talks. (*See in* CE: Mongolia.)

MOROCCO.

During 1969 Morocco took steps to settle long-standing territorial disputes with three of its neighbors. In January King Hassan II and Revolutionary Council President Houari Boumedienne of Algeria signed a treaty of friendship and cooperation that ended six years of hostile relations and eased conflicting claims to the Tindouf mining region. The treaty provided for Algeria to mine Tindouf's iron ore for export to Morocco, where it would be processed and used. Six months later Morocco regained the enclave of Ifni, which Spain had occupied since 1934.

The first direct contact between Morocco and Mauritania since 1960 occurred in September, when Mauritania's President Mokhtar Ould Daddah attended an Islamic conference in Rabat, Morocco's capital. After talks with Ould Daddah, King Hassan indicated willingness to sign a treaty of friendship.

The Islamic conference brought together leaders of 25 Muslim nations who were concerned for the safety of Islamic shrines after fire damaged a mosque in Israeli-held Jerusalem. The conferees declared support for the Palestinian liberation movement and demanded Israel's withdrawal from Arab lands.

Morocco took a major economic step in 1969 by signing an accord of association with the European Economic Community (EEC), or Common Market. Under the accord Moroccan agricultural products receive preferential treatment in EEC countries; in exchange, Morocco gives tariff and quota concessions to manufactured goods from EEC nations. The economy was also aided by a second consecutive year of good crops.

Morocco's first communal and municipal elections in six years, held in October, were boycotted by leftists and opposition groups who demanded legislative elections and a new constitution. (*See in* CE: Morocco.)

MOTION PICTURES. Sex and violence in motion pictures during 1969 became an ever greater attraction for the public. Films rated "X" under the year-old rating system seemed to generate more interest rather than to deter audiences from viewing films with such a rating. Directors in 1969 continued to gradually replace actors and actresses as the stars of motion pictures, and low-budget films often had greater success than the star-studded extravaganzas. The new elements of independent producer-directors and their low-budget films did nothing to alleviate the financial difficulties of the once-great Hollywood (Calif.) studios. Several studios were sold to large corporations.

'I Am Curious (Yellow)', a Swedish import, was not well received by the U.S. customs officials, but it was an undeniable box-office success in 1969. The motion picture dealt with problems of Swedish politics. Of perhaps more interest to adult U.S. audiences, however, were the film's explicit sex scenes—for which it received an "X" rating. The film was called everything from pornographic to antierotic. Equally opposite reactions to its quality were voiced by film critics, some of whom thought the foreign film interesting, while others thought it formless and boring.

'Midnight Cowboy' received critical acclaim for its unusually touching treatment of deviant sexual subjects. In the movie an all-American innocent played by Jon Voight made his way from Texas to New York City where he intended to win his fortune as a male prostitute. In the city he met a crippled petty thief, played by Dustin Hoffman. A warm alliance developed between the two even though they were a part of and surrounded by the squalor of big-city street life.

In the area of Westerns 'The Wild Bunch' was widely criticized for its excessive portrayal of violence. In the film, which starred William Holden and Ernest Borgnine, two towns were destroyed and several hundred persons killed by a gang of outlaws. Popular singer Glen Campbell made his motion-picture debut in another Western, 'True Grit', which starred John Wayne. The aging Wayne portrayed an aging, one-eyed federal marshal who joined a young girl (played by Kim Darby) in the search for her father's killer.

'Battle of Britain', a film three years in the making, employing an air force of more than a hundred planes and a cast of no fewer than 14 stars, was released in the fall of 1969. The motion picture paid homage to the Allied air heroes who thwarted the threatened Nazi invasion of Great Britain during World War II. An antiwar movie, 'Oh! What a Lovely War', satirically took up the subject of World War I.

In 1969 a popular song became an equally popular motion picture. 'Alice's Restaurant', directed by Arthur Penn, was based partly on Arlo Guthrie's talking-blues song of the same name and told of a communal "family" living in a deconsecrated church at Stockbridge, Mass. Many of the episodes in the film actually happened, and several of the characters, including Arlo, were played by the real-life persons.

Philip Roth's novella 'Goodbye, Columbus' was adapted for the screen and released as a motion picture early in 1969. The successful film starred Richard Benjamin and a newcomer to motion pictures, Ali MacGraw.

The musicals released during the year included 'Sweet Charity' and 'Paint Your Wagon'. Some film critics found both motion pictures overdone and poorly directed. The leading roles in 'Sweet Charity' were played by Shirley MacLaine and Ricardo Montalban; in 'Paint Your Wagon', by Lee Marvin, Clint Eastwood, and Jean Seberg. 'The Loves of Isadora' was a biographical account of the dancer Isadora Duncan, portrayed by Vanessa Redgrave.

For younger audiences Walt Disney Productions released 'The Love Bug', the story of a Volkswagen and a race-car driver. One critic described the film as a long, sentimental commercial. 'Popi', starring Alan Arkin, was a humorous film about a Puerto Rican family and its problems of living in New York City's Spanish Harlem.

Shooting Stars

In Europe motion-picture directors were firmly entrenched as the new stars of films, and during the year this trend toward elevating the status of the director became more evident in the United States. Mike Nichols, who won fame as a director with his films 'Who's Afraid of Virginia Woolf?' and 'The Graduate', was busy completing the film version of Joseph Heller's World War II novel 'Catch-22'. The studio producing the film, Paramount Pictures Corp., gave Nichols total control over the motion picture.

Cinematographer Haskell Wexler found a ready-made cast of thousands for a motion picture that he wrote, directed, and photographed—'Medium Cool'. The film was set in the events surrounding the 1968 Democratic National Convention at Chicago, Ill., and dealt with the relationship between a television cameraman and the events he was recording. An unusual *cinéma-vérité* quality of the film was that rather than being a documentary it combined actual recorded events with a fictional plot. 'American Revolution 2' also was a film featuring events at the convention, but in a purely documentary form.

Another film that combined reality with fiction was 'The Rain People'. This film about a runaway housewife employed such typical U.S. settings as motels and roadside diners. Writer-director Francis Ford Coppola filmed the entire production on the road.

Searching for and interpreting "America" was a popular theme with directors during the year. 'Easy Rider', produced by Peter Fonda and directed by Dennis Hopper, was the story of two young men on a motorcycle trip across the Southwestern United States. Fonda and Hopper played the leading roles. By, for, and about the younger generation, the film attempted to contrast the gentle hippie society with the brutality and violence of ordinary U.S. society. The Italian director Michelangelo Antonioni also sought to capture the "deepest and truest aspects" of America in his film 'Zabriskie Point'.

Two great foreign directors, Federico Fellini of Italy and Ingmar Bergman of Sweden, announced in January that they would make a film together. Fellini and Bergman planned a two-part film about love, entitled 'Love Duet'.

'Satyricon', the first full-length motion picture made by Fellini in four years, was presented at the Venice (Italy) Film Festival in September. The film was based on a satire by Petronius Arbiter about the decadence of the ancient Roman Empire. One lengthy sequence centered around a Roman banquet. The film offered by French director François Truffaut in 1969 was 'Stolen Kisses', a sympathetic chronicle of a Frenchman's young adulthood.

Best of the Year

An unusual development at the 41st annual awards presentation of the Academy of Motion Picture Arts and Sciences was the tie vote for best

(*continued on page 357*)

FRED LYON FROM RAPHO GUILLUMETTE

COURTESY, UNITED ARTISTS CORP.

COURTESY, UNITED ARTISTS CORP.

Three of the most talked-about motion pictures of 1969 were Frank and Eleanor Perry's 'Last Summer' (left), a drama, adapted from Evan Hunter's novel, about confused adolescents; 'Midnight Cowboy' (top), featuring Jon Voight (left) and Dustin Hoffman, created for the screen by Waldo Salt from a novel by James Leo Herlihy and concerned with two drifters on the make in New York City; and 'Stolen Kisses' (above), starring Jean-Pierre Léaud, about a young man uneasy in life and love.

Special Report: How Far Can We Go?

by John Trevelyan, Secretary,
British Board of Film Censors

COURTESY, GROVE PRESS

Lena Nyman and Borje Ahlstedt star as young lovers in 'I Am Curious (Yellow)', a controversial Swedish-made film that contained very frank sexual scenes.

While the motion-picture industry in the United States celebrated its 75th anniversary in 1969, around the world the problems of censorship remained largely unresolved. The years 1968–69 were years of significant change in the field of censorship, with marked effects on motion pictures and on the live theater. New demands for freedom of expression in the arts produced increasing pressures on all forms of restraint.

New freedoms opened new markets. Sex and pornography in books, films, and theater began to spread to areas where formerly they had been unacceptable. Films that in the past had been shown in only a few underground theaters were given general theatrical distribution. Sex and nudity in the live theater suddenly became acceptable to the main theatergoing public.

In live theater, 'Hair', a musical peppered with four-letter words and having a scene in which several actors removed all their clothes, continued to be a sensational success. The Living Theater, directed by Julian Beck, employed the same technique mixed with political protest. Straight plays such as 'The Beard' showed sexual acts on the stage and used dialogue that was totally uninhibited. In 1969 this trend toward utter freedom culminated in Kenneth Tynan's production of a musical with nudity, sex, and eroticism called 'Oh! Calcutta!' Motion pictures from Hollywood, Calif., as well as from foreign countries explored themes that before had been considered taboo, such as homosexuality in 'The Sergeant', 'Midnight Cowboy', and in several other films.

Censorship by Self-Regulation

The mainstream of the U.S. film industry reacted to these developments and for the first time in nearly 40 years felt it necessary to protect itself from public criticism. Precensorship of films until only a few years before had been practiced in some cities and states. After legal battles extending over many years such precensorship had been judged illegal by the Supreme Court and had ceased to exist. The only control left was the film industry's self-regulation, which had been established in 1930 by Will Hays.

This self-regulation was operated from Hollywood by a division of the Motion Picture Association of America (MPAA) called the Production Code Administration. Film producers working for the major U.S. studios were bound to observe the standards set by the administration's Production Code. The original 1930 code was a very restrictive document. In 1966 it was completely revised and considerably shortened by the MPAA president, Jack Valenti. Finally, in 1968 the association introduced a system for classifying motion pictures according to audiences.

The Commercial Value of X

Since increasing freedom for film makers produced the risk of further public criticism of the film industry and the risk of harm to children, the MPAA in 1968 introduced its own system of rating films. Films that were approved by the Production Code Administration were rated as follows: G, suitable for general audiences; M, suitable for adults and children of 16 years and under who have permission from parents or guardian; and R, suitable for adults and for children of 16 years and under only when accompanied by a parent or other adult.

In addition to these ratings, films not approved by the Production Code Administration—or not submitted for approval—could be shown under an X rating. This rating recommends that no person under 16 years of age be admitted to see a film.

The operation of this system of classification is voluntary. Cities or states may enact enforcement legislation, however, and may vary the minimum age. Valenti said the introduction of the system was motivated by two concerns—a desire to give film makers greater freedom of expression and a concern for safeguarding children.

One result of this rating system is that films rated X are a special attraction to the public. Two prime examples of the success of films with an X rating are 'I Am Curious (Yellow)' and 'The Killing of Sister George'. This latest turn in public taste is also reflected toward films rated "condemned" by an organization of the Roman Catholic church. For many years films shown in the United States have been given a rating by the National Catholic Office for Motion Pictures (formerly the National Legion of Decency). Some years ago a film condemned by this organization suffered considerable commercial disadvantage. At the present time, however, the effects appear to be minimal.

Time will show whether the commercial attraction of X-rated films is enduring or short-lived. Since the film industry is fighting for survival in the highly competitive field of entertainment, it is reasonable to expect that profitability will dictate production policies.

Foreign Films

Scandinavian countries, particularly Denmark and Sweden, are commonly regarded as leaders in the trend toward complete freedom of expression in the arts. In Sweden books and magazines displayed in shop windows and on newsstands, not only in Stockholm but even in small towns, would be cause for prosecution in most other countries. In Denmark the parliament removed all legal restrictions on written pornography in 1967. In 1969 it also removed all legal restrictions on pictorial pornography as well as all censorship of films for adults (persons 16 years of age and older). Film censorship in Sweden has become increasingly permissive with scenes of sex but has maintained a restrictive policy with scenes of violence.

In 1967 the Swedish film 'I, a Woman', which many people regarded as pornographic, was distributed to theaters throughout the United States. This set a precedent for other such films. Perhaps the most controversial film of 1969 was another Swedish import, 'I Am Curious (Yellow)'. The film showed complete nudity of both sexes and included graphic sexual scenes.

When attempts were made to bring 'I Am Curious (Yellow)' into the United States, the film was

'Satyricon', Federico Fellini's first full-length motion picture in four years, was very well received at its first showing at the Venice (Italy) Film Festival, in September 1969. The film's source was a satire of the same name by Petronius Arbiter.

FRANCO PINNA FROM RAPHO GUILLUMETTE

held by U.S. customs officers at New York City. A federal court ruled the film obscene, but the verdict was reversed by a higher court on appeal. Eventually the film was shown in its complete form at two New York City theaters, where it became a huge commercial success. Then it was distributed to theaters in other U.S. cities. In Boston, Mass., an exhibitor was given a short prison sentence for showing this film, and police action was taken in some other U.S. cities and states. Nevertheless, 'I Am Curious (Yellow)' continued to be distributed in many U.S. cities.

A West German film called 'Helga', though it was originally intended for educational use in schools and colleges, proved to be a great box-office success in Western Europe and the United States. Since sex education seemed to be a certain commercial success, other West German films were made along these lines.

In recent years Italy has probably produced more sex films than any other country. The increasingly liberal policies of the Italian Ministry of Entertainment's censorship board led to the resignation of several members in protest. The liberality of the self-policing Japanese film industry in producing scenes of sex and violence has created the possibility of intervention by the Japanese government. However, in India, a country with relatively restrictive censorship policies, a committee recommended in 1969 that "if in telling the story it is logical, relevant, or necessary to depict a passionate kiss . . . there should be no question of excluding the shot." (*See also* Literature; Theater.)

The Great Censorship Debate

In most free societies censorship will probably remain a controversial subject for some years. The chief protagonists in each country will be virtually the same: the liberal intellectual who demands freedom of expression for the artist and freedom of choice for the adult, and the conservative who believes that the average adult does not know what is good or bad for himself, but must have other people decide that for him.

There are two different issues involved in the censorship problem. One is a legal issue; the other, a social issue. The legal issue is concerned with the interpretation in exact terms of such words as "obscenity" and "pornography" and of phrases such as "tend to deprave and corrupt." Unless the law is specific and can establish exactly what is to be prohibited and punished it can lead only to confusion and injustices.

The social issue is concerned with the well-being of the individual and of society. Although research has as yet produced no definite findings about the good or bad influence of the mass media, there are indications that people are influenced by what they see and hear and by what they read. It should be noted that what may be a right solution to the legal issue may prove to be a wrong solution to the social issue. The aim should be to find a way of giving freedom to the artist without doing social harm by giving freedom also to the pornographers who intend to make money by exploiting human weakness.

The motion picture 'The Killing of Sister George' was another controversial film in 1969. It starred Beryl Reid, Susannah York, and Coral Browne and was directed by Robert Aldrich. Miss Reid (second from right) dances with Miss York; both are in men's costumes.

COURTESY, CINERAMA RELEASING CORP.

In the film 'Easy Rider' Dennis Hopper (left) and Peter Fonda set out on their motorcycles to explore the United States. In their travels they pick up Jack Nicholson, a small-town lawyer who decides, on the spur of the moment, to don his gold football helmet and join the adventure. The film ends with stunning violence.
AUTHENTICATED NEWS INTERNATIONAL

(*continued from page 353*)
actress of 1968. Best-actress awards were presented to Katharine Hepburn for her role in 'The Lion in Winter' and to Barbra Streisand for 'Funny Girl'. The Oscar for best performance by an actor went to Cliff Robertson for his role in 'Charly'.

The musical 'Oliver!' was voted best picture of the year and won four other Oscars, including one for Sir Carol Reed as best director. The Oscar for the best foreign film went to the Soviet Union's 'War and Peace'. 'The Windmills of Your Mind' from 'The Thomas Crown Affair' was selected as the best song. Other films that won Oscars were 'Bullitt', 'The Producers', '2001: a Space Odyssey', 'Rosemary's Baby', 'Romeo and Juliet', and 'The Subject Was Roses'.

The National Catholic Office for Motion Pictures and the Broadcasting and Film Commission of the National Council of Churches chose 'Rachel, Rachel' and 'The Heart Is a Lonely Hunter' as the best films of 1968. Ingmar Bergman's 'Shame' was named the best film of 1968 by the National Society of Film Critics, and Bergman won the society's best-director award. Late in December 1968 the New York Film Critics voted 'The Lion in Winter' the best picture of the year. The critics chose Paul Newman as best director for 'Rachel, Rachel'.

The Hollywood Scene

Financial difficulties beset the major U.S. studios during 1969. The realities of valuable real estate and a nonprofit-making studio forced Gulf & Western Industries, Inc., owner of Paramount Pictures Corp., to put the Paramount movie lot up for sale. Metro-Goldwyn-Mayer, Inc., sold in 1968 to Edgar M. Bronfman, was again sold in 1969. The studio, which had three different presidents during 1969, was purchased by Las Vegas (Nev.) hotel owner Kirk Kerkorian. Kinney National Service, Inc., purchased Warner Bros.-Seven Arts, and Joseph E. Levine's Embassy Pictures Corp. was sold to the AVCO Corp.

In New York City the birthplace of U.S. motion pictures was declared a historic site as part of the celebrations of the 75th anniversary of the U.S. film industry. The legendary actress Mae West in 1969 planned to play a comeback role in the film version of Gore Vidal's novel 'Myra Breckinridge'. Boris Karloff, the master monster of horror films, died in February. (*See* Obituaries.)

The Film Generation

The American Film Institute's 'Guide to College Film Courses 1969–70' showed that 219 institutions of higher education had courses in film making. By 1969, 51 schools of higher education offered degrees ranging from B.A. (Bachelor of Arts) to Ph.D. (Doctor of Philosophy) in motion pictures.

The Center for Advanced Film Studies awarded its first fellowships in 1969 to 15 aspiring film makers. The founders of the center hoped to create an institution comparable to European film schools.

A grant by the Ford Foundation helped young Negro film makers in New York City gain experience as apprentices in a motion picture being made by Harry Belafonte Enterprises. (*See also* Motion Pictures Special Report. *See in* CE: Motion Pictures.)

MOUNTAIN CLIMBING. Mountaineering was starting to take on the look of a popular sport. At Yosemite National Park in California a fledgling climber could purchase a day's instruction for $10. Additional instruction was available as skills

JACK WILKINS

The interest in mountain climbing in the United States has been increasing yearly, and some observers believe it could become a craze. Women, as well as men, are participating in this recreation.

and stamina improved. Some 2,000 climbers scaled Washington's Mount Rainier in 1969, about 600 more than in the preceding year. Aided by guide-instructors who gave on-the-spot training, participants paid $125 for the climb, a cost that included meals and lodging but excluded equipment rental. More climbers were noted at the Grand Tetons and at the Colorado Rockies, as well as at many Eastern U.S. peaks.

High-mountain areas once visited only by full-scale expeditions began to attract tourists. Sole requirements were good physical condition and the ability to walk over rough country. For example, a typical Himalayan tour started in Katmandu, Nepal, moved to the base of Mount Everest on the Tibet-Nepal border, and then backtracked.

Alpine, Himalayan Climbs

First winter climbs in the Alps were made of the northeast faces of the Obergabelhorn and the Bishorn, the north face of Mont Collon, and the southeast face of the Lenzspitze. The north face of the Droites was challenged but unclimbed during the winter. However, R. Messner tackled this route in the summer and scored a solo ascent. A guided climb of the Walker Spur of the Grandes Jorasses was made by 62-year-old Jean Juges. And a Polish team found a new route up the Pilier d'Angle of Mont Blanc, near Courmayeur, Italy.

Although Nepal lifted its ban on mountain climbing in 1969, Himalayan ventures were slow to start. A centennial expedition of the German Alpine Club failed to reach the top of Annapurna. The U.S. expedition to Dhaulagiri ended in disaster—a massive avalanche buried famed U.S. climber Boyd N. Everett, Jr., and six others, including two Sherpa guides. Swiss climbers, however, were able to scale Tukucha Peak (22,703 feet) in the Dhaulagiri area. A Japanese party reached the South Col of Everest by ski during the year.

Ascents in the Western Hemisphere

In Alaska, several U.S. parties reached the top of Mount McKinley from a new eastern route. In addition, first ascents were made of Mount Kimball (East Alaska Range), Paradise Peak (Kenai Peninsula), and peaks in the Cathedral (Kichatna) Spires. In Canada, Mount Robson was reached by the north face. Also, the first winter ascent of Mount Waddington was achieved.

South America was again a major region for climbers. Few important new routes, however, were climbed in Peru in 1969. There, Pumahuacanca, the southeast ridge of Chopicalqui, the west ridge of Huascarán, the east ridge of Jirishanca, and the northeast spur of Cerro Yerupaja were climbed for the first time in 1969. In Bolivia, a German expedition climbed 16 peaks in the Cordillera Apolobamba, and a Japanese party scaled seven peaks in the Cordillera Quisma Cruz.

MUSEUMS.

In 1969 U.S. museums were faced with a serious financial threat in the form of various tax-law revisions proposed in the U.S. Congress. According to the Association of Art Museum Directors and many concerned nonprofessional bodies, the proposed tax revisions would disastrously affect the day-to-day operations and future acquisitions of the country's museums and worsen their already grave financial plight. The major revision under consideration was one that would have eliminated any tax advantage for art donors. However, the final tax bill did not include the threatening revisions.

In ironic contrast this same year saw the appearance of *The Belmont Report: America's Museums,* a federally sponsored study begun some two years before to ascertain the state of U.S. museums. The report concluded that federal support for the country's museums was the only solution to their financial crisis and urged that the National Museum Act of 1966 be funded immediately with at least $1 million.

The "Open" Museum versus the "Object" Museum

The financial crisis was one of two current dilemmas faced by U.S. museums. The other was the

The University of Iowa Museum of Art, in Iowa City, features "carpeted" walls and an open plan of galleries. Ulfert Wilke is director of the museum.

COURTESY, THE UNIVERSITY OF IOWA

controversy raging over the museum's purpose and function, a subject that was widely discussed during the year. There were two schools of thought. One was the "open" museum concept, which saw the museum as an up-to-date community service center for all artistic manifestations. In opposition to this was the concept of the traditional "object-oriented" museum, the repository of art objects of the past and the present.

One major exponent of the open policy was Thomas P. F. Hoving, the director of New York City's Metropolitan Museum of Art, who presented the multimedia exhibition "Harlem on My Mind" early in the year. The exhibition, a sociopsychological survey of the Negro community in upper Manhattan, dragged the august Metropolitan into a community fracas. Some groups objected to the exhibit's content; other groups objected to its catalog for presumed racist remarks; and finally some groups objected to the very concept of the Metropolitan as anything but a repository for "high art." The exhibit opening was marked by picketing and also by an act of vandalism—several major museum paintings were marked with a small "H." Despite the controversy, the experimental exhibit proved a success in achieving heavy attendance, particularly among the city's Negro community.

General Events

Exhibitions devoted to old masters during 1969 centered around Rembrandt and the commemoration of the 300th anniversary of his death. In modern art there was exhibition emphasis on the great men of American art in the post-World War II period. Some U.S. museums also began to document the avant-garde "process" or "concept" art, which involved only ideas and their realization in a situation, or series of events, that did not always produce objects or traditional works of art.

The year was marked by the initiation of centennial anniversaries by three of the nation's largest art museums—New York City's Metropolitan Mu-

A British Columbian headdress ornament (left); a Tlingit (Alaska) dead man's mask (center); and an Olmec (Mexico) clay figure are in New York City's Museum of Primitive Art.

LEFT: JOHN T. HILL—COURTESY, THE MUSEUM OF PRIMITIVE ART
CENTER AND RIGHT: ELIZABETH LITTLE—COURTESY, THE MUSEUM OF PRIMITIVE ART

COURTESY, THE ART INSTITUTE OF CHICAGO

Included in the "Rembrandt and His Pupils" exhibition in 1969 was the painter's 'Young Girl at an Open Half-Door' (1645), an oil on canvas. A number of museums commemorated the tercentenary of Rembrandt's death in 1969.

seum of Art and American Museum of Natural History and the Museum of Fine Arts in Boston, Mass. Among the major museum gifts during 1969 were two given to the Metropolitan in New York—the Robert Lehman collection of European art and the Nelson Rockefeller collection of primitive art. (*See also* Painting and Sculpture.)

MUSIC. New York City's famous 64-year-old Juilliard School of Music got a new name and a new home in 1969. The institution moved into $30-million quarters at the Lincoln Center for the Performing Arts. Its name was changed to Juilliard School to fit its new role as the world's first conservatory for all performing arts. The old building at 120 Claremont Ave. was remodeled and taken over by the Manhattan School of Music. Another innovation at Lincoln Center was the completion of acoustical adjustments at Philharmonic Hall; for the first time the sound of music there satisfied musicians and patrons alike.

New sounds and new adaptations of old music enlivened the 1969 scene in the United States and Europe. The works of Johann Sebastian Bach, which have been arranged and rearranged to suit contemporary composers for the last 200 years, were recorded on the Moog electronic music synthesizer. The Moog version, arranged by Walter Carlos with the assistance of Benjamin Folkman, included the 'Brandenburg Concerto No. 3' and other favorites in an all-new interpretation of the old master. In tune with the times Baldwin Piano and Organ Co. put out an electronic piano with two extra pedals to control volume and knobs that permit filtering out or boosting of bass or treble.

Bach in a Mod mood was presented in concert at Philharmonic Hall by the Jacques Loussier Trio in 1969. The highly successful pieces started with straight Bach and then swung into jazz.

Music in 1969 also reflected the controversies of the time. Ned Rorem's 'War Scenes', a five-part song cycle adapted from Walt Whitman's poem 'Specimen Days', successfully portrayed the stupidities of war. Sung by Gérard Souzay, the work was premiered in Philharmonic Hall in November. In London, England, Hans Werner Henze's 'Versuch über Scheine', with text by Gaston Salvatore, showed *schweine* ("pigs," or rioting students) proudly flaunting the epithet attached to them by police and bourgeois.

The highlight of the Gulbenkian Festival in Lisbon, Portugal, was Olivier Messiaen's full-scale oratorio 'The Transfiguration of Our Lord Jesus Christ', a setting of New and Old Testament text for a large orchestra and 105-voice choir. The London Sinfonietta presented an unusual first performance in John Tavener's 'Celtic Requiem', based in part on children's singing games.

Symphony orchestras suffered severe financial woes in 1969, due largely to rising labor costs. The Buffalo and Rochester symphonies considered mergers, as did Cincinnati and Indianapolis groups. Detroit suffered a 34-day musicians' strike, and the Chicago and Cleveland orchestras were forced to

Hungarian Georg Solti became the new music director of the Chicago Symphony Orchestra in September 1969. He was previously the director of the Covent Garden Opera in London, England.

COURTESY, CHICAGO SYMPHONY ORCHESTRA

The famed Juilliard School opened its new quarters at the Lincoln Center for the Performing Arts in New York City in October 1969.

MARC & EVELYNE BERNHEIM FROM RAPHO GUILLUMETTE

dip into their endowments. San Francisco's orchestra was also in financial straits, and labor trouble forced the postponement of the National Symphony season in Washington, D.C.

Prizewinners for the year included James Frazier of Detroit, Mich., the Cantelli prize for conductors at Rome, Italy, and Okko Kamu of Finland, the international conductors' competition at Berlin, West Germany. Cristina Ortiz of Brazil won the Van Cliburn prize at Fort Worth, Tex.

Pierre Boulez, the French composer-conductor, will succeed Leonard Bernstein as conductor of the New York Philharmonic Orchestra in 1971. Bernstein, 51, retired in 1969 after 26 years with the orchestra. (*See also* Opera; Popular Music; Popular Music Special Report. *See in* CE: Music.)

NATIONAL PARK SERVICE. Areas added to the U.S. national park system in the first eight months of 1969 were Marble Canyon National Monument, in Arizona; Mar-A-Lago National Historic Site, in Florida; and Florissant Fossil Beds National Monument, in Colorado. Legislation to authorize several other areas was pending as the year ended.

In January U.S. President Lyndon B. Johnson set aside the 26,000-acre Marble Canyon National Monument gorge, long earmarked for a Colorado River dam site. Presidential proclamations also added 358,500 acres to three national monuments: Capitol Reef and Arches, in Utah; and Katmai, in Alaska.

The U.S. Congress acted quickly to save Florissant Fossil Beds when its private owners were about to bulldoze an area rich in fossils. By September the Senate also had approved bills to establish Apostle Islands National Lakeshore, in Wisconsin; Sawtooth National Recreation Area, in Idaho; and Buffalo National River, in Arkansas. Bills to authorize two new national historic sites honoring former Presidents William Howard Taft in Ohio and Lyndon B. Johnson in Texas were well through the legislative process, along with a bill to authorize development of Eisenhower National Historic Site, in Pennsylvania, designated by secretarial proclamation in 1967 as an area of the national park system.

The new secretary of the interior, Walter J. Hickel, reappointed George B. Hartzog, Jr., as director of the National Park Service, a position he had held since January 1964. Secretary Hickel cited 11 guidelines for management of the national park system. He stressed that the service, rather than concessioners, should operate campgrounds.

A National Park Service study published in 1969 reported that visitors to the national park system spent an estimated $6.4 billion in 1967. Attendance in 1967 was about 140 million. This spending benefited the nation, according to Ernst W. Swanson, North Carolina State University economist, in the form of $4.76 billion in personal income, $5.71 billion added to the gross national product, and $952 million in federal taxes. He estimated the capitalized value of the national park system at $142.7 billion. "Dollar signs cannot be attached to values" derived from the parks, Swanson said, "but the economic value alone justifies our continued care of these assets." Visits in 1969 were expected to reach 160 million.

Virgin Islands National Park was the site of a record scientific achievement—an underwater marine study conducted for 60 consecutive days by four Department of Interior aquanauts on the bottom of Lameshur Bay. The National Park Service also provided the base campsite for the project. Participating with the department were the U.S. Navy, National Aeronautics and Space Administration, and General Electric Co., the manufacturer of the underwater living quarters. (*See* Oceanography.)

"Summer in the Parks," a creative program to use the parks of metropolitan Washington, D.C., to capacity for community enjoyment, surpassed its opening year of 1968. Approximately 1,300 events

TOP: WILLIAM KELLER—COURTESY, NATIONAL PARK SERVICE
ABOVE: COURTESY, NATIONAL PARK SERVICE

The Lady Bird Johnson Grove (top) in Redwood National Park, California, was dedicated by U.S. President Richard M. Nixon in August 1969. Earlier in the year the Wawona Tunnel Tree in Yosemite National Park, California, fell to the ground (above). The tree stood 234 feet high and its tunnel was 9 feet high.

were held, attracting 400,000 participants—an increase of 100,000 over the preceding year. Mrs. Richard M. Nixon launched the program and later was hostess to Washington children on two Potomac River cruises aboard the presidential yacht. The National Park Service took youngsters to parks in the District of Columbia, Maryland, and Virginia throughout the summer. Puppet shows, artmobiles, pottery demonstrations, concerts, movies, and dances blended entertainment with educational programs.

Environmental education continued to receive emphasis. The National Environmental Education Development program broadened its pilot program, begun in 1968. By September the service had 23 pilot schools serving 27 schools and school systems, compared to five the preceding year. The pilot schools are devoted to the fifth- and sixth-grade levels of a kindergarten-through-high-school curriculum on environmental education designed by the University of California, at Davis.

The National Park Service increased to 48 the number of Environmental Study Areas operating in 26 states and the District of Columbia. These areas are National Park Service lands serving schools, adult groups, workshops, and clubs as outdoor laboratories for teaching environmental principles. In the planning stage were 54 more study areas.

Conservation; Other Developments

Secretary Hickel strongly opposed construction of a 39-square-mile jetport just north of the 1,400,000-acre Everglades National Park, in southern Florida, on the grounds that massive water and air pollution, noise, access routes, and other results would be ruinous to the park. He reached an agreement with Secretary of Transportation John A. Volpe and Florida's Gov. Claude R. Kirk, Jr., that an alternative site must be found. In an equally crucial agreement, Hickel and the governor pledged to work toward a plan that would assure the park the overland flow of fresh water that it needs to exist. The secretary also strengthened protection of the Florida alligator by reinforcing the park's antipoaching activities directed at hide hunters.

During the year the Sierra Club, backed by other conservation groups, intensified their opposition to a proposed building of a multimillion-dollar resort in the Mineral King area of the Sierra Nevada range. The conservationists contended that the project would endanger the wilderness setting of parts of Sequoia National Park, which surrounds Mineral King on three sides.

The National Park Service took a significant step to preserve rare natural areas from automobile traffic by limiting Yosemite National Park's Mariposa Grove of sequoia trees (*Sequoia gigantea*), in California, to tramway visitors and hikers. Visitors park near the grove and board tramways equipped with sound narratives that provide background data on the big trees. Each tram carries about 60 passengers and makes the tour at 15-minute intervals.

The tour passes the famous Wawona Tunnel Tree, which fell in the spring of 1969. One of the world's best-known trees, the 2,000-year-old sequoia bestrode the Mariposa road.

In August U.S. President Richard M. Nixon dedicated the Lady Bird Johnson Grove in Redwood National Park, California, in honor of the former first lady, "who has done so much," he said, "on behalf of the natural beauty of the land." Mrs. Johnson, Mrs. Nixon, and former President Johnson attended. The ex-president had signed the Redwood National Park Act in 1968, and Mrs. Johnson later dedicated the park at the grove bearing her name.

A new jetport (bottom) under construction in 1969, 45 miles west of Miami, Fla., was the subject of much controversy. Environmental scientists claim that if it is completed for use it will virtually destroy the wildlife of Everglades National Park (below).

BELOW AND BOTTOM: COURTESY, NATIONAL PARK SERVICE

The park service entered into a cooperative agreement with the American Society of Civil Engineers and the Library of Congress to prepare a Historic Engineering Record of American engineering sites, structures, and antiquities. Many early American canals, locks, bridges, and buildings were to be surveyed, mapped, and photographed. These records would be preserved in the Library of Congress in a program similar to, and allied with, the Historic American Buildings Survey.

The National Park Service Registry of National Historic Landmarks increased its number to 808. Landmarks are not units of the national park system. The National Registry of Natural Landmarks added Dinosaur Valley in Somervell County, Texas, because of the valley's excellent limestone tracks of sauropods, the largest of the dinosaurs. (*See in* CE: National Parks articles.)

NAURU. In 1969 Nauru celebrated its first full year of independence. President Hammer de RobURT described the first year as free of major difficulties but added that more progress could have been made with the help of Australia, Great Britain, and New Zealand—the countries that had administered Nauru as a colony.

Efforts to transfer control of the phosphate industry to Nauruans continued in 1969. In June De Roburt participated in negotiations with the British Phosphate Commission (BPC) and the Nauru Phosphate Commission (NPC). Nauru was willing to renew a partial contract with the BPC but also wanted the NPC to sell directly to Australia and other countries and thereby reap the profits that would have gone to British interests. The BPC paid $9.80 a ton for phosphate in 1969, but Nauru was able to sell 300,000 tons directly to Japan at a considerably higher price, $12.40 a ton.

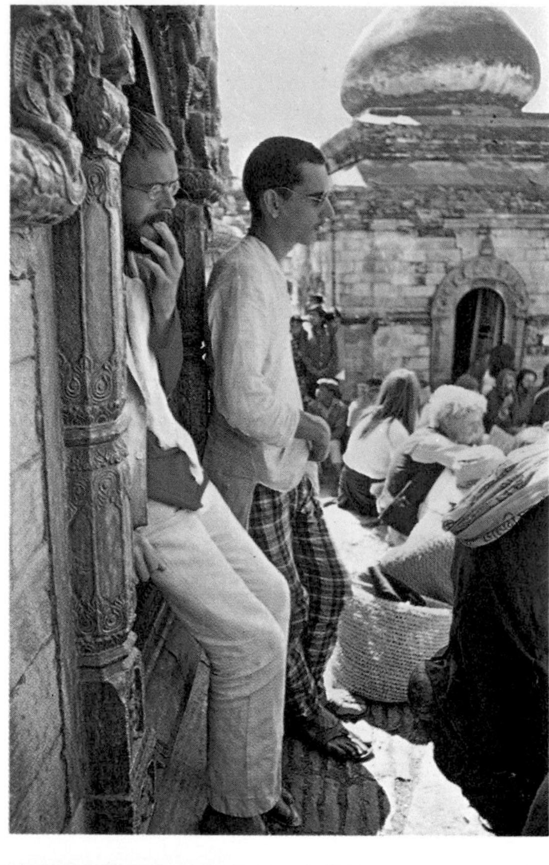

TOP: LIAISON AGENCY. ABOVE: HARRISON FORMAN

Hippies pass the time in Katmandu, the capital of Nepal (top). Drugs are easily obtained there and the city draws an international clientele. Part of the 1969 grain harvest is shown drying at Bhadgaon, Nepal (above).

NEPAL. In the face of pressure from India and Communist China, Nepal remained sensitive about its neutrality in 1969. When India's Foreign Minister Dinesh Singh visited Katmandu, the capital, in June he stressed Nepal's "special relationship" with India. The Nepalese government promptly reasserted its sovereignty by demanding the withdrawal of Indian radio operators from checkpoints on the Tibetan border and of the 40-man Indian military liaison group. Nepal also announced that it had canceled its 1965 arms agreement with India.

The release in October 1968 of B. P. Koirala and other Nepali Congress leaders did not bring political stability. King Mahendra still considered the *panchayat* system of elected councils indispensable, despite student dissatisfaction. Kirti Nidhi Bista, who succeeded Surya Bahadur Thapa as prime minister on April 7, strengthened the royalist membership of the cabinet and suspended the controversial land taxes. (*See in* CE: Nepal.)

NETHERLANDS. The composition of the government of the Netherlands in 1969 remained at six members of the Catholic People's party, three members of the People's Party for Freedom and Democracy (Liberals), three members of the Antirevolutionary party, and two members of the Christian Historical Union. Thirteen parties were represented in the parliament.

On July 2 the Upper House was elected by the members of the provincial states. The new House was divided as follows: Catholic People's party 24; Labor party 20; People's Party for Freedom and Democracy 8; Antirevolutionary party 7; Christian Historical Union 8; and others 8.

Economic developments in early 1969 began with the introduction on January 1 of a new system of purchase tax—the value-added tax—causing a rapid rise in prices. At the end of March the price index for family consumption had risen by 5.5%. On April 8 the government announced a general price freeze, which was revoked on September 4.

The execution of the Delta Plan (the closing of the sea arms in the southwestern part of the country) continued throughout 1969. On April 28 the Volkerak, a sea arm between the isle of Overflakkee and the province of North Brabant, was closed. On July 22 near Heinenoord a tunnel under the Maas River was opened, completing a high road right across the delta area from Rotterdam to Zeeland. In the north a new project of land reclamation was started by the closing of the Lauwers Zee. In the presence of Queen Juliana on May 23 the last of 25 caissons was sunk; together the caissons had a length of 900 meters (2,952 feet).

In June the nation was alarmed by a serious poisoning of the Rhine River by an insecticide accidentally dumped into the waters. Hasty measures had to be taken to protect the supply of drinking water for large areas of the country. (*See also* Conservation. *See in* CE: Netherlands.)

NEWSPAPERS. The press in 1969 was severely criticized by U.S. Vice-President Spiro T. Agnew. Agnew broadly attacked television networks and newspapers alike for what he termed unfairness in their coverage of the Administration of U.S. Presi-

The first issue of *Chicago Today,* a new version of an old afternoon daily, was published on April 28, 1969. It is owned by the Chicago Tribune Co. and was previously called *Chicago's American.*

COURTESY, "CHICAGO TODAY"

dent Richard M. Nixon. Although the vice-president's criticism touched on certain problems in television and the press that had long troubled conscientious journalists, his sweeping denunciations were widely challenged. Many felt that the main thrust of Agnew's remarks was not directed at the media's genuine faults but was a partisan attempt to stifle legitimate criticism of the Administration's policies.

Diplomatic blows were traded by the Soviet Union and the United States in April and May on behalf of the journalistic function. Travel restrictions placed on correspondents for *The New York Times* and the *Washington Post* in the Soviet Union brought similar restrictions on two Soviet newsmen representing *Pravda* and *NOVOSTI* (news and feature agency) in Washington, D.C., and New York City, respectively. The Soviet Union then responded by expelling the *Washington Post* man, Anatole Shub; *TASS* correspondent Victor Kopytin, who was assigned to Washington, D.C., was then asked to leave the United States.

An agreement was reached in September between the Times Mirror Co. of Los Angeles, Calif., and the Times Herald Co. of Dallas, Tex., for an exchange of stock that would make the Los Angeles publisher the new owner of the *Dallas Times Herald* and its affiliated broadcasting stations. The market value of the transaction was placed at $91.5 million. Completion of the agreement was subject to the approval of the Times Herald stockholders and the Federal Communications Commission, which must approve all transfers of broadcast licenses.

Another major purchase was announced in October by Knight Newspapers Inc. The Knight chain agreed to buy the *Philadelphia Inquirer* and the *Philadelphia Daily News* from Triangle Publications for a reported $55 million. Triangle owns several major magazines as well as broadcasting stations; these were not involved in the transaction. Walter H. Annenberg, head of Triangle Publications, became the U.S. ambassador to Great Britain on April 30, 1969.

In Chicago, Ill., personnel of the news media continued to publish a critical review of their employers' journalistic efforts under the title of *Chicago Journalism Review.* The enterprise was precipitated by coverage of the Democratic National Convention in 1968. Some Chicago newspapermen felt that their newspapers had not done an entirely honest job of handling the situation and its aftermath.

The *Los Angeles Times* won two Pulitzer prizes—for meritorious public service and international reporting. The latter prize was presented to William Tuohy for his work in Vietnam.

Daily newspaper circulation in the United States reached 62,535,394 copies during 1968 for a gain of 1.5% over the preceding year. At a meeting of the American Newspaper Publishers Association in April 1969 it was also noted that 492 of the 1,753 dailies in the United States were printing by offset by the end of 1968. This represented 89 more newspapers in offset in 1968 than in 1967.

In the United States two widely known and widely read public-affairs columnists died. Westbrook Pegler, a nationally syndicated columnist until his retirement in 1962, died in June at the age of 74. The winner of a Pulitzer prize in 1941, Pegler was best known for his acid criticism of important public figures. Drew Pearson, whose Washington, D.C., column was carried by more than 650 daily and weekly newspapers, died in September. Pearson specialized in Washington exposés. (*See also* Magazines; Obituaries. *See in* CE: Newspapers.)

NEW ZEALAND. In the general elections of Nov. 29, 1969, the National party government resisted a strong challenge from the Labor party and was expected to command 45 seats in the 84-seat Parliament. With the defeat of its chief, V. F. Cracknell, the Social Credit party lost its lone seat. The government decided in February that New Zealand troops would remain in Malaysia and Singapore after the British withdrawal in 1971.

Economic recovery from a slump in exports, mainly wool, two years previously continued in

1969. Unemployment, which reached 8,665 in mid-1968, was down to 3,358 by mid-1969 and still falling. The brightest economic development was the discovery of oil offshore that looked promising enough for a Sedco 135F rig to be towed to the South Pacific to explore the field fully. It began drilling 30 miles off Opunake early in October.

New Zealand dairy farmers, hit by gluts in importing countries, were urged to move more into beef production. The annual budget, constructed mainly on recommendations of the National Development Conference organized by the government the preceding year, made special provision for these farmers. Wool growers who saw the possibility of their reserves' running out by the mid-1970's failed to obtain direct government assistance in paying their levy to the International Wool Board.

The voting and liquor-drinking age was reduced from 21 to 20. Archbishop Peter McKeefrey of Wellington, the capital, became New Zealand's first Roman Catholic cardinal. The divorce rate increased as a result of speeding up liberalized provisions of the Matrimonial Amendment Act of 1968. (*See in* CE: New Zealand.)

NICARAGUA. The booming economy that characterized the first year of President Anastasio Somoza Debayle's administration tapered off to a standstill during 1969. The gross national product dropped, from between 6% and 8%, to less than 1%. Cotton, the number one export and principal indicator of the nation's economy, produced well after three dry years, but unfortunately this advantage was offset by a 2¢-to-3¢ drop in price due to foreign competition.

Coffee, the second most important export, also produced well both locally and worldwide. Nicaragua's quota was cut 7.5% by the International Coffee Agreement, and this cut, accompanied by a 30% drop in price, definitely affected the nation's economy. The growing meat industry increased 4.5%, and meat ranked as the third most important export; however, the United States cut its quota of imported Nicaragua beef.

Because of a heavy trade deficit, Nicaragua had some reservations about its position in the Central American Common Market. In 1969 Nicaragua bought heavily of manufactured goods from its neighbors, and, in line with its hope to become the breadbasket of Central America, expected to pay with agricultural goods. However, there was no Common Market policy on bartering agricultural produce and, as a result, Nicaragua was not able to maintain a favorable balance of trade. The 1969 war between El Salvador and Honduras put a critical strain on the delicately balanced Common Market, with much trade shut off entirely.

The austerity program presented by the president to cope with the recession found few supporters. The cost of living sharply increased and the standard of living dropped. (*See in* CE: Nicaragua.)

NIGER. Throughout 1969 President Hamani Diori maintained an intense level of diplomatic activity, as much in the name of Niger as in that of the Afro-Malagasy Common Organization, of which he was reelected president on January 27. The first international conference of French-speaking countries was held at Niamey, the capital of Niger, in February. It was attended by 29 delegations from Africa, Asia, Europe, Canada, and, notably, from Quebec province. An agency for cultural and technical cooperation was created, and President Diori was made its provisional head.

Problems facing Niger's economy in 1969 included a fall in peanut prices, the consequences of the French currency devaluation, tax evasion, high transport costs, and the loss of customs duties through fraud. The lack of highly trained executives and the growth of population presented difficulties. In addition, the effects of the prolonged 1968 drought proved to be catastrophic. In the Sahel region 50% of the livestock, a major source of income, were wiped out, and in the extreme east 75% of the livestock died. (*See also* Africa. *See in* CE: Niger.)

NIGERIA. Efforts by international organizations and influential individuals failed again in 1969 to produce any concrete hope of ending the civil war in Nigeria. The Ibo tribesmen of secessionist Biafra continued to starve while federal and Biafran government officials alike quarreled over the legal technicalities of allowing emergency airlifts into Biafra, the former Eastern Region of Nigeria. Throughout the year the starvation problem in Biafra worsened as federal forces fought for control of the remaining rebel-held territory.

The greatest problem of getting food and medical supplies into Biafra continued to be that of finding an acceptable route into the region. The Nigerian federal government, concerned that the supplies would be distributed to Biafran troops and that arms could be smuggled to the rebels, insisted on inspecting all shipments. The Biafrans, fearing the food would be poisoned, refused to accept shipments coming from federal territory.

In June the Swiss-run International Committee of the Red Cross suspended all relief flights into Biafra after a Swedish Red Cross plane was shot down by federal forces. Earlier in the year the federal government had tolerated the night flights to Biafra's Uli airstrip. The federal government announced later in June that it was taking over the responsibility for all relief efforts in both Nigeria and Biafra. The Red Cross coordinator was expelled from Nigeria. The federal government warned that it would shoot down any unauthorized planes attempting to reach Biafra. Another relief group, Joint Church Aid, continued to send relief flights to Biafra by night despite the danger.

Both Biafra and Nigeria accused the Red Cross of having less than humanitarian aims. The Nigerians unofficially charged that the Red Cross was

Starving Biafrans are aided at feeding stations like this one at Nguru, Nigeria.
JEFF GRALNICK FROM BLACK STAR

part of a "subversive conspiracy," and the Biafrans claimed that the Red Cross ran spy networks inside rebel-held areas.

The federal government in November had to cut food distribution within Nigeria. Some observers felt that the federal government, by taking over the efforts of the Red Cross, was inviting food-shortage problems as severe in Nigeria as they were in Biafra. The federal government was not equipped to handle massive relief programs, and the financial burden was enormous. The Red Cross had been spending $3.5 million a month for relief efforts in Nigeria and Biafra.

In March Great Britain's Prime Minister Harold Wilson visited Lagos, the federal capital. There were reports that Wilson had intended to protest the bombing of civilian targets in Biafra, seek ways for initiating peace moves, and find a way for expediting relief-supply shipments. The Nigerian head of government, Maj. Gen. Yakubu Gowon, in his welcoming speech cautioned Wilson against making any attempts to interfere in Nigerian affairs. During his visit to Uganda in July Pope Paul VI also made fruitless attempts at mediation between Biafra and Nigeria. (*See also* Commonwealth of Nations; International Relations.)

The Organization of African Unity (OAU) made attempts during the year to aid Biafra and Nigeria in resolving their differences. In April the OAU consultative committee met at Monrovia, Liberia, to draft a proposal calling for a cease-fire and recognition by the Biafrans of the concept of a united Nigeria. The Nigerian federal government accepted the proposal; the Biafrans rejected it.

The leaders of the member nations in the OAU, meeting in September at Addis Ababa, Ethiopia, again took up the Nigerian-Biafran problem. A resolution passed by the OAU conference called for a cease-fire and the opening of peace talks and endorsed the concept of a united Nigeria. Gowon, while not agreeing to the cease-fire proposal, indicated that he was willing to begin negotiations without demanding any preconditions from Biafra.

In October Biafra's leader, Lieut. Col. C. Odumegwu Ojukwu, communicated to Gowon through Emperor Haile Selassie I of Ethiopia his willingness to hold unconditional peace talks. A Biafran spokesman early in November indicated that Biafra would ease the demands for complete independence if Nigeria would guarantee the safety of all Biafrans at the end of the civil war. Another Biafran, however, denounced the overture as ridiculous; and Ojukwu said the war would have a military end.

The stalemate reached between Nigerian and Biafran forces in late 1968 continued into early 1969. In February federal air force planes bombed

This is a Biafran oil refinery, located somewhere in the jungles of Nigeria. The Nigerian civil war began on July 6, 1967, and at the end of 1969 there was some evidence that it would end soon.
JEFF GRALNICK FROM BLACK STAR

two market towns, killing more than 400 civilians. Biafran troops, after receiving new supplies of arms from France, managed to hold federal troops at bay until April 23, when federal forces captured Umuahia, the provisional capital of Biafra.

A few days later, however, the federally-held town of Owerri was retaken by Biafran troops. Owerri had been under siege by the Biafrans since February. The Biafrans also crossed the Niger River to the west and captured a town in the Mid-Western Region. In the fall federal and Biafran forces, using gunboats, fought for control of the oil fields around the Orashi River.

Early in the year the Nigerian government hoped that oil production would reach a new high of a million barrels a day in 1969. Air raids by Biafrans flying small Swedish planes, however, severely hampered the oil industry, and production dropped to an estimated 440,000 barrels a day.

The civilian population in Nigeria became increasingly impatient with the federal government and called for an end to the war. Student and labor groups demanded that civilians be protected against Biafran air raids. Antitax riots in the Western Region forced the government to lower taxes. The Kainji Dam on the Niger River opened during the year. (*See also* Africa. *See in* CE: Nigeria.)

President Richard M. Nixon

NIXON, RICHARD M. The president of the United States should be an "activist" who would "bring dissenters into policy discussions" and build his Administration on the "broadest possible base," Republican presidential candidate Richard M. Nixon declared in 1968. One year later, President Nixon's performance was being judged by candidate Nixon's standard and, in the opinion of some critics, was falling short of meeting it. The problems besetting the new president were basically those which plagued his predecessor: the Vietnam conflict, inflation, and racial unrest. While these burdens were inherited, others were of Nixon's own making.

No discernible progress toward a negotiated settlement of the Vietnam conflict had been made by the end of 1969. The peace talks in Paris, France, were stalemated. The resignation of the chief U.S. negotiator at the talks, Henry Cabot Lodge, and the lack of a replacement of equivalent rank was interpreted as a turning away from negotiation as a method of achieving peace. The Nixon Administration seemed to be placing emphasis instead on its "Vietnamization" policy—the gradual withdrawal of U.S. troops and the turning over of more of the fighting to the South Vietnamese.

Although most of the nation was content to let Nixon handle the conflict in his own way, by autumn a substantial number of U.S. citizens began feeling impatience and disillusionment with the effectiveness of Nixon's policy. In moratorium marches and demonstrations in October, November, and December many indicated their desire for "peace now." Nixon stressed that he would not be swayed by their appeal, that U.S. foreign policy should not be made "in the street." In a nationally televised speech on November 3, Nixon appealed directly to the "silent majority" of the people for support for his Vietnam policies. Nixon's gamble for more time in which to make his policies effective seemed to work. In a Gallup Poll conducted after the president's speech, 68% of those interviewed felt the president was handling his job well —a 12% increase over the previous rating.

Nixon made other attempts to weld together public support for his Administration mainly by isolating his major critics—youth, war protesters, and the news media. He directed his appeal for support to what he called the "silent majority"—never defined but taken to be the conservative, middle-aged, nonblack, and nonpoor—where the Republican party had its greatest potential for strength. One major element in this strategy was the vice-president, Spiro T. Agnew, who in a number of highly provocative speeches attacked war protesters, rebellious youth, and the news media.

On the domestic front, Nixon strove to combat inflation by applying strong brakes to the economy, which was going through its worst inflationary crisis since the Korean War. It was not clear at year's end whether the president's efforts at curbing inflation were attaining success.

Nixon seemed to have no civil rights program; in fact, Negroes complained that the Nixon Administration was basically hostile to black aspirations. Nixon did support proposals to establish a federal minimum standard of welfare assistance and to create more opportunities for blacks in craft unions.

However, blacks were alienated by his attempt at a slowdown in school desegregation and his nomination of Judge Clement F. Haynsworth, Jr., a Southern conservative with an anti-civil rights record, for Supreme Court associate justice.

The Senate's stinging rejection of Nixon's nomination of Haynsworth was considered the president's major defeat in Congress. Nixon's chief victories were in draft reform and the passage of the controversial ABM (antiballistic missile) program. (*See* Congress, U.S.; Defense; Selective Service.)

Two highlights of Nixon's first year in office were his journey to Europe in February and March and his tour of Asia and Europe in July and August. The latter journey included a visit to Romania, where Nixon received a tumultuous welcome. It was the first trip by a U.S. president to a Communist country in almost a quarter of a century.

Nixon's general approach in U.S. foreign policy was low-key and cautious. During his Asian tour he enunciated a new policy of U.S. disengagement and of encouraging "Asian solutions to Asian problems." In his major speech on Latin American policy, he emphasized that the United States would decrease its leadership role in the region.

Most observers felt that the president had ended his first year in office in a stronger position than that in which he had begun. How long Nixon would be able to retain support, however, without making more substantial progress in ending the Vietnam conflict and inflation, remained in doubt. (*See also* Foreign Policy, U.S.; Latin America; United States. *See in* CE: Nixon.)

NORWAY. The four non-Socialist coalition parties were returned to power in Norway's 1969 parliamentary elections. The coalition majority in the Storting (parliament) was reduced to two with 76 seats as opposed to 74 held by the Labor party. Per Borten continued as prime minister.

Shortly after the election, a price freeze was announced in anticipation of rises that would undoubtedly follow the 20% value-added tax scheduled to begin Jan. 1, 1970. Budgetary provisions were made for increased social benefits to help compensate low-income groups.

To compensate for the gap between Norwegian interest rates and those abroad, which had decreased Norway's gold and currency holdings, the discount rate was raised from 3.5% to 4.5%—the first such rise in 14 years. The balance of payments for the first seven months of 1969 showed a surplus of $170.4 million. Imports increased 19% as against a .5% export rise; total production rose 4%, and exports to the European Economic Community (EEC), or Common Market, countries increased 23% in the first six months of 1969. There was, however, a steep rise in labor costs, and imports of heavy goods and chemical products rose.

Industrial, commercial, and shipping circles generally opposed participation in Nordek, the proposed Scandinavian customs union, as the possibility of EEC membership grew. The government urged suspension of Greece from the Council of Europe. (*See also* Europe. *See in* CE: Norway.)

NUCLEAR ENERGY. Electric utilities were reconsidering their commitment to nuclear power in 1969. Sales of conventionally powered plants outstripped those of nuclear plants, or "nukes," by some three to one during the year. The cost of electricity produced by nuclear plants was to have been 4 mills (.4¢) per kilowatt-hour (kw-hr) by 1969, a competitive price. But the actual cost, affected by inflation and high interest rates for building funds, proved to be about 6 mills (.6¢).

Conservationists proved adept at stalling construction of nuclear plants. Waters used to cool nuclear reactors pollute rivers and lakes when reintroduced, argued conservationists. They also charged that radioactive gases periodically vented from the nuclear plants posed another environmental hazard. Such venting, utilities' officials countered, did not exceed safety limits set by the Atomic Energy Commission (AEC).

The AEC was retiring from the enriched-uranium business. In November U.S. President

Prior to detonation, engineers with Project Rulison gather at Colorado's first nuclear test site. The blast, on September 10, used a 40-kiloton nuclear bomb to free natural gas trapped in underground rock.

WIDE WORLD

TOP AND ABOVE: WIDE WORLD

Canadians gather at the U.S. border (top) to protest a nuclear blast on tiny Amchitka, a remote Alaskan island. The Atomic Energy Commission's underground test of a one-megaton bomb, in October, cracked a road on the island (above).

Richard M. Nixon ordered the AEC to operate its three gaseous-diffusion plants, which make all U.S. nuclear fuel, as separate entities. They would eventually be sold to private operators.

Nuclear engineers from 12 West European nations cooperated in developing a nuclear reactor, code-named Project Dragon, capable of generating electricity at about 3.6 mills (.36¢) per kw-hr. The reactor will be cooled by a gas like helium rather than water or sodium. The gas would also drive the power turbines, thus eliminating the uneconomical steam generators ordinarily employed.

French scientists reported they used the energy of the world's most powerful laser to fuse the nuclei of deuterium (heavy water) atoms, an action that can release an enormous amount of energy, as in the hydrogen bomb. Although the experiment resulted only in a series of tiny explosions with minimal energy release, it was an initial step toward possible laser control of fusion.

An older approach toward harnessing fusion was the "magnetic bottle"—strong magnetic fields that confine high-temperature gases, or plasmas, long enough for fusion to take place. Soviet scientists were working with Tokamak 3, a magnetic bottle that confined plasma for 50 thousandths of a second at 18,000,000° F. British scientists confirmed these results in a 1969 report. (*See also* Fuel and Power. *See in* CE: Atomic Energy and Structure.)

NURSING. The ranks of practicing registered nurses (R.N.s) were beginning to enlarge, according to the American Nurses' Association (ANA). An estimated 680,000 R.N.s were practicing in the United States by 1969. This meant that there were 338 nurses per 100,000 population. This figure, however, still fell short of the 850,000 R.N.s the U.S. Public Health Service said would be needed by 1970.

Recent efforts to make nursing more attractive to youth appeared to be paying off. The National League for Nursing reported there were some 61,400 admissions in schools with R.N. programs during academic 1968, a gain of more than 2,600 over the preceding year's total. Graduations rose by about 3,300 to provide some 41,500 new R.N.s by 1969. The rapid expansion of associate-degree

A faculty member of the University of Rochester School of Medicine talks of the school's first black graduate nurse to the accompaniment of "soul" music, as part of a drive to recruit black student nurses.

COURTESY, AMERICAN NURSES' ASSOCIATION

nursing programs, usually offered by junior and community colleges, was primarily responsible for the upsurge of nursing candidates.

The ANA looked ahead to the 1970's, predicting that improved health care would be a major focus of nursing. The profession was expected to participate actively with other health groups in encouraging health legislation.

Demands for higher wages and better working conditions continued to be voiced by nurses in 1969. A recent ANA study of salary ranges for staff nurses in nonfederal, short-term hospitals with at least 200 beds showed that the average starting salary was $6,900. This represented only a $500-a-year advance in nurses' starting wages since early 1968.

Most R.N.s again were employed in hospitals and other health institutions. The remainder, about one third, were employed as private-duty nurses or worked for physicians and dentists or in public-health agencies and nursing schools, in industry, and in schools. (*See also* Hospitals; Medicine. *See in* CE: Nursing.)

OBITUARIES. The following is a selected list of notable people who died in 1969:

Earl Alexander of Tunis (Harold Rupert Leofric George Alexander), British field marshal, one of the major Allied military commanders in World War II, governor-general of Canada 1946–52; June 16, in Slough, England, age 77.

Emilio Arenales Catalán, Guatemalan diplomat, president of the United Nations (UN) General Assembly from 1968 and foreign affairs minister of Guatemala; April 17, in Guatemala City, Guatemala, age 46.

Baroness Asquith of Yarnbury (Lady Violet Bonham Carter), daughter of Herbert Henry Asquith, Great Britain's prime minister 1908–16, Liberal party leader, and first member of Liberal party to be made a life peer in the House of Lords; February 19, in London, England, age 81.

René Barrientos Ortuño, president of Bolivia from 1966; April 27, in a helicopter crash near Cochabamba, Bolivia, age 49.

Josef Cardinal Beran, Roman Catholic primate of Czechoslovakia, imprisoned both by the Nazis and by the Communist government for his unswerving criticism of them, in exile in Rome, Italy, since 1965; May 17, in Rome, age 80.

Philip Blaiberg, a dentist who had been the world's longest-surviving heart-transplant recipient to date—19 months and 15 days; August 17, in Cape Town, South Africa, age 60.

Robert Briscoe, Irish nationalist and one of the founders of the Fianna Fail party, first Jewish lord mayor of Dublin, Ireland, 1956–57 and 1961–62; May 30, in Dublin, Ireland, age 74.

Ailsa Mellon Bruce, philanthropist who was considered the richest woman in the United States with a fortune estimated at $500 million; August 25, in New York City, age 68.

PICTORIAL PARADE

DIRKSEN

UPI (UK) LTD.

ESHKOL

UPI COMPIX

EISENHOWER

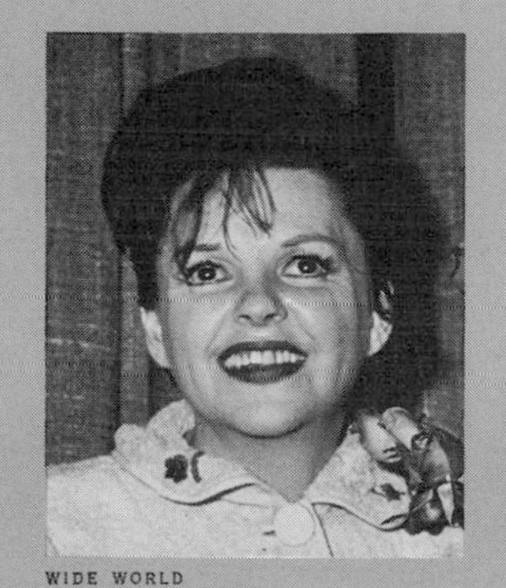

WIDE WORLD

GARLAND

KEYSTONE
JONES

KEYSTONE
KARLOFF

WIDE WORLD
KENNEDY

MARCIANO
WIDE WORLD

MC GILL
WIDE WORLD

Irene Castle, ballroom dancer who, teamed with her husband Vernon, popularized such dance steps as the "Castle Walk" and "Maxixe"; January 25, in Eureka Springs, Ark., age 75.

Bud Collyer, popular television host; September 8, in Greenwich, Conn., age 61.

Dame Ivy Compton-Burnett, English author, known for her novels depicting the Edwardian period ('The Mighty and Their Fall'); August 27, in London, age 77.

Maureen (Little Mo) Connolly, tennis champion who, in 1953, captured the national championships of Australia, France, Great Britain, and the United States—the first woman ever to do so; June 21, in Dallas, Tex., age 34.

Amos De-Shalit, one of the world's most eminent nuclear physicists; September 2, in Rehovot, Israel, age 42.

Everett M. Dirksen, U.S. senator (R, Ill.) from 1951, Senate minority leader from 1959, and member of House of Representatives 1933–49; September 7, in Washington, D.C., age 73.

Dorothy Draper, interior decorator, early advocate of total color coordination and bright color combinations; March 10, in Cleveland, Ohio, age 79.

Vernon Duke (Vladimir Dukelsky), Russian-born composer known for his stage and popular music ('April in Paris', 'Autumn in New York') as well as his serious compositions ('Emperor Norton'); January 17, in Santa Monica, Calif., age 65.

Allen W. Dulles, director of the Central Intelligence Agency 1953–61; January 29, in Washington, D.C., age 75.

Dwight D. Eisenhower, U.S. president 1953–61, five-star general of the Army, and during World War II Supreme Commander, Allied Expeditionary Forces in Europe; March 28, in Washington, D.C., age 78.

Levi Eshkol, prime minister of Israel from 1963; February 26, in Jerusalem, Israel, age 73.

PICTORIAL PARADE
HO CHI MINH
WIDE WORLD
PIKE

Harry Emerson Fosdick, leader in the development of liberal Protestantism in the 1920's, author; October 5, in Bronxville, N.Y., age 91.

William Freyse, cartoonist of "Our Boarding House," syndicated cartoon panel; March 3, in Tucson, Ariz., age 70.

Judy Garland, teen-age star ('The Wizard of Oz'), actress ('A Star Is Born'), and singer; June 22, in London, age 47.

Josef Gerstmann, internationally respected neurologist and psychiatrist known for his work on a brain disorder named after him—Gerstmann syndrome; March 23, in New York City, age 81.

Adam L. Gimbel, developer of the largest chain of U.S. specialty stores—Saks Fifth Avenue; September 9, New York City, age 75.

Walter Gropius, architect and designer who founded the innovative Bauhaus school in Weimar, Germany, which had a major influence on the development of modern design; July 5, in Boston, Mass., age 86.

Nicolas Grunitsky, Togo's president 1963–67; September 27, in Paris, France, age 56.

Coleman Hawkins, saxophonist who was a pioneer of jazz; May 19, in New York City, age 64.

George Francis (Gabby) Hayes, character actor who played in 200 Westerns, known for his role as the sidekick of cowboy Hopalong Cassidy; February 9, in Burbank, Calif., age 83.

Sonja Henie, three times Olympic Games figure-skating champion and later a producer of ice-revue shows and a motion-picture star; October 12, in a plane flying from Paris to Oslo, Norway, age 57.

Conrad (Nicky) Hilton, Jr., playboy son of hotel magnate Conrad N. Hilton and first husband of actress Elizabeth Taylor; February 5, in West Los Angeles, Calif., age 42.

Ho Chi Minh, Vietnamese Communist leader, president of North Vietnam from 1954; September 3, in Hanoi, North Vietnam, age 79.

Jeffrey Hunter, actor ('King of Kings'); May 27, in Hollywood, Calif., age 43.

Zakir Husain, educator and president of India from 1967, the first Muslim ever to be elected to the position; May 3, in New Delhi, India, age 72.

Karl Jaspers, psychiatrist and one of the world's leading existentialist philosophers; February 26, in Basel, Switzerland, age 86.

(Lewis) Brian Jones, guitarist-singer for the Rolling Stones (until June 1969); July 3, in Hartfield, England, age 26.

Boris Karloff, actor best known for his movie role as Frankenstein's monster; February 2, in Midhurst, England, age 81.

David A. Karnofsky, medical specialist in cancer research whose work helped initiate several drug treatments for cancer; August 31, in Ellsworth, Me., age 55.

Joseph Kasavubu, first president of the Democratic Republic of the Congo 1960–65 and father of Congolese independence; March 24, in Boma, Democratic Republic of the Congo, age uncertain.

Joseph P. Kennedy, wealthy financier and founding father of U.S. political dynasty; his sons included the late U.S. President John F. Kennedy, the late Senator Robert F. Kennedy (D, N.Y.), and Senator Edward M. Kennedy (D, Mass.); November 18, in Hyannis Port, Mass., age 81.

Jack Kerouac, novelist of the "Beat Generation"; October 21, in St. Petersburg, Fla., age 47.

A(lfred) D(aniel) Williams King, Baptist minister, civil rights activist, and younger brother of the Rev. Martin Luther King, Jr.; July 21, in Atlanta, Ga., age 38.

Frank King, cartoonist who created comic-strip series "Gasoline Alley"; June 24, in Winter Park, Fla., age 86.

Rod La Rocque, silent-screen star ('The Love Pirate') who also achieved success in the talkies; October 15, Beverly Hills, Calif., age 70.

Robert Lehman, wealthy investment banker and partner in Lehman Brothers, a major U.S. underwriter; August 9, in Sands Point, N.Y., age 76.

William H. Lennon, father of the singing Lennon Sisters; August 12, in Venice, Calif., age 53.

William Lescaze, architect and urban planner, an early leader in the U.S. modernist school of design; February 9, in New York City, age 72.

John L. Lewis, labor leader, one of the cofounders of the Congress of Industrial Organizations (CIO) and president emeritus of the United Mine Workers of America; June 11, in Washington, D.C., age 89.

Willy Ley, rocket expert and author of natural-science and science-fiction works; June 24, in New York City, age 62.

Diane Linkletter, television actress and youngest daughter of television personality Art Linkletter; October 4, in West Hollywood, Calif., age 20.

Frank Loesser, composer and lyricist who wrote Broadway shows ('Guys and Dolls', 'How to Succeed in Business Without Really Trying') and

WIDE WORLD
RITTER

TSHOMBE
KEYSTONE

UPI COMPIX
TATE

MIES VAN DER ROHE
KARSH OF OTTAWA—RAPHO GUILLUMETTE

WHITE
WIDE WORLD

many popular songs ('Baby, It's Cold Outside'); July 28, in New York City, age 59.

Adolfo López Mateos, president of Mexico 1958–64; September 22, in Mexico City, Mexico, age 59.

Warren S. McCulloch, scientist in the specialty of cybernetics; September 24, in Old Lyme, Conn., age 70.

Ralph E. McGill, Southern journalist and publisher who won the Pulitzer prize in 1958 for his editorials denouncing the Ku Klux Klan for its opposition to racial equality in the South; February 4, in Atlanta, age 70.

Jimmy McHugh, composer of many popular songs ('The Sunny Side of the Street'); May 23, in Beverly Hills, age 74.

Norman Washington Manley, prime minister of Jamaica 1959–62 and father of the now-defunct West Indies Federation; September 2, in Kingston, Jamaica, age 76.

Rocky Marciano, former world heavyweight champion who retired unbeaten in 49 professional fights; August 31, in a plane crash en route to Des Moines, Iowa, age 45.

Giovanni Martinelli, during 1913–46 a leading dramatic tenor for the Metropolitan Opera Company, of New York City; February 2, in New York City, age 83.

Tom Mboya, Kenya's minister of economic planning and development and one of its leading politicians; July 5, in Nairobi, Kenya, age 38.

Ludwig Mies van der Rohe, one of the greatest architects of the 20th century (Seagram Building in New York City, Illinois Institute of Technology's Crown Hall in Chicago, Ill.); August 17, in Chicago, age 83.

Douglas Stuart Moore, composer and author, best known for his folk operas ('The Ballad of Baby Doe', 'Giants in the Earth'); July 25, in Greenport, N.Y., age 75.

Sir Edward Frederick Mutesa II, exiled king of Buganda, now part of Uganda; November 21, in London, age 44.

Drew Pearson, political columnist ("Washington Merry-Go-Round"); September 1, in Washington, D.C., age 71.

Westbrook Pegler, retired newspaper columnist, who won the Pulitzer prize in 1941 for disclosures of labor-union corruption, also known for his vitriolic attacks on public figures; June 24, in Tucson, age 74.

James A. Pike, theologian, previously Episcopal bishop of California; found September 7, in the Judean wilderness two miles from the Dead Sea, in Israel, age 56.

The Rev. (Dominique) Georges (Henri) Pire, Belgian Dominican priest, winner of the 1958 Nobel peace prize for his work to aid refugees in Eastern Europe after World War II; January 30, in Louvain, Belgium, age 58.

Hans Rademacher, one of the world's leading mathematicians and professor emeritus of mathematics at the University of Pennsylvania; February 7, in Haverford, Pa., age 76.

Thelma Ritter, character actress known for her roles as a woman with a tough shell and a heart of gold; February 5, in New York City, age 63.

Charles Ellsworth (Pee Wee) Russell, jazz clarinetist who played with Louis Armstrong, Red Nichols, and others; February 15, in Alexandria, Va., age 62.

Saud Ibn Abdul-Aziz al-Saud, king of Saudi Arabia from 1953 until 1964 (when he was deposed by his half brother Faisal) and one of the world's richest men; February 23, in Athens, Greece, age 67.

Ben(jamin) Shahn, painter and lithographer, primarily known for his social themes (Sacco and Vanzetti, nuclear disarmament); March 14, in New York City, age 70.

The Most Rev. Bernard J. Sheil, former auxiliary archbishop of Chicago, who was an activist in civil rights and social causes, founder of Catholic Youth Organization; September 13, Tucson, age 83.

Sir Osbert Sitwell, English novelist, poet, and essayist, member of famed Sitwell literary family; May 4, in Montagnana, Italy, age 76.

Mongi Slim, Tunisian nationalist, politician, and diplomat, a key figure in his country's fight for independence, first African president of the UN General Assembly 1961–62; October 23, in Tunis, Tunisia, age 61.

Gladys Swarthout, opera star who sang with New York City's Metropolitan Opera Company 1929–45; July 7, in Florence, Italy, age 64.

Sharon Tate, motion-picture actress ('Valley of the Dolls') and wife of Polish-born film director Roman Polanski; August 9, in Benedict Canyon, near Bel Air, Calif., age 26.

Robert Taylor, popular movie star of the 1930's and '40's ('Magnificent Obsession'); June 8, in Santa Monica, age 57.

B. Traven, pen name for **Traven Torsvan,** mysterious author of several novels ('Treasure of the Sierra Madre'); March 27, in Mexico City, age 79.

Moise Tshombe, former premier of the Democratic Republic of the Congo and previously leader of the breakaway Katanga Province during 1960–63 Congolese political crisis; June 29, in captivity near Algiers, Algeria, age 49.

Victoria Eugenie Julia Ena, Queen Ena of Spain, widow of King Alfonso XIII of Spain, in exile from 1931, at the birth of the Spanish republic, to 1968; April 15, in Lausanne, Switzerland, age 81.

Kliment E. Voroshilov, Soviet Communist leader for half a century; holder of numerous government and party posts including that of president of the Presidium of the Supreme Soviet 1953–1960; December 2, in Moscow, U.S.S.R., age 88.

Josh White, folk and blues singer ('John Henry'); September 5, in Manhasset, N.Y., age 61.

Robert E. Wood, who made Sears, Roebuck and Co. the world's largest merchandising organization; November 6, in Lake Forest, Ill., age 90.

OCEANOGRAPHY. In January the Commission on Marine Science, Engineering, and Resources, a panel urged by former U.S. President Lyndon B. Johnson to examine national needs in oceanography, concluded that large-scale, long-range U.S. oceanic research projects were called for. The panel also suggested the creation of a national oceanic and atmospheric agency, which in turn would absorb the Environmental Science Services Administration, the U.S. Coast Guard, and the Bureau of Commercial Fisheries.

Hopes for a major U.S. oceanographic effort diminished somewhat when Vice-President Spiro T. Agnew told a June gathering of oceanographers at Miami Beach, Fla., that budgetary problems would limit the scope of research. This verdict came at a time when impetus in oceanography was suffering from waning industrial commitment and defections of marine scientists who sought other areas of research. By October, however, the Administration of President Richard M. Nixon had second thoughts and assembled a task force of oceanographers to develop marine policy for 1970.

Clues on Seabed Origin; Weather

The Deep Sea Drilling Project, financed with $12.6 million of National Science Foundation funds, completed a yearlong quest for ocean-basin cores in August. Conducted aboard the research vessel *Glomar Challenger,* the drilling unearthed 140-million-year-old sediments in the western Pacific Ocean, perhaps the oldest in any ocean. Other sediment cores were increasingly younger as the drilling progressed eastward.

Findings of the *Glomar Challenger* undertaking suggested that the sea floor in the traversed region grew from the subsurface East Pacific Rise, extending from California past New Zealand. According to the hypothesis of continental drift (or sea-floor spreading), young rocks formed in the earth's mantle, surfaced at the rises, and spread outward. The

The *Ben Franklin* spent 30 days drifting underwater in the Gulf Stream. Scientists aboard, including Swiss oceanographer Jacques Piccard, were engaged in the first sweeping study of ocean current.

COURTESY, GRUMMAN AEROSPACE CORP.

Sealab III, the U.S. Navy's underwater habitat (foreground), is shown prior to a 620-foot descent off California. Its occupants were to spend 60 days in it, but a diver's death caused delay of the ambitious project.
COURTESY, U.S. NAVY

rocks grew older as they were pushed along by the moving seabed.

In May the Barbados Oceanographic and Meteorological Experiment (BOMEX) was under way to improve weather forecasts by studying air-sea interaction. In more than 90,000 square miles of ocean east of Barbados, BOMEX workers gathered data on how energy stored in upper ocean layers was transferred to the atmosphere bounding the water's surface. Then in July, aircraft and satellites kept tabs on tropical storms to help BOMEX scientists learn how the energy was further moved by convection to the upper atmosphere, later to be carried toward the poles.

The effect of air-sea interchange on deep water was also probed in 1969. Vessels from France, Great Britain, Italy, the United States, and the North Atlantic Treaty Organization were used to study the influence of cooling and evaporation on the density of the Mediterranean Sea's surface water. A continual overturn occurred in the Mediterranean because its surface water was dense enough to sink and mix with deeper water.

Man Beneath the Sea

Four aquanauts of Project Tektite I, a joint U.S.-industrial effort, "splashed up" in April after spending 60 days in a 160-ton habitat, 42 feet under the Caribbean Sea. Their feat was a record.

A more ambitious attempt at underwater living, the U.S. Navy's *Sealab III,* was temporarily stayed after one of the aquanauts died while on a repair dive. (*See also* Armed Forces, U.S.: Navy; Earth Sciences; Weather. *See in* CE: Oceanography.)

OLDER PEOPLE.

On Sept. 17, 1969, U.S. President Richard M. Nixon signed a bill that extended the Older Americans Act for three years, 1970–72. The new bill not only extended the old law but also added some new features to the national legislation on the aged—including a strengthening of state agencies that deal with the problems of the aged.

The law has a new Title VI, which creates a new Retired Senior Volunteers Program (RSVP). John B. Martin, U.S. commissioner on aging, said of the new program: "Because the legislation authorizes payment of out-of-pocket expenses for RSVP volunteers, it opens an opportunity of community service to many men and women who could not previously afford to volunteer." Also under the new provisions of the law, the Foster Grandparent Program was transferred from the Office of Economic Opportunity (the antipoverty agency) to the Administration on Aging (AOA).

The Older Americans Act calls for a total expenditure of $247 million over the three-year period, but actual appropriations had not yet been made by Congress. During fiscal 1969 Congress appropriated $23 million for AOA programs.

President Nixon asked Congress for a 10% increase in all social security benefits, to help meet the rising cost of living. (*See* Congress, U.S.; Social Services.)

State and Local Programs

A reduced transit fare of 10¢ was put into operation in New York City on July 1 for persons over 65. About 50,000 older people took advantage of the reduced fare on buses and subways during the first two weeks the new fare was available. The discount was applicable only during nonrush hours.

The Eastern Idaho Special Services Agency started an unusual program to provide useful occupation and supplemental income for its senior citizens. In the program, called "To Encourage Programs Employing Elderly" (TEPEE), senior citizens made two-foot authentic scale models of an Arapaho Indian shelter. The models, which sold for $7.77, went primarily to tourists. The TEPEE program was funded under Title III of the Older Americans Act.

Poverty Among the Aged

Senator Harrison A. Williams, Jr. (D, N.J.), testified before a Congressional committee that more than one third of all Americans 65 years old or more live in a state of poverty. This would include about 7 million people. Senator Williams, chairman of the Senate Special Committee on Aging, said the situation is deteriorating.

The North Carolina Governor's Council on Aging estimated that 50% of the state's male senior citizens had incomes of $1,000 or less per year—and 50% of its female aged lived on less than $500. In Inkster, Mich., the Senior Citizens Center formed a food-buying cooperative that reduced the cost of food by as much as 40% for some items. (*See also* Medicine.)

OPERA. Opera lovers were concerned by the failure of New York City's Metropolitan Opera Company to open its 1969–70 season on schedule because of a prolonged labor dispute, primarily over salaries, between the company's management and unions representing its performers and employees. Despite numerous attempts at negotiations through the fall of 1969, no settlement was achieved until December. The Met was finally able to open its season on December 29, nearly three months late. The labor dispute, the fourth in eight years, had threatened the survival of the famed opera house, which along with many other U.S. cultural institutions was suffering severe financial woes.

The New York City Opera opened its fall season with new productions of Gaetano Donizetti's 'Lucia di Lammermoor'—with the much-acclaimed U.S. soprano Beverly Sills in the title role—and Arrigo Boito's 'Mefistofele'. The 'Mefistofele' was praised for Tito Capobianco's imaginative staging, which employed spectacular multimedia effects.

The rarely performed 'Khovanshchina', an unfinished work by the Russian composer Modest Musorgski, opened the 1969–70 season of the Lyric Opera of Chicago. Nicolai Ghiaurov sang the role of Prince Ivan Khovansky. The San Francisco Opera offered notable productions of Daniel Auber's 'Fra Diavolo' in November 1968 and Richard Wagner's 'Götterdämmerung' in October 1969. The Santa Fe Opera presented the U.S. premiere of Krzysztof Penderecki's 'The Devils of Loudun'.

Some of the smaller U.S. companies provided a number of novelty productions. The Center Opera Company of Minneapolis, Minn., had four new operas in its 1969–70 schedule, among them 'Oedipus and the Sphinx', by Wesley Balk and Yale Marshall, and a modern folk opera by Paul and Martha Boesing, 'The Wanderer: a Ballad of Now'. Indiana University's Opera Theater in Bloomington opened its fall season with George Frederick Handel's 'Deidamia'. The New Orleans Opera House Association produced Giuseppe Verdi's 'Attila'.

Opera Abroad

Humphrey Searles's 'Hamlet' had its first British performance in April at Covent Garden in London, England. In May Birgit Nilsson sang the title role of Richard Strauss's 'Elektra', and in September a lavish new production of Hector Berlioz' 'Les Troyens' was given at Covent Garden. The summer Glyndebourne Festival featured Claude Debussy's 'Pelléas et Mélisande'.

In West Germany the Hamburg State Opera, thought by some critics "one of the most creative companies in the world," gave the first performance of Lars Johan Werle's 'Die Reise'. The Hamburg company also presented Mikhail Ivanovich Glinka's 'Russlan and Ludmilla'. At the Bayreuth Festival a new production of Wagner's 'The Flying Dutchman', produced by August Everding, was given. It was the first production at Bayreuth by someone outside the Wagner family since 1951. Austria's Vienna State Opera ended its centenary celebrations in May with Ludwig van Beethoven's 'Fidelio'.

In August, New Mexico's Santa Fe Opera staged the U.S. debut of 'The Devils of Loudun', a bold and unorthodox opera written by Krzysztof Penderecki. The Santa Fe company received plaudits for its readiness to offer contemporary opera.

MICHAEL MOUCHETTE

During the year the state opera also presented Luchino Visconti's new production of Verdi's 'Simon Boccanegra', labeled "eccentric" by critics.

In Italy Renata Scotto inaugurated the 1968–69 Teatro Massimo season at Palermo with a critically acclaimed performance in Vincenzo Bellini's 'La Straniera'. She had a further success in Scotland's Edinburgh Festival in August when she appeared with the Florence Opera Company in Verdi's 'Rigoletto'. (*See in* CE: Opera.)

PAINTING AND SCULPTURE. To mark the 300th anniversary of the death of the Dutch master Rembrandt van Rijn, a number of museums organized commemorative exhibitions in 1969. The first of these was a Canadian exhibit, "Rembrandt and His Pupils," displayed at the beginning of the year at the Montreal (Que.) Museum of Fine Arts and the Art Gallery of Ontario in Toronto. The exhibition included 18 paintings by Rembrandt and 90 by his forerunners, pupils, and contemporaries. Later in the spring the British Museum in London, England, mounted a show of Rembrandt's late etchings. London's Colnaghi Gallery held a related print exhibition, "The Age of Rembrandt."

Perhaps the most important commemorative exhibition was the one held in the autumn at the Rijksmuseum in Amsterdam, Netherlands, the city where Rembrandt spent most of his life. Paintings, drawings, and etchings, representing the three media in which the artist worked, were included.

One of the largest shows of the year was the exhibition of frescoes from Florence, Italy. The exhibit, intended as a gesture of gratitude for aid given to Florence following the disastrous floods of 1966, was seen in New York City, Amsterdam, and London. Entitled "The Great Age of Fresco: Giotto to Pontormo," the show consisted of 70 frescoes and fresco fragments, many that previously could be examined only with difficulty in dimly lit churches. Modern techniques developed in Florence in the last 20 years had made possible the removal of the pigmented surface of old frescoes. In many cases the frescoes were removed from walls out of necessity to arrest decay and preserve the frescoes. This process has made it possible to expose the *sinopia,* or first underdrawing, of a mural. Many such preliminary drawings were included in the show and could be studied in relation to the finished design.

U.S. Shows

An important event in the U.S. art world in 1969 was the showing at New York City's Solomon R. Guggenheim Museum of 125 selected works from the famous collection of art patron Peggy Guggenheim, after whose uncle the museum is named. Mrs. Guggenheim's collection is generally considered one of the outstanding collections of 20th-century art in the world. Great modern artists including Pablo Picasso, Georges Braque, Max Ernst, and Fernand Léger are represented.

A retrospective exhibit of the work of the U.S. abstract expressionist painter Willem de Kooning was organized by the Museum of Modern Art in New York City and seen there as well as in Chicago, Ill.; Los Angeles, Calif.; and abroad in Amsterdam and London. The 149 items included dated from the 1920's to 1967.

Other U.S. exhibitions in 1969 covered a wide range of subjects. At the Baltimore (Md.) Museum of Art a show of masterpieces "From El Greco to Pollock: Early and Late Works" brought together works by a whole range of artists. Forty-five paintings and 16 drawings by William Sidney Mount, founder of the American school of genre paintings, were shown at the National Gallery of Art in Washington, D.C. The show traveled to St. Louis, Mo.; New York City; and San Francisco, Calif. The National Gallery also began a series of small, intimate shows of paintings from the collection of English art owned by Paul Mellon. The first of these shows was devoted to the 19th-century English master Joseph Mallord William Turner.

A monumental exhibition of the graphic art of the 19th-century U.S. artist Winslow Homer, organized by the Museum of Graphic Art of New York City, was circulated to 14 cities. The mu-

In 'Seascape Number Fifteen', contemporary artist Tom Wesselman persisted in his use of human forms. This "seascape" was fashioned with synthetic polymer applied to canvas.

AUTHENTICATED NEWS INTERNATIONAL

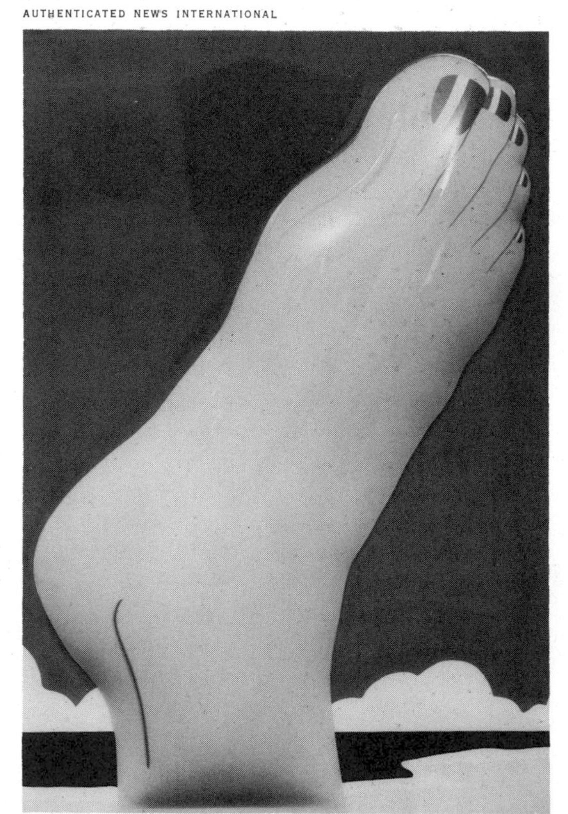

'Chicago', a gouache done by Ben Shahn in 1955, was one of the paintings shown in an exhibit of his works at the New Jersey State Museum, September 20 through November 16. The show was a tribute to Shahn, who died early in the year.

COURTESY, KENNEDY GALLERIES, INC., COLLECTION OF MR. AND MRS. ROBERT H. SMITH

seum also organized "American Printmaking—the First 150 Years," covering the period 1670–1821. Among the works displayed was the oldest known American print, John Foster's woodcut done in 1670 of the Congregational clergyman Richard Mather, who died in 1669.

The Philadelphia (Pa.) Museum of Art featured an exhibition of Mexican art covering the period from the 16th to the 20th century. The William Hayes Fogg Art Museum in Cambridge, Mass., held a show, "Daumier Sculpture, a Critical and Comparative Study," which brought together many works by Honoré Daumier, the 19th-century artist noted for his caricatures.

Japanese wood-block prints were featured in the exhibit "Master Prints of Japan, Ukiyo-e Hanga" sponsored by the University of California at Los Angeles and the Los Angeles Art Council and mounted at that city's Dickson Art Center. The *Ukiyo-e* or "Floating World" school of Japan produced masterly wood-block prints, meant for the average man, depicting simple Japanese pleasures. The show traced the development of the *Ukiyo-e* print from the 17th to the mid-19th century.

The Metropolitan Museum of Art in New York City held a spring exhibit of Florentine baroque art. The 40 paintings and several sculptures, drawings, and prints made it the largest show of Florentine 17th-century works ever held. At the end of 1969 the Metropolitan inaugurated its 1970 centennial celebration with an ambitious show, "New York Painting and Sculpture: 1940–70." Organized by the museum's curator of contemporary arts, Henry Geldzahler, the exhibit displayed more than 400 works of 43 major U.S. artists whose work had attracted critical attention in the last three decades. Among those represented in this survey of recent American art were Jackson Pollock, Arshile Gorky, Edward Hopper, De Kooning, Alexander Calder, Hans Hofmann, Josef Albers, Isamu Noguchi, and David Smith. Although the show was criticized for the selections included as well as for those left out, it nevertheless represented a major venture into contemporary art for the traditionalist museum.

A bigger-than-life sculpture by Edward Kienholz was exhibited at a pop-art show assembled by the Hayward Gallery, London, England. The sculpture was entitled 'Walter Hopps, Hopps, Hopps'.

"THE TIMES," LONDON

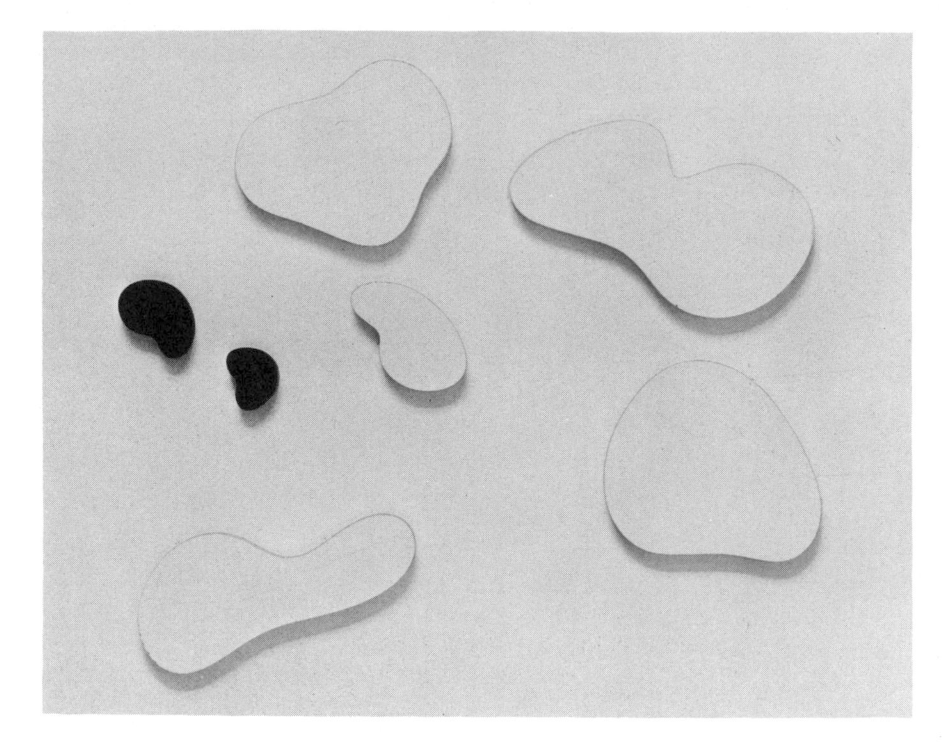

'Constellation in Five White Forms and Two Black, Variation III', an oil-on-wood relief done by Jean Arp in 1932, was shown at a recent retrospective exhibit of the artist's works. The showing was held at the Solomon R. Guggenheim Museum in New York City.

AUTHENTICATED NEWS INTERNATIONAL

Major London Exhibits

One of the major winter exhibitions in London in 1968–69 was the Bicentenary Exhibition of the Royal Academy of Arts staged to commemorate the 200th anniversary of its founding. The exhibit was large, with over 1,000 items including paintings, sculptures, drawings, prints, and miniatures.

An exhibition of work by contemporary U.S. artists, "Art of the Real," was organized by New York City's Museum of Modern Art and mounted at London's Tate Gallery. Works by Ellsworth Kelly, Tony Smith, and Robert Morris were included. The Tate also held an exhibition of the work of the Belgian surrealist René Magritte and a large retrospective of works by the pioneer British modern painter Ben Nicholson.

A comprehensive pop-art show was displayed at the Hayward Gallery in London. Artists represented included Peter Blake, Nicholas Munro, and Roy Lichtenstein. The more than 160 items in the exhibition were arranged according to formal themes: household objects, cinema images, comic-strip images, food, clothing, and images drawn from art. The Victoria and Albert Museum featured an exhibition of Czechoslovak art, "Baroque in Bohemia."

French Exhibits

The 200th anniversary of the birth of Napoleon I was marked by exhibitions at the Grand Palais and the Petit Palais in Paris. There were also exhibits in Corsica, Napoleon's birthplace.

A large-scale exhibit entitled "1,000 Years of Polish Art" was also mounted at the Petit Palais. Polish art, rarely seen in large quantities in the West, is known for its successive absorption of German, French, and Russian influences. The Polish exhibition was the largest of its kind ever sent abroad. It consisted of 350 works lent by 24 museums, churches, and other institutions in Poland.

An exhibition of the graphic works of the Norwegian expressionist Edvard Munch was displayed in the early spring at the Musée des Arts Decoratifs in Paris. The city of Strasbourg museum organized a second exhibition of modern European art with the support of the Council of Europe on the theme "The Russian Ballets of Sergei Diaghilev."

Le Havre's Musée des Beaux-Arts mounted "Masterpieces from the Hermitage" (the famed Soviet museum) representing artists from Rembrandt to Ingres. In return the State Pushkin Museum of Fine Arts in Moscow, U.S.S.R., exhibited about 100 paintings lent by French museums on the subject of romanticism in France.

Art Events Elsewhere

At Mannheim, West Germany, brightly colored abstract canvases by the Danish-born Hamburg artist K. Sönderborg were exhibited at the Städtische Kunsthalle. Work by the English sculptor Henry Moore was shown at the Staatliche Kunsthalle at the West German resort city of Baden-Baden. The Galleria di Palazzo Bianco in Genoa, Italy, held an exhibit of 17th- and 18th-century Genoese painters.

In Sweden at Stockholm's Moderna Museet a major retrospective was held of the work of Max Ernst. Among the works displayed were three paintings done in 1922 that had only recently been discovered, along with a number of others, in a house owned by a friend of the artist.

In Brazil the Tenth Bienal of São Paulo opened late in the year. Before the opening several countries, including the United States, had withdrawn their delegations. Part of the protest against the Bienal was directed at the harsh repression by Brazil's military regime of the country's leading political and intellectual figures. (*See* Brazil.) The Bienal's $10,000 Grand Prize was given to the German artist Erich Hauser, maker of smooth steel constructions, although many observers believed that British sculptor Anthony Caro deserved it.

Art Sales

In 1969 one more Rembrandt self-portrait passed into museum ownership when the Norton Simon Museum of Art of Los Angeles bought an early signed portrait belonging to a private owner for about $1.16 million. During the year French impressionist paintings once again rose in value. Particular works by Camille Pissarro and Alfred Sisley fetched exceptionally high prices. Interest also increased in drawings and watercolors by old masters. Fine old silver was in demand.

Jewelry played a larger part than usual in the year's sales. The actor Richard Burton paid somewhat more than $1 million for a large diamond for his wife, actress Elizabeth Taylor. Huge crowds in New York City and Chicago viewed the diamond before it was turned over to its new owner.

In 1969, London auctioneers began to hold sales in Tokyo, Japan. There the auction house of Christie's sold a 14th-century jar for $61,423, the highest price ever paid for a single piece of porcelain. (*See* Feature Article: "Color Fun, Function, Illusion." *See also* Museums. *See in* CE: Painting; Sculpture.)

PAKISTAN. The serious domestic upheaval that had developed in Pakistan during the last three months of 1968 attained increased momentum in the early months of 1969. Student unrest in West Pakistan, the main part of the divided country, sparked riots in several cities. In East Pakistan the student community, acting as the spearhead of general discontent, virtually displaced governmental authorities. Pakistan's President Mohammed Ayub Khan made some concessions and announced that he would not seek reelection. Demonstrations, however, increased in intensity. Widespread strikes occurred and economic life became paralyzed. In East Pakistan the situation grew increasingly unmanageable, and orderly government ground to a halt. On March 25 President Ayub Khan resigned, calling on the armed forces under the command of Gen. Agha Mohammed Yahya Khan to take control. Martial law was proclaimed, and on March 31 Yahya Khan became president.

The new president announced that his aim was to narrow the gaps separating various sections of the country and, particularly, to remove the economic disparities between East and West Pakistan. Political activity was not suppressed. The president announced that a new constitution would be framed and appointed an election commissioner to make some preparations for a return to civilian rule.

In another retrospective held at the Guggenheim, the welded metal constructions of David Smith were shown. Smith, who died in 1965 at the age of 59, created massive stainless steel pieces in the 'Cubi' series—as well as painted weldings in his bold 'Zig' series.

WIDE WORLD

Yahya Khan also made efforts to increase East Pakistan's participation in the national life. The president's determination to reform economic and political abuses quickly restored public confidence.

The overall economic progress of the country was hardly disturbed by the political unrest. The total number of goods and services produced showed a growth of 9.8% in 1968–69 compared with 5.9% in 1967–68.

Pakistan maintained cordial relations in 1969 with the People's Republic of China, the Soviet Union, the United States, and Great Britain. A visit by U.S. President Richard M. Nixon in August revitalized Pakistan's friendship with the United States. Pakistan and its partners in the organization of Regional Cooperation for Development, Iran and Turkey, continued to achieve closer economic and political cooperation during the year. Only with India was there real antagonism. Even so, a long-standing border dispute between the two countries ended in July with the finalized partition of the Rann of Kutch. (*See in* CE: Pakistan.)

PANAMA. During 1969 the people of Panama tolerated the military regime of Col. José María Pinilla, the provisional president. The regime was actually run by Brig. Gen. Omar Torrijos Herrera. Early in the year Col. Boris Martínez, who had shared power with Torrijos, was forced to leave the country. Supporters of ex-President Arnulfo Arias engaged in some guerrilla activity, mostly confined to areas along the Costa Rica-Panama border. In January five civilian members of Pinilla's cabinet resigned in protest over the harsh measures taken by the regime against its opponents. The National University of Panama was temporarily closed, and thus the opportunity for student unrest was lessened.

Panama's relations with Costa Rica were tense during the year. The pro-Arias guerrillas used Costa Rica as a refuge and as a supply base. In the spring the Costa Rican government threatened to break diplomatic relations with Panama again, charging that Panamanian national guard troops had pursued guerrillas across the border and opened fire in a Costa Rican town. (*See* Costa Rica.)

The junta was careful to emphasize its program of planned reforms and to stress the temporary nature of the military regime. In January Torrijos announced that a presidential election would be held in 1970. Electoral reforms were instituted to ensure honest voting procedures, and stricter rules were set up to govern the formation of political parties. Torrijos indicated that he would not be a presidential candidate.

Among the regime's other reforms were improved methods of tax collecting. Tax collections had risen by 11% one year after the military coup of October 1968, and there had been no increase in tax rates. The military regime also attempted administrative and economic reforms and conducted a campaign to improve public morality.

In May Gov. Nelson A. Rockefeller of New York visited Panama on the first part of his Latin American fact-finding tour. Rockefeller discussed the problems of forming new Panama Canal treaties with Torrijos.

In the fall Torrijos paid a visit to New York City and told businessmen there of Panama's recent progress. Torrijos hoped to stimulate new U.S. investments in Panama. The U.S. government approved a new loan to Panama in May but continued to withhold military aid. In December two colonels in the country's national guard attempted to overthrow the Torrijos regime. The guard, however, remained loyal to Torrijos and the coup was unsuccessful. (*See also* Latin America. *See in* CE: Panama.)

PARAGUAY. Throughout 1969 President Alfredo Stroessner retained full authoritarian power in Paraguay with the unequivocal support of both his Colorado party and the army; the main opposition continued to come from the Roman Catholic church. In the 1968 presidential elections a "restricted democracy" had been heralded when Stroessner allowed three opposition parties to participate, largely in compensation for his changing the constitution in order to succeed to another five-year term. This apparent political liberalization was reversed early in 1969 when opposition radio broadcasts were prohibited following the "Farias affair," in which a street vendor died while undergoing police interrogation.

In June Gov. Nelson A. Rockefeller of New York visited Paraguay. His reception was the least stormy of his South American tour with only minor student demonstrations—a reflection of Paraguay's severe national-security measures. (*See also* Foreign Policy, U.S.; Latin America.)

A serious recession in meat-packing, Paraguay's foremost export industry, continued all year. Cattle slaughtering had decreased in 1968 because of low world prices. However, increased exports of cotton, tobacco, and coffee offset the decline in beef export earnings.

The wheat acreage in the 1968–69 season was greatly expanded under an import-saving national wheat plan. The September harvest was 50,000 tons, sufficient for half the domestic needs. The first stage of the Acaray River hydroelectric project was completed in December 1968, and in 1969 road building continued.

In August an international commission redefined the northwest frontier, giving Paraguay more than 300 square miles of the Chaco territory. This land formerly belonged to Bolivia. (*See in* CE: Paraguay.)

PEACE CORPS. In its first eight years, the Peace Corps grew from 578 volunteers in 8 countries to 11,453 in 60 countries in July 1969. In May 1969, U.S. President Richard M. Nixon appointed Joseph H. Blatchford to succeed Jack H.

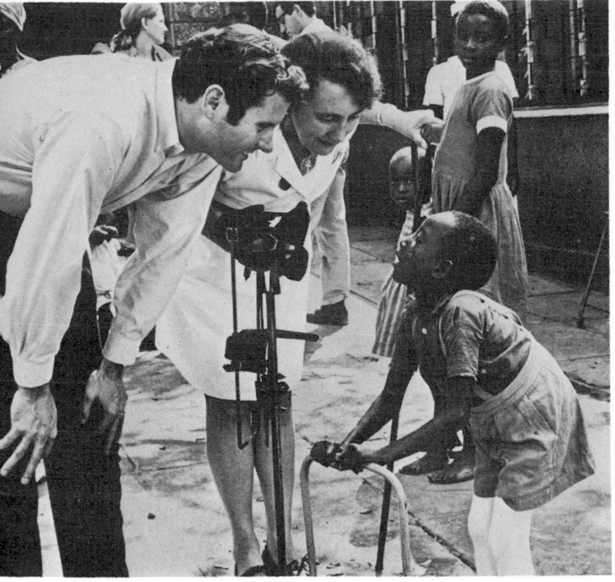

MOHAMED AMIN FROM KEYSTONE

Joseph H. Blatchford toured Kenya shortly after his appointment as director of the Peace Corps. Here he chats with a child at an orthopedic clinic in Nairobi.

Vaughn as director. This marked the beginning of a reexamination of the Peace Corps "directions," the reorganization of its Washington, D.C., headquarters, and the implementation of new pilot projects. Among the new programs for 1969 were an accounting program in Malaysia, a tourism program in South Korea, a rehabilitation program for lepers in Thailand, an orphanage program in Ceylon, and a vocational education program in Jamaica.

Emphasis was placed on the recruitment of technically skilled volunteers: carpenters, plumbers, electricians, mechanics, welders, masons, physical therapists, engineers, machinists, and a host of others. In the summer of 1969, a group of mechanics skilled in the maintenance and repair of heavy vehicles was sent on request to Guinea, which had asked the volunteers to leave in 1966.

A setback, however, occurred early in the year when Tanzania (the first country selected for a Peace Corps delegation) decided to do away with the program. Government officials there were reported to be dissatisfied with the corps workers, complaining that too many were teachers and not enough were skilled technicians. All volunteers were expected to be gone by the end of 1969.

In Liberia, squabbles between the local corps administration and a group of volunteers broke out, and dissidents organized the Volunteer Action Committee to protest existing policies (there were frequent complaints about living conditions). The chief of the Peace Corps in Liberia, William E. Gaymon, denounced the committee leaders.

In 1969 almost half the volunteers overseas served as teachers. About 22% were in community development programs, 11% in health and agriculture, and 3% in public works and public administration.

Of returned volunteers, one in five was teaching, many in ghetto schools. About one third of the returned volunteers worked for the government, the largest number in community action programs. It was estimated that by December 1971 about 54,000 Americans aged 18 to 80 would have served as Peace Corps volunteers. Their impact would inevitably be felt in the United States as more and more of them became involved.

In June 1969, the Peace Corps was granted authority by the U.S. Congress to administer the Volunteers to America. This program, sometimes called the "reverse Peace Corps" or the "exchange Peace Corps," calls for volunteers from other countries to serve in the United States. After a tour of duty there, they would presumably return home better equipped to mount community action and volunteer programs in their own countries. At the same time, U.S. citizens would have an opportunity to learn about other countries and their own communities from people who came great distances to help.

Peace Corps volunteer Douglas Sloane helped the people of Sara Kawa, a village in Togo, build a new school. Funds for the project were donated by the Mohave County Union High School, Kingman, Ariz.

COURTESY, PEACE CORPS

In 1969 the School Partnership Program sponsored the 1,000th school to be built overseas with funds collected by students in the United States. Schools are constructed in foreign countries by local citizens working with a Peace Corps volunteer. The funds for part of the school are collected and contributed by students in a "partner" school in the United States. Almost every state is represented in Asia, Africa, South America, and in the Pacific in the form of a school constructed under the auspices of the School Partnership Program. (*See in* CE: Peace Corps.)

PEOPLE OF THE YEAR. During 1969 tragedy, laudable accomplishment, acts of dissent, or crime brought the following people before the public eye. For other notable persons of 1969 see individual biographies by name.

A nationwide controversy was provoked by U.S. **Vice-President Spiro T. Agnew** after he attacked first the major television networks and then two prominent newspapers, charging that they presented one-sided coverage of the news. In the wake of this criticism **Dean Burch,** chairman of the Federal Communications Commission, asked the networks to submit transcripts of commentaries that followed a presidential speech on November 3.

Penelope Ashe was actually a group of writers who conspired together to write a risqué novel, 'Naked Came the Stranger'. When the public discovered who the "writer" was, the novel sold more copies than before.

In May **Leonard Bernstein** retired as music director of the New York Philharmonic Orchestra, a post he had held for 11 years. He was appointed laureate conductor of the orchestra.

The former child star **Shirley Temple Black** was named as a member of the U.S. delegation to the United Nations (UN) General Assembly in August.

The **Black Panther party** lost several prominent leaders in 1969. **Stokely Carmichael** resigned as the party's prime minister, and **Eldridge Cleaver** was in self-imposed exile. **Fred Hampton** was shot and killed during a police raid.

Jimmy Breslin traded his career as a newspaper columnist for that of a novelist and unsuccessful politician. He and **Norman Mailer** ran for the top two positions in the New York City mayoral election. **John V. Lindsay** was reelected mayor.

Former U.S. **Senator Daniel B. Brewster** (D, Md.) was indicted by a jury for allegedly accepting bribes from a mail-order firm while serving on a Senate post-office committee.

Angie E. Brooks, who had represented Liberia in the United Nations for 15 years, became the president of the 24th UN General Assembly. She was the second woman and the third African to be elected to that office.

Bunnies from 19 Playboy Clubs participated in a brand-new beauty contest, the Bunny Beauty Pageant. The winner of the title "Bunny of the Year—1970" was **Gina Byrams** of the Baltimore, Md., Playboy Club.

William L. Calley, Jr., a first lieutenant in the U.S. Army, was charged with the murder of at least 109 South Vietnamese villagers. **Staff Sgt. David Mitchell** also faced murder charges. The company commander **Capt. Ernest L. Medina** was under investigation.

Cassius Clay, or **Muhammad Ali,** made his Broadway debut in 'Buck White', a musical about black power. The former heavyweight boxing champion was also scheduled to fight **Joe Frazier** sometime during 1970 in Florida, but the bout was canceled.

Richard M. Daley, the son of Chicago's **Mayor Richard J. Daley,** entered politics as a delegate to the Illinois State Constitutional Convention.

Fiery orators rose up on both sides of the religious conflict in Northern Ireland. **Bernadette Devlin,** a 22-year-old member of the British Parliament, fought for the Roman Catholic cause and traveled to the United States seeking funds for refugees. **The Rev. Ian Paisley,** an extremist Protestant minister, was convicted of unlawful assembly in January and sentenced to three months in prison.

(James) Charles Evers, a field secretary for the National Association for the Advancement of Colored People, won the mayoral election in Fayette, Miss. He became the first black mayor in the town's history.

The "black manifesto" was presented by **James Forman** at a meeting with Episcopal church leaders in New York City. The manifesto demanded that U.S. religious institutions pay reparations to the nation's blacks for racial injustices.

Comedian and impressionist **David Frye** won acclaim in 1969 for his imitations of U.S. **President Richard M. Nixon,** former U.S. **President Lyndon B. Johnson,** and others.

A sensational memoir, 'My Life with Jacqueline Kennedy', by **Mary Barelli Gallagher,** was released during the year. The book portrayed the former U.S. first lady as a rather petty and bad-tempered person.

New Orleans, La., **District Attorney James Garrison** finally brought to trial his case of alleged conspiracy in the assassination of John F. Kennedy. The defendant **Clay Shaw** was acquitted by the jury after less than one hour's deliberation.

Former astronaut **John H. Glenn, Jr.,** made plans during the year to reenter politics, perhaps as a candidate in the 1970 Ohio election for the U.S. Senate.

The Rev. James E. Groppi, a militant Roman Catholic priest, was found guilty of violating his parole and was imprisoned by a judge in Milwaukee, Wis., after the priest had led a demonstration by welfare recipients at the State Capitol in Madison, Wis.

Goldie Hawn, the line-flubbing blonde on the television show Laugh-In, made a movie ('Cactus Flower') during the year and announced she would

"The Conspiracy" posed for this picture in December. The group included Jerry Rubin (wearing headband) and Abbie Hoffman (right). Judge Julius J. Hoffman is above.

LEFT: AVEDON. ABOVE: WIDE WORLD

leave the show. Other Laugh-In regulars who planned to quit were **Arte Johnson, Judy Carne,** and **Joanne Worley.**

Nancy Hanks was appointed the new chairman of the National Council on the Arts. The National Endowment for the Arts, of which she also became chairman, issued more than $200,000 in grants to assist performing artists.

President Nixon's nominee for the position of associate justice of the U.S. Supreme Court, **Clement F. Haynsworth, Jr.,** was rejected by the U.S. Senate after a bitter debate. He would have replaced **Justice Abe Fortas,** who resigned as the result of a conflict-of-interest scandal.

Federal Judge Julius J. Hoffman presided over the "conspiracy" trial of the so-called "Chicago Eight," a group of defendants—including Abbie Hoffman and Jerry Rubin—accused of conspiring to incite riots during the 1968 Democratic National Convention. The "Chicago Eight" were reduced to seven after the judge sentenced Black Panther **Bobby Seale** to prison for contempt of court.

Former **Vice-President Hubert H. Humphrey** returned to private life in 1969. He became an instructor at the University of Minnesota and at Macalester College. He also joined Encyclopædia Britannica, Inc., and its affiliate Encyclopædia Britannica Educational Corp. as a member of the board of directors.

The Rev. Jesse L. Jackson waged a war against hunger among the nation's poor through his Chicago-based Operation Breadbasket.

Sam Houston Johnson, the brother of former **President Johnson,** wrote a book about his brother simply entitled 'My Brother Lyndon'.

There was yet another tragedy in the life of **Senator Edward M. Kennedy** (D, Mass.) when the car he was driving plunged off a bridge and a passenger, **Mary Jo Kopechne,** died. The senator failed to report the accident immediately, and there was speculation that the incident may have ruined his political future.

Coretta Scott King, widow of the slain civil rights leader **the Rev. Martin Luther King, Jr.,** became the first woman ever to preach at an official service in St. Paul's Cathedral in London, England.

Virginia H. Knauer was named U.S. President Richard M. Nixon's special assistant for consumer affairs. (*See* Consumer Protection.)

While on a visit to Great Britain, Soviet writer **Anatoli P. Kuznetsov** defected from the Soviet Union and was granted asylum by British authorities. (*See* Literature.)

John Lennon of the singing Beatles married Japanese film director **Yoko Ono.** On their honeymoon John and Yoko held a "bed-in" for peace. Lennon also returned his Member of the Order of the British Empire award "in protest against Britain's involvement in the Nigeria-Biafra thing, against our support of America in Vietnam, and against 'Cold Turkey' (recorded by John and Yoko) slipping down the charts."

Mickey Mantle, one of baseball's all-time greats, retired at 37 after an 18-year career with the New York Yankees.

Rumors swept the Beatle-loving world that **Paul McCartney** had died in an auto accident in 1966 and that an imposter replaced him. The rumors, which seemed to have originated on U.S. college campuses, were based on supposed clues on album jackets and in the lyrics of the Beatles' latest record album, 'Abbey Road'. When queried, Beatle McCartney said, "I am alive and well, but if I were dead I would be the last to know." (*See also* Marriages.)

AGNEW
WHITE HOUSE
CLEAVER
SHAMES FROM BLACK STAR
FRYE
DAVID GAHR
ALI
WIDE WORLD
DEVLIN
CAMERA PRESS—PIX FROM PUBLIX

Famed 67-year-old anthropologist **Margaret Mead** testified before a U.S. Senate subcommittee that marihuana is "not nearly as bad as alcohol . . . not harmful unless it is taken in enormously excessive amounts."

Martha Mitchell, the wife of **U.S. Attorney General John N. Mitchell,** revealed in a television interview after the November antiwar demonstrations that her husband had "said many times, some of the liberals in this country, he'd like to take them and change them for the Russian Communists."

Daniel Patrick Moynihan, originally named presidential assistant for urban affairs for Nixon, emerged as one of the Administration's major policy makers in domestic affairs. He was made "counselor to the president," given Cabinet rank, and assigned the task of developing a "long-term urban strategy."

"Broadway Joe" Namath, colorful New York Jets football quarterback, "retired" from football after a quarrel with **National Football League Commissioner Pete Rozelle** over his part interest in the bar Bachelors III, which Rozelle said had become a gamblers' hangout. But Namath later sold his interest in the bar and returned to football.

Jacqueline Kennedy Onassis was accused by news photographer Mel Finkelstein of throwing him to the sidewalk with a judo flip after he had photographed her leaving a theater that was showing the movie 'I Am Curious (Yellow)'. Other bystanders said Finkelstein wasn't flipped—he just slipped.

The New York Mets became the heralded heroes of baseball when they captured the World Series after having suffered the status of underdogs during their seven years of existence.

Great Britain's **Prince Philip,** the duke of Edinburgh, admitted that the royal family's finances were in poor straits. Not only would Prince Philip have to give up polo but the royal family also "may have to move into smaller premises," he quipped.

Joining the ranks of U.S. literary folk heroes in 1969 was **Alexander Portnoy** of **Philip Roth's** book 'Portnoy's Complaint'.

The commander of U.S. Army Special Forces troops in Vietnam, **Col. Robert B. Rheault,** was charged, along with seven other "Green Berets," with murder and conspiracy to commit murder in the alleged slaying of a Vietnamese man thought to be a counterspy. The charges were eventually dropped. (*See* United States.)

Barbara Jo Rubin broke through another barrier and became the first U.S. woman jockey to win a regular pari-mutuel flat horse race.

Pamela Anne Eldred was selected Miss America in 1969 and **Gloria Smith** was chosen Miss Black America.

Soviet author **Aleksandr I. Solzhenitsyn** ('The First Circle', 'The Cancer Ward'), considered by many critics as "the greatest living Soviet novelist," was expelled from the Soviet Writers' Union, an action which effectively stripped him of official status as a writer.

The convictions of pediatrician and war critic **Benjamin M. Spock** and his codefendant **Michael Ferber** for counseling young men to avoid the draft were overturned by the U.S. Court of Appeals for the First Circuit in Boston, Mass. The court ordered the cases of other defendants, **the Rev. William Sloane Coffin, Jr.,** and **Mitchell Goodman,** to be re-tried by a lower court.

Martin Sweig was suspended from his job as chief assistant to **Speaker of the House John W. McCormack** (D, Mass.) after McCormack learned that his aide had been involved in influence peddling.

FRANK LEONARD FROM PICTORIAL PARADE

BRESLIN AND MAILER

COURTESY, NATIONAL BROADCASTING CO.

HAWN

UPI COMPIX

HUMPHREY

NAMATH

FRED BAUMANN—PIX FROM PUBLIX

KENNEDY

PICTORIAL PARADE

A 69.42-carat diamond, the most expensive precious stone ever auctioned, turned up on the hand of **Elizabeth Taylor.** Her husband, **Richard Burton,** purchased the $1.05-million gem for her from Cartier, Inc.

Two Army men came under Congressional scrutiny for allegedly unethical activities. **Retired Maj. Gen. Carl C. Turner,** a former provost marshal general of the Army, was alleged to have received weapons from the police departments of Chicago, Ill., and Kansas City, Mo., for official use but instead sold them for personal profit. In another incident the first sergeant major of the Army, **William O. Wooldridge,** was alleged, along with several other sergeants, to have profited personally in the course of managing servicemen's clubs.

Author **Gore Vidal** ('Myra Breckinridge'), a political liberal, and columnist and magazine publisher **William F. Buckley, Jr.** (*National Review*), a political ultraconservative, carried their feud dating from the 1968 Democratic National Convention into a war of words in 1969 in a series of lively articles in *Esquire* magazine.

Screen star **Mae West,** 77, came out of retirement to star in the filmed version of Gore Vidal's 'Myra Breckinridge', joining sex symbol **Raquel Welch** and film critic **Rex Reed** already in the cast.

U.S. black separatist **Robert F. Williams** returned to the United States to face criminal charges after having lived abroad in exile since 1961 in Cuba, Tanzania, and the People's Republic of China. He had fled the United States while under indictment for kidnapping.

WITCH (Women's International Terrorist Conspiracy from Hell) and other militant feminist groups began to publicize the unequal rights and status of women in U.S. society.

UPI COMPIX

MC CARTNEY

WIDE WORLD

MITCHELL

WIDE WORLD

RUBIN

UPI COMPIX

SEALE

PERU. The military government that took power in Peru under the leadership of Gen. Juan Velasco Alvarado on Oct. 3, 1968, immediately began to implement a series of reforms that it regarded as fundamental for the future development of the country. The government's first significant act was to expropriate the installations and assets belonging to the International Petroleum Co., Ltd. (IPC), a subsidiary of Standard Oil of New Jersey, on the grounds that the company owed the state about $690 million in tax arrears. This immediately caused U.S.-Peruvian relations to deteriorate; the U.S. State Department threatened to apply the 1962 amendment—sponsored by Senator Bourke B. Hickenlooper (R, Iowa)—by which the U.S. sugar quota and all economic aid to Peru would be canceled. The U.S. government also suspended military aid. Application of the Hickenlooper amendment was twice postponed for negotiations.

UPI COMPIX

Peruvian girls use balloons with anti-U.S. slogans to make their protest in front of the U.S. Embassy in Lima. The protests came in the wake of Peru's expropriation of a U.S. oil company.

Meanwhile, Peru attempted to enforce its 200-mile offshore fishing limit, seizing several U.S. tuna-fishing boats within the claimed waters. The boats were released later after their captains paid substantial fines. Relations mellowed as the year progressed, particularly with the appointment of a new U.S. ambassador, Taylor Garrison Belcher, who was not associated with any Peruvian interests. The entire installations of IPC were placed under the administration of Petroperú, the state petroleum agency. (*See in* CE: Peru.)

PETS. Cats and dogs remained the most popular household pets in the United States in 1969, though animal dealers reported mounting demand for unusual pets. (*See* Animals and Wildlife.) It was estimated that there were 34 million cats and 25 million dogs in the United States.

COURTESY, QUAKER OATS CO.

Top, a Great Dane, was Ken-L Ration's dog hero of the year. A broken leg resulted when Top rushed in front of a truck to save an 11-year-old girl. While the leg was healing, Top saved a baby from drowning by barking for help.

Cats in the News

Health, both feline and human, stole most of the cat headlines in 1969. Scientists in Glasgow, Scotland, reported that their experiments seemed to indicate that a leukemia virus was transmissible from cat cells to human cell cultures. There was, however, no evidence that such a process could occur under other than laboratory conditions.

In the area of cat health, other scientists disclosed evidence that a combination of viral and bacterial agents is the primary cause of urinary blockage, one of the deadliest of cat diseases. It was also announced that artificial insemination had been carried out successfully for the first time in cats and that gestation periods for cats average 69 days, rather than 63 days as was previously thought.

Both of 1969's top-winning show cats were Persian females. Conalon's Miss Prettee of Walhall, a black owned by Theodore Napolski of Redondo Beach, Calif., was All-American Cat of the Year; Misty Morning Meg, a tortoiseshell owned by Charles Milwain and William Nix of Smyrna, Ga., was the Cat Fanciers' Association's All-Star Best Cat.

Cat-show activity reached an all-time high in 1969. Entries in the 189 U.S. shows totaled 38,677, and attendance was 310,000. Three shows had more than 500 entries apiece, thus becoming the first in the United States to reach or surpass that mark.

During 1969 some 47,000 cats were registered, bringing the total number of living registered cats in the United States to 205,000. Siamese remained the most popular of purebreds, closely followed by Persians. During the year cat-food sales exceeded $275 million.

Dog Registration Rises

The American Kennel Club reported in 1969 that in the preceding year registrations of purebred dogs numbered 909,300. The club expected that new registrations in 1969 would exceed the one-million mark for the first time.

Among registered purebred dogs, poodles remained the most popular for a ninth consecutive year. Registrations of standard, miniature, and toy varieties totaled 263,700 in 1968, some 7,000 more than in 1967. German shepherds, Chihuahuas, and collies, respectively, maintained their positions as second, fifth, and eighth in popularity. Dachshunds and miniature schnauzers both moved up one place in the "top ten" to rank third and sixth.

This pet helps his master earn money. Honda, a pinto pony, is very important to his young owner, Peter Reading, 12, of Pembroke, Mass. Peter rides bareback on Honda to deliver newspapers.

WIDE WORLD

Beagles, Pekingese, and cocker spaniels each dropped a notch, ranking fourth, seventh, and tenth. Labrador retrievers were ninth in public favor, moving up from eleventh place.

Although terriers remained relatively low in overall popularity—despite an 11% registration increase in 1968—a silver-haired Skye terrier in 1969 won best-of-show honors at the prestigious 93d annual Westminster Kennel Club dog show in New York City. The dog, Champion Glamoor Good News, was owned by Walter and Adele Goodman of Center Island, Long Island, N.Y.

Dogs also remained a large and growing business. In 1968, for instance, dog owners spent some $655 million for commercial dog foods in more than 27,000 retail outlets. (*See in* CE: Cat; Dogs; Pets.)

KEYSTONE

The Philippines' President Ferdinand E. Marcos gestures to the crowds who came to see and hear him on his campaign tour. He was reelected in November, in the wake of election violence.

PHILIPPINES. In the bloodiest election in the history of the Philippines, President Ferdinand E. Marcos won an unprecedented second four-year term in 1969. Marcos, of the Nationalist party, defeated Liberal party candidate Sergio Osmena, Jr., 4,451,766 to 2,754,130—breaking the record for the winning margin set by Ramón Magsaysay, who won by 1,599,000 votes in 1953.

From the time the campaign started in July, 67 persons were killed and there were assassination threats from a band of Philippine Muslims, allegedly instigated by the Communist-oriented Hukbalahap (Huks) guerrillas operating in central Luzon island. Following the election, Marcos announced that he would withdraw the Philippines' 1,500 noncombat troops from Vietnam and redeploy them against the Huks.

Other difficulties were harder to combat. Lack of land reform, unemployment, and the underemployment of professional people also plagued the island nation. The per-capita income for 70% of the people was less than $100; 70% of the population were under 25 years old, and the population was increasing at 3.5% a year. During his campaign Marcos promised a review of military and economic treaties with the United States, whose many military bases bring considerable cash into the country. While the 1955 Laurel-Langley trade agreement, due to expire in 1974, guarantees Philippine access (within a quota) to U.S. markets for sugar, cordage, and other products, it also grants special privileges to U.S. investors.

Another problem was a deficit budget for 1969 brought about by overspending on public works. The government lost millions of dollars through corruption, tax evasion, and smuggling.

In 1969, stringent measures were taken to curb inflation. The gross national product rose 6.3% in 1968, and income from agriculture rose 9% as against a 3.5% increase in consumer prices. New rice strains, diversification of agriculture, and development of underground steam power improved the outlook. Diplomatic ties with Malaysia were renewed in December. (*See also* Asia; Malaysia. *See in* CE: Philippines.)

COURTESY, GENERAL ELECTRIC CO.

A locomotive (above) is depicted in three different ways: (top) in a photograph, (center) in an X-ray picture, and (bottom) in a neutron radiograph, created by directing a high-intensity beam of neutrons at the locomotive. Another neutron radiograph (below) reveals the inner parts of a stopwatch.

PHOTOGRAPHY.

An international exhibit of camera wares—Photo Expo 69—took place at New York City's Coliseum on June 8–15. Although manufacturers displayed a number of items, nothing of major photographic innovation was seen.

Camera Equipment for 1969

Among new lenses shown at Photo Expo 69 was the 500-mm. f/8 Reflex Nikkor. This new Nikkor had a mirror optics system of unusually short length and light weight. It was designed to fit all Nikon F and Nikkormat cameras. An 80-mm. f/4 telephoto lens and close-up system for the Nikonos underwater camera was also on display.

One of the updated cameras shown at the exhibit was the Leicaflex SL-Mot. Designed for use with this power-focused single-lens-reflex (SLR) camera were the 45–90-mm. Angenieux f/2.8 zoom lens and the 21-mm. Super Angulon f/3.4 lens. Yashica showed its new reflex camera, the TL Electro-X. This model featured an electronic shutter and electronic exposure readout.

The GAF Corp. announced a new color film at the June show. Made for 126-size instant-loading cassettes, the new GAF daylight color film had a speed of ASA 80. It was available later in the year in other film sizes, including 35 mm.

Polaroid Corp. released a new line of instant-print cameras. They ranged from the Colorpak II, a $30 camera with a cadmium sulfide (CdS) electric eye for exact setting during flashbulb use, to the Model 360, a $200 camera with an electronic timer that "beeped" when the picture was developed.

Warner Products made available a new SLR. The Warner 6x6 looked and felt somewhat like a 35-mm. camera but it used 120 or 220 roll film. It boasted ease of handling, along with the large picture area of a 2¼-inch-square format. With an 80-mm. f/2 lens the Warner 6x6 sold for $495.

Recent Photographic Trends

Nearly all movie cameras sold in 1969 used Super 8 cartridge film. Kodak's dominance of the worldwide amateur movie market more than assured success of its Super 8 film.

Electronic shutters were incorporated into a growing number of cameras. It seemed likely they would eventually supersede mechanical shutters.

The advent of Ciba paper was an interesting development in color printing. Working through a process of bleach reversal, colors were produced by subtraction from black rather than by addition to white. Stable hues and purer colors resulted.

The Bell Telephone Laboratories had discovered a new material capable of large-scale storage of digital or visual information for holography, or laser photography. A single crystal of lithium niobate had up to a thousand times the holographic storage capacity of the film plates ordinarily used in laser photography. Data could be erased by heating the crystal, thus allowing its reuse. (*See in* CE: Photography articles.)

PHOTOGRAPHY EXHIBITIONS. The most publicized show of 1969 was "Harlem on My Mind," a multimedia exhibit featuring photography, at New York City's Metropolitan Museum of Art. The show was a sociopsychological study of

UPI COMPIX

A large photograph of Harlem during the early 20th century towers over a young viewer at the "Harlem on My Mind" multimedia exhibition sponsored by New York City's Metropolitan Museum of Art. The exhibit was a sociopsychological survey of the Negro community in upper Manhattan.

A time-exposure photograph of a young boy twirling sparkling firecrackers in a circle won Graham Ellingford the award of Junior Photographer of the Year in Great Britain in 1969. The photo was judged the best of nearly 2,000 entries from all over the country.

"LONDON DAILY EXPRESS" FROM PICTORIAL PARADE

"the cultural capital of Black America" from 1900 to 1969. It combined blown-up photos, slides, and film projections with recordings of voices and sounds of the Harlem community. (*See* Museums.)

Another experiment in multimedia presentation was "America in Crisis," mounted at New York City's Riverside Museum. Featuring the work of 21 photographers, the show depicted the United States in the strife-torn decade of the 1960's.

Among other major events of the year was Photo Expo 69, held at New York City's Coliseum. It was primarily a trade show for photographic manufacturers, but it also displayed more than 3,000 photos. In Chicago, Ill., the Exchange National Bank continued its program of photographic exhibitions with an imaginatively displayed presentation, "The World of Underwater Photography." An exhibition of the work of the early French documentary photographer Eugene Atgét was mounted at New York City's Museum of Modern Art in 1969. The 120 prints included detailed everyday scenes of the streets of Paris, France. (*See in* CE: Photography.)

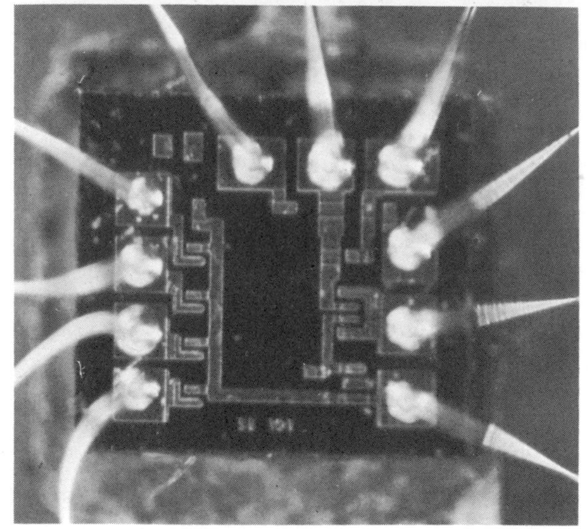

COURTESY, BARNES ENGINEERING CO.

An integrated circuit smaller than the size of a pinhead is shown (above) in a regular photograph and (top) in a thermomicrograph, which depicts an image of the heat emitted by the circuit.

PHYSICS. Physicists in 1969 reported controversial evidence of the existence of a fundamental subatomic particle and of gravity waves. Discovery of the particle—the quark—was announced by an Australian physicist. A University of Maryland physicist announced detection of the gravitational waves predicted in Albert Einstein's general theory of relativity.

The Quest for the Quark

The quark was "invented" in the mid-1960's by Murray Gell-Mann and George Zweig in independent efforts to simplify theories of the fundamental nature of matter. Carrying one third or two thirds of the normal charge on a proton, the quark is a particle from which all other subatomic particles could be made. The postulators of the quark regarded it as a mathematical concept, not as a physical reality; other physicists, however, sought to prove its existence.

Apparent success in detecting the quark was announced in September by Charles B. A. McCusker of the University of Sydney (Australia). In previous experiments, the most powerful particle accelerators had proved unable to split a proton into the three quarks that theoretically constitute it. McCusker and his co-workers reasoned, however, that cosmic rays, which possess far greater energy than particles accelerated in atom smashers, might be able to produce quarks. In a year, they photographed more than 60,000 cloud-chamber tracks produced during cosmic-ray showers. Five of the tracks appeared to have been made by particles with two thirds of the normal charge of an electron. "I am 99 percent sure," McCusker said, "the tracks are those of quarks of two-thirds primary charge." He added that the next step was to find the quark of one-third charge. Many physicists, however, were skeptical, maintaining that the five tracks might have been produced by known particles that for some reason did not behave normally.

Weighing Way-Out Waves

Discovery of gravitational waves was announced by Joseph Weber of the University of Maryland. Einstein had predicted that such waves—extremely weak—would be generated when massive bodies such as stars, gigantic masses of gas, or entire galaxies stop or start suddenly, oscillate, or otherwise accelerate.

Because of the weakness of gravitational waves, few physicists thought they could be demonstrated. Weber and his associates, however, reasoned that the waves should be able to set a mass into oscillation, just as electromagnetic waves set electric charges into motion. Weber's sensing devices were one-ton aluminum cylinders, to which supersensitive vibration detectors were attached. Two were at the University of Maryland, and another was at the Argonne National Laboratory in Illinois.

Though the cylinders were always jiggling slightly, due to random background disturbances such as natural earth tremors and passing trucks, the scientists reasoned that a sudden marked increase in the activity of all cylinders at once would indicate the arrival of genuine gravitational waves. A number of such coincidences were observed, leading Weber to believe he had detected gravitational waves. If the waves indeed exist and can be detected, they may give astronomers a new source of information about distant cosmic events. Many scientists, however, were unconvinced of the validity of Weber's findings. (*See also* Astronomy; Chemistry; Electronics; Space Exploration. *See in* CE: Physics; Radiation; Radioactivity.)

POLAND. In 1969 Poland solemnly commemorated the 30th anniversary of the outbreak of World War II and the 25th anniversary of the foundation of the Polish People's Republic. Also during the year a new *Sejm* (parliament) was elected, a new government constituted, and a new five-year economic development plan outlined. Polish Jews, persecuted by the Communist regime, continued to leave the country. In foreign affairs Poland made friendly overtures to West Germany.

CAMERA PRESS—PIX FROM PUBLIX

Soviet Communist Party General Secretary Leonid I. Brezhnev's call for unity in the 'socialist commonwealth' is applauded at a Polish Communist party meeting.

Elections to the Sejm were held in June. There were 618 candidates, but as only 460 deputies could be elected, the voters had some opportunity to show their preference. Out of the valid votes cast, 99.2% were cast for candidates on the lists of the National Unity Front, made up of the Polish United Workers' (Communist) party and parties allied with it. The new Sejm elected a Council of State, the supreme organ of state authority in Poland. Jozef Cyrankiewicz was again made chairman of the Council of Ministers (premier).

Communist Party First Secretary Wladyslaw Gomulka made a major speech in May on the German problem. He indicated that West Germany had so far blocked every initiative aimed at détente. With pending West German elections in mind, Gomulka stressed that one of the candidates, Willy Brandt, had recently made a realistic assessment of the European situation. Brandt had, for instance, stated the necessity of recognizing the Oder-Neisse frontier (the de facto post-World War II western Polish boundary). Gomulka thus took the occasion to indicate that Poland was ready to conclude an agreement with West Germany recognizing the Oder-Neisse frontier as final.

When Brandt became head of the new West German government, he proposed to the Polish government the opening of negotiations on issues touched on by Gomulka in his May speech. The Polish government accepted the proposal. (*See also* West Germany. *See in* CE: Poland.)

POLICE. In 1969 for the second consecutive year in the United States there was an increase in police strength. According to the Federal Bureau of Investigation's Uniform Crime Reports—1968, the average number of police employees per 1,000 inhabitants in 1968 was 2.1 as compared with 2.0 in 1967, which represents an increase of 5%. In the larger cities of over 250,000, the average rate was 2.9, an increase of 7% over the 1967 rate of 2.7. In suburban areas the rate stayed at 1.5.

Salaries for policemen had increased appreciably over the past decade. The 1969 Municipal Year Book reported that as of Jan. 1, 1969, the highest median-maximum salary for American policemen was $8,819 per annum in cities of 250,000 to 500,000 population, 37% higher than the figure reported ten years earlier. Over the period since

A three-way fight broke out at the University of Wisconsin. Demonstrators for heavier recruiting of black students were attacked by counter demonstrators, then fought the police.

IRA BLOCK—PIX FROM PUBLIX

Toronto, Ont., authorities advertised that a reward would be given to anyone with information "leading to the arrest and conviction" of the killer of police constable David Goldsworthy.

"THE GLOBE AND MAIL," TORONTO, ONT.

1959, the per capita expenditures on salaries and wages for police departments increased 44%.

Civil disorders stemming from racial tensions or student uprisings continued to be major problems for police throughout the United States in 1969. On March 29, in Detroit, Mich., one policeman was killed and another officer and four civilians wounded during a shoot-out between police and a black separatist group, the Republic of New Africa. In July five policemen were shot in Chicago, Ill., in a confrontation with members of the Black Panther party. Forty-five persons, including 12 policemen, were injured in Pittsburgh, Pa., in August. In September two policemen in St. Louis, Mo., were wounded by a sniper who was hiding in a housing project.

Policemen picket the town hall in Weymouth, Mass., in January to get popular support for a pay raise. The police said that the town refused to enter into collective bargaining.

UPI COMPIX

In the United States, 64 law-enforcement officers were killed by criminal action in 1968. From 1960 through 1968, 475 officers were killed; of the 626 offenders involved in those murders, 76% had been arrested previously on some criminal charge. Assaults on police increased 17% in 1968 over 1967. Nationally there were 15.8 assaults per 100 officers in 1968 as compared with 13.5 in 1967 and 12.2 in 1966. (*See also* Crime. *See in* CE: Police.)

POLITICAL PARTIES. In 1969 U.S. political parties sought to resolve a virtual deadlock between Republicans and Democrats—a deadlock reflected in the close presidential election of 1968 and in continuing Democratic control of Congress under a new Republican Administration. The results included changes in the structures of both parties, as well as a series of hard-fought election contests.

Democratic Party

The Democratic National Committee in January elected Senator Fred R. Harris (D, Okla.), as its chairman. He succeeded Lawrence F. O'Brien, a former John F. Kennedy aide and campaign manager of the unsuccessful presidential bid of Hubert H. Humphrey in 1968.

The Democratic National Convention in 1968 authorized two reform efforts, one to make the selection of a presidential nominee more democratic, the other to revise the party's rules. Harris appointed Senator George McGovern (D, S.D.) to head a 27-member commission on presidential nominations and Representative James G. O'Hara (D, Mich.) to head a second 27-member group on party rules.

In late November, the McGovern commission adopted a series of 20 guidelines for reform to be submitted to party leaders in each state. Among the proposals was a formula to assure that future delegations to national conventions would reflect the actual population and politics of each area. Some of the proposals would require changes in state laws governing presidential primaries.

Republican Party

For the Republicans, the main problem in 1969 was to shape a party responsive to its newly elected leader, U.S. President Richard M. Nixon, and to win additional seats in Congress. Nixon's nomination of Judge Clement F. Haynsworth, Jr., to the U.S. Supreme Court presented problems in unity; 17 Republicans joined 38 Democrats to defeat the nomination in the U.S. Senate. (*See* Supreme Court of the U.S.)

The resignation of Ray C. Bliss, who had served as national chairman for four years, was announced on February 18. Bliss stayed in office until April to give the party time to choose a successor. He was succeeded by Representative Rogers C. B. Morton (R, Md.), who is the brother of Thruston B. Morton, a former Republican chairman.

Morton, like his Democratic counterpart, Senator Harris, combined the roles of legislator and party chairman. During his four years as party chairman, Bliss avoided public positions on political issues; as a legislator, that course was clearly impossible for Morton. As his first major step after taking over the chairmanship, he announced that he would lead a campaign for the president's ABM (antiballistic missile) program. He also announced that he would end the separate role of the Republican party's minorities division, terming it a "Jim Crow" operation.

Election Trends in 1969

Off-year elections, eagerly watched but often unreliable barometers of voter sentiment, provided their usual collection of contradictory signs during 1969. The Democrats won four out of five early Congressional contests but lost two governorships in the November elections.

An incumbent liberal Republican mayor was reelected in New York City, and an incumbent conservative Democratic mayor was reelected in Los Angeles, Calif. Both campaigns involved the issues of law enforcement and of rights for blacks.

Congressional Elections

On March 25, Ed Jones of Tennessee was elected to a district already held by the Democrats. On April 1, David R. Obey, a Democrat, won the normally Republican Wisconsin district vacated by Secretary of Defense Melvin R. Laird.

On April 29, Barry M. Goldwater, Jr., son of the 1964 presidential candidate, was elected in a normally Republican California district. On June 24, John Melcher, a Democrat, was elected in a previously Republican Montana district. On October 1 Michael Harrington, a Democrat, was elected in a Massachusetts district not held by a Democrat since 1877.

In New Jersey, in the one Congressional election on November 4, Robert A. Roe, a Democrat, was elected to succeed Charles S. Joelson in a contest so close that his Republican opponent, Gene Boyle, demanded a recount. In the last House of Representatives contest of the year, Philip M. Crane, a conservative Republican, was elected in Illinois to succeed Donald Rumsfeld, also a Republican, appointed to head the Office of Economic Opportunity.

WIDE WORLD

Representative Rogers C. B. Morton (R, Md.) was appointed chairman of the Republican National Committee in February. His brother Thruston is a former chairman.

Mayoral Elections

The political potential of racial issues was starkly demonstrated in Los Angeles. Incumbent Mayor Sam Yorty, who was far behind in the primary, staged a sensational comeback in a runoff election against Thomas Bradley, a black former policeman and a city-council member. Yorty's campaign stressed racial issues.

HOWARD HARRISON FROM NANCY PALMER AGENCY

Radical political groups held a "counter-Inaugural" ceremony in Washington, D.C., in January—as President Nixon was inaugurated. The protester in the foreground holds a mask of Nixon.

By contrast Carl B. Stokes, the Negro mayor of Cleveland, Ohio, won a resounding victory in the Democratic primary September 30 and went on to win the November election. A black candidate for mayor of Detroit, Mich., Wayne County Auditor Richard Austin, lost a nonpartisan election to Sheriff Roman S. Gribbs. While the campaign appeared to have significant racial overtones, both campaigned as moderates. Both were Democrats.

Sam H. Massell, Jr., a liberal Jewish Democrat, was elected mayor of Atlanta, Ga., over Republican Alderman Rodney Cook in October. Massell received massive backing from Atlanta's black community. The campaign took a sensational turn when Mayor Ivan Allen, Jr., a Democrat, accused Massell of corruption in soliciting financial support from nightclub owners. Maynard Jackson was elected vice-mayor, the first Negro to hold that office in the city's history.

In a nonpartisan election in Dayton, Ohio, millionaire Dave Hall was chosen mayor over Lawrence Nelson, a Negro foundry worker, in November. It was Dayton's first mayoral election since 1913. Previously, the post was filled by a member of the city commission.

In Louisville, Ky., former Representative Frank Burke defeated John Sawyer for mayor, ending eight years of Republican control. In Boston, Mass., Louise Day Hicks, a law-and-order candidate for mayor two years before and a strong opponent of school bussing to achieve integration, led a list of nine candidates elected to the city council. She hinted that she would campaign again for mayor in 1971.

In Pittsburgh, Pa., a Democrat, Peter F. Flaherty, defeated his party's regular candidate in the primary and went on to a November victory. Another Democrat, Frank A. Sedita, was elected in Buffalo, N.Y.

Charles S. Stenvig, a police detective who ran as an independent, was elected mayor of Minneapolis, Minn. He ran on a law-and-order platform and said that he would "take the handcuffs off the police." Stenvig defeated Republican Dan Cohen, who had been endorsed by President Nixon and Senator Eugene J. McCarthy (D, Minn.). Stenvig captured approximately 62% of the total votes cast.

Spectacular Upset by Lindsay

By far the most publicized campaign for mayor, however, was in New York City. Incumbent Mayor John V. Lindsay staged an upset and won reelection to another four-year term. Defeated in the Republican primary by state Senator John J. Marchi, Lindsay ran as the candidate of the Liberal party and the Independent party. Mario A. Procaccino, the Democratic candidate, was a heavy favorite early in the race. Marchi and Procaccino stressed law-and-order issues in their campaign. Lindsay stressed the importance of urban problems in national priorities, and he strongly opposed the Vietnam conflict.

Lindsay won with 41.8% of the votes cast. He drew strong support from the city's poor—especially blacks and Puerto Ricans—and from the wealthy. (*See* Lindsay.)

Republican Triumphs

Despite continued Democratic domination of many large cities and Republican losses in scattered Congressional districts, the Republicans had a significant triumph in the November elections. The party captured the only two governorships at stake in the November elections—in Virginia and New Jersey.

The victory of Representative William T. Cahill over former Gov. Robert B. Meyner ended 16 years of Democratic administration in New Jersey. A. Linwood Holton's victory over William C. Battle, son of a former Democratic governor, was the first Republican victory in Virginia in 84 years.

The victories represented personal triumphs for President Nixon, who campaigned in Roanoke, Va., and in Bergen and Morris counties, N.J., during October. The results brought the number of Republican governors to 32, the most the party had held since 1920.

A Clouded Political Future

The promising political career of Senator Edward M. Kennedy (D, Mass.) was suddenly placed in jeopardy by a tragic accident. Mary Jo Kopechne, a secretary for the late Senator Robert F. Kennedy (D, N.Y.), was found dead in Kennedy's car in a pond on Chappaquiddick Island in Massachusetts.

At the inquest into Miss Kopechne's death, Kennedy admitted driving the car and pleaded guilty to charges of leaving the scene of an accident after causing "injury" to her. He had delayed reporting the accident for about ten hours. Many aspects of the complicated incident remained a mystery to the press and the public.

Kennedy had often been mentioned as a possible Democratic candidate for president in 1972. Some observers thought that the accident removed this possibility; others thought Kennedy could regain the confidence of the voters before 1972. (*See* People of the Year.)

Third-Party Developments

One of the big questions in U.S. politics during 1969 was the future of the American Independent party, the group which under various names backed George C. Wallace, former governor of Alabama, for president in 1968. As the result of Wallace's showing, the party was entitled to a place on the ballot in several states.

A meeting in Dallas, Tex., in February failed to set up a national party but one of the organizers, Bob Walters of Los Angeles, asserted that the group established a national committee and authorized formation of an interim national organization. Another, apparently separate group also met in February and announced the formation of a national committee with a long name incorporating the names of many local groups.

Dissension Among the New Left

Students for a Democratic Society (SDS), the organization that spearheaded many militant—and sometimes violent—protests in recent years, literally ripped itself apart during a Chicago, Ill., convention in mid-June. The convention brought frank avowals that SDS was a revolutionary movement designed to overthrow the existing U.S. government by force if necessary. The split came over tactics. A group affiliated with the Progressive Labor party (PLP), which identifies with the Chinese version of Communism, advocated a shift from campus demonstrations to agitation among labor groups. Eventually, the PLP set up a national headquarters in Boston.

A second, "regular" faction, which took control of the national SDS headquarters in Chicago, pushed for direct political action and campus strife sponsored by SDS. Later, the regulars split into two Chicago-based groups, one the ultraviolent "Weatherman" faction. An effort by the militant

Charles Evers (left) shakes hands with Carl B. Stokes, the mayor of Cleveland, Ohio. Many persons, including Stokes, traveled to Fayette, Miss., from other states to attend Evers' inauguration as mayor of Fayette.

WIDE WORLD

WIDE WORLD

Barry M. Goldwater, Jr., was elected to a seat in the U.S. House of Representatives in 1969. He represents California's 27th district. His father was the Republican presidential nominee in 1964.

Weatherman group, also known as Revolutionary Youth Movement I, failed to create a major riot in October.

An effort to disrupt a massive, peaceful antiwar demonstration staged by moderate groups in mid-November in Washington, D.C., was an even more abject failure. Those seeking violence in the antiwar rally were subdued largely by the demonstrators themselves. (*See also* Cities and Urban Affairs; Congress, U.S.; United States.)

POMPIDOU, GEORGES. The irresistible rise of Georges Pompidou, who was elected president of France on June 15, 1969, clearly shows that, though politics may be defined as the art of the possible, it also leaves a considerable amount to luck and to obstinacy. At the age of nearly 50, in 1961, this former grammar-school teacher, who later became a jurist and then a bank director, was unknown to the general public. When, to the amazement of the country, President Charles de Gaulle appointed him prime minister in April 1962, he had never held an elective office though he had exercised governmental responsibility, and he had never even set foot in the Chamber of Deputies, except in the public gallery.

For six years, Pompidou's prudent conduct of the government, his nerve, and his skill increasingly confirmed him as a major public figure. He was referred to as the "crown prince," the successor to the aging De Gaulle. Pompidou organized the Gaullist electoral victory in 1968, and for his pains he was dismissed.

This could have been the end of his career, but luck came to the aid of obstinacy. De Gaulle staked his future on an ill-conceived referendum in April 1969, was defeated, and stepped down. Just 38 hours after the general had retired, Georges Pompidou announced his candidacy. All the public-opinion polls and all other forecasts put him in the lead.

However, his victory was not yet won. An opponent emerged: the president of the Senate, Alain Poher, who held temporary responsibility for the presidency of the republic. The battle was fierce, but day by day Pompidou's stock rose. He spoke of continuity, but also of change; of loyalty, but also of a determination to remain open-minded. At the polls he won 58.21% of the vote, and so less than ten years after first entering politics, he moved into the Élysée Palace as the successor to De Gaulle and president of the republic.

Georges Pompidou was born at Montboudif, France, on July 5, 1911. His father was a schoolteacher, and Georges himself later taught school in Marseilles and Paris. During World War II he served with an infantry regiment and then took an active part in the resistance. In 1944 Pompidou joined the personal staff of General De Gaulle. After a series of government and banking jobs, he helped draft the constitution of the Fifth Republic. He married Claude Cahour in 1935. They have one son, Alain, a medical student. (*See also* France.)

POPULAR MUSIC. The most spectacular "happening" in popular music during 1969 was the Woodstock Music and Art Fair held on a farm at Bethel, N.Y., in August. An estimated 400,000 youths made their way to the Woodstock festival, a crowd four times larger than anticipated. Roads leading to the site were clogged with cars. Many youths abandoned their vehicles and hiked as far as 15 miles to the festival grounds.

Facilities were not adequate to accommodate the enormous crowd. There was a shortage of food, water, and sanitary facilities. Cases of illness and accidents were so numerous that 50 doctors had to be flown in from New York City. Food was airlifted in by U.S. Army helicopters. Local residents helped out by offering the youths free food and water.

Heavy rains added to the woes of the spectators at the three-day festival. Nevertheless, the crowd were exceptionally well-behaved and good-humored as they sat in the mud listening to such performers as Ravi Shankar, Arlo Guthrie, Joan Baez, the Who, and the Jefferson Airplane.

The Beatles managed to make news all year long. In March John Lennon turned his honeymoon with Japanese film director Yoko Ono into a demonstration for peace when the couple staged a weeklong "bed-in" at a hotel in Amsterdam, Netherlands.

The Beatles recorded a hit song, 'The Ballad of John and Yoko', about Lennon's honeymoon difficulties.

In the fall a rumor sprang up that Paul McCartney was dead. Ambitious fans found "clues" everywhere—on Beatle album covers, hidden in song lyrics, and even in some songs when played in reverse. This "evidence" showed that McCartney had died in an auto accident in November 1966. Paul McCartney, who was married in March and whose daughter was born in August, denied that he was dead. The rumor, however, remained alive. A professor at the University of Miami (Fla.) analyzed Beatle recordings on a sound spectrograph and claimed to have found three different voices that were supposed to belong to Paul McCartney.

The Beatles recorded and released a new album during the year, 'Abbey Road'. Two songs from the album, 'Something' and 'Come Together', were released as a single record. Both sides became hits.

From all over the world 100,000 devoted fans went to the Isle of Wight off the coast of England in September for the first concert by Bob Dylan since his motorcycle accident in 1966. 'Nashville Skyline', an album reflecting Dylan's new country-and-Western style, was released in the spring. His 1969 hit song 'Lay, Lady, Lay' was on the album along with a Dylan-Johnny Cash duet.

In January, Cream, a blues-rock group from Great Britain, released its fourth and last album, entitled 'Goodbye'. Two Cream musicians joined a British "supergroup," Blind Faith, which made its U.S. debut in 1969 to a crowd of 20,000 listeners at New York City's Madison Square Garden Center. Pillars of the popular-music world Diana Ross and the Supremes cut their last record together in 1969.

Several songs from the rock musical 'Hair' were released as singles and became hit records: 'Hair' by the Cowsills; 'Aquarius-Let the Sunshine In' by the 5th Dimension; and 'Good Morning Starshine' by Oliver. The Broadway-cast recording of 'Hair' was the top-selling album in the United States for many weeks. (*See also* Music.)

This girl is really "turned on" at the Woodstock Music and Art Fair in Bethel, N.Y., held in August. Massive crowds of young people peacefully assembled to enjoy the pop music.

WIDE WORLD

The Rolling Stones gave a free rock concert in London, England, in July; a tribal dance was performed to this number. Mick Jagger (behind dancer) and the other Stones delighted huge audiences on their U.S. tour in the fall of 1969.

UPI (UK) LTD.

Popular Music

Special Report: Today's Rock Sound

by Richard Kostelanetz,
Author, Critic, and Cultural Historian

A new popular music, known mostly as "rock," has swept the United States, if not the entire Western world, in the past half dozen years, and it has conclusively distinguished itself from the old by a few crucial differences. The old pop music was decidedly sentimental—about falling in love at first sight, sexless emotions, general good feelings—while the new pop strives to be unsentimental about a greater range of attitudes and experience, including such previously taboo subjects as politics, alienation, psychedelic drugs, the terrors of violence, unfulfilled sensuality, seduction, promiscuity, and, most especially, sexual intercourse.

The music itself is also different, flirting more with unusual harmonies, if not outright dissonance (which is usually resolved, nonetheless)—also looking to the possibilities of loud volume and aural feed-back afforded by electronic amplification equipment. The loudness is partially an attempt, analogous to much environmental art and psychedelic drugs, to overwhelm the listener's perceptual system, particularly his neural mechanisms, with unusual external stimuli. The new pop music has also largely rejected the rhymed couplet for a less restricted verse and has avoided the decade-old conventions of pop musical phrasing, mostly derived from the sonata form, for more freely formed structures. It has also overthrown the three-minute limit on pop songs established first by the 10-inch 78-rpm record, and later, the commercial radio stations, for pieces running seven minutes and beyond. Also intrinsic in the new music is an emphasis on groups, rather than individuals, partly because more than one performer is needed to project that ear-shattering volume. In the new pop, most of the musicians write their own melodies and lyrics, and the predominant instrument is the guitar, usually accompanied by drums and a bass, sometimes by an organist, and occasionally by horns, a tambourine, or other percussion instruments, all of which are either attached to amplification equipment or played directly into microphones.

Similarly, the performers of the new pop hardly resemble their predecessors, as nearly all of them are young, wear their hair long, and feature outlandish nonmatching costumes. Their group names cultivate outrageousness: the Grateful Dead, the Creedence Clearwater Revival, the Vanilla Fudge, Steppenwolf, and so on.

One major reason why the new pop music is so different from the old is that rock grows out of contrary musical traditions. If the old pop music came from neoclassical compositions, Broadway show tunes, and advertising jingles, the singing styles and unsentimentality of the new pop music descend primarily from Negro American music—urban folk blues, to which have been added a dash of gospel and a pinch of jazz.

KEN REGAN FOR CAMERA 5

Singer Janis Joplin and her group, Big Brother and the Holding Company, reached the top in rock with their white "soul" music.

The first era of rock came in the middle 1950's with Elvis Presley, a singer-guitarist who appropriated (perhaps imported) the earthiness of Negro blues for a white audience, and Bill Haley and the Comets, whose best-selling single 'Rock Around the Clock' helped bring into the common language a new phrase, "rock 'n' roll." The early 1960's witnessed the increasing popularity of both guitar-oriented folk music, represented at its best by white solo singers like Bob Dylan and Joan Baez, and Negro "rhythm and blues" performers like Ray Charles and Antoine (Fats) Domino. There was also a new dance called "the twist," invented by the Negro singer Chubby Checker, as well as a new kind of dancing place where the twist was emphasized and unconventional dress was allowed and even encouraged; but not until 1963 did the new music really begin to flourish.

At that time, there were two complementary developments, one in England and the other in the United States—one associated with the unorthodox appearance and highly amplified instruments of the Beatles, the other with several new Negro groups linked with a Detroit, Mich., Negro-owned record company, Motown. The Beatles and the Motown groups—among them, the Supremes, Stevie Wonder, Martha and the Vandellas, Smokey Robinson and the Miracles—all gained their earliest success not with the established commissars of popular music but with the large and newly affluent audience of teen-agers.

Following the inaugurations of new rock (1963–64) was the arrival in 1964–65 of a second generation of new groups—the Rolling Stones and the

RALPH GARCIA FOR CAMERA 5

Singer-guitarist Jimi Hendrix is credited with being one of the most important of the rock innovators. His music uses the blues for its foundation.

In action at New York City's Fillmore East is the Creedence Clearwater Revival, one of the most highly regarded rock groups to be heard in the 1960's. The Fillmores East and West were centers of rock music.

KEN REGAN FOR CAMERA 5

Masters of "sensual rock," the Doors give one of their lively performances at the Fillmore East.

KEN REGAN FOR CAMERA 5

Who in England, the Beach Boys and Sonny and Cher, among others, in the United States. The next year saw the Beatles' shift (followed by others) away from the hard-driving rock with a regular beat to more rhythmically free, more repetitious, more psychedelic music. Also, there was a growing pop-related enthusiasm for Indian music, particularly that of the sitarist Ravi Shankar. In 1966–67 came the first great U.S. hard-rock groups—the Doors, the Jefferson Airplane, the Mothers of Invention, Big Brother and the Holding Company, and others; and it was precisely on the issue of psychedelics (and concomitantly, Indian music) that white rock began to diverge drastically from Negro music and achieve full realization during 1967–69.

The music of Texas-born singer-guitarist Johnny Winter was one of the reasons why the blues revival in the United States continued to gain momentum in 1969.

KEN REGAN FOR CAMERA 5

Among the great American rock performers are Simon and Garfunkel (who supplied the musical background for the motion picture 'The Graduate'), the Mamas and the Papas, the Beach Boys, the Association, the Monkees, the defunct Buffalo Springfield, and the original Byrds, all prime exponents of a kind of "clean rock"; the Doors, masters of "sensual rock" and probably the creators of more bona-fide memorable music than any other American group; Aretha Franklin, whose songs of desire and frustration evoke that mysteriously sublime realm of feeling known as "soul"; and Big Brother and the Holding Company (starring Janis Joplin) and the Jefferson Airplane (featuring Grace Slick), groups that perform what can be called "co-ed rock."

What is rock's place in contemporary music? Rock in performance may make for great theater—few examples of literary drama exploit the performer-audience relationship so successfully. But, as music, not even the best rock is as artistically adventurous or as intrinsically rich as avant-garde music, largely because, by contemporary standards, the musical ideas are too elementary, the structures too repetitious, the pieces too short, and the means too obvious. It is, therefore, probably valid to say that rock stands to contemporary music as journalism stands to literature, for the former item in both pairs is unashamedly transient and stylistically derivative, rather than innovative and possibly permanent. (*See also* Fashion Special Report; Popular Music.)

POPULATION. In the final months of 1969 the U.S. population topped the 203.8-million-person mark, according to U.S. Bureau of the Census estimates. By the time the 19th decennial census was compiled—as of April 1, 1970—the population was expected to jump to about 205 million. By contrast, the first U.S. census, taken in 1790, registered a total of only 4 million people. The Census Bureau was inaugurating a census by mail for 1970. Only in about 35% of the cases would an "enumerator" personally collect the data.

Although the U.S. population continued its upward movement, the national rate of growth was at its lowest level since 1940. At the onset of 1969 the citizenry had increased by 2 million people in a year's time, a net gain of 1% of the total population. The high point of growth was in 1955–56, when the rate was some 1.8%.

Numbers of whites and blacks in the U.S. population rose by mid-1969. Estimates were that, of the total populace, 22.7 million were Negroes, an increase of 20.1% over the 1960 census count. The white population jumped 11.8% in the same period.

There was a continuing downslide of the U.S. farm population. Between mid-1967 and mid-1968, rural population dropped about 4% to a total of 10.5 million persons. The 1969 farm census, tabulated in January 1970, was expected to show that for the first time since 1870 there were fewer than 3 million farms and ranches in the United States. (*See* Agriculture.)

As 1969 began it was noted that the median family income in the United States was $8,600. This was an increase of $600 from the start of the preceding year. Also, a nonfarm family of four headed by a male was officially considered to be in poverty if its annual income was $3,553 or less. By this standard there were 25.4 million poor in the nation by 1969. (*See in* CE: Population.)

PORTUGAL. During 1969 Portugal enjoyed political stability and made some economic progress. Premier Marcello José das Neves Alves Caetano, who took office in September 1968 following the illness of former Premier António de Oliveira Salazar, succeeded in introducing political reforms that led to some liberalization.

Caetano visited Angola, Mozambique, and Portuguese Guinea in April (the first time that a Portuguese premier had done so) and later the United States and Brazil. He also sponsored measures to liberalize press censorship, reform the leadership of trade unions and professional societies, and curb the powers of the secret police. He expressed support for allowing prominent exiles to return to Portugal, reforming the electoral law, and allowing the opposition more freedom to express their views. The official party, the National Union, was reorganized. Many officials and parliamentary representatives were replaced; Caetano appointed several young technocrats, including João Augusta Dias Rosas as minister of finance and economy and Xavier Pintado as minister of commerce.

The political scene during the year was dominated by the elections for 130 deputies in the National Assembly, held on October 26; deputies for the new session would have the power to change the constitution, an opportunity that occurred only once in ten years. The National Union won all the seats, as it had done in previous elections during the preceding 50 years. The campaign, which began on September 27, was lively; opposition groups of socialists and Catholics were granted equal opportunities to campaign, but they were not allowed to function as political parties.

The most important political event in the overseas provinces was the assassination in February of Eduardo Chivambo Mondlane. He was the leader of the anticolonial Mozambique Liberation Front. (*See* Africa. *See in* CE: Portugal.)

WIDE WORLD

On Feb. 28, 1969, an earthquake shook northern Africa and the Iberian Peninsula. In Lisbon, Portugal, power service was disrupted for about 15 minutes and falling debris destroyed several parked automobiles.

POST OFFICE, UNITED STATES. Early in the year U.S. President Richard M. Nixon, in an effort to take the postal system "out of politics" and place it on a businesslike basis, asked Congress to establish a postal corporation—the United States Postal Service—to take the place of the Post Office Department. Management of the more than $7-billion-a-year enterprise would rest in the hands of a nine-man board of directors.

Even before the reform measure was submitted, President Nixon moved to further cut long-standing political ties between the department and Congress by asking the Senate to end its historic prerogative of confirming nominations of postmasters. The Senate, without debate, consented to the president's recommendation that, henceforth, postmasters in the nation's first-, second-, and third-class post of-

PIEROTTI FROM BEN ROTH AGENCY

"May I suggest something?"

fices would be chosen on the basis of civil service examinations. The move would eventually affect most of the nation's 32,200 postmasters and 31,000 rural letter carriers.

The sweeping postal reform plan was introduced in Congress on May 27. Other key provisions of the reform measure included authorization to issue up to $10 billion in bonds.

Despite widespread support, and a belief that Congress would be happy to be rid of the pressures generated practically every session by demands placed by and against the department, President Nixon's proposal was not uniformly welcomed. Some members of Congress wished to retain ultimate control of the department, and leaders of the giant postal employees' unions feared the changes in labor-management relations that could develop. Representative Thaddeus J. Dulski (D, N.Y.) submitted his own reform measure that, while adopting many of the changes proposed in the Administration bill, would keep the postal service as a government agency. The House Post Office Committee split 13–13 over the presidential measure, which was thus defeated. (*See in* CE: Postal Services.)

POVERTY, WAR ON. In 1969 some 25 million Americans, about 17 million of them white, lived in poverty. The poverty threshold for a nonfarm family of four, by official designation, was a yearly income of $3,553.

The Office of Economic Opportunity (OEO), the federal agency charged with eradicating U.S. poverty, received a new director in 1969, Donald Rumsfeld. Formerly an Illinois congressman, Rumsfeld was chosen by U.S. President Richard M. Nixon early in the year to head the agency.

In December OEO opponents in Congress tried to shift control of the federal poverty programs to the states. Rumsfeld, a Republican, waged a successful fight to retain control, even without support from many Republican leaders.

Additional legislation was under consideration at year's end to give state governors veto power over budget appropriations for the OEO's Legal Services Program. Working from nearly 900 regional offices, the 1,800 lawyers in the nationwide program furnished legal aid to those ordinarily unable to attain it. The inhibiting legislation, originating in the Senate, was an apparent attempt to minimize the number of court suits being brought against local and state governments by Legal Services lawyers on behalf of the poor.

Most of the antipoverty programs of the OEO were administered at local levels through Community Action Agencies (CAAs). By mid-1969 there were 962 locally controlled CAAs in the United States and its dependencies. They offered legal aid, health care, and emergency food and medical services to eligible persons.

Health centers sponsored by the OEO provided care for 400,000 persons in 36 urban and 13 rural locations. Through its emergency food and medical services the OEO provided temporary relief to the needy in crisis locales. Particular attention was

A Volunteers in Service to America (VISTA) worker tutors a child in Botkin, Ala. VISTA, established in 1965, claimed more than 18,100 workers as of mid-1969.

RICHARD BELLAK

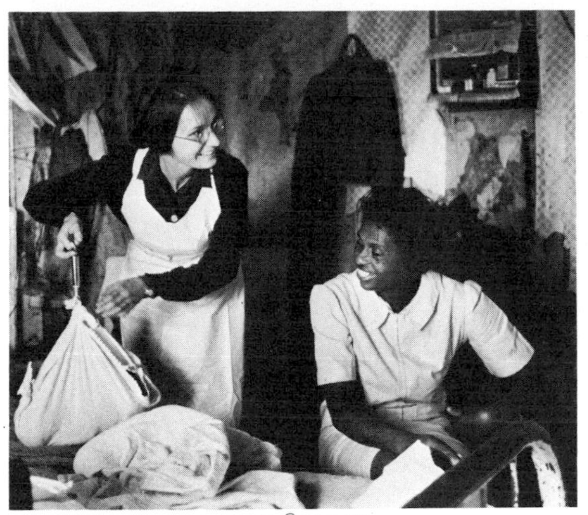

HOWARD BINGHAM, "LIFE" MAGAZINE © TIME INC.

Poverty-stricken people in Bolivar County, Miss., are helped by the Tufts-Delta Health Center. Here a project nurse and an aide are about to weigh a baby.

given to the 255 lowest-income counties of the United States.

By mid-1969 the total number of workers in Volunteers in Service to America (VISTA) since its inception in 1965 had risen to more than 18,100. The VISTA volunteers, mostly in the 20–24 age group, were placed in cities, small towns, and rural areas to live with poverty victims and to help them find ways of attaining financial independence.

One of the OEO's most recent projects was New Gate, which encouraged prison inmates to pursue college studies. The philosophy of OEO was changed to delegate successful projects to other federal agencies. For example, Project Head Start, the popular educational program for preschoolers, and Project Upward Bound, which helped poverty-stricken youth get college educations, were transferred in 1969 to the U.S. Department of Health, Education, and Welfare. Also, the Job Corps and other OEO manpower programs were shifted to the U.S. Department of Labor.

PRISONS. On the whole, the period 1968–69 was one of consolidation rather than of innovation in the field of prisons and penology. Despite prison-building programs, especially in highly developed countries with old jails such as France and Great Britain, overcrowding got worse. Modern industrial work in prisons was on the increase and was most highly developed in the U.S. federal prison system. Work for prisoners and security were still two of the main preoccupations of penal administrators everywhere. But they also considered such questions as the problem of sexuality in prisons and the relationship between penal administrations and the public.

The treatment of offenders with special problems such as drunkenness received much attention during the year. Prisons can usually do little more than withhold alcohol. The underlying personality and social difficulties often remain untouched. At an international symposium on this subject held in London, England, in May 1968 there was general agreement that the alcoholic should be considered as sick, often with a whole combination of adverse factors working against him. The symposium noted that in a number of countries drunkards were no longer even taken to court by the police but rather to other places, such as sobering-up centers (Warsaw, Poland), a medical detention center (Milan, Italy), a university psychiatric clinic (Vienna, Austria), or the police medical service (Paris, France). The Supreme Court of the United States had gone so far as to rule that it was a "cruel and unusual punishment" (and thus a violation of the Constitution) to convict an alcoholic for being publicly intoxicated.

Paving the Way to the Outside

Hostels and halfway houses were being started in many places to ease the transition from prison to the outside. One of the most interesting halfway-house programs in the United States was that of Crofton House in San Diego, Calif. It was named after Sir Walter Crofton, an early penal reformer. Inmates were carefully selected, and the regime differed from other halfway houses—for

On February 14 friends flew birthday greetings to former teamsters union president James R. Hoffa, who was serving an eight-year term in the federal prison at Lewisburg, Pa.

WIDE WORLD

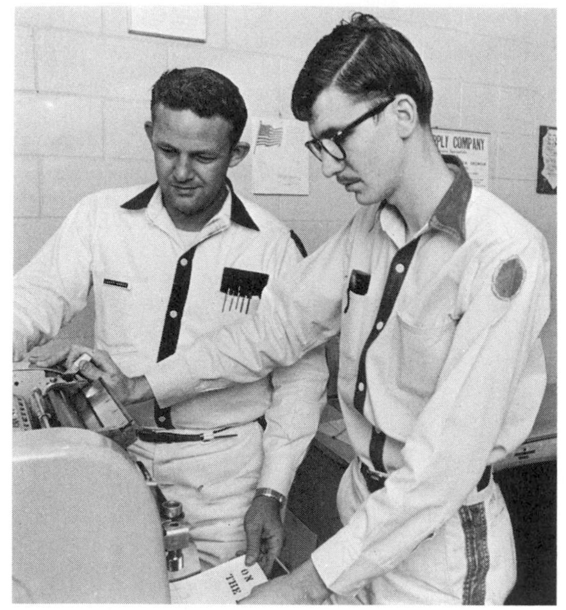

"THE AUGUSTA (GA.) CHRONICLE-HERALD"

Two inmates at the Richmond County correctional camp, in Augusta, Ga., are working to bring out another issue of their newspaper. The camp has won wide acclaim for its successful rehabilitation of prisoners.

example, in West Germany or in Great Britain—in that there was a strong emphasis on group counseling, with a trained supervisor and his wife on the premises. The accent was on an open expression of feelings, a "pulling off of the covers" where a resident evaded or distorted the need to face problems head-on, and, at the same time, there was a continued acceptance and mutual support.

The work-release program, whereby certain lesser offenders continued to live in penal institutions but were allowed to hold down regular jobs on the outside, gained wider approval throughout the United States in 1969. As of early 1969 at least 24 states and most of the federal government's 36 prisons had adopted the plan. (*See also* Crime. *See in* CE: Prisons and Punishments.)

PSYCHOLOGY. The controversy over the psychologist's role in today's society was brought into sharp focus in 1969. Conflict centered around whether the psychologist should be a scientist-investigator confined to office practice and laboratory work or an activist working in the community with involvement in "real problems."

The most dramatic confrontation came at the meeting of the American Psychological Association when black graduate students in psychology disrupted the affair with demands to be heard. A spokesman for the radical group charged that "psychologists and sociologists go into the black community and do research but refuse to specify and push major programs for improvement in the black community."

The year also saw the rekindling of the old dispute over heredity versus environment—this time intensified by racial overtones. The storm centered around a study by Arthur R. Jensen, educational psychologist at the University of California, at Berkeley. Jensen supported the theory that intelligence is determined largely by heredity and cannot be altered significantly by environmental changes. He suggested that differences in racial and ethnic groups are chiefly hereditary and may account for the 15-point average advantage of whites over blacks in intelligence quotient (IQ) scores. The article was, Jensen said, a plea for research to determine differences. He declared that if his theories could be substantiated more effective techniques may be developed to achieve learning with different patterns of ability. He discounted the value of programs such as Project Head

(*continued on page 409*)

On Sept. 2, 1969, black psychology students won a round in their attempt to gain financial and educational aid from the American Psychological Association.

UPI COMPIX

Psychology

Special Report: If Stars Could Talk . . .

by Loriene Eck Chase, Clinical Psychologist

Not since the heyday of the occult sciences in the later Middle Ages and the Renaissance has interest in the supernatural been so animated as during the late 1960's. Astrology, extrasensory perception (ESP), reincarnation, fortune-telling, witchcraft, and spiritualism have all enjoyed a revival in the minds of young and old alike—but especially among youth. In an age of unmatched scientific advances and technological gains, people are turning in greater numbers to ancient, mysterious practices.

The search into the world of imagination confounds the three-dimensional confines of scientific procedure. This phenomenon cannot be explained away with clichés or by means of simple moralizing. People are more and more seeking the answers to things they do not understand in the so-called "fifth dimension."

In our technologically advanced society the term "alienation" has become a household word. Mankind is witnessing a period of scientific, or outer-world, advancement such as has never been known before. Nevertheless, man remains through one means or another the essential author of this "knowledge explosion" outside himself. He must struggle to maintain a stable condition in a fast-moving world and find a means of affirming his sense of individuality. Many persons seek their individual destinies in horoscope charts, by consulting fortune-tellers, or by attempts to communicate with the spirits of the dead.

One reason offered for why the occult is so popular is that organized religion has failed to fulfill the spiritual needs of modern man. This explanation is particularly aimed at young persons of college age. Along with the advances being made in the external world many youths feel a need to explore the inner world of the mind. Hallucinatory drugs, alcohol, disciplined meditation, and the occult arts are increasingly popular—this popularity may be motivated by something larger than, or even opposite to, the simple explanation of escapism. These experiments with the mysterious might be an attempt to find a new and more meaningful form of religious experience. They could also be related to man's innate desire to uncover the mysteries of life and of the self.

Psychology and psychiatry have been delving and probing for years into the confines of the human mind in an effort to penetrate its mysteries. These sciences have made attempts to define the conscious responses of the human mind and to "crack the code" of the subconscious mind. Many people still hold steadfastly to the physical, material, and conditioned-response approach to solving these human mysteries, but their opposite numbers seek answers in mystical experiences and in parapsychology and psychic phenomena.

LAURENCE B. FINK FROM NANCY PALMER AGENCY

Dark Side of the Mind

The most respectable of all supernormal phenomena is ESP—telepathy, clairvoyance, precognition. For more than 40 years scientific research has been conducted at Duke University, Durham, N.C., and at other centers to determine if such phenomena do exist. In 1968 the first "premonitions laboratory" in the United States opened at the Maimonides Medical Center in Brooklyn,

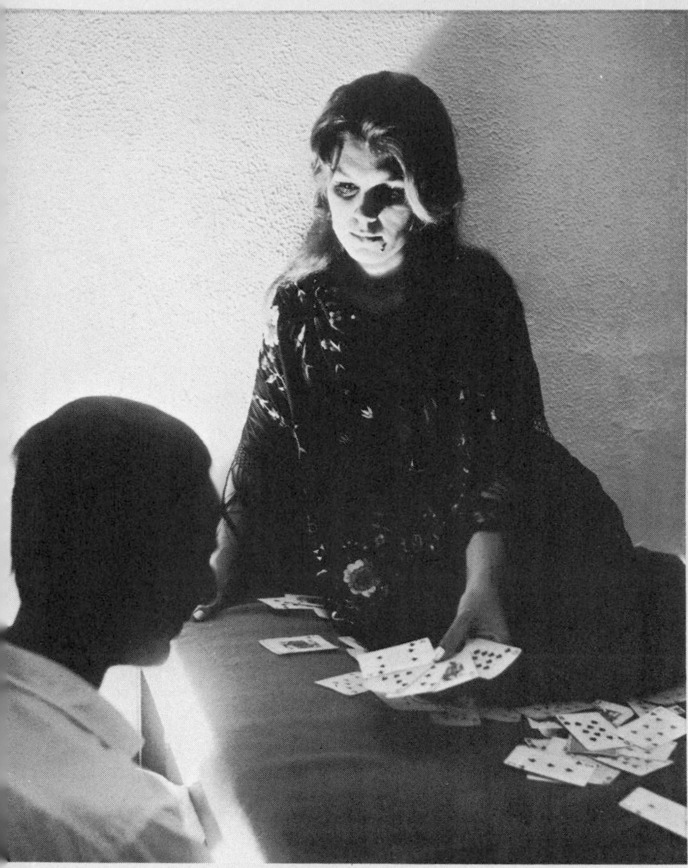

MANCHETE FROM PICTORIAL PARADE

In many countries, occultism has become extremely popular as well as profitable. In Brazil the playing-card reader is patronized more than anyone else, and the experience costs less.

N.Y. Many researchers are convinced that ESP does exist, and research procedures have become increasingly complex.

Tests for determining whether a person has ESP range from having the person predict the order of cards in a special deck to having him predict the selections of numbers made by an electronic random-number generator. When a subject consistently predicts the correct outcome of these tests this is considered beyond the laws of chance, and the person is said to possess powers of ESP.

Not everyone can display psychic ability at will, and tests seem to show that persons of high intelligence are less likely to be "psychic." Some parapsychologists feel this is a psychological reaction causing skepticism to block out the psychic powers that these intelligent people do in fact possess. Many psychologists believe, however, that the successes in parapsychological research are due to factors other than careful scientific investigation—statistical errors, the unconscious wishes of the tester, or outright fraud. Many laymen simply want to believe.

Twilight Zones

One step beyond ESP and related psychic phenomena is the practice called spiritualism, emphasizing communication with the dead. Spiritualism, a shadowy practice, came to wide public attention in 1968 when the late James A. Pike, formerly the Episcopal bishop of California, claimed he had communicated with his dead son. In addition to receiving messages from his son, Pike reported that physical objects in his home and office had been moved on a number of occasions, allegedly by his son's spirit.

Many young people refused to accept the traditional scientific belief that reason can explain the world and all of life. They felt there was more to it than that. Eastern religions with their strong mystical basis have attracted many young people, but so has witchcraft. Beginning with the hippies, beads and amulets, potions and spells, have found their way to most college campuses. Lectures and courses that have been offered in witchcraft and other occult areas have had an overwhelming response from young people.

The new popularity of witchcraft is not limited to the young. Los Angeles County, Calif., has an official county witch. 'Rosemary's Baby', a very popular novel that was later made into a motion picture, told a story of demonology and the practice of black magic by a coven of witches in New York City.

Much of the emphasis on ghosts and witchcraft among the young, on television, and in motion pictures is a put-on. Nevertheless, it is still a preoccupation, and a pervasive one.

In the Ascendant

Perhaps leading all other occult pursuits in popularity is astrology. In a world of chaos, many people are seeking order in the stars. Some amateur astrologers do it for fun; others take it quite seriously. Professional astrologers claim that the stars are right for astrology and say that we are entering an age of faith and high-mindedness—the Age of Aquarius.

As astrology gained popularity with increasing numbers of people, enterprising "soothsayers" gradually turned this occult study into big business. Astrology had become a full-blown fad by 1969. Almost every daily newspaper in the United States was carrying a daily horoscope column. The general predictions in these columns for the millions of individuals that fell under each sign were, however, little more than common-sense advice. In addition to the newspaper columns there were dozens of astrology magazines, an astrology-inspired cookbook, dieters' guide, and marriage guide. Astrology even appeared as a theme in the rock musical 'Hair', with its opening tribute to the dawning of the new Aquarian Age.

Astrological designs appeared on clothing. Personalized zodiacal symbols such as the Aries ram, the Gemini twins, the Leo lion, the Pisces fish, and the Taurus bull were imprinted on drinking cups, ash trays, glassware, pillows, and jewelry. Even service industries were affected. Astrology-oriented marriage counseling services were set up. Astrologically compatible partners could be found through special dating services.

The very basis of astrology, the horoscope itself, was affected by modern technology and the methods of mass production. One organization fed 19 million bits of astrological information into a computer and programmed it to churn out 10,000-word character analyses at a cost of $20 each. For those who preferred a human touch in their horoscopes there were about 5,000 professional astrologers throughout the United States. The most successful of these astrologers was Zolar. One of his individual horoscopes cost $200.

In casting a horoscope, astrologers determine the position of the sun, moon, and planets at the moment of an individual's birth. The technicalities of astrology are a set routine, but the interpretation of the influence of the planets on a person's character and destiny is largely a matter of the astrologer's intuition. Quite often different astrologers will have different interpretations of the same horoscope.

Some astrologers dare to predict the future by interpreting the stars just as fortune-tellers do with crystal balls and tarot cards. Sometimes they are right and sometimes they are wrong, but they can usually justify what appears to be an error in their prophecies. So in spite of wide credibility gaps, belief in astrology remains unshaken among the faithful.

LAURENCE B. FINK FROM NANCY PALMER AGENCY

Jeane Dixon's predictions of future happenings cover a multitude of topics, from elections to athletic events, and her prophecies are always widely reported by the press, radio, and TV.

(*continued from page 406*)

Start in altering learning ability. His premise was challenged as unwarranted under present knowledge of the subject. Opponents pointed out that the IQ test-score gaps between whites and blacks diminish among those of comparable cultural backgrounds regardless of race. The report was also condemned as being inflammatory.

The attempt to improve man's ability to communicate was approached from many angles in 1969. Nonverbal communication, the almost subconscious everyday sign language used universally but differently in various cultures, was the subject of several studies. Psychologists said that people who fail to learn the mannerisms and signals of nonverbal communication are unable to maintain regular social relationships. The signals may also be a source of misunderstanding between those on different social levels, it was concluded. For example, mannerisms used to maintain rapport in middle-class circles might be misunderstood as flirtations by those in lower-class brackets.

Sensitivity groups came into increasing use as a means of improving communicative skills. One aim was to utilize the technique to develop ways of resolving conflict situations through problem-solving behavior rather than by power plays, coercion, or manipulation. Better communication was also the object of a number of psychological parlor games marketed in 1969.

Investigations continued into the nonmedical use of drugs, notably the hallucinogens, in an effort to solve some of the complicated psychological, social, medical, and legal questions involved. (*See also* Drugs. *See in* CE: Psychology.)

PUBLISHING, BOOK. The pattern of corporate mergers that had dominated book publishing in recent years continued in 1969. The Dell Publishing Co., Inc., completed its acquisition of The Dial Press, Inc.; Barnes & Noble, Inc., became a subsidiary of Amtel Inc.; Harcourt, Brace & World, Inc. acquired Academic Press, Inc., owners of the Johnson Reprint Corp.; and Harrison Blaine, Inc., which owns *The New Republic,* bought the Liveright Publishing Corp. Cass Canfield, Jr., an editor at Harper & Row, Publishers, set up a European affiliate to be operated jointly by himself and Etas Kompass of Milan, Italy, for publication of college-level works in the social and behavioral sciences. McGraw-Hill, Inc., acquired the American Heritage Publishing Co. and also entered into a joint venture with Far Eastern Publishers Ltd. for printing and publishing in Singapore and Malaysia.

Time-Life Books announced a joint venture with Salvat Editores of Barcelona, Spain, for a book club to be known as Salvat Club de Ediciones. Time-Life Books was publishing in 19 languages for distribution in 85 countries, with annual sales of 5 million books. A new group was set up to handle the company's relations with affiliated enterprises, which included Rowohlt books (West Germany), Éditions Robert Laffont (France), and Organización Editorial Novaro (Mexico). In October Time-Life's acquisition of André Deutsch Ltd. (Great Britain) was announced.

In April Sir William Haley resigned as editor in chief of 'Encyclopædia Britannica', a post which he had assumed in January 1968. Earlier in the year former U.S. Vice-President Hubert H. Humphrey was made a member of the boards of directors of Encyclopædia Britannica, Inc., and the Encyclopædia Britannica Educational Corp.

Censorship continued to be a problem in the United States at both federal and state levels. The House of Representatives Subcommittee on Postal Operations heard proposals to curb a reported increase in the flow of pornography through the mail. Already publishers had to contend with new legislation under which, if a citizen complained of receiving unsolicited mail he regarded as obscene, the mailer was liable to prosecution if he sent the same person another mailing. The U.S. Supreme Court ruled that states had the right to enact statutes imposing "variable censorship"—that is, for adults and children—and publishers and distributors were opposing restrictive legislation.

The year was noteworthy in the United States and elsewhere for the publishing activity surrounding the successful journey of the Apollo 11 astronauts to the moon. A number of books and atlases were prepared to cover the event. The best-known of these projects was the account of the moon landing by novelist Norman Mailer, for which Little, Brown and Co. paid an advance of $150,000 for the book rights and *Life* magazine $100,000 for magazine rights. Both were owned by Time Inc. It was estimated that Mailer's books would probably earn $1 million in sales of U.S. and foreign rights.

In 1968 the number of new U.S. titles was 30,387, an increase of 5.6% over the preceding year. The best-selling novel was 'Airport', by Arthur Hailey, with 250,000 copies. The 'Better Homes and Gardens New Cook Book' was the top nonfiction work with 433,000 copies. Total sale of textbooks in 1968 was $782.43 million, an increase of 7.8% over 1967. 'The Chairman', a novel by Jay Richard Kennedy, achieved the curious distinction of appearing first as a film, then as a paperback, and finally, in 1969, as a hard-cover book. The author had written the screenplay first and had not completed the novel before the release of the film. Another rarity was the publishing by the Macmillan Co. of the 2,337-page 'Baseball Encyclopedia'. (*See also* Literature. *See in* CE: Books and Bookmaking.)

PUERTO RICO. On Jan. 2, 1969, Luis A. Ferré took the oath of office as the new governor of Puerto Rico. As a member of the New Progressive party (the Puerto Rican equivalent of the Republican party in the United States), Ferré supported the idea of statehood for Puerto Rico, a self-governing commonwealth.

The new governor made many public speeches during the year to promote statehood and announced he would tell U.S. President Richard M. Nixon that Puerto Ricans should be allowed to vote in presidential elections. Ferré's critics, those who favored continuing the commonwealth status and those who favored independence, denounced his tactics. Ferré was accused of conducting an "assimilation" campaign, ignoring the will of the majority of Puerto Ricans who supported commonwealth status.

In 1969 there were demonstrations by procommonwealth and by proindependence Puerto Ricans alike. In September proindependence students at the University of Puerto Rico in Rió Piedras burned the school's Reserve Officers Training Corps building. They were against the U.S. Selective Service System.

In an effort to improve the 1970 sugarcane harvest over the declining harvests of previous years, cutting operations began in mid-November 1969. The 1969 agricultural work force had about 9,000 men fewer than the force of 1968.

In the fiscal year 1968–69 Operation Bootstrap enlisted 551 new factory projects to provide 42,000 more jobs. (*See in* CE: Puerto Rico.)

RACE RELATIONS. Fear was a major and growing characteristic of race relations in the United States during 1969. The white population feared militant black groups, and police action against militants increased fear and mistrust of the white community among Negroes. Black demands became more specific during the year as Negroes sought real power in politics, economics, and education.

"All Power to the People"

The fate of the Black Panther party was a focus of attention for black and white Americans alike. During the year the Black Panthers were stripped of almost all their leaders, who were either killed or arrested. Eldridge Cleaver, the party's minister of information, remained in exile in Algeria.

Police raids on local Black Panther party headquarters were frequent in 1969. The police claimed that the Panthers were storing illegal arms and ammunition; the Panthers claimed the police were conducting a genocide campaign against party members.

On December 4 the nation began to pay serious attention to the Panthers' charges against law-enforcement agencies. In Chicago, Ill., Fred Hampton and Mark Clark were killed and four other Black Panthers were wounded during an early-morning police raid on their apartment. The raid was carried out by Chicago police assigned to the office of State's Attorney Edward V. Hanrahan.

The police claimed that the Black Panthers opened fire on them when the officers tried to enter

"CHICAGO SUN-TIMES" PHOTO

At the Cook County Jail, in Chicago, Ill., Dick Gregory, a civil rights activist and a comedian, gives a "peace" sign to a group of his supporters who came to the jail to demand his immediate release.

the apartment and search it for an alleged cache of illegal weapons. The police stated that a gun battle ensued,lasting for 10 or 12 minutes with about 200 rounds of ammunition being fired. There were few bullet holes, however, in most of the rooms and none at the doorway where the police had entered. The lack of physical evidence raised suspicions among members of the white community as well as the black about the believability of the police version. Black Panthers charged that Hampton had been murdered in his bed. They stated that an independent autopsy of the body also indicated that Hampton had been murdered. Hampton was the Illinois chairman of the Black Panther party.

The Panthers conducted public tours through the apartment, pointing out that the bullet holes were concentrated in areas where party members had been shot. Finally, 13 days after the raid, police sealed off the apartment.

In the controversy that erupted after the raid several groups called for an independent investigation of the incident—among them the Afro-American Patrolmen's League, the American Civil Liberties Union, and several city councilmen. The police action was condemned by a group of Roman Catholic priests in Chicago. Nine congressmen wrote U.S. President Richard M. Nixon, urging him to have the incident investigated by the National Commission on the Causes and Prevention of Violence. The U.S. Department of Justice denied that there was a nationwide police conspiracy to eliminate the Black Panthers and ordered a federal investigation of the incident.

The party claimed that the Chicago police raid brought the total number of Black Panthers killed through police action to 28 since January 1968. Other Black Panther-police confrontations in 1969 included a raid on the party's headquarters in Los Angeles, Calif., later in December. About 300 policemen battled with the Panthers. The police said the headquarters building was reinforced like a bunker and that a huge cache of weapons was found inside. Also in December, the party's national chief of staff, David Hilliard, was arrested on charges of threatening the U.S. president's life during a moratorium day speech on November 15 at San Francisco, Calif.

As typified by their new slogan "all power to the people," the Black Panthers broadened their approach to social problems from that of a racial struggle to that of a class struggle. This was evident at the Black Panthers' National Conference Against Fascism held at Oakland, Calif., in July. The Black Panthers hoped to enlist the support of young white radicals. At the conference Panther leader Bobby Seale denounced black racism as being as bad as white racism.

In racially torn Cairo, Ill., the Rev. Gerald Montroy talks with Negro youths on March 27, 1969. The Roman Catholic priest was an outspoken critic of a local citizens' group known as the "White Hats."

WIDE WORLD

Black militants are brought to court in manacles in Detroit, Mich., in March. They were 4 of 135 persons arrested after a shooting incident in which a policeman died. The blacks said police fired first, and police said they were fired on first from a church. Similar incidents occurred in other cities.

UPI COMPIX

Later in the year Seale was convicted of contempt of court by Judge Julius J. Hoffman during the "conspiracy" trial in Chicago, stemming from the disturbances that surrounded the 1968 Democratic National Convention. (*See* United States.)

In urban areas throughout the United States the Black Panthers in 1969 conducted a program of providing hot breakfasts to children. They drew praise from some quarters for feeding the hungry and criticism from others who accused the Panthers of using the breakfast sessions to indoctrinate young children with radical ideas.

Race, Religion, and Politics

The civil rights movement in 1969 was fragmented, and its influence on the federal government declined. At the same time, the power of Negroes on the national level had increased. The more militant groups, particularly, experienced considerable internal struggles. Although no one leader appeared to unite the blacks, several new and powerful voices were heard during the year.

The Rev. Jesse L. Jackson from his base in Chicago continued to conduct a campaign against certain food stores and food products. His Operation Breadbasket waged a war against hunger among the poor, black and white alike.

James Forman took the religious community by surprise in May 1969 when he presented the "black manifesto" at a meeting of church leaders. The manifesto originally demanded that U.S. Protestant churches and Jewish synagogues pay Negroes $500 million in reparations for past racial injustices. Forman later raised the figure to $3 billion. He also demanded reparations from the Roman Catholic church. (*See* Religion.)

The Black Panther party's ideological differences with US, a militant organization based in the Watts section of Los Angeles, allegedly led to violence. In January two Black Panthers were shot and killed by members of US. The shootings occurred on the Los Angeles campus of the University of California. Police arrested two suspects in the shootings, allegedly on the basis of information released by the Black Panthers. One Black Panther leader, however, denied that the killings were the result of a power struggle and said they were political assassinations carried out by US members at the instigation of "the big power structure."

In July Eldridge Cleaver met with Stokely Carmichael at Algiers, Algeria, during the Pan-African Cultural Festival. Carmichael had resigned as prime minister of the Black Panther party in June. Carmichael and Cleaver were reported to have differed over the issue of cooperation with white people. Carmichael took a black-separatist stand, advocating armed struggle.

In the mainstream of U.S. politics Negroes made substantial gains in the South. In Birmingham, Ala., black civil rights leader Arthur D. Shores was elected to the city council. In Greene County, Ala., Negroes won control of the county commission and the school board. Another civil rights leader, Charles Evers, was elected mayor of Fayette, Miss.

There was also white opposition to the Negroes' gains. Three men were arrested in Fayette on charges of plotting to assassinate Mayor Evers. In Cairo, Ill., a group of white vigilantes patrolled the streets, and there were sporadic outbreaks of violence in Cairo throughout the year. (*See* Cities and Urban Affairs.)

A controversial issue in U.S. race relations in 1969 was a proposed new voting-rights bill that would extend the Voting Rights Act of 1965 for an additional five years. The Administration opposed the bill and presented a new law that would apply to all states rather than just the Southern states. Critics of the Administration said that such a law would actually be weaker than the present voting-rights law.

ELAINE TOMLIN

The first "soul saint," a black counterpart to Santa Claus, was introduced in 1969 by Operation Breadbasket in Chicago, Ill., under the direction of the Rev. Jesse Jackson.

Negroes Versus Nixon

A breach developed between Negroes and the new Nixon Administration and widened during the year. Perhaps the one Administration action that did the most toward alienating Negroes involved the issue of school desegregation. When the Nixon Administration took office, the deadline for total desegregation of Southern schools had already been set for September 1969. A few districts had been given until 1970.

The desegregation guidelines drawn up by the Administration in July, however, seemed to pose a threat to rapid school desegregation. Attorney General John N. Mitchell and Secretary of Health, Education, and Welfare Robert H. Finch favored court action against districts that refused to desegregate rather than cutting off federal funds to those districts. They also recommended granting delays in the desegregation deadline to 33 Mississippi school districts.

The Administration's position drew strong protests from the National Association for the Advancement of Colored People, a group of lawyers in the Justice Department, and the U.S. Commission on Civil Rights. The U.S. Supreme Court overruled the Administration's plan and upheld the deadline for immediate desegregation.

Black-studies programs were instituted in many colleges and universities and at some high schools. Clifton R. Wharton, Jr., was appointed president of Michigan State University. He was the first Negro ever named to head a major, predominantly white U.S. university. (*See also* Colleges and Universities; Education.)

Many Negroes were disappointed in President Nixon's program for black capitalism and turned to more direct forms of action. Negroes demanded membership in trade unions and demonstrated on construction sites in several U.S. cities. In November the Administration announced that $500 million would be available for financing Negro businesses by June 1970.

On Sept. 21, 1969, Harlem's U.S. Representative Adam Clayton Powell and Shirley Chisholm, U.S. representative from Brooklyn, N.Y., give black-power salutes during a parade in New York City.

UPI COMPIX

UPI COMPIX

Black militant James Forman presented a "black manifesto" to U.S. religious groups in 1969, demanding financial reparations for past racial injustices. Here he speaks at the Riverside Church in New York City.

Charges of anti-Semitism were made against black militant groups by the heads of the American Jewish Congress and of B'nai B'rith. An attack on Jewish teachers was printed in an Afro-American teachers' publication, and an allegedly anti-Semitic poem was broadcast from a New York City radio station.

There were charges of racism in the U.S. armed forces during 1969. To ease tensions the Marine Corps allowed Negro servicemen to wear modified Afro hair styles and give the clenched-fist salute.

Great Britain also had racial problems during 1969. There were demonstrations against the British immigration policy and against the white-minority regimes in Africa. (*See also* Great Britain; Indians, American; Poverty, War on.)

RECREATION. Recreation in 1969 appeared to be the fastest-growing business in the United States. Figures compiled by the American Automobile Association, the Recreational Vehicle Institute, and other private and government organizations indicated that $83 billion—some 10% of the gross national product—was spent in the pursuit of pleasure. The greatest expenditures were for travel and for recreational equipment—including color television sets.

Among items of recreational equipment the snowmobile was the fastest-growing seller. An estimated one million were in use by year-end. Priced at $700 and up, snowmobiles open previously inaccessible areas for winter trail rides and camping and are also used by forest rangers and police. Demands for registration and control of snowmobiles increased during the year as some drivers used them to pursue animals, either shooting their prey or simply running it to death.

Also gaining in popularity was the trail cycle, a lightweight, quiet "mechanical pony." It can carry people into areas previously accessible only to the hiker or horseback rider, and it offers a great deal more comfort.

Raft trips down Western rivers continued to grow in popularity during the year. An estimated 12,000 people, according to the National Park Service, braved the rapids of the Colorado and Green rivers. For some $30 per person per day, professional guides provided outboard-powered rubber rafts, necessary camping equipment, and some of the luxuries of life. Water flow—and therefore boating conditions—in the rivers was often regulated by varying the release of water from dams.

At the annual congress of the National Recreation and Park Association, held in Chicago, Ill.,

In Tokyo, Japan, children climb all over a 24-foot-high "monster," which quickly became the most popular attraction in that city's newest playground, Tire Park.

UPI COMPIX

Children attend school at a tent camp that shelters about 40,000 Arab refugees at Baqua, Jordan. The youngsters are taught that Israel is responsible for seizing their homeland and that they must prepare to help take it back.

GAMMA—PIX FROM PUBLIX

U.S. Secretary of the Interior Walter J. Hickel reported that his department was considering a $6.3-billion program to increase recreational resources in and near major cities. (*See also* Camping; Hobbies; Travel; other sports articles.)

REFUGEES. In 1969 the displaced persons of the world numbered more than 17 million. People of all races, colors, and creeds continued their flight from religious and political oppression, war, and starvation imposed on them by their fellow men.

By September 1969 the number of Czechoslovak refugees reached an estimated 90,000, many of them highly qualified workers and professional people who were easily resettled. Most, however, found a hard life in Austria, where they lived in crowded quarters, working for low salaries and paying high prices as they awaited visas. Polish Jews, Romanians, and East Germans added to the European refugee roles in 1969.

Cubans continued their influx to Miami, Fla., at about 1,000 a week, with 25% settling there. The Latin American population in Dade County, Fla., reached almost 300,000 with an annual buying power of $350 million.

Africa, with 5 million, had the highest number of refugees. In the Nigerian civil war, much of the relief for secessionist Biafra came from private agencies. Tibetan settlements in India and Sudanese refugee areas in the Central African Republic proved successful. Conditions were somewhat improved for 1.3 million refugees in South Vietnam as they settled into rehabilitation rather than emergency programs, but the plight of uprooted village families thrust into city slum conditions brought human problems like theft and prostitution. In May Israel announced two pilot projects for the resettlement of Arab refugees. The United Nations Relief and Works Agency for Palestine Refugees had pledges of $41 million for 1969, with expenditures of $44.3 million forecast for the year.

This woman and child were among the 20 refugees forced to live in concrete drainpipes in the Cholon section of Saigon, South Vietnam, because of the Communist shelling of the area in May 1969.

UPI COMPIX

RELIGION. Perhaps the most controversial issue in U.S. church life of 1969 was introduced to the public during May, when the National Black Economic Development Conference (NBEDC) presented startling economic demands in the form of a "black manifesto." The manifesto had been developed by the NBEDC in Detroit, Mich. Spokesman for the group was James Forman, a former leader of the Student Nonviolent Coordinating Committee. Basically, the manifesto articulated the idea that the black people of the United States are entitled to some $500 million in reparations from whites for racial and economic exploitation. The manifesto also discussed some ways in which the money would be spent. Plans included a Southern land bank to secure land for black farmers, black-controlled publishing and broadcasting enterprises, and a fund to develop cooperative businesses in the United States and in Africa. Following the initial presentation of the manifesto, the sum demanded was later increased to a total of $3 billion to be paid by U.S. religious institutions.

The manifesto elicited an understandably wide range of responses. Groups of black churchmen all over the country joined the National Committee of Black Churchmen in endorsing the manifesto's principles and demands. At a special convention of the Protestant Episcopal church delegates voted to give $200,000 to the National Committee of Black Churchmen for community organization projects. It was understood that most of the money was destined for the NBEDC. Orthodox rabbis voted unanimously to reject "categorically" any demands on Jewish institutions. The bishops' council of the United Methodist church repudiated the ideology of the manifesto and further pointed out that their church had already set up a $20-million Fund for Reconciliation, designed to aid minority groups. Christian Scientists, during their annual meeting in Boston, Mass., also rejected the manifesto's demands. In September, however, the general board of the National Council of Churches asked its member bodies to join in raising not less than $500,000 for economic development of U.S. black communities. Arthur S. Flemming, president of the Council, stated that, though the ideology of the black manifesto was unacceptable, the goals of the NBEDC could not be ignored.

Liturgical dances are performed by Sister Ann Taylor (above) at Newton College of the Sacred Heart in Newton, Mass., and Wray Taylor (right) in Calvary Episcopal Church in New York City. Using dance as a part of worship revives an ancient Hebrew custom.

ABOVE: UPI COMPIX
RIGHT: WIDE WORLD

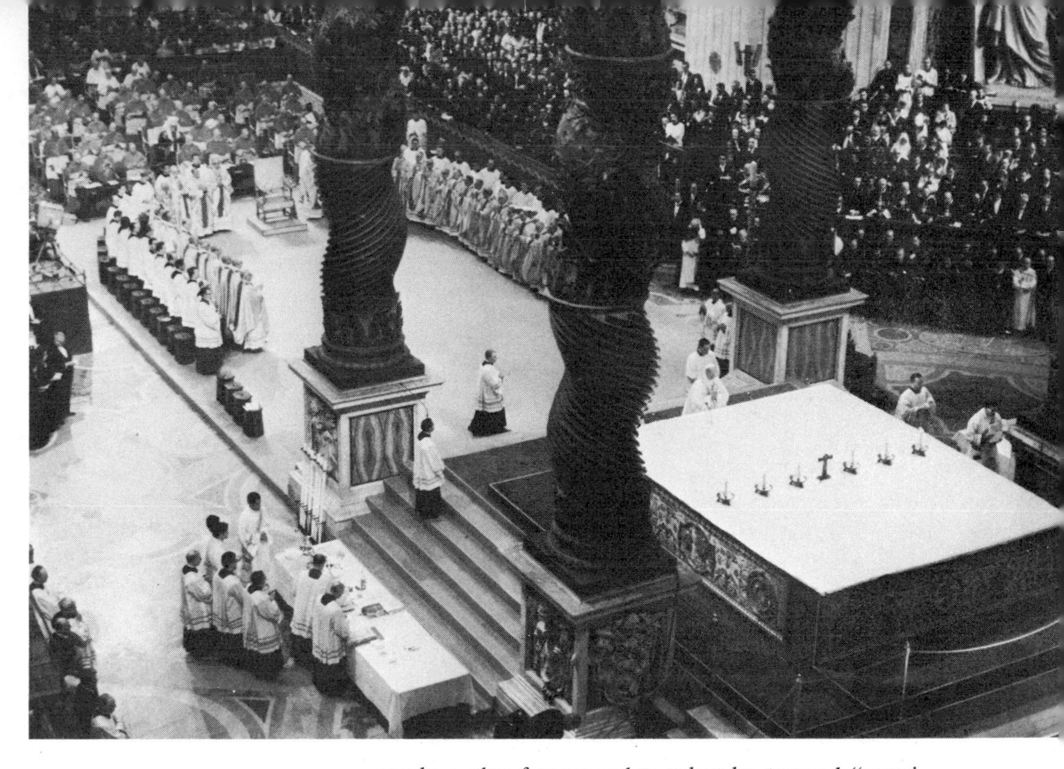

Pope Paul VI celebrates mass with the 33 newly nominated cardinals in Vatican City on Jan. 5, 1969.

KEYSTONE

Ecumenism

In international religious affairs, the ecumenical movement of past years continued to gain momentum in 1969. The Consultation on Church Union, involved in achieving the eventual merger of ten major Protestant bodies, held its annual meeting in March. A proposed outline for the merger was made public for the first time at this session. The outline represented seven years of work and planning by leaders of the participating denominations.

Efforts to achieve closer rapprochement between various Protestant bodies and the Roman Catholic church were continued. A visit by Pope Paul VI to the World Council of Churches headquarters at Geneva, Switzerland, marked a major effort to increase understanding among the various Christian churches of the world. In the meantime, the first Baptist-Catholic dialogue in the United States was held at Wake Forest University's Ecumenical Institute. Nineteen Roman Catholics and 39 Southern Baptists adopted a resolution emphasizing the "overwhelming fact that we are brothers in Christ." In December the Vatican issued a startling document redefining the Catholic attitude toward Judaism and setting forth a series of guidelines for improved relations between the two faiths.

The Lutheran Council in the U.S.A. and the Protestant Episcopal church began the first of what were expected to be semiannual discussions to explore the divisions between the two faiths. Lutheran meetings were also progressing in similar joint consultations with Roman Catholic, Eastern Orthodox, and Jewish theologians.

ROMAN CATHOLICISM

The year 1969 was marked by continued internal struggles over the reforms initiated by the second Vatican council. In his Easter message Pope Paul made a plea for an end to what he termed "crucifixion" of the church by criticism. On Maundy Thursday he had warned of the danger of schism and accused critics of the 1968 encyclical *Humanae Vitae* (Of Human Life) of "seeking the easy way."

A revised liturgical calendar, made public in May, aroused interest in the Catholic and non-Catholic worlds alike. The existence of many saints was deemed dubious, and the feast days of others were made optional. Two popular saints, Valentine and Christopher, were dropped from the official calendar. Altogether, the traditional anniversary celebrations of 200 saints were declared optional. Many new saints from Africa, Japan, Oceania, and the Americas were introduced into the calendar for the first time.

The threatened crisis over the issue of celibacy at last materialized, most seriously in Western Europe—particularly the Netherlands and the Americas. Thirty-one priests of the Diocese of Brooklyn rejected the papal view outright, declaring that they considered themselves free to marry. In one of the year's most publicized incidents, Msgr. Giovanni Musante, a Vatican aide, left his post to marry. In the United States, the resignation and marriage of former Bishop James P. Shannon had a dramatic impact. Shannon, who had been auxiliary bishop of Minneapolis-St. Paul, Minn., resigned from the church in June. He stated that he was unable to reconcile his views on birth control with those set forth by the pope. Two months later, former Bishop Shannon was married in a Protestant ceremony. It was believed to be the first time a U.S. bishop of the Roman Catholic church had married.

Many of the problems of 1969 were discussed in a new book, 'Coresponsibility in the Church', by Belgium's Leon Joseph Cardinal Suenens. The much-publicized book called for an honest reappraisal of authority at all levels of the church. It called particular attention to the problem of collegiality, or the collective sharing of church rule by all the bishops. Despite his affirmations of loyalty to the Holy See, Cardinal Suenens was viewed with suspicion from many quarters in the church. Suenens found himself becoming a focal point of Catholic dissent.

A two-week meeting of the Synod of Bishops began in Rome, Italy, on October 11. The meeting was one of the most important events in the Catholic world during 1969. The main questions on the group's agenda concerned collegiality and relations between bishops and the Holy See. Also at issue was the decentralization of church power in favor of greater concentration at local and regional levels. At the closing session of the synod, the pope agreed to grant the bishops' plea for greater participation in church government. He also agreed to their request that the synod be convened every two years on a regular basis. In addition, he promised to give consideration to the demands for permanent episcopal representation in Rome. Nevertheless, the pontiff made it clear that his authority on all doctrinal matters would remain immune from dispute.

Earlier in the year Pope Paul nominated 33 to the College of Cardinals, bringing the membership of that body to 134—the largest in its history. Among the newly appointed cardinals were four from the United States: Archbishop Terence J. Cooke of New York City; Archbishop John F. Dearden of Detroit, Mich.; Archbishop John J. Carberry of St. Louis, Mo.; and Bishop John J. Wright of Pittsburgh, Pa.

JUDAISM

The precarious position of Jews in the Arab countries, the U.S.S.R., Poland, and Czechoslovakia was a prime matter of Jewish concern during 1969. Some 75,000 Jews were still living within the Arab world and bearing the brunt of anti-Israeli and anti-Zionist animosity. While no blatant forms of discrimination were noticeable in Tunisia and Morocco (estimated Jewish population 60,000), hundreds of Jews arrested in Syria, Iraq, and the United Arab Republic (UAR), or Egypt, during June 1967 remained imprisoned in 1969. Those not in jail were virtual prisoners in their homes.

Very tragic was the plight of the remnants of the Jewish community in Iraq. During January a group of Iraqi Jews and Arabs accused of spying for Israel were executed in a public hanging. These summary executions produced a wave of revulsion throughout the world. Hundreds of Iraqi Jews were arrested and imprisoned without benefit of legal aid or contact with relatives. No Jew was allowed to leave his town of residence or change his domicile without permission. The venerable chief rabbi of Iraq, 93-year-old Sasson Khadouri, whose own son had been in prison since the beginning of the year, was forced to call a conference of Jewish leaders in Arab countries to denounce Israel and Zionism.

Another event that shocked both the secular and religious worlds was the fire of August 21 that swept through a wing of the Al Aksa Mosque in Israeli-occupied Jerusalem. An Australian Christian fundamentalist, Denis Michael Rohan, later confessed to the crime and was charged with arson, as well as violation of a holy place. Although no member of the Jewish faith was connected with the tragedy, Arab propagandists took advantage of the situation to arouse anger in the Muslim world. Demonstrations against Israel took place in Jerusalem, Syria, Jordan, Iraq, Lebanon, the UAR, and the Philippines. A Soviet statement issued on Au-

Burial services are held on July 7, 1969, in Masada, Israel, for 27 ancient Jewish heroes who died defending Masada against invading Romans. The 2,000-year-old remains were discovered during a 1965 excavation.

WIDE WORLD

gust 29 declared that Israel and its allies would have to bear responsibility for the fire.

Hostility and distrust toward Jews continued in the U.S.S.R. The type of discrimination practiced against Soviet Jewry, while not of a physical nature, was a subtle combination of economic, cultural, and social pressures. Jews were barred from upper-echelon jobs and were not allowed to attain positions of prestige. Thus, the number of Jewish members of the Soviet Academy of Sciences, as well as of regional and republic academies, was greatly reduced.

In June Polish authorities announced a strict tightening of existing emigration procedures for Jews. It was officially stated that since July 1967 about 5,000 Jews had left the country (though in all probability the number was much greater). Despite the many Jews who had already fled from Poland, thousands more were waiting for exit visas. Hundreds of Jews were dismissed from their posts in the Polish military, civil service, and institutions of higher learning.

The largest and most influential segment of the Jewish people, those of the United States, witnessed the continuation and increase of black anti-Semitism. The New York City school system remained a focal point in the conflict. A public school in Brooklyn, N.Y., broke into the news when a social-studies teacher distributed an obscene and anti-Jewish poem to his class. Several incidents of vandalism to Jewish schools and synagogues in New York occurred during the year. Similar reports came from Boston and other U.S. cities.

Another example of racial and religious conflict in the United States was the publication by the African-American Teachers Association of an anti-Jewish editorial in *Forum*, the organization's official publication. The editorial accused Jews of exploiting Negroes and Puerto Ricans in the schools.

PROTESTANTISM

The central committee of the World Council of Churches, a group composed of Protestant and Orthodox Christians, met in England during 1969 and asserted that "growing tensions and conflicts between the races demanded urgent action." Recommendations to the 235 member denominations included a vote in favor of a "massive transfer" of economic resources to the victims of racial injustice. This action on the part of the council seemed in part to endorse the demands put forth in the United States by the NBEDC.

The National Council of Churches, a federation of 33 U.S. Protestant denominations, experienced serious financial difficulties during 1969. According to a national poll, more than 50% of the people familiar with the organization did not approve of its social and political activities. The sharp decline in contributions from member bodies undoubtedly reflected these feelings. As a result of decreased funds, six programs of various council departments—including the departments of social justice and church renewal—had to be substantially reduced. In addition, the council was forced to relinquish its support of several projects. Among those to be dropped was the Delta Ministry in Mississippi, a civil rights project. Contributions to national agencies of many Protestant churches also declined in 1969.

In December Cynthia Clark Wedel became the first woman ever to be elected president of the National Council of Churches. The position was considered to be the "highest symbolic post of American Protestantism."

A six-day Congress on Evangelism drew representatives from 93 Protestant denominations. The participating churches were predominantly fundamentalist in nature. Evangelist Billy Graham served as honorary chairman of the congress. Among the attending church groups were such traditionally isolationist bodies as the Church of the Nazarene, the Churches of Christ, and the Lutheran Church-Missouri Synod. It was the first such interdenominational meeting for these conservative Protestant groups.

The congress was dominated by discussion of social issues, perhaps another first for a major evangelical gathering. Many of the normally conservative evangelicals adopted what might be described as a liberal Protestant policy of responsiveness and cooperation. Much of the discussion centered around plans for action on such social problems as race, peace, and poverty.

Deaths in the Protestant world during 1969 included Karl Barth, the prominent Swiss theologian, and James A. Pike, formerly the Protestant Episcopal bishop of California. Pike, long a controversial figure in Protestant circles, died while lost in the Judean wilderness of Israel.

RETAIL TRADE.

In dollar terms, retail sales in the United States reached all-time highs in each quarter of 1969. The steady rise of dollar volume, however, was largely a result of inflation-bred price increases; the quantity of merchandise sold grew but little. In Canada, consumer demand—which had picked up momentum in the last half of 1968 —continued at a high level through 1969.

Retailers in the United States believed that there were two major reasons for the lack of increase in the quantity of goods sold. Continuation of the income-tax surcharge made buyers more conservative in their purchases, and an influenza epidemic that swept the United States early in the year kept many people out of stores.

The prices of most goods and services rose under the impact of inflation. Consumer spending during the year was highest for nondurable goods. By the third quarter, for instance, apparel and department-store sales jumped approximately 7.5% higher than in the first half of 1968; drugstore sales rose 3.1%. Spending for durables was up in the first half of the year but dropped slightly in the third quarter.

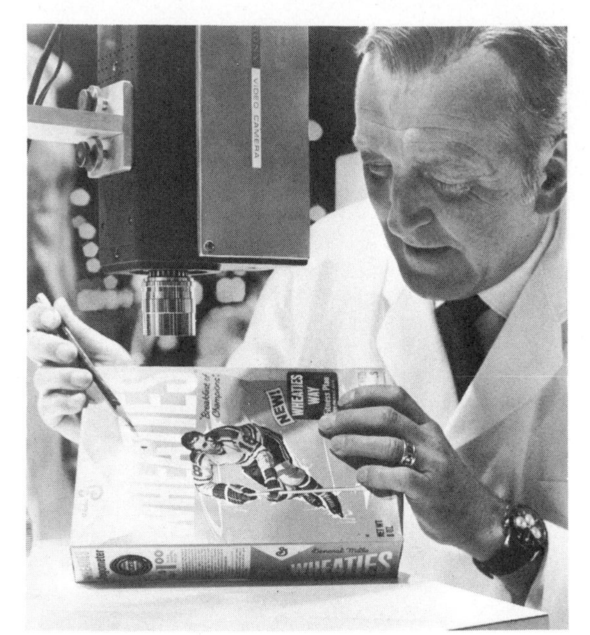

UPI COMPIX

On May 6, 1969, St. Regis Paper Co. announced the development of a package with a microcircuit that is designed to be price-coded and translated instantly by a computer at the check-out counter.

Consumers spent more money on services in 1969 than in any previous year. Although the costs of medical, maintenance, and other services rose sharply, consumers paid the higher fees instead of doing without.

The fastest-growing business in the United States in 1969 was the business of leisure. Affluent Americans, with more spare time and money than ever, spent $83 billion on leisure. The money went into travel, sports equipment, campers, boats, summerhouses, and a host of related items. (*See also* Camping; Hobbies; Recreation; Travel.)

Young people spent a large proportion of the consumer dollars. Many of the young were spending all the money they earned and taking great advantage of installment credit. Outstanding installment credit rose to about $93 billion in the second quarter of the year.

"Consumerism" gained in importance as a social movement in the United States during the year. Aid to consumers became a major concern of the federal government. More than 100 bills to protect buyers were introduced in the first session of the 91st Congress. More than 100 members of the House of Representatives sponsored a bill to set up a Cabinet-level Department of Consumer Affairs. (*See also* Consumer Protection; Economy; Food.)

RHODESIA. The Union Jack—the British flag—flew officially in Rhodesia for the last time July 6, 1969. On that day the governor, Sir Humphrey Gibbs, left Salisbury, the capital, for retirement. On November 11 the former colony observed the fourth anniversary of its unilateral declaration of independence from Great Britain. Shortly after, a bill was signed that would make Rhodesia a republic in mid-1970 and thus complete the long process of breaking away from Britain.

Rhodesian voters on June 20 had approved a new white-supremacist constitution and a proposal for breaking of final ties with Great Britain. The controversial *apartheid*-slanted constitution won the voters' consent despite condemnation by 12 Protestant denominations and councils and the Roman Catholic church in Rhodesia. Only the Dutch Reformed church refrained from comment. In the June referendum only 6,645 of the 90,704 voters were Africans, though Rhodesia had a black population of more than 4.5 million and a white population of some 230,000. Rigid income and educational qualifications, stiffened in February, kept most Rhodesian blacks from voting. The U.S. consulate remained open after the voting, still officially accredited to Great Britain.

Opposition to the referendum proposals was widespread both among Rhodesian Africans and in the United Nations (UN). Meetings arranged by the African Trade Union Council to discuss the referendum were banned. A number of tribal chiefs were against both parts of the question. At the UN in June there were demands that economic sanctions be strengthened, and a resolution by African and Asian members urging action, even force, by Great Britain was passed.

Ian D. Smith continued as prime minister of Rhodesia in 1969. He was expected to become president under the new constitution in 1970.

GAMMA—PIX FROM PUBLIX

There was criticism of the economic sanctions from Rhodesia's business community. In letters to the press E. S. Newson, chairman of the Rhodesia Iron and Steel Corp., and Evan Campbell, chairman of the Standard Bank in Rhodesia, emphasized the disastrous effects of the economic sanctions. In June and July it became clear that ships were violating the sanctions. Economic activity was higher than in 1965. However, according to Great Britain, the sanctions were having serious effects on exports. In March Rhodesia announced large cutbacks in import quotas to help offset its foreign currency shortage.

CAMERA PRESS—PIX FROM PUBLIX

At a ceremony in Salisbury on Jan. 11, 1969, the British flag and the old Rhodesian flag fly together for the last time as officials prepare to replace them with the new Rhodesian flag. Ian D. Smith and his wife are in attendance.

The 1969 budget cut direct taxation and increased indirect taxation. The adverse effects were felt more strongly by the black African population. Although food costs were not changed, clothing and minor luxuries cost more.

Legislation was enacted to extend the state of emergency for another year starting April 12. Leaders of the African nationalist movement suffered setbacks. Joshua Nkomo began another five years in prison and Ndabaningi Sithole was sentenced to six years hard labor for conspiracy to murder the prime minister. On March 7, however, 49 Africans under death sentence were granted a reprieve, and in August another 19 had sentences commuted to life imprisonment. In September government troops evicted some 1,500 members of the Tangwena tribe from its homeland, a territory near Mozambique designated for whites only. (*See also* Africa. *See in* CE: Rhodesia.)

ROGERS, WILLIAM P. On Jan. 22, 1969, William P. Rogers was sworn in as secretary of state in the new Administration of U.S. President Richard M. Nixon. Later in the year observers noted that Nixon was "his own secretary of state" and that Henry A. Kissinger, his foreign policy adviser, also played a chief role in formulating U.S. foreign policy. (*See* Kissinger.)

During a six-nation tour of Asia July 28–August 8, Rogers stressed U.S. readiness to resume ambassadorial talks with Communist China. He acknowledged the "reality of the Communist rule on the mainland" and thus hinted at a possible "two China" policy officially recognizing both Communist China and the Nationalist Chinese regime on Taiwan. (*See* Feature Article: "China and the United States: Distorted Images.")

In May Rogers visited South Vietnam and other Asian countries to promote Nixon's peace plan for the Vietnam conflict. He conferred with South Vietnam's President Nguyen Van Thieu on troop replacement. In June Rogers said that the United States was "not wedded to any government in Saigon."

Rogers was born June 23, 1913, in Norfolk, N.Y. He received degrees from Colgate University and Cornell Law School. He practiced law privately and has held various government positions, including U.S. attorney general, 1957–61. He is married and has four children. (*See* Foreign Policy, U.S.)

William P. Rogers, U.S. secretary of state, speaks with reporters about combat activity in Vietnam. During 1969 the Vietnam conflict continued to be the most important issue in U.S. foreign policy.

WIDE WORLD

ROMANIA. During 1969, under the leadership of Romanian Communist Party First Secretary Nicolae Ceausescu, Romania made further progress on the road toward socialism and national sovereignty. In the Romanian Communist party (RCP) and the government, the men of the old guard, steeped in Stalinist traditions, lost ground almost entirely. Romania expanded its political contacts and economic agreements with capitalist countries while remaining a genuine member of the socialist community.

On March 2 a new Grand National Assembly was elected. Out of 13,577,143 votes, 13,543,499 (more than 99%) were given to the candidates of the Socialist Unity Front. Among 465 deputies there were 41 Magyars, 12 Germans, and 9 of other nationalities. On March 13 the Assembly elected Stefan Voitec as its chairman and reelected Ceausescu as president of the State Council; it also elected 4 vice-presidents and 22 members of the Council, the supreme state body. Supported by

CAMERA PRESS—PIX FROM PUBLIX

Nicolae Ceausescu (center), first secretary of Romania's Communist party, reviews a parade in Bucharest, Romania's capital, on the occasion of the 25th anniversary of the country's Communist revolution. A representative from the Soviet Union (far left) and one from Communist China (far right) attended but avoided each other.

Ceausescu, Ion Gheorghe Maurer was again invested by the Assembly with the office of chairman of the Council of Ministers. In the new government Ilie Verdet continued to occupy the position of first vice-chairman.

The tenth congress of the RCP was held in Bucharest, the capital, on August 6–12. Addressing 1,915 delegates representing more than 1.9 million party members, Ceausescu reaffirmed Romania's friendship with the Soviet Union.

Romanians gave an enthusiastic welcome to U.S. President Richard M. Nixon (standing in car, left) during his historic visit in August. Ceausescu accompanies Nixon in the car.

KEYSTONE

The congress elected the Central Committee of full and alternate members and reelected Ceausescu as first secretary. On August 12 the Central Committee approved the composition of Ceausescu's Executive Committee, of the Permanent Presidium, and of the Secretariat.

As a European country, Romania was particularly interested in European security. Together with other member states of the Warsaw Pact, meeting in Budapest, Hungary, in March, Romania called for the recognition of the "realities created after World War II," namely the two German states and the existing frontiers. Ceausescu called for "strengthening the defensive capacity of Romania" and for perfecting the organization and equipment of the armed forces "called upon to defend the independence and sovereignty of the homeland."

The most sensational event in the domain of Romania's foreign relations was the visit in Bucharest, on August 2–3, of Richard M. Nixon, the first visit by a U.S. president to a Communist country in peacetime. More than a million people turned out to greet President Nixon, who danced the hora with Romanian girls in a city square and also had a long talk with Ceausescu. (*See* Communist Movement.)

During the year Ceausescu visited Turkey in March, Poland in May, and Iran in September, and he met twice with Yugoslavia's President Tito, in February and September. In March Romanian troops took part in maneuvers in Bulgaria involving also Soviet and Bulgarian ground forces. (*See in* CE: Rumania.)

RUBBER. World production of natural rubber in 1968 was estimated at more than 2.9 million tons, an increase of some 168,000 tons over the 1967 figure. Production for the first six months of 1969 was estimated at more than 1.37 million tons, up 25,000 tons from the first half of 1968.

World production of all types of synthetic rubber for 1968 (excluding the Soviet Union and other countries not reporting) was some 4.42 million tons (including latices), of which the United States produced more than 2.38 million tons (including oil content). World production of synthetic rubber in the first six months of 1969 was estimated at nearly 2.44 million tons, compared with 2.19 million tons for the corresponding period of 1968. In the reporting countries of the United States, Great Britain, West Germany, Australia, Canada, and Brazil, production of reclaimed rubber for 1968 totaled some 413,000 tons. For the first six months of 1969, production was estimated at 210,000 tons, compared with 218,000 tons for the first half of 1968.

World consumption of new rubber—natural and synthetic—in 1968 was again at a new high of nearly 7.5 million tons, of which 64.6% was synthetic rubber. The world's consumption of new rubber in the first six months of 1969 was estimated at slightly more than 4 million tons, of which 65.4% was synthetic rubber.

Meeting in London, England, in July, the Management Committee of the International Rubber Study Group estimated non-Communist world production and consumption of new rubber as follows: supply of natural rubber, 3.16 million tons in 1969 and 3.26 million tons in 1970; supply of synthetic rubber, 4.96 million tons in 1969 and 5.32 million tons in 1970. It was estimated that the world would consume some 3.2 million tons of natural rubber and about 4.8 million tons of synthetic rubber in 1969. (*See in* CE: Rubber.)

RWANDA. Relations with the Democratic Republic of the Congo (Kinshasa), broken off in 1968 after Rwanda's refusal to hand over European mercenaries, improved in 1969. The border was reopened in February following a conciliation move at the meeting of the heads of state of the Afro-Malagasy Common Organization in Kinshasa in January. The first Rwandan ambassador was accepted by the Congo in August. The most pressing problem remained the refugees from Rwanda, of whom some 24,000 were reported in the Congo. Financial provision for a number of Rwandan refugees was made in Tanzania and Uganda.

In June the foreign ministers of the Congo (Kinshasa), Rwanda, and Burundi met in Kinshasa to discuss a regional economic grouping to be called the Common Organization for Economic Cooperation in Central Africa. Suggested projects included a joint power plant, exploitation of natural gas from Lake Kivu, and an increase in commercial exchanges. Three commissions were established: economic and technical (Burundi), political and judicial (the Congo), and social and cultural (Rwanda).

Economic aid from Belgium in 1968 totaled $5.76 million. Development aid was also received from the European Economic Community, or Common Market, for regional development and power projects, including a hydroelectric plant at Mukungwa. (*See in* CE: Rwanda.)

SAFETY. The National Safety Council (NSC) reported 115,000 accidental deaths in the United States in 1968, an increase of 2% over the total for 1967. Accidents claimed the lives of 54,800 Americans in the first six months of 1969. The accidental-death rate was 57 per 100,000 persons.

Motor-Vehicle Deaths

Motor-vehicle accidents in the United States resulted in 25,890 fatalities during the first six months of 1969, an increase of 3% over the same period in 1968. The death rate per 100,000 persons was 28.2; the rate per 100 million vehicle miles was 5. Motor-vehicle accidents claimed 55,200 lives in 1968, an increase of 4% over the 1967 figure. The U.S. Department of Transportation's report to Congress on "Alcohol and Highway Safety" concluded that "alcohol has been the largest single factor leading to fatal crashes."

In an effort to reduce highway deaths, the National Highway Safety Bureau issued several new standards for motor vehicles and state highway-safety programs. Standards for 1969 cars dealt with lamps and reflective devices, latch systems for hoods, and head restraints to minimize whiplash injuries. Other standards governed headlight-con-

A cockpit instrument designed by Bendix Corp. to instruct airline pilots on how to avoid possible collisions was being tested in 1969.

WIDE WORLD

CANADIAN PRESS

The Toronto (Ont.) Transit Commission demonstrates water-cushion bumpers, which are being installed on 30 Toronto transit buses. The new safety bumpers are designed to cushion the impact in collisions.

cealment devices, door locks, and tires. As of January 1970 automakers were required to equip new cars with antitheft locking devices, safer windshield mountings, and protection against impact with glove-compartment doors.

New standards for state highway-safety programs dealt with improvement of police traffic services, pedestrian safety, and postcrash hazard control and cleanup. The NSC coordinated a program designed to help states adjust their safety programs to new federal standards.

Accidents at Work and Home

Home accidents claimed the lives of 13,700 persons during the first six months of 1969, a decrease of 7% from the same period of 1968. Accidental deaths in public places totaled 10,000 for the period, and deaths from work accidents rose to 6,900. The occupational-injury rate had risen steadily during the 1960's. The increase was attributed in part to more complex industrial processes and to high labor turnover.

In an effort to insure optimum on-the-job safety, Congress considered several versions of the Occupational Safety and Health Act of 1969. All included programs to insure safe working conditions, to authorize appropriate authorities to set health and safety standards, to offer assistance to states in their efforts to eliminate on-the-job accidents, and to provide for research, education, and training in the field of occupational safety and health. In October Congress passed a Federal Coal Mine Health and Safety Act extending federal jurisdiction to surface mines, establishing standards for coal-dust levels, and streamlining enforcement procedures. New standards dealing with general occupational safety and noise were promulgated by Secretary of Labor George P. Shultz.

The National Commission on Product Safety, established to warn consumers of commonly used products involving unreasonable risk, recommended legislation affecting refrigerators and children's toys. Several products were recalled or improved by manufacturers as a result of commission hearings. Secretary of Commerce Maurice H. Stans reported that new or amended flammability standards might be needed for wearing apparel, rugs, and carpets. (*See in* CE: Safety.)

SAUDI ARABIA. Throughout 1969 King Faisal's Saudi Arabian government continued to pursue conservative Islamic policies and to oppose spreading leftist influences on the Arabian Peninsula. With the uncovering in June of a leftist plot to overthrow the government, arrests were begun that culminated in a purge of 200 to 300 military officers, civil servants, and others in September. While the June plot involved primarily members of the air force, the revolutionary movement exposed in September was the largest ever to be found in Saudi Arabia. The plots were attributed to elements of the Arab-nationalist movement seeking to end the monarchy and to establish a republic on the Arabian Peninsula.

Although King Faisal remained opposed to any summit conference to determine Arab policy toward Israel, he scored a diplomatic success among Arab nations by sponsoring an Islamic summit meeting at Rabat, Morocco, in September. At the meeting efforts were made to bring about normal relations between Saudi Arabia and Yemen, but Saudi Arabia did not take the step on the grounds that the Yemeni civil war remained unsettled. The Saudi government continued to refuse recognition to Southern Yemen, and late in the year fighting broke out along their common border.

Saudi Arabian relations with other Arab socialist states, including the United Arab Republic, or Egypt, were cool but correct. Relations with the

United States were endangered by continuing U.S. support for Israel. After France's President Charles de Gaulle resigned, King Faisal warned a delegation of French businessmen that their interests would be threatened if France modified its Middle East policy in favor of Israel. Saudi Arabia remained a quiet but substantial contributor of funds to the Palestinian guerrilla organizations operating against Israel. (*See also* Middle East; Morocco; Yemen. *See in* CE: Saudi Arabia.)

SELECTIVE SERVICE. On Oct. 10, 1969, U.S. President Richard M. Nixon announced that Lieut. Gen. Lewis B. Hershey would be removed as director of the selective service system. Hershey, 76, would be promoted to four-star general and appointed as adviser to the president on mobilization of manpower on the date of his retirement, Feb. 16, 1970.

General Hershey had been director of selective service since 1941; he became a controversial figure in the 1960's for his policies in dealing with draft resisters. In addition, some observers criticized Hershey for not striving to make uniform, nationwide standards for the more than 4,000 local draft boards in the United States.

Draft calls for 1969 totaled 290,400, down more than 5,000 from the 1968 total. President Nixon eliminated the draft calls for November and December and instead spread the call for October—29,000 men—over the last three months of the year. Late in 1969 the Nixon Administration estimated that the 1970 draft calls would total 250,000.

Lottery Determines Fate of Young Men

The first national draft lottery since 1942 was held on Dec. 1, 1969. The U.S. Congress cleared the way for the lottery, at the request of the Administration, with a one-sentence bill repealing a 1967 law that forbade such random selection.

All 366 days of the year, including February 29, were drawn from a large glass bowl; thus each young man's birthday determined his number in the lottery. The 26 letters of the alphabet were drawn to determine alphabetical order, by last name, within the group of men with a given birth date.

Administration officials estimated that young men whose birthdays were among the first one-third drawn from the bowl would almost certainly be drafted; those in the last third were almost certainly safe; and those in the middle third would take their chances, depending on the distribution of birth-date lottery numbers within their draft board areas and the national draft calls. The first five dates drawn were September 14, April 24, December 30, February 14, and October 18. Each local draft board will exhaust its supply of eligible men born September 14 before moving to those born April 24, and so on.

For the first year only, the lottery included all eligible men 19 through 25—those with birth dates between Jan. 1, 1944, and Dec. 31, 1950. However, there will be a new lottery every year that will include only 19-year-olds.

UPI COMPIX

Representative Alexander Pirnie (R, N.Y.) draws the first capsule during the national draft lottery on Dec. 1, 1969. The lottery was the first to be held in the United States in 27 years.

This does not mean, however, that all future draftees will be 19 years old. A man with a deferment is not subject to the lottery while his deferment is valid; when the deferment is removed and he is reclassified 1A, he enters the lottery with the number drawn for him in the year he was 19 (or in 1969 for those 19–25 in that year).

For example, a sophomore in college in 1969 probably held a 2S, or student, deferment; when he graduates in June 1972 he becomes subject to the

Two hundred antiwar demonstrators, marking the first anniversary of the 1968 arrest of the "Milwaukee 14" group, watch a policeman slam the lid on a newspaper fire in an imitation coffin.

WIDE WORLD

lottery with the number drawn for him in 1969. If this hypothetical sophomore was born September 14, his lottery number is one and he knows already that he certainly *will* be drafted in 1972 or whenever he loses his deferment.

Protest, Dissent, and Disruption

In Chicago, Ill., 18 persons were arrested in May for burning the records of a local draft board. Convictions were returned in 1969 for two groups arrested on similar charges in 1968—11 of the "Milwaukee (Wis.) 14" and the "Catonsville (Md.) 9." The Milwaukee group, including several Roman Catholic priests, were sentenced to two years in prison. (*See* Defense Special Report.)

A Boston, Mass., federal district judge ruled that "profound moral beliefs" could be the basis for a deferment as a conscientious objector—membership in a religious denomination was not legally necessary for such a deferment. In July a U.S. circuit court of appeals overturned the 1968 conviction of pediatrician Benjamin M. Spock for conspiring to counsel draft evasion; codefendant Michael Ferber, a graduate student, was also acquitted. Retrials were ordered for their codefendants William Sloane Coffin, Jr., chaplain of Yale University, and Mitchell Goodman.

SENEGAL. Civil unrest and economic difficulties made 1969 a trying year for President Léopold S. Senghor's government in Senegal. Schoolchildren, older students, and labor unions staged strikes. However, a call in May by a student organization for a general strike was unsuccessful, as was a June strike call by the unions. Dissension in the trade unions, however, resulted in a two-week state of emergency. In August the National Union of Senegalese Workers lodged a complaint against the government with the International Labor Organization, charging that the government had confiscated its property.

On September 16 a draft bill of a new constitution was adopted by the cabinet. The document provided for a prime minister responsible to the head of state and the national assembly; it was to

Senegal's President Léopold S. Senghor (right) is greeted by Jacques Foccart, France's general secretary of African affairs, in March.

AFP FROM PICTORIAL PARADE

be submitted for referendum in 1970. Diplomatic relations with Nationalist China, terminated in 1965, were resumed in July. An African peace program was presented by President Senghor. (*See in* CE: Senegal.)

SHIPS AND SHIPPING. Shipyards around the world hit a new high in the production of giant ships in 1969. In March the 253,000-ton tanker *Esso Scotia* was launched in Bremen, West Germany. The ship, 1,140 feet long, was the largest vessel ever built in Europe. In May the *Esso Northumbria* was launched at Newcastle-on-Tyne, England. This tanker, also 253,000 tons, was the largest ship ever built in Great Britain.

In July the sixth in a series of 326,000-ton tankers was launched in Japan. Christened the *Universe Iran,* the new tanker shared with five sister ships the distinction of being the largest vessels afloat. Each of the supertankers has a capacity of 2.4 million barrels of oil and was intended to transport crude oil from the Middle East to Ireland.

The new luxury liner *Queen Elizabeth 2* completed her maiden voyage to the United States on May 7. The voyage was from Le Havre, France, to New York City and took 4 days, 16 hours, and 35 minutes. Her average speed was about 28 knots, or about 32.23 mph. The vessel's top speed was about 32 knots, or about 36.80 mph. The ship carried 1,451 passengers. Her total capacity, however, is 2,025 passengers. The weight of the *Queen Elizabeth 2* is 65,863 tons and its length 963 feet. The $71-million vessel was originally scheduled to make her maiden voyage in January but was delayed because of trouble with its turbine engines.

The first transatlantic liner to be built in West Germany since before World War II made its maiden voyage in June. The 25,000-ton *Hamburg,* with a cruising speed of 24 knots, or about 27.6 mph, arrived in the New York City harbor after an eight-day crossing from Germany. The $25-million liner carried 330 passengers. The ship's total passenger capacity is 600.

Ice-Breaking Oil Tanker

In September the giant oil tanker SS *Manhattan* traversed the Northwest Passage—the sea route north of Canada. The 1,005-foot vessel was sent on the voyage by the Humble Oil and Refining Co. to prove that such a venture was not only physically possible but also economically feasible.

Accompanying the tanker was a Canadian icebreaker, which helped to plow through ice that was 15 feet thick in some places. A pair of helicopters, based on the *Manhattan's* deck, flew ahead occasionally and landed men who took core samples of the ice. (*See* Arctic.)

Higher Speeds and Quicker Stops

In February the British Admiralty reported the use of a chemical that could have a radical effect on water transport in the future. The substance, polyethylene oxide, in a water solution, was poured into the seawater from holes near the bow of the minesweeper HMS *Highburton.* The molecular structure of the chemical is such that it reduces the friction of water against a ship's hull by about 20%. As a consequence, the ship traveled faster than it had ever gone before. At the same time, reported Admiralty officials, fuel consumption was reduced by 15%.

In Japan, engineers were testing parachutes as braking devices for supertankers, which normally travel for at least two miles before coming to a complete stop. The engineers estimated that nylon parachutes, dragged in the water, could reduce this distance by some 25%. The device had already been used with success on smaller vessels. (*See also* Transportation. *See in* CE: Ship and Shipping.)

West Germany's first home-built transatlantic liner since prewar days, the *Hamburg,* rests in her home port before beginning her maiden voyages to western Africa, South America, and New York.

AUTHENTICATED NEWS INTERNATIONAL

SIERRA LEONE. The state of emergency in Sierra Leone, imposed in November 1968, was lifted in March 1969. Special elections took place in which the All-People's Congress (APC) and the Sierra Leone People's party (SLPP) each won five seats. This brought the division in the House of Representatives to 48 seats for the APC and 12 for the SLPP.

The Consolidated African Selection Trust reported that illicit diamond mining was on the increase within leases granted by the Sierra Leone Selection Trust. The unchecked influx of thousands of outside dealers provided a ready market for stolen diamonds, and corruption was spreading. Tax revenues and legitimate trading by the selection trust were suffering as a result. Diamonds accounted for 60% to 70% of Sierra Leone's exports and some 15% of its revenue. The selection trust paid about $6 million, and the government collected $1.6 million from small miners. Much potential revenue was lost through smuggling, mostly to Liberia.

A national oil refinery was completed toward the end of 1968 at a cost of $7.26 million. On Jan. 3, 1969, the government signed an agreement with five oil companies under which both the government and the companies would hold 50% of the shares. (*See also* Africa. *See in* CE: Sierra Leone.)

SINGAPORE. The city of Singapore, hub of the island republic, in 1969 marked its 150th anniversary and the fourth anniversary of the nation's independence, with an eye to the future. On August 9 some 30,000 people marched in a celebration that emphasized the building of the country's defense forces. The new stress on military strength was designed to insure Singapore's safety after the pullout of British forces in 1971. (*See also* Asia; Commonwealth of Nations.)

Uncertainty about the U.S. presence in Asia after the cessation of the Vietnam conflict also contributed to the buildup. Budgets for the following few years were to provide a 10% expenditure of the gross national product for defense. Israel, France, Great Britain, and others were providing technical training and equipment for the fast-developing defense system.

The multiracial nation meanwhile continued to maintain civil peace and economic prosperity. Economic gains included 8.8% in per-capita income; 16.6% in foreign trade; 11.9% in cargo; 21.25% in total revenue; 24% in bank deposits; and 22% in tourism. Employment rose by 16,000 persons. It was estimated that one apartment was built every 36 minutes. Economic growth, up 13%, was achieved in an atmosphere of monetary stability despite the nearly 20% increase in the money supply. During the year Prime Minister Lee Kuan Yew visited the United States, Canada, Great Britain, Hong Kong, and Japan. (*See in* CE: Singapore.)

SKIING. There was a sizable increase in the number of pleasure skiers in 1969, both in traditional areas and in lands previously less closely associated with the sport. Australia attracted more European and U.S. instructors as some 85,000 skiers converged on the newly developed Thredbo Village of Mount Kosciusko in New South Wales. South American facilities expanded around Portillo, Chile, the scene of the 1966 world Alpine championships; and Japanese participation increased notably around Sapporo, site of the 1972 Winter Olympics. New resorts drew more skiers to the Spanish Pyrenees, while in Switzerland additional mechanized lifts to higher slopes resulted in a longer season in several districts.

In ski equipment, the increasing popularity of plastic boots and fiber-glass skis appeared to be signaling the end of an era of leather and wood. Another transformation was the decline in the popularity of bootlaces in favor of various clip fastenings.

Ski bobbing, a sport using a wooden or metal bicycle frame with miniature skis instead of wheels, also exhibited a growth in popularity, particularly in Europe, where more than 100,000 units were sold. In the world ski-bobbing championships held at Montana-Crans, Switzerland, the combined downhill and slalom winners were P. Bonvin of Switzerland and Miss G. Schiffkorn of Austria.

The Fédération Internationale de Ski meeting in Barcelona, Spain, in May relaxed amateur rules to the extent that racers were permitted to receive commercial backing provided they were not paid for actual racing. (*See* Feature Article: "Run for Your Supper.")

Kiki Cutter of Bend, Ore., is racing through the gates in the Women's Giant Slalom at Oberstaufen in the Bavarian Alps. She won that event in the Fédération Internationale de Ski's World Cup slalom competition, on Jan. 3, 1969.

WIDE WORLD

Karl Schranz won the men's title at the Swiss ski championships in Wengen. He broke the old record for this title by more than a second.

KEYSTONE

Alpine Racing

The Alpine World Cup competition enjoyed a highly successful third season. Public interest was stimulated by providing a continuity of competition at some 15 top international meetings at different sites. The first ten skiers earned points, each racer's highest aggregate score in any three downhill, slalom, and giant slalom events counting toward his final tally. Winner of the men's division was Karl Schranz of Austria, with Gertrud Gabl, his compatriot, annexing women's honors. They won trophies that were undefended by Jean-Claude Killy of France and Nancy Greene of Canada, both of whom had retired from amateur competition.

Schranz and Miss Gabl took the combined titles in the 34th Arlberg-Kandahar competition at St. Anton, Austria, January 31–February 2, still widely regarded as the major international meet between biennial world championships. Schranz gained his fifth overall title in 13 years and his sixth downhill triumph, three more than anyone else since the competition began in 1928. In the final World Cup placings, second and third to Schranz were Jean-Noel Augert of France and Reinhard Tritscher of Austria. In scoring her triumph, Miss Gabl performed brilliantly in slalom and giant slalom. The women's runner-up was Florence Steurer of France, with Wiltrud Drexel of Austria finishing third.

The U.S. Nationals were held at Bear Valley, Calif., late in February. Barbara and Bob Cochran of Richmond, Vt., won their divisions' giant slalom and slalom.

Nordic Events

In a season without world championships in cross-country racing, attention switched to the biathlon and jumping. The biathlon remained very much the preserve of Eastern Europe. In the major meet held at Zakopane, Poland, February 22–March 3, the Soviet Union retained the team title, and Aleksandr Tikhonov, whose rifle marksmanship matched his dexterity on skis, the individual award.

Björn Wirkola of Norway retained his prestige as an outstanding jumper by winning overall honors in West German and Austrian tournaments in January. Jiri Raska of Czechoslovakia was runner-up. (*See in* CE: Skiing.)

SOCCER. Twin headlines dominated the soccer news in 1969—qualification for World Cup matches, to be held at four centers in Mexico in June 1970, and widespread violence on and off the field before, during, and after matches. An extreme example was the limited-scale war that broke out between Honduras and El Salvador after the World Cup deciding match in Group 13 (played in neutral Mexico). El Salvador had won the deciding match, defeating Honduras 3–2.

In Turkey, all-night riots followed the 1–1 draw game between Kirikkale and Idmanyurdu of Tarsus, in which three fans were killed, more than 50 injured, and buses set ablaze. In the Soviet Union one World Cup star, Anatoli Banishevski, was banned from playing for two years following a drunken street brawl, and another, Eduard Streltsev, was suspended from five matches. In Poland, Stefan Florenski was sentenced to a two-year ban for striking a referee. Other European cities were warned that particularly violent actions by fans could result in their club grounds' being barred from competition.

One of the major shocks in the play-offs was the elimination of Argentina from the 16 finalists.

"LONDON DAILY EXPRESS" FROM PICTORIAL PARADE

Martin Peters (extreme left) is turning away after putting a shot past Scotland's goalkeeper, the first of four English goals (to Scotland's one) that secured the British Isles championship for England at Wembley on Dec. 5, 1969.

Generally regarded as the most powerful team in South America, it finished third behind Peru and Bolivia. Meanwhile, Belgium, former titleholders Brazil and Uruguay, Mexico (the host country), and England, the champion, had already qualified for the 1970 finals. North Korea was ruled out of the contest for protesting the distance its team was forced to travel, leaving New Zealand and Israel to decide the winner of Group 15A for a place in Mexico.

In Inter-Continental Club Championship Cup play, a two-part affair regarded by many as the world club championship, the Estudiantes of Argentina beat Manchester United of England in the first leg in 1968. The Argentines then followed up their advantage in October 1969.

In European Cup play AC Milan regained the trophy it had previously won in 1963, by downing Ajax of Amsterdam 4–1 in Madrid, Spain, on May 28. The European Cup-Winners' Cup went to Czechoslovakia in a masterful defeat of Barcelona 3–2, in Basel, Switzerland, on May 21.

Newcastle United defeated Ujpest Dozsa of Budapest, Hungary, 6–2, in a two-leg final of the Inter-Cities Fairs' Cup in Budapest on June 11, after taking the first leg 3–0 at St. James's Park in England on May 29. Also in May, the British Isles championship was won outright for the 27th time by England 4–1 in a tense final against Scotland, after earlier upsets of Wales 2–1 and Northern Ireland 3–1.

There was little to cheer about in U.S. soccer during the year. Early in May the U.S. World Cup soccer team was edged 1–0 by Haiti in the semifinals of the North American-Central American-Caribbean series, played at San Diego, Calif. In professional soccer, the North American Soccer League (formed by merging the National Professional Soccer League and the United Soccer Association after the 1967 season) was disbanded in 1969, so there were no league games played.

SOCIAL SERVICES. In December 1969 the U.S. Congress passed a bill increasing social security benefits by 15%. President Richard M. Nixon had threatened to veto any increase over 10% as inflationary, but he signed the bill into law. Under the law the increase was effective Jan. 1, 1970. However, recipients were not to receive increased checks until April 1970.

Upgrading of Social Security Benefits Seen

While calling for a 10% increase in social security benefits for April 1970, President Nixon, on September 25, urged that all future increases be automatically tied in with the cost of living. This move was an attempt to remove social security from political haggling during election times. Congress put off all social security reform, except for the benefit increase, until 1970.

Nixon suggested using as the basis for social security benefits for men the work periods they amassed to age 62 rather than to age 65. He also proposed noncontributory wage credits for military personnel who served between January 1957 and December 1967. Benefits for widows were also to be improved.

Social Security Administration figures showed that 90% of employed or self-employed persons in the United States were covered by social security in 1969. By the end of July, monthly social security payments went to about 25 million persons—retired or disabled workers and their dependents, or the survivors of deceased workers.

Virtually all the nation's elderly were protected by medicare. In the year ending June 1969, nearly 6 million medicare patients had hospital care, and more than .5 million took advantage of extended-care provisions of the program.

Medicare administrators pondered why elderly patients most often left the hospital on the 14th or 21st day of their stay. After no medical reason was found, it was finally recalled that those were the times when physicians had to reassess the need for continued confinement. Effective Jan. 1, 1970, physicians would recertify confinement of a medicare patient on the 12th or no later than the 18th day of his hospital stay. This procedural change was expected to shorten the average length of hospitalization of medicare beneficiaries.

Several thousand social workers, welfare recipients, and sympathizers demonstrated against welfare cuts in New York City in April. Police moved in to stop the protest.

"NEW YORK DAILY NEWS"

Hard Times for Welfare

Relief programs, never too popular with many taxpayers, often were the first to suffer revenue cuts by cost-conscious state legislatures in 1969. Some large-scale welfare cutbacks were effected in New York, long a leader in social legislation. The Wisconsin legislature trimmed its welfare budget and then refused to enact a supplemental budget that would have restored $24 million in welfare funds. These actions provoked the Rev. James E. Groppi, the Roman Catholic civil rights leader, and others into occupying the assembly chambers, resulting in the militant priest's arrest.

In November a commission appointed by former President Lyndon B. Johnson made public a report on poverty. The commission, composed of prominent businessmen, argued that a guaranteed annual income would be a sound approach toward alleviating poverty in the United States. A nonfarm family of four, they said, should receive $2,400 a year. This amount was some $1,100 less than the index of poverty ascertained by the government—$3,553 a year for a family of four. The guaranteed income suggested by the commission, however, was larger than the $1,600 annual income figure espoused by the Nixon Administration.

During 1969 some 9.6 million people in the United States were in one of the four major federally funded welfare programs. These included help for the blind and disabled, relief for the aged, aid to families with dependent children, and assistance to mothers of preschool children. (*See also* Poverty, War on. *See in* CE: Social Security.)

The first bachelor father in San Francisco, Calif., William Jones, 40, and his newly adopted son Aaron Hunter Jones are taking one of their Sunday strolls. Hunter adopted Aaron through the city's social-service agency.

UPI COMPIX

SOMALIA. On Oct. 15, 1969, Abdirashid Ali Shermarke, who had been president of Somalia (Somali Democratic Republic) since 1967, was assassinated. His death occurred at a time of widespread public discontent following the results of the allegedly rigged elections in March. The Somali Youth League party had again proved its invincibility, winning 73 of the 124 seats in the National Assembly. Discontent at the election results was aggravated by the High Court's decision in June that, contrary to previous rulings, it had no authority to decide a large number of election petitions. On hearing of the president's death, Premier Muhammad Haji Ibrahim Egal returned from a visit to the United States.

On October 21, the day following Shermarke's funeral, the army and police staged a coup, finally ending Somalia's nearly ten years of democratic government. Premier Egal and his cabinet were arrested and charged with corruption. The constitution was abolished, the National Assembly was dissolved, and the name of the republic was changed to the Somali Democratic Republic.

The National Revolutionary Council, led by Gen. Muhammad Siyad, commander in chief of the armed forces, declared its neutrality, its respect for existing treaties and interstate relations, and its desire for peaceful coexistence. It gave assurances of respect for human rights and individual liberty and of noninterference in the internal affairs of other states. On October 25 Italy and the United Arab Republic, or Egypt, officially recognized the new regime. On November 1 a 14-man cabinet was appointed; all but the minister of the interior were civilians. (*See in* CE: Somali Republic.)

SOUTH AFRICA. The major political development in South Africa in 1969 was the split that occurred in the country's ruling Nationalist party. The extreme right-wing minority faction of the party, often referred to as the *verkramptes* or "narrow-thinking" ones, bolted the Nationalist party because of dissatisfaction with Prime Minister (and party leader) Balthazar J. Vorster's *verligte* or "enlightened or outward-looking" policies. The verkrampte faction specifically opposed Vorster's policies of offering friendship to black African countries and allowing the admission of multiracial sports teams into the country. Vorster considered his policies as merely pragmatic attempts to bring South Africa's rigid policy of apartheid, or racial separation, into line with the demands of the modern world. The verkrampte faction, however, felt these policies were a dilution of traditional apartheid. Its members formed a new party, the Reconstituted National party, which adopted a program politically to the right of the Nationalist party.

In September Prime Minister Vorster's government announced that a general election would be held in April 1970—a full year ahead of schedule. The move was interpreted as an attempt by Vorster to nip the new party in the bud and to achieve a strong endorsement for his policies from the 4 million whites who alone would vote in the election.

In June the government established a Bureau of State Security (BOSS), a secret agency responsible only to Vorster, which was given far-reaching powers to "coordinate" all security work in the country. Among the powers granted to the BOSS was the right to withhold evidence from the courts in the interests of the state or of public security. The BOSS was criticized by liberal groups, by the ultraright Reconstituted National party, and by almost the country's entire legal profession. The opposition to law made by a Nationalist party government was unprecedented.

After a trial in Johannesburg that attracted worldwide attention, Laurence Gandar, the editor in chief of the city's *Rand Daily Mail,* and Benjamin Pogrund, a senior reporter for the *Daily Mail,* were found guilty of having published information about conditions in South African prisons without having made "reasonable efforts" to ensure that the facts were correct. The articles written by Gandar and Pogrund, published in 1965, were based on testimony from wardens and former prisoners. They described brutal conditions that existed in the prisons—among them, torture by electric shock. Gandar and Pogrund were given suspended sentences and fined. They planned further appeals.

South Africa continued to promote its policy of "separate development of the races" in 1969. The first nationwide election for "coloreds"—the South African designation for persons of mixed racial ancestry—was held in September to choose 40 of the 60 members of the newly constituted Colored People's Representative Council. The council replaced parliamentary representation for the coloreds. In a surprise outcome, the anti-apartheid Labor party won 26 of the 40 elected seats; the pro-apartheid Federal party and smaller pro-apartheid parties won the remaining seats. The government nominated 20 additional members to the council, all belonging to the Federal party, which thus secured a majority and appointed the council's executive. The council was to have limited powers in matters concerning coloreds (education, welfare, etc.) but the white parliament was to have final authority.

Partial self-government was granted to various Bantu tribal authorities. (Bantu is South Africa's designation for all black South Africans.) Bantu tribal communities in Natal and Transvaal, areas designated for white settlement only, were removed to other areas. The government continued to give some aid for industrial development near the Bantu homelands—land set aside by the South African government for Bantu use.

The Trade Union Council of South Africa reversed an earlier decision under pressure from some of its member bodies and decided not to allow Bantu labor unions to become affiliated members. Bantu labor unions were already banned by the government from legal registration.

The creation of separate Bantu reserves in South Africa is the keystone of the government apartheid program. In March 1969 the United Nations Commission on Human Rights passed a resolution condemning this program.

MARVIN E. NEWMAN FROM MULTI-MEDIA PHOTOGRAPHY

The black South African nationalist movement continued to be suppressed by the government. Robert Mangaliso Sobukwe, a black nationalist leader, was released after six years' detention without trial on charges of incitement to subversion, but he remained under restriction. In October the trial began of 22 Bantu suspects, charged under the Suppression of Communism Act. Among them was Winifred Mandela, the wife of Nelson Mandela, a black nationalist leader currently imprisoned under the Suppression of Communism Act.

The United Nations (UN) continued to criticize South Africa's apartheid policy and its continued administration of South-West Africa, called Namibia by the UN. With the major Western powers abstaining, the UN Security Council passed a resolution calling on South Africa to withdraw from Namibia and hand over control to the UN by Oct. 4, 1969. South Africa rejected the demand.

South Africa's balance of payments took a downward turn as a result of a poor agricultural season and a drop in exports. Unspecified quantities of newly mined gold were sold by the government on the free market. South Africa's stock prices, which had risen spectacularly in the first half of the year, dropped sharply in the second half. The widespread losses led to public agitation for a relaxation of a credit squeeze. South Africa increased its outlays for defense to record heights and continued to develop new defense weapons and programs. (*See in* CE: South Africa.)

SOUTHERN YEMEN. In June 1969 Southern Yemen's relatively moderate president, Qahtan al-Shaabi, was replaced by a five-man Presidential Council appointed by the ruling National Liberation Front. The move brought into power a more radically leftist faction that had the backing of most of the armed forces and of the Soviet Union. Al-Shaabi's power had been reduced earlier in the year when he had been forced to give up the premiership to his brother-in-law.

The coup against Al-Shaabi occurred while half of the army was occupied in a campaign against rebellious Aulaqi tribesmen. The Aulaqis were supported by deposed sultans and sheikhs, the Saudi Arabian monarchy, and the Front for the Liberation of Occupied Southern Yemen, a terrorist group operating from Yemen. The campaign against the Aulaqis created a rift between

Miners extract gold from the Western Reef mines near Johannesburg. Gold production in South Africa reached a record high of 31.168 million ounces in 1968.

MARVIN E. NEWMAN FROM MULTI-MEDIA PHOTOGRAPHY

extremists and moderates in the government and in the army.

Relations with Yemen worsened during the year. Southern Yemen accused the Yemeni government of aiding its enemies, and each of the two governments called for the destruction of the other. As a result, the possibility of the unification of the two Yemens was weakened.

Southern Yemen suffered another year of acute economic difficulties in 1969 as a result of the continued closure of the Suez Canal and the general decline in the port of Aden. Although President Al-Shaabi received a pledge of Soviet aid in February, the Soviets had provided only emergency economic aid and some arms by August, and they had refused to undertake the dredging of Aden's harbor.

In October Southern Yemen severed diplomatic relations with the United States and barred the entry of U.S. citizens. The Southern Yemeni government accused the United States of favoritism for Israel and of plotting against Palestinian commandos in Lebanon. (*See in* CE: Aden; Yemen.)

SPACE EXPLORATION.

Two landings on the moon by manned spacecraft—Apollo 11 and Apollo 12 of the United States—made 1969 the most momentous year to date in the history of astronautics. As usual, however—while manned spacecraft commanded the widest public attention—unmanned vehicles in growing number continued to perform a host of scientific and practical tasks.

The Flight of Apollo 11

No event in the history of the world had so vast an audience as did the flight of Apollo 11, the first spacecraft to carry men to the surface of the moon. From lift-off to splashdown, almost every major aspect of the flight was seen on television or followed on radio by hundreds of millions of people in nations around the world (Communist China was the major exception).

At Cape Kennedy, Fla., at 9:32 A.M. (EDT) on the morning of July 16, hundreds of thousands of spectators watched as the 363-foot-tall Apollo/-Saturn V assembly, weighing nearly 6.5 million pounds, roared away from launch pad 39A. Aboard were astronauts Neil A. Armstrong, commander; Edwin E. Aldrin, Jr., lunar-module pilot; and Michael Collins, command-module pilot. The spacecraft first entered earth "parking" orbit, then was injected into translunar trajectory so accurately that a planned mid-course correction was canceled.

Soon after departure from earth orbit, the astronauts performed their transposition and docking maneuvers, turning the command/service module combination around and withdrawing the lunar module from the third stage of the Saturn V launch vehicle. Early in the morning of July 19, Apollo 11 smoothly entered lunar orbit.

On the morning of July 20 Armstrong and Aldrin entered the lunar module (code-named "Eagle"; the command module was called "Columbia") and prepared for descent to the lunar surface. Early in the afternoon, with the words "The Eagle has wings," Armstrong separated the lunar module from the mother craft, in which Collins remained in lunar orbit. Soon thereafter Eagle entered its descent orbit, with a low point of only 50,000 feet above the moon. At this point its engine was again fired to brake the craft for final descent and landing. About 300 feet above the lunar surface Armstrong began semimanually maneuvering Eagle with its reaction-control thrusters, moving laterally to avoid a rock-strewn crater and find a smooth landing site.

Aldrin called out "Contact light!" as one of the probes beneath Eagle's footpads touched the surface. From Houston, Tex., Mission Control replied, "We copy you down, Eagle," and Armstrong answered, "Houston, Tranquillity Base here. The Eagle has landed." At 4:17:41 P.M. EDT—a minute and 19 seconds ahead of schedule—man had reached the moon. The site was near the edge of the Sea of Tranquillity, south of the crater Sabine D and northwest of the crater Moltke.

Six and a half hours later, at 10:56:20, Armstrong stepped onto the lunar soil, earlier than planned. As he moved from Eagle's footpad to the surface, Armstrong said, "That's one small step for a man, one giant leap for mankind." Nineteen minutes later Aldrin joined him.

The astronauts experienced no difficulty in walking on the moon. They set up a television camera to cover their extravehicular activity (EVA) and talked by radio with U.S. President Richard M. Nixon. Armstrong remained on the surface for 2 hours 21 minutes; Aldrin, for a shorter time. During that time they set up a device to measure the composition of solar radiation reaching the moon, a laser-beam reflector to permit precise measurement of the distance of the moon from the earth, and a seismometer system to measure moonquakes and meteor impacts. They also put up a U.S. flag, picked up about 50 pounds of rock and soil samples, and took photographs.

After a rest period, the astronauts prepared to return to lunar orbit and rejoin Collins in Columbia. Lift-off from the lunar surface came at 1:54 P.M. on July 21, after 21 hours and 42 minutes on the moon. The ascent stage of Eagle rose smoothly, entered orbit, and docked with Columbia. It was discarded after Armstrong and Aldrin transferred to Columbia. The return to earth of Columbia was uneventful. Splashdown came at 12:50 P.M. on July 24, about 950 miles southwest of Hawaii and 11 miles from the prime recovery ship, USS *Hornet*.

Conveyed to Houston in a sealed van, the astronauts were kept in quarantine for 18 days, to prevent the spread of any disease organisms they might have brought back from the moon. Examination of the astronauts and of the lunar material they collected, however, yielded no evidence of any form of life. Upon release from isolation, the astronauts were given heroes' welcomes—first during a one-

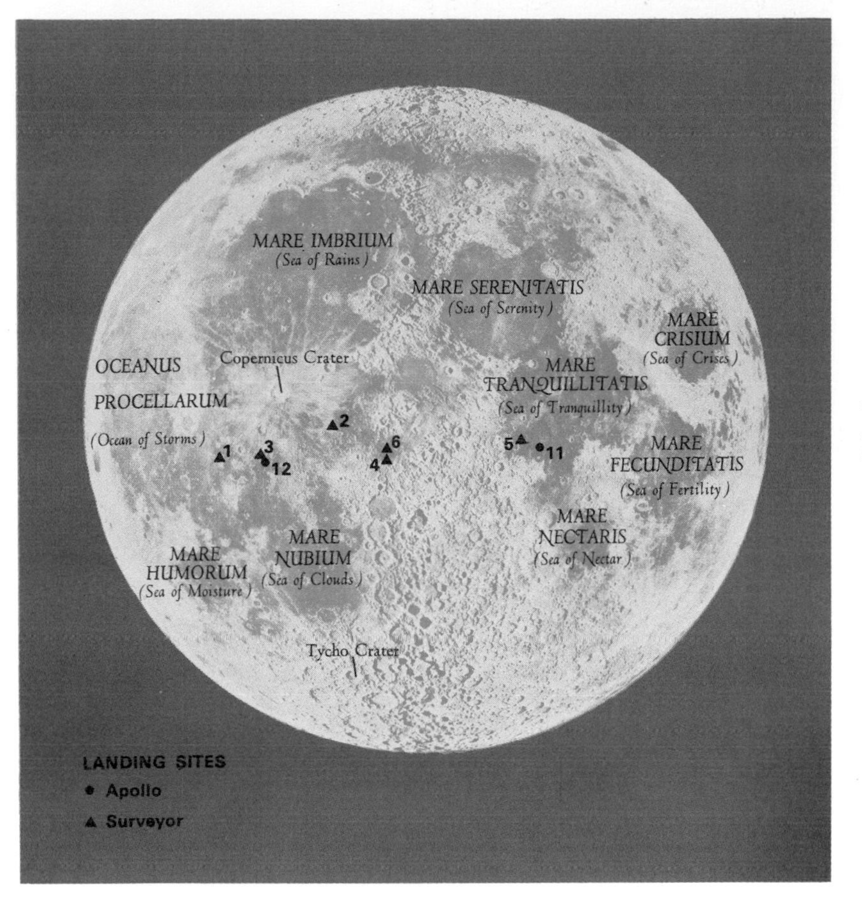

The lunar landing sites of Apollo and Surveyor are pinpointed here.

day whirlwind tour of New York City; Chicago, Ill.; and Los Angeles, Calif., and later during a tour of the world.

The Moon Revisited

The second manned lunar-landing spacecraft—Apollo 12—was launched into low-lying clouds from Cape Kennedy at 11:22 A.M. EST November 14, with Charles (Pete) Conrad, Jr., in command. Richard F. Gordon, Jr., was command-module pilot, and Alan L. Bean was lunar-module pilot.

There were anxious moments early in the flight. Little more than half a minute after lift-off, a heavy discharge of static electricity passed through the Saturn V, overloading electrical circuits in the spacecraft and causing a temporary loss of power. Fortunately, the guidance system of the launch vehicle itself was not affected, and the astronauts quickly restored power in the Apollo by resetting circuit breakers.

Apollo 12 thereafter continued smoothly toward the moon and entered lunar orbit, where the lunar module ("Intrepid") separated from the command module ("Yankee Clipper") and prepared for descent. Conrad and Bean skillfully brought Intrepid down on target at 1:54:43 A.M. EST on November 19—a minute and 43 seconds behind schedule. The landing in the Ocean of Storms was made within 600 feet of Surveyor 3, an unmanned spacecraft that had soft-landed on the moon in April 1967.

During their 31½-hour stay on the moon, Conrad and Gordon conducted two "moon walks," one of 4 hours, the other of 4½. A color-television camera deployed during their first EVA failed after 20 minutes, but the world followed the astronauts' activities through their radio descriptions.

In their first EVA the astronauts took conventional and stereo pictures, gathered rock and soil samples, and made visual and photographic geological surveys in the neighborhood of their spacecraft. They also deployed a nuclear-powered experiments package that included a seismometer, a magnetometer, a dust detector, ionosphere and atmosphere detectors, and a solar-wind spectrometer.

After resting, eating, and recharging their life-support-system backpacks, the astronauts began a second EVA some 12½ hours after the end of the first. They tested the instruments they had deployed previously, then proceeded to Surveyor 3, gathering more rock and soil samples on the way. From the Surveyor they removed some tubing and cable, as well as its television camera and soil scoop, for study on earth, where scientists wished to determine the effects upon the vehicle of 2½ years' exposure to the lunar environment.

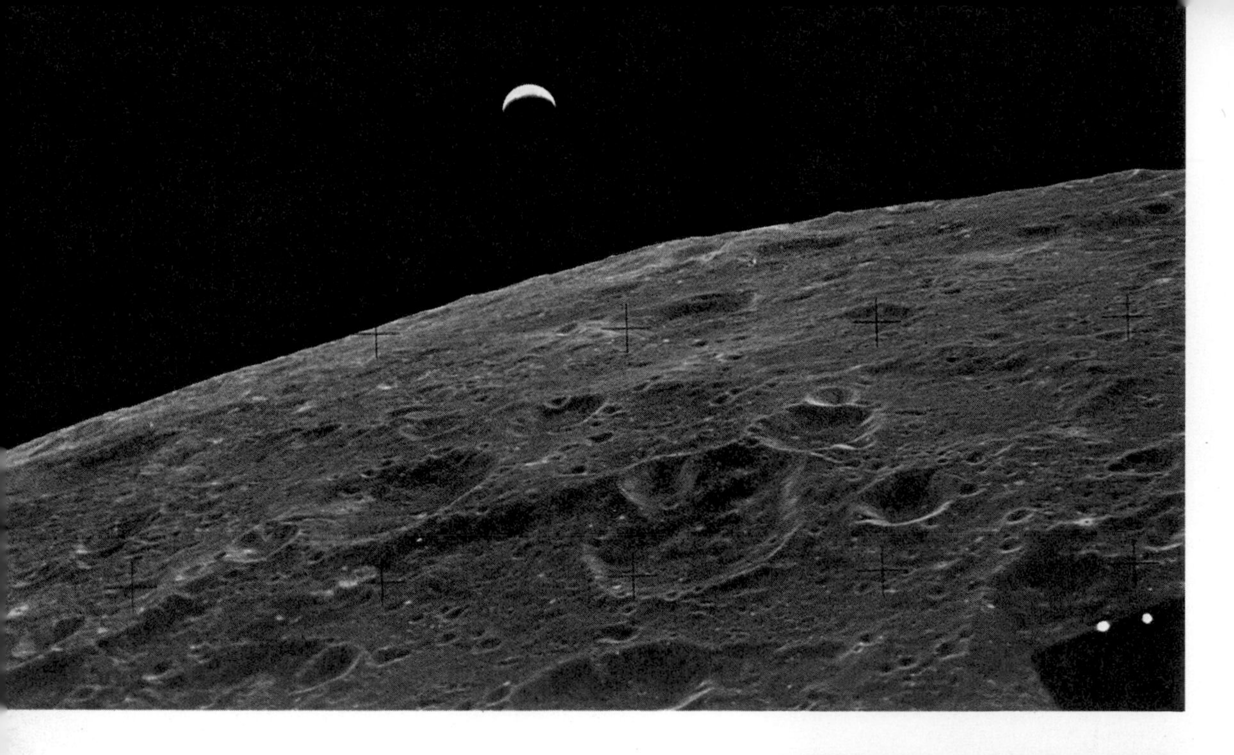

The earthrise is seen (above) over the lunar horizon from the Apollo 12 spacecraft, and the moon's surface is viewed in detail (right) from the Apollo 11 spacecraft. Walking on the moon for the first time, Apollo 11 astronaut Edwin E. Aldrin, Jr., deploys the Passive Seismic Experiments Package (below, left) and the Solar Wind Composition Experiment (below, right).

COURTESY, NASA

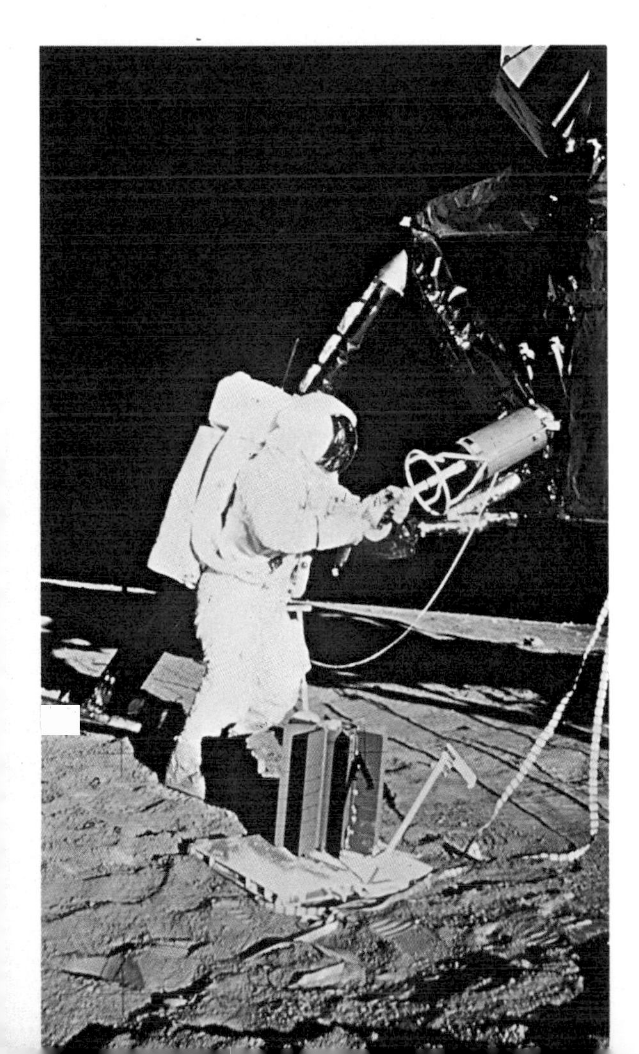

Apollo 12 astronauts Charles Conrad, Jr., and Alan L. Bean land on the moon while astronaut Richard F. Gordon, Jr., remains with the Apollo 12 command/service module in lunar orbit. Standing at the foot of the lunar module near the erectable S-band antenna (above, left) and walking from the TV camera (above), the astronauts prepare to deploy a number of scientific experiments to enable further study of the moon's surface. Alan Bean (left) prepares to traverse with the two ALSEP (Apollo Lunar Surface Experiments Package) subpackages.

COURTESY, NASA

Takeoff from the moon and return to "Yankee Clipper," waiting in orbit above with astronaut Gordon in charge, was accomplished without incident. Return to earth and splashdown in the Pacific Ocean—at 3:58 P.M. EST on November 24—went according to plan. After recovery the astronauts entered a period of quarantine similar to that of the Apollo 11 astronauts. They were released early in December after tests again indicated absolutely no evidence of disease resulting from exposure to the lunar environment.

Preliminary Apollo Flights

Two developmental flights of Apollo spacecraft preceded the lunar-landing missions in the year. Apollo 9, launched from Cape Kennedy on March 3 with astronauts James A. McDivitt, David R. Scott, and Russell L. Schweickart aboard, completed a ten-day earth-orbital mission. During its flight the lunar module received its first manned test in space. The astronauts performed rendezvous and docking of the command/service module and the lunar module, EVA, earth-resources photography, and landmark tracking.

Apollo 10, carrying astronauts Thomas P. Stafford, John W. Young, and Eugene A. Cernan, was launched toward lunar orbit on May 18. From lunar orbit, in a final prelanding test of the lunar module, Stafford and Cernan descended to within 50,000 feet of the lunar surface, then rose and rejoined the command module, in which Young had remained in a higher orbit. The lunar module vibrated heavily as its ascent and descent stages separated, but Stafford quickly brought his craft under control. It was found later that the vibration had been caused by a changeover from one mode of automatic control to another.

Apollo Findings and Plans

Ultimately, it is hoped, lunar exploration will yield new information about both the moon and the solar system as a whole. Analysis of the lunar material collected by the Apollo 11 and 12 astronauts and of data from the experiments left on the moon, however, does not permit firm conclusions.

The lunar rocks brought back by Apollo 12 differed greatly from those returned by Apollo 11, leading scientists to speculate that the moon may be far more complex than previously thought. Questions about its substructure were raised when the seismometer left by Apollo 12 recorded vibrations lasting 30 minutes after the lunar module's ascent stage was deliberately crashed on the moon about 45 miles from the instrument. It was estimated that a similar impact on the earth—equivalent to the explosion of about a ton of TNT—would have generated shock waves lasting for less than a minute.

Other instruments detected a lunar-magnetic field that—while far weaker than that of the earth—was many times stronger than expected. (*See* Earth Sciences.)

After the Apollo 11 flight, the National Aeronautics and Space Administration (NASA) announced that it planned to launch subsequent Apollo lunar missions at the rate of three a year, about four months apart. Apollo 13, scheduled for launch in March 1970, was to land in the Fra Mauro, a rugged highland structure about 110 miles east-southeast of the Apollo 12 landing site.

Soviet Manned Space Flights

There were indications during the year that the Soviet Union would concentrate in the near future on large-scale earth-orbital operations rather than on efforts to send a manned spacecraft to the moon. It was announced in October that a state committee had been formed to coordinate the development of an experimental manned-orbital laboratory.

The Soviet Union orbited five manned spacecraft during the year. Soyuz 4, with cosmonaut Vladimir A. Shatalov, was lofted on January 14. Soyuz 5 carried Boris Volynov, Yevgeni Khrunov, and Aleksei S. Yeliseyev. The two spacecraft rendezvoused on January 16 and successfully docked under the manual control of Shatalov. Yeliseyev and Khrunov transferred to Soyuz 4, in which they returned to earth, becoming the first men to enter space in one craft and return in another.

Three more Soyuz spacecraft were launched in October. Soyuz 6 was orbited from Tyuratam on October 11, carrying Georgi S. Shonin and Valeri N. Kubasov. Soyuz 7 followed on October 12, carrying Anatoli V. Filipchenko, Viktor V. Gorbatko, and Vladislav N. Volkov; and Soyuz 8 was launched on October 13 with Shatalov and Yeliseyev aboard.

Wide speculation that the Russians were attempting to establish a large space station was reinforced by the announcement that the Soyuz 6 cosmonauts conducted in-space welding experiments. Although the spacecraft approached each other closely, no docking took place. Soyuz 6 returned to earth on October 16, Soyuz 7 on October 17, and Soyuz 8 on October 18. The Russians announced only that all assigned tasks had been completed.

Important Artificial Satellites

Orbiting Astronomical Observatory (OAO) 2, the heaviest and most complex unmanned satellite ever launched by the United States, operated from Dec. 7, 1968, to April 12, 1969. In its first 20 days of operation it collected 20 times the amount of data that had been gathered during 15 years of sounding-rocket firings to collect data on ultraviolet radiation from stars.

Intelsat 3 (F-2), launched on Dec. 18, 1968, and maneuvered into a 22,300-mile-high synchronous orbit over Brazil, began commercial service on Jan. 2, 1969. It provided 1,200 voice channels and 4 television channels. Intelsat 3C (Pacific 3) was orbited on February 5. It more than doubled the number of available trans-Pacific telephone and

COURTESY, NASA

The Apollo 12 lunar module (background) stands about 600 feet from the Surveyor 3 spacecraft in the Ocean of Storms on the surface of the moon.

television circuits. On February 9 the 1,600-pound Tactical Communications Satellite (Tacomsat), the world's largest and most complex military communications satellite, was placed in synchronous orbit over the Galápagos Islands in the Pacific Ocean.

ESSA 9, the last of the familiar drum-shaped Tiros weather satellites, was launched on February 26. Nimbus 2, an advanced weather satellite that also carried other scientific instruments, was orbited on April 14. It was the first nonmilitary satellite to carry a nuclear power supply.

Biosatellite 3 was launched from Cape Kennedy on June 28. The 1,536-pound spacecraft carried a small pigtail monkey named Bonny. Scheduled for 30 days, the mission was aborted after nine days because the monkey had begun to show signs of deterioration. It died 12 hours after the capsule was recovered from the Pacific Ocean. Autopsy findings indicated that the effects of weightlessness had contributed to the monkey's death.

During the year the Soviet Union also launched a variety of military, communications, and scientific satellites. On June 27 the Soviet Union launched its 1,000th payload since Sputnik 1 in 1957. It was Cosmos 288, a military reconnaissance satellite. On October 14 the Soviet Union announced the beginning of a new series of scientific satellites with the launching of Intercosmos 1, a solar-observatory satellite.

Deep-Space Probes

Both Mars and Venus were again targets for deep-space probes in 1969. The Soviet Union chose to investigate Venus, while the United States studied Mars.

The Soviet Venera 5 was launched from Tyuratam on January 5, and Venera 6 followed on January 10. Both of the 2,486-pound probes—scheduled to arrive at Venus within a day of each other—carried 891-pound soft-landing pods intended to land on the dark side of Venus. As the pods descended through the thick Venusian atmosphere in mid-May, they transmitted data on its temperature, pressure, and chemical makeup. Although they were heavily protected, both pods were thought to have been crushed by the atmosphere before they reached the surface. Venera 5, which ceased to transmit at an altitude of 21.6 miles, indicated a surface temperature of 986° F. and a pressure of 2,058 pounds per square inch (psi). Venera 6, which ceased transmission at 22.8 miles, indicated surface conditions of 752° and 882 pounds psi. Scientists felt that the differing values could be accounted for by a very rugged surface, with Venera 5 descending over a deep basin and Venera 6 over a high plateau.

The 850-pound Mars probes by the United States—Mariner 6 and Mariner 7—were launched from Cape Kennedy by Atlas/Centaur rockets. Both were flyby probes, intended neither to land on Mars nor go into orbit around it. Each carried two television cameras—one wide-angle, one narrow; an infrared and an ultraviolet spectrometer, to identify components of the Martian atmosphere; and an infrared radiometer, to determine temperature.

Mariner 6, launched on February 24, passed Mars at a distance of 2,120 miles on July 30. In all, it took 74 pictures, 24 of them during its nearest approach to Mars. Its instruments failed to detect nitrogen in Mars's upper atmosphere—bad news for those who felt that life might exist upon the red planet.

Mariner 7 was launched on March 27 on a trajectory that took it across Mars's south pole on August 5. It took 91 pictures, 33 of them at nearest approach. While there was some difference between its measurements and those of Mariner 6, they were in general agreement.

Temperature measurements of Mars ranged from −253° at the south pole to 75° at the equator. The planet's apparent surface atmospheric pressure was 6.5 millibars, compared with 1,000 millibars at the earth's surface. If the measurement is correct, future astronauts will have to wear pressure suits while on the surface.

Photographs taken by the Mariners indicated that, despite the presence of craters, the surface of Mars is quite different from that of the moon. There is extremely rough terrain near the south pole, with snowdrifts some three feet deep. (*See in* CE: Space Travel.)

ABOVE: DAVID LEES, "LIFE" MAGAZINE © TIME INC. BELOW: LIAISON AGENCY

Generalissimo Francisco Franco (right) watches as his appointed successor, Prince Juan Carlos of Bourbon, takes the oath of succession in the grand hall of Cortes. Juan Carlos will reign with his wife, Princess Sophie (below).

SPAIN. The liberal trend that had been developing in Spain was suddenly halted in 1969 by a series of dramatic political events. Repressive actions by the Spanish government silenced outspoken critics. The aging head of government, Generalissimo Francisco Franco, named his heir.

On January 24 the government of Spain declared a "state of exception," suspending five articles of the constitution and establishing semimartial law. Full censorship of the press was reinstated after about three years of relative freedom. Under these emergency measures the police were given almost unlimited powers of search and seizure.

The justification the government gave for instituting the repressive rule was that student disorders were growing out of control. Government spokesmen stated that Spain wanted to prevent the type of disruption that temporarily crippled France in May 1968. Even the Spanish government, however, did not deny that the repressive measures were aimed at liberal government critics in all walks of life—not only students.

The blame for instituting the emergency powers was laid directly to pressure exerted by Spanish military leaders. Military leaders were said to have been disturbed by students' displaying red flags of revolution and the flag of the old Spanish Republic, by a petition calling for an investigation of alleged torture of prisoners, and by pressure from lawyers to have repressive legislation revoked. They saw these liberal trends as a subversive threat to the government. Three military ministers were reported to have called for the declaration of an internal state of war. The Spanish cabinet compromised by proclaiming the state of exception. After the state of exception was declared, a series of political arrests followed—students, labor leaders, clergy, and others who opposed the government in recent months.

On March 24 the state of exception was ended. Newspapers, though without official censorship, remained subject to strict press laws. Universities were reopened under heavy police guard, and classes were infiltrated by plainclothes policemen.

Francisco Franco looked to the future when in July 1969 he named Prince Juan Carlos of Bourbon to be his successor. The pretender to the throne of Spain was the prince's father, Don Juan of Bourbon. After the Franco regime ends, Spain will once again become a monarchy. Don Juan, who had been classified as a moderate liberal, held political views that were unacceptable to Franco.

In October Franco made another dramatic move by dismissing 14 of Spain's 19 cabinet members. The new cabinet members were generally younger than those dismissed, most of their ages ranging from 43 to 53. The cabinet reshuffle reduced the power of the Fascist Falange. This brought violent demonstrations from young Falangists.

A major political scandal was created earlier in the year when it was discovered that a highly successful textile-machinery company had illegally used about $140 million in official export credits. The machinery that was supposedly exported was in fact stored in company warehouses outside of Spain. The export credits were invested in foreign businesses. When the fraud was uncovered, in August, several company executives were arrested.

In the press there were demands for the resignations of several cabinet ministers.

Spain and the United States failed to negotiate a new military-base pact during the year. There was no progress between Spain and Great Britain toward settling their conflicting claims to Gibraltar. (*See in* CE: Spain.)

SPORTS CHAMPIONS OF 1969.

Archery. World champions (target): men, Hardy Ward (Mt. Pleasant, Tex.); women, Dorothy Lidstone (Vancouver, B.C.); men's team, U.S.; women's team, U.S.S.R. World champions (field): freestyle, Richard Branstetter (Creve Coeur, Ill.); instinctive, Warren Cowles (Herndon, Va.).

Badminton. All-England championships (unofficial world champions): men's singles—Rudy Hartono (Indonesia); women's singles—Hiroe Yuki (Japan); men's doubles—Henning Borch-Erland Kops (Denmark); women's doubles—Sue Boxall-Margaret Whetnall (England); mixed doubles—Roger Mills-Gillian Perrin (England). Uber Cup (women's world championship): final—Indonesia; challenge round (for championship)—Japan.

Billiards (Pocket). World champion: L. Dielis (Belgium); world three-cushion: R. Ceulemans (Belgium); world professional snooker: J. Spencer (Great Britain).

Bobsledding. World champions: 2-man—N. De Zordo-A. Frassinelli (Italy); 4-man—W. Zimmerer, S. Geisreiter, W. Steinbauer, P. Utzschneider (West Germany).

Canoeing. World champions: kayak singles, 500 meters—A. Tishenko (U.S.S.R.); 1,000 meters—A. Schaparenko (U.S.S.R.); 10,000 meters—V. Tsaryev (U.S.S.R.); kayak pairs, 500 meters—A. Vernescu-A. Sciotnic (Romania); 1,000 meters—A. Schaparenko-V. Morozov (U.S.S.R.); 10,000 meters—J. Szaba-I. Timar (Hungary); kayak fours, 1,000 meters—East Germany; 10,000 meters—Norway. Canadian singles, 1,000 meters—T. Wichman (Hungary); 10,000 meters—Wichman; Canadian pairs, 1,000 meters—I. Patzaichin-S. Covaliov (Romania); 10,000 meters—S. Szerna-J. Hingi (Hungary).

Cross-Country. International senior champions: individual—G. Roelants (Belgium); team—England.

Curling. World champion: Canada.

Cycling. World champions: professional—sprint, P. Sercu (Belgium); pursuit, F. Bracke (Belgium); motor-paced, J. Oudkerk (Netherlands); road, H. Ottenbros (Netherlands). World champions: amateur—sprint, D. Morelon (France); pursuit, X. Kurmann (Switzerland); motor-paced, A. Broom (Netherlands); road, L. Mortensen (Denmark).

Fencing. World champions: men—foil, F. Wessel (West Germany); épée, B. Andrejewski (Poland); saber, V. Sydiak (U.S.S.R.); team—foil, U.S.S.R.; épée, U.S.S.R.; saber, U.S.S.R.; women—foil, E. Novikova (U.S.S.R.); women's team—foil, Romania.

Gymnastics. National AAU champions: all-around—Mauno Nissinen (Seattle, Wash.); free exercise—Toby Towson (Michigan State University); rings—Robert Emery (Penn State University); parallel bars—Yoshi Hoyasaki (Seattle); horizontal bar—John Ellas (Northwestern Louisiana State); long horse—Paul Tickenoff (Northwestern Louisiana State); side horse—Dave Thor (Reseda, Calif.); team—Husky Gym Club (Seattle). Women's AAU champions: all-around—Joyce Tanac (Downtown YMCA, Seattle); free exercise—J. Tanac; side horse—J. Tanac; balance beam—J. Tanac; uneven parallel bars—J. Tanac; team—Downtown YMCA (Seattle). NCAA champions: all-around—M. Nissinen (Washington); team—Iowa.

Winning pitcher Jerry Koosman (right) praises Ron Swoboda whose eighth-inning double brought in the winning run in the fifth game of the World Series, ensuring the New York Mets of the 1969 championship.

WALTER IOOSS, JR., "SPORTS ILLUSTRATED" © TIME INC.

Handball. U.S. Handball Association 4-wall champions: singles—Paul Haber (Milwaukee, Wis.); doubles—Lou Kramberg-Lou Russo (New York City); masters singles—John Scopis (Detroit, Mich.); masters doubles—Ken Schneider-Gus Lewis (Chicago, Ill.). National AAU one-wall champions: singles—Steve Sandler (92d St. YMHA, New York City); doubles—Sandler-Marty Decatur (New York City); masters doubles—Al Goldstein-Nat Schifter (Brooklyn, N.Y.).

Horse Racing. Thoroughbred winners: Kentucky Derby, Churchill Downs—Majestic Prince (W. Hartack); Preakness Stakes, Pimlico, Md.—Majestic Prince (Hartack); Belmont Stakes, Belmont Park, N.Y.—Arts and Letters (B. Baeza); Santa Anita (Calif.) Handicap—Nodouble (Belmonte); American Derby, Arlington, Ill.—Fast Hilarious (Pincay); Arlington-Washington Futurity—Silent Screen (Rotz); Flamingo Stakes, Hialeah, Fla.—Top Knight (M. Ycaza); Hollywood Gold Cup, Hollywood Park, Calif.—Figonero (Pinedo); Yankee Gold Cup, Suffolk Downs—Jean-Pierre (Blum); Epsom Derby, England—Blakeney; Grand National Steeplechase, England—Highland Wedding (Hatky); Grand Prix de Paris, France—Chapparal (Head); Irish Sweeps Derby, Dublin—Prince Regent (Lewis); Prix de l'Arc de Triomphe, Paris—Levmoss (Williamson). Harness winners: Hambletonian, Du Quoin, Ill.—Lindy's Pride (H. Beissinger); Yonkers Futurity Trot, Yonkers, N.Y.—Lindy's Pride (Beissinger); Roosevelt International Trot, New York—Unde de Mai (J. Gougeron, France); Little Brown Jug, Delaware, Ohio—Laverne Hanover (Billy Haughton).

Horseshoe Pitching. World champions: men—Dan Kuchcinski (Erie, Pa.); women—Vicki Winston (Lamonte, Mo.); senior—John Paxton (Ottumwa, Iowa); junior—Mark Siebold (Huntington, Ind.).

Lacrosse. World champions: women—British Pioneers (Great Britain). U.S. champions: intercollegiate—Army and Johns Hopkins University (tie); club—Long Island Athletic Club; Collegiate All-Stars—South 12, North 11.

Motorcycling. World champions: 50-cc class—A. Nieto (Spain); 125-cc—D. Simmonds (Great Britain); 250-cc—K. Carruthers (Australia); 350-cc—G. Agostini (Italy); 500-cc—G. Agostini; sidecar—K. Enders (West Germany). U.S. Grand National champion—Mert Lawwill (San Francisco, Calif.).

Polo. Cup of the Americas: Argentina. Cowdray Gold Cup (England): Windsor Park.

Roller Skating. North American champions: men's singles—Michael Jacques (Norwood, Mass.); women's singles—Mary Sue Wilcox (Greeley, Colo.); pairs—Ron Robovitsky-Gail Robovitsky (Detroit); dance—Marc Parker-Vicki Freeman (Pleasanton, Calif.). U.S. champions: men's singles—Jack Courtney (Marion, Ind.); women's singles—Dorothy Cochrane (Marion); pairs—Jack Courtney-Sheryl Trueman (Marion); dance—Thomas Straker-Bonnie Lambert (Grand Rapids, Mich.). European champions (figure skating): men—M. Obrecht (West Germany); women—C. Kreutzfeld (West Germany).

Sailboat Racing. Mallory Cup (men)—Graham Hall (Larchmont, N.Y.); Adams Cup (women)—Jan O'Malley (Mantoloking Y.C., N.J.). Chicago-to-Mackinac—*Norsaga,* Harry Zieman (Milwaukee). Transpacific (San Pedro, Calif.-Honolulu, Hawaii)—*Argonaut,* Jon Andron (Santa Barbara, Calif.). Transatlantic (Newport, R.I.-Cork, Ireland)—*Kialoa II,* John B. Kilroy (Los Angeles, Calif.).

Shooting. World champions: Olympic trench—men, E. Matarelli (Italy); women, N. Avril (Italy); team, Italy. World champions: skeet—men, Y. Tsuranov (U.S.S.R.); women, N. Ortiz (Mexico); team, U.S.S.R. U.S. skeet all-around—men, Robert F. Shuley (Roselle, Ill.); women, Sgt. Margarett Burdett, RCAF (Angus, Ont.). U.S. trapshooting, Grand American Handicap—men, Bernard Bonn, Jr., (Dayton, Ohio); women, JoAnn Nelson (Lone Tree, Iowa).

Army (left) and Navy compete in a 7–7 tie game during the lacrosse season. Army shared the 1969 intercollegiate championship with Johns Hopkins University.

ARTHUR RICKERBY, "LIFE" MAGAZINE © TIME INC.

TONY TRIOLO, "SPORTS ILLUSTRATED" © TIME INC.

Mike Suyderhoud (left) and Elizabeth Allan lead the U.S. team to their tenth straight victory in the 11th World Water Ski Championship in Copenhagen, Denmark. Miss Allan won the overall women's championship by placing first in all three preliminary events, and Suyderhoud won the overall men's championship.

Softball. Amateur Softball Association champions: fast pitch—men, Raybestos Cardinals (Stratford, Conn.); women, Lionettes (Orange, Calif.); slow pitch—men, Copper Hearth (Milwaukee); women, Converse Dots (Hialeah); industrial, Avco Lycoming (Stratford).

Speedboat Racing. Unlimited hydroplanes: world champion—*Miss U.S.* (Bill Muncey); Gold Cup—*Miss Budweiser* (Bill Sterett); high-point champion—*Miss Budweiser.* Distance races: Bahamas 500 (512 mi.)—Don Aronow (Miami, Fla.); Cowes-Torquay (239 mi.)—D. Aronow; Sam Griffith Memorial (216.6 mi.)—Bill Wishnick (New York); Viareggio-Bastia, Italy (214 mi.)—D. Aronow.

Squash Racquets. World championship—Australia. U.S. champions: singles—Anil Nayar (Bombay, India); doubles—Sam Howe (Philadelphia)-Ralph Howe (New York); veterans—H. Salaun (Boston, Mass.); seniors—Ed Hahn (New York); team—Ontario; intercollegiate team—Harvard.

Table Tennis. World champions: men's singles—S. Ito (Japan); doubles—H. Alser-K. Johansson (Sweden); team (Swaythling Cup)—Japan; women's singles—T. Kowada (Japan); doubles—S. Grinberg-Z. Rudnova (U.S.S.R.); team (Corbillon Cup)—U.S.S.R.

Volleyball. World Cup (men): East Germany. Inter-Continental Cup (men): East Germany. National AAU: men—U.S. Armed Forces; women—Mayor Daley Youth Foundation (Chicago). U.S. Volleyball Association: men—Downtown YMCA (Los Angeles); women—Shamrocks (Long Beach); collegiate—University of California (Santa Barbara). Canadian Volleyball Association: men—Hamilton YMCA (Ont.); women—Colonas (Vancouver, B.C.); collegiate—University of Winnipeg.

Water Polo. European Champion Clubs Cup: Mladost Zagreb (Yugoslavia). U.S. (AAU) champions: indoor—Corona del Mar (Calif.); outdoor—De Anza Aquatic Foundation (Cupertino, Calif.).

Water Skiing. World champions: men—overall, M. Suyderhoud (San Anselmo, Calif.); slalom, V. Palomo (Spain); jumping, W. Grimditch (Pompano Beach, Fla.); tricks, B. Cockburn (Australia); women—overall, Elizabeth Allan (Winter Park, Fla.); slalom, E. Allan; jumping, E. Allan; tricks, E. Allan.

Weight Lifting. World champions: flyweight—V. Krishinin (U.S.S.R.), 744 lbs.; bantamweight—M. Nassiri (Iran), 793 lbs.; featherweight—Yoshiyuki Miyake (Japan), 848 lbs.; lightweight—W. Baszanowski (Poland), 981 lbs.; middleweight—V. Kurentsov (U.S.S.R.), 1,030 lbs.; light heavyweight—M. Ohuchi (Japan), 1,075 lbs.; middle heavyweight—K. Kangasniemi (Finland), 1,135 lbs.; heavyweight—J. Talts (U.S.S.R.), 1,207 lbs.; super-heavyweight—J. Dube (U.S.), 1,273 lbs.

Special Report: The Art of Self-Defense

by Jonathan R. Eley, Black Belt (2d degree) in Aikido and Brown Belt (3d degree) in Judo, and Martin Patrick Myrieckes, Black Belt (1st degree) in Kendo and Karate

EARL HOKENS

To stop aggression is the foremost philosophy of karate. A system of blocks, punches, and kicks is used for this purpose.

Throughout the 1960's the Far Eastern systems of martial arts rapidly gained popularity in the United States. Special gymnasiums, called *dojos,* were set up to give private lessons in such martial arts as judo and karate. High schools, colleges, civic associations, and some programs in adult education began offering courses in these subjects. The special appeal of these martial arts to the general public lies mainly in their success as a method of self-defense, and so they appeal to women as well as to men. With the proper judo techniques even a small woman can defend herself against a much stronger male opponent. Judo also has wide appeal as a sport and is a good way to exercise. In spite of their apparent violence, however, the martial arts were not intended to be a form of aggressive behavior.

Tea and Swords

A Japanese story tells of a master of the tea ceremony who was challenged to a sword duel by a samurai. The master had two days to prepare and called on a sword master to teach him how to fight. While visiting the sword master, the tea master performed the tea ceremony. The sword master saw the extreme concentration of the tea master as he performed the tea ceremony and noted how his every movement was made with all of his being. The sword master told the tea master there was nothing he could teach him. If only the tea master would face the samurai with the same concentration he had shown during the tea ceremony, he would have no trouble.

On the day of the duel the tea master took up the sword in the same way he had taken up the ceremonial teacup. He faced his antagonist and, forgetting himself entirely, he waited. The samurai was terrified; he could see no opening for attack. He pleaded for forgiveness and left.

The common problems of fear and violence are presented in this story, but the solution to these problems is one unique to the Far East. It is basically an internal solution using self-control.

When the techniques of judo are perfected, even a small woman can defend herself successfully against a much larger and stronger male.

EARL HOKENS

Defending against danger is a part of life, and fear can be an aid to self-defense. The feeling of fear in animals can motivate them into action. Extreme fear, however, is a danger itself. Too often the immediate fear produces images of old fears and an expectation of disaster. A person in this state could become "frozen" with fear, and this could prevent even the most elementary response to danger. All of the Eastern systems of martial arts stress this point. No matter what techniques a person may have learned, they will be of little or no use if fear renders the person unable to employ them. Very little or no technique may be needed, however, if the person is free enough from fear to respond to the situation.

This is basically what the sword master said to the tea master. He merely had to maintain an attitude of calm and detachment to ward off or defeat the brute strength of the samurai. Training in the Eastern system of martial arts centers around the internal ability to deal with the problems of fear and violence.

EARL HOKENS

Some karate experts become so proficient at their art that, in some localities, they must have their hands registered as deadly weapons.

How Not to Fight

All the Eastern martial arts are designed to teach a person how to stop aggression. When the tea master faced the samurai calmly and without fear, there was no fight. The Japanese word for these martial arts is *budo* ("the way of life to stop aggression"). Budo has many different forms.

Kendo is a sword-fighting technique; *kyudo,* a type of archery. *Aikido* is a system of holds and throws utilizing strong powers of concentration along with a harmonious coordination of body movements. To avoid the danger of developing a fighting mental attitude, there are no competitive matches in the art of aikido and kyudo. In those martial arts where opponents are competitively matched, such as judo and karate, the object of the matches is to develop a strong—that is, nonfighting or nonaggressive—mind.

Two of the most popular martial arts in the United States are judo and karate. Judo, meaning "the gentle way; the way of Confucius," is a system of throws, chokes, and pins. Competitive judo matches have done much to add to this art's popularity in the United States. Modern judo was developed from the ancient art of ju-jitsu by Jigoro Kano, a Japanese professor, in 1882. Judo's underlying philosophy stresses nonaggression, courtesy, and mutual welfare and benefit for the opponents. The basic principle of judo technique is to use the attacker's force and momentum against him rather than to resist the attack.

Reputable, well-qualified judo instructors concentrate on training the mind as well as the body, instilling both emotional and physical control. As a sport judo helps develop self-confidence, poise, and physical dexterity. Judo has been approved as an event for the 1972 Summer Olympics. There are three basic grades of judo proficiency recognized by the United States Judo Federation and signified by colored belts: white for beginners, brown for intermediates, and black for experts.

Karate or karate-do, meaning "the way of the empty hand," is a system of blocks, punches, and kicks. Karate can be used either to kill or to maim, and karate experts who have reached a high degree of proficiency are in some places even required to register their hands as deadly weapons. In karate classes opponents are not allowed to strike one another, for the force of a kick or punch would break bones. Nevertheless, the basic philosophy underlying karate is still that of stopping aggression. Defense in karate is based on blocking the attack of an opponent.

Karate, though not as popular as judo, gained many followers during the late 1960's. By the end of the decade there were about 750 karate schools throughout the United States. Karate is a more strenuous practice than judo, and some class sessions include exercises and sparring matches ending with a period of meditation.

The martial arts can be of great benefit to those who practice them. Many new students, however, see only a fascinating and effective form of fighting. To practice and teach these martial arts without understanding and practicing their underlying philosophy of nonaggression is meaningless. Without this philosophy the essence of the arts is lost, and what remains is merely another method of aggression and violence. Properly practiced, the martial arts of the East bring about a unification of body and mind. To those who have the strength and the will, there is much peace to be found in the way of not fighting.

STAMPS. For the first time in philatelic history, Sofia, Bulgaria, was chosen as the site for the major international philatelic exhibition of the year. The International Grand Prix was won by an Italian collector who, under the name "Emanuela," entered a collection of Italian stamps. The Grand Prix Nationale (restricted to collections of Bulgarian stamps) was won by T. Popov Velislavov of Bulgaria.

British participation in the exhibition was the strongest among non-Communist countries. Awards to British collectors included three gold medals. Collectors from the United States carried home a number of lesser awards.

In April the Royal Philatelic Society in London, England, became the first philatelic organization to celebrate its centenary. An exhibition of classic stamps of the world issued by the date of the society's founding in 1869 was held at the society's headquarters. The stamps were valued at about $5 million.

Queen Elizabeth II opened the British National Postal Museum at the London Chief Office of the Post Office in February. The museum was especially built to house the Reginald M. Phillips collection of stamps of the world, as well as rare materials from the post office archives. Periodic exhibitions were given under strict security conditions in humidity-controlled galleries.

The United States issued a stamp (left) to focus attention on the need to help crippled children.

Newsmaking Issues

The first-day covers carrying the U.S. Apollo 11 moon-landing commemorative stamp generated unprecedented demand among collectors. The stamps were printed from plates made from a master die that was actually carried to the moon by astronauts Neil A. Armstrong and Edwin E. Aldrin, Jr. At 1.05 by 1.80 inches, the moon-landing stamp was the largest ever issued by the United States (later, a Dwight D. Eisenhower commemorative stamp was issued in the same size).

The Apollo 11 astronauts also carried with them an envelope bearing a die proof of the new stamp. It was to have been canceled by Armstrong and Aldrin on the lunar surface—but they were too busy there and actually canceled it on the way back to earth. Postmaster General Winton M. Blount remarked, "This was probably the most expensive letter we ever delivered."

A number of other nations also issued Apollo 11 commemorative stamps. Many were intended to make money from collectors, not for use as postage.

Beginning October 4, United Nations (UN) organizations based in Switzerland, which previously used Swiss stamps of special design, were permitted to issue their own stamps, valued in Swiss currency, for use on mail posted from the Palace of Nations in Geneva. Previously, UN stamps—since their first issue in 1951—had been valid only for use from UN headquarters in New York City.

The U.S. Post Office Department in 1969 offered to collectors an album containing all U.S. stamps issued in 1968. It was thought probable that such albums would be issued annually in the future. Similar collectors' albums of stamps have been issued by the UN Postal Administration at various intervals since 1958.

Major Stamp Sales

Although the stamp market in general remained depressed, scarce philatelic items and valuable collections continued to sell at high prices in 1969. The sale of the Josiah K. Lilly collection set a record for a single collection of $3,145,298.50. Realizations from the continuing dispersal of the Dale-Liechtenstein collection in New York City mounted to more than $2 million, all profits going to philanthropic societies named in the will of Louise Boyd Dale. A single 1918 U.S. 24¢ airmail stamp with an inverted center sold for $31,000 in May. The price was a record for the stamp, which had sold for $15,500 in 1964. A block of four of the stamps realized $115,000. The block of four was one of 264 lots of rare stamps auctioned in New York City in March at a sale that realized $911,935, thought to be the largest amount ever realized at a single stamp-auction session.

A pair of twelvepenny 1851 Canadian stamps sold for $38,400. The famous "Pack" strip of three 1843 Brazilian stamps, consisting of two 30-reis stamps and one 60-reis stamp, was sold in Great Britain for $27,600. An 1858 cover with a pair of sixpenny scarlet vermilion Newfoundland stamps of the 1857 series sold for $11,000.

Philatelic Miscellany

At its congress in Tokyo, Japan, late in the year the Universal Postal Union (UPU) of the UN was expected to consider action against the postage stamps that some nations issue mainly for revenue

The United States commemorated Christmas in 1969 with a traditional winter scene (left).

A Swedish stamp (left) commemorates the birth of artist Ivan Aguéli.

To commemorate the Apollo 11 moon landing the United States issued this stamp (right).

purposes. The UPU had previously opposed such "exploitative" issues but had not attempted to influence the stamp-issuing policies of its member nations. For some time, the American Philatelic Society has published "Black Blot" ratings for any new issues that appear to be of limited printing, or limited "on sale" time in the issuing country; that seem excessively extended; that include stamps of unwarrantedly high value; that have no direct relationship to the issuing country; or that have "oddities" intentionally included.

The U.S. Treasury Department's Office of Foreign Assets Control banned future importation of Rhodesian postage stamps into the United States. The action brought to five the number of nations whose stamps cannot be imported into the United States. The other four are North Korea, Communist China, Cuba, and North Vietnam.

Two boxes of 10¢ airmail stamps shipped by air from Finland and scheduled for sale by the UN in mid-March were missing for several weeks. Late in February, about two months after the stamps were lost, the UN Postal Administration notified major philatelic publications of the loss and promised to reprint the stamps in different colors if they were not found. Early in March, however, the UN reported that the stamps had been found and would be released for sale in April.

The U.S. Bureau of Engraving and Printing expected to have in operation sometime in 1970 a web (roll)-fed rotary photogravure press. The Italian-built press is intended mainly for the production of air-letter sheets, though it could also be used for printing stamps. Ultimately the bureau hoped to have a similar press to produce stamps from a combination of photogravure and line-engraving plates. (*See also* Coin Collecting. *See in* CE: Stamp and Stamp Collecting.)

Sweden, Australia and Greece issued stamps (right and below) to commemorate the 50th anniversary of the International Labor Organization.

MORLEY BAER

WERNER STOY FROM CAMERA HAWAII

The new State Capitol of Hawaii, dedicated on March 15, 1969, replaces the historic Iolani Palace (bottom, foreground). In the central court (top), the sky takes the place of the traditional dome.

STATE GOVERNMENTS, UNITED STATES.

During 1969 state governments in the United States grappled with the problems of crime, urban decay, and student unrest and with finding the financial means to deal with these problems. The legislatures of almost all the states met during the year. Several states took steps toward revising their constitutions and toward generally modernizing state administration. Soon after taking office U.S. President Richard M. Nixon announced that Vice-President Spiro T. Agnew would be the Nixon Administration's liaison between the state and federal governments.

Tax Increases

Efforts by state governments to collect more taxes were greater during 1969 than at any other time since World War II. During the year about half the states either imposed new taxes or increased the existing ones. Many state officials charged that the federal government had imposed so many taxes that any effort by the states to collect more money would spur a taxpayers' revolt. In Massachusetts a militant organization was formed with the purpose of preventing further tax increases.

State income taxes were introduced for the first time in Maine and Illinois during the year. Existing income taxes were increased in Mississippi and New Mexico. In Arkansas and Connecticut taxes were raised on the income of corporations. An increase in sales tax was effected in Mississippi, Maryland, Maine, and Connecticut.

Tax increases on specific items such as gasoline, liquor, and cigarettes were approved by the legislatures of Louisiana, Indiana, Maine, Illinois, Arkansas, Connecticut, New Jersey, and Nevada. In West Virginia sales and use taxes were expanded to cover more items. Connecticut imposed a 2% tax on health insurance premiums and a 10% amusement tax. North Carolina adopted a 2% cigarette tax. It was the last state in the Union to place a tax on cigarettes.

Campuses, Crime, and Cities

Campus disorders had a high priority on the lists of problems taken up by state legislatures in 1969. Several states passed new antiriot laws and strengthened penalties for violation of existing laws. New York passed a law barring unregistered firearms from campuses and cut off all state aid to colleges that did not file a plan for controlling campus disorders. The Georgia legislature made it a misdemeanor to interfere with the use of college buildings. Tennessee declared it a felony for nonstudents to incite campus riots, and Idaho deemed it a misdemeanor to participate in campus disorders.

There were two opposite trends in dealing with drug abuse, particularly marihuana. Indiana, Maine, and Wyoming toughened their narcotics laws. In Connecticut, however, possession of marihuana was reduced from a felony to a misdemeanor.

Arkansas and New Mexico passed laws expanding the grounds for therapeutic abortion. Similar measures failed in the legislatures of New York, New Hampshire, Illinois, and other states. Maryland passed a preventive detention act which provides that a person freed on bail for committing a violent crime can be denied new bail if he commits a similar crime while awaiting trial. Various types of prison reforms were instituted by New York, Georgia, and Vermont.

Rising welfare costs continued to burden state budgets. The Nixon Administration proposed a revenue-sharing program that would allot federal funds to local and state governments. One provision of this program (called the "New Federalism") was a guaranteed minimum family income of $1,600 a year. In a speech at the National Governors Conference, held at Colorado Springs, Colo., Nixon asked the governors to endorse and support his new federal-state program. The governors endorsed the president's revenue-sharing plan but expressed reservations about the ultimate value of the New Federalism. The governors also passed a resolution urging the federal government to take over all welfare costs and institute national compulsory health insurance. (*See* Medicine; Social Services.)

During 1969 the states moved in various ways to confront the problems that arise from a heavy concentration of low-income families living in cities. New Jersey set up a State Council on Urban Affairs and appropriated $12 million to extend programs for disadvantaged persons living in urban areas. In Connecticut a $5-million fund was established to guarantee mortgages for low- and moderate-income families wishing to purchase a home. The New Mexico legislature passed a human-rights law barring discrimination in housing, employment, and accommodations. Georgia created a low-cost-housing authority. In New Jersey, storefront "street academies" were set up to aid high-school dropouts in earning a diploma.

The states showed increasing concern over the plight of private education. Ohio, Connecticut, New York, and Rhode Island approved state aid to private schools, and several other states approved aid to students attending private schools. Connecticut and Rhode Island agreed to pay part of the secular teachers' salaries in nonpublic elementary and secondary schools. (*See* Education.)

Cleaning the Houses

The trend toward legislative, administrative, and judicial reform in state governments gathered momentum during 1969. Committees studying the shortcomings of state governments suggested a wide range of improvements including smaller legislative bodies and salary increases for legislators.

By 1969 the legislatures of 31 states were meeting in annual sessions. Some states had adopted constitutional amendments that permitted annual sessions. Legislative bodies in other states simply did not adjourn. Constitutional amendments allowing for annual sessions were proposed in Indiana, Oregon, Nevada, and Connecticut. The Delaware legislature amended the state constitution to provide for annual six-month legislative sessions.

Salary increases for state legislators became effective in Nebraska, Indiana, South Dakota, Massachusetts, and Iowa. Idaho legislators, unable to obtain a salary increase, voted an increase in their expense allowances and added $200 a month for maintaining offices.

There was considerable administrative reorganization in several states during the year. New Mex-

About 3,000 demonstrators mass in the winter cold on the steps of New York's Capitol to protest Gov. Nelson A. Rockefeller's proposed cuts in welfare spending for the state. The demonstrators—welfare recipients, students, and social workers—had come from cities throughout New York.

UPI COMPIX

GOVERNORS OF THE STATES

(With Party Affiliations and Current Terms)

State	Governor
Ala.	Albert P. Brewer (D), 1968–71
Alaska*	Keith H. Miller (R), 1969–70
Ariz.	Jack Williams (R), 1969–71
Ark.	Winthrop Rockefeller (R), 1969–71
Calif.	Ronald Reagan (R), 1967–71
Colo.	John A. Love (R), 1967–71
Conn.	John N. Dempsey (D), 1967–71
Del.	Russell W. Peterson (R), 1969–73
Fla.	Claude R. Kirk, Jr. (R), 1967–71
Ga.	Lester G. Maddox (D), 1967–71
Hawaii	John A. Burns (D), 1966–70
Idaho	Don Samuelson (R), 1967–71
Ill.	Richard B. Ogilvie (R), 1969–73
Ind.	Edgar D. Whitcomb (R), 1969–73
Iowa	Robert D. Ray (R), 1969–71
Kan.	Robert B. Docking (D), 1969–71
Ky.	Louie B. Nunn (R), 1967–71
La.	John J. McKeithen (D), 1968–72
Me.	Kenneth M. Curtis (D), 1967–71
Md.†	Marvin Mandel (D), 1969–71
Mass.‡	Francis W. Sargent (R), 1969–71
Mich.§	William G. Milliken (R), 1969–71
Minn.	Harold LeVander (R), 1967–71
Miss.	John B. Williams (D), 1968–72
Mo.	Warren E. Hearnes (D), 1969–73
Mont.	Forrest H. Anderson (D), 1969–73
Neb.	Norbert T. Tiemann (R), 1967–71
Nev.	Paul Laxalt (R), 1967–71
N.H.	Walter Peterson (R), 1969–71
N.J.◆	Richard J. Hughes (D), 1966–70
N.M.	David F. Cargo (R), 1969–71
N.Y.	Nelson A. Rockefeller (R), 1967–71
N.C.	Robert W. Scott (D), 1969–73
N.D.	William L. Guy (D), 1967–71
Ohio	James A. Rhodes (R), 1967–71
Okla.	Dewey F. Bartlett (R), 1967–71
Ore.	Tom L. McCall (R), 1967–71
Pa.	Raymond P. Shafer (R), 1967–71
R.I.	Frank Licht (D), 1969–71
S.C.	Robert E. McNair (D), 1967–71
S.D.	Frank L. Farrar (R), 1969–71
Tenn.	Buford Ellington (D), 1967–71
Tex.	Preston E. Smith (D), 1969–71
Utah	Calvin L. Rampton (D), 1969–73
Vt.	Deane C. Davis (R), 1969–71
Va.¶	Mills E. Godwin, Jr. (D), 1966–70
Wash.	Daniel J. Evans (R), 1969–73
W.Va.	Arch A. Moore, Jr. (R), 1969–73
Wis.	Warren P. Knowles (R), 1969–71
Wyo.	Stanley K. Hathaway (R), 1967–71

* Former Secretary of State of Alaska Keith H. Miller took office to fill the unexpired term of Walter J. Hickel, who was appointed to the U.S. Cabinet.

† Upon the resignation of Vice-President-elect Spiro T. Agnew in January, Marvin Mandel, speaker of the Maryland House of Delegates, was selected by the Maryland General Assembly to fill Agnew's unexpired term.

‡ Former Lieut. Gov. Francis W. Sargent took office to fill the unexpired term of John A. Volpe, who was appointed to the U.S. Cabinet.

§ Former Lieut. Gov. William G. Milliken took office to fill the unexpired term of George Romney, who was appointed to the U.S. Cabinet.

◆ In the November 1969 election William T. Cahill (R) was elected governor, to take office January 1970.

¶ In the November 1969 election Linwood Holton (R) was elected governor, to take office January 1970.

ico established several new departments including a State Department of Corrections and a State Judicial Council. The Arkansas legislature authorized $36,000 for indexing and standardizing the state's administrative rules and regulations. New Hampshire's legislature appointed a task force to study and recommend changes in the state's administration. Kentucky received 380 recommendations for changes from a committee of businessmen and educators. Major administrative changes were proposed for Minnesota's state government. Maryland began a project of reshaping its 250 government agencies into 20 departments.

There was also activity surrounding the judicial branches of some state governments. Idaho reorganized its court system to eliminate justices of the peace. Utah set up a judicial qualification committee to rule on judicial requirements. The Illinois Supreme Court was plagued by scandal that led to the resignation of two judges.

The trend toward updating state constitutions continued throughout 1969. Major revisions of the existing constitution or the drafting of a new constitution were proposed in the states of Oklahoma, Virginia, and North Dakota. A new constitution was drafted for South Carolina. North Dakota prepared for a constitutional convention. Conventions were held during the year in Massachusetts and New Mexico. Illinois's constitutional convention opened in December. Voters in Vermont rejected the proposal to hold a constitutional convention.

Many states took steps to strengthen antipollution legislation. In March Hawaii's new $28-million state Capitol was dedicated. New state capitols were proposed during the year for California and Michigan. A project to put all the laws of the 50 states on a computer was completed in 1969. (*See in* CE: State Governments.)

STOCKS AND BONDS. The average investor in stocks and bonds had more cause to complain than to rejoice in 1969. The Dow-Jones industrial average, the most closely followed stock market indicator, fell from 943.75 at the start of the year to 800.36 on December 31. This was a decline of 15.2%, compared to an increase of 4.3% for the previous calendar year.

The year's Dow-Jones high was 968.85, reached on May 14. The low for the year was 769.93, reached on December 17. This was the lowest mark the average had hit in more than three years. The traditional year-end rally of stock prices occurred for the 36th time in 42 years as the industrial average surged upward 5.68 points on the final day of trading.

While stock-price averages fell, trading volume also declined throughout the year. On the floor of the New York Stock Exchange (NYSE) some 100 million fewer shares of stock were traded than in 1968, while some 200 million fewer shares were traded at the American Stock Exchange. October

A new trading room was added to the New York Stock Exchange in 1969, the first major expansion in nearly half a century. The room was equipped with horseshoe-shaped trading posts, about twice the size of old stock-exchange posts, and new equipment including a computerized price board.
WIDE WORLD

14 was the busiest day at the NYSE, when 19.95 million shares were traded.

Blue Chips and Glamour Stocks Suffer

Many of the so-called "blue chip" stocks tumbled in value from the beginning to the end of 1969. E. I. du Pont de Nemours & Co. fell from 165 to 105; United States Steel Corp., from 43 to 34; General Electric Co., from 94 to 77; General Motors Corp., from 79 to 69; and Standard Oil Co. (New Jersey), from 79 to 62.

Some of the most highly touted "glamour" stocks fell even more sharply in 1969. Occidental Petroleum Corp. plummeted from 47 to 24; Litton Industries, Inc., from 72 to 36; Gulf and Western Industries, Inc., from 50 to 19; and Ling-Temco-Vought, Inc., from 95 to 25.

The bond market, on the whole, also suffered during the year. Many bond issues fell 20% or more in value. The large mutual funds almost without exception declined in 1969.

The year-end rally was largely due to a December 18 statement by Arthur F. Burns, whose appointment as chairman of the Federal Reserve Board had been confirmed by the U.S. Senate that day. "Under normal circumstances," said Burns, "I would say the time has definitely come for some easing of credit conditions." Following Burns's statement, the Dow-Jones industrial average jumped 13.86 points in a single day, its sharpest upswing in eight months. He referred to an existing tight monetary policy which, for the previous 12 months, had tended to keep stock prices depressed. Other factors also contributed to the general decline of stock and bond prices during 1969. Among them were inflation, the inconclusiveness of peace talks on the Vietnam conflict, and the uncertainty of the year ahead.

Seat Prices Fall, Security Thefts Increase

The year's "bear" market, or falling market, affected the price of seats on the NYSE. On Jan. 2, 1969, two seats sold for a record price of $515,000 each. By August, however, the price had fallen to $300,000—the lowest sum in more than two years.

DOBBINS, "BOSTON (MASS.) HERALD-TRAVELER," FROM BEN ROTH AGENCY

The world viewed with uneasiness the downward price trend of U.S. stocks.

The theft of securities came to be recognized as a serious problem in 1969. It was estimated that some $45 million in securities would be reported by brokerage firms as lost or missing during the year. Thefts from the mails and from airports were becoming increasingly common as was counterfeiting. Law-enforcement agencies believed that organized crime was responsible for many of the losses. (*See also* Business and Industry; Economy. *See in* CE: Stocks and Bonds.)

SUDAN. The attempt by Sudan's coalition government to pursue parliamentary rule was brought to an end in 1969 when leftist army officers seized power on May 25. The government, headed by Ismail al-Azhari, president of the Supreme Council, and Mohammed Ahmed Mahgoub, prime minister, had created widespread dissatisfaction by its political and economic mismanagement. The nation was heavily in debt both at home and abroad, and political rifts splintered the coalition.

The timing of the coup was prompted by an agreement between the Unionist Democratic and Umma political parties on the draft of a permanent constitution to replace the provisional constitution of 1964. The draft, which provided for a presidential system based on Islam, was to have been submitted to a popular referendum. The coup was staged to prevent promulgation of the new permanent constitution.

LEFT AND RIGHT: CAMERA PRESS—PIX FROM PUBLIX

A coup in Sudan in May put into power a Revolutionary Council, headed by Maj. Gen. Jaafar Mohammed al-Nimeiry (right), with Abubakr Awadallah (left) serving as prime minister. Later al-Nimeiry himself took over the post of prime minister.

The nine officers who organized the coup formed a Revolutionary Council that dissolved the Supreme Council and the Constituent Assembly, imprisoned or dismissed leading political figures and senior officials, and appointed a Communist sympathizer, Abubakr Awadallah, as prime minister in a largely civilian cabinet. Differences between Communist-oriented and Arab-nationalist cabinet members led Maj. Gen. Jaafar Mohammed al-Nimeiry, chairman of the Revolutionary Council, to replace Awadallah as prime minister in October.

The new regime abolished local administration by tribal chiefs and nationalized some sectors of the export-import trade. Three southern provinces were promised regional autonomy, but long-rebellious blacks there continued to hold out against Arab domination even though their strength was waning.

In foreign affairs the new regime moved toward closer ties with Eastern Europe and the Arab nationalists. A Sudanese military mission to the Soviet Union was followed by the arrival in Sudan of a Soviet planning mission. (*See in* CE: Sudan.)

SUPREME COURT OF THE UNITED STATES. The U.S. Supreme Court received a new chief justice in June 1969 when Warren Earl Burger was sworn into office by retiring Chief Justice Earl Warren. Burger, the nominee of U.S. President Richard M. Nixon, had been approved by the U.S. Senate in a 74–3 vote.

The president had described Burger as a "strict constructionist" and obviously had hoped that his nominee would change the pace if not the direction the court had been taking under Earl Warren. Burger, however, dramatically demonstrated his independence when, in his first important decision as chief justice, he voted with his colleagues to end the delay in fulfilling the landmark 1954 Supreme Court decision against school segregation and to begin desegregation "at once." With this unanimous decision the court removed the last escape clause open to Southern states for maneuvering against school desegregation. Whether the U.S. Department of Justice would take an active role in speeding the implementation of the decision, however, remained undetermined in view of the policy of the Nixon Administration to go slow on desegregation. (*See also* Burger.)

The Fortas Resignation and the Haynsworth Nomination

In May Associate Justice Abe Fortas resigned from the court after a public uproar concerning disclosure of his acceptance of $20,000 from financier Louis E. Wolfson, who was later imprisoned for stock manipulation. Fortas was the first justice in the court's history to resign because of public criticism.

To fill the vacated seat Nixon nominated a Southerner and judicial conservative, Judge Clement F. Haynsworth, Jr., chief judge of the U.S. Court of Appeals for the Fourth Circuit. The nomination, considered part of Nixon's strategy to build Republican party strength in the South, became a matter of deep contention. Haynsworth's record was denounced by a number of senators as strongly anti-civil rights and antilabor. Opposition to his nomination, however, centered on judicial ethics and conflict-of-interest charges. President Nixon strongly defended Haynsworth, and his Administration waged a hard campaign to have the nomination approved. The Senate, however, rejected the president's choice in a 55–45 vote.

Major Supreme Court Decisions

In one of the last major decisions under Chief Justice Warren, the court ruled unconstitutional the U.S. House of Representatives' exclusion of Representative Adam Clayton Powell (D, N.Y.) from the 90th Congress. Other major decisions by the Warren court included matters involving freedom of speech and expression, the right of privacy, and the application of military law.

Several cases were decided concerning freedom of speech. In Stanley *vs.* Georgia, a case involving

LEFT: "THE NEW YORK TIMES" FROM WIDE WORLD. CENTER AND RIGHT: WIDE WORLD

Earl Warren (left), the 14th chief justice of the United States, resigned and was replaced by Warren Earl Burger (center). After a bitter controversy the U.S. Senate rejected President Nixon's nominee for an associate justice of the Supreme Court, Judge Clement F. Haynsworth, Jr. (right, with Nixon).

obscenity, the court unanimously ruled unconstitutional a state statute making private possession of obscene materials a crime. "If the 1st Amendment means anything," wrote Justice Thurgood Marshall in the principal opinion, "it means that a state has no business telling a man, sitting alone in his own house, what books he may read or what films he may watch. Our whole constitutional heritage rebels at the thought of giving government the power to control men's minds."

In Brandenburg *vs.* Ohio the court reversed the conviction of a Ku Klux Klan leader who had been charged with violating Ohio's criminal-syndicalism law. This statute made it a crime to "advocate or teach the duty, necessity, or propriety" of violence "as a means of accomplishing industrial or political reform." The court held the decision unconstitutional because it prohibited mere advocacy of, as distinguished from incitement to, lawless action. In Tinker *vs.* Des Moines Independent Community School District, the court upheld the right of students in public schools to protest the Vietnam conflict by wearing black armbands, as long as such action had no disrupting effect on the operation of the school.

The Right of Privacy

In Chimel *vs.* California the court defined the area of permissible search incidental to a valid arrest. The court's definition rejected a view widely accepted in police circles that it was permissible to search a person's house without a warrant when he was validly arrested there. The court held that a police officer might search a person arrested, in order to remove any weapons and to seize evidence on his person. An officer could also search the area within the immediate control of the accused, who might otherwise gain possession of a weapon or destroy evidence. Further searching of the premises, however, required the authority of a search warrant.

In what was considered to be a remarkable case, Alderman *vs.* United States, the court decided that in a criminal case the government may use evidence obtained by unlawful electronic surveillance only against a defendant who does not have "standing to object." The court said that a defendant has standing to object if he was a party to the overheard conversation or if it took place on his premises. Illegally obtained surveillance records to which a defendant has standing to object must be submitted to him so that their relevance may be determined in adversary proceedings.

Military Law

A significant decision involving the selective-service law was handed down during the 1968–69 session. In Oestereich *vs.* Selective Service Local Board No. 11, the court interpreted a section of the Military Selective Service Act of 1967 providing that "no judicial review shall be made of the classification or processing of any registrant . . . except as a defense to criminal prosecution. . . ." It was thought that under this section there was only one recourse open to someone who felt he was wrongly classified and wished to challenge his draft classification in court before being inducted. This was to refuse induction, undergo criminal prosecution for doing so, and use the allegedly erroneous classification as a defense. The Supreme Court rejected this interpretation.

James J. Oestereich was a divinity student classified 4D by his draft board—a classification that exempted him from military service. He returned his draft card to the government to express dissent from U.S. participation in the Vietnam conflict. Before long, his draft board declared him delinquent for failure to have a draft card in his possession and reclassified him 1A, making him liable for immediate induction. He took an administrative appeal, lost, and was ordered to report for induction. At that point he brought suit to restrain induction, but a federal district court held that it had no power to review the classification. A federal court of appeals affirmed this decision, but the Supreme Court reversed it.

Justice William O. Douglas pointed out in the majority opinion that nothing in the selective-service statute authorized the local board to reclassify Oestereich. "We deal with conduct of a local board that is basically lawless," said Douglas. Since Oestereich had established that he was entitled to an exemption as a divinity student, the court said, it would be harsh to require him to test the validity of the classification in a criminal proceeding. Accordingly, a preinduction review should be permitted. Justices Potter Stewart, William J. Brennan, and Byron R. White strongly dissented from the decision. (*See also* Law. *See in* CE: Supreme Court of the U.S.)

SWAZILAND. In 1969, the first full year of independence, Swaziland's economic situation remained satisfactory and political stability was maintained. Agricultural exports were hit by drought, and the World Food Programme approved $373,000 worth of aid for famine relief. Crop failure for corn was estimated at between 60% and 80% of the average harvest. The drop in agricultural exports was compensated for by increased exports of processed products and mineral ores. Swaziland's principal customers remained Great Britain, Japan, and South Africa. About 90% of Swaziland's imports—of which the most important were machinery and transport equipment—came from South Africa. A close economic relationship was maintained with South Africa.

With the population growing rapidly, the government was under increasing pressure to demand the return of land held by European settlers (approximately 50% of the total land). During a visit to Kenya in June, Prime Minister Prince Makhosini Dlamini said that the transfer of land to African ownership in Swaziland would follow the Kenyan pattern. (*See also* Africa; South Africa. *See in* CE: Swaziland.)

SWEDEN. In 1969 Sweden became the first nation of Western Europe to establish full diplomatic relations with North Vietnam. In September the Swedish government announced that it would send $40 million in aid and credits to North Vietnam for reconstruction and other purposes, possibly before the end of the conflict in South Vietnam. During the year U.S. military deserters continued to find a haven in Sweden.

WIDE WORLD

A member of the Swedish labor market board (left) interviews a U.S. military deserter, one of four trainees at Sweden's new job-training camp for U.S. defectors. Most of the approximately 300 U.S. defectors who have found haven in Sweden seem to prefer life in the city to life in the remote camp.

The U.S. government was critical of Sweden's recognition of North Vietnam and left the U.S. ambassador's post in Sweden unfilled. Swedish business executives complained to their government that pro-North Vietnam policies were damaging export sales.

In October 68-year-old Tage Erlander retired as prime minister and head of the ruling Social Democratic party after 23 years at the head of the government. Succeeding him was 42-year-old Olof Palme, the minister of education. The new prime minister had attracted public notice by his participation in a march in 1968 protesting U.S. involvement in the Vietnam conflict and for his appearance in the film 'I Am Curious (Yellow)'.

Reports issued early in 1969 showed a 3.5% rise in the gross national product for 1968 and a continued balance-of-payments deficit. The 1969 budget was slightly higher than the 1968 budget. The Social Welfare Department requested $2.3 billion of the $8.39 billion estimated as expenditures for 1969. State ownership of industry increased in 1969. The government stepped up its program to purchase more than 50% of the building-materials industry.

Sweden was in 1969 an enthusiastic supporter of Nordek, the proposed Scandinavian economic union. At the United Nations (UN) General Assembly the Swedes introduced a resolution proposing a UN Conference on Human Environment for 1972, which was endorsed without dissent. The pesticide DDT was banned in Sweden as part of a multifaceted domestic pollution-control program. (*See also* Europe. *See in* CE: Sweden.)

SWIMMING. Post-Olympic years traditionally bring a letdown in swimming performances. Measured by the standard of world records, that was only half true in 1969. Of the 13 world records for men's individual races, nine were broken, two equaled officially, and one tied unofficially. However, only 3 of the 13 women's individual world records were bettered.

The best of the male swimmers were Gary Hall, Mike Burton, Mark Spitz, and Don Havens of the United States; Hans Fassnacht of West Germany; Roland Matthes of East Germany; and Nikolai Pankin of the Soviet Union. The leading females were Debbie Meyer and Susie Atwood of the United States, Karen Muir of South Africa, and Gabriella Wetzko of East Germany.

Outstanding Men

In the Amateur Athletic Union (AAU) national long-course (outdoor) championships, held August 12–17 at Louisville, Ky., Hall broke three world records in four days. The 18-year-old high-school senior from Garden Grove, Calif., set the records in the 200-meter individual medley (2:09.6), 400-meter individual medley (4:33.9), and 200-meter backstroke (2:06.6, a record that stood only 15 days). In the AAU national short-course (indoor) championships, April 8–13 at Long Beach, Calif., Hall won two races in U.S.-record time.

Burton, a 22-year-old University of California at Los Angeles junior—swimming for the Arden Hills Swim Club of Sacramento, Calif.—won the AAU 1,500-meter freestyle for a fourth consecutive year, lowering his world record to 16:04.5 and setting, en route, a world mark of 8:28.8 for 800 meters. Also for a fourth consecutive year, he won the AAU 1,650-yard freestyle indoors in U.S.-record time of 15:40.1. (The indoor meets were swum in 25-yard pools; world records could be set only in 50-meter or 55-yard pools.)

In the July 11–13 Santa Clara (Calif.) invitational meet, which attracted many foreign stars, Spitz—a 19-year-old Indiana University freshman from Santa Clara—tied two world records: his own 0:55.6 for the 100-meter butterfly and the retired Don Schollander's 1:54.3 for the 200-meter freestyle. In the same meet, Spitz tied the U.S. record of 0:52.6 for the 100-meter freestyle. He was also the only three-event winner in the National Collegiate Athletic Association (NCAA) championships March 27–29 at Bloomington, Ind., where his Indiana team won overall honors.

"LONDON DAILY EXPRESS" FROM PICTORIAL PARADE

U.S. swimmer Jon Erikson, 14, comes ashore at Dover, England, after swimming across the English Channel from Cape Griz-Nez, France, in 11 hours 23 minutes. He was the youngest ever to swim the channel.

Havens, a University of Southern California senior, captured the AAU 100-yard indoor title for a third straight year. Outdoors, he won the AAU 100-meter title.

Gary Hall, 17, wins the 400-yard individual medley, in 4:00.85, a new U.S. record, in the national AAU swimming and diving championships in Long Beach, Calif., in April.

WIDE WORLD

WORLD SWIMMING RECORDS SET IN 1969 (through September 15)

	Event	Name	Country	Time
MEN	200-meter freestyle	Mark Spitz	United States	1 minute 54.3 seconds*
	400-meter freestyle	Hans Fassnacht	West Germany	4 minutes 4.0 seconds
	800-meter freestyle	Mike Burton	United States	8 minutes 28.8 seconds
	1,500-meter freestyle	Mike Burton	United States	16 minutes 4.5 seconds
	100-meter breaststroke	Nikolai Pankin	U.S.S.R.	1 minute 5.8 seconds
	200-meter breaststroke	Nikolai Pankin	U.S.S.R.	2 minutes 25.4 seconds
	100-meter butterfly	Mark Spitz	United States	55.6 seconds*
	100-meter backstroke	Roland Matthes	East Germany	57.8 seconds
	200-meter backstroke	Roland Matthes	East Germany	2 minutes 6.4 seconds
	200-meter individual medley	Gary Hall	United States	2 minutes 9.6 seconds
	400-meter individual medley	Gary Hall	United States	4 minutes 33.9 seconds
WOMEN	1,500-meter freestyle	Debbie Meyer	United States	17 minutes 19.9 seconds
	100-meter backstroke	Karen Muir	South Africa	1 minute 5.6 seconds
	200-meter backstroke	Susie Atwood	United States	2 minutes 21.5 seconds

Equaled record

Fassnacht, an 18-year-old freshman at Long Beach State College in California, won the 200-meter and 400-meter freestyles in the AAU outdoor meet, setting a world record of 4:04.0 for 400 meters. He won the same two races and both individual-medley titles in the European Cup meet for men, held August 23–24 at Würzburg, West Germany.

The 18-year-old Matthes, winner of two Olympic titles in 1968, continued his domination of the backstroke. He set world records of 0:57.8 for 100 meters and 2:06.4 for 200 meters.

The Soviet Union continued to produce outstanding breaststrokers. The 20-year-old Pankin was the best, setting world records of 1:05.8 for 100 meters and 2:25.4 for 200 meters.

Jim Henry, a 21-year-old Indiana University senior from Dallas, Tex., was the outstanding U.S. diver. In the three major championships—AAU outdoor, AAU indoor, and NCAA—he won five of the eight diving titles.

Marvelous Mermaids

Miss Meyer, a 17-year-old high-school junior from Sacramento, won three AAU titles outdoors and one indoors. In 1968 she had broken four women's world freestyle records and won three Olympic gold medals.

The 16-year-old Miss Atwood, from Long Beach, won four AAU backstroke titles—two outdoors and two indoors. She set U.S. records in all four races and a world record of 2:21.5 for 200 meters outdoors. Miss Muir, 16, set a world 100-meter backstroke record of 1:05.6.

Miss Wetzko, a 15-year-old freestyler, was the star of the European Cup women's meet, August 23–24 at Budapest, Hungary. She won the 100-meter final in 0:59.6 and the 200-meter title in 2:08.9, both European records, and anchored her East German medley relay team to victory and another European record.

Cynthia Potter, an 18-year-old Indiana University sophomore from Houston, Tex., captured three of the six AAU diving titles for women. Micki King, 25, captured two AAU outdoor titles. (*See in* CE: Diving, Sport; Swimming.)

SWITZERLAND. Religious freedom and voting rights for women were among the main domestic issues debated in Switzerland in 1969. In anticipation of the constitutional revision expected by 1974, a questionnaire concerning the abrogation or replacement of anti-Catholic articles was submitted to cantons, political parties, churches, and other or-

"LONDON DAILY EXPRESS" FROM PICTORIAL PARADE

A Swiss woman wearing a placard demanding "No Discrimination" joins with other Swiss women in a demonstration for female rights, particularly the right to vote. Little progress was made in enfranchising women in 1969.

One unit (upper left) of Switzerland's first nuclear power plant was completed in 1969. The plant, located on Beznau Island in the Aare River near the city of Baden, is the first dual commercial nuclear power station in Europe. It was scheduled for full completion in 1972.
PICTORIAL PARADE

ganizations. Little progress was made in voting rights for women. By October, six of the 22 cantons had granted women's suffrage, and three had authorized the communes to enfranchise women.

The autonomy-seeking citizens in the French speaking Catholic Jura region of the canton of Bern remained dissatisfied with progress on their behalf. A report commissioned by the federal government proposed a "Jura statute" allowing considerable autonomy, followed by plebiscites in the districts, to decide for the status quo, greater autonomy, or establishment of a new canton.

In December the Federal Council elected Hans-Peter Tschudi as president of the Confederation for 1970. Pierre Graber replaced Willy Spühler as foreign minister, and Ernst Brugger succeeded Hans Schaffner, minister of economic affairs.

In November the council decided to sign the international nuclear nonproliferation treaty. Parliament approved a new defense law in 1969 providing for coordination of all defense activities.

The balance-of-payments surplus in 1968 was $540 million, and the gross national product rose by 3.5%. In the 1970 budget federal expenditure amounted to only one third of total public expenditure, a cut made to head off inflation threats. In the first quarter of 1969, exports rose by 14%. (*See in* CE: Switzerland.)

SYNTHETICS. During 1969 synthetics found new applications in automobile production, in the aerospace program, and in recreational equipment. The headlong expansion of plastics production continued. The world output of plastics was estimated at 27.5 million tons. The United States led production with 9.15 million tons followed by West Germany and Japan, each with 3.58 million tons.

The automobile industry made increased use of plastics in 1969. The typical 1970-model U.S. car was estimated to contain an average of 100 pounds of plastics, or 15 pounds more than the 1969 models. In France, Citroën increased production of its Mehari runabout model to 100 per day, making it the first car with a thermoplastic body to be mass produced.

Early in the year an indoor "ice" rink of vinyl plastic was installed at the Vanderbilt Athletic Club in New York City. The rink requires little maintenance with only weekly applications of a conditioner and a room temperature of between 45° and 85° F. needed to preserve its hardness. The club also has two plastic tennis courts and a plastic ski slope.

Teflon, a fluorocarbon substance used to line kitchen utensils, was woven into a fabric that was used in the space suits worn by the Apollo 11 crew on their moon flight. Teflon is completely inert to chemical attack and will withstand temperatures of up to 500°. (*See in* CE: Fibers, Man-Made; Plastics.)

SYRIA. During 1969 there were no major changes in Syria's uncompromising, independent policies in spite of a reorganization of the ruling Ba'athist regime and a broadening of the government's base. The changes in government resulted from a long-smoldering power struggle between one faction of the Ba'athist party headed by Lieut. Gen. Hafez al-Asaad, the defense minister, and a second faction led by Syria's President Nureddin al-Attassi and Maj. Gen. Salah Jedid. To settle the dispute an emergency party congress was called late in March. The congress selected a new 16-man party leadership reflecting a compromise between the factions. Al-Attassi, Al-Asaad, and Jedid retained their positions, but new policies announced in April—calling for closer cooperation with other Arab states—reflected the aims of General Al-Asaad. Also announced was a relaxation of the political system and the promise of a new provisional constitution. When a new cabinet was formed in May it included Arab nationalists, unionists, independents, and Ba'athists but the Ba'athists held the key spots.

The new regime maintained the hard line against a political settlement of Arab-Israeli issues. Syria's detention of two male Israeli passengers from a hijacked U.S. airliner in August stirred international protests.

In an effort to pressure the Soviet Union into speeding up arms deliveries, President Al-Attassi delayed a scheduled visit to the Soviet Union while a Syrian general sought Chinese Communist aid. Al-Attassi finally visited the Soviet Union in July, obtaining an agreement for further Soviet scientific and technical cooperation.

During the year Syria attempted to coordinate its defense policies with those of its Arab neighbors. A joint Syrian-Iraqi-Jordanian Eastern Command was established, a Syrian-Iraqi defense pact was signed in July in spite of continued distrust between the two nations' opposing Ba'athist regimes, and Syria sought a revival of the Syrian-Egyptian defense pact as a step toward political unity.

Syria's relations with Lebanon were severely strained in the fall when Syrian-backed Palestinian guerrillas clashed with Lebanese forces trying to contain them. Syria, supporting the right of the guerrillas to operate against Israel from bases in Lebanon, closed its border with Lebanon in October as a retaliatory measure.

Syria's economy in 1969 was bolstered by excellent cotton and cereal crops, an expanding oil industry, and rising exports. A large international airport was opened in Damascus, the capital, in September. During 1969 Syria lifted its ban on U.S., British, and West German visitors; the ban was imposed after the Arab-Israeli war of 1967. (*See also* Lebanon. *See in* CE: Syria.)

TAIWAN. In 1969 the 57-year-old Republic of China (or Nationalist China), which has its seat in Taiwan, celebrated its 20th anniversary in exile. The year brought the Nationalist Chinese government no closer to its avowed aim, the recovery of the Chinese mainland, now controlled by the People's Republic of China (or Communist China). The disunity within the Chinese Communist party, however, gave encouragement to the Nationalist aim. Nationalist China's President Chiang Kai-shek continued his attempt to reap benefit from the disunity by indicating that he would cooperate with any opposition group on the mainland against Politburo Chairman Mao Tse-tung. Chiang's policy, however, met with no success.

The Nationalist Chinese government was greatly concerned by U.S. President Richard M. Nixon's declared policy of reducing U.S. involvement in Asia after the Vietnam conflict ends and by U.S. overtures to Communist China. The statement by U.S. Secretary of State William P. Rogers that "we recognize the Republic of China on Taiwan and Communist China on the mainland as facts of life" was regarded by Nationalist China as the clear definition of a two-China policy by the Nixon Administration.

After the meeting of the Tenth National Congress of the Kuomintang, Chiang's political party, the president appointed his son Chiang Ching-kuo as deputy premier. Young Chiang's appointment strengthened his position as heir apparent to his father. (*See also* Feature Article: "China and the United States: Distorted Images." *See in* CE: Formosa.)

TANZANIA. At the Tanganyika African National Union (TANU) national conference in June 1969 President Julius K. Nyerere outlined Tanzania's second five-year development plan. The keynote was self-reliance, with 60% of government expenditure to be financed from within Tanzania itself. The East African Community was expected to provide some $69.6 million. The aim of the plan was to produce a 6.5% growth in the gross domestic product in each year. In spite of the long-term plans for industrial expansion, most of the

Tanzanian citizens march in a procession through the streets of Dar es Salaam, the capital, during Biafra Day celebrations. Tanzania was the first country to recognize Biafra, the breakaway state of Nigeria.

KEYSTONE

Recruits for Tanzania's Women's National Service march through the National Stadium in Dar es Salaam. They are each equipped with the latest in automatic rifles. Despite its small population—about 12 million—Tanzania maintains both an army and an air force.

CAMERA PRESS—PIX FROM PUBLIX

country's economic growth would depend upon the rural workers, who would be encouraged to improve methods of cultivation.

In anticipation of the development plan, 100 Soviet geologists arrived in Tanzania in February to speed prospecting and geological investigations. Italy agreed in June to lend $9.6 million to build an airport at the foot of Mount Kilimanjaro. The survey for the Tanzania-Zambia railway to be built by Communist Chinese engineers was almost done.

At the TANU national conference Nyerere was reelected president of Tanzania; he ran unopposed. Rashidi M. Kawawa was elected second vice-president.

In December 1968 Nyerere reassured the Asians of Tanzania that they would be judged by performance and not by racial origins. In January 1969 he warned Great Britain against forbidding the entry of East African Asians possessing British passports.

The government arrested Abdulla Kassim Hanga, former vice-president of Zanzibar; Othman Shariff, formerly ambassador to the United States; and Ali Mwange Tambwe, a junior minister, on charges of plotting against the Zanzibar government. The three men, all former members of the Zanzibar revolutionary council, were flown to the island in September and were later executed.

In February, Eduardo Mondlane was assassinated in Dar es Salaam, the capital. He was the head of the anti-Portuguese guerrilla movement in Mozambique. (*See in* CE: Tanzania.)

TELEPHONES. The number of telephones in service throughout the world climbed to nearly 225 million in 1969. More than 114 million of the telephones were in the United States. The number of transoceanic telephone calls continued to increase at an annual rate of 20%; more than 16 million were completed in 1968, and nearly 140 million are expected to be completed in 1980.

The American Telephone and Telegraph Co. (AT&T), which serves most of the telephones in the United States, handled some 105 billion messages in 1968. Long-distance calls increased some 11% to almost 6 billion. Telephone companies continued to make substantial investments in new equipment to meet ever-mounting demands for

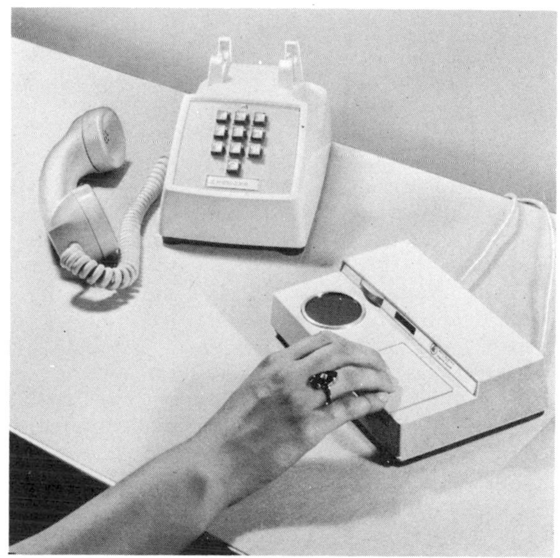

AUTHENTICATED NEWS INTERNATIONAL

The new "Code-Com" set being developed by Bell Telephone Laboratories will, when connected to a conventional telephone, allow a deaf person to "see" phone messages in coded flashes of light or "feel" them in the vibrations of a finger pad.

telephone service. In 1969 AT&T said that it plans to introduce intercontinental direct-distance dialing between the United States and Great Britain, permitting overseas calls to be made without the aid of an operator. The new system will permit an overall 25% rate reduction. With the completion of a new submarine cable to Spain, AT&T said all rates to Europe would be reduced by about one fourth.

The quality of telephone service in the United States—long touted as the world's finest—came into serious question in 1969. In some locations —notably the Wall Street section of New York City and parts of Florida—service deficiencies reached crisis proportions. Some affected business firms took newspaper advertisements to complain about bad service and to chide the telephone companies—mainly AT&T. The difficulties were widely attributed to a failure by the telephone companies to anticipate demand for their services. The U.S. Federal Communications Commission (FCC) began an investigation of AT&T's facility-planning procedures. Meanwhile, AT&T requested FCC permission to increase its profits on interstate service from 7–7.5% to 8.5–9%.

In November AT&T, after negotiations with the FCC, consented to reduce its long-distance rates by the largest amount ever. The rate reductions—to average about 4% and to total $150 million annually—were scheduled to become effective on Jan. 1, 1970. Despite the rate cut, however, the company was expected to continue to make larger profits than the maximum permissible under the FCC rules, which were drawn up in 1967. (*See in* CE: Telephone.)

TELEVISION AND RADIO.

With television service already established in more than 100 nations and radio in almost all countries and dependencies, there was less room for growth in 1969. Expansion continued, but on a more modest scale than in earlier years. The broadcasting industry estimated that 223 million television sets and 606 million radios were in use in the world. About 81 million of the television sets—more than a third—were in the United States. Great Britain followed with 30 million, and the Soviet Union was third with 25 million. There were about 6.7 million in Canada. Half of the world's radios—303.4 million —were in the United States. The rest were spread among other countries in densities that ranged from one set for every two persons to less than one set for every 100 persons.

Television stations on the air or under construction in the world in 1969 totaled about 6,350; 1,042 were in the United States. The world's radio stations, in operation or under construction, numbered about 12,700; of these, 6,957 were in the United States. Most of the stations were AM (amplitude modulation), though in the United States nearly 40% were estimated to be FM (frequency modulation).

Satellites and Television

In 1969 the global network of communications-satellite ground stations grew to 29 in countries around the world. By the end of 1972, it was expected that at least 78 ground stations would be in operation in 53 countries. In 1965, when the U.S. Communications Satellite Corp. (COMSAT) placed its first satellite in operation, ground stations had totaled three—one each in the United States, Great Britain, and France.

Television's usage of communications satellites also increased. In 1965, satellites had been used for only 80 hours of international television transmission; in 1968 they were so used for 666 hours, and COMSAT in 1969 put into effect a 40% rate reduction that it thought would double television's use of satellites. More than 230 hours of satellite time—and a network of 20 ground stations around the world—were used for worldwide distribution of telecasts from the Apollo 11 moon-landing spacecraft in July 1969. A similar network provided around-the-world coverage of the investiture of Prince Charles as prince of Wales.

Commercial communications satellites themselves continued to improve. Each of the Intelsat 3 satellites launched in 1968–69 provided 1,200 voice circuits, as well as 300 channels for television and other occasional uses, and each satellite had a life expectancy of five years. Satellites of the Intelsat 4 generation, planned for launch beginning in 1971, were to have even greater capacities. It was thought that by 1975 it would be possible to transmit television directly from satellites to home receivers, bypassing ground facilities. However,

YARDLEY JONES, "TORONTO (ONT.) TELEGRAM," FROM BEN ROTH AGENCY

"Mom says it's okay as long as we don't watch the newscasts . . . "

WIDE WORLD

One of television's most promising new shows in 1969 was Sesame Street, an experimental educational program for preschool children using puppets, cartoons, and live action film as teaching devices. Four adults (foreground) hosted the show.

it was also felt that costs and other problems would delay the introduction of such a system for an additional ten years—by which time conventional distribution systems might well be so sophisticated that satellite-to-home transmission would be unnecessary or uneconomic.

Television Under Fire

Commercial-television broadcasters in the United States came increasingly under attack in 1969. In January the Federal Communications Commission (FCC), pursuing a policy designed to foster diversification of mass-media ownership, took the license of WHDH-TV in Boston, Mass., from the owners of the *Boston Herald Traveler* newspaper and awarded it to Boston Broadcasters, Inc., one of several challengers for the license. The FCC held that the former owners had paid insufficient attention "to the public's needs and interests."

In June the U.S. Supreme Court upheld the FCC's "fairness doctrine" and "personal attack" rules, which broadcasters had challenged as unconstitutional. Soon thereafter a U.S. court of appeals took the license of WLBT-TV in Jackson, Miss., from its owners and ordered the FCC to invite new applicants for the license. The station had long been involved in litigation over viewers' charges of racism in its programming. A number of other license holders across the nation were under similar pressures. The U.S. Department of Justice also continued its efforts to break up multiple media holdings.

Sex and violence in programming were criticized both in Congress and by the President's National Commission on the Causes and Prevention of Violence. Many broadcasters, however, had already moved programs containing such matter to times at which children were unlikely to be watching. In the face of mounting opposition to cigarette advertising on television, broadcasters offered to "phase out" cigarette commercials over a four-year period; cigarette makers countered with an offer to stop advertising their product on television and radio by September 1970.

The most spectacular of broadcasters' troubles, however, came from U.S. Vice-President Spiro T. Agnew in a mid-November speech denouncing network television news as biased and unfair. Agnew's speech—carried live by all three major networks, which knew its content in advance—generated intense controversy. Mail and telephone

In The Bill Cosby Show, a television series beginning in the 1969 fall season, comedian Cosby starred in the role of a high-school coach. The series was one of the few on U.S. television that featured blacks.

COURTESY, NATIONAL BROADCASTING CO.

Leonard Nimoy was a new member of the "Impossible Missions Force" in the popular television series Mission: Impossible during its fourth season, in the fall of 1969.
COURTESY, COLUMBIA BROADCASTING CO.

response to the speech was strongly favorable. However, network executives, many newspapers and news magazines (which became Agnew's target in a later speech), and a substantial number of private citizens called the speech an attempt to intimidate a news medium dependent upon federal licensing for its existence. (*See also* Newspapers; People of the Year.)

Television Programming

In the United States and throughout the world, news remained a primary service of television and radio broadcasters in 1969. The year's most spectacular event—man's first landing on the moon, the Apollo 11 mission in July—was carried by a global television network with a potential audience of 625 million.

A survey revealed that in the United States, television—despite the criticism leveled at it—remained, for most people, the primary and most credible news medium. Another survey revealed that more than 3,000 U.S. radio stations carried news provided by one or more of the established radio networks or by the increasing number of specialized audio-news services.

Television entertainment programming in the United States in 1969 was marked by decreased violence—in new series, an almost total absence of violence—and by a diminishing emphasis on sex as broadcasters responded to criticism. Individual television and radio stations, as well as networks, gave increased attention—and air time—to racial and social problems. They offered, for instance, more and more programs designed to find jobs and training for unemployed members of minority groups.

The three major U.S. television networks spent approximately $275 million to produce regularly scheduled nighttime programs for the 1969–70 season, about $15 million more than in 1968–69. Sports also continued to attract big audiences—and ever-higher prices. In 1969, television and radio stations and networks paid $37.2 million for major-league baseball rights, up almost 20% from 1968; almost $54.2 million for professional and college football, about 1% more than in 1968; and lesser but increasing sums for other sports.

Comedies, Westerns, and mysteries produced in the United States remained staples in most television countries, and U.S.-made motion pictures became increasingly popular. Conversely, foreign programs became more popular in the United States. Overall, it was estimated that, in 1969, overseas sales of U.S. programs would reach $100 million for the first time, while U.S. purchases of foreign programs would total a record $30 million. (*See in* CE: Radio; Television.)

TENNIS. The year 1969, the first full season of open tournaments with major individual meets open to all categories of players, was highlighted by brilliant performances. Particularly outstanding was Rod Laver of Queensland, Australia, whose left-handed skill made him open-singles champion of Australia, South Africa, France, the United States, and Wimbledon, England. Margaret Smith Court, also an Australian, became the women's singles champion of Australia, France, and the United States.

The player categories, differing from one nation to another, presented a confused picture. The two broadest classes, however, were no longer amateur and professional but "contracted" professionals (players under contract to promoters and, to that extent, beyond national association authority) and others. The former group was barred from all traditional events except tournaments specifically designated as "opens." Efforts to make the Davis Cup, the men's team championship of the world, open to all classes of players were unsuccessful. (*See* Feature Article: "Run for Your Supper.")

At the annual meeting of the International Lawn Tennis Federation (ILTF), Sweden—in disapproval of South Africa's apartheid policy—proposed a motion that would have barred both South Africa and Rhodesia from international participation as teams and individuals. Although the motion failed, the ILTF management committee was empowered to exclude South Africans from such events if they deemed such action prudent. In the European Zone of the Davis Cup, Poland and Czechoslovakia defaulted to South Africa in protest against apartheid.

A new organization, the International Tennis Players' Association, formed under the chairmanship of the Australian player John Newcombe, quickly reached a membership of 96. The new group was open to all categories of men who competed widely in international events.

In Davis Cup play, the United States retained the trophy without difficulty against Romania, a surprise challenger, at Cleveland, Ohio, in September. With Arthur Ashe and Stan Smith in the singles, and Smith and Bob Lutz in the doubles, the U.S. squad easily overwhelmed the challenging team of Ion Tiriac and Ilie Nastase 5–0. Australia failed to reach the challenge round for the first time since 1937, losing to Mexico in Mexico City 3–2 in the American Zone. India was an easy victor in the

CENTRAL PRESS FROM PICTORIAL PARADE

English tennis player Ann Jones leaps to return a shot to Billie Jean King of the United States during the women's singles final at Wimbledon. Mrs. Jones won, becoming the first Englishwoman to hold the singles title in eight years.

Eastern Zone, and Great Britain and Romania came through with interzone ties as winners of the two European Zone sections. Before losing to Romania 3–2, Britain had beaten Switzerland, Ireland, West Germany, South Africa, and finally Brazil in an interzone final. Romania reached the European finals by beating the United Arab Republic, Israel, Spain, and the Soviet Union, before downing India in the interzone.

In open play in 1969, Laver scored his second "grand slam" (his first was in 1962) by winning the Australian, French, Wimbledon, and U.S. open championships, as well as the South African title. In the doubles, Newcombe and Tony Roche took the honors at Wimbledon and France; Roy Emerson and Laver, the Australian doubles and runner-up honors in France; Tom Okker of the Netherlands and Marty Riessen of the United States, the German title and runner-up honors at Wimbledon; and Ken Rosewall and Fred Stolle, of Australia, the U.S. open title.

The National Collegiate Athletic Association singles title was captured by Joaquin Loyo Mayo of the University of Southern California (USC) from Mike Ester of Rice University in three straight sets in June. Mayo also teamed with Marcello Lara for the doubles title, as USC won the team championship.

Women's Competition

Although Mrs. Court dominated the singles competition in 1969 and took the U.S. National grass-courts title, Billie Jean King of the United States, top woman player of 1968, won the South African singles, and Julie Heldman of the United States, the Italian title. Ann Jones of Britain and Françoise Durr of France dominated the women's doubles, winning in South Africa, France, and Italy.

Mrs. Court and Judy Tegart, of Australia, took the honors at Australia and Wimbledon. Miss Durr then teamed with Darlene Hard of the United States to win the U.S. Open doubles. In Wightman Cup play, the U.S. beat Britain 5–2 at Cleveland in August to regain the trophy, with Miss Heldman playing a stellar role.

The tennis world was saddened in June by the death of Maureen (Little Mo) Connolly, top performer on the world's courts in the 1950's. A three-time winner of both the Wimbledon and U.S. titles, she took all four major championships (U.S., Wimbledon, France, and Australia) for an unprecedented grand slam in 1953. (*See in* CE: Tennis.)

Australian Rod Laver displays his powerful form against fellow countryman John Newcombe in the semifinals of the London Grass Court Championships in London, England. Laver was one of the outstanding tennis players of 1969.

CENTRAL PRESS FROM PICTORIAL PARADE

TEXTILES. The world's textile industry continued to expand in 1969. The year also saw advances in textile-making machinery and in the development of artificial fibers.

Wool consumption in 1969 continued the rise begun in 1968. World wool production in the 1969–70 season was expected to reach a record 6.177 billion pounds, greasy basis, up from the 6.098 billion pounds of 1968–69. Wool prices remained relatively stable during the year, moving in general very gradually downward.

World cotton production in the 1968–69 season, ending in July, reached 52.7 million bales. Production was expected to rise slightly from this figure in 1969–70. In the United States, the 1969–70 cotton output was at first expected to reach almost 12 million bales, but hurricane damage in the growing areas cut the forecast to 11 million bales. At the end of the 1968–69 season, cotton production and consumption were roughly in balance for the first time in many years, because the smaller crops of recent seasons had permitted the reduction of accumulated surpluses. Like those of wool, cotton prices drifted slowly downward.

Cotton continued to be challenged by man-made fibers. In 1968 man-made fibers accounted for an estimated 47% of the total market for fibers. Researchers continued to develop products with improved wearing characteristics from artificial fibers. Manufacturing methods were also being streamlined.

World production of raw silk continued its steady advance in 1969. Over a five-year period, it moved from 32,800 metric tons to 37,600 metric tons. Demand, however, continued to outrun supply.

New textile-making machinery promised more efficient production of better-quality textiles. Developments included higher speeds, increased automation, and more sophisticated control devices. (*See also* Fashion. *See in* CE: Textiles.)

THAILAND. Rule by martial law ended in Thailand in 1969 when the Thais went to the polls for their first general election in more than 11 years. Elephants carried ballot boxes to the remote rural areas of the north. To return the results, elephants, carrier pigeons, ponies, and small boats were pressed into service.

When the votes were counted Premier Thanom Kittikachorn's newly formed United Thai People's party won 75 of the 219 seats in the House of Representatives, or lower house. The party had heavy rural support. The Democrats, led by M. R. Seni Pramoj, took 56 seats including all 21 in Bangkok, the capital, and its twin city of Thonburi. The remainder went to minor parties and independents. In his first policy speech after the election, Premier Kittikachorn told the parliament that Communism was the biggest threat to Thailand's security and pledged to continue to fight it with help from the United States.

However, on a visit to Thailand in July, U.S. President Richard M. Nixon announced that the bulk of U.S. forces in Thailand would be withdrawn as the Vietnam conflict was resolved. He said that Thailand itself should shoulder the major responsibility for defense against Communist subversion. In September it was agreed that the disposition of the 49,000 U.S. troops in Thailand would depend on the outcome of the Vietnam conflict. On Sep-

Thai infantrymen are firing heavily as they battle Communist guerrillas in the rugged mountainous jungle north of Bangkok, opening a third front in January 1969.
WIDE WORLD

tember 30 the United States announced withdrawal of 6,000 troops, to begin within a few weeks and to be completed by July 1970. There were six U.S. air bases and one U.S. naval base in Thailand. These bases provided jobs for some 150,000 Thais and poured about $200 million into the economy, while Thailand served as an operations site for military action against Communist forces in Laos and Vietnam.

Meanwhile, Communist activity in the north and northeast continued, and there was some difficulty with Meo tribesmen, believed to be Communist-led. In the region bordering Malaysia, however, the Communist guerrillas' strength grew to nearly 1,000. A new separatist threat loomed in the south where fanatical Muslims stepped up their campaign to secede from Thailand and join Malaysia. The two governments agreed on some measures to reduce both problems.

The rate of economic growth slowed from a three-year average of more than 7.2% to 6%, largely because of reduced agricultural exports and low world prices. Rice exports were the lowest since World War II; tin and rubber exports declined in volume and price, but corn showed some gain. The government called for drastic measures to halt the mounting trade deficit. A record deficit budget was planned for fiscal 1969–70 as national defense and internal security expenses increased some 16%. (*See also* Asia. *See in* CE: Thailand.)

THE PLAY HOUSE

Elizabeth Lowry and Stuart Levin are playing the title roles in 'The United States vs. Julius and Ethel Rosenberg', the preseason opener in autumn 1969, at the Play House Euclid-77th Theatre.

THEATER. In 1969 U.S. theater continued to be characterized by an assault on tradition, a breaking of barriers, and change and innovation. Among the year's most discernible trends were the nudity fad, the emergence of black playwrights, the development of the resident professional theaters, and the renewed strength of off-Broadway as a theatrical breeding ground and, with it, the continued decline of Broadway theater. Although these and similar tendencies had all been in evidence for some time, they seemed to dominate the U.S. theatrical scene more than ever in 1969.

The Nudity Fad

The trend toward sexual freedom in the theater was significant as a reflection, in whatever extreme and distorted fashion, of some of the changes taking place in U.S. life. Initiating the trend was the Broadway version of 'Hair' (first performed in April 1968), which had a brief and dimly lit nude scene. In 'Sweet Eros', by Terrence McNally (produced off-Broadway in November 1968), an actress performed nude during the entire length of a one-act play. In January 1969 came 'Geese', by Gus Weill, a pair of off-Broadway one-act plays featuring both boys and girls in the nude. In March 1969 an off-off-Broadway attraction called 'Che!', by Lennox Raphael, was raided by the police for using nudity and simulated sex acts as metaphors to represent the relations between the United States and worldwide revolutionary movements. The play continued its run in a somewhat toned-down form. In May came two competing off-Broadway adaptations from the sexually oriented works of the Marquis de Sade.

The month of June brought 'Oh! Calcutta!', devised by Kenneth Tynan and directed by Jacques Levy, with material written by (among others) Samuel Beckett, Jules Feiffer, and John Lennon. The sketches, songs, and dances that comprised 'Oh! Calcutta!' were exclusively concerned with sex, and much of the show was performed in the nude. Offered frankly as "elegant erotica," the revue was a tremendous success, establishing a precedent by charging a top price of $25 a ticket.

The sex trend continued during the 1969 fall season with the opening of 'And Puppy Dog Tails' by David Gaard, an off-Broadway play that functioned mainly as an all-male nude show for homosexuals. It made back its entire investment and began to show a profit before it had even finished previewing.

The Emergence of Black Playwrights

A very different manifestation in the theater of the recent changes in U.S. society has been the emergence of talented new black playwrights. As with the nudity fad, this trend too was far more evident in 1969 in off-Broadway theater than on Broadway.

The Negro Ensemble Company (NEC) had the greatest success of its career with 'Ceremonies in Dark Old Men', a realistic comedy-drama of Harlem (New York City) life by Lonne Elder III. After the play concluded its run at the NEC theater in lower Manhattan, it was recast and presented successfully at a regular off-Broadway house by a commercial producer. During its 1968–69 season the NEC also offered 'God Is a (Guess What?)', a satirical minstrel show in reverse by Ray McIver; a triple bill of one-act plays by Alice Childress, Ted Shine, and Derek Walcott; and a Trinidadian musical called 'Man Better Man', by Errol Hill. All of these playwrights were black.

Other off-Broadway managements offered more works by black playwrights, among them 'To Be Young, Gifted, and Black', a compilation from the works of the late Lorraine Hansberry, and 'A Black Quartet', a bill of one-act plays by Ben Caldwell, Ronald Milner, Ed Bullins, and LeRoi Jones. The New York Shakespeare Festival Public Theater presented 'No Place to Be Somebody', a comedy-melodrama set in a barroom in Greenwich Village (New York City), written by another new black playwright, Charles Gordone.

Although these black playwrights were more or less united in expressing a sense of the difficulty of life for the black man in a predominantly white society, it was difficult in other respects to generalize about them. Their works ranged from realistic to expressionistic to poetic and from apolitical to militant.

Baiko is enacting a scene from 'Kagami Jishi', a production of the Grand Kabuki Theatre of Japan, during the company's first national tour of the United States since 1959.
PICTORIAL PARADE

The Avant-Garde

On the avant-garde front, the most important event of 1969 was the brief visit to New York City of the Polish Laboratory Theater, headed by Jerzy Grotowski. Grotowski's exercises, methods, and pronouncements have had considerable influence on such U.S. avant-garde companies as the Living Theater, the Open Theater, and the Performance Group. At Grotowski's insistence only 100 people at most were allowed in at each performance, and even these favored ones had difficulty in following the action, unless they knew Polish. Despite these problems, U.S. critics greatly admired the intensity and precision of the company's physical and vocal work.

Nothing produced during the year by the U.S. avant-garde proved very popular or influential, with one exception—'The Serpent', an account of the events in the Garden of Eden with a text by Jean-Claude van Itallie, which was presented by the Open Theater. The institutionalization of the avant-garde, however, took a long step forward with the opening of the new headquarters of the La Mama Experimental Theatre Club. The new quarters contained two theaters that had been bought and renovated with the aid of grants from major U.S. foundations.

Off-Broadway Theater

Off-Broadway, after a few lean years, was becoming increasingly popular and prolific as a commercially viable alternative to Broadway, and new theaters were proliferating rapidly. Two factors were mainly responsible for off-Broadway's rebirth. First, the costs of Broadway production had been increasing astronomically, making off-Broadway look good by comparison. Second, a national market for off-Broadway-type material had been discovered. The income from touring productions, movie sales, and record albums helped to make off-Broadway production economically feasible.

Among the major off-Broadway successes was 'Little Murders', Jules Feiffer's black comedy about violence and fear as they impinge on the life of an "ordinary" New York City family. The play had been a Broadway failure in 1967. Revived at the Circle in the Square in January 1969, it was a moderate success, able to attract a substantial audience. Another of the season's off-Broadway highlights was a pair of one-act comedies, 'Adaptation', by Elaine May, and 'Next', by McNally. A new play by Tennessee Williams, 'In the Bar of a Tokyo Hotel', was unfavorably received, and it quickly vanished.

There were a number of successful small-scale off-Broadway musicals during the 1968–69 season. 'Dames at Sea' (book and lyrics by George Haimsohn and Robin Miller, music by Jim Wise) was a

MICHAEL CHILDERS FROM SANTORO STUDIO

'Oh! Calcutta!', devised by Kenneth Tynan and directed by Jacques Levy, was an immediate success in its off-Broadway opening in June 1969, with much of the show being performed in the nude.

parody of a Busby Berkeley film musical. Two other musical successes had scores by Al Carmines: 'Peace', an adaptation from Aristophanes with a book by Tim Reynolds, and 'Promenade', with a book by Maria Irene Fornes. The first commercially successful off-Broadway musical of the 1969–70 season was 'Salvation', an imitation of 'Hair', written by and starring Peter Link and C. C. Courtney.

Broadway Offerings

Although Broadway retained a good measure of its old prestige and prominence, it originated little—if any—critical significance. It continued to turn out light comedies and musicals but in smaller numbers than formerly. In the 1968–69 season one notable musical was 'Promises, Promises', a big, slick, well-crafted dazzler, produced by David Merrick. Harold Prince produced and directed 'Zorbá', based on the novel and movie 'Zorba the Greek'. Another popular success was the musical '1776', which succeeded in making popular show business out of the events leading up to the signing of the American Declaration of Independence.

In the way of light comedy, the best that Broadway had to offer was 'Jimmy Shine', by Murray Schisgal, considered a flimsy pretext for Dustin Hoffman's star performance; 'Forty Carats' starring Julie Harris; and 'Play It Again, Sam', a vehicle for Woody Allen written by Allen himself. Since good new comedies were scarce, there were revivals of old ones. 'The Front Page' and 'Three Men on a Horse' both returned to Broadway in 1969.

The few serious Broadway plays came almost entirely from Great Britain or from U.S. regional theaters. From Great Britain in 1968–69 there were two notable successes: 'The Man in the Glass Booth', by Robert Shaw, and 'Hadrian VII', adapted by Peter Luke from the novel by Frederick William Rolfe, in which Alec McCowen starred as the man who would be pope. British playwright John Osborne's 'A Patriot for Me', a chronicle of homosexuality under the Hapsburgs, opened and closed in the fall season of 1969.

The regional theaters made their presence felt on Broadway. The Minnesota Theatre Company of Minneapolis and the American Conservatory Theatre of San Francisco, Calif., both played guest engagements on Broadway, but their reception was disappointing. During the 1968–69 season, however, there were no fewer than eight Broadway productions of plays that had had previous productions in regional theaters. Following the great dramatic success of 'The Great White Hope', imported from the Arena Stage in Washington, D.C., was another critical success from the Arena—'Indians', by Arthur Kopit. Kopit's play examined Buffalo Bill (William F. Cody) as a prototypical white liberal.

The Negro Ensemble Company of lower Manhattan was a successful attempt at total black theater in 1969.

UPI COMPIX

These theatrical presentations helped induce more U.S. regional companies to risk offering new plays.

New York City's Lincoln Center Repertory Theater probably had its most successful season to date. Its most popular offering was 'In the Matter of J. Robert Oppenheimer', a documentary play by Heinar Kipphardt. The APA (Association of Producing Artists)-Phoenix Repertory Company, which had become a fixture on Broadway, proved unable to sustain itself financially in New York City any longer. At the end of its 1968–69 season it was forced to take to the road. (*See in* CE: Drama.)

TOBACCO. The world's consumption of tobacco products rose slowly in 1969. In a number of developed countries, however, the tobacco market failed to share in the general uplift as sales were affected by both rising cigarette prices and increasingly intense antismoking campaigns.

Tobacco firms in the United States felt perhaps the most acute pressures. Cigarette consumption in the United States in 1969 continued the decline it had begun in 1968, the first year in which it had dropped since the 1964 release of the surgeon general's report linking cigarette smoking to lung cancer and other diseases. Efforts to halt the decline with stepped-up advertising met little success. Continuing increases in tobacco prices and taxes were thought to contribute to the decline. Another factor was thought to be the Federal Communications Commission requirement that radio and television stations give antismoking announcements one third as much time as they devote to cigarette advertising.

A tobacco planter in the north of France is hanging up part of the year's satisfactory but not outstanding harvest crop to dry in the sun.

AGIP FROM PICTORIAL PARADE

Cigarette advertising faced curtailment in the future. In July the National Association of Broadcasters—to whose advertising codes most U.S. radio and television stations subscribe—announced that cooperating stations would begin to cut down cigarette commercials in 1970 and eliminate them by Sept. 1, 1973. Soon after the announcement, the U.S. tobacco industry announced that it would not advertise cigarettes on radio or television after September 1970. In September several newspapers announced that they would no longer accept cigarette advertising. Meanwhile, the U.S. Congress considered measures that would place yet further restrictions upon cigarette ads. Similar antismoking campaigns were starting in Canada.

Tobacco firms continued to take out economic insurance by diversifying into other businesses. In May, for instance, when the American Tobacco Co. announced that it was changing its name to American Brands, Inc., officers of the firm reported that 28% of its nearly $430 million in domestic sales came from nontobacco products.

Tobacco growers also felt economic pressures. First estimates of the total U.S. tobacco crop in 1969 stood at 1.851 billion pounds, 444 million pounds below the annual average during the peak tobacco-production period of 1962–64. (*See in* CE: Tobacco.)

TOGO. Togo's military regime in 1969 seemed to be preparing the country for an eventual return to civil rule. Hardly any political activists, however, showed any interest in replacing the military. One exception was Bonito Herbert Olympio, son of a former president, who was expelled from Ghana on charges of conspiring to overthrow the Togo regime.

Togo's President Étienne Eyadema announced in January that political activities could be resumed, but after public protests in favor of the political status quo, the decision was reversed. In September the country's traditional chiefs pledged support for Eyadema's policies, approving his plan for a single political party. The death of former President Nicolas Grunitsky in 1969 marked the end of an older generation of administrators.

Togo received aid from France and other sources during the year for development projects. The country continued to suffer a trade deficit despite an increase in exports. (*See in* CE: Togo.)

TOYS AND GAMES. More than 10,000 toy buyers registered for the annual American Toy Fair held in New York City in March 1969, an increase of 1,000 over the number visiting the 1968 fair. The president of the Toy Manufacturers of America, Inc., Lionel Weintraub, predicted a 10% increase in sales over the 1968 wholesale figure of $1.824 billion. The 1968 total, an increase of about 20% over 1967, was the biggest jump ever

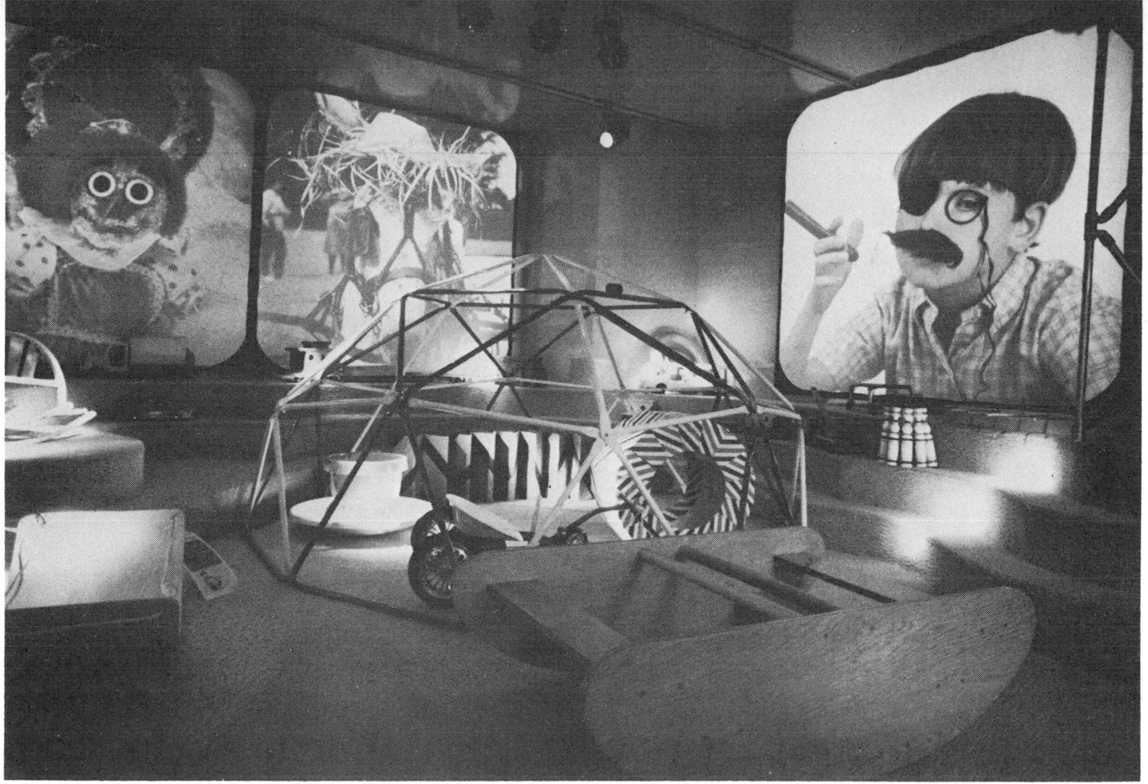

WIDE WORLD

By allowing children to play with toys in this room, called Creative Playthings, a new toy store in New York City is giving parents a chance to shop for toys in the pre-Christmas rush.

made in the history of the industry and concluded a five-year period in which the industry's gains exceeded increases in population, gross national product, and disposable personal income. Prices averaging 5% to 10% higher accompanied the expanding market. Prices for dolls, the largest single toy category, soared in 1969—the average prices ranging from $15 to $20.

Some of the toy industry's more than 100,000 items have been found to be potentially dangerous, either because they contain substances harmful to children or because of certain electrical, mechanical, or thermal hazards. United States Senator Frank E. Moss (D, Utah) introduced a bill into Congress that would give the secretary of health, education, and welfare the authority to remove dangerous toys from the market. The bill, the Child Protection Act of 1969, passed both houses and was signed into law in November.

A survey of toy manufacturers in 1969 indicated that educational and scientific toys were expected to show the greatest increase in sales over the following five years. Space toys—including space suits, lunar explorers, and battery-powered rocket cars that can travel upside down and in and out of water along specially constructed tracks—were very popular in 1969. Chemistry sets, following a resurgence that began in 1967, continued to grow in demand.

In 1968 toy manufacturers developed and produced a number of toys that demonstrated scientific principles or that were "computerized"; this trend continued in 1969. One "computer" football game, for example, was actually a binary read-

Large inflatable toys are a specialty of Two Plus Three, a company in New Rochelle, N.Y. Children are hard at work (or is it play?) helping fill orders and inflate toys.

UPI COMPIX

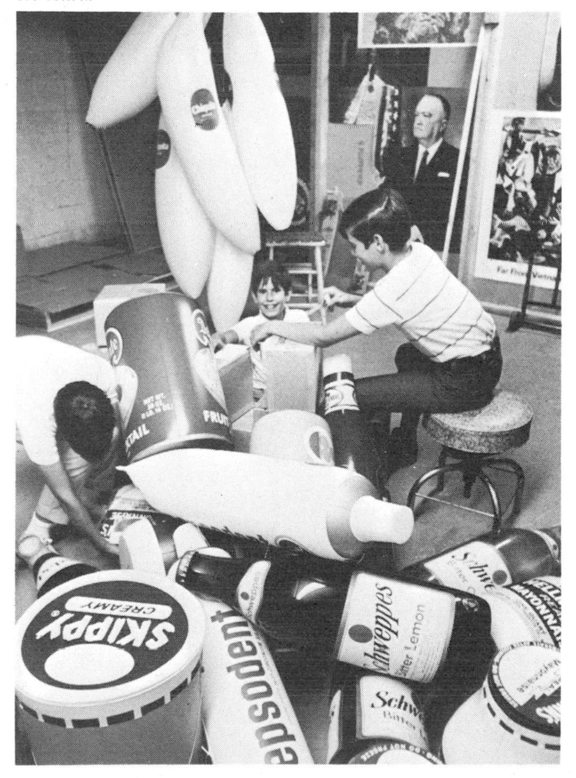

out device operating on the same principle as computers: after information was introduced by pressing various selector buttons, 16 indicator lights would give results of play on a selection chart. A scientific toy, called "Tork," that also serves as a kinetic sculpture was marketed in 1969. It is simply a colorful ball mounted on a thin twisted metal rod. When set in motion, it demonstrates the varying direction principle of torque. The first big seller among the scientific demonstration toys was "The Swinging Wonder," which illustrates the conservation of momentum principle.

Guns and other war toys had received much adverse publicity, and sales were slow in 1969. The trend toward authentic scale-model reproduction of boats, cars, and trains continued. (*See also* Hobbies. *See in* CE: Toys.)

TRACK AND FIELD. The U.S. track and field season in 1969 was distinguished only by a scarcity of new world records and an unusually large number of retirees from the sport. American male athletes accounted for only two new international marks (pole vault and 440-yard run), far fewer than in an average year, and ties in the frequently matched standards for the 100-yard run, 120-yard hurdles, and 110-meter hurdles. American women athletes were shut out on the world-record front.

Among Olympic champions stepping down were Jim Hines (100-meter); Tommie Smith (200-meter), who planned to enter professional football; and Al Oerter, four-time discus winner in his 15-year career. Bronze medalists Tom Farrell (800-meter) and George Young (steeplechase) also ended long careers, as did hammer thrower Ed Burke. Triple jumper Art Walker chose to sit out the season. But the most spectacular retirement was that of Jim Ryun, world record holder in the 880-yard, mile, and 1,500-meter and a silver medalist in the 1968 Olympics. Besieged by injury and committed to marriage and a new career, Ryun not only lost in the collegiate championships but also stepped from the track during the Amateur Athletic Union (AAU) title race to announce his retirement for the season, perhaps for all time. Only partly active because of slackened interest or injury were Olympic winners Bob Beamon (long jump), Dick Fosbury (high jump), and Randy Matson (shot put) and the U.S. intermediate-hurdles champion, Geoff Vanderstock.

A number of Olympic champions distinguished themselves during the year, however. Willie Dav-

At the Continent Track and Field Meet between Europe and the Western Hemisphere on July 31, 1969, in Stuttgart, West Germany, Lee Evans (above) of the United States finished first in the 400-meter sprint, and Karin Balzer (left) took the women's 100-meter hurdles for East Germany.

ABOVE AND LEFT: DPA FROM PICTORIAL PARADE

WIDE WORLD

Olympic gold medalist Bill Toomey of the United States is winning the 100-meter dash of the decathlon event of the West German-U.S. Track and Field Meet at Augsburg, West Germany, on Aug. 5, 1969.

enport, high-hurdles champion, chalked up a 13.2-second race at Zurich, Switzerland, to equal the ten-year-old record in the 120-yard and 110-meter races, and he also had a brilliant year in indoor competition. Bill Toomey, Olympic decathlon champion, came back to score 8,277 points for a U.S. record. He chalked up an all-time high of 4,123 points in the pentathlon, for which there is no official world record.

Javelin thrower Mark Murro established a new U.S. mark of 292 ft. 8 in. Olympic winner Lee Evans was surprised in the 440-yard race in the National Collegiate Athletic Association (NCAA) meet by Curtis Mills, a young Texas A & M sophomore, who not only scored an upset but also set a new international mark of 44.7 seconds. Olympic pole-vault titlist Bob Seagren lost out to the former record holder, John Pennel, who cleared 17 ft. 10¼ in. at Sacramento, Calif., on June 21.

Performances matching world records included a 9.1-second mark in the 100-yard run by John Carlos of San Jose State and a 13.2 clocking by Erv Hall of Villanova in the 120-yard hurdles at the NCAA meet at Knoxville, Tenn. New U.S. marks were also established by San Jose State, which trimmed the 440-yard relay standard to 38.8 seconds, and by the University of California, at Los Angeles, with a 3:03.4 performance in the mile relay. Ralph Mann of Brigham Young matched the U.S. record of 49.6 for the 440-yard hurdles.

Indoor Track and Field

In 1969 indoor competition was far more impressive than outdoor, even though there were many nonstandard events on the schedule. Several Olympic competitors performed brilliantly during the January-March indoor season but were not around for the outdoor campaign.

Most impressive was George Young, third in the Olympic steeplechase, who equaled the world's best (there are no official indoor marks) in the two-mile run with 8:27.2 and followed up with a new low of 13:09.8 in the three-mile before announcing his retirement. Indoor marks were also set by Villanova's Larry James, who covered 500 yards in 55.4; Ralph Doubell, Australian Olympic winner, who ran 880 yards in 1:47.9; Villanova, with a two-mile relay timing of 7:22.8; and Seagren, with a mark of 17 ft. 5¾ in. in the pole vault. All-time bests were equaled or bettered in the 70-yard, 100-yard, 60-yard low hurdles, 70-yard high hurdles, and 35-pound weight.

Championship Meets

Team titles in major U.S. meets went to Prairie View in the National Association of Intercollegiate Athletics; San Jose State in the NCAA at Knoxville; and the Southern California Striders in the National AAU meet at Miami, Fla. In international competition at Los Angeles the United States easily out-

DPA FROM PICTORIAL PARADE

Lisl Westermann of West Germany is throwing her winning toss in the discus-throwing event at the Continent Track and Field Meet in July.

scored the Soviet Union 125–111, and the British Commonwealth, 137–96, in the first such meet held in four years. In midsummer, the U.S. triumph was repeated in a dual meet with West Germany, 127–96, at Augsburg, and with Britain, 131–90, at London. But a Western Hemisphere team, made up mostly of U.S. athletes, lost 113–97 to a European team at Stuttgart, West Germany, in July.

In the IX European championships, held at Athens, Greece, in September, East Germany emerged triumphant with 11 gold medals, followed by the Soviet Union with 9 and Great Britain with 6. Five world marks were broken at the meet, mostly by women. World marks set by European athletes during the year included a javelin toss of 304 ft. 1½ in. by Jorma Kinnunen of Finland on June 18 at Tampere, Finland, and a hammer toss of 245 ft. by Antoli Bondarchuk of the Soviet Union on September 20 at Athens.

In the two-day Pacific Games at Tokyo, Japan, in September, Australia defeated the United States 15 gold medals to 11. A surprise was the defeat of Bob Seagren in the pole vault by Kyoichiro Inooe of Japan with a leap of 16 ft. 9½ in.

Women's Competition; Other Developments

American women were limited during the year to three new national records outdoors. Eleanor Montgomery high-jumped 5 ft. 11 in. in the women's outdoor AAU meet at Dayton, Ohio. Doris Brown and Frances Larrieu shared a new record of 4:16.8 in the 1,500-meter, and 17-year-old Kathy Hammond ran the 400-meter in 52.1. Indoors, Tennessee State's Madeline Manning established a national record of 2:07.9 for the half mile.

Tennessee State captured both the indoor and outdoor AAU titles. Highlight of the season was the U.S. women's win over the Russians, 70–67, and the British Commonwealth, 81–54, in Los Angeles. But in Europe the U.S. women were soundly trounced, 81–54, by the European team, then lost close meets to West Germany, 68–66, and to Great Britain, 67–66.

New world marks established by European women athletes included a time of 51.7 by Nicole Duclos of France in the 400-meter; 12.9 by Karin Balzer of East Germany in the 100-meter hurdles; 26.0 by Pam Kilborn of Australia in the 200-meter hurdles; and 4:10.7 by Jaroslava Jehlichova of Czechoslovakia in the 1,500-meter. Liese Prokop of Austria compiled 5,352 points in the pentathlon.

In May the International Amateur Athletic Federation ruled that all track athletes would be required to wear plain white shoes after May 1, 1970, as a result of the Olympic shoe scandal of 1968. The ban on brush spikes was continued. (*See* Feature Article: "Run for Your Supper." *See in* CE: Track and Field Sports.)

TRANSPORTATION. Mass transportation needs in the world's major cities continued to grow. But plans to ease urban transportation problems were only in initial stages or needed adequate funding for development. Since 1945, users of city transportation—buses, subways, and elevated railways—declined from 23 billion persons a year to 8 billion a year in 1969. Meanwhile, the use of the automobile for urban transportation rose significantly. Early in 1969 the U.S. Urban Mass Transportation Administration received a $37.4-million Congressional mandate to investigate high-speed ground transportation systems as a way of untangling the urban traffic snarl.

Lack of money was the perennial rationale of urban transportation planners for the slow pace in modernizing city-transit systems. However, some avenues of financing had opened up. In 1969 New York City and Chicago, Ill., were in the process of updating and extending their subway systems. Mexico City, Mexico's capital, saw a portion of its first subway system in operation during the year. The $1.3-billion Bay Area Rapid Transit (BART) that will operate in a 75-mile-wide area in the Oakland-San Francisco, Calif., area

At Southampton, England, coaches and cars are driving on the "Atlantic Causeway" container vessel on Dec. 3, 1969, as Atlantic Container Line introduces roll-on, roll-off weekly trips between Great Britain and North America.
UPI (UK) LTD.

was expected to be the most advanced urban transportation system in the world. Features of BART, hopefully to be running by 1971, included: completely computerized ticket distribution, including fare rebates; an 88-foot-long electronic control panel at the system's Oakland headquarters capable of pinpointing the immediate location of all trains; and computer control of the entire system, except for certain emergency situations in which a motorman could halt the train.

High-Speed Interurbans Sought

Fast trains were seen as a way of expediting interurban travel. At present, intercity air traffic was as congested as its highway counterpart. Development of short-takeoff-and-landing aircraft might relieve some of the burdens of sky travel by shunting a portion of air traffic away from major airports to smaller fields. In the opinion of some experts, however, interurban trains traveling at speeds in excess of 100 mph would greatly reduce intercity transportation strains.

Two interurbans—the Metroliner and the TurboTrain—were on test runs during the year. The Metroliner, powered electrically, operated at a top speed of 110 mph. It plied a route between New York City and Washington, D.C. The TurboTrain, by contrast, used gas turbine engines for its power. It hit speeds of 120 mph. TurboTrains were test run by the Canadian National Railway between Toronto, Ont., and Montreal, Que., for a short time. Other TurboTrains were on experimental runs on U.S. rails between New York City and Boston, Mass. However, mechanical troubles plagued both interurban rail projects, and by year-end the effectiveness of the Metroliner and the TurboTrain was still in question.

Plans were also made to look into the practicality of elevated monorail transportation. One such device was the French-designed Aerotrain. It rode on a cushion of air and was driven by two turbojet engines. The Aerotrain, under franchised construction in the United States by the U.S. Rohr Corp., had a projected top speed of 250 mph.

The most revolutionary new idea for interurban travel centered around a gravity rail system. According to the scheme, trains would operate in somewhat V-shaped, airless tunnels that linked the cities. The technique was fairly simple. A train, operating in the frictionless medium, would build up speed on the downward slope of the first half of the journey and then slow down as it approached the station at the end of the tunnel's upward slope. As the train neared the terminal the tunnel in back of it would be sealed and air would then be pumped into the station area so that passengers could leave the train. The plan was so promising that the U.S. government was supporting a full-scale experiment.

Low-Pollution Auto Engines Tested

The gasoline-burning internal-combustion automobile engine was accused of being a prime cause of air pollution. Unburned hydrocarbons emitted in auto exhaust contributed measurably to the mass of pollutants fouling the air. In 1969 engineers were exploring alternatives to the gasoline engine. One idea was to revert back to the steam engine, which had its heyday in the early 20th century. Steam engines burn fuel almost totally and thus emit few pollutants.

Industrialist William P. Lear, famed for his compact executive jets, invested $5.5 million in the production of a steam-powered car. However, by year-end Lear admitted that his steam car was too complicated for reliable and economic use. Lear then turned his attention to the development of a gas-turbine automobile engine.

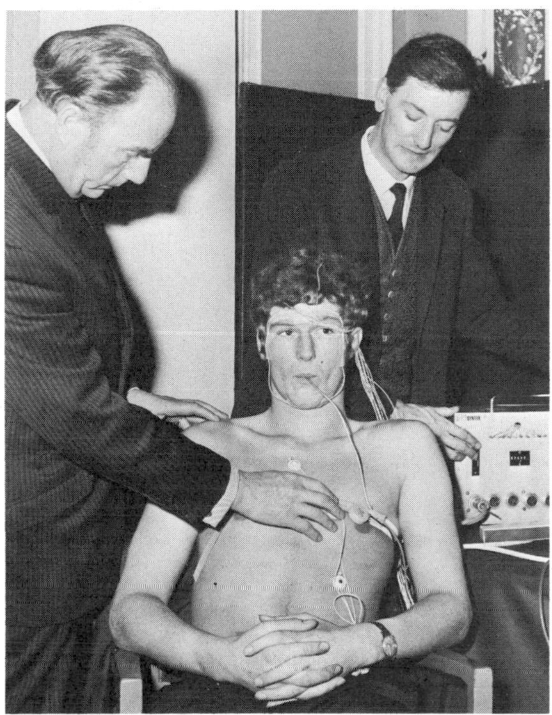

KEYSTONE

Kenneth Bergin (left) is adjusting the equipment fitted to a volunteer for Project Pegasus, a unique study of the changes in human physiology induced by high-speed jet travel between time zones. The study was announced in November.

The California Highway Commission, however, scheduled 1970 tests for a Lear steam-powered highway-patrol car. Another steam engine, tested earlier in the year, was expected to operate at speeds up to 130 mph.

AIRLINES

Airlines throughout the world, especially those in the United States, experienced a disappointing 1969. Traffic growth was faltering, and the load factor (the ratio of available seats to passengers carried) was low on many trunk routes. In the wake of slow traffic growth, increasing numbers of the huge Boeing 747 would be introduced into service in 1970 and 1971 (*see* Aircraft). Fears were that use of the 350-passenger jets would produce a situation far more serious than the airline profit recession of the early 1960's, when the first commercial jets entered service in large numbers and increased the available seat-mile capacity beyond possible traffic growth.

Costs were greatly cutting into profits among the U.S. airlines in 1969. Relatively small domestic fare increases approved by the Civil Aeronautics Board (CAB) early in the year were not enough to alleviate the profit slump. However, the larger farcs asked for by the airlines and approved by the CAB in September could possibly inhibit traffic growth.

The U.S. scheduled airlines comprised 38 domestic and international carriers that operated some 2,300 aircraft. Even with dwindling profits, they amassed large enough operating revenues. The leading means of intercity transportation, the airlines provided 72% of all passenger-miles traveled between the U.S. cities.

New Air Routes

A hassle grew over awarding a second South Pacific route to a U.S. airline. Pan American World Airways, Inc., held the sole license for the area until July, when the CAB finally nominated American Airlines as the second U.S. carrier in the South Pacific. In 1968 the CAB selected Continental Airlines, a domestic trunk carrier with Pacific interests, to ply the route to Australia and New Zealand. The choice was approved by former U.S. President Lyndon B. Johnson late in 1968 but was rescinded by President Richard M. Nixon when he took office. After the case was returned to the CAB, American Airlines won out over Eastern Air Lines, the other alternative. However, there were considerable misgivings among Australians about the need for another U.S. airline operation in the South Pacific.

The Federal Aviation Administration (FAA) set forth a plan late in the year to realign the air routes in and out of New York City. The plan was scheduled for implementation by April 1970. The reshifting of the New York air lanes used by jetliners was expected to minimize congestion in the sky, speed up takeoffs and landings, and lessen the intensity of jet noise heard at ground level.

Skyjackings Continue

Although a U.S. capital offense, jetliner piracy continued unabated in 1969. The most spectacular involved the late October hijacking of a Trans World Airlines flight from San Francisco, Calif., to Rome, Italy. A distraught U.S. serviceman forced the plane's crew to make four stops before the Boeing 707 eventually touched down at Rome's Fiumicino Airport. (*See* Crime.)

The airlines were hard pressed for an effective method of detecting possible "skyjackers." Some of the companies rigged detection devices at entrance ramps or resorted to checks of hand baggage. Most airlines officials, however, glumly conceded that the checks were ineffective and felt that only extradition of the skyjackers and imposition of severe penalties would be a deterrent to future skyjackers.

RAILROADS

The 100th anniversary of the meeting of the westbound Union Pacific and the eastbound Central Pacific, on May 10, 1869, was celebrated at the original site at Promontory, Utah, during the year. Railroad officials used the occasion, honoring the historic uniting of both coasts of the United States, to voice their conviction that the nation still needed the railroads.

The Penn Central Turbo Train, operative in April 1969, is rounding a curve typical of those that prevent the vehicle from reaching its maximum speed of 170 mph on its daily round trips between Boston, Mass., and New York City.
WIDE WORLD

The capabilities of the Mercedes-Benz UNIMOG road-rail machine are being demonstrated in Kew Bridge South, England. The road-traveling machine transforms itself into a miniature locomotive able to haul 300 tons.
KEYSTONE

The opening of the potentially valuable oil fields in Alaska's Arctic Slope was expected to place new demands on transportation in the region. In 1969 the U.S. government allocated funds for an engineering survey to determine the feasibility of extending the government-owned rail line from Fairbanks to the Arctic Slope, with a Kobuk branch.

Traffic Volume Up; Profits Squeezed

Railroad freight traffic reached a record high in 1969. Freight haulage totaled an estimated 758 billion ton-miles, 14 billion ton-miles more than the 1968 high. More than 50% of the 1969 automobile inventory was delivered to dealers throughout the United States by rail. Passenger traffic, however, continued to drop off. Passenger-miles fell to about 12 billion, only half that of a decade ago. Railroad commuter traffic was still on the upswing, though.

Passenger service stoppages accelerated despite Interstate Commerce Commission (ICC) refusal of permission in some cases. By 1969 barely 500 regular intercity trains were running. As a result, the ICC urged federal study into the preservation of a national rail passenger service.

Despite a record volume of freight traffic in 1969, the railroads experienced a profit dip due to inflation. Also, wage demands by most rail unions at year-end were a portent of future profit losses on the part of railroads. At the close of 1969 an increase in rates was under consideration by the rail firms.

Railroad Mergers

Mergers continued to reshape the profile of the U.S. rail system. The New Orleans & Northeastern merged with the Alabama Great Southern. In another merger, the Piedmont & Northern linked with the Seaboard Coast Line.

Final decision from the ICC was pending on several mergers. These included: the Chicago & North Western with the Chicago, Milwaukee, St. Paul & Pacific; the Illinois Central and Gulf, Mobile & Ohio; and the Chicago, Rock Island and Pacific with a number of railroads. Also pending was a U.S. Supreme Court decision on the merger of the Great Northern, the Northern Pacific, and the Chicago, Burlington & Quincy with lease of the Spokane, Portland & Seattle into a new company—The Great Northern Burlington Lines.

A Rail Innovation

By the close of 1969 nearly every freight car in the United States bore a set of "service stripes." These colored strips found on the sides of each car indicated its identification number, owner, weight, and capacity, as well as other information. Scanners to be installed at strategic points along the main lines will periodically pick up pertinent data from the side markings and relay the information to the Washington, D.C., office of the Association of American Railroads. The gathered data will be stored for quick retrieval. The information would thus indicate where freight cars were located and whether they should be sent to other locations.

TRUCKS AND TRUCKING

The trucking industry in the United States grew at a slower pace in 1969 than it did in the preceding year. The ICC-regulated trucking firms, totaling about 15,000, reported that annual revenues rose to nearly $13 billion. Trucking continued to be the foremost common-carrier transport, accounting for half of the revenues of all modes of transit.

Truck Use Increases

The number of trucks on U.S. highways rose again. Total number of trucks in 1969 operation hit a record high of 16.8 million vehicles. And as truck numbers soared and trucking revenues grew, the highway-use taxes paid by the industry increased proportionally. With levies for the approximately 41,000-mile National System of Interstate and Defense Highways included, truckers paid a total of nearly $5 billion in federal, state, and local road-user taxes in 1969; this total was expected to rise in 1970.

Although trucking use increased, the demand for new trucks dropped somewhat during the year. Estimates of 1969 truck sales were 2% lower than the record high of 1968. On the other hand, truck-trailer sales were considerable, 10% higher than in 1968. This demand was generally considered a reflection of greater transport flexibility required by U.S. shippers.

Packaging Gains

Containerization of shipped goods, particularly those moved internationally, was becoming more prevalent. It permitted extraordinary flexibility of transfer from one mode of transportation to another. Container use allowed land, sea, and air shipment of goods without costly repacking, loading, and unloading. Standardization of container sizes was still unresolved but the trucking industry was hopeful that a standard scheme of packaging would eventually be worked out by manufacturers and shippers.

Equipment enlargement to meet shippers' needs was an effort made by the transportation industry as a whole in 1969. Motor carriers sought allowance to operate larger and heavier trucks on the interstate highways to match the larger aircraft and railroad cars in current use. Size and weight increases would permit, in the view of truckers, heightened coordination of truck, rail, and air transport facilities. This would most likely improve all shipping services, they said. (*See also* Cities and Urban Affairs. *See in* CE: Transportation; Airlines; Railroads; Truck.)

TRAVEL.

TRAVEL. A significant event in the history of modern travel took place in May 1969 when an intergovernmental conference on travel convened in Sofia, Bulgaria. The conference met to discuss the future of travel and to consider means of strengthening the International Union of Official Travel Organizations, which represented the world's 103 national tourist organizations.

The key to the fortunes of international travel in 1968 was the decline—for the first time in more than 20 years—of U.S. expenditure on foreign travel. Receipts earned from the foreign travel of U.S. residents amounted to $3.9 billion, some $100 million less than in 1967. Although it is clear that certain short-term factors were involved, such as former U.S. President Lyndon B. Johnson's call for restriction of nonessential travel outside the Western Hemisphere, there was also evidence of some redistribution of U.S. travel spending, mainly in favor of destinations nearer to home—for example, Mexico, Central and South America, and the Caribbean islands. However, the predominant factor was the decline in U.S. travel spending in Canada—U.S. travelers spent $250 million less in Canada during 1968 than during the 1967 Expo year. While this factor more than accounts for the net decline of $100 million in spending, it should also be observed that receipts from U.S. tourists declined in several European countries in 1968. In Western Europe, total spending amounted to $925 million, 2% below the 1967 figure of $944 million. The effects of civil disturbances abroad seem to have caused widespread cancellations of planned trips.

While the volume and value of international travel were easily measured, the growth rate of domestic travel was harder to assess. This was because no border crossings or exchange transactions were involved. Domestic travel expenditure had been estimated to account for 75% of total world tourist expenditures, with international travel representing the other 25%. Because of its size and

The new seaport passenger terminal, designed by David Volkert and John Andrews and constructed by International Builders of Florida, is now operating for the new Port of Miami, Fla., for the convenience of travelers.

MIAMI-METRO DEPARTMENT OF PUBLICITY AND TOURISM

"LONDON DAILY EXPRESS" FROM PICTORIAL PARADE

In July 1969 the William Parry family prepared for their trip from England to Australia in an ex-army amphibious vehicle by way of France, Italy, Greece, Cyprus, Turkey, Iran, Pakistan, India, Burma, Java, and New Guinea.

geography, the United States is the world's largest single spender on domestic travel.

A hopeful note was struck by the newly appointed director of the U.S. Travel Service at the beginning of 1969 when he declared: "U.S. President Richard M. Nixon firmly believes in the role of travel in promoting international understanding." He added that the new U.S. secretary of commerce was confident in the country's ability to overcome the balance-of-payments deficit without resorting to restrictions on the freedom of U.S. citizens to travel abroad.

Available data suggested that 1969 was a better year for travel than was predicted. Improvement was forecast for a number of reasons, notably the absence of political unrest that had upset the travel picture in 1968, the renewed travel of North Americans to Europe, and a spell of comparatively fine weather in Europe through the peak summer months. In the first half of 1969, arrivals in Greece, Italy, Spain, and Great Britain were well above 1968 levels; and during August, London, England, found itself with a temporary shortage of accommodations as foreign tourists arrived in numbers far exceeding expectations. Outside Europe, the U.S. Travel Service was predicting an increase of 20% in foreign visitors to the United States through 1969.

TRUDEAU, PIERRE ELLIOTT. Prime Minister Pierre Elliott Trudeau consolidated his position at the head of Canada's government and as a commanding figure in Parliament in 1969. Much of his work was aimed at reorganization of the federal government. During the year, the prime minister revamped his 29-man Cabinet into committees, each with its own specific powers. His government pushed a measure through Parliament that shortened the time needed for passage of a bill and for debate. This action, along with a successful government move to adjourn Parliament, led to a bitter squabble in the House of Commons, where Trudeau was accused of trying to throttle the Opposition.

Some of the government's efforts to stem inflation proved unpopular, among them cuts in make-work, welfare, and medicare programs. An enormous raise in postal rates upset magazine and newspaper publishers and editorial writers. Prime Minister Trudeau ended an era of very liberal government spending by establishing rigid overall guidelines and planning a 10% attrition in the strength of public service. Policies on foreign affairs, defense, and welfare were all subjected to comprehensive review.

In April he weathered the resignation of Paul T. Hellyer, a senior minister who quit over Trudeau's approach to a new Canadian constitution. At home, another of Trudeau's biggest tasks remained the maintenance of a unified Canada in spite of separatist agitation in Quebec.

In January the leader attended a Commonwealth of Nations prime ministers' conference in London, England. During the year he insisted on meeting demonstrators and exchanging arguments wherever he went. After a visit with U.S. President Richard M. Nixon in Washington, D.C., he announced his opposition to the U.S. ABM (antiballistic missile) system on moral grounds. (*See also* Canada.)

Pierre Elliott Trudeau, prime minister of Canada, continued to be a vigorous and controversial leader. One of his biggest problems in 1969 was Quebec nationalism.

UPI COMPIX

TUNISIA. The dominating event in Tunisia in 1969 was the national election held in November. With President Habib Bourguiba in poor health and constitutionally permitted to succeed himself only once more, the question of an eventual successor to his leadership became a vital issue.

Several potential successors figured in the year's events. Ahmed Ben Salah was dismissed as minister of planning and economics in September when Bourguiba became convinced that his program to reform agriculture through cooperatives was a failure. Later, Ben Salah was ousted from Bourguiba's Neo-Destour Socialist party. In October former Defense Minister Ahmed Mestiri, ejected from the party earlier, made Tunisian political history by publicly criticizing Bourguiba's policies.

Running without opposition, Bourguiba and the Neo-Destour candidates for the National Assembly were elected in November. Bourguiba subsequently named Bahi Ladgham to the newly created post of prime minister—a step seen by some as indicating Bourguiba's choice of a successor.

In economic affairs, Tunisia took an important step by becoming an associate member of the European Economic Community (EEC), or Common Market. The move gave certain Tunisian products preferential treatment in EEC countries in exchange for tariff reductions for some EEC goods imported by Tunisia. The opening of a chemical industry near the port of Gabès in southern Tunisia inaugurated a new development program for the region. As a result of steps taken to erase bitter relations with France, Tunisia received a substantial development loan. Tunisia also signed a cooperative agreement with Algeria.

In October Tunisia was devastated by ten days of torrential rains. Half the country was buried in mud, thousands of people were isolated, and the vital phosphate industry was badly crippled. (*See also* Africa. *See in* CE: Tunisia.)

"LONDON DAILY EXPRESS" FROM PICTORIAL PARADE

Female students at the University of Istanbul are lining up for their march protesting the presence of four vessels from the U.S. Sixth Fleet in Istanbul harbor. The march was one of the demonstrations promoted by left-wing student organizations.

TURKEY. Violence by students and militants, anti-U.S. actions, and a political crisis that threatened parliamentary rule marked the first six months of 1969 in Turkey. Student violence began in January when the U.S. ambassador's car was burned at the Middle East Technical University in Ankara, the capital. A month later a street battle

Turkey's March 1969 earthquake left grieved people waiting atop piles of rubbish to find out if their relatives, who are buried beneath them, are dead or alive.

"LONDON DAILY EXPRESS" FROM PICTORIAL PARADE

erupted in Istanbul when leftist demonstrators, protesting a visit of the U.S. Sixth Fleet, were attacked by right-wing militants. The fleet's planned visit to Izmir was canceled. When a new U.S. ambassador was appointed in April, a strike by Turkish workers at U.S. military installations was under way, accompanied by violence between Turks and Americans. The strike was settled in June.

In May the Justice party administration of Prime Minister Suleyman Demirel faced a serious political crisis when the opposition Republican People's party obtained National Assembly approval of a constitutional amendment providing for political rehabilitation for former Democratic party leaders. The army, which had ousted the Democrats from power in 1960, threatened to seize control if the bill became law. To avert a showdown, the bill was shelved in the Senate, and parliament was recessed until October.

Parliament's early recess brought immediate responses from groups awaiting action on legislation. Students demanding passage of a university reform bill staged protest demonstrations, occupied university buildings, fought with police, and forced the closing of several universities. Workers seeking passage of a pension improvement bill threatened to follow the student example, but workers' rallies held in August proved to be peaceful.

Demirel and his Justice party succeeded in preserving broad electoral support in national elections in October, when they won a clear majority in parliament. Under new electoral laws, extremist parties of both the right and the left lost some parliamentary seats. A new, more moderate cabinet was appointed in November, and the disqualifications of former Democrats were removed.

In foreign affairs Turkey continued as an active member of the Western defense alliances while maintaining a policy of friendly relations with all nations. In November President Cevdet Sunay became the first Turkish chief of state to visit the Soviet Union; the Soviets agreed to provide aid for various Turkish industrial development projects. (*See in* CE: Turkey.)

UGANDA. National problems in Uganda were forgotten momentarily in 1969 when that nation became the first modern African state to be visited by a Roman Catholic pope. In August Pope Paul VI went to Kampala, the capital, where he visited shrines honoring 45 Ugandan martyrs of the 19th century. The pontiff attended services for the 23 Protestant martyrs at a $300 reed replica of the executioner's hut and funeral pyre at the scene of the massacres. Later he said mass at a $280,000 shrine built in memory of the 22 Catholic martyrs. The Uganda government paved a new highway, issued memorial coins, and manufactured souvenir clothing to mark the visit. Schools were closed and turned into hotels to accommodate visitors, and restaurants and food stands were set up to accommodate the huge crowds.

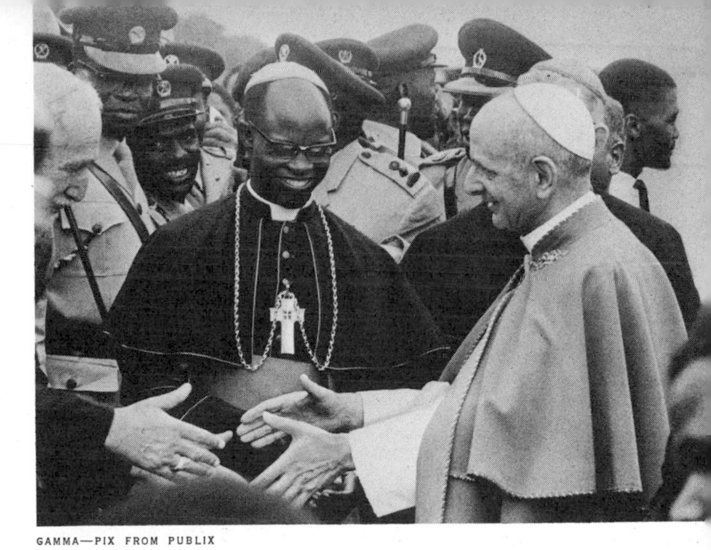

GAMMA—PIX FROM PUBLIX

Pope Paul VI is greeted by African bishops on his unprecedented trip to Uganda in 1969. He discussed "Africanization" of the church there.

President Milton Obote's government extended the state of emergency in Uganda for six-month periods in April and in October 1969. Through the year a number of government opponents were detained under the emergency regulations. In January Princess Victoria, sister of the deposed King Mutesa II of Buganda, was arrested. Rajat Neogy, a magazine editor, and Abubakar K. Mayanja, a controversial member of parliament, were tried on sedition charges and acquitted but were rearrested immediately. Neogy was released in March. In September Benedicto Kiwanuka, Uganda's first prime minister and later an opposition leader, was arrested on charges of libel and sedition. The opposition party accused Obote of using the state of emergency as a political tool.

The 40,000 Asians in Uganda on British passports were told during the year they would have to leave the country. The government later amended the statement, saying the Asians would be replaced professionally only as qualified Ugandans became available, a process expected to take some five years.

After two prominent Ugandan schools were closed because of student disorders, President Obote warned that student power did not mean destruction of property. Taking a hard line against student dissidents, he emphasized that their aim should be to advance the cause of African revolution. The schools, he said, should produce men and women dedicated to the cause of African development.

In October Obote issued his "Charter for the Common Man." The document outlined the future of Uganda along a socialist economic pattern.

Political tension increased at year's end. One cause was the death in exile of King Mutesa II, who had been banished by Obote since 1966. Another cause was the demand by Obote's ruling party that the opposition party be banned entirely. On December 19, Obote was wounded in an assassination attempt. (*See in* CE: Uganda.)

UNION OF SOVIET SOCIALIST REPUBLICS (U.S.S.R.).

In 1969 the collective leadership of the Union of Soviet Socialist Republics was devoted to maintaining the political status quo. Despite rumors during the preceding year of power struggles among the rulers, there were no changes in leadership. An example of the conservative nature of the government was presented early in the year when Soviet ideologists called for a "balanced" portrayal of the late Joseph Stalin. On December 21, for the first time in 13 years, there were observances of Stalin's birthday.

Dissenters in the Soviet Union were effectively dealt with by Soviet "law and order." The dissenters were, however, a very small minority, and the vast majority of Soviet citizens remained silent about government policies. While the Soviet Union in 1969 was still wary of independent moves in East European nations, an even greater concern arose over the military threat of Communist China.

The Silenced Minority

The greatest controversy of the year over the treatment of dissident Soviet intellectuals was created after the Union of Soviet Writers expelled Aleksandr I. Solzhenitsyn in November, thereby banning his works from publication within the Soviet Union. Solzhenitsyn, the author of 'The Cancer Ward' and 'The First Circle', was considered by many to be the greatest living Russian writer. The union accused him of antisocial behavior and of showing only the bad side of Soviet life in his novels about the excesses of the Stalinist era. He was also accused of aiding "bourgeois propaganda" by allowing his works to be published in the West.

Solzhenitsyn replied that he had asked Western publishers not to print unauthorized versions of his works. In a letter protesting the action of the union Solzhenitsyn described Soviet society as seriously sick and asked why he had not been allowed to defend himself. In its reply the writers' union suggested that Solzhenitsyn leave the Soviet Union.

During the year there were also attacks on the press. In July three liberal writers (including the poet Yevgeni Yevtushenko) who criticized the 1968 invasion of Czechoslovakia were removed from the editorial board of *Yunost* magazine. In December the editor of a Soviet theater journal was removed from his post following charges that the journal was not being guided by the "correct ideology." The liberal magazine *Novy Mir* was criticized for the same reason.

In October it was revealed that three Soviet naval officers had been arrested in June 1969 for attempting to distribute copies of an appeal for democracy in the Soviet Union. During the year a Jewish engineer was charged with slandering the Soviet Union and sentenced to three years in prison. At a memorial service at Babi Yar he had referred to the victims of the Nazi massacre as Jews rather than as Soviet citizens. This was considered to be bourgeois, Zionist propaganda.

In July Soviet writer Anatoli P. Kuznetsov, the author of 'Babi Yar', defected to Great Britain. Kuznetsov said that it was impossible for him to work in the rigid Soviet system, and he told how the secret police expected writers to inform on one another.

The Red Dragon

After a long series of minor border incidents involving Soviet and Communist Chinese troops along the Amur and Ussuri rivers, a major military engagement occurred in March over possession of Damanskiy (Chenpao) Island in the Ussuri River. The Russians claimed that Chinese troops crossed

The *Severnoye Siyanie* is the Soviet Union's first floating power station. The station will provide 20,000 kilowatts of power.

"LONDON DAILY EXPRESS" FROM PICTORIAL PARADE

ABOVE: "LONDON DAILY EXPRESS" FROM PICTORIAL PARADE. BELOW: UPI COMPIX

The Soviet Union held a dramatic viewing of the bodies of 31 border guards who were killed, the U.S.S.R. said, in border clashes with the Communist Chinese. Russians demonstrate (below) against the Chinese outside the Chinese Embassy in Moscow, the Soviet capital.

over the border and fired at Soviet guards who were about to ask the Chinese to leave. The Russians claimed that 31 Soviet guards were killed. Demonstrations protesting the incident were staged outside the Chinese Embassy in Moscow, the capital.

There was a second battle on the Ussuri River in March, and in July Soviet and Chinese troops clashed on the Amur River. In August there were reports of serious trouble on the Soviet border with China's Sinkiang-Uigur Autonomous Region. In September the Soviet Union charged China with 488 border violations in June, July, and August. The military buildup on the Soviet and Mongolian frontiers with China continued throughout the year. There were rumors during the year that the Soviet Union might launch a preventive nuclear attack on China.

In addition to the military measures the Soviet Union took serious diplomatic steps to deal with the problem of China. The Russians attempted to use the conference of world Communist parties as a means for isolating China from the international Communist movement. The conference was held in Moscow during June. At the conference Soviet Communist Party General Secretary Leonid I. Brezhnev made a controversial proposal for an Asian security system. Many national delegations, however, were reluctant to criticize the Chinese, and 14 parties refused to endorse completely the conference's final document. (*See* Communist Movement.)

Some progress toward easing tensions was made in September when Soviet Premier Aleksei N. Kosygin met with Chinese Premier Chou En-lai at Peking, the Chinese capital. After the meeting the Chinese agreed to border negotiations, and the talks began on October 20. Brezhnev later also

proposed that the Chinese and the Russians enter into negotiations to solve their ideological differences and to avoid further conflict. (*See* China, People's Republic of.)

The conflict with China compelled the Soviet Union to establish closer relations with Western countries, in the view of some observers. The Soviet Union took a major step toward easing tensions in central Europe by urging members of the Warsaw Pact to propose a European security conference in which Eastern and Western nations alike would participate. (*See* Europe.)

Willy Brandt, the new chancellor of West Germany, proposed entering negotiations with the Soviet Union on the renunciation of the threat or use of force in settling disputes. After considering the West German proposal at a Warsaw Pact meeting in Moscow on December 3–4, the Soviet Union accepted the offer, and the talks began on December 8. (*See* Germany, West.)

In mid-November preliminary talks between the United States and the Soviet Union on strategic arms limitation began at Helsinki, Finland. Earlier in the year there was evidence of a new conciliatory tone toward the United States. There was an absence of military display in the May Day parade, and the traditional speech, delivered by Brezhnev rather than the defense minister, stressed peaceful coexistence. In July former U.S. Vice-President Hubert H. Humphrey met with Kosygin in Moscow. Kosygin stressed the Soviet Union's desire for peaceful cooperation with the United States.

In the aftermath of the 1968 invasion of Czechoslovakia the Soviets emphasized "normalization." The new Czechoslovak leadership was generally in favor of Soviet policies, and the Russians made no concessions to liberal demands.

In the Middle East crisis the Soviet Union continued to support the Arabs and to denounce "Israeli aggression." The Russians repeatedly called for the withdrawal of Israeli troops from occupied Arab areas. While calling for a political settlement and attempting to restrain the Arabs from using force to regain their lands, the Soviet Union continued to send military aid to the Arab states. (*See* Middle East; United Nations.)

Relations between the Soviet Union and Cuba showed a marked improvement during the year. There were reports that the Cuban government had agreed to stop instigating revolution in other Latin American countries and to end criticism of the Soviet Union in return for continued economic aid. Soviet aid to Cuba was estimated at $1 million a day. In July a fleet of Soviet naval vessels visited Cuba as a show of friendship, and in November Soviet Defense Minister Andrei A. Grechko arrived for talks with Cuban leaders. (*See* Cuba.)

Russians in Space

Soviet space triumphs during the year were eclipsed by the two U.S. moon landings. The Russians did, however, make important contributions to space technology during the year.

In January Soyuz 4 and Soyuz 5 completed a successful docking operation between two manned space vehicles. In May the Venera 5 and Venera 6 spacecraft, which had been launched in January, began relaying information from the planet Venus. One major Soviet space failure was the crash landing on the moon of the Luna 15 in July when the first U.S. astronauts were landing on the moon.

During a motorcade honoring the Soyuz 4 and Soyuz 5 cosmonauts in Moscow, a man fired several shots at the car carrying the Soviet spacemen. Two persons were injured, and the assailant was immediately arrested. He was later described as mentally deranged. (*See* Space Exploration.)

Economic Affairs

Bad weather in 1969 had an adverse effect on agriculture and food production in the Soviet Union. Heavy snows and cold temperatures hampered transportation, and industrial production was also affected. There were serious losses of live-

During a lull in the May Day parade in Moscow, Russians dance to the music of a brass band. The figure represents a "scorpion" and is crowned by a U.S. dollar sign.

UPI COMPIX

stock, and in the Ukraine the winter wheat crop was severely damaged. The spring planting was supposed to offset the winter losses, but farmers were hampered by broken-down equipment. The fall wheat harvest also ran behind schedule. Wheat production for 1969 was 10% lower than in 1968.

In a report issued in January the Soviet Union conceded that the industrial growth rate had declined in 1968. In July it was revealed that the economy was still lagging behind the planned growth rate. Industry expanded by 6.9% in the first six months of 1969 as compared to 9% for the same period in 1968. The proposed national budget for 1970, presented to the Supreme Soviet in December, again emphasized consumer goods over heavy industry.

In October the Soviet Communist party endorsed a plan for eliminating surplus workers, improving labor productivity, and raising the pay of the remaining workers. The new plan, some analysts felt, would cause an increase in unemployment. Plans were being made to redistribute the Soviet work force, and centers for employment information were to be opened in 200 cities. Some government workers were to be laid off in 1970, cutting the payroll by $1.8 billion. (*See in* CE: Russia.)

PIEROTTI FROM BEN ROTH AGENCY

"Somehow he doesn't look Egyptian."

UNITED ARAB REPUBLIC (UAR). At the beginning of 1969 the UAR, or Egypt, was still recovering from the effects of student violence that had occurred late in 1968. In January the government announced that students arrested during the riots would be released for disciplinary action by their universities, and the universities, closed for two months, were reopened. Compulsory military training for all students was introduced.

Also in January, new elections were held for the National Assembly, dissolved by presidential decree in November 1968. Candidates of the ruling Arab Socialist Union were elected to fill most seats. The election was the last stage of political reform promised by President Gamal Abdel Nasser after the 1967 Arab-Israeli war.

In 1969 the strength of the UAR's military arms and equipment was restored to the level that had existed before the 1967 war. Under the guidance of Soviet advisers, the quality of military training and personnel was improved. In March, skirmishes with Israeli forces on the eastern bank of the Suez Canal escalated when UAR commandos began crossing the canal to raid Israeli positions. Throughout the rest of the year fighting along the canal intensified steadily on the ground and in the air. A new phase of military action began in September when Israeli commandos landed and swept unopposed along the UAR's Gulf of Suez coastline for ten hours. The UAR responded with a massive air attack on Israeli targets in Sinai. Israeli attacks along the length of the canal and the Gulf of Suez continued almost daily in the fall in spite of increasing Egyptian air, sea, and ground attacks on Sinai. Israeli and UAR reports on the results of the fighting were conflicting.

During the early part of the year Nasser's statements indicated that he was still hopeful for a political solution to the Arab-Israeli conflict. As the year wore on, and attempts by the United States, the Soviet Union, France, and Great Britain to reach a solution made no progress, Nasser became increasingly militant. In July he declared that the UAR had reached a "stage of liberation" in which Arabs should regain their occupied lands by a "war of attrition" against Israel. In November he told the National Assembly that Arabs could free their lands only "over a sea of blood with horizons of fire." He also came out firmly in support of the Palestinian guerrilla organizations, including *al Fatah*. (*See also* Middle East.)

The Soviet Union continued its strong support of the UAR but showed some concern with Nasser's militancy. The Russians emphasized their desire for a political settlement in the Middle East when an important UAR delegation visited the Soviet Union in December.

Nasser gained considerable prestige in the Arab world by successfully mediating a crisis involving the Lebanese government and Palestinian guerrillas seeking Lebanese bases. He also obtained approval from the Arab League Defense Council for an Arab summit meeting, long opposed by Saudi Arabia. An offer of increased aid from Libya's new regime promised to reduce the UAR's dependence on Saudi Arabia.

UPI COMPIX

This view through barbed wire on the Israeli border shows severely damaged buildings on the UAR side of the Suez Canal. The area was shelled and bombed heavily by Israeli forces in the spring.

Throughout most of 1969, however, the UAR's economy remained dependent on Saudi Arabia and Kuwait to make up for revenues lost by the continued closure of the Suez Canal. The most hopeful development was a rapid increase in oil production, mainly at the Al Morgan oil field on the Red Sea. A contract for the construction of an oil pipeline between Suez and Alexandria was awarded to an international consortium in July. (*See also* Israel; Lebanon; Libya. *See in* CE: Egypt.)

UNITED NATIONS (UN). As the United Nations in 1969 prepared for the Second Development Decade, Secretary-General U Thant expressed deep concern over the world situation. During celebrations marking the 24th anniversary of the UN, U Thant issued a statement criticizing the arms race, violations of human rights, and the hunger, poverty, and "plain misery" in all parts of the world. The conflict in Vietnam and the civil war in Nigeria remained outside UN jurisdiction. The most serious and seemingly unsolvable problem before the UN in 1969 was the virtual state of war between Arabs and Israelis in the Middle East.

The Middle East

The UN continued its search for a settlement to the Middle East crisis by calling on the "big four" powers—Great Britain, France, the United States, and the Soviet Union—to place moral pressure on the Arabs and Israelis and to work together toward finding a solution to the problem. The formal talks among the four permanent members of the UN Security Council began on April 3 and recessed from July 2 until December 2. Bilateral talks between the United States and the Soviet Union continued throughout the summer and fall. Hope for accord between the United States and the Soviet Union on establishing guidelines for a settlement appeared on December 9 when the U.S. secretary of state said that the United States favored the withdrawal of Israeli troops to the frontiers that had existed before the war of June 1967. In the U.S. view this would be in exchange for an agreement binding the Arabs to a peace settlement. Combat operations between Israelis and Arabs continued throughout 1969 on an almost daily basis.

The Security Council censured Israel for its actions several times in 1969. Israel was censured in April for an air attack on Jordan in which 18 civilians were killed. In July the Security Council censured Israel for attempting to annex the Arab section of Jerusalem. Another censure vote followed Israeli air raids on Lebanese villages. A resolution in September condemned the burning of the Al Aksa Mosque in Jerusalem. Israel objected to these actions, charging that Arab terrorism was ignored while Israeli retaliation was censured. (*See* Israel.)

In spite of Israeli efforts Syria was elected to the Security Council in October. The other new members elected were Poland, Burundi, Nicaragua, and Sierra Leone. In January Iraq's permanent UN representative resigned but denied that his action was related to the execution of alleged Israeli spies in Iraq. (*See* Iraq.)

Along the Suez Canal UN truce observers were in constant danger as Egyptians and Israelis bombed and shelled one another. There were several casualties among the observers during the year, and in July an observer from Sweden was killed.

In November Arab guerrillas took control of 14 of the 15 refugee camps in Lebanon operated by the UN Relief and Works Agency for Palestine Refugees. There were rumors that the camps were being used as centers for guerrilla training. (*See* Middle East; Refugees.)

In a speech at the UN in September, Jordan's Foreign Minister Abdel Monem Rifai criticized the United States for supporting Israel and said that such support is obstructing peace in the Middle East.

WIDE WORLD

Demonstrators burn the Iraqi flag in front of Iraq's mission to the UN in New York City. They were protesting the hanging of 14 alleged Israeli spies in Iraq.
UPI COMPIX

Chemical and Germ Warfare

A UN report on chemical and biological weapons released in July concluded that such weapons were not vital to any nation's security. The report further stated that these weapons could affect human society and the environment in dangerous and unpredictable ways. U Thant urged all nations to stop the development and stockpiling of chemical and biological weapons.

While the United States in November pledged not to engage in offensive chemical or biological warfare, it still maintained the right to use tear gas and defoliants in the Vietnam conflict. The Political Committee of the General Assembly declared that tear gas and defoliants were prohibited by the 1925 Geneva Protocol against the use of chemical and biological weapons. The United States claimed that the General Assembly had no right to rule on points of international law. A World Health Organization report presented in December showed that the defoliants may have caused birth defects in Vietnamese children.

Protecting the Oceans

The United States and the Soviet Union in 1969 proposed a treaty for banning the installation of nuclear weapons and other weapons of mass destruction on the ocean floor. The draft was not endorsed by the General Assembly because smaller nations were suspicious of Soviet and U.S. motives. The smaller nations pointed out that not all weapons were included in the joint proposal, that no adequate method of inspection was provided, and that they feared that the resources of the seabed would be exploited by U.S. and Soviet interests. In another area of disarmament, however, the General Assembly approved a resolution urging the United States and the Soviet Union to halt the nuclear arms race immediately. The Soviet Union and the United States both objected to what they regarded as outside pressure by the General Assembly on the two-way arms-limitation talks then under way in Helsinki, Finland. (*See* Disarmament.)

The General Assembly also considered the peaceful uses of the world's oceans. This, too, raised monumental problems concerning territorial waters and the exploitation of mineral wealth in seabeds under international waters. The smaller nations feared that the great powers with their advanced technology would seize the wealth in the seabeds. As a result, a resolution was adopted urging all nations to stop undersea development until an international regulatory commission could be set up. The United States objected, saying that such action would cause some nations to file unreasonable claims to territorial waters.

Developing Nations

The UN in 1969 began outlining its programs for the Second Development Decade beginning in 1971. Strong emphasis was placed on agriculture, birth control, and self-help programs. A 15-year agricultural plan called for concentration on wheat and rice production to feed the one billion additional people expected to be living in developing nations by 1985. As sources of protein, chicken and hogs were recommended, since these animals have a relatively fast reproduction rate.

Another UN report urged that the UN Development Programme be given more efficient control over aid being channeled to poorer nations. A UN economic committee recommended an annual growth rate of 6% for developing nations during the 1970's and called on wealthier nations to contribute 1% of their gross national product in aid. In January $226.7 million in financial aid was approved for 84 developing nations.

The UN Educational, Scientific, and Cultural Organization reported in September that the number of illiterate adults in the world had increased by about 70 million during the 1960's. This was caused by the high birthrates and inadequate educational programs in underdeveloped nations. In December the General Assembly authorized U Thant to begin working on plans for an international university. It was thought that such a school would be of great benefit to nations having no university of their own.

Resolutions condemning the apartheid policies of Rhodesia and South Africa were sponsored by other African nations and adopted by the General Assembly in November. The resolutions called for a stoppage of air and sea transport to South Africa, urged Great Britain to overthrow forcibly the white-minority government in Rhodesia, and demanded that Portugal relinquish control of African territories.

During the year the UN sponsored a sea search aimed at preventing ships from evading the 1968 sanctions against Rhodesia. In December Portugal was censured for shelling a village in Senegal. Black African nations also urged UN aid and support for African guerrilla movements.

Other Actions

In November, for the 20th consecutive year, the General Assembly voted against allowing Communist China a seat at the UN to replace the Nationalist Chinese. In 1969, however, there were 48 votes in favor of the move, 4 more than in 1968. There was a marked change in attitude toward Communist China, even among the nations that voted against the proposal or abstained. (*See* Feature Article: "China and the United States: Distorted Images.")

In December the Security Council extended the UN peace-keeping force on Cyprus for another six months to June 1970. The presence of 55,000 U.S. troops under the UN flag in South Korea was also approved for another year.

The General Assembly passed a resolution calling for more severe punishment of airline hijackers. The resolution urged all nations to support the International Civil Aviation Organization in its efforts to halt air piracy.

Former child film star Shirley Temple Black was appointed a U.S. delegate to the UN by U.S. President Richard M. Nixon. Mrs. Black expressed interest in social and economic issues. Other new delegates appointed by Nixon included Representatives Dante B. Fascell (D, Fla.) and J. Irving Whalley (R, Pa.).

WIDE WORLD

David A. Morse, director general of the International Labor Organization (ILO), addresses the UN in October after the ILO was awarded the Nobel peace prize. The ILO is a specialized agency of the UN.

A UN-sponsored treaty to end racial discrimination went into effect on March 13. Angie E. Brooks of Liberia was elected president of the General Assembly, becoming the second woman to hold that post. (*See in* CE: United Nations.)

UNITED STATES.

"Polarized" was a word frequently used to describe U.S. society during 1969. Differences of opinion between radicals and conservatives, black and white, young and old reached new extremes. The "silent majority" of middle-class citizens adopted U.S. flag decals as their symbol—in opposition to peace buttons and black armbands, the symbols of antiwar protesters and other antiestablishment groups. Even the monumental achievement of landing the first man on the moon failed to win unanimous acclaim in the United States. Some people felt that the enormous outlay of funds on the U.S. space program could have been better used in solving the earthly problems of crime, poverty, and pollution.

While the number of incidents of violence rose, so did the cost of living. A new Administration fought to curb a serious inflation but, with its policies, created fears of a recession.

The Coming of Nixon

The year began with a new president, Richard M. Nixon, who was inaugurated as the 37th U.S. president on January 20. Spiro T. Agnew took office as the 39th vice-president.

The first conflict-of-interest issue of 1969 surrounded the nominations of David M. Kennedy for secretary of the treasury and of David R. Packard for deputy secretary of defense. Both were given Senate approval after Kennedy agreed to diversify his bank holdings and Packard placed his stock in a charitable trust.

The most controversial Cabinet nominee was Alaska's Gov. Walter J. Hickel for secretary of the interior. Strong doubts were raised about the wisdom of the choice of Hickel after he stated that strong controls against water pollution would hamper industry and that he saw no merit in "conservation for conservation's sake." Also, as governor of Alaska he had prevented an Eskimo cooperative from selling fish to a Japanese firm and forced them to sell to local buyers at lower prices. Hickel was the last Nixon Cabinet member to be confirmed by the Senate.

Soon after taking office Nixon made an eight-day tour of Western Europe, visiting Belgium, Great Britain, West Germany, Italy, and France. He encountered some anti-U.S. demonstrations—especially in Rome, Italy—but generally the president was well received. (*See* Nixon.)

The strategic-arms-limitation talks opened in November at Helsinki, Finland. The opening sessions were noted for their cordiality and lack of propaganda. Within three weeks the U.S. and Soviet negotiators had worked out broad areas for substantive talks covering offensive and defensive weapons and ways of carrying out inspections. While the preliminary talks were in progress the Soviet Union and the United States ratified the nuclear nonproliferation treaty.

In July Nixon made a brief tour of several Asian nations and was on hand for the splashdown of the Apollo 11 crew in the Pacific Ocean. He made a stopover in South Vietnam and also paid a visit to Romania. (*See* Foreign Policy, U.S.)

Nixon sent New York's Gov. Nelson A. Rockefeller on a series of four fact-finding tours of Latin American nations in 1969. At almost every stop on the Rockefeller trips there were demonstrations and anti-U.S. riots. In September the U.S. ambassador to Brazil, Charles Burke Elbrick, was kidnapped by leftist guerrillas. He was released after the Brazilian government freed 15 political prisoners—part of the ransom for the U.S. ambassador. (*See* Brazil.)

President Nixon suffered a major defeat when the U.S. Congress refused to confirm Judge Clement F. Haynsworth, Jr., as an associate justice of the Supreme Court to replace Abe Fortas. Fortas resigned under pressure after evidence was disclosed that he had engaged in fee taking. Fortas

BELOW: UPI COMPIX. ABOVE: PICTORIAL PARADE

Hurricane Camille smashed the Mississippi Gulf Coast area in August. National Guardsmen (above) unload food for hurricane victims. A boat was deposited against a house in Biloxi, Miss., by the storm. President Nixon declared disaster areas in Mississippi and Louisiana.

ABOVE: HOWARD HARRISON FROM NANCY PALMER AGENCY. BELOW: JIM ANDERSON FROM NANCY PALMER AGENCY

The "Weatherman" faction of the Students for a Democratic Society (left) begins a march that ended in violence in Chicago, Ill., in October. Peaceful protest (below) took place at Fort Dix, N.J., in October. Some 5,000 people protesting conditions in the post stockade were turned back by Military Police.

had been former President Lyndon B. Johnson's choice for chief justice. Judge Warren E. Burger of the U.S. Court of Appeals in Washington, D.C. —Nixon's nominee—became the new chief justice in 1969. The Supreme Court under Burger handed down its first important decision late in the year by ordering the immediate desegregation of 33 Mississippi school districts. The Administration had asked for a delay. (*See* Supreme Court of the U.S.)

One of the major proposals of the new Administration was the "new Federalism," a program for sharing federal revenue with the states. The program was opposed by the mayors of a number of major U.S. cities. (*See* Cities and Urban Affairs.)

Profound Divisions

Beginning in October the Nixon Administration was faced with "moratoriums" against the U.S. involvement in Vietnam. President Nixon stated that he would not be influenced by the Vietnam moratorium or antiwar demonstrations.

On October 15, rallies were held in cities and on college campuses throughout the United States. In Washington, D.C., the U.S. capital, thousands of protesters wearing black armbands marched past the White House. Mrs. Martin Luther King, Jr., addressed a rally at the Washington Monument. The moratorium was supported by students, unions such as the United Auto Workers, many professional people, and also some members of Congress. New York City's Mayor John V. Lindsay decreed a day of mourning there and ordered that flags be flown at half-staff. Supporters of the Administration flew flags at full staff. All demonstrations were generally peaceful.

In a speech referring to the October moratorium Vice-President Agnew stirred controversy by stating, "A spirit of national masochism prevails, encouraged by an effete corps of impudent snobs who characterize themselves as intellectuals." Agnew predicted "wilder" demonstrations in November.

On November 3 Nixon delivered a much-publicized and long-awaited speech on U.S. policy in Vietnam. Nixon stated that an immediate withdrawal of U.S. troops would be disastrous for the people of South Vietnam. Instead he favored a program of "Vietnamization," or the gradual withdrawal of U.S. troops as the South Vietnamese became better able to defend themselves. He also made public the contents of secret communications with the government of North Vietnam. Immediately after the president's address, television news commentators pointed out that Nixon had announced no major change in the existing Vietnam policy.

On November 13, in perhaps his most memorable speech of the year, Agnew attacked the major television networks that had allowed criticism of the president's November 3 address. Agnew charged that public opinion was manipulated by "a tiny, enclosed fraternity of privileged men" who controlled the televised news medium. He said they failed to present the views of the majority of U.S. citizens. Dean Burch, chairman of the Federal Communications Commission, requested transcripts from the networks of the commentaries that followed Nixon's speech. Burch stated that Agnew's speech was a warning to the major networks but said also that he saw no signs of intimidation in either Agnew's speech or the request for the transcripts. Later Agnew broadened his attack on the press to include *The New York Times,* the *Washington Post,* and *Newsweek* magazine.

President Nixon commented that the "great silent majority" supported his Vietnam policy. As evidence he presented thousands of letters and telegrams expressing support. Also, 77% of the persons interviewed in a special Gallup Poll supported the president's policy.

The November moratorium, endorsed by Senators Charles E. Goodell and George S. McGovern, drew hundreds of thousands of protesters to Washington, D.C. The symbolic "March Against Death," with marchers carrying cards bearing the names of servicemen who had died in Vietnam, was conducted on November 14–15. Several clergymen were arrested while attempting to conduct an "Ecumenical Mass for Peace" at the Pentagon. A small band of militants provoked a confrontation with police at the Department of Justice building. In many parts of the nation, supporters of the Nixon policy displayed their feelings by driving with headlights turned on.

Attorney General John N. Mitchell stated that the demonstration was not peaceful. Other government officials, however, praised the demonstrators for their dignity and orderliness.

In the aftermath of the moratorium the Justice Department announced that some organizers of the demonstrations were being investigated for possible violations of the federal antiriot law. A group of former government officials and the deans of 11 law schools issued a statement expressing alarm at inflammatory remarks made by some Administration leaders and at attempts to discredit critics.

Earlier in the fall, criticism of the U.S. policy in Vietnam had appeared to subside. In November, however, new controversy was stirred by a report of an alleged massacre of South Vietnamese villagers by a company of U.S. soldiers. (*See* Armed Forces, U.S.: Army.)

In September the trial of the so-called "Chicago eight" began in Chicago, Ill. Federal Judge Julius J. Hoffman presided over the trial, in which eight defendants, including Abbie Hoffman, Jerry Rubin, David Dellinger, and Bobby Seale, were accused of conspiring to cross state lines to incite a riot during the 1968 Democratic National Convention.

The defense attempted to prove that the violence was caused by the Chicago police acting under the orders of Mayor Richard J. Daley. Defense witnesses testified that they saw some policemen beat, club, and kick people. (*See* Law.)

Judge Hoffman ordered the chairman of the Black Panther party, Bobby Seale, gagged and chained to his chair in the courtroom after repeated outbursts by Seale. Seale contended that he was denied constitutional rights by not being allowed to conduct his own defense. Earlier Judge Hoffman had refused to postpone the trial while Seale's attorney was recuperating from an operation. On November 5 Judge Hoffman declared a mistrial for Seale, convicted him of contempt of court, and sentenced him to four years in prison.

In October the National Guard was called into Chicago to put down a disturbance caused by the

THE 12 EXECUTIVE DEPARTMENTS

(December 1969)

Secretary of State	William P. Rogers
Secretary of the Treasury	David M. Kennedy
Secretary of Defense	Melvin R. Laird
Attorney General	John N. Mitchell
Postmaster General	Winton M. Blount
Secretary of the Interior	Walter J. Hickel
Secretary of Agriculture	Clifford M. Hardin
Secretary of Commerce	Maurice H. Stans
Secretary of Labor	George P. Shultz
Secretary of Health, Education, and Welfare	Robert H. Finch
Secretary of Housing and Urban Development	George Romney
Secretary of Transportation	John A. Volpe

New York City gave an enthusiastic welcome to the Apollo 11 astronauts in August. Edwin E. Aldrin, Jr., Michael Collins, and Neil A. Armstrong wave to the crowds.

WIDE WORLD

radical "Weatherman" faction of the Students for a Democratic Society. Hundreds of windows were broken, several persons were injured, and more than 200 demonstrators were arrested. In New York City bombs planted by other political radicals exploded in several office buildings.

The National Commission on the Causes and Prevention of Violence issued its final report in December and called for a massive national commitment to end the sociological causes of crime and violence. The commission urged a reordering of national priorities and recommended that domestic needs take precedence over military considerations. (*See also* Colleges and Universities; Crime; Economy; Employment; Vietnam. *See in* CE: United States.)

UPPER VOLTA. In 1969 the military regime of Upper Volta, undoubtedly influenced by events in neighboring Dahomey and Ghana, seriously considered restoring power to civil authorities. Upper Volta's President Sangoulé Lamizana even drew up a schedule indicating that progressive steps would be taken to restore civil rule by late 1970. (*See* Dahomey; Ghana.)

In April former President Maurice Yaméogo was brought to trial on the charge of embezzling government funds and was found guilty. In October Joseph Conombo was also tried on the same charge but was acquitted. Conombo appeared to be the sole political leader who could take power if the military withdrew in favor of a civil regime.

President Lamizana's program of economic austerity achieved a budget surplus of almost $1 million in 1969. Much of the government's debt to private business was paid, and the country's exports rose slightly. (*See in* CE: Upper Volta.)

URUGUAY. The acute economic and political disorder experienced in Uruguay during 1968 continued into 1969, highlighted by a series of paralyzing strikes, periods of emergency rule, a further deterioration of the nation's economy, and the intensification of terrorist activities by the left-wing Tupamaru National Liberation Front. Reaction by labor to a determined government program to halt Uruguay's runaway inflation and the strong political measures taken by the administration to ensure its success were largely responsible for the social unrest. Meanwhile, a British ban on Uruguayan meat imports, which resulted in an estimated $10-million loss in foreign exchange, slowed the nation's economic recovery. Together, these factors shook the foundations of Uruguay's economic stability and democratic tradition.

As a result of strikes, associated violence, and economic disruption, Uruguay was placed under a state of emergency by President Jorge Pacheco Areco on June 24. A distinct possibility existed that Uruguay's long tradition of democratic government might be in jeopardy for the first time since a short-lived military dictatorship ended in 1934. A fight for power involving the executive (with military backing) and the legislative branches of government emerged over the proper ways to bring order to the nation's chaotic political, economic, and social situation. This was underscored by political events surrounding the resignations of the labor minister in March and the minister of industry and trade in June, the 25th and 26th cabinet resignations since March 1967.

Despite the strikes, political difficulties, and terrorism, in June Finance Minister Cesár Chalone claimed that President Pacheco's stringent program for economic stabilization was paying off. The

The marketplace in Ouagadougou, Upper Volta, contains a modern shopping arcade (background) as well as the traditional street vendors' stalls and carts.
"THE NEW YORK TIMES" FROM WIDE WORLD

cost of living, which rose 136% in 1967 and 77% in 1968, was held in check. During the first half of 1969 the rate of inflation was less than 10%, as compared to 63.7% during the first half of 1968. (*See also* Latin America. *See in* CE: Uruguay.)

VENEZUELA. In 1969, for the first time in the history of Venezuela, the government changed hands peacefully—following the elections held in December 1968. Rafael Caldera Rodriguez took over the office of president from his predecessor Raúl Leoni on March 11, 1969.

Caldera initiated sweeping changes in Venezuela's foreign policy, including recognizing Latin American dictatorships and courting closer ties with Communist nations. During the year Venezuela resumed diplomatic relations with Argentina, Panama, and Peru in spite of their military regimes. Legal status was restored to the Venezuelan Communist party.

The government concentrated on bringing more revenue to Venezuela's economy by revising the national policy on foreign oil rights. Caldera announced that any new drilling operations by foreign oil companies would be on the basis of service contracts rather than concessions. The government also went ahead with plans to establish a petrochemical industry centered around Lake Maracaibo.

In an effort to eliminate the terrorist activities that have plagued Venezuela for ten years, Caldera opened talks with leftist guerrillas in April. In the fall battles erupted between soldiers and students at Central University in Caracas, the capital. The students were protesting the alleged torture and slaying of a student by antiguerrilla forces. (*See also* Latin America. *See in* CE: Venezuela.)

VETERINARY MEDICINE. Widespread efforts to eradicate foot-and-mouth disease, rinderpest, and other enzootic diseases continued in 1969. The diseases remained major deterrents to efficient production of food animals in South America, Asia, Africa, and Eastern Europe. More than 90% of Argentina's 50 million cattle were vaccinated against foot-and-mouth disease, and in Uruguay a compulsory vaccination program begun in 1968 was expected to include all cattle by the end of 1969. In Europe the overall incidence of the disease was reduced from some 12,850 farms affected in 1966 to 3,650 in 1968.

A significant stage in the ten-year program begun in 1962 to eradicate hog cholera (swine fever) in the United States was reached in July. The U.S. Department of Agriculture prohibited interstate shipment of vaccine into Puerto Rico and the 43 states that had reached the "stamping-out" phase—slaughter of all affected and in-contact animals. Although vaccination—beginning about 60 years before—had been the only means of saving the swine industry from destruction, in more recent years the vaccine had served to perpetuate the

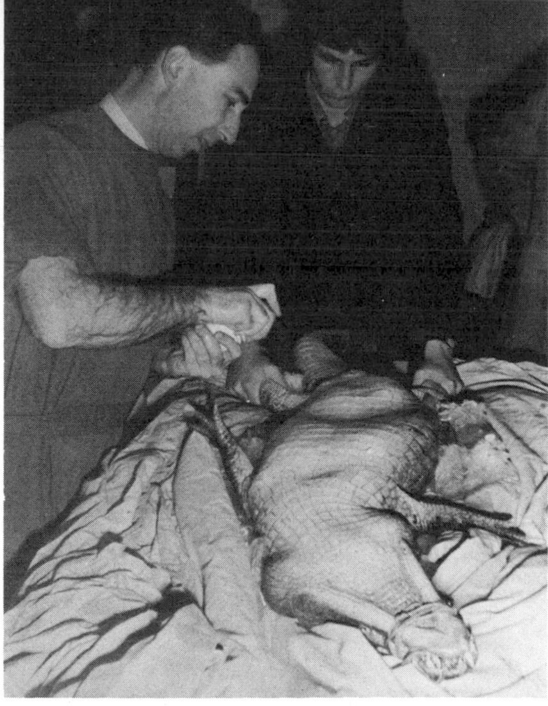

"LONDON DAILY EXPRESS" FROM PICTORIAL PARADE

English veterinary surgeons performed a risky "first" in 1969—the first heart surgery on a man-eating crocodile. Since anesthetics cannot be used on a croc, it was frozen and its jaws were tied.

disease. By August 1969, 12 states were cholera-free and 29 others nearly so. Complete eradication of the disease was expected by 1972.

Veterinarians in the United States continued to expand their activities in diverse areas, notably in laboratory-animal medicine, in aerospace research, and in projects having potential application in human medicine—such as the implantation of nuclear-powered cardiac pacemakers in dogs. The search for animals in which rare human diseases could be simulated was intensified.

A U.S. Air Force veterinarian was the first scientist at the Manned Spacecraft Center in Houston, Tex., to study the effects of lunar soil upon germ-free animals. Other veterinarians assisted in microbiological, radiological, and nutritional aspects of the space program. The Texas A & M University's College of Veterinary Medicine instituted a program for the study of fish diseases.

Increasing numbers of U.S. veterinarians served in the Peace Corps, VISTA programs, and voluntary missions. Their work ranged from providing veterinary services for Indian tribes in the Andes mountains to involvement in large-scale measures for increasing food-animal production in Africa.

The first class from the new veterinary school in Saskatchewan—the third such college in Canada—graduated in 1969. In the United States a faculty was appointed for a school in Louisiana and money appropriated for one in Florida. With a school in the planning stages in Connecticut, these would bring the total of veterinary colleges in the United States to 21, double the pre-World War II number. (*See also* Agriculture; Animals and Wildlife. *See in* CE: Diseases, Plant and Animal; Zoo.)

VIETNAM. The conflict in Vietnam between Communist and non-Communist forces continued in 1969 despite intensive peace efforts and rising opposition in the United States to U.S. involvement. In September Ho Chi Minh, the president of North Vietnam, died. Political problems, economic inflation, and Communist spies troubled the regime in South Vietnam. Hope for a negotiated settlement of the conflict dwindled during the year, and a new word, "Vietnamization," entered the vocabulary of the conflict. Late in the year a former U.S. serviceman revealed details of an alleged massacre of South Vietnamese villagers by a company of U.S. soldiers.

The North

On September 3 North Vietnam's President Ho died of a heart attack at the age of 79. September 4–11 was declared a time of mourning in North Vietnam, and in South Vietnam the Viet Cong called a three-day truce in honor of President Ho's memory. The South Vietnamese government would not honor the truce.

Notables of the Communist world attended the funeral rites in Hanoi, the capital. Communist China's Premier Chou En-lai left Hanoi before Premier Aleksei N. Kosygin of the Soviet Union arrived. President Ho's will, which was read during a memorial service, contained a request for the North Vietnamese Communist party to aid in lessening the ideological differences between the People's Republic of China and the Soviet Union that had divided the Communist world. In this final message to the people, Ho also predicted "total victory" over the government forces of South Vietnam and the "U.S. imperialists." (*See* Communist Movement.)

Soon after Ho's death Hanoi radio announced that North Vietnam would be ruled by a collective leadership. Although the members were not publicly named, many observers believed that those included were Premier Pham Van Dong; Le Duan, first secretary of the North Vietnamese Communist party; Truong Chinh, chairman of the National Assembly; and possibly Defense Minister Vo Nguyen Giap.

In December there were reports that the new government was attempting to strengthen party control over North Vietnamese life. The press accused the Communist party of poor management of national enterprises and of a lack of vigor in building socialism within North Vietnam. Some analysts speculated on the possibility that the new hard line could be a buildup to a power struggle between the North Vietnamese leaders and an eventual party purge. The rhetoric resembled that employed by Maoists during the Chinese "cultural revolution."

Food and labor shortages plagued the economy of North Vietnam during 1969. In November the economic ministries were reorganized and emphasis was placed on centralizing many operations. In

In Hue, South Vietnam, young boys and girls go through a "self-defense" night training course. Such self-defense units were formed beginning in 1968 after the Tet offensive. The units enrolled an estimated one million persons by the fall of 1969.

WIDE WORLD

WIDE WORLD

Some 385 houses were destroyed in Bo Kinh hamlet, in South Vietnam, in a raging battle in May. Some Vietnamese children contemplate the ruins of their hamlet. At least 19 civilians were killed and 50 wounded.

urban areas a youthful subculture similar to that of Western hippies was reported to have arisen in recent months.

During 1969 the North Vietnamese government managed to keep in suspense the families of about 1,300 U.S. servicemen, thought to be held as prisoners of war. The North Vietnamese released three U.S. prisoners on August 4, following a July 3 announcement that prisoners would be released as a humanitarian gesture and in recognition of the U.S. Independence Day.

In June U.S. Senator J. W. Fulbright (D, Ark.) sent a secret letter to President Ho asking for a list of the U.S. prisoners. Ho refused the request, saying the issue of prisoners could not be considered separately from the settlement of the conflict based on the Communist plan. A U.S. antiwar group and the Rev. Paul D. Lindstrom of the Remember the *Pueblo* Committee both released lists of prisoners allegedly sent from North Vietnam through private sources. Department of Defense officials, however, said the lists were meaningless because the information was outdated and up to five years old. The North Vietnamese would not agree to a prisoner exchange because they continued to deny the presence of North Vietnamese troops in South Vietnam.

The South

During the year there were some new political developments in South Vietnam. President Nguyen Van Thieu reversed his previous position by announcing that his government was willing to enter into direct negotiations with the Viet Cong and that the National Liberation Front (NLF)—the political arm of the Viet Cong—could compete in South Vietnam's elections. Thieu, however, was strongly opposed to a coalition government with the Communists.

In June the NLF established a provisional revolutionary government, declaring itself to be the legitimate ruler of South Vietnam. On July 11 President Thieu called on the Communists to compete in free elections supervised by an international commission. The NLF responded to all of Thieu's proposals by reiterating their demand that the "puppet regime" in Saigon, the capital, be dissolved before any further action could be taken.

Aware of the NLF's efforts to expand its political base, President Thieu sought to improve his government's position among the masses. His first step was the creation of the National Social Democratic Front to bring together the deeply divided political elements in a non-Communist alliance. Only six major parties were able to unite under Thieu's plan, primarily conservatives and hard-line refugees from North Vietnam. Even this unity, however, was short-lived, and Thieu recognized the need for further steps to broaden his political base.

In August Premier Tran Van Huong resigned his post under pressure from Thieu. Huong was replaced by Gen. Tran Thien Khiem. In July Thieu had announced that a major reshuffle of the cabinet would be undertaken. He stated that politicians of "real force" would be added to the government.

On September 1 Thieu announced the formation of a new 31-man cabinet, the largest in the nation's history. It included 6 members from the military, 16 bureaucratic functionaries, and 9 members of the old cabinet. Notably absent from the new administration were members of the Buddhist elements and representatives of the non-Communist opposition. It was felt that the new cabinet actually represented a narrower political base.

In November, 43 persons were tried on charges of being Communist spies. Among those on trial were President Thieu's special assistant for political affairs and Vu Ngoc Nha, who was reported to have close ties with the president.

Supplies are dropped on a remote airstrip in South Vietnam by a U.S. Air Force C-130. By making such parachute drops, the huge C-130 can deliver supplies to bases where the airstrips could accommodate only smaller planes.

PICTORIAL PARADE

WIDE WORLD

A military version of the U.S. motorcycle gang was employed on an experimental basis in South Vietnam in 1969. Four "bike" riders of the U.S. 25th Infantry Division check with their platoon leader in the jeep. The four are about to embark on a reconnaissance patrol near Tay Ninh, South Vietnam.

The economy of South Vietnam in 1969 continued to be caught up in a serious inflation. The U.S. government pressured the South Vietnamese to curb the inflation, and $40 million in U.S. aid was withheld during April and May. The South Vietnamese agreed to reduce imports of luxury items and to increase imports of essential products. Also, they levied tariffs to equalize the prices of imports from different foreign sources.

In October heavy duties were imposed on about a thousand luxury imports in an effort to reduce the national budget deficit. Overnight the price of a small car rose from about $4,000 to almost $19,000. An undesirable result of the new luxury taxes was an immediate ten-point rise in the price index, bringing the cost of living to 30% higher than in 1968. On October 31 President Thieu made an emotional plea for austerity.

A Round Table

On January 16, after weeks of negotiating the issue, the participants in the peace talks being held at Paris, France, finally decided on the shape of the conference table, and the expanded talks began. On January 20 U.S. President Richard M. Nixon replaced the chief U.S. negotiator, W. Averell Harriman, with Henry Cabot Lodge.

The first serious proposals were presented in May. The NLF presented a ten-point program calling for the unconditional withdrawal of U.S. forces, free elections, a new South Vietnamese constitution, a coalition government, and a policy of neutrality for South Vietnam.

In response President Nixon outlined an eight-point program calling for the phased withdrawal of all non-South Vietnamese troops, for the confinement of any remaining troops to designated base areas, and for free elections. The moves proposed by Nixon were to be carried out under the supervision of an international body.

The NLF denounced Nixon's plan as "unjust and unreasonable" but did not completely reject it. The areas of possible understanding in the two offers, however, were too narrow to allow development of a basis for serious negotiation.

In October the North Vietnamese proposed secret two-way peace talks between the United States and the new provisional revolutionary government of South Vietnam. Lodge rejected the proposal, but said that the United States would agree to secret four-way talks. The Communist side remained firm in its position, and a new impasse developed. Each side blamed the other for the lack of progress at the peace table. On November 20 Lodge resigned as the chief U.S. negotiator, and at the end of 1969 Nixon had not yet named Lodge's successor.

Vietnamization

Noting the lack of progress at the Paris peace talks the United States earnestly began its program of "Vietnamization." In March U.S. Secretary of Defense Melvin R. Laird first announced that additional funds would be requested for a plan to modernize the South Vietnamese forces. The object was to replace U.S. troops with South Vietnamese troops. United States military commanders in the field were instructed to keep casualties to an absolute minimum.

President Nixon publicly defined the Vietnamization plan in his televised speech on November 3. Troop withdrawals, however, began earlier in the year. The first withdrawal announcement, involving 25,000 U.S. troops, was made by Nixon during talks with President Thieu on Midway island in June. In September Nixon announced that 35,000 more U.S. military personnel would be pulled out by December 15. Later in December 50,000 U.S. troops were scheduled to be withdrawn from Vietnam by April 15, 1970. A timetable for further withdrawals was suggested by Nixon in his November 3 speech, but he did not give any details. He said the unannounced withdrawal schedule would depend on the level of North Vietnamese infiltration and on the reduction of U.S. casualties.

Thieu objected to the term "Vietnamization" because he felt it implied that all the fighting was being done by U.S. troops. In September Thieu declared that it would be impossible for South Vietnamese troops to replace all U.S. troops by the end of 1970, as had earlier been suggested. The U.S. commanders felt that all U.S. ground troops could safely be withdrawn by mid-1971. In the last six months of 1969, South Vietnamese forces were increased by 88,000 men.

Vietnamization was unsatisfactory to some critics of the Nixon Administration on the grounds that the plan would not end the basic conflict in South Vietnam. Other critics of the plan wanted an immediate withdrawal of U.S. troops. Harriman objected to Nixon's reasoning that a Communist-led massacre would result if U.S. troops were immediately withdrawn on the grounds "there's a massacre going on right now." The North Vietnamese and the Viet Cong also denounced the slow withdrawal as a means of prolonging the U.S. "occupation" of South Vietnam.

Realities of Conflict

Battle actions were irregular during the year and seemed to be related to political events and to the Paris peace talks. Military activity was relatively low until after Tet, the Lunar New Year, in February. The day after the Tet holiday ended Communist forces launched mortar attacks on more than a hundred cities, towns, and military targets, including Saigon. About 300 U.S. soldiers and 6,000 Communist troops were killed. There was speculation that the action was staged to strengthen the Communist bargaining position in Paris.

Of all the major battles in 1969, the one that commanded the most attention in the United States was the fight for "Hamburger Hill," or Ap Bia Mountain, in the A Shau Valley. The peak was seized by U.S. forces in a ten-day battle that resulted in at least 50 dead and 270 wounded U.S. troops. It came at a time of de-escalatory gestures when U.S. commanders were under orders to hold casualties to a minimum. The battle for the hill began on May 10, and on May 28 the U.S. troops abandoned the hill, which was eventually reoccupied by the North Vietnamese. Senator Edward M. Kennedy (D, Mass.) denounced the effort as "senseless and irresponsible."

Early in the fall there was a lull in enemy actions that in some areas amounted almost to a cease-fire. Enemy action increased again in November with significant attacks on South Vietnamese troops.

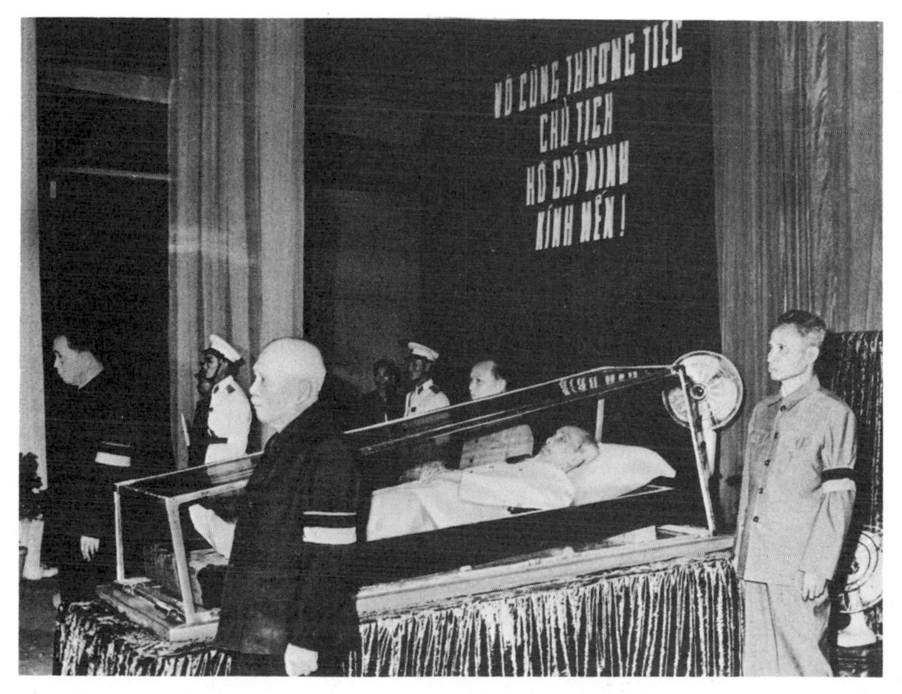

North Vietnam's President Ho Chi Minh lies in state in Hanoi. He died in September. Premier Pham Van Dong (right) and other party and government officials serve as an honor guard.

INTERFOTO MTI, HUNGARY—PIX FROM PUBLIX

This was thought to be a reaction against Nixon's Vietnamization plan. Toward the end of the year South Vietnamese deaths were about 80% higher than those of other allied troops. By the end of 1969 the total number of U.S. troops killed in the Vietnam conflict since Jan. 1, 1961, had risen to more than 39,700.

In November an account of an alleged massacre of South Vietnamese villagers by U.S. soldiers became public. Soldiers who had participated in the alleged massacre in March 1968 then came forward and told how unarmed women, children, and old men had been rounded up and shot by U.S. soldiers. An Army photographer released pictures showing dead bodies at My Lai 4 hamlet in the village of Song My, site of the alleged incident. Agents of the U.S. Army's Criminal Investigation Division found three mass graves at My Lai and a ditch full of bodies and estimated that between 450 and 500 people had been killed. (*See also* Armed Forces, U.S. *See in* CE: Vietnam.)

WEATHER. The Global Atmospheric Research Program (GARP), the investigative side of the World Weather Program, reached major milestones in 1969. Early in the year, research ships from the United States, Great Britain, and West Germany conducted extensive air-sea boundary-layer measurements in the Atlantic trade-wind belt, and they also tested sensors and data systems needed for a larger undertaking in the tropical Atlantic.

The latter experiment—called BOMEX (Barbados Oceanographic and Meteorological Experiment)—was led by the Environmental Science Services Administration (ESSA) of the U.S. Department of Commerce. Participants included 7 federal agencies, 22 universities, 6 industrial laboratories, and the government of Barbados. Data were gathered by aircraft, ships, satellites, and buoys from a parcel of atmosphere and ocean covering 90,000 square miles from the sea floor to an altitude of 100,000 feet. A larger, follow-up experiment was planned for the 1970's; it was expected to be conducted in the Pacific Ocean. (*See* Earth Sciences.)

Changing the Weather; ESSA

Progress was also made in weather-modification experiments. During the 1968–69 winter, the effects of seeding upon lake-effect snowstorms—which deliver enormous quantities of snow to the lee shores of some Great Lakes each winter—were investigated. Hurricane Debbie was also seeded with silver iodide; analysis of its effects, however, remained incomplete at year-end.

ESSA 9, the last of a series of first-generation operational weather satellites, was launched in February. An infrared spectrometer aboard the Nimbus 3 satellite provided the first vertical temperature profiles of the atmosphere ever obtained from a satellite.

Bad Weather

The winter of 1968–69 was one of the worst of record across the northern states. This "year of the big snows" brought the coldest temperatures in 40 years to Oregon and the coldest winter in 90 years to Helena, Mont. Sioux Falls, S.D., had a record 95-inch season snowfall, and a 100-year-old record for snowfall was broken in New England.

The Pacific coast received unusually heavy rainfall in January and February. Catastrophic flooding and mudslides accompanied the rains in Southern California, where stations reported rainfall as much as 800% above normal.

Winter's heavy snowfall brought extensive spring floods to the Midwest. Although considerable damage was done, early warnings permitted sub-

A mud slide, loosened by recent winter floods, covered one side of the Pomona Freeway near Los Angeles, Calif., on Feb. 13, 1969. The driver of the car caught in the slide was released by other motorists.

WIDE WORLD

WIDE WORLD

Abandoned cars remained stranded in snowdrifts on the intersection of the Belt Parkway and Van Wyck Expressway in New York City's Borough of Queens the morning after a massive snowstorm hit the area on Feb. 10, 1969, completely disrupting movement in the city.

stantial deflection of any potential flood disaster.

Hurricane Camille, the most violent tropical storm ever recorded on the U.S. mainland, struck the Gulf coast in mid-August, causing widespread destruction and more than 200 deaths. Camille's remnants, combining with other storms near the Virginia-West Virginia boundary, brought torrential rains and catastrophic flash floods to the Appalachian foothills and the James River basin early in the morning of August 20, killing more than 100 persons and causing extensive damage.

Seasonal floods plagued Brazil, Chile, Venezuela, and Mexico, and storms brought disastrous flooding to coastal India and South Korea. An April day in Pakistan brought a destructive hurricane that killed more than 500 and injured thousands, according to reports, causing heavy damage as well. A day later "a dreadful tornado" caused deaths reported in the hundreds. Other destructive typhoons struck the Philippines, Japan, and Taiwan. (*See also* Disasters of 1969; Space Exploration. *See in* CE: Weather.)

WEST INDIES. The odd assortment of islands that make up the West Indies experienced in 1969 the usual diversity of conditions, ranging from peace and prosperity to poverty and revolt. The small island of Anguilla became a problem for Great Britain, and social problems caused unrest on Curaçao. The Bahamas, however, were in a period of unusual financial growth.

The British Are Coming

On March 19 a task force of British paratroopers invaded Anguilla. The Anguillans offered no armed resistance, but anti-British sentiment ran high among the island's native population.

The events that led to the 1969 invasion began in 1967 when Anguilla unilaterally withdrew from the associated state of St. Kitts-Nevis-Anguilla and declared itself an independent republic. In a referendum held in February 1969 the islanders voted to break all ties with Great Britain and elected Ronald Webster as the island's acting president. In March Great Britain decided to restore "lawful government" to Anguilla and sent a British official, William Whitlock, to Anguilla with a proposition to install a British administrator to run the island's affairs while the Anguillans worked out their difficulties. The proposal was not popular with the Anguillans.

Whitlock claimed he was forced off the island by an armed band of U.S. Mafia-style gangsters. Webster denied any gangster influence on the island. Nevertheless, Great Britain launched the invasion and also left itself open to critics who pointed out that the British had not intervened militarily in the larger nation of Rhodesia, which—like Anguilla—had proclaimed unilateral independence.

After the invasion a British commissioner was sent to govern Anguilla. The commissioner and Webster, who represented the Anguillans, finally came to an agreement, pledging mutual cooperation. (*See* Commonwealth of Nations.)

Rioting broke out on the island of Curaçao in the Netherlands Antilles during the year. Political rivalries, inflation, and increasing unemployment created the tensions that exploded into violence, causing an estimated $40 million damage to the town of Willemstad, the capital of Curaçao.

Boom Islands

The Bahamas continued to prosper in 1969 as a result of the growing tourist trade and a real-estate boom. An estimated 500,000 tourists visited Grand Bahama Island during the year. The land boom that began in the mid-1960's after the opening of gambling casinos reached new heights in 1969. Land on Paradise Island, across from Nassau, the capital of the Bahamas, sold for as much as $300,000 an acre.

The real-estate boom aided the construction industry, which in turn provided new employment opportunities. During the year an additional 2,500 hotel rooms were either planned or under construction at Freeport.

A hotel chain based in Great Britain announced plans during the year to construct hotels in the Caribbean area at a cost of up to $28.8 million. Barbados, Jamaica, Grenada, and St. Lucia were among the islands proposed for the new hotel sites.

In March Barbados joined the Inter-American Development Bank. Jamaica, while retaining economic ties with Cuba, was accepted as the 24th member of the Organization of American States (OAS). Barbados and Trinidad and Tobago were already members. Trinidad, in fact, hosted two important meetings of the OAS during the year. All of these activities were symbolic of the growing involvement and participation of the West Indies region in Latin American and hemispheric affairs. (*See also* Cuba; Jamaica; Puerto Rico. *See in* CE: West Indies.)

CAMERA PRESS—PIX FROM PUBLIX

Harold Wilson, prime minister of Great Britain, looks weary as he addresses Parliament during a year filled with economic problems.

WILSON, HAROLD. "It was the best of times, it was the worst of times" for Harold Wilson, prime minister of Great Britain, in 1969. His triumph came in the balance-of-payments surplus at the end of the year—a goal he had pursued with an almost religious fervor since taking office in 1964. His troubles took many forms.

For the first time Wilson faced a real threat to his power. There was opposition within his own Labor party and from the unions when he backed legal measures to curb the wildcat strikes that paralyzed trade and services in Britain throughout the year. Challenging him was Home Secretary James Callaghan, a man with powerful union support.

After a series of financial crises, Wilson's popularity poll ratings slipped; the discontented "man on the street" chafed under spiraling taxes, soaring interest rates, scarce credit, and austerity spending designed to pull Great Britain out of the red-ink column. The Labor government lost election after election at local levels, retaining control in virtually no city of any size.

However, as the year ended, British reserves were up $2.52 billion, some foreign debts had been paid, and Wilson's tactics had brought Britain back to prestige in international financial circles. France had promised to negotiate by mid-1970 on Britain's entry into the European Economic Community, or Common Market; and Labor's prestige climbed. Wilson was expected to call elections in 1970 rather than wait for the April 1971 deadline. (*See also* Great Britain and Northern Ireland, United Kingdom of. *See in* CE: Wilson, Harold.)

WORLD TRADE. During 1969 the revival of economic growth among the major industrial nations that was initiated in 1968 continued to contribute to the acceleration of world trade. At the beginning of 1969 the total volume of world trade was growing at a rate of 13%, compared to a rate of 5% in 1967.

Such a healthy trade situation theoretically might have led to a universal relaxation of commercial policies. However, several of the major industrial nations were struggling to overcome an unfavorable balance of payments and were reluctant to ease policies appreciably. The United States and Great Britain were able to boast trade surpluses only in the latter quarters of the year after registering deficits during the early months of 1969. The balance of payments in France, which had been weakened by a run on the franc beginning in the summer of 1968, was still deteriorating. West Germany, on the other hand, continued to amass a sizable trade surplus—though the October revaluation of the mark threatened to reduce export traffic by making West German products less competitive.

Trade Activities and Policies of the Industrial Nations

At the end of the third quarter, the United States had accumulated a trade surplus that was larger than the surplus on hand during the same period in 1968 but was small by traditional standards. Ex-

IVEY, FROM BEN ROTH AGENCY

A Texas cattle rancher prepares his cattle for air transport to Chile, where they were sent to help alleviate a serious beef shortage.
WIDE WORLD

ports reached an annual rate of $36.85 billion and imports an annual rate of $35.78 billion. The increase in both imports and exports for the first three quarters was 9%. The figure, however, indicated a dramatic falloff in import demand. During a comparable period in 1968, imports had grown by 23%.

During the year U.S. trade policies indicated a willingness to establish freer commerce with the Communist bloc of nations. In July U.S. President Richard M. Nixon announced that the United States would unilaterally ease a 19-year-old trade curb that had barred Communist Chinese goods from entering the country. Beginning on July 23, U.S. tourists were permitted to bring home $100 worth of products from China's mainland.

By year-end, trade restrictions had been relaxed even further. The $100 maximum was completely removed and regulations loosened to allow foreign subsidiaries of U.S. firms to trade with Communist China in nonstrategic goods such as radios or razor blades. Restrictions on banks, insurance companies, and transport companies located in other foreign countries against dealing with Chinese Communists were also lifted.

In December the U.S. Congress passed a new version of the Export Control Act that extended the authority of the president to control export legislation. Under the new law, which would be in effect until July 1971, a list of commodities that require export licenses for security reasons would come up for reevaluation. Many items are expected to be removed from the list, an action that will lead to more open trade with Communist nations.

In September President Nixon asked the U.S. Tariff Commission to look into the effect on the balance of payments of the tariff privileges granted on the reentry of American goods shipped abroad for processing, finishing, or assembly. The primary concern was over transportation equipment returned from Canada, West Germany, Sweden, and Great Britain.

West Germany, in an effort to reduce its huge payments surplus, bought proportionately more from other countries and sold proportionately less during 1969. In the first half of the year, it registered $12 billion in imports, up $4.5 billion from the same period in 1968. At the same time, its exports stood at $13.5 billion, up from $11.5 billion in the first half of 1968.

One of the most significant areas of expansion was in trade with East Germany. At the end of the second quarter the volume of trade between the two nations was at an annual rate of $875 million, compared to $725 million in 1968. This represented an increase of 20.6%.

Canada put into full effect the tariff reductions agreed to in the "Kennedy round" of negotiations under the General Agreement on Tariffs and Trade. Although the reductions were not due to come into force until 1972, they were made effective in June in an effort to contain rising Canadian manufacturing costs. The act reduced duties on $2 billion worth of imports by 3%.

In October the Japanese government conferred with representatives of the U.S. government to discuss liberalizing trade between the two nations. The talks produced only limited concessions that were not wholly satisfactory to the United States. Among the products discussed were grapefruit, tangerines, lima beans, helicopters, light aircraft, and diesel engines. In the past, the United States had exported much more to Japan than it imported from Japan. However, the situation was recently reversed when Japan piled up a $1-billion surplus in trade with the United States during 1968.

The Communist Nations

On the whole, established attitudes toward foreign trade prevailed within the Communist bloc throughout 1969. The Soviet Union remained basically self-sufficient, and while the other countries of Eastern Europe tended to rely more on foreign trade, trading was primarily with the Soviet Union. However, a number of advances were made toward loosening trade policies with other nations.

Communist China signed a one-year pact with Japan that provided for $70 million in foreign trade; this was a drop of over 30% from 1968. As in the preceding year, the actual value of trade between the two countries was expected to be far in excess of the sum agreed upon. In 1968 China sold almost $225 million in goods to Japan while buying $325 million.

At a meeting of the Communist bloc's Council for Mutual Economic Assistance (Comecon) in the spring, the Soviet Union withdrew its objections to expanded exchanges between its East European allies and West Germany. Trade between Moscow and Bonn during the year was thought to be in excess of the $567-million figure recorded in 1968.

During the spring Peru signed trade pacts with the Soviet Union and Bulgaria. The South American country hailed the agreements as major advances in expanding its foreign trade. In the past, 50% of Peru's foreign commerce had been with the United States.

A thaw in Soviet-Iranian relations produced a sizable increase in Iran's export trade. In mid-1969, trade with Eastern Europe accounted for approximately 27% of Iran's exports and 7% of its imports.

International and Regional Trade Organizations

The European Economic Community (EEC), or Common Market, which had been plagued by high agricultural prices and great commodity surpluses, agreed to a common farm-support policy shortly before year-end. The farm supports will be financed mainly by contributions from national treasuries during 1970. Following that will be a four-year transition period during which members will pay to the common farm fund all the proceeds of levies on agricultural imports. The proportion of customs duties on industrial goods paid into the community budget will also be gradually increased. The achievement of the farm agreement lifted the last procedural roadblock to Great Britain's entry into the EEC. (*See* Europe.)

In March Morocco signed an accord of association with the EEC after nearly six years of negotiations. Under the accord, about 75% of existing Moroccan exports to EEC members get preferential treatment or tariff concessions. In return, Morocco agreed to grant tariff and quota concessions to the members of the EEC for manufactured goods. The new status as an associate member of the EEC was especially advantageous to Morocco because it gave the country an advantage over its two strongest competitors in the production of citrus fruit—Spain and Israel—neither of which had yet signed accords with the EEC.

A new container terminal was opened on Jan. 15, 1969, in Duisburg, West Germany, on the Rhine, to further facilitate world trade.

DPA FROM PICTORIAL PARADE

In July the EEC renewed an agreement for an association with 18 African states to extend over another five-year period. Under the terms of the convention, the EEC will make a grant totaling $1 billion to the European Development Fund. Although the sum is 25% higher than the amount allocated over the preceding five years, it was considerably lower than the $1.5 billion that the African states had requested.

In November the 18 members of the Organization for Economic Cooperation and Development (OECD) submitted proposals for special tariff preferences to developing nations. The preferences would help to attract industry to the poor countries, provide jobs, and contribute to the national income. The proposals were part of a long-range plan to help the less developed countries increase their national wealth.

A treaty for the establishment of a Nordic customs union, Nordek, was drawn up in mid-July but was not to be considered for approval until February 1970. The nations involved—Sweden, Denmark, Norway, and Finland—faced a number of obstacles in reaching an agreement. Norway and Denmark, both applicants for membership in the EEC, felt that Nordek membership might be an impediment to getting into the EEC. They also believed that Nordek was designed to favor the interests of industrial Sweden while neglecting problems of farm surpluses in Denmark and fish prices in Norway. Sweden and Finland, both neutral nations, enthusiastically favored the alliance. (*See also* Europe; Sweden.)

Latin American Trade

The Central American Common Market recorded a 25% increase in trade over 1968. However, the year was marked by internal dissent. Costa Rica failed to follow the Protocol of San José, under which each member nation was required to increase import duties by 30% on luxury goods originating outside of the area. Nicaragua cited Costa Rica's violation to justify its reinstatement of duties on products from member nations. Nicaragua's action, taken in an effort to reverse an unfavorable balance-of-payments position, brought retaliatory measures from other member nations.

In September representatives of the government banks and fiscal institutions of 18 Latin American countries met to take steps toward integrating their economies and expanding trade. In the Santo Domingo Pact, the nations agreed that their central banks would come to the aid of one another when shortages of funds were brought about by trading among members. The group also worked on plans for the development of a Latin American traveler's check and for the establishment of machinery to enable member nations to clear each other's trade debits and credits. (*See also* Feature Article: "China and the United States: Distorted Images"; Latin America; Money and International Finance. *See in* CE: International Trade.)

YEMEN.

After almost seven years of intermittent civil war, Yemen experienced a year of relative peace and stability in 1969. Leaders of Yemen's republican regime, which had been fighting royalist forces since an Egyptian-supported army coup had overthrown the monarchy in 1962, declared that the civil war had ended.

Only minor tribal skirmishes continued around the former royalist stronghold of Sa'ada in the north. Saudi Arabian aid to the royalists was withheld during most of the year, though in November the republicans accused Saudi Arabia of stirring up new trouble in the north, and there were reports that Saudi Arabia had resumed supplying arms and money to the royalists. At an Islamic summit meeting in Morocco in September mediation between Yemeni republicans and Saudi Arabia's King Faisal was attempted, but the king refused to recognize the republican government on the grounds that it was not freely chosen by the Yemeni people. (*See also* Middle East; Saudi Arabia.)

The New National Assembly

Yemen ended one thousand years of religious, colonial, and military rule in March when the National Assembly was formed as the beginning of parliamentary government. Two thirds of the assembly's 45 members were elected; the other third was appointed. Members included tribal chiefs, military and business leaders, and educated youths. An additional 12 seats were left vacant for representatives of Southern Yemen, with which Yemen still hopes to unite in spite of opposition to such unity by the Southern Yemeni regime.

The National Assembly elected a three-man republican Presidential Council that included President Abdul Rahman al-Iryani, Gen. Hassan al-Amri, a republican center group leader and former premier, and Muhammad Ali Uthman. Al-Iryani remained in the presidency in spite of a constitutional provision requiring the office to rotate among members of the council. As premier, General Al-Amri formed a new government, but after a disagreement over policies of reconciliation with the royalists, he resigned in July. A new cabinet was formed in September by Abdullah al-Karshumi, a former minister of communications.

Other News, Foreign and Domestic

In domestic matters the Al-Iryani government directed its efforts toward building internal strength to prevent the kind of extreme leftist take-overs that had occurred in Southern Yemen and Sudan. Some opposition from Soviet-trained army officers and leftist exiles in Aden had to be dealt with during the year.

In foreign affairs the government attempted to reduce its dependence on the Communist bloc and to reestablish relations with Western nations under a policy of friendly nonalignment. Normal relations were established with West Germany, which provided Yemen with a $5-million development loan. Diplomatic efforts to obtain financial aid and diplomatic recognition from other Western nations were unsuccessful.

In spite of the attitude of Western governments, Yemen's economic activity increased in 1969 as private Western businesses began to take advantage of renewed stability. However, a severe drought was expected to affect agricultural production for the year. (*See also* Southern Yemen. *See in* CE: Yemen.)

YOUTH ORGANIZATIONS. In the United States youth organizations continued to gain in membership during 1969. Many redirected their policics and programs with thc aim of increasing their members' interest in contemporary concerns.

Boys' Clubs of America

The Boys' Clubs of America in 1969 inaugurated new programs—including job counseling and training—to aid inner-city youths. Employing more than 3,000 full-time salaried professional workers, the clubs reached more youngsters than ever before. The number of clubs increased at the rate of one per week as the organization spent more than $30 million on new construction and development in an effort to keep pace with the need for new facilities. As the year drew to a close, more than 850 Boys' Clubs were providing daily services and guidance to well over 850,000 youngsters in more than 500 cities and towns.

In March, Perry J. Ludy, 17, a top student and all-state athlete from Oxnard, Calif., was the first Negro to become the Boy of the Year in the 23-year history of the award. The award was presented by U.S. President Richard M. Nixon, who at the start of the year had stepped down after four years as Boys' Clubs board chairman. He was succeeded by business executive A. L. Cole; John L. Burns was named president, and A. Boyd Hinds continued as national director.

Boy Scouts of America

The Boy Scouts of America reelected Irving Feist, a national realtor, as its president at the National Council's 59th annual meeting, held at Boston, Mass., in May. Gilbert R. Pirrung was reelected international commissioner, and Robert W. Reneker and Roger Firestone were named vice-presidents.

The emphasis of the annual meeting was implementation of Boypower '76, a long-range plan launched January 1. Its goals were to increase Boy Scout membership by 50%, involve a representative one third of U.S. boys in Scouting, penetrate poverty areas, and provide an improved program "relevant to the needs of today's youth."

Honor medals—awarded to Scouts who have demonstrated unusual heroism in efforts to save lives—were presented by aquanaut-astronaut M. Scott Carpenter to John W. Borkowski, Jr., of Baltimore, Md.; Nelson Crosby of Marcus Hook, Pa.; and Michael DeMauro of Princeton, N.J. Ten men received awards for outstanding service to boyhood.

Late in July more than 33,000 Scouts and leaders attended the 7th National Jamboree. It was held at Farragut State Park, in Idaho. (*See in* CE: Boy Scouts of America.)

Camp Fire Girls

Membership in the Camp Fire Girls totaled more than 600,000 in 1969. The organization's program was carried out by more than 400 chartered councils and associations in all 50 states.

The results of a Metropolitan Critical Areas Project, tested in highly congested urban areas, led

Mayor Carl B. Stokes of Cleveland, Ohio, urges the YMCA to form "Youth Now" organizations during the 1969 YMCA convention in St. Louis, Mo.

COURTESY, YMCA

to the incorporation into the Camp Fire Girls of special services to meet the needs of low-income girls living in restricting neighborhoods. A creative-arts project generated art exhibits across the nation. (*See in* CE: Camp Fire Girls.)

4-H Clubs

As 4-H Club membership increased across the United States in 1969, the number of Head-Heart-Hands-Health youth in towns and cities grew markedly. Of a total of nearly 3.5 million members, nearly one in three lived in a town or metropolitan area, more than one in three in a rural nonfarm area, and about one in three on a farm. Members represented all cultural and economic backgrounds.

About one of every 11 members received special recognition for outstanding work during the year. Some 1,650, for example, received expense-paid trips to the National 4-H Congress in Chicago, Ill. Of these, 220 received national 4-H college scholarships with an aggregate value of $150,000.

In April, 225 top-ranking 4-H Club members—four to five from each of the 50 states, the District of Columbia, and Puerto Rico met in Washington, D.C., for the 39th National 4-H Conference. The delegates suggested and considered methods for expanding 4-H in town as well as country and reviewed issues and programs. During the year about 700 4-Hers had experiences as International Farm Youth exchangees and as members of Teen Caravans abroad. At year-end 4-H Clubs existed in some 75 nations around the world. (*See in* CE: 4-H Clubs.)

Future Farmers of America

In 1969 membership in the Future Farmers of America (FFA), the national organization of vocational-agriculture students, totaled more than 449,000. Members belonged to nearly 8,500 high-school chapters in all states except Alaska, in Puerto Rico, the Virgin Islands, and Guam.

At their 42d national convention, FFA members voted to allow female membership in the national organization, sharing all rights and privileges, and to establish an alumni category of membership. Harry Wayne Birdwell, 20, of Fletcher, Okla., was elected 1969–70 national president.

Winners of the FFA's most coveted awards—the Star Farmer and the Star Agri-Businessman of America—were Oscar J. Manbeck, a 21-year-old dairy farmer from Bethel, Pa., and Ken Dunagan, 20, a custom sprayer and harvester operator from Willcox, Ariz. Each received a $1,000 cash award.

In 1969 the FFA initiated a student-exchange program. In the first year, 31 FFA members were placed on farms in eight European countries, while 44 foreign students were received on U.S. farms. (*See in* CE: Future Farmers of America.)

Future Homemakers of America

Membership in the Future Homemakers of America (FHA) rose to 604,000 in 1969, making the FHA the largest U.S. youth organization devoted to vocational and technical education. Its annual national meeting, held in July on the campus of Colorado State University, was attended by 2,000 youth delegates and 400 adult advisers from across the country.

COURTESY, YWCA

Representatives from (left to right) Ethiopia, the United States, and Malaysia discuss geography. They took part in the leadership program of the International Training Institute of the YWCA in the United States.

Luck Hendrix, a 17-year-old high-school senior from Metter, Ga., was elected FHA national president for 1969–70. Regional and major-program vice-presidents and administrative officers were also chosen.

Girls Clubs of America

In 1969, its 24th year, the Girls Clubs of America, Inc., offered approximately 100,000 school-age girls opportunities for education and recreation not available elsewhere in their communities. Its 157 Girls Club centers, or clubhouses, across the nation were located largely in crowded urban areas.

Nine members of the organization received national awards for citizenship, art, sewing, and cooking. Eight college scholarships were awarded to girls in the Career Key program.

For a third year the Girls Clubs continued its "Fit for Life" physical-fitness program, offering both exercise and basic information on health and nutrition. The program was expanded to include courses for adults and training for new instructors. For 1970, the organization's 25th year, Girls Clubs throughout the United States prepared to carry out youth-planned community-service projects in their communities.

Girl Scouts of the United States of America

Membership in the Girl Scouts totaled more than 3,750,000 in 1969. Included were some 3,160,000 Scouts and about 600,000 adults. During the year the Girl Scouts expanded their efforts to reach more members of minority groups, to provide assistance to the poor and elderly in urban areas, and to promote conservation.

COURTESY, BOYS' CLUBS OF AMERICA

President Nixon congratulates Perry J. Ludy of Oxnard, Calif., who received the 1969 Boy of the Year award from the Boys' Clubs of America.

Girl Scouts in Cleveland, Ohio—in cooperation with Boy Scouts—planned and conducted a camping program for a group of inner-city children. Girl Scout camping facilities were employed. Among those attending dedication ceremonies at a new Girl Scout camp near Cuba, N.M., were members of Junior Girl Scout Troop 72 from Lukachukai on the Navajo reservation west of Window Rock, Ariz. At a day camp near Phoenix, Ariz., a Navajo instructor taught Girl Scouts how to make Indian bread.

In the central cities, Girl Scout volunteers worked among the poor and elderly. The youthful volunteers provided such services as shopping, washing and ironing, and assistance in personal grooming.

The new Girl Scout National Center West near Worland, Wyo., was the site of an "All States Rendezvous" in 1969. During the summer of 1970, when the new center was to operate continuously for two months, it was expected to serve some 4,000 Girl Scouts. (*See in* CE: Girl Scouts.)

Junior Achievement

More than 145,000 high-school students operated 6,900 miniature business enterprises during the 1968–69 program year of Junior Achievement. During the year the nonprofit business-education program celebrated its 50th anniversary. It expanded to 20 cities a pilot project, begun in 1968, for educating and training inner-city youths who are considered potential high-school dropouts.

Nearly 1,400 teen-agers from city ghettos, both black and white, participated in an expanded Junior Achievement summer program. For a period of eight weeks, the program provided summer employment for participants, as well as instruction in the workings of a private-enterprise economy.

More than 2,000 Achievers, representing all 50 states, attended the organization's 26th annual conference at Indiana University. Gregory Perczak of Chicago, Ill., was named President of the Year. Leslie Marchello of Omaha, Neb., was selected as Miss Junior Achievement. Helco, a New Orleans, La., Junior Achievement company, was named Company of the Year.

Young Men's Christian Association

The Young Men's Christian Association (YMCA) in 1969 celebrated the 125th anniversary of its founding with its first national convention, held in St. Louis, Mo., in June. The 5,500 delegates—including some 1,000 youths—considered means of modifying YMCA programs to meet contemporary needs. Meeting just before the convention, the YMCA's National Council voted to raise its membership from 60 to 75 and to require that at least 15 memberships "be equally distributed among persons under 36 years of age . . . (including) . . . women and girls and persons from minority groups."

The YMCA reported that in 1968 its membership had increased by 7.4%. The organization conducted more than 1,200 programs in inner cities and needy communities. (*See in* CE: Young Men's Christian Association.)

Young Women's Christian Association

In 1969 the Young Women's Christian Association (YWCA) strengthened its emphasis upon work with economically deprived and socially isolated persons. Employability programs were among its major efforts. They included a Business Office Culture Project, which prepared young women for business jobs, and a renewal through June 1970 of the

COURTESY, CAMP FIRE GIRLS, INC.

A young girl discovers a turtle at a Camp Fire Girls camp. Camp Fire Girls camps often provide city children with their only real access to nature.

Job Corps-YWCA extension residence program. (*See also* Poverty, War on.)

Numerous YWCA programs were implemented through local funds. They variously included consumer education for poverty-area mothers; services to the aged and infirm; and instruction for teen-age girls in cooking, sewing, and crafts. (*See in* CE: Young Women's Christian Association; Juvenile Organizations.)

YUGOSLAVIA. Continued economic reform and changes in party organization were highlights of 1969. Curbs on artistic expression were renewed as national divergencies increased, and relations with the Soviet Union seemed to improve by midyear.

Domestic Affairs

In March the 9th Congress of the League of Communists adopted new statutes guaranteeing the right of party members to hold minority opinions. It also approved a Central Committee report calling for further curbs on bureaucracy, the extension of workers' self-management in industry, and greater decision-making roles for the Socialist Alliance, the trade unions, and other sanctioned social organizations. A new 15-member Executive Bureau consisting of President Tito, the two top political figures from each of the six republics, and one from each of the two autonomous provinces, was established in place of the 11-man Executive Committee. A new 52-member Presidium based on geographic representation replaced the Central Committee's former 35-man Presidium. The former Central Committee of 154 was abolished to make way for the 300-member annual Party Conference.

In the April-May elections more than 43,000 candidates ran for half as many seats in parliament and posts in local government, and there were a record number of independent candidates. In May Mirko Tepavac became secretary for foreign affairs, Mitja Ribicic was elected president of the Federal Executive Council, and Milentije Popovic was reelected as president of the Federal Assembly.

Curbing Dissent

Between March and July the courts in the Kosovo-Mitohiyan autonomous province and the Macedonian republic convicted more than 30 people of Albanian origin for "fomenting national hatred." Some were accused of conspiring with Albanian officials to bring about the secession of certain Yugoslav towns. In August President Tito made a bitter attack on "undisciplined party leaders" after the Slovenian government had repeatedly challenged the federal government's decision to withhold from it foreign credits for road and highway modernization.

In April Dragoljub Golubovic, a writer for the weekly journal *Nin,* was expelled from the party for publishing a letter criticizing existing press restrictions. In June Tanjug news agency editor Momcilo Pudar was forced to resign after printing an unauthorized article critical of the world Communist conference. At the end of August, shortly before the visit of the Soviet foreign minister, Andrei A. Gromyko, the literary paper *Knjizevne Novine* was banned for including an article condemning the be-

Yugoslav workers participate in their own management through a "workers' council," a rotating group of 15 or more employees whose function is similar to that of a board of directors. Economic enterprises in Yugoslavia legally belong to all the people, and the workers act as "trustees" for society in managing their respective enterprises.

COURTESY, YUGOSLAV INFORMATION CENTER

Residents of Banja Luka, Yugoslavia, survey the damage caused by the earthquake that destroyed their city on Oct. 27, 1969.
WIDE WORLD

havior of Soviet troops in Czechoslovakia. Its author, Zoran Gluscevic, was dismissed from his editorship of the paper. In October he was given a six-month prison sentence. During the same month a play portraying the predicament of the pro-Stalin Yugoslavs in 1948 was closed down, and a ban was put on the distribution in Yugoslavia of a book published abroad by Milovan Djilas, a former vice-president. Djilas' book, 'The Unperfect Society', was published in the United States.

Economic Affairs

The success of the automobile firm Crvena Zastaya in attracting bondholders induced several other firms to follow suit, including Yugoslav Railways. In October Yugoslav, U.S., and West European bankers combined to establish an international investment bank to help prospective foreign investors find suitable Yugoslav partners for joint ventures and to give financial help to Yugoslav exporters. By October industrial production was 13.5% above the level for the same period in the preceding year, but there were serious imbalances in the economy.

Serious delays in the payment of salaries and some wage cuts caused several strikes. An earthquake at Banja Luka in October, which killed at least 20 people and injured about 660 others, was an economic as well as a social catastrophe. By October Yugoslavia's trade deficit was sufficiently grave to produce a government tightening of credit facilities. But there was optimism regarding trade with such countries as Communist China, the Soviet Union, Czechoslovakia, Hungary, Romania, and the countries of the European Economic Community, or Common Market.

Foreign Affairs

During the first half of the year relations with the Soviet Union and its allies were strained. In January the Yugoslav delegation walked out of the European Student Conference at Budapest, Hungary, after being accused of "subversion" by Soviet, Polish, and Hungarian participants. At the Italian Communist congress in February, a Yugoslav speaker attacked the Soviet concept of "limited sovereignty." Although Yugoslavia was represented at the Council for Mutual Economic Assistance meeting in Moscow, in April, it boycotted most of the other Soviet-sponsored meetings. Yugoslavia did not send delegates to the world Communist conference in Moscow in June.

The Yugoslav Communist congress was, in turn, boycotted by all the Soviet-bloc countries except Romania. Following a report in the Macedonian National Assembly that Bulgaria was intensifying its subversion of Macedonia, there was a large anti-Bulgarian demonstration in Skopje in March.

Relations with Romania continued to improve. President Tito conferred with President Nicolae Ceausescu in February and September, and a Romanian army delegation was warmly received in Belgrade, the capital, in June. There was little improvement in relations with Albania, even though in April the Albanian press pledged solidarity with Yugoslavia in the event of a conflict with the Soviet Union. However, relations with Communist China thawed after February when the two countries opened their first bilateral economic exchanges in nine years.

Late in April the Soviet press muted its criticisms of Yugoslavia, and in May the Yugoslavs were handed specific proposals for a Soviet-Yugoslav détente. Although Yugoslavia made no immediate reply, the government toned down its attacks on Soviet policies and in September the Soviet foreign minister visited Yugoslavia, agreeing to the principle of "noninterference."

President Giuseppe Saragat of Italy visited Yugoslavia in October. In July a 51-nation consultative conference of nonaligned nations was held in Belgrade. Yugoslav officials were inclined to blame the Algerians for the failure of the conference to draw up a timetable for a further nonaligned summit conference; but President Tito's visit to Algiers, Algeria, in November was thought to have reduced existing frictions between the two countries. (*See in* CE: Yugoslavia.)

ZAMBIA. On Aug. 11, 1969, President Kenneth Kaunda announced that in order to safeguard Zambia's economic independence the copper industry was being nationalized. The two major mining companies were to consign 51% of their shares to the government, and compensation would be paid out of future profits. New mining companies would be invited to cooperate with the state in mining development. At the same time the president announced a new mineral tax of 51% on gross profits.

On January 30 Vice-President Simon Kapwepwe introduced a stiff budget for fiscal 1969 aimed at checking inflation and steadying the balance-of-payments position. Income-tax rates were increased, and wives were to be taxed on the same basis as their husbands. Taxes on luxury goods were increased, while government expenditure was to be cut. In February a government white paper on nationalization in the mining industry forecast that by 1972 more than 5,500 Zambians would have replaced expatriates.

In April the World Bank announced a loan of $17.4 million for educational development, and in August it came to a preliminary arrangement with the governments of Great Britain and Zambia on a $20-million plan to end the Zambian copper industry's dependence upon power supplies from the Rhodesian side of the Kariba Gorge Dam. On November 15 Zambia, Tanzania, and the People's Republic of China signed a joint agreement to proceed

In an attempt to save the wildlife in Zambia, Herwig Sekotill (below) uses a helicopter to apprehend poachers and quickly dispatch a game guide to handle the arrest. As one of the major targets for Zambian poachers, the once abundant red lechwe antelope (above) has been reduced in number to 30,000.

ABOVE AND BELOW: COURTESY, FRED DUCKWORTH

with the construction of a 1,200-mile railway linking Zambia and Tanzania.

President Kaunda was sworn in for a second term on Dec. 21, 1968, after the electoral victory of the United National Independence party (UNIP). Polling was heavy, and the UNIP won 81 seats to the 23 of the African National Congress party (ANC), with one seat going to an independent. The ANC made gains in Barotse Province (renamed Western Province in August), where the Lozi resented the government ban on their working in South Africa. A successful candidate was Nalumino Mundia, the restricted leader of the banned United party, many of whose followers voted for the ANC candidates. Kaunda appointed eight new ministers, responsible for individual provinces, to promote rural development. Robinson Nabulyato was elected speaker of the second National Assembly. He ruled that the ANC would not be recognized as the official opposition.

On June 17 a referendum empowered the parliament to amend the constitution without recourse to the electorate. In July the president clashed with the white judiciary when he rebuked a judge, Ifor Evans, for quashing sentences of two Portuguese soldiers convicted of illegal entry into Zambia from Angola. Evans had earlier ruled elections in 15 seats invalid because UNIP supporters had physically prevented ANC candidates from handing in nomination papers. He was supported by Chief Justice James Skinner and the judiciary. Rioting youths ransacked the High Court in Lusaka, the capital, and both Evans and Skinner left the country and subsequently resigned. On November 3 Godfrey Muwo was sworn in as Zambia's first African High Court judge.

On August 25 Kapwepwe resigned, claiming that he and his Bemba supporters had been abused and persecuted. Kaunda announced that he was taking personal control of the UNIP and would rule the country as party secretary-general. He had been urged to adopt more extreme programs to win the support of the Bemba radicals who were critical of Kaunda's policy and who had sought to control the UNIP. On August 27 Kapwepwe withdrew his resignation at the president's request. In September Kaunda ordered the temporary suppression of all public meetings of the UNIP, but in October a number of political prisoners were released. (*See also* Feature Article: "Black Africa Saves the Game"; Africa. *See in* CE: Zambia.)

ZOO.

Zoos in many parts of the world continued in 1969 to give aid to endangered species by supporting the World Wildlife Fund. In a further effort to protect endangered species, many zoos operated under a self-imposed ban on importing them. The zoo in Frankfurt-am-Main, West Germany, aided in establishing wildlife colleges in Africa and gave generously to the Serengeti National Park, in Tanzania. (*See* Feature Article: "Black Africa Saves the Game.")

Rare Species Bred or Acquired

With increasing success, zoos continued to breed rare and endangered species. Antwerp, Belgium, made zoo history by breeding the first captive-born mountain gorilla. Duisburg, West Germany, bred five bat-eared foxes; this species had been born in captivity previously, but the offspring were not successfully reared.

The zoo on Jersey, Channel Islands, for the first time bred the volcano rabbit in captivity. Another first was a spectacled penguin hatched at Stuttgart, West Germany. Philadelphia, Pa., bred American mergansers for the second time on record; and both

Triplet tiger cubs, born in the Glenwood Zoo in Erie, Pa., pose with their mother. Triplet births among tigers are rare.
UPI COMPIX

CANADIAN PRESS

The baby hippopotamus, named Apollo after the U.S. lunar-landing project, was born in Toronto's Riverdale Zoo. Apollo was believed to be the first hippopotamus born in captivity in Canada.

Frankfurt and Edinburgh, Scotland, bred cassowaries—an extremely rare occurrence.

Zoos acquired a number of rarities during the year. Three Cameroon bareheaded rock fowl (*Picathartes oreas*) arrived at Frankfurt; only one of this species had ever been in captivity before. Washington, D.C., was presented with two kiwis, the first at the zoo since 1925, by the prime minister of New Zealand. The San Diego (Calif.) Zoo was also given a pair of these birds to honor the city's 200th anniversary.

Zoo Developments

As zoos continued to become larger, transporting increasing numbers of visitors through them became of prime importance. Two U.S. zoos approached this problem similarly. Philadelphia offered a monorail tour of its zoo, and the San Diego Zoo had a "Skyfari" chair lift.

Zoo history was made when a 576-pound male gorilla was transported uncaged by air from the Como Park Zoo, in St. Paul, Minn., to the Henry Dooly Zoo, in Omaha, Neb. The animal was given tranquilizing drugs for the trip.

Throughout the world, zoos were constructing more spacious and natural enclosures for their animals. At the Bronx Zoo, in New York City, a building called "The World of Darkness" was opened. Instead of cages, 32 "environmental enclosures" accommodated up to 300 animals. A new idea to give reptiles more freedom in captivity was put into practice at Rapid City, S.D. Three huge underground viewing dens, connected to a one-acre paddock surrounded by a snake- and rodentproof fence, were constructed. At Chester, England, a new ape house was opened to accommodate orangutans and lowland gorillas. Indoors, visitors viewed the apes through armor-plated glass windows; the animals had free access to outside moated islands.

San Diego planned to open an 1,800-acre wild-animal park at San Pasqual, Calif. The site was chosen for its similarity in vegetation and topography to the plains of East Africa. Huge enclosures were to be incorporated. A $750,000 home was constructed for the five species of penguins at the Detroit (Mich.) Zoo. The birds could be viewed from either above or below the water while they were swimming. (*See also* Animals and Wildlife. *See in* CE: Zoo.)

New arrivals to the Windsor Safari Park Zoo wear earmuffs to muffle the noise from the London Airport, which is only a few minutes' flying time from the zoo. The first time a low-flying jet airliner flew over the elephants, which had recently arrived from Bangkok, Thailand, they became frightened and stampeded into Windsor Great Park.

"LONDON DAILY EXPRESS" FROM PICTORIAL PARADE

CALENDAR FOR 1970

JANUARY

1 Thursday. New Year's Day. Football bowl games. National Blood Donor Month begins.
4 Sunday. Save the Pun Week begins.
5 Monday. Twelfth Night.
6 Tuesday. Twelfth Day, or Epiphany.
9 Friday. Richard M. Nixon's birthday.
11 Sunday. Super Bowl game. Printing Week begins.
13 Tuesday. Stephen Foster Memorial Week begins.
14 Wednesday. Ratification Day.
17 Saturday. Benjamin Franklin's birthday.
18 Sunday. Cuckoo Dancing Week begins.
19 Monday. Robert E. Lee's birthday.
21 Wednesday. Anniversary of the launching of the first nuclear submarine (USS *Nautilus*).
29 Thursday. Kansas admitted to the Union, 1861. William McKinley's birthday.
30 Friday. Franklin D. Roosevelt's birthday.

FEBRUARY

1 Sunday. American Heart Month and National Cherry Month begin.
2 Monday. Groundhog Day. Candlemas.
3 Tuesday. Four Chaplains Memorial Day.
7 Saturday. Boy Scout Week begins.
8 Sunday. National Crime Prevention Week and National Negro History Week begin.
9 Monday. William Henry Harrison's birthday.
10 Tuesday. Shrove Tuesday. International Pancake Race. Mardi Gras.
11 Wednesday. Ash Wednesday. Lent begins.
12 Thursday. Abraham Lincoln's birthday.
14 Saturday. Saint Valentine's Day.
15 Sunday. Susan B. Anthony Day.
21 Saturday. Future Farmers of America Week begins.
22 Sunday. George Washington's birthday. Book Week and Brotherhood Week begin.

MARCH

2 Monday. Texas Independence Day. National Housing for Handicapped Week begins.
3 Tuesday. National Procrastination Week begins.
8 Sunday. Girl Scout Week begins.
15 Sunday. Andrew Jackson's birthday. National Poison Prevention Week and National Wildlife Week begin.
16 Monday. James Madison's birthday. National Boys' Club Week begins.
17 Tuesday. Saint Patrick's Day.
20 Friday. Spring begins.
22 Sunday. Palm Sunday. Air Age Education Week, Art Week, and Camp Fire Girls Birthday Week begin.
25 Wednesday. Feast of the Annunciation.
27 Friday. Good Friday.
29 Sunday. Easter Sunday.

APRIL

1 Wednesday. April Fools' Day. National Laugh Week begins. Cancer Control Month and Freedom Shrine Month begin.
5 Sunday. Mother-in-Law Day.
7 Tuesday. National Cherry Blossom Festival.
9 Thursday. Sir Winston Churchill Day.
10 Friday. Salvation Army Founder's Day.
12 Sunday. National Library Week begins.
13 Monday. Thomas Jefferson's birthday.
19 Sunday. Free World Friendship Week, National Coin Week, and National Young Women's Christian Association Week begin.
20 Monday. Good Human Relations Week begins.
21 Tuesday. Passover begins.
24 Friday. Penn Relays.
25 Saturday. National Baby Week begins.
26 Sunday. Daylight saving time begins.

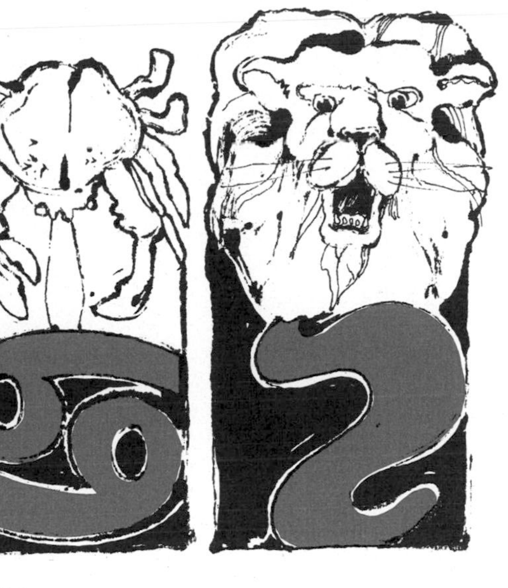

MAY

1 Friday. May Day. Law Day. Loyalty Day. Mental Health Week begins. National Tavern Month, Radio Month, and Senior Citizens Month begin.
3 Sunday. Humane Sunday. National Be Kind to Animals Week and National Goodwill Week begin.
6 Wednesday. Birthday of the first postage stamp (1840).
7 Thursday. Ascension Day.
8 Friday. Harry S Truman's birthday. World Red Cross Day.
10 Sunday. Mother's Day. Let's Go Fishing Week, National Hospital Week, National Transportation Week, and Police Week begin.
15 Friday. National Defense Transportation Day.
16 Saturday. Armed Forces Day.
17 Sunday. Whitsunday, or Pentecost.
21 Thursday. International Pickle Week begins.
22 Friday. National Maritime Day.
29 Friday. John F. Kennedy's birthday.
30 Saturday. Memorial Day.

JUNE

1 Monday. Fight the Filthy Fly Month, National Ragweed Control Month, National Recreation Month, National Rose Month, and National Seat Belt Month begin.
3 Wednesday. Jefferson Davis' birthday.
6 Saturday. D-Day Anniversary. National Pioneer Settler's Day.
7 Sunday. Freedom of the Press Day. National Humor Week begins.
8 Monday. National Little League Baseball Week begins.
11 Thursday. Kamehameha Day, Hawaii.
14 Sunday. Flag Day. Race Unity Day. National Root Beer Week begins.
21 Sunday. Summer begins. Father's Day. Amateur Radio Week begins.
24 Wednesday. Saint John the Baptist Day.
28 Sunday. National Safe Boating Week begins.
29 Monday. National Tom Sawyer Days begin.
30 Tuesday. Old Milwaukee Days begin.

JULY

1 Wednesday. Dominion Day, Canada. Battle of Gettysburg Annual Commemorative Ceremonies. National Barbecue Month and National Hot Dog Month begin.
4 Saturday. Independence Day. Calvin Coolidge's birthday.
6 Monday. National Cherry Festival begins. John Paul Jones's birthday.
11 Saturday. John Quincy Adams' birthday.
12 Sunday. Orangeman's Day, Northern Ireland.
14 Tuesday. Bastille Day, France.
15 Wednesday. Saint Swithin's Day.
17 Friday. Luis Muñoz-Rivera's birthday.
19 Sunday. International Railway Day. National Farm Safety Week begins.
20 Monday. Moon Day.
24 Friday. Simón Bolívar's birthday.
25 Saturday. Constitution Day, Puerto Rico.
27 Monday. Hall of Fame Baseball Game.
31 Friday. Maine Seafoods Festival begins.

AUGUST

1 Saturday. National Sandwich Month begins.
2 Sunday. Beauty Queen Week begins.
3 Monday. National Smile Week begins.
4 Tuesday. Coast Guard Day. Lizzie Borden Liberation Day.
8 Saturday. International Character Day.
9 Sunday. Family Reunion Day.
10 Monday. Herbert Clark Hoover's birthday.
11 Tuesday. Tishah b'Ab, or Fast of Ab.
14 Friday. V-J Day. Atlantic Charter Day.
15 Saturday. Assumption of the Virgin Mary. National Allergy Month begins.
16 Sunday. Bennington Battle Day, Vermont.
19 Wednesday. National Aviation Day.
20 Thursday. Benjamin Harrison's birthday.
21 Friday. Iowa State Fair begins.
25 Tuesday. Independence Day, Uruguay.
27 Thursday. Lyndon B. Johnson's birthday.
30 Sunday. Freedom of Enterprise Week begins.
31 Monday. Federation of Malaysia Independence Day.

SEPTEMBER

1 Tuesday. American Youth Month, Bourbon Month, Home Sweet Home Month, National Better Breakfast Month, National Bowling Month, and National Pancake Month begin.
3 Thursday. National Green Olive Week begins.
7 Monday. Labor Day.
8 Tuesday. Miss America Beauty Pageant begins.
13 Sunday. Granddad's Day. National Hispanic Heritage Week and National Home Week begin.
15 Tuesday. William Howard Taft's birthday.
17 Thursday. Citizenship Day. Constitution Week and Oktoberfest begin.
19 Saturday. International Police Day.
20 Sunday. World Peace Day. National Dog Week begins.
23 Wednesday. Autumn begins.
25 Friday. American Indian Day.
27 Sunday. Gold Star Mother's Day.
29 Tuesday. Michaelmas.

OCTOBER

1 Thursday. Rosh Hashanah, or Jewish New Year. March Against Muscular Dystrophy begins. National Employ the Physically Handicapped Week and National Lighthouse Week begin.
4 Sunday. Fire Prevention Week, International Letter Writing Week, National 4-H Week, and National Pharmacy Week begin.
5 Monday. Child Health Day.
9 Friday. Leif Ericson Day.
10 Saturday. Yom Kippur, or Day of Atonement.
11 Sunday. National School Lunch Week begins.
12 Monday. Columbus Day.
14 Wednesday. Dwight D. Eisenhower's birthday.
17 Saturday. Sweetest Day.
19 Monday. National Cleaner Air Week begins.
24 Saturday. United Nations Day. National Honey Week and National Popcorn Week begin.
25 Sunday. Daylight saving time ends.
27 Tuesday. Theodore Roosevelt's birthday.
31 Saturday. Halloween. Reformation Day.

NOVEMBER

1 Sunday. All Saints' Day. International Cat Week begins. Retarded Children's Month begins.
2 Monday. All Souls' Day.
3 Tuesday. General Election Day.
5 Thursday. Guy Fawkes Day.
8 Sunday. World Fellowship Week begins.
9 Monday. Spiro T. Agnew's birthday. Youth Appreciation Week begins.
10 Tuesday. Marine Corps birthday.
11 Wednesday. Veterans Day. Remembrance Day.
12 Thursday. Christmas Seal campaign begins.
14 Saturday. Sadie Hawkins Day.
15 Sunday. National Children's Book Week begins.
16 Monday. Asparagus Week and Diabetes Week begin.
17 Tuesday. National Stamp Collecting Week begins.
22 Sunday. Bible Week and Latin America Week begin.
24 Tuesday. Zachary Taylor's birthday.
26 Thursday. Thanksgiving Day.

DECEMBER

1 Tuesday. Civil Air Patrol Week begins.
2 Wednesday. Pan American Health Day and World Community Day.
6 Sunday. National Mimicry Week begins.
7 Monday. Pearl Harbor Day.
8 Tuesday. Feast of the Immaculate Conception.
10 Thursday. United Nations Human Rights Day. Human Rights Week begins.
15 Tuesday. Bill of Rights Day.
16 Wednesday. Ludwig van Beethoven's birthday.
17 Thursday. Wright Brothers Day. Pan American Aviation Day. Kitty Hawk Day.
21 Monday. Forefathers' Day.
22 Tuesday. Winter begins. International Arbor Day.
23 Wednesday. Hanuka, or Festival of Lights, begins.
25 Friday. Christmas Day.
26 Saturday. Boxing Day.
28 Monday. Childermas. Woodrow Wilson's birthday.
31 Thursday. New Year's Eve.

New Words

This New Words section consists of two parts. The first part is a list of new words officially accepted for use in Merriam-Webster dictionaries. The second part is more informal—it is an essay on new words of the 1960's; some of these words might not endure but they *are* a reflection of the influence of current events on the language.

New Words from

Merriam-Webster

REG. U. S. PAT. OFF.

The list of new words and new meanings on the following pages has been prepared by the permanent editorial staff of G. & C. Merriam Company of Springfield, Massachusetts, publishers of *Webster's Third New International Dictionary* and *Webster's Seventh New Collegiate Dictionary* and other dictionaries in the Merriam-Webster Series.

A

Acapulco gold *n* : a marijuana grown in Mexico

accommodationist *n* : one who seeks accommodation with a conflicting point of view; *specif* : a Negro willing to cooperate with whites

affinity rate *n* : a reduced fare for persons traveling by air in a group (as of 25)

affirmation law *n* : a state law requiring liquor manufacturers to give assurance that prices for their products in a designated state are no higher than in any other state

Afram *adj* : AFRO-AMERICAN

agrichemical *or* **agrochemical** *n* : a chemical (as a fungicide, herbicide, or insecticide) used in agriculture

aircab *n* : a helicopter that serves as a taxi for a small number of passengers (as between an airport and the business section of a city)

airshed *n* : a region having a common air supply

airway *n* : an overhead walkway connecting buildings

ambisextrous *adj* **1** : not distinguishable as male or female : common to males and females ⟨*ambisextrous* clothing⟩ **2** : involving males and females ⟨an *ambisextrous* party⟩

Ameriachi *n* : a style of popular music characterized especially by the use of brass instruments, a pulsing often Latin rhythm, and short bursts of melody—called also *cucaracha-rock*, *Mexiland*

anthropoktony *n* : the inclination of human beings to kill their own kind (as in murder or war)

antifertility *adj* : reducing or destroying fertility ⟨a mammalian *antifertility* agent⟩

B

banana hash *n* : the dried scrapings of the inner skin of banana peel said to be smoked for its euphoric effect

barbecue maneuver *n* : the rolling of a spacecraft about its long axis so that all sides are equally exposed to the heat of the sun and the cold of space—called also *barbecuing*

bashful bunny *n* : a mixed drink made of gin, rum, grenadine, and lemon juice

belted-bias tire *n* : a pneumatic tire that has a hooplike belt of cord running around the tire underneath the tread and on top of the ply cords laid at an acute angle to the center line of the tread

bias-belted tire *n* : BELTED-BIAS TIRE

bioresearch *n* : research in biological science

black studies *n* : studies (as sociology and history) dealing with Afro-Americans

blindgating *n* : driving close enough behind another vehicle to be taken unawares by an obstacle that unexpectedly appears in front of and is avoided by the preceding vehicle

blip *vb*, *specif* : to remove recorded sound from a videotape so that in the received television program there is an interruption in the sound ⟨a censor *blipped* the swearwords⟩

block parent *n* : one who offers his place of residence or business as a refuge for children in distress and far from help

bodyshirt *n* : a woman's fitted blouse often with a high collar and deep cuffs

bounceball *n* : volleyball played by two players or pairs of players on a trampoline

brain bank *n* : a pool of academic talent

braindrain *vb* : to hire in such a manner as to result in a brain drain—**brain drainer** *n*

branchheading *n* : the practice of speaking (as by a politician) in a folksy style characterized by ostensibly naïve mistakes in pronouncing polysyllabic words

buffet *n*, *specif* : a one-room apartment with cooking facilities

bugler *n*, *specif* : a member of the armed forces who brags loudly especially in a public place about the virtues of his unit

C

cat suit *n* : a one-piece or two-piece formfitting bell-bottomed woman's garment for casual wear ⟨flowered cotton *cat suit*⟩

centralizer *n*, *specif* : one who buys stolen traveler's checks and sells them at a profit

cherry sheet *n* : a report of the distribution of state tax revenue to the cities and towns of the state

Chinese restaurant syndrome *n* : a set of symptoms including numbness of the neck, arms, and back, headaches, dizziness, and palpitations that affects susceptible persons after eating Chinese food in a Chinese restaurant and that has been attributed to various causative agents including monosodium glutamate

Christmas tree *n*, *specif* : a set of flashing red, yellow, and green lights used to start drag races

Christmas-tree bill *n* : a legislative bill that includes various riders relating to pet projects of individual legislators

cockamamy *n* : NONSENSE, INANITY

coffee-tabler *n* : an expensive, illustrated oversize book suitable for display on a coffee table

cortico-centrism *n* : the theory or practice of assuming that everyone has the same attitudes and viewpoints as one's own

crash-program *vb* : to intensify by swift action and maximum effort

crunch *n*, *specif* **1** : pressure on banks and other financial institutions for cash as opposed to credit ⟨a *crunch* cripples home mortgages and cuts employment as credit evaporates⟩ **2** : a critical point in the buildup of pressure between opposing elements : CRISIS, SHOWDOWN, CONFRONTATION ⟨to be prepared when the military *crunch* comes⟩

cryochemistry *n* : chemistry dealing with processes carried out at low temperatures—**cryochemical** *adj*—**cryochemically** *adv*

cucaracha-rock *n* : AMERIACHI

curdler *n* : a high-frequency noisemaker used to control unruly crowds

D

dancercises *n pl* : exercises in dance form set to music

dashiki *or* **daishiki** *n* : a usually brightly colored pullover garment for men that hangs loose over the upper body and midriff

[1]**deorbit** *vb* : to go out of an orbit or cause to go out of an orbit ⟨*deorbit* a spacecraft⟩

[2]**deorbit** *n* : the process of deorbiting

E

earthrise *n* : the apparent rising of the earth above the horizon of the moon as seen from the moon or its vicinity

F

fail *n, specif* : a failure (as by a broker) to deliver or receive securities within a prescribed period after a purchase or sale

falsie *n, specif* : a piece of false hair (as a moustache) worn on the face by men

fantasy *vb, specif* : to imagine a sexually stimulating situation especially as an adjunct to autoerotism

G

geezer *n* : an injected dose of a narcotic

G job *n* : a personal project carried on by a worker on company time with company machinery

H

hairweaving *n* : the covering of a bald spot with a wig whose nylon base is sewn to the wearer's remaining hair—**hairweave** *n*—**hair weaver** *n*

headhunter *n, specif* : a recruiter of senior personnel (as executives for a corporation)

headrest *n, specif* : an extension attached to the top of an automobile seat for restraining the movement of the head to prevent whiplash injury in case of a collision

head restraint *n* : HEADREST

hedge fund *n* : an investing group usually in the form of a limited partnership that employs speculative techniques (as short selling and leverage) in the hope of obtaining large capital gains

Hong Kong flu *n* : a relatively mild pandemic influenza caused by a variant strain of the influenza virus

hydrairport *n* : an airport designed as a floating structure (as on Long Island Sound)

I

inertia welding *n* : the welding of metals by means of the heat produced by friction when one metallic piece is pressed while spinning against another

internationalite *n* : a person of international social prominence

investment letter stock *n* : stock not registered with the Securities and Exchange Commission which is sold at a discount to an institutional investor under a written agreement that it is being purchased for investment and not for resale to the general investing public

J

jazzcotheque *n* : a dance that combines jazz and discotheque styles

jazzotheque *n* : a discotheque in which jazz music is played

jet belt *n* : a beltlike harness on which a jet engine is mounted to provide a wearer with aerial propulsion

jumblescape *n* : a landscape marked by a jumble of buildings of varied colors and architectural forms

K

kamagraphy *n* : a process for making multiple copies of a painting produced by an artist on a specially treated canvas in which the copies retain the texture of the brushstrokes of the original but the original is destroyed in the process—**kamagraph** *n*—**kamagrapher** *n*—**kamagraphic** *adj*

khiva *n* : an indoor lounging area furnished only with pillows

kickout *n, specif* : a student who leaves school against his will

knockoff *n* : a copy (as of the design of a textile or apparel product) that sells for less than the original

knock off *vb, specif* **1** : to make a knockoff of **2** : to undersell by means of knockoffs

L

L'aubina *n* : a protein-rich powder developed in Lebanon as a diet supplement that consists of chick-peas, parboiled wheat, dried skimmed milk, vitamins, and calcium

litter lady *n* : a woman who issues tickets to violators of laws against littering

LM *n* : LUNAR MODULE

[1]**loid** *n* : a strip of celluloid used (as by a burglar) to open a door

[2]**loid** *vb* : to unlock (a door) by using a strip of celluloid to retract the spring bolt

loid man *n* : a burglar who unlocks a door by using a strip of celluloid to retract the spring bolt

luminal art *n* : an art form created by electric lighting (as in projected still or moving patterns of colored light or an arrangement of flashing colored light bulbs)—called also *lumia*—**luminism** *n*—**luminist** *n*

lunar excursion module *n* : the part of a space vehicle assembly that can be detached for carrying passengers to the surface of the moon

lunar module *n* : LUNAR EXCURSION MODULE

M

magnicide *n* : the murder of a prominent leader or ruler

mascon *n* : one of the concentrations of large mass under the surface of the moon in the maria thought to cause perturbations of the paths of spacecraft orbiting the moon

megapark *n* : a large park within a megalopolis

megaversity *n* : a multiversity with divisions at widely separate locations

Mexiland *n* : AMERIACHI

milker *n, specif* : one who steals a few traveler's checks from the middle of a book of checks

mind-blowing *adj* **1** : PSYCHEDELIC; *also* : of, relating to, or causing a psychic state similar to that produced by a psychedelic drug **2** : mentally or emotionally stimulating : OVERWHELMING

mini *vb* : to wear miniskirts

minibike *n* : a small one-passenger motorcycle having a low frame and elevated handlebars

minibuster *n* : a filibuster of short duration

minisub *n* : a very small submarine used especially in research (as on the ocean bottom)

MIRV *n* : multiple independently targeted reentry vehicle—used of a missile with two or more warheads designed to reenter the atmosphere on the way to separate enemy targets or of any of the warheads themselves

motique *n* : a vehicle from which merchandise (as women's clothing) is sold on suburban streets

N

negative income tax *n* : a government payment to individuals whose income falls below a prescribed level—called also *negative tax*

noise pollution *n* : pollution consisting of annoying noise ⟨*noise pollution* caused by automobile traffic, a jet airplane, or a vacuum cleaner⟩—called also *sound pollution*

nosewarmer *n* : a cover that fits over the nose and is attached by a band around the head for wear especially in skiing

O

Okun's law *n* : a statement in economics : a rise in the unemployment rate is correlated with a fall in the gross national product

P

pacey *adj* : appropriate to the times : UP-TO-DATE—**paceyness** *n*

Panama red *n* : a marijuana grown in Panama that is darker than Acapulco gold

paper gold *n* : SPECIAL DRAWING RIGHTS

people sniffer *n* : a device for detecting concealed persons (as enemy troops) by bodily odors (as of ammonia) in the air

piggybacking *n* **1** : the broadcasting of commercials for two products of a company in the time regularly allotted to one **2** : the establishing of the state income tax rate at a specified percentage of one's federal income tax

R

ranchero *n* : a casual necktie designed for wear with an open-collared or collarless shirt

registered player *n* : an amateur tennis player authorized to compete for prize money in open tournaments

rejective art *n* : a simplified and often depersonalized art (as painting or sculpture) based on the principle of the artist's rejecting various options open to him—called also *reductive art, reductivism, rejectivism*

S

sand surfing *n* : the sport of sliding down a sand slope while standing on a small board—**sand surfer** *n*

SDR *abbr* special drawing rights

self-destruct *vb* : to destroy itself ⟨a device designed to **self-destruct**⟩

shrink *n, specif, slang* : PSYCHOANALYST, PSYCHIATRIST

smokeout *n* : a gathering at which persons smoke the dried scrapings of the inner skin of banana peel

sound pollution *n* : NOISE POLLUTION

special drawing rights *n pl* : a proposed artificial international money intended to supplement gold as a medium of exchange for the settlement of debts between nations—called also *paper gold*

stagorium *n* : an establishment (as a resort hotel or a bar) that serves as a meeting place for unmarried men and women

starfish *vb* : to bend in the sides of a food container so as to make it hold less

strike force *n* : a team of federal agents assigned to investigate organized crime in a specific area (as a city)

T

technetronic *adj* : of or being a society shaped by the impact of technology and electronics and especially of computers and communications on its structure, culture, psychology, and economics

technologism *n* : the doctrine or practice of subordinating man to the technological apparatus of his society

tetrahydrocannabinol *n* : a physiologically active liquid derived from a resin of the hemp plant and believed to be the chief intoxicant in marijuana

THC *n* : TETRAHYDROCANNABINOL

Thurmondize *vb* : to bring into conformity with the attitudes of Senator Strom Thurmond of South Carolina

transcreation *n* : a modified translation of a literary work

transearth *adj* : of or relating to the entry of a spacecraft into a trajectory between the earth and a celestial body (as the moon) and to the travel of the spacecraft in the direction of the earth ⟨*transearth* injection⟩ ⟨*transearth* burn⟩ ⟨*transearth* coast⟩

tube *n, specif* : television tube; also : TELEVISION—usually used with *the*

tube suit *n* : a wet suit that circulates warm water over a diver's body

tye-dye *n* : a circular design to be gazed at especially while under the influence of a psychedelic drug

U

ultramicrofiche *n* : a photographic reproduction of printed matter in greatly reduced form ⟨a four-by-six inch *ultramicrofiche* card containing images of 3000 pages⟩

undergroundling *n* : a moviegoer especially interested in underground productions

¹unisex *n* : a group of males and females not distinguishable (as by hair or clothing styles) as to sex

²unisex *adj* : AMBISEXTROUS ⟨*unisex* fashions⟩

uppies *n pl* : AMPHETAMINES

urbanology *n* : a study that deals with the physical, social, and economic problems of cities—**urbanologist** *n*

Y

yippie *n* : a person affiliated or identified with an activist hippie group

youthquake *n* : the impact of the values, tastes, and mores of youth on the established norms of society

Special Essay: New Words of the 1960's

by Simeon Potter, Professor Emeritus of the English Language and Philology, University of Liverpool, England

The Apollo 11 moon landing, the most dramatic event of 1969, brought many new terms into the language, many of which would undoubtedly survive. The *command module* of the three-man spacecraft Apollo 11 was named "Columbia." Its detachable *lunar module* called "Eagle" touched down on the Sea of Tranquillity on July 20. The *space probe,* or *extraterrestrial exploration,* went ahead and plans were made to launch an *earth-orbiting laboratory* in 1972; but a *lunar receiving laboratory* was an urgent necessity in 1969. At Houston, Tex., it took shape as a mobile silver caravan, a specially constructed quarantine facility "to keep what is outside out and what is inside in." At Houston, too, was located the headquarters of the *CAPCOM,* or Command Communicator.

The year closed with no proof that any life existed outside the *biosphere* of earth. This "life-globe," or realm of living organisms, was limited to the earth's crust (*lithosphere*), waters (*hydrosphere*), and air blanket (*atmosphere*). Nevertheless, the terms *astrobiologist,* student of life on stars, and *exobiologist,* student of life outside earth, gained wide currency. *Selenologists,* students of the moon's physical characteristics, especially its surface features, began to speak of *mascons* and *astroblemes.* Mascons, discovered by orbiting spacecraft late in 1968, are massive concentrations of rock embedded beneath the moon's circular *maria.* Astroblemes, literally "star-wounds," are mysterious depressions, of which the Meteor Crater of Arizona is the best known.

The moon-landing missions produced important acronyms like *COSPAR,* Committee on Space Research (International Council of Scientific Unions), and *EVA* (extravehicular activity). It also produced the acronym *PLSS* (portable life-support system).

Word formation was conspicuously active in the 1960's. The International Scientific Vocabulary, defined and described in 'Webster's Third New International Dictionary' of 1961, went more and more to neo-Hellenic sources for its new terms. The prefixes *macro-*, long, large; *micro-*, small; *para-*, alongside; and *poly-*, many, were frequently used to form words. A valuable distinction was drawn between *macroeconomics,* concerned at the broadest level with the gross national product, and *microeconomics,* concerned with the price-cost relationships of individual undertakings. *Microcircuitry, microclimatology,* and *microengineering* denoted new spheres of invention and discovery.

Parabibliographical studies were concerned with catalogs and collections of manuscripts. In a jocular mood, psychologists invented *parasynonyms* to denote those differing qualities ascribed by the speaker to his esteemed self, to the person addressed, and to the person spoken about—for example: I am firm, you are obstinate, he is pig-headed; I am dignified, you are self-important, he is pompous.

The prefix *mini-* originally was an abbreviation for *miniature.* In an overcrowded world *mini-* formations flourished endlessly; the popular *miniskirt* was joined by *minibag, minibicycle, minibus, minicam* (*era*), and scores of others. The prefix *mini-* merely took the place of the old epithet *small.* Its opposite was *maxi-*, a clipped form of the Latin *maximus.*

Derivatives using *-wise* were criticized by purists, but they continued to multiply: *fashionwise,* with an eye to fashion, and *moneywise,* from a monetary point of view. The Russian suffix *-nik* also continued its existence (at least informally) in *beatnik,* member of the beat generation, and *peacenik,* pacifist.

The adverb-preposition *in,* used as a suffix in the *sit-in* or *stay-in* strikes of the 19th century, had assumed new life in *teach-in,* a prolonged series of lectures and seminars held in defiance of university authorities, and *pray-in,* a service of supplication held by a Roman Catholic lay congregation in protest against the encyclical *Humanae Vitae,* banning birth-control devices. Moreover, *in* functioned as an adjective in *in crowd,* people in the swim and in the know; *in thing,* the most fashionable pursuit of the day; *in word,* the most avant-garde expression among the elite.

In the evolution of verbs the year saw a striking increase in the use of progressive forms consisting of some tense-form of the verb *to be* + present participle (*I am going*). Progressive forms denote that an action or state is (a) actually in progress or (b) of short duration or (c) vividly pictured in the speaker's mind. Until recently, many verbs expressing mental states and attitudes—*believe, forget, hate, hear, hope, imagine, know, like, love, mean, remember, seem, smell, taste,* and *understand*–had seldom or never been used in their progressive forms. This remained valid in principle, but of these 15 verbs only 4–*believe, hate, know,* and *seem*–resisted this growing preference for *-ing* forms. "The kind of music we are hearing today" is a typical example of the new usage. People wanted to make what they said (were saying) more arresting, more lively, and more vivid. Maybe it was only a transient fashion.

It would seem, however, that *going to* (slang, *gounta* and *gonna*), expressing an immediate future, had come to stay. "Apollo 12 *is going to* cost $12 million" sounded more urgent, more definite, and more impressive than plain *will cost.*

The past year also saw a marked increase in the choice of phrasal verbs like *break down* and *set up* instead of their classical synonyms *analyze* and *establish.* In a rapidly changing world *phase out* became a special favorite; it was used both transitively, in the sense "to ease something gently out of service," and intransitively, meaning "to withdraw gradually."

The noun *phaseout* suggested a less painful transition than *changeover* or *layoff.* So, too, *breakthrough* in the sense of "forceful advance," originally a military term, was applied to the sudden overcoming of an obstruction to progress in research, the unexpected move forward after a prolonged *buildup* of resources and power. Such nouns derived from verb phrases were used more than ever before. They were felt to be more vigorous, more down-to-earth, and less abstract than their traditional counterparts. Among the commonest were *breakaway,* secession; *dropout,* one who rejects; *followup,* sequel; *frameup,* conspiracy; *leftover,* remnant; *letup,* relaxation; *stepup,* escalation; and *tieup,* connection. The next stage was seen in the functional shift of these phrasal-verb nouns into attributive adjectives as in *breakaway group, getby makeshift,* and *takeover bid.*

Fashionable words, highly significant for students of psycholinguistics, were exceptionally interesting: *ambience,* "total environment, milieu"; *charisma,* "that special grace which gives its possessor power and influence over others"; *confrontation,* a solemn and ponderous word denoting "direct and open encounter between rival powers"; *dialogue* (in depth), more impressive than *negotiations* and more dignified than mere *talks; image,* already on its way out before being resuscitated by J. B. Priestley in his novel 'The Image Men' with its Institute of Social Imagistics; and *monolith,* literally "single block of stone" but metaphorically "something (especially an institution) massive, uniform, and immovable."

Adjectives in vogue included *rebarbative,* repellent, evoking annoyance and irritation (like a prickly beard), and *open-ended,* permissive, not restrictive, allowing the broadest possible interpretation. Outstanding among vogue phrases were *areas of agreement,* especially in collective bargaining; *corridors of power,* echoing the title of C. P. Snow's novel; *golden handshake,* the formal dismissal (with a gift) of an unwanted chairman or an aging director; *grassroots facts,* basic or fundamental realities, right down to earth, stated without embellishment or humbug; *moment of truth,* that critical instant when a person or a society is put to the supreme test, originally the point in a bullfight at which the matador makes (or fails to make) the kill; *pressure group,* any body of people bent on deflecting legislation through lobbying techniques and propaganda; and *status symbol,* any object by which the position of its possessor is judged by contemporary society.

Vogue phrases also abounded. *Let's face it!* said the realists. Perhaps *it's just one of those things,* and certainly it's better to *spell it out* if we really wish to *bridge the gap.*

Reprints from the 1970 Compton's

This section consists of six new or fully revised articles selected from the new edition of Compton's Encyclopedia. The articles are reprinted here to help the reader keep his home reference library complete and up-to-date.

Reprinted are the following:

EGYPT (UNITED ARAB REPUBLIC)
EGYPT, ANCIENT
PORTUGAL
REPRODUCTION
SPACE TRAVEL
SPAIN

Today, as in the times when the pyramids were built, the life of Egypt depends upon the irrigating waters of the Nile River and the labors of the Egyptian peasant. The Nile also supplies some industrial power.

EGYPT—Land of the Nile

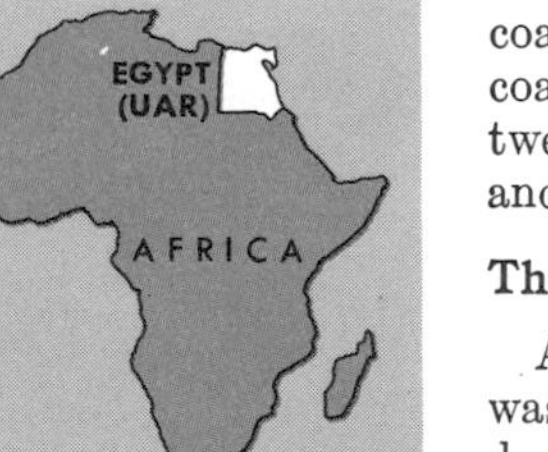

EGYPT (UNITED ARAB REPUBLIC). In the northeastern corner of the African continent the Nile River cuts a fertile valley through desert lands as it empties into the Mediterranean Sea. For 5,000 years the Nile Valley, a fountainhead of Western civilization, has been the heart of Egypt.

Modern Egypt is a socialist state, known officially as the United Arab Republic (UAR). About 90 percent of its people are Arabs of the Islamic faith. The nation's capital is Cairo, located on the Nile about 80 miles from the Mediterranean. Egypt's population (1966 census) is 30,083,419.

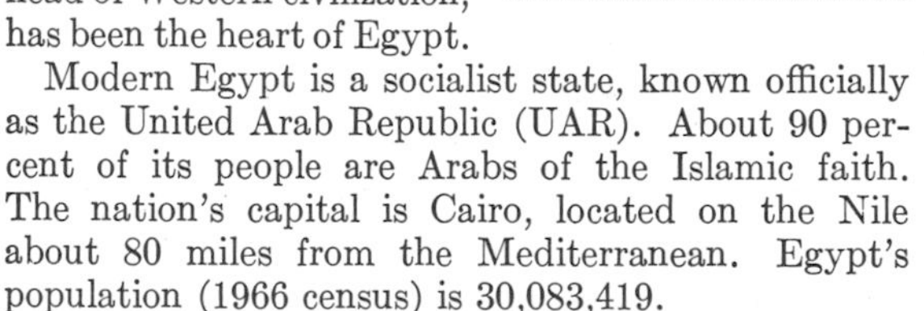

Egypt occupies both northeastern Africa and the Sinai Peninsula of Asia, which links the two continents. The land area is 386,101 square miles, including the 23,200 square miles of Sinai. Egypt is bordered on the west by Libya, on the south by the Sudan, and on the northeast by Israel. Its northern coast lies on the Mediterranean, and its eastern coasts on the Red Sea and the Gulf of Aqaba. Between Sinai and African Egypt lie the Gulf of Suez and the Suez Canal (*see* Suez Canal).

The World's Largest Oasis

Almost 97 percent of Egypt's terrain is desert wasteland, inhospitable to life or settlement. Underlying the desert is a plateau of limestone and sandstone, through which the Nile runs a 960-mile course from the Sudan border. The Aswan High Dam created the vast Lake Nasser, extending from Aswân (Syene) into the Sudan some 200 miles to the south. Between Aswân and Cairo the Nile Valley broadens into a plain ranging in width from about 3 to 15 miles. A branch of the Nile, the Bahr Yusef, flows through a gap in the Nile's western cliffs to water the fertile Faiyûm. North of Cairo the valley fans out into a wide delta. The delta area is called Lower Egypt; the valley south of Cairo is called Upper Egypt. (*See also* Aswan High Dam; Nile River.)

The Nile Delta and Valley make up the world's largest oasis. In this area, comprising less than 4 percent of Egypt's territory, live 99 percent of its people. It has one of the highest population densities for an agricultural area—some 1,900 persons to the square mile. In the delta are Egypt's most fertile lands and its industrial centers.

The Nile Valley separates two vast desert regions. The Western Desert, a part of the great Libyan Desert, is one of the world's driest areas. In five oases where water is available and in small towns along the northern coast about 100,000 people live. Near the Siwa Oasis, on the edge of the Libyan Plateau, is the arid Qattara Depression, which drops 436 feet below sea level. Mountains rise to 7,000 feet in the extreme southwest.

The area between the Nile River and the Red Sea is known as the Arabian, or Eastern, Desert. Along the Red Sea coast, mountains inhabited by nomadic Bedouin shepherds rise to heights of over 7,000 feet. Some 15,000 people live in villages and mining camps along the coast.

Near the tip of the triangular Sinai Peninsula is Egypt's highest point—Jebel (Mount) Katherina (8,651 feet). Both Katherina and nearby Mount Sinai (7,497 feet) are in the Musa mountain group that dominates the southern part of the peninsula. In the north is a more open plateau, where most of Sinai's sparse population lives. Some nomads live in the mountains.

A Dry Climate

Egypt's climate is generally dry and sunny. Winds from the Mediterranean make the area along the northern coast cooler in summer and warmer in winter than the rest of the country. Average monthly temperatures there may range from about 55° F. in January to about 90° in August. South of Cairo a desert climate prevails, with temperatures rising above 100° in the daytime and dropping sharply at night. In the spring a hot desert wind, the *khamsin*, blows from the south to the delta.

Rainfall of up to eight inches a year occurs along the Mediterranean coast. Cairo gets less than an inch a year. In the south, after many years without rain a deluge may suddenly occur. A little rain falls in Sinai.

The People of Egypt

Most of Egypt's population today is made up of Hamitic Arabs—descendants of the Arab settlers who followed the Moslem invasion of Africa in the 7th century and of the Hamites who lived in ancient Egypt. The south, between Aswân and the Sudan, is largely inhabited by Nubians, a people related to the Berber tribes of North Africa. Thousands of Nubians were resettled in new villages near Kôm Ombo when the formation of Lake Nasser flooded their homelands. Small groups of Armenians, Greeks, and other Europeans live in Egypt's cities. (*See also* Egypt, Ancient; Africa, section "African Peoples and Where They Live.")

The Egyptians, including the Nubians, generally adhere to the Moslem faith. The largest religious minority are members of the Coptic church, one of the oldest Christian churches. The Copts, descended from the ancient Egyptians, constitute about 10 percent of the people.

Classic Arabic, one of the many Arabic dialects spoken in Egypt, is used in books and other printed matter. It is not understood by many of the people, of whom some 70 percent are illiterate. Through

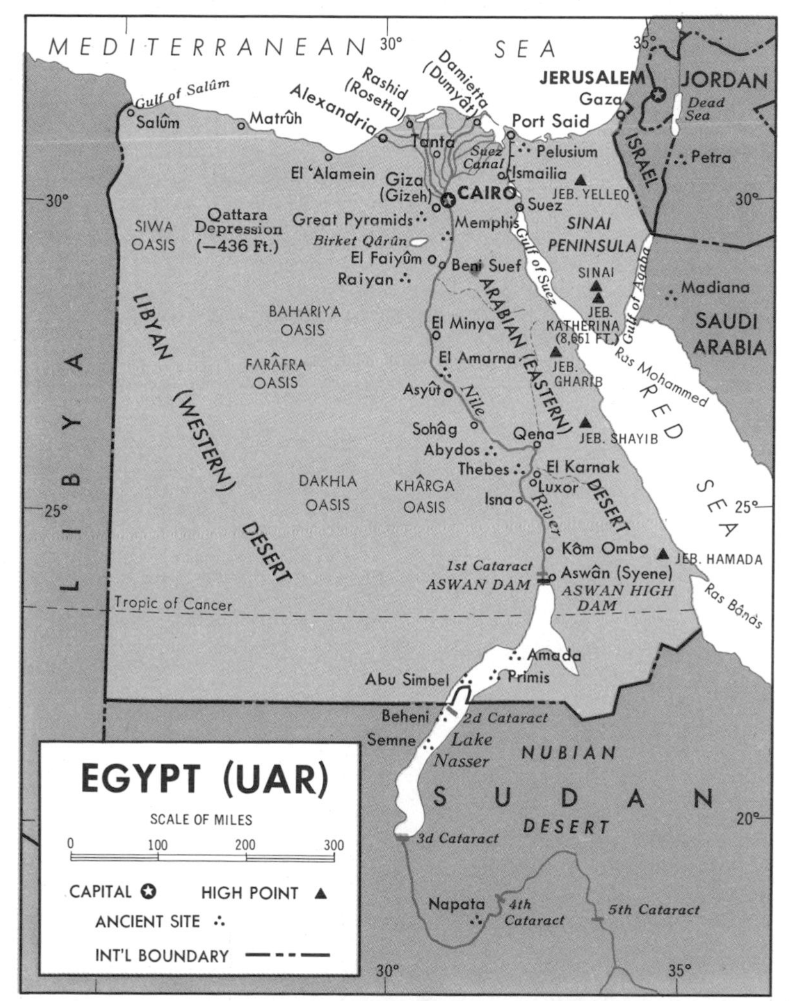

Egypt, now called the United Arab Republic, occupies the northeastern corner of Africa and the Sinai Peninsula of Asia—a crossroads of the ancient Middle Eastern world. Since the 1967 war between a number of the Arab states and Israel, Israel has occupied the peninsula. Almost all of Egypt's people—some 99 percent—live in the fertile Nile River valley and delta.

MODERN TECHNOLOGY

In Egypt's long-barren deserts, pumping equipment now taps precious reserves of oil. Although slow to change from ancient ways, Egypt has begun to industrialize.

radio and television the government has tried to develop a vernacular Arabic as the country's common language. The Coptic language, related to ancient Egyptian, is used only in church liturgies. The Nubian dialect, while spoken, is no longer written.

Agriculture and the Farmer

From ancient times through the 19th century Egyptian farmers planted their crops in the rich soil left by the annual midsummer flooding of the Nile. Then each field produced only one crop a year. Today barrages and dams built on the Nile allow large quantities of water to be stored for use when the river level is low. Canals distribute the water where it is needed throughout the year. Under this system of irrigation, a field may yield two or three crops a year. Since dams filter out the Nile's enriching silt, artificial fertilizers are used.

More than half of the Egyptian people live by farming. The peasant farmer is called a *fellah,* meaning "one who tills the soil." Because land is precious, farm families live in crowded villages. Their homes are built of bricks made from mud and straw, with small shuttered openings for windows and floors of packed earth. Many houses have only two bare rooms, furnished with a brick oven, a chest for

IRRIGATING THE LAND

Farmers still use the ancient waterwheel, or *sakieh,* to lift water from canals to their fields. As a water buffalo turns a horizontal wheel, an underground shaft connected to a vertical wheel (foreground) also turns, causing that wheel to revolve. Jars on the vertical wheel scoop water from the canal and dump it into a trough, from which it flows to the fields.

clothing, and earthenware jars for storing food and water. The family sleeps on matting atop the oven.

The fellah wears a long white robe, called a *galabia*, and a small cap. Married women wear black galabias over their brightly colored dresses and cover their heads and faces with black veils when in public. The children wear cotton dresses.

The whole family works long hours in the fields. Their work animals—water buffalo, oxen, camels, and donkeys—carry farm implements to and from the fields. The people still use tools similar to those of the ancient Egyptians—a wooden plow with an iron-tipped share, a hoe that also serves as a spade, and a hand sickle for reaping.

The peasant diet consists of vegetables grown on the farm and salted cheese made from the milk of the water buffalo. Meat is a luxury eaten only on feast days. Most of the farm produce—including chickens, eggs, and butter made from water buffalo milk—is sold in the marketplace.

Nearly all the farmers are very poor, and their farms are only a few acres in size. After 1953, when land reforms were introduced, the large farming estates were broken up and redistributed among the peasants. Since 1961, farms have been limited to a maximum size of 103 acres. Laws protect the fellah's land tenure. Cooperatives aid the farmer by renting implements and distributing seeds, fertilizer, and pesticides. Agricultural reforms and modern methods such as crop rotation have greatly increased the yield of Egypt's land.

The most valuable crop is long-staple cotton, which is grown on about one fourth of the farmland and is the leading export. Next in importance is rice. Other crops are grains, fodder, fruits, and vegetables. Most cattle are used as draft animals, but there is some livestock breeding. Sheep and goats are raised for wool and hair. Water buffalo provide most of the dairy products.

A SIMPLE WATER-LIFTING DEVICE
With this device, called a *shadoof*, a water bucket is filled, then released. The weight on the end of the shaft raises the leather bucket to the level of the farmer's ditch.

Industry and Trade

After Egypt became a republic in 1952, the new government began an intensified drive toward industrialization, which had been attempted earlier on a small scale. Since 1961 all industries have been nationalized. Under Egypt's socialist policies only agriculture and urban real estate remain free from complete government control. By law 25 percent of industrial profits are distributed to the workers as pensions or other benefits. Workers are represented on the boards of directors of all industries.

Power for industry comes from hydroelectric generators at the Aswan High Dam and from oil. Egypt's petroleum industry has a great potential for growth. Oil wells are located along the Red Sea coast, in Sinai, and offshore in the Gulf of Suez. In 1968 oil production was begun in the Western Desert, near El 'Alamein, and a new offshore field was discovered in the Red Sea. Refineries are situated at Suez and near Cairo and Alexandria; a pipeline links the Suez refineries with Cairo.

Other mineral resources include phosphates along the Red Sea coast, manganese and nitrates in Sinai, salt in the delta and the Red Sea area, and iron ore near Aswân and the Bahariya Oasis. There are iron and steel plants at Helwân, near Cairo. Other minerals obtained in Egypt include gypsum, talc, lead, and asbestos. Granite is quarried near Aswân and limestone from the cliffs along the Nile.

The most important industry is textiles—cotton, wool, and synthetic goods. Food processing, including the refining of sugarcane and the canning and dehydration of fruits and vegetables, is the second largest industry. Manufactures include industrial chemicals, soap, fertilizers, drugs, cement, rubber, leather, and glass.

Agricultural products and minerals account for most of Egypt's exports. After raw cotton, the chief agricultural exports are rice, fresh fruit, and vegetables. Crude petroleum, manganese, and phosphates are the leading mineral exports. Among the manufactured goods exported are textiles, refined sugarcane, printed matter, films, and cement.

The principal imports are foods, including cereals and animal and vegetable oils. Mineral products, machinery, chemical products, and transportation equipment are also major imports.

Leading Cities

Egypt's largest cities, Cairo and Alexandria, are commercial and industrial centers. Cairo, which with its suburbs occupies both banks of the Nile just south of the delta, is the largest city in Africa. Alexandria, on the Mediterranean, is the chief seaport. The Suez Canal made international ports of Suez, at the south entrance, and Port Said, at the north. (*See also* Cairo; Alexandria.)

A farm labor surplus has led many fellahin to seek work away from the fields. Because there are not enough industrial jobs, however, the cities are burdened with large numbers of unemployed people. Peasant migration also contributes to an urban housing shortage. Near some industrial centers federal housing for workers has been built.

Transportation and Communication

Canals are as important for transportation in Egypt as they are for agriculture. On the Nile and on the major canals, flat-bottomed sailboats, called *feluccas*, carry most of the nation's heavy goods and much of its produce. There are some 1,000 miles of navigable canals, mostly in the delta. Passenger steamers ply the Nile between Cairo and Aswân. The Suez Canal handles mainly international shipping.

Egypt has about 2,600 miles of railroads. From Cairo lines extend along the Nile to Aswân, across the northern coast to Salûm, and to Alexandria, Port Said, and Suez. Smaller lines connect the delta towns. A railroad parallels the western bank of the Suez Canal between Suez and Ismailia.

Most of Egypt's 12,600 miles of roads are packed-earth tracks suitable only for carts and animals. Paved roads connect Cairo with Alexandria, Suez, Ismailia, El Faiyûm, and Asyût. Other roads follow the Suez Canal's western bank and cross the northern coast between Alexandria and Salûm. Airlines provide service within the country and link Egypt with other Middle Eastern nations.

Egypt's newspapers and motion pictures are the most highly developed and influential in the Arab world. The press is strictly censored and reflects government policies on domestic and international issues. Motion pictures produced in Giza (Gizeh) are distributed throughout Arabic-speaking lands. Through radio and television the government can communicate with illiterate Egyptians.

Education, Welfare, and Culture

Under the educational system established during the 1950's, Egyptian children must attend free pri-

A VILLAGE IN RURAL EGYPT
The flat roof of the farmer's village home is almost as important as a room. Here straw is stored for use as fuel and chickens are raised for the market.

GROWING CITIES FOR AN EXPANDING POPULATION

Behind an old wall, a modern apartment complex rises in Cairo. The rapid increase in Egypt's population and the influx of workers to industrial centers have led the government to build vast housing developments in the cities. Many slums have been cleared and replaced by blocks of inexpensive apartments. New housing is pushing Cairo's limits into the desert.

mary schools for six years. Those who qualify are prepared for three-year general or technical courses in secondary schools. Postprimary courses in domestic, commercial, or agricultural subjects are also available. Secondary-school graduates may take examinations for the universities or go on to technical institutes. Over a third of the primary- and secondary-school students are women.

Egypt has four major state universities, all coeducational. The largest of these is the University of Cairo, at Giza, founded as the Egyptian University in 1908. It has been government operated since 1925, and there is a branch at Khartoum, in the Sudan. Universities were opened at Alexandria in 1942 and at Asyût in 1957. Ain Shams University, incorporating several other schools near Cairo, was established in 1950.

One of the world's oldest centers of Islamic education, El Azhar University, was founded in Cairo in A.D. 970. Since 1961 it has also provided secular education. The American University in Cairo was founded in 1919.

The Ministry of Education operates about 40 technical institutes. Over 700 Combined Rural Centers offer training in agriculture and crafts.

Due to the poverty, ignorance, and high birthrates in rural Egypt, health standards there differ widely from those in the urban areas. The Combined Rural Centers operate health clinics and conduct programs to reduce and control the diseases that have long plagued the Egyptian peasant—tuberculosis, malaria, amebic dysentery, hookworm, and schistosomiasis. The government has installed pumps in most villages to provide pure water. Because the peasants cling to their age-old ways, however, improvements in their health can be accomplished only gradually.

Agricultural workers are also benefited by rent controls and other agrarian reforms. Since the 1930's laws have provided industrial workers with minimum wages, medical benefits and compensation, and pensions and have limited their working hours.

The government supports cultural activities aimed at furthering the development of Egyptian nationalism. Writers, playwrights, and artists who cooperate with government goals are well paid. A number of theatrical companies tour the country. One of Egypt's most important businesses is publishing.

Government and Politics

Since 1952, when a military junta overthrew the monarchy, Egypt has evolved into a socialist state. The constitution of 1964 provides for a strong presidency and a unicameral National Assembly. The president, elected for a six-year term, has complete executive power, including the right to appoint and dismiss cabinet ministers, vice-presidents, prime ministers, civil servants, and military officers; to decree, suggest, and protest laws; to convene, terminate, and dissolve the National Assembly; and to issue security and law-enforcement regulations. The National Assembly has 350 members, of whom half are workers or farmers. Its primary functions are to initiate and amend legislation and to approve budgets and government programs.

Egypt is divided into 25 districts, called governorates. Each is headed by an official appointed by the president and governed by a council elected from government-approved candidates. Village councils also carry out national policies.

The only legal political party in Egypt is the Arab Socialist Union. It was founded in 1962 to create a popular political base for the socialist regime. It has representatives on all the government councils down to the village level. Through the district councils and the Arab Socialist Union, Egyptians of all classes have been able to participate in the political process for the first time. Opponents of the regime are not permitted to take part in the nation's political life.

Moslem, Turkish, and British Control

The history of Egypt up to the early Middle Ages is told in the article Egypt, Ancient. That period ended with the 7th-century conquest of Arabia by the Islamic prophet Mohammed. The caliphs who succeeded him after his death in 632 conquered Egypt in 639–41 (*see* Mohammed and Mohammedanism).

At the time of the invasion the Egyptians were a Christian people, but the Arabs succeeded in converting most of them to Islam (*see* Islam). Those who held out despite persecution were called Copts, from an Arabic word meaning "Egyptian." With the coming of Arabic culture, the Egyptian language passed out of use except in the Coptic church.

When Egypt was conquered by the Turkish sultan Selim I in 1517, it became part of the Ottoman Empire (*see* Turkey). Napoleon I, invading Egypt in 1798, defeated the Turks in the battle of the Pyramids, but his fleet was destroyed by Britain's Admiral Horatio Nelson in the battle of the Nile (*see* Napoleon I; Nelson).

The British and French had left Egypt by 1803. Mehemet (Mohammed) Ali, an Ottoman army officer, took control and rebuilt the Egyptian army and navy. In 1805 he was recognized as governor (pasha) of Egypt. During his rule irrigation was improved and many acres were reclaimed from the desert. The fellahin were given land to raise cotton, sugarcane, and rice. About 1819 Mehemet Ali conquered the Sudan.

In 1856 Said Pasha, Mehemet Ali's son, granted a French company the right to build the Suez Canal (*see* Suez Canal). It was opened in 1869 during the reign of Khedive Ismail Pasha. To repay his debts to British and French bankers, Ismail Pasha sold Egypt's shares of Suez stock to Britain, giving the British control of the canal. In 1876, again in debt, he allowed British and French officials to supervise Egypt's finances. When the Egyptian people revolted in 1882, the French withdrew and British forces occupied Egypt. Egypt was in effect a British dependency while still a part of the Ottoman Empire.

Egypt prospered under the British, who reduced taxes, introduced industry, developed trade, and stabilized finances. They modernized the irrigation system with canals and dams, such as the first Aswan Dam project (1898–1902). In 1899 the Anglo-Egyptian Sudan was established under joint British and Egyptian rule (*see* Sudan).

LEARNING THE CRAFT OF WEAVING

Although Egypt's textile plants use modern spinning and weaving techniques, handweaving is still taught in some schools. Weavers sell handmade blankets and shawls in town markets. There other craftsmen also sell their wares—jars and bowls of pottery, baskets and mats woven from rushes and palm leaves, and ornaments and utensils made of silver, gold, and brass.

In World War I Turkey sided with Germany but Egypt supported the British. In 1914 Britain declared Egypt free of Turkish rule and formally proclaimed it a British protectorate.

Egypt as an Independent Nation

Egyptian riots for independence ended the protectorate in 1922. The British recognized Egypt as a sovereign state but reserved the right to keep troops there. In 1923 a constitutional monarchy was established with Sultan Fuad as king. He was succeeded in 1936 by his son Farouk. A treaty that year confirmed Britain's military control of the canal zone and joint rule of the Sudan. In World War II Egypt was invaded by German and Italian troops.

When the British left Palestine in 1948, Egypt and its Arab allies invaded the area proclaimed as the state of Israel (*see* Israel). Although defeated, Egypt kept the Gaza coast, called the Gaza Strip.

In 1952 Farouk was overthrown by a military junta. An army council, led by Maj. Gen. Mohammed Naguib and Col. Gamal Abdel Nasser, declared Egypt a republic (*see* Nasser). Nasser became premier in 1954 and president in 1956. In July 1956, after the British left Suez, he declared the internationally owned canal Egyptian property. As a result, Israel invaded Sinai in October and British and French forces landed in the canal zone in November. United Nations pressure brought a cease-fire and withdrawal of troops. Egypt kept the canal.

In 1958 Egypt and Syria merged as the United Arab Republic (UAR), and the UAR and Yemen formed the United Arab States. After Syria withdrew from the union in 1961, Egypt retained the name UAR. Also in 1961, Egypt ousted Yemen from their federation. When Yemen's civil war began in 1962, Egypt aided the republican side. (*See also* Arab Federations; Syria; Yemen.)

As an advocate of Arab unity and the destruction of Israel, Nasser was recognized as the leader of the Arab world. In 1967 he forced the United Nations peace-keeping forces to withdraw from Sinai and the Gaza Strip and blockaded the Gulf of Aqaba against Israeli shipping. In the six-day war that ensued, Israel defeated the allied Arab forces and occupied Sinai and Gaza. The Suez Canal, closed by Egypt, was blocked by damaged ships. United Nations patrols were stationed along the cease-fire line at the canal in July 1967.

Egypt's economy survived through massive financial aid from wealthier Arab nations and Russian technical and military assistance and trade. As dependence on Communist states grew, Western influence in Egypt weakened. Since 1967, Egyptian forces—retrained and reequipped by the Russians—have clashed often with Israel along the canal. (For a detailed account of Arab-Israeli relations, *see* Israel.)

WORSHIPING MOSLEMS

On the richly designed carpets inside the Sultan Hasan mosque in Cairo, Moslem worshipers kneel in the traditional praying position. Most Egyptian towns have a mosque.

Egypt Fact Summary

THE LAND

Area: 386,101 square miles.
Chief River: Nile.
Highest Point: Jebel Katherina (8,651 feet), on the Sinai Peninsula.
Climate: Arid, with scanty rainfall on Mediterranean coast; summers, hot and dry; winters, mild.

THE PEOPLE

Population (1966 census): 30,083,419.
Density: 78 persons per square mile.
Language: Arabic.
Religion: Moslem; Coptic Christian.
Largest Cities (1960 census): Cairo, 3,348,779; Alexandria, 1,516,234; Giza, 250,534; Port Said, 245,318; Suez, 203,610; Tanta, 184,299.

GOVERNMENT

Capital: Cairo.
Form: Socialist republic; unicameral National Assembly elected by national suffrage; president of the republic may appoint up to ten additional members.
Constitution: Adopted 1964.
Monetary Unit: Egyptian pound.
Weights and Measures: Metric system.

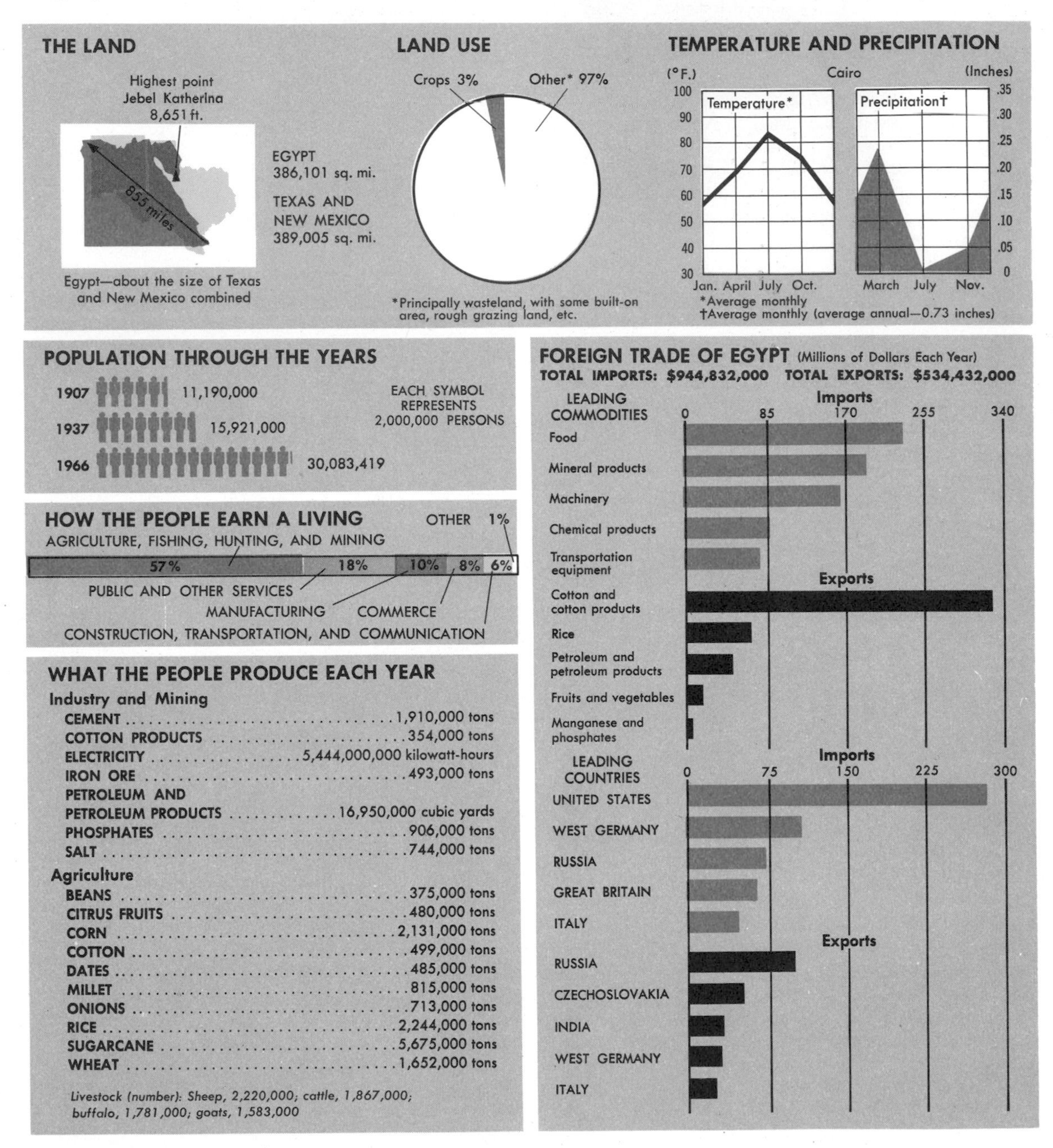

For 45 centuries the Great Sphinx and the pyramids at Giza (Gizeh) have symbolized the wealth and power of ancient Egypt, where the seeds of Western civilization were planted. Egypt has had a longer continuous history than any other country.

EGYPT, ANCIENT. No other country—not even China or India—has such a long unbroken history as Egypt. Nearly 3,000 years before the birth of Christ, the Egyptians had reached a high stage of civilization. They lived under an orderly government; they carried on commerce in ships; they built great stone structures; and, most important of all, they had acquired the art of writing.

Because they lived so long ago, the Egyptian people had to find out for themselves how to do many things that are easily done today. They adopted some inventions of the Sumerians but made more extensive use of them. In the Nile Valley the early development of the arts and crafts that formed the foundation of Western civilization can be traced. (*See also* Babylonia and Assyria.)

The traveler along the Nile sees many majestic monuments that reveal the achievements of ancient Egypt. Most of these monuments are tombs and temples. The ancient Egyptians were very religious. They believed in a life after death—at first only for kings and nobles—if the body could be preserved. So they carefully embalmed the body and walled it up in a massive tomb (*see* Mummy). On the walls of the tomb they carved pictures and inscriptions. Some private tombs were decorated with paintings. They put into the tomb the man's statue and any objects they thought he would want when his soul returned to the body. The hot sand and dry air of Egypt preserved many of these objects through the centuries. Thousands of them are now in museums all over the world. Together with written documents, they show how people lived in Egypt thousands of years ago.

The desert sands have also preserved the remains of prehistoric people. By their sides, in the burial pits, lie stone tools and weapons, carved figures, and decorated pottery. These artifacts help archaeologists and historians piece together the story of life in the Nile Valley centuries before the beginning of the historical period. (*See also* Archaeology.)

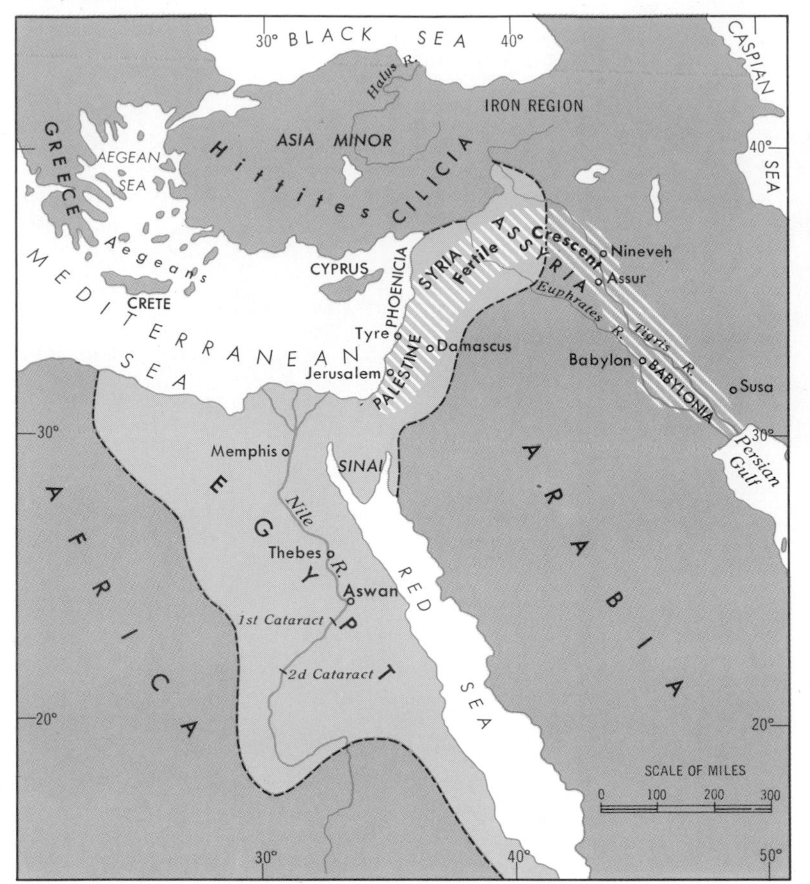

During the New Kingdom period Egypt became a Mediterranean empire. Around 1479 B.C. Thutmose III, riding "in a chariot of fine gold," led his armies out of Egypt into Phoenicia, Palestine, and Syria. In later campaigns he extended the empire to the Euphrates Valley in Mesopotamia. Earlier rulers had already pushed the frontiers south into Nubia, beyond the First Cataract of the Nile.

Prehistoric Era

Ages ago the land of Egypt was very different from what it is today. There was rain. There was no delta, and the sea extended far up the Nile Valley. The plateau on each side of the water was grassland. The people wandered over the plateau in search of game and fresh pastures and had no permanent home. They hunted with a crude stone hand ax and with a bow and arrow. Their arrows were made of chipped flint. (*See also* Egypt; Stone Age.)

Very gradually the rains decreased and the grasslands dried up. The Nile began to deposit silt in the valley and to build up the delta. The animals went down to the valley. The hunters followed them and settled at the edge of the jungle that lined the river.

In the Nile Valley the people's way of life underwent a great change. They settled down in more or less permanent homes and progressed from food gathering to food producing. They still hunted the elephant and hippopotamus and wild fowl, and they fished in the river. More and more, however, they relied for meat on the animals they bred—long-horned cattle, sheep, goats, and geese.

The early Egyptians learned that the vegetables and wild grain they gathered grew from seeds. When the Nile floodwater drained away, they dug up the ground with a wooden hoe, scattered seeds over the wet soil, and waited for the harvest. They cut the grain with a sharp-toothed flint sickle set in a straight wooden holder and then ground it between two flat millstones. The people raised emmer (wheat), barley, a few vegetables, and flax. From the grain they made bread and beer, and they spun and wove the flax for linen garments.

The first houses were round or oval, built over a hole in the ground. The walls were lumps of mud, and the roofs were matting. Later houses were rectangular, made of shaped bricks, with wooden frames for doors and windows—much like the houses the Egyptian farmers live in today. To work the lumber, the people used ground stone axheads and flint saws. Beautiful clay pottery was created, without the wheel, to hold food and drink. They fashioned ornaments of ivory, made beads and baskets, and carved in stone the figures of people and animals. They built ships that had oars, and they carried on trade with nearby countries. Instead of names, the ships had simple signs, probably indicating the home port. These signs were an early step in the invention of writing.

Good farmland was scarce. The desert came down close to the marshes that edged the river. To gain more land, the people rooted out the jungle, filled in marshes, and built mud walls to keep out floodwater. In time they engaged in large-scale irrigation work, digging canals that cut across miles of land. This required the cooperation of many people living in different places. Leaders became necessary to plan the work and direct the workers. Because of this need, orderly government arose.

Population and wealth grew with the increase in farmland. There was food enough to support a professional class, who worked at crafts instead of farming. Villages grew into towns. Large towns spread their rule over nearby villages and became states. At the end of the prehistoric period, there were only two political units—Lower Egypt (the delta) and Upper Egypt (the valley). Later, when Egypt was united, the people still called it the Two Lands, and the king of all Egypt wore a double crown combining the white crown of the south with the red crown of the north.

Before the prehistoric period ended, the Egyptians were stimulated by their contact with people who lived in a Mesopotamian river valley in Asia. These people were more advanced than the Egyptians in working metal, and they also had writing. Although this was probably the inspiration for Egyptian writing, the Egyptians did not take over the Mesopotamian script but developed a script of their own. This great invention brought Egypt abruptly to the threshold of history, for history begins with written records. (*See also* Mesopotamia.)

DYNASTIES OF EGYPT

The beginnings of writing in Egypt go back to about 3100 B.C., when the Two Lands became united in a single kingdom. According to tradition, it was Menes, a king of Upper Egypt, who brought about the union. He stands first in the long line of kings who ruled Egypt for about 3,000 years. Egyptian priests made lists of their kings, or pharaohs, and noted the most important events of their reigns. About 280 B.C. one of these priests, Manetho, grouped the pharaohs into 30 dynasties. (A dynasty is a succession of rulers of the same line of descent.)

Modern historians group the dynasties into periods. The periods when Egyptian civilization flourished are the Old Kingdom, the Middle Kingdom, and the New Kingdom. These are separated by periods of decline called the First Intermediate Period and the Second Intermediate Period. The final period of decline is called the Late Period.

The Old Kingdom

Little is known of Menes' successors until the reign of King Zoser, or Djoser, at the end of the 3d dynasty. Zoser's capital was located at Memphis, on the Nile's west bank near the point where the Two Lands met. Imhotep, a master builder, erected Zoser's tomb, the step pyramid of Saqqara, on high ground overlooking the city. This monument—the first great building in the country made entirely of stone—marked the beginning of Egypt's most creative period, the Pyramid Age.

Later kings built their tombs in true pyramidal form. Each pyramid guarded the body of one king, housed in a chamber deep within the pile. The climax of pyramid building was reached in the three gigantic tombs erected for Kings Khufu (Cheops), Khafre, and Menkure at Giza (Gizeh). Near them in the sand lies the Great Sphinx, a stone lion with the head of King Khafre. (*See also* Pyramids; Sphinx.)

The Old Kingdom lasted about 500 years. It was an active, optimistic age, an age of peace and splendor. Art reached a brilliant flowering. Sculpture achieved a grandeur never later attained. The pharaoh kept a splendid court. The people worshiped him as a god on earth, for they believed him to be the son of Ra, or Re, the great sun-god. They called him *pr-'o* (in the Bible, *pharaoh*), meaning "great house."

About 2200 B.C. the Old Kingdom came to an end. Nobles became independent and ruled as if they were kings. The country was split up into small warring states. Irrigation systems fell into disrepair. According to writers of the time: "The desert is spread throughout the land. The robbers are now in the possession of riches. Men sit in the bushes until the benighted traveler comes to . . . steal what is upon him." Thieves broke into the pyramids and robbed them of their treasures.

The Middle Kingdom

The Middle Kingdom period began about 2050 B.C. After a long struggle, the rulers of Thebes won out over their enemies and once again united Egypt into a single state. Thebes was then a little town on the Nile in Upper Egypt. In the New Kingdom it became one of the ancient world's greatest capitals.

The pharaohs of the Middle Kingdom constructed enormous irrigation works in the Faiyûm. Noting the annual heights of the Nile flood at Aswân, they laid plans to use the Nile water wisely. They sent trading ships up the Nile to Nubia and across the sea to Mediterranean lands. They got gold from Nubia and copper from the mines in Sinai. Construction of the most colossal temple of all time, the Temple of Amen (Amon) at El Karnak, was begun.

After two centuries of peace and prosperity, Egypt entered another dark age. About 1800 B.C. it fell for the first time to foreign invaders. Down from the north came the Hyksos, a barbarian people who used horses and chariots in combat and also had superior bows. The Egyptians, fighting on foot, were no match for them. The Hyksos occupied Lower Egypt, living in fortified camps behind great earthen walls. They failed to conquer Upper Egypt, and the pharaohs stayed on at Thebes. When the Egyptians had learned the new methods of warfare, the ruler Kamose began a successful war of liberation.

PERIODS IN EARLY EGYPTIAN HISTORY*

Prehistoric Period	Before 3100 B.C.
Archaic Period	
Dynasties I–II	3100–2700 B.C.
Old Kingdom	
Dynasties III–VI	2700–2200 B.C.
First Intermediate Period	
Dynasties VII–X	2200–2050 B.C.
Middle Kingdom	
Dynasties XI–XII	2050–1800 B.C.
Second Intermediate Period	
Dynasties XIII–XVII	1800–1570 B.C.
New Kingdom	
Dynasties XVIII–XX	1570–1090 B.C.
Late Period	
Dynasties XXI–XXX	1090–332 B.C.
Ptolemaic Period	332–30 B.C.
Roman Period	30 B.C.–A.D. 395
Byzantine Period	A.D. 395–640

*Dates are approximate until about 500 B.C. For the earliest period, about 3000 B.C., historians estimate the margin of error may be up to 100 years. At about 1000 B.C. the margin narrows to 10 to 15 years.

THE COLOSSI OF MEMNON IN THEBES
These statues of Amenhotep III—all that remains of his temple—once weighed over 700 tons each and were nearly 70 feet high. The Romans thought they depicted Memnon, a Trojan hero.

The New Kingdom

A new era dawned for Egypt after the Hyksos had been expelled. This period, the New Kingdom, was the age of empire. The once-peaceful Egyptians, having learned new techniques of warfare, embarked on foreign conquest on a large scale. The empire reached its peak under Thutmose III, one of the first great generals in history. He fought many campaigns in Asia and extended Egypt's rule to the Euphrates.

Slaves and tribute poured into Egypt from the conquered nations. The tribute was paid in goods, for the ancient world still did not have money. Wall paintings show people from Nubia, Babylonia, Syria, and Palestine bearing presents on their backs and bowing humbly before the pharaoh.

The Egyptian rulers used their new wealth and slaves to repair the old temples and build new ones. Hatshepsut, Egypt's first great queen, enlarged the great Temple of Amen at El Karnak. She also built her own beautiful temple at Deir el Bahri.

Amenhotep III built the wonderful temple at Luxor and put up the famous pair of colossal seated statues called the Colossi of Memnon (*see* Memnon). In the Middle Kingdom period, the pharaohs of Thebes had built modest brick pyramids for their tombs. In the New Kingdom period they broke with this tradition and began to hew tombs deep in the cliffs of an isolated valley west of Thebes. About 40 kings were buried in this "Valley of the Tombs of the Kings."

In the last years of his reign Amenhotep III paid little attention to the empire. It was already decaying when his son Amenhotep IV came to the throne. This king was more interested in religion than in warfare. Even before his father's death, he began to promote a new religious doctrine. He wanted the people to give up all their old gods and worship only the radiant sun, which was then called Aten. He changed his name from Amenhotep ("Amen is satisfied") to Ikhnaton (Akhenaton) ("It is well with Aten"). He left Thebes and built a splendid new capital sacred to Aten at El Amarna in middle Egypt. Throughout the land he had the word "gods" and the name "Amen" removed from tombs and monuments.

Ikhnaton's idea of a single god gained no hold on the Egyptian people. His successor, Tutankhamen, moved the capital back to Thebes and restored the name of Amen on monuments. Tutankhamen is famous chiefly for his lavishly furnished tomb, discovered in 1922. Its treasures reveal the luxury of the most magnificent period of Egyptian history.

Half a century later Ramses II completed the gigantic hall at El Karnak and set up many statues of himself. He also had his name carved on monuments built by earlier rulers, so that he became better known than any other king. He regained part of Egypt's Asian empire. But the kings who followed him had to use the army to defend Egypt against invaders.

The Late Period

In the Late Period, the final decline of Egypt's power set in. The treasury had been drained by extensive building projects and by the army. Hungry workers had to resort to strikes to get their wages in grain. The central government weakened, and the country split up once more into small states.

About 730 B.C., Ethiopian invaders entered Egypt and established a strong, new dynasty. However, they were unable to withstand an invasion from the north by the Assyrians. When Assyria's power waned, a new Egyptian dynasty reorganized the country. Persia conquered Egypt in 525 B.C. and held it until 404 B.C. Three brief Egyptian dynasties followed, ending with the 30th, which fell to a second Persian conquest in 341 B.C.

Postdynastic Periods

Persian rule lasted until Alexander the Great invaded Egypt in 332 B.C. After Alexander's death, Ptolemy, one of his generals, seized the throne. The Ptolemys introduced Greek manners and ideas into Egypt. The city of Alexandria, founded by Alexander, became the center of Greek civilization in the Near East (*see* Alexandria).

The rule of Egypt by the Ptolemaic line ended with the beautiful Queen Cleopatra, who reigned first with her brother Ptolemy XIII, then with her brother Ptolemy XIV, and finally with Caesarion, her son by Julius Caesar (*see* Cleopatra). In 30 B.C. Egypt was proclaimed a province of Rome.

After the Roman Empire was divided in half in the 4th century A.D., Egypt was ruled from Constantinople by the Byzantine emperors (*see* Byzantine Empire). During this period most Egyptians were converted to Christianity. In the 7th century, Egypt fell to the Arabs. (For later Egyptian history, *see* Egypt, subhead "Moslem, Turkish, and British Control.")

Everyday Life in Ancient Egypt

PEOPLE TODAY live in an age when every year brings forth new inventions and discoveries, new fads and fashions that affect everyday life. Through communications, migration, and travel, foreign cultures merge into new life styles. The Egyptians had their greatest creative period at the very beginning of their long history. After that, their way of living changed very little. It is therefore possible to describe their homelife and their art without reference to the historical periods of Egyptian history.

Upper-Class Homelife and Dress

Of all the early peoples, the Egyptians were the least warlike. Their country was protected by the sea on the north and by deserts to the east and west. For many centuries they could develop their own way of life without fear of invasion by foreign armies. Their interests were centered in their homes and families and in their work. Their stone tombs were a kind of insurance against death. They loved life and wanted it to go on forever.

Villages and towns were situated near the Nile because it was the chief highway as well as the only source of water. Even the rich lived in houses of mud brick. The walls were richly colored. Windows were small, high openings covered with loosely woven matting to keep out the heat and glare of the sun. The most fashionable district was near the king's palace. Even here, houses were crowded close together to leave more space for farmland. Some dwellings were two stories high. Usually houses were built back to back to save space. Some opened onto a narrow street; others faced a small walled garden.

The walls were decorated with bright frescoes. Straw matting and rugs covered the floors. Lamps were saucers of oil with a floating wick. Rich people had beds, chairs, and stools but no real dining tables (*see* Furniture, subhead "Furniture's Heritage"). They kept their clothes and linen sheets in box chests or in baskets. The linen was sent to professional laundrymen to be washed in the river.

The ancient Egyptians stored their water and food in huge pottery jars. The cook used pottery bowls, placing them directly on the fire or in a clay oven. She baked bread and cake and roasted beef, mutton, goose, or wildfowl. The common drinks were beer, wine, and milk. Honey and dates were the only sweets. Almost everything the family needed was grown or made by workers belonging to the estate.

The members of Egypt's upper classes spent much of their time tending to their appearance. They bathed with soda instead of soap and then rubbed perfumed oil into the skin. Men shaved with a bronze razor. They cut their hair short and wore wigs. Women also wore wigs or added false braids to their own hair. They had combs and hairpins and mirrors of polished bronze or silver. Both men and women darkened their eyelids with black or green paint. Women rouged their cheeks and lips and stained their nails with henna. They kept their cosmetics in beautiful box chests.

Because of the hot climate, both men and women wore white linen clothes. Men usually wore only a skirt. In the early centuries the skirts were short and narrow; later they were long and full. Women wore low-cut white dresses with bands over the shoulders. Young children wore nothing at all. Both men and women wore jewelry—collars and necklaces, strings of beads, bracelets, anklets, earrings, and finger rings. Silver was more precious than gold.

Peasants and Craftsmen

The luxurious life of the pharaoh and the nobles was made possible by the continual labor of the peas-

USEFUL OBJECTS FROM AN EGYPTIAN NOBLEMAN'S HOUSE

In contrast to the bare home of the peasant, that of the noble was well furnished. He used vessels of pottery, glass, and faience (upper left and far right); a bed with a raised headrest (bottom left); and chairs with seats of hide or rope (bottom right). His children played with "paddle dolls" with hair of clay beads (top center) and with shell beads (top right).

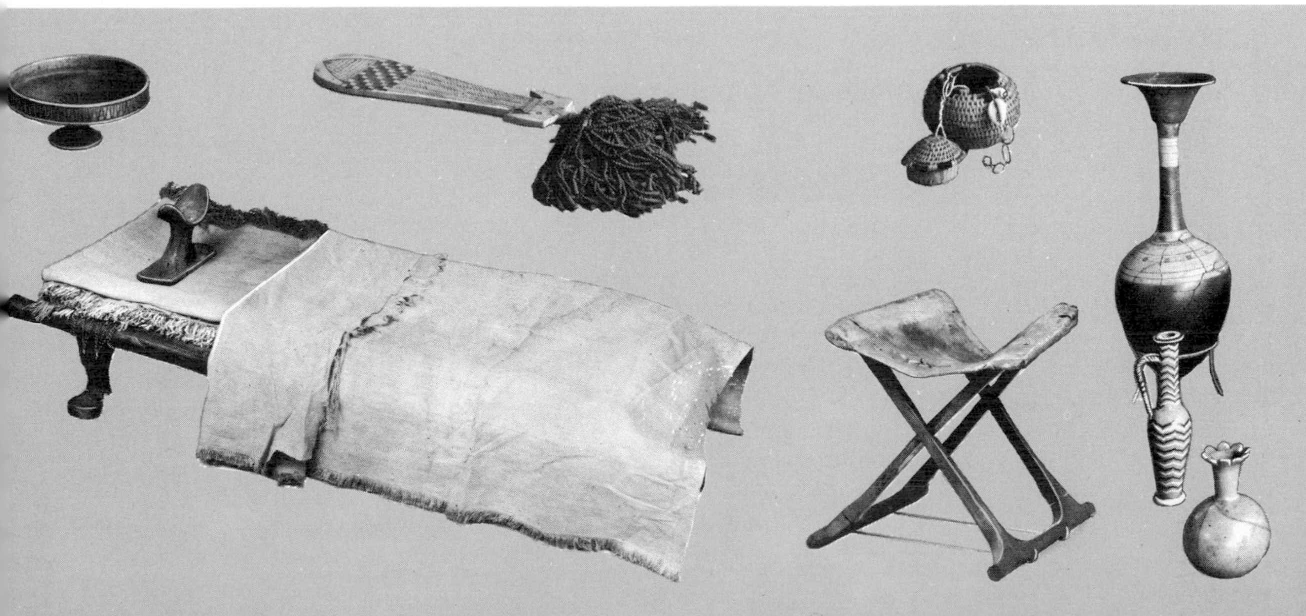

ants who tilled the soil. After the crops were harvested, the pharaoh could call on them to leave their village huts and go off to labor on irrigation works, to quarry stone with primitive tools, or to build tombs and temples. Their only pay was grain from the state granaries, oil, fish, vegetables, and clothing.

The craftsmen and artists had an easier life. They worked in shops close to the palace of the pharaoh or on the estates of priests and nobles. Their professions were hereditary, passed down from father to son. An artist was never hurried. If he could produce a masterpiece, it did not matter whether he worked on it for one year or ten.

The smiths forged bronze tools and weapons and made fine copper and bronze dishes for the homes of the rich. Goldsmiths and silversmiths also made tableware as well as richly wrought jewelry set with turquoise, carnelian, lapis lazuli, and other semiprecious stones. Craftsmen in stone ground out vases, jars, bowls, and platters in hard diorite and porphyry or in soft, cream-colored alabaster, which could be ground so thin it let the light through.

Potters turned clay vessels on a potter's wheel and then baked them in closed clay furnaces as tall as a man. They covered some of the pottery with a blue glaze. Women wove sheer fabrics of linen for clothing and for tapestries and awnings to decorate the houses of the rich.

Egypt then as now had little timber. Cedar and cypress were imported from Lebanon and tropical woods from Nubia. Cabinetmakers fashioned chairs and couches. Other craftsmen overlaid the furniture with precious metals or inlaid it with ebony or ivory. The leatherworker contributed cushions. Shipbuilders made Nile vessels with curving hulls and tall sails and cargo ships to sail to foreign lands (*see* Ship and Shipping). Paperworkers took the papyrus reeds gathered from the Nile marshes, split them, and pasted them crosswise into double sheets of pale yellow writing paper (*see* Papyrus Plant).

MUSIC AND DANCE
This painting from a tomb of the 18th dynasty shows musicians entertaining at a banquet. The performers are playing (left to right) a harp, a lute, a double-reed pipe, and a lyre. The three girls in the center are also dancing.

Religion and Culture of Ancient Egypt

IN VERY EARLY times each town had its own town-god as well as a number of lesser gods. There were also gods that everybody worshiped. The most important of these were Ra, the sun-god; Horus, the sky-god; and Osiris, the god of the dead.

When a town grew in influence, its town-god became more important too. People worshiped him as part of their allegiance to the town. After Thebes became the capital, the worship of its town-god, Amen, spread throughout Egypt. The people combined his worship with that of Ra, and in this form called him Amen-Ra. Temples were raised to Amen throughout Egypt. The most splendid was the temple at El Karnak, in Thebes.

The Story of Ra and Osiris

The people believed that every day Ra, the sun, sailed across the sky in his boat. Every night he disappeared into the underworld, in the west. In the underworld, they thought, was another Nile River. Osiris, the ruler of the underworld, had the sun's boat pulled along this river until at last it crossed the horizon and the sun rose again.

Osiris had been murdered by his brother Set but lived again in the underworld as king of the dead. The people looked to Osiris to give them, too, a life after death. Osiris was usually shown in human form, tightly swathed in linen like a mummy and wearing a high crown. (*See also* Osiris; Isis; Mummy.)

Other Gods and Sacred Animals

Other important deities were Nut and Hathor, goddesses of the sky and of joy; Ptah, master artist and craftsman; Thoth, the moon-god, who was also scribe of the gods and the inventor of writing; and Khnemu, who fashioned men and women on a

MAKING WINE AND ROPE
Grapes are gathered from the vine (top) and then pressed for juice for wine making (center). In the bottom panel, wine jars are brought into port (left), and rope is made from papyrus reeds (right).

A FAMILY EXCURSION IN THE NILE MARSHES
In this tomb painting, a sportsman aims his serpent-headed throwing stick at fowl hidden among the lotus and papyrus plants in a marsh. The figure clinging to his leg in the skiff is his daughter.

potter's wheel. Some gods, such as Amen and Osiris, were always represented in purely human form. Others were pictured as animals or with human bodies and animal heads. Thus Horus was worshiped in the form of a hawk, or falcon, or of a hawk-headed man. Thoth was an ibis, Khnemu was a ram, and Hathor was a cow. The sun had various symbols —the obelisk, the sacred scarab beetle, the uraeus cobra, and the sun disk.

Certain sacred animals were carefully kept in the temples. When Egyptian civilization decayed in its very late days, the people came to regard every animal of these species as sacred. They embalmed thousands of crocodiles, cats, and ibis and buried them in special cemeteries. Bulls were buried in stone vaults in an underground cemetery called the *Serapeum*, at Memphis. (*See also* Cat, subhead "The Origin of Cats.")

Architecture of the Temples

Egyptian architecture was designed to blend into the setting of the Nile Valley, which is as level as a floor and is walled in on both sides by sheer limestone cliffs. The temples erected by the Egyptians are gigantic; their surfaces, flat. The form is rectangular, like that of the flat-topped cliffs. The only decorations are reliefs and inscriptions that do not break the straight lines of the stone surfaces on which they are carved. Private tombs were decorated and inscribed in the same way.

Temples were built on a grand scale. The front wall consisted of two massive sloping towers, together called a pylon, with a door between them. The door gave entrance to a huge unroofed court, bordered on two or three sides by colonnades. Here the public

A RELIGIOUS PILGRIMAGE TO THE UNDERWORLD
In ancient Egypt, even the dead had to make religious pilgrimages, as shown in this depiction of a voyage to a temple of Osiris. In the prow of the boat the captain directs his crew. Overseers with whips, posted atop either end of the cabin, urge the oarsmen on to greater effort. The oars are decorated with painted eyes to help the men find their way through the water.

A QUEEN'S TERRACED TEMPLE
Queen Hatshepsut, the greatest of Egypt's women rulers, built this temple against the stone cliffs of Deir el Bahri. She ruled during the 18th dynasty in the New Kingdom period.

assembled for worship. Beyond the court rose the hypostyle hall—a forest of huge pillars holding up a roof. Past the hall was the sanctuary of the temple-god. Only priests and the pharaoh were allowed to enter the sanctuary. There were many variations of this plan. Large temples—particularly the great temple at El Karnak—had a series of courts, each faced by a pylon. An avenue of sphinxes led from El Karnak to the temple at Luxor.

Painting and Sculpture

Wall paintings took the place of reliefs in many private tombs of the New Kingdom. Some of the paintings and reliefs of this period rank with the world's finest masterpieces in art. In order to appreciate them, it is necessary to understand the principles upon which Egyptian artists worked.

Like other early peoples, the Egyptians did not use perspective. Figures at different distances from the observer were drawn in the same size. Humble people and servants, however, were pictured smaller than the great lord. Furthermore, the artist did not limit himself to a single point of view. He drew what he knew, not merely what he saw. A fisherman in a boat might be sketched as if the artist were looking at the scene from the shore, but fish would be shown swimming under the water. The same picture might even outline the pond as if seen from above. Nevertheless, Egyptian paintings are beautiful and harmonious, and they reveal more than they would if drawn from a single point of view.

In sketching the human figure, the artist usually followed conventions established in early times. Since he wanted to show all the principal parts of the body, he combined front and side views. The head is always in profile, but the eye is drawn as it appears from the front. The shoulders and skirt are front view, but the legs and feet are side view.

Sculptors carved thousands of statues in all sizes, from colossal figures to miniatures. In addition to gods, kings, and nobles, their works included animals and sphinxes. The pharaoh is always shown in a dignified pose, never in movement. The face is often an expressive portrait. The sculptor painted the bodies of men red and women pale yellow and set in eyeballs of colored stone or crystal.

Three Ways of Writing

The ancient Egyptians had three different ways of writing. They are called hieroglyphic, hieratic, and demotic. Hieroglyphs were chiseled on a stone surface. The word comes from two Greek words—

A KING'S TEMPLE FOR HIS GOD
This temple in honor of the supreme god Amen-Ra was erected at El Karnak by Ramses III, one of the rulers of the 20th dynasty, who reigned during the 12th century B.C. The view here is from the top of a pylon into the main hall of the temple.

A KING IN COMMAND
Carved on a wall of the Medinet Habu temple at Luxor, this relief portrays Ramses III reviewing prisoners taken in battle.

hieros, meaning "sacred," and *glyphein*, meaning "to carve." From hieroglyphs the Egyptians developed a cursive writing. Called hieratic, this was written on papyrus with a pen. Out of hieratic a much more rapid script—demotic—developed in the Late Period.

Hieroglyphic writing developed out of picture writing toward the end of the prehistoric period. Until then the only way to record an event had been to draw a picture of it, but only the simplest facts could be told in this way. Picture recording evolved into writing with the realization that pictures of objects could be used to express all kinds of ideas if the words for these ideas had the same sounds as the names of the objects pictured. The picture of a house meant *house;* but it could also stand for the sound of the word for *house*, *pr*. The Egyptians did not write vowels. Because the word for *to go* also consisted of the consonants *pr* with a different vowel sound, the sign for *house* could be used to write *to go* by adding to it a pair of walking legs. The legs sign—called a determinative—was not pronounced but indicated a verb of motion. Hieroglyphic writing was therefore sound writing, though it used pictures. Some of the pictures stood for one consonant and were thus alphabetic, while others were used to represent two or three consonants.

In hieratic and demotic writing, the signs no longer resembled the pictures from which they were developed. Rapid cursive writing with a pen on the soft surface of papyrus led to shortening the signs.

The Rosetta Stone—Key to the Hieroglyphs

The ability to read hieroglyphics died out with the Egyptian religion. Throughout the Middle Ages people thought the inscriptions on monuments were not writing but symbols with some deep religious meaning.

When Napoleon went to Egypt in 1798, he took with him a large staff of scholars and scientists to study the civilization of ancient Egypt. Near Rashid (Rosetta) one of his officers discovered a stone inscribed with three kinds of writing. Napoleon's scholars recognized the writing as Greek at the bottom, demotic in the middle, and hieroglyphic at the top. They could read the ancient Greek and guessed that the other sections must have the same content.

The stone fell into the hands of the British, who sent copies to scholars throughout the world. In 1822 Jean François Champollion deciphered the hieroglyphs. Written about 196 B.C., they commemorate the accession of Ptolemy V Epiphanes, about 205 B.C. Champollion's work was the basis of the science of Egyptology. (*See also* Writing.)

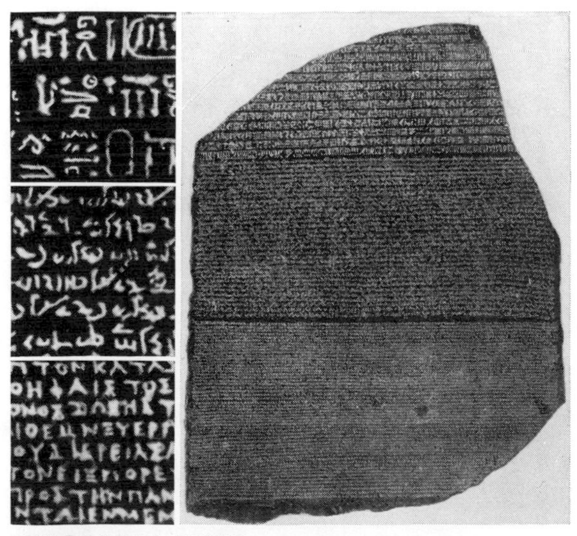

THE ROSETTA STONE
The stone's text, magnified at left, is written in hieroglyphics at the top, demotic script in the middle, and Greek at the bottom.

The Literature of Ancient Egypt

Ancient Egyptian literature consists of both religious and nonreligious texts. The principal religious texts were designed to guide the dead into the underworld. In the Old Kingdom period such texts were for the use of the king only. They were written on the burial chamber walls in the pyramids of the 5th and 6th dynasties and are called Pyramid Texts. There are no inscriptions in the three great pyramids of Giza. Later, "coffin texts" were written on the coffins of private citizens. Still later, religious texts—now called 'Book of the Dead'—were written on papyrus rolls and buried with the dead. (For a description of a papyrus roll, *see* Books and Bookmaking.)

Nonreligious writings relate events in the lives of kings or citizens. Purely literary compositions include poetry and tales of adventure. (For Reference-Outline and Bibliography, *see* Ancient History.)

Carl Frank from Photo Researchers

Harrison Forman

George Holton from Photo Researchers

Erich Lessing from Magnum

Nat and Yanna Brandt from Photo Researchers

EGYPTIAN ART

Much of the art of ancient Egypt centered around temples and the tombs of noblemen. One of the greatest temples ever built was the Temple of Amen, or Amon, at El Karnak. At the far left is a statue amid the ruins of this temple. Sphinxes with the heads of rams (lower left) line the way to the temple at El Karnak. At the upper left is a gold mask molded from the sarcophagus of King Tutankhamen. Above is a model, found in a tomb, of a cattle inspection in ancient Egypt. In the center of the picture a slave is being brought before his owner, probably for punishment. At the right is an example of the paintings found inside the tombs at Thebes.

The temperate climate of Algarve, the southernmost province of Portugal, makes it one of Europe's most popular summer resort areas. The freshly scrubbed appearance of the houses and hotels adds to the charm of its coastal towns.

The Tiny Nation with the Last Big Empire

PORTUGAL. One of the smallest and poorest countries in Europe, Portugal commands a more important place in history than it does in modern world affairs. During the 15th and 16th centuries Portugal's prestige grew as it accumulated a vast overseas empire through exploration and conquest. Although it was subsequently stripped of many of its colonial holdings, there are still Portuguese provinces in both hemispheres. However, neglect of the resources abroad, coupled with a lagging development of industry at home, has held Portugal to the status of a minor power.

In some respects, Portugal's underdevelopment has become an asset. With a countryside still free of industrial blemish, Portugal is a popular resort area. The picturesque quality of its cities and the preservation of provincial customs and festivals in its villages have helped build a thriving tourism. The Shrine of Our Lady of Fátima and other shrines also attract many visitors on annual pilgrimages.

Portugal occupies the southwestern corner of the Iberian Peninsula. Its capital, Lisbon (Lisboa), is the westernmost seaport of continental Europe. The nation's land area of 35,340 square miles includes two island groups in the Atlantic—the Azores, to the west, and Madeira, to the southwest (*see* Azores; Madeira). In Portugal's empire are Macao, on the South China Sea; Portuguese Timor, in the East Indies; and the African provinces of Angola (including Cabinda), Cape Verde Islands, Mozambique, Portuguese Guinea, and São Tomé é Príncipe (*see* Angola; Cape Verde Islands; Mozambique). On the Arabian Sea, Portuguese India (Goa, Damão, and Diu) remained in the empire until 1961, when the territory was seized by India. The scattered overseas provinces total some 805,000 square miles in area.

Natural Features and Climate

Like a deep pocket patched onto Spain, the mainland of Portugal is largely the western continuation of the rugged plateau (Meseta) of central Spain (*see* Spain). No major natural boundaries divide the two nations. The only considerable stretch of level land in the somewhat mountainous country is a narrow plain that extends the length of the Atlantic coastline. On this plain are Portugal's two major cities, Lisbon and Oporto (Porto). Here also live most of the population of 9,440,000 (1967 official estimate).

The highest peak in Portugal, Malhão in the Serra da Estrêla, rises only 6,532 feet. The relatively low mountain ranges are cut with deep and twisting valleys. Through many of them, mountain streams—rising chiefly in Spain—race westward into the Atlantic. The principal rivers are the Douro, the Tagus (Tejo), the Minho, and the Guadiana, which flows south to form part of the Spanish boundary.

Portugal's sunny and moderate climate encourages rich vegetation and easy living. Its long coastline is open to the Atlantic westerlies, which provide ample rainfall for farming. The mean temperature at Lisbon and Oporto is about the same as that at San Diego, Calif. The sheltered valleys of Portugal are very hot in the summer, however.

Varied Products of Land and Sea

The favorable climate and location provide many natural resources. The land along the coastal plain is easy to work. Great forests in the south produce enough cork oak to make Portugal the world's chief source of cork. Portuguese pines, which grow in the northern half of the nation, are used in the manufacture of paper and naval stores.

Portugal has a wide variety of mineral deposits, but they have remained largely unexploited. Sizable amounts of tungsten (concentrate), tin, copper pyrites, sulfur, kaolin, slate, lead, manganese, marble,

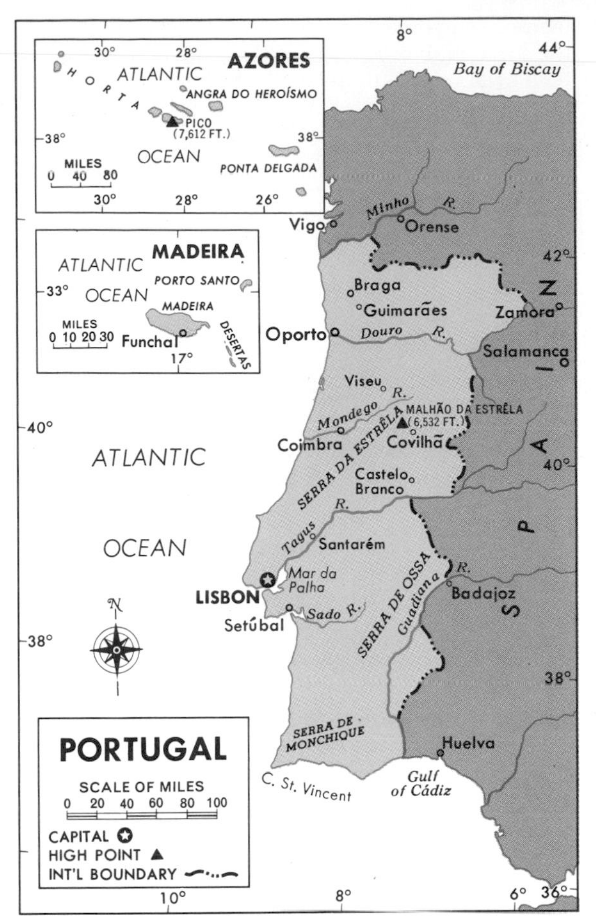

Portugal occupies about one sixth of the Iberian Peninsula. Its mountainous terrain levels off near the Atlantic coast. Many of the nation's rivers originate in the mountains of Spain.

PORTUGUESE FISHING VILLAGE
The port of Nazaré is typical of the many picturesque towns along the coast of Portugal. Nearly all the inhabitants of this village make their living from the sea.

and gypsum have been discovered. Most of the coal used domestically must be imported.

At least a third of the land of continental Portugal is arable, but crop yields are low. Wheat is the chief field crop, followed by rye, barley, oats, corn, potatoes, and rice. Fruits and nuts—notably carobs, figs, and almonds—are grown, as well as citrus fruits. The most valuable commercial crops are grapes and olives. The vineyards on the terraced slopes of the Douro River valley yield most of the grapes from which the celebrated Portuguese wines are made. Portugal is the third largest producer of olive oil, used chiefly in canning sardines.

Although the seacoast is dotted with fishing villages, only 10 percent of the people make their living as fishermen. Sardines are the major catch, with the sardine-canning industry centered at Setúbal. Cod is important in the native diet, and tuna and oysters are also caught.

Industry and Commerce in Portugal

Despite intensified government efforts to boost the output of manufactures, Portugal is considered an industrially underdeveloped nation. The rapid expansion of hydroelectric power production, harnessing the force of Portugal's many swift rivers, has benefited even remote rural areas. An industry that grew markedly during the 1960's was the refinement of nonmetallic minerals. Increasing emphasis has been placed on the production of steel and industrial equipment. Corkware is the leading manufacture, followed closely by wines, sardines, and olive oil. Sizable quantities of paper, shoes, textiles, china, glass, and sugar are also produced.

Transportation and communications in Portugal are still rather primitive. Since most native travel is by oxcart, many roads are little more than unpaved ruts. There are about 18,750 miles of highway, used primarily for commercial transport as few Portuguese families have private automobiles. Most of the nation's 2,235 miles of railroad track were constructed wider than standard gauge to facilitate shipments from Spain. Portugal is serviced by a number of international airlines at the Lisbon airport.

The Portuguese People and Their Culture

In appearance, the Portuguese people closely resemble the Spanish. Although somewhat shorter than their neighbors, they have dark, wavy hair and olive complexions. The Portuguese language is also closely related to the Spanish. However, its nasal vowels give it a melodic quality like that of spoken French.

Portugal is primarily an agrarian nation of small villages. The illiteracy rate is over 40 percent. Only a minority of the people have more than the compulsory six years of education. Comparatively few attend college, though there are three universities—at Coimbra, Lisbon, and Oporto—and a technical university, at Lisbon. The University of Portugal, now at Coimbra, was founded at Lisbon in 1290.

A simple people, the Portuguese center most of their social activities around the home and family. Since the majority are Roman Catholics, they celebrate many saints' days and religious holidays. These are marked by elaborate dinners, singing, and dancing. Villagers may dress in bright costumes that are traditional in their communities. A less joyous aspect of Portuguese culture is embodied in its *fados*. These melancholy folk songs convey the spirit of *saudades*, an untranslatable Portuguese word whose meaning falls somewhere between sorrow and a longing for the past.

Entertainment outside the home is infrequent and usually consists of going to cafés to hear fado singers or to bullfights. More humane than the Spanish version, the Portuguese bullfight never ends with serious injury to the animal; instead, the bull is regarded as a "team" contesting human opponents. *Futebol*, a game similar to soccer, is especially popular among university students.

The most significant cultural achievements came during the era of exploration. The 16th century produced the finest works in Portuguese literature, the most important being 'The Lusiads', a national epic by Luíz Vaz de Camões. A distinctive architectural style—the Manueline—emerged in the ornate cathedrals and monasteries at Belém and Coimbra. It was named for Manuel (Emanuel) I, the Fortunate, who dispatched several successful expeditions to the Orient and to South America. The paintings of Nuno

AN ANTIQUATED METHOD OF PLOWING USED BY PORTUGUESE FARMERS

Although Portugal is a predominantly agricultural country, almost half the farming tools and methods used there have remained relatively primitive. Horses, mules, and oxen are employed as beasts of burden in the fields.

FLEA MARKET IN LISBON
Vendors display their wares at a street market in one of Lisbon's picturesque neighborhoods. The vivid ceramic tiles seen here are common throughout the city.

OPORTO'S HISTORIC CATHEDRAL
The Sé stands on the highest point of eastern Oporto. Its Romanesque architecture is representative of the 12th century in which it was originally constructed.

Gonçalves immortalized the navigators, peasants, and fishermen of the time.

Portugal's capital, a contemporary city, presents a stunning contrast to its timeless countryside. Lisbon was almost leveled by a severe earthquake in 1755. The 18th-century charm of flower vendors, flea markets, and buildings adorned with tiles has survived in the area of the Rossio, a colorful square. Lisbon is the nation's largest port and the hub of commercial activity, but it moves at a slower pace than other major cities. (*See also* Lisbon.)

History of Portugal

The early history of Portugal is the history of Spain (*see* Spain). Under Roman rule, Portugal was merely the western part of the province of Lusitania, an area originally occupied by an Ibero-Celtic tribe. Its present name was derived from Portus Cale, a Roman settlement on the banks of the Douro.

The first step toward independence was taken in 1094, when the land was given to Henry of Burgundy as part of the dowry of his wife, Teresa, a princess of León and Castile. In 1131, a year after her death, her son Afonso Henriques began a series of wars to win freedom. He proclaimed himself the first king of Portugal in 1139, and in 1179 Portugal was recognized as an independent kingdom by Pope Alexander III.

The kingdom's strategic position on the Atlantic coast gave Portugal an advantage when European nations began seeking new sea routes to the Orient. The Golden Age of Discovery began with exploratory expeditions under the patronage of Prince Henry of Portugal (*see* Henry the Navigator). Among the navigators who later sailed under the Portuguese flag were Bartholomew Diaz, Vasco da Gama, and, on his early voyages, Christopher Columbus. By discovery, conquest, and colonization Portugal amassed a great empire in the Orient, Africa, and South America. During the 16th century Portugal dominated European trade with its colonial riches. (*See also* Brazil; Columbus, Christopher; Diaz, Bartholomew; Gama.)

The Portuguese proved unable to cope with their far-flung empire. They tried to hold their colonies with garrisons alone. They failed to send out men to develop the natural resources of their holdings. Other nations coveted their possessions.

In 1580 the Portuguese royal family died out. The throne was seized by Philip II of Spain in the same year. Not until 1640 did the "years of captivity" end, when Portugal threw off the Spanish yoke. By then only fragments of the empire were left. In 1642 a treaty with Charles I of England reestablished an earlier pact that has become one of the longest-lived alliances in European history.

When Napoleon Bonaparte overran the Iberian Peninsula in 1807, the Portuguese king, John VI, fled to Brazil with his family and court. The British under the duke of Wellington defeated the French in the

Peninsular War (1808–14), but the king did not return to Portugal until 1821. Brazil declared its independence, ending Portuguese power in the New World.

By 1892 Portugal had been plunged into bankruptcy. Internal dissension culminated in the assassination of Carlos I and his eldest son, Luis, in 1908. Two years later his successor, Manuel II, was forced to abdicate, and Portugal was proclaimed a republic.

The Republic of Portugal

The civil strife persisted until 1926, when a military dictatorship gained control. António de Oliveira Salazar, a professor of economics at the University of Portugal, was appointed minister of finance. In 1932 he became premier, and in 1933, with the establishment of the "New State," he acquired dictatorial powers.

Under Salazar the government was reorganized as a unitary and corporative republic. The 1933 constitution provides for the election of a president every seven years. The president chooses the functional head of government, the premier, and the Council of Ministers, or cabinet. Laws are proposed by the National Assembly of 130 members, elected for four-year terms. A Corporative Chamber represents economic, cultural, religious, and administrative interests. All branches of the government have advisory powers only.

In 1968 Salazar's authoritarian rule ended when he suffered a stroke. He was replaced as premier by Marcello Caetano, a law professor and former minister of colonies, who had helped create the "New State."

Portugal has kept its traditional ties with Great Britain and Spain, though it remained neutral through World War II. It is a charter member of the North Atlantic Treaty Organization and was admitted into the United Nations in 1955.

Ironically, maintenance of the last big colonial empire is still Portugal's greatest problem. Its overseas possessions cover an area 23 times the size of the mother country, with a population of 12,680,000 (1960 estimate). Thus, Portugal is reluctant to part with its provinces even though military suppression of revolts in Portuguese Guinea, Mozambique, and Angola takes 40 percent of the national budget. Angola—with its rich petroleum, diamond, and iron-ore deposits—is making a positive contribution to the national wealth, however.

REFERENCE-OUTLINE FOR STUDY OF PORTUGAL

THE LAND AND THE PEOPLE

I. **Location and size** P-454: location in world, map W-242; in Europe, map E-334; air distances, map A-794
- A. **Azores and Madeira** A-808, M-23–4, map W-242
- B. **Overseas provinces,** maps A-94–5, A-637: Angola A-399; Cape Verde Islands C-130b; Mozambique M-538; Portuguese Guinea A-89; São Tomé é Príncipe A-89; Macao and Portuguese Timor (Fact-Index)

II. **Land structure** P-454–5, 457b, maps P-455, E-306
- A. **Mountains, plateaus, and coastal plain** P-454–5
- B. **Coastline and islands** P-454, A-808, M-23: Atlantic Ocean A-669

III. **Climate** P-455, 457b: rainfall, map E-308

IV. **The people** P-456–7, 457b, R-27, color pictures P-454–7: rural life P-456; city life L-302, P-457; language P-456; religion P-456, color picture P-457; holidays and festivals P-456

V. **Resources and industries** P-455–6, color pictures P-455–6, table P-457b: land use, chart P-457b
- A. **Agriculture and fisheries** P-455: olives O-450
- B. **Forest products** P-455: cork C-573
- C. **Manufacturing** P-455–6
- D. **Minerals and mining** P-455
- E. **Tourism** P-454, color pictures P-454, 457

VI. **Trade and transportation** P-456, L-302, B-327, I-243, E-326, chart P-457b

VII. **Principal cities** P-455: Lisbon L-302, P-457, color picture P-457; Oporto (Fact-Index)

VIII. **Education and the arts** P-456–7: libraries L-239

IX. **Government** P-457a: flag F-204, color picture F-203

HISTORY

I. **General** P-457–457a

II. **Early history and establishment of kingdom** P-457

III. **Portuguese explorations and growth of colonial empire** P-457, E-355, I-245, table E-358
- A. **Henry the Navigator** H-140: Madeira M-24; Azores A-808; Cape Verde Islands C-130b
- B. **Diaz rounds Cape of Good Hope** D-105, A-81
- C. **Columbus in Portugal** C-475, 476
- D. **Spain and Portugal divide New World (1493–94)** A-298, S-290
- E. **Vasco da Gama** G-7–8: discovers Mozambique M-538; reaches India I-79–80, A-298
- F. **Far East explorations** A-631, C-202, E-42, 43
- G. **Exploration in the Americas** A-298, 300, L-134: Brazil colonized B-309, S-290–1
- H. **Disputed claim to Spice Islands** A-299, M-36

IV. **Decline of Portuguese empire** P-457–457a
- A. **Throne seized by Philip II of Spain (1580); independence regained (1640)** P-457
- B. **Treaty with England (1642), reestablishing earlier pact, becomes one of Europe's longest** P-457
- C. **Peninsular War (1808–14)** P-457–457a, W-99: royal family flees to Brazil B-309
- D. **Brazil declares its independence (1822)** B-309

V. **Revolution of 1910; republic declared** L-302: civil strife and military dictatorship P-457a

VI. **Salazar civilian dictator (1933–68)** P-457a
- A. **Portugal neutral in World War II** L-302
- B. **North Atlantic Treaty Organization** E-326
- C. **Unrest in African provinces** P-457a, A-399
- D. **Diu, Damão, and Goa seized by India** I-83

VII. **New leaders and the colonial problem** P-457a

BIBLIOGRAPHY FOR PORTUGAL

Buehr, Walter. Portuguese Explorers (Putnam, 1966).

Déon, Michel. The Portugal I Love (Tudor, 1964).

Kimbrough, Emily. Pleasure by the Busload (Harper, 1961).

Livermore, H. V. A New History of Portugal (Cambridge, 1966).

Nach, James. Portugal in Pictures (Sterling, 1965).

Wohlrabe, R. A. and Krusch, W. E. The Land and People of Portugal (Lippincott, 1960).

Portugal Fact Summary

THE LAND

Area: 35,340 square miles (including Madeira and the Azores).
Chief Rivers: Douro, Tagus, Guadiana, Minho.
Highest Points: Malhão (6,532 feet), on the mainland; Pico (7,612 feet), in the Azores.
Chief Islands: Azores Archipelago (905 square miles); Madeira Archipelago (308 square miles).
Climate: Mild, moist winters and dry summers; interior is hotter and drier than coastal region.

THE PEOPLE

Population (1967 official estimate): 9,440,000.
Density: 267 persons per square mile.
Language: Portuguese.
Religion: Roman Catholic.
Largest Cities (1966 estimate): Lisbon (822,000); Oporto (319,000).

GOVERNMENT

Capital: Lisbon.
Form: Unitary, corporative republic; president popularly elected for seven years through electoral college.
Constitution: Adopted by plebiscite 1933; frequently amended.
Monetary Unit: Escudo.
Weights and Measures: Metric system.

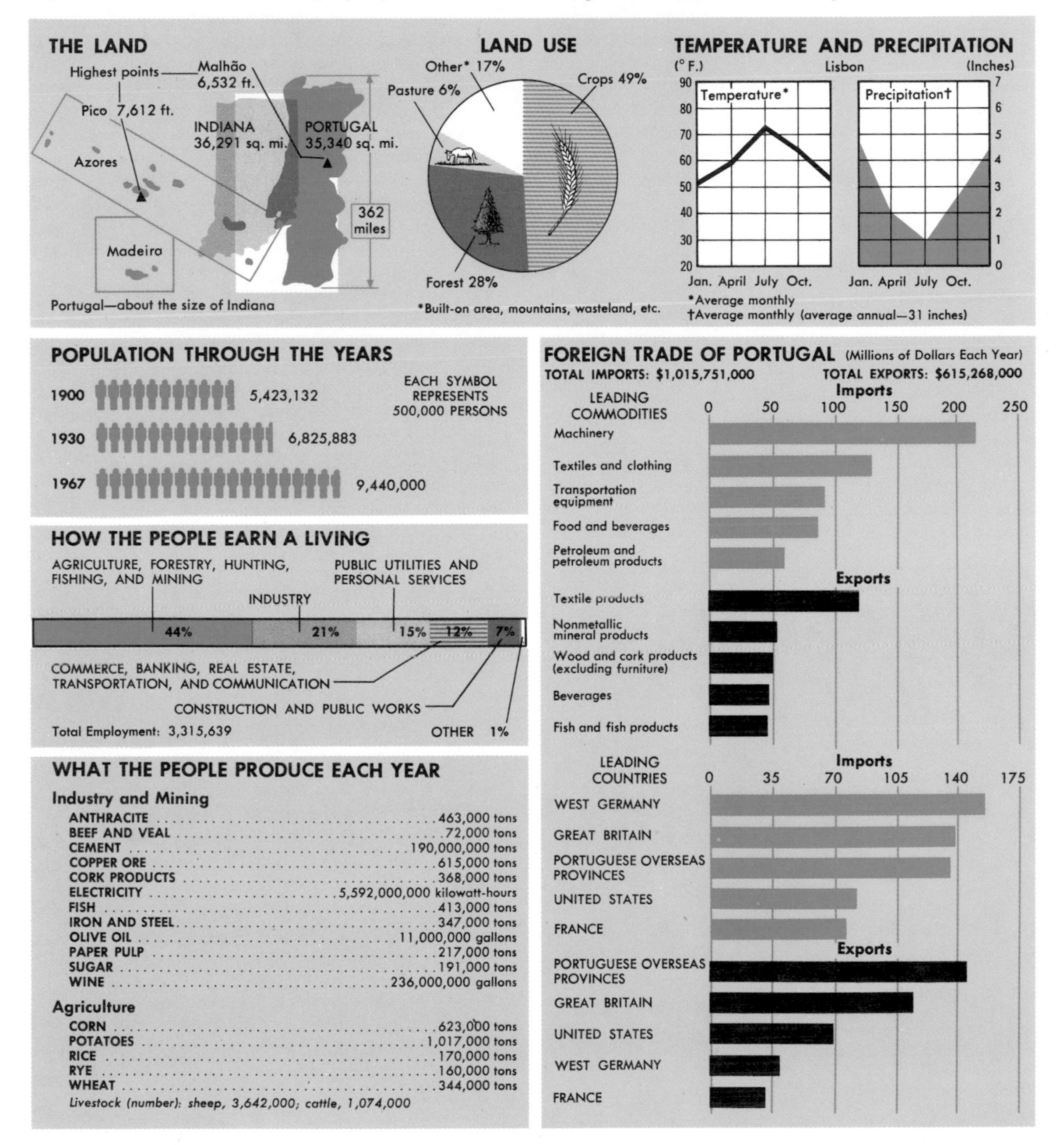

REPRODUCTION—The Perpetuation of Life

REPRODUCTION AND REPRODUCTIVE ORGANS. All living things reproduce, or give rise to offspring similar to themselves. Since no organisms live forever, members of a species must reproduce for the species to survive. Among human beings, reproduction is accompanied by the establishment of closely knit family groups and is ordinarily accomplished by partners who have chosen to share their lives (*see* Marriage; Family).

One-celled plants and animals and some other lower forms of life reproduce asexually. Either they split in two or their young develop from body buds. However, most advanced animals and complex plants reproduce sexually. They possess sex cells whose sole function is reproduction (*see* Cell). Some plants reproduce in both ways. In one generation they reproduce from asexual spores and in the next from sexual spores (*see* Spore).

Sexual reproduction provides the variety that enables complex living things to survive in ever-changing surroundings. It affords almost limitless combinations of hereditary traits. The young that result from sexual reproduction are not merely blends of their parents' traits, because the sex cells from which they develop transmit somewhat differing body-building instructions than did those from which their parents developed (*see* Genetics).

Special body parts called reproductive organs house the sex cells. The primary reproductive organs, or *gonads*, are the *ovaries* and the *testes*. The ovaries contain eggs—the female sex cells. The testes produce sperm—the male sex cells. Accessory organs play an important part in reproduction. The individual members of some species have both sets of reproductive organs and so are both male and female, or hermaphrodites. However, the members of most species that reproduce sexually are either males or females.

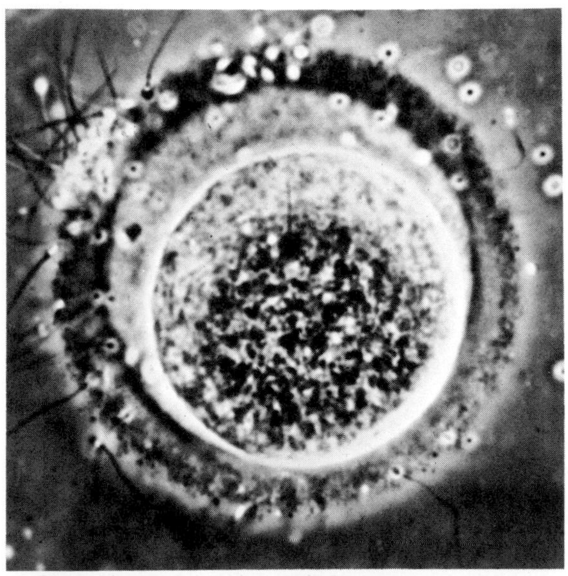

AT THE MOMENT OF CONCEPTION
Human sperm swarm at the edge of a human egg. One will shed its tail as it penetrates the egg. A tough outer membrane will then form around the egg to prevent other sperm from entering.

Human Female Reproductive Organs

Girls are born with two tiny ovaries which contain thousands of eggs. When a girl becomes sexually mature—usually between the ages of 12 and 15—the ovaries, enlarged to the size of almonds, begin to release eggs. About once a month an egg breaks out of its cellular enclosure and begins a journey that ends either in its fertilization by a sperm, a process called conception, or in its degeneration. The release of an egg is controlled by hormones, secreted by the pituitary gland (*see* Hormones). Rarely is more than one egg released at a time.

After leaving an ovary, the egg is caught by the fingery projections at the tip of a nearby *oviduct*. There are two of these four-inch-long tubes. With the help of contractions of the oviduct, special cells in the wall of the tube move the egg along. Conception takes place in the oviduct.

The oviduct ends in the *uterus*, a chamber surrounded by a tough, muscular wall. If fertilized, the egg becomes embedded in the uterine wall. The uterus is about three inches long, two inches wide, and an inch deep. During the later stages of pregnancy, however, it expands greatly to accommodate the growing baby.

Connected to the uterus is a firm but expandable three-inch-long muscular tube called the *vagina*. This tube and the uterine opening are commonly called the "birth canal," because the baby emerges from these passages during birth.

Human Male Reproductive Organs

At birth boys have two oval testes (singular, testis). The testes are suspended from the body in the *scrotum*, a skin-covered sac. If they were not suspended, the internal heat of the body would destroy the testes' ability to produce sperm. When a boy becomes sexually mature, at about his 12th birthday, the testes begin their lifelong manufacture of sperm. Through a series of changes, fledgling sperm cells become fully developed sperm with characteristic tails. At any given time a male human may harbor more than 225 million sperm. Only one of this vast number is used in the fertilization of a single egg.

Sperm are stored in the *epididymis*, a C-shaped structure linked with each testis. From the epididymis they are passed through tubes to the short *ejaculatory ducts*. Nearby are the twin *seminal vesicles* and the *prostate gland*. These structures secrete lubricants that combine with the sperm to form semen. The ejaculatory ducts empty into the *urethra*, the tube through which semen is ejected from the body. (Urine also passes through this tube.)

Enclosing the urethra is the *penis*, a skin-covered,

spongy organ with a rich nerve supply, loose inner tissue, and numerous spaces. By a complex action that involves the nervous system, blood can fill these spaces, making the penis firm and erect.

Reproductive Behavior

Females of most aquatic groups release their eggs by the millions into surrounding water. Males then deposit sperm over the eggs. This process is called external fertilization. Eggs fertilized externally develop in a hazardous environment.

Such higher animals as reptiles, birds, and mammals reproduce by internal fertilization. In this process sperm fertilize eggs inside the female body. Humans and other mammals *copulate* to achieve internal fertilization. During copulation the erect penis of the male is inserted into the vagina of the female. Then contractions of the seminal vesicles and prostate gland ejaculate, or eject, semen through the penis into the uterus. Propelled by their whipping tails, the sperm swim into the oviducts. If an egg is present, one of the millions of ejaculated sperm will probably fertilize it. All other sperm eventually die.

The fertilized egg is transported from the oviduct to the uterine lining, where it becomes embedded. Soon after fertilization, the egg begins to undergo the marvelous series of cell divisions by which a baby is formed. (For a discussion of the growth and development of a fertilized egg, *see* Embryology.)

Birth of a Baby

The gestation period, or length of pregnancy, of humans is about nine months. During that time the growing baby lies snug within the mother's body, protected from outside dangers. It receives oxygen and nourishment and expels wastes through the umbilical cord. This lifeline is linked with the placenta, a blood-filled organ that develops during pregnancy. The placenta makes possible the exchanges that take place between the mother and the baby. (For illustrations of the umbilical cord and the placenta, *see* Embryology; Multiple Births.)

At the close of the gestation period the mother begins to experience "labor pains." These signal the onset of birth. In most cases the baby moves to a head-down position in the uterus in readiness for its passage through the birth canal. Extremely strong contractions of the uterine muscles begin to push the baby through the canal. The woman's labor may be brief or may last for many hours, depending upon the difficulty of the birth.

After the baby emerges from the birth canal, the umbilical cord is cut and the baby takes its first breath. Then the placenta, is passed from the mother with the remaining portion of umbilical cord. Although now a separate organism, the new infant requires maternal nourishment—mother's milk—or its equivalent during its early months. (*See also* Animals, subheads on reproduction; Plants, subheads on reproduction; Mammals; Child Development; Maturity.)

FEMALE REPRODUCTIVE PARTS

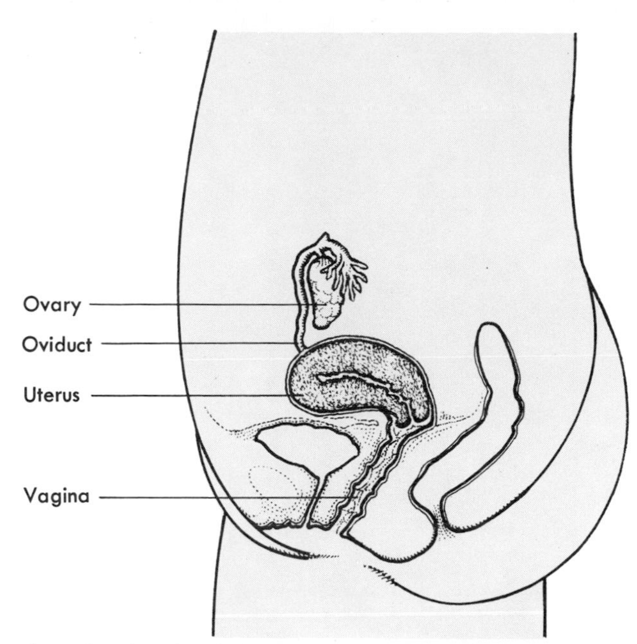

Shown here is a side view of the female sex organs. Eggs, the female sex cells, are stored in the ovaries. An egg released from an ovary moves down an oviduct. If fertilized, the egg becomes implanted in the uterus to develop into a baby.

MALE REPRODUCTIVE PARTS

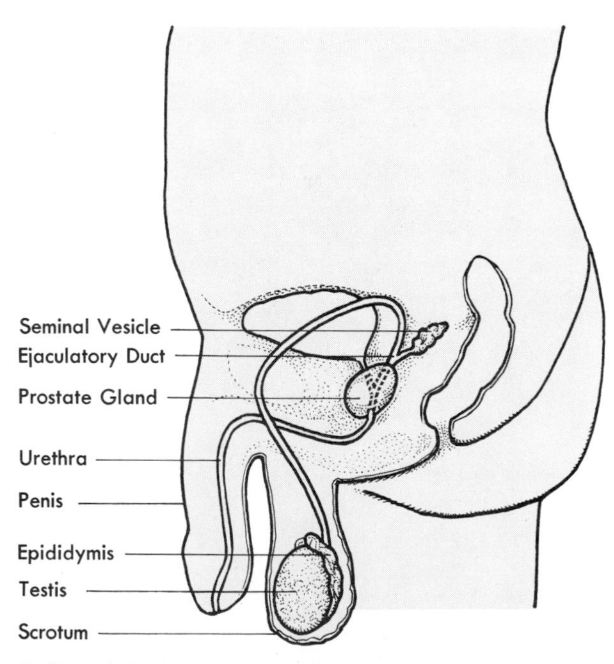

Unlike their female counterparts, the male sex organs are mostly external. Sperm, the male sex cells, are produced in the testes. Sperm move from the testes to the urethra, from which they are ejected during the reproductive act.

UNIT
STAT

SPACE TRAVEL

Exploring Beyond The Earth

SPACE TRAVEL. "That's one small step for a man, one giant leap for mankind." With those words, on July 20, 1969, United States astronaut Neil A. Armstrong stepped from the lunar landing vehicle "Eagle" onto the surface of the moon. Minutes later he was joined by Edwin E. Aldrin, Jr. They were the first men to land on the moon. A third astronaut, Michael Collins, remained in orbit above them in the command module "Columbia" of the Apollo 11 spacecraft.

Moving with unexpected ease over the lunar surface, Armstrong and Aldrin (pictured here) took pictures, set up experiments, and collected samples of moon soil and rock. After 21 hours and 42 minutes on the lunar surface, they rejoined Collins for a safe return to earth.

The epic journey of Apollo 11—and the other manned space flights of the 1960's—were a climax to centuries of speculation and study and to decades of work on the practical problems of space exploration. They were a prelude to longer voyages of the future, which will carry men to Mars and other planets and ultimately, perhaps, beyond the solar system.

Facing Page: Courtesy National Aeronautics and Space Administration

Space—The Newest Frontier

MAN'S REACH into space is among the most fascinating ventures of modern times. It has carried first his instruments, then man himself, into a remoteness that until recent years was hardly known or understood. Although its borders have already been crossed, space still holds mysteries and, undoubtedly, surprises beyond number.

The Realm Beyond the Earth

Space is the region beyond the earth's atmosphere (*see* Atmosphere). Its beginning is hard to define, for the atmosphere does not end abruptly but simply grows thinner and thinner with increasing height.

For man, the conditions of space begin at about 45,000 feet. Above this level, he requires a sealed, pressurized suit or cabin for breathing. Winged, air-breathing jet aircraft can operate at sustained altitudes of a little more than 80,000 feet. Balloons have risen to about 150,000 feet. Rocket-powered aircraft, not requiring oxygen from the air, have ascended to more than 354,000 feet, or some 67 miles, a level above 99 percent of the atmosphere.

WEIGHTLESSNESS—A SPACE-FLIGHT EXPERIENCE
Weightlessness—envisioned (below) by such writers as Jules Verne—is common in space flight. It can be experienced briefly in aircraft flying elliptical trajectories (right).

At an altitude of about 100 miles, satellites can orbit the earth. Here, true space may be said to begin. The farther regions of space are described by the bodies that limit them. *Cislunar* space is the area between the earth and the moon. *Interplanetary* space lies between the sun and the planets of the solar system. *Interstellar* space lies between the stars of a galaxy. *Intergalactic* space—unimaginably huge—lies between the myriad galaxies of the universe (for diagram, *see* Aerospace).

Although it contains less matter per unit of volume than do the highest vacuums that can be produced in laboratories, space is far from empty (*see* Vacuum). The vast reaches between major celestial bodies are permeated by radiation and swept by charged particles and varieties of matter ranging from large meteoroids to the tiny grains known as "cosmic dust." (*See also* Comet; Meteorites and Meteors; Radiation; Van Allen.)

Why Explore Space?

Clearly, for man and his machines space is a hostile environment. Great ingenuity and lavish expenditure of time, talent, and money are required to permit them to survive there. The effort to explore space, however, is being made—and will continue.

A principal reason for the exploration of space is to extend knowledge about the earth, the solar system, and the universe beyond. Artificial satellites have yielded much new information about the earth (*see* Earth; Van Allen). "Observation posts" above the earth's atmosphere permit astronomers to observe radiation that does not penetrate the earth's atmosphere. Spacecraft voyaging far from the earth have gathered new data about the moon and the planets (*see* Moon; Planets).

The exploration of space also has practical value. Meteorological satellites aid in weather forecasting. Communications satellites multiply international communications channels and make possible the intercontinental transmission of television. Navigation satellites guide ships. Military satellites perform vital reconnaissance. Geodetic satellites make possible maps of unprecedented accuracy. Finally, many products of space technology find employment on earth (*see* last section of this article).

Perhaps the greatest and most compelling reason for exploring space, however, is man's insatiable curiosity. Today's space explorers probe beyond their planet in response to the same irresistible lure of the unknown that impelled their predecessors to cross the oceans and the continents, to seek out the poles of the earth, to ply the air, to climb the mountains, and to pierce the depths of the sea. Quite simply, man explores space because he must.

ACTIVITY IN SPACE
Such spacewalkers as David R. Scott (right) demonstrated that men could work effectively while weightless in space.

SOME TERMS USED IN SPACE TRAVEL

Apogee: the point in an earth orbit farthest from the earth's center. *Apolune* and *aphelion* are the similar points in lunar and solar orbits.

Astronaut: a United States spacecraft pilot or crewman.

Astronautics: a term for space travel; from the Greek *astron*, for "star," and *nautes*, for "sailor."

Attitude: the orientation of a spacecraft to its flight path or to an external reference.

Circular velocity: the minimum velocity needed for one body to stay in orbit around another.

Cosmonaut: a Russian spacecraft pilot or crewman.

Countdown: the precisely timed sequence of events preceding the launch of a spacecraft.

Escape velocity, or parabolic velocity: the minimum speed a spacecraft must attain to overcome the gravitational attraction of a primary and proceed into space, without orbiting or returning to the primary.

Free fall: the motion of an unsupported body being drawn by gravitation toward the earth or another primary; produces weightlessness.

g: the symbol and term for the acceleration—approximately 32.2 feet per second per second—produced by the earth's gravity at the earth's surface.

Guidance: the control of a spacecraft's flight path.

Hypoxia: a deficiency of oxygen in the blood sufficient to impair mental and physical faculties.

Launch vehicle: a rocket used to launch a spacecraft.

Micrometeoroids: tiny particles of matter that are found in outer space.

Orbit: the closed path of a satellite about a primary; a complete trip of a satellite about its primary; the act of placing a satellite into orbit.

Orbital decay: the gradual shrinking of an orbit due to friction between a satellite and the upper atmosphere of its primary.

Orbital period: the time a satellite requires to complete an orbit about its primary.

Perigee: the point in an earth orbit nearest to the earth's center. *Perilune* and *perihelion* are the similar points in lunar and solar orbits.

Primary: the body about which another body orbits, from which it escapes, or toward which it falls.

Probe: a nonorbiting spacecraft.

Reentry: return to the earth's atmosphere after flight above it.

Satellite: a body that is in orbit around a primary.

Spacecraft: a vehicle designed for flight beyond the earth's atmosphere.

Telemetry: the automatic radio transmission of data.

Trajectory: the flight path of a nonorbiting spacecraft.

Weightlessness, or zero-g: a condition in which acceleration, whether produced by gravity or any other force, cannot be detected by an observer within a system.

The Prehistory of Space Travel

IN A SENSE, the history of space exploration began when early man first looked upward and wondered at what he saw in the sky. Wonder, as always, prompted a quest for knowledge. The study of astronomy—mingled with astrology and religion—was a feature of every civilization of which there is record (*see* Astronomy). As a realistic picture of the solar system and the universe evolved, man's urge to travel beyond his planet became stronger. That urge found its first expression in literature.

Science and Science Fiction

Science fiction—usually thought of as a 20th-century literary form—actually made its first appearance in the 2d century A.D. Most educated people of that

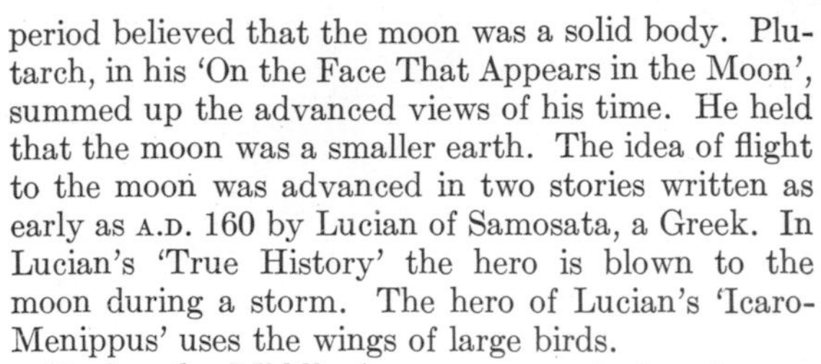

period believed that the moon was a solid body. Plutarch, in his 'On the Face That Appears in the Moon', summed up the advanced views of his time. He held that the moon was a smaller earth. The idea of flight to the moon was advanced in two stories written as early as A.D. 160 by Lucian of Samosata, a Greek. In Lucian's 'True History' the hero is blown to the moon during a storm. The hero of Lucian's 'Icaro-Menippus' uses the wings of large birds.

During the Middle Ages no more stories of space travel were written. Late in the Renaissance, however, as scientific interests revived, interest in space also reawakened.

In the 17th century the invention of the telescope and the work of Johannes Kepler in Germany and Isaac Newton in England yielded knowledge of the solar system. Kepler accurately described the orbits of the planets. Newton set forth mathematically the laws of gravitation and motion. He also broached the idea of an artificial satellite and calculated the "escape velocity" needed to leave the earth's gravitational field. (*See also* Gravitation; Jet Propulsion; Kepler; Newton; Rockets.)

THE QUEST FOR PROPULSION IN SPACE
Novelist Jules Verne's space travelers (left) were fired to the moon by a giant cannon, a method now known to be unworkable. The rockets built by Robert H. Goddard in the 1920's and 1930's (above) were the forerunners of modern launch vehicles.

PIONEER UNITED STATES LAUNCH VEHICLES

In 1958 a modified Jupiter C rocket (left) launched Explorer 1, the first United States artificial satellite of the earth. The Saturn V rockets (right) of Project Apollo propelled into space the first manned vehicles to reach the moon.

Kepler was an author of science fiction as well as an astronomer. His 'Sleep', a tale of a trip to the moon, was published in 1634, after his death. The rocket as a device for space travel made its first appearance in a 1657 moon-trip novel written by Savinien Cyrano de Bergerac of France.

Perhaps the most famous of space-travel novels, the Frenchman Jules Verne's 'From the Earth to the Moon', appeared in 1865. The idea of an artificial earth satellite entered fiction in 'The Brick Moon', a magazine serial of 1869–70 by the American Edward Everett Hale. Hale's satellite was to be a navigational aid. The concept of manned artificial satellites remained a key theme in early 20th-century fictional works on space exploration.

Space-Travel Pioneers

Toward the close of the 19th century and in the first decades of the 20th century, science began to overtake fiction. In a number of nations serious attempts were made to solve the theoretical and technical problems of space exploration. During this period several individuals and groups made contributions that are still of value.

In point of time, Konstantin E. Tsiolkovsky, a Russian schoolteacher, was foremost among the pioneer theoreticians. He was the first to derive the fundamental rocket equation, by means of which it is possible to calculate the ultimate velocity of a rocket if the mass of the rocket, the mass of its propellants, and the velocity of its exhaust are known. Tsiolkovsky also suggested the use of liquid fuels and of multistage, or "step," rockets.

A second theoretician, Hermann Oberth, a German, had perhaps the greatest vision. Possibly because he sought publicity, Oberth's work had the greatest impact of all in exciting new interest in rocketry and space exploration. His first and most famous book, 'The Rocket into Interplanetary Space', was published in 1923. Like other pioneering works, it contained an exposition of the fundamentals of rocket propulsion. It also included proofs that a rocket can both operate in a vacuum and exceed the velocity of its own exhaust. Oberth also speculated upon the problems of manned space flight.

The work of an American physicist, Robert Hutchings Goddard, earned him the name "father of modern rocketry." Early in life, through reading the works of Jules Verne and others, Goddard acquired an interest in space and its exploration that shaped his career. He devoted his life to rocket design.

Late in 1919, Goddard's most influential publication was issued by the Smithsonian Institution, which had in 1916 begun to subsidize his experimental work. Entitled 'A Method of Reaching Extreme Altitudes', the booklet set forth the principles of rocketry in mathematical terms. It also furnished calculations of the rocket masses that would be required to lift loads to varying heights. One section—"Calculation of Minimum Mass Required to Raise One Pound to an 'Infinite' Altitude"—discussed the possibility of sending a rocket to the moon.

"EARTHRISE"—A VIEW FROM THE MOON
The camera helps astronauts share experiences with the world. This spectacular view of the cloudy earth rising above the lunar horizon was taken in December 1968 from Apollo 8, the first manned spacecraft to reach the vicinity of the moon.

Early in the 1920's Goddard began work on the development of liquid-propellant rockets. By 1926 he had developed a workable small motor. On the morning of March 16, in a field on his aunt's farm near Auburn, Mass., Goddard launched the world's first successful liquid-propellant rocket—a spidery contrivance of tanks and tubes that rose to a height of 41 feet and traveled 184 feet horizontally (for picture, *see* Rockets).

Through the 1930's Goddard continued to develop liquid-propellant rockets, eventually producing models that reached heights of a mile and a half. Goddard conceived, and patented, virtually all the fundamental components of modern rockets.

The Rocket Societies

In the 1920's and 1930's, inspired and guided by the work of the theoreticians and their popularizers, rocket enthusiasts throughout the world formed societies to study the possibilities of space exploration. Many of today's most noted space scientists began their work in these groups.

The Soviet Union's Society for the Study of Interplanetary Travel was founded in 1924. After it was suppressed by the Communist government, a second organization—the Group for the Study of Reactive Propulsion—was formed in 1931; ultimately it provided the nucleus of the Russian government's rocket-research agency. By the mid-1930's the Soviet society had produced liquid-propellant sounding rockets that reached heights of about six miles.

In the United States the American Interplanetary Society was formed in 1930. Later renamed the American Rocket Society, it joined the Institute of Aerospace Sciences in 1962 to form the American Institute of Aeronautics and Astronautics. During the 1930's members of the society built and tested a number of small liquid-propellant rockets. In England the British Interplanetary Society was formed in 1933. Space science also became an important study of the Astronomical Society of France.

In Germany the Society for Space Travel was organized in 1927. Experiments conducted by the group in the 1930's paved the way for the development of the V-2. This ballistic missile, a weapon used against the Allies during World War II, contributed greatly to the production of today's space boosters (*see* Guided Missiles). The principal developers of the V-2, led by Wernher von Braun, came to the United States after the war. Many of them played key roles in the engineering of United States military rockets and space vehicles.

In the years after World War II, space flight became an activity of governments. By that time it had become too expensive for private individuals, societies, or corporations to undertake.

Reaching into Space

DESPITE HIS dreams, it was many centuries before man could rise even a short distance above the surface of the earth. His first steps toward space were taken with kites and balloons (*see* Balloon; Kites). Early in the 20th century, the airplane began its rapid evolution (*see* Airplane History). Man was still confined to the earth's atmosphere, however, because all these devices depend upon the air for support—and the airplane requires oxygen from the air to burn its fuel.

The Rocket—Key to Space

For flight above the earth's atmosphere a device is needed that carries both its fuel and its oxidizer and that is not dependent upon the air for support. That device is the rocket. The rocket motor is a reaction engine. It operates in accordance with Newton's third law of motion, which states that "for every action there is an equal and opposite reaction." A rocket is driven forward by the pressure of expanding gases against the walls of the combustion chamber, or thrust chamber, of its motor. (The principles of reaction engines are discussed in the articles Jet Propulsion and Rockets.)

Most of the rockets employed in space exploration are multistage, or "step," rockets. They are constructed by placing one rocket, or stage, atop another. Successive stages are discarded as they exhaust their propellants. This process increases the efficiency of the vehicle because, as each exhausted stage falls away, the mass that must be accelerated by the next stage is reduced.

The power of a rocket is called its *thrust*. In the United States, thrust is ordinarily expressed in pounds. It is theoretically equal to the mass that the rocket would be able to lift upward against the pull of the earth's gravity. Actually, in most rockets thrust exceeds weight by 20 percent or more. The thrust-to-weight ratio increases as propellants are consumed, permitting the rocket to accelerate faster and faster as it rises.

The hot gases that drive a rocket are produced by the combustion of its propellants—fuel and oxidizer. Propellants may be either solid or liquid. Solids are easier to handle and store than are liquids, but they are generally less efficient—that is, they produce less thrust per pound. Liquid propellants, therefore, have been chosen for most large space-launch vehicles. A common combination is liquid oxygen (oxidizer) and kerosine (fuel).

While the chemical rockets of today are suitable for propelling spacecraft into orbit and to the moon and the nearer planets, more efficient engines will be required for the longer flights of the future. One possibility now being explored is the nuclear engine. In it, heat generated by a nuclear reaction would be transmitted to a light gas (preferably hydrogen). The gas would then be expelled through a nozzle to provide thrust.

Sounding Rockets and Launch Vehicles

The rockets employed in space exploration today may be divided into two groups: *sounding rockets* and *launch vehicles*. Sounding rockets carry packages of instruments into the upper atmosphere and space. Ordinarily the instrument package is detached at the desired altitude and returns to earth by parachute, telemetering data as it descends (*see* Telemetry).

Sounding rockets are perhaps most useful for studying the region between about 20 and 100 miles above the earth, where the atmosphere is too thin to support airplanes or balloons but too dense to permit the economical operation of satellites. Thousands of sounding rockets are launched each year. Most are employed to study the weather. Others carry instruments to study such phenomena as the ultraviolet and X rays that emanate from the sun.

AMERICA'S FOREMOST LAUNCH CENTER

The principal United States "spaceport" is at Cape Kennedy (formerly Cape Canaveral), Fla. Its major launch complexes (launching pads and supporting facilities) and the rockets for which they are used are indicated on the map below.

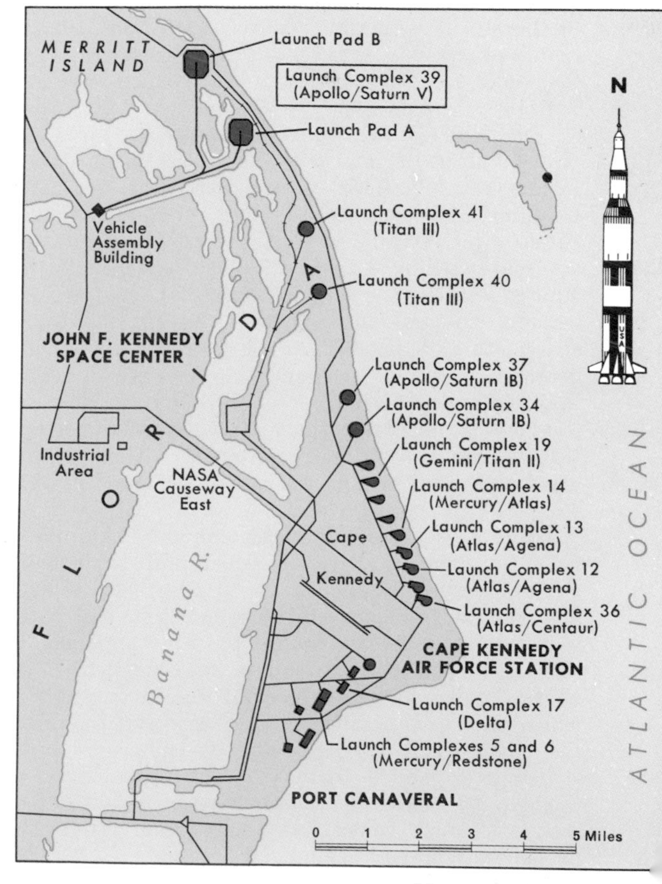

CONTROL CENTER FOR MANNNED SPACE FLIGHTS

Seconds after the launch vehicle begins to rise from its pad at Cape Kennedy, Fla., control of a United States manned space flight is taken over by NASA's Manned Spacecraft Center near Houston, Tex. From this room, controllers monitor the flight and relay information and instructions to the astronauts. Data for the controllers are displayed on their individual television consoles. Information may also be projected on the large screens at top right.

A typical sounding rocket is the United States Nike Apache. This two-stage, solid-propellant vehicle is 25 feet long, weighs 1,600 pounds, and is capable of lifting a 50-pound payload to an altitude of about 800,000 feet. Since sounding rockets are relatively inexpensive, they permit less wealthy nations, which cannot afford to orbit satellites or send spacecraft to the moon and the planets, to have modest space-research programs.

Launch vehicles are rockets that are employed to propel spacecraft into orbits or trajectories. The earliest launch vehicles were derived from the ballistic missiles developed by the United States and Russia after World War II. The first United States artificial satellite—Explorer 1—was launched by a Jupiter C missile. Modified Atlas intercontinental ballistic missiles launched the one-man Mercury spacecraft. Modified Titan II missiles orbited the two-man Gemini spacecraft. Vostoks—Russia's first manned spacecraft—were orbited by derivatives of a Soviet intercontinental missile. Many recent launch vehicles were developed specifically for space exploration and not as weapons. (*See also* Guided Missiles.)

While most launch vehicles employ liquid propellants, some are driven by solid propellants and others have both liquid- and solid-propellant stages. United States launch vehicles range from the four-stage, solid-propellant Scout, which is capable of placing a 300-pound payload in an earth orbit 300 nautical miles high, to the liquid-fueled Saturn V, which propelled the first manned spacecraft to reach the moon. The Soviet Union has launch vehicles similar in capability to those of the United States, though it releases little information about their design. Launch vehicles have also been developed by such nations as England and France.

Major Rocket-Launching Centers

For reasons of safety, space-launch centers are usually so located that rockets may be fired over large open spaces, either oceans or sparsely populated land regions. The two largest launch centers in regular use are in the United States and in Russia.

The principal United States center, commonly called Cape Kennedy, is on the Atlantic coast of Florida, some 60 miles east of Orlando. Personnel at the major installation, the John F. Kennedy Space Center of the National Aeronautics and Space Administration (NASA), and the United States Air Force's Eastern Test Range at Patrick Air Force Base work closely together. Cape Kennedy's principal facilities include a headquarters, a flight crew training building, a manned-spacecraft operations building, and a central instrumentation facility. In its huge Vehicle Assembly Building the 363-foot-tall Saturn V rockets are assembled on a mobile launcher. Apollo/Saturn V missions depart from its launch pads. The Kennedy Space Center is on Merritt Island. The control of a manned space mission is taken over by NASA's Manned Spacecraft Center near Houston, Tex., seconds after the launching.

Cape Kennedy proper—formerly Cape Canaveral—is separated from Merritt Island by the Banana River. Both NASA and the Air Force maintain launch complexes on the cape. These are employed in the launching of various scientific and military satellites and deep-space probes. The cape also has facilities for the testing of military missiles.

Russia's principal space-launch complex is also a center for the launching of intercontinental ballistic missiles and other military missiles. It is near the small town of Tyuratam, east of the Aral Sea on the steppes of the Kazakh Soviet Socialist Republic.

The missile-launching facilities, largely underground, are widely dispersed throughout the desert. Space-launching pads, however, are aboveground. Supporting facilities are similar to those at Cape Kennedy and Houston, though they are somewhat less lavish.

Both the United States and Russia have large military launching sites in addition to Cape Kennedy and Tyuratam. These include the United States Western Test Range at Vandenberg Air Force Base near Lompoc, Calif., and the White Sands Missile Range in southern New Mexico. The civilian NASA maintains an installation on Wallops Island, Va., from which small satellites are orbited. The Soviet Union has a major military rocket facility at Kapustin Yar, near Volgograd north of the Caspian Sea, and another launch facility near Plesetsk, some 125 miles south of the White Sea port of Archangel. Outside the United States and Russia, important space-launch facilities include France's site at Kourou, French Guiana; Australia's site at Woomera; and Japan's site at Kagoshima.

Spacecraft Launching Operations

The process of launching a spacecraft may be said to begin with the mating of the spacecraft and its launch vehicle. This is usually done at or near the *launching pad,* the sturdy base that supports the rocket before it is launched. Beside the pad is a scaffold, the "gantry," from which the rocket and its payload are serviced.

Prelaunch operations are carried out according to a schedule called the *countdown.* The countdown is similar to the familiar "check list" employed by airplane pilots. It ensures the performance of all essential operations in the proper sequence and at the proper times. It also assures maximum safety for ground crewmen and astronauts; avoids unnecessary wear on equipment before it is really needed; permits the launch director to begin vehicle lift-off at a precise moment dictated by such events as the relative position of celestial bodies or other spacecraft; and ensures that all elements of the launch operation —such as tracking cameras and radars, telemetry receivers, and tracking and recovery ships and aircraft—are working properly and are coordinated.

Time preceding lift-off of the rocket is called *minus time. T-time,* or *zero time,* is the time scheduled for lift-off. The count continues throughout the mission. Time after lift-off is called *plus time,* or *ground elapsed time* (GET). Time preceding and following lift-off is expressed in days, hours, minutes, and seconds: "T minus three hours," "T minus four seconds," "T plus five minutes."

Ordinarily, a countdown may be stopped at any point and later resumed from the same point. Thus, if a part of the rocket fails at T minus 20 minutes, the countdown is stopped until the faulty part is repaired or replaced. Then the count is resumed at T minus 20 minutes, even though several hours may have been required to make the repair. Such a pause in a countdown is called a *hold.* The countdowns for large space-launch vehicles usually contain built-in holds to allow time for the elimination of the minor malfunctions that almost inevitably occur.

The length of minus time in a countdown varies with the type of launch vehicle and its mission. Some unmanned test flights require only eight to ten hours of minus time, while an Apollo/Saturn V lunar launch requires six days. The last few events in a countdown are usually controlled by an automatic sequencer. This electronic, computer-controlled device issues commands to the space vehicle during a period when things must happen too fast for human beings to make the necessary decisions.

THE FIRST LEG OF A JOURNEY TO THE MOON

A Saturn V rocket bearing an Apollo craft leaves the huge Vehicle Assembly Building on Merritt Island, in Florida. The rocket-spacecraft combination is assembled on a mobile launcher, then carried by a massive transporter to its pad.

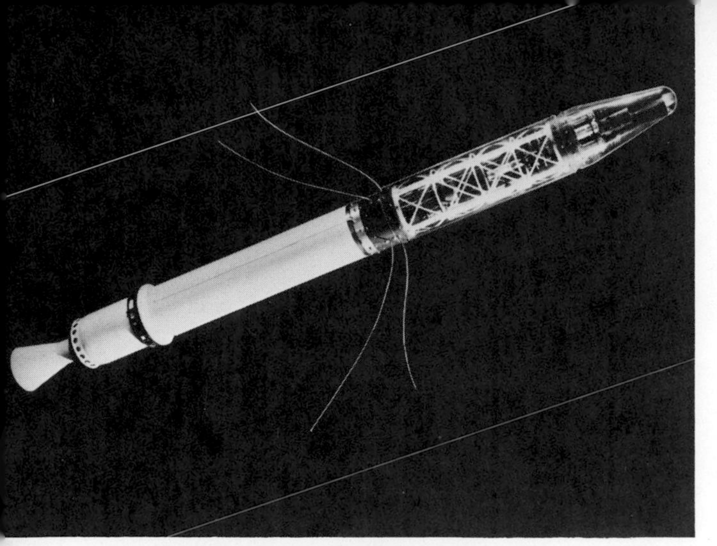

THE FIRST UNITED STATES SATELLITE
This is a model of Explorer 1, orbited on Jan. 31, 1958. It detected the earth-circling Van Allen radiation belts.

Artificial Satellites and Deep-Space Probes

SINCE the orbiting of the first artificial earth satellite—Russia's Sputnik 1—on Oct. 4, 1957, hundreds of spacecraft have been launched to perform a great variety of tasks. However varied they may be in purpose, all spacecraft move through space in accordance with fundamental physical laws, and all are made up of similar basic components.

ORBITS AND TRAJECTORIES

The paths of spacecraft are governed by the laws of gravitation and planetary motion first set forth by Newton and Kepler. They are the same laws that govern the motion of all bodies in the universe—for instance, the moon about the earth, and the earth about the sun. If the path of a spacecraft is closed and repetitive, it is an *orbit*. A spacecraft in an orbit is a *satellite*. If the path of a spacecraft has definite starting and ending points, it is a *trajectory*. A spacecraft that follows a trajectory is called a *probe*.

Orbital Velocity

A satellite is held in orbit about the earth—or any other primary—by the interaction of its own inertia and the gravitational attraction between it and the primary. Inertia tends to keep a satellite moving in a straight line (*see* Mechanics). Gravitation tends to deflect it from that straight line and cause it to follow a curved path (*see* Gravitation). If the curvature of the path parallels the curvature of the primary, the satellite will remain in orbit (*see* diagram on this page). In effect, the surface of the primary "falls away" from the satellite just as fast as the satellite falls toward the surface.

A satellite and its primary actually revolve around their common center of gravity. If, however, the mass of the satellite is very small in comparison with the mass of the primary, the center of gravity of the primary may be regarded as the point about which the satellite orbits, and approximate calculations of orbital characteristics are then greatly simplified.

The minimum velocity required to sustain a satellite in orbit around a primary would produce a circular orbit. It is called the *circular velocity*, and may be expressed by the equation $V=\sqrt{\frac{GM}{R}}$, in which V is the velocity, G the universal constant of gravitation, M the mass of the primary, and R the radius of the orbit, measured from the center of gravity of the primary. For the common United States units of miles and minutes, with mass in slugs, $G=8.4\times 10^{-16}$. Slugs are found by dividing the weight in pounds by the acceleration due to gravity—approximately 32.17 feet per second per second. For the metric units of kilometers and minutes, with mass in kilograms, $G=2.4\times 10^{-16}$. For earth orbits, the circular-velocity equation may be simplified to $V=\frac{K}{\sqrt{R_e+h}}$, in which K is $\sqrt{GM}$ (1.85×10^4 for the United States units, 3.78×10^4 for the metric), R_e is the radius of the earth (3,960 miles, or 6,370 kilometers), and h is the height of the orbit above the surface of the earth. (The mass of the earth is 4.08×10^{23} slugs, or 5.96×10^{24} kilograms.) It may be seen, for instance, that the velocity required to sustain a satellite in circular earth orbit at the minimum practical height

WHY A SATELLITE STAYS IN ORBIT

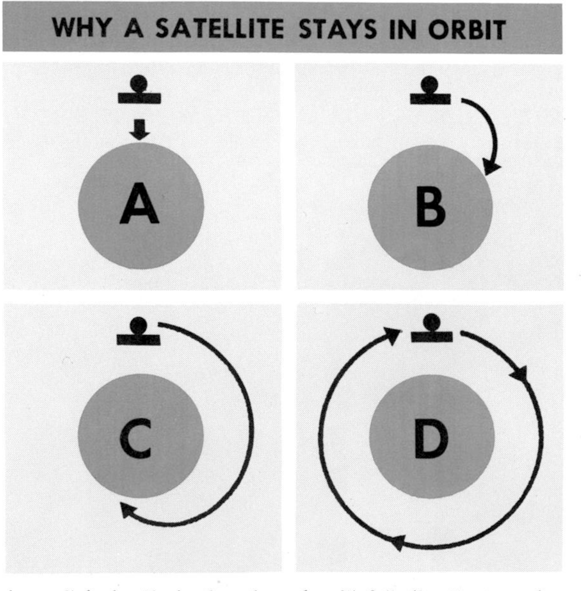

A small body, if simply released, will fall directly toward a larger body, or primary (A). If given a horizontal velocity as well, the small body will reach the primary at a point removed from the line of direct fall (B). The greater its horizontal velocity, the farther the small body will travel (C). If the small body has sufficient horizontal velocity, the curvature of its path will match the curvature of the surface of its primary, and it will stay in orbit about the primary (D).

of about 100 miles is some 290 miles per minute, or 17,400 miles per hour.

For several reasons—including the difficulty of precise adjustment of velocity—exactly circular orbits are not achieved in practice. Noncircular orbits are elliptical, with the primary at one focus of the ellipse. The closest point to earth of a satellite in elliptical orbit is the *perigee;* the greatest distance, the *apogee.* Elliptical orbits result when the velocity of the satellite at perigee is greater than the circular velocity for that height.

The velocity of a satellite at any point in an elliptical orbit may be determined by $V=\sqrt{GM\left(\frac{2}{R}-\frac{1}{a}\right)}$, where R is the distance from the satellite to the center of gravity of the primary (R_e+h, for earth orbits) and a is one half the major (long) axis of the ellipse (R_e plus half the sum of apogee and perigee, for earth orbits). The velocity at perigee is $V_{per}=\sqrt{GM\left(\frac{2a-R}{aR}\right)}$; the velocity at apogee, $V_{apo}=\sqrt{\frac{GMR}{a(2a-R)}}$. In both of these equations, R is the distance from the perigee to the center of the primary. Again, for earth orbits, $\sqrt{GM}=K$.

Periods and Escape Velocity

The time required for a satellite to complete one *sidereal,* or Keplerian, orbit (defined in reference to the "fixed," or apparently motionless, stars in distant space) is called its *period.* For a circular orbit, the period is $P=2\pi\sqrt{\frac{R^3}{GM}}$. For an elliptical orbit, the period is $P=2\pi\sqrt{\frac{a^3}{GM}}$. Thus, the time required to complete a 100-mile-high circular earth orbit would be about 1 hour 28 minutes. Interestingly, a satellite in a nearly circular orbit some

VELOCITY AND PATH

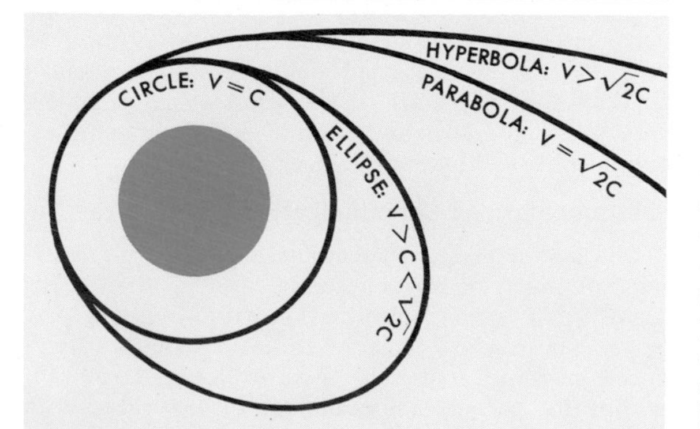

The minimum velocity (V) required to sustain a spacecraft in orbit is called the circular velocity (C). If V is greater than C but less than √2 multiplied by C (√2 C), the orbit will be elliptical. When V equals √2 C, the eccentricity of the ellipse becomes unity, and the flight path of the spacecraft is no longer closed; it is a parabola. The spacecraft has reached escape velocity and will not return to its primary. Velocities greater than √2 C produce hyperbolic paths.

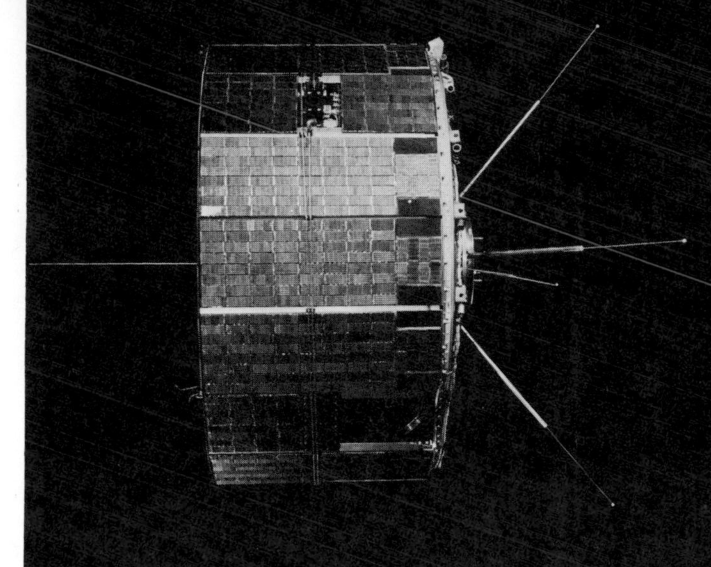

A "WORKING" ARTIFICIAL SATELLITE

Typical of applied satellites are meteorological satellites of the Tiros (ESSA) series. They televise cloud-cover pictures to earth and also provide data on reflected solar radiation.

22,300 miles above the earth's equator will have a period of 24 hours—the time required for the earth to rotate once on its axis—and will appear to hover motionless above one point on earth. Such an orbit is called a *synchronous* orbit.

During the flights of manned Gemini spacecraft, the term "revolution" was introduced. The period of a revolution is the time elapsed between successive passes over a given meridian of earth longitude. It is called the *synodic* period. The synodic period of a satellite will usually differ from its sidereal period because the earth rotates beneath the satellite. The time difference is influenced by the height of the orbit, its inclination (the angle between the plane of the orbit and that of the equator), and whether it is posigrade (in the direction of the earth's rotation) or retrograde (against that direction).

As the velocity of a satellite at a given perigee is increased, the ellipse of its orbit will become more and more eccentric. When the eccentricity reaches unity, the orbit is no longer a closed path, but an open-ended parabola. A spacecraft in a parabolic trajectory will not return to its primary; it has sufficient inertia to overcome the gravitational attraction of the primary and continue on, or escape, into space. Thus the velocity required to place a spacecraft into a parabolic trajectory is called the *parabolic velocity,* or *escape velocity.* At any given height above a primary, the parabolic velocity is $\sqrt{2}$ (approximately 1.414) times the circular velocity. Escape velocity from the surface of the earth, then, is about 420 miles per minute, or 25,000 miles per hour. For various reasons, however, actual escape trajectories are hyperbolic curves. A hyperbolic path is produced by any velocity greater than $\sqrt{2}$ times the circular velocity.

The fundamental relations given above consider only the gravitational attraction between a spacecraft and its primary. When applied, for example, to the data of an actual satellite in earth orbit, they will yield results that are approximately correct, but not exact. Such a spacecraft would actually be influenced, for instance, by the gravity of the sun and the moon as well as by that of the earth. The equations that describe actual spacecraft motions are very complex. No general solutions are known, but they may be solved to any desired degree of accuracy by successive-approximation methods. Only the calculating speed of the electronic computer has made such computations possible.

SPACECRAFT FUNDAMENTALS

Any satellite or probe may be considered as a single system composed of several subsystems—an assembly of components which, together, can perform a desired task. A number of basic subsystems are common to most spacecraft, regardless of their missions. Among these are power supply; on-board propulsion; environmental control; attitude control; on-board computer; guidance and control; instrumentation; communications; and structure.

Power; Propulsion; Environmental Control

The power-supply subsystem provides the electricity for other subsystems. Power for most satellites today is generated by solar cells, which convert energy from the sun into electricity (*see* Photoelectric Devices). They are lightweight, reasonably inexpensive, reliable, and long lived—all essential requirements for a spacecraft power subsystem. Batteries—recharged by the solar cells—may provide power when the solar cells are in the dark.

Thermoelectric power supplies, employing radioisotopes as heat sources, have been used in some satellites. They are long lived but very expensive. Fuel cells, in which oxygen and hydrogen are combined to yield electricity, water, and heat, are used in United States manned spacecraft.

The on-board propulsion subsystem is variously employed to change the orbit of a satellite or the trajectory of a probe, to "keep station" with other objects, to remove a spacecraft from orbit, or to brake a probe for landing. It consists of one or more liquid- or solid-propellant rockets.

The environmental-control subsystem protects spacecraft components and astronauts. The crew of a manned spacecraft must have a gas for breathing, food, water, and some means of disposing of human waste. Cabin temperature and pressure must be kept within certain limits, and some shielding from radiation must be provided. The less complex subsystem of an unmanned spacecraft is usually designed to control temperature and radiation, to which some electronic components are as sensitive as is man. Temperature control may be achieved by reflective or absorptive external coatings or by such means as electric heaters.

Attitude; Computation; Guidance

The attitude-control subsystem keeps the spacecraft oriented with respect to an external reference. For example, solar cells must be kept pointed toward the sun, communications antennas toward the earth, and cameras toward their subjects. Small rockets or compressed-gas jets are often used for attitude control. Other devices include magnets that interact with the earth's magnetic field. The subsystem usually responds to on-board sensors, such as gyroscopes or sun- or star-trackers.

The on-board computer subsystem provides computing service for other subsystems. It may variously store engineering data, commands for other subsystems, and scientific data from sensors. It can also serve as an event timer, or clock.

The guidance-and-control subsystem monitors the spacecraft's attitude and velocity. It may also receive information from ground stations in order to issue to other subsystems the appropriate commands to keep the spacecraft in a desired orbit or trajectory. The guidance-and-control, computer, and attitude-control subsystems are closely related.

Instrumentation; Communications; Structure

The instrumentation subsystem is the data-gathering equipment of the spacecraft. Among the instruments that gather information from without the spacecraft may be cameras, radiation counters, and spectrometers. Instruments to collect information within the spacecraft may include biomedical sensors that measure such phenomena as the temperature and heartbeat of astronauts. Other instruments may monitor the operation of the spacecraft itself.

The communications subsystem transmits and receives information by radio. Information transmitted includes data from scientific, biological, and

A HUGE ANTENNA IN THE MOJAVE DESERT
Spacecraft control is maintained through such devices as this 210-foot-diameter tracking and communications antenna.

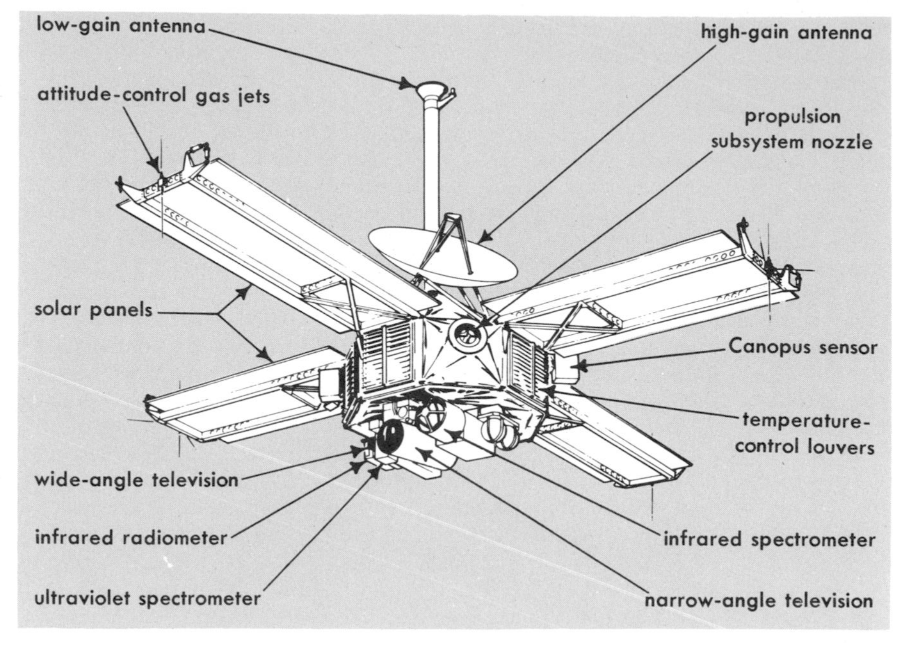

INVESTIGATOR OF THE PLANET MARS
Some principal components of a typical deep-space probe are labeled in this diagram of Mariners 6 and 7, which in the summer of 1969 flew by Mars. The twin spacecraft returned to earth data that included the best pictures yet of the red planet. After flying by the planet, both Mariners entered solar orbit, themselves becoming miniature "planets."

engineering instruments. Commands are received from control stations on earth to start or stop various functions of the spacecraft.

The structure, or skeleton, of a spacecraft may also be regarded as a subsystem. It supports and holds together the other subsystems.

GROUND SUPPORT FACILITIES

Information is received from—and transmitted to—spacecraft through elaborate networks of tracking stations on earth. Communication with unmanned satellites launched by the United States is carried out by NASA's Space Tracking and Data Acquisition Network (STADAN). It operates 26 radio and optical stations worldwide and is headquartered at Goddard Space Flight Center in Greenbelt, Md.

Contact with deep-space probes millions of miles from the earth is maintained by NASA's Deep Space Network (DSN). Its major permanent stations are located about 120 degrees apart—at Woomera and near Canberra, Australia; near China Lake, Calif.; and at Johannesburg, South Africa; on Ascension; and near Madrid, Spain. The DSN facilities are generally equipped with 85-foot-diameter antennas.

A special 11-station Manned Space Flight Network maintains communication with manned spacecraft. The DSN stations assist when manned spacecraft are far from the earth. There are also four tracking ships and eight tracking aircraft. All the stations are tied to the Manned Spacecraft Center in Texas, by radio, telephone, and teletype circuits.

The United States Department of Defense also operates space-tracking facilities to communicate with military spacecraft. The Soviet Union has a network of facilities across its territory. France and ESRO also have tracking networks. They cooperate with both the United States and the Soviet Union.

TYPES OF SATELLITES AND PROBES

Two general categories of artificial satellites are in use today. They may be called *working,* or *applied,* satellites and *scientific* satellites. Deep-space probes are scientific spacecraft. Some important unmanned satellites and probes are listed in the table on the following page.

Working satellites include communications, meteorological, geodetic, navigation, and military spacecraft. Communications satellites relay radio and television signals. Meteorological, or weather, satellites send cloud-cover pictures and other data. Geodetic satellites make possible maps of greater accuracy. Navigation satellites help ships find their way. Military satellites perform photographic and electronic reconnaissance.

Each satellite is built to perform a specific task or tasks. The meteorological satellite Tiros E, or ESSA (Environmental Science Services Administration) 7, provides an example of a "typical" applied satellite. (Tiros stands for Television and Infra Red Observation Satellite.) The 325-pound spacecraft, resembling a hatbox, was launched on Aug. 16, 1968, into a nearly circular polar orbit some 900 miles high. From this orbit the cameras that are its principal instruments can take pictures of the entire earth daily. Power is provided by solar cells and storage batteries. Attitude is maintained by spinning the satellite—in effect, the entire satellite is a gyroscope. The guidance-and-control subsystem includes a tape recorder that stores television pictures for transmission to earth upon demand and a timer that governs the operation of other subsystems.

Scientific satellites are designed to gather information on physical phenomena in space. The hundreds already launched have, for instance, yielded data on radiation, magnetic and gravitational fields, and the prevalence of micrometeoroids.

Explorer 38—Radio Astronomy Explorer 1—is a typical scientific satellite. It was launched on July 4, 1968, into a nearly circular orbit some 3,600 miles high, inclined at about 60 degrees to the earth's equator. Its instruments detect and measure the intensity and direction of cosmic radio signals of frequencies too low to penetrate the earth's atmosphere. Sensors include four 750-foot-long antennas, deployed after the satellite was in orbit and arranged in an acute double V. The 420-pound Explorer 38 is powered by solar cells and storage batteries. It is stabilized by slow rotation and by interaction with the earth's gravitational field. Data gathered by the satellite may be transmitted to earth instantly or stored in a tape recorder.

Deep-space probes are designed to study space phenomena at great distances from the earth and to investigate such other bodies as the moon and planets. Structurally, they are similar to artificial satellites, though often they must be built to operate longer. Major components of a typical deep-space probe are shown in the diagram on the preceding page.

Lunar and planetary probes are variously designed to fly by, crash on, orbit, or land softly on their targets. Russia and the United States have successfully launched all four types to the moon. Probes to Venus and Mars—the only planets to be investigated by spacecraft to date—have usually been designed to fly by their targets, though Russia has launched probes that impacted upon Venus. Many flyby probes, their missions accomplished, end their careers as satellites of the sun. (*See also* Moon; Planets.)

Soft-landing planetary probes of the future will carry devices designed to detect any form of life that may exist upon their targets, as well as instruments to measure physical phenomena. In yet more distant years, it may become possible to launch probes to targets beyond the solar system.

SOME IMPORTANT UNMANNED SATELLITES AND SPACE PROBES

Satellite or Probe	Date Launched	Initial Apogee/ Perigee (miles)	Remarks
			UNITED STATES
Explorer 1	Jan. 31, 1958	1,584/224	First United States artificial satellite.
Vanguard 1	March 17, 1958	2,462/405	Provided data on pear shape of earth.
Score	Dec. 18, 1958	914/115	First communications satellite; transmitted taped messages.
Pioneer 4	March 3, 1959	in solar orbit	First United States lunar probe; missed moon by 37,300 miles.
Explorer 6	Aug. 7, 1959	26,366/157	Returned first television photo of earth.
Tiros 1	April 1, 1960	468/430	First weather satellite; transmitted 22,952 cloud-cover pictures.
Transit 1B	April 13, 1960	463/232	First navigational satellite.
Discoverer 13	Aug. 10, 1960	431/157	Carried first payload to be recovered from orbit.
Courier 1B	Oct. 4, 1960	767/586	First active-repeater communications satellite.
Samos 2	Jan. 31, 1961	350/300	First successful United States military reconnaissance satellite.
Ranger 4	April 23, 1962	in flight 64 hrs.	First United States lunar probe to reach moon; crashed.
Telstar 1	July 10, 1962	3,503/593	First privately built communications satellite.
Syncom 2	July 26, 1963	22,750/22,062	First synchronous-orbit communications satellite.
Ranger 7	July 28, 1964	in flight 68.6 hrs.	Took first closeup photographs of lunar surface; transmitted 4,316 pictures; impacted on moon.
Mariner 4	Nov. 28, 1964	in solar orbit	First successful Mars probe; returned 21 pictures.
Early Bird	April 6, 1965	22,733/21,748	First commercial communications satellite; in synchronous orbit.
Surveyor 1	May 30, 1966	in flight 63.6 hrs.	First of Surveyor series to land softly on moon; returned 11,150 lunar-surface pictures.
Lunar Orbiter 1	Aug. 10, 1966	1,159/117	First of series; photographed potential lunar-landing sites.
Mariner 5	June 14, 1967	in solar orbit	Successful Venus probe passed within 2,480 miles of planet.
Mariner 6	Feb. 24, 1969	in solar	Twin Mars probes; returned best pictures of planet to date.
Mariner 7	March 27, 1969	orbits	
			SOVIET UNION
Sputnik 1	Oct. 4, 1957	588/141	First artificial satellite of earth.
Sputnik 2	Nov. 3, 1957	1,038/140	First biological satellite; carried dog Laika.
Luna 1	Jan. 2, 1959	in solar orbit	First lunar probe; missed moon by 4,660 miles.
Luna 2	Sept. 12, 1959	in flight 33.5 hrs.	First probe to impact on the moon; no instrumentation on moon.
Luna 3	Oct. 4, 1959	291,439/25,257	Took first pictures of back side of moon.
Polyot 1	Nov. 1, 1963	893/213	First Soviet satellite to maneuver in orbit.
Molniya 1	April 23, 1965	24,470/309	First Soviet communications satellite; capable of color TV.
Luna 9	Jan. 31, 1966	in flight 79 hrs.	First probe to land softly on moon; returned surface pictures.
Luna 10	March 31, 1966	632/217	First moon-orbiting satellite.
Zond 5	Sept. 15, 1968	min. alt. 1,212 mi. above moon	First lunar flyby probe to return to earth and be recovered; recovered in Indian Ocean on Sept. 21.
			OTHER NATIONS
Ariel 1	April 26, 1962	754/242	First international satellite; made in England, launched by United States.
Alouette 1	Sept. 28, 1962	638/620	First Canadian satellite; launched by United States.
San Marco 1	Dec. 15, 1964	510/128	First Italian satellite; launched by United States.
A 1	Nov. 26, 1965	1,099/328	First French satellite.
WRESAT 1	Nov. 29, 1967	777/106	First Australian satellite.
ESRO 2B	May 17, 1968	677/205	First successful satellite built by European Space Research Organization; launched by United States.

Animal Pioneers in Space

IN THE JOURNEY into space, man was preceded by animals. Experiments conducted both on earth and beyond demonstrated that biological organisms, properly protected, could survive a space environment. The information gained through these experiments directed the design of spacecraft in which men could function efficiently. Continuing experiments are devised to investigate the effects of prolonged exposure to the conditions of space flight.

Early Experiments

In the United States, the first opportunity for biologists to use rockets in their research came in 1947, when captured German V-2 ballistic missiles were being tested at the White Sands proving ground in New Mexico. Flights involving monkeys demonstrated that the animals could withstand the acceleration inherent in rocket flight and could endure brief periods of weightlessness. In the Soviet Union, known experiments began in 1951 with the launching of a small dog in the nose cone of a sounding rocket.

On Nov. 3, 1957, the Soviet Union became the first nation to place a living creature in earth orbit in an artificial satellite. The female dog Laika, accustomed by special training to the acceleration and noise of rocket flight, was launched in the satellite Sputnik 2. Instruments telemetered data on Laika's breathing, heartbeat, and blood pressure. The dog lived for nearly a week, until its air supply ran out; no provision had been made for recovering the craft. Laika's adaptation to acceleration and weightlessness firmly indicated that man too could function in space.

As the tempo of preparations for manned space flight increased in Russia and the United States, a number of dogs and chimpanzees orbited the earth. The journey of Enos, a chimpanzee, was typical of these flights. The $5\frac{1}{2}$-year-old primate made two orbits in a Mercury spacecraft on Nov. 29, 1961. While in flight, it ate, drank, and performed psychomotor tests for which it had been trained. Enos was safely recovered, as were the dogs and other organisms carried on Soviet spacecraft after Sputnik 2. Space flight had no apparent effect upon the animals' ability to bear normal offspring.

Current Research

Typical of continuing research projects is the United States Biosatellite program. The Biosatellites afford a means to study the effects upon living things—plant and animal—of such phenomena as weightlessness, radiation, and elimination of the normal day-night cycle. Among early Biosatellite findings was that plants are—to a greater degree than had been anticipated—dependent upon earth's gravity for normal growth. Biosatellites carrying monkeys for periods of up to 30 days are intended to provide data on the effects of long-term exposure to space-flight phenomena.

Other animals, large and small, play an important role in space medical research without leaving the earth. In both the United States and Russia a variety of life is used in laboratories to study the biodynamics of acceleration and vibration and the effects of temperature, various breathing gases, and radiation on biological systems. Dogs and mice are most commonly employed in Russian experiments, while United States scientists favor mice and such larger animals as monkeys, chimpanzees, hogs, and bears. For example, dogs are widely used in centrifuge and vibrating-table experiments in Russia, while in the United States bears and hogs have been employed in rocket-sled studies of the effects of deceleration. (*See also* Aerospace Medicine.)

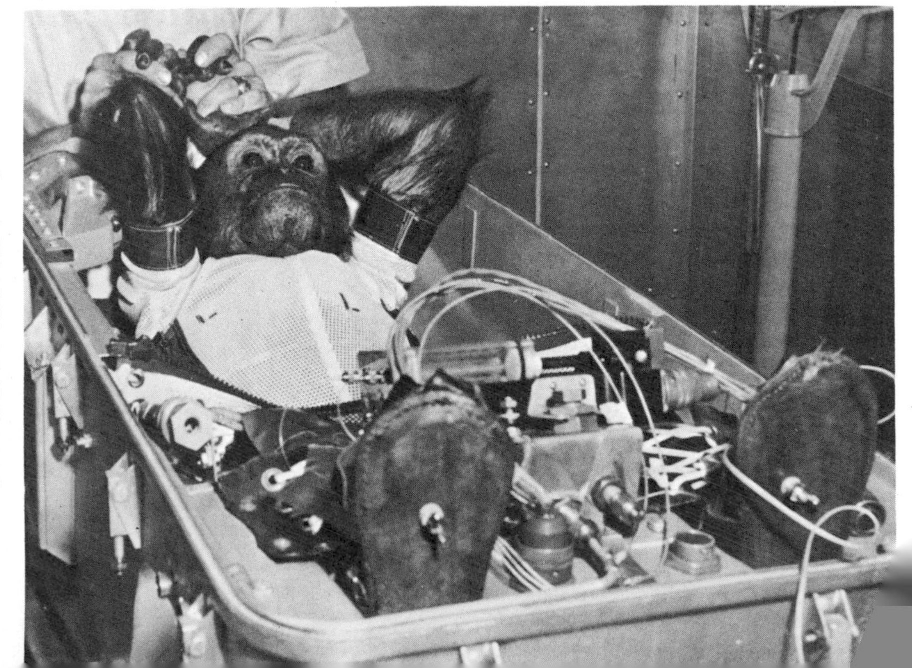

"ASTROCHIMP" READY FOR SPACE FLIGHT
Enos, a 42-pound chimpanzee, reclines in the couch it occupied during two orbits of the earth in November 1961. The animal's successful flight proved the readiness of the Mercury spacecraft for manned orbital missions. Less than three months later, in the next Mercury flight, John H. Glenn, Jr., became the first American to orbit the earth. Data gathered through animal experiments have contributed greatly to the success of manned space missions.

THE FIRST MAN IN SPACE
The world's first true space flight was made by Russia's Yuri A. Gagarin in the spacecraft Vostok 1 on April 12, 1961.

Man's Venture into Space

MAN EVOLVED on the surface of the earth and is naturally fitted for life on it or only a few feet above it. Space is an alien environment. In his journey into space, man has overcome obstacles perhaps more formidable than any he has faced before.

MAN AND SPACE

The barriers to manned space flight are both physical and psychological. They arise from both the nature of space and the means employed to reach space. They have been overcome by a combination of protective devices and rigorous training.

The Functional Borders of Space

The altitudes at which man can no longer exist naturally are the functional borders of space. They are the heights at which various vital functions of the human organism fail to operate because of the nature of the ambient physical environment.

For man, space begins at an altitude of less than three miles. At this height he suffers oxygen deficiency in the blood, or hypoxia, because of the low partial pressure of oxygen in the air (*see* Gas). Here he requires an auxiliary supply of oxygen.

Only a mile and a half or so farther up, man becomes subject to "the bends," or dysbarism. Nitrogen in his tissues is released because of the low atmospheric pressure. Bubbles collect in his blood and tissues, causing great pain and, in some cases, death. Some ten miles from earth, man encounters anoxia, or an absence of oxygen in the body. At this altitude the atmospheric pressure is so low that his lungs can no longer exchange water vapor and carbon dioxide for oxygen, even though there is oxygen in the air. Positive-pressure breathing apparatus is required.

At an altitude of about 12 miles, the atmospheric pressure is so low—about 47 millimeters of mercury—that it equals the vapor pressure of the fluids in the body. Bubbling of these fluids, or ebullism, from the eyes, mouth, nose, and other orifices occurs. A pressurized cabin or suit is necessary.

Stresses and Hazards of Space Flight

The men who travel into space successfully cross the functional borders because they are protected by the environmental-control subsystems of their spacecraft and space suits. They must, however, also overcome other stresses and hazards.

The first stress of space flight is acceleration, produced as the launch vehicle leaves the pad and rapidly builds up velocity. In a few minutes, for instance, the apparent weight of Apollo astronauts increases from its usual value at the earth's surface (1g) to seven or eight times that value (7 or 8g). Acceleration affects voluntary muscular activity, blood circulation, and visual acuity. Critical controls are therefore placed within easy reach of astronauts' couches. These are so placed that the astronauts lie on their backs, facing in the direction of flight. In this "eyeballs in" position, the heart can supply the brain with blood at accelerations of up to 10g, preventing dimming or loss of consciousness. The same supine position is adopted during reentry, when high deceleration (negative acceleration) is experienced. Lighting of twice the normal intensity is provided during high acceleration to counteract dimming of vision.

Vibration and noise—primarily produced by rocket engines, propellant sloshing, engine movements, wind gusts, and air turbulence as the spacecraft passes transonic speed—can cause nausea, choking sensations, difficulty in breathing and seeing, headaches, and deafness. Although these stresses largely cease after the powered stage of flight, spacecraft and space suits are designed to attenuate noise and cushion vibration.

Temperature is also important. Man can operate efficiently within only a narrow range of temperatures—about 50° to 80°F. Around 70° is ideal. Temperature control in spacecraft is maintained by powered heating-and-cooling systems and by such passive means as reflective exterior coatings. United States spacecraft are protected from the heat of reentry into the earth's atmosphere by ablative heat shields. By charring and melting, these dissipate the heat generated by atmospheric friction. Thus, though temperatures of up to 5,000° are generated by reentering Apollo lunar spacecraft, the cabin temperature seldom rises above 75°.

Too much light can also be a serious hazard to an astronaut. In particular, excess ultraviolet—to which the eye is especially sensitive but to which the iris does not respond—can cause eye damage.

AMERICANS ENTER SPACE

The suborbital flight of Alan B. Shepard, Jr., entering a helicopter after his ocean landing (left), was the first United States manned space flight. John H. Glenn, Jr. (right), made the first United States orbital flight on Feb. 20, 1962.

Normally, the spacecraft provides protection. Astronauts who venture outside it wear visors that screen out all but 4 percent of ultraviolet light.

Radiation poses the greatest hazard to man in space. It includes cosmic rays, X rays, gamma rays, alpha particles, beta particles, neutrons, protons, and electrons. It comes from the sun, from other stars in the galaxy, and from distant space (*see* Radiation; Radioactivity). Radiation damages the cells of organisms in a manner not fully understood. Spacecraft and space suits are designed to provide protection from radiation.

The possibility of sudden decompression, exposing the occupants of a spacecraft to the effects of extremely low pressures, is a further hazard. Small leaks may be detected by sensors and, in some instances, repaired if necessary. Should repair be impossible, astronauts may have time to put on space suits. Sudden decompression—which could be caused, for example, by collision with a meteoroid—is probably not survivable by the occupants of present-day spacecraft. Fortunately, the chances that a spacecraft will strike an object large enough to cause explosive decompression are very small. Future spacecraft, designed for long-term missions, may have double walls for additional protection.

The Effects of Weightlessness

The effects of weightlessness, or zero-g, have not been fully evaluated. It is known, however, that weightlessness—the absence of any sensation of acceleration—produces changes in human physiology. All space fliers have lost weight during their flights. The losses, which ranged from 2 to 6 percent, seemed to be unrelated to the time spent in weightlessness. Most space travelers regain the weight they lost within a day or two of their return to earth.

Disorientation, greatly feared before the first manned space flights, occurred only once during the first eight years of manned flight. Russian cosmonaut Gherman S. Titov, the second man to orbit the earth, became severely disoriented and mildly nauseated. Some later space fliers—particularly those who had had little previous training or experience—had the sensation of being suspended upside down.

All astronauts and cosmonauts have experienced orthostatic collapse, or "lazy heart." The heart and vascular system lose their normal tone because the heart does not work as hard as usual when it is pumping weightless blood. The result is a temporary decrease in work-load tolerance. In-flight exercises provide partial control of this effect.

A softening of the bones, or osteoporosis, is another result of weightlessness. It is caused by the loss of calcium and other minerals. Total blood volume and red-cell mass also decrease during weightlessness. Lesser consequences of weightlessness have included a "feeling of a stuffy head" similar to a common cold. This lasts for only a few hours.

The limitations weightlessness places upon physical activity are counteracted by various devices, including special handholds and footholds. Without such aids, a man attempting to turn a nut with a wrench would merely turn himself, as he could offer no resistance to the force he applied to the wrench. Compressed-gas jets have helped space fliers maneuver outside their craft.

Psychological Stress

The unaccustomed environment of space may also produce psychological stresses. These are more difficult to define and evaluate—and probably more difficult to overcome—than are the physical stresses. Isolation could be an important psychological stress, but little is as yet known about the effects of long-term social, cultural, and perceptual isolation.

In the space flights conducted to date, isolation has produced no incapacitating mental stress—pos-

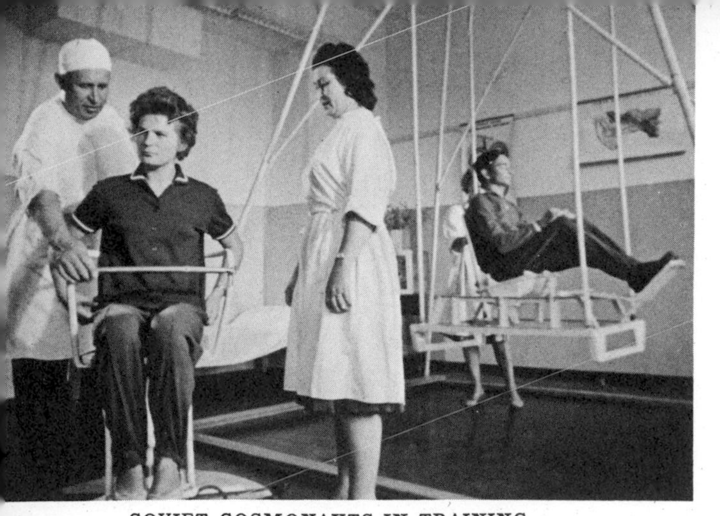

SOVIET COSMONAUTS IN TRAINING
Valentina V. Tereshkova, the first woman in space (seated, front), and Valery F. Bykovsky (rear) undergo balance tests. Training procedures are similar in the United States and Russia.

sibly because astronauts have been very busy and because they also have been in almost constant radio contact with earth. Possible effects of isolation, however, include states of anxiety, indifference, exhilaration, and euphoria. Such reactions could be disastrous.

ASTRONAUT SELECTION AND TRAINING

The men and the woman who have flown in space have been carefully selected and rigorously trained to withstand—and work efficiently in—the environment of space. The selection and training procedures of the United States and Russia are largely similar.

In the United States, an astronaut candidate must be a citizen; be no more than 36 years old; be six feet or less in height; have a bachelor's degree in engineering or science; be a pilot with 1,000 hours of jet time or a qualified test pilot; be recommended by his present organization; and be in excellent physical condition. A scientist-astronaut candidate must have a doctorate or its equivalent but need not be a pilot. Otherwise, he must meet the same requirements.

The United States training program combines academic studies, field trips, physical training, and aircraft piloting. Scientist-astronaut candidates are trained to fly jet aircraft. Jet pilots take basic courses in such areas as astronomy, geology, physiology, rocket propulsion, computer principles, and celestial mechanics. More advanced courses follow. Each astronaut also becomes a specialist in some area of space engineering associated with his spacecraft, launch vehicle, or tracking system. He then becomes a teacher, keeping his fellow astronauts up-to-date on developments in his specialty.

Astronauts make use of a number of training devices. These include the human centrifuge, upon which they are accustomed to acceleration (for picture, *see* Aerospace Medicine). Audiovisual devices assist in teaching astronauts to operate spacecraft subsystems. Weightlessness is introduced in aircraft flying ballistic paths and is simulated in neutral-buoyancy exercises underwater. More complicated devices permit astronauts to practice such intricate maneuvers as rendezvous and docking.

Once selected for a specific mission, an astronaut and his fellow crew members begin an intensive six-month training period. Much of the period is spent in very elaborate and realistic training devices. Typical are the mission simulators at the Manned Spacecraft Center in Texas and at the Kennedy Space Center in Florida.

The computer-controlled mission simulator is called "the great train wreck" because of its jumbled appearance. It has a cabin that looks exactly like the one in which the astronauts will fly. Outside its windows, star patterns and views of the earth and moon move past just as the astronauts will see them during their flight. Instructors at consoles monitor the actions of the astronauts as they rehearse their mission. The computer relays problems to the astronauts through their instruments, notes their responses and adjusts the instruments appropriately. The instructors and the computer also introduce emergencies to train the astronauts to respond correctly. In effect, men who fly in space have already been there many times. (*See also* Aerospace Careers; "Space Pilots and Astronauts of the United States" table in Fact-Index.)

THE MODERN MANNED SPACECRAFT

The astronaut's spacecraft provides him with both transportation and the means to sustain life. Manned spacecraft are among the most complex devices ever built. The three-man Apollo spacecraft of the United States, which carries men to the moon, is a good example of a modern manned spacecraft.

The Apollo has three basic components: the command module (CM), the service module (SM), and the lunar module (LM). The CM is the spacecraft's control center and its crew's basic working and living area. The SM provides propulsion, power, and storage for consumables. The LM is the lunar-landing vehicle. The launch vehicle is a three-stage Saturn V rocket (*see* diagram on the next page).

The spacecraft is launched first into earth (parking) orbit, then into lunar trajectory. En route, the combined CM and SM (C/SM) draw the LM from its compartment atop the third Saturn V stage, then discard the stage. Upon reaching the moon, the SM's engine places the spacecraft in lunar orbit. From lunar orbit the LM—with two astronauts aboard—descends to the surface. The third astronaut remains in lunar orbit in the C/SM. After the astronauts complete their surface activities, the LM's upper stage returns them to lunar orbit for rendezvous and docking with the C/SM. All three astronauts again aboard, the C/SM engine boosts the spacecraft into earth-return trajectory. A landing is made in the ocean (*see* diagram on a following page).

The Command Module

Conical in shape, the CM is 12 feet 10 inches in diameter and 10 feet 7 inches high. It weighs about 13,000 pounds. Its two shells are constructed and joined to withstand the stresses of launch, in-flight maneuvers, and reentry. The inner shell, primarily of aluminum honeycomb, is the astronauts' pressure cabin. The outer shell is a heat shield of stainless steel honeycomb. Atop the CM, at launch, are a protective cover and the rocket tower of the launch-escape system, which would lift the CM to safety in an emergency. The cover and escape system are jettisoned at about 295,000 feet. The base of the CM—the only module that returns to earth—is covered by the ablative reentry heat shield of fiber glass and epoxy resin. The CM has two hatches, one in the side and another in the apex of the cone. Astronauts enter the LM through the second. There are five windows. Couches—one of which may be stowed away during flight to provide extra room—are provided for the three astronauts.

The principal spacecraft subsystems are located in the CM. The guidance-and-control subsystem includes both inertial and optical navigational devices. The on-board computer stores flight programs and aids in navigational calculations. The communications subsystem provides voice, television, and telemetry links between the spacecraft and earth.

The instrumentation subsystem monitors the condition of both spacecraft and crew. The environmental-control subsystem provides an atmosphere, food, water, and human-waste management for the crew. The atmosphere is pure oxygen, maintained at a pressure of five pounds per square inch. Temperature is kept between 70° and 75°. Food is prepared and packaged for easy handling in weightlessness. Water is provided for drinking, hygiene, and the rehydration of food. Urine is dumped overboard with waste water, while solid wastes are stored in plastic bags. Also in the CM are storage batteries, which are part of the total spacecraft power-supply subsystem.

Space suits, or pressure suits, are worn during launch, recovery, and extravehicular activity (EVA). They may be regarded as part of the environmental-control subsystem. A backpack portable life-support system (PLSS) provides moon-walking astronauts with oxygen and temperature control for up to four hours of activity outside the spacecraft.

The recovery, or reentry, subsystem includes two drogue parachutes which are deployed at a height of 23,000 feet to slow the spacecraft so that the three main parachutes may be deployed at 10,000 feet. These lower the spacecraft gently into the ocean.

Service and Lunar Modules; Launch Vehicle

The SM contains the spacecraft's on-board propulsion subsystem, a 20,500-pound-thrust liquid-propellant rocket engine. It is used for mid-course corrections, braking the spacecraft into lunar orbit, and thrusting it out of lunar orbit into earth-return trajectory. Also in the SM are attitude-control subsystem components, oxygen for the environmental-control subsystem, and three fuel cells which are the Apollo's basic power supply.

The LM is designed to operate only in the hard vacuum of space. It cannot reenter the earth's at-

The Apollo/Saturn V Lunar Spacecraft

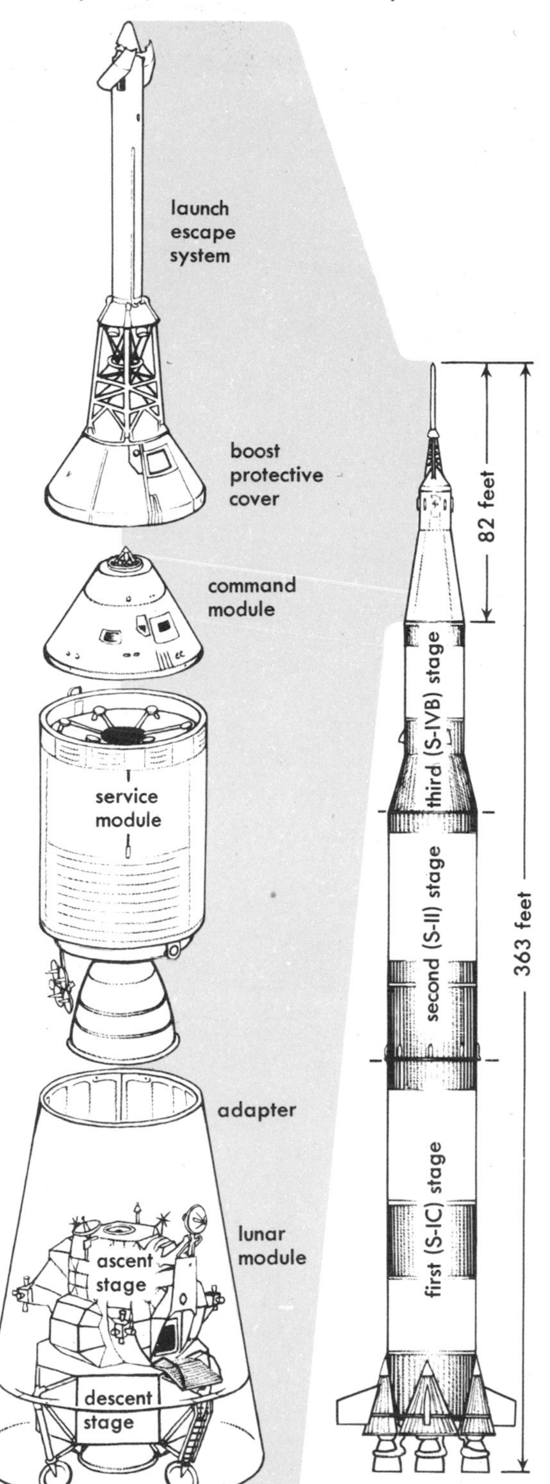

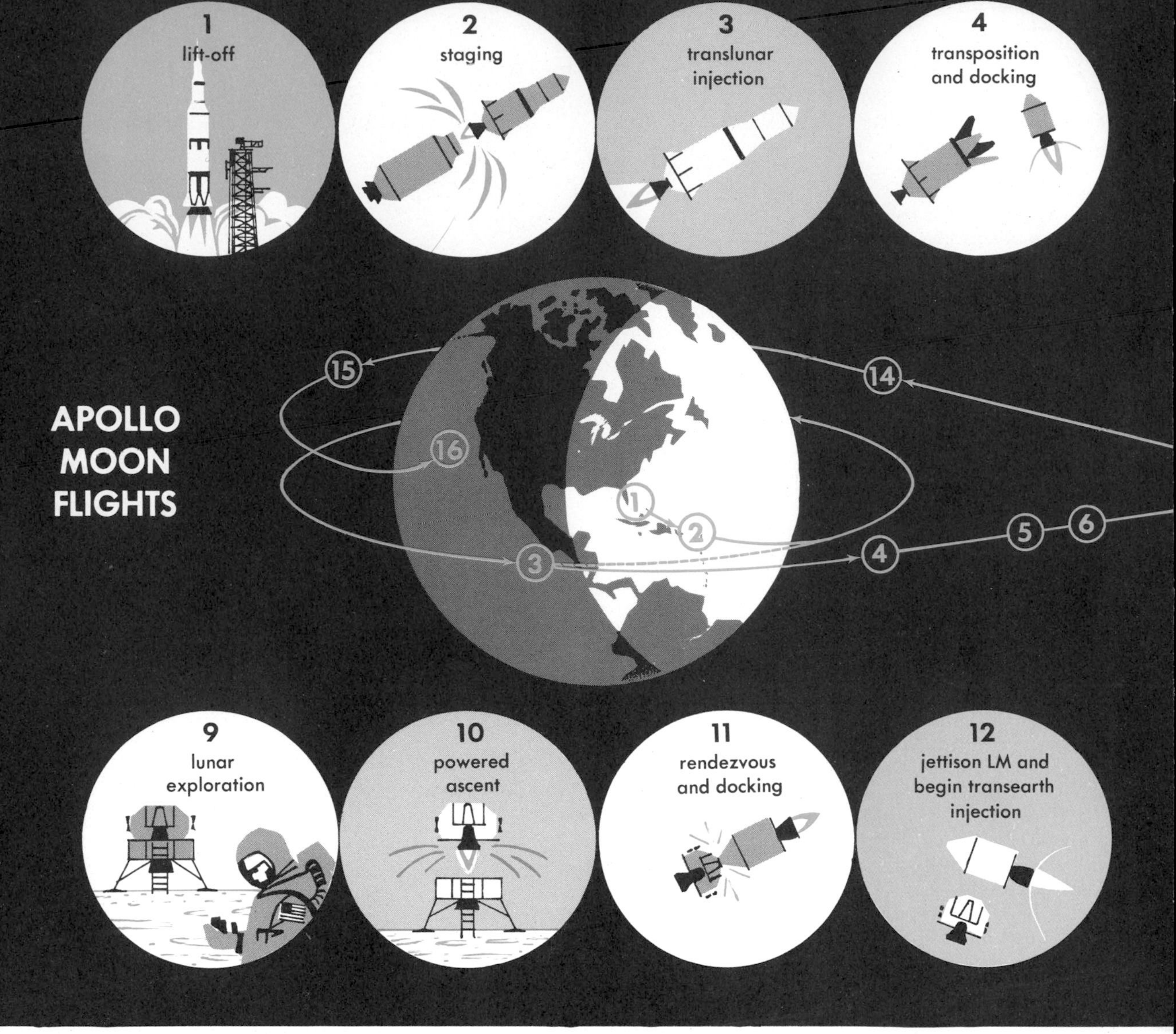

Apollo lunar spacecraft are launched by Saturn V rockets from Cape Kennedy, Fla. Rocket stages are discarded as exhausted. From parking orbit the spacecraft is boosted into lunar trajectory. The command and service modules (C/SM) separate from the third rocket stage, turn around, dock with the lunar module (LM), and withdraw it from its adapter. The third stage is then discarded. Mid-course corrections are made as needed. The spacecraft enters lunar orbit, from which the LM carries

mosphere. It has two major parts: the descent stage and the ascent stage.

The descent stage carries a rocket engine, propellant tanks, and landing gear. The engine, which is variable in thrust, is used to brake the LM from lunar orbit and lower it gently to the surface. The landing gear consists of four shock-absorbing struts with yard-wide, saucer-shaped "foot pads" at their ends. The descent stage also serves as a "launch pad" for the ascent stage.

The ascent stage is the "command module" of the LM. It contains life-support, communications, and other subsystems similar to those of the CM. It also carries the rocket engine that boosts it back into lunar orbit for rendezvous and docking with the orbiting CM. It has windows for both landing and docking operations. A hatch at the top is used to transfer astronauts between it and the CM; another at the front opens onto a ladder leading down a landing strut to the lunar surface.

Apollo lunar spacecraft are launched by three-stage Saturn V rockets. Ready for launch, the spacecraft/launch vehicle assembly is 363 feet tall and weighs some 6 million pounds. The first (S-IC) stage contains five F-1 engines which together develop some 7.6 million pounds of thrust at sea level. They burn kerosine and liquid oxygen. The stage boosts the upper stages to an altitude of more than 40 miles and a velocity of more than 6,000 miles per hour. The second (S-II) stage is powered by five J-2 engines which together develop more than one million pounds of thrust. They burn liquid oxygen and liquid hydrogen. The S-II boosts the third stage and spacecraft to parking-orbit height (nearly

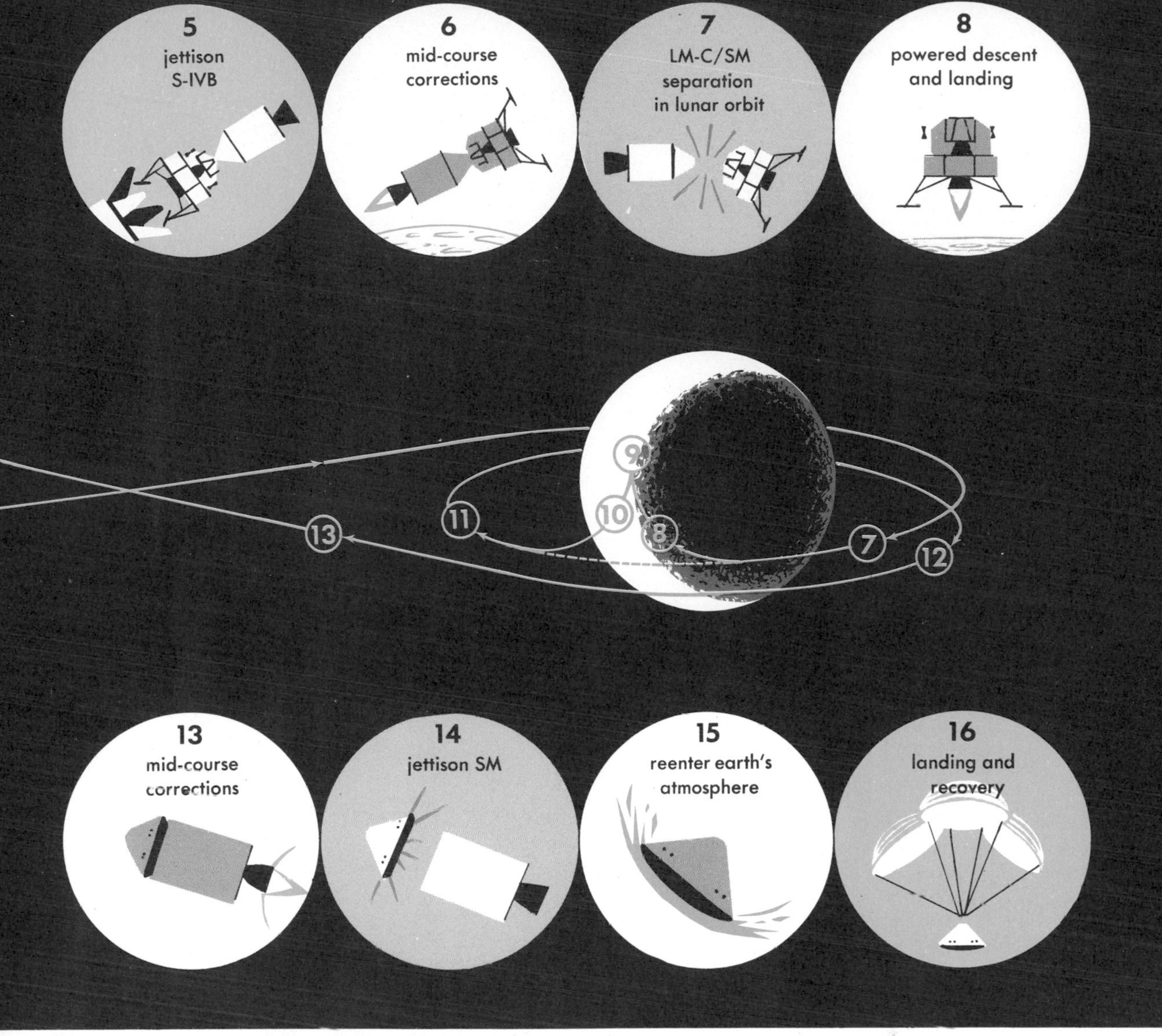

two astronauts to the moon's surface while the third remains in the C/SM. After the astronauts complete their work on the moon, the LM's ascent stage carries them back to the orbiting C/SM. The LM is jettisoned and the C/SM's engine boosts the spacecraft into earth-return trajectory. Mid-course corrections are made. Near earth, the SM is jettisoned and the CM reenters the earth's atmosphere and lands by parachute in the ocean. Ships and helicopters recover the astronauts and CM.

120 miles) and to a near-orbital velocity of more than 15,000 miles per hour.

The third (S-IVB) stage has one J-2 engine with a thrust of more than 200,000 pounds. It is fired twice—to insert the spacecraft into parking orbit and to inject it into lunar trajectory. It is discarded en route to the moon after the C/SM has withdrawn the LM from the adapter at its upper end.

MAN'S JOURNEYS INTO SPACE

Man's venture into space is perhaps the most complex and costly of all his undertakings. It is also surely among the most fascinating and successful—less than two decades after man first brushed the edges of space, he walked upon the surface of the moon. Manned space flights are summarized in the table at the end of this section.

To the Fringe of Space—The X-15

Man first crossed the border of space in a curious vehicle that was neither wholly spacecraft nor wholly airplane. It functioned as a manned rocket, capable of arcing briefly into the very lowest fringes of space, and as an airplane, landing with wings, rudder, stabilizer, and wheels. It was the X-15.

Conceived in the early 1950's and designed to reach altitudes of more than 50 miles and speeds of more than 4,000 miles per hour, the X-15 first flew in September 1959. Three were built. (For illustrations, *see* Aerospace Research and Development.)

In nearly 200 flights between 1959 and the end of the program in 1968, the X-15 returned information that was of great value in the design of both spacecraft and supersonic aircraft. It reached an altitude of 67 miles and a speed of more than 4,500 miles per hour. Military pilots who flew the X-15 higher than 50 miles were regarded as astronauts.

Russian Manned Space Flights

The one-earth-orbit flight of Russia's Yuri A. Gagarin in the spacecraft Vostok 1 on April 12, 1961, is regarded as man's first true space flight. Five more flights of single-seat Vostok spacecraft were made before the program's end in 1963. The flights of Vostoks 3 and 4 and Vostoks 5 and 6 were "group" flights—two spacecraft were aloft at the same time in similar orbits, sometimes within sight of each other. The Vostok was not maneuverable, however, and attempts at rendezvous and docking were not made. The pilot of Vostok 6 was Valentina V. Tereshkova, the first woman to fly in space.

Two flights of multiman Voskhod spacecraft—derivatives of the Vostok—were made in 1964 and 1965. Voskhod 1 carried three cosmonauts. Voskhod 2 carried two, one of whom—Aleksei A. Leonov—left the orbiting spacecraft for some ten minutes to become the first space flier to perform a space walk, or extravehicular activity.

Flights of multiman Soyuz spacecraft began in 1967. The first ended in tragedy. Cosmonaut Vladimir M. Komarov, a veteran of Voskhod 1, was killed in a crash when the parachute lines of Soyuz 1 fouled upon reentry into the earth's atmosphere. The first man to be killed in space flight, Komarov was the spacecraft's sole occupant.

In October 1968 cosmonaut Georgi T. Beregovoy, the sole occupant of Soyuz 3, completed Russia's first rendezvous in space. He came within 650 feet of the unmanned Soyuz 2. Rendezvous and docking were accomplished by Soyuz 4 and 5 in January 1969. Soyuz 4 was launched with one cosmonaut, Soyuz 5 with three. Two cosmonauts made extravehicular transfers to Soyuz 4, becoming the first men to leave earth in one spacecraft and return in another.

". . .ONE SMALL STEP . . ."
On July 20, 1969, Neil A. Armstrong became the first man to walk on the moon. This television image shows him descending toward the surface. He was accompanied by Edwin E. Aldrin, Jr. Michael Collins remained in the orbiting command module.

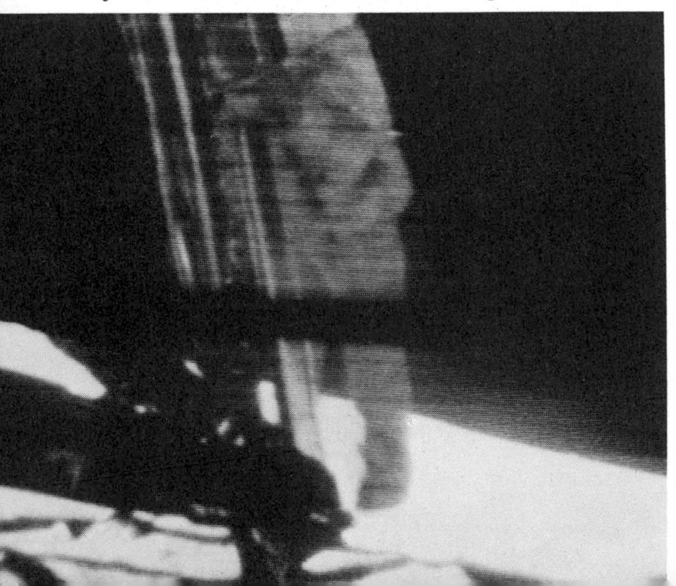

United States Mercury and Gemini Flights

The first United States astronaut to enter space was Alan B. Shepard, Jr. His suborbital flight, on May 5, 1961, in a one-man Mercury spacecraft carried him 115 miles high. He landed in the Atlantic Ocean as planned, 302 miles from the launching site at Cape Canaveral (now Cape Kennedy).

On Feb. 20, 1962, John H. Glenn, Jr., became the first American to orbit the earth. He completed three orbits in 4 hours 55 minutes. Three more flights completed the Mercury program. Suborbital Mercury flights were launched by modified Redstone missiles, orbital flights by modified Atlas missiles.

The two-man vehicles of Project Gemini, capable of changing the size, shape, and plane of their orbits, were the world's first maneuverable manned spacecraft. In the first manned Gemini flight—that of Gemini 3—Virgil I. Grissom and John W. Young completed three orbits. On June 3, 1965, during the flight of Gemini 4, Edward H. White II became the first American to walk in space. During his 20-minute EVA, White maneuvered outside the spacecraft with the aid of a hand-held compressed-gas jet.

The first rendezvous between two orbiting spacecraft was accomplished on Dec. 15, 1965. Command pilot Walter M. Schirra maneuvered Gemini 6 to within a foot of Gemini 7, in which Frank Borman and James A. Lovell, Jr., set a space flight endurance record of 330 hours 35 minutes. In the succeeding Gemini flights, rendezvous and dockings were achieved with unmanned Agena target vehicles and EVA techniques were perfected. The program ended in November 1966 with the flight of Gemini 12. Gemini flights were launched by modified Titan II missiles.

Project Apollo—Man to the Moon

Mercury and Gemini were a prelude to Project Apollo, the goal of which was manned exploration of the moon. Development of the three-man, three-module Apollo spacecraft and its massive Saturn V launch vehicle began in the early 1960's. Potential lunar landing sites were selected on the basis of data returned by unmanned Ranger, Surveyor, and Lunar Orbiter spacecraft. Meanwhile, unmanned developmental flights of Apollo components were conducted.

The first manned test of the Apollo spacecraft was scheduled for the spring of 1967, but tragedy intervened. On Jan. 27, 1967, during a practice countdown at Cape Kennedy, Grissom, White, and Roger B. Chaffee were killed when a flash fire swept the command module in which they sat atop a Saturn IB launch vehicle. The Apollo program was delayed while the module was modified for greater safety.

The first manned Apollo spacecraft—Apollo 7—was launched on Oct. 11, 1968, by a Saturn IB rocket. In it Schirra, Donn F. Eisele, and Walter Cunningham conducted a thorough and successful 11-day checkout of the command and service modules in earth orbit. The first telecasts from United States manned spacecraft were made during the flight.

HIGHLIGHTS FROM THE FLIGHT OF APOLLO 11

Pictured before lift-off on July 16, 1969, are the astronauts of Apollo 11 (from left): Neil A. Armstrong, Edwin E. Aldrin, Jr., and Michael Collins.

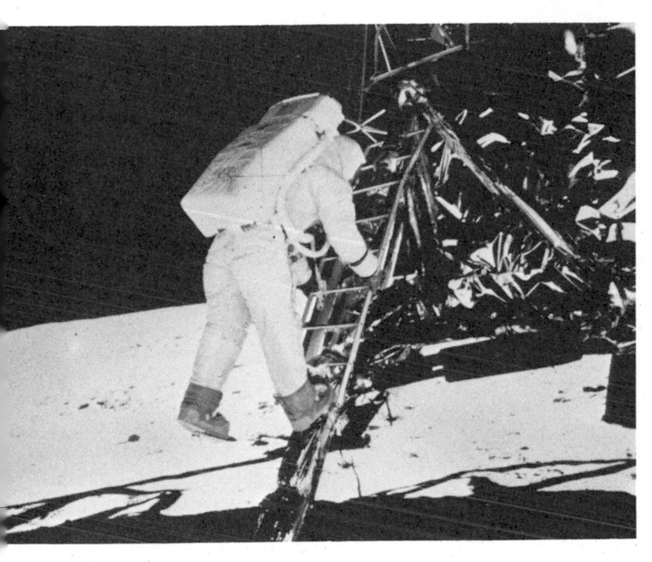

The Apollo 11 lunar module (LM) landed on the moon on the afternoon of July 20. Near 10 P.M. CDT Armstrong stepped onto the lunar surface. Soon afterward Aldrin descended the LM's ladder to join him (left). The two emplaced a United States flag (above), stiffened by wire to "fly" above the airless moon.

The earth beckoned above the lunar horizon (below) on July 21 as the LM lifted toward rendezvous with the command module.

Aldrin moved easily across the lunar surface, carrying a laser-beam reflector and a seismometer (above). These were left on the moon. After splashdown in the Pacific Ocean on July 24, the astronauts (in raft, below) awaited helicopters.

In Apollo 8, launched by a Saturn V on Dec. 21, 1968, Borman, Lovell, and William Anders became the first men to orbit the moon. They completed ten lunar orbits on December 24 and 25, then returned to earth for a safe landing in the Pacific Ocean on December 27. The Apollo lunar module was tested in earth orbit during the ten-day flight of Apollo 9, launched on March 3, 1969. Apollo 10, launched on May 18, again carried three men—Thomas P. Stafford, Eugene A. Cernan, and John W. Young—into lunar orbit. They completed 31 lunar orbits, and the lunar module—carrying Stafford and Cernan—descended to within nine miles of the lunar surface. No landing was planned or attempted.

Apollo 11, launched on July 16, 1969, carried the first men to land on the moon. It entered lunar orbit on July 19. In the afternoon of July 20 command pilot Neil A. Armstrong and lunar module pilot Edwin E. Aldrin, Jr., began their descent to the surface. They landed in the Mare Tranquillitatis at 3:17 P.M. CDT. At 9:56 P.M. CDT Armstrong became the first man to step onto the moon. He was followed by Aldrin. (*See also* first page of this article.) On July 21 they rendezvoused with Michael Collins, who had remained in the moon-orbiting command module, then returned to earth, landing in the Pacific Ocean at 11:50 A.M. CDT July 24. (*See also* Moon.)

Beyond Apollo

Apollo lunar missions are expected to continue into the early 1970's. Extensive exploration of the moon is expected to yield information on its age and structure—and to shed light as well upon the age and evolution of the earth and solar system.

Plans for post-Apollo missions include the orbiting of large scientific laboratories, capable of supporting several men for long periods—and possibly of being serviced by reusable shuttle vehicles. For the more distant future, manned missions to Mars and other planets have been suggested.

MANNED SPACE FLIGHTS

Spacecraft	Crew	Date Launched	Duration (hrs.: mins.)	Remarks
		SOVIET UNION		
Vostok 1	Y. Gagarin	April 12, 1961	1:48	World's first manned space flight; one orbit.
Vostok 2	G. Titov	Aug. 6, 1961	25:11	Earth orbited 17 times.
Vostok 3	A. Nikolayev	Aug. 11, 1962	94:22	First Soviet "group" flight; craft came within
Vostok 4	P. Popovich	Aug. 12, 1962	70:57	3.1 miles of each other.
Vostok 5	V. Bykovsky	June 14, 1963	119:06	Craft came within 3 miles of each other; V.
Vostok 6	V. Tereshkova	June 16, 1963	70:50	Tereshkova first woman in space.
Voskhod 1	V. Komarov, K. Feoktistov, B. Yegorov	Oct. 12, 1964	24:17	First spacecraft with multiman crew.
Voskhod 2	P. Belyayev, A. Leonov	March 18, 1965	26:02	Leonov first space walker; out of craft 10 min.
Soyuz 1	V. Komarov	April 23, 1967	25:37	Parachute fouled in reentry; cosmonaut killed.
Soyuz 3	G. Beregovoy	Oct. 26, 1968	94:51	Rendezvous made in space with unmanned Soyuz 2.
Soyuz 4	V. Shatalov	Jan. 14, 1969	71:14	First docking of Soviet manned spacecraft;
Soyuz 5	B. Volynov, A. Yeliseyev, Y. Khrunov	Jan. 15, 1969	72:46	Yeliseyev and Khrunov made extravehicular transfer from Soyuz 5, returned to earth in Soyuz 4.
		UNITED STATES		
Mercury 3	A. Shepard	May 5, 1961	0:15	Shepard first American astronaut to fly in space; suborbital flight, ballistic trajectory.
Mercury 4	V. Grissom	July 21, 1961	0:16	Suborbital; craft sank in recovery attempt.
Mercury 6	J. Glenn	Feb. 20, 1962	4:55	Glenn first United States astronaut to orbit earth; 3 orbits completed.
Mercury 7	S. Carpenter	May 24, 1962	4:56	Retro-rockets late; landed 250 miles from target.
Mercury 8	W. Schirra	Oct. 3, 1962	9:13	Landed within 5 miles of target after 6 orbits.
Mercury 9	G. Cooper	May 15, 1963	34:20	Last and longest of Project Mercury flights.
Gemini 3	V. Grissom, J. Young	March 23, 1965	4:53	First maneuverable manned spacecraft.
Gemini 4	J. McDivitt, E. White	June 3, 1965	97:56	White first United States spacewalker.
Gemini 5	G. Cooper, C. Conrad	Aug. 21, 1965	190:55	Long-duration test; in orbit nearly 8 days.
Gemini 7	F. Borman, J. Lovell	Dec. 4, 1965	330:35	Longest flight; was Gemini 6A rendezvous target.
Gemini 6A	W. Schirra, T. Stafford	Dec. 15, 1965	25:51	Came within one foot of Gemini 7.
Gemini 8	N. Armstrong, D. Scott	March 16, 1966	10:41	First spacecraft to dock with another (Agena).
Gemini 9A	T. Stafford, E. Cernan	June 3, 1966	72:21	Rendezvous with target; space walk (Cernan).
Gemini 10	J. Young, M. Collins	July 18, 1966	70:47	Rendezvous and docking; space walk (Collins).
Gemini 11	C. Conrad, R. Gordon	Sept. 12, 1966	71:17	Rendezvous and docking; space walk (Gordon).
Gemini 12	J. Lovell, E. Aldrin	Nov. 11, 1966	94:35	Rendezvous and docking; space walk (Aldrin).
Apollo 7	W. Schirra, D. Eisele, W. Cunningham	Oct. 11, 1968	260:09	First manned flight of Apollo command module; in earth orbit.
Apollo 8	F. Borman, J. Lovell, W. Anders	Dec. 21, 1968	147:00	First manned craft to orbit moon; made 10 lunar orbits at height of 70 miles.
Apollo 9	J. McDivitt, D. Scott, R. Schweickart	March 3, 1969	241:01	Successful test in earth orbit of Apollo lunar module designed for landing on moon.
Apollo 10	T. Stafford, E. Cernan, J. Young	May 18, 1969	192:03	Second manned lunar-orbital flight; lunar module came within 50,000 feet of moon.
Apollo 11	N. Armstrong, E. Aldrin, M. Collins	July 16, 1969	195:18	Armstrong, Aldrin first men to land on moon; deployed experiments, collected soil samples.

International Cooperation in Space

ON THE WHOLE, the nations of the world have cooperated in exploring space. Many organizations promote such cooperation. These include international scientific bodies, national professional bodies, and industrial concerns.

International cooperation in the exploration of space takes many forms. Among nations it has involved financial assistance, the donation of rockets and instruments, and the training of foreign scientists, technicians, and teachers in colleges and laboratories. Scientists foster the free exchange of ideas and the results of space research. Businesses cooperate in building and selling space-research equipment.

The United Nations and Other Groups

Several organizations of the United Nations (UN) encourage international cooperation in space. The International Telecommunication Union allocates radio frequencies on a worldwide scale to avoid confusion and interference. The World Meteorological Organization, which sponsors the World Weather Watch, collects and distributes to all nations data from United States and Russian meteorological satellites, together with information gathered by sounding rockets, balloons, and ground-based observations.

The UN Educational, Scientific, and Cultural Organization concerns itself with all scientific research, including research connected with space exploration. The World Health Organization finds many uses on earth for medical knowledge gained in space research. The Inter-Governmental Maritime Consultative Organization is investigating the potential uses of navigation satellites. The International Atomic Energy Agency is interested in the use of nuclear energy for propulsion in space. The International Civil Aviation Organization seeks to eliminate the possibility that space vehicles leaving or entering the earth's atmosphere might interfere with or endanger civil aircraft. It is also exploring the use of communications satellites to solve the problems of civil aviation.

In addition to the UN bodies, international space-research organizations include the European Space Research Organization (ESRO) and the European Space Vehicle Launcher Development Organization (ELDO). ESRO, formed in 1962, is engaged in both fundamental research and the development of spacecraft. ELDO has built the Europa 1 launch vehicle, which combines a British first stage, a French second stage, a German third stage, and an Italian satellite. Belgium and the Netherlands provide supporting ground facilities, and early versions of the rocket were launched from Woomera, Australia.

CANADIAN SATELLITE—UNITED STATES ROCKET
Canada's Alouette 2 (above), designed for studies of the ionosphere, was placed in orbit by a United States rocket. The United States often launches satellites built abroad.

Nonpolitical Organizations

Many influential nonpolitical bodies also further international cooperation in space. Perhaps the most active is the Committee on Space Research (COSPAR) of the International Council of Scientific Unions. COSPAR was formed in 1959. Composed of representatives from 11 international organizations and 35 scientific bodies, it confines its attention to the basic problems of space research and disregards its engineering aspects.

COSPAR is an international clearinghouse for the results of experiments and research in space science. In addition, it studies proposed space experiments with a view to deciding which ones might have adverse effects upon other research. COSPAR also operates Spacewarn, an international network for the rapid transmission of information on newly launched rockets and spacecraft.

Other nonpolitical international professional organizations devote their efforts to more limited areas of space research. These specialized groups further the free exchange of information within specific fields. Typical are the International Academy of Aviation and Space Medicine, the International Association for Cybernetics, the International Institute of Space Law, the International Institute of Communications, and the International Federation of Aerospace Technology and Engineering.

National organizations that foster the free exchange of space information have been established in most of the countries of Western Europe and the Americas. Among them are the British Interplanetary Society, the American Institute of Aeronautics and Astronautics, the American Astronautical Society, Inc., the French Astronautical Society, the Hermann Oberth Society (West Germany), the Canadian Aeronautics and Space Institute, the Society for Rocketry Technique and Space Travel (West Germany), and the Italian Rocket Association. There is also a Japan Astronautical Society.

In most countries—among others, the United States, Russia, Poland, West Germany, France, Bulgaria, England, and Czechoslovakia—there are also amateur rocket societies for young people. Many future space scientists and astronauts will come from these clubs. Amateur groups in the United States and Australia, for instance, have constructed inexpensive but functional satellites which were launched for them by the United States Air Force.

Industrial Cooperation Among Nations

Industrialists of the United States, Western Europe, and other areas also spur cooperation in space research and technology. They not only seek markets for space vehicles but also encourage the development of other applications and markets for the materials and products of space research.

The best known and most active of the international industrial organizations that sponsor cooperation in space research and technology is Eurospace, which was formed in 1961. Its membership consists of some 150 Western European industrial concerns. About a dozen firms in the United States have been admitted as associate members. Typical of Eurospace's projects is the development of an aerospace transporter—a reusable vehicle capable of taking off from the earth, delivering personnel and cargo to a space station, and returning to earth.

Valuable By-Products of Space Research

AS SPACE technology progressed after World War II, a curious development occurred. From the research that produced the rocket motors, liquid propellants, space suits, and other necessities of space flight emerged by-products that no one had anticipated. These were unexpected applications—in medicine, industry, and the home—for materials, equipment, and services that had been created for use in space. Such by-products are called "spin-off" or "fallout." Only a few of hundreds can be named here.

Boons to Medicine

Perhaps the best-known examples of spin-off are found in hospitals and doctors' offices. Some of these stem from space medical research. Many are adaptations from other areas of space technology. Typical of spun-off implements is a sight switch that permits handicapped people to operate devices they could not otherwise use. They do this by using their eye movements to interrupt a light beam. The switch was developed to give astronauts a means of controlling their spacecraft while their arms and legs were rendered useless by high acceleration.

Another device, developed to enable astronauts to steer spacecraft by voice command, can help the retarded learn to speak, the deaf to speak more clearly, and stutterers to improve their speech. The device permits the user to compare the oscilloscope trace of his voice with a trace of the desired sound.

Microminiature electronic components—required

A MULTINATIONAL SPACE VEHICLE

A Europa 1 launch vehicle, built by the European Space Vehicle Launcher Development Organization, awaits testing in Australia. Great Britain built the first stage of the rocket, France the second, Germany the third, and Italy the satellite.

because spacecraft devices must be small and light and use little power, yet be very rugged—have made many new instruments available to the doctor and his patient. There are now hearing aids, not much larger than aspirin tablets, that are worn entirely within the ear. A television camera the size of a cigarette package is mounted on the surgeon's head to give students a closeup view of an operation. Other small cameras, equipped with flexible light-transmitting devices, take pictures inside such body organs as the stomach.

Biotelemetry, which was developed to monitor the temperature, brain-wave activity, breathing rate, and heartbeat of astronauts, offers a new means of monitoring hospital patients. Biosensors attached to the body send data by wire or radio. This information may be displayed on oscilloscopes for doctors to analyze. It can also be fed into a computer that "watches" the patient and sounds an alarm if the results indicate that he requires medical assistance. Some biosensors, called endoradiosondes, can be implanted in the body. The tiny batteries that power them can be recharged by radio waves.

Not all spin-off of value in medicine involves electronics. Thus, a special stretcher developed to immobilize and remove injured workmen from the huge propellant tanks of the Saturn V rocket is now widely employed to remove injured men from mines, offshore oil-drilling rigs, and boats. The rigid aluminum device permits a man to be moved through an opening 18 inches in diameter.

The search for a better insulating material for rocket-propellant tanks produced a plastic polymer gel with the density of human fat at body temperature. Used as a padding for bedridden patients, it prevents bedsores. Aerospace scientists in England developed a special bed which enables burn patients literally to float on a cushion of air. The burns heal more quickly because they do not rub against bedclothes.

The scientists who developed the Surveyor lunar probe found that they could make the Surveyor pictures clearer by using a computer to control printing. This technique applied to X-ray pictures reveals anatomical details that were previously invisible.

Benefits in Other Areas

Many items developed in space research are now being used in factories, offices, and homes. Some may seem trivial; others have been of great benefit. A very valuable industrial application was found for an infrared earth-horizon sensor developed to orient spacecraft. It continuously monitors ribbons of steel moving at up to 50 miles an hour and maintains the desired product thickness.

The requirement for small, accurate, and rugged timing devices in spacecraft led to the development of a very small tuning fork that vibrates at 360 cycles per second, some 144 times as fast as the balance wheel in a conventional watch. The device is now a component of highly accurate wristwatches that run for a year on a battery as small as a dime.

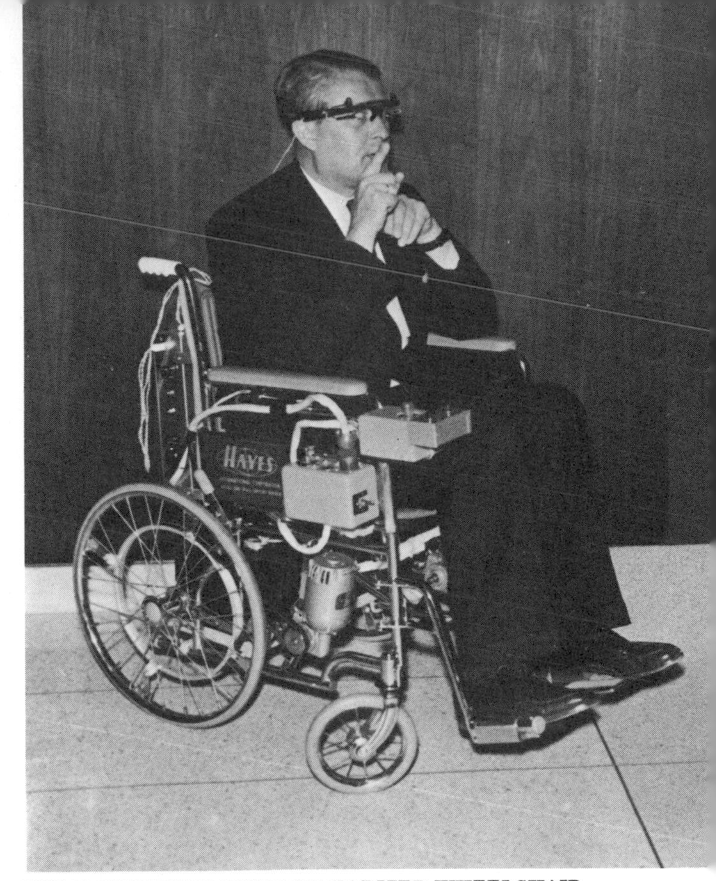

EYE MOVEMENTS GUIDE MOTORIZED WHEELCHAIR
Wernher von Braun, rocket pioneer and director of NASA's George C. Marshall Space Flight Center, demonstrates a wheelchair controlled by eye movements sensed by special glasses. Such devices are by-products of space research.

Fiber-glass materials for rocket-fuel tanks are now employed to make lightweight, high-strength storage tanks, railway tank cars, and highway tankers. A magnetic hammer that originally served to eliminate small imperfections from metal surfaces of the Saturn V rocket is being adapted for use in the automotive and shipbuilding industries.

Hundreds of other items could be mentioned. There are, for example, an aluminized plastic blanket that can be folded small enough to be carried in a pocket; a cooler-smoking tobacco pipe, lined with a material developed for nuclear rocket engines; an ultrasonic testing device that can reveal hidden earthquake damage in masonry structures; and an improved caulking compound for tiles, derived from sealants used in spacecraft.

One of the most valuable contributions of aerospace technology to industry in general is a management technique called the *systems approach,* or *systems engineering.* With the aid of computers, this technique brings together all the elements of a complex project—people, money, materials—so that everything is ready at the optimum time. It has been applied to a variety of problems unrelated to space exploration. Among them are cancer research, hospital design and management, city planning, crime detection and prevention, pollution control, building construction, and transportation.

SPACE TRAVEL—FROM DREAM TO REALITY

A.D. 160—Lucian of Samosata, Greek satirist, writes 'True History', the first fictional account of a trip to the moon.

1634—'Sleep', a moon-trip fantasy, by German astronomer Johannes Kepler, is published.

1865—Jules Verne, French author, writes classic novel 'From the Earth to the Moon'.

1900—Konstantin E. Tsiolkovsky of Russia evolves the idea of large piloted rockets.

1919—Robert H. Goddard, professor at Clark University, Worcester, Mass., publishes 'A Method of Reaching Extreme Altitudes'.

1923—Professor Hermann Oberth, German mathematician, publishes 'The Rocket into Interplanetary Space', the cornerstone for all later space-travel ideas.

1926—Goddard fires first liquid-fuel rocket.

1938–44—Peenemünde Research Institute on Usedom Island in the Baltic develops V-2 rocket weapon used in World War II.

1945–49—German V-2 parts are shipped to the United States and Russia; United States starts rocket program at White Sands Proving Grounds in New Mexico. First shot into space is made in 1949 with V-2 as first stage and WAC Corporal rocket as second stage.

1957—Russia launches Sputnik 1, the first man-made earth satellite, and Sputnik 2, which carries a dog, Laika, the first space traveler.

1958—United States launches its first satellites, Explorer 1 and Vanguard 1.

1959—United States recovers monkeys unharmed after space flight; Russian probe hits moon.

1960—United States launches television-equipped satellite, Tiros 1, to photograph the earth's cloud cover. United States makes first recovery of satellite that has been in orbit.

1961—First man is sent into space, by Russia, and orbits earth; United States astronauts make first suborbital space flights.

1962—First United States astronauts make orbital flights; X-15 rocket plane penetrates outer space; communications satellite Telstar 1 orbited. Two Russian manned spaceships stay in twin orbits for three days.

1963—First woman is launched into space, by Russia; makes 48-orbit flight.

1964—Russia orbits three cosmonauts in the Voskhod 1, first multipassenger spaceship.

1965—Russian cosmonaut is first man to walk in space. United States orbits Gemini 3, the first maneuverable manned spaceship. United States spacecraft Gemini 6 and Gemini 7 achieve first rendezvous in orbit.

1966—United States Gemini 8 spacecraft docks with Agena rocket. Russian and United States probes land intact on the moon.

1967—Three United States astronauts, one Russian cosmonaut die in spacecraft accidents; lunar-landing programs delayed.

1968—United States astronauts make man's first lunar-orbital flight.

1969—United States astronauts are first men on the moon; return safely.

BIBLIOGRAPHY FOR ROCKETS, GUIDED MISSILES, AND SPACE TRAVEL

Books for Younger Readers

Bendick, Jeanne. The First Book of Space Travel (Watts, 1963).

Bergaust, Erik. Rocket Power (Putnam, 1962).

Bergaust, Erik. Saturn Story (Putnam, 1962).

Bergwin, C. R. and Coleman, W. T. Animal Astronauts (Prentice-Hall, 1963).

Bova, Benjamin. The Uses of Space (Holt, 1965).

Chester, Michael. Let's Go to the Moon (Putnam, 1965).

Coombs, C. I. Lift-Off (Morrow, 1963).

Coombs, C. I. Project Apollo (Morrow, 1965).

Dille, John. Americans in Space (American Heritage, 1965).

Elting, Mary. Spacecraft at Work (Harvey, 1965).

Gilmore, H. H. Model Rockets for Beginners (Harper, 1961).

Goodwin, H. L. All About Rockets and Space Flight (Random, 1964).

Gottlieb, W. P. Space Flight and How It Works (Doubleday, 1963).

Hirsch, S. C. The Globe for the Space Age (Viking, 1963).

Keen, Martin. The Wonders of Space (Grosset, 1967).

Lauber, Patricia. Big Dreams and Small Rockets: a Short History of Space Travel (Crowell, 1965).

Lent, H. B. Your Place in America's Space Program (Macmillan, 1964).

Sonneborn, R. A. The Question and Answer Book of Space (Random, 1965).

Stambler, Irwin. Breath of Life (Putnam, 1963).

Throneburg, James. Man on the Moon (Knopf, 1961).

Wells, Robert. Alive in Space (Little, 1961).

Books for Advanced Students and Teachers

Alexander, Tom. Project Apollo: Man to the Moon (Harper, 1964).

Caidin, Martin. Wings Into Space (Holt, 1964).

Chester, Michael. Rockets and Spacecraft of the World (Norton, 1964).

Clarke, A. C. The Promise of Space (Harper, 1968).

Coombs, C. I. Rocketmen and What They Do (Watts, 1962).

Drake, F. D. Intelligent Life in Space (Macmillan, 1962).

Freedman, Russell. 2000 Years of Space Travel (Holiday, 1963).

Goodwin, H. L. The Images of Space (Holt, 1965).

Hendrickson, W. B., Jr. Reach for the Moon (Bobbs, 1962).

Henry, J. P. Biomedical Aspects of Space Flight (Holt, 1966).

Hyde, Wayne. The Men Behind the Astronauts (Dodd, 1965).

Ley, Willy. Beyond the Solar System (Viking, 1964).

Ley, Willy. Rockets, Missiles, and Men in Space (Viking, 1968).

Meitner, J. G., ed. Astronautics for Science Teachers (Wiley, 1965).

Nayler, J. L. A Dictionary of Astronautics (Hart, 1965).

Newell, H. E. Space Book for Young People (Whittlesey, 1968).

Ordway, F. I. and others. Basic Astronautics (Prentice-Hall, 1962).

Pizer, Vernon. Rockets, Missiles and Space (Lippincott, 1962).

Posin, D. Q. Life Beyond Our Planet (Whittlesey, 1962).

Sharpe, M. R. Living in Space (Doubleday, 1969).

Sharpe, M. R. Yuri Gagarin: First Man into Space (Strode, 1969).

Simak, C. D. The Solar System (St. Martin's, 1962).

Stern, P. D. Our Space Environment (Holt, 1966).

Stoiko, Michael. Project Gemini (Holt, 1964).

Sullivan, Walter. We Are Not Alone (McGraw, 1966).

von Braun, Wernher and Ordway, F. I. History of Rocketry and Space Travel (Crowell, 1967).

Woodbury, D. O. Outward Bound for Space (Little, 1961).

The grandeur of medieval Spain lives on in Toledo. The city was the seat of the Visigothic court, a Moorish cultural center, and in the early 16th century the capital of a unified Spain.

SPAIN—Once Europe's Greatest Power

SPAIN. To the Western European nations of the 16th century, the kingdom of Spain was known as the Mistress of the World and as the Queen of the Sea. Spain's graceful galleons sailed into its ports laden with treasures from its colonies in the New World. Most of Europe paid tribute to this powerful nation on the Iberian Peninsula. While Spain's explorers raised their nation's flag in the Americas, its priests, laboring among the natives, raised the cross of Roman Catholicism at countless missions on the new Spanish soil. The daring Spaniards, however, were unable to hold on to their vast realm. They had spread too far in an effort to extend their political power and the sway of Catholicism, not only abroad but also in Europe. Civil strife and wars with other countries weakened Spain's economy and destroyed its power. One by one Spain lost its possessions across the seas, and eventually its influence in Europe waned.

In recent years Spain has achieved significant industrial advances and agricultural improvements as well as a broadening of educational opportunity. Nevertheless, it remains a poor country. In addition, a great gap exists between its few very rich people and its many very poor people. Spain has also been saddled by decades of dictatorial rule, and its people have less political power and less personal freedom than those of other Western nations. These shortcomings have aroused considerable discontent, particularly among the workers and the intellectuals.

The three chief causes for Spain's difficulties are such natural characteristics as poor soil, erratic weather, and many mountains; regionalism; and the Civil War of the 1930's. Spain is an agricultural country, but much of its land is unfruitful, and rainfall is variable and uncertain. The mountains make communication and transportation costly and difficult. They have fostered and help maintain cultural regional barriers in this land of many heritages. The brutal Civil War, which raged from 1936 to 1939, further divided and demoralized an already discontented people and sapped the Spanish economy.

Spain's Natural Features

Spain occupies five sixths of the Iberian Peninsula in southwestern Europe. The rest of the peninsula is occupied by Portugal. Including the Balearic Islands in the Mediterranean and the Canary Islands in the Atlantic, Spain has an area of 194,884 square miles and a population of 32,411,000 (1968 estimate). Spain is about the size of Illinois, Iowa, and Missouri combined and has twice as many people. The population of the Canaries totals 1,017,361; of the Balearics, 451,343 (1965 estimates).

The greatest extent is 635 miles, east to west. The country is about 550 miles long. The total area of continental Spain is 189,652 square miles. Spanish possessions in Africa include Spanish Sahara, on the northwestern coast, with an area of 102,703 square miles and a population of 23,793.

The geography of Spain has played an important part in its history. In the north the massive snow-crested Pyrenees rise in a jagged wall from the Bay of Biscay to the Mediterranean, cutting Spain off from France and the rest of Europe. The mountains and rivers of the interior have divided the country into a number of separate regions with diversified cultures. Since Spain was at one time divided into a number of geographically isolated kingdoms, the official title of the monarch of unified Spain became *Rex Hispanarum*, meaning "King of Spains." The southern tip of Spain is only 12 miles from the African continent. It has been said that Europe ends in the Pyrenees and that Africa begins there. Spain has a long but regular coastline, with few good natural harbors. Spain's Atlantic coastline is about 600 miles long; its Mediterranean coastline, about 1,700 miles long. The ratio of its coastline to its land surface is one mile to 95 square miles.

Mountains, Plateau, Rivers, and Lakes

Most of the population of Spain is crowded into the narrow coastal strips of lowland along the Bay of Biscay to the north and the Mediterranean Sea to the south and east. Rising abruptly from the ribbons of lowlands, the mountains encircle the interior of the country like a ring. A vast central plateau—the Meseta—occupies about half the land area of Spain. The altitude of the Meseta averages about 2,200 feet above sea level, and the plateau is ribbed with mountains and hills.

The chief mountains are the giant Pyrenees (*see* Pyrenees). Their craggy line of summits tower to more than 10,000 feet. In the northwest rise the Cantabrian Mountains, whose peaks reach more than 8,000 feet in height. Ranges ridging the Meseta are the Sierra de Guadarrama, Sierra de Gredos, and Sierra de Guadalupe. In Spanish *sierra* means "saw," a name frequently given to a mountain range because of its saw-toothed crest line. The Sierra Nevada plunge from Mulhacén—at 11,417 feet, the highest point on the mainland—south to the Mediterranean. Between these ranges loom abrupt hills, dusty brown highlands, and sharp valleys.

The principal rivers are the Ebro, Duero (Douro), Tagus, Guadiana, and Guadalquivir. Only the Ebro, in the north, and the Guadalquivir, in the south, are wholly inside Spain. The Duero, in the northwest, and the Tagus, in central Spain, flow through Portugal to empty into the Atlantic Ocean. The Guadiana sprawls over the southern part of the Meseta, then flows south to drain into the Gulf of Cádiz. The prefix *guad* in the names of some Spanish rivers comes from the Moorish *wadi*, meaning a stream that is dry for much of the year.

Spanish rivers have little value for transportation. The mouths of the Tagus and Duero, which are in

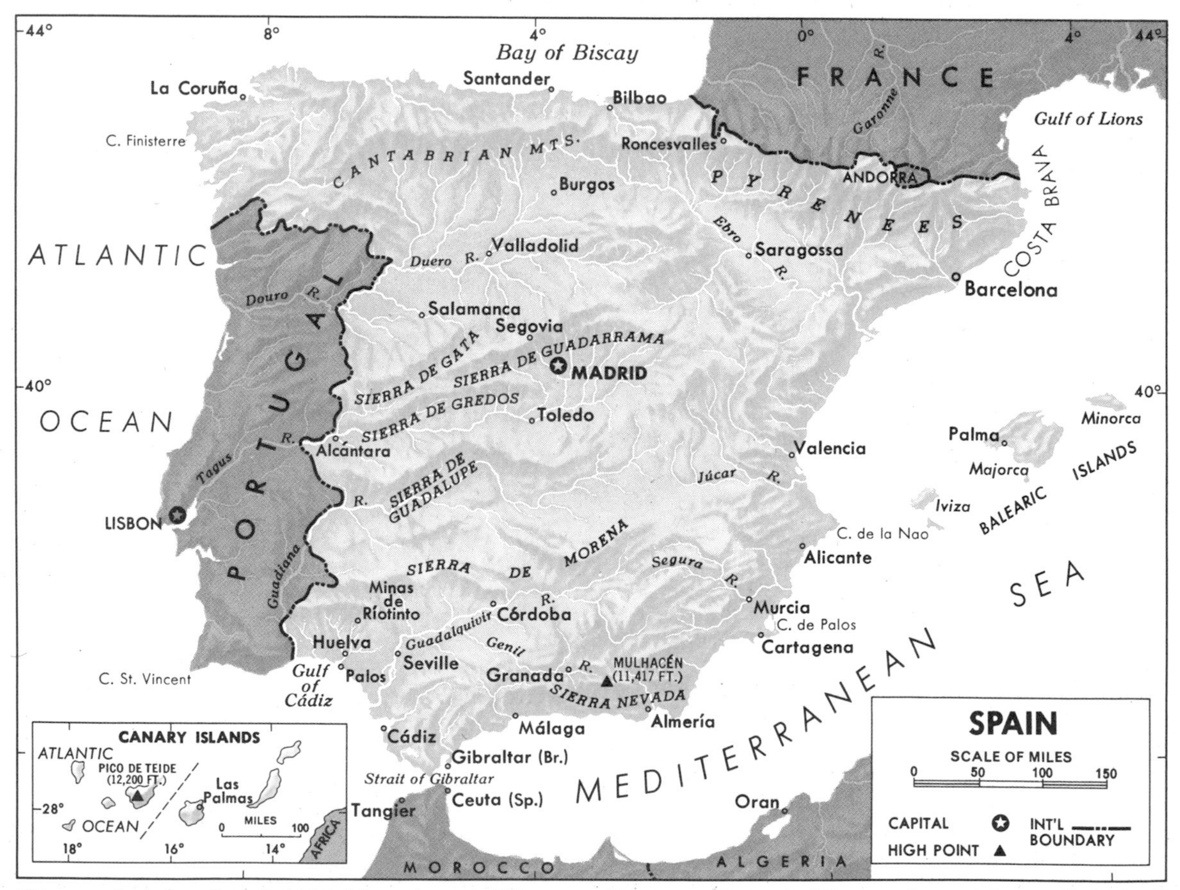

This map shows how Spain is isolated from the rest of Europe. At the north are the Pyrenees and to the west mountains bar the way to Portugal. Rivers and mountains cut Spain itself into many regions, each with its own heritage and customs.

Portugal, provide good harbors. Of the wholly Spanish rivers, however, only the Guadalquivir is navigable for any considerable distance from the sea. Ships sail the Guadalquivir as far as Seville. The twisting gorge of the Ebro makes it useless for navigation. The valleys of other rivers also wind in deep, rocky clefts as they cut across the Meseta.

Spain has only two really large lakes, and they are actually lagoons of the Mediterranean in the east coast provinces of Valencia and Murcia. Small Alpine lakes dot the mountains, and little salt lakes break the brown monotony of the steppe regions of the Meseta.

A Varied Climate

Considering its moderate size, Spain has a surprising variety of climate. It differs in four general regions—northern Spain around the Bay of Biscay and the Atlantic coast; central Spain, or the Meseta; southernmost Spain; and the Mediterranean coast.

Northern Spain has a marine climate, with mild, damp winters and cool summers. The western slopes of the mountains, facing the Atlantic, receive the heaviest rainfall in Spain and are one of the wettest areas in Europe. Overall the slopes receive about 35 inches of rain annually, but in some places average annual rainfall is as high as 60 inches. Most of the rain falls in winter, but it is ample throughout the year for agriculture and forestry.

The climate of the rest of Spain may be called generally Mediterranean—hot, dry summers and mild winters with light rainfall. There are, however, regional differences. The climate of the Meseta is harsh. Winter is bitter, with occasional heavy snowstorms. Summer is intensely hot in the daytime, quite chilly at night. Sudden blasting winds frequently blow the dust in choking clouds. A wall of mountains cuts the Meseta off from the moisture-bearing westerlies. The scanty rainfall ordinarily waters the sunbaked plateau with only 12 to 14 inches a year. Occasional below-average rainfall causes tragic droughts.

The southern tip of Spain is semidesert, with virtually no winter. The eastern coast has the typical Mediterranean climate—brief, mild winters and long, rather hot summers. Rainfall ranges from about 12 to 22 inches annually.

Plant and Animal Life

Because of the diversity of its climate and terrain, Spain is able to have a rich variety of vegetation. Much of the forest cover has been destroyed by ruthless land clearing. However, reforestation programs are being undertaken.

The damp northern forests have oak, pine, black poplar, elm, beech, and chestnut trees. Pines, junipers, a variety of evergreens, and cork oak grow in the dry areas of the south, where date palms also flourish. Among the plants of the Mediterranean area are laurel, olive, orange, lemon, fig, and carob trees. Esparto grass covers large stretches of the plains. Of the 10,000 species of flowers found in Europe, more than half grow in Spain.

A LAND DIVIDED BY MOUNTAINS
Spain is one of the most mountainous nations in Europe. The great ranges keep the rainy sea winds from reaching the interior, where a shortage of water is a perennial problem.

Few species of wild animals remain in the country. Vultures and eagles soar high in the mountains. In the Sierra de Gredos a unique species of mountain goat, *Capra hispanica*, is found. Salmon and trout abound in the swift northern rivers. The waters of the Atlantic yield anchovies, tuna, whitings, sardines, and sea bream. Crayfish, halibut, lobsters, and salmon abound in the Mediterranean.

A Lagging Agriculture

One third of Spain's people live in rural areas. In recent decades Spain has directed much effort to increasing its agricultural productivity. However, despite the growing mechanization of farms, large-scale irrigation projects, the increased use of fertilizer, and intense reforestation to halt soil erosion, the Spanish farmer has not been able to keep pace with the needs of a growing population.

Somewhat less than half the total land area is arable. In many parts of the country scant rain falls on scorched, shallow, unirrigated soil. Dry farming is practiced on most of the fertile soil, and wheat—cultivated by dry farming since Roman times—is the most widespread crop. With oats, rye, and barley, it is grown on the vast central plateau. Rice is grown in the strips of marshy lowlands along the Valencian coast. The fertile Valencia area also raises oranges, Spain's chief export crop; onions; and a variety of other fruits and vegetables.

Olives and grapes are raised mainly in the east and south. Spain ranks second only to Italy in the production of olive oil. Its grapes are used chiefly to

OLIVE GROVES IN CENTRAL SPAIN
Spain is a major producer of olives and olive oil. Its olive groves cover about one tenth of the cultivated land. Olives are often grown together with other crops.

make wine. Other important crops are potatoes, cotton, tobacco, tomatoes, hemp, and such subtropical crops as bananas, which thrive on the islands.

The only real ranches in Europe are in Andalusia, where bulls for the arena and the famous Andalusian horses are raised. More sheep are raised in Spain than any other type of livestock. They are able to withstand the arid climate and not only provide meat but also support a thriving woolen industry. Merino sheep, native to Spain, are noted for their fine wool. Sheep are grazed chiefly in the northeast and along the northern coast. Cattle and hogs are raised in northwestern Spain. Goats, the source of most of Spain's dairy products, are raised along the southern coast and in central Spain. Because of the mountainous terrain and the scarcity of good roads, donkeys are used for transportation in many parts of the country. Donkeys and mules are still important as farm work animals.

Forestry and Fishing

Although forests comprise nearly a fourth of Spain's area, only 10 percent of it is usable. The most important forested areas are in the Pyrenees, Asturias, and Galicia. However, cork, the principal forest product, grows in the east-central and southeastern coastal regions. Spain ranks second only to Portugal as a source of cork. Other commercially important forest products are resin and turpentine. The forests, badly depleted by unplanned cutting, are inadequate for Spain's lumber needs, and timber must be imported. Reforestation projects, often hampered by grazing animals, are being undertaken.

Much of the coastline of Spain is dotted with fishing villages. Most of the commercial fleet, however, is concentrated on the northern coast. In the 1960's the Spanish government allocated nearly one billion dollars for a ten-year program to modernize the fishing fleet. Many of the country's commercial fishing boats have since been motorized.

Seafood is an important source of protein in the Spanish diet. Fresh fish is a favorite domestic food, while most of the fish processed in Spain's 700-odd fish canneries is exported. The chief catches are sardines, tuna, and cod. Salmon are caught in the Mediterranean and in the cascading rivers of the north.

Spain's Mineral Wealth

The mountains of Spain are rich in minerals, and the mining and metallurgical industries employ more than 300,000 workers. The country's mines, quarries, and mineral subsoil rights are state controlled.

Mines at Almadén contain some of the world's richest mercury deposits. Iron ore is produced in Andalusia and in the Basque provinces. Copper is the leading mineral export. Lead is mined at Jaén; potash, in the province of Barcelona. In 1960 oil was discovered near Burgos, and a uranium-processing plant was opened at Andújar. Other important mineral products are iron pyrites, lignite, zinc, and sulfur.

Industry and Trade

The manufacture of cotton and woolen goods, most of which are made in Catalonia, is one of Spain's leading industries. Other textiles include silk, linen, jute yarn, and rayon fabrics. The manufacture of paper and cardboard products and of cement are fast-growing industries.

Most of Spain's large factories are centered in cities. Barcelona produces textiles, machinery, automobiles, chemicals, and paper products; Bilbao, iron and steel, machinery, and chemicals; Madrid, machinery and chemicals; Seville, tobacco products; Cartagena, iron and steel, ships, and nonferrous metals. Such Spanish specialties as lace, jewelry, and pottery are often made in small workshops or in

LANDING A TUNA
Fishing villages dot the shores of Spain, but most of the commercial fleet is concentrated on the northern coast. Sardines, cod, tuna, and anchovies are the chief catches.

ASSEMBLING AUTOMOBILES
The manufacture of automobiles is one of Spain's newer industries. Barcelona is the principal center for the production of automobiles. As Spanish industry expanded in the 1960's, many farm workers moved to the cities to take factory jobs.

homes. Over one fourth of the Spanish people are employed by its manufacturing industries.

Spain's chief exports are oranges, machinery, petroleum products, olive oil, and copper. Its main imports are machinery, crude oil, iron and steel, and chemicals. Spain's most important trading is with the United States, West Germany, France, and Great Britain.

Power, Transportation, and Communication

An ambitious dam-building program has benefited the Spanish economy by providing irrigation water for agriculture and electric power for homes, offices, and industry. In 1935, just before the Civil War, Spain produced only 3.3 billion kilowatt-hours of electricity. By the mid-1960's the amount had increased more than tenfold. Well over half of Spain's power is hydroelectric.

The mountains of Spain have long made the construction of both roads and railways difficult and expensive. Spain has more than 80,000 miles of highways, of which about two thirds are paved. The Spanish railways were almost completely destroyed during the Civil War but have since been rebuilt. Most of Spain's railroad lines are broad-gauge. In 1964 a plan was initiated to modernize the railway system over a ten-year period. Spain maintains air service among its cities as well as with other nations. It has 37 civil and 7 military airports. Spain's merchant fleet comprises some 2,500 vessels.

Telephone, telegraph, radio, and television facilities are controlled by the government. However, nearly all of the more than 9,500 telephone exchanges are privately operated. There are several television stations and some 250 radio stations.

The People and Their Differences

The Spanish people have one of the oldest and most mixed heritages in Europe. They are descended from the ancient Iberians, who were invaded by the Carthaginians, Celts, Romans, Vandals, Visigoths, and Moors. Many Jews also entered Spain. All the proud, strong invaders helped mold the Spaniards of today.

There is no "typical Spaniard." Spaniards of different regions differ in traits, customs, and language. Spanish, the national language of Spain, is a Romance language—it comes from the spoken Latin of the Romans. The five principal cultural regions of Spain are Castile, Andalusia, Galicia, the Basque country, and Catalonia. The people of Castile, on the Meseta, are usually thought of as the "true Spaniards." The educated Castilian is poised, sensitive, courtly, gracious, very individualistic, and intensely proud. Castilian Spanish is the literary language of Spain and the Spanish usually taught in the United States and in the diplomatic service.

The people of Andalusia, on the sunny southern coast, are gayer and quicker to show their feelings.

A SHEPHERD AT WORK
Sheep, raised mainly in the northern mountain regions, are the most common type of livestock in Spain. They provide wool for a thriving textile industry as well as meat.

APRIL IN SEVILLE
Every Spanish city has its favorite fiesta. Seville's features parades with Andalusian horses and street dancing to the accompaniment of guitar music.

They have more Jewish and Moorish blood, and they speak an Andalusian dialect of Spanish. On the damp, temperate northern coast live the people of Galicia, called Gallegos. They are hardworking, frugal, and somewhat stolid. The language of the Gallegos mingles Portuguese with Spanish.

The three Basque provinces are almost a world apart from Spain. Basque villages nestle on the northern coastline and in the Pyrenees. The sturdy, aloof Basques do not call themselves Spaniards, but Iberians. They speak a language of their own. Scholars have not been able to trace the origin of the strange Basque language, one of the oldest in Europe. It is gradually giving way to Spanish, partly because its use for public purposes has been forbidden. The Basques have long sought independence.

The people of Catalonia, who live along the northeastern Mediterranean, have also sought to break away from Spain. Time and again, they have demanded autonomy. Nevertheless, the Catalonian workers fought stoutly to preserve the Spanish republic during the Civil War. The Catalonians, a practical, brisk people, form the hard core of Spanish business and industry. Their language is a branch of the old Provençal dialect of southern France.

Despite their regional differences, the Spanish people possess many common characteristics. They are proud, courteous, brave, and individualistic.

How the People Live

About one third of the Spanish people live in rural areas. Spain has a number of large landowners, but many families own their own small farms. Near Barcelona and along the Atlantic coast farmhouses are often on the farmers' fields. On the Meseta, where most of Spain's farms are located, the farmers live in villages several miles from their fields.

Two-story houses are common in some rural areas. Livestock is kept on the lower floor, while living quarters are on the upper floor. Granaries on pillars are used to store cereals and meats. In the villages of the Meseta houses are usually built of adobe or stone. Andalusian homes are often built around patios bright with flowers and fountains. In many areas houses are whitewashed. The stone houses of the Pyrenees have slanted roofs to shed the snow.

Charcoal burners heat the homes of southern Spain. Elsewhere straw-burning hearths, with ducts to distribute the heat, are used. Much housing of modern design, with running water and central heating, has appeared in recent years, especially in the cities.

GYPSY CAVE IN GRANADA
One of Spain's most picturesque cities, Granada was the last Moorish stronghold on the Iberian Peninsula. Its Gypsies are a popular tourist attraction.

Traditional clothing has been largely replaced with modern dress, though folk costumes are still worn on festive occasions. The straw cape, the mantilla, and the cummerbund are traditional accessories. Aragonese women wear kerchiefs; Galician men, cloth caps; Basque men, berets. Leggings are worn on ranches.

At the Spanish table, seafood is more plentiful than meat. Olive oil is used in cooking. Every Spanish cook seasons with garlic, saffron, and peppers. Rice is popular along the Mediterranean. A basic part of the Spanish diet is pulse—dried beans, lentils, and chick peas—cooked with fish, chicken, or pork.

Every city and town has its sidewalk cafés, where citizens meet to discuss the issues of the day over a cup of coffee or a glass of wine. In the villages, community life centers upon the plaza or square, where local festivals are held. The marketplaces are social as well as business centers. There are many motion-picture theaters in Spain; admission is cheap; and moviegoing is a favorite pastime.

Religious and holiday observances are an important part of Spanish recreation, and the Spanish fiestas are famous throughout the world. Although there are many local variations in the conduct of these celebrations, they generally begin with a High Mass. Seville's fiestas are famous for their horse parades, guitar music, and street dancing. Murcia has a battle of flowers. The Asturians make pilgrimages to the cornfields and hold sea parades in flower-decked boats. Bagpipe music is played at Galician festivals. Choral singing, games, and contests are features of the Basque fiestas.

Every large city and nearly every town has a bullring. Although foreigners generally think of bullfighting as Spain's "national sport," the Spanish do not regard it as a sport but as a test of bravery, skill, and grace. Soccer now rivals bullfighting as a spectator attraction.

Spain's Cultural Heritage

Beauty literally crowds Spain's great museums, cathedrals, and monasteries. Spanish kings collected masterpieces of art from all over Europe, but none surpassed the great works of Spain's own painters—Murillo, Velasquez, and Goya (*see* Murillo; Velasquez). El Greco, who was born in Greece, is also considered a Spanish painter, because he did his greatest work in Toledo. Prominent Spanish-born painters of the 20th century include Pablo Picasso, Joan Miró, and Salvador Dali (*see* Painting; Picasso).

Spain has also developed notable writers. Cervantes' 'Don Quixote' has been translated into all the major languages. Lope de Vega and Pedro Calderón de la Barca wrote brilliant plays. Miguel de Unamuno was an inspiring philosopher. (*See also* Spanish Literature; Cervantes; Calderón de la Barca.)

Cities and Tourism

Madrid, the capital, is the distribution center for central Spain. The population of the commune is 2,900,000 (1967 estimate). The second largest city is Barcelona, on the northeastern coast, Spain's most important manufacturing center. Other large cities include Bilbao, a port and industrial center; the major overseas ports of Seville, Santander, and Valencia; and Saragossa, Málaga, Murcia, and Córdoba (*see* Madrid; Barcelona; Seville; Valencia).

Many of Spain's cities are rich in history and in the treasures of bygone days. Tourists from all over the world visit Spain each year to see their magnif-

THE BULLS OF PAMPLONA

At Pamplona, during the festivities of San Fermín, youths run through the streets, chased by the animals that will appear in the bullring later in the day.

icent castles, mosques, and cathedrals. At picturesque Granada is the Alhambra and the cathedral housing the tombs of King Ferdinand and Queen Isabella (*see* Alhambra). Salamanca's university was founded about 1215; Saragossa's, in 1474. The most elaborate Gothic cathedral in Spain is at Burgos. The monastery of San Pedro de Cardeña, near Burgos, holds the remains of the Cid, the knight whose deeds are celebrated in song and story. Cádiz, on the south Atlantic coast, is one of the oldest cities in Europe. It was founded by the Phoenicians about 1100 B.C.

Such cultural attractions, as well as the bullfights and fiestas, fine beaches, and facilities for winter sports, help bring millions of visitors to Spain each year. An equally important reason is that favorable exchange rates have made Spain one of the most inexpensive tourist centers in Europe. Tourism is now Spain's largest source of foreign currency.

Social Welfare and Labor

The social-welfare programs of the government place great emphasis on family life. Since March 1939, workers have received subsidies based on the size of their families. A marriage-loan plan is available for the poor. Compulsory health and maternity benefits, old-age pensions, and disability benefits have been in effect since 1949. They are subsidized by contributions of both employers and employees. A voluntary public collection taken every two weeks helps supply food and clothing for the needy and maintains public day-care centers and infirmaries.

A system of national syndicates, 26 in all, controls the various branches of industry and agriculture. The syndicates represent workers, management, and owners. Through these syndicates the government controls prices, wages, and the distribution of goods. In 1965 the power of the syndicates was weakened somewhat by the enactment of a law allowing workers to strike for economic improvements.

Religion and Education

Roman Catholicism is the state religion of Spain. The decrees of the church govern marriage, divorce, and other matters which are the province of the civil government in most Western countries. Before 1967 the few Protestants and Jews in Spain were not permitted to conduct public religious services or to hold public office. Since then, restrictions on non-Catholics have eased. In 1968 the Spanish government rescinded a 476-year-old order expelling the Jews from the country, and the first synagogue to be built in Spain in six centuries was dedicated in Madrid.

Education is free and compulsory for all children between the ages of 6 and 14. About three fourths of Spain's primary schools are run by the state. The Roman Catholic religion is taught in all schools, and the Roman Catholic church has the right to review the teaching of religion in the schools. Secondary schools have two divisions—elementary and senior —with a choice of programs in science or the humanities. Of Spain's 14 universities, 12 are operated by the government.

Government

Nominally, the government of Spain is a monarchy. In practice it has been a dictatorship under the rule of Gen. Francisco Franco since 1939. Gen-

A RELIGIOUS PROCESSION
Religious observances are important to the Spanish people. This typical First Communion procession is passing through a modern working-class neighborhood near Seville.

eral Franco, who is known as "El Caudillo" (The Leader), has been the head of state, commander of the armed forces, and leader of the country's one legal political party, the Falange (Phalanx). In 1947 Franco secured the approval of a Law of Succession which provided for the reinstitution of the Spanish monarchy upon his death (*see* Franco).

Spain's government is based upon a series of fundamental laws. In 1966 these were modified somewhat and incorporated into the Organic Law of the Spanish State, a constitution approved by referendum. The Organic Law provides for the selection of a premier, chosen from three candidates submitted to the head of state by the 17-member Council of the Realm. Three of the council's members are appointed by the head of state. The remainder are elected by the 567-member Cortes, the Spanish legislature. The Organic Law also provides for the appointment of a Council of Ministers by the head of state. Its members head the various government departments.

The Cortes has little power except to ratify the proposals of the head of state. An electorate confined to heads of families and their wives votes only 104 of its members into office. The remaining members include government officials; members of the Council of the Realm; and representatives of the armed forces, the trade unions, city and provincial councils, universities, and the professions.

The Supreme Court heads the judicial branch of the government. There are 50 provinces, each governed by a state-appointed governor and an assembly. Mayors of cities are also appointed.

Spain's Early History

The pageant of Spain's history is as picturesque and as full of contrasts as the country itself. The first records left by inhabitants of Spain are paintings dating to the Old Stone Age. These paintings were discovered in 1879 in a cave near Altamira. Deer, bison, horses, and boar are skillfully depicted in yellow, brown, red, and black.

As early as 1100 B.C. the Phoenicians sailed their tiny ships to Spain, seeking its iron and tin. Carthaginians colonized the land about 500 B.C. and held it until Roman galleys and armies drove them out in 201 B.C. Then came six centuries of Roman colonization and government. During that time most of the Spanish cities were founded, and the population of Spain may have reached 9 million. Three Roman emperors, Trajan, Hadrian, and Theodosius, were born in Spain. Many of the more notable writers of the "silver age" of Latin literature were of Spanish origin (*see* Latin Language and Literature).

In the 5th century A.D. began 300 years of subjection to Teutonic tribes. Spain was invaded by the Suevi, Alans, and Vandals. In A.D. 415 Rome sent the Visigoths, another Teutonic tribe, to regain Spain for the empire. The Visigoths defeated the invaders, but some Vandals reached Andalusia, giving their name—Vandalusia—to that region. The Visigoths ruled Spain from 415 to 711.

VIADUCT AT MADRID
Madrid, the capital and largest city of Spain, has undergone great changes in recent years. Freeways and parking lots are replacing its promenades and plazas.

Moorish Invasion

Moorish invaders from Africa overthrew the Visigoths at the battle of Guadalete in 711. Thus began seven centuries of Mohammedan power in Spain. Córdoba was transformed into a Moorish center of learning. Moorish Spain produced distinguished scientists, mathematicians, philosophers, and writers, while Christian northern Spain remained divided into

SPAIN'S HEAD OF STATE
From the center of the receiving stand, Gen. Francisco Franco salutes his troops. General Franco exercised a dictatorial rule over Spain for more than three decades.

small barbaric kingdoms. The splendid irrigation projects of the Moors made a garden land out of the arid coastlands and southern hills of Spain. The Moors rebuilt the old Roman cities on Arabic lines, with graceful palaces and vast mosques. Fine metalwork and silk and leather goods, as beautiful as any from the Orient, were made in Moorish Spain. Toledo blades became as famous as those from Damascus.

The Rise of Christian Kingdoms

While a succession of weak caliphs weakened Moorish rule, Christian kingdoms were being formed in the northern mountain regions. Bit by bit they wrested territory from the Moors. The kingdom of Asturias on the Bay of Biscay, which later expanded into the kingdom of León and Castile, was the birthplace of Spanish liberty. Almost from the beginning of the Moorish invasion, Asturias struck back at the Mohammedans.

Later it was joined by Aragon, Navarre, Catalonia, and Portugal. Together they waged the long battle to "free Spain from the infidel." After the victory of León and Castile in the battle of the plains of Tolosa in 1212, Moorish rule was restricted to the small kingdom of Granada in southern Spain.

The Spanish Empire

In 1469 the marriage of Ferdinand of Aragon and Isabella of Castile united most of Spain. The final

BARCELONA'S FAMOUS CHURCH
La Familia Sagrada, one of the most famous and bizarre churches in the world, was designed by Antonio Gaudí. The church, begun in 1884, is still unfinished.

THE COURT OF THE LIONS
The Court of the Lions, with its playing fountains, is one of many courts in the Alhambra at Granada. The palace is the finest example of Moorish architecture in Europe.

blow at Moorish power in Spain was the conquest of Granada in 1492. In 1512 the Spanish part of Navarre was conquered. Philip II seized Portugal in 1580, and Spain held it for 60 years. Only Andorra in the Pyrenees was able to maintain independence.

The grandson of Ferdinand and Isabella became the most powerful ruler in Europe. He was Charles I of Spain, better known as the Holy Roman Emperor Charles V. In the reign of Charles V, Spain became mistress of nearly half the world. Charles ruled Spain, Naples and Sicily, the duchy of Milan, and the Netherlands and was the imperial lord of Germany as well as of the New World (*see* Charles V, Holy Roman Emperor).

Under his son, Philip II, Spain championed Catholicism against the march of the Protestant Reformation (*see* Reformation). Tragically, Spain spread the institution of the Inquisition (*see* Inquisition). Many Jews and Moors were expelled. Protestants and heretical Catholic Spaniards were tortured and burned at the stake in *autos-da-fé* ("acts of faith"). The persecution crushed the Spanish people's initiative and freedom of thought. At the same time, Philip tried to stamp out Protestantism abroad by attempting to conquer England. Sir Francis Drake's defeat of his invasion fleet smashed Spain's rule of the seas (*see* Armada, Spanish). Philip's futile efforts at conquest permanently impaired the resources of the kingdom.

After the reign of Philip II, Spain steadily declined in power and riches. The final expulsion of the Moors in 1609–14 by his son, Philip III, seriously weakened Spain, because the Moors had been energetic builders and businessmen. The death of Charles II in 1700 ended the Hapsburg line of Spanish kings. Many European countries fought for the vacant throne in the War of the Spanish Succession (1701–13).

The war stripped Spain of most of its outlying possessions in Europe and seated a French Bourbon prince on the throne as Philip V. From 1714 to the outbreak of the French Revolution, Spain was little more than a satellite of France. In 1808 Napoleon placed his brother Joseph on the throne of Spain. The outraged Spaniards revolted. Aided by the British, they freed Spain from Bonaparte's rule in the Peninsular War (1808–14). Meanwhile, in 1812, Spain had adopted a liberal constitution. However, when Ferdinand VII was restored to the throne, in 1814, he abolished it. By the end of Ferdinand's reign, in 1833, Spain had lost its vast empire in the New World except Cuba and Puerto Rico. These were lost in the Spanish-American War of 1898, which also cost Spain the Philippines.

The Establishment of the Spanish Republic

As the old Spain—the Spain of grandees and absolute royal power—declined, a new and more liberal Spain was struggling forward. Conflicts between liberals and reactionaries brought years of revolutionary movements interspersed with periods of constitutional government. From 1873 to 1875 Spain was a republic, but in 1875, when Alfonso XII ascended the throne, the Bourbon monarchy was restored to power. In 1876 a new constitution was adopted.

A ROMAN AQUEDUCT
The aqueduct at Segovia was built by the Romans. Although it dates to the 1st century A.D., it is still bringing water to the city. No mortar was used in its construction.

During World War I Spain was neutral. This stimulated its few industries, as it sold supplies to the Allied nations. Peace brought the loss of foreign markets, and Spain fell into economic depression. The weak Bourbon government of Alfonso XIII could not cope with the depression. It also failed to put down an old, costly rebellion in Spanish Morocco. In 1923 Gen. Primo de Rivera seized power with Alfonso's consent and set up a dictatorial government. He made many improvements, but the worldwide depression of 1929 again plunged Spain into poverty. De

AN ANCIENT BRIDGE
This Roman bridge, restored by the Moors, crosses the Guadalquivir at Córdoba. A statue of St. Raphael now surmounts the bridge. At left is Córdoba cathedral.

TOMB OF KINGS
The Escorial, once a monastery and royal residence, now shelters an art collection and the tombs of Spanish monarchs since Charles V. It is located near Madrid.

Rivera resigned in 1930. Opposition to the dictatorship shifted to dislike of the monarchy. Republican parties overwhelmingly won the elections held in 1931, and Alfonso went into exile. (*See also* Alfonso XIII.)

A provisional republican government under President Niceto Alcalá Zamora took control. A new liberal constitution, which separated the church from the state, was adopted. New reforms were initiated.

At the start of the republic nearly half the Spanish people could not read or write. Poverty was widespread, and industrial wages were low. In Madrid many workers had become socialists. In Barcelona many had turned to anarchism and syndicalism.

The republic struggled to reconcile the conflicting movements and to push its reforms, but it lacked influence and money. In 1936 the many leftist parties formed a Popular Front and overwhelmed the conservatives and moderate liberals in a national election.

Civil War and Dictatorship

Civil war followed. The rebels, who called themselves Nationalists, were led by General Franco and were supported by the conservatives and the army. The defenders of the republic were known as the Loyalists. Nazi Germany and Fascist Italy supported the rebels, while the Soviet Union gave limited aid to the Loyalists. The war was incredibly fierce. The hostilities ended on March 28, 1939, with the surrender of starving Madrid, the last Loyalist stronghold. It has been estimated that the conflict cost Spain about 600,000 lives, 700,000 wounded, and some 40 billion dollars.

Out of the Civil War emerged the dictatorship of General Franco. Franco restored the privileges of the church and placed the economy of the country under the control of the syndicates. He banned all political parties except the Falange. Although the Cortes was reestablished in 1942, Franco continued to dominate the government.

During World War II Spain was ostensibly neutral. Actually, however, it gave undercover aid to Germany and Italy. On the pretext of keeping the international zone of Tangier neutral, Spain occupied the region. The demands of the Allied powers forced it to withdraw in 1945 (*see* Tangier). These unfriendly acts, combined with Franco's harsh rule, kept Spain out of the United Nations until 1955.

THE ALCÁZAR OF SEGOVIA
Queen Isabella lived in this castle when she was crowned ruler of Castile. The structure was originally built in the 11th century, was almost completely rebuilt in the 14th century, and had to be restored after it was damaged by fire in the mid-19th century. It has been called a perfect example of the medieval Spanish castle.

Spain Under the Franco Regime

Under Franco, Spain made some economic progress, but recovery from the ruinous Civil War was slow. Factories, railroads, and shipping all needed large quantities of new equipment. Housing was an especially grave problem, for thousands of homes had been destroyed during the conflict. Workers demonstrated in protest against the high cost of living. Franco sought economic assistance from other nations. The United States considered Spain a key to Europe's defense against Communism and came to its aid in 1950.

In 1947 a controlled plebiscite approved Franco's Law of Succession. This established a council which, at the death of Franco, would name a king or regent. By a two-thirds vote of the Cortes, the king or regent would become ruler of Spain. Franco trained Juan Carlos of Bourbon, a grandson of Alfonso XIII, to serve as his successor. In 1969 the Cortes approved the future crowning of Juan Carlos when Franco's rule should end. Other contenders for the throne had included the father of Juan Carlos, Don Juan, and members of the house of Bourbon-Parma.

In 1953 the United States agreed to give Spain economic and military aid in exchange for air- and naval-base sites. A 400-million-dollar network of United States military bases was completed in 1959. Later, some of the installations were closed, and a submarine base was opened. In 1969 a new pact was signed with the United States in which the remaining bases would become exclusively Spanish.

By the end of the 1960's Spain had relinquished most of its African possessions. Spanish Morocco, now part of Morocco, was granted independence in 1956. Equatorial Guinea, comprising the former provinces of Fernando Po and Río Muni, achieved independence in 1968. Ifni was ceded to Morocco in 1969. Only the Spanish Sahara and two enclaves in Morocco—the cities of Melilla and Ceuta—remained under Spanish control. (*See also* Africa Fact Summary.)

Prepublication censorship was abolished in April 1966, though the press was still subject to restrictions. A referendum held in December 1966 endorsed a new constitution presented by General Franco. Effective in 1967, it created the office of premier, provided for the election of 108 Cortes members, made religious liberty a legal right, eased restrictions on labor unions, and permitted married women to vote.

In 1968 unrest among the Basques, who sought to separate their provinces from Spain, resulted in a declaration—the "state of exception"—which severely curtailed their civil rights. Franco imposed the same restrictions on the entire nation in the early months of 1969 after widespread strikes had broken out among workers and students. The state of exception superceded civil rights provisions of the constitution.

CIVIL WAR MEMORIAL

On the southern slopes of the Sierra de Guadarrama is the Valley of the Fallen, a huge mausoleum for the Civil War dead. The cross is over 500 feet in height.

Spain Fact Summary

THE LAND

Area: 194,884 squarc miles (including the Canary Islands and the Balearic Islands).
Chief Rivers: Tagus, Ebro, Duero, Guadalquivir.
Highest Points: Mulhacén (11,417 feet), on the mainland; Pico de Teide (12,200 feet), in the Canaries.
Climate: Marine, continental, mountain, and Mediterranean.

THE PEOPLE

Population (1968 estimate): 32,411,000.
Density: 166 persons per square mile.
Language: Spanish; Catalan; Basque.
Religion: Roman Catholic.
Largest Cities: Madrid, 2,900,000; Barcelona, 1,700,000; Valencia, 601,000; Seville, 598,000.

GOVERNMENT

Capital: Madrid.
Form: Officially a monarchy; Cortes discusses and proposes legislation; Council of Ministers initiates legislation; head of state has absolute veto power.
Constitution: (None written.) Legal foundation of state formed by fundamental laws and charters.
Monetary Unit: Peseta.
Weights and Measures: Metric system.

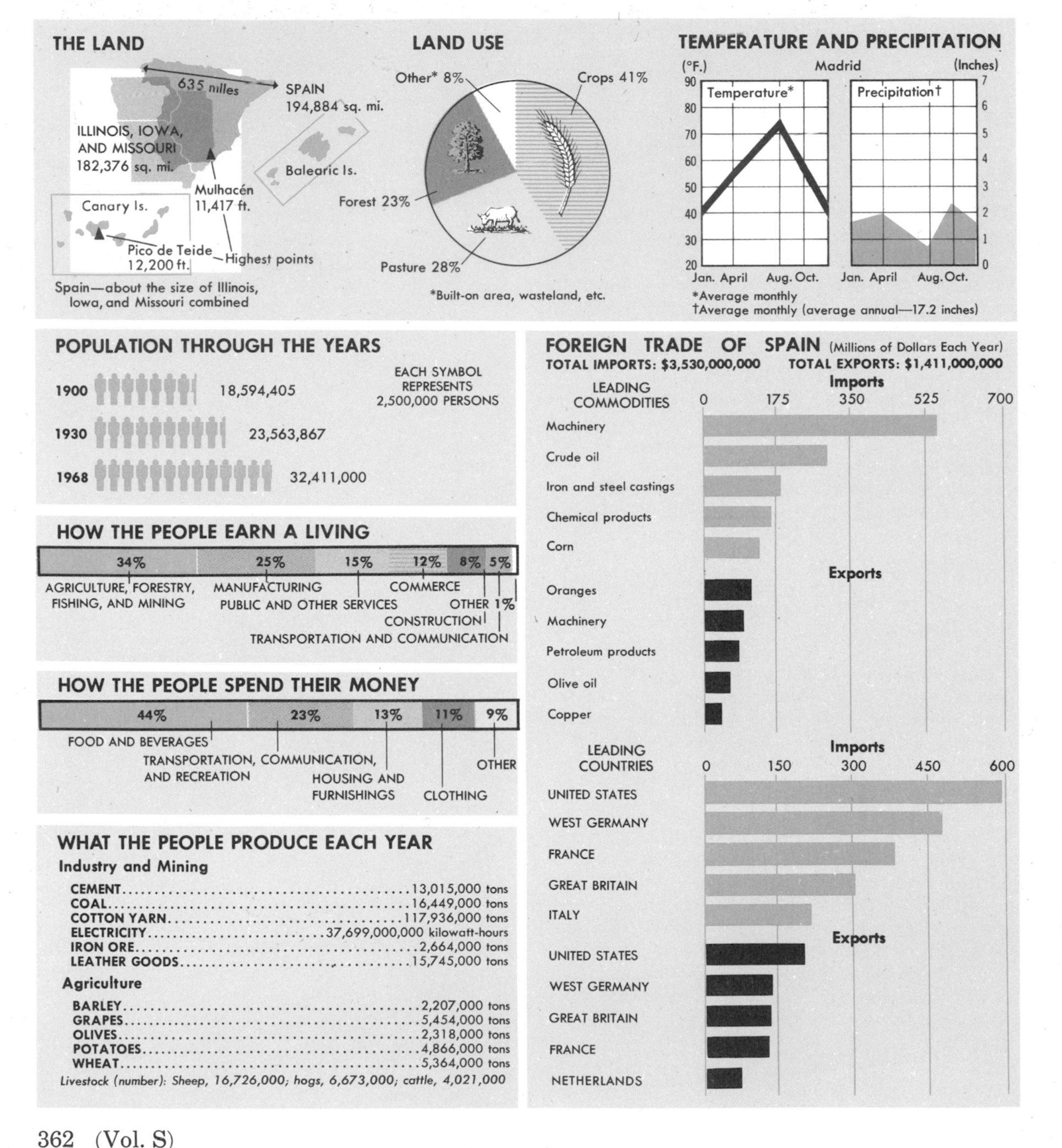

REFERENCE-OUTLINE FOR STUDY OF SPAIN

THE LAND AND THE PEOPLE

I. **Location and size** S-349, 362: location in the world, map W-242–3; in Europe, map E-334
  A. **Island provinces** S-349: Balearic Islands B-22, map S-350; Canary Islands C-122, map A-94
  B. **African possessions** S-349, map A-94: Spanish Sahara A-90; Ceuta A-86; Melilla A-88

II. **Structure of the land** S-349–50, 362, S-365, E-312, 313, maps S-350, E-306, pictures S-351–3
  A. **Mountains and central plateau (Meseta)** S-349–50, picture S-351: Pyrenees P-543, E-312
  B. **Rivers and lakes** S-350–1
  C. **Coastline and islands** S-350, B-22, C-122: Atlantic Ocean A-669; Gibraltar G-123, picture G-124; Mediterranean Sea M-216

III. **Climate** S-351: rainfall, graph S-362, map E-308

IV. **Plants and animals** S-351: vegetation, map E-309

V. **The people** S-350, 351, 353–4, 362, pictures F-288, S-352–4, 356: Andalusians, Basques, Castilians, Catalonians, Gallegos, Moriscos (Moors) S-353–4, M-486; population S-349, chart S-362, map E-312; immigration I-60; names N-4

VI. **How the people live** S-354–5: clothing S-355, pictures F-288, S-354, 356; food S-355; shelter S-354, M-30–1, S-118; social welfare S-356
  A. **Farm and village life** S-354–5, picture S-353
  B. **City life** S-355, M-30–1, S-118–19, color picture M-31, pictures S-354, 356, V-256
  C. **Education and religion** S-356, 362, M-30, V-256, picture S-356: libraries L-239
  D. **Recreation, fiestas, and holidays** S-355, F-94, 95, pictures F-288, S-354–6: bullfighting S-355, M-31; Christmas C-329

VII. **Resources and industries** S-351–3, tables S-362: land use, chart S-362; government controls S-356
  A. **Agriculture** S-351–2, V-256, picture S-352: grape S-352 (raisin R-90); lemon L-187; olive O-450; orange O-472; rice R-201; wheat S-352; livestock S-352 (sheep S-147, picture S-353)
  B. **Fisheries** S-351, 352, F-167: tuna T-287
  C. **Forests and forest products** S-351, 352, C-573
  D. **Manufacturing** S-352–3, M-32, B-64, S-119, V-256, picture S-353: lace L-97
  E. **Minerals and mining** S-352, P-543, map O-497: copper C-567; mercury M-225
  F. **Tourism** S-355–6, pictures S-354–5, 358–61
  G. **Waterpower** S-353, P-543, B-64

VIII. **Trade** S-353, B-64, charts S-362

IX. **Transportation and communication** S-349, 352, 353, B-64, M-30, S-119, picture S-357

X. **Principal cities** S-355: Madrid M-30, pictures M-31, S-357; Barcelona B-64, picture S-358; Seville S-118, picture S-354; Valencia V-256

XI. **Spain's cultural heritage—the arts** S-355, M-31–2
  A. **Architecture,** pictures M-31, S-358–60, S-119: Alhambra A-275, picture S-358; Alcázar of Segovia, picture S-360; Escorial, picture S-360
  B. **Language and literature** S-353, 354, L-114, S-365–8, S-475, L-149, lists S-366–8, S-480, outline L-119: drama D-171
  C. **Music** M-560
  D. **Painting** P-39, 41, 50, 58, 60–1, color pictures P-40–1, 50, 56, 59, pictures M-548, D-93d, P-318: El Greco P-39; Goya P-50; Murillo M-547; Picasso P-318; Velasquez V-271

XII. **Government** S-356–7, 361, 362, D-112 (Franco F-419, picture S-357): flag, color picture F-203

HISTORY

I. **General** S-349, 357–61, P-457: Spain's rulers, table (Fact-Index)

II. **Early history** S-357: Phoenicians P-267 (Cádiz founded S-356); Carthaginians C-145, B-64, H-21–2; Roman colonization and government R-246, 248, C-14, map R-242, pictures A-465, S-359

III. **Barbarian invasions** S-357, E-318: rule of the Visigoths G-161, S-119: Vandals V-265

IV. **Moorish invasion** S-357–8, M-421, E-318, M-486

V. **The rise of Christian kingdoms** S-358, E-318: Moors expelled M-486, S-358, M-32, S-119

VI. **The Spanish Empire** S-358–9
  A. **Union under Ferdinand and Isabella** S-358, I-317: Inquisition I-191; Ximenes de Cisneros X-329–30; Columbus discovers America C-474–9, A-298, I-317, D-163–4, picture A-295
  B. **Charles V (Charles I of Spain) as Holy Roman Emperor rules half of the known world** C-211–12, S-358, E-319: Loyola founds Jesuit order R-135, L-383; Saint Francis Xavier X-329
  C. **Spain and Portugal divide the New World (1493–94)** A-298, S-290
  D. **New World exploration and conquests** A-298–300, A-303, E-355, G-151, L-139, map A-297, picture A-301, table E-358: Columbus C-479; Vespucius V-304; Magellan M-35–6
    1. West Indies W-101, C-627, D-163–4, H-7, J-360, P-530: Las Casas L-129
    2. North America N-317, U-167–8, S-337–9, F-66, C-40, F-237, O-483, T-117: Ponce de León P-444; Cabeza de Vaca C-3; De Soto D-95; Coronado C-580; Aztecs in Mexico A-808, M-253 (Cortez C-582–3)
    3. Central America C-197, H-213, S-33, C-584, N-283, P-86: Balboa B-21; Mayas in Yucatán M-178, G-248b, Y-347
    4. South America S-290: Incas in Peru and Bolivia I-62, P-224, B-240 (Pizarro P-349). See also history sections in articles on South American republics
  E. **Philip II inherits Spain, the Netherlands, parts of Italy, and Spanish possessions in the New World** P-253, S-358–9: Madrid becomes capital M-30; marriage with Mary Tudor of England M-121; seizes Portuguese crown and East Indian trade P-457, E-42–3; Philippines conquered and colonized P-260

VII. **Decline of the Spanish Empire** S-359–60
  A. **Catholic Spain attempts to stem the spread of Protestantism** S-358–9: loss of the Netherlands N-138–9, W-165
  B. **Defeat of the Armada (1588)** A-566–7, E-185
  C. **Portugal regains independence (1640)** P-457
  D. **Blake defeats Spanish fleet in 1657** B-219
  E. **War of the Spanish Succession (1701–13)** A-741, S-359: Bourbon Philip V gains Spanish throne B-280, P-253, L-360: Gibraltar lost G-124; Treaty of Utrecht U-236, A-741, I-343a
  F. **War of the Austrian Succession (1740–48)** A-741–2, E-240: King George's War K-56 (battle of Bloody Marsh G-83, picture G-85)

G. **Seven Years' War (1756–63)** S-117–18, F-435

H. **Napoleon and the Peninsular War (1808–14)** N-12, S-359, W-99: Joseph Bonaparte made king of Spain S-359, B-241

I. **New World possessions lost** S-359, L-139–40: boundary settlements with United States W-24; Louisiana Territory L-379; Florida F-238; Mexico M-254, H-155–6; Central America C-197; South America S-291, B-236, S-44b

J. **Spanish-American War (1898)** S-364–5: Cuba C-628; Philippines, Guam, and Puerto Rico ceded to the United States P-17, P-260, G-245, P-530

VIII. **The struggle for liberal government** S-359, E-321

IX. **World War I, economic depression, and dictatorship** S-359–60: Alfonso XIII A-260

X. **Revolution of 1931 and the Spanish Republic** S-360

XI. **Spanish Civil War (1936–39) and fascist dictatorship** S-349, 360, M-32, B-65, F-71, D-112, E-324, W-267, G-105, I-343d: Franco F-419

XII. **World War II** S-360, T-15

XIII. **Postwar economic progress** S-361: United States economic and military aid S-361; causes of Spain's chronic economic difficulties S-349

XIV. **Spanish Morocco (1956) and Equatorial Guinea (1968) gain independence; Ifni ceded to Morocco (1969)** S-361, A-84, M-489

XV. **Spain's new constitution (1967)** S-361

XVI. **Prince Juan Carlos is approved as Franco's chosen successor by the Cortes** S-361

BIBLIOGRAPHY FOR SPAIN

Books and Films for Younger Readers

Cervantes Saavedra, Miguel de. The Adventures of Don Quixote de la Mancha (Macmillan, 1957).

Daly, Maureen. Spain: Wonderland of Contrasts (Dodd, 1965).

Gidal, Sonia and Tim. My Village in Spain (Pantheon, 1962).

Goldston, Robert. Spain (Macmillan, 1967).

Manning, Jack. Young Spain (Dodd, 1963).

People of Spain, film (Encyclopaedia Britannica Films).

Books for Advanced Students and Teachers

Belso, Ramiro. Living Spain (Crown, 1968).

Bottineau, Yves. Spain (Oxford, 1960).

Brossard, Chandler. The Spanish Scene (Viking, 1968).

Clark, S. A. All the Best in Spain and Portugal (Dodd, 1966).

Crow, J. A. Spain: the Root and the Flower (Harper, 1963).

Daly, Maureen. Spanish Roundabout (Dodd, 1960).

Fodor, Eugene, ed. Spain (McKay, 1969).

Goldston, Robert. The Civil War in Spain (Bobbs, 1966).

Irving, Washington. The Alhambra (Macmillan, 1953).

Loder, Dorothy. The Land and People of Spain (Lippincott, 1963).

Madariaga, Salvador de. Spain (Praeger, 1960).

Michener, J. A. Iberia (Random, 1968).

Morton, H. C. V. A Stranger in Spain (Dodd, 1955).

Payne, S. G. Franco's Spain (Crowell, 1967).

Sawyer, Ruth. My Spain (Viking, 1967).

Snellgrove, L. E. Franco and the Spanish Civil War (McGraw, 1968).

Thomas, Hugh. Spain (Time, 1966).

Index

This index is arranged in alphabetical order. Words beginning with "Mc" are alphabetized as "Mac," and "St." is alphabetized as "Saint."

The figures in brackets [66, 68] indicate earlier editions of THE COMPTON YEARBOOK in which the topic has appeared since 1966.

The first page reference is the main discussion.

Cross-references refer to index entries in this volume.

The reprints from the 1970 COMPTON'S ENCYCLOPEDIA are usually indexed by title only unless they contain events of 1969.

Major sections of the Yearbook appear on the following pages:

Compton's Pictured Highlights and Chronology of 1969, 10–29

Feature articles—China and the United States: Distorted Images, by Senator J. W. Fulbright, 30–39; Run for Your Supper, by William Barry Furlong, 40–53; Black Africa Saves the Game, by Marion Kaplan, 54–77; What Are We Laughing At?, by Steve Allen, 78–87; Color, by Max Kozloff (in part), 88–105

Special reports—Business and Industry: The Conglomerate, 161–3; Cities and Urban Affairs: The Trash Crisis, 184–5; Defense: Military Values Revisited, 218–20; Fashion: The Peacock Revolution, 250–2; Japan: Expo '70, 308–9; Motion Pictures: How Far Can We Go?, 354–6; Popular Music: Today's Rock Sound, 400–2; Psychology: If Stars Could Talk . . . , 407–9; Sports Champions: The Art of Self-Defense, 444–5

Events of the Year 1969, 106–509

Calendar for 1970, 510–12

New Words, 513–18

Reprints from the 1970 edition of COMPTON'S ENCYCLOPEDIA, 519–92

The Family Record follows the index.

D

I

M

O

Q

R

T

V

OUR FAMILY RECORD FOR 1970

What we did and how we looked

This space for family group photo

Each year important events highlight the life of every family. Year after year these events may be noted in the Family Record pages of your Compton Yearbooks. You will then have a permanent record of your family's significant achievements, celebrations, and activities.

OUR FAMILY TREE

Family name

Children

Children

Father

Mother

Grandmother

Grandfather

Great-Grandmother

Great-Grandfather

Great-Grandmother

Great-Grandfather

Grandmother

Grandfather

Great-Grandmother

Great-Grandfather

Great-Grandmother

Great-Grandfather

DATES TO REMEMBER

Birthdays, weddings, anniversaries, graduations, gifts sent

JANUARY	FEBRUARY	MARCH
APRIL	**MAY**	**JUNE**
JULY	**AUGUST**	**SEPTEMBER**
OCTOBER	**NOVEMBER**	**DECEMBER**

FAMILY CELEBRATIONS IN 1970

PASTE PHOTO HERE

BIRTHDAYS

NAME

DATE

NAME

DATE

NAME

DATE

NAME

DATE

NAME

DATE

NAME

DATE

WEDDINGS

NAMES

DATE

NAMES

DATE

NAMES

DATE

ANNIVERSARIES

NAMES

DATE

NAMES

DATE

PROMOTIONS

FIRM

TITLE

DATE

FIRM

TITLE

DATE

HOLIDAYS

OCCASION

OCCASION

OCCASION

OCCASION

BIRTHS

NAME
DATE
PARENTS

NAME
DATE
PARENTS

NAME
DATE
PARENTS

NAME
DATE
PARENTS

SPIRITUAL MILESTONES

NAME
MILESTONE

NAME
MILESTONE

NAME
MILESTONE

NAME
MILESTONE

NAME
MILESTONE

NAME
MILESTONE

NAME
MILESTONE

NAME
MILESTONE

PASTE PHOTO HERE

SCHOOL ACTIVITIES AND ACHIEVEMENTS

NAME ______________________

SCHOOL ______________ GRADE ____

NAME ______________________

SCHOOL ______________ GRADE ____

SPORTS

NAME ______________________

SPORT ______________________

ACHIEVEMENT ______________________

NAME ______________________

SPORT ______________________

ACHIEVEMENT ______________________

NAME ______________________

SPORT ______________________

ACHIEVEMENT ______________________

NAME ______________________

SPORT ______________________

ACHIEVEMENT ______________________

NAME ______________________

SPORT ______________________

ACHIEVEMENT ______________________

CLUB ACTIVITIES

NAME ______________________

CLUB ______________________

ACHIEVEMENT ______________________

NAME ______________________

CLUB ______________________

ACHIEVEMENT ______________________

NAME ______________________

CLUB ______________________

ACHIEVEMENT ______________________

NAME ______________________

CLUB ______________________

ACHIEVEMENT ______________________

NAME ______________________

CLUB ______________________

ACHIEVEMENT ______________________

PASTE PHOTO HERE

NAME ______
SCHOOL ______ GRADE ____
NAME ______
SCHOOL ______ GRADE ____

PASTE PHOTO HERE

SCHOOL PARTIES

DATE ______
OCCASION ______

DATE ______
OCCASION ______

DATE ______
OCCASION ______

DATE ______
OCCASION ______

DATE ______
OCCASION ______

DATE ______
OCCASION ______

DATE ______
OCCASION ______

DATE ______
OCCASION ______

EDUCATIONAL HONORS AND PRIZES

Scholarships, Awards, Honor Societies

NAME ______
GRADE ______
HONOR ______
NAME ______
GRADE ______
HONOR ______
NAME ______
GRADE ______
HONOR ______
NAME ______
GRADE ______
HONOR ______

GRADUATIONS

NAME ______
SCHOOL ______
NAME ______
SCHOOL ______
NAME ______
SCHOOL ______

OUR FAMILY HEALTH RECORD

DOCTOR'S NAME ______________________

ADDRESS ______________________

____

TELEPHONE NUMBER ______________________

____

DENTIST'S NAME ______________________

ADDRESS ______________________

____

TELEPHONE NUMBER ______________________

____

DOCTOR'S NAME ______________________

ADDRESS ______________________

____

TELEPHONE NUMBER ______________________

DENTIST'S NAME ______________________

ADDRESS ______________________

____

TELEPHONE NUMBER ______________________

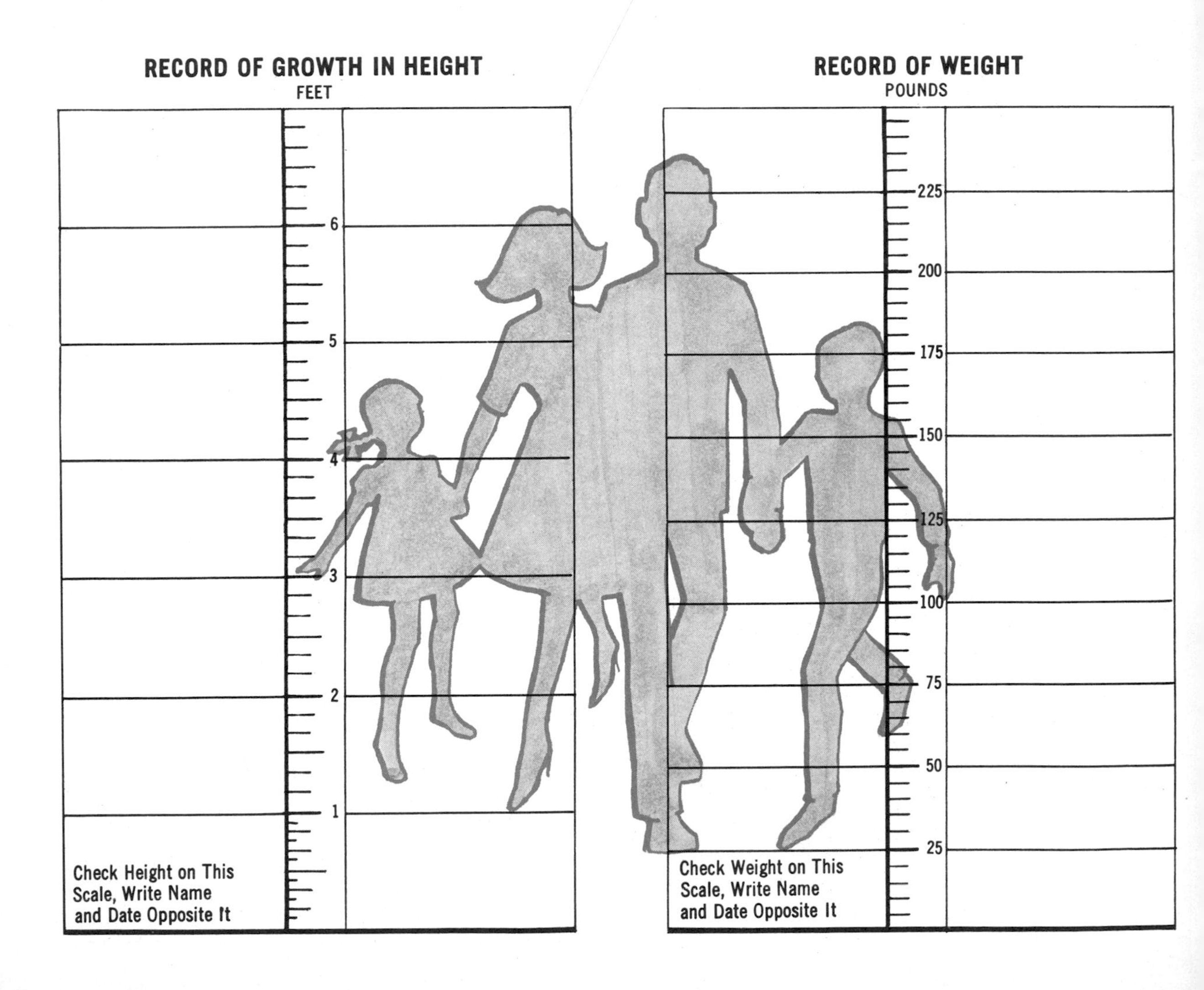

NAME ____________________

HEIGHT ____________ WEIGHT ________

VISITS TO DENTIST ____________________

VISITS TO DOCTOR ____________________

INOCULATIONS ____________________

TYPE ____________ DATE ________

TYPE ____________ DATE ________

ACCIDENTS, ILLNESSES ____________________

OPERATIONS ____________________

NAME ____________________

HEIGHT ____________ WEIGHT ________

VISITS TO DENTIST ____________________

VISITS TO DOCTOR ____________________

INOCULATIONS ____________________

TYPE ____________ DATE ________

TYPE ____________ DATE ________

ACCIDENTS, ILLNESSES ____________________

OPERATIONS ____________________

NAME ____________________

HEIGHT ____________ WEIGHT ________

VISITS TO DENTIST ____________________

VISITS TO DOCTOR ____________________

INOCULATIONS ____________________

TYPE ____________ DATE ________

TYPE ____________ DATE ________

ACCIDENTS, ILLNESSES ____________________

OPERATIONS ____________________

NAME ____________________

HEIGHT ____________ WEIGHT ________

VISITS TO DENTIST ____________________

VISITS TO DOCTOR ____________________

INOCULATIONS ____________________

TYPE ____________ DATE ________

TYPE ____________ DATE ________

ACCIDENTS, ILLNESSES ____________________

OPERATIONS ____________________

LEISURE HOURS INDOORS

BOOKS WE ENJOYED

AUTHOR

TITLE

WHO READ IT

WHY IT WAS LIKED

AUTHOR

TITLE

WHO READ IT

WHY IT WAS LIKED

AUTHOR

TITLE

WHO READ IT

WHY IT WAS LIKED

FAVORITE RECORDS

FAVORITE PLAYS, MOVIES, TV PROGRAMS

NAME

WHO SAW IT

WHY IT WAS LIKED

NAME

WHO SAW IT

WHY IT WAS LIKED

NAME

WHO SAW IT

WHY IT WAS LIKED

HOBBIES AND GAMES WE LIKED

COMPTON ARTICLES WE LIKED